AF660057

3e

Physics Galaxy

Volume III A

Electrostatics & Current Electricity

Ashish Arora
Mentor & Founder

PHYSICSGALAXY.COM

World's largest encyclopedia of online video courses on High School Students preparing for

* JEE Main * JEE Advanced * NEET * NSEP/INPhO/IPhO

GKP

First Edition : December, 2000

Second Edition : May, 2016

Revised Edition : March, 2023

Title : Physics Galaxy : Vol. IIIA - Electrostatics & Current Electricity (3rd edition)

Language : English

Author's Name : Ashish Arora

Copyright © : 2026 Ashish Arora

No part of this book may be reproduced in a retrieval system or transmitted, in any form or by any means, electronics, mechanical, photocopying, recording, scanning and or without the written permission of the Author/Publisher.

Typeset & Published by :

Career Launcher Infrastructure (P) Ltd.

A-45, Mohan Cooperative Industrial Area, Near Mohan Estate Metro Station, New Delhi - 110044

Marketed by :

CL Educate (Publication Division)

14/4, Mathura Road, Faridabad, Haryana, 121003

ISBN : **978-93-94168-59-6**

Printer's Details : Printed in India, New Delhi.

For product information :

Visit ***www.gkpublications.com*** or email to ***gkp@gkpublications.com***

Dedicated

to

My Parents, Son, Daughter

and

My beloved wife

In his teaching career since 1992 Ashish Arora personally mentored more than 10000 IITians and students who reached global heights in various career and profession chosen. It is his helping attitude toward students with which all his students remember him in life for his contribution in their success and keep connections with him live. Below is the list of some of the successful students in International Olympiad personally taught by him.

NAVNEET LOIWAL	*International GOLD Medal in IPhO-2000 at LONDON*, Also secured **AIR-4** in **IIT JEE 2000**
	PROUD FOR INDIA : Navneet Loiwal was the first Indian Student who won first International GOLD Medal for our country in International Physics Olympiad.
DUNGRA RAM CHOUDHARY	**AIR-1** in **IIT JEE 2002**
HARSHIT CHOPRA	*National Gold Medal in INPhO-2002* and got **AIR-2** in **IIT JEE-2002**
KUNTAL LOYA	A Girl Student got position **AIR-8** in **IIT JEE 2002**
LUV KUMAR	*National Gold Medal in INPhO-2003* and got **AIR-3** in **IIT JEE-2003**
RAJHANS SAMDANI	*National Gold Medal in INPhO-2003* and got **AIR-5** in **IIT JEE-2003**
SHANTANU BHARDWAJ	*International SILVER Medal in IPhO-2002 at INDONESIA*
SHALEEN HARLALKA	*International GOLD Medal in IPhO-2003 at CHINA* and got **AIR-46** in **IIT JEE-2003**
TARUN GUPTA	*National GOLD Medal in INPhO-2005*
APEKSHA KHANDELWAL	*National GOLD Medal in INPhO-2005*
ABHINAV SINHA	*Hon'ble Mension Award in APhO-2006* at *KAZAKHSTAN*
RAMAN SHARMA	*International GOLD Medal in IPhO-2007* at *IRAN* and got **AIR-20** in **IIT JEE-2007**
PRATYUSH PANDEY	*International SILVER Medal in IPhO-2007* at *IRAN* and got **AIR-85 in IIT JEE-2007**
GARVIT JUNIWAL	*International GOLD Medal in IPhO-2008* **at** *VIETNAM* and got **AIR-10** in **IIT JEE-2008**
ANKIT PARASHAR	*National GOLD Medal in INPhO-2008*
HEMANT NOVAL	*National GOLD Medal in INPhO-2008* and got **AIR-25** in **IIT JEE-2008**
ABHISHEK MITRUKA	*National GOLD Medal in INPhO-2009*
SARTHAK KALANI	*National GOLD Medal in INPhO-2009*
ASTHA AGARWAL	*International SILVER Medal in IJSO-2009* **at** *AZERBAIJAN*
RAHUL GURNANI	*International SILVER Medal in IJSO-2009* **at** *AZERBAIJAN*
AYUSH SINGHAL	*International SILVER Medal in IJSO-2009* **at** *AZERBAIJAN*
MEHUL KUMAR	*International SILVER Medal in IPhO-2010* at *CROATIA* and got **AIR-19** in **IIT JEE-2010**
ABHIROOP BHATNAGAR	*National GOLD Medal in INPhO-2010*
AYUSH SHARMA	*International Double GOLD Medal in IJSO-2010* at *NIGERIA*
AASTHA AGRAWAL	*Hon'ble Mension Award in APhO-2011* at *ISRAEL* and got **AIR-93** in **IIT JEE 2011**
ABHISHEK BANSAL	*National GOLD Medal in INPhO-2011*
SAMYAK DAGA	*National GOLD Medal in INPhO-2011*
SHREY GOYAL	*National GOLD Medal in INPhO-2012* and secured **AIR-24** in **IIT JEE 2012**
RAHUL GURNANI	*National GOLD Medal in INPhO-2012*
JASPREET SINGH JHEETA	*National GOLD Medal in INPhO-2012*
DIVYANSHU MUND	*National GOLD Medal in INPhO-2012*
SHESHANSH AGARWAL	*International SILVER Medal in IAO-2012 at KOREA*
SWATI GUPTA	*International SILVER Medal in IJSO-2012 at IRAN*
PRATYUSH RAJPUT	*International SILVER Medal in IJSO-2012 at IRAN*
SHESHANSH AGARWAL	*International BRONZE Medal in IOAA-2013 at GREECE*
SHESHANSH AGARWAL	*International GOLD Medal in IOAA-2014 at ROMANIA*
SHESHANSH AGARWAL	*International SILVER Medal in IPhO-2015 at INDIA* and secured **AIR-58** in **JEE(Advanced)-2015**
VIDUSHI VARSHNEY	*International SILVER Medal in IJSO-2015 at SOUTH KOREA*
AMAN BANSAL	**AIR-1 in JEE Advanced 2016**
KUNAL GOYAL	**AIR-3 in JEE Advanced 2016**
GOURAV DIDWANIA	**AIR-9 in JEE Advanced 2016**
DIVYANSH GARG	*International SILVER Medal in IPhO-2016 at SWITZERLAND*
NALIN KHANDELWAL	**AIR-1 in NEET 2019**
MRIDUL AGARWAL	**AIR-1 in JEE Advanced 2021**

ABOUT THE AUTHOR

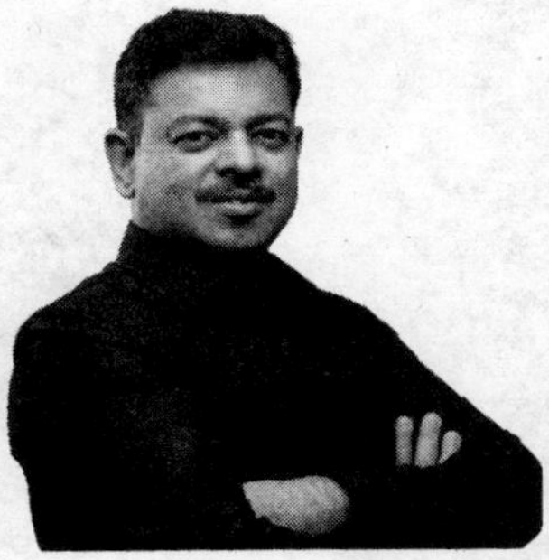

The complexities of Physics have given nightmares to many, but the homegrown genius of Jaipur- Ashish Arora has helped millions of students to live their dreams by decoding it.

Newton Law of Gravitation and Faraday's Magnetic induction force apply perfectly well with this unassuming genius. A Pied Piper of students, his webportal https://www.physicsgalaxy.com, The world's largest encyclopedia of video lectures on high school Physics possesses strong gravitational pull and magnetic attraction for students who want to make it big in life.

Ashish Arora, gifted with rare ability to train masterminds, has mentored over 10,000 IITians and Medicos in his past over three decades of teaching sojourn including lots of students made it to Top 100 in IIT-JEE/JEE(Advance) including multiple times AIR-1 and many in Top-10. Apart from that, he has also groomed hundreds of students for cracking International Physics Olympiad. No wonder his student Navneet Loiwal brought laurel to the country by becoming the first Indian to win a Gold medal at the 2000 - International Physics Olympiad in London (UK).

His special ability to simplify the toughest of the Physics theorems and applications rates him as one among the best Physics teachers in the world. With this, Arora simply defies the logic that perfection comes with age. Even at 18 when he started teaching Physics while pursuing engineering, he was as engaging as he is now. Experience, besides graying his hair, has just widened his horizon.

Now after encountering all tribes of students - some brilliant and some not-so-intelligent - this celebrated teacher has embarked upon a noble mission to make the entire galaxy of Physics inform of his webportal PHYSICSGALAXY.COM to serve and help global students in the subject. Today students from 183 countries are connected with this webportal. On any topic of physics students can post their queries in INTERACT tab of the webportal on which many global experts with Ashish Arora reply to several queries posted online by students.

Dedicated to global students of middle and high school level, his website *www.physicsgalaxy.com* also has teaching sessions dubbed in American accent and subtitles in 87 languages. For students in India preparing for JEE & NEET, his online courses will be available soon on PHYSICSGALAXY.COM.

Subscribe to

Physics Galaxy Mobile App — GET IT ON Google Play — Download on the App Store

PG Telegram
https://t.me/physicsgalaxyworld
High Quality Academic Resources for JEE(Main+Adv) & NEET

YouTube Channel
World's Largest Youtube Channel of 9000+ Video Lectures on High School Physics

Courses on Mobile App

- Complete JEE & NEET Concept Videos on Physics
- Complete Pre-Foundation Physics for Class 6-7-8
- Complete Foundation Physics for Class 9-10
- Complete NCERT Class 11 & 12 Physics Solutions
- Complete JEE Main 2002-2020 Video Solutions (Online & Offline)
- 700+ Advance Illustration Videos for JEE Advanced
- Tips & Tricks Guidance Videos for Competitive Exams
- Revision Checklist Videos for JEE Main & NEET
- Exam Memory Maps Videos for JEE Main & NEET

and much more...

FOREWORD

It has been pleasure for me to follow the progress Er. Ashish Arora has made in teaching and professional career. In the last about three decades he has actively contributed in developing several new techniques for teaching & learning of Physics and driven important contribution to Science domain through nurturing young students and budding scientists. Physics Galaxy is one such example of numerous efforts he has undertaken.

The third edition of Physics Galaxy provides a good coverage of various topics of Mechanics, Thermodynamics and Waves, Optics & Modern Physics and Electricity & Magnetism through dedicated volumes and many new questions included. It would be an important resource for students appearing in competitive examination for seeking admission in engineering and medical streams.

The structure of book is logical and the presentation is innovative. Importantly the book covers some of the concepts on the basis of realistic experiments and examples. The book has been written in an informal style to help students learn faster and more interactively with better diagrams and visual appeal of the content. Each chapter has variety of theoretical and numerical problems to test the knowledge acquired by students. The book also includes solution to all practice exercises with several new illustrations and problems for deeper learning.

I am sure the book will widen the horizons of knowledge in Physics and will be found very useful by the students for developing in-depth understanding of the subject.

Date : June 25, 2024

Prof. Sandeep Sancheti
Ph. D. (U.K.), B.Tech. FIETE, FIE (I), SMIEEE
Vice-Chancellor (Provost) Marwadi University, Rajkot
Member Executive Council, Association of Commonwealth Universities, London
Former President, AIU, New Delhi
Former Vice-Chancellor, SRMIST, Chennai
Former President, Manipal University, Jaipur
Former-Director NIT Surathkal, NIT New Delhi, NIT Trichy,
NIT Calicut, SPA Delhi; Former-Mentor Director NIT Goa,
NIT Sikkim, NIT Puducherry
Former-Member JEE Apex Board (JAB), MHRD, GoI
Former-Chairman, Central Counselling Board (CCB), AIEEE, MHRD, GoI
Former-Chairman, Direct Admission of Students Abroad (DASA), MHRD, GoI

PREFACE

For a science student, Physics is the most important subject, unlike to other subjects it requires logical reasoning and high imagination of brain. Without improving the level of physics it is very difficult to achieve a goal in the present age of competitions. To score better, one does not require hard working at least in physics. It just requires a simple understanding and approach to think a physical situation. Actually physics is the surrounding of our everyday life. All the six parts of general physics-Mechanics, Heat, Sound, Light, Electromagnetism and Modern Physics are the constituents of our surroundings. If you wish to make the concepts of physics strong, you should try to understand core concepts of physics in practical approach rather than theoretical. Whenever you try to solve a physics problem, first create a hypothetical approach rather than theoretical. Whenever you try to solve a physics problem, first create a hypothetical world in your imagination about the problem and try to think psychologically, what the next step should be, the best answer would be given by your brain psychology. For making physics strong in all respects and you should try to merge and understand all the concepts with the brain psychologically.

The book PHYSICS GALAXY is designed in a totally different and friendly approach to develop the physics concepts psychologically. The book is presented in five volumes, which covers almost all the core branches of general physics. This part of book, volume 3A covers Electrostatics, Capacitance and Current Electricity. These are most critical topics of Physics for building strong calculus based applications. The things you will learn in this book will form a major foundation for understanding of the branch electricity and magnetism as a core fundamental. In this book every chapter is explained in a simple, interactive and experimental way. The book is divided in the three major chapters, first two chapters covering all the complete applications of electric field and electric potential due to charged bodies including the applications of electrical interaction energy as well as field energy associated with different configuration of conductors. Third chapter covers the understanding and applications of electric current in different types of electric circuits with several applications on heating effects of current and devices used to measure electrical properties in a circuit.

The best way of understanding physics is the experiments and this methodology I am using in my lectures and I found that it helps students a lot in concept visualization. In this book I have tried to translate the things as I used in lectures. After every important section there are several solved examples included with simple and interactive explanations. It might help a student in a way that the student does not require to consult any thing with the teacher. Everything is self explanatory and in simple language.

One important factor in preparation of physics I wish to highlight that most of the student after reading the theory of a concept start working out the numerical problems. This is not the efficient way of developing concepts in brain. To get the maximum benefit of the book students should read carefully the whole chapter at least three or four times with all the illustrative examples and with more stress on some illustrative examples included in the chapter. Practice exercises included after every theory section in each chapter is for the purpose of in-depth understanding of the applications of concepts covered. Illustrative examples are explaining some theoretical concept in the form of an example. After a thorough reading of the chapter students can start thinking on discussion questions and start working on numerical problems.

Exercises given at the end of each chapter are for circulation of all the concepts in mind. There are two sections, first is the discussion questions, which are theoretical and help in understanding the concepts at root level. Second section is of conceptual MCQs which helps in enhancing the theoretical thinking of students and building logical skills in the chapter. Third section of numerical MCQs helps in the developing scientific and analytical application of concepts. Fourth section of advance MCQs with one or more options correct type questions is for developing advance and comprehensive thoughts. Last section is the Unsolved Numerical Problems which includes some simple problems and some tough problems which require the building fundamentals of physics from basics to advance level problems which are useful in preparation of NSEP, INPhO or IPhO.

In this third edition of the book I have included many new questions and solutions in different exercises at practice, conceptual, numerical and advance MCQs to support students who are dependent on their self study and not getting access to teachers for their preparation.

This book has taken a shape just because of motivational inspiration by my mother in 1997 when I just thought to write something for my students. She always motivated and was on my side whenever I thought to develop some new learning methodology for my students.

I don't have words for my best friend my wife Anuja for always being together with me to complete this book in the unique style and format.

I would like to pay my gratitude to Sh. Dayashankar Prajapati in assisting me to complete the task in Design Labs of PHYSICSGALAXY.COM and presenting the book in totally new format of third edition.

At last but the most important person, my father who has devoted his valuable time in finally presenting the book in such a format and a simple language, thanks is a very small word for his dedication in building the base structure of this book.

In this third edition I have tried my best to make this book error free but owing to the nature of work, inadvertently, there is possibility of errors left untouched. I shall be grateful to the readers, if they point out me regarding errors and oblige me by giving their valuable and constructive suggestions via emails for further improvement of the book.

Date : June 25, 2024

Ashish Arora

PHYSICSGALAXY.COM
B-80, Model Town, Malviya Nagar, Jaipur-302017
e-mails: ashisharora@physicsgalaxy.com
ashash12345@gmail.com

CONTENTS

Chapter 3 Current Electricity 303-430

ANSWERS & SOLUTIONS

1 Electrostatics

FEW WORDS FOR STUDENTS

You know without electricity our life will be very limited and the foundation of electricity is based on behaviour and analysis of charges. To understand the roots of topic we need to understand these in detail. To understand charges its essential to study their behaviour and effects in surrounding in state of rest as well as in motion. In this chapter we will discuss everything that forms the basis for our knowledge in relation to static charges. This chapter is going to build foundation of all types of effects produced by charges whether at rest or in motion which includes electric current and magnetism.

CHAPTER CONTENTS

COVER APPLICATION

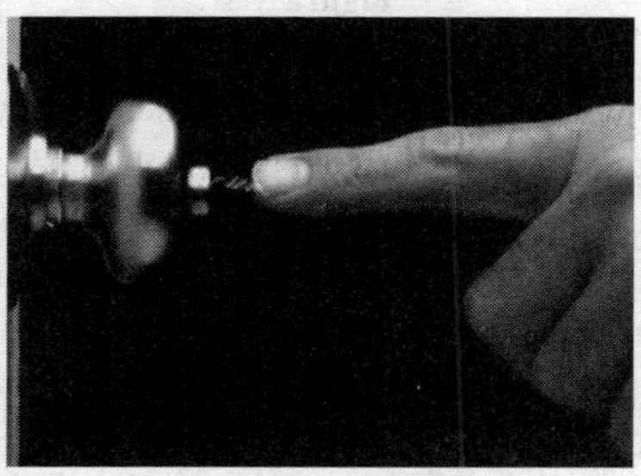

Figure-(a)

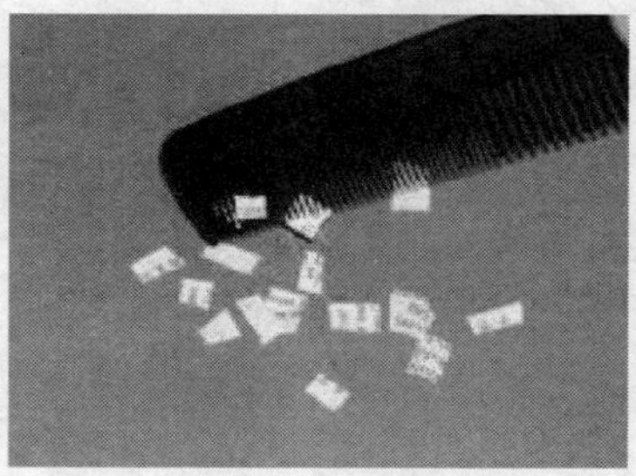

Figure-(b)

We experience static electricity in our day to day life. Figure-(a) shows a door knob being touched by a finger charged with static charges due to friction in normal routine thats is why in dry weather touching a metal body causes electric discharge from body and we feel a slight electric shock. Figure-(b) shows small pieces of paper which are attracted by a comb charged with static electricity after combing hairs. Its due to friction comb receives charges and by induction pieces if paper are attracted.

All matter is made up of tiny units called atoms. Naturally all atoms are electrically neutral having equal amount of positive charge on protons and same charge on its electrons. Electrons are loosely bound particles in an atom of any material whereas protons are tightly fused and confined within the nucleus only. The simplest way to charge a body is to add or extract electrons from it.

When a body is charged in state of rest or in motion it exhibits several different phenomenon and effects, applications of which are used in many practical cases in our surrounding. All the phenomenon concerned to charges including electricity and magnetism are divided in two parts - Electrostatics and Electrodynamics. This chapter of electrostatics deals only with study, effects and applications of charges at rest.

1.1 Charge & its Characteristics

Charge is a property of physical matter due to which all types of electric and magnetic phenomenon are produced. Every body is made up of atoms in which both positive and negative charge are there in form of electrons and protons in equal quantity that's why by nature every body is electrically neutral. In common practice a body can be charged by exchange of electrons as protons are confined within the nucleus of atom and in general cases it requires high amount of energy to extract or add a proton from the nucleus of an atom which is not possible in normal practical and natural conditions whereas extraction of electron require very small amount of energy which is possible in practical conditions.

When electrons are added to a body, it gets negatively charged and when electrons are extracted from a body, it gets positively charged as shown in figure-1.1(a) and (b).

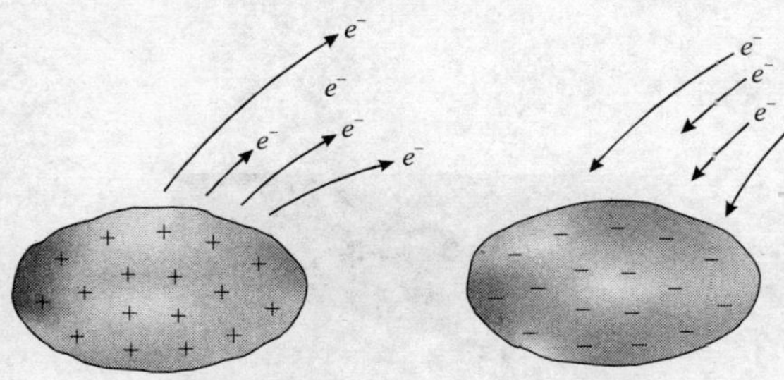

(a) (b)

Figure 1.1

In general whenever we talk about a positively charged body then it means the body is electron deficient and if we talk about a negatively charged body then we consider there are excess electrons on the body. In this chapter by charged body we will mean that the body is charged by either addition or removal of electrons from it.

1.1.1 Charging of Metallic and Non-metallic Bodies

In a metal body charges are free to move due to free electrons in it whereas in non metals charges are not allowed to move or flow within the body volume.

When charge is supplied to a metallic body, due to its conducting behaviour, the charges (excess electrons as negative charges or electron deficiency as positive charge) within the volume of body repel each other and spread outward till these all charges reach the outer surface of the body as shown in figure-1.2. Always remember that in case of a charged metallic body whole of its charge resides only on its outer surface in normal conditions.

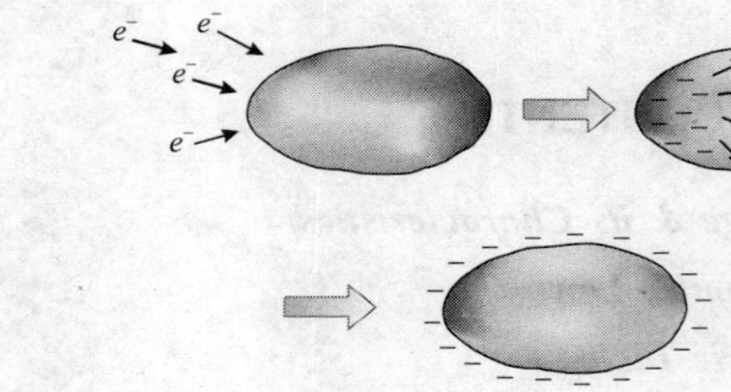

Figure 1.2

Figure-1.2 shows a body on which excess electrons are supplied to make it negatively charged. When the electrons are placed on the metal body, inside the body volume these electrons repel each other and spread out till all these reach on the outer surface of the body where the charge distribution becomes stable.

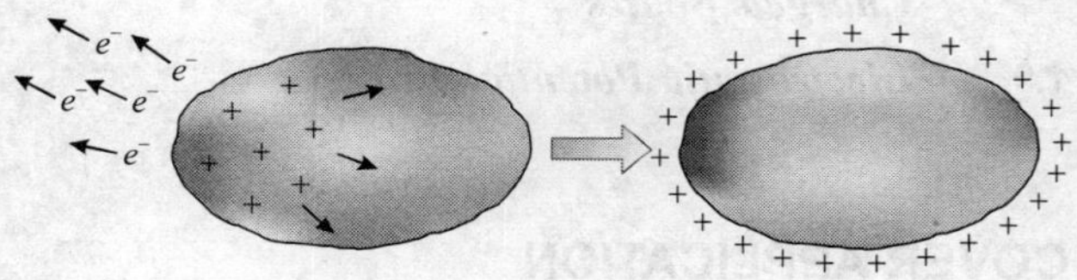

Figure 1.3

Similarly in figure-1.3 we can see a metal body from which electrons are extracted to make it positively charged after which the positive charges on body which can be considered as electron deficient places, will repel each other (or attract other free electrons of the body from outside) and finally in stable state whole positive charge will distribute on the outer surface of the body.

In case of a non metal body as charges are not free to move within its volume, the supplied charge whether positive or negative will remain within the volume of body at the location where the charge is supplied by removal or addition of electrons to it.

Charge is a scalar physical quantity so on supplying more charge to an already charged body, its total charge will be the sum of algebraic addition of all the total charges supplied to it.

1.1.2 Friction Electricity

Atoms of different materials hold their orbiting electrons with different strengths so when the two bodies of different materials are rubbed against each other, due to friction electrons from one body will get transferred to the other body which has more electron affinity and due to transfer of these electrons, one body gets positively charged and other gets negatively charged. Figure-1.4(a) shows the case when a glass rod is rubbed with silk cloth then due to higher electron affinity of silk it extracts electrons from the glass rod and gets negatively charged and the glass rod becomes positively charged. Similarly figure-1.4(b) shows a case when an ebonite rod which is a very hard rubber is rubbed with fur, the ebonite rod gets negatively charged and fur becomes positively charged. This process of charging bodies by friction is called "*Friction Electricity*".

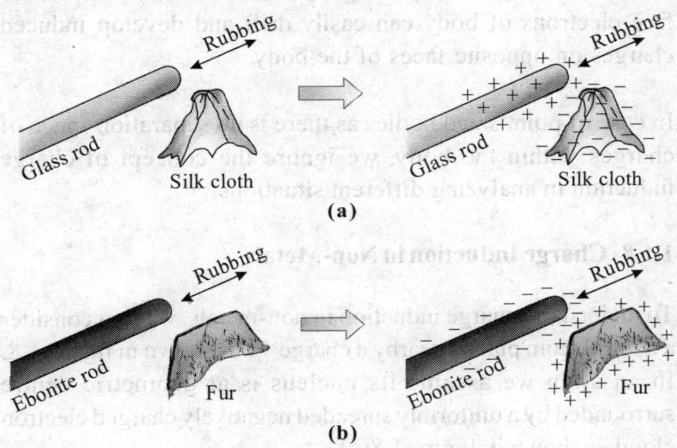

Figure 1.4

By friction electricity only non metallic bodies can be charged as if metal bodies are rubbed against each other, some transfer of electrons may take place due to different materials but due to conductivity of both bodies in contact charges will flow back and neutralize each other that's why metal bodies cannot be charged by rubbing them. At least one body must be non metal so that after electron transfer due to contact bodies will not get neutralized.

It is also important to note that two identical bodies having different charges will have different masses. This is because the difference in number of electrons on the bodies as these have different charges.

1.1.3 Quantization of Charge

The magnitude of charge of an electron is $e = 1.6 \times 10^{-19}$ C which is also called elementary or fundamental charge. Whenever a body is charged, always it can attain charge in multiples of elementary charge only as electrons cannot be exchanged in fractions so charge can vary on a body in steps of e. Thus any charge on a body in nature can be expressed as an integral multiple of elementary charge as

$$q = Ne \quad (N \in I)$$

Thus the charge of any object can be increased or decreased in steps of e only. This is called '*Quantization of Charge*' as any physical quantity which varies in discrete steps is called a '*Quantized Quantity*' and something which can vary continuously such as time at macroscopic level is called '*Continuous Quantity*'.

1.1.4 Conservation of Charge

It is considered that for an isolated system, the net charge of system is always constant. Within the system charge may be transferred from one body to another which does not affect the net charge of the system. Thus charge can neither be created nor be destroyed and this is called '*Conservation of Charge*'.

It is also important to note that in a mechanical system the charge on a body does not affect the inertial properties of the body. Charge on a body is invariant i.e. it does not depend on the reference frame from which a body and its different mechanical parameters are observed.

1.1.5 Charging by Conduction

When a charged metal body is connected to a uncharged metal body then charge flows from charged body to the neutral body until the potential energy of the charges on both bodies become equal. Figure-1.5(a) shows a charged metal body which is connected to a neutral metal body via a switch. When switch is closed charge flows to the neutral body and charge is distributed on the outer surface of both the bodies. In later part of this chapter we will discuss about the numerical calculation of amount of charge after redistribution between the two bodies.

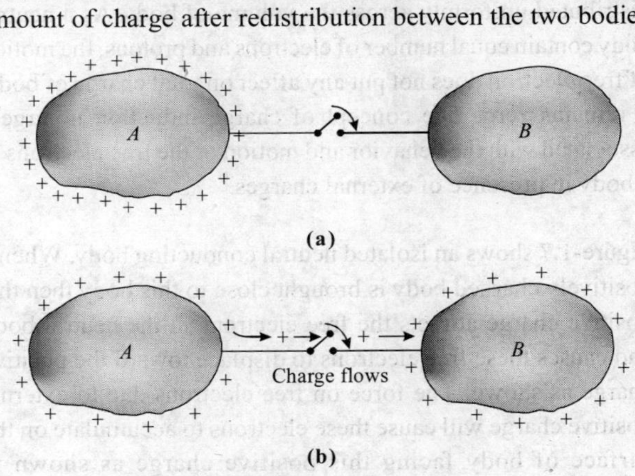

Figure 1.5

1.1.6 Charge Distribution on an Isolated Conductor

When some charge is supplied to an isolated conductor then due to mutual repulsion within the volume of the body charge is distributed on the outer surface of the conductor in such a way that the surface charge density (C/m^2) remain inversely proportional to the local radius of curvature of the body surface at any point. Figure-1.6 shows a conductor which is having a random shape and at different points on the surface it has different radii of curvature. When charge is supplied to this conductor, it is distributed on its outer surface with varying surface charge density given as σ C/m^2. At different points of the surface where radius of curvature is r, under isolated conductions the surface charge density is observed to be given as

$$\sigma \propto \frac{1}{r} \qquad \ldots(1.1)$$

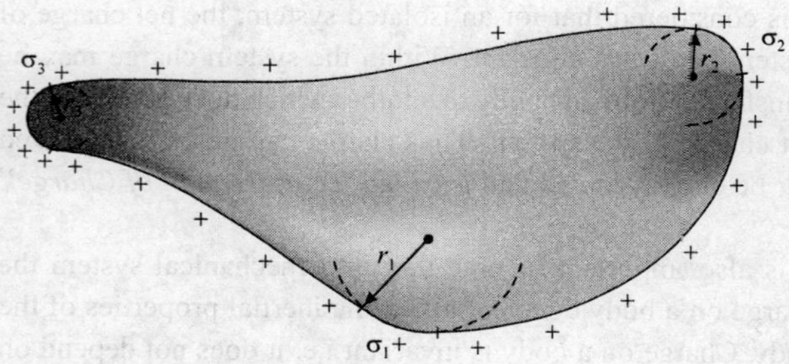

Figure 1.6

NOTE: ***Proof of above expression*** in equation-(1.1) is explained in section-1.11.5 but for various applications in different questions it is essential to understand and remember above result and standard observation as a fact given here.

1.1.7 Concept of Charge Induction in Metal Bodies

To understand the concept of charge induction first we need to understand the behaviour of free electrons in a metal body. In a metal body we can consider free electrons behave like gas atoms in a container which are in random Brownian motion and all distributed uniformly across the volume of body. As a neutral body contain equal number of electrons and protons, the motion of free electron does not put any affect on total charge of body, it remains zero. The concept of charge induction is largely associated with the behavior and motion of the free electrons in a body in presence of external charges.

Figure-1.7 shows an isolated neutral conducting body. When a positively charged body is brought close to this body then this positive charge attracts the free electrons in the neutral body and causes these free electrons to displace toward the positive charge as shown. The force on free electrons due to external positive charge will cause these electrons to accumulate on the surface of body facing this positive charge as shown in figure-1.7. As the electrons are displacing toward this surface, the opposite side of body the surface will become electron deficient and this surface will get negatively charged as shown in figure but the overall charge of the body remain zero as it is neutral. In the process the charges appearing on the two surface of the body are called induced charges and the phenomenon of separation of charges in a body by some external factor is called '*Charge Induction*'.

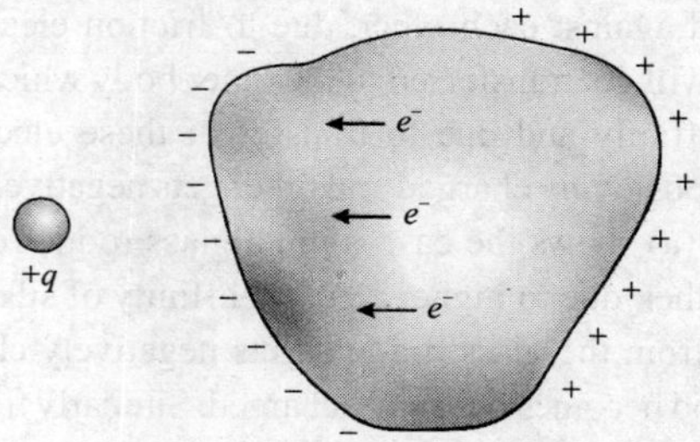

Figure 1.7

In extended conducting bodies which are not point sized (also called extended bodies) charge induction is very common as free electrons of body can easily drift and develop induced charges on opposite faces of the body.

In case of point sized bodies as there is no separation space of charges within the body, we ignore the concept of charge induction in analyzing different situations.

1.1.8 Charge Induction in Non-Metals

To understand charge induction in non-metals, we first consider a neutral atom placed nearby a charge $+q$ as shown in figure-1.8. In an atom we assume its nucleus is at geometric centre surrounded by a uniformly spreaded negatively charged electron cloud as shown in figure-1.8(a).

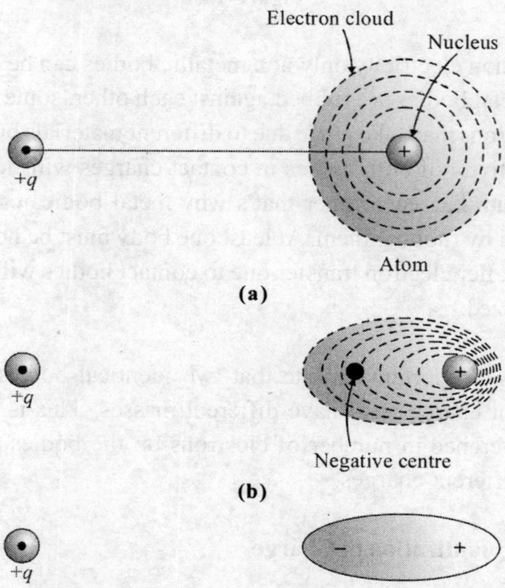

Figure 1.8

When a point charge is brought close to an atom, it will attract electron cloud of the atom and repel the nucleus, due to which the electron cloud gets distorted in the shape shown in figure-1.8(b). We can say that earlier electron cloud was uniformly spreaded in a spherical volume so that the negative centre of charge for this electron cloud was at nucleus but after distortion of electron cloud as shown in figure-1.8(b), the negative centre of charge is displaced toward left. Thus due to the presence of an external charge $+q$, an atom gets transformed into an electric dipole as shown in figure-1.8(c). Thus when we place a charge near a non-conducting body, almost all of its atoms (dipoles) get aligned toward the external charge as shown in figure-1.9.

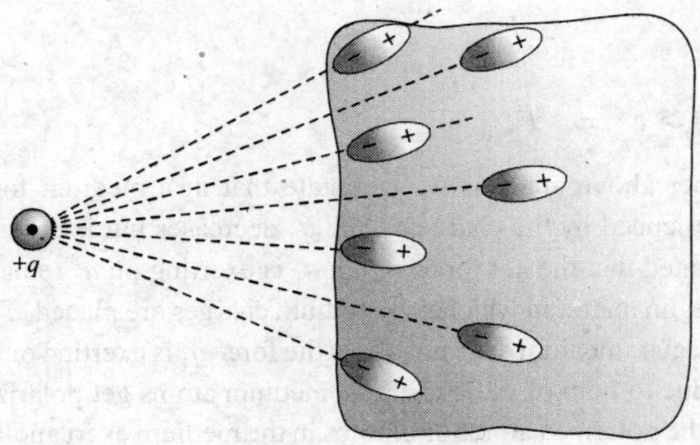

Figure 1.9

This alignment of dipoles in a non-conducting body due to an external charge is called induction in non-conducting bodies or '*Polarization*' of non-conducting bodies. As the separation of charges in a non conducting body is by a very small distance at atomic level only so in many numerical cases we ignore the effect of charge induction unless a specified question requires it to be considered.

Thus in both the cases of conducting and non-conducting bodies when a positive charge is brought closer, opposite charges are developed in the bodies due to charge induction and the negative induced charge is close to the external positive charge as compared to positive induced charge hence always the body is attracted toward the external charge.

This phenomenon also explains why always a charged body attracts a neutral body. It is also obvious that in conductors induction is more due to drift of free electrons hence attractive force on neutral conducting body will be more due to any external charge.

1.1.9 Gold Leaf Electroscope

An electroscope is an early scientific instrument that is used to detect the presence and magnitude of electric charge on a body. Several electroscopes were made with low and high sensitivity for measurement of charges on bodies. Gold Leaf Electroscope was one such instrument. It consists of a vertical metal rod, made up of brass. At the end of which two parallel strips of thin flexible gold leaves are attached as shown in figure-1.10. A metal ball terminal is attached to the top of the rod. When an external charged body is brought close to the ball terminal, due to induction opposite charges are induced on the ball and same polarity charges are induced on the gold leaves as shown in figure-1.10. Due to the similar charge on flexible gold leaves these repel each other and diverge. The angle of divergence of gold leaves is dependent on the magnitude of charge. More charge will cause more diverging angle and less charge causes less diverging angle. By proper calibration of instrument it can be used to measure the charge on the external body by measuring diverging angle of gold leaves.

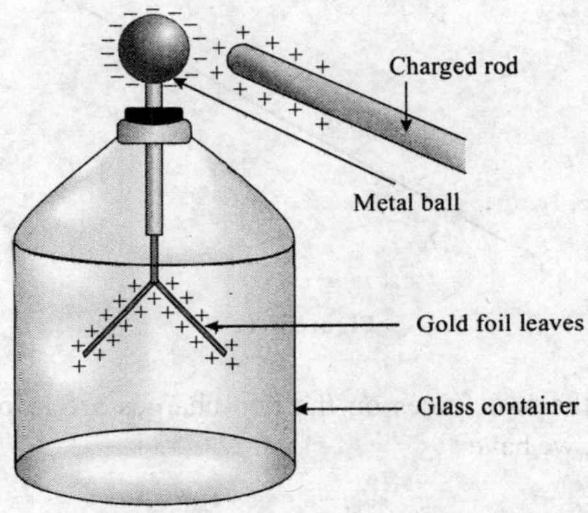

Figure 1.10

1.2 Coulomb's Law

Coulomb, through his experiments found out that the two charges 'q_1' and 'q_2' kept at distance 'r' in a medium as shown in figure-1.11 exert a force 'F' on each other and the magnitude of the force F is given as

$$F = \frac{K\, q_1 q_2}{r^2} \qquad \ldots(1.2)$$

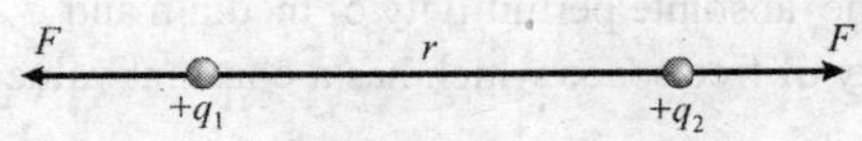

Figure 1.11

This law gives the net force experienced by each of the charges q_1 and q_2. This law also accounts for the surrounding medium in which charges are submerged. In above equation-(1.2), K is electrostatic constant which depends upon the surrounding medium. About electrostatic constant K we will discuss further in section-1.2.2 and also in section 1.20.

This force F acts along the line joining the two charges and is repulsive if q_1 and q_2 are of same sign and is attractive if they are of opposite sign.

1.2.1 Coulomb's Law in Vector Form

As the Coulombic force acts along the line joining the two charges, in vector form the expression of force by Coulomb's law for the two charges separated by the position vector $\vec{r}$ as shown in figure-1.12 can be written as

$$\vec{F}_2 = \frac{Kq_1q_2}{r^2}\hat{r}$$

$$\Rightarrow \quad \vec{F}_2 = \frac{Kq_1q_2}{r^3}\vec{r}$$

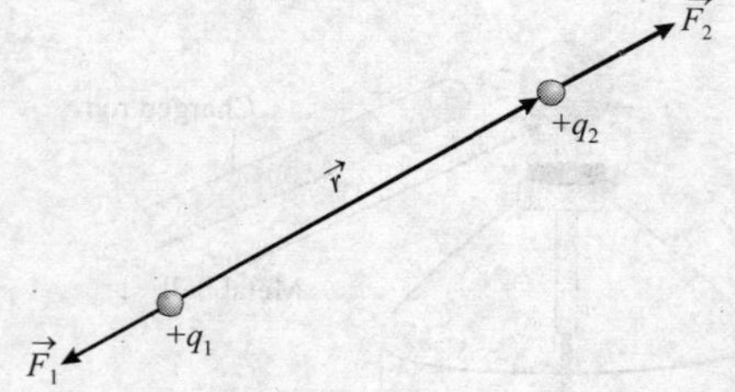

Figure 1.12

Here as the two forces on the two charges are in opposite direction, we have

$$\vec{F}_1 = -\vec{F}_2$$

1.2.2 Force Dependency on Medium

When two charges are placed in vacuum or when the same set of charges are fully submerged in a medium, the net force experienced by the charges will be different. The effect of presence of medium is accounted in the proportionality constant K. This electrostatic constant K is defined as

$$K = \frac{1}{4\pi \in}$$

where $\quad \in = \in_0 \in_r$

Here $\in$ is the absolute permittivity of medium and $\in_0$ is called permittivity of free space which has a constant value given as

$$\in_0 = 8.85 \times 10^{-12}\ \text{C}^2/\text{N-m}^2$$

Here $\in_r$ is called relative permittivity of medium with respect to free space, it is also termed as dielectric constant and is given as

$$\in_r = \frac{\in}{\in_0}$$

For free space $\in_r = 1$ and $K = \dfrac{1}{4\pi\in_0} = 9 \times 10^9\ \text{N-m}^2/\text{C}^2$

Here we can say when two charges are placed in vacuum (or air) the force experienced by the charges can be given as

$$F_{\text{air}} = \frac{1}{4\pi\in_0}\frac{q_1q_2}{r^2}$$

When these charges are submerged in a medium, having dielectric constant $\in_r$, then force becomes

$$F_{\text{med}} = \frac{1}{4\pi\in_0\in_r}\frac{q_1q_2}{r^2}$$

$$\Rightarrow \quad F_{\text{med}} = \frac{F_{air}}{\in_r}$$

as $\in_r > 1 \quad \Rightarrow \quad F_{\text{med}} < F_{\text{air}}$

As per above analysis we can state that in a medium force experienced by the charge q_1 and q_2 decreases but it can also be stated that the net force which q_1 is exerting on q_2 remains same, no matter in whichever medium charges are placed. This is because medium does not affect the force q_1 is exerting on q_2, but due to both of these charges, medium atoms get polarized and the polarized atoms or dipoles in the medium exert another force on these charges which is always in opposition to the force between the two charges in free space thats why in a medium net force between the two charges is always less than that compared to free space and Coulomb's law gives this net force and as already explained that electrostatic constant K or the dielectric constant of medium in it accounts for the effect of medium on the net interaction between the two charges.

As analyzed and explained above the net force between the two charges decreases when the charges are submerged fully in a medium at same separation. The force may also increase if medium exist only between two opposite polarity charges and not occupying the whole surrounding of charges. This can be easily explained as shown in figure-1.13.

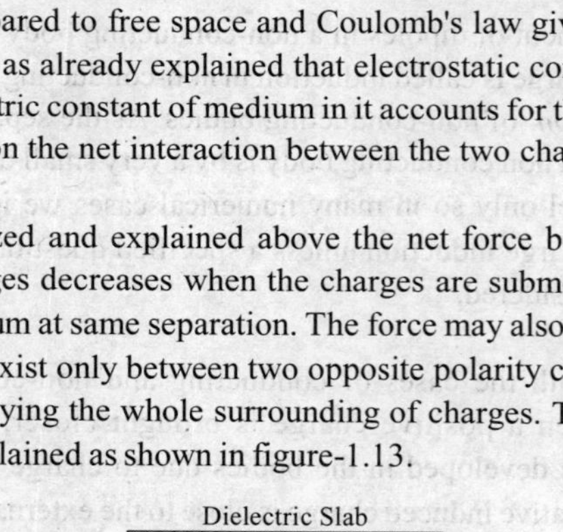

Figure 1.13

As shown in figure if there exist a dielectric slab between the two charges then we can see that both the charges being of opposite polarity attract each other, say with a force F_1 and both of the charges will polarize the medium diploes on the facing slab of the dielectric as shown and due to which these dipoles will exert an attractive force F_m on these charges in the same direction of F_1 and this increases the net force on the two charges.

Similar to this we can easily prove and explain that if a dielectric slab is inserted between two same polarity charges then the net force between the two charges decreases as shown in figure-1.14 as force F_m by medium on the charges acts in opposite direction to the force F_1 between the charges.

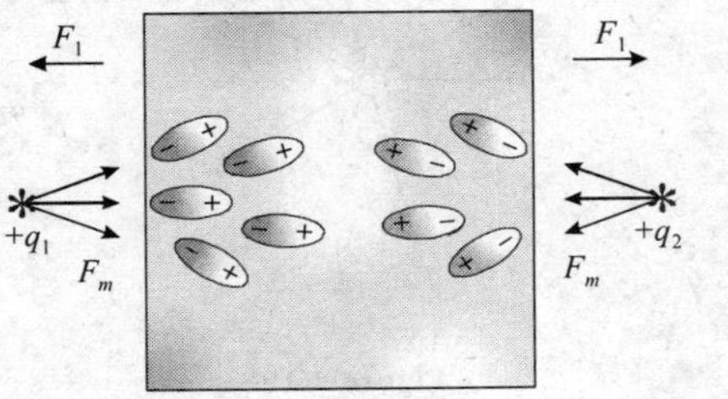

Figure 1.14

Thus we can state that on inserting a dielectric slab between two point charges the net interaction between the charges increases if the charges are of opposite sign and it decreases if charges are of same sign.

1.2.3 Limitations of Coulomb's Law

As analyzed in previous article Coulomb's law gives the net interaction between two charges. Applications of this law have some limitations which must be understood carefully before applying this law in different physical situations. There are two specific limitations or conditions in which this law cannot be applied which are explained below in detail.

(i) Limitation for Point Charges : Coulomb's Law is only valid for point charges i.e. if we have two large conducting spheres having charges q_1 and q_2, then we cannot use Coulomb's law to determine the interaction force between the two. This is because of charge induction on extended bodies.

Figure-1.15 shows two uniformly charged spheres with charges q_1 and q_2 placed at large separation. At large separation the effect of charge on one sphere on another is negligible so no charge induction take place and we can consider the two spheres to be having uniform charge distribution as shown in figure-1.15

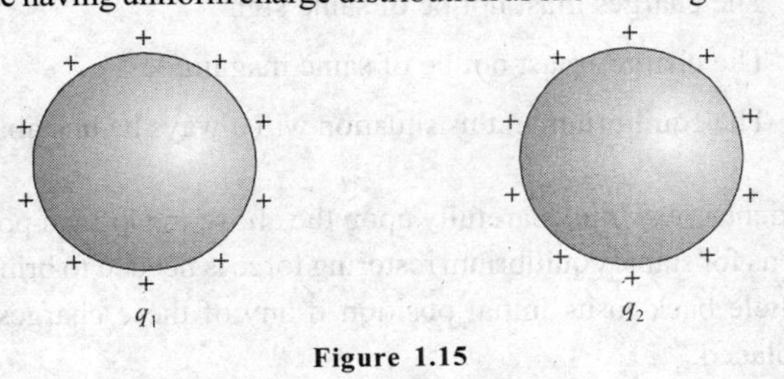

Figure 1.15

As these spheres are brought closer, due to charge induction effect of one on another the effective centres of the charge of spheres will shift from centre of spheres to points P_1 and P_2 as shown in figure-1.16 due to their mutual repulsion, and now the distance between the two charge centres is not taken as r. It will be considered as r_{eff} $(r_{eff} > r)$.

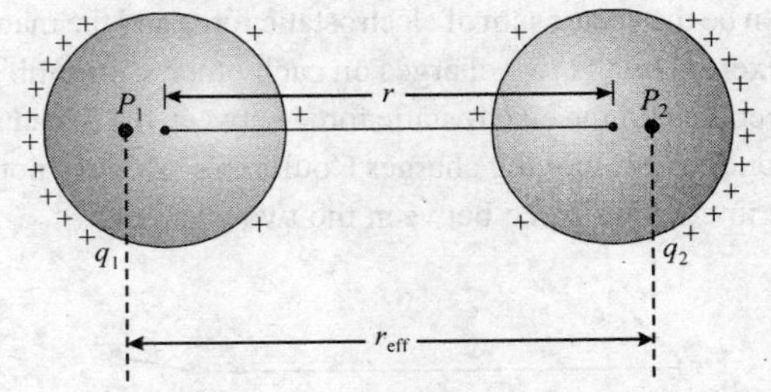

Figure 1.16

Thus the actual force acting between the two sphere shown in figure-1.16 is given as

$$F_{actual} = \frac{K\, q_1 q_2}{r_{eff}^2}$$

Where by Coulomb's law it is given as

$$F_{Coulomb} = \frac{K\, q_1 q_2}{r^2}$$

Here it is more than F_{actual}, thats why if charged bodies are not point sized or extended in dimensions then we avoid using Coulomb's law as the charge distribution on the bodies get modified due to charge induction and in such cases effective charge centers do not coincides with geometric centers of bodies.

In above case if sphere 1 is positively charged and sphere 2 is negatively charged, then the separation between the charge centers decreases and actual force becomes more than that given by Coulomb's law as shown in figure-1.17.

$$F_{actual} > F_{coulomb} \text{ as } r_{eff} < r$$

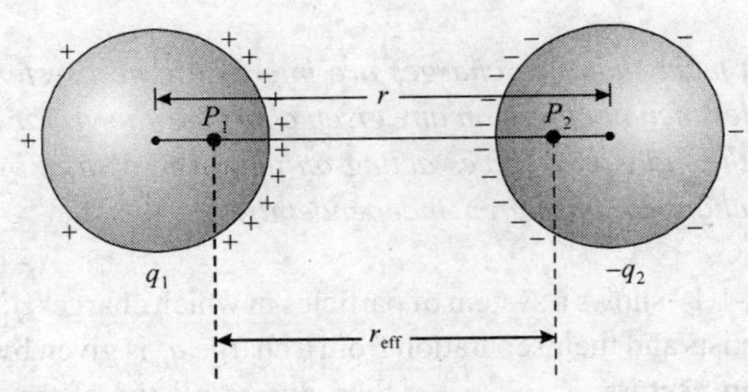

Figure 1.17

(ii) Limitation for Static Charges : Coulomb's law is considered to be valid only for static charges because moving charges may involve magnetic interaction which is not accounted by Coulomb's law.

If the two charges are moving, both the charges will also have an associated magnetic field in their surrounding. The net force will then be the vector sum of electrostatic force and the magnetic force exerted by the two charges on each other. Coulomb's law only accounts for the electrostatic force between the two charges so in condition of moving charges Coulomb's law does not give the net interaction force between the two charges.

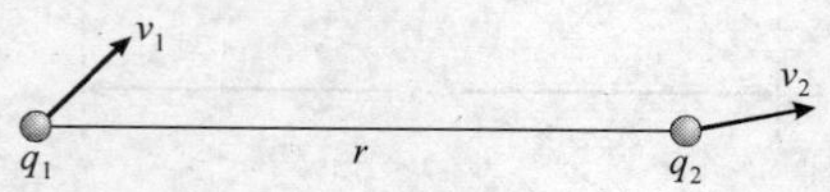

Figure 1.18

In figure-1.18 two charges q_1 and q_2 are moving with velocities v_1 and v_2 respectively and due to their motion they will also exert a magnetic force on each other. The electric interaction between the two charges is given as

$$F_{\text{Coulomb}} = \frac{K\, q_1 q_2}{r^2}$$

But the net interaction between the two charges is given as

$$\vec{F}_{\text{actual}} = \vec{F}_{\text{Coulomb}} + \vec{F}_{\text{magnetic}}$$

In above case or in similar cases if one of the charges is at rest, then $\vec{F}_{\text{magnetic}} = 0$ and under this condition Coulomb's law can be used for determining the net interaction between the charges. Thus we can state that Coulomb's law can be applied to point charges only if at least one of these charges is at rest.

1.2.4 Principle of Superposition for Electric Forces

As already discussed that Coulomb's law gives the net interaction force between two charge particles. When in a system there are more than two charges then net electric force on any charge due to all other charges is given by '*Principle of Superposition*' stated as given below.

"*When more than two charges are interacting in a system of particles then net force on any given charge is the vector sum of all the individual forces acting on the given charge by all other charges considered independently.*"

Figure-1.19 shows a system of particles in which charges q_1, q_2, q_3.... exists and their separation from a charge q_0 is given by the position vectors $\vec{r}_1, \vec{r}_2, \vec{r}_3$.... then due to all the charges in system the net force experienced by the charge q_0 is given by Principle of Superposition as

$$\vec{F}_{\text{Net}} = \vec{F}_1 + \vec{F}_2 + \vec{F}_3 + \ldots\ldots$$

$$\Rightarrow \quad \vec{F}_{\text{Net}} = \frac{Kq_1q_2}{r_1^2}\hat{r}_1 + \frac{Kq_1q_2}{r_2^2}\hat{r}_2 + \frac{Kq_1q_2}{r_3^2}\hat{r}_3 + \ldots\ldots$$

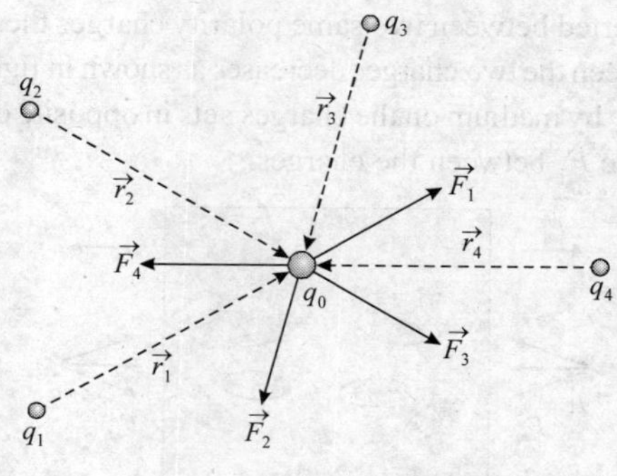

Figure 1.19

1.2.5 Equilibrium of three particles under Electrostatic Forces

Figure-1.20 shows three charge particles in equilibrium under their mutual electrostatic forces only. In this situation each charge will be experiencing two forces due to other two charges and for equilibrium of the system on each charge both the forces must cancel each other. If we carefully see the system and analyze then it is possible only if q_1 and q_2 are of same sign and q_3 is of opposite sign. Students can consider various possibilities and analyze the cases also.

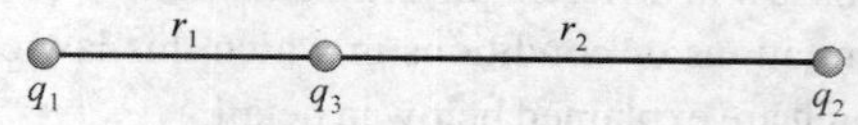

Figure 1.20

With the above explanation and analysis of situation for a system of three charge particles to be in equilibrium only under electrostatic forces some conditions can be stated which are given below.

Conditions for equilibrium of three charge particles only under electrostatic forces-

(i) The charges must be collinear

(ii) The charges must not be of same sign

(iii) The charges must not be of same magnitude

(iv) The equilibrium in this situation will always be unstable

Students must think carefully upon the above mentioned point (iv) as for stable equilibrium restoring force is needed to bring a particle back to its initial position if any of these charges is displaced.

1.2.6 Stable and Unstable Equilibrium of a Charge Particle between Two Fixed Charges

When two equal magnitude charges of same sign are fixed at a given separation and a third charge is placed exactly midway between these two charges then we can discuss different cases of equilibrium of the middle particle based on the sign of middle charge.

Case-I : When middle charge is of Same Sign

Figure-1.21 shows two fixed positive charges q_1 at a separation $2r$ and a third charge $+q_2$ is placed midway between the two charges. In this case in figure-1.21(a) we can see that the middle charge on displacing along the bisector of the line joining the side charges, the force on q_2 due to both q_1 will push it away from the equilibrium position and we can state that at mid point for displacement along the bisector of line joining the side charges middle charge is in unstable equilibrium.

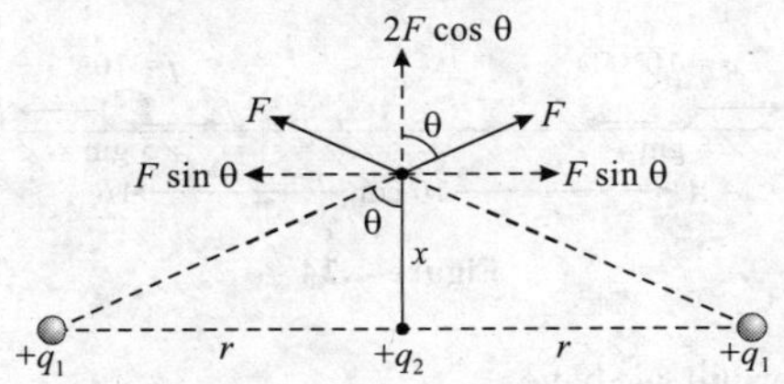

$$F = \frac{Kq_1q_2}{(r^2+x^2)}$$

(a)

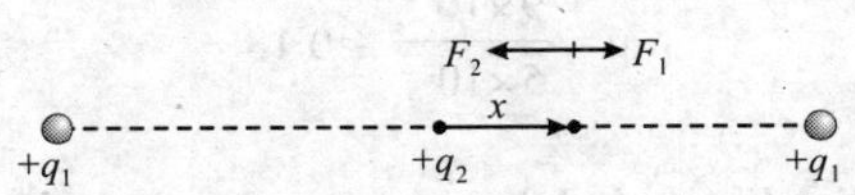

$$F_1 = \frac{Kq_1q_2}{(r+x)^2} \text{ and } F_2 = \frac{Kq_1q_2}{(r-x)^2}$$

(b)

Figure 1.21

Similarly from figure-1.21(b) we can see that the middle charge when displaced along the line joining the two charges, the repulsive force on it due to the nearer charge is more than that due to the other side charge hence net force on it will be the restoring force which tend to bring it back to the equilibrium position and we can state that at the mid point for displacement along the line joining the side charges the middle charge is in stable equilibrium.

Case-II : When middle charge is of Opposite Sign

Figure-1.22 shows two side fixed side charges $+q_1$ and middle free charge $-q_2$ for which we analyze the type of equilibrium for its displacement along the line joining the side charges and along the perpendicular bisector of this line. Figure-1.22(a) shows the case when the middle charge is displaced along the bisector of the line joining the side charges. Due to opposite sign the forces on middle charge due to side charges are attractive and thus the resulting force will be toward the equilibrium position and the equilibrium of middle charge for its displacement along the bisector is stable equilibrium.

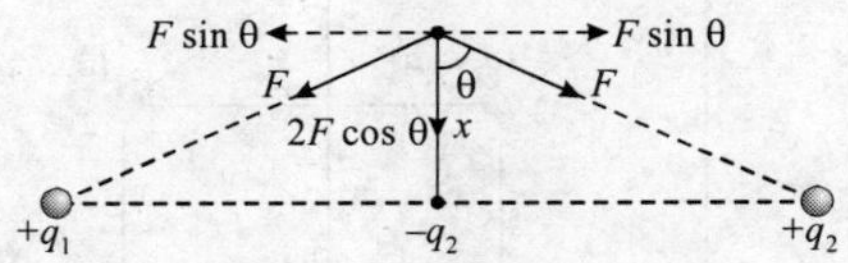

$$F = \frac{Kq_1q_2}{r^2+x^2}$$

(a)

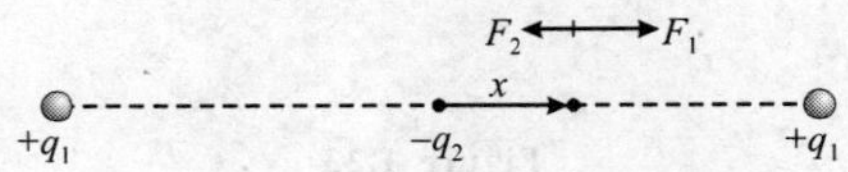

$$F_1 = \frac{Kq_1q_2}{(r-x)^2} \text{ and } F_2 = \frac{Kq_1q_2}{(r+x)^2}$$

(b)

Figure 1.22

Similarly from figure-1.22(b) we can see that the middle charge when displaced along the line joining the two charges, the attractive force on it due to the nearer charge is more than that due to the other side charge hence net force on it will be acting on it away from the equilibrium position and its equilibrium for displacement along the line joining the side charges is unstable equilibrium.

 # Illustrative Example 1.1

A cube is given with eight point charges q on each of its vertices. Calculate the force exerted on any of the charges due to rest of the seven charges.

Solution

The cube with the charges on its vertices is shown in figure-1.23. We will calculate the net force on charge at vertex A which can be given by vector sum of force experienced by this charge due to all the other charges on different vertices of the cube.

For this we use vector form of coulomb's law as

$$\vec{F}_{Ai} = \frac{K\, q_1q_2}{|\vec{r}_1 - \vec{r}_i|^3}(\vec{r}_1 - \vec{r}_i) \qquad \ldots(1.3)$$

Where $\vec{r_1}$ is the position vector of point A and $\vec{r_i}$ is the position vector of the vertex due to which force on charge at A is given by the force vector given in above equation-(1.3)

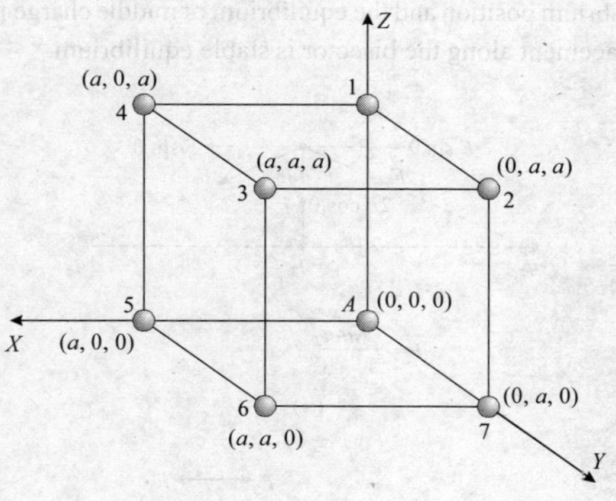

Figure 1.23

From the figure-1.23 the different forces acting on A are given as

$$\vec{F}_{A1} = \frac{Kq^2(-a\hat{k})}{a^3}$$

$$\vec{F}_{A2} = \frac{Kq^2(-a\hat{j} - a\hat{k})}{(\sqrt{2}a)^3}$$

$$\vec{F}_{A3} = \frac{Kq^2(-a\hat{i} - a\hat{j} - a\hat{k})}{(\sqrt{3}a)^3}$$

$$\vec{F}_{A4} = \frac{Kq^2(-a\hat{j} - a\hat{k})}{(\sqrt{2}a)^3}$$

$$\vec{F}_{A5} = \frac{Kq^2(-a\hat{j})}{a^3}$$

$$\vec{F}_{A6} = \frac{Kq^2(-a\hat{i} - a\hat{j})}{(\sqrt{2}a)^3}$$

$$\vec{F}_{A7} = \frac{Kq^2(-a\hat{j})}{a^3}$$

The net force experienced by A can be given as

$$\vec{F}_{net} = \vec{F}_{A1} + \vec{F}_{A2} + \vec{F}_{A3} + \vec{F}_{A4} + \vec{F}_{A5} + \vec{F}_{A6} + \vec{F}_{A7}$$

$$\Rightarrow \quad \vec{F}_{net} = \frac{-Kq^2}{a^2}\left[\left(\frac{1}{3\sqrt{3}} + \frac{1}{\sqrt{2}} + 1\right)(\hat{i} + \hat{j} + \hat{k})\right]$$

 # Illustrative Example 1.2

Two particles, each of mass of 5 gm and charged with charge 1.0×10^{-7} C each stay in equilibrium at the verge of sliding on a horizontal table with a separation of 10 cm between them. The coefficient of friction μ between each particle and the table is the same. Find μ.

Solution

Figure-1.24 shows the situation described in the problem. The forces acting on A are coulombic force and frictional force and at the limiting equilibrium limiting friction acting on it will be equal to the coulombic force by other particle which are given as

$$F_c = \frac{Kq^2}{r^2} = \frac{9 \times 10^9 \times (10^{-7})^2}{(10 \times 10^{-2})^2} = 9 \times 10^{-3}\,\text{N}$$

and $\quad f = \mu N = \mu mg = \mu\,(5 \times 10^{-3} \times 10) = \mu\,(5 \times 10^{-2})$ N

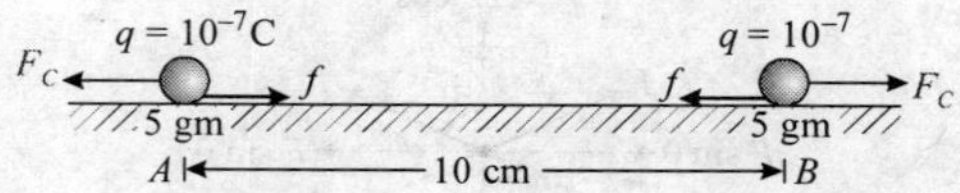

Figure 1.24

For equilibrium, we have

$$F_c = f$$

$$\Rightarrow \quad 9 \times 10^{-3} = \mu\,(5 \times 10^{-2})$$

$$\Rightarrow \quad \mu = \frac{9 \times 10^{-3}}{5 \times 10^{-2}} = 0{\cdot}18$$

 # Illustrative Example 1.3

Two particles A and B having charges q and $2q$ respectively are placed on a smooth table at separation d. A third particle C is to be clamped on the table in such a way that the particles A and B will be in equilibrium on the table under electrical forces only. What should be the charge on C and where should it be clamped for this ?

Solution

For the charges to be in equilibrium forces should be balanced an A on well as on B. Figure-1.25 shows the situation described in the question.

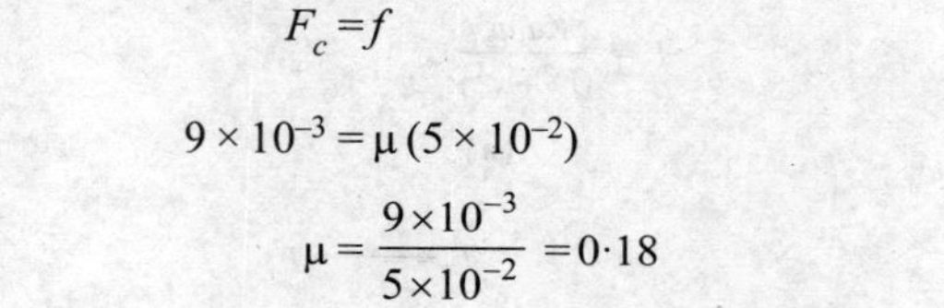

Figure 1.25

Forces acting on particle A are shown in figure-1.26 and given as

$$F_{AB} = \frac{Kq(2q)}{d^2}$$

$$F_{AC} = \frac{KqQ}{x^2}$$

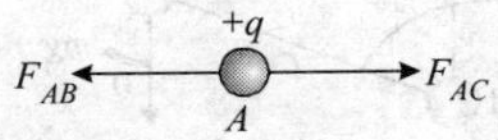

Figure 1.26

For equilibrium of A these forces are balanced so we use

$$F_{AB} = F_{AC}$$

$$\Rightarrow \quad \frac{2q}{d^2} = \frac{Q}{x^2}$$

$$\Rightarrow \quad Q = \frac{2qx^2}{d^2} \qquad \ldots(1.4)$$

Forces acting on particle B are shown in figure-1.27 and given as

$$F_{AB} = \frac{Kq(2q)}{d^2}$$

$$F_{BC} = \frac{2Kq(Q)}{(d-x)^2}$$

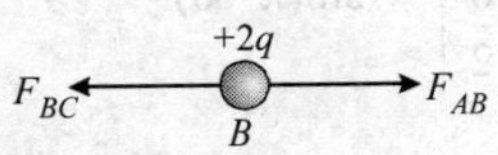

Figure 1.27

For equilibrium of B these forces are balanced so we use

$$F_{AB} = F_{BC}$$

$$\Rightarrow \quad \frac{2KqQ}{(d-x)^2} = \frac{Kq(2q)}{d^2}$$

$$\Rightarrow \quad \frac{Q}{(d-x)^2} = \frac{q}{d^2} \qquad \ldots(1.5)$$

Solving equation-(1.4) and (1.5), we get

$$\frac{2qx^2}{d^2} = \frac{q}{d^2}(d-x)^2$$

$$\Rightarrow \quad 2x^2 = (d-x)^2$$

$$\Rightarrow \quad 2x^2 = d^2 + x^2 - 2xd$$

$$\Rightarrow \quad x^2 + 2xd - d^2 = 0$$

$$\Rightarrow \quad x = (\sqrt{2}-1)d \quad \text{or} \quad -d(1+\sqrt{2})$$

The negative value of x implies that the particle C will lie toward left of A at a distance $(\sqrt{2}-1)d$ from A (as x was measured from A)

For the position $x = x_1 = (\sqrt{2}-1)d$, $Q = Q_1 = -q(6-\sqrt{2})$

and for $x = x_2 = -d(\sqrt{2}+1)$, $Q = Q_2 = -q(6+4\sqrt{2})$

Thus the two possibilities obtained above are shown in figure-1.28 below

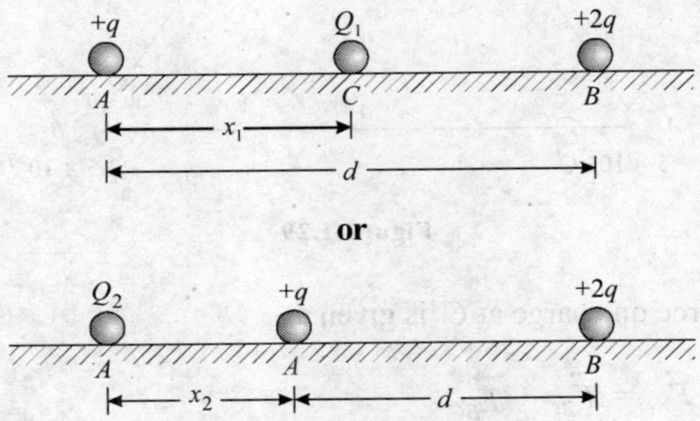

Figure 1.28

But second possibility will not be correct for equilibrium of both charges A and B as direction of forces are not opposite on A as Q_2 is negative.

Illustrative Example 1.4

Three charges of magnitudes 5.0×10^{-7} C, -2.5×10^{-7} C and 1.0×10^{-7} C are fixed at the three corners A, B and C of an equilateral triangle of side 5.0 cm. Find the electric force on the charge at vertex C due to the rest two.

Solution

Figure-1.29 shows the situation described in the question in which forces acting on charge at C are also shown. These forces are given by Coulomb's law as

$$F_{AC} = \frac{Kq_Aq_C}{d^2}$$

$$\Rightarrow \quad F_{AC} = \frac{9\times10^9 \times 5\times10^{-7} \times 1\times10^{-7}}{(.05)^2}$$

$$\Rightarrow \quad F_{AC} = 0.18\,\text{N}$$

Force on C due to B is given as

$$F_{BC} = \frac{Kq_Bq_C}{d^2}$$

$$\Rightarrow \quad F_{BC} = \frac{9\times10^9 \times -2.5\times10^{-7} \times 1\times10^{-7}}{(.05)^2}$$

$$\Rightarrow \quad F_{BC} = -0{\cdot}09\,\text{N}$$

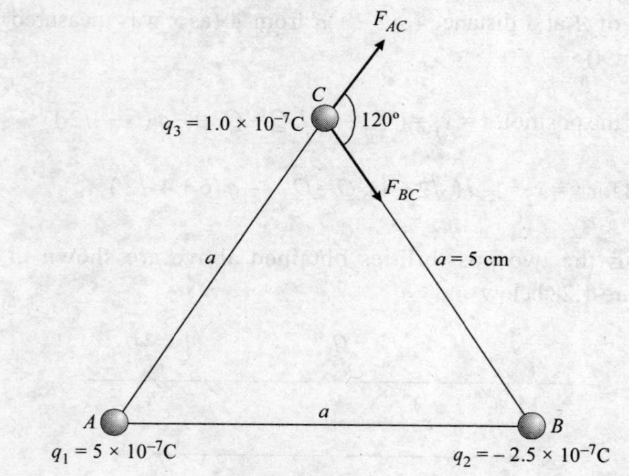

Figure 1.29

Net force on charge at C is given as

$$\vec{F}_{Net} = \vec{F}_{AC} + \vec{F}_{BC}$$

$$\Rightarrow \quad \left|\vec{F}_{Net}\right| = \sqrt{(F_{AC})^2 + (F_{BC})^2 + 2(F_{AC})(F_{BC})\cos(120^\circ)}$$

$$\Rightarrow \quad \left|\vec{F}_{Net}\right| = 0.156\,\text{N}$$

Illustrative Example 1.5

A particle A having with a charge $q = 5 \times 10^{-7}$ C is clamped in a vertical wall. A small ball B of mass 100 g and having equal charge is suspended by an insulating thread of length 30 cm from the wall. The point of suspension is 30 cm above the particle A as shown in figure-1.30. Find the angle θ which the thread makes with the wall in equilibrium. Take $g = 10$ m/s^2.

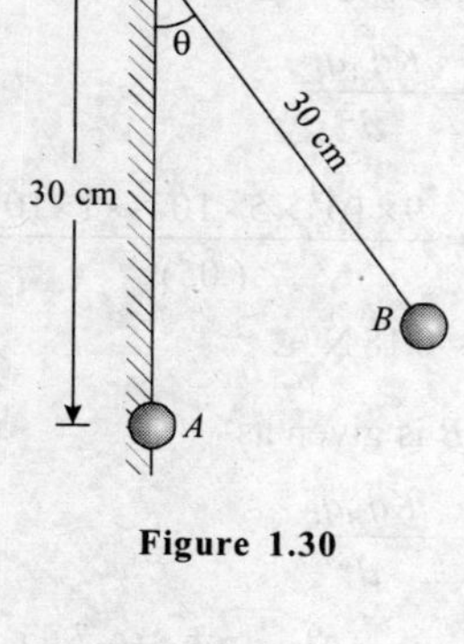

Figure 1.30

Solution

The forces acting on the ball B in equilibrium are shown in figure-1.31(a) and FBD of ball B is shown in figure-1.31(b).

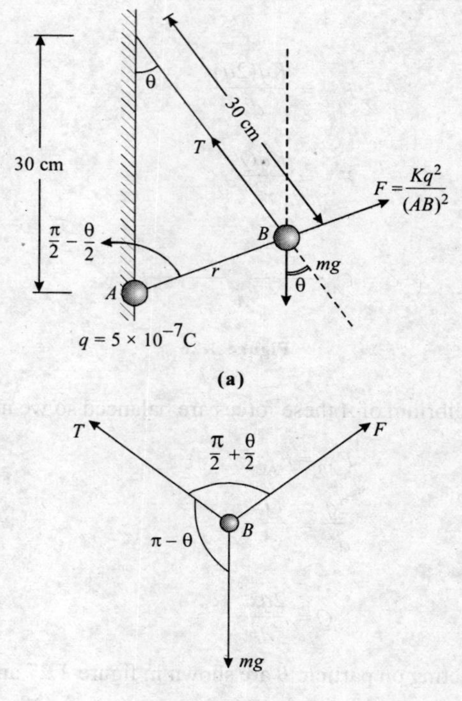

Figure 1.31

In FBD of ball B as it is in equilibrium under the influence of three forces, we use Lami's theorem, which gives

$$\frac{mg}{\sin\left(\frac{\pi}{2} + \frac{\theta}{2}\right)} = \frac{F}{\sin(\pi - \theta)}$$

$$\Rightarrow \quad \frac{mg}{\cos\frac{\theta}{2}} = \frac{Kq^2}{(2 \times 0\cdot 30) \times \sin\frac{\theta}{2} \times \sin\theta}$$

$$\Rightarrow \quad \frac{mg}{\cos\frac{\theta}{2}} = \frac{Kq^2}{(0\cdot 60)\sin\frac{\theta}{2} \times 2\sin\frac{\theta}{2}\cos\frac{\theta}{2}}$$

$$\Rightarrow \quad \sin^2\frac{\theta}{2} = \frac{Kq^2}{2\text{mg}(0\cdot 60)}$$

$$\Rightarrow \quad \sin\left(\frac{\theta}{2}\right) = \sqrt{\left(\frac{9 \times 10^9 \times \left(5 \times 10^{-7}\right)^2}{2 \times 0.1 \times 10 \times 0.60}\right)}$$

$$\Rightarrow \quad \theta = 17^\circ$$

Illustrative Example 1.6

Ten charged particles are kept fixed clamped on the X axis at points $x = 10$ mm, 20 mm, 30 mm, … 100 mm. The first particle has a charge 10^{-8} C, the second 8×10^{-8} C, the third 27×10^{-8} C and so on. The tenth particle has a charge 100×10^{-8} C. Find the magnitude of electric force acting on a 1 C charge placed at the origin.

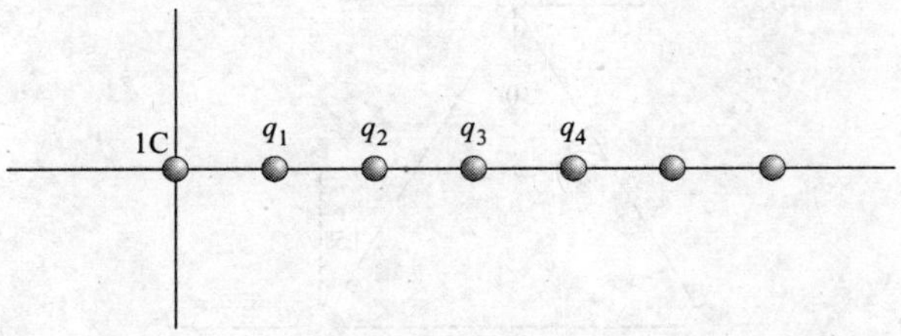

Figure 1.32

Solution

Force on 1 C charge at origin can be given by sum of forces acting on it due to all the ten charges by Coulomb's law as

$$F_{net} = \frac{Kq_1 \times 1}{(10\times10^{-3})^2} + \frac{Kq_2 \times 1}{(20\times10^{-3})^2} + \frac{Kq_3 \times 1}{(30\times10^{-3})^2} + \ldots$$

$$\Rightarrow \quad F_{net} = \frac{K\times10^{-8}}{10^{-4}}\left[\frac{1^3}{1^2}+\frac{2^3}{2^2}+\frac{3^3}{3^2}+\ldots\frac{10^3}{10^2}\right)$$

$$\Rightarrow \quad F_{net} = 9\times10^9\times10^{-4}\times55$$

$$\Rightarrow \quad F_{net} = 4.95\times10^7\,\text{N}$$

 # Illustrative Example 1.7

Two positive charges q_1 and q_2 are located at the points with position vectors $\vec{r}_1$ and $\vec{r}_2$. Find the magnitude of a negative charge q_3 and the position vector $\vec{r}_3$ of the point at which it is to be placed for the force acting on each of the three charges to be equal to zero.

Solution

Figure-1.33 shows the situation described in the question. As already discussed for equilibrium under electrostatic forces three charges must be collinear.

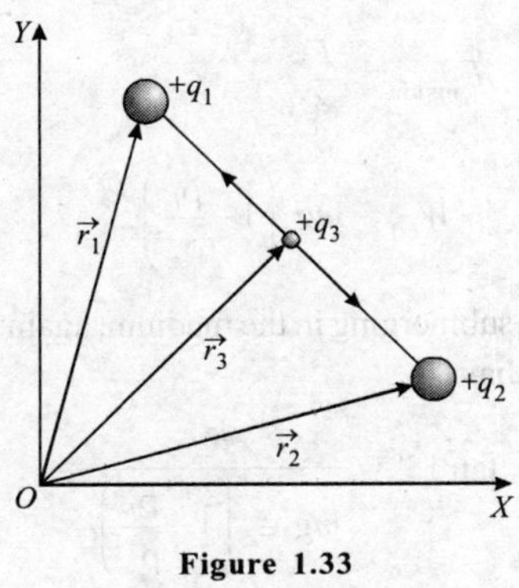

Figure 1.33

In above situation for equilibrium of q_3 force on it due to the two side charges must be zero, so we have

$$\frac{Kq_2q_3(\vec{r}_2-\vec{r}_3)}{|r_2-r_3|^3} + \frac{Kq_1q_3(\vec{r}_1-\vec{r}_3)}{|r_1-r_3|^3} = 0 \qquad \ldots(1.6)$$

As the charges are collinear, we have

$$\frac{\vec{r}_2-\vec{r}_3}{|r_2-r_3|} = -\frac{\vec{r}_1-\vec{r}_3}{|r_1-r_3|}$$

Thus from equation-(1.6), we get

$$\frac{q_2}{|r_2-r_3|^2} = \frac{q_1}{|r_1-r_3|^2}$$

$$\Rightarrow \quad \sqrt{q_2}\,(\vec{r}_1-\vec{r}_3) = \sqrt{q_1}\,(\vec{r}_3-\vec{r}_2)$$

$$\Rightarrow \quad \vec{r}_3 = \frac{\sqrt{q_2}\,\vec{r}_1+\sqrt{q_1}\,\vec{r}_2}{\sqrt{q_1}+\sqrt{q_2}}$$

Now for equilibrium of q_1, force on it due to other two charges must be zero so we have

$$\frac{Kq_1q_3(\vec{r}_1-\vec{r}_3)}{|r_1-r_3|^3} + \frac{Kq_1q_2(\vec{r}_2-\vec{r}_1)}{|r_2-r_1|^3} = 0$$

$$\Rightarrow \quad q_3 = \frac{q_2}{|r_2-r_1|^2}\times|r_1-r_3|^2 \qquad \ldots(1.7)$$

Substituting the value of r_3 in above equation, we get

$$q_3 = \frac{-q_1q_2}{(\sqrt{q_1}+\sqrt{q_2})^2}$$

 # Illustrative Example 1.8

Three small balls, each of mass 10 gm are suspended separately from common point by silk threads, each one meter long. The balls are identically charged and hang at the corners of an equilateral triangle of side 0.1 metre. Find the charge on each ball ?

Solution

Figure-1.34 shows the situation described in the question. The different forces on ball A are also shown in figure-1.34.

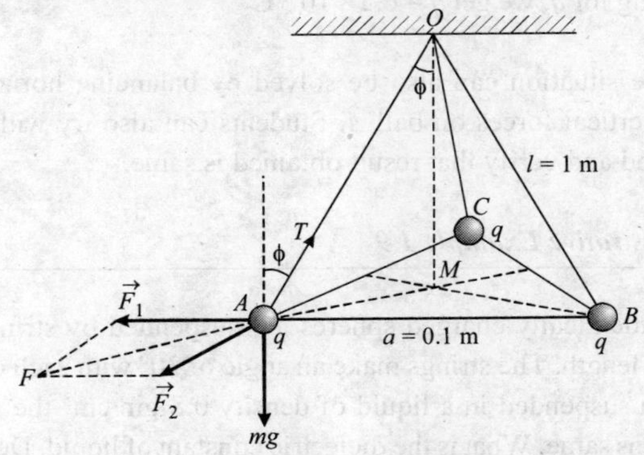

Figure 1.34

The force of repulsion on A due to charge q at B is given as

$$F_1 = \frac{Kqq}{(AB)^2}$$

$$\Rightarrow \quad F_1 = \frac{Kq^2}{(0.1)^2} \text{ along } BA \qquad \ldots(1.8)$$

The force of repulsion on A due to charge q at C is given as

$$F_2 = \frac{Kq^2}{(0.1)^2} \text{ along } CA \qquad \ldots(1.9)$$

The force of gravity acting downward is given as

$$W = mg$$

$$\Rightarrow \quad W = 0.01 \times 9.8 = 0.098\text{ N} \qquad \ldots(1.10)$$

The tension T in the thread is along AO

The resultant of F_1 and F_2 is F which is acting along MA and it is given as

$$F = F_1 \cos 30 + F_2 \cos 30 = \sqrt{3}\, F \qquad [F = |\vec{F}_1| \neq |\vec{F}_2|]$$

Here M is the centroid of equilateral triangle ABC.

If we drop a perpendicular on the base of triangle ABC from O, then it passes through M. Taking moments of all the forces about O, we have

$$(mg) \cdot AM = F \cdot OM \qquad \ldots(1.11)$$

Substituting the values, we get

$$(0.01 \times 9.8)\left(\frac{2}{3} \times 0.1 \times \cos 30\right)$$

$$= \frac{K\sqrt{3}q^2}{(0.1)^2} \times \left\{(1)^2 - \left(\frac{2}{3} \times 0.1 \times \cos 30\right)^2\right\}^{1/2}$$

and we also have

$$OM = [(OA)^2 - (AM)^2]^{1/2}$$

Solving for q, we get $q = 6.2 \times 10^{-8}$ C

Above situation can also be solved by balancing horizontal and vertical forces on ball A. Students can also try with that method and verify that result obtained is same.

Illustrative Example 1.9

Two identically charged spheres are suspended by strings of equal length. The strings make an angle of 30° with each other. When suspended in a liquid of density 0.8 gm/cm^3 the angle remains same. What is the dielectric constant of liquid. Density of sphere = 1.6 gm/cm^3.

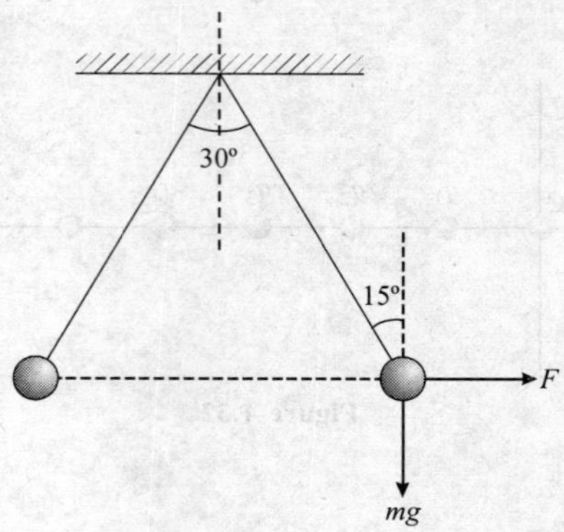

Figure 1.35

Solution

When set up shown in figure-1.35 is in air, we have

$$\tan 15° = \frac{F}{mg} \qquad \ldots(1.12)$$

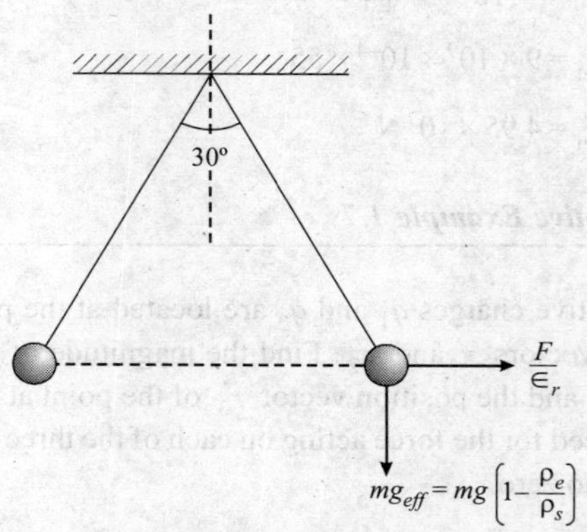

Figure 1.36

When set up is immersed in the medium as shown in figure-1.36, the electric force experienced by the ball will reduce to F_{inside} and the effective gravitational force will be changed to W_{eff} given as

$$F_{\text{inside}} = \frac{F}{\epsilon_r}$$

and

$$W_{\text{eff}} = mg\left(1 - \frac{\rho_l}{\rho_s}\right).$$

Thus now after submerging in the medium, again for equilibrium of spheres we have

$$\tan 15° = \frac{F}{mg\,\epsilon_r\left(1 - \frac{\rho_l}{\rho_s}\right)}$$

$$\Rightarrow \quad \epsilon_r = \frac{1}{1 - \frac{\rho_l}{\rho_s}} = 2$$

Illustrative Example 1.10

A ring of radius R with a uniformly distributed charge q as shown in figure-1.37. A charge q_0 is now placed at the centre of the ring. Find the increment in the tension in ring.

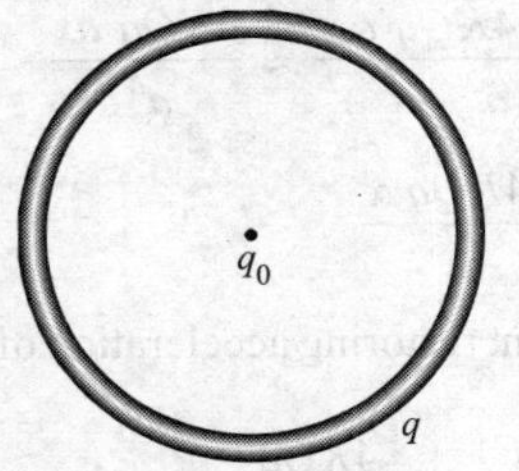

Figure 1.37

Solution

Initially when q_0 was not placed there was some tension in the ring. This was due to the repulsion of the already present charges on ring. When q_0 is placed the repulsion will increase. And hence tension will increase. The increment in tension ΔT will therefore balance the repulsion due to q_0.

To determine the tension increment we consider an infinitesimal element of ring subtending angle $d\theta$ at centre as shown in figure-1.38.

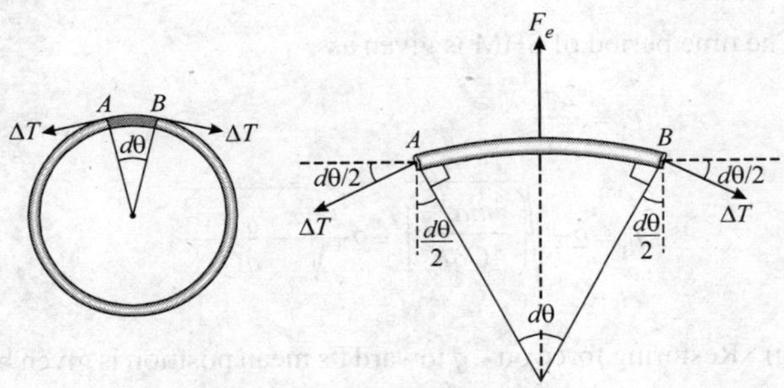

Figure 1.38

The element is now shown exaggerated. For equilibrium of this segment, we have

$$F_e = 2\Delta T \sin\left(\frac{d\theta}{2}\right) \qquad \ldots(1.13)$$

Where F_e is the electric repulsion on the element due to the charge q_0

Charge on element is given as

$$dq = \frac{q}{2\pi R} \times R d\theta$$

The electric outward force on element is given by Coulomb's law as

$$F_e = \frac{Kq_0 dq}{R^2}$$

$$\Rightarrow \qquad F_e = \frac{K\left(\frac{q}{2\pi R}\right) R d\theta\, q_0}{R^2}$$

Now from equation-(1.13), we can use $\sin(\theta/2) \approx \theta/2$ for $\theta/2$ to be very small, we get

$$\frac{Kqq_0 d\theta}{2\pi R^2} \approx 2\Delta T \frac{d\theta}{2}$$

$$\Rightarrow \qquad \Delta T = \frac{Kqq_0}{2\pi R^2}$$

Illustrative Example 1.11

Four small particles charged with equal positive charges Q each are arranged at the four corners of a horizontal square of side a. A unit positive charge mass m is placed at a point P, at a height h above the centre of the square. What should be the magnitude of charge Q in order that the unit charge remain in equilibrium.

Solution

The situation is shown in figure-1.39(a).

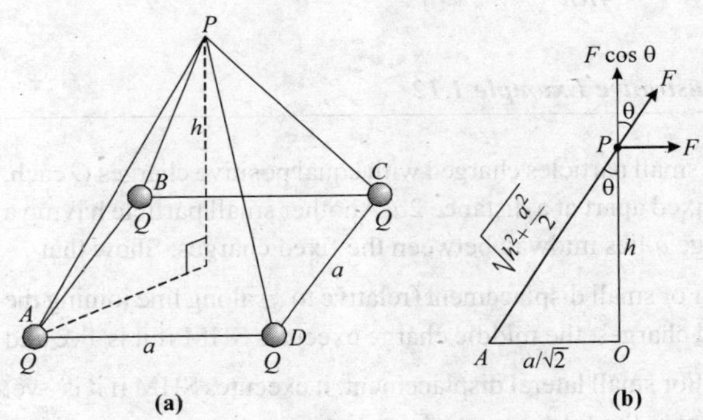

Figure 1.39

Force experienced by unit positive charge placed at P due to a charge Q at vertex A is given by Coulomb's law as

$$F = \frac{K(Q \times 1)}{\left(h^2 + \frac{a^2}{2}\right)}$$

Similarly, equal forces also act on unit positive charge at P due to charge at B, C and D. When these forces are resolved in horizontal and vertical directions, the horizontal components ($F \sin\theta$) cancel each other due to their opposite directions and the net vertical upward force on the unit charge is added up to $4F\cos\theta$.

Thus net upward force on the unit charge is given as

$$F_V = \frac{4KQ}{\left(h^2+\frac{a^2}{2}\right)}\cdot\cos\theta$$

For the equilibrium of unit positive charge at P,

$$F_V = mg$$

$$\Rightarrow \quad \frac{4KQ}{\left(h^2+\frac{a^2}{2}\right)}\cdot\cos\theta = mg \qquad \ldots(1.14)$$

From figure-1.39(b), we have

$$\cos\theta = \left\{\frac{h}{\sqrt{(h^2+a^2/2)}}\right\}$$

Substituting the value of cosθ in equation-(1.14), we get

$$\frac{4KQh}{\left(h^2+\frac{a^2}{2}\right)^{3/2}} = mg$$

$$\Rightarrow \quad Q = \frac{mg}{4Kh}\left(h^2+\frac{a^2}{2}\right)^{3/2} = \frac{\pi\epsilon_0 mg}{h}\left(h^2+\frac{a^2}{2}\right)^{3/2}$$

Illustrative Example 1.12

Two small particles charged with equal positive charges Q each, are fixed apart at a distance $2a$. Another small particle having a charge q lies midway between the fixed charges. Show that

(i) For small displacement (relative to a) along line joining the fixed charges, the middle charge executes SHM if it is +ve and

(ii) For small lateral displacement, it executes SHM if it is –ve. Compare the frequencies of oscillation in the two cases.

Solution

The two situations are shown in figure-1.40 in which the middle charge is displaced along the line joining or normal to it laterally.

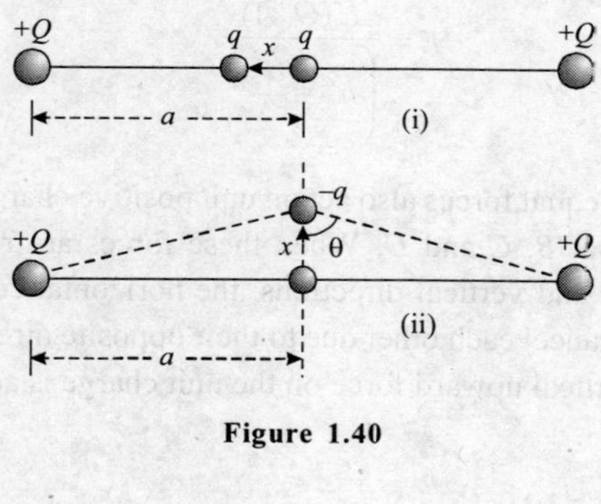

Figure 1.40

(i) Let x be the displacement of the charge $+q$ from the mean position. Now net force acting on the charge q toward its equilibrium position is

$$F = \frac{KQq}{(a-x)^2} - \frac{KQq}{(a+x)^2}$$

$$\Rightarrow \quad F = \frac{4KQq\,ax}{(a^2-x^2)^2} \approx \frac{4KQq\,ax}{a^4} \qquad [\text{As } x \ll a]$$

$$\Rightarrow \quad F = \frac{4KQq\,x}{a^3}$$

After displacement restoring acceleration of particle is given as

$$a = \frac{F}{m} = -\frac{4KQq}{ma^3}x \qquad \ldots(1.15)$$

In above expression we've included a negative sign which shows restoring tendency of acceleration. As acceleration in above equation-(1.15) is directly proportional to displacement of the particle, it verifies that particle is executing SHM. For SHM of a particle, its acceleration is given as

$$a = -\omega^2 x \qquad \ldots(1.16)$$

Comparing equations-(1.15) and (1.16) we get angular frequency of SHM, given as

$$\omega = \sqrt{\left(\frac{4QqK}{ma^3}\right)}.$$

The time period of SHM is given as

$$T_1 = \frac{2\pi}{\omega}$$

$$T_1 = 2\pi\sqrt{\left(\frac{ma^3}{4QqK}\right)} = 2\pi\sqrt{\frac{\pi\epsilon_0 ma^3}{qQ}}$$

(ii) Restoring force on $-q$ toward its mean position is given by the vertical components of the Coulombic forces on it due to the two clamped charges, given as

$$F = \frac{2KQq}{(a^2+x^2)}\cos\theta$$

$$\Rightarrow \quad F = \frac{2KQq}{(a^2+x^2)}\cdot\frac{x}{\sqrt{(a^2+x^2)}}$$

$$\Rightarrow \quad F = \frac{2KQqx}{(a^2+x^2)^{3/2}} \approx \frac{2KQqx}{a^3} \qquad [\text{As } x \ll a]$$

After displacement restoring acceleration of particle is given as

$$a = \frac{F}{m} = -\frac{2KQq}{ma^3}x \qquad \ldots(1.17)$$

In above expression we've included a negative sign which shows restoring tendency of acceleration. As acceleration in above equation-(1.17) is directly proportional to displacement of the particle, it verifies that particle is executing SHM. For SHM of a particle, its acceleration is given as

$$a = -\omega^2 x \quad \ldots (1.18)$$

Comparing equations-(1.17) and (1.18) we get angular frequency of SHM, given as

$$\omega = \sqrt{\left(\frac{2QqK}{ma^3}\right)}$$

Hence the time period of SHM is given as

$$T_2 = \frac{2\pi}{\omega}$$

$$T_2 = 2\pi\sqrt{\left(\frac{ma^3}{2QqK}\right)} = 2\pi\sqrt{\frac{2\pi \in_0 ma^3}{qQ}} \quad \ldots (1.19)$$

Comparing the two frequencies of SHM in cases (i) and (ii) we have

$$\frac{n_1}{n_2} = \frac{T_1}{T_2} = \sqrt{2}$$

Web Reference at www.physicsgalaxy.com

Age Group - Grade 11 & 12 | Age 17-19 Years
Section - ELECTROSTATICS
Topic - Electrostatics
Module Number - 1 to 18

Practice Exercise 1.1

(i) Two identical small non conducting balls are charged by rubbing against each other. They are suspended from ceiling rod through two strings of length $L = 20$ cm each. The separation between the suspension points being $d = 5$ cm. In equilibrium the separation between the balls is $r = 3$ cm. Find the mass m of each ball and the tension in the strings. The charge on each ball has magnitude 2×10^{-8} C.

[7.96g, 7.72×10^{-2} N]

(ii) Two positively charged small particles, each of mass 1.7×10^{-27} kg and carrying a charge of 1.6×10^{-19} C are placed apart at a separation r. If each one experiences a repulsive force equal to its weight, find their separation.

[0.117 m]

(iii) Two free particles carrying charges $+q$ and $+4q$ are placed apart at a distance l. Find the magnitude, sign and location of a third charge which makes the system in equilibrium.

[$\frac{l}{3}, \frac{4q}{9}$]

(iv) A charge Q is to be divided on two small objects. What should be the value of the charges on the objects so that the force between the objects will be maximum.

[$\frac{Q}{2}, \frac{Q}{2}$]

(v) Three charges q_1, q_2 and q_3 are shown in figure-1.41. Determine the net force acting on charge q_1. The charges and separation are given as $q_1 = -1.0 \times 10^{-6}$ C, $q_2 = +3.0 \times 10^{-6}$ C, and $q_3 = -2.0 \times 10^{-6}$ C, $r_{12} = 15$ cm, $r_{13} = 10$ cm and $\theta = 30°$.

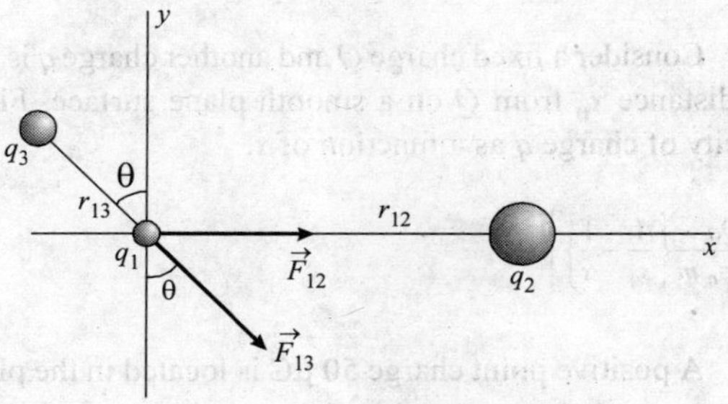

Figure 1.41

[2.64 N]

(vi) Three Charges of magnitude 100 μC are placed at the corners A, B and C of an equilateral triangle of side 4 m. If the charge at A and C are positive and the one at point B is negative, what is the magnitude and direction of total force acting on charge at C?

[5.625 N]

(vii) Two negative charges of unit magnitude and a positive charge q are placed along a straight line. At what position and for what value of q will the system be in equilibrium ? Check whether it is stable, unstable or neutral equilibrium.

[mid point, 0.25 C]

(viii) A charge Q is placed at each of two opposite corners of a square and a charge $-q$ is placed at each of the remaining two corners. If the resultant force on Q is zero, how are Q and q related.

[$Q = -2\sqrt{2}\,q$]

(ix) Two balls of the same radius and weight are suspended on threads so that their surface are in contact. A charge of $q_0 = 4 \times 10^{-7}$ C is given to the balls which makes them repel each other and diverge to an angle of 60°. Find the mass of the balls if the distance of balls from the point of suspension to the centre of ball is 20 cm. Find the density of the material of the balls if the angle of divergence becomes 54° when the balls are immersed in kerosene of density 800 kg m^{-3}. dielectric constant of kerosene is $\varepsilon_r = 2$

[1.592 g, 2559 kg/m^3]

(x) Two equal positive point charges are separated by a distance $2a$. A point test charge is located in a plane which is normal to the line joining these charges and midway between them.

(a) Calculate the radius r of the circle of symmetry in this plane for which the force on the test charge has a maximum value.

(b) What is the direction of this force, assuming a positive test charge ?

[$a/\sqrt{2}$, radial and away from the center]

(xi) Consider a fixed charge Q and another charge q is placed at a distance x_0 from Q on a smooth plane surface. Find the velocity of charge q as a function of x.

[$\left[\dfrac{Qq}{2\pi\epsilon_0 m}\left\{\dfrac{1}{x_0}-\dfrac{1}{x}\right\}\right]^{1/2}$]

(xii) A positive point charge 50 μC is located in the plane xy at the position vector $r_0 = 2\hat{i} + 3\hat{j}$, where $\hat{i}$ and $\hat{j}$ are the unit vectors of the x and y axis. Find the vector of the electric field strength $\vec{E}$ and its magnitude at the point with radius vector $\vec{r} = 8\hat{i} - 5\hat{j}$. Here $\vec{r}_0$ and $\vec{r}$ are expressed in meter.

[4.5 kV/m]

(xiii) Four point charges, each of charge $+q$, are rigidly fixed at the four corners of a square planar soap film of side 'a'. The surface tension of the soap film is σ. If the he system of charges and planar film are in equilibrium, then side of square is given as

$$a = k\left[\frac{q^2}{\sigma}\right]^{1/N}$$, find the values of k and N.

[$\left[\dfrac{1}{4\pi\epsilon_0}\left(1+\dfrac{1}{2\sqrt{2}}\right)\right]^{1/3}$, 3]

(xiv) Two identical beads each having a mass m and charge q. When placed in a hemispherical bowl of radius R with frictionless, non-conducting walls, the beads move, and at equilibrium they are a distance R apart (figure-1.42). Determine the charge on each bead.

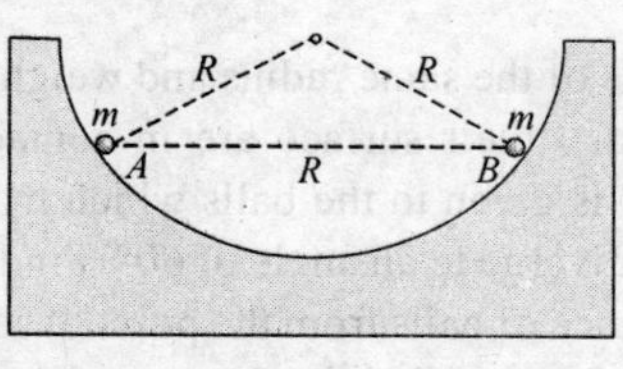

Figure 1.42

[$\left(\dfrac{4\pi\epsilon_0 mgR^2}{\sqrt{3}}\right)^{1/2}$]

1.3 Electric Field

When a charge is brought close to another fixed charge then it experiences some force on it due to the presence of the fixed charge. This region in surrounding of a charge where any other charge experiences a force is called the electric field of the charge. In other words we can say that electric field is the space surrounding an electric charge q in which another charge q' experiences an electrostatic force of attraction, or repulsion.

Electric field is measured as a vector quantity which has a direction and magnitude which is called strength or intensity of electric field. The direction of electric field is radially outwards in surrounding of a positive charge and is radially inwards for a negative charge as shown in the figure-1.43.

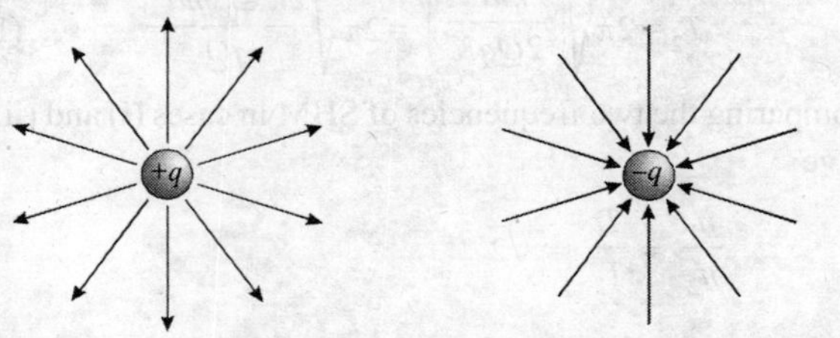

Electric field for a positive charge Electric field for a negative charge

Figure 1.43

For electric field there are some points always to be kept in mind for understanding its applications in different situations. These are

(1) Electric field can be defined as a space surrounding a charge in which another '*static*' charge experiences a force on it.

(2) A moving charge can experience a force by magnetic fields also thus moving charges cannot be used to detect the presence of electric field whereas magnetic field does not exert force on static charges.

(3) In a region of electric field if a positive charge is placed, it exerts a force on the charge in the direction of electric field whereas on a negative charge the direction of force is opposite to the direction of electric field as shown in figure-1.44

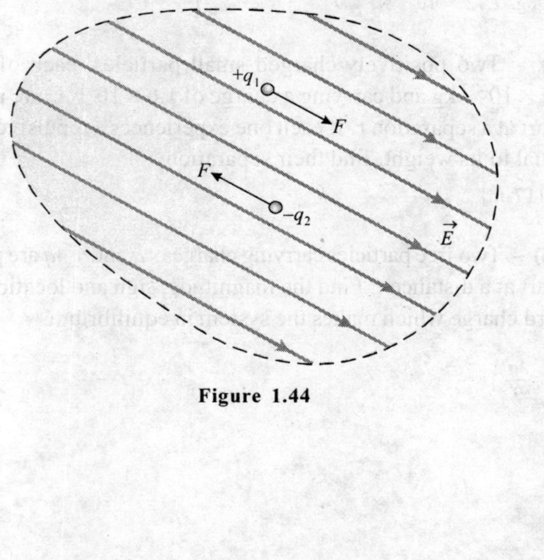

Figure 1.44

(4) It is important to note that with every charge particle, there is an electric field associated which extends up to infinity and this field is not affected by presence of any other charges or bodies in surrounding.

(5) No charged particle experiences force due to its own electric field.

1.3.1 Strength of Electric Field

Intensity or strength of electric field at a point in a region where electric field is present can be defined as the force experienced by a unit charge placed at that point. The unit used for measurement of electric field strength is newton per coulomb or N/C. Another unit used for electric field strength is volt per meter or V/m which we will discuss and analyze later.

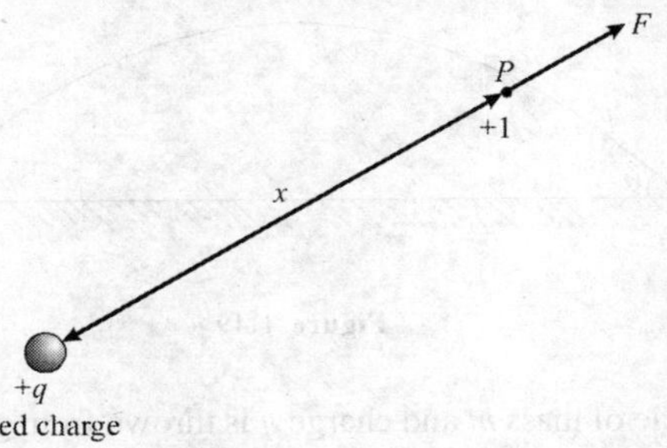

Figure 1.45

As shown in figure-1.45, at a distance x from a fixed point charge q, if we wish to find the electric field strength at point P which is located at a distance x from the charge, we place $a + 1$C charge at P and find a force on it due to $+q$ which can be given as

$$F = \frac{Kq(+1)}{x^2} = \frac{Kq}{x^2} \qquad \dots(1.20)$$

Here equation-(1.20) gives the magnitude of electric field strength at point P due to charge $+q$. But calculation of electric field is not very easy like this if it is not a point charge. Let us consider the an example to understand this.

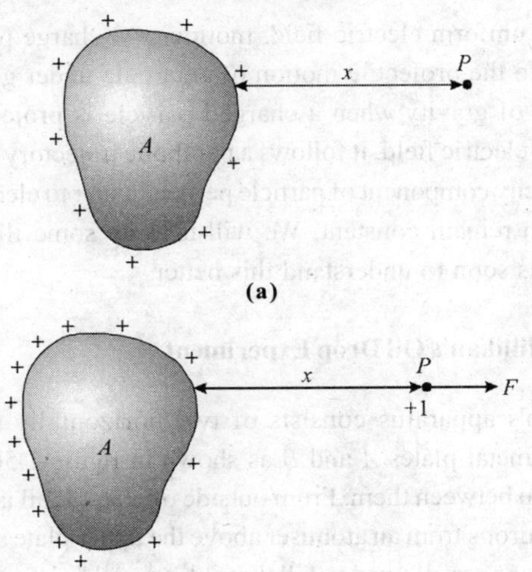

Figure 1.46

Figure-1.46(a) shows a metal body A, which has charges distributed on its surface. Here we wish to calculate electric field strength at point P at a distance x from its surface. For this if we place +1C charge at point P, as shown in figure-1.46(b), we can see that due to repulsion of +1C charge, charge induction takes place on the body and the distribution of charge on body surface changes. As most of the positive charges are shifted to back surface of the body due to repulsion, the net force experienced by +1C charge in this case will not give the electric field at point P which was to be determined due to original distribution of charges as shown in figure-1.46(a).

Thus if we want to determine electric field strength at a point due to a point charge such as explained for figure-1.45, the force on +1C charge will give the desired result but if we want to calculate the electric field strength at a point due to charges distributed on a metal body, use of +1C charge at that point will change the distribution of charges on body because of charge induction on the body and it changes the electric field at the point where it was to be determined, and the force on +1C charge in this case will give the electric field strength due to this new charge distribution and not due to the original distribution.

Thus for calculation of electric field at a point in surrounding of extended charged bodies, this method is not appropriate. Now we'll discuss another method of electric field calculation in surrounding of charged metal bodies. Consider the following situation shown in figure-1.47.

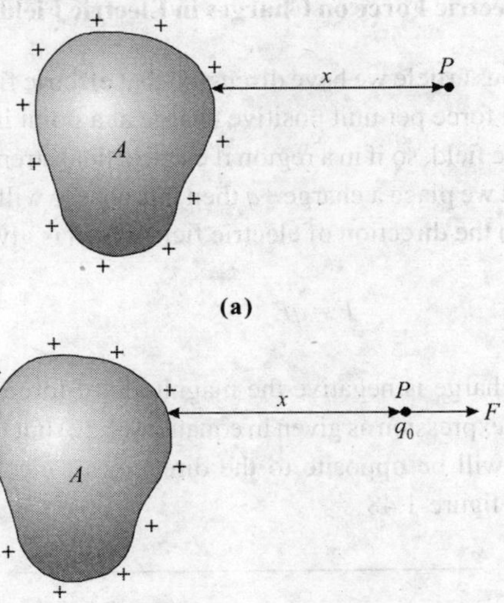

Figure 1.47

The situation shown above is similar to that of previous case. Now at point P we wish to determine the electric field strength, for this at point P we place a very small positive charge q_0 as shown in figure-1.47(b). This charge q_0 is considered to be so small that it can not produce any significant force on any charge on body to change its charge distribution. Now if we find force on this charge due to the body, if it is F then the force per unit charge at point P can be given as

$$E_P = \frac{F}{q_0} \quad \ldots(1.21)$$

As the charge q_0 is not producing any induction effects on the body, the electric field calculated as given in equation-(1.21) will be the electric field due to original charge distribution on the body. Here the charge q_0 used in this analysis is called a test charge. So we can define as test charge as *"a very small positive charge which does not produce its significant electric field in surrounding"*.

Thus electric field strength at point in space can be defined in general as *"Electric field strength at any point in space to be the electrostatic force per unit charge on a test charge."*

If a charge q placed at a point in electric field, experiences a net force F on it, then electric field strength at that point can be expressed as

$$\vec{E} = \lim_{q \to 0} \frac{\vec{F}}{q}$$

$$\Rightarrow \quad \vec{E} = \frac{\vec{F}}{q_0}$$

Here q_0 is the test charge.

1.3.2 Electric Force on Charges in Electric Field

In previous article we have discussed that electric field strength gives the force per unit positive charge at a point in the region of electric field, so if in a region if electric field strength is E and at a point we place a charge $+q$ then this charge will experience a force in the direction of electric field which is given as

$$F = qE \quad \ldots(1.22)$$

Even if charge is negative the magnitude of force is given by the same expression as given in equation-(1.22) but the direction of force will be opposite to the direction of electric field as shown in figure-1.48

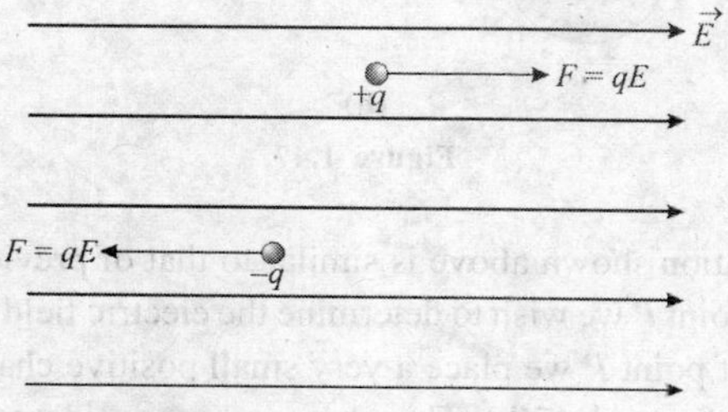

Figure 1.48

1.3.3 Motion of Charge Particle in Electric Field

In uniform electric field when a positively charge particle is released from rest it starts moving in the direction of electric field with uniform acceleration given as

$$a = \frac{qE}{m}$$

If a particle is moving in a uniform electric field along the direction of electric field then we can use speed equations for constant acceleration for analysis of its motion. If particle is thrown in a uniform electric field in the direction different from the direction of electric field, it will follow a parabolic trajectory like a projectile motion. Consider the example shown in figure-1.49.

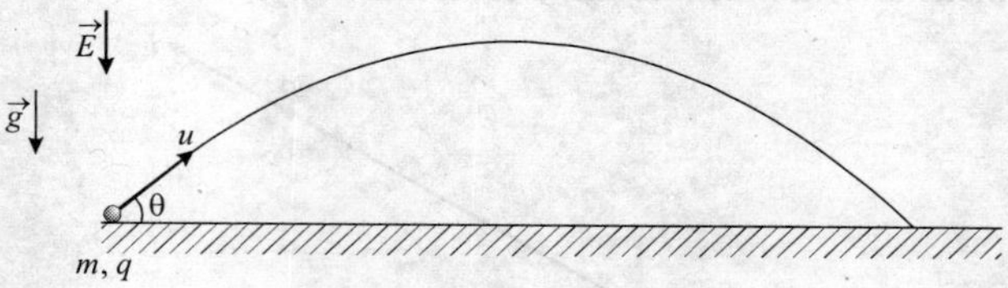

Figure 1.49

A particle of mass m and charge q is thrown from ground at an angle θ with initial speed u. In space a uniform electric field strength E exist in vertically downward direction as shown. After projection during motion we can consider the effective gravitational acceleration on the particle can be given as

$$g_{eff} = g + \frac{qE}{m} \quad \ldots(1.23)$$

In above case we can use all the concepts of projectile motion by replacing g by g_{eff}. If electric field in space exist in upward direction, effective acceleration due to gravity can be given as

$$g_{eff} = g - \frac{qE}{m} \quad \ldots(1.24)$$

Thus in uniform electric field, motion of a charge particle is similar to the projectile motion of a particle under gravity. In absence of gravity when a charged particle is projected in a uniform electric field, it follows a parabolic trajectory such that the velocity component of particle perpendicular to electric field direction remain constant. We will take up some illustrative examples soon to understand this better.

1.3.4 Millikan's Oil Drop Experiment

Millikan's apparatus consists of two horizontally mounted parallel metal plates A and B as shown in figure-1.50, with a small gap between them. From outside of plate A, oil is sprayed in small drops from an atomiser above the upper plate and a few of the drops are allowed to fall through a small hole in this plate as shown. A light beam is incident between the plates, and a telescope is used to see this motion of oil drops between the plates. In free fall motion oil drops attains terminal velocity due to air friction. It is found that some of the oil drops are electrically charged because of friction at orifice of atomiser. The drops can also be charged by many other ways. The drops are usually negatively charged in this experiment.

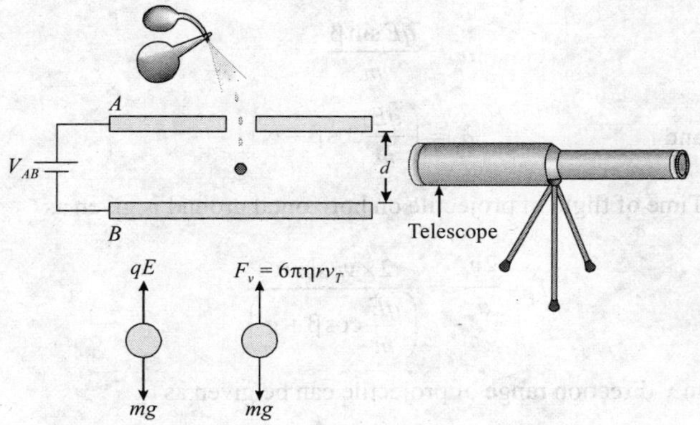

Figure 1.50

Suppose a drop has a negative charge q and plates are maintained at a potential difference by a battery which produces a downward electric field $E = V_{AB}/d$ between the plates. The forces on the drop are its weight mg and the upward force qE, Battery voltage is adjusted in such a way that the drop comes in equilibrium between the plates. So when stationary drops are observed by telescope then we can use

$$qE = mg$$

$$\Rightarrow \quad q = \frac{mg}{E}$$

If r be the radius of the drop and ρ be the density of oil, then mass of oil drop is given as

$$m = \rho \times \frac{4}{3}\pi r^3$$

$$\Rightarrow \quad q = \frac{4\pi}{3}\frac{\rho r^3 gd}{V_{AB}} \quad \ldots(1.25)$$

Now we switch off the field and allow the drop to fall freely then due to viscosity of air these drops attain terminal velocity very soon. If v_T is the terminal velocity of the oil drop, then by Stoke's law, viscous force on drops is given as

$$F_v = 6\pi\eta r v_T \quad \ldots(1.26)$$

As oil drop falls freely and due to low air density we can neglect the buoyant force exerted by air so in steady motion of drops we can use

$$mg = F_v$$

$$\Rightarrow \quad \frac{4}{3}\pi r^3 \rho g = 6\pi\eta r v_T$$

$$\Rightarrow \quad r = 3\sqrt{\eta v_T / 2\rho g}$$

Substituting the value of r in equation-(1.25), we get

$$q = 18\pi\frac{d}{V_{AB}}\sqrt{\frac{\eta^3 v_T^3}{2\rho g}} \quad \ldots(1.27)$$

Thus by above analysis using Millikan's Experiment the charges on the different drops of different oils can be measured and in this experiment it is found that every drop had a charge equal to some small integral multiple of charge e. That is, drops were observed with charges of e, $2e$, $3e$, ...etc. that verifies the phenomenon of '*Quantisation of Charge*' we've studied in article-1.1.3.

1.4 Electric Field Strength due to a Point Charge

As discussed earlier that every charge produces electric field in its surrounding space, if we consider a point charge $+q$ then in its surrounding at every point electric field exist in radially outward direction. As shown in figure-1.51 if we consider a point P at a distance x from the charge q, the electric field strength at this point P due to the charge is given as

$$E = \frac{F}{q_0} = \frac{1}{q_0}\left(\frac{Kqq_0}{x^2}\right) = \frac{Kq}{x^2} \quad \ldots(1.28)$$

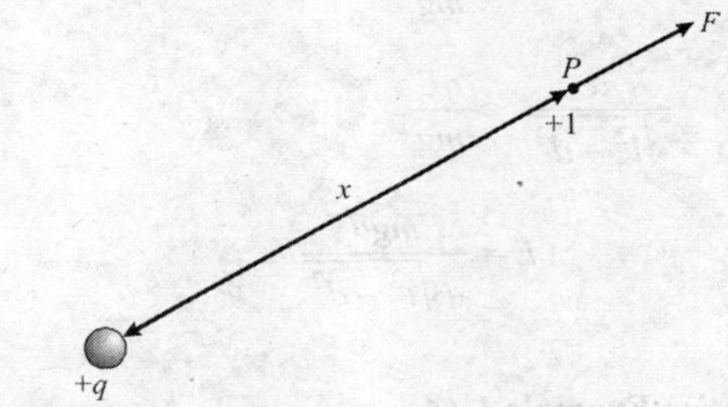

Figure 1.51

If the position vector of point P from the location of charge is given as $\vec{x}$ then the electric field vector at point P due to the charge is given as

$$\vec{E} = \frac{Kq}{x^3}\vec{x} \quad \ldots(1.29)$$

Illustrative Example 1.13

A wooden ball covered with an aluminimum foil having a mass m hangs by a fine silk thread l metre long in a horizontal electric field E. When the ball is given an electric charge q coulomb, it stands out d metre from the vertical line passing through the suspension point of thread. Show that the electric field is given by

$$E = \frac{mgd}{q\sqrt{l^2 - d^2}}$$

Solution

From figure-1.52 we can write for equilibrium of ball

$$T\sin\theta = qE \qquad \ldots(1.30)$$

$$T\cos\theta = mg \qquad \ldots(1.31)$$

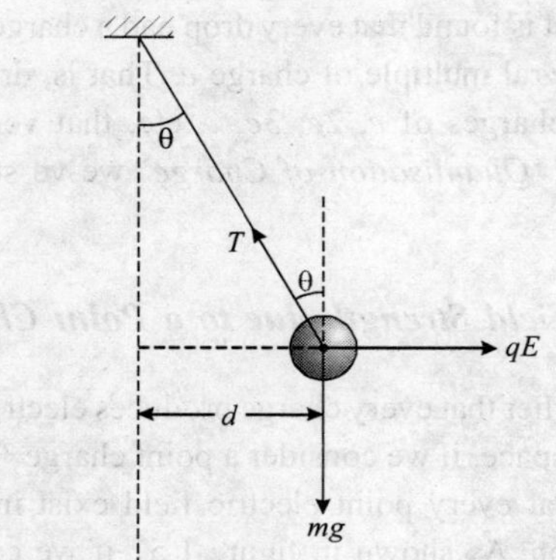

Figure 1.52

From equations-(1.30) and (1.31), we have

$$\tan\theta = \frac{qE}{mg}$$

$$\Rightarrow \quad \frac{d}{\sqrt{l^2-d^2}} = \frac{qE}{mg}$$

$$\Rightarrow \quad E = \frac{mgd}{q\sqrt{l^2-d^2}}$$

Illustrative Example 1.14

A particle of mass m and charge q is thrown with initial velocity v_0 at an angle α with the horizontal. In space there exist an electric field of strength E at angle β with the downward vertical away from the point of projection. Find the time of flight and range of projectile on horizontal ground.

Solution

Figure-1.53 shows the situation described in the question.

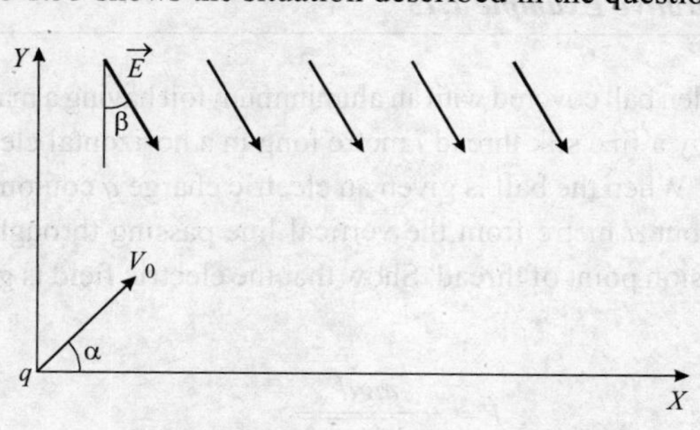

Figure 1.53

In x and y-direction the components of initial velocity of particle v_x and v_y is given as

$$v_x = v_0\cos\alpha$$

$$v_y = v_0\sin\alpha$$

Acceleration of particle in x and y-direction are given as

$$a_x = \frac{qE\sin\beta}{m}$$

and
$$a_y = \left(\frac{qE}{m}\cos\beta + g\right)$$

Time of flight of projectile on horizontal ground is given as

$$T_f = \frac{2v_y}{a_y} = \frac{2\times v_0\sin\alpha}{\left(\frac{qE}{m}\cos\beta+g\right)}$$

In x-direction range of projectile can be given as

$$R = ut + \frac{1}{2}at^2$$

We on substituting the values $u = v_x$ and $a = a_x$, we get the range as

$$R = v_0\cos\alpha\left(\frac{2v_0\sin\alpha}{\frac{qE}{m}\cos\beta+g}\right) + \frac{1}{2}\left(\frac{qE\sin\beta}{m}\right)\left[\left(\frac{2v_0\sin\alpha}{\frac{qE}{m}\cos\beta+g}\right)^2\right]$$

Illustrative Example 1.15

An inclined plane making an angle $\theta = 30°$ with the horizontal is placed in a uniform horizontal electric field E of 100 V/m as shown in figure-1.54. A small block of mass 1 kg and charge 0.01 C is allowed to slide down from rest from a height $h = 1$ m. If the coefficient of friction is 0.2, find the time it will take the block to reach the bottom of incline.

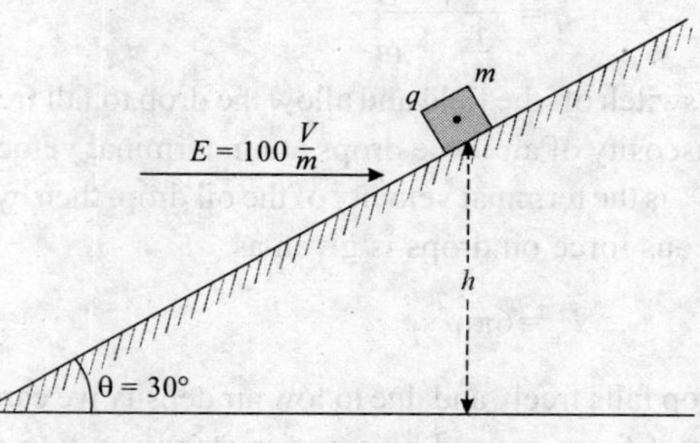

Figure 1.54

Solution

During sliding along the inclined plane, different forces on the block are shown in figure-1.55.

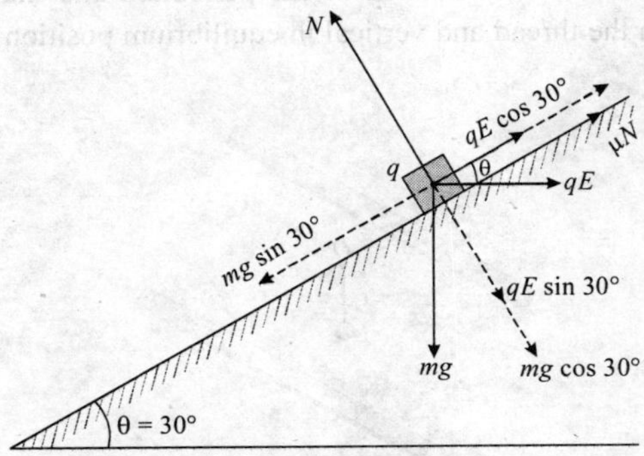

Figure 1.55

As the block is sliding along the incline, all forces on it normal to incline are balanced so we use

$$N = mg\cos 30° + qE\cos 60°$$

During sliding the friction on the block is given as

$$f = \mu N = \mu\, mg\cos 30° + \mu\, qE\cos 60°$$

If a be the acceleration of block during sliding, we can write its motion equation as

$$mg\sin 30° - \mu N - qE\cos 30° = ma$$

$$\Rightarrow \quad a = g\sin 30° - \mu g\cos 30° - \frac{\mu qE}{m}\cos 60° - \frac{qE}{m}\cos 30°$$

$$\Rightarrow \quad a = 9.8\times 0.5 - 0.2\times 9.8\times(\sqrt{3}/2)$$

$$-\frac{0.2\times 0.01\times 100}{1}\times 0.5 - \frac{0.01\times 100}{1}\times\frac{\sqrt{3}}{2}$$

$$\Rightarrow \quad a = 4.9 - 0.98\times 1.732 - 0.10 - 0.5\,5\,1.732$$

$$\Rightarrow \quad a = 4.9 - 1.697 - 0.10 - 0.866 = 2.237\ \text{m/s}^2$$

If the block takes a time t in sliding the distance along incline which is $s = 1/\sin(30°) = 2$, it is given as

$$s = 0 + \frac{1}{2}at^2$$

$$\Rightarrow \quad t = \sqrt{\left(\frac{2\times 2}{a}\right)}$$

$$\Rightarrow \quad t = \sqrt{\left(\frac{4}{2.237}\right)} = 1.345\ \text{s}$$

Illustrative Example 1.16

A ball of mass m with a charge q can rotate in a vertical plane at the end of a string of length l in a uniform electrostatic field whose lines of force are directed upwards. What horizontal velocity must be imparted to the ball in the upper position so that the tension in the string in the lower position of the ball is 15 times than the weight of the ball ?

Solution

The situation described in question is shown in figure-1.56.

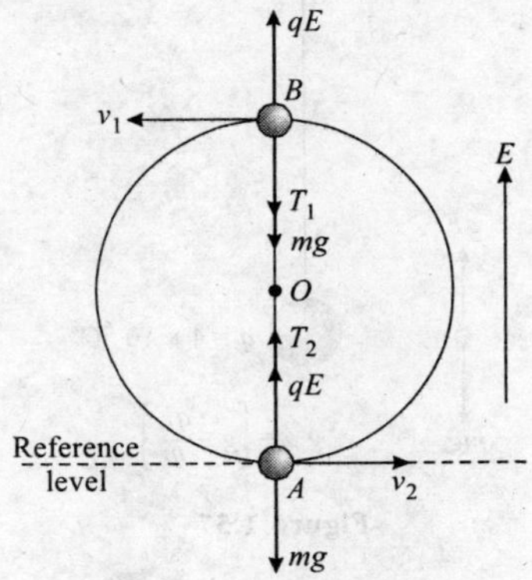

Figure 1.56

By using work energy theorem between position B and A, we have

$$\frac{1}{2}mv_1^2 + 2mgl - 2qEl = \frac{1}{2}mv_2^2 \qquad \text{...(1.32)}$$

For the forces acting on ball at position A we have

$$T + qE = \frac{mv_2^2}{l} + mg$$

$$\Rightarrow \quad lqE = mv_2^2 - 14\,mgl$$

From equation-(1.32) we have

$$qEl + 14\,mgl = mv_1^2 + 4\,mgl - 4\,qEl$$

$$\Rightarrow \quad v_1^2 = \frac{5qE}{m} + \frac{10mg}{m}$$

$$\Rightarrow \quad v_1 = \sqrt{\frac{5qEl}{m} + 10gl}$$

$$\Rightarrow \quad v_1 = \left[\frac{5l}{m}(qE + 2mg)\right]^{1/2}$$

Illustrative Example 1.17

A simple pendulum has a bob of mass $m = 40$ gm and a positive charge $q = 4\times 10^{-6}$ C. It makes 20 oscillation in 45 s. A vertical upward electric field of magnitude $E = 2.5\times 10^4$ N/C is switched on in space. How much time will the simple pendulum now take to complete 20 oscillation.

Solution

Figure-1.57 shows the simple pendulum and the forces acting on the its bob in presence of electric field.

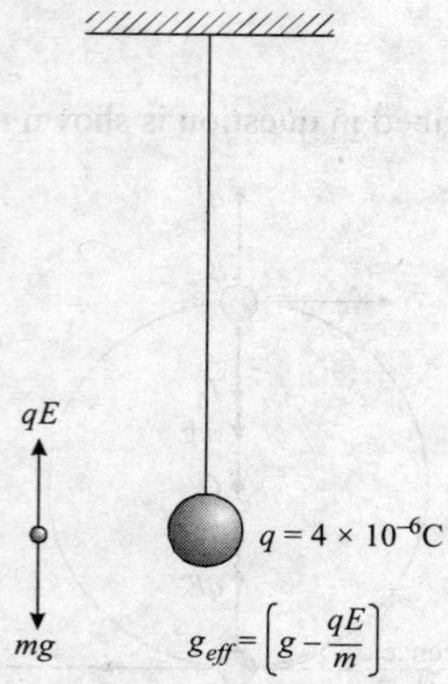

Figure 1.57

Initially when no electric field is present, time period of pendulum is given as

$$T = 2\pi\sqrt{\frac{L}{g}} = \frac{45}{20} \quad \ldots(1.33)$$

After switching on the electric field in the region effective gravity on bob will be given as

$$g_{\text{eff}} = g - \frac{qE}{m}$$

Thus using effective gravity as given above, the new time period of oscillation is given as

$$T' = 2\pi\sqrt{\frac{L}{\left(g - \frac{qE}{m}\right)}} \quad \ldots(1.34)$$

Dividing equation-(1.33) and (1.34), we get

$$\frac{T}{T'} = \sqrt{\frac{g - \frac{qE}{m}}{g}} = \sqrt{1 - \frac{qE}{mg}} = \sqrt{1 - \frac{4\times10^{-6}\times2.5\times10^{4}}{40\times10^{-3}\times10}}$$

$$\Rightarrow \quad T' = 2.6 \text{ s}$$

For 20 oscillation, time taken is given as

$$t = 20 \times 2.6$$

$$t = 52 \text{ s}$$

Illustrative Example 1.18

A bob of mass m carrying a positive charge q is suspended from a light insulating string of length l inside a parallel plate capacitor with its plates making an angle β with the horizontal as shown in figure-1.58. The plates of the capacitor are connected with a battery to establish an electric field E between the plates with its upper plate negatively charged. Find the period of small oscillations of the pendulum and the angle between the thread and vertical in equilibrium position of the bob.

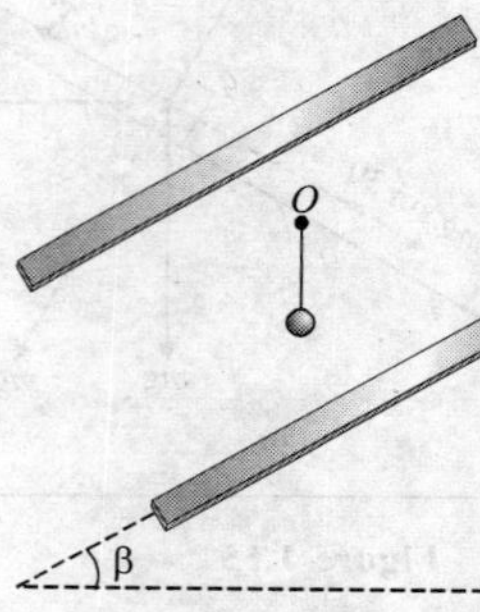

Figure 1.58

Solution

Different forces acting on pendulum bob are shown in figure-1.59.

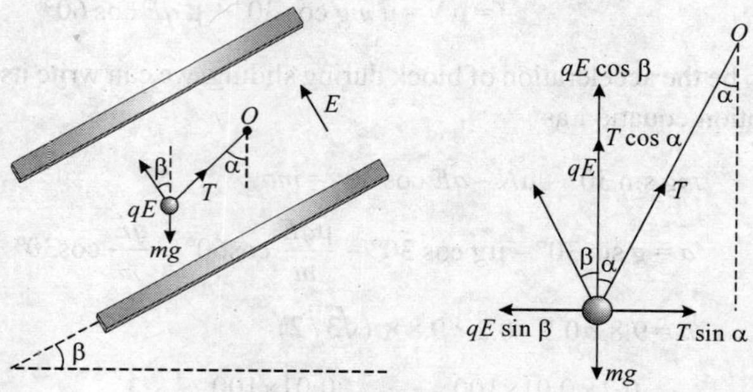

Figure 1.59

For equilibrium of bob, from its FBD in figure-1.59(b), we balance forces on bob in horizontal direction as

$$T\sin\alpha = qE\sin\beta \quad \ldots(1.35)$$

In vertical direction we balance forces which gives

$$T\cos\alpha + qE\cos\beta = mg$$

$$\Rightarrow \quad T\cos\alpha = mg - qE\cos\beta \quad \ldots(1.36)$$

From equations-(1.35) and (1.36), we have

$$\tan\alpha = \frac{qE\sin\beta}{mg - qE\cos\beta}$$

$$\Rightarrow \quad \alpha = \tan^{-1}\left(\frac{qE\sin\beta}{mg - qE\cos\beta}\right) \quad \ldots(1.37)$$

The effective acceleration on the bob due to mg and qE is given as,

$$a = \sqrt{\left[g^2 + \left(\frac{qE}{m}\right)^2 + 2g\left(\frac{qe}{m}\right)\cos(180 - \beta)\right]}$$

$$\Rightarrow \quad a = \sqrt{g^2 + \left(\frac{qE}{m}\right)^2 - 2g\left(\frac{qe}{m}\right)\cos\beta}$$

Time period of pendulum in this state can be given as

$$T = 2\pi\sqrt{\left(\frac{l}{a}\right)}$$

$$\Rightarrow \quad T = 2\pi\left[\frac{l}{\sqrt{\left\{g^2 + \left(\frac{qE}{m}\right)^2 - 2g\left(\frac{qe}{m}\right)\cos\beta\right\}}}\right]^{1/2}$$

Illustrative Example 1.19

A rectangular tank of mass m_0 and charge Q is placed over a smooth horizontal floor. A horizontal electric field E exist in the region. Rain drops are falling vertically in the tank at the constant rate of n drops per second. Mass of each drop is m. Find velocity of tank as function of time.

Solution

In above situation there are two forces acting on the tank during motion. First is the electric force which is the driving force on tank and other is the opposing force due to increase in weight of the tank. If v be the velocity of tank at an instant $t = t$ then the extra momentum gained per second by the tank due to rain fall is mnv which can be considered here the opposition force on tank due to thrust of rainfall on it. Thus net force on tank during motion can be given as

$$F_{net} = QE - mnv$$

$$\Rightarrow \quad (m_0 + mnt)\frac{dv}{dt} = QE - mnv$$

$$\Rightarrow \quad \int_0^v \frac{dv}{QE - mnv} = \int_0^t \frac{dt}{m_0 + mnt}$$

$$\Rightarrow \quad \ln\left(\frac{QE}{QE - mnv}\right) = \ln\left(\frac{m_0 + mnt}{m_0}\right)$$

$$\Rightarrow \quad \frac{QE}{QE - mnv} = \frac{m_0 + mnt}{m_0}$$

$$\Rightarrow \quad v = QE\left(\frac{t}{m_0 + mnt}\right)$$

Students can also try solving this question with the method of impulse momentum equation explained in the chapter of system of particle by considering momentum of tank at time t and $t + dt$ and then integrate the equation thus obtained. That will also give the same result as above.

Web Reference at www.physicsgalaxy.com
Age Group - Grade 11 & 12 | Age 17-19 Years
Section - ELECTROSTATICS
Topic - Electrostatics
Module Number - 19 to 26

Practice Exercise 1.2

(i) A block of mass m with a positive charge q is placed on a smooth horizontal table which terminates in a vertical wall as shown in figure-1.60. The distance of the block from the wall is d. A horizontal electric field E is switched on in the space in rightward direction. Consider elastic collisions with the wall, find the time period of resulting oscillatory motion of the block. Analyse the motion and state if it is a simple harmonic motion.

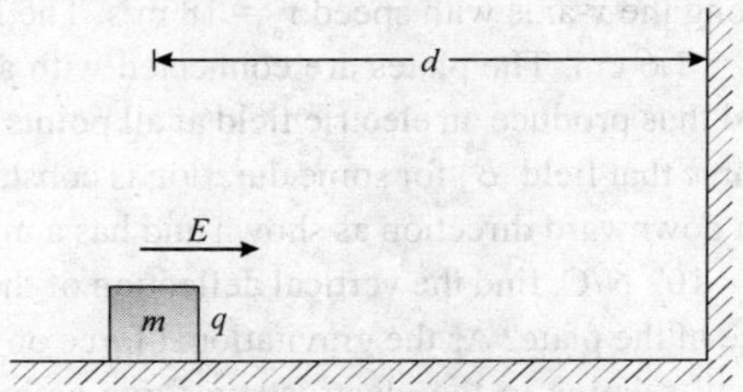

Figure 1.60

$[2\sqrt{\frac{2md}{qE}}]$

(ii) Two horizontal parallel conducting plates are kept at a separation $d = 1.5 \times 10^{-2}$ m apart one above the other in air as shown in figure-1.61. The upper plate is maintained at a positive potential of 1.5 kV while the other plate is earthed which maintains it at zero potential. Calculate the number of electrons which must be attached to a small oil drop of mass $m = 4.9 \times 10^{-15}$ kg between the plates to maintain it at rest. Consider density of air is negligible in comparison with that of oil. If the potential of above plate is suddenly changed to –1.5 kV, what will be the initial acceleration of the charged drop? Also calculate the terminal velocity of the drop if its radius is $r = 5.0 \times 10^{-6}$ m and the coefficient of viscosity of air is $\eta = 1.8 \times 10^{-5}$ N-s/m^2.

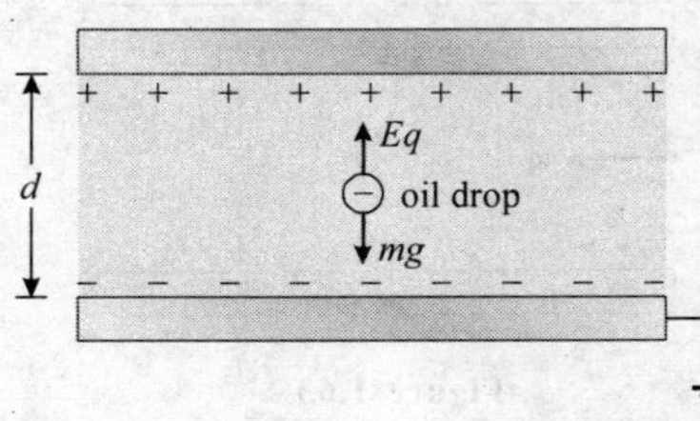

Figure 1.61

[3, 2 g, 5.7×10^{-5} m/s^2]

(iii) A uniform electric field of intensity $E = 10^6$ V/m exist in vertically downwards direction in a region. A particle of mass $m = 0.01$ kg and charge $q = 10^{-6}$ C is suspended by an inextensible thread of length $l = 1$ m. The particle is displaced slightly from its mean position and released. Calculate the time period of its oscillation. What minimum velocity should be given to the particle at rest from its equilibrium position so that it completes a full circle in vertical plane? Calculate the maximum and minimum tension in the thread in its circular motion in vertical plane.

[0.6 s, 23.42 m/s, 6.59 N, 0]

(iv) Figure-1.62 shows an assembly of deflecting plates A and B of an ink-jet printer which causes moving ink droplets to deflect at desired displacements by continuously varying electric field between the plates. An ink drop with a mass $m = 1.3 \times 10^{-10}$ kg and a negative charge of magnitude $q = 1.5 \times 10^{-13}$ C enters the region between the plates, initially moving along the x-axis with speed $v_x = 18$ m/s. The length of plates is $L = 1.6$ cm. The plates are connected with a varying voltage and thus produce an electric field at all points between them. Assume that field $\vec{E}$ for some duration is constant and it is acting in downward direction as shown and has a magnitude of $E = 1.4 \times 10^6$ N/C, find the vertical deflection of the drop at the far edge of the plate? As the gravitational force on the drop is very small relative to the electrostatic force acting on the drop, it can be neglected for this analysis.

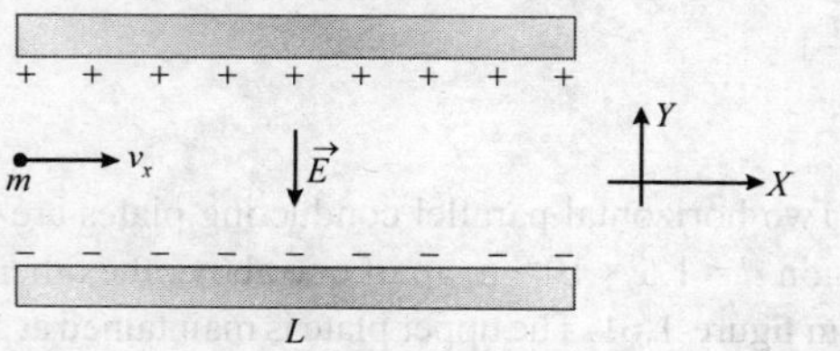

Figure 1.62

[6.4×10^{-4} m]

(v) A uniform electric field E is established between two parallel charged plates as shown in figure-1.63. An electron enter the field symmetrically between the plates with a speed u. The length of each plate is l. If the electron does not strike any of the plates, find the angle of deviation of the electron as it comes out of the field at the other end of plates.

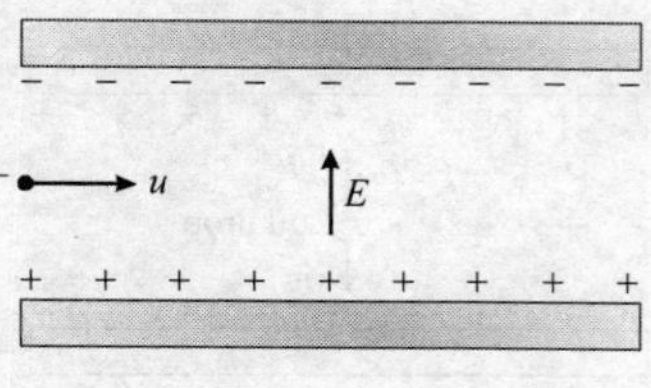

Figure 1.63

[$\tan^{-1}\left(\frac{eEl}{mu^2}\right)$]

(vi) In a region an electric field is setup with its strength $E = 15$ N/C and it makes an angle of 30° with the horizontal plane as shown in figure-1.64. A ball having a charge 2C, mass 3 kg and coefficient of restitution with ground 0.5 is projected at an angle of 30° with the horizontal along the direction of electric field with speed 20 m/s. Find the horizontal distance travelled by ball from first hit with the ground to the second time when it hits the ground.

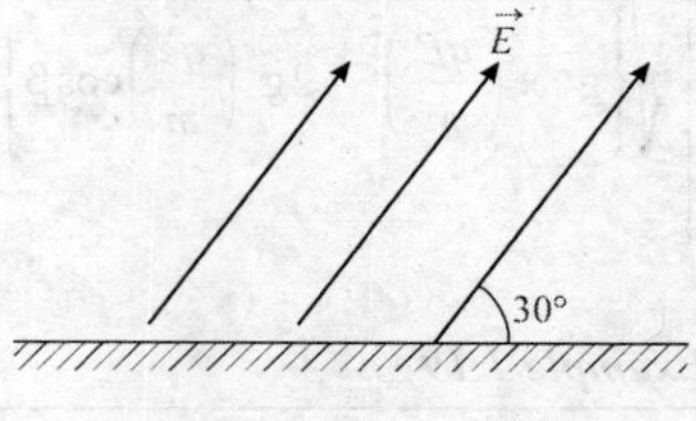

Figure 1.64

[$70\sqrt{3}$m]

(vii) In a hydrogen atom an electron of mass 9.1×10^{-31} kg revolves about a proton in circular orbit of radius 0.53 Å. Calculate the radial acceleration and angular velocity of electron.

[8.9×10^{22} m/s², 4.1×10^{16} s⁻¹]

(viii) An electron is released with a velocity of 5×10^6 m/s in an electric field of 10^3 N/C in same direction of its motion. What distance would the electron travel and how much time would it take before it is brought to rest ?

[0.07 m, 2.9×10^{-8} s]

(ix) A particle is thrown vertically upward from ground level with a speed of $5\sqrt{5}$ m/s in a region of space having uniform electric field. As a result, it attains a maximum height h. The particle is then given a positive charge q and it reaches the same maximum height h when thrown vertically upward with a speed of 13 m/s. Next, the particle is given a negative charge q. Ignoring air resistance, determine the speed with which the negatively charged particle must be thrown vertically upward so that it attains the same maximum height h.

[9 m/s]

(x) A particle of charge q and mass m is suspended from a point on the wall by a rigid massless rod of length $L = 3$ m as shown. Above the point of suspension another particle is clamped which has a charge $-q$ at a distance L from point of suspension. On slight displacement from the mean position, the suspended particle is observed to executes SHM. Find the time period of SHM. (For calculations consider $Kq^2 = 2$ mgL² and $g = \pi^2$)

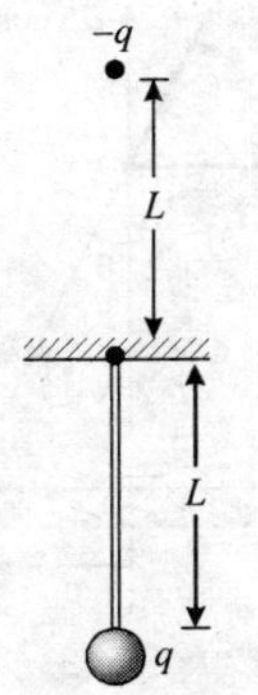

Figure 1.65

[4 s]

(xi) A non-conducting ring of mass m and radius R is charged as shown in figure-1.66 and placed on a rough horizontal non conducting plane. The charge per unit length on the charged quadrants of ring is λ. At time $t = 0$, a uniform electric field $\vec{E} = E_0\hat{i}$ is switched on and the ring starts rolling without sliding. Determine the magnitude and direction of friction force acting on the ring when it starts rolling.

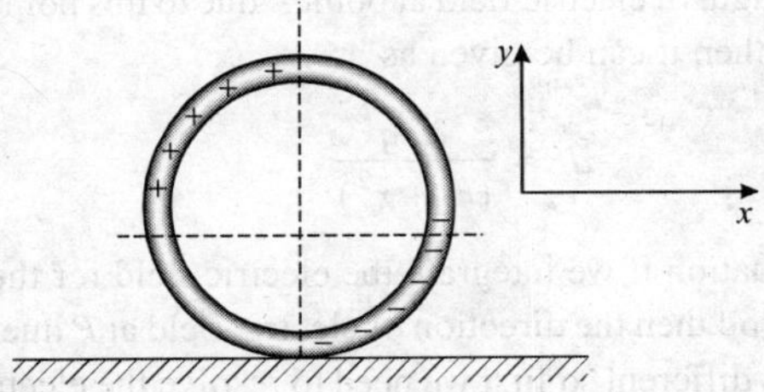

Figure 1.66

[λRE_0 along positive x-axis]

1.5 Electric Field Strength due to an Extended Body

Figure-1.67(a) shows an extended non conducting body which is charged in its volume and if wish to find the electric field due to this body at a point P as shown in figure then for this we consider an elemental charge dq within the body as shown in figure-1.67(b) which is located at the distance x from the point P. Now we find the electric field $\overrightarrow{dE}$ due to dq at P using the result of the point charge as given in equation-(1.29) which is given as

$$\overrightarrow{dE} = \frac{Kdq}{x^3}\vec{x} \qquad \ldots(1.38)$$

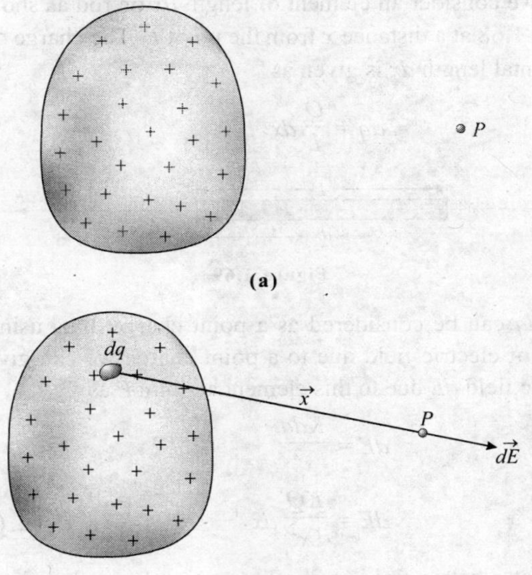

Figure 1.67

Thus net electric field strength at P due to whole body is given by integrating the expression in equation-(1.38).

$$\vec{E} = \int\overrightarrow{dE} = \int\frac{Kdq}{x^3}\vec{x}$$

In above integration we substitute limits according to the charge distribution and shape of the extended body. This will be clarified better with the different cases explained in upcoming articles.

Next we will first discuss some standard cases of electric field calculation due to uniform line charge distribution on different bodies such a rod, long wire, ring and a circular arc.

1.5.1 Electric Field Strength due to a Uniformly Charged Rod

For a uniformly charged rod here we will discuss two cases of determining electric field in its surrounding - at a point on the axis of rod and at a point on its bisector which is also called the equator of rod.

Case-I : Electric Field at an Axial Point

Figure-1.68 shows a rod of length L, uniformly charged with a charge Q. Now we wish to determine the electric field strength at a point P located at a distance r from one end of it as shown in figure. Here the extended line along the length of rod is called the axis of rod and here point P is the axial point of this rod.

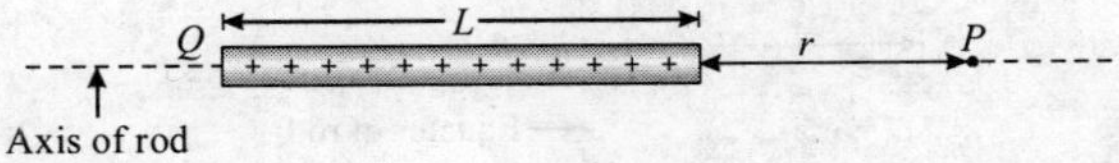

Figure 1.68

Now we consider an element of length dx on rod as shown in figure-1.68 at a distance x from the point P. The charge on the elemental length dx is given as

$$dq = \frac{Q}{L}\,dx$$

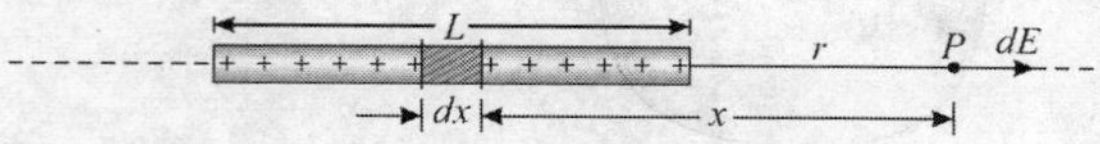

Figure 1.69

This dq can be considered as a point charge, thus using the result of electric field due to a point charge we can give the electric field dE due to this element at point P as

$$dE = \frac{Kdq}{x^2}$$

$$\Rightarrow \quad dE = \frac{KQ}{Lx^2}\,dx \qquad \ldots(1.39)$$

The net electric field strength at point P can be given by integrating this expression over the whole length of rod. Here due to all elements of the rod the direction of electric field at point P are in same direction so directly we can integrate the expression given in equation-(1.39) as

$$E_P = \int dE = \int_r^{r+L} \frac{KQ}{Lx^2}\,dx$$

$$\Rightarrow \quad E_P = \frac{KQ}{L}\int_r^{r+L} \frac{1}{x^2}\,dx$$

$$\Rightarrow \quad E_P = \frac{KQ}{L}\left[-\frac{1}{x}\right]_r^{r+L}$$

$$\Rightarrow \quad E_P = \frac{KQ}{L}\left[\frac{1}{r} - \frac{1}{r+L}\right] \qquad \ldots(1.40)$$

Case-II : Electric Field at an Equatorial Point

Figure-1.70(a) shows a rod of length L, uniformly charged with the charge Q. Now we wish to determine the electric field strength due to the rod at a point P situated at a distance r from center of the rod along the perpendicular bisector of the rod which is also known as equator of the rod.

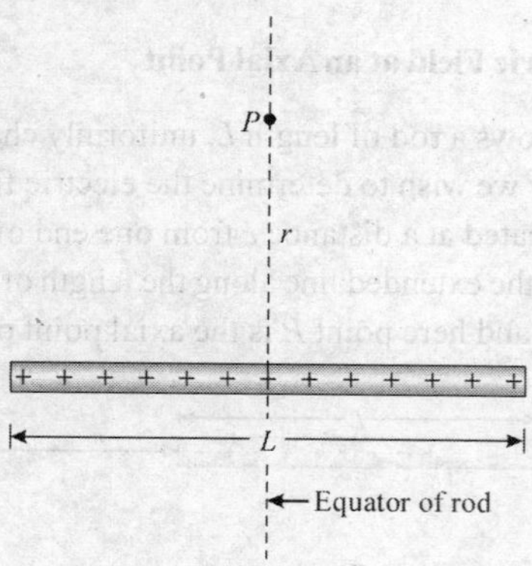

(a)

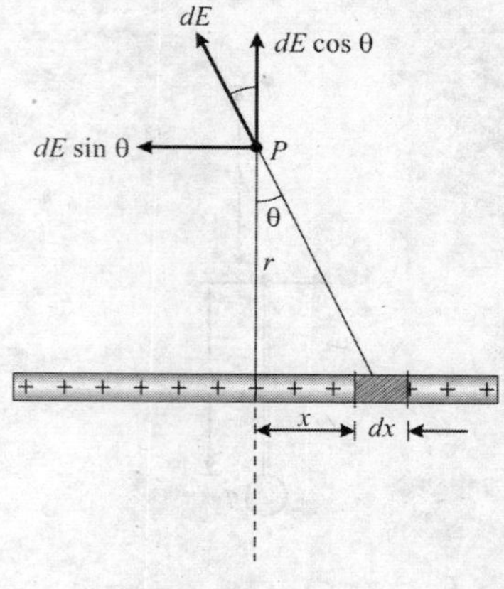

(b)

Figure 1.70

To calculate the electric field due to whole rod at P, first we consider an element of length dx at a distance x from centre of rod as shown in figure-1.70(b).

The charge on this element can be considered as a point charge which is given as

$$dq = \frac{Q}{L}\,dx$$

If the strength of electric field at point P due to this point charge dq is dE, then it can be given as

$$dE = \frac{Kdq}{(r^2 + x^2)}$$

In this situation if we integrate the electric field for the whole length of rod then the direction of electric field at P due to each element is different so first we need to resolve the electric field dE into its rectangular components as shown in figure-1.70(b). the component $dE \sin\theta$ will get cancelled because of equal and opposite components due to elements of the rod on the two sides of its center and net electric field at point P will be due to the component $dE \cos\theta$ which will all be added up.

Thus net electric field strength at point P can be given as

$$E_P = \int dE \cos\theta$$

$$\Rightarrow \quad E_P = \int_{-L/2}^{+L/2} \frac{KQdx}{L(r^2 + x^2)} \times \frac{r}{\sqrt{r^2 + x^2}}$$

$$\Rightarrow \quad E_P = \frac{KQr}{L}\int_{-L/2}^{+L/2} \frac{dx}{(r^2 + x^2)^{3/2}}$$

For integration we substitute

$$x = r\tan\theta$$

$$\Rightarrow \quad dx = r\sec^2\theta\, d\theta$$

Substituting above values in the integrand, we get

$$E_P = \frac{KQr}{L}\int \frac{r\sec^2\theta\, d\theta}{r^3\sec^3\theta}$$

$$\Rightarrow \quad = \frac{KQ}{Lr}\int \cos\theta\, d\theta$$

$$\Rightarrow \quad = \frac{KQ}{Lr}[\sin\theta]$$

Substituting $\theta = \tan^{-1}\frac{x}{r} = \sin^{-1}\frac{x}{\sqrt{x^2+r^2}}$, we get

$$E_P = \frac{KQ}{Lr}\left[\frac{x}{\sqrt{x^2+r^2}}\right]_{-L/2}^{+L/2}$$

$$\Rightarrow \quad E_P = \frac{KQ}{Lr}\left[\frac{L/2}{\sqrt{(L/2)^2+r^2}} + \frac{L/2}{\sqrt{(L/2)^2+r^2}}\right]$$

$$\Rightarrow \quad E_P = \frac{2kQ}{r\sqrt{L^2+4r^2}} \quad \ldots(1.41)$$

1.5.2 Electric Field due to a Uniformly Charged Long Thread

Figure-1.71 shows an infinitely long wire/thread which is uniformly charged with linear charge density λ C/m. Here we wish to determine electric field at a point P located at a normal distance r from the wire as shown.

For this we consider an element of length dx at a distance x from point O. This element we consider as a point charge and the charge on this element is given as

$$dq = \lambda dx$$

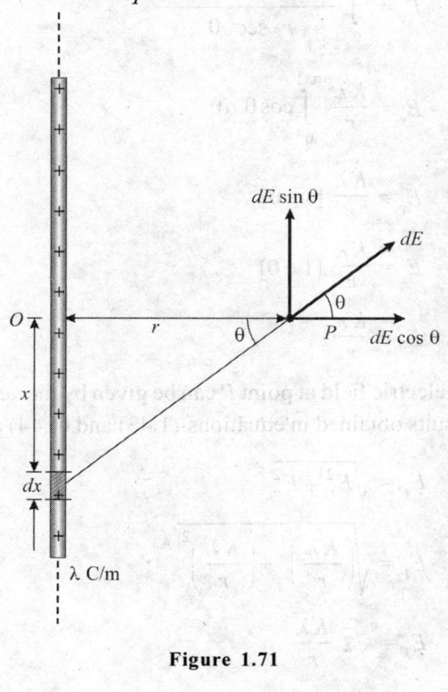

Figure 1.71

Due to this elemental charge dq, the electric field at point P can be given as

$$dE = \frac{Kdq}{(x^2+r^2)}$$

As discussed in previous article, here also due to symmetry of thread the component of electric field $dE\sin\theta$ will get cancelled and net electric field at P will be due to the component of electric field $dE\cos\theta$ in direction normal to wire.

Thus net electric field strength at point P can be given by integrating $dE\cos\theta$ for the whole length of wire as

$$E_P = \int dE\cos\theta$$

$$\Rightarrow \quad E_P = \int_{-\infty}^{+\infty} \frac{K\lambda\, dx}{(x^2+r^2)} \times \frac{r}{\sqrt{x^2+r^2}}$$

$$\Rightarrow \quad E_P = \int_{-\infty}^{+\infty} \frac{K\lambda\, r}{(x^2+r^2)^{3/2}}\, dx$$

To integrate we substitute $x = r\tan\theta$

$$\Rightarrow \quad dx = r\sec^2\theta\, d\theta$$

Changing the limits of integration according to the above substitution, we get

at $x = -\infty$, $\theta = -\frac{\pi}{2}$

and at $x = \infty$, $\theta = +\frac{\pi}{2}$

Thus by transforming limits of integration after substitution we get

$$E_P = \int_{-\pi/2}^{+\pi/2} \frac{K\lambda r}{r^3\sec^3\theta} \times r^2\sec^2\theta\, d\theta$$

$$\Rightarrow \quad E_P = \frac{K\lambda}{r}\int_{-\pi/2}^{+\pi/2}\cos\theta\, d\theta$$

$$\Rightarrow \quad E_P = \frac{K\lambda}{r}[+\sin\theta]_{-\pi/2}^{+\pi/2}$$

$$\Rightarrow \quad E_P = \frac{2K\lambda}{r} \quad \ldots(1.42)$$

1.5.3 Electric Field due to a Uniformly Charged Semi-infinite Thread

Figure-1.72 shows a semi-infinite uniformly charged wire/thread with linear charge density λ C/m. Here we wish to determine the electric field strength at point P at a distance r from the end O of wire as shown.

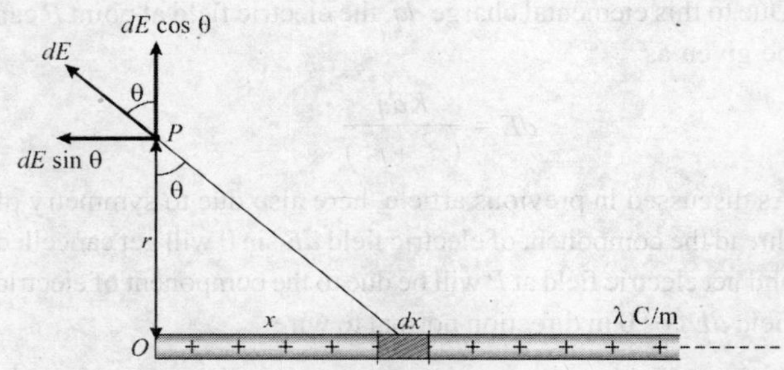

Figure 1.72

For this we consider an element of length dx at a distance x from end O. The charge on this element dq, can be given as

$$dq = \lambda dx$$

Due to the elemental charge dq, the electric field strength dE at point P can be given as

$$dE = \frac{Kdq}{(x^2 + r^2)}$$

Similar to previous articles here also to calculate the net electric field at point P, we resolve the electric field strength dE along X and Y direction and in this case we need to integrate both the components separately as none of these will get cancelled. Thus in x-direction electric field strength due to dq can be given as

$$dE_x = dE \sin\theta$$

The net electric field in x-direction is given by integrating above component as

$$E_x = \int dE_x = \int dE \sin\theta$$

$$\Rightarrow \quad E_x = \int_0^\infty \frac{Kdq}{(r^2 + x^2)} \times \frac{x}{\sqrt{r^2 + x^2}}$$

$$\Rightarrow \quad E_x = \int_0^\infty \frac{K\lambda x\, dx}{(r^2 + x^2)^{3/2}}$$

For integration we use substitution

$$x = r\tan\theta$$

and $\quad dx = r\sec^2\theta\, d\theta$

For changing the limits of integration, we use

at $x = 0, \theta = 0$

and at $x = \infty, \theta = \dfrac{\pi}{2}$

By substituting the above values in above integrand, we get

$$E_x = \int_0^{\pi/2} \frac{K\lambda \cdot r\tan\theta \times r\sec^2\theta\, d\theta}{r^3 \sec^3\theta}$$

$$\Rightarrow \quad E_x = \frac{K\lambda}{r} \int_0^{\pi/2} \sin\theta\, d\theta$$

$$\Rightarrow \quad E_x = \frac{K\lambda}{r} [-\cos\theta]_0^{\pi/2}$$

$$\Rightarrow \quad E_x = \frac{K\lambda}{r} [0 + 1]$$

$$\Rightarrow \quad E_x = \frac{K\lambda}{r} \qquad \ldots(1.43)$$

Similarly in y-direction net electric field at point P can be given by integrating the component $dE \cos\theta$ as

$$E_y = \int dE \cos\theta$$

$$\Rightarrow \quad E_y = \int_0^\infty \frac{K\lambda dx}{(r^2 + x^2)} \times \frac{x}{\sqrt{r^2 + x^2}}$$

$$\Rightarrow \quad E_y = \int_0^\infty \frac{K\lambda r\, dx}{(r^2 + x^2)^{3/2}}$$

For integration we use substitution

$$x = r\tan\theta$$

and $\quad dx = r\sec^2\theta\, d\theta$

For changing the limits of integration, we use

at $x = 0, \theta = 0$

and at $x = \infty, \theta = \dfrac{\pi}{2}$

By substituting the above values in above integrand, we get

$$E_y = \int_0^{\pi/2} \frac{K\lambda r \times r\sec^2\theta\, d\theta}{r^3 \sec^3\theta}$$

$$\Rightarrow \quad E_y = \frac{K\lambda}{r} \int_0^{\pi/2} \cos\theta\, d\theta$$

$$\Rightarrow \quad E_y = \frac{K\lambda}{r} [\sin\theta]_0^{\pi/2}$$

$$\Rightarrow \quad E_y = \frac{K\lambda}{r} [1 + 0]$$

$$\Rightarrow \quad E_y = \frac{K\lambda}{r} \qquad \ldots(1.44)$$

Thus net electric field at point P can be given by the vector sum of the results obtained in equations-(1.43) and (1.44) as

$$E_P = \sqrt{E_x^2 + E_y^2}$$

$$\Rightarrow \quad E_P = \sqrt{\left(\frac{K\lambda}{r}\right)^2 + \left(\frac{K\lambda}{r}\right)^2}$$

$$\Rightarrow \quad E_P = \sqrt{2}\, \frac{K\lambda}{r} \qquad \ldots(1.45)$$

The net electric field strength vector is at an angle θ with horizontal, which can be given as

$$\theta = \tan^{-1}\frac{E_y}{E_x} = \tan^{-1}(1) = 45°$$

Following figure-1.73 shows the direction of electric field due to a uniformly charged semi infinite straight wire.

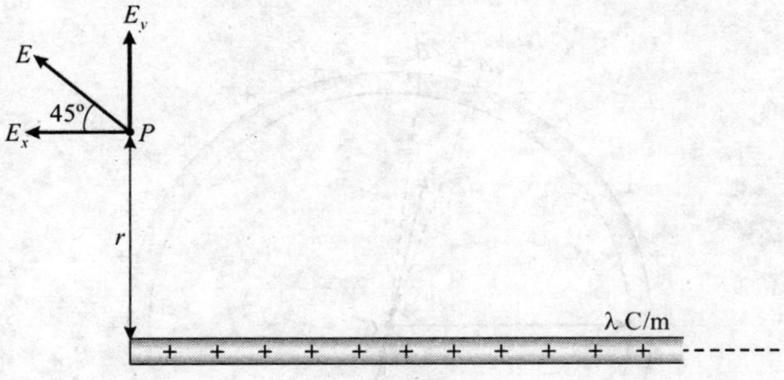

Figure 1.73

1.5.4 Electric Field Strength at a General Point due to a Uniformly Charged Rod

Figure-1.74(a) shows a uniformly charged rod and P is a general point in surrounding of rod, to determine electric field strength at P, like previous articles we consider an element on rod of length dx at a distance x from point O as shown in figure-1.74(b). The charge on this element can be considered as a point charge which is given as

$$dq = \frac{Q}{L}dx$$

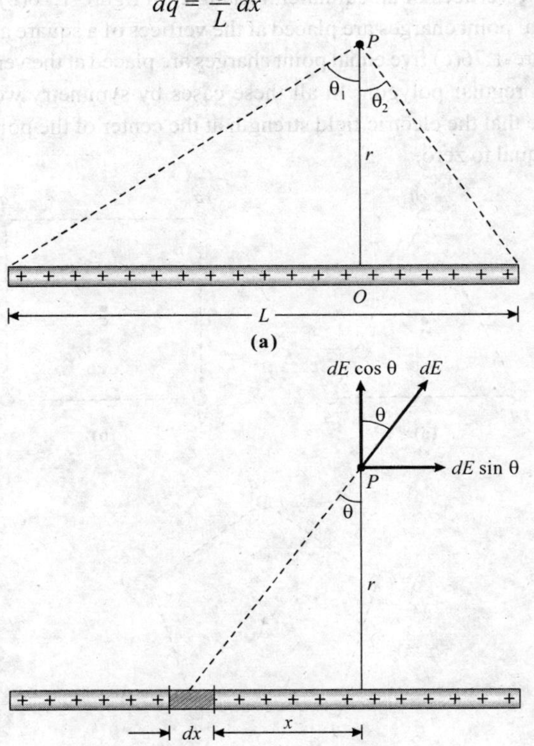

Figure 1.74

The electric field dE due to the elemental charge dq at point P can be given as

$$dE = \frac{Kdq}{(x^2 + r^2)}$$

As point P is not symmetric with respect to rod here also we resolve the electric field dE in rectangular components as shown in figure-1.74(b). The electric field strength in x-direction will be given by integrating the component $dE \sin\theta$ as

$$E_x = \int dE_x = \int dE \sin\theta$$

$$\Rightarrow \quad E_x = \int \frac{Kdq}{(r^2 + x^2)} \times \frac{x}{\sqrt{r^2 + x^2}}$$

$$\Rightarrow \quad E_x = \int \frac{K\lambda x\, dx}{(r^2 + x^2)^{3/2}}$$

For integration we use substitution

$$x = r\tan\theta$$

and $\quad dx = r\sec^2\theta\, d\theta$

After substitution in above integrand, we get

$$dE_x = \int \frac{KQ}{L}\frac{r\tan\theta . r\sec^2\theta\, d\theta}{r^3\sec^3\theta}$$

$$\Rightarrow \quad dE_x = \int \frac{KQ}{Lr}\sin\theta d\theta \qquad \ldots(1.46)$$

As shown in figure-1.74(a) the angles subtended by the end points of the rod at point P are θ_1 and θ_2, correspondingly we substitute the limits of integration for θ in equation-(1.46) as

$$E_x = \frac{KQ}{Lr}\int_{-\theta_2}^{+\theta_1} \sin\theta\, d\theta$$

$$\Rightarrow \quad E_x = \frac{KQ}{Lr}\left[-\cos\theta\right]_{-\theta_2}^{+\theta_1}$$

$$\Rightarrow \quad E_x = \frac{KQ}{Lr}\left[\cos\theta_2 - \cos\theta_1\right]$$

Similarly, electric field strength at point P due to dq in y-direction is given as

$$E_y = \int dE_y = \int dE\cos\theta$$

$$\Rightarrow \quad E_y = \int \frac{KQ\, dx}{L(r^2 + x^2)} \times \cos\theta$$

For integration we use substitution

$$x = r\tan\theta$$

and $\quad dx = r\sec^2\theta\, d\theta$

After substitution in above integrand, we get

$$E_y = \int \frac{KQr\sec^2\theta d\theta}{Lr^2\sec^2\theta} \times \cos\theta$$

$$\Rightarrow \qquad E_y = \int \frac{KQ}{Lr}\cos\theta d\theta$$

For calculating net electric field strength at P due to dq in y-direction again we use the limits of integration from θ_1 and θ_2 which gives

$$E_y = \frac{KQ}{Lr}\int_{-\theta_2}^{+\theta_1}\cos\theta\, d\theta$$

$$\Rightarrow \qquad E_y = \frac{KQ}{Lr}\left[+\sin\theta\right]_{-\theta_2}^{+\theta_1}$$

$$\Rightarrow \qquad E_y = \frac{KQ}{Lr}\left[\sin\theta_1 + \sin\theta_2\right]$$

Thus net electric field components at a general point in the surrounding of a uniformly charged rod which subtend angles θ_1 and θ_2 at the two corners of rod can be given as

In x-direction or along the length of rod

$$E_x = \frac{KQ}{Lr}(\cos\theta_2 - \cos\theta_1) \qquad \ldots(1.47)$$

In y-direction or perpendicular to length of rod

$$E_y = \frac{KQ}{Lr}(\sin\theta_1 + \sin\theta_2) \qquad \ldots(1.48)$$

Net electric field at point P due to rod is given by vector sum of the field components given in equations-(1.47) and (1.48).

Using the results of equations-(1.47) and (1.48) we can directly obtain the electric field strength due to a long uniformly charged wire by substituting $\theta_1 = \theta_2 = \pi/2$. Using these values the expression in equation-(1.47) becomes zero and expression in equation-(1.48) becomes

$$E_y = \frac{KQ}{Lr}(\sin\theta_1 + \sin\theta_2)$$

For a uniformly charged long wire of linear charge density λ, we use $\frac{Q}{L} = \lambda$, thus we get

$$E_y = \frac{K\lambda}{r}(1+1) = \frac{2K\lambda}{r}$$

Above expression is same as obtained in equation-(1.42) in article-1.5.2.

1.5.5 Electric Field due to a Uniformly Charged Ring at its Center

Figure-1.75 shows a uniformly charged ring of radius R and charge Q. By symmetry we can say that electric field strength at centre due to every small segment on ring is cancelled by that due to the segment diametrically opposite to it as shown. The electric field strength at centre due to segment AB is cancelled by that due to segment CD and same is valid for all segments on the ring. Thus net electric field strength at the centre of a uniformly charged ring can be given as zero.

$$E_C = 0$$

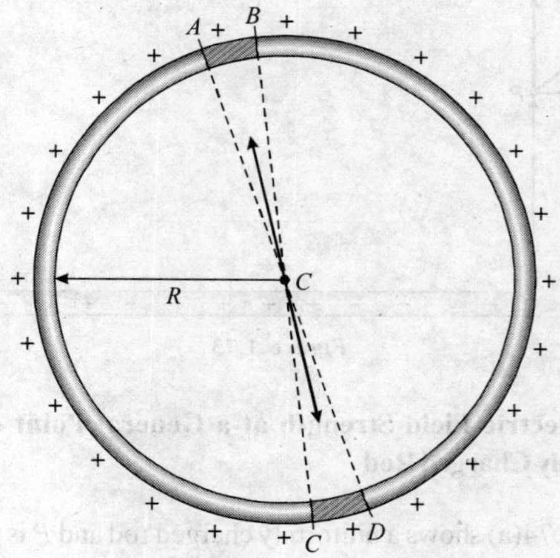

Figure 1.75

Above analysis of a ring can be extended to any symmetric uniformly charge distribution in a plane like the cases shown in figure-1.75. In figure-1.76(a) three equal point charges are placed at the vertices of an equilateral triangle, in figure-1.76(b) four equal point charges are placed at the vertices of a square and in figure-1.76(c) five equal point charges are placed at the vertices of a regular polygon. In all these cases by symmetry we can state that the electric field strength at the center of the polygon is equal to zero.

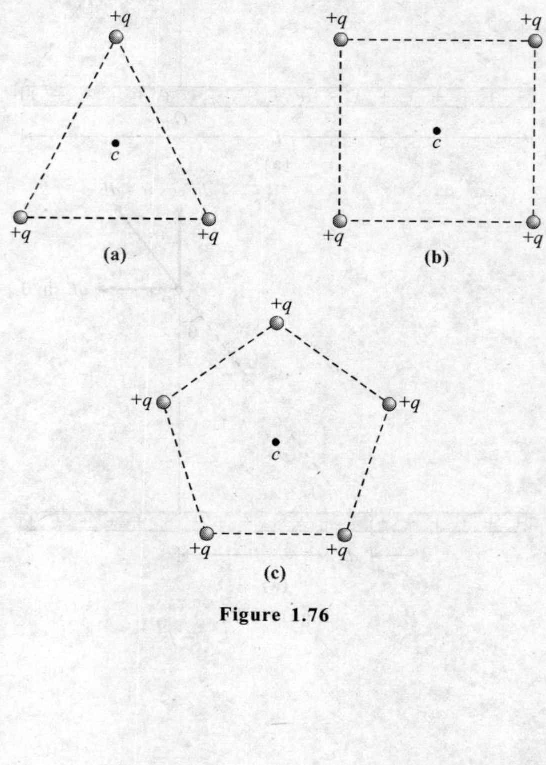

Figure 1.76

1.5.6 Electric Field due to a Uniformly Charged Ring with a cut

Figure-1.77 shows a uniformly charged ring of radius R and charge Q with a small cut of width w ($w << R$) in it. If cut is not there then we have already analyzed in previous article that the electric field at the center will be zero due to symmetry but in this case, the electric field due to the element on the ring diametrically opposite to the cut will not get cancelled out and will remain present at the center of ring. Other than this all other elements of ring will produce net zero electric field at center. If we consider the element is of same width 'w' as that of cut then charge on this element of ring is given as

$$q' = \frac{Q}{2\pi R} \times w$$

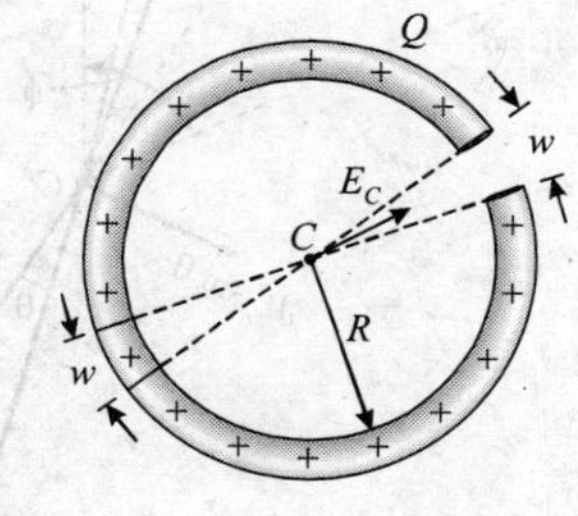

Figure 1.77

Electric field due to the above discussed element at center of ring is given as

$$E_C = \frac{Kq'}{R^2} = \frac{KQw}{2\pi R^3}$$

Above analysis can also be extended for the symmetric charge distribution of equal point charges placed at the vertices of a regular polygon. Figure-1.78 shows a regular pentagon with four equal point charges placed at the vertices of the pentagon. If the distance of each charge from the center of pentagon is a then in this case the net electric field due to the four charges present can be considered to be equal to that of the fifth charge which is absent at the vacant vertex of the pentagon because if there were all five charges present then the net electric field at center would have been zero.

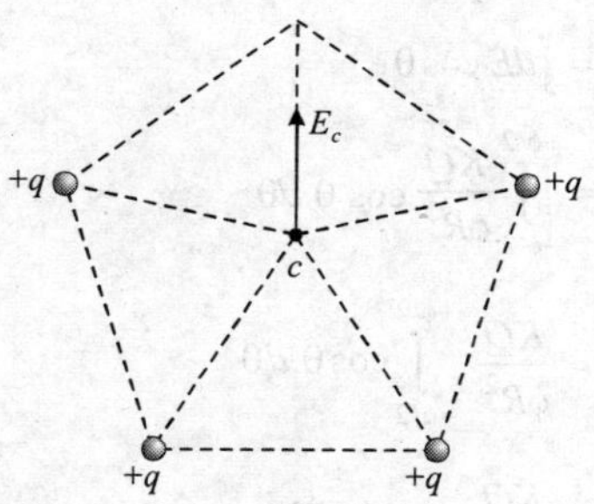

Figure 1.78

Thus the net electric field due to the four charges present at center is given as

$$E_C = \frac{Kq}{a^2}$$

1.5.7 Electric Field due to a Uniformly Charged Ring at its Axial Point

Figure-1.79 shows a uniformly charged ring of radius R and with a charge Q. P is a point on the axis of ring at a distance x from the center of the ring. We will calculate the electric field strength at point P due to the ring. Now we consider a small element of length dl on ring as shown. As total charge is uniformly distributed on right, the charge on this elemental section is given as

$$dq = \frac{Q}{2\pi R} dl$$

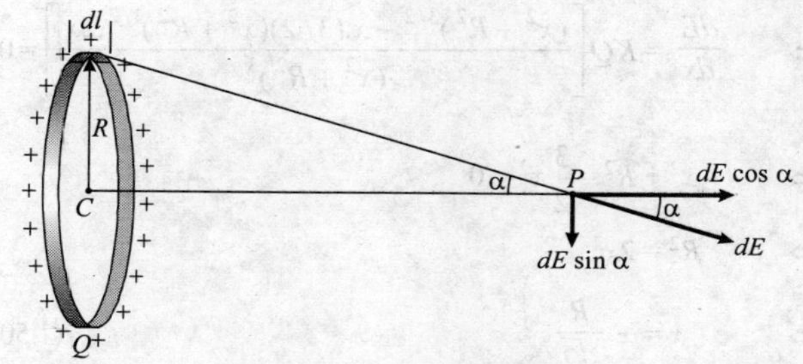

Figure 1.79

Due to the elemental charge dq, electric field strength dE at point P can be given as

$$dE = \frac{Kdq}{(R^2 + x^2)}$$

As shown in figure, we can see that the component of this field strength dE sinα which is normal to the axis of ring will be cancelled out due to element on ring located diametrically opposite to dl whereas the component of electric field strength along the axis of ring dE cosα due to all the elements on right will be added up. Hence net electric field strength at point P due to the ring is given by integration of this component of the electric field for the whole circumference of the ring, given as

$$E_P = \int dE \cos\alpha$$

$$\Rightarrow \quad E_P = \int_0^{2\pi R} \frac{Kdq}{(R^2 + x^2)} \times \frac{x}{\sqrt{R^2 + x^2}}$$

$$\Rightarrow \quad E_P = \int_0^{2\pi R} \frac{KQx}{2\pi R(R^2 + x^2)^{3/2}} dl$$

$$\Rightarrow \quad E_P = \frac{KQx}{2\pi R(R^2 + x^2)^{3/2}} \int_0^{2\pi R} dl$$

$$\Rightarrow \quad E_P = \frac{KQx}{2\pi R(R^2 + x^2)^{3/2}} [2\pi R]$$

$$\Rightarrow \quad E_P = \frac{KQx}{(R^2 + x^2)^{3/2}} \quad \ldots(1.49)$$

The above expression of electric field varies with the distance x from center of ring along axis. In this expression we can see that at $x = 0$, $E = 0$ at the center of ring and at very large values of x we will use $x^2 >> R^2$ and then also electric field approaches to zero value for $x -> \infty$ thus as x increases, electric field strength also increases, approaches to a maximum value and then again decreases for higher values of x. The maximum electric field can be determined using maxima-minima for the function given in equation-(1.49) as

$$\frac{dE}{dx} = 0$$

$$\Rightarrow \quad \frac{dE}{dx} = KQ\left[\frac{(x^2 + R^2)^{3/2} - x.(3/2)(x^2 + R^2)^{1/2}.2x}{(x^2 + R^2)^3}\right] = 0$$

$$\Rightarrow \quad x^2 + R^2 - \frac{3}{2}x^2 = 0$$

$$\Rightarrow \quad R^2 = 2x^2$$

$$\Rightarrow \quad x = \pm \frac{R}{\sqrt{2}} \quad \ldots(1.50)$$

Thus on both sides of ring at its axis at $x = \pm R/\sqrt{2}$, electric field has its maximum magnitude which is given as

$$E_{\max} = \frac{KQ(R/\sqrt{2})}{((R/\sqrt{2})^2 + R^2)^{3/2}} = \frac{2KQ}{\sqrt{27}R^2} \quad \ldots(1.51)$$

The variation of electric field given by the expression in equation-(1.49) is shown in figure-1.80.

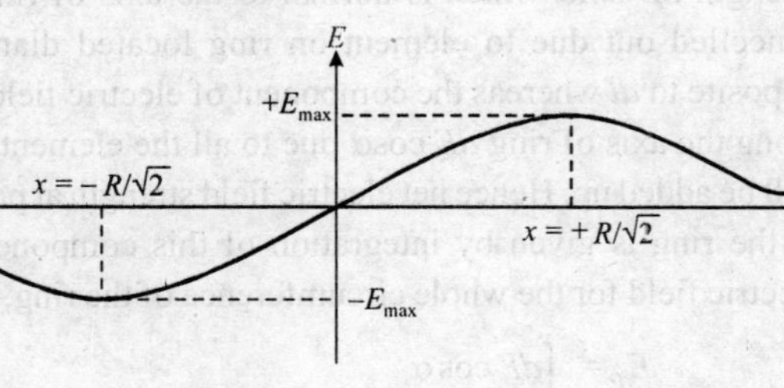

Figure 1.80

1.5.8 Electric Field due to a Charged Circular Arc

Figure-1.81 shows a circular arc of radius R having a uniformly distributed charge Q which subtend an angle ϕ at its centre. To determine the electric field strength due to charge on arc at its center C, we consider a polar elemental segment on arc of angular width $d\theta$ at an angle θ from the angle bisector XY as shown.

The length of elemental segment is $Rd\theta$ and the charge on this element dq is given as

$$dq = \frac{Q}{\phi} d\theta$$

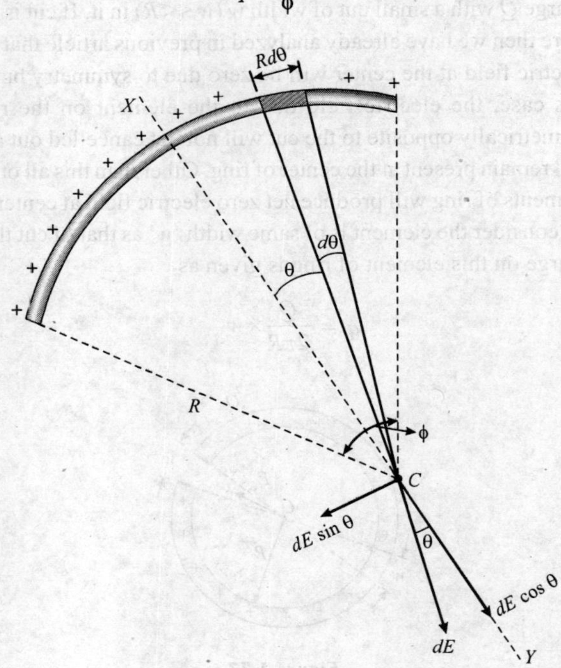

Figure 1.81

The electric field dE due to the elemental charge dq on the segment at centre of arc C is given as

$$dE = \frac{Kdq}{R^2}$$

As shown in figure here we resolve the electric field dE in two rectangular components, along the angle bisector and normal to it. The component $dE \sin\theta$ which is normal to the angle bisector gets cancelled due to symmetry of arc because of a similar element on the other side of bisector and net electric field at centre will be along angle bisector which can be calculated by integrating $dE \cos\theta$ within limits from $-\phi/2$ to $+\phi/2$.

Thus net electric field strength at centre of the arch is given as

$$E_C = \int dE \cos\theta$$

$$\Rightarrow \quad E_C = \int_{-\phi/2}^{+\phi/2} \frac{KQ}{\phi R^2} \cos\theta \, d\theta$$

$$\Rightarrow \quad E_C = \frac{KQ}{\phi R^2} \int_{-\phi/2}^{+\phi/2} \cos\theta \, d\theta$$

$$\Rightarrow \quad E_C = \frac{KQ}{\phi R^2} [\sin\theta]_{-\phi/2}^{+\phi/2}$$

$$\Rightarrow \qquad E_C = \frac{KQ}{\phi R^2}\left[\sin\frac{\phi}{2} + \sin\frac{\phi}{2}\right]$$

$$\Rightarrow \qquad E_C = \frac{2KQ\sin\left(\frac{\phi}{2}\right)}{\phi R^2} \qquad ...(1.52)$$

Using the above expression given in equation-(1.52) we can directly find the electric field strength due to a uniformly charged half ring or quarter ring by substituting the value of angle ϕ as π or $\pi/2$.

 # Illustrative Example 1.20

Four particles each having a charge q are placed on the four vertices of a regular pentagon. The distance of each corner from the centre is 'a'. Find the electric field at the centre of pentagon.

Solution

We can calculate the electric field at centre by the superposition method i.e. by adding vectorially the electric field due to all the 4 charges at centre which will come out to be :

$$\vec{F}_{\text{centre}} = \vec{F}_1 + \vec{F}_2 + \vec{F}_3 + \vec{F}_4 = \frac{Kq}{a^2}$$

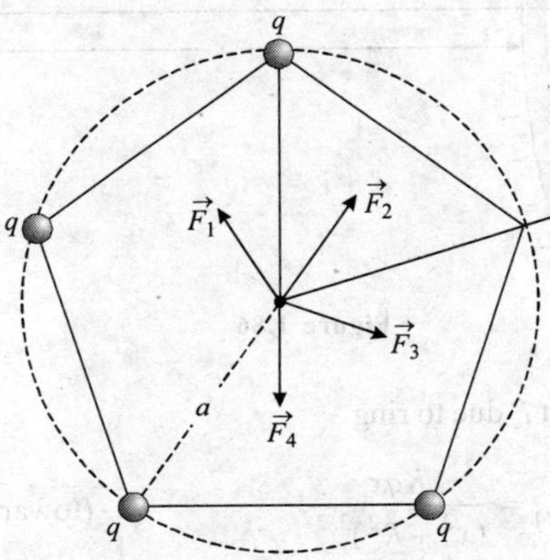

Figure 1.82

in the direction of the vertex with no charge as shown in figure-1.82.

Alternate :

Consider pentagon with charges on all vertex.

The electric field at centre must be zero due to symmetry

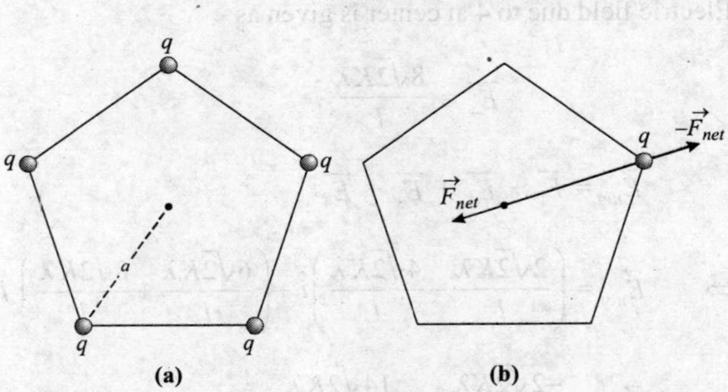

Figure 1.83

Thus EF due to 4 charges + EF due to 1 charge = 0

$\Rightarrow$ EF due to 4 charges = – EF due to 1 charge

Where '–' sign denotes that both the forces are in opposite direction.

Thus EF due to 4 charges $= \dfrac{Kq}{a^2}$

 # Illustrative Example 1.21

In the given arrangement of a charged square frame made up of four wires 1, 2, 3 and 4 charged with the linear charge density as mentioned in figure-1.84. Find electric field at centre due to this frame.

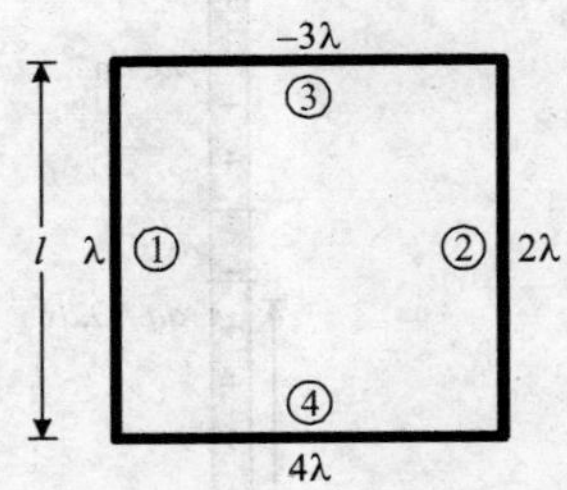

Figure 1.84

Solution

Electric field due to 1 at center is given as

$$\overline{E_1} = \frac{2K\lambda}{l}(\cos 45° + \cos 45°)\,\hat{i}$$

$$\Rightarrow \qquad \overline{E_1} = \frac{2\sqrt{2}K\lambda}{l}\hat{i}$$

Electric field due to 2 at center is given as

$$\overline{E_2} = -\frac{4\sqrt{2}K\lambda}{l}\hat{i}$$

Electric field due to 3 at center is given as

$$\overline{E_3} = \frac{6\sqrt{2}K\lambda}{l}\hat{j}$$

Electric field due to 4 at center is given as

$$\overline{E_4} = \frac{8\sqrt{2}K\lambda}{l}\hat{j}$$

$$\vec{E}_{net} = \overline{E_1} + \overline{E_2} + \overline{E_3} + \overline{E_4}$$

$$\Rightarrow \quad \vec{E}_{net} = \left(\frac{2\sqrt{2}K\lambda}{l} - \frac{4\sqrt{2}K\lambda}{l}\right)\hat{i} + \left(\frac{6\sqrt{2}K\lambda}{l} + \frac{8\sqrt{2}K\lambda}{l}\right)\hat{j}$$

$$\Rightarrow \quad \vec{E}_{net} = \frac{-2\sqrt{2}K\lambda}{l}\hat{i} + \frac{14\sqrt{2}K\lambda}{l}\hat{j}$$

Illustrative Example 1.22

A system consists of a thin charged wire ring of radius R and a very long uniformly charged thread oriented along the axis of the ring, with one of its ends coinciding with the centre of the ring. The total charge of the ring is equal to q. The charge of the thread (per unit length) is equal to λ. Find the interaction force between the ring and the thread.

Solution

Force dF on the wire = $dq\,\vec{E}$

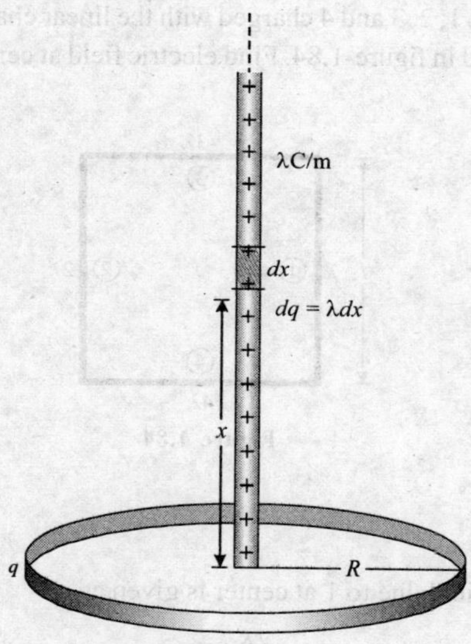

Figure 1.85

$$dF = \frac{Kqx}{(x^2 + R^2)^{3/2}} \cdot \lambda dx$$

$$F = Kq\lambda \int_0^\infty \frac{x\,dx}{(R^2 + x^2)^{3/2}}$$

$$F = \frac{\lambda q}{4\pi \epsilon_0 R}$$

Alternate :

Due to wire electric field on the points of ring in y-direction is

$$E_y = \frac{K\lambda}{R}$$

Thus force on ring due to wire is

$$q\frac{K\lambda}{R} = \frac{Kq\lambda}{R} = \frac{\lambda q}{4\pi \epsilon_0 R}$$

and $\quad E_x = 0 \quad$ [As cancelled out]

(Here x components of forces on small elements of rings are cancelled by the x component of diametrically opposite elements).

Illustrative Example 1.23

A point charge q is located at the centre of a thin ring of radius R with uniformly distributed charge $-q$. Find the magnitude of the electric field strength vector at the point lying on the axis of the ring at a distance x from its centre if $x >> R$.

Solution

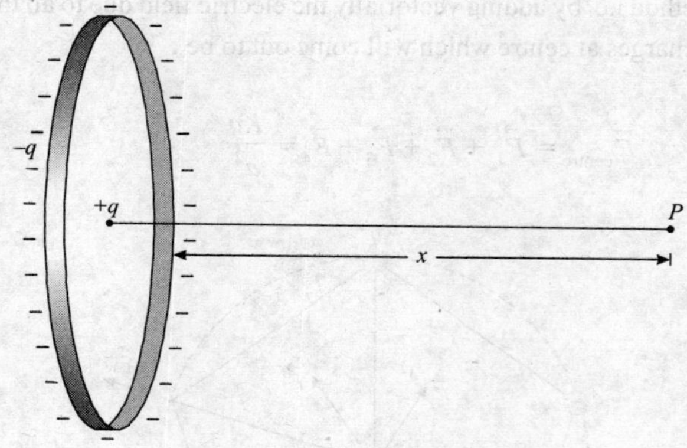

Figure 1.86

Electric field at P due to ring

$$E_1 = \frac{Kqx}{(x^2 + R^2)^{3/2}} \quad \text{(toward centre)}$$

Electric field at P due to $+q$

$$E_2 = \frac{Kq}{x^2} \quad \text{(away from centre)}$$

Thus net field at P is

$$E_{net} = E_2 + E_1$$

$$\Rightarrow \quad E_{net} = Kq\left(\frac{1}{x^2} - \frac{x}{(x^2 + R^2)^{3/2}}\right)$$

For $x >> R$

$$E_{\text{net}} = Kq\frac{(x^2+R^2)^{3/2}-x^3}{x^2(x^2+R^2)^{3/2}} = \frac{3KqR^2}{2x^4}$$

(using binomial approximation)

Illustrative Example 1.24

A thin fixed ring of radius 1 meter has a positive charge 1×10^{-5} C uniformly distributed over it. A particle of mass 0.9 gm and having a negative charge of 1×10^{-6} coulomb is placed on the axis at a distance of 1 cm from the centre of the ring. Show that the motion of the negatively charged particle is approximately simple harmonic. Calculate the time period of oscillations.

Solution

Let us first find the force on a $-q$ charge placed at a distance x from centre of ring along its axis.

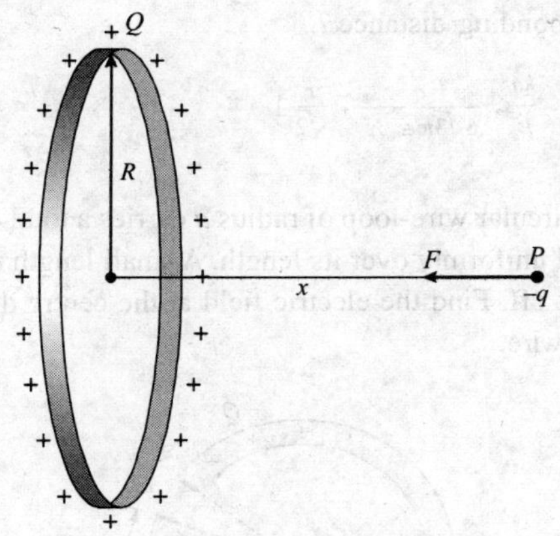

Figure 1.87

Figure-1.87 shows the respective situation. In this case force on particle P is

$$F_P = -qE$$

$$\Rightarrow \quad F_P = -q \cdot \frac{KQx}{(x^2+R^2)^{3/2}}$$

For small x, $x << R$, we can neglect x, compared to R, we have

$$F = -\frac{KqQx}{R^3}$$

Acceleration of particle is

$$a = -\frac{KqQ}{mR^3}x$$

[Here we have $x = 1$ cm and $R = 1$ m hence $x << R$ can be used]

This shows that particle P executes SHM, know comparing this acceleration with $a = -\omega^2 x$

We get $$\omega = \sqrt{\frac{KqQ}{mR^3}}$$

Thus time period of SHM is

$$T = \frac{2\pi}{\omega} = 2\pi\sqrt{\frac{mR^3}{KqQ}}$$

$$\Rightarrow \quad T = 2\pi\sqrt{\frac{0.9\times10^{-3}\times(1)^3}{9\times10^9\times10^{-5}\times10^{-6}}}$$

$$\Rightarrow \quad T = \frac{\pi}{5}\text{ s}$$

Illustrative Example 1.25

A clock face has charges $-q, -2q, -3q, \ldots -12q$ fixed at the position of the corresponding numerals on the dial. The clock hands do not disturb the net field due to point charges. At what time does the hour hand point in the direction of the electric field at the centre of the dial.

Solution

Six vectors of equal magnitudes are as shown in figure-1.88.

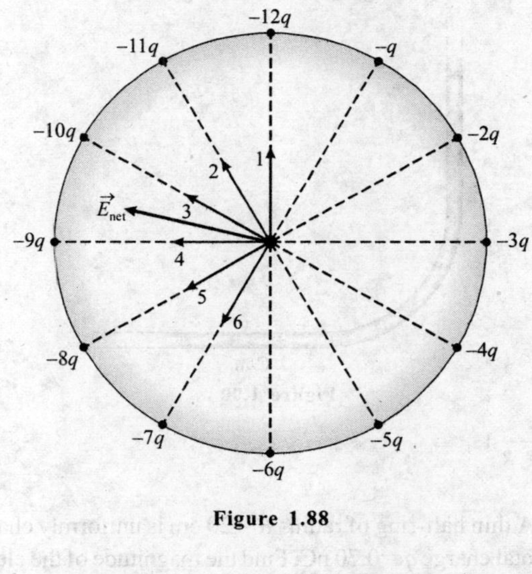

Figure 1.88

Now resultant of two vectors of equal magnitudes (= E say) at 120° is also E and passing through their bisector line.

So, resultant of 1 and 5 is also E in the direction of 3. Similarly resultant of 2 and 6 is also E is the direction of 4.

Finally resultant of $2E$ in the direction of 3 and $2E$ in the direction of 4 passes through the bisector line of 3 and 4 (or 9.30).

Web Reference at www.physicsgalaxy.com
Age Group - Grade 11 & 12 | Age 17-19 Years
Section - ELECTROSTATICS
Topic - Electrostatics
Module Number - 27 to 38

Practice Exercise 1.3

(i) In the given arrangement find the electric field at C in the figure-1.89. Here the U-shaped wire is uniformly charged with linear charge density λ.

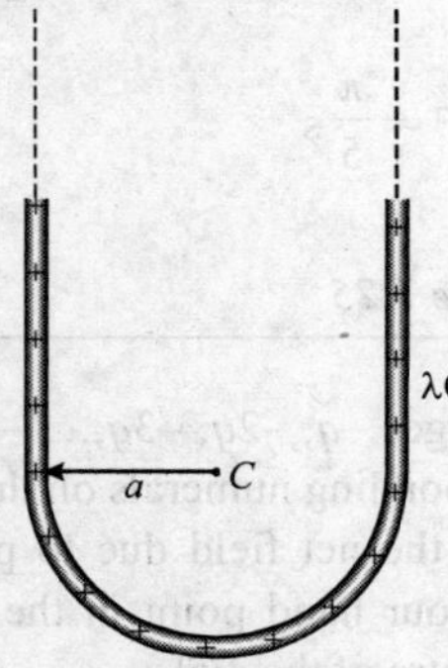

Figure 1.89

[0]

(ii) In the given arrangement find electric field at C. Complete wire is uniformly charged at linear charge density λ.

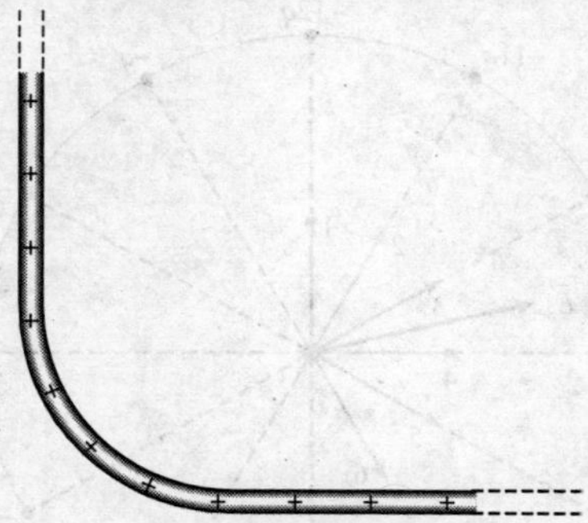

Figure 1.90

$[\frac{\lambda}{2\sqrt{2}\pi\epsilon_0 R}]$

(iii) A thin half-ring of radius $R = 20$ cm is uniformly charged with a total charge $q = 0.70$ nC. Find the magnitude of the electric field strength at the curvature centre of this half-ring.

[100 V/m]

(iv) Given an equilateral triangle mode up of three rods each of length l. Find electric field strength at the centroid of triangle. The linear charge density on the sides of triangle are as shown in figure-1.91.

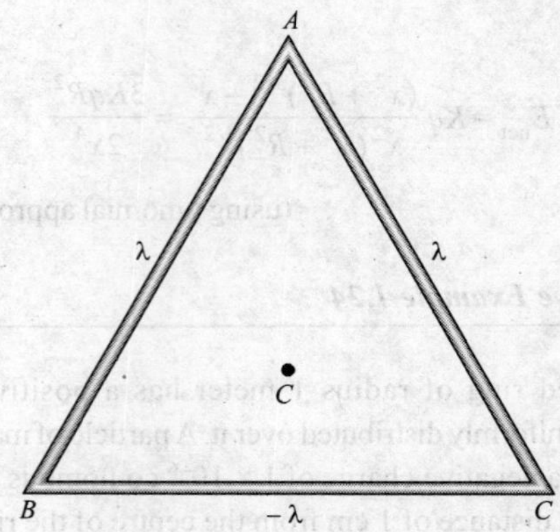

Figure 1.91

$[\frac{\lambda}{2\pi\epsilon_0 l}$ in vertically downward direction]

(v) A thin wire ring of radius r carries a charge q. Find the magnitude of the electric field strength on the axis of the ring as a function of distance l from the centre. Investigate the obtained function at $l >> r$. Find the maximum strength magnitude and the corresponding distance l.

$[\frac{Kql}{(l^2+r^2)^{3/2}}, \frac{kq}{l^2}, \frac{q}{6\sqrt{3}\pi\epsilon_0 r^2}, \frac{r}{\sqrt{2}}]$

(vi) A circular wire-loop of radius a carries a total charge Q distributed uniformly over its length. A small length dL of the wire is cut off. Find the electric field at the centre due to the remaining wire.

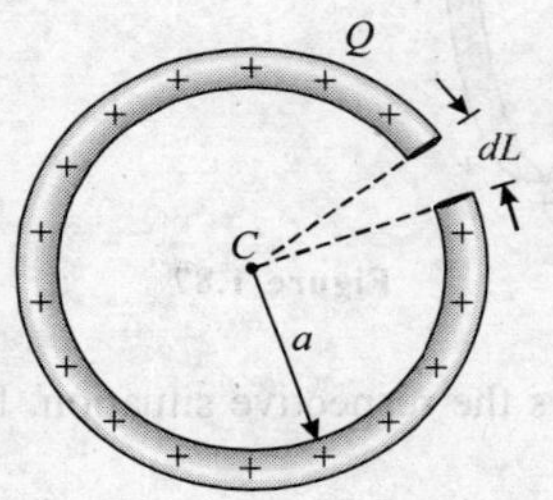

Figure 1.92

$[\frac{QdL}{8\pi^2\varepsilon_0 a^3}]$

(vii) An electron is constrained to move along the central axis of a ring of radius R having uniformly distributed charge q. Show that the electrostatic force exerted on the electron can cause it to oscillate through the centre of the ring with an angular frequency of $\omega = \sqrt{(eq/4\pi\varepsilon_0 mR^3)}$, where m is the mass of the electron.

$[\sqrt{\frac{qe}{4\pi\epsilon_0 mR^3}}]$

(viii) Two point charges Q_1 and Q_2 are positioned at points 1 and 2. The field intensity to the right of the charge Q_2 on the line that passes through the two charges varies according to a law that is represented in the figure-1.93. The field intensity is assumed to be positive if its direction coincides with the positive direction on the *x*-axis. The distance between the charges is *l*.

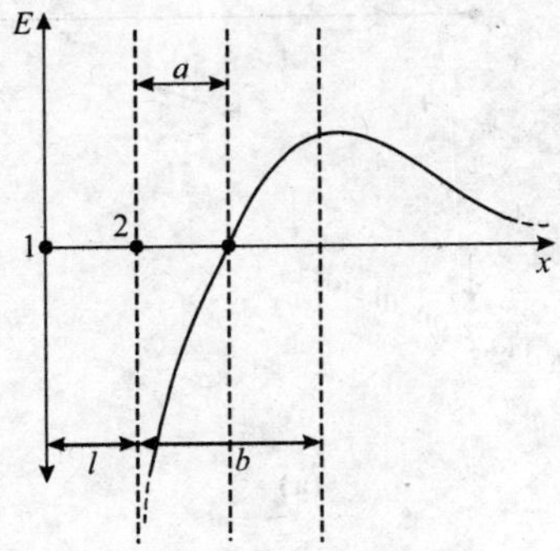

Figure 1.93

(a) Find the sign of each charge

(b) Find the ratio of the absolute values of the charges $\left|\frac{Q_1}{Q_2}\right|$

(c) Find the value of *b* where the field intensity is maximum

[(a) Q_2 is negative and Q_1 is positive; (b) $\left(\frac{l+a}{a}\right)^2$; (c) $\frac{l}{\left(\frac{l+a}{a}\right)^{2/3}-1}$]

(ix) Two wires *AB* & *CD*, each 1 m length, carry a total charge of 0.2 microcoulomb each and are placed as shown in figure-1.94. The ends *B* & *C* are separated 1 m distance. Determine the value of electric intensity at the mid point *P* in terms of unit vector $\hat{i}$ and $\hat{j}$.

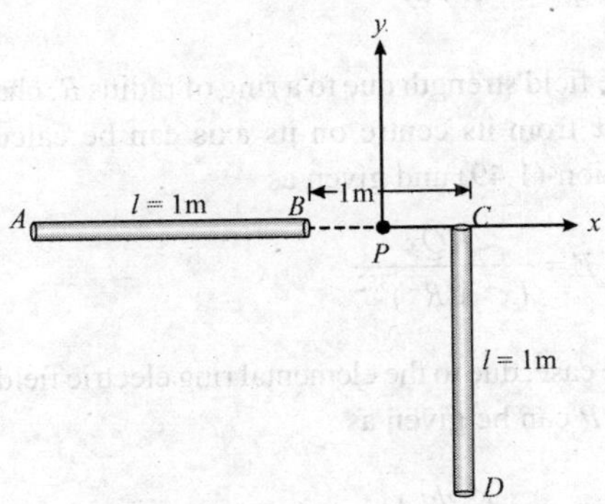

Figure 1.94

[$(-839\,\hat{i} + 1980\,\hat{j})$V/m]

1.6 Electric Field Strength due to Surface and Volume charge distributions

In previous article we've discussed and analyzed that electric field strengths due to a charge uniformly distributed on a line in form of a rod, long wire, ring and a circular arc. These results of electric field strengths are basic building blocks for calculation of electric field strengths due to charges distributed on surface and volume of an extended body as explained in further articles.

1.6.1 Electric Field Strength due to a Uniformly Surface Charged Disc

Figure-1.95(a) shows a disc of radius *R*, charged on its surface with surface charge density σ C/m². Now we will determine electric field strength due to this disc at a distance *x* from the centre of disc on its axis at point *P* as shown.

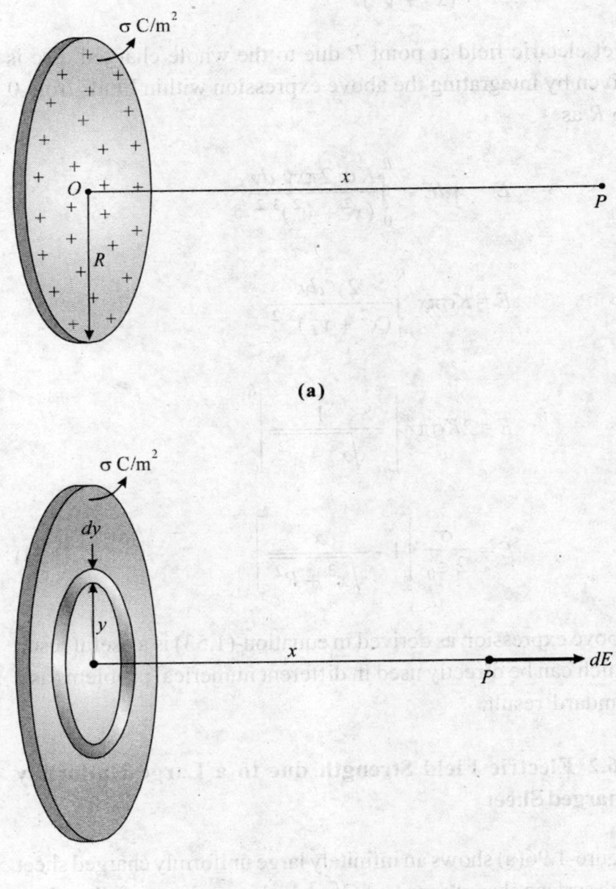

Figure 1.95

To find electric field at point *P* due to this disc, we consider an elemental ring of radius *y* and width *dy* in the disc as shown in figure-1.95(b). The surface area of the elemental ring on disc surface is $2\pi y.dy$ thus the charge dq on this elemental ring can be given as

$$dq = \sigma \cdot 2\pi y\, dy$$

The electric field strength due to a ring of radius R, charge Q, at a distance x from its centre on its axis can be calculated by using equation-(1.49) and given as

$$E = \frac{KQx}{(x^2 + R^2)^{3/2}}$$

In the above case, due to the elemental ring electric field strength dE at point P can be given as

$$dE = \frac{K\, dq\, x}{(x^2 + y^2)^{3/2}}$$

$$\Rightarrow \qquad dE = \frac{K\sigma\, 2\pi y\, dy\, x}{(x^2 + y^2)^{3/2}}$$

Net electric field at point P due to the whole charged disc is given by integrating the above expression within limits from 0 to R as

$$E = \int dE = \int_0^R \frac{K\sigma\, 2\pi xy\, dy}{(x^2 + y^2)^{3/2}}$$

$$\Rightarrow \qquad E = K\sigma\pi x \int_0^R \frac{2y\, dy}{(x^2 + y^2)^{3/2}}$$

$$\Rightarrow \qquad E = 2K\sigma\pi x \left[-\frac{1}{\sqrt{x^2 + y^2}} \right]_0^R$$

$$\Rightarrow \qquad E = \frac{\sigma}{2\epsilon_0} \left[1 - \frac{x}{\sqrt{x^2 + R^2}} \right] \qquad \ldots (1.53)$$

Above expression as derived in equation-(1.53) is a useful result which can be directly used in different numerical problems as a standard result.

1.6.2 Electric Field Strength due to a Large Uniformly Charged Sheet

Figure-1.96(a) shows an infinitely large uniformly charged sheet with surface charge density σ C/m^2. In this section we will analyze and determine the electric field strength due the charge on sheet at a point P which is located at a distance x from the sheet as shown in figure. For this again like the previous article we consider an elemental ring of radius y and width dy with centre O as shown in figure-1.96(b).

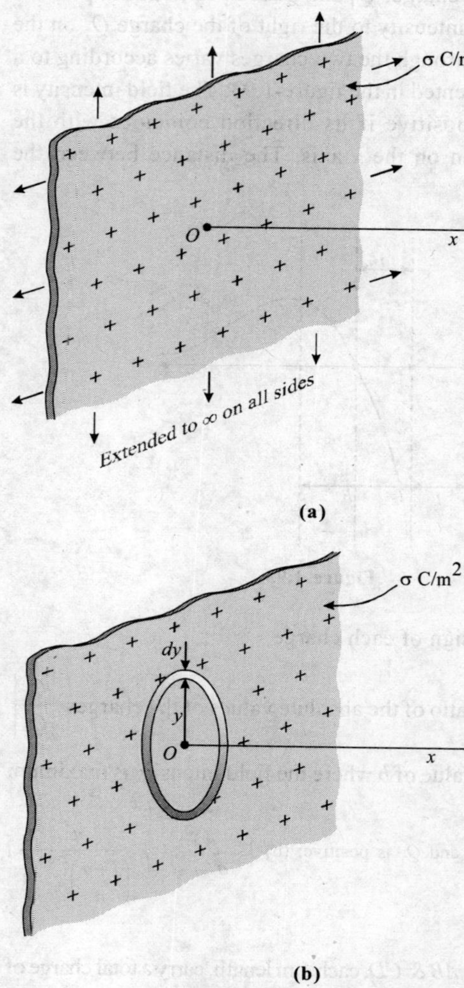

Figure 1.96

The charge dq on this elemental ring is given as

$$dq = \sigma \cdot 2\pi y\, dy$$

The electric field strength due to a ring of radius R, charge Q, at a distance x from its centre on its axis can be calculated by using equation-(1.49) and given as

$$E = \frac{KQx}{(x^2 + R^2)^{3/2}}$$

In the above case, due to the elemental ring electric field strength dE at point P can be given as

$$dE = \frac{K\, dq\, x}{(x^2 + y^2)^{3/2}}$$

$$\Rightarrow \qquad dE = \frac{K\sigma\, 2\pi y\, dy\, x}{(x^2 + y^2)^{3/2}}$$

Net electric field at point P due to the whole infinite sheet is given by integrating the above expression within limits from 0 to ∞ as

$$E = \int dE = \int_0^\infty \frac{K\sigma\, 2\pi xy\, dy}{(x^2+y^2)^{3/2}}$$

$$\Rightarrow \quad E = K\sigma\pi x \int_0^\infty \frac{2y\, dy}{(x^2+y^2)^{3/2}}$$

$$\Rightarrow \quad E = 2K\sigma\pi x\left[-\frac{1}{\sqrt{x^2+y^2}}\right]_0^\infty$$

On simplifying we get

$$\Rightarrow \quad E = \frac{\sigma}{2\epsilon_0} \qquad \ldots(1.54)$$

Above expression of electric field due to a uniformly charged infinite sheet can also be obtained directly by substituting the limit $x \to \infty$ in the equation-(1.53) and the same result can also be derived by considering long wire elements in the sheet instead of circular rings as explained next in alternative method.

1.6.3 Alternative Method of Electric Field Calculation by a Large Uniformly Charged Sheet

To calculate electric field at the point P in front of the sheet, we consider on elemental strip of width dx at a distance x from the point O as shown in figure-1.97. This elemental strip behaves like a long straight wire having charge per unit length given as

$$\lambda = \sigma dx \text{ C/m}$$

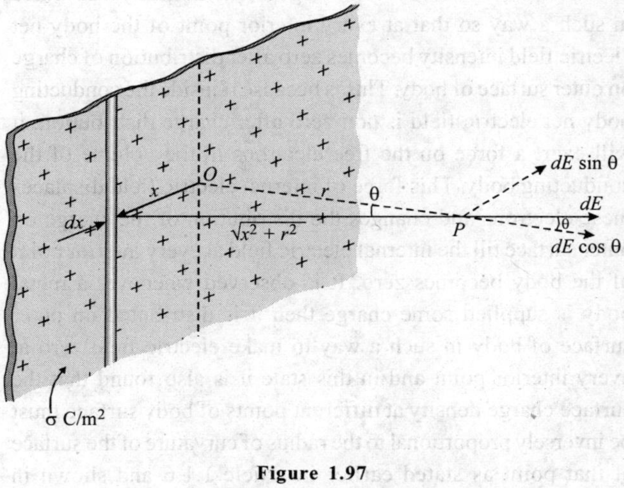

Figure 1.97

Now due to this elemental strip the electric field dE at point P can be given by equations-(1.42) as already explained in article-1.4.2 and shown in above figure. This is given as

$$dE = \frac{2K\lambda}{\sqrt{x^2+r^2}}$$

By symmetry the component of electric field $dE \sin\theta$ gets cancelled and thus net electric field at point P can be calculated by integration of the field component $dE \cos\theta$ given as

$$E_P = \int dE \cos\theta$$

$$\Rightarrow \quad E_P = \int_{-\infty}^{+\infty} \frac{2K\sigma dx}{\sqrt{x^2+r^2}} \times \frac{x}{\sqrt{x^2+r^2}}$$

$$\Rightarrow \quad E_P = \int_{-\infty}^{+\infty} \frac{2K\sigma\, r}{(x^2+r^2)}\, dx$$

$$\Rightarrow \quad E_P = \frac{\sigma r}{2\pi\epsilon_0} \int_{-\infty}^{+\infty} \frac{dx}{x^2+r^2}$$

$$\Rightarrow \quad E_P = \frac{\sigma r}{2\pi\epsilon_0} \frac{1}{r}\left[\tan^{-1}\frac{x}{r}\right]_{-\infty}^{+\infty}$$

$$\Rightarrow \quad E_P = \frac{\sigma}{2\pi\epsilon_0}\left[\frac{\pi}{2}+\frac{\pi}{2}\right]$$

$$\Rightarrow \quad E_P = \frac{\sigma}{2\epsilon_0} \qquad \ldots(1.55)$$

Above expression in equation-(1.55) is same as obtained in equation-(1.54).

1.6.4 Electric Field Strength in Vicinity of Center of a Uniformly Charged Disc

Figure-1.95(a) shows a uniformly charged disc of radius R with surface charge density σ C/m². By symmetry of the disc we can say that the electric field strength at the center of disc is zero as if we consider elemental rings in the disc then due to each elemental ring at center electric field is zero thus net field strength due to whole disc at center will also come out to be zero.

Now we carefully analyze the same situation in a different way. As already discussed and analyzed in article-1.6.1 the electric field strength due to a uniformly charged disc at a distance x from its surface along the axis is given as

$$E = \frac{\sigma}{2\epsilon_0}\left[1 - \frac{x}{\sqrt{x^2+R^2}}\right]$$

If in above expression of electric field we put $x = 0$, we get

$$E = \frac{\sigma}{2\epsilon_0}$$

In above expression $x = 0$ stands for the center of the disc and the result is not zero. This is because if we are approaching the disc surface from a distant point along the axis of disc then $x = 0$ corresponds to a point which is just outside the disc surface in the vicinity of its center as shown in figure-1.98

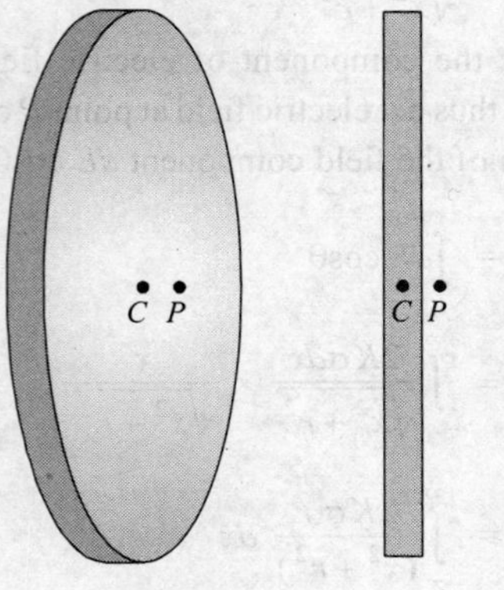

Figure 1.98

Thus for a point very close to the disc surface, we get electric field strength same as that of a large sheet, but this result is only for the points outside the disc surface as shown in figure-1.98. Here electric field strength at point P, just outside the disc surface is given as $\sigma/2\varepsilon_0$ because for a point very close to surface, the disc may act like a very large sheet for this point and if we calculate electric field at point C, inside the disc at its centre, electric field strength will be zero due to symmetry.

1.6.5 Electric Field Strength due to a Uniformly Charged Hollow Hemispherical Cup

Figure-1.99 shows a hollow hemisphere, uniformly charged with surface charge density σ C/m^2. To determine the electric field strength at its centre C, we consider an elemental ring on its surface of angular width $d\theta$ at an angle θ from its axis as shown. The surface area of this elemental ring is given as

$$dS = 2\pi R\sin\theta \times Rd\theta$$

Charge on this elemental ring is given as

$$dq = \sigma dS = \sigma \cdot 2\pi R^2 \sin\theta\, d\theta$$

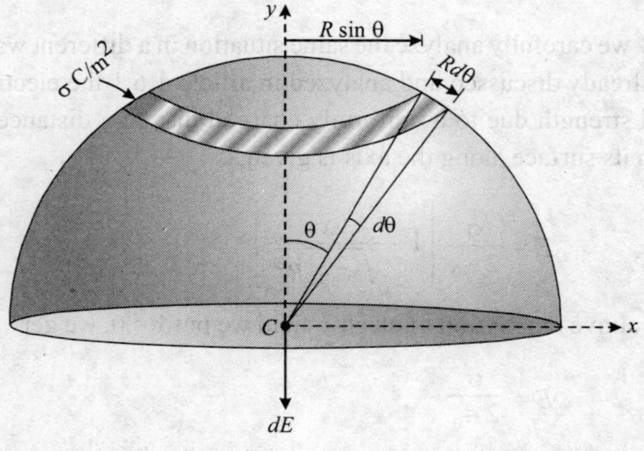

Figure 1.99

The electric field strength dE due to this elemental ring at centre C can be given by using the result of electric field strength due to a uniformly charged ring at its axis point from equation-(1.49) in article-1.5.7 as

$$dE = \frac{Kdq(R\cos\theta)}{(R^2\sin^2\theta + R^2\cos^2\theta)^{3/2}}$$

$$\Rightarrow \quad dE = \frac{K\sigma \cdot 2\pi R^2 \sin\theta\, d\theta \cdot R\cos\theta}{R^3}$$

$$\Rightarrow \quad dE = \pi K\sigma \sin 2\theta\, d\theta$$

Thus net electric field at the centre of the hemispherical shell can be obtained by integrating this expression between limits from 0 to $\pi/2$ as given below

$$E_C = \int dE$$

$$\Rightarrow \quad E_C = \pi K\sigma \int_0^{\pi/2} \sin 2\theta\, d\theta$$

$$\Rightarrow \quad E_C = \frac{\sigma}{4\epsilon_0}\left[-\frac{\cos 2\theta}{2}\right]_0^{\pi/2}$$

$$\Rightarrow \quad E_C = \frac{\sigma}{4\epsilon_0}\left[\frac{1}{2} + \frac{1}{2}\right]$$

$$\Rightarrow \quad E_C = \frac{\sigma}{4\epsilon_0} \quad \text{...(1.56)}$$

1.7 Charge Distribution on a Metal Body

As already discussed whenever charge is given to a conducting body, due to mutual repulsion whole of its charge spread on the outer surface of the body. The charge is automatically distributed in such a way so that at every interior point of the body net electric field intensity becomes zero after distribution of charge on outer surface of body. This is because if inside the conducting body net electric field is non-zero after charge distribution, it will exert a force on the free electrons in the volume of the conducting body. This force of internal electric field displaces these electrons and changes the distribution of the charge on outer surface till the internal electric field at every interior point of the body becomes zero. It is observed whenever a metal body is supplied some charge then it is distributed on outer surface of body in such a way to make electric field zero at every interior point and in this state it is also found that the surface charge density at different points of body surface must be inversely proportional to the radius of curvature of the surface at that point as stated earlier in article-1.1.6 and shown in figure-1.6. Based on above analysis we can state the law of charge distribution on isolated metal bodies as

"Whenever charge is given to a metal body it distributes on the outer surface in such a manner to make net electric field inside the body equal to zero."

In this article we have not derived the expression given in equation-(1.1) but it is explained that if expression given in equation-(1.1) is true then at every interior point of the body electric field will be zero. In article-1.11.5 in later sections of this chapter we will also discuss the proof of equation-(1.1).

1.7.1 Electric Field Strength due to a Large Uniformly Charged Conducting Sheet

We've discussed earlier that in a metal body whenever, we supply some charge, it will automatically spread on its outer surface due to mutual repulsion between charges. If some charge is given to a large metal sheet, it will spread on both of its surfaces as shown in figure-1.100 which shows the cross-section of a large metal sheet. If charge density on both of its surfaces is considered to be σ C/m^2, the electric field strength at a point out side the sheet, due to both the surfaces is in same direction hence added up. Thus electric field strength at point B, outside the sheet can be given as

$$E_B = \frac{\sigma}{2\epsilon_0} + \frac{\sigma}{2\epsilon_0} = \frac{\sigma}{\epsilon_0}$$

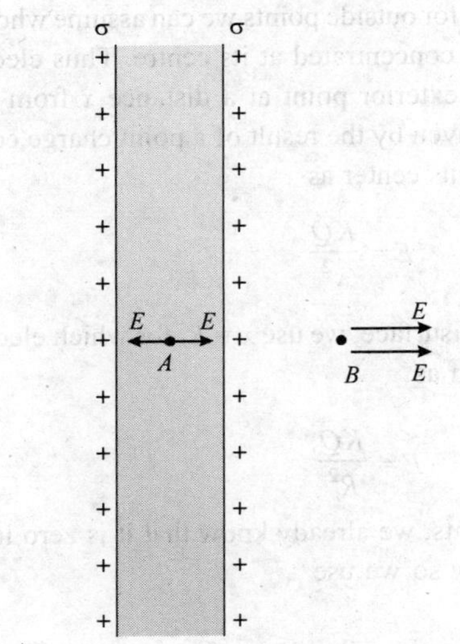

Figure 1.100

For an interior point of the sheet, we've already discussed that electric field strength inside a metal body is always zero. Here at point A also we can see that due to both the surfaces, electric field is in opposite direction hence get cancelled.

1.7.2 Charge Induction in Metal Bodies

Whenever a metal body is placed in an electric field, the free electrons in the body experiences an electric force eE in opposite direction as shown in figure-1.101(a). Due to this force, these electrons start drifting toward the left surface of the body as shown in figure and develop negative and positive charges on the body as shown in figure-1.101(b).

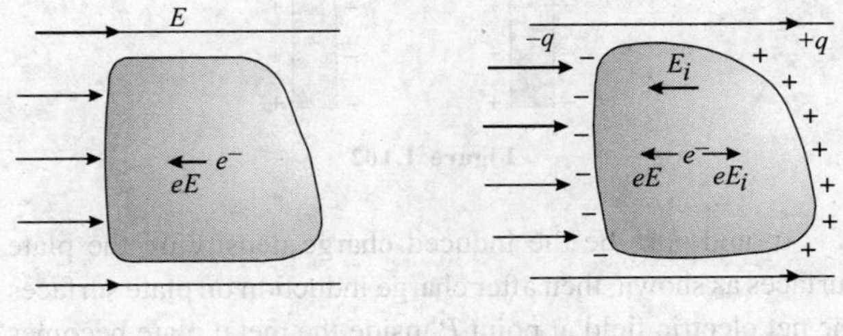

Figure 1.101

Due to the induced charges on the surface of body an electric field E_i is developed in the direction opposite to external electric field as shown. If $E_i < E$, free electrons in the body still experience a force toward left and drift in that direction due to which induced charges q_i increase and hence the induced electric field E_i also increases. This in the whole process due to external electric field charge induction takes place and the induced charges continuously increase till E_i balances E after which at every interior point of body net electric field becomes zero and no force on any free electron will act so no more separation of charges will take place in the body and induction stops.

In other words we can say, if a metal body is placed in an electric field, charge induction on the body surface starts and continuous flow of electrons inside the body takes place till the net electric field inside the body becomes zero.

Hence $E - E_i = 0$

Thus we can say when all charges in a metal body are at rest, net electric field at every interior point of the metal body is zero or the electric field inside the body due to the charges on its surface always balances the external electric field in the body.

1.7.3 Charge Induction in Parallel Metal Plates in Uniform Electric Field

Figure-1.102 shows two large uncharged metal plates placed normal to an external electric field. Due to electric field charges are induced on surfaces of plates in such a way that at every interior point electric field becomes zero after induction.

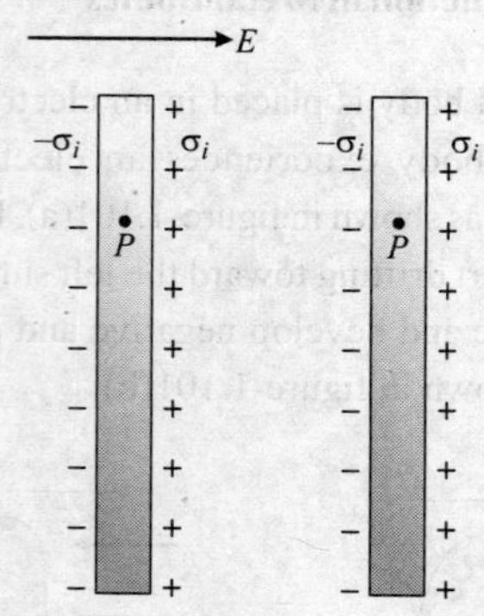

Figure 1.102

If $-\sigma_i$ and $+\sigma_i$ be the induced charge density on the plate surfaces as shown, then after charge induction on plate surfaces the net electric field at point P inside the metal plate becomes zero. Thus at point P we can say that the external electric field E is balanced by the electric field due to induced charges. At point P inside one plate internal electric field will only exist due to the induced charges on this plate as because of other plate due to opposite charges on the two surfaces it gets cancelled. Due to opposite charges on the two surfaces electric field inside the plate will be in same direction so it will be added up and given as

$$E_i = \frac{\sigma_i}{2\epsilon_0} + \frac{\sigma_i}{2\epsilon_0} = \frac{\sigma_i}{\epsilon_0}$$

$$\Rightarrow \quad \sigma_i = \epsilon_0 E \qquad \ldots(1.57)$$

Equation-(1.57) gives the surface density of induced charges on the plate surfaces which are placed normally in an external electric field.

1.7.4 Electric Field Strength due to a Uniformly Charged Conducting Sphere

We've already discussed that charge supplied to an isolated conducting body is distributed automatically on the outer surface of the body in such a manner that its surface charge density is given as

$$\sigma \propto \frac{1}{r}$$

In above expression r is the local radius of curvature of body surface at different points.

For a sphere, at every point on its surface radius of curvature is constant and same as that of the radius of sphere, hence the charge given to an isolated metal sphere will always have uniform surface charge density on the surface and the surface charge density on a sphere of radius R due to a charge Q supplied to it is given as

$$\sigma = \frac{Q}{4\pi R^2}$$

From the figure-1.103, we can see that a positive charge supplied to it is uniformly spreaded on its surface. As a positive charge produces outward electric field, here by symmetry we can see that the direction of electric field is in radially outward direction in the surrounding of sphere. From the radially symmetric direction of electric field in the surrounding of sphere we can consider that for outside points of the sphere the charge appears to be concentrated at the center of sphere from which the electric field is appear to be originating.

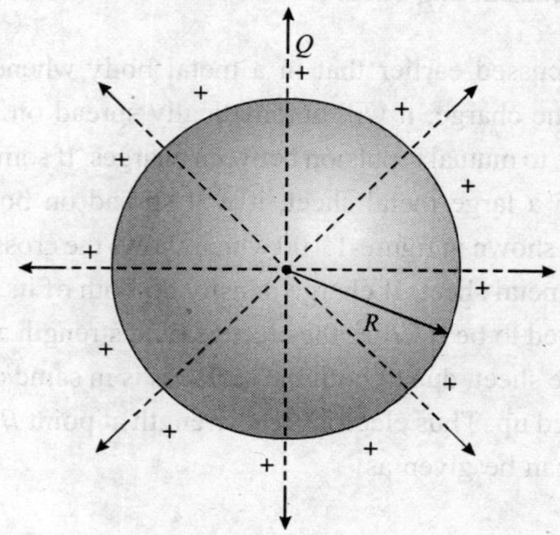

Figure 1.103

This is an important point to be noted that for a uniformly charged sphere, for outside points we can assume whole charge of the sphere is concentrated at its centre. Thus electric field strength at any exterior point at a distance x from centre of sphere can be given by the result of a point charge considered to be located at its center as

$$\text{For } x > R \qquad E = \frac{KQ}{x^2} \qquad \ldots(1.58)$$

For points on its surface, we use $x = R$, for which electric field strength is given as

$$\text{For } x = R \qquad E = \frac{KQ}{R^2} \qquad \ldots(1.59)$$

For interior points, we already know that it is zero inside any conducting body so we use

$$\text{For } x < R \qquad E_{in} = 0 \qquad \ldots(1.60)$$

1.7.5 Variation Curve of Electric Field Strength with Distance for a Uniformly Charged Conducting Sphere

We can plot the electric field strength due to a uniformly charged conducting sphere using the equations-(1.58), (1.59) and (1.60), the graph is shown in figure-1.104.

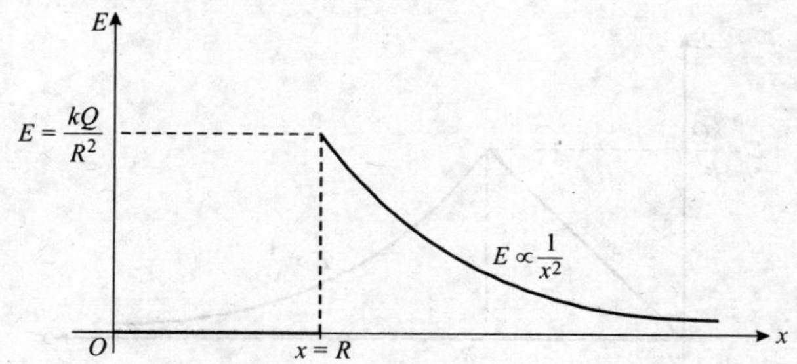

Figure 1.104

1.7.6 Electric Field Strength due to a Uniformly Charged Hollow Sphere

For a conducting body we've discussed that whether it is a solid body or hollow, it won't make any difference as charge only reside on outer surface in such a fashion so as to make net electric field zero at every interior point. Thus electric field strength due to a uniformly charged hollow conducting sphere will be exactly same as that due to a solid conducting charged sphere. If a thin walled hollow sphere is non-conducting and uniformly charged then also we can use the same results because in case of solid metal sphere charge is distributed only on the outer surface and for a non-conducting hollow sphere also charge is only there in the only thin wall of radius R and electric field exist due to the charge distribution, no matter if it is on a metal or non-metal. Figure-1.105 shows a solid conducting, hollow conducting and a hollow non-conducting uniformly charged sphere of equal radius R and charged with same charge Q. The electric field due to all these will be same in their surrounding with values given below.

For $x>R$ $\quad E_{out}=\frac{KQ}{x^2}$

For $x=R$ $\quad E_s=\frac{KQ}{R^2}$

For $x<R$ $\quad E_{in}=0$

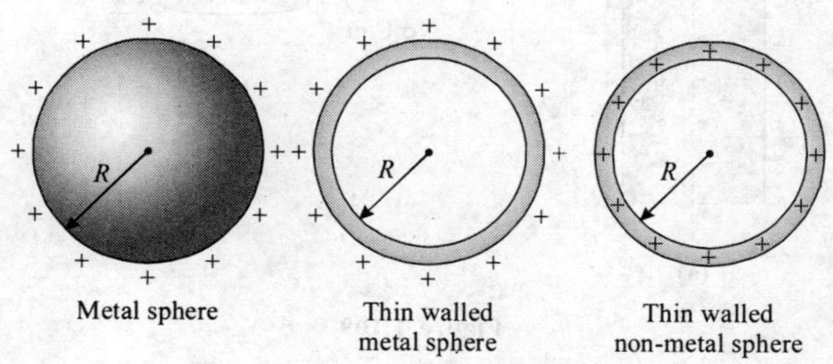

Figure 1.105

Thus for all these cases of a uniformly surface charges sphere, variation of electric field strength with distance from center is given by the curve shown in figure-1.104.

1.7.7 Electric Field Strength due to a Uniformly Charged Non-conducting Sphere

Figur-1.106 shows a non-conducting uniformly volume charged sphere of radius R and charge Q. By symmetry of charge distribution again we can say that everywhere in surrounding of sphere the electric field strength is radially outward as it is positively charged and if it were negative then electric field direction would be radially inward. For outside points we can say by symmetry that electric field can be determined by treating its charge at centre as field as radial symmetry and it appear to be originating from center. Thus for exterior points electric field strength at a point at a distance x from centre can be given as

For $x>R$ $\quad E_{out}=\frac{KQ}{x^2}$ ...(1.61)

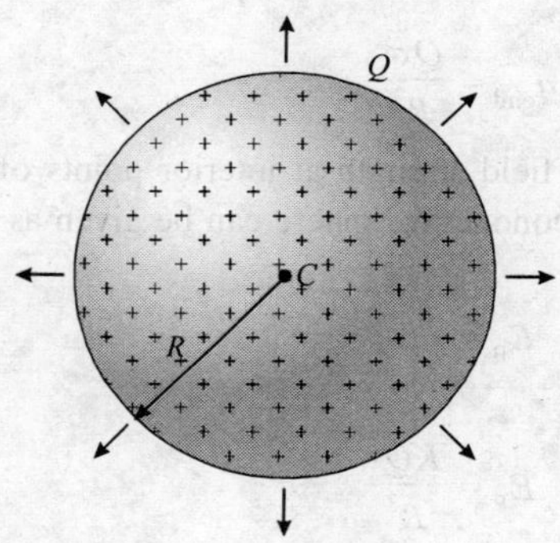

Figure 1.106

Similarly for surface points we'll use

For $x=R$ $\quad E_S=\frac{KQ}{R^2}$ ...(1.62)

For interior points, say we calculate electric field at a point P as shown in figure-1.107 which is located at a distance x from centre of sphere. For this we divide the sphere in two parts. A solid sphere of radius x, on the surface of which point P is located. Another is a shell of inner radius x and outer radius R for which point P is a point on its inner surface.

In this situation the electric field strength at point P is only due to the inner sphere of radius x as due to the shell, which is uniformly charged, we've already analyzed in article-1.7.6 that at interior points electric field strength is zero. Thus electric field strength at point P can be given as

$$E_P=\frac{Kq_{encl}}{x^2}$$

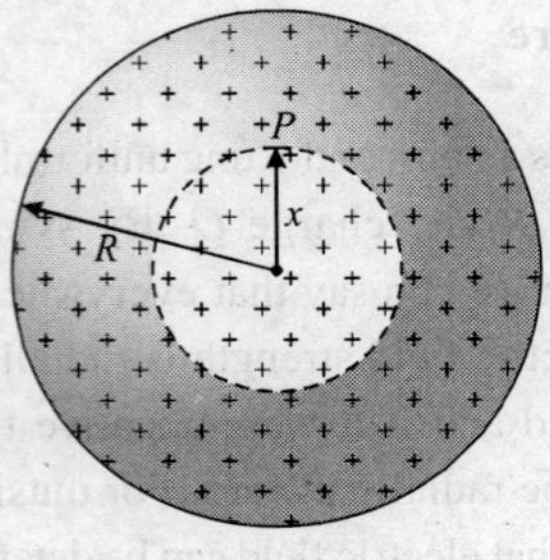

Figure 1.107

Where q_{encl} is the charge enclosed in the inner sphere of radius x which can be given as

$$q_{end} = \frac{Q}{\frac{4}{3}\pi R^3} \times \frac{4}{3}\pi x^3$$

$$\Rightarrow \quad q_{end} = \frac{Qx^3}{R^3}$$

Thus electric field strength at interior points of a uniformly charged non conducting sphere can be given as

$$E_P = \frac{K}{x^2}\left(\frac{Qx^3}{R^3}\right)$$

$$\Rightarrow \quad E_P = \frac{KQx}{R^3} \qquad \ldots(1.63)$$

Sometime in some cases instead of total charge of sphere, volume charge density is given. If ρ C/m^3 be the volume charge density of charge distribution in sphere then total charge of sphere can be given as

$$Q = \rho \times \frac{4}{3}\, pR^3$$

Thus electric field strength at interior points of sphere can be given as

$$E_P = \frac{Kx}{R^3} \times \left[\rho \times \frac{4}{3}\pi R^3\right]$$

$$\Rightarrow \quad E_P = \frac{1}{4\pi\epsilon_0} \cdot \frac{x}{R^3} \times r \times \frac{4}{3}\, pR^3$$

$$\Rightarrow \quad E_P = \frac{\rho x}{3\epsilon_0} \qquad \ldots(1.64)$$

1.7.8 Variation Curve of Electric Field due to a Uniformly Charged Non-conducting Sphere with Distance

We can plot the electric field strength due to a uniformly charged non-conducting sphere using the equations-(1.61), (1.62) and (1.63), the graph is shown in figure-1.108.

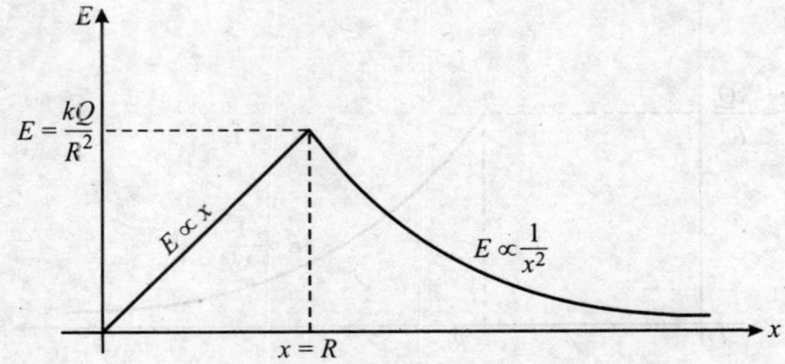

Figure 1.108

1.7.9 Electric Field Strength due to a Long Uniformly Charged Conducting Cylinder

Figure-1.109(a) shows a long conducting cylinder charged uniformly on its surface with surface density σ C/m^2. Due to uniform charge distribution on cylinder surface, by symmetry the electric field direction can be considered radially outward as shown. Here for exterior points it can be considered that electric field is originating or appear to be originating from the central axis of the cylinder. Thus for outer points we can calculate electric field strength due to the charge on cylinder by using the result of a uniformly charged long wire in which the electric field configuration is exactly the same. Thus the electric field strength due to the cylinder at a distance x from the central axis of cylinder is given by equation-(1.42) as

$$E_P = \frac{2K\lambda}{x}$$

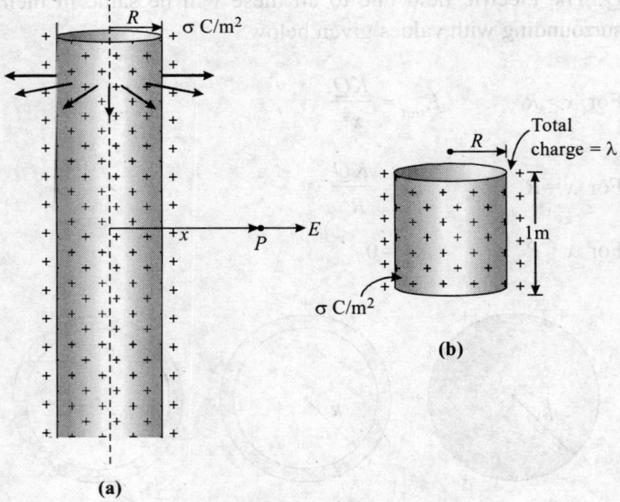

Figure 1.109

Where λ is charge per unit length on the cylinder which can be calculated from the 1 m length of a segment of the conducting cylinder as shown in figure-1.109(b), given as

$$\lambda = \sigma \times 2\pi R \times 1$$

Thus E_P is given as

$$E_P = \frac{2 \times \sigma \cdot 2\pi R}{4\pi \epsilon_0 x}$$

$$\Rightarrow \qquad E_P = \frac{\sigma R}{\epsilon_0 x} \qquad \ldots(1.65)$$

For points on surface, we use $x = R$ so electric field strength on the surface points can be given by using equation-(65) as

$$E_S = \frac{\sigma}{\epsilon_0} \qquad \ldots(1.66)$$

For interior points, we know inside a metal body due to static charges electric field strength is always zero, thus we have

$$E_{in} = 0 \qquad \ldots(1.67)$$

A solid metal cylinder when uniformly charged, its whole charge is distributed on its surface uniformly. If there is a thin walled hollow cylindrical shell whether conducting or non conducting and it is uniformly charged then also the charge is distributed only on its surface so the electric field strength in such cases of a hollow uniformly charged sphere can also be given by the above equations-(1.65), (1.66) and (1.67).

1.7.10 Electric Field Strength due to a Long Uniformly Charged Non-conducting Cylinder

Figure-1.110 shows a long non-conducting cylinder uniformly charged with a volume charge density ρ C/m^3. The electric field strength due to symmetry of charges in this case is also in radially outward direction in such a way that it appears to be originating from the axis of cylinder.

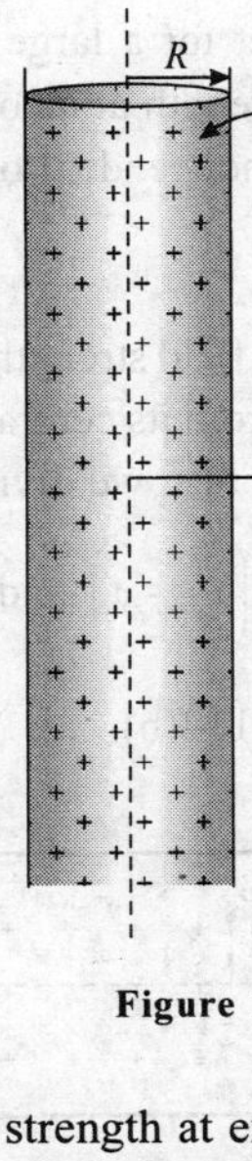

Figure 1.110

Thus electric field strength at exterior points of cylinder at a distance x from the axis of cylinder can be given by the result of a long uniformly charged wire as

$$E_P = \frac{2K\lambda}{x}$$

Where λ is the charge per unit on the cylinder which can be given as

$$\lambda = \rho \times \pi R^2 \times 1$$

Thus we have

$$E_P = \frac{2K(\rho \pi R^2)}{x}$$

$$\Rightarrow \qquad E_P = \frac{\rho R^2}{2 \epsilon_0 x} \qquad \ldots(1.68)$$

Electric field strength on the surface of this cylinder is given by using $x = R$ in above equation-(1.68) as

$$E_S = \frac{\rho R}{2 \epsilon_0} \qquad \ldots(1.69)$$

Now if we calculate the electric field strength at interior points of the cylinder, such as a point P located at a distance x from the axis of cylinder as shown in figure-1.111. To calculate this, we divide the cylinder in two parts in the same way we did for interior points of a uniformly charged solid non conducting sphere. One part is an inner solid cylinder of radius x for which point P is on its outer surface. Another is a cylindrical shell of inner radius x and outer radius R and point P is on its inner surface.

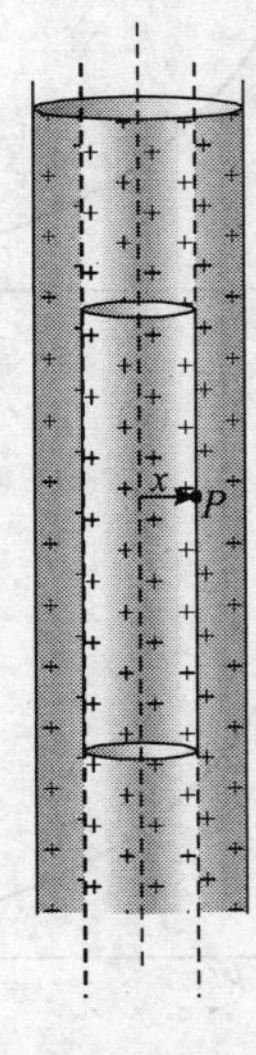

Figure 1.111

Now due to uniform charge distribution in a hollow cylinder it is already discussed that electric field does not exist at any interior point, thus the electric field at point P will only be due to the inner cylinder of radius x. For determining this we again assume that the inner cylinder behaves like a long line of charge and whole charge of inner cylinder is concentrated at its axis, whose charge per unit length λ can be given as

$$\lambda = \rho \times \pi x^2 \times 1 \quad \ldots(1.70)$$

Thus electric field strength at point P can be given by using the result of electric field of a line charge as

$$E_{\text{in}} = \frac{2K\lambda}{x}$$

Substituting the value of l from equation-(1.70) we get

$$E_{\text{in}} = \frac{1}{2\pi \epsilon_0} \times \frac{\rho \pi x^2}{x}$$

$$\Rightarrow \quad E_{\text{in}} = \frac{\rho x}{2 \epsilon_0} \quad \ldots(1.71)$$

1.7.11 Variation of Electric Field Strength for a Uniformly Charged Long Cylinder

Figure-1.112(a) shows the variation of electric field strength due to a long uniformly charged solid conducting or a hollow non conducting cylinder which is plotted by using equations-(1.65), (1.66) and (1.67) and figure-1.112(b) shows the variation of electric field strength due to a long uniformly charged solid non conducting cylinder which is plotted by using equations-(1.68), (1.69) and (1.71).

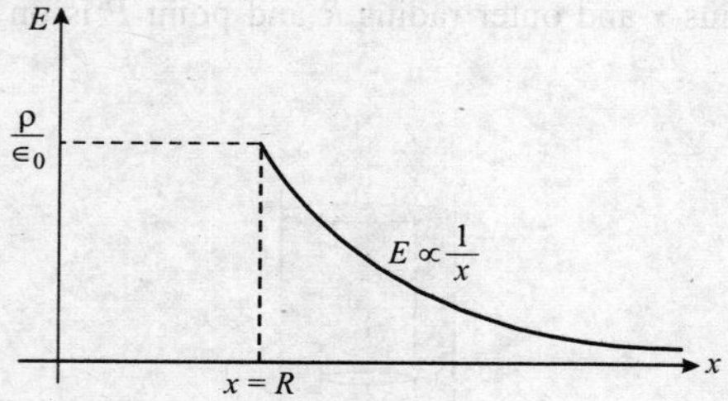

(a)

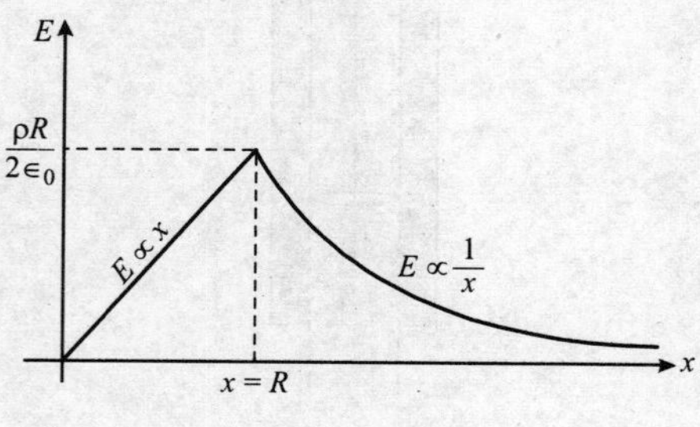

(b)

Figure 1.112

1.7.12 Electric Field due to a Large Thick Charged Sheet

Figure-1.113 shows a large non conducting sheet of thickness d, uniformly charged at charge density ρ C/m³. On both sides of sheet due to this charge electric field strength is directed, away from the sheet as shown in figure. On both the sides at outer points of the sheet electric field configuration is such that it appears to be originating from the central plane of the sheet and for outer points we can consider that whole charge of the sheet is concentrated at its central plane.

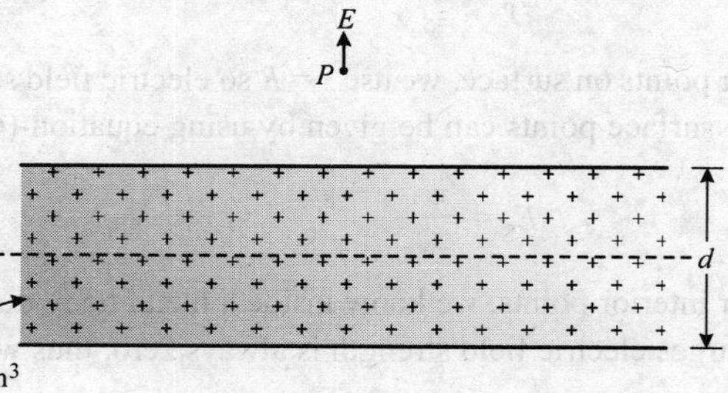

Figure 1.113

The electric field strength at a point P in front of the sheet as shown in figure-1.113 can be given by using the result of a large sheet of charge as already calculated in equation-(1.54) in article-1.5.2 and 1.5.3 which is given as

$$E_{\text{P}} = \frac{\sigma}{2 \epsilon_0}$$

Where σ is the charge per unit surface area of the sheet which can be calculated by considering unit area on this sheet surface having thickness d as

$$\sigma = \rho \times d \times 1 \quad \ldots(1.72)$$

Substituting the value of s in above expression of electric field, we get

$$E_{\text{P}} = \frac{\rho d}{2 \epsilon_0} \quad \ldots(1.73)$$

Similar to the large thin sheet for a large uniformly charged sheet also the electric field strength at its outer points is given by equation-(1.73) and it is independent of the distance from the sheet.

Now we will calculate electric field strength at an interior point P of the sheet at a distance x from its central plane as shown in figure-1.114(a). To determine this, we divide the sheet in two large sheets, one of thickness $\left(\frac{d}{2} - x\right)$ and other of thickness $\left(\frac{d}{2} + x\right)$ as shown in figure-1.114(b).

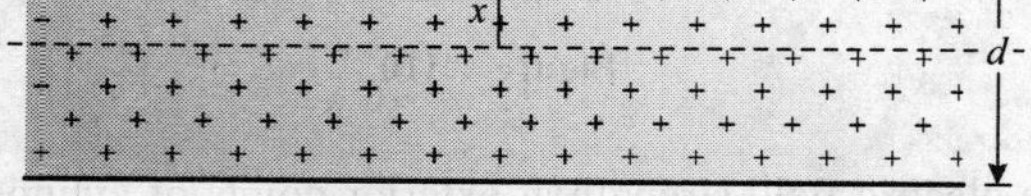

(a)

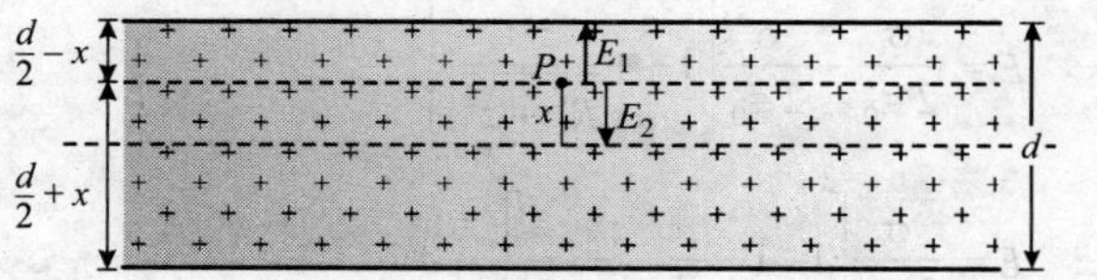

(b)

Figure 1.114

Due the thin part of sheet of thickness $(d/2 - x)$, the electric field at point P is in downward direction, say if it is considered as E_2 then it is given by the expression in equation-(1.73) as

$$E_2 = \frac{\rho\left(\frac{d}{2} - x\right)}{2\epsilon_0} \quad \ldots(1.74)$$

Similarly due to thick part of sheet electric field at P is in upward direction, say if it is considered as E_1 then again it is given by equation-(1.73) as

$$E_1 = \frac{\rho\left(\frac{d}{2} + x\right)}{2\epsilon_0} \quad \ldots(1.75)$$

Net electric field at point P can be given by the difference of the two electric field strengths given in equations-(1.74) and (1.75) as

$$E_P = E_1 - E_2$$

$$\Rightarrow \quad E_P = \frac{\rho\left(\frac{d}{2} + x\right)}{2\epsilon_0} - \frac{\rho\left(\frac{d}{2} - x\right)}{2\epsilon_0}$$

$$\Rightarrow \quad E_P = \frac{\rho x}{\epsilon_0} \quad \ldots(1.76)$$

 # Illustrative Example 1.26

Consider the classical model of an electron such that a nucleus of charge $+e$ is uniformly distributed within a sphere of radius 2Å. An electron of charge $-e$ at a radial distance 1Å moves inside this sphere. Find the force attracting the electron to the centre of the sphere. Calculate the frequency with which the electron would oscillate about the centre of the sphere, if released from rest at this radial distance.

Solution

Figure-1.115 shows the situation described in the question.

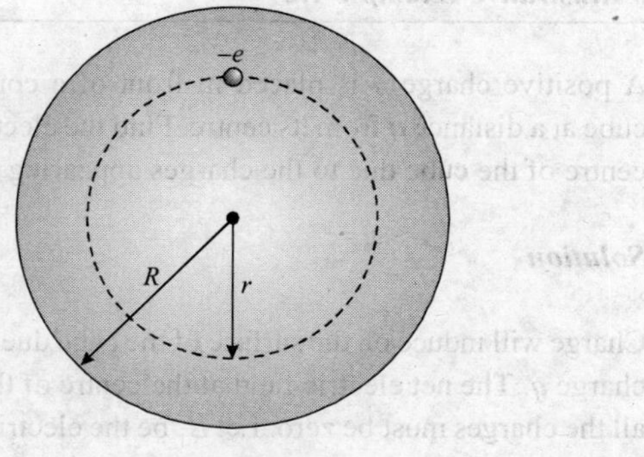

Figure 1.115

We know the electric field inside a uniformly charged sphere at a radial distance r is given as

$$E = \frac{K e r}{R^3}$$

Thus inward restoring force on electron is

$$F = -eE$$

$$\Rightarrow \quad F = -Ke^2 \frac{r}{R^3}$$

$$\Rightarrow \quad F = -\frac{(1.6\times10^{-19})^2 \times (9\times10^9)\times(1\times10^{-10})}{(2\times10^{-10})^3}$$

$$\Rightarrow \quad F = -\frac{(1.6\times10^{-19})^2 \times (9\times10^9)\times(1\times10^{-10})}{8\times10^{-30}}$$

$$\Rightarrow \quad F = -2.88 \times 10^{-9}\,\text{N}$$

Acceleration of electron is given as

$$a = \frac{F}{m} = -\frac{Ke^2 r}{mR} \quad \ldots(1.77)$$

As the acceleration is proportional to the displacement from the mean position this verifies that the motion of electron will be simple harmonic. For SHM acceleration of a particle is given as

$$a = -\omega^2 r \quad \ldots(1.78)$$

Comparing equations-(1.77) and (1.78), we get

$$\omega^2 = \frac{Ke^2}{mR^3}$$

$$\Rightarrow \quad \omega = \sqrt{\left[\frac{(1.6\times10^{-19})\times(9\times10^9)}{(9\times10^{-31})\times(8\times10^{-10})^3}\right]}$$

$$\Rightarrow \quad \nu = \frac{1}{2\pi}\sqrt{\left[\frac{(1.6\times10^{-19})\times(9\times10^9)}{(9\times10^{-31})\times(8\times10^{-30})}\right]}$$

$$\Rightarrow \quad \nu = 8.7 \times 10^{14}\,\text{s}^{-1}$$

Illustrative Example 1.27

A positive charge q is placed in front of a conducting solid cube at a distance d from its centre. Find the electric field at the centre of the cube due to the charges appearing on its surface.

Solution

Charge will induce on the surface of the cube due to the positive charge q. The net electric field at the centre of the cube due to all the charges must be zero. Let E_1 be the electric field due the charges appearing on the surface of the cube and if E_2 is the electric field due to charge q, then we have

$$\vec{E}_1 + \vec{E}_2 = 0$$

$$\Rightarrow \quad \vec{E}_1 = -\vec{E}_2$$

$$\Rightarrow \quad E_1 = E_2$$

The electric field due to charge q at the centre of the cube,

$$E_2 = \left(\frac{1}{4\pi \epsilon_0}\right)\frac{q}{d^2}$$

$$\Rightarrow \quad E_1 = \left(\frac{1}{4\pi \epsilon_0}\right)\frac{q}{d^2}$$

Illustrative Example 1.28

A large nonconducting surface has a uniform charge density σ. A small circular hole of radius R is cut in the middle of the sheet, as shown in figure-1.116. Ignore fringing of the field lines around all edges calculate the electric field at point P, a distance z from the centre of the hole along its axis.

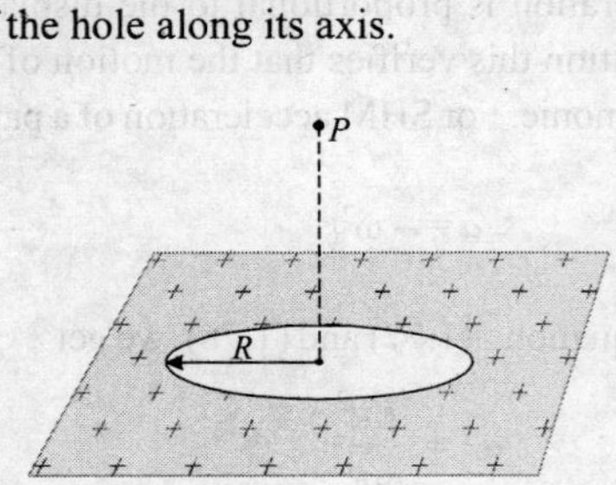

Figure 1.116

Solution

The electric field due to the given charge sheet is

$$E = E_{\text{conducting surface}} - E_{\text{hole}}$$

$$\Rightarrow \quad E = \frac{\sigma}{2\epsilon_0} - \frac{\sigma}{2\epsilon_0}\left[1 - \frac{z}{\sqrt{R^2+z^2}}\right]$$

$$\Rightarrow \quad E = \frac{\sigma}{2\epsilon_0}\left[1 - 1 + \frac{z}{\sqrt{R^2+z^2}}\right]$$

$$\Rightarrow \quad E = \frac{\sigma z}{2\epsilon_0 (R^2+z^2)^{1/2}}$$

Illustrative Example 1.29

A thin insulating wire is stretched along the diameter of an insulated circular hoop of radius R. A small bead of mass m and charge $-q$ is threaded onto the wire. Two small identical charges are tied to the hoop at points opposite to each other, so that the diameter passing through them is perpendicular to the thread as shown in figure-1.117. The bead is released at a point which is located at a distance x_0 from the centre of the hoop. Assume that $x_0 << R$.

(a) What is the resultant force acting on the charged bead?

(b) Describe the motion of the bead after it is released

(c) Use the assumption that $\frac{x}{R} << 1$ to obtain an approximate equation of motion, and find the displacement and velocity of the bead as functions of time

(d) When will the velocity of the bead will become zero for the first time ?

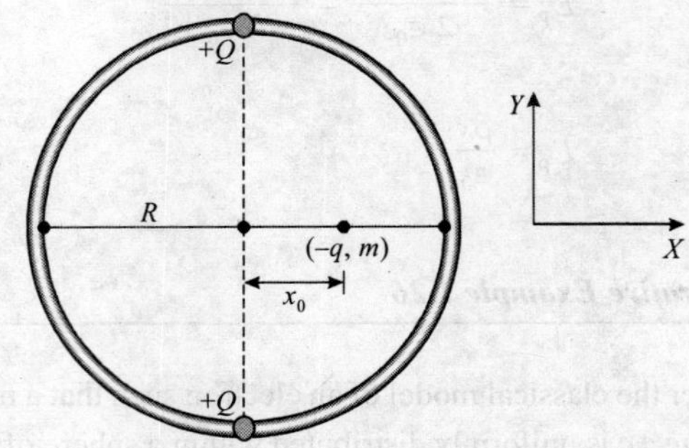

Figure 1.117

Solution

(a) Figure-1.118 shows the forces acting on the bead due to the two fixed charges. Components of these forces in y-direction gets cancelled out and along x-direction will be added up so net force acting on the bead is given as

$$F_{\text{net}} = 2F\cos\theta$$

$$\Rightarrow \quad F_{net} = \frac{2KQ.q}{(\sqrt{R^2+x_0^2})^2} \cdot \frac{x_0}{\sqrt{R^2+x_0^2}} \left(K = \frac{1}{4\pi\varepsilon_0}\right)$$

$$\Rightarrow \quad F_{net} = \frac{2KQqx_0}{(R^2+x_0^2)^{3/2}}$$

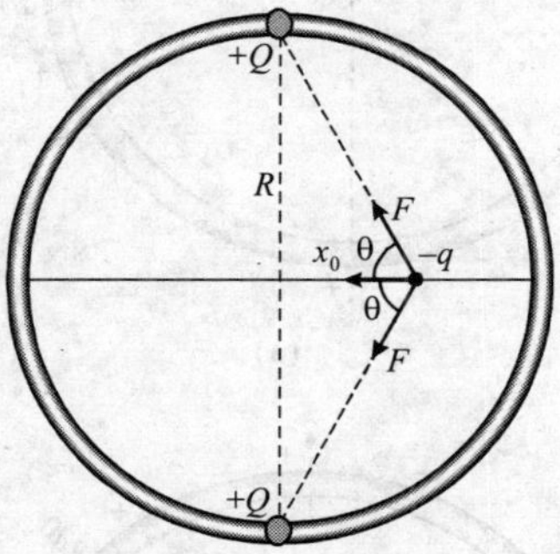

Figure 1.118

We can generalised the force by putting $x_0 = x$, which gives

$$F = -\frac{2KQqx}{(R^2+x^2)^{3/2}} \quad \ldots(1.79)$$

(b) Equation-(1.79) shows that the force on the bead is directed toward the center of the circular hoop and it is directly proportional to the displacement of the bead from mean position thus particle's motion is SHM. As particle is released from $x = x_0$, motion of bead will be periodic between $x = \pm x_0$

(c) For $\frac{x}{R} << 1$, we can use $R^2 + x^2 \approx R^2$

Thus equation-(1.79) can be rewritten as

$$F = -\left(\frac{2KQq}{R^3}\right)x$$

Acceleration of bead is given as

$$a = \frac{F}{m} = -\left(\frac{2KQq}{mR^3}\right)x \quad \ldots(1.80)$$

Since $a \propto -x$, motion will be simple harmonic in nature and for SHM acceleration is given as

$$a = -\omega^2 x \quad \ldots(1.81)$$

Comparing equations-(1.80) and (1.81) we get

$$\omega = \sqrt{\frac{2KQq}{mR}}$$

As particle starts from extreme position at $t = 0$, SHM equation is given as

$$x = x_0 \cos \omega t$$

$$\Rightarrow \quad v = \frac{dx}{dt} = -\omega x_0 \sin \omega t.$$

(d) Velocity will become zero again when bead will reach the other extreme position which will happen at $t = T/2 = \pi/\omega$ which is given as

$$t = \pi\sqrt{\frac{mR^3}{2KQq}}$$

1.8 Electric Field Strength due to Non Uniformly Charged Bodies

Till now upto previous article we've discussed about calculation of electric field strength due to uniformly charged bodies. If the charge is supplied to a body or bodies of different shapes in such a way that the charge distribution is not uniform throughout the volume of body then the electric field strength due to such a body at a point in its surrounding can be calculated by integrating the electric field strength at that point due to an elemental section of body. If $\overline{dE}$ be the electric field strength due to an elemental charge dq of the body then the net electric field strength at that point due to the whole body can be given by integrating $\overline{dE}$ over the surface or volume of the body depending upon its charge distribution as

$$\vec{E} = \int d\vec{E}$$

1.8.1 Electric Field Strength due to a Non-uniformly Charged Rod

The rod AB shown in figure-1.119 is of length L, charged with a linear charge density which depends on distance x from end A of rod, given as

$$\lambda = cx \text{ C/m} \quad \ldots(1.82)$$

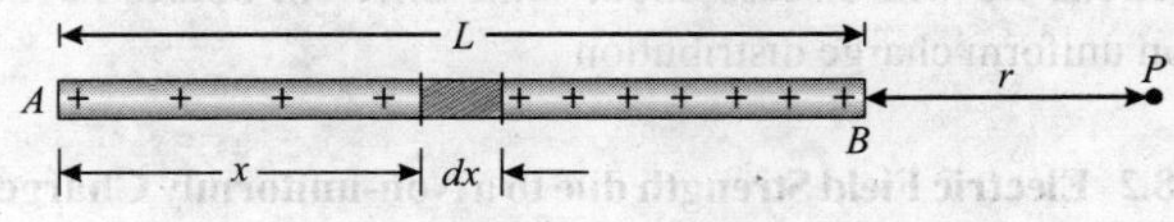

Figure 1.119

Due to this rod we wish to determine electric field strength at point P, shown in figure-1.66. For this we consider an element of width dx at a distance x from the end A of rod as shown. The charge on this element is given as

$$dq = \lambda dx = cx\, dx$$

As dq is a very small sized elemental charge, it can be treated as a point charge thus electric field strength dE at point P due to the elemental charge dq can be given as

$$dE = \frac{Kdq}{(L+r-x)^2}$$

Net electric field at P due to charge on whole rod can be calculated by integrating the above expression within limits from 0 to L, given as

$$E = \int dE = \int_0^L \frac{Kc\,x\,dx}{(L+r-x)^2}$$

For integration we substitute

$$t = L + r - x$$

$$\Rightarrow \quad dt = -dx$$

Changing the limits, we get

at $x = 0, \quad t = L + r$

at $x = L, \quad t = r$

Substituting the above values in the integrand, we get

$$E = \int_{L+r}^{r} \frac{Kc(L+r-t)dt}{t^2}$$

$$\Rightarrow \quad E = -Kc \int_{L+r}^{r} \left(\frac{L+r}{t^2}dt - \frac{1}{t}dt\right)$$

$$\Rightarrow \quad E = Kc\,(L+r)\left[\frac{1}{t}\right]_{L+r}^{r} + Kc\,[\ln t]_{L+r}^{r}$$

$$\Rightarrow \quad E = Kc\left[\frac{L+r}{r} - 1\right] + Kc\ln\left(\frac{r}{L+r}\right)$$

$$\Rightarrow \quad E = \frac{KcL}{r} - \text{Kc}\ln\left(\frac{r+L}{r}\right) \qquad \ldots(1.83)$$

Above expression of electric field obtained in equation-(1.83) is corresponding to the charge distribution on the given rod as provided in equation-(1.82). If the charge distribution changes then the electric field will also change accordingly. In further sections we will discuss about some different bodies having non uniform charge distribution.

1.8.2 Electric Field Strength due to a Non-uniformly Charged Ring

As shown in the figure-1.120(a), the ring is non-uniformly charged with linear charge density varying as a function of polar angle θ from x-axis as

$$\lambda = \lambda_0 \cos\theta \text{ C/m} \qquad \ldots(1.84)$$

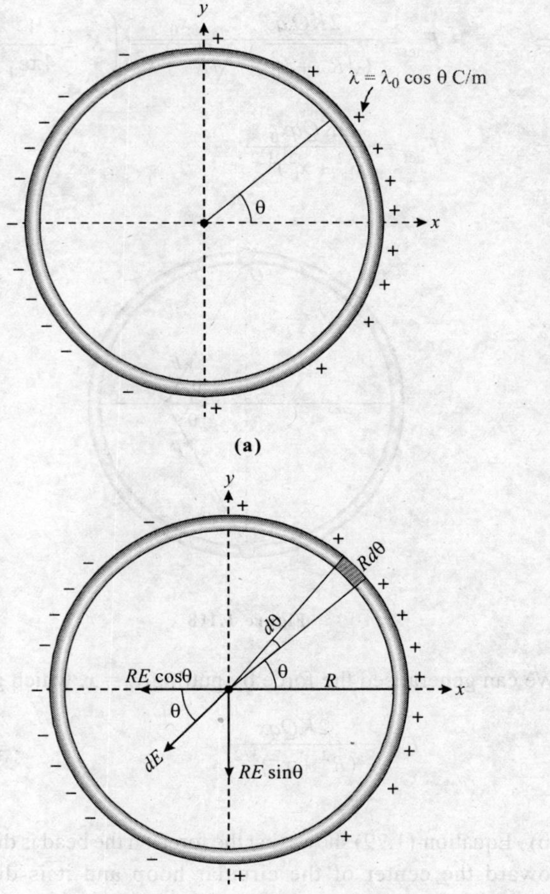

Figure 1.120

If we carefully analyze the function of linear charge density as given in equation-(1.84), we can state that due to cosine function, in the ring first and fourth quadrant are positively charged and second and third quadrant are negatively charged as shown in figure-1.120(a) with higher charge density at $\theta = 0°$ and π on x-axis which decreases as we move toward y-axis.

To determine electric field strength at the centre of ring due to this non uniform charge distribution on ring, we consider an element of polar width $d\theta$ at an angle θ on ring from x-axis as shown in figure-1.120(b). The charge on this element can be given as

$$dq = \lambda \times Rd\theta$$

$$= \lambda_0 \cos\theta \times Rd\theta$$

The electric field strength at centre of ring due to this element can be given by the result of electric field strength of a point charge as

$$dE = \frac{Kdq}{R^2}$$

To calculate the net electric field strength at centre of ring we integrate the components of this electric field for the circumference of ring. All the components $dE \sin\theta$ due to different elements on ring will cancel each other due to symmetry and the components $dE \cos\theta$ will all be added up as in same direction due to all the elements. Thus net electric field strength at centre will be given by

$$E_C = 2\int_{-\pi/2}^{+\pi/2} dE\cos\theta$$

$$\Rightarrow \quad E_C = 2\int_{-\pi/2}^{+\pi/2} \frac{K\lambda_0 \cos\theta \cdot Rd\theta}{R^2}\cos\theta$$

$$\Rightarrow \quad E_C = \frac{2K\lambda_0}{R}\int_{-\pi/2}^{+\pi/2} \cos^2\theta\, d\theta$$

$$\Rightarrow \quad E_C = \frac{2K\lambda_0}{R}\int_{-\pi/2}^{+\pi/2} \frac{1+\cos 2\theta}{2}\, d\theta$$

$$\Rightarrow \quad E_C = \frac{2K\lambda_0}{R}\int_{-\pi/2}^{+\pi/2} \frac{1+\cos 2\theta}{2}\, d\theta$$

$$\Rightarrow \quad E_C = \frac{K\lambda_0}{R}\left[\theta + \frac{\sin 2\theta}{2}\right]_{-\pi/2}^{+\pi/2}$$

$$\Rightarrow \quad E_C = \frac{\lambda_0}{4\epsilon_0 R} \qquad \ldots(1.85)$$

Above expression of electric field in equation-(1.85) is corresponding to the already provided charge distribution given in equation-(1.84).

1.8.3 Electric Field due to a Non-uniformly Charged Sphere

If a solid non conducting sphere of radius R is charged with a non uniform radially symmetric charge distribution of which the charge density varies with the distance from centre x as

$$\rho = \frac{\rho_0}{x}\ \text{C/m}^3 \qquad \ldots(1.86)$$

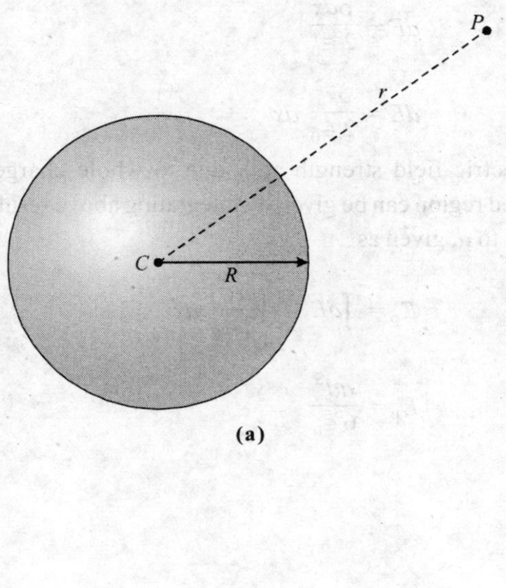

(a)

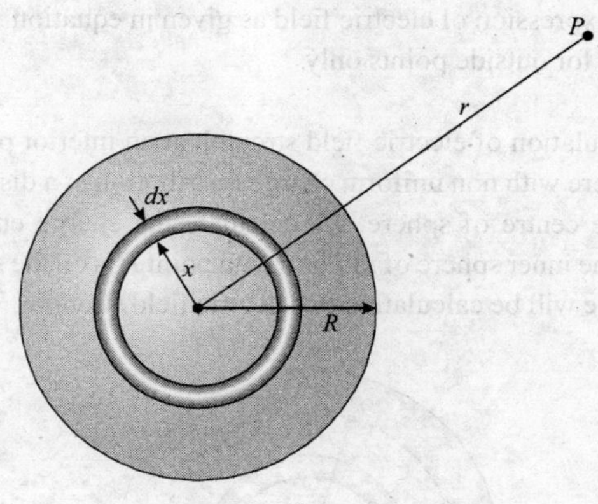

(b)

Figure 1.121

In this case we will calculate the electric field strength at a point P located at a distance r from centre of sphere outside it as shown in figure-1.121. Due to radially symmetric charge distribution in the spherical volume, the electric field will be in radially outward direction and for outer points the electric field appear to be originating from the center of sphere thus we can use the result of electric field due to a point charge for outer points as

$$E_P = \frac{KQ}{r^2} \qquad \ldots(1.87)$$

Where Q is the total charge of the sphere. For outer points as discussed we are considering that whole charge of sphere is concentrated at its centre. The total charge of sphere Q can be calculated by integrating the charge of an elemental shell of radius x and width dx as shown in figure-1.121(b). The charge dq in this elemental shall can be given as

$$dq = \rho \cdot 4\pi x^2 dx$$

$$\Rightarrow \quad dq = \frac{\rho_0}{x} \times 4\pi x^2 dx$$

$$\Rightarrow \quad dq = 4\pi\rho_0 x\, dx$$

Total charge of sphere can be given as

$$Q = \int dq$$

$$\Rightarrow \quad Q = \int_0^R 4\pi\rho_0 x\, dx$$

$$\Rightarrow \quad Q = 4\pi\rho_0\left[\frac{x^2}{2}\right]_0^R$$

$$\Rightarrow \quad Q = 2\pi\rho_0 R^2$$

Substituting the above charge in equation-(1.87), the electric field strength at outer points of the sphere can be given as

$$E_P = \frac{K(2\pi\rho_0 R^2)}{r^2} = \frac{\rho_0 R^2}{2\epsilon_0 r^2} \qquad \ldots(1.88)$$

Above expression of electric field as given in equation is valid for $r > R$ for outside points only.

For calculation of electric field strength at an interior point of this sphere with non uniform charge distribution at a distance r from the centre of sphere, we calculate the charge enclosed within the inner sphere of radius r with point P is on the surface where we will be calculating the electric field strength.

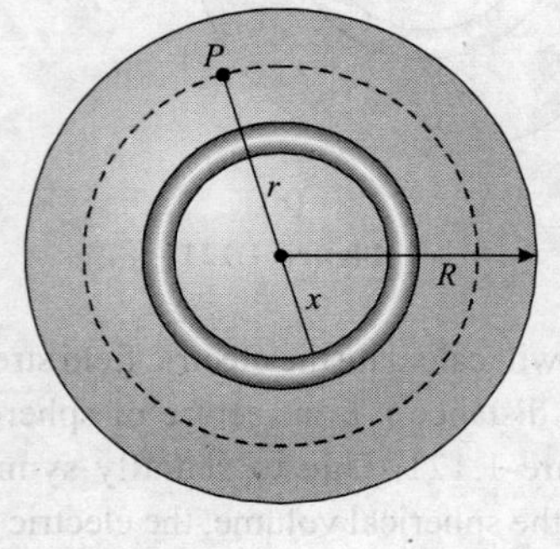

Figure 1.122

To find the enclosed charge within the inner solid sphere of radius r ($<R$), we consider an elemental spherical shell inside of radius x and width dx as shown in figure-1.122. The charge enclosed dq within the thin wall of this elemental shell is given as

$$dq = \rho \cdot 4\pi x^2 dx$$

$$\Rightarrow \quad dq = \frac{\rho_0}{x} \times 4\pi x^2 dx$$

$$\Rightarrow \quad dq = 4\pi\rho_0 x\, dx$$

Total charge enclosed within the inner solid sphere of radius r is given by integrating above elemental charge within limits from 0 to r ($<R$) as

$$q_{\text{encl}} = \int_0^r \frac{\rho_0}{R} \cdot 4\pi x^2 dx$$

$$\Rightarrow \quad q_{\text{encl}} = 2\pi\rho_0 r^2$$

Here electric field strength at point P can be given by considering the charge in this inner sphere as center as

$$E_P = \frac{Kq_{encl}}{r^2} = \frac{K(2\pi\rho_0 r^2)}{r^2}$$

$$\Rightarrow \quad E_P = \frac{\rho_0}{2\epsilon_0} \qquad \ldots(1.89)$$

The above expression of electric field as given in equation we can see that the above expression is independent of distance from centre. This is because of the specific charge distribution as specified in equation-(1.86). This is not a standard result but we can note that if in a region if charge distribution is radially symmetric and charge density is inversely proportional to the distance from a fixed point then electric field in the region is constant and does not vary with the radial distance from the fixed point.

1.8.4 Electric Field due to a Large Non Uniformly Charged Slab

Figure-1.123 shows a region between yz plane and a plane parallel to yz plane at $x = d$ which is charged with a non uniform distribution of charge of which charge density varies with x and it is given as

$$\rho = ax^2 \text{ C/m}^3 \qquad \ldots(1.90)$$

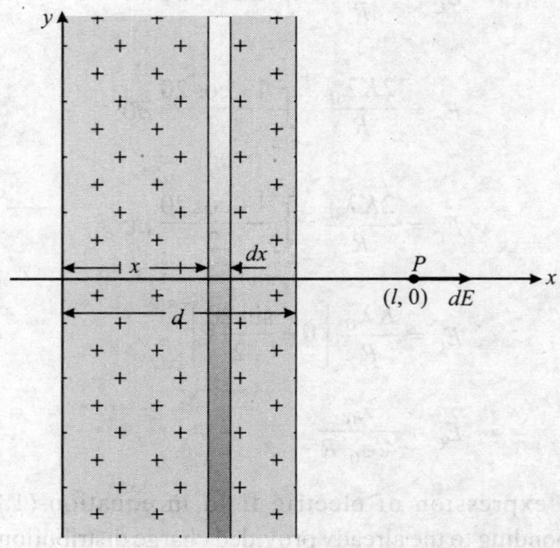

Figure 1.123

In this case we will calculate the electric field strength due to this slab at an outside point P (l, 0). To calculate this electric field strength first we consider an elemental sheet of width dx at a distance x from the yz plane within the specified charged region as shown. Electric field strength at P due to this elemental sheet of charge can be given by the result already obtained in equation-(1.73) in article-1.7.12 given as

$$dE = \frac{\rho dx}{2\epsilon_0}$$

$$\Rightarrow \quad dE = \frac{ax^2}{2\epsilon_0} dx$$

Net electric field strength at P due to whole charge in the specified region can be given by integrating above result within limits 0 to d, given as

$$E_P = \int dE = \int_0^d \frac{ax^2}{2\epsilon_0} dx$$

$$\Rightarrow \quad E_P = \frac{ad^3}{6\epsilon_0} \qquad \ldots(1.91)$$

The above electric field strength obtained in equation-(1.91) is corresponding to the charge distribution in the region as given by the equation-(1.90).

1.8.5 Electric Field Inside a Cavity of Charged Body

Consider a non-conducting sphere shown in figure-1.124. which is charged uniformly with charge density ρ C/m^3. Inside the sphere a spherical cavity is made with centre at C which is displaced from the center of the sphere by a position vector $\vec{a}$ as shown.

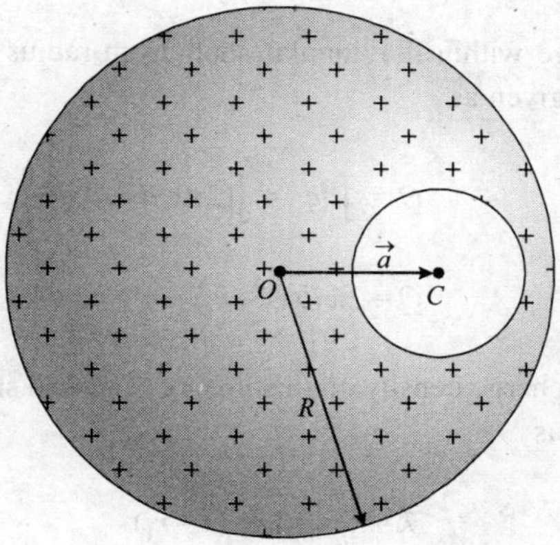

Figure 1.124

In above case, we will determine the electric field strength inside the above cavity in sphere as mentioned. For this we consider a point P in the cavity such that it is located at a position vector $\vec{x}$ from the centre of sphere and at a position vector $\vec{y}$ from the centre of cavity as shown in figure-1.125.

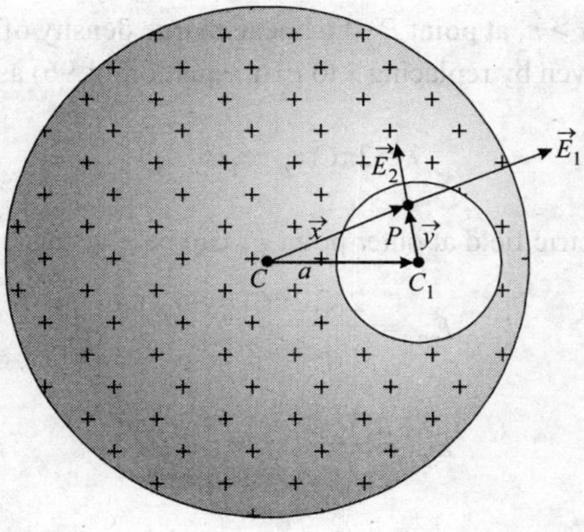

Figure 1.125

If $\vec{E_1}$ is considered to be the electric field strength at P due to the complete charge of the sphere (including the charges inside cavity also of same charge density) then as already discussed in article-1.7.7 we know that electric field strength inside a uniformly charged sphere can be given by the result from equation-(1.64) given as

$$\vec{E_1} = \frac{\rho \vec{x}}{3 \epsilon_0} \quad \ldots(1.92)$$

Similarly if we determine the electric field at point P only due to the uniform charge distribution in the region of cavity then the electric field at point P due to cavity charges can also be given by the equation-(1.64). If $\vec{E_2}$ be the electric field at point P only due to the cavity charge then it can be given as

$$\vec{E_2} = \frac{\rho \vec{y}}{3 \epsilon_0} \quad \ldots(1.93)$$

Thus net electric field due to the charged sphere in the cavity at point P can be obtained by vectorially subtracting the electric field strength at point P due to whole charge in sphere (including cavity region) and the electric field strength at P only due to the charge in cavity region. This can be calculated by using the field values in equations-(1.92) and (1.93), given as

$$\vec{E_2} = \vec{E_1} - \vec{E_2}$$

$$\Rightarrow \quad \vec{E_2} = \frac{\rho}{3 \epsilon_0} (\vec{x} - \vec{y})$$

From figure-1.125 we can see that $\vec{x} - \vec{y} = \vec{a}$ thus above equation can be written as

$$\vec{E_2} = \frac{\rho \vec{a}}{3 \epsilon_0} \quad \ldots(1.94)$$

Above expression of electric field strength in equation-(1.94) shows that the net electric field inside the cavity is uniform and in the direction of $\vec{a}$ i.e. along the line joining the centre of spheres and cavity.

By doing similar to above analysis for a long cylinder, we can also calculate the electric field strength inside a cylindrical cavity of a long uniformly charged cylinder. If cavity axis is displaced from axis of cylinder by a displacement vector $\vec{a}$ as shown in figure-1.126, then by the similar analysis which we've done above for a sphere, we can calculate and show that the electric field strength inside the cylindrical cavity is uniform and can be given as

$$\vec{E} = \frac{\rho \vec{a}}{2 \epsilon_0} \quad \ldots(1.95)$$

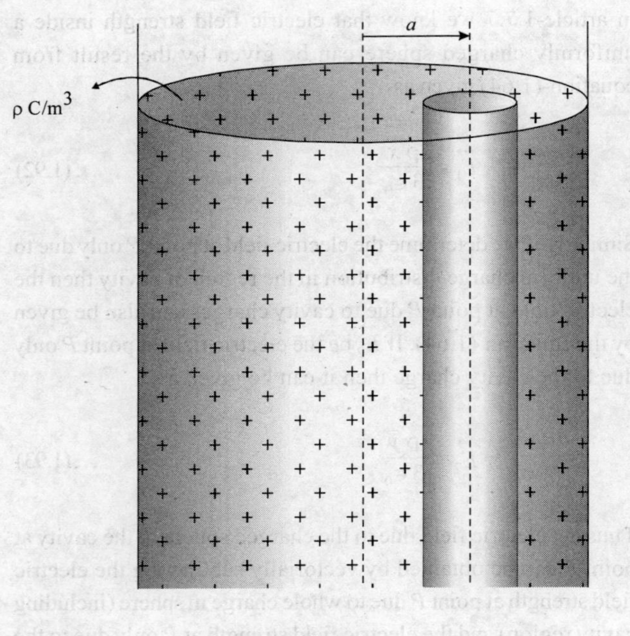

Figure 1.126

Illustrative Example 1.30

An infinitely long cylindrical shell of inner radius r_1 and outer radius r_2 is charged in its volume with a volume charge density which varies with distance from axis of cylinder as $\rho = b/r$ C/m³ which C is a positive constant and r is the distance from axis of cylinder. Find the electric field intensity at a point P at a distance x from axis of cylinder.

Solution

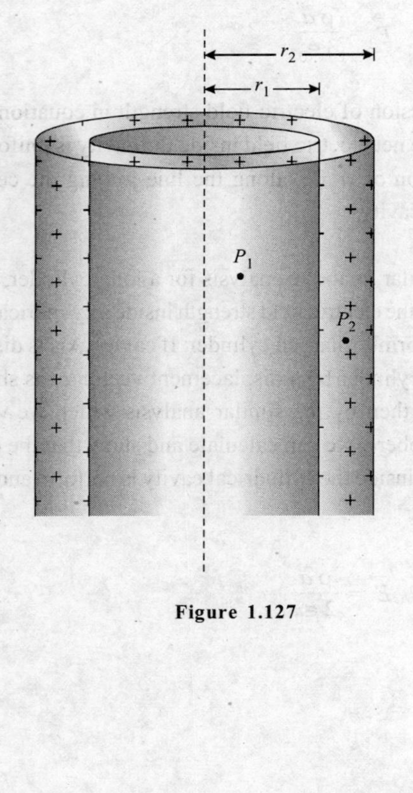

Figure 1.127

(a) At $x < r_1$

as there is no charge enclosed for $x < r_1$

hence electric field at $P_1 = 0$

(b) At x such that $r_1 < x < r_2$

We can calculate the charge enclosed for a length l of cylindrical shell by considering an elemental cylindrical shell of length l, radius x and width dx. The charge dq in the elemental shell is given as

$$dq = \rho \times 2\pi x\, dx \times l$$

Total charge within the annular shell from radius r_1 to x of length l is given as

$$Q = \int dq = \int_{r_1}^{x} (2\pi x\, dx \times l) \times \frac{b}{x}$$

$$\Rightarrow \quad Q = 2\pi\, lb\, (x - r_1)$$

The linear charge density on this inner cylindrical shell can be calculated as

$$\lambda = \frac{Q}{l} = 2\pi b\, (x - r_1) \qquad \ldots(1.96)$$

Thus electric field at a distance x from axis of this shell is given by considering whole charge concentrated at its axis by using the result of line charge as

$$E_{P_2} = \frac{2K\lambda}{x} = \frac{2K\left[2\pi b(x - r_1)\right]}{x}$$

$$\Rightarrow \quad E_{P_2} = \frac{4K\ \pi C(x - r_1)}{x}$$

(c) For $x > r_2$ at point P_3 the linear charge density of cylinder can be given by replacing x to r_2 in equation-(1.96) as

$$\lambda = 2\pi C(r_2 - r_1)$$

Thus electric field at outer point P_3 can be given as

$$E_{P_3} = \frac{2K(2\pi C(r_2 - r_1))}{x}$$

$$\Rightarrow \quad E_{P_3} = \frac{4K\pi C(r_2 - r_1)}{x}$$

Illustrative Example 1.31

An infinitely long cylindrical surface of circular cross-section is uniformly charged lengthwise with the surface charged density $\sigma = \sigma_0 \cos\phi$, where ϕ is the polar angle of the cylindrical coordinate system whose z-axis coincides with the axis of the given surface. Find the magnitude and direction of the electric field strength vector on the z-axis.

Solution

Let ρ be the radius of the cylinder. The surface charge density varies as $\sigma = \sigma_0 \cos\phi$.

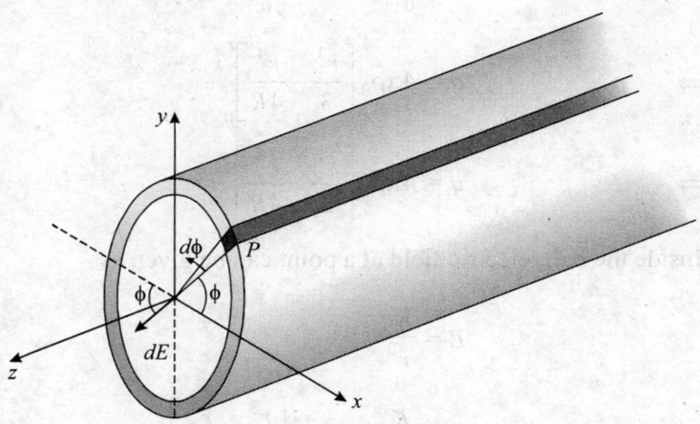

Figure 1.128

Thus it is maximum along the x-axis and goes on decreasing towards y-axis and becoming zero there. Consider a strip at point P on the cross section of the cylindrical surface whose length is parallel to the axis of the cylinder and whose width is $Rd\phi$.

Charge per unit length on the elemental strip is given as

$$\lambda = \sigma_0 \cos\phi \,.\, Rd\phi$$

Electric field at point O on the axis of cylinder due to the strip is given as

$$dE = \frac{2K\lambda}{R} = \frac{\sigma \cos\phi . Rd\phi}{2\pi\varepsilon_0 R}$$

Resolving above electric field along x and y axes, we get

$$dE_x = -\frac{\sigma_0 \cos^2\phi}{2\pi\varepsilon_0} d\phi$$

and $$dE_y = -\frac{\sigma_0 \cos\phi \sin\phi d\phi}{2\pi\varepsilon_0}$$

$$\Rightarrow \quad dE_x = -\frac{\sigma_0}{4\pi\varepsilon_0}(1+\cos 2\phi)d\phi;$$

$$\Rightarrow \quad dE_y = -\frac{\sigma_0}{4\pi\varepsilon_0}\sin 2\phi d\phi$$

Integrating above expressions between limits of ϕ from 0 to 2π gives

$$E_x = \int dE_x = -\frac{\sigma}{2\varepsilon_0}$$

and $$E_y = 0$$

 # Illustrative Example 1.32

A thin non-conducting ring of radius R has linear charge density $\lambda = \lambda_0 \cos\phi$, where λ_0 is a constant, ϕ is the azimuthal angle. Find the magnitude of the electric field strength on the axis of the ring as a function of the distance x from its centre. Investigate the obtained function at $x >> R$.

Solution

Figure-1.129 shows the charge distribution on the ring. We consider an element of length dl on ring at an azimuthal angle ϕ. This element subtends an angle $d\phi$ at the centre O. The charge on this element is given as

$$dq = \lambda\, dl$$

$$\Rightarrow \quad dq = \lambda_0 \cos\phi \,.\, Rd\phi$$

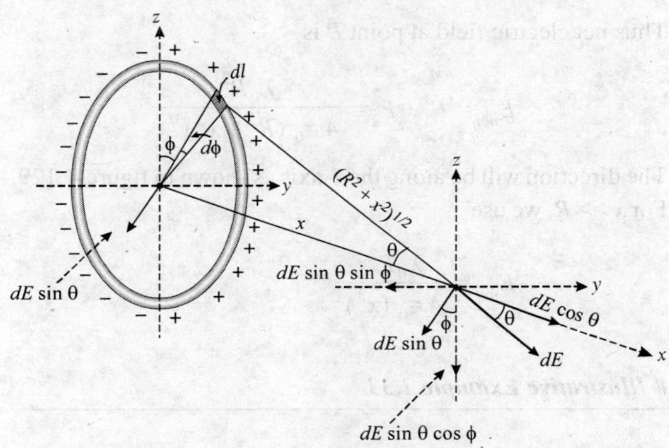

Figure 1.129

The electric field due to the charge on element at an axial point as shown in figure is given as

$$dE = \frac{Kdq}{(R^2+x^2)}$$

Figure-1.129 shows the components of electric field along and normal to the axis of ring. Due to positive half and negative half of ring along y and z directions, electric field components will get cancelled out. The components of electric fields due to positive and negative half rings along x direction will be in same direction so will get added up. Thus electric field due to positive half ring

$$E_1 = \int_{-\pi/2}^{+\pi/2} dE \sin\theta \sin\phi$$

$$\Rightarrow \quad E_1 = \int_{-\pi/2}^{+\pi/2} \frac{Kdq}{(R^2+x^2)} \times \frac{R}{(R^2+x^2)^{1/2}} \sin\phi$$

$$\Rightarrow \quad E_1 = \int_{-\pi/2}^{+\pi/2} \frac{K\lambda_0 R\cos\phi \, d\phi \times R\sin\phi}{(R^2+x^2)^{3/2}}$$

$$\Rightarrow \quad E_1 = \frac{K\lambda_0 R^2}{(R^2+x^2)^{3/2}} \times 2\int_0^{\pi/2} \left[\frac{1-\cos 2\phi}{2}\right] d\phi$$

$$\Rightarrow \quad E_1 = \frac{2K\lambda_0 R^2}{(R^2+x^2)^{3/2}}\left[\frac{\pi}{4}\right]$$

$$\Rightarrow \quad E_1 = \frac{\lambda_0 R^2}{8\in_0 (R^2+x^2)^{3/2}}$$

For negative part of ring also the field at point P will be same and in same direction, if it is E_2 then this is given as

$$E_2 = \frac{\lambda_0 R^2}{8\in_0 (R^2+x^2)^{3/2}}$$

Thus net electric field at point P is

$$E_{net} = E_1 + E_2 = \frac{\lambda_0 R^2}{4\in_0 (R^2+x^2)^{3/2}}$$

The direction will be along the x-axis as shown in figure-1.129. For $x >> R$, we use

$$E_{net} = \frac{\lambda_0 R^2}{4\in_0 (x^3)}$$

Illustrative Example 1.33

A ball of radius R carries a positive charge whose volume density depends on a separation r from the ball's centre as $\rho = \rho_0 (1 - r/R)$, where ρ_0 is a constant. Assuming the permittivities of the ball and the environment is equal to unity, find :

(a) The magnitude of the electric field strength as a function of the distance r both inside and outside the ball,

(b) The maximum intensity E_{max} and the corresponding distance r_m.

Solution

(a) As the charge distribution is spherically symmetric, electric field will be radially outward and at any point interior spherical charge can be considered at center. If we consider an elemental shell inside the ball at a radius r of width dr then charge within the shell volume is given as

$$dq = \rho dV$$

$$\Rightarrow \quad dq = \rho 4\pi r^2 dr$$

$$\Rightarrow \quad dq = \rho_0\left(1-\frac{r}{R}\right) \times 4\pi r^2 dr$$

Now total charge enclosed in the sphere of radius r can be determined by integrating the above expression from 0 to r, given as

$$q = \int_0^q dq = 4\pi\rho_0 \int_0^r \left(1-\frac{r}{R}\right) r^2 dr$$

$$\Rightarrow \quad q = 4\pi\rho_0 \left[\frac{r^3}{3} - \frac{r^4}{4R}\right]_0^r$$

$$\Rightarrow \quad q = 4\pi\rho_0 \left[\frac{r^3}{3} - \frac{r^4}{4R}\right]$$

Inside the ball, electric field at a point can be given as

$$E = \frac{Kq}{r^2}$$

$$\Rightarrow \quad E = \frac{K}{r^2} \times 4\pi\rho_0 \left[\frac{r^3}{3} - \frac{r^4}{4R}\right]$$

$$\Rightarrow \quad E = \frac{\rho_0 r}{3\in_0}\left(1-\frac{3r}{4R}\right) \quad \ldots(1.97)$$

When $r > R$, we use the total charge of ball which is distributed from 0 to R, given as

$$q_{\text{ball}} = \int_0^R \rho_0\left(r-\frac{r}{R}\right) 4\pi r^2 dr = \frac{4\pi\rho_0 R^3}{12}$$

The electric field outside the ball at a distance r from the center of ball is given as

$$E = \frac{Kq_{ball}}{r^2}$$

$$\Rightarrow \quad E = \frac{\rho_0 R^3}{12\in_0 r^2}$$

(b) For maximum electric field we use the inside electric field as a function of distance r as given in equation-(1.97) and use maxima-minima as

$$\frac{dE}{dr} = 0$$

$$\Rightarrow \quad \frac{dE}{dr} = \frac{\rho_0 R}{9\in_0}\left(1-\frac{6r}{4R}\right) = 0$$

$$\Rightarrow \quad \left(1-\frac{6r}{4R}\right) = 0$$

$$\Rightarrow \quad r = \frac{2R}{3}$$

Thus maximum electric field can be given by substituting the above value of r in equation-(1.106) as

$$E_{\max} = \frac{\rho_0}{3\epsilon_0}\left(\frac{2R}{3} - \frac{3}{4R} \times \frac{4R^2}{9}\right) = \frac{\rho_0 R}{9\epsilon_0}$$

Web Reference at www.physicsgalaxy.com

Age Group - Grade 11 & 12 | Age 17-19 Years

Section - ELECTROSTATICS

Topic - Electrostatics

Module Number - 39 to 54

Practice Exercise 1.4

(i) A solid sphere of radius R has a charge Q distributed in its volume with a charge density $\rho = kr^a$, where k and a are constants and r is the distance from its centre. If the electric field at $r = R/2$ is 1/8 times that at $r = R$, find the value of a.

[2]

(ii) The diagram shows a uniformly charged hemisphere of radius R. It has volume charge density ρ. If the magnitude of electric field at a point A located a distance $2R$ above its centre is E then what is the electric field at the point B which is $2R$ below its centre as shown in figure-1.130.

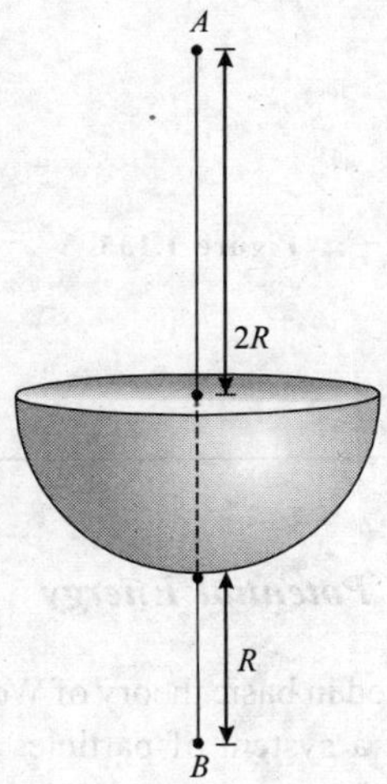

Figure 1.130

$[\frac{\rho R}{12\epsilon_0} - E]$

(iii) An infinitely long solid cylinder of radius R has a uniform volume charge density ρ. It has a spherical cavity of radius $R/2$ with its centre on the axis of the cylinder, as shown in the figure-1.131. Find the magnitude of the electric field at the point P, which is at a distance $2R$ from the axis of the cylinder.

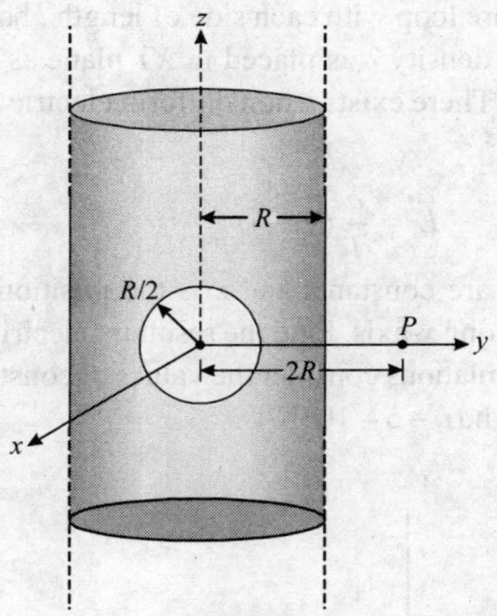

Figure 1.131

$[\frac{23\rho R}{96\epsilon_0}]$

(iv) Figure-1.132 shows two uniformly and oppositely charged spheres with volume charge density $+\rho$ and $-\rho$ are intersecting with some overlapped neutral region with their centres at a separation a, find the electric field strength in the overlapped region between the two spheres.

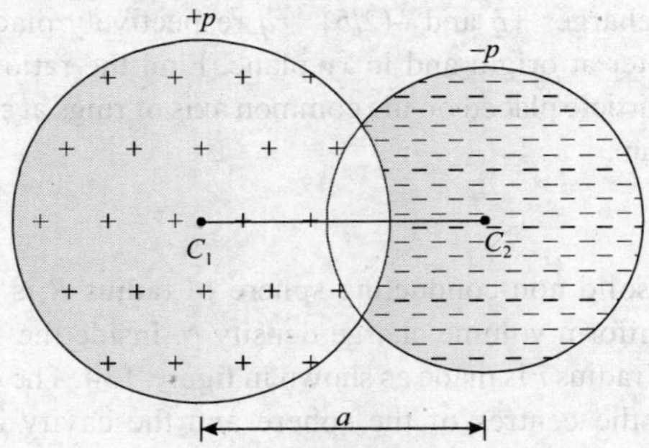

Figure 1.132

$[\frac{\rho a}{3\epsilon_0}]$

(v) Suppose the surface charge density over a sphere of radius R depends on a polar angle θ as $\sigma = \sigma_0 \cos\theta$, where σ_0 is a positive constant. Show that such a charge distribution can be represented as a result of a small relative shift of two uniformly charged balls of radius R whose charges are equal in magnitude and opposite in sign. Resorting to this representation, find the electric field strength vector inside the given sphere.

$[\frac{\sigma_0}{3\epsilon_0}]$

(vi) A nonconducting spherical shell, of inner radius a and outer radius b, has a volume charge density $\rho = A/r$, where A is a constant and r is the distance from the centre of the shell. At the centre of shell a positive point charge q is placed. What should be the value of constant A such that the electric field in the shell ($a \le r \le b$) is to be uniform.

$[q/2\pi a^2]$

(vii) A square loop with each side of length l having uniform linear charge density λ is placed in XY plane as shown in the figure-1.133. There exists a non uniform electric field in space given as

$$\vec{E} = \frac{a}{l}(x+l)\hat{i}$$

Here a and l are constants and x is the position of the point from origin along x-axis. Find the resultant electric force on the loop. For calculations consider the values of constant $l = 10$ cm, $\lambda = 20\ \mu$C/m and $a = 5 \times 10^5$ N/C.

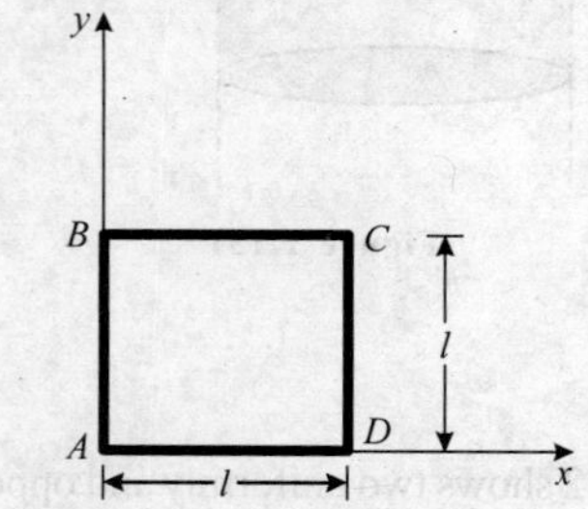

Figure 1.133

[6 N]

(viii) Two concentric rings, one of radius a and other of radius b have charges $+q$ and $-(2/5)^{-3/2}q$ respectively placed with their center at origin and in xy plane. Find the ratio b/a if a charge particle placed on the common axis of rings at $z = a$ is in equilibrium.

[2]

(ix) A solid non-conducting sphere of radius R is charged with a uniform volume charge density ρ. Inside the sphere a cavity of radius r is made as shown in figure-134. The distance between the centres of the sphere and the cavity is a. An electron e is kept inside the cavity at angle $\theta = 45°$ as shown. If at $t = 0$ this electron is released from point P, calculate the time it will take to touch the sphere on inner wall of cavity again.

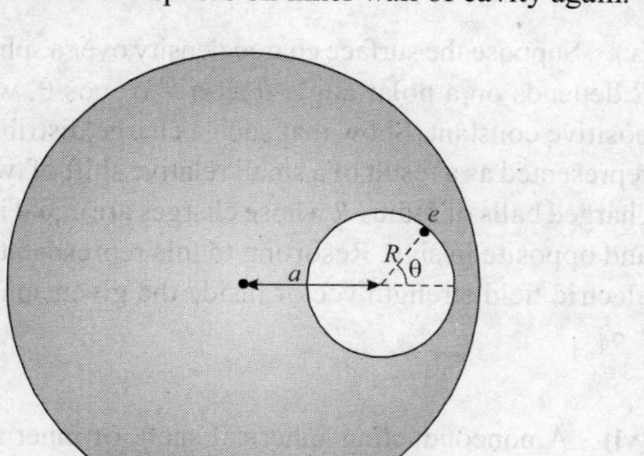

Figure 1.134

$\left[\sqrt{\frac{6\sqrt{2}mr\epsilon_0}{e\rho a}}\right]$

(x) An infinite non-conducting sheet having surface charge density σ has a hole of radius R in it. An electron with charge e and mass m is released on the axis of the hole at a distance $\sqrt{3}R$ from the centre. What will be the velocity with which it crosses the plane of sheet.

$\left[2\sqrt{\frac{\sigma eR}{m\epsilon_0}}\right]$

(xi) A uniform rod AB of mass m and length l is hinged at its mid point C as shown in figure-1.135. The left half (AC) of the rod has linear charge density $-\lambda$ and the right half (CB) has $+\lambda$ where λ is constant. A large non conducting sheet of uniform surface charge density σ is also present near the rod. Initially the rod is kept perpendicular to the sheet. The end A of the rod is initially at a distance d. Now the rod is rotated by a small angle in the plane of the paper and released. Prove that the rod will perform SHM and find its time period.

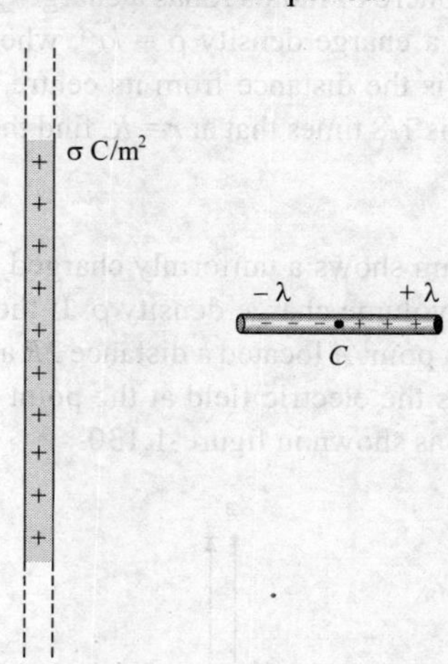

Figure 1.135

$\left[2\pi\sqrt{\frac{2m\epsilon_0}{3\lambda\sigma}}\right]$

1.9 Electrostatic Potential Energy

We've already studied in basic theory of Work and Energy that potential energy of a system of particles is defined only in conservative fields where work done against the force of system in assembling a system of particles in a given configuration and shape is stored in form of potential energy of system.

As electric field is also conservative, we define potential energy in it. Before proceeding on further discussion and analysis of electrostatic potential energy, first we should review and keep in mind the following fundamental points, which are useful in understanding potential energy in electric fields.

(i) Doing work implies supply of energy

(ii) Energy can neither be transferred nor be transformed into any other form without doing work.

(iii) Kinetic energy implies utilization of energy where as potential energy implies storage of energy.

(iv) Whenever work is done on a system of bodies, the supplied energy to the system is either used in form of kinetic energy of its particles or it will be stored in the system in some form, which increases the potential energy of system.

(v) When all particles of a system are separated far apart by infinite distance there will be no interaction between them. In general this state of no interaction we consider as reference state of zero potential energy.

(vi) Potential energy of a given system of particles is defined as the work done in assembling the particles in a given configuration against the interaction forces of particles.

Based on above points in electric field, the potential energy due to electrostatic interaction between particle which is called electrostatic potential energy can be defined in two ways

(i) Interaction energy of charged particles of a system

(ii) Self energy of a charged object

In this section, first we will discuss and analyze only about the interaction energy of charged particles of a system and different situations related to this. Self energy of a charged object we will discuss and analyze in upcoming articles.

1.9.1 Electrostatic Interaction Energy

Electrostatic interaction energy of a system of charged particles is defined as the external work required to assemble the particles from infinity to a given configuration.

When some charged particles are at infinite or very large separation, their potential energy is considered zero as a reference because no interaction is there between these particles at large separation. When these charges are brought close to each other in a given specified configuration, external work is required if the force between these particles is repulsive and energy is supplied to the system and final potential energy of system will be positive. If the force between the particles is attractive, work will be done by the system and final potential energy of system will be negative.

In next article using the same process, we will calculate the interaction potential energy of two charged bodies at a fixed separation.

1.9.2 Interaction Energy of a System of Two Charged Particles

Figure-1.136(a) shows two point charges $+q_1$ and $+q_2$ are kept at a separation r. In this state when these charges are brought from very large separation or from the state of no interaction then these will repel each other and in the process of brining these charges from no interaction state to the state shown in figure-1.136 some external work is required to be done again the electric repulsion between the charges. This work is considered to be stored in form of electrostatic potential energy of this system. We can calculate the work in the process of assembling these charges as explained below.

As electric forces are conservative forces which does not depend upon the path or process. The work can be calculated by considering initial and final state to be same. Figure-1.136(b) shows the process of bringing the two charges from large separation to the state shown in figure-1.136(b). We can consider that initially the charge q_1 is at rest which is kept fixed and charge q_2 is brought from far away point to the final separation r from q_1 as shown in figure.

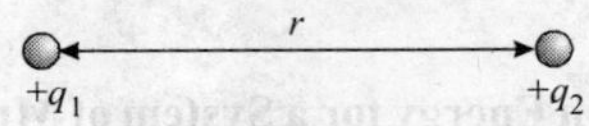

(a)

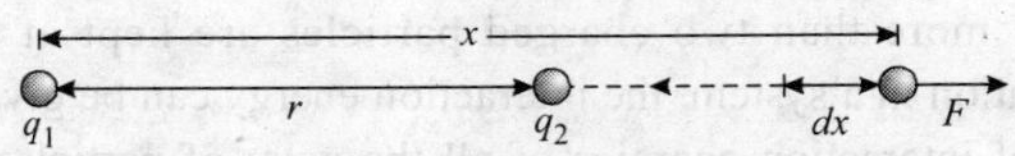

Figure 1.136

If we consider an intermediate state in the above process as shown in figure-1.136(b) when q_2 is located at a distance x from q_1 and it is being displaced toward q_1 by an elemental distance dx then work done by external agent in this elemental displacement of charge q_2 can be given as

$$dW = \vec{F}_{ext} . \vec{dx} \quad \ldots(1.98)$$

If we consider very slow displacement of the charge as it is not supposed to gain any kinetic energy then the external force will be almost balancing the electric coulombian repulsion between the two charges, thus we can use

$$\vec{F}_{ext} = -\frac{Kq_1q_2}{x^2}\hat{x}$$

From equation-(1.107), on substituting the force, we get

$$W = \int dW = \int_{\infty}^{r} \vec{F} . \vec{dx}$$

$$\Rightarrow \quad W = -\int_{\infty}^{r} \left(\frac{Kq_1q_2}{x^2}\hat{x}\right) . \vec{dx}$$

$$\Rightarrow \quad W = \int_{\infty}^{r} \frac{Kq_1q_2}{x^2} . dx$$

$$\Rightarrow \qquad W = -Kq_1q_2\left[-\frac{1}{x}\right]_{\infty}^{r} = \frac{Kq_1q_2}{r} \qquad \ldots(1.99)$$

The work done in the process of bringing the two charges from the state of no interaction to the state shown in figure-1.136(a) is calculated as given in equation-(1.99). This work is the energy spent by the external agent in execution of the process which is gained by the electric system of two charges. This amount of energy is stored as potential energy and called as "*Interaction Energy of the system of two charges*". Thus we use

$$W = U = \frac{Kq_1q_2}{r} \qquad \ldots(1.100)$$

If the two charges used in situation shown in figure-1.136(a) are of opposite sign, the potential energy will be negative as the work will be required to oppose the electrostatic attraction between the two charges when brought close from large separation to the final separation at state of rest.

$$U = -\frac{Kq_1q_2}{r}$$

1.9.3 Interaction Energy for a System of Multiple Charged Particles

When more than two charged particles are kept at some separation in a system, the interaction energy can be given by sum of interaction energies of all the pairs of particles. For example if a system of three particles having charges q_1, q_2 and q_3 is given as shown in figure-1.137. The total interaction energy of this system can be given as

$$U = \frac{Kq_1q_2}{r_3} + \frac{Kq_1q_3}{r_2} + \frac{Kq_2q_3}{r_1} \qquad \ldots(1.101)$$

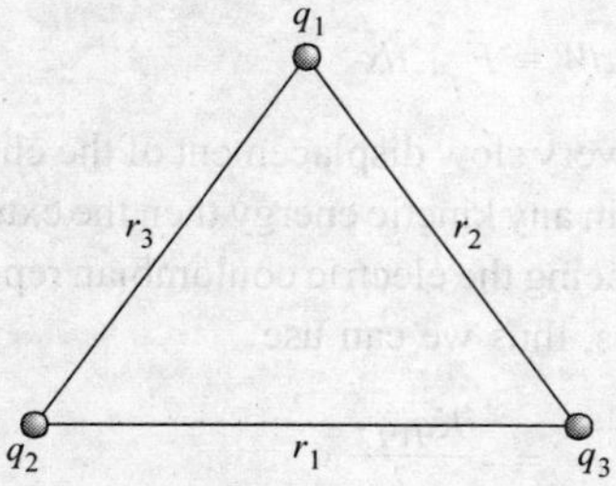

Figure 1.137

The expression in above equation-(1.101) is the interaction energy of the system of three charges as shown in figure-1.137. First term in this equation is the work done in bringing the charges q_1 and q_2 from infinity or large separation to a distance r_3 apart. Then second and third term of the equation are giving the work done in bringing the charge q_3 from infinity to the given position against the field forces of q_1 and q_2 respectively.

As electric forces are conservative in nature, it does not make any difference if we calculate the work done separately by individual forces or it is done simultaneously. Eventually final state must be same. For N charged particles in space total interaction energy can also be calculated by considering sum of all pair of particles considered independently.

When there are N charges $q_1, q_2, q_3, \ldots q_N$ placed in a region of space such that the separation between q_1 and q_2 is r_{12}, between q_1 and q_3 is r_{13} and similarly separation between i^{th} and j^{th} charge separation is r_{ij} then the interaction energy of such a multi particle system is given as

$$U = \frac{1}{2}\sum_{j=1}^{N}\sum_{i=1}^{N}\frac{Kq_iq_j}{r_{ij}} \qquad \ldots(1.102)$$

In above equation-(1.102) the factor of 1/2 is taken because in the two summations each terms of potential energy between i^{th} and j^{th} charge particle is considered twice.

1.9.4 Closest Distance of Approach between Two Charges

When two charged particles having same polarity charges are projected toward each other along same line of motion then due to their mutual repulsive force their speed decreases and they get closer to a minimum separation between the two particles when their final speed becomes zero and then they will repel. Using the concept of interaction energy we can find their closest distance of approach in this and in many other cases of projections. Next we will discuss some similar cases of projection of two charged particles and analyse these situations using the concept of interaction energy.

Case-I : One Charge is kept Fixed

Figure-1.138(a) shows a fixed charge q_1 and from a large distance another charge particle having mass m and charge q_2 is projected toward it with an initial speed v_0. If due to repulsion, charge q_2 gets close to the fixed charge q_1 upto a minimum distance r_{min} as shown in figure-1.138(b) then this closest distance of approach can be calculated by using conservation of energy between initial state when charge was projected and at the state of minimum separation, given as

$$\frac{1}{2}mv_0^2 = \frac{Kq_1q_2}{r_{min}} \qquad \ldots(1.103)$$

$$\Rightarrow \qquad r_{min} = \frac{2Kq_1q_2}{mv_0^2}$$

$$\Rightarrow \qquad r_{min} = \frac{q_1q_2}{2\pi\epsilon_0 mv_0^2} \qquad \ldots(1.104)$$

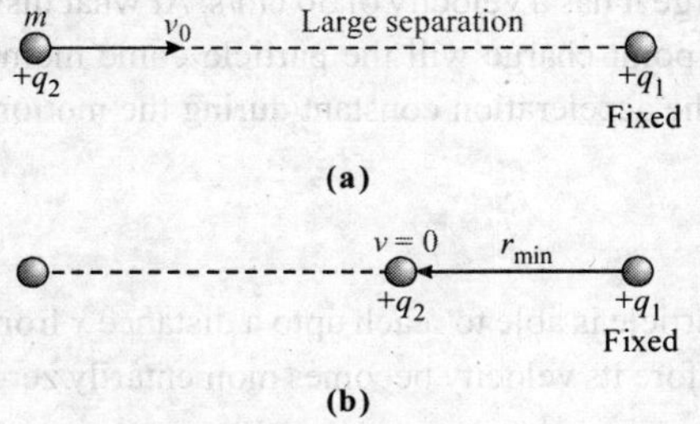

Figure 1.138

Above equation-(1.103) shows that initially at large separation there was no interaction energy between the two charges and there was kinetic energy in the charge which is projected. At the state of closest approach charge q_2 will come to rest and whole of its kinetic energy will transform into the electrostatic interaction energy of the system of these charges.

Case-II : No charge is fixed but moving along same line

Figure-1.139(a) shows a charge q_1 and of mass m_1 at rest and another charge q_2 of mass m_2 is projected toward it from a large separation with initial speed v_0. In this case as charge q_2 gets close to q_1, due to mutual repulsion q_1 also starts moving and because of electric force its speed increases and that of q_2 decreases. As the separation between the two charges decreases their interaction energy increases and interaction energy will be maximum when they will be at the distance of closest approach r_{min}. At this state the kinetic energy of the two charges will be minimum and as already analyzed in the topic of linear momentum conservation that at the point of maximum potential energy in collision the speeds of particles are equal. By conservation of energy and linear momentum of the two moving charges we can find the closest distance of approach as explained below.

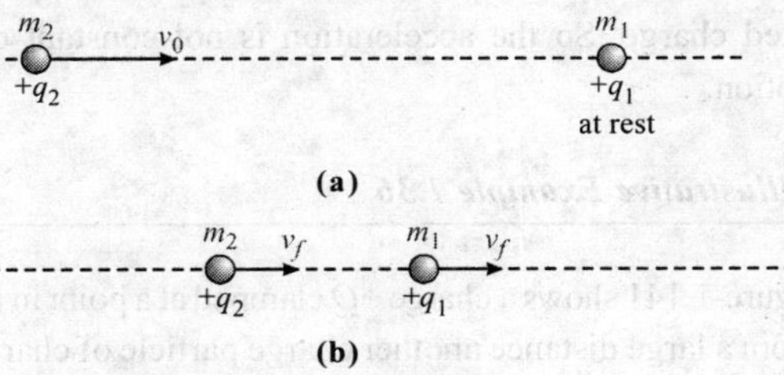

Figure 1.139

If at the distance of closest approach the speed of particles is v_f then by conservation of linear momentum, we have

$$m_2 v_0 = (m_1 + m_2)\, v_f \qquad \ldots(1.105)$$

By using energy conservation, we have

$$\frac{1}{2} m_2 v_0^2 = \frac{1}{2}(m_1 + m_2) v_f^2 + \frac{Kq_1 q_2}{r_{min}} \qquad \ldots(1.106)$$

Solving equations-(1.105) and (1.106), we get

$$r_{min} = \frac{2Kq_1 q_2 (m_1 + m_2)}{m_1 m_2 v_0^2}$$

$$\Rightarrow \quad r_{min} = \frac{q_1 q_2 (m_1 + m_2)}{2\pi \in_0 m_1 m_2 v_0^2} \qquad \ldots(1.107)$$

Case-III : One Charge is fixed and other moving not in line

Figure-1.140(a) shows a fixed charge q_1 and another charge q_2 of mass m is projected toward it with initial speed v_0 at an impact parameter d from large separation. Due to mutual repulsion the path of q_2 gets deviated as shown in figure-1.140(b) and it moves in the curved path as shown. The separation between the two charges is minimum during motion will be the normal distance between charge q_1 and the trajectory of q_2 as shown. If at the point of closest approach the speed of q_2 is v_f then by conservation of angular momentum we can write

$$mv_0 d = mv_f\, r_{min}$$

$$\Rightarrow \quad v_f = \frac{v_0 d}{r_{min}} \qquad \ldots(1.108)$$

By conservation of energy, we have

$$\frac{1}{2} mv_0^2 = \frac{1}{2} mv_f^2 + \frac{Kq_1 q_2}{r_{min}} \qquad \ldots(1.109)$$

Using equations-(1.108) and (1.109), we can solve these for calculating the value of r_{min}.

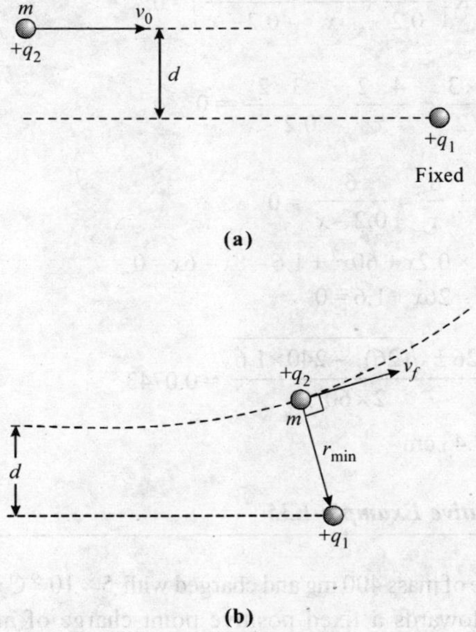

Figure 1.140

Illustrative Example 1.34

A point charge q_1 = 4.00 nC is placed at the origin, and a second point charge q_2 = – 3.00 nC is placed on the x-axis at x = + 20.0 cm. A third point charge q_3 = 2.00 nC is placed on the x-axis between q_1 and q_2.

(a) What is the potential energy of the system of the three charges if q_3 is placed at x = + 10.0 cm?

(b) Where should q_3 be placed to make the potential energy of the system to be equal to zero?

Solution

(a) For a three particle system as discussed in article-1.9.3 the interaction energy is given as

$$U = K\left(\frac{q_1q_2}{r_{12}} + \frac{q_1q_3}{r_{13}} + \frac{q_2q_3}{r_{23}}\right) \quad \text{...(1.110)}$$

$$\Rightarrow \quad U = 9 \times 10^9 \left(-\frac{4\times3}{0.2} + \frac{4\times2}{0.1} - \frac{3\times2}{0.1}\right) \times 10^{-18}$$

$$\Rightarrow \quad U = 9 \times 10^{-9}\,[-60 + 80 - 60]$$

$$\Rightarrow \quad U = -3.6 \times 10^{-7}\text{ J.}$$

(b) If charge q_3 is placed at a position x (< 20 cm), then in equation-(1.110) of part (a), use

$$U = 0,\ r_{12} = 0.2\text{ m},\ r_{13} = x \text{ and } r_{23} = (0.2 - x)$$

That gives

$$U = K\left(\frac{q_1q_2}{0.2} + \frac{q_1q_3}{x} + \frac{q_2q_3}{0.2 - x}\right) = 0$$

$$\Rightarrow \quad -\frac{4\times3}{0.2} + \frac{4\times2}{x} - \frac{3\times2}{0.2 - x} = 0$$

$$\Rightarrow \quad -60 + \frac{8}{x} - \frac{6}{0.2 - x} = 0$$

$$\Rightarrow \quad -60 \times 0.2x + 60x^2 + 1.6 - 8x - 6x = 0$$

$$\Rightarrow \quad 60x^2 - 26x + 1.6 = 0$$

$$\Rightarrow \quad x = \frac{26 \pm \sqrt{(26)^2 - 240\times1.6}}{2\times60} = 0.0743$$

$$\Rightarrow \quad x = 7.43\text{ cm}$$

Illustrative Example 1.35

A particle of mass 400 mg and charged with 5×10^{-9} C is moving directly towards a fixed positive point charge of magnitude 10^{-8} C. When it is at a distance of 10 cm from the fixed positive point charge it has a velocity of 50 cm/s. At what distance from the fixed point charge will the particle come momentarily to rest ? Is the acceleration constant during the motion ?

Solution

Let the particle is able to reach upto a distance x from the fixed charge before its velocity becomes momentarily zero.

The initial kinetic energy of the particle

$$\frac{1}{2}mv^2 = \frac{1}{2} \times (40 \times 10^{-6})\left(\frac{1}{2}\right)^2 = 50 \times 10^{-7}\text{ J}$$

The potential energy at 10 cm is given as

$$U_{10\text{ cm}} = (9 \times 10^9)\frac{(5\times10^{-9})(10^{-8})}{(0.1)} = 45 \times 10^{-7}\text{ J}$$

The potential energy at x metre is given by

$$U_{x\text{ cm}} = (9 \times 10^9)\frac{(5\times10^{-9})(10^{-8})}{x} = \frac{45\times10^{-8}}{x}\text{ J}$$

Gain in potential energy is given as

$$\Delta U = \frac{45\times10^{-8}}{x} - 45 \times 10^{-7} = \left(\frac{4.5}{x} - 45\right)10^{-7}\text{ J}$$

This must be equal to the total kinetic energy lost, thus we have

$$\left(\frac{4.5}{x} - 45\right)10^{-7} = 50 \times 10^{-7}$$

$$\Rightarrow \quad x = 0.0473\text{ m} = 4.73\text{ cm}$$

The force of repulsion increases as the particle approaches the fixed charge. So the acceleration is not constant during the motion.

Illustrative Example 1.36

Figure-1.141 shows a charge +Q clamped at a point in free space. From a large distance another charge particle of charge – q and mass m is thrown toward +Q with an impact parameter d as shown with speed v. Find the distance of closest approach of the two particles.

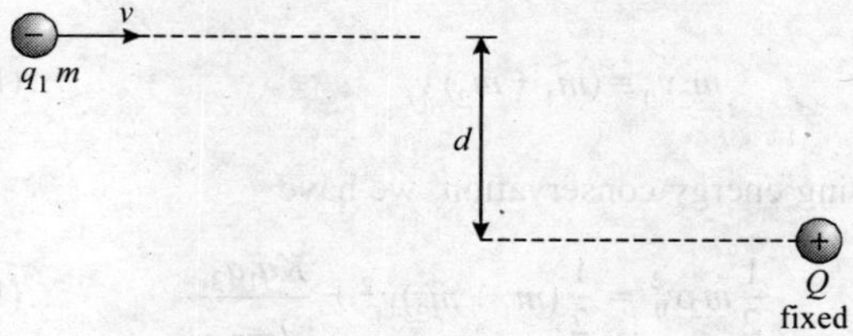

Figure 1.141

Solution

In this situation we can see that as $-q$ moves toward $+Q$, an attractive force acts on $-q$ toward $+Q$. Here as the line of action of force passes through the fix charge, no torque act on $-q$ relative to the fix point charge $+Q$, thus here we can say that with respect to $+Q$, the angular momentum of $-q$ must remain constant. Here we can say that $-q$ will be closest to $+Q$ when it is moving perpendicularly to the line joining the two charges as shown in figure-1.142.

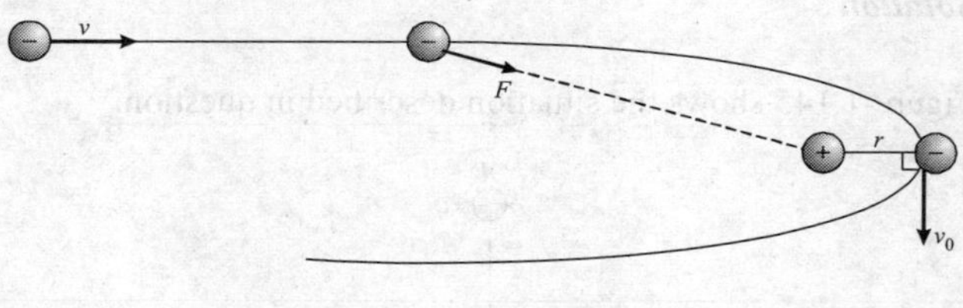

Figure 1.142

If the closest separation in the two charges is r_{min}, from conservation of angular momentum we can write

$$mvd = mv_0 r_{min} \quad \ldots(1.111)$$

Now from energy conservation, we have

$$\frac{1}{2}mv^2 = \frac{1}{2}mv_0^2 - \frac{KqQ}{r_{min}} \quad \ldots(1.112)$$

From equation-(1.111), we have

$$v_0 = \frac{vd}{r_{min}}$$

Substituting the above value of v_0 in equation-(1.112), we get

$$\frac{1}{2}mv^2 = \frac{1}{2}mv^2\frac{d^2}{r_{min}^2} - \frac{KqQ}{r_{min}} \quad \ldots(1.113)$$

$$\Rightarrow \quad \frac{1}{r_{min}^2} - \left(\frac{qQ}{2\pi \epsilon_0 mv^2 d^2}\right)\frac{1}{r_{min}} - \frac{1}{d^2} = 0$$

$$\Rightarrow \quad \frac{1}{r_{min}} = \frac{1}{2}\left(\frac{qQ}{2\pi \epsilon_0 mv^2 d^2} \pm \sqrt{\left(\frac{qQ}{2\pi \epsilon_0 mv^2 d^2}\right)^2 + \frac{4}{d^2}}\right)$$

$$\Rightarrow \quad r_{min} = \frac{2}{\left(\frac{qQ}{2\pi \epsilon_0 mv^2 d^2} \pm \sqrt{\left(\frac{qQ}{2\pi \epsilon_0 mv^2 d^2}\right)^2 + \frac{4}{d^2}}\right)}$$

 # Illustrative Example 1.37

A particle of mass 40 mg and carrying a charge 5×10^{-9} C is moving directly towards a fixed positive point charge on magnitude 10^{-8} C. When it is at a distance of 10 cm from the fixed positive point charge it has a velocity of 50 cm s^{-1}. at what distance from the fixed point charge will the particle come momentarily to rest ? Is the acceleration constant during motion ?

Solution

Let r be the distance of q from Q when it comes to rest as shown in figure-1.143.

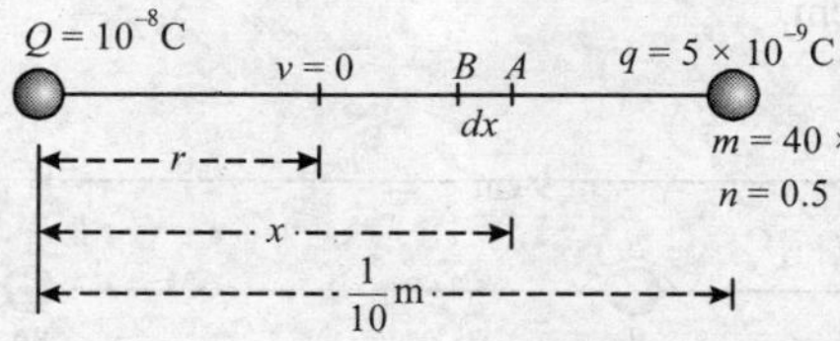

Figure 1.143

The loss of kinetic energy given by

$$\Delta K = \frac{1}{2}mu^2 - \frac{1}{2}mv^2 = \frac{1}{2}\cdot 40\times10^{-6}\left(\frac{1}{2}\right)^2 - \frac{1}{2}\times 40\times10^{-6}\times(0)^2$$

$$\Rightarrow \quad \Delta K = 5\times10^{-6}\text{ J}$$

By conservation of energy this loss of kinetic energy is the gain in electrostatic interaction energy of the system which is given as

$$\Delta U = \frac{Kq_1q_2}{r_1} - \frac{Kq_1q_2}{r_2}$$

$$\Rightarrow \quad \Delta U = Kq_1q_2\left(\frac{1}{r} - \frac{1}{0.1}\right)$$

$$\Rightarrow \quad \Delta U = 9\times10^9\times5\times10^{-9}\times10^{-8}\times\left(\frac{1}{r} - 10\right)\text{ J}$$

$$\Rightarrow \quad \Delta U = 45\times10^{-8}\times\left(\frac{1}{r} - 10\right)\text{ J}$$

By energy conservation we use $\Delta K = \Delta U$ which gives

$$5\times10^{-6} = 45\times10^{-8}\times\left(\frac{1}{r} - 10\right)$$

$$\Rightarrow \quad 100r = 9 - 90r$$

$$\Rightarrow \quad r = 4.737\times10^{-2}\text{ m}$$

As at different positions of particle during motion the Coulombic force on it is varying due to changing distance, its acceleration will not remain constant during motion.

Illustrative Example 1.38

Three point charges q, $2q$ and $8q$ are to be placed on a 9 cm long straight line. Find the positions on the line where the charges should be placed such that the electrostatic interaction energy of this system is minimum. In this situation, what is the electric field strength at the position of the charge q on line due to the other two charges.

Solution

For minimum interaction energy, the charges of greater magnitudes should be placed at the extreme ends. The situation is shown in figure-1.144. Let the distance of charge $2q$ from charge q be x cm.

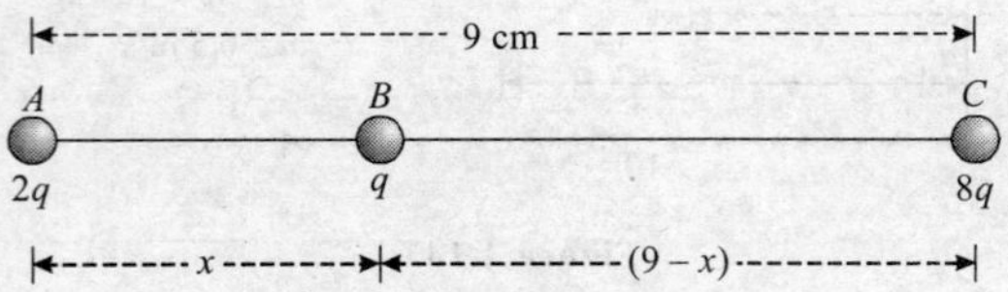

Figure 1.144

The electrostatic interaction energy of this system is given as

$$U = K\left[\frac{2q\times q}{x\times 10^{-2}} + \frac{q\times 8q}{(9-x)10^{-2}} + \frac{2q\times 8q}{9\times 10^{-2}}\right]$$

For minimum interaction potential energy, we use

$$\frac{dU}{dx} = 0$$

$$\Rightarrow \quad \frac{dU}{dx} = K\frac{d}{dx}\left[\frac{2q^2}{x\times 10^{-2}} + \frac{8q^2}{(9-x)10^{-2}} + \frac{16q^2}{9\times 10^{-2}}\right] = 0$$

$$\Rightarrow \quad x = 3 \text{ cm}$$

Thus the charge q should be placed at a distance of 3 cm from the charge $2q$.

The electric field strength at the location of charge q is

$$E = E_1 + E_2$$

$$\Rightarrow \quad E = \frac{K(2q\times q)}{(3\times 10^{-2})^2} - \frac{K(q\times 8q)}{(6\times 10^{-2})^2}$$

$$\Rightarrow \quad E = \frac{K(2q^2)}{(3\times 10^{-2})^2} - \frac{K(2q^2)}{(3\times 10^{-2})^2} = 0$$

Illustrative Example 1.39

Two fixed, equal positive charges, each of magnitude 5×10^{-5} C, are located at points A and B separated by a distance of 6 m. An equal and opposite charge moves towards them along the line COD, the perpendicular bisector of the line AB. The moving charge, when reaches the point C at a distance of 4 m from O, has a kinetic energy of 4 J. Calculate the distance x of the farthest point D at which the negative charge will reach before returning towards C.

Solution

Figure-1.145 shows the situation described in question.

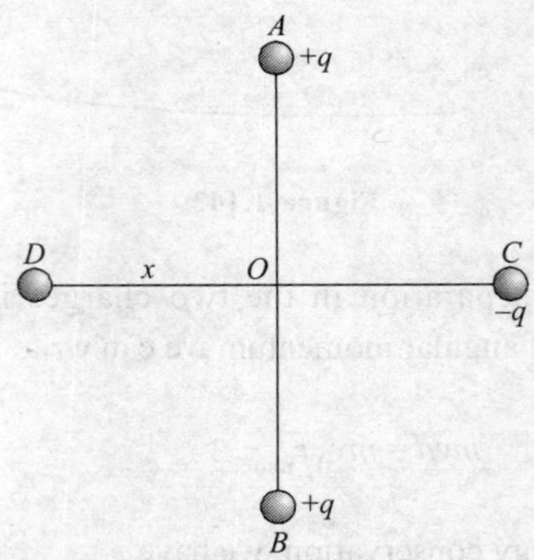

Figure 1.145

From figure, we have

$$AC = \sqrt{(AO)^2 + (OC)^2}$$

$$\Rightarrow \quad AC = \sqrt{(3)^2 + (4)^2} = 5 \text{ m}$$

Similarly we have

$$BC = 5 \text{ m}$$

Potential energy of charge $-q$ at point C is given as

$$U_C = -\frac{2Kq^2}{(AC)} = -2\times(9\times 10^9)\times\frac{q^2}{AC}$$

$$\Rightarrow \quad U_C = -2\times(9\times 10^9)\,\frac{(5\times 10^{-5})^2}{5}$$

$$\Rightarrow \quad U_C = -9 \text{ J}$$

Kinetic energy of charge at C is given as

$$K_C = 4 \text{ J}$$

Total energy of charge at C is given as

$$\text{T.E.} = \text{P.E.} + \text{K.E.}$$

$$\Rightarrow \quad \text{T.E.} = -9 + 4 = -5 \text{ J}$$

If we use $AD = BD = r$ then potential energy of charge at point D is given as

$$U_D = -\frac{2Kq^2}{r}$$

$$\Rightarrow \quad U_D = \frac{-2\times(9\times10^9)(5\times10^{-5})^2}{r}$$

$$\Rightarrow \quad U_D = \frac{-45}{r}\ \text{J}$$

As kinetic energy of charge at point D is zero, by conservation of energy at point C and D, we use

$$\frac{-45}{r} = -5,$$

$$\Rightarrow \quad r = 9\ \text{m}$$

From figure-1.145, we use

$$x = OD = \sqrt{(AD)^2 - (AO)^2}$$

$$\Rightarrow \quad x = \sqrt{(9)^2 - (3)^2} = 6\sqrt{2}\ \text{m}.$$

Illustrative Example 1.40

Two small identical balls lying on a smooth horizontal plane are connected by a weightless spring - one ball is fixed at point O and the other is free. The balls are charged identically, as a result of which the spring length increases two fold. Determine the change in the frequency of harmonic vibration of the system due to the charges present on balls.

Solution

If l be the length of the spring, then extension of the spring becomes $2l$ in state of equilibrium.

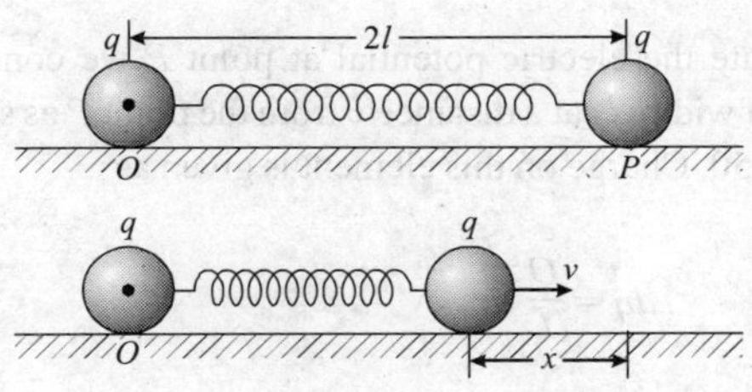

Figure 1.146

Let at any instant free ball is displaced from the mean position by a distance x which is very small comparison to l.

The total mechanical energy of the system at the instant when ball is at a distance x from the mean position and moving at speed v is given as

$$E = \frac{1}{2}k(l-x)^2 + \frac{1}{4\pi\epsilon_0}\frac{q^2}{(2l-x)} + \frac{1}{2}mv^2$$

$$\Rightarrow \quad E = \frac{1}{2}k(l-x)^2 + \frac{1}{4\pi\epsilon_0}q^2(2l-x)^{-1} + \frac{1}{2}mv^2$$

$$\Rightarrow \quad E = \frac{1}{2}k(l-x)^2 + \frac{1}{4\pi\epsilon_0}q^2\left[(2l)^{-1}\left\{1-\frac{x}{2l}\right\}^{-1}\right] + \frac{1}{2}mv^2$$

$$\Rightarrow \quad E = \frac{1}{2}k(l-x)^2 + \frac{q^2}{4\pi\epsilon_0}\left[\frac{1}{2l}\left\{1+\frac{x}{2l}\right\}\right] + \frac{1}{2}mv^2$$

$$\Rightarrow \quad E = \frac{1}{2}k(l-x)^2 + \frac{q^2}{4\pi\epsilon_0}\left[\frac{1}{2l}+\frac{x}{4l^2}\right] + \frac{1}{2}mv^2 \quad \ldots(1.114)$$

At the mean position of one of the ball, we use

$$kl = \frac{q^2}{4\pi\epsilon_0(2l)^2} \quad \ldots(1.115)$$

On solving equation-(1.114) and (1.115) and simplifying, we get

$$E = \frac{5}{2}kl^2 + kx^2 + \frac{1}{2}mv^2 \quad \ldots(1.116)$$

For free oscillation,

$$\frac{dE}{dt} = 0$$

$$\Rightarrow \quad \frac{d}{dt}\left[\frac{5}{2}kl^2 + kx^2 + \frac{1}{2}mv^2\right] = 0$$

$$\Rightarrow \quad 2kx\frac{dx}{dt} + \frac{m}{2}\times 2v\times\frac{dv}{dt} = 0$$

$$\Rightarrow \quad a = \frac{dv}{dt} = -\frac{2k}{m}x$$

On comparing above acceleration with standard equation of SHM, $a = -\omega^2 x$, we get $\omega = \sqrt{\frac{2k}{m}}$. The frequency without charge $\omega_0 = \sqrt{\frac{k}{m}}$. Thus we have $\omega = \sqrt{2}\omega_0$.

1.10 Electric Potential

Electric potential is a characteristic property at every point in the region of electric field. At a point in the region of electric field, electric potential is defined as the interaction energy of a unit positive charge due to the field.

If at a point P in an electric field shown in figure-1.147, a charge q_0 has interaction potential energy U, then electric potential at that point can be given as

$$V_P = \frac{U}{q_0}\ \text{J/C} \quad \ldots(1.117)$$

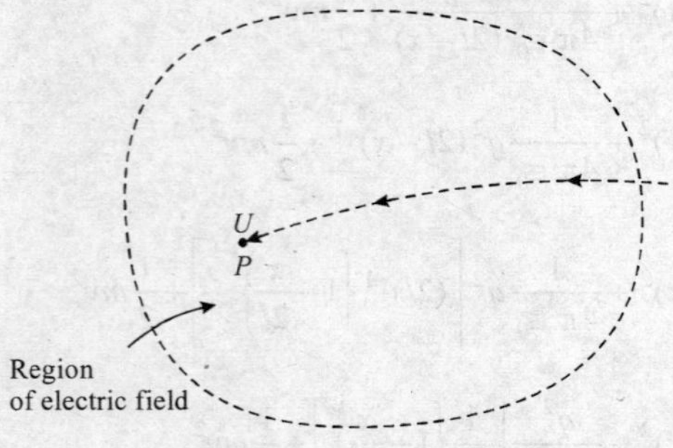

Figure 1.147

We have already discussed that electrostatic potential energy of a point charge at a point in electric field is defined as the work done in bringing the charge from infinity to the given point in electric field. Thus we can defined electric potential at a point in space as "*work done in bringing a unit positive charge from infinity to the given point against the electric forces.*"

1.10.1 Electric Potential due to a Point Charge in its Surrounding

We have already discussed that in the region in surrounding of every charge is electric field thus we can also define electric potential in the surrounding of every charge. Figure-1.148 shows a point charge $+q$ and now we will determine the electric potential at a point P located a distance x from the charge.

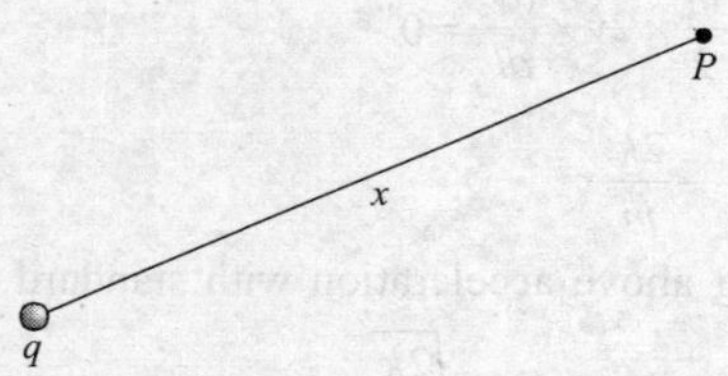

Figure 1.148

If at point P, we place a charge q_0 and find the interaction energy of the charge q_0 in the field of charge q then it is given as

$$U = \frac{Kq_1 q_0}{x}$$

The potential at a point P due to the charge q can be given by equation-(1.126) as

$$V_P = \frac{U}{q_0}$$

$$V_P = \frac{Kq}{x} \quad \ldots(1.118)$$

The above expression of potential is only valid for electric potential in the surrounding of a point charge. If we wish to determine electric potential in the surrounding of a charged extended body as shown in figure-1.149 then we need to find the potential dV at a specific point due to an elemental charge dq in the body as shown by using the above result and then integrate the expression for the whole body. It is important to note as potential is a scalar quantity so integration is carried out directly without considering any components unlike to the cases we've discussed for integration of electric field. Next few articles are based on calculation of electric potential due to charged extended bodies.

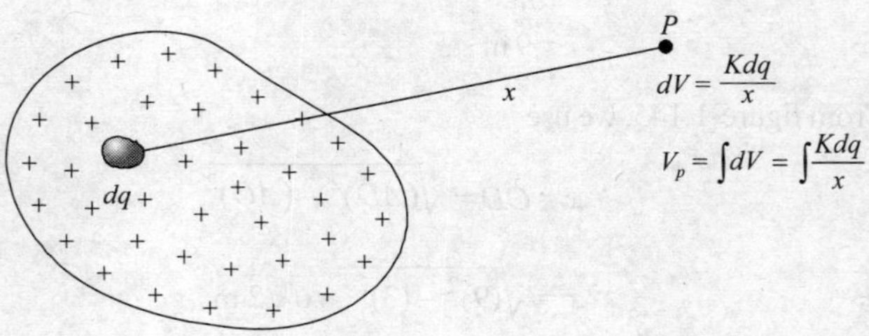

Figure 1.149

1.10.2 Electric Potential due to a Charge Rod

Figure-1.150 shows a charged rod of length L which is uniformly charged with a charge Q. Due to this rod we will determine the electric potential at a point P located at a distance r from one end of the rod shown.

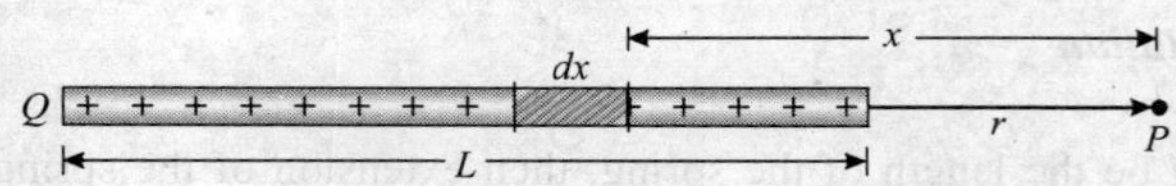

Figure 1.150

To calculate the electric potential at point P we consider an element of width dx at a distance x from the point P as shown in figure-1.150. Charge on this element is given as

$$dq = \frac{Q}{L}dx$$

The potential dV due to this elemental charge at point P can be given by using the result of a point charge from equation-(1.118) given as

$$dV = \frac{Kdq}{x}$$

$$\Rightarrow \quad dV = \frac{KQ}{Lx}dx$$

Net electric potential at point P can be given by integrating the above expression for the whole length of rod within limits of x from r to $r + L$, given as

$$V = \int dV = \int_{r}^{r+L} \frac{KQ}{Lx} dx$$

$$\Rightarrow \quad V = \frac{KQ}{L} [\ln x]_r^{r+L}$$

$$\Rightarrow \quad V = \frac{KQ}{L} \ln\left(\frac{r+L}{r}\right) \quad \ldots(1.119)$$

1.10.3 Electric Potential due to a Charged Ring at its center

To find potential at the centre C of the ring as shown in figure-1.151, we first find potential dV at centre due to an elemental charge dq on ring which is given as

$$dV = \frac{Kdq}{R}$$

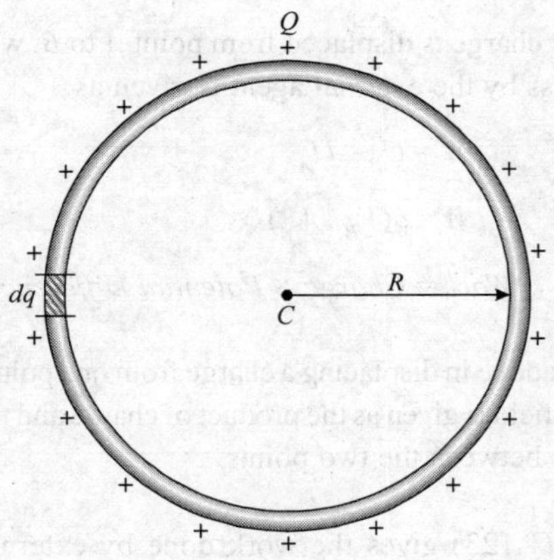

Figure 1.151

Total potential at C is

$$V = \int dV$$

$$\Rightarrow \quad V = \int \frac{Kdq}{R}$$

$$\Rightarrow \quad V = \frac{KQ}{R}$$

In figure we can see that all dq's of the ring are situated at same distance R from the ring centre C and being a scalar quantity the electric potential due to all elemental charges at center will be added up. Thus the total electric potential at ring centre is given by equation-(1.101). Here we can also state that even if charge Q is non-uniformly distributed on ring, the electric potential C will remain same as charge is a scalar quantity and all elemental charges are at same distance from the center and potential due to all elements will remain same so all will be simply added up and it does not make any difference if charge is uniformly or non uniformly distributed on the ring.

1.10.4 Electric Potential due to a Charged Ring at its Axial Point

Figure-1.152 shows a uniformly charged ring of radius R and charge Q. P is a point on the axis of ring at a distance x from the center of the ring. To calculate the electric potential at point P we can use the same direct logic which is explained in the previous article used for direct calculation of electric potential at center of a charged ring.

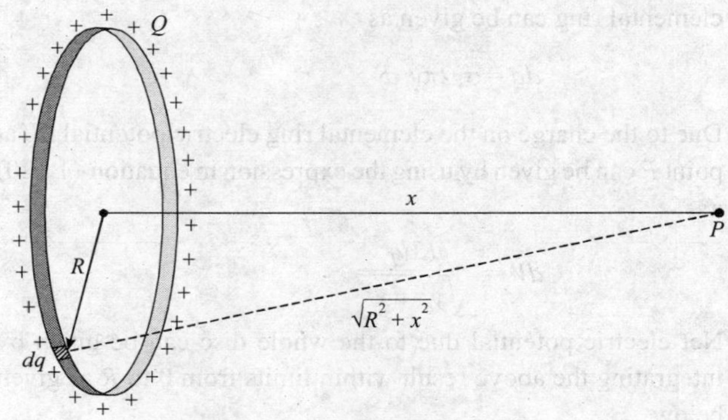

Figure 1.152

If in figure-1.152, we consider a small element on the ring with a charge dq then the distance of this element form the point P is given as $\sqrt{R^2+x^2}$ and the electric potential due to this elemental charge dq at point P will be given as

$$dV = \frac{Kdq}{\sqrt{R^2+x^2}}$$

As all elements on the ring are at same distance from point P, potential due to all will be simply added up and the net electric potential due to whole ring at point P is given by

$$V_P = \frac{KQ}{\sqrt{R^2+x^2}} \quad \ldots(1.120)$$

The result given in equation-(1.120) will remain same even if the ring is non uniformly charged as already discussed in article 1.9.3.

1.10.5 Electric Potential due to a Uniformly Charged Disc

Figure-1.153 shows a circular disc of radius R, charged uniformly with a surface charge density σ C/m^2. P is a point on the axis of the disc at a distance x from the center of the disc as shown. Now we will calculate the electric potential due to disc charges at point P.

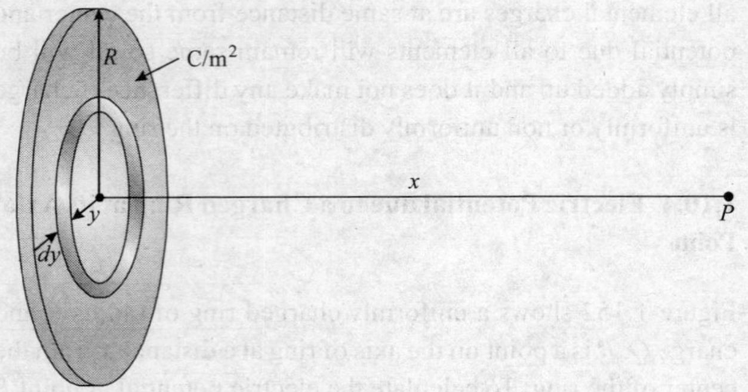

Figure 1.153

As shown in figure above we consider an elemental ring on the surface of the disc of radius y and width dy. The charge on the elemental ring can be given as

$$dq = \sigma . 2\pi y . dy$$

Due to the charge on the elemental ring electric potential dV at point P can be given by using the expression in equation-(1.120) as

$$dV = \frac{Kdq}{\sqrt{y^2 + x^2}}$$

Net electric potential due to the whole disc can be given by integrating the above result within limits from 0 to R as given below

$$V = \int dV = \int_0^R \frac{Kdq}{\sqrt{y^2 + x^2}}$$

$$\Rightarrow \quad V = \int_0^R \frac{K\sigma . 2\pi y . dy}{\sqrt{y^2 + x^2}}$$

$$\Rightarrow \quad V = \int_0^R \frac{\sigma}{2\varepsilon_0} . \frac{y . dy}{\sqrt{y^2 + x^2}}$$

$$\Rightarrow \quad V = \frac{\sigma}{2\varepsilon_0}\left[\sqrt{y^2 + x^2}\right]_0^R$$

$$\Rightarrow \quad V = \frac{\sigma}{2\varepsilon_0}\left[\sqrt{x^2 + R^2} - x\right] \quad \ldots(1.121)$$

To find the electric potential at the center of the disc we can put $x = 0$ which gives

$$V_C = \frac{\sigma R}{2\varepsilon_0} \quad \ldots(1.122)$$

1.10.6 Potential Difference between two points B in Electric Field

Consider two points A and B in a region of electric field as shown in figure-1.154. The potentials at points A and B are considered V_A and V_B respectively then the potential energy of a charge $+q$ placed at these points are given as

$$U_A = qV_A$$

$$U_B = qV_B$$

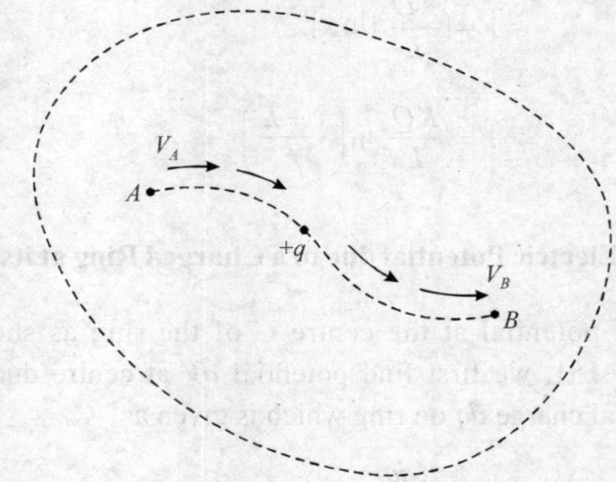

Figure 1.154

When this charge is displaced from point A to B, work done in this process by the external agent is given as

$$W = U_B - U_A$$

$$\Rightarrow \quad W = q(V_B - V_A) \quad \ldots(1.123)$$

$$\Rightarrow \quad Work = Charge \times Potential\ Difference$$

Thus work done in displacing a charge from one point to another in electric field is given as the product of charge and the potential difference between the two points.

Equation-(1.123) gives the work done by external agent in displacing the charge against the electric forces of the field. If we calculate the work done by electric field in this displacement then it is given as

$$W = q(V_A - V_B) \quad \ldots(1.124)$$

Above equation-(1.124) is the negative of equation-(1.123). From equation-(1.123) we can calculate the potential difference between two points in electric field as

$$V_A - V_B = \frac{W}{q} \quad \ldots(1.125)$$

From the above equation-(1.125) we can define the potential difference between two points in electric field as "*Work done in displacing a unit positive charge from one point to another against electric forces is called the potential difference between these points.*"

1.10.7 Calculation of Potential Difference by Electric Field

The potential difference between two points can also be calculated by using the electric field strength. Figure-1.155 shows a region of electric field in which a unit positive point charge is displaced from a point A to B. As electric field strength gives the force per unit positive charge so the work done in displacing a charge against an electric field $\vec{E}$ for an elemental displacement $\vec{dr}$ can be given as

$$dW = -\vec{E}\cdot\vec{dr} \quad \ldots(1.126)$$

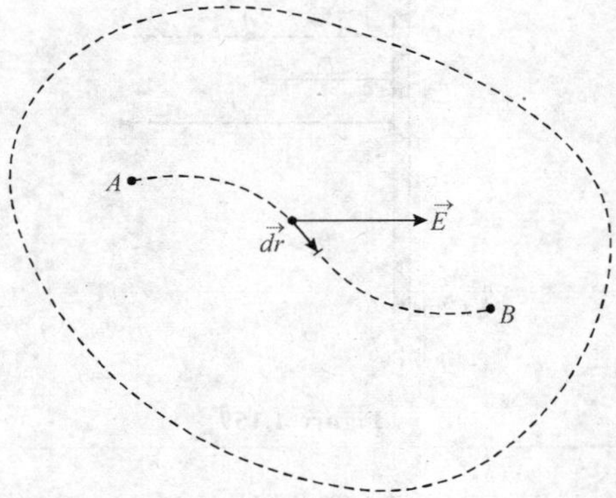

Figure 1.155

In above expression negative sign shows that work is done against electric field by an external agent. Thus the potential difference between two points A and B can be given by integrating the above expression in equation-(1.126) from A to B as given below

$$V_B - V_A = -\int_A^B \vec{E}\cdot\vec{dr} \quad \ldots(1.127)$$

As the electric field is conservative in nature, above expression will remain independent from the path along which the charge is displaced. We know that a positive charge has a tendency to move toward low potential point or we can say that electric forces acts on a positive charge such that the direction of force is toward low potential region. Thus electric field direction always points from the side of high potential to low potential or in other words we can say that in the direction of electric field always electric potential decreases.

In general cases of calculation of potential we bring a unit positive charge from infinity to a specific point and evaluate the work done in the process as explained above. In the analysis we consider infinity is the reference point where charges are in state of no interaction or it is the reference of zero potential energy thus in general cases for potential calculation we consider electric potential at infinity is zero. But for calculation of potential difference between two points it is irrelevant to choose reference at infinity or in other words we can say that potential difference between two points in an electric field can always be calculated by using equation-(1.127) and will remain same whether we choose reference at infinity or not.

1.10.8 Potential Difference in Uniform Electric Field

Figure-1.156 shows a region of uniform electric field in which everywhere the strength of electric field is same in magnitude as well as in direction.

Thus for two points A and B along the direction of electric field separated by a distance d, we can calculate the potential difference by using equation-(1.127) as

$$V_B - V_A = -\int_A^B \vec{E}\cdot\vec{dr} \quad \ldots(1.128)$$

$$\Rightarrow \quad V_B - V_A = -Ed \quad \ldots(1.129)$$

$$\Rightarrow \quad V_A - V_B = Ed \quad \ldots(1.130)$$

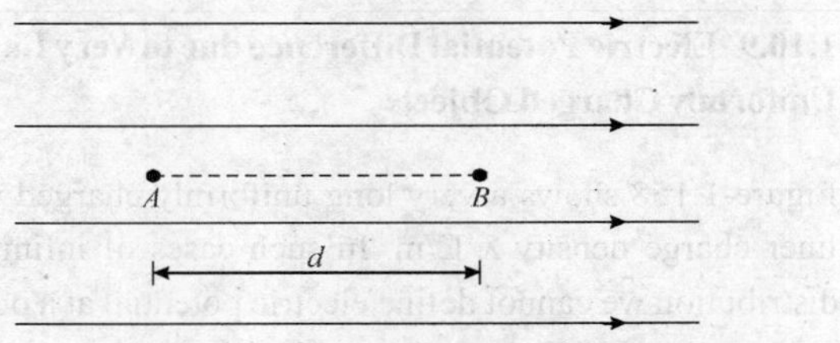

Figure 1.156

Negative sign in equation-(1.129) is because at point B potential is less than potential at point A. This we can directly analyze as we've studied that in the direction of electric field, electric potential decreases. Equation-(1.130) shows that in uniform electric field potential varies linearly with distance along the direction of electric field. If at any point in uniform electric field potential is known say V_0 then at a distance x along the direction of electric field potential at a point P can be given as

$$V_P = V_0 - Ex \quad \ldots(1.131)$$

Even in non uniform electric fields, by looking at the field direction, the potential difference can be calculated with proper sign. Figure-1.157 shows a non uniform electric field of which magnitude and direction both are changing in space. If we look at the two points M and N here, we can see that point N is ahead of M along the direction of electric field so potential at N is less than that of M so we can rewrite the equation-(1.128) for this case as

$$V_M - V_N = \left|\int_A^B \vec{E}\cdot\vec{dr}\right| \quad \ldots(1.132)$$

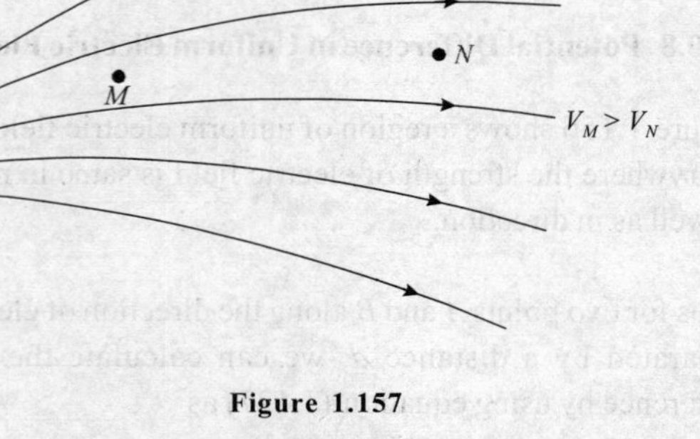

Figure 1.157

Here as we've analysed that potential at M is higher so right hand side of equality in above equation must be positive thats why without bothering the signs in dot product of integrand or any other factor we consider modulus of the right hand side of equation-(1.141).

1.10.9 Electric Potential Difference due to Very Large Sized Uniformly Charged Objects

Figure-1.158 shows a very long uniformly charged wire with liner charge density λ C/m. In such cases of infinite charge distribution we cannot define electric potential at a point in the surrounding of the given charge distribution (say at P in figure shown), because potential at a point is always defined relative to infinity by taking the potential at infinity to be zero. Here the wire is very long and its charges are extended up to infinity so it is not reasonable in such cases to take potential at infinity to be zero and without zero reference we can not define the potential of any point in electric field.

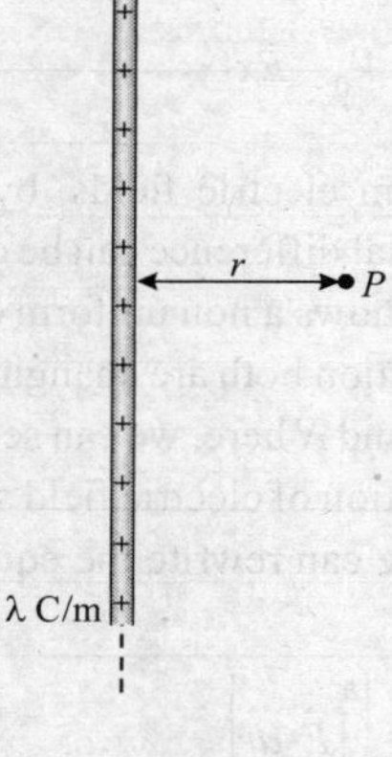

Figure 1.158

As specified and explained in article-1.10.6, in electric field we can always define potential difference between two points as electric field is a conservative field and potential difference between two points in electric field does not depend on choice of zero reference.

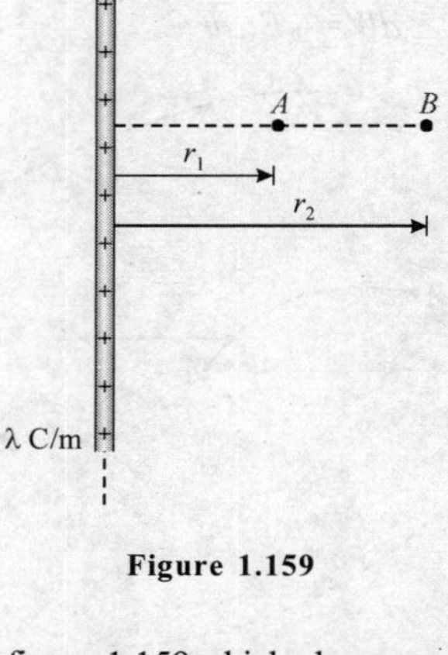

Figure 1.159

Thus if we look at figure-1.159 which show a very long uniformly charged wire with liner charge density λ C/m similar to figure-1.158. Points A and B are located at a radial distance r_1 and r_2 from the wire as shown. We know that electric field due to a uniformly charged wire is in radial direction and due to positive charge on wire it is in direction from point A to B. Thus in this case potential of point B is less than that of A and we can calculate this potential difference using equation-(1.132) as

$$V_A - V_B = \left| \int_A^B \vec{E} \cdot \vec{dx} \right|$$

$$\Rightarrow \quad V_A - V_B = \int_{r_1}^{r_2} \frac{2K\lambda}{x} \cdot dx$$

$$\Rightarrow \quad V_A - V_B = 2K\lambda [\ln x]_{r_1}^{r_2}$$

$$\Rightarrow \quad V_A - V_B = 2K\lambda [\ln r_2 - \ln r_1]$$

$$\Rightarrow \quad V_A - V_B = 2K\lambda \ln\left(\frac{r_2}{r_1}\right) \quad \ldots(1.133)$$

1.10.10 Equipotential Surfaces

As shown in figure-1.160 if a charge is shifted from a point A to B on a surface M which is perpendicular to the direction of electric field, the work done in shifting will obviously, be zero as electric force is normal to the direction of displacement.

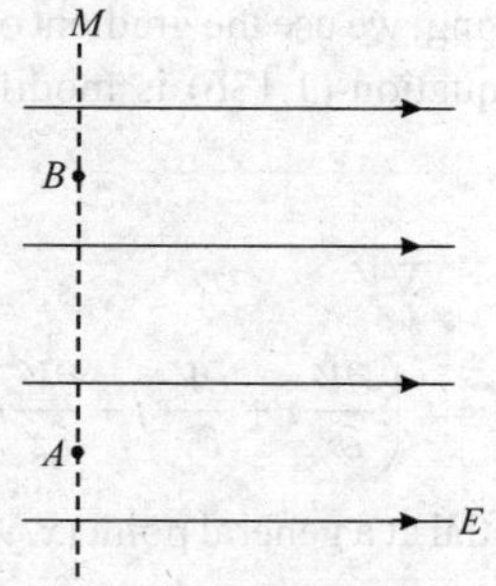

Figure 1.160

We've studied that work done in displacing a charge from one point to another is given by product of charge and potential difference between the two points. As no work is done in moving the charge from A to B, we can say that potential difference between these points is zero or points A and B are at same potentials or by analysing the above situation carefully we can say that all the points of surface M are at same potential or we call surface M as an "*Equipotential Surface*".

In a region of electric field, a surface can be equipotential if at every point of the surface direction of electric field is perpendicular to it so that work done in displacing any charge on this surface from one point to another will remain zero.

Figures-1.161 and 1.162 show equipotential surfaces in the surrounding of point charge and a long charged wire.

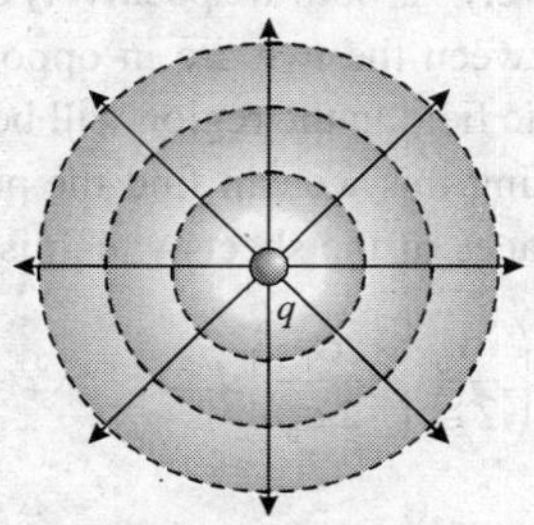

Spherical equipotential surfaces due to point charge

Figure 1.161

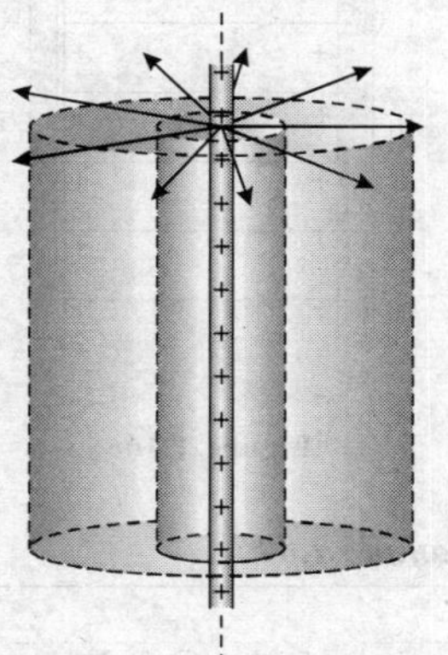

Cylindrical equipotential surfaces due to line charge

Figure 1.162

Figure-1.163 shows two equipotential surfaces in a uniform electric field E. If we wish to determine the potential difference between two points A and B in this situation then it can be calculated by the potential difference between the two equipotential surfaces on which these points lie which can be calculated by using equation-(1.130), given as

$$V_A - V_B = Ed$$

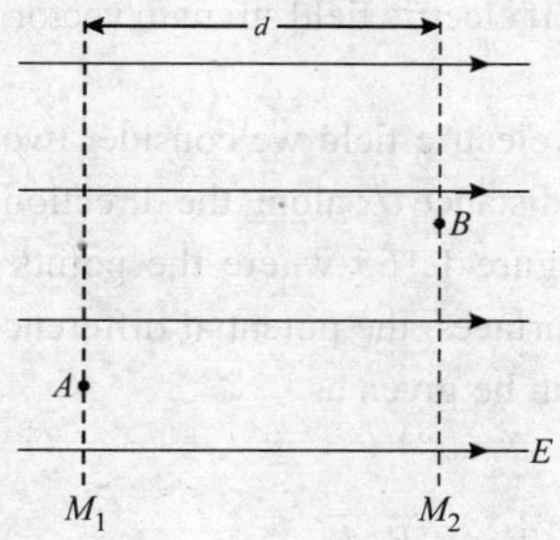

Figure 1.163

Figure-1.164 shows a long line charge with linear charge density λ C/m. If we wish to determine the potential difference between two points X and Y as shown which lie on equipotential surfaces M_1 & M_2 then the potential difference between these surfaces can be directly given by equation-(1.133) as

$$V_X - V_Y = 2K\lambda \ln\left(\frac{r_2}{r_1}\right)$$

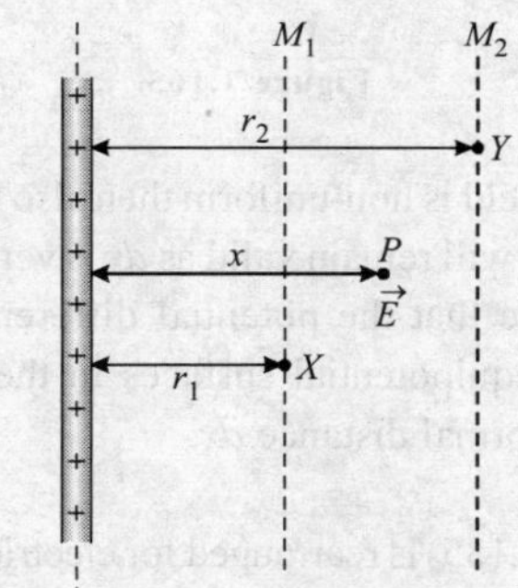

Figure 1.164

1.10.11 Relation in Electric Field and Electric Potential in a Region

We have studied in article-1.10.6 that in electric field, potential difference between two points is defined as

$$V_B - V_A = -\int_A^B \vec{E} \cdot \vec{dx}$$

Above equation gives the work done in displacing a unit positive charge from a point A to B. If we bring a charge from infinity to a point B then above equation can be written as

$$V_B = -\int_{\infty}^{B} \vec{E}\cdot\vec{dx} \quad \ldots(1.134)$$

In above equation at infinity we consider $V_A = 0$. Using above equation we can calculate the potential at a point in the region of electric field if electric field strength vector $\vec{E}$ is known.

If in a uniform electric field we consider two points A and B separated by a distance dx along the direction of electric field as shown in figure-1.165 where the points are on the two equipotential surfaces, the potential difference between these two surfaces can be given as

$$dV = -\vec{E}.\vec{dx} \quad \ldots(1.135)$$

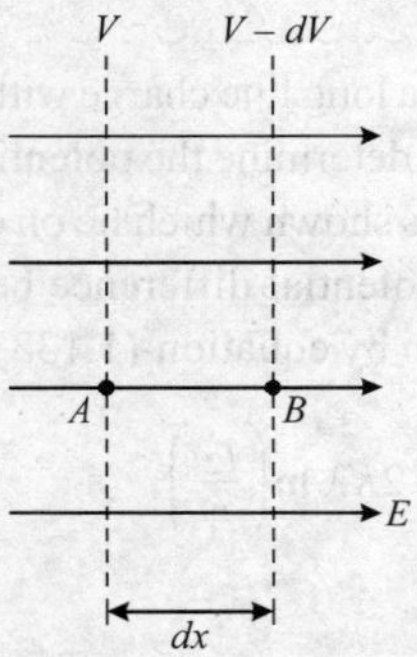

Figure 1.165

Even if electric field is non-uniform then also this expression in equation-(1.135) will remain valid as dx is very small. Here it is important to note that the potential difference dV is always across the two equipotential surfaces in the field which are separated by a normal distance dx.

If the equation-(1.135) is rearranged for electric field vector then it can be given as

$$\vec{E} = -\frac{dV}{dx}\hat{i} \quad \ldots(1.136)$$

Here $\hat{i}$ is the unit vector along the direction of dx or the direction normal to the equipotential surfaces across which the potential difference is dV which will be the direction of electric field at that point. Negative sign in above equation-(1.136) shows that along the direction of electric field potential decreases which we've already studied. In unidirectional electric field, equation-(1.136) gives the magnitude of electric field in direction normal to the equipotential surface. If electric field is three dimensionally varying, we use the gradient of potential to define electric field so equation-(1.136) is modified to the gradient equation given as

$$\vec{E} = -\nabla V \quad \ldots(1.137)$$

$$\Rightarrow \quad \vec{E} = -\left(\frac{\partial V}{\partial x}\hat{i} + \frac{\partial V}{\partial y}\hat{j} + \frac{\partial V}{\partial z}\hat{k}\right) \quad \ldots(1.138)$$

Here V is the potential at a general point (x, y, z) in the space. We can understand this with an example as if in a region the electric potential at a general point (x, y, z) is given as

$$V = (3x^2 + 4xy + y^3 z) \text{ volt}$$

For the above potential in space, the electric field vector in that region can be given by using equation-(1.138) as

$$\vec{E} = [(6x + 4y)\hat{i} + (4x + 3y^2 z)\hat{j} + (y^3)\hat{k}] \text{ V/m}$$

1.10.12 Potential difference between two Large Plane Sheets

As already discussed that electric field due to a uniformly charged large metal plate is uniform in its surrounding so potential decreases linearly with distance from the plates as we move away from the plate. Figure-1.166 shows two large planer sheets X and Y, charged with surface charge densities σ_1 and σ_2 ($\sigma_2 > \sigma_1$) respectively. As both are positively charged the electric field strength between the two are in opposite directions. As $\sigma_2 > \sigma_1$ net electric field in the region will be leftward between the plates and using this we can find the potential difference between the surfaces of the sheets which is given as

$$V_Y - V_X = \left(\frac{\sigma_2}{2\epsilon_0} - \frac{\sigma_1}{2\epsilon_0}\right)d \quad \ldots(1.139)$$

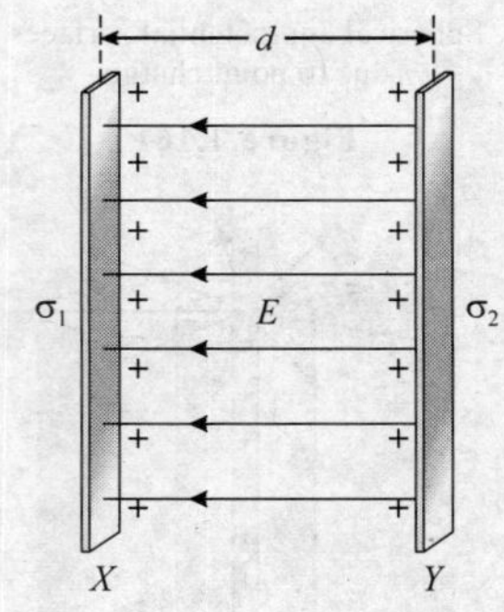

Figure 1.166

Illustrative Example 1.41

A particle has charge – 5.00 μC and mass 2.00 × 10^{-4} kg. It moves from point A, where the electric potential is V_A = +200 V, to point B, where the electric potential is V_B = + 800 V. During motion of the particle electric force is the only force acting on the particle. The particle has speed 5 m/s at point A. What is its speed at point B? It is moving faster or slower at B than at A? Explain.

Solution

By conservation of energy, we use

$$KE_A + U_A = KE_B + U_B$$

$$\Rightarrow \quad \frac{1}{2}mv_A^2 + qV_A = \frac{1}{2}mv_B^2 + qV_B$$

$$\Rightarrow \quad v_B = \sqrt{V_A^2 + \frac{2}{m}q(V_A - V_B)}$$

$$\Rightarrow \quad v_B = \sqrt{(5)^2 + \frac{2\times(-5\times10^{-6})}{2\times10^{-4}}(200-800)}$$

$$\Rightarrow \quad v_B = 7.42 \text{ m/s}$$

As $V_B > V_A$, the negative charge moving (freely) from lower potential at A to higher potential at B will gain energy as electric force is doing work on it so its electrostatic potential energy will decrease at B and kinetic energy will increase.

Illustrative Example 1.42

A particle having a charge $+3 \times 10^{-9}$ C is placed in a uniform electric field directed toward left. It is released from rest and moves a distance of 5 cm after which its kinetic energy is found to be 4.5×10^{-5} J.

(a) Calculate the work done by the electrical force on the particle

(b) Calculate the magnitude of the electric field.

(c) Calculate the potential of starting point with respect to the end point of particle's motion.

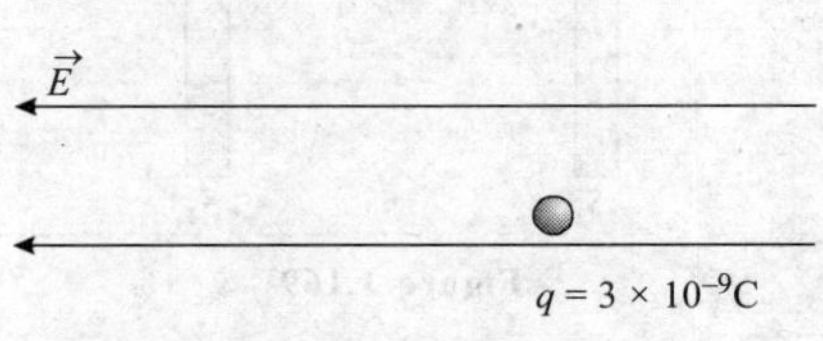

Figure 1.167

Solution

(a) Work done by electric forces on a charge particle is the gain in its kinetic energy, thus work done by electric forces can be given as

$$W = \Delta KE = 4.5 \times 10^{-5} \text{ J}$$

(b) Work done by electric forces can also be given as

$$W = qE.l$$

$$\Rightarrow \quad 4.5 \times 10^{-5} = 3 \times 10^{-9} \times 5 \times 10^{-2} \times E$$

$$\Rightarrow \quad E = 3 \times 10^5 \text{ N/C}$$

(c) By using work energy theorem again, we have

$$q(V_1 - V_2) = \frac{1}{2}mv^2$$

$$\Rightarrow \quad V_1 - V_2 = \frac{\frac{1}{2}mv^2}{q}$$

$$\Rightarrow \quad V_1 - V_2 = \frac{4.5\times10^{-5}}{3\times10^{-9}}$$

$$\Rightarrow \quad V_1 - V_2 = 1.5 \times 10^4 \text{ V}$$

Illustrative Example 1.43

An electric field $\vec{E} = Ax\hat{i}$ exist in the space, where $A = 10$ V/m². Consider the potential at (10 m, 20 m) to be zero. Find the potential at the origin.

Solution

Figure-1.168 shows the situation described in question. Here BC is the equipotential line so we can use

$$V_C = V_B = 0$$

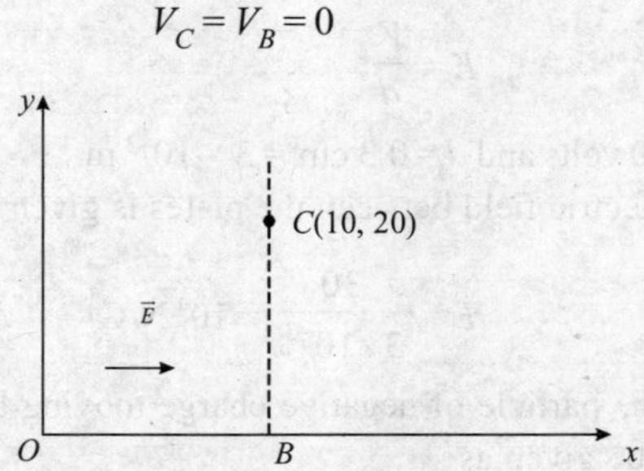

Figure 1.168

If V_0 be the potential at the origin, we can use

$$V_0 - V_B = \int_A^B E dx = \int_0^{10} Ax dx$$

$$\Rightarrow \quad V_0 - 0 = A\left|\frac{x^2}{2}\right|_0^{10} = 10 \times \frac{10^2}{2}$$

$$\Rightarrow \quad V_0 = 500 \text{ V}$$

Illustrative Example 1.44

12 J of work has to be done against an existing electric field to take a charge of 0.01 C from A to B. Find the potential difference $V_B - V_A$?

Solution

Using work energy theorem, we can calculate the work done in displacing a charge from point A to B which is given as

$$W = q(V_B - V_A)$$

$$\Rightarrow \quad V_B - V_A = \frac{W}{q} = \frac{12}{0.01} = 1.2 \times 10^3\ V$$

Illustrative Example 1.45

A particle of mass 9×10^{-31} kg and a negative charge of 1.6×10^{-19} C is projected horizontally with a velocity of 10^5 m/s into a region between two infinite horizontal parallel plates of metal. The distance between the plates is 0.3 cm and the particle enter 0.1 cm below the top plate. The top and bottom plates are connected respectively to the positive and negative terminals of a 30 V battery. Find the component of the velocity of the particle just before it hits one on the plates in direction perpendicular to plates.

Solution

Between the two parallel plates electric field will be uniform and it can be given as

$$E = \frac{V}{d}$$

Here $V = 30$ volts and $d = 0.3$ cm $= 3 \times 10^{-3}$ m
Thus the electric field between the plates is given as

$$E = \frac{30}{3 \times 10^{-3}} = 10^4\ \text{N/C}$$

Force on the particle of negative charge moving between the plates can be given as

$$F = eE = 1.6 \times 10^{-19} \times 10^4 = 1.6 \times 10^{-15}\ \text{N}$$

The direction of force will be towards the positive plate i.e. upward in the above given situation.

The acceleration of the particle between the plates is given as

$$a = \frac{eE}{m}$$

$$\Rightarrow \quad a = (1.6 \times 10^{-15})/(9 \times 10^{-31})$$

$$\Rightarrow \quad a = 1.77 \times 10^{15}\ \text{m/s}^2$$

As the electric intensity E is acting in the vertical direction the horizontal velocity v of the particle remains same. If y is the displacement of the particle, in upward direction, we have

$$y = \frac{1}{2}at^2$$

Here, $\quad y = 0.1$ cm $= 10^{-3}$ m, $a = 1.77 \times 10^{15}$ m/s^2

$$\Rightarrow \quad 10^{-3} = \frac{1}{2} \times (1.77 \times 10^{-15})(t^2)$$

Solving we get $t = 1.063 \times 10^{-10}$ s

Component of velocity in the direction of field is given by,

$$v_y = at$$

$$\Rightarrow \quad v_y = (1.77 \times 10^{15})(1.063 \times 10^{-10})$$

$$\Rightarrow \quad v_y = 1.881 \times 10^4\ \text{m/s}$$

Illustrative Example 1.46

There are two large metallic plates S_1 and S_2 carrying surface charge densities σ_1 and σ_2 respectively ($\sigma_1 > \sigma_2$) placed at a distance d apart in vacuum. Find the work done by the electric field in moving a point charge q distant a ($a < d$) from S_1 towards S_2 along a line making an angle $\pi/4$ with the normal to the plates.

Solution

If E_1 and E_2 are the respective fields produced by the plates, then net field between the plates is given as

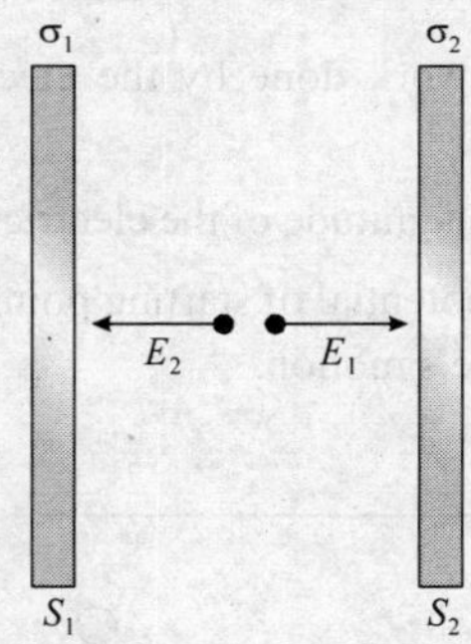

Figure 1.169

$$E = E_1 - E_2$$

$$\Rightarrow \quad E = \frac{\sigma_1}{\epsilon_0} - \frac{\sigma_2}{\epsilon_0} = \frac{\sigma_1 - \sigma_2}{\epsilon_0}$$

Force on the point charge due to the field between the plates is given as

$$F = qE = \frac{q}{\epsilon_0}(\sigma_1 - \sigma_2)$$

Work done by the electric field

$$W = Fs\cos\theta$$

$$\Rightarrow \quad W = \frac{q}{\epsilon_0}(\sigma_1 - \sigma_2)a\cos\frac{\pi}{4}$$

$$\Rightarrow \quad W = \frac{qa}{\sqrt{2}\,\epsilon_0}(\sigma_1 - \sigma_2)$$

Illustrative Example 1.47

A charge q_0 is transported from point A to B along the arc AB with centre at C as shown in figure-1.170 near a long charged wire with linear density λ lying in the same plane. Find the work done in doing so.

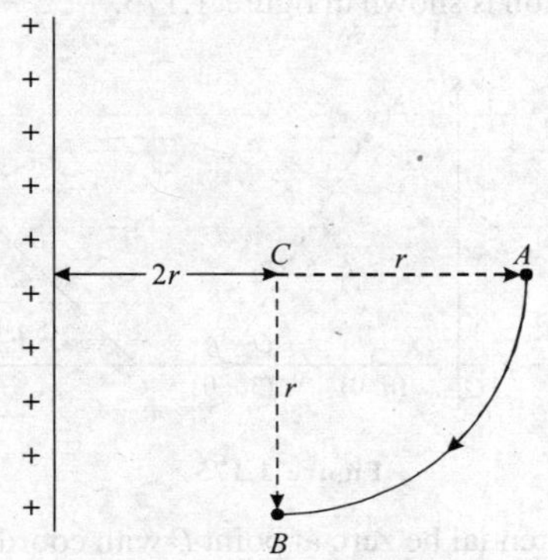

Figure 1.170

Solution

As electric field is a conservative field work doesn't depend upon the path so in above case work done in transporting the particle from point A to B is same as if it is shifted from A to C as points B and C are lying on same equipotential surface. Thus we have

$$W_{AB} = W_{AC}$$

$$W_{AC} = -q\int_{3r}^{2r} E \cdot dr$$

$$\Rightarrow \quad W_{AC} = q\int_{2r}^{3r} \frac{2K\lambda}{r}\, dr$$

$$\Rightarrow \quad W_{AC} = 2Kq\lambda \ln\left(\frac{3}{2}\right)$$

Illustrative Example 1.48

Some equipotential surfaces are shown in figure-1.171. Determine the magnitude and direction of electric field ?

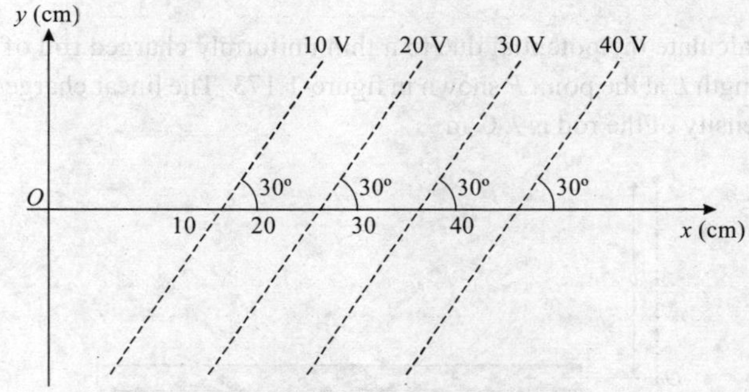

Figure 1.171

Solution

As we know that the direction of electric field is perpendicular to the equipotential surfaces and in the direction of electric field potential decreases. With these facts we get direction of electric field is 120° from x-axis as shown is figure-1.172.

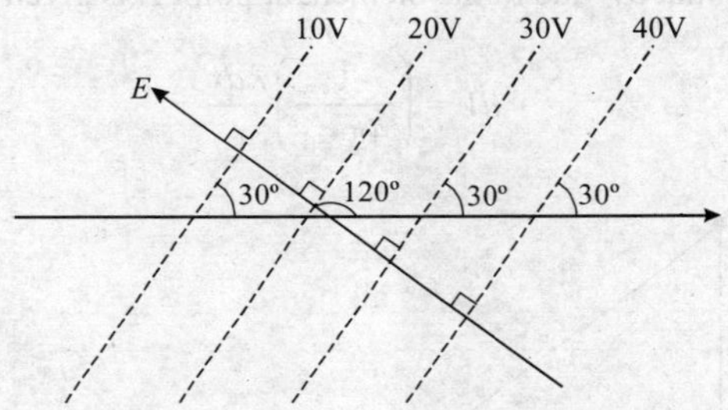

Figure 1.172

As already discussed that magnitude of electric field is given as

$$E = \frac{dV}{dx}$$

For uniform electric field, we can also write

$$E = \frac{\Delta V}{\Delta x}$$

Here ΔV is potential difference and Δx is the normal distance between equipotential surfaces, thus we use

$$E = \frac{20 - 10}{10\sin 30^\circ}$$

$$\Rightarrow \quad E = \frac{10}{5} = 2\ \text{V/m}$$

Illustrative Example 1.49

Calculate the potential due to a thin uniformly charged rod of length L at the point P shown in figure-1.173. The linear charge density of the rod is λ C/m.

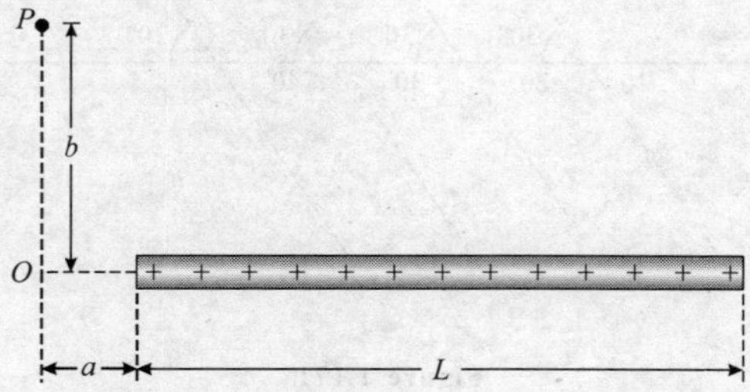

Figure 1.173

Solution

To find potential at point P, we consider an element of thickness dx as shown. The charge on the element is

$$dq = \lambda\, dx$$

The potential dV due to the element at point P is given as

$$dV = \left(\frac{1}{4\pi \epsilon_0}\right)\frac{\lambda dx}{r}$$

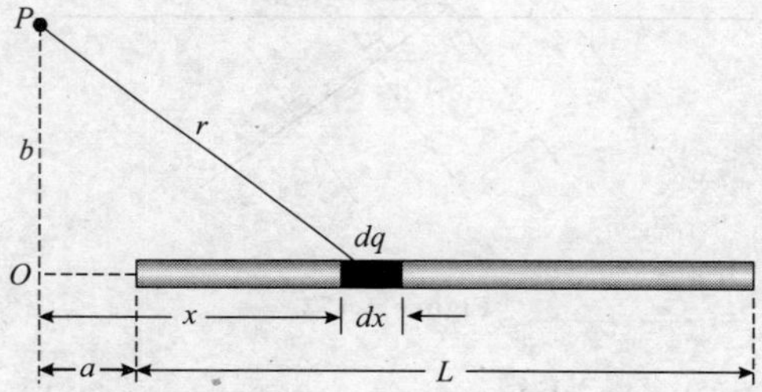

Figure 1.174

The potential due to the entire rod at point P can be given by integrating the above result due to the element as

$$V = \left(\frac{1}{4\pi \epsilon_0}\right)\int_a^{(L+a)} \frac{\lambda dx}{r}$$

$$\Rightarrow \quad V = \left(\frac{1}{4\pi \epsilon_0}\right)\int_a^{(L+a)} \frac{\lambda dx}{(b^2+x^2)^{1/2}}$$

$$\Rightarrow \quad V = \left(\frac{\lambda}{4\pi \epsilon_0}\right)\left[\ln\{x+\sqrt{b^2+x^2}\}\right]_a^{L+a}$$

$$\Rightarrow \quad V = \left(\frac{\lambda}{4\pi \epsilon_0}\right)\ln\left[\frac{(L+a)+\sqrt{b^2+(L+a)^2}}{a+\sqrt{b^2+a^2}}\right]$$

Illustrative Example 1.50

Two fixed charges $-2Q$ and Q are located at the points with coordinates $(-3a, 0)$ and $(+3a, 0)$ respectively in the x-y plane.

(a) Show that all the points in the x-y plane where the electric potential due to the two charges is zero, lie on a circle. Find its radius and the location of its centre.

(b) Give the expression for the potential $V(x)$ at a general point on the x-axis and sketch the function $V(x)$ on the whole x-axis.

(c) If particle of charge $+q$ starts from rest at the centre of the circle, show by a short qualitative argument that the particle eventually crosses the circle. Find its speed when it does so.

Solution

(a) The situation is shown in figure-1.175.

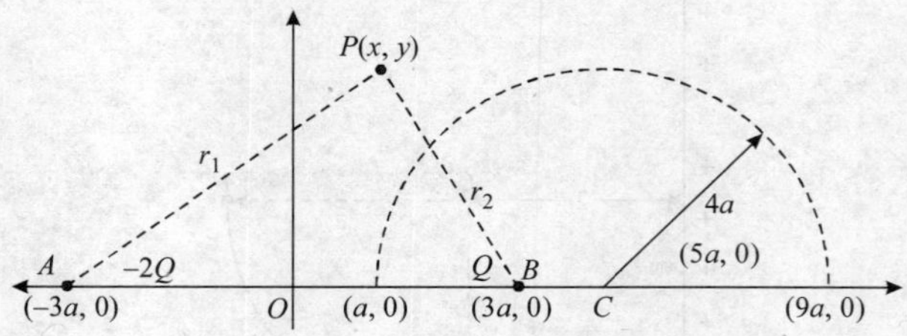

Figure 1.175

Let electric potential be zero at point P with coordinates (x, y). The electric potential at P is given by

$$V = K\left[-\frac{2Q}{r_1}+\frac{Q}{r_2}\right] = 0$$

Where r_1 and r_2 are the distances of P from $-2Q$ and Q respectively. Then,

$$r_1 = \sqrt{[(3a+x)^2+y^2]}$$

and

$$r_2 = \sqrt{[(3a-x)^2+y^2]}$$

Here the potential is

$$V = K\left[-\frac{2Q}{\sqrt{[(3a+x)^2+y^2]}}+\frac{Q}{\sqrt{[(3a-x)^2+y^2]}}\right] = 0$$

$$\Rightarrow \quad \frac{2}{\sqrt{[(3a+x)^2+y^2]}} = \frac{Q}{\sqrt{[(3a-x)^2+y^2]}}$$

Solving this equation, we get

$$x^2+y^2-10ax+9a^2 = 0$$

$$\Rightarrow \quad (x-5a)^2+y^2 = (4a)^2$$

This is an equation of a circle in XY plane having a radius $4a$ and coordinates of centre at $(5a, 0)$.

(b) The potential at any general point on X-axis is given by,

$$V(x) = K\left[\frac{Q}{(3a-x)} - \frac{2Q}{(3a+x)}\right] \quad \text{for } 0 < x < 3a$$

$$V(x) = K\left[\frac{Q}{(x-3a)} - \frac{2Q}{(3a+x)}\right] \quad \text{for } x > 3a$$

Sketch of potential $V(x)$ versus distance x is shown in figure-154.

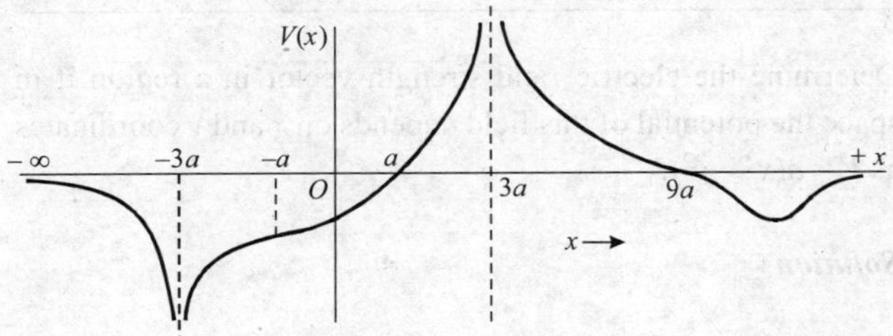

Figure 1.176

We now sketch the potential function $V(x)$ on the whole X-axis. Now for sketching the curve we have

(i) $V(x) = 0$ for $x = a$ and $x = 9a$.

(ii) From the expression of $V(x)$, it is clear that $V(x) \to \infty$ as $x \to 3a$ and $V(x) \to -\infty$ when $x \to -3a$.

(iii) $V(x) \to 0$ as $x \to \pm\infty$.

(iv) in general $V(x)$ varies as $1/x$.

The sketch is shown in figure-1.176.

(c) When the particle of charge q is at the centre of the circle $(5a, 0)$, the force on the particle is given by

$$F = K\left[\frac{Qq}{(2a)^2} - \frac{2Qq}{(8a)^2}\right] = \frac{K\,Qq}{4a^2}\left[1 - \frac{1}{8}\right]$$

$$\Rightarrow \quad F = K\left(\frac{7}{32}\right)\frac{Qq}{a^2} \text{ along } +X\text{-axis.}$$

Thus the particle moves along X-axis. When it reaches at the point on the periphery of the circle i.e., at $x = 5a + 4a = 9a$, the force on the particle is given by

$$F = K\left[\frac{Qq}{(6a)^2} - \frac{2Qq}{(12a)^2}\right] = \frac{K\,Qq}{(6a)^2}\left(1 - \frac{1}{2}\right)$$

$$\Rightarrow \quad F = \frac{K\,Qq}{36a^2}\,\frac{1}{2} = \frac{K\,Qq}{(72a^2)} \text{ along } +X\text{-axis.}$$

This expression shows that still there is a force on he particle along X-axis, so the particle crosses the circle.

Let v be the velocity of particle when it crosses the circle. From the law of conservation of energy, we have

(K.E. + P.E.) at the centre = (K.E. + P.E.) at periphery

$$0 + K\left(\frac{Qq}{2a} - \frac{2Qq}{8a}\right) = \frac{1}{2}mv^2 + K\left(\frac{Qq}{6a} - \frac{2Qq}{12a}\right)$$

$$\frac{K\,Qq}{a}\left(\frac{1}{2} - \frac{1}{4}\right) = \frac{1}{2}mv^2 + 0$$

$$\Rightarrow \quad v = \sqrt{\left[K\left(\frac{Qq}{2ma}\right)\right]}$$

Illustrative Example 1.51

There is an infinite chain of alternating charges q and $-q$ with the distance between the neighbouring charges is equal to a. Calculate the interaction energy of each charge with all the other charges.

Solution

Electric potential energy of one $+q$ charge with other is given as

$$U = 2\left[-\frac{Kq^2}{a} + \frac{Kq^2}{2a} - \frac{Kq^2}{3a} + \frac{Kq^2}{4a} + \ldots\ldots\right]$$

$$\Rightarrow \quad U = -2\,\frac{Kq^2}{a}\left[1 - \frac{1}{2} + \frac{1}{3} - \frac{1}{4} + \ldots\ldots\right]$$

$$\Rightarrow \quad U = -2\,\frac{Kq^2}{a}\ln 2$$

Illustrative Example 1.52

A uniform electric field of 100 V/m is directed at 30° with the positive x-axis as shown in figure-1.177. Find the potential difference V_{BA} if $OA = 2$ m and $OB = 4$ m.

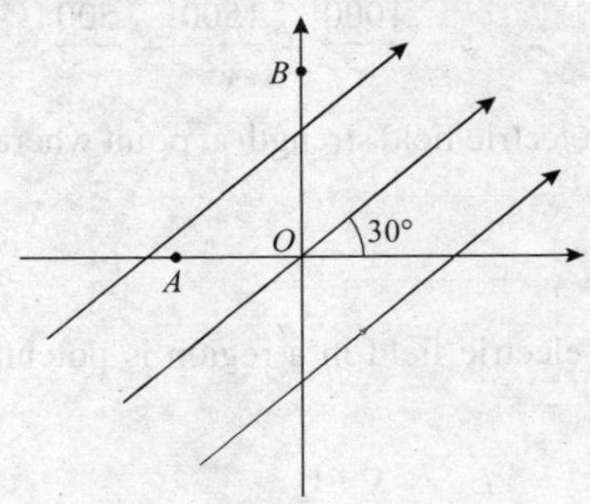

Figure 1.177

Solution

Electric field vector can be written from the figure as

$$\vec{E} = (100\cos 30°\,\hat{i} + 100\sin 30°\,\hat{j})\text{ V/m}$$

$$\Rightarrow \quad \vec{E} = (50\sqrt{3}i + 50\hat{j})\ \text{V/m}$$

Potential difference between points B and A can be given as

$$V_{BA} = V_B - V_A = -\int_A^B \vec{E}\cdot d\vec{r}$$

$$\Rightarrow \quad V_{BA} = \int_{(-2m,0,0)}^{(0,4m,0)} (50\sqrt{3}i + 50\hat{j})\cdot(dx\hat{i} + dy\hat{j} + dz\hat{k})$$

$$\Rightarrow \quad V_{BA} = -[50\sqrt{3}x + 50y]_{(-2m,0,0)}^{(0,4m,0)}$$

$$\Rightarrow \quad V_{BA} = -100(2+\sqrt{3})\ \text{V}$$

In this case point B is at lower potential as along the direction of electric field potential decreases.

Alternative Method:

As the given electric field is uniform in space, we can use the potential difference in uniform electric field is given as

$$V = Ed$$

As $V_A > V_B$ the potential difference $V_B - V_A$ will be negative.

We also have

$$d_{AB} = OA\cos 30° + OB\sin 30°$$

$$\Rightarrow \quad d_{AB} = 2\times\frac{\sqrt{3}}{2} + 4\times\frac{1}{2} = (\sqrt{3}+2)\ \text{m}$$

$$\Rightarrow \quad V_B - V_A = -Ed_{AB} = -100(2+\sqrt{3})\ \text{V}$$

 # Illustrative Example 1.53

The potential at a point in space depends only upon the x-coordinate and it is given as

$$V = \frac{1000}{x} + \frac{1500}{x^2} + \frac{500}{x^3}$$

Determine the electric field strength at point where $x = 1$ m.

Solution

We know that electric field in a region is potential gradient, given as

$$\vec{E} = -\nabla\cdot V$$

$$\Rightarrow \quad \vec{E} = -\left(\frac{\partial V}{\partial x}\hat{i} + \frac{\partial V}{\partial y}\hat{j} + \frac{\partial V}{\partial z}\hat{k}\right)$$

As the given relation is only a function of x we use

$$\vec{E} = -\frac{dV}{dx}\hat{i}$$

$$\Rightarrow \quad \vec{E} = -\left[-\frac{1000}{x^2} - 2\cdot\frac{1500}{x^3} - 3\cdot\frac{500}{x^4}\right]\hat{i}$$

At $x = 1$ m, we have

$$\vec{E} = -[-1000 - 3000 - 1500]$$

$$\Rightarrow \quad \vec{E} = +5500\ \hat{i}\ \text{V/m}$$

 # Illustrative Example 1.54

Determine the electric field strength vector in a region if in space the potential of this field depends on x and y coordinates as $V = a(x^2 - y^2)$.

Solution

As we know that for three dimensional variation of electric field in a region electric field and potential are related as

$$\vec{E} = -\left(\frac{\partial V}{\partial x}\hat{i} + \frac{\partial V}{\partial y}\hat{j} + \frac{\partial V}{\partial z}\hat{k}\right)$$

Using the given value of potential, we have

$$E_x = -\frac{\partial V}{\partial x} = -2ax,$$

and $$E_y = -\frac{\partial V}{\partial y} = 2ay$$

$$\Rightarrow \quad \vec{E} = E_x\hat{i} + E_y\hat{j}$$

$$\Rightarrow \quad \vec{E} = 2a(x\hat{i} + y\hat{j})$$

Web Reference at www.physicsgalaxy.com

Age Group - Grade 11 & 12 | Age 17-19 Years
Section - ELECTROSTATICS
Topic - Electric Potential
Module Number - 1 to 30

Practice Exercise 1.5

(i) Four particles with charges $+q, +q, -q, -q$ are placed respectively at the corners. A, B, C, D of a square of side 'a' arranged in given order. Calculate the electric potential and intensity at point O, the center of the square. If E and F are the midpoints of the sides BC and CD respectively, what will be the work done in displacing a charge Q from O to E and from O to F?

$\left[0, -\frac{4KqQ}{a}\left(\frac{\sqrt{5}-1}{\sqrt{5}}\right)\right]$

(ii) Two particles each charged with a charge $+q$ are clamped on the y axis at the points $(0, a)$ and $(0, -a)$. If a positively charged particle of charge q_0 and mass m is slightly displaced from origin in the direction of negative x-axis.

(a) What will be its speed at infinity ?

(b) If the particle is projected towards the left along the x-axis from a point at a large distance on the right of the origin with a velocity half that acquired in part (a), at what distance from origin will it come to rest ?

[$2\sqrt{\dfrac{Kqq_0}{ma}}$, $\sqrt{15}a$]

(iii) An infinite number of charges each equal to q are placed along the x-axis at $x = 1$ m, $x = 4$m, $x = 8$ m, ... and so on. Find the potential and electric field at the point $x = 0$ due to this set of charges. What will be potential and electric field if in the above set up if the consecutive charge have opposite sign?

[$\dfrac{q}{2\pi\epsilon_0}$, $\dfrac{q}{3\pi\epsilon_0}$, $\dfrac{q}{6\pi\epsilon_0}$, $\dfrac{q}{5\pi\epsilon_0}$]

(iv) A particle having a charge of 1.6×10^{-19} C enters midway between the two plates of a parallel plate capacitor. The initial velocity of particle is parallel to the plates. A potential difference of 300 V is applied between the two plates. If the length of the plates is 10 cm and they are separated by 2 cm, calculate the greatest initial velocity for which the particle will not be able to come out of the plates. The mass of the particle is 12×10^{-24} kg.

[10^4 m/s]

(v) A circular ring of radius R with uniform positive charge density λ per unit length is located in the Y-Z plane with its centre at the origin O. A particle of mass m and positive charge q is projected from the point P $(R\sqrt{3}, 0, 0)$ on the positive X-axis directly towards O, with initial velocity v. Find the smallest (non-zero) value of the speed v such that the particle does not return to P.

[$\sqrt{\dfrac{\lambda q}{4\epsilon_0 m}}$]

(vi) There are two thin wire rings, each of radius R, whose axes coincide. The charges of the rings are q and $-q$. Find the potential difference between the centres of the rings separated by a distance a.

[$\dfrac{q}{2\pi\epsilon_0}\left(1 - \dfrac{1}{\sqrt{1+(a/R)^2}}\right)$]

(vii) A positive charge Q is uniformly distributed throughout the volume of a dielectric sphere of radius R. A point mass having charge $+q$ and mass m is fired towards the centre of the sphere with velocity v from a point at distance x $(x > R)$ from the centre of the sphere. Find the minimum velocity v so that it can penetrate $R/2$ distance of the sphere. Neglect any resistance other that electric interaction. Charge on small mass remains constant through out the motion.

[$\sqrt{\dfrac{2KQq}{m}\left(\dfrac{11}{8R} - \dfrac{1}{x}\right)}$]

(viii) The electric potential at surface of thin non-conducting sheet with charge density σ is V_0. Show that the electric potential at a distance x from infinite sheet can be written as

$$V = V_0 - \frac{\sigma}{2\epsilon_0}x$$

(ix) Two identical circular rings A and B of radius 30 cm are placed coaxially with their axes horizontal in a uniform electric field $E = 10^5$ N/C directed vertically upward as shown in figure-1.178. Distance between centres of these rings A and B is 40 cm. Ring A has a positive charge 10 μC while ring B has a negative charge of magnitude 20 μC. A particle of mass 100 g and carrying a positive charge 10 μC is released from rest at the centre of the ring A. Calculate its velocity when it has moved a distance of 40 cm. Take $g = 10$ m/s^2.

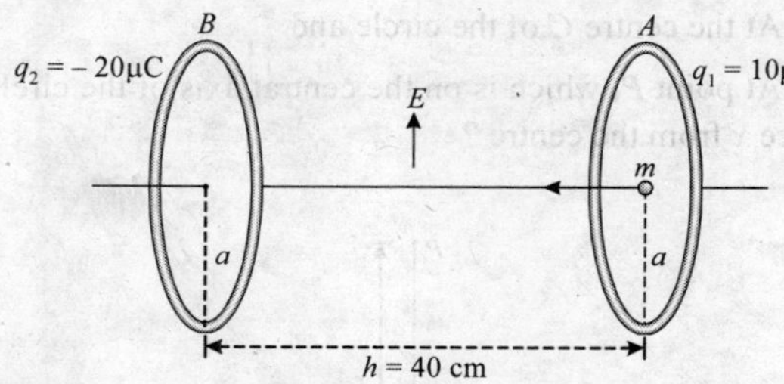

Figure 1.178

[$6\sqrt{2}$ m/s]

(x) A non-conducting disc of radius a and uniform surface charge density σ is placed on the ground, with its axis vertical. A particle of mass m and positive charge q is dropped, along the axis of the disc, from a height H above the center of disc with zero initial velocity. The particle has $q/m = 4\pi\varepsilon_0 g/\sigma$.

(a) Find the value of H if the particle just reaches the disc.

(b) Sketch the potential energy of the particle as a function of its height and find its equilibrium position.

[$\dfrac{4a}{3}$,  $\dfrac{a}{\sqrt{3}}$]

(xi) Determine the potential $\phi(x, y, z)$ of an electrostatic field $\vec{E} = ay\,\hat{i} + (ax + bz)\,\hat{j} + by\,\hat{k}$, where a and b are constants; $\hat{i} \cdot \hat{j}$ are the unit vectors of the axes x, y, z.

[$-y(ax + bz)$ + constant]

(xii) Find the potential difference between points a and b in an electric field of which strength in the region is given by the vector as

$$\vec{E} = (2\hat{i} + 3\hat{j} + 4\hat{k})\ \text{N/C}$$

The position vectors of points a and b are given as

$$\vec{r}_a = (\hat{i} - 2\hat{j} + \hat{k})m \text{ and } \vec{r}_b = (2\hat{i} + \hat{j} - 2\hat{k})m$$

[–1V]

(xiii) Consider a spherical surface of radius 4 m centred at the origin. Two point charges $+q$ and $-2q$ are clamped at points A(2 m, 0, 0) and B(8 m, 0, 0). Show that every point on the spherical surface is potential is zero.

(xiv) A plastic rod has been formed into a circle of radius R. It has a positive charge $+Q$ uniformly distributed along one-quarter of its circumference and a negative charge of $-6Q$ uniformly distributed along the rest of the circumference (figure-1.179). With $V = 0$ at infinity, what is the electric potential.

(a) At the centre C of the circle and

(b) At point P, which is on the central axis of the circle at distance x from the centre ?

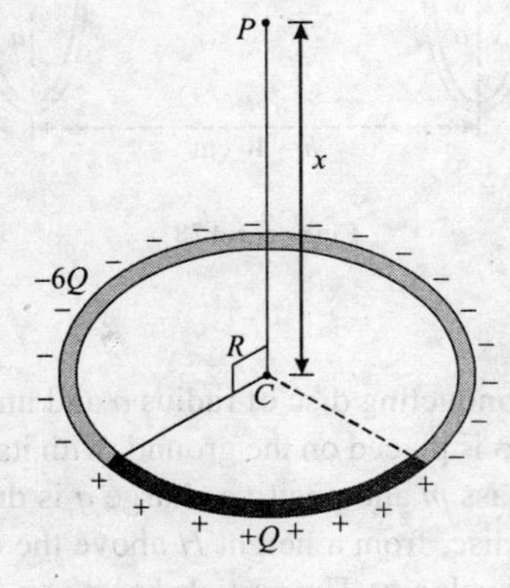

Figure 1.179

[(a) $\frac{-5Q}{4\pi\epsilon_0 R}$; (b) $\frac{-5Q}{4\pi\epsilon_0\sqrt{R^2 + x^2}}$]

(xv) A ring of radius R is having two charges q and $2q$ distributed on its two half parts. Find the electric potential at a point on its axis at a distance $2\sqrt{2}R$ from its centre.

[$\frac{q}{4\pi\epsilon_0 R}$]

1.11 Electric Potential Inside a Metal Body

As we've already discussed whenever charge is given to a metal body, it is distributed on its outer surface in such a way that net electric field at every interior point of body is zero. Thus if inside a metal body, a charge is displaced, no work is done in the process as electric field at every point is zero. Hence we can say that the whole metal body is equipotential. Based on this discussion we can also define an equipotential region as

"In a region of space if at every point electric field strength is zero then all points of this region will be having same potential and the region is said to be Equipotential."

Always remember that all points in a metal body whether charged or uncharged, within its volume or on its surface are at same potential. If the body is charged then electric field originates from its surface in perpendicular direction as surface of a metal body is always an equipotential surface as shown in figure-1.180.

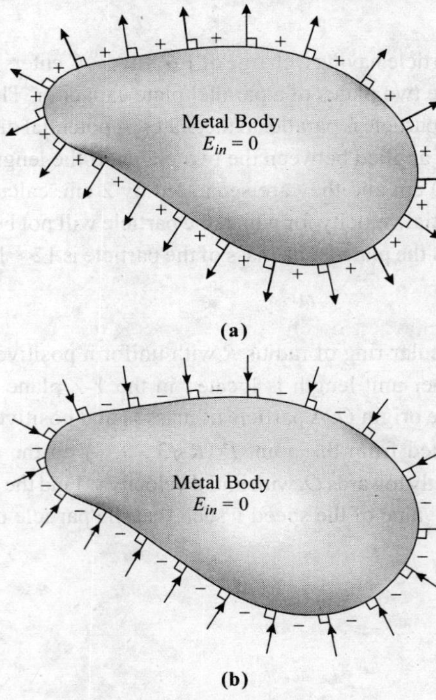

Figure 1.180

1.11.1 Electric Potential due to a Charged Conducting Sphere

We've already discussed in article-1.7.4 that for exterior points of a uniformly charged sphere we can consider whole charge of sphere is concentrated at its centre thus electric potential at a distance x from the centre of sphere outside can be given by the result of a point charge as

$$\text{For } x > R \qquad V = \frac{KQ}{x} \qquad \ldots(1.140)$$

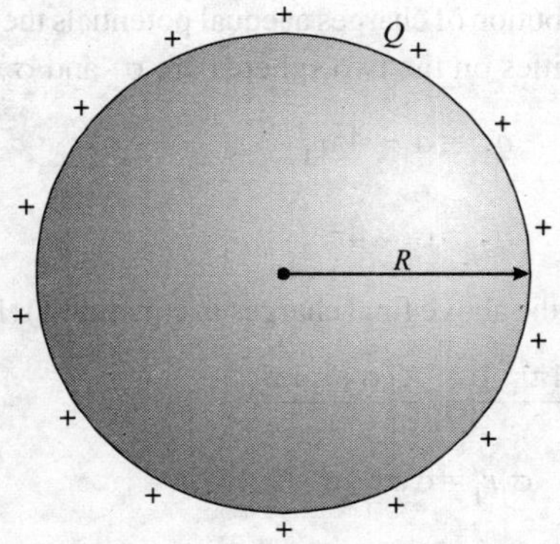

Figure 1.181

At the points on surface of sphere we use $x = R$ for which the potential can be given as

For $x = R$ $\quad V_S = \dfrac{KQ}{R}$ ...(1.141)

At interior points of sphere at every point electric field is zero so we can state that this is an equipotential region and at every interior point potential is same as that of its surface. Thus for interior points we use

For $x < R$ $\quad V_{in} = \dfrac{KQ}{R}$ ...(1.142)

1.11.2 Variation Curve of Electric Potential for a Uniformly Charged Conducting Sphere

Using equations-(1.140), (1.141) and (1.142) we can plot the curve of electric potential with distance from the center of a uniformly charged conducting sphere which is shown in figure-1.182.

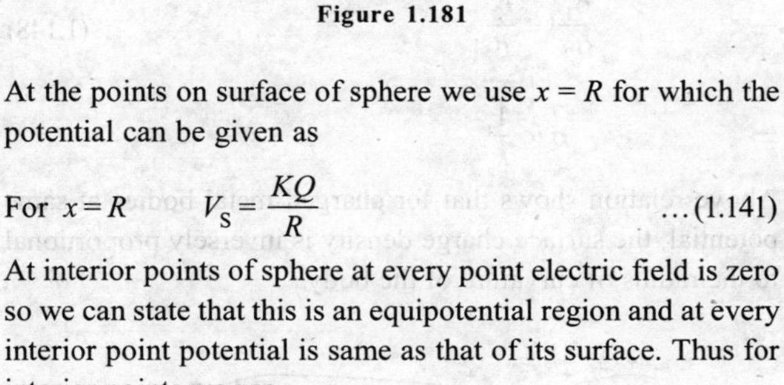

Figure 1.182

As already discussed in article-1.7.6 above graph as well as the relations in equation-(1.140), (1.141) and (1.142) are valid also for a uniformly charged thin walled non conducting sphere.

1.11.3 Electric Potential due to a Non-conducting Uniformly Charged Sphere

For outer and surface points due to symmetry again we consider the charge of sphere is concentrated at its center so the results of potential remains same as that of a conducting sphere, given as

For $x > R$ $\quad V = \dfrac{KQ}{x}$ ...(1.143)

For $x = R$ $\quad V_S = \dfrac{KQ}{R}$ ...(1.144)

(for $x > R$)

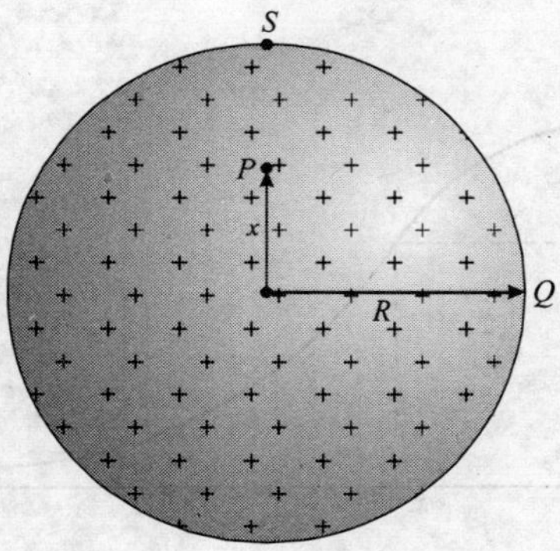

Figure 1.183

For interior points unlike to a conducting sphere, potential will not remain uniform as electric field exists in inside region of a solid uniformly charged sphere. We know inside a uniformly charged sphere electric field is in radial direction thus for a positive charge as we move away from centre, in the direction of electric field potential decreases.

As shown in figure-1.183, if we consider an interior point P at a distance x from the centre of sphere, the potential difference between points P and S can be given by equation-(1.127) as

$$V_P - V_S = \int_P^S \vec{E}\cdot\vec{dx}$$

$$\Rightarrow \quad V_P - V_S = \int_x^R \frac{KQx}{R^3}\,dx$$

$$\Rightarrow \quad V_P - \frac{KQ}{2R^3} = \frac{KQ}{2R^3}(R^2 - x^2)$$

$$\Rightarrow \quad V_P = \frac{KQ}{2R^3}(R^2 - x^2) + \frac{KQ}{R}$$

$$\Rightarrow \quad V_P = \frac{KQ}{2R^3}(3R^2 - x^2) \qquad \text{...(1.145)}$$

In above equation-(1.145) if we substitute $x = 0$, we get the potential at centre of sphere, given as

$$V_C = \frac{3KQ}{2R} = \frac{3}{2}V_S \qquad \text{...(1.146)}$$

Thus at centre of a uniformly charged non conducting spheres electric potential is maximum and it is equal to 1.5 times that on its surface.

1.11.4 Variation Curve of Electric Potential for a Uniformly Charged Non Conducting Sphere

Using equations-(1.143), (1.144) and (1.145) we can plot the curve of electric potential with distance from the center of a uniformly charged conducting sphere which is shown in figure-1.184.

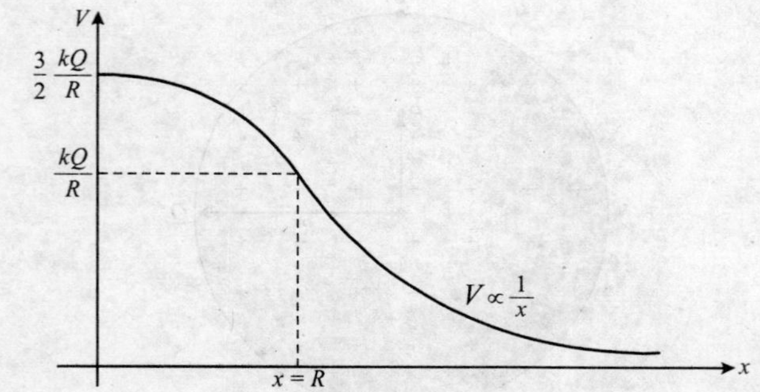

Figure 1.184

1.11.5 Charge Distribution on Metal Objects

We've earlier discussed that whenever a charge is given to a metal body, due to mutual repulsion, it automatically spreads on the outer surface of the body. Let us consider an illustration for understanding the distribution of charges in detail on metal bodies.

Figure-1.185 shows two conducting metal spheres of radii r_1 and r_2 at large separation having charges q_1 and q_2 initially.

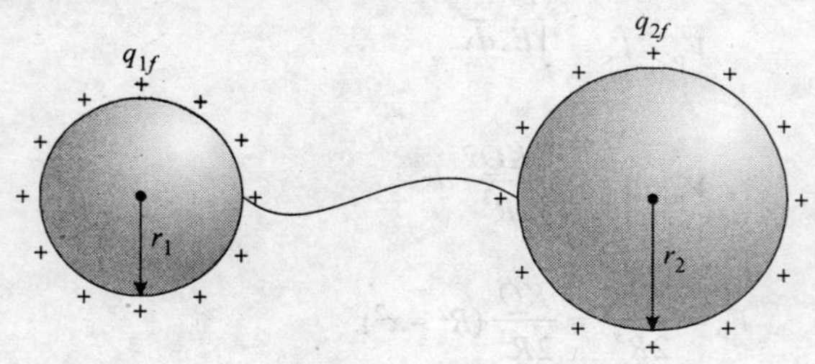

Figure 1.185

If the two spheres are connected by a metal wire as shown, charge flows from higher potential one to the lower potential one till final potential of the two spheres will become equal.

We consider that after final distribution of charges on the two sphere final charges are q_{1_f} and q_{2_f} respectively. Then we can relate these final charges with the radii of the two spheres such that

$$\frac{Kq_{1_f}}{r_1} = \frac{Kq_{2_f}}{r_2} \quad \ldots(1.147)$$

If after distribution of charges at equal potentials the final surface charge densities on the two spheres are σ_1 and σ_2, we have

$$q_{1_f} = \sigma_1 \times 4\pi r_1^2$$

and $$q_{2_f} = \sigma_2 \times 4\pi r_2^2$$

Substituting the above final charges in equation-(1.147) we have

$$\frac{K(\sigma_1 \times 4\pi r_1^2)}{r_1} = \frac{K(\sigma_2 \times 4\pi r_2^2)}{r_2}$$

$$\Rightarrow \quad \sigma_1 r_1 = \sigma_2 r_2$$

$$\Rightarrow \quad \frac{\sigma_1}{\sigma_2} = \frac{r_2}{r_1} \quad \ldots(1.148)$$

$$\Rightarrow \quad \sigma \propto \frac{1}{r}$$

Above relation shows that for charged metal bodies at same potential, the surface charge density is inversely proportional to the radius of curvature of the body.

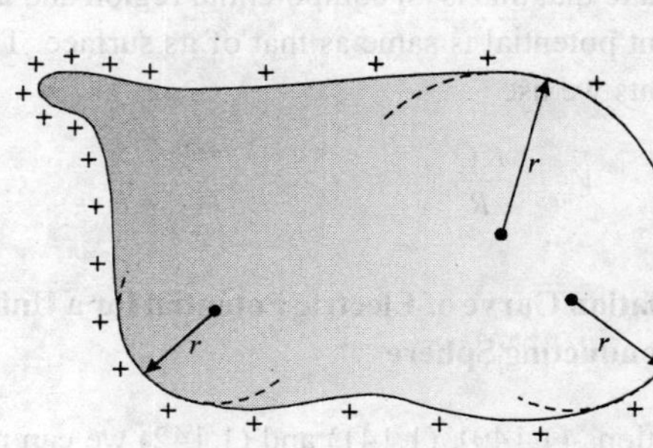

Figure 1.186

Figure-1.186 shows a random shaped metal body. If it is given some charge then it is distributed on the outer surface of this body in such a way that at sharp edges of body where radius of curvature is less, charge density is more and on the broader parts of body, where radius of curvature is large, charge density is less as we have already studied in article-1.11 that all points of a metal body within its volume and surface are equipotential.

1.11.6 Van de Graaff Generator

Whatever charge is given to a metal body it spreads on the outer surface of it due to which whole body is maintained at a constant potential in it. When this body is connected with some other neutral metal body then charge from this charged body flows to the neutral body until the two bodies will attain same potential. In this process of charge transfer or redistribution of charge between two bodies a very common questions comes in mind – "*Can we transfer complete charge of a metal body to another metal body by connecting the two ?*" The answer is simple. If we put the charged body inside a hollow metal body and the two are connected by a wire, whole of the charge of inner body will flow to the outer surface of the hollow body as shown in figure-1.187.

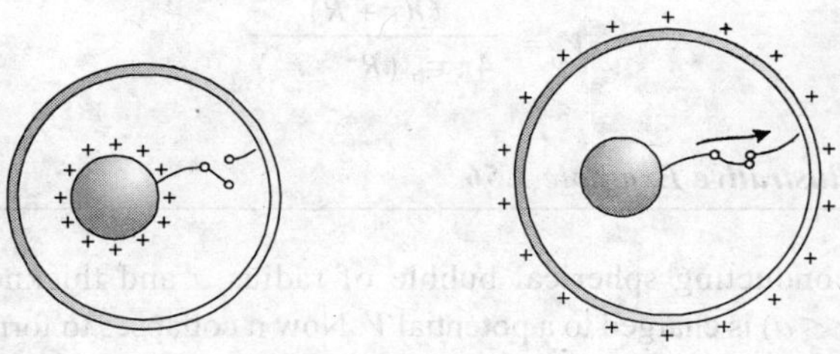

Figure 1.187

We've already discussed that whole of the charge given to a metal body spreads on its outer surface, no matter how large charge is as by this way only net electric field inside a conducting body becomes zero. This concept can be used to develop very high charges in a device called "*Van de Graaff generator*".

A Van de Graaff generator produces intense electric field to build up high voltages of a few million volt. To understand its working consider a small conductor carrying a positive charge q kept inside the cavity of a large conductor. The electric field that originates from the positive charge q must end on the inner surface of the large conductor irrespective of charge on the outer surface and the electric field inside the metal body of outer conductor is again zero. The potential on the inner conductor must be higher because electric field direction begin from it and end on the larger conductor. If the two conductors are now connected by a conducting wire, all the charges originally on the smaller conductor will flow to the larger one as it is always at lower potential until whole charge of inner conductor goes out. The positive charge transferred to the larger sphere resides completely on the outside surface of the larger conductor. Again the inner conductor can be given more charge and this process can be repeated indefinitely to produce large potential on the outer conductor.

Consider a shell of radius R and charge Q enclosing a smaller sphere of radius and r and charge q. The potentials of the two spheres are

$$V_{\text{outer}} = \frac{1}{4\pi \epsilon_0}\left(\frac{Q}{R}+\frac{q}{R}\right)$$

and $$V_{\text{inner}} = \frac{1}{4\pi \epsilon_0}\left(\frac{Q}{R}+\frac{q}{R}\right)$$

The potential difference between the two inner and outer spheres is

$$V_{\text{inner}} - V_{\text{outer}} = \frac{1}{4\pi \epsilon_0}\left[\frac{1}{r}-\frac{1}{R}\right]$$

Thus for positive q, whatever be the magnitude and sign of Q, the small sphere is at a higher potential than the shell. When an electric contact is provided the charge would flow from the small sphere to the shell. This is the way how a Van de Graaff Generator works.

Figure-1.188 shows a structural diagram of a Van de Graaff Generator. These are invented for the purpose of generating static electricity. It uses a moving rubber belt on two rollers to accumulate charge on a big hollow spherical conducting globe. Using this assembly a common table top Van de Graaff generator can produce potentials of the order of 10^5 V. Broadly we can discuss here the working of a Van de Graaff generator.

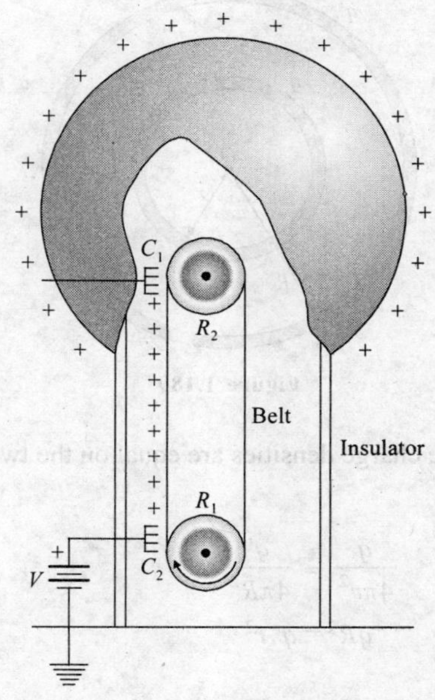

Figure 1.188

One of the rollers on which belt is moving is kept inside the globe and other is mounted at the bottom. Two comb shaped electrodes C_1 and C_2 are kept in touch with the rubber belt as shown. C_1 is connected to a grounded battery near bottom roller and C_2 is connected to the globe and kept near to upper roller. By friction charges are deposited on the belt by lower roller R_1 as the material of belt and roller is different. By the sharp edges of the comb C_1 charge is supplied to the outer surface of belt by air ionization. Belt carries these charges up and these are collected by C_2 and spread on the outer surface of the globe. In this way high charges can be accumulated on the outer surface of globe and belt carries a net charging current.

In practical conditions metal rollers and charges on inside surface of belt also play a role in net current through the belt but not important to be discussed here in the working of this generator. By selecting the specific materials for rollers and belt the globe of generator can be charged positively or negatively.

Illustrative Example 1.55

A charge Q is distributed over two concentric hollow spheres of radii r and R ($> r$) such that the surface densities are equal. Find the potential at the common centre.

Solution

Let q and q' be the charges on inner and outer sphere. Then we have

$$q + q' = Q \quad \dots (1.149)$$

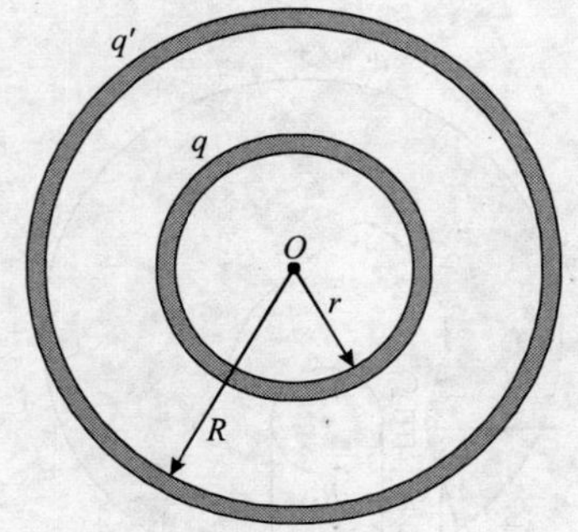

Figure 1.189

As the surface charge densities are equal on the two shells, we use

$$\frac{q}{4\pi r^2} = \frac{q'}{4\pi R^2}$$

$$\Rightarrow \quad qR^2 = q' r^2 \quad \dots (1.150)$$

From equation-(1.149) $q' = (Q - q)$, we have

$$qR^2 = (Q - q)r^2$$

$$\Rightarrow \quad q(R^2 + r^2) = Qr^2$$

$$\Rightarrow \quad q = \frac{Qr^2}{R^2 + r^2}$$

and $\quad q' = Q - q = \dfrac{QR^2}{R^2 + r^2}$

Potential at common centre O can be given as

$$V_0 = \frac{Kq}{r} + \frac{Kq'}{R}$$

$$\Rightarrow \quad V_0 = \frac{K\,Qr^2}{(R^2 + r^2)r} + \frac{K\,QR^2}{(R^2 + r^2)R}$$

$$\Rightarrow \quad V_0 = \frac{Q(r + R)}{4\pi \in_0 (R^2 + r^2)}$$

Illustrative Example 1.56

A conducting spherical bubble of radius a and thickness t ($t << a$) is charged to a potential V. Now it collapses to form a spherical droplet. Find the potential of the droplet.

Solution

As mass and charge of the bubble remain conserved, and if r be the radius of the resulting drop, so

$$\left(\frac{4}{3}\pi r^3\right)\rho = (4\pi a^2 t)\rho$$

$$\Rightarrow \quad r = (3a^2 t)^{1/3}$$

The potential of the bubble

$$V = \frac{1}{4\pi \in_0} \frac{q}{a},$$

Which gives

$$q = 4\pi \in aV$$

Now potential of the resulting drop

$$V' = \frac{1}{4\pi \in_0} \frac{q}{r}$$

$$\Rightarrow \quad V' = \frac{1}{4\pi \in_0} \frac{4\pi \in_0 aV}{(3a^2 t)^{1/3}}$$

$$\Rightarrow \quad V' = \left(\frac{a}{3t}\right)^{1/3} V$$

Illustrative Example 1.57

Find the electric field strength and potential at the centre of a hemisphere of radius R charged uniformly with the surface density σ.

Solution

The hemisphere is shown in figure-1.190. We consider a an elemental ring over the surface of this hemisphere as shown. The charge on this element is given as

$$dq = (2\pi R \sin\theta)(R\,d\theta)\,\sigma$$

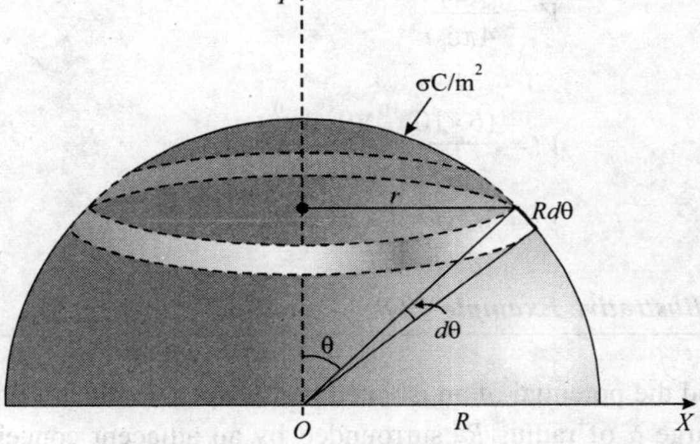

Figure 1.190

The potential due to this element at the centre O of the hemisphere is given as

$$dV = \frac{Kdq}{R} = \frac{1}{4\pi\epsilon_0} \times (2\pi R\,\sigma \sin\theta)\,d\theta$$

$$\Rightarrow \quad dV = \frac{\sigma R}{2\epsilon_0}\sin\theta\,d\theta$$

Potential due to whole hemisphere can be calculated by integrating the above expression within limits of θ from 0 to π/2.

$$V = \frac{R\sigma}{2\epsilon_0}\int_0^{\pi/2}\sin\theta\,d\theta = \frac{R\sigma}{2\epsilon_0}[-\cos\theta]_0^{\pi/2}$$

$$\Rightarrow \quad V = \frac{R\sigma}{2\epsilon_0}$$

From the symmetry of the problem, the net electric field at the hemisphere is directed towards negative y-axis. Thus the electric field due to the elemental ring at O along negative y-direction is given as

$$dE_y = \frac{1}{4\pi\epsilon_0}\times\frac{dq\cos\theta}{R^2} = \frac{\sigma}{2\epsilon_0}\sin\theta\cos\theta\,d\theta$$

$$E_y = \int dE_y = \frac{\sigma}{2\epsilon_0}\int_0^{\pi/2}\sin\theta\cos\theta\,d\theta$$

$$\Rightarrow \quad E_y = \frac{\sigma}{2\epsilon_0}\int_0^{\pi/2}\left[\frac{\sin 2\theta\,d\theta}{2}\right]$$

$$\Rightarrow \quad E_y = \frac{\sigma}{2\epsilon_0}\left[-\frac{\cos 2\theta}{2}\right]_0^{\pi/2} = \frac{\sigma}{4\epsilon_0}$$

Above result of electric field can also be obtained by integrating the electric field due to the elemental ring at the center of the hemisphere. Students can try calculating this and verify the above result.

Illustrative Example 1.58

On a thin rod of length $l = 1$ m, lying along the x-axis with one end at the origin $x = 0$, there is uniformly distributed charge per unit length $\lambda = Kx$, where K = constant = 10^{-9} cm^{-2}. Find the work done in displacing a charge q = 1000 μC from a point $(0, \sqrt{0.44}$ m) to (0, 1 m).

Solution

The situation described in question is shown in figure-1.191. We consider a small element of length dx on the rod at a distance x from the origin as shown in figure. Then potential dV_P at a general point P at a distance y from origin due to this element is given by

$$dV_P = \frac{1}{4\pi\epsilon_0}\frac{\lambda dx}{r} = \frac{Kxdx}{4\pi\epsilon_0 r}$$

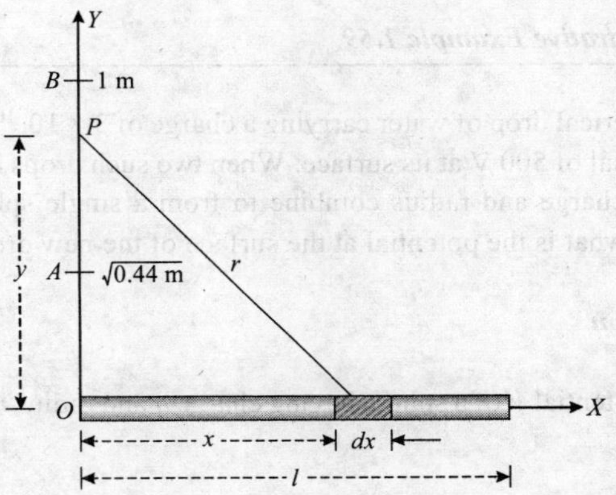

Figure 1.191

From figure-1.191 we have

$$r^2 = x^2 + y^2$$

$$\Rightarrow \quad 2rdr = 2xdx$$

$$\Rightarrow \quad dV_P = \frac{Kr\,dr}{4\pi\epsilon_0 r} = \frac{K}{4\pi\epsilon_0}dr$$

Integrating above expression for the length of rod, we get the potential at point P which is given as

$$V_P = \frac{K}{4\pi\epsilon_0}\int_y^{\sqrt{(l^2+y^2)}} dr$$

$$\Rightarrow \quad V_P = \frac{K}{4\pi\epsilon_0}\left[\sqrt{(l^2+y^2)} - y\right]$$

Potential at point A is given as

$$V_A = \frac{K}{4\pi \epsilon_0}[\sqrt{1.44} - \sqrt{0.44}]$$

$$\Rightarrow \quad V_A = 0.5366\frac{K}{4\pi \epsilon_0}$$

$$\Rightarrow \quad V_A = (9 \times 10^9) \times 10^{-9} \times 0.5366 = 4.83 \text{ V}$$

Potential at point B is given as

$$V_B = \frac{K}{4\pi \epsilon_0}[\sqrt{2} - 1] = 0.4142 = 3.728 \text{ V}$$

Work done in displacing the charge is given as

$$W = q(V_B - V_A)$$

$$\Rightarrow \quad W = 1000 \times 10^{-6}[3.728 - 4.83]$$

$$\Rightarrow \quad W = -1.1 \times 10^{-3} \text{J}$$

Illustrative Example 1.59

A spherical drop of water carrying a charge of 3×10^{-10} C has potential of 500 V at its surface. When two such drops having same charge and radius combine to from a single spherical drop, what is the potential at the surface of the new drop?

Solution

The potential V of a sphere having charge q and radius r given by

$$V = \frac{q}{4\pi\varepsilon_0 r}$$

For the drop we use $V = 500$ and $q = 3 \times 10^{-10}$ C

$$\Rightarrow \quad 500 = \frac{3\times10^{-10}}{r} \times (9 \times 10^9)$$

$$\Rightarrow \quad r = 0.0054 \text{ m} = 0.54 \text{ cm}$$

If r' be the radius of the new drop formed after combining two drops of radius r then we have

$$\frac{4}{3}\pi r'^3 = \frac{8}{3}\pi r^3$$

$$\Rightarrow \quad r' = (2)^{1/3} r$$

Charge on new drop is given as

$$q' = 2q = 2 \times (3 \times 10^{-10}) = 6 \times 10^{-10} \text{C}$$

Potential of the new drop formed is given as

$$V' = \frac{2q}{4\pi\varepsilon_0 r'}$$

$$\Rightarrow \quad V' = \frac{(6\times10^{-10})(9\times10^9)}{(2)^{1/3}\times 0.0054}$$

$$\Rightarrow \quad V' = 794 \text{ V}$$

Illustrative Example 1.60

Find the potential of an isolated ball-shaped conductor with a charge q of radius R_1 surrounded by an adjacent concentric layer of dielectric with dielectric constant k and outer radius R_2.

Solution

Situation described in question is shown in figure-1.192. The potential on the conductor can be obtained as

$$V = -\int E \cdot dr$$

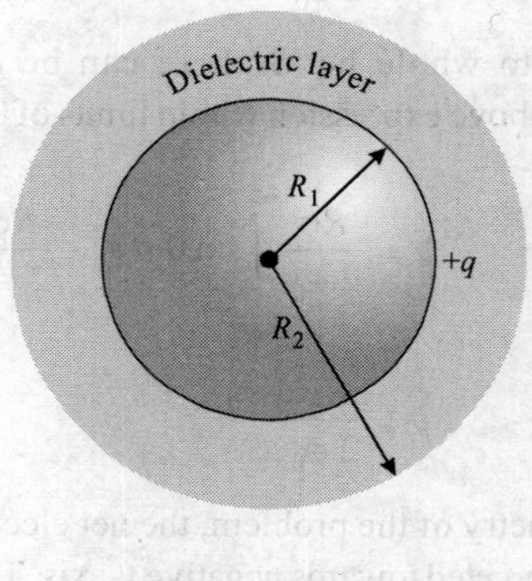

Figure 1.192

We need to split the integral in above equation in two parts, one for the region inside the dielectric and other for the outer space and solve within proper limits as

$$V = -\left[\int_{\infty}^{R_2} \frac{1}{4\pi \epsilon_0}\frac{q}{r^2}dr + \int_{R_2}^{R_1} \frac{1}{4\pi \epsilon_0 R}\frac{q}{r^2}dr\right]$$

$$\Rightarrow \quad V = -\frac{q}{4\pi \epsilon_0}\left[\int_{\infty}^{R_2}\frac{dr}{r^2} + \int_{R_2}^{R_1}\frac{dr}{kr^2}\right]$$

$$\Rightarrow \quad V = Kq\left[\left(-\frac{1}{r}\right)_{\infty}^{R_2} + \left(-\frac{1}{kr}\right)_{R_2}^{R_1}\right]$$

$$\Rightarrow \quad V = +Kq\left[\frac{1}{R_2} + \frac{1}{kR_1} - \frac{1}{kR_2}\right]$$

$$\Rightarrow \quad V = Kq\left[\frac{kR_1 + R_2 - R_1}{kR_1R_2}\right]$$

$$\Rightarrow \quad V = Kq\left[\frac{R_1(k-1) + R_2}{kR_1R_2}\right]$$

Illustrative Example 1.61

Three concentric metallic shells A, B and C of radii a, b and c $(a < b < c)$ have surface charge densities σ, $-\sigma$ and σ respectively.

(a) Find the potential of three shells A, B and C

(b) If the shells A and C are at the same potential, obtain the relation between the radii a, b and c.

Solution

(a) The three shells are shown in figure-1.193

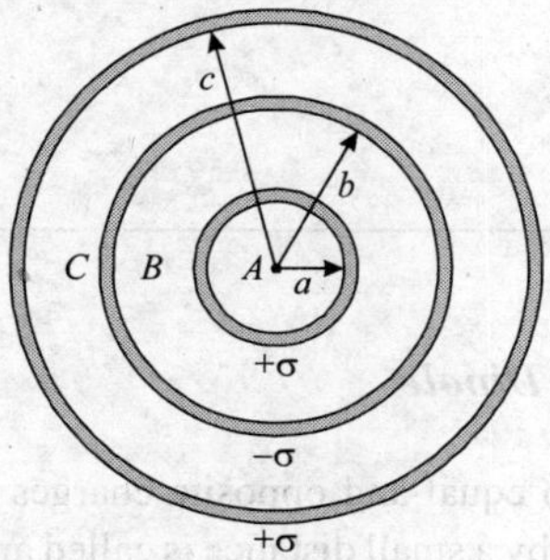

Figure 1.193

(1) Potential of A

V_A = (Potential of A due to $+\sigma$ on A)

+ (Potential of A due to $-\sigma$ on B)

+ (Potential of A due to $+\sigma$ on C)

$$\Rightarrow \quad V_A = \frac{1}{4\pi\varepsilon_0}\left[\frac{4\pi a^2\sigma}{a} - \frac{4\pi b^2\sigma}{b} + \frac{4\pi c^2\sigma}{c}\right]$$

$$\Rightarrow \quad V_A = \frac{\sigma}{\varepsilon_0}[a - b + c]$$

(2) Potential of B

V_B = (Potential due to $+\sigma$ on A)

+ (Potential due to $-\sigma$ on B)

+ (Potential due to $+\sigma$ on C)

$$\Rightarrow \quad V_B = \frac{4}{4\pi\varepsilon_0}\left[\frac{4\pi a^2\sigma}{b} - \frac{4\pi b^2\sigma}{b} + \frac{4\pi c^2\sigma}{c}\right]$$

$$\Rightarrow \quad V_B = \frac{\sigma}{\varepsilon_0}\left[\frac{a^2}{b} - b + c\right]$$

(3) Potential of C

V_C = (Potential due to $+\sigma$ on A)

+ (Potential due to $-\sigma$ on B)

+ (Potential due to $+\sigma$ on C)

$$\Rightarrow \quad V_C = \frac{1}{4\pi\varepsilon_0}\left[\frac{4\pi a^2\sigma}{c} - \frac{4\pi b^2\sigma}{c} + \frac{4\pi c^2\sigma}{c}\right]$$

$$\Rightarrow \quad V_C = \frac{\sigma}{\varepsilon_0}\left[\frac{a^2}{c} - \frac{b^2}{c} + c\right]$$

(b) Given that $V_A = V_C$

$$\Rightarrow \quad \frac{\sigma}{\varepsilon_0}[a - b + c] = \frac{\sigma}{\varepsilon_0}\left[\frac{a^2}{c} - \frac{b^2}{c} + c\right]$$

$$\Rightarrow \quad a - b - c = \frac{a^2}{c} - \frac{b^2}{c} + c$$

$$\Rightarrow \quad c = (a + b)$$

Web Reference at www.physicsgalaxy.com
Age Group - Grade 11 & 12 | Age 17-19 Years
Section - ELECTROSTATICS
Topic - Electric Potential
Module Number - 31 to 38

Practice Exercise 1.6

(i) Two concentric spheres of radii R and $2R$ are charged. The inner sphere has a charge of 1 μC and the outer sphere has a charge of 2 μC of the same sign. The potential is 9000 V at a distance $3R$ from the common centre. What is the value of R?

[1 m]

(ii) A spherical oil drop, radius 10^{-4} cm has on it at a certain time a total charge of 40 electrons. Calculate the energy that would be required to place an additional electron on the drop. Charge on an electron is 1.6×10^{-19} C.

[9.21×10^{-21} J]

(iii) Three charges 0.1 C each are placed on the corners of an equilateral triangle of side 1.0 m. If the energy is supplied to this system at the rate of 1.0 kW, how much time would be required to move one of the charges onto the midpoint of the line joining the other two?

[1.8×10^5 s]

(iv) A system consists of two conducting concentric spherical shells with the inside spherical of radius a carrying a positive charge q_1. What charge q_2 has to be deposited on the outside sphere of radius b to reduce the potential of the inside spherical to zero? How does the potential V depend in this case on a distance r from the centre of the system? Draw the approximate plot of this dependence.

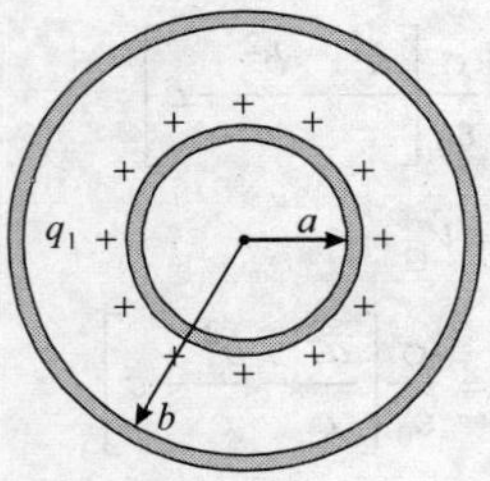

Figure 1.194

[$-(b/a)q_1$, 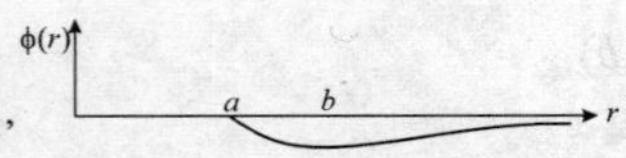]

(v) At the end points of a line segment of a length of $d = \frac{\sqrt{337}}{84}$ m there are two identical positive electric charges q. What is the ratio of the electric field strength and the electric potential magnitudes in *SI* units at a point located by an angle α = 37° on the circle drawn around the line segment as a diameter ?

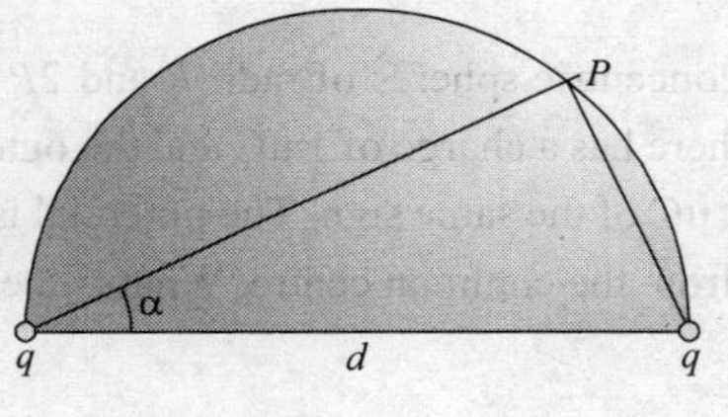

Figure 1.195

[≈5]

(vi) A conducting sphere S_1, of radius r is attached to an insulating handle. Another conducting sphere S_2 of radius R is mounted as an insulating stand. S_2 is initially uncharged. S_1 is given a charge Q, brought into contact with S_2 and removed. S_1 is recharged such that the charge on it is again Q and is again brought into contact with S_2 and removed. This procedure is repeated n times.

(a) Find the electrostatic energy of S_2 after n such contacts with S_1.

(b) What is the limiting value of this energy as $n \to \infty$.

[$\left(\frac{Q^2}{8\pi\epsilon_0 R(1+r/R)^2}\right)\left[\frac{1-\frac{1}{[1+(r/R)]^n}}{1-\frac{1}{[1+(r/R)]}}\right]^2$, $\frac{Q^2R}{8\pi\epsilon_0 r^2}$]

(vii) A uniform disc of radius R is charged with a uniform surface charge density σ. Find the electric potential due to the charges on the disc at a point on its edge.

[$\frac{\sigma R}{\pi\epsilon_0}$]

(viii) A dielectric cylinder of radius a is infinitely long. It is non-uniformly charged such that volume charge density ρ varies directly as the distance from the cylinder. Calculate the electric field intensity due to it at a point located at a distance r from the axis of the cylinder. Given that ρ is zero at the axis and it is equal to ρ on the surface of cylinder. Also calculate the potential difference between the axis and the surface.

[$\frac{\rho r^2}{3\epsilon_0 a}$, $\frac{\rho a^2}{9\epsilon_0}$]

1.12 Electric Dipole

A system of two equal and opposite charges maintained at a fixed separation by a small distance is called an electric dipole, shown in figure-1.196. Every dipole has a characteristic property called dipole moment which gives an idea about its behaviour, response and strength of diploe, we'll discuss later. Dipole moment of an electric dipole is defined as the product of magnitude of either charge and the separation between the charges, given as

$$\vec{p} = q\vec{d}$$

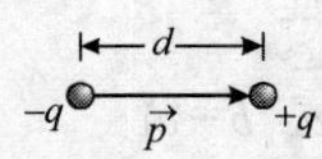

Figure 1.196

Dipole moment is a vector quantity and conventionally its direction is given from negative charge to positive charge.

1.12.1 Electric Dipole placed in a Uniform Electric Field

Figure-1.197 shows an electric dipole of dipole moment p placed at an angle θ to the direction of electric field in a region of uniform electric field of strength $\vec{E}$. In this case the charges of dipole experience forces qE in opposite direction on the two charges as shown.

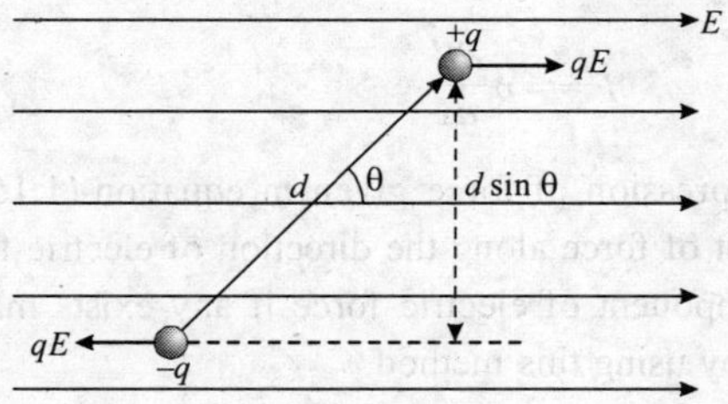

Figure 1.197

In such situations we can state when a dipole is placed in a uniform electric field, net force on the dipole is zero but as equal and opposite forces act with some separation in their lines of action, these forces produce a couple which tend to align the dipole along the direction of electric field. The torque due to this couple can be given as

$$\tau = \text{Force} \times \text{separation between lines of actions of forces}$$

$$\Rightarrow \quad \tau = qE \times d \sin\theta$$

$$\Rightarrow \quad \tau = pE \sin\theta \qquad \ldots(1.151)$$

Vectorially equation-(1.151) can be written as

$$\vec{\tau} = \vec{p} \times \vec{E} \qquad \ldots(1.162)$$

1.12.2 Work done in Rotation of a Dipole in Electric Field

When a dipole is placed in an electric field at an angle θ, the torque on it due to electric field is given as

$$\tau = pE \sin\theta$$

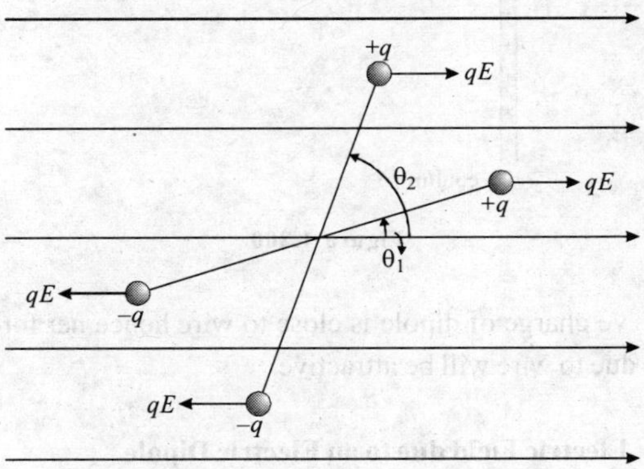

Figure 1.198

Figure-1.198 shows a dipole placed at an angle θ_1 to the direction of electric field, the torque on it acts in clockwise direction. If we rotate the dipole in anticlockwise direction from an angle θ_1 to θ_2 slowly, we have to apply an anticlockwise torque equal to that applied by the electric field, then the work done by external agent in this process will be given as

$$W = \int dW = \int \tau d\theta$$

$$\Rightarrow \quad W = \int_{\theta_1}^{\theta_2} pE \sin\theta d\theta$$

$$\Rightarrow \quad W = pE\,[-\cos\theta]_{\theta_1}^{\theta_2}$$

$$\Rightarrow \quad W = pE\,(\cos\theta_1 - \cos\theta_2) \qquad \ldots(1.153)$$

The expression of work done given in above equation-(1.153) is valid even if a dipole orientation is changed from θ_1 to θ_2 by any means not only by rotation as in conservative field initial and final orientation is of concern and work is independent of the path or the process by which it is changed.

1.12.3 Interaction Energy of a Dipole in Electric Field

Figure-1.199 shows a dipole placed at an angle θ with the direction of electric field. In this situation we consider that the two charges of dipoles are located on two equipotential surfaces having potentials V_1 and V_2, which can be related as

$$V_1 - V_2 = Ed\cos\theta \qquad \ldots(1.154)$$

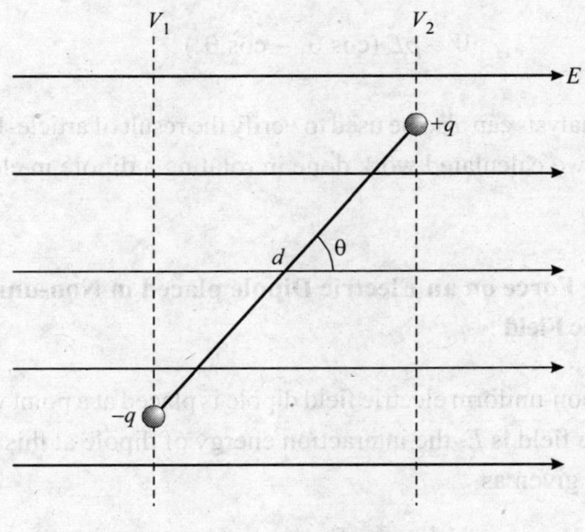

Figure 1.199

The interaction energy of the dipole with electric field can be given as

$$U = -qV_1 + qV_2$$

$$\Rightarrow \quad U = q\,(V_2 - V_1)$$

$$\Rightarrow \quad U = -q\,Ed\cos\theta$$

$$\Rightarrow \quad U = -pE\cos\theta \qquad \ldots(1.155)$$

In vector notations we can write interaction energy of dipole in electric field from equation-(1.164) as

$$U = -\vec{p} \cdot \vec{E} \quad \ldots(1.156)$$

1.12.4 Work done in Changing the Orientation of a Dipole in Electric Field using Interaction Energy

If in a uniform electric field, a dipole is placed such that its dipole moment vector makes an angle θ_1 with the direction of electric field, the interaction energy of the dipole with electric field can be given by equation-(1.156) as

$$U_i = -pE\cos\theta_1 \quad \ldots(1.157)$$

If dipole is displaced to another position in same electric field where it is oriented such that the dipole moment vector makes an angle θ_2 with the direction of electric field, then the final interaction energy of dipole is given as

$$U_f = -pE\cos\theta_2$$

Now we can calculate the work required in displacing the dipole and changing its orientation as

$$W = U_f - U_i$$

$$\Rightarrow \quad W = pE(\cos\theta_1 - \cos\theta_2)$$

This analysis can also be used to verify the result of article-1.12.2 where we calculated work done in rotating a dipole in electric field.

1.12.5 Force on an Electric Dipole placed in Non-uniform Electric Field

If in a non-uniform electric field dipole is placed at a point where electric field is E, the interaction energy of dipole at this point can be given as

$$U = -\vec{p} \cdot \vec{E}$$

The force on dipole due to electric field can be given as

$$\vec{F} = -\nabla U$$

For unidirectional variation in electric field say in x-direction, we can calculate the x-component of electric force as

$$\vec{F} = -\frac{d}{dx}(\vec{p} \cdot \vec{E})\,\hat{i}$$

If dipole is placed in the direction of electric field we can use

$$F = -p\frac{dE}{dx} \quad \ldots(1.158)$$

Above expression of force given in equation-(1.158) is the component of force along the direction of electric field only. Other component of electric force if any exists may not be obtained by using this method.

1.12.6 Force on a Dipole placed in Surrounding of a Long Charged Wire

In the situation shown in figure-1.200, the electric field strength due to the wire, at the position of dipole located at a distance r can be given as

$$E = \frac{2k\lambda}{r}$$

Thus force on dipole (along the in the direction of electric field is

$$F = -p \cdot \frac{dE}{dr} = -p\left[-\frac{2K\lambda}{r^2}\right]$$

$$\Rightarrow \quad F = \frac{2Kp\lambda}{r^2} \quad \ldots(1.159)$$

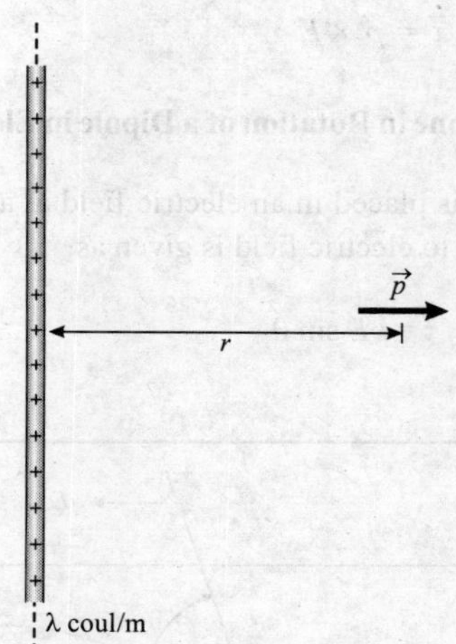

Figure 1.200

Here – ve charge of dipole is close to wire hence net force on dipole due to wire will be attractive.

1.12.7 Electric Field due to an Electric Dipole

Figure-1.201 shows an electric dipole placed on y-axis at origin. We need to determine the electric field and potential at a point P having coordinates (r, θ). Due to the positive charge of dipole electric field at P is in radially outward direction and due to the negative charge it is radially inward as shown.

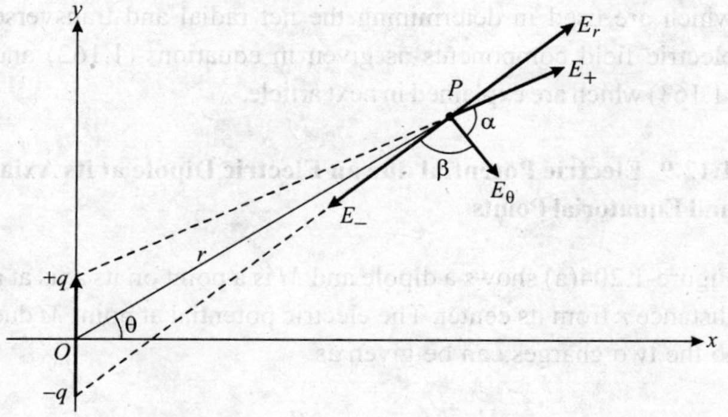

Figure 1.201

To find net electric field at point P, we resolve E_+ and E_- along radial and transverse direction. These electric fields at point P in radial and transverse direction are termed as radial and transverse components of electric field and given as

Radial Electric Field at point P

$$E_r = E_+ \sin\alpha - E_- \sin\beta \qquad \dots(1.160)$$

Transverse Electric Field at point P

$$E_\theta = E_+ \cos\alpha + E_- \cos\beta \qquad \dots(1.161)$$

Solving equations-(1.160) and (1.161) we get the magnitudes of radial and transverse components of electric fields due to dipole at point P. Final results of the magnitudes of E_r and E_θ are given below. Students are advised to learn these results on tips as

$$E_r = \frac{2Kp\sin\theta}{r^3} \qquad \dots(1.162)$$

and

$$E_\theta = \frac{Kp\cos\theta}{r^3} \qquad \dots(1.163)$$

Thus net electric field at point P can be given as

$$E_P = \sqrt{E_r^2 + E_\theta^2}$$

$$\Rightarrow \quad E_P = \frac{Kp}{r^3}\sqrt{1+3\sin^2\theta}$$

The direction of E_P is at an angle ϕ from radial direction, from figure-1.201 and 1.202, we have

$$\phi = \tan^{-1}\frac{E_\theta}{E_r}$$

$$\Rightarrow \quad \phi = \tan^{-1}\left(\frac{1}{2}\cot\theta\right)$$

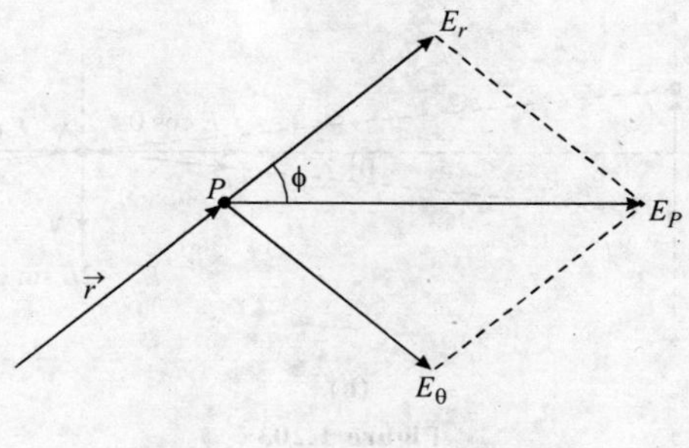

Figure 1.202

Thus the slope of net electric field at point P is $(\theta - \phi)$. Depending upon the orientation of dipole placed at origin the direction of radial electric fields could be in either direction along the position vector away from origin or toward origin, similarly the direction of transverse electric field can also be in either of the two directions along normal to position vector of the point P.

1.12.8 Electric Field at Axial and Equatorial Point of a Dipole

The extended line joining the two charges of a dipole is called '*Axis of Dipole*'. If we consider a point M at a distance r from the dipole center as shown in figure-1.203(a) and we calculate the electric field strength due to dipole charges at this point, then it can be given as

$$E_{M \text{ on Axis}} = \frac{Kq}{\left(r-\frac{d}{2}\right)^2} - \frac{Kq}{\left(r+\frac{d}{2}\right)^2}$$

$$\Rightarrow \quad E_{M \text{ on Axis}} = \frac{Kq}{r^2}\left[\left(1-\frac{d}{2r}\right)^{-2} - \left(1+\frac{d}{2r}\right)^{-2}\right]$$

In above equation as $\frac{d}{2r} << 1$ we can use binomial expansion as $(1+x)^n = 1 + nx$ for $x << 1$, this gives

$$E_{M \text{ on Axis}} = \frac{Kq}{r^2}\left[\left(1+\frac{2d}{2r}\right) - \left(1-\frac{2d}{2r}\right)\right]$$

$$\Rightarrow \quad E_{M \text{ on Axis}} = \frac{Kq}{r^2}\left[1+\frac{d}{r}-1+\frac{d}{r}\right]$$

$$\Rightarrow \quad E_{M \text{ on Axis}} = \frac{2Kqd}{r^3} = \frac{2Kp}{r^3} \qquad \dots(1.164)$$

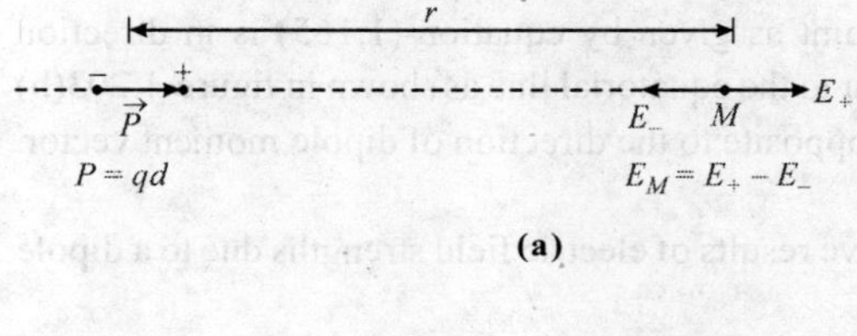

(a)

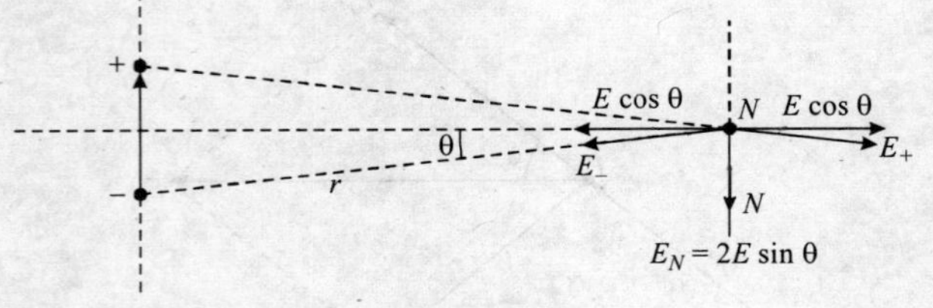

(b)

Figure 1.203

Figure-1.203(b) shows another point N located at a distance r from the dipole on its equatorial line which is the perpendicular bisector of the line joining charges of dipole. In this figure we can see that the electric field due to both the charges of dipole will have same magnitude at point N due to equal separation, which is given as

$$E_N = E_+ = E_- = \frac{Kq}{\left(r^2 + \left(\frac{d}{2}\right)^2\right)}$$

To find net electric field at point N due to dipole we resolve the electric field in its rectangular components as shown. We can see that the component $E_N\cos\theta$ due to both charges are in opposite direction and get cancelled and the other component $E_N\sin\theta$ will be added up and gives the net field strength at point N as

$$E_{N\text{ on Equatorial Line}} = 2E_N \sin\theta$$

$$\Rightarrow \quad E_{N\text{ on Equatorial Line}} = 2\times\frac{Kq}{\left(r^2+\left(\frac{d}{2}\right)^2\right)}\times\frac{d/2}{\sqrt{r^2+\left(\frac{d}{2}\right)^2}}$$

$$\Rightarrow \quad E_{N\text{ on Equatorial Line}} = \frac{Kqd}{\left(r^2+\left(\frac{d}{2}\right)^2\right)^{3/2}}$$

As $\frac{d}{2} << r$, we can neglect the second term in denominator which gives

$$\Rightarrow \quad E_{N\text{ on Equatorial Line}} = \frac{Kp}{r^3} \qquad \ldots(1.165)$$

The direction of electric field strength due to dipole at its equatorial point as given by equation-(1.165) is in direction perpendicular to the equatorial line as shown in figure-1.203(b) in direction opposite to the direction of dipole moment vector.

Both the above results of electric field strengths due to a dipole on its axial and equatorial points are considered standard results which are used in determining the net radial and transverse electric field components as given in equations-(1.162) and (1.163) which are explained in next article.

1.12.9 Electric Potential due an Electric Dipole at its Axial and Equatorial Points

Figure-1.204(a) shows a dipole and M is a point on its axis at a distance r from its center. The electric potential at point M due to the two charges can be given as

$$V_M = \frac{Kq}{\left(r-\frac{d}{2}\right)} - \frac{Kq}{\left(r+\frac{d}{2}\right)}$$

$$\Rightarrow \quad V_M = \frac{Kq}{r}\left(\left(1-\frac{d}{2r}\right)^{-1} - \left(1+\frac{d}{2r}\right)^{-1}\right)$$

In above equation as $\frac{d}{2r} << 1$ we can use binomial expansion as $(1+x)^n = 1 + nx$ for $x << 1$, this gives

$$V_M = \frac{Kq}{r}\left(\left(1+\frac{d}{2r}\right)-\left(1-\frac{d}{2r}\right)\right)$$

$$\Rightarrow \quad V_M = \frac{Kq}{r}\left(1+\frac{d}{2r}-1+\frac{d}{2r}\right)$$

$$\Rightarrow \quad V_M = \frac{Kqd}{r^2} = \frac{Kp}{r^2} \qquad \ldots(1.166)$$

Equation-(1.166) gives the electric potential due to an electric dipole at its axial point as shown in figure-1.204(a).

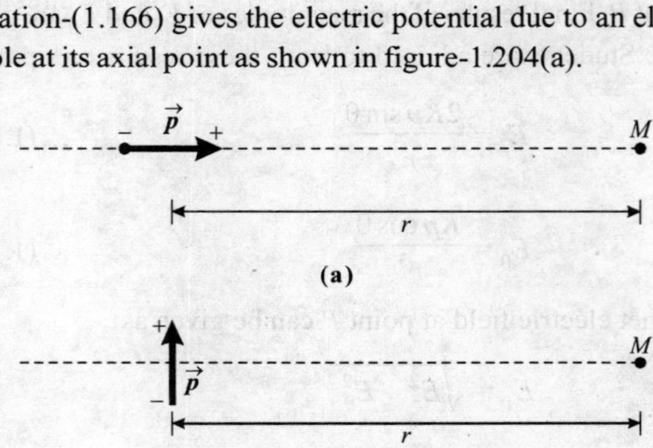

(b)

Figure 1.204

Figure-1.204(b) shows a point M located at a distance r from a dipole on its equatorial point. As the positive and negative charges of the dipole are situated at same distance from the point M, the potential due to these charges will be equal and of opposite sign which nullify each other and net potential due to dipole at its equatorial point will be zero.

1.12.10 Proof of Radial and Transverse Electric Field Strengths due to a Dipole using Axial and Equatorial Electric Fields

Figure-1.205 shows a dipole oriented along y-axis of a coordinate system due to which we will determine electric field strength at a general point P in space having polar coordinates (r, θ). To determine the field strength at point P we resolve the dipole moment in two rectangular components, one along the radial direction of position vector of point P and other normal to it. The two components are $p\cos\theta$ and $p\sin\theta$ respectively as shown in figure.

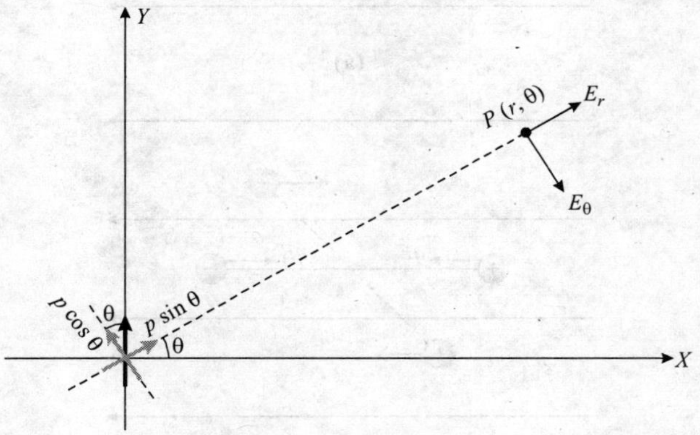

Figure 1.205

From above figure we can see that point P is located on the axis of the dipole component $p\sin\theta$ and it is located on the equatorial line of the dipole component $p\cos\theta$. Due to the dipole component $p\sin\theta$, we can calculate the electric field strength at point P by using equation-(1.164) which is along the direction of position vector of the point P, given as

$$E_r = \frac{2K(p\sin\theta)}{r^3} \qquad \ldots(1.167)$$

Similarly if we determine the electric field strength at point P due to the other dipole component $p\cos\theta$ then it can be calculated by the equation-(1.165), given as

$$E_\theta = \frac{K(p\cos\theta)}{r^3} \qquad \ldots(1.168)$$

Above two expressions of electric field strengths as given in equations-(1.167) and (1.168) are same as stated in equations-(1.162) and (1.163) which are the results of radial and transverse electric field components of electric field strength at a point in surrounding of an electric dipole as discussed in article-1.12.7

1.12.11 Direction of E_r and E_θ in the Surrounding of a Dipole

As discussed in previous article, both the electric field E_r and E_θ can have two directions as shown in figure-1.206. Exact direction depends on the orientation of dipole moment.

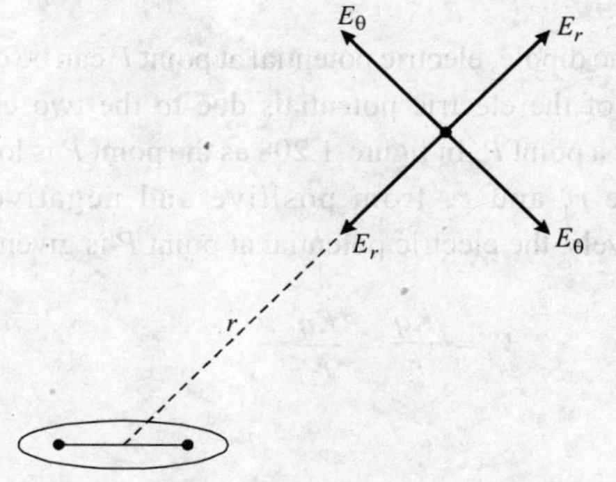

Figure 1.206

While analyzing the directions of E_r and E_θ at a point P in surrounding of diploe we need to be careful as which charge of dipole is close to the point P. If positive charge of dipole is closer to P then radial electric field will be away along the position vector of P and if negative charge of dipole is closer to P then radial electric field will be toward the dipole along the position vector. This is because the electric field magnitude at P due to the closer charge will be more. Similarly the direction of transverse magnetic field will be in direction away from the positive charge along normal to the position vector. Consider the following examples in figures-1.207 which explain the different directions of E_r and E_θ for different orientations of dipole.

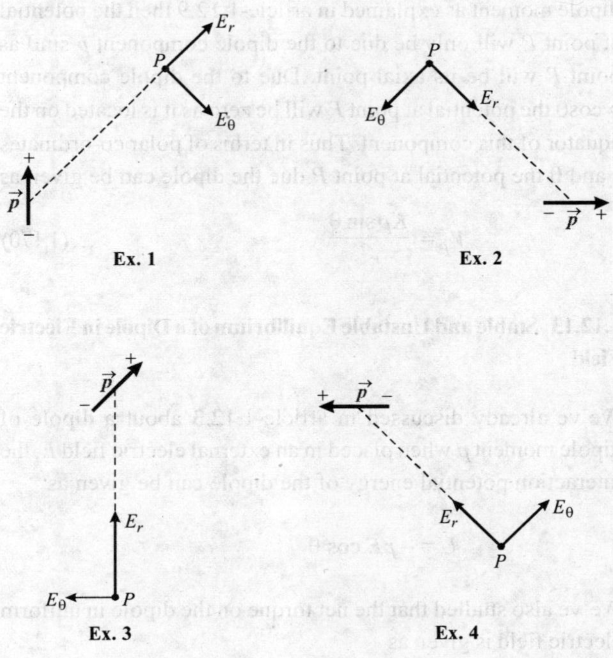

Figure 1.207

1.12.12 Electric Potential due to a Dipole in its Surrounding

Due to the dipole, electric potential at point P can be calculated by sum of the electric potentials due to the two charges of dipole at a point P. In figure-1.208 as the point P is located at a distance r_1 and r_2 from positive and negative charge respectively, the electric potential at point P is given as

$$V_P = \frac{Kq}{r_1} - \frac{Kq}{r_2} \quad \ldots(1.169)$$

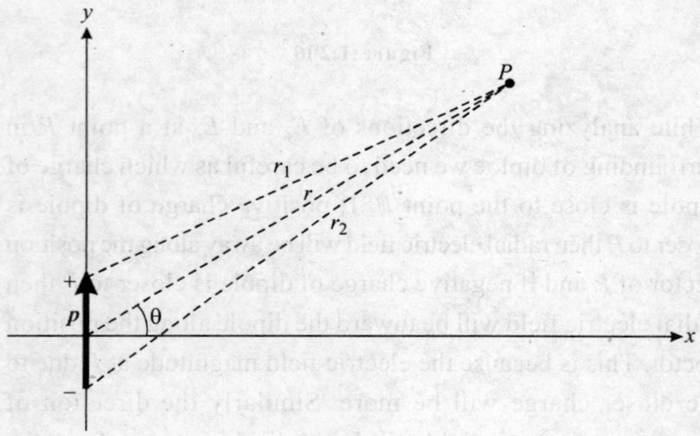

Figure 1.208

In above expression given in equation-(1.169) if we substitute the values of r_1 and r_2 in polar form or we take components of dipole moment as explained in article-1.12.9 then the potential at point P will only be due to the dipole component $p \sin\theta$ as point P will be its axial point. Due to the dipole component $p \cos\theta$ the potential at point P will be zero as it is located on the equator of this component. Thus in terms of polar co-ordinates r and θ the potential at point P due the dipole can be given as

$$V_P = \frac{Kp\sin\theta}{r^2} \quad \ldots(1.170)$$

1.12.13 Stable and Unstable Equilibrium of a Dipole in Electric Field

We've already discussed in article-1.12.3 about a dipole of dipole moment p when placed in an external electric field E, the interaction potential energy of the dipole can be given as

$$U = -pE\cos\theta$$

We've also studied that the net torque on the dipole in uniform electric field is given as

$$\tau = pE\sin\theta$$

From above equation, we can see that net torque on dipole in electric field is zero in two situations when $\theta = 0°$ and $\theta = 180°$ as shown in figures-1.209.

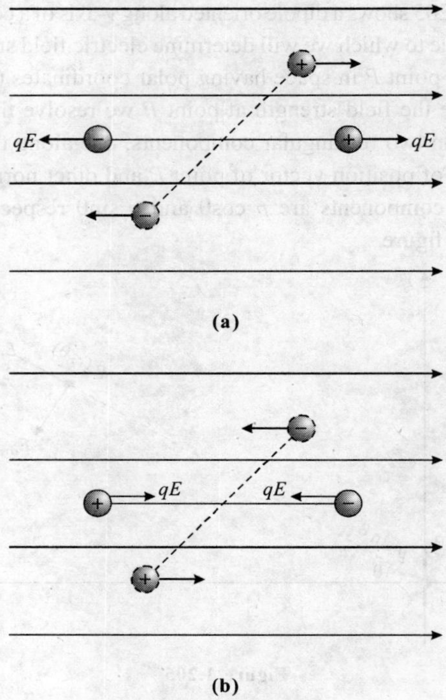

Figure 1.209

We can see that when $\theta = 0°$ as shown in figure-1.209(a) when torque on dipole is zero, the dipole is in equilibrium. We can analyze and understand that here equilibrium is stable. If we slightly tilt the dipole from its equilibrium position in anticlockwise direction as shown by dotted position, the dipole experiences a clockwise torque due to the electric forces by electric field which tend to rotate the dipole back to its equilibrium position. Thus at $\theta = 0°$, dipole is in stable equilibrium. We can also find the potential energy of dipole at $\theta = 0°$, which can be given as

$$U = -pE \quad \ldots(1.171)$$

Here from above equation-(1.171) we can see that at $\theta = 0°$, potential energy of dipole in electric field is minimum which favours the position of stable equilibrium.

Similarly when $\theta = 180°$, net torque on dipole is again zero and potential energy of dipole in this state is given as

$$U = pE \quad \ldots(1.172)$$

Thus at $\theta = 180°$, dipole potential energy is maximum and it is in unstable equilibrium. This can also be shown by figure-1.209(b). From equilibrium position if dipole is slightly displaced in anticlockwise direction, we can see that torque on dipole due to electric forces also acts in anticlockwise direction away from equilibrium position. Thus the dipole is in unstable equilibrium in this state.

1.12.14 Distributed Dipole

An electric dipole is a system of two equal and opposite charges fixed at a small separation. Sometimes these charges may not be point charges. A charge $+q$ is a point charge and another charge $-q$ is uniformly distributed over a semicircle of small radius R at the center of which $+q$ is placed. Such a system of two charges in which one or both the charges are distributed on a small length, area or a region is called a '*Distributed Dipole*'. In such cases on the body over which charge is distributed, we can consider element charges on the two charges and calculate the dipole moment dp of these elemental charges $+dq$ and $-dq$. Integrating the dipole moment of elemental charges we can calculate the dipole moment of the distributed dipole.

 # Illustrative Example 1.62

An electric dipole is situated at the origin of coordinate axis with its axis along x-axis and equator along y-axis. It is found that the magnitudes of the electric intensity and electric potential due to the dipole are equal at a point distant $r = \sqrt{5}$ m from origin. Find the position vector of this point.

Solution

Let P be such a point at distance r and angle θ from equator as shown in figure-1.210.

Now $$|E_P| = |V_P|$$

$$\Rightarrow \quad \frac{Kp}{r^3}\sqrt{1+3\sin^2\theta} = \frac{Kp\sin\theta}{r^2}$$

$$\Rightarrow \quad \frac{\sqrt{1+3\sin^2\theta}}{\sqrt{5}} = \sin\theta$$

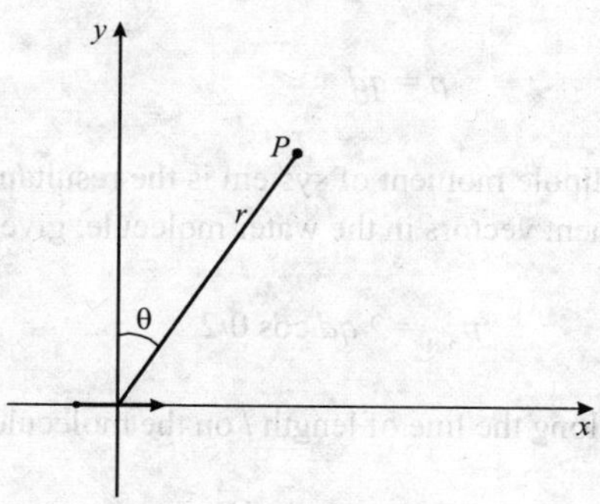

Figure 1.210

Squaring both sides of above equation gives

$$1 + 3\sin^2\theta = 5\sin^2\theta$$

$$\Rightarrow \quad \sin\theta = \frac{1}{\sqrt{2}}$$

$$\Rightarrow \quad \theta = 45^\circ$$

Positive vector $\vec{r}$ of point P is given as

$$\vec{r} = \frac{\sqrt{5}}{2}(\hat{i} + \hat{j})$$

 # Illustrative Example 1.63

Prove that the frequency of oscillation of an electric dipole of moment p and moment of inertia I for small angular displacements about its equilibrium position in a uniform electric field strength E is given as

$$\frac{1}{2\pi}\sqrt{\left(\frac{pE}{I}\right)}$$

Solution

Let us consider the case of an electric dipole with charges q and $-q$ at a distance $2a$ apart, placed in a uniform external electric field of strength E as shown in figure-1.211.

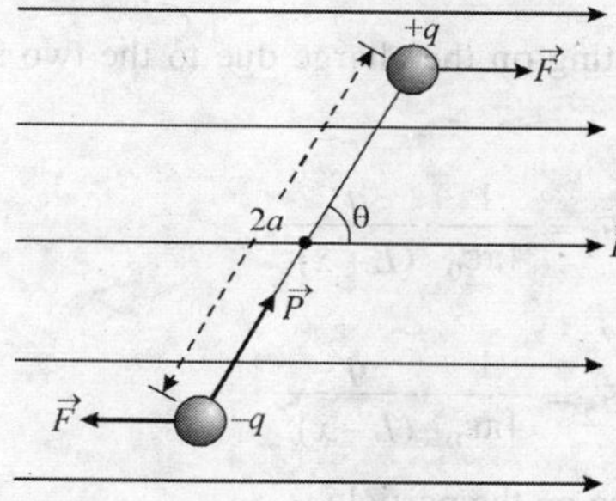

Figure 1.211

We know that restoring torque on dipole in uniform electric field is given as

$$\tau = -pE\sin\theta \approx -pE\theta \qquad \text{(as } \theta \text{ is small)}$$

Here negative sign is included to show the restoring tendency of torque.

Now angular acceleration of dipole can be given as

$$\alpha = -\frac{\tau}{I} = -\frac{pE}{I}$$

As we know for angular SHM angular acceleration is given as

$$\alpha = -\omega^2\theta$$

Comparing above two angular accelerations, we get

$$\omega = \sqrt{\frac{pE}{I}}$$

Thus frequency of oscillations of dipole can be given as

$$n = \frac{\omega}{2\pi} = \frac{1}{2\pi}\sqrt{\left(\frac{pE}{I}\right)}$$

Illustrative Example 1.64

A particle of mass m and charge $+q$ is located midway between two fixed charged particles each having a charge $+q$ and at a distance $2L$ apart. Assuming that the middle charge moves along the line joining the fixed charges, calculate the frequency of oscillation when it is displaced slightly.

Solution

The situation described in question is shown in figure-1.212.

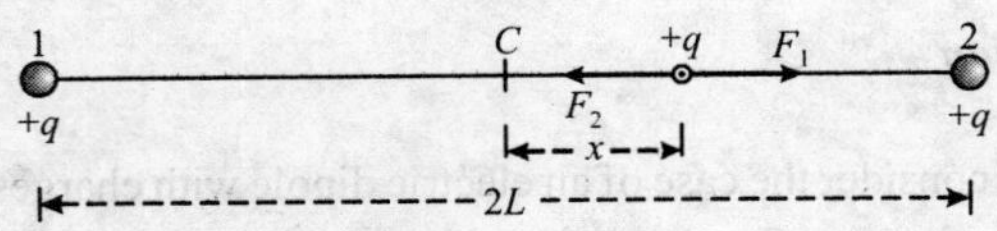

Figure 1.212

The forces acting on the charge due to the two side charges are given as

$$F_1 = \frac{1}{4\pi\varepsilon_0}\cdot\frac{q^2}{(L+x)^2}$$

and $$F_2 = \frac{1}{4\pi\varepsilon_0}\cdot\frac{q^2}{(L-x)^2}$$

Resultant force on the particle is

$$F = F_1 - F_2$$

$$\Rightarrow \quad F = \frac{q^2 \cdot 4Lx}{4\pi\varepsilon_0 (L^2 - x^2)^2}$$

for $L >> x$, we can consider $L^2 - x^2 \approx L^2$ thus above expression will be reduced to

$$F = -\frac{q^2 x}{\pi\varepsilon_0 L^3}$$

In above expression we've included a negative sign to show that it is a restoring force on particle and as this force is directly proportional to the displacement x, it can be considered as SHM for which acceleration can be considered as $\omega^2 x$ as given below.

$$\text{Acceleration} \quad a = \frac{-q^2 x}{m\pi\varepsilon_0 L^3} = -\omega^2 x$$

$$\Rightarrow \quad \omega^2 = \frac{q^2}{m\pi\varepsilon_0 L^3}$$

Thus frequency of oscillations can be given as

$$n = \frac{\omega}{2\pi} = \frac{q}{2\pi}\sqrt{\left(\frac{1}{m\pi\varepsilon_0 L^3}\right)}$$

Illustrative Example 1.65

A water molecule is placed at a distance l from the line carrying linear charge density λ. Find the maximum force exerted on the water molecule. The shape of water molecule and the partial charges on H and O atoms are shown in figure-213.

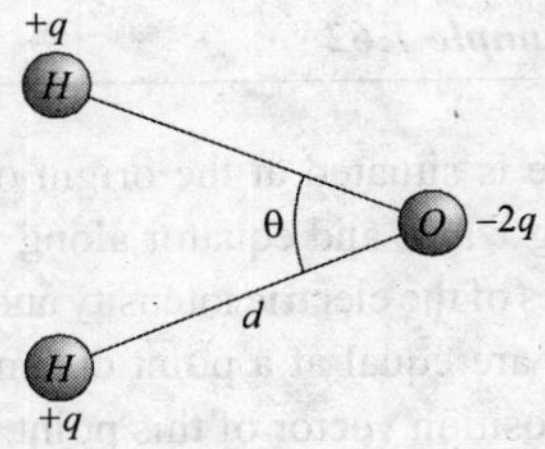

Figure 1.213

Solution

The figure can be resolved as combination of 2 dipoles.

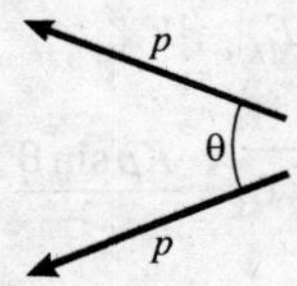

Figure 1.214

Dipole moments of each dipole is given as

$$p = qd$$

Here total dipole moment of system is the resultant of the two dipole moment vectors in the water molecule, given as

$$p_{\text{net}} = 2\,qd\cos\theta/2$$

The force along the line of length l on the molecule is given as

$$\vec{F} = \vec{p}_{\text{net}} \cdot \frac{d\vec{E}}{dx}\,\hat{n}$$

For maximum force, the angle between $\vec{p}_{net}$ and $\frac{d\vec{E}}{dx}$ should be 0° for which the force is given as

$$F_{max} = 2qd\cos\frac{\theta}{2} \times \frac{d}{dx}\left(\frac{2K\lambda}{x}\right)$$

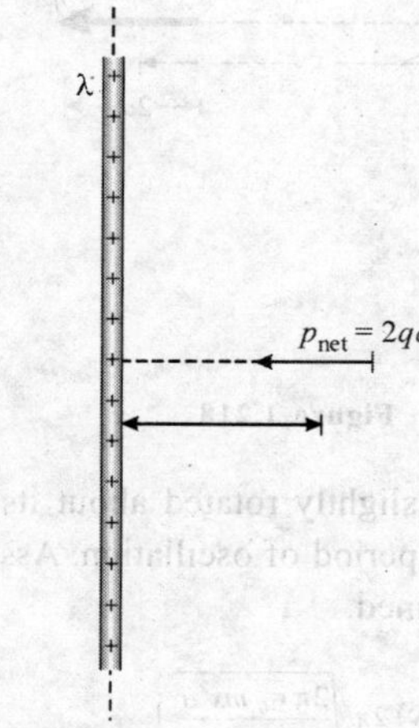

Figure 1.215

$$\Rightarrow \quad F_{max} = 2qd\cos\frac{\theta}{2} \times 2k\lambda\left(\frac{-1}{x^2}\right)$$

$$\Rightarrow \quad F_{max} = \frac{-4Kqd\lambda\cos\theta/2}{x^2}$$

$$\Rightarrow \quad |\vec{F}_{max}| = \frac{4Kqd\lambda\cos\theta/2}{x^2}$$

$$\text{at } x = l \quad |\vec{F}_{max}| = \frac{4Kqd\lambda\cos\theta/2}{l^2}$$

Illustrative Example 1.66

Two thin parallel threads carry a uniform charge with linear charge densities λ and – λ. The distance between the threads is equal to l. Find the potential of the electric field and the magnitude of its strength at the distance $r >> l$ at the angle θ to the line of length l which is perpendicular to both the threads and joining the two threads. Angle θ is measured from the side of positively charged thread as shown in figure-1.216.

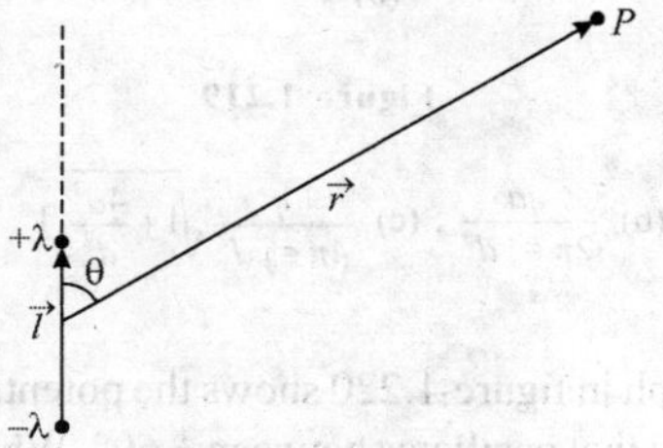

Figure 1.216

Solution

The electric field at point P (where $r >> l$) in the figure shown in given as

$$\vec{E} = \frac{\lambda}{2\pi\varepsilon_0}\left[\frac{\vec{r}+\frac{\vec{l}}{2}}{\left|\vec{r}+\frac{\vec{l}}{2}\right|^2} - \frac{\vec{r}-\frac{\vec{l}}{2}}{\left|\vec{r}+\frac{\vec{l}}{2}\right|^2}\right]$$

$$\Rightarrow \quad \vec{E} = \frac{\lambda}{2\pi\varepsilon_0}\left[\frac{\vec{r}+\frac{\vec{i}}{2}}{r^2+\frac{l^2}{4}+rl\cos\theta} - \frac{\vec{r}-\frac{\vec{i}}{2}}{r^2+\frac{l^2}{4}-rl\cos\theta}\right]$$

$$\Rightarrow \quad \vec{E} = \frac{\lambda}{2\pi\varepsilon_0}\left[\frac{\vec{r}+\frac{\vec{i}}{2}}{r(r+l\cos\theta)} - \frac{\vec{r}-\frac{\vec{i}}{2}}{r(r-l\cos\theta)}\right]$$

$$\Rightarrow \quad \vec{E} = \frac{\lambda}{2\pi\varepsilon_0}\left[\frac{\vec{i}}{r^2} - \frac{2r\vec{i}}{r^3}\cos\theta\right]$$

$$\Rightarrow \quad \vec{E} = \frac{\lambda l}{2\pi\varepsilon_0 r^2}, \text{ if } r >> l$$

Similarly, potential at point P can be given by the sum of the two components of the discus

$$V = \frac{\lambda}{2\pi\varepsilon_0}\left[\log_e\left|\vec{r}+\frac{\vec{l}}{2}\right| - \log_e\left|\vec{r}-\frac{\vec{l}}{2}\right|\right]$$

For $r >> l$, we can expand the logarithmic series and thus the above expression will reduce to

$$V = \frac{\lambda l\cos\theta}{2\pi\varepsilon_0 r}$$

Illustrative Example 1.67

Show that, for a given dipole, V & E cannot have the same magnitude at distances less than 2 m from the dipole. Suppose that the distance is $\sqrt{5}$ m, determine the directions along which V & E are equal in magnitude.

Solution

The situation here is same which is discussed in Illustration 1.64 which we reanalyze. Equating the magnitudes of potential and field strength due to the dipole gives

$$|V_P| = |E_P|$$

$$\frac{KP\cos\theta}{r^2} = \frac{KP}{r^3}\sqrt{1+3\cos^2\theta}$$

$$\Rightarrow \quad \cos\theta = \frac{1}{\sqrt{r^2-3}} \quad \ldots (1.173)$$

$$\Rightarrow \quad r^2 - 3 \geq 1$$

$$\Rightarrow \quad r \geq 2\,\text{m}$$

We substitute $r = \sqrt{5}$ m in equation-(1.173), gives

$$\cos\theta = \frac{1}{\sqrt{r^2-3}} = \frac{1}{\sqrt{2}}$$

$$\Rightarrow \quad \theta = 45°, 135°, 225° \text{ and } 315°$$

Web Reference at www.physicsgalaxy.com

Age Group - Grade 11 & 12 | Age 17-19 Years

Section - ELECTROSTATICS

Topic - Electric Potential

Module Number - 39 to 53

Practice Exercise 1.7

(i) A dipole is placed at origin of coordinate system as shown in figure-1.217, find the electric field at point $P(0, y)$.

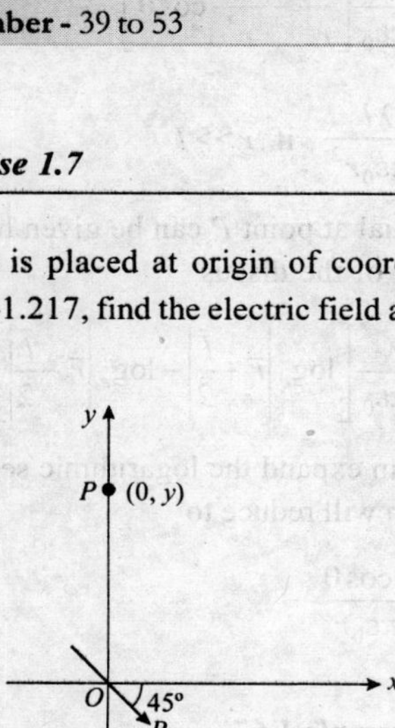

Figure 1.217

$[\frac{KP}{\sqrt{2}y^3}(-\hat{i}-2\hat{j})]$

(ii) In figure-1.218, an electric dipole is placed at a distance x from an infinitely long rod of linear charge density λ.

(a) Find the net force acting on the dipole

(b) What is the work done in rotating the dipole through 180°.

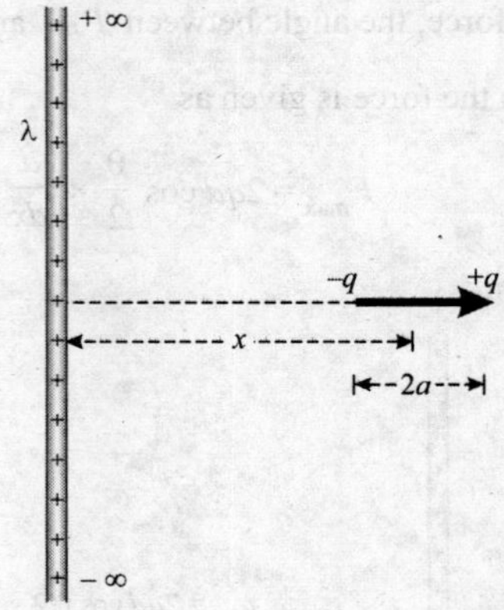

Figure 1.218

(c) If the dipole is slightly rotated about its equilibrium position, find the time period of oscillation. Assume that the dipole is linearly restrained.

[(a) $\frac{\lambda aq}{\pi\epsilon_0 x^2}$, (b) $\frac{2\lambda aq}{\pi\epsilon_0 x}$, (c) $2\pi\sqrt{\frac{2\pi\epsilon_0 mx^2a}{\lambda q}}$]

(iii) Two point dipoles $p\hat{k}$ and $\frac{P}{2}\hat{k}$ are located at (0, 0, 0) and (1 m, 0, 2 m) respectively. Find the resultant electric field due to the two dipoles at the point M(1 m, 0, 0).

$[-\left(\frac{7p}{32\pi\epsilon_0}\right)\hat{k}]$

(iv) Find the magnitude of the electric field at the point P in the configuration shown in figure-1.219 (a), (b) and (c) for $d >> a$ take $2qa = p$.

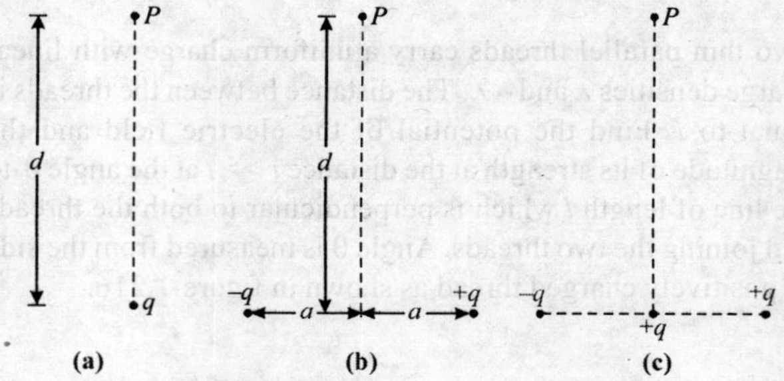

Figure 1.219

[(a) $\frac{q}{4\pi\epsilon_0 d^2}$, (b) $\frac{qa}{2\pi\epsilon_0 d^3}$, (c) $\frac{q}{4\pi\epsilon_0 d^2}\sqrt{1+\frac{4a^2}{d^2}}$]

(v) The graph in figure-1.220 shows the potential energy of an electric dipole that oscillates between ± 60°. What is the kinetic energy of dipole when it is aligned with the field?

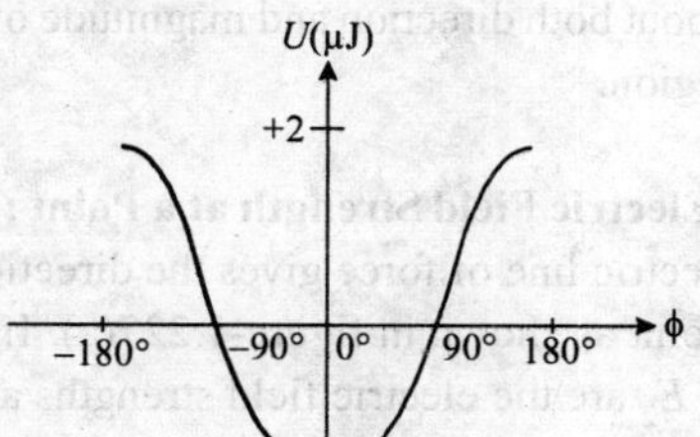

Figure 1.220

[1 μJ]

(vi) An electric dipole with dipole moment p oriented in the positive direction of z-axis is located at the origin of a three dimensional coordinate system. Find the projections of electric field E_x and E_y of the electric field strength vector at a point $P(r, \theta)$. Also find out the angle θ at which electric field vector is perpendicular to the dipole moment.

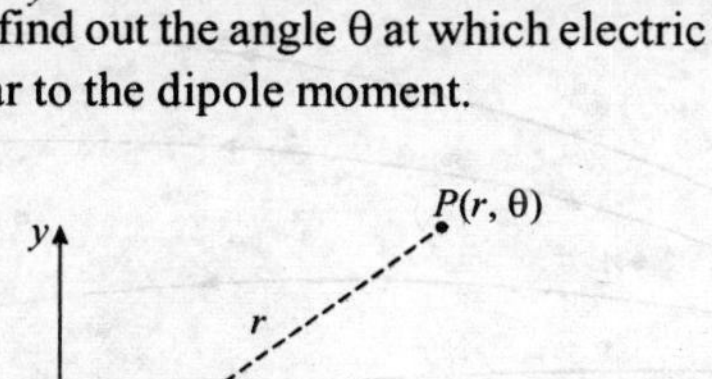

Figure 1.221

[$\frac{p}{4\pi\epsilon_0 r^3}(3\cos^3\theta - 1)$, $\frac{3p\sin\theta\cos\theta}{4\pi\epsilon_0 r^3}$, $\cos^{-1}\left(\frac{1}{\sqrt{3}}\right)$]

(vii) An electric dipole is placed at a distance x from centre O on the axis of a charged ring of radius R and charge Q uniformly distributed over it.

(a) Find the net force acting on the dipole

(b) What is the work done in rotating the dipole through 180°?

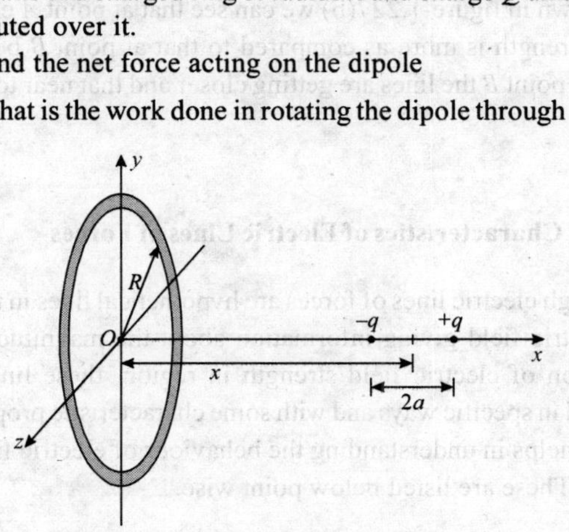

Figure 1.222

[(a) $\frac{aqQ}{2\pi\varepsilon_0}\left(\frac{R^2 - 2x^2}{(R^2 + x^2)^{5/2}}\right)$; (b) $\frac{aqQx}{\pi\varepsilon_0(R^2 + x^2)^{3/2}}$]

(viii) A dipole with an electric moment $\vec{p}$ is located at a distance r from a long uniformly charged thread as shown in figure-1.223

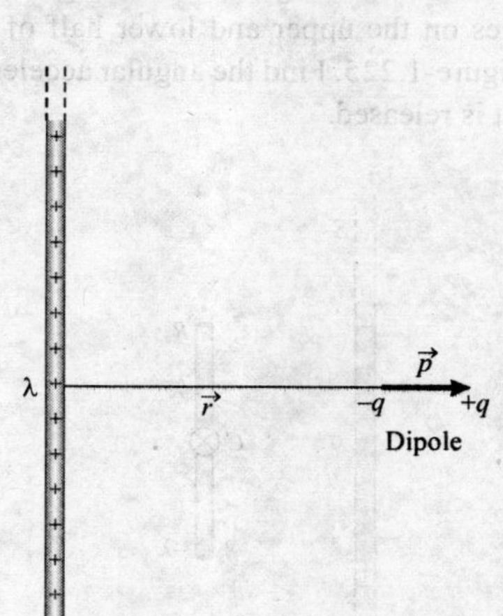

Figure 1.223

The linear charge density on thread is λ. Find the force $\vec{F}$ acting on the dipole under three different orientations given below.

(a) The vector $\vec{p}$ is oriented along the thread

(b) The vector $\vec{p}$ is oriented along the radius vector $\vec{r}$

(c) The vector $\vec{p}$ is oriented at right angles to the thread and the radius vector $\vec{r}$

[(a) 0; (b) $\frac{\lambda p}{2\pi\epsilon_0 r^2}$ along the dipole moment vector; (c) $\frac{\lambda p}{2\pi\epsilon_0 r^2}$ along the dipole moment vector]

(ix) Two short electric dipoles are placed as shown in figure-1.224. Find the potential energy of electric interaction between these dipoles.

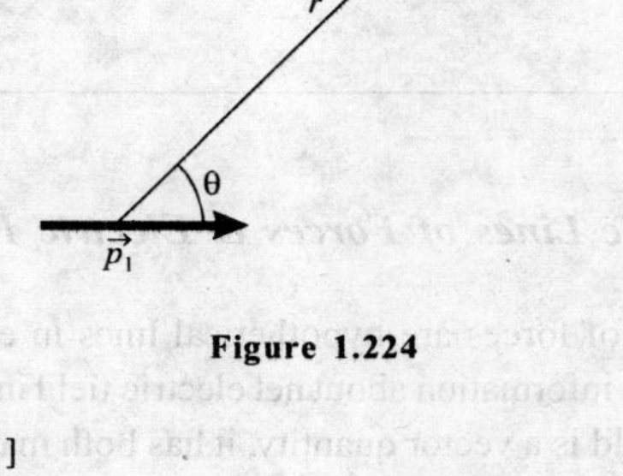

Figure 1.224

[$-\frac{2Kp_1p_2\cos\theta}{r^3}$]

(x) In the figure shown S is a large non-conducting sheet of uniform charge density σ. A rod R of length l and mass 'm' is parallel to the sheet and hinged at its mid point. The linear charge densities on the upper and lower half of the rod are shown in the figure-1.225. Find the angular acceleration of the rod just after it is released.

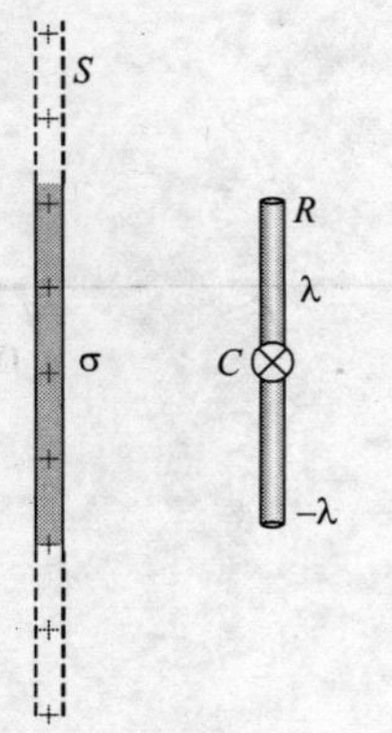

Figure 1.225

$[\frac{3\sigma\lambda}{2m\epsilon_0}]$

(xi) Point charges q and $-q$ are located at the vertices of a square with diagonals $2l$ as shown in figure-1.226. Find the magnitude of the electric field at a point located symmetrically with respect to the vertices of the square at a distance x from its centre. Consider $x >> l_0$.

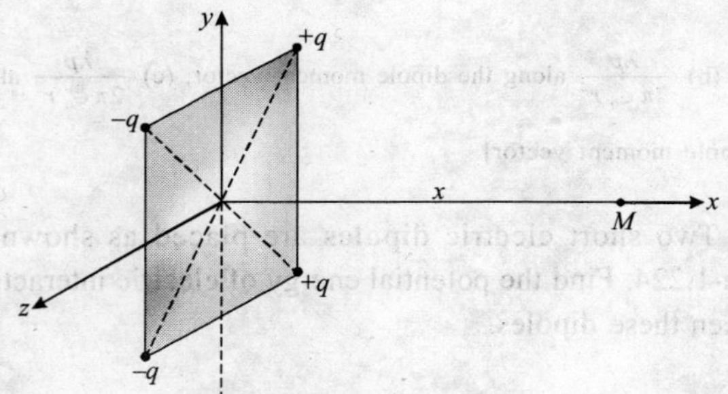

Figure 1.226

$[\frac{ql}{\sqrt{2}\pi\varepsilon_0 x^3}]$

1.13 Electric Lines of Forces & Electric Flux

Electric lines of forces are hypothetical lines in electric field which give the information about net electric field in that region. As electric field is a vector quantity, it has both magnitude and direction. In a region of electric field, electric lines give information about both direction and magnitude of the field at a point in the region.

Direction of Electric Field Strength at a Point : Tangent at a point on an electric line of force gives the direction of electric field at that point as shown in figure-1.227(a). If in the figure shown E_1 and E_2 are the electric field strengths at point P and Q respectively then the directions of these electric field at these points is given along the tangent of the electric line curve as shown.

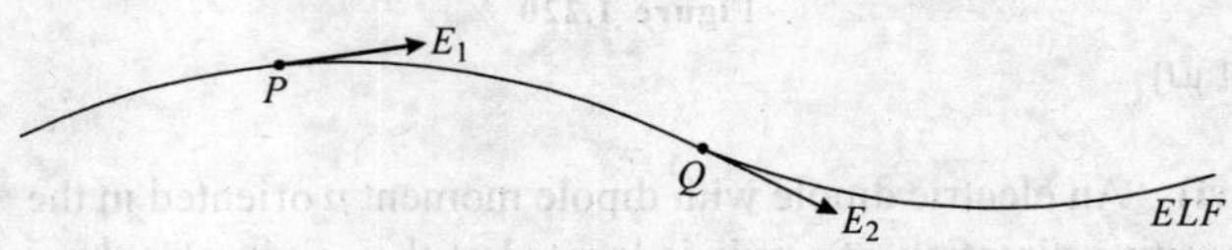

(a)

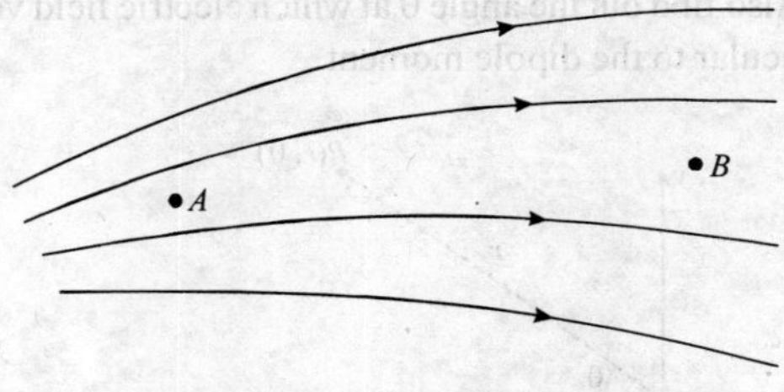

(b)

Figure 1.227

Magnitude of Electric Field Strength at a Point : In the region where electric field is present we draw electric lines of forces in such a way that the density of electric lines at a point gives the magnitude of electric field strength at that point in the region.

As shown in figure-1.227(b) we can see that at point A electric field strength is more as compared to that at point B because near to point B the lines are getting closer and that near to point A.

1.13.1 Characteristics of Electric Lines of Forces

Although electric lines of forces are hypothetical lines in region of electric field giving information about the magnitude and direction of electric field strength in region, these lines are defined in specific ways and with some characteristic properties which helps in understanding the behaviour of electric field in space. These are listed below point wise.

(i) *Two electric lines can never intersect in space at a point.* If we consider two electric lines are intersecting at one point in space, there will be two directions of electric field strength as shown in figure-1.228 which is not possible.

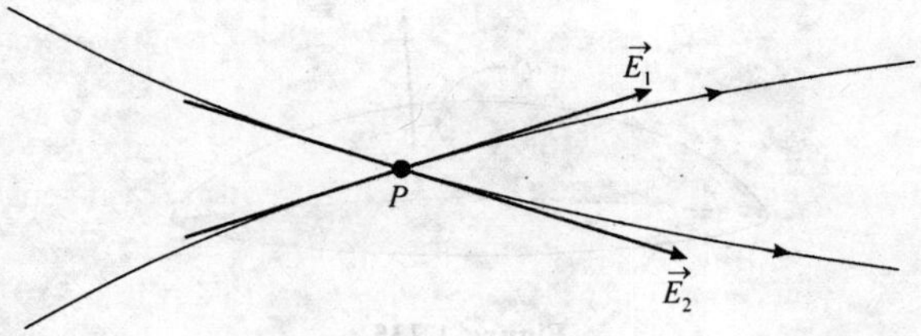

Figure 1.228

(ii) *Electric lines always originate either from a positive charge or infinity and terminate on a negative charge or infinity*. Figure-1.229 shows the configuration of *ELFs* due to point charges.

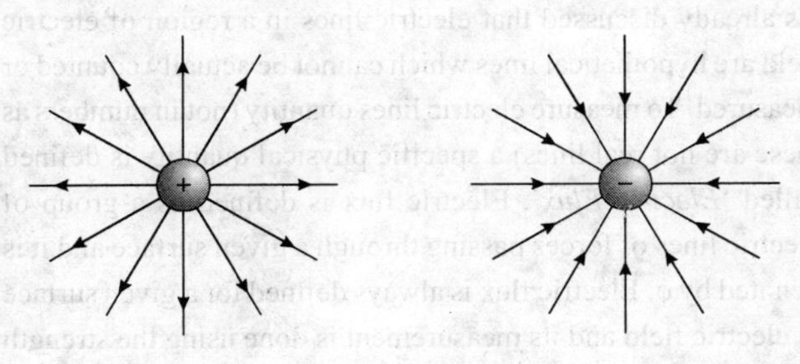

Figure 1.229

As shown in above figure-1.229 due to an isolated point charge, if it is positive, the electric lines originate from it and terminate at infinity and for a negative point charge electric lines originate from infinity and terminate on the charge in radially inward direction.

(iii) *Always the preference of termination of electric lines is toward a negative charge rather at infinity*. For example if we consider there is a positive point charge, in its surrounding electric lines exist in radially outward direction. If a negative charge is placed in its surrounding, electric lines have a tendency of termination toward the negative charge rather going toward infinity, thus lines will bend and terminate toward the negative charge. If charge magnitude is more, bending will be more as shown in figure-1.230.

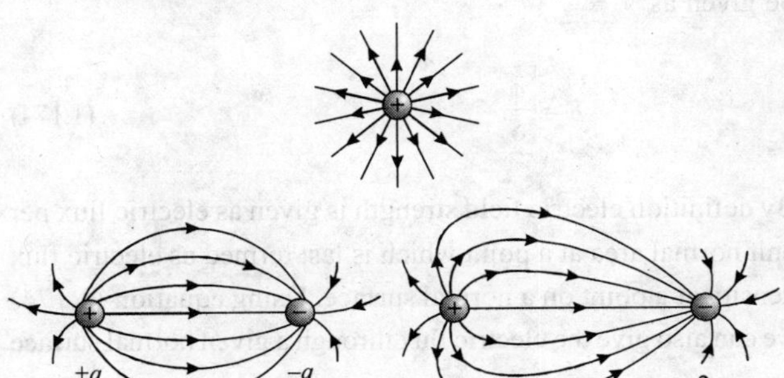

Figure 1.230

As electric lines have tendency to bend toward negative charges, similarly electric lines also have tendency to bend away from the positive charges in space. The configuration of electric lines due to two positive charges is shown in figure-1.231.

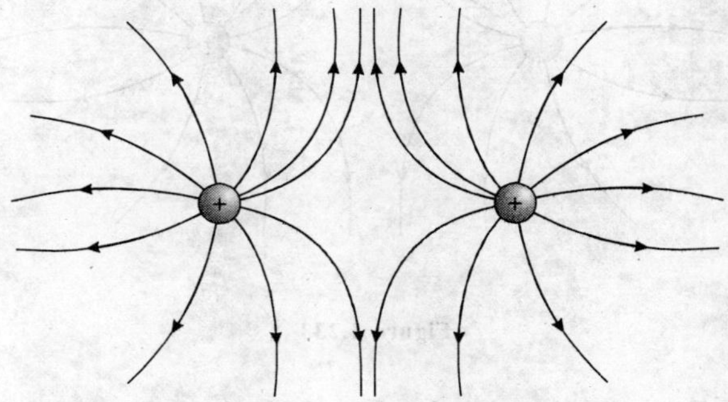

Figure 1.231

In the region of electric field the configuration of electric lines of forces gives the net electric field of the region. Let us consider some charge configuration to understand this concept.

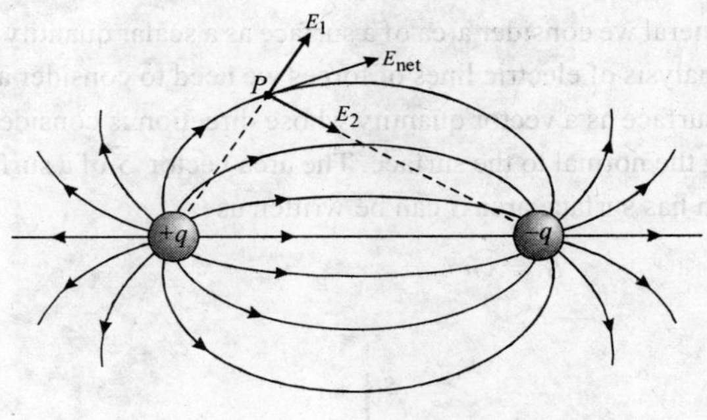

Figure 1.232

As shown in figure-1.232 we consider a point P on an electric line of force. At point P due to the positive charge $+q$ electric field is $\overrightarrow{E_1}$ in the direction shown and at the same point $\overrightarrow{E_2}$ is the electric field strength due to the negative charge $-q$ as shown in figure-1.232. The resultant electric field strength at point P is $\vec{E}_{net}$ in the direction along the tangent at P as the electric line of force is passing through point P. Thus we can say that at every point in electric field, tangent to an electric line of force gives the direction of net electric field of system and not due to the charge from which the lines are originating. Following figure shows the net electric field distribution due to two equal positive charges.

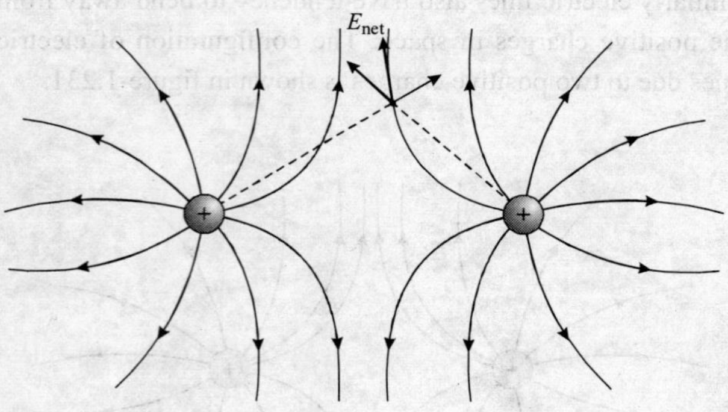

Figure 1.233

(iv) *Total quantity of electric lines of forces originating from a positive charge or terminating on a negative charge are considered to be directly proportional to the magnitude of the charge.* Thus in surrounding of a higher magnitude charge the density of field lines is more as it produces stronger electric field in surrounding.

1.13.2 Area considered as a Vector

In general we consider area of a surface as a scalar quantity but for analysis of electric lines of forces we need to consider area of a surface as a vector quantity whose direction is considered along the normal to the surface. The area vector $\vec{S}$ of a surface which has surface area S can be written as

$$\vec{S} = S\hat{n}$$

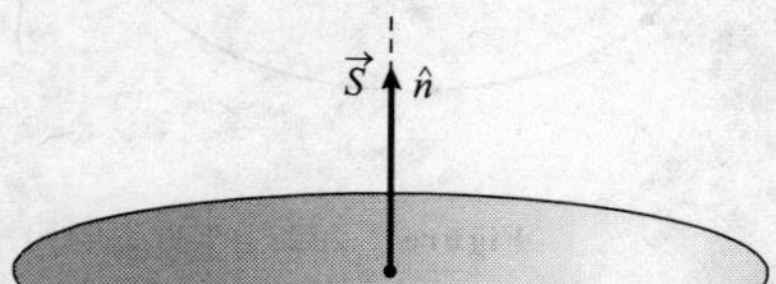

Figure 1.234

Where $\hat{n}$ is the unit vector in the direction along normal to the surface as shown-1.234.

If a surface is three dimensional we consider a small elemental area $\overrightarrow{dS}$ on this surface and direction of this elemental area vector is along the local normal of the surface at the point where elemental area is chosen as shown in figure-1.235. Such an elemental area vectorially is written as

$$\overrightarrow{dS} = dS\,\hat{a}$$

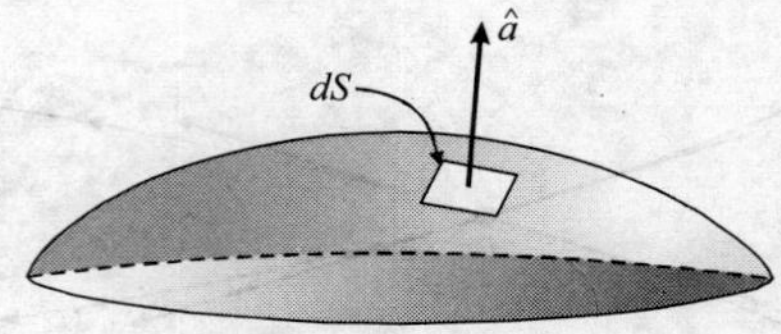

Figure 1.235

Here $\hat{a}$ is the unit vector in the direction along the normal at the location of elemental area dS.

1.13.3 Electric Flux

As already discussed that electric lines in a region of electric field are hypothetical lines which cannot be actually counted or measured. To measure electric lines quantity (not in numbers as these are not real lines) a specific physical quantity is defined called '*Electric Flux*'. Electric flux is defined as a group of electric lines of forces passing through a given surface and it is denoted by ϕ. Electric flux is always defined for a given surface in electric field and its measurement is done using the strength of electric field in the region. In upcoming article we will be discussing about the measurement of electric flux by using electric field strength in the region as well as we will discuss about calculation of electric field in a region using electric flux.

1.13.4 Electric Flux Measurement by Electric Flux

We've already discussed that the density of electric lines gives the magnitude of electric field strength at any point in a region. Mathematically the numerical value of electric field strength at a point in the region of electric field can be given as the electric flux passing through a unit normal area at that point.

In a uniform electric field shown in figure-1.236 if ϕ be the electric flux passing through an area S which is normal to the electric field lines, the value of electric field strength at this surface can be given as

$$E = \frac{\phi}{S} \quad \ldots(1.174)$$

By definition electric field strength is given as electric flux per unit normal area at a point which is last termed as electric flux density at a point on a normal surface. Using equation-(1.174) we can also give the electric flux through a given normal surface as

$$\phi = ES \quad \ldots(1.175)$$

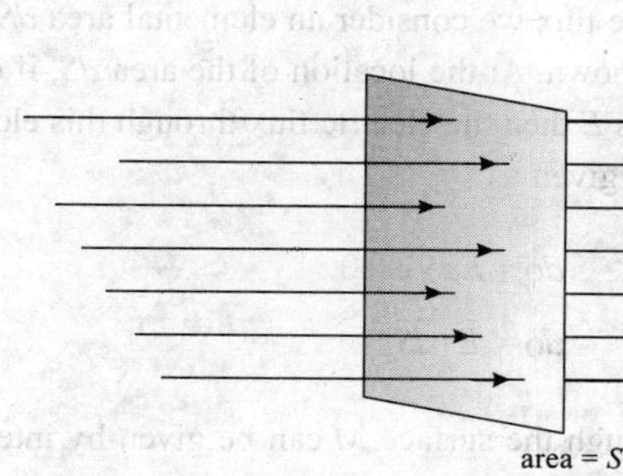

Figure 1.236

If in an electric field, surface is not normal as shown in figure-1.237 then in such a case we consider the component of area which has surface normal to the direction of electric field. In the figure-1.237 the actual area *ABCD* is inclined at an angle θ from the direction normal to electric field. We resolve this area *ABCD* in two perpendicular components as shown in figure. One is $S\cos\theta$, which is area *ABC'D'* normal to electric field direction and other is $S\sin\theta$, which is area *CDC'D'* along the direction of electric field.

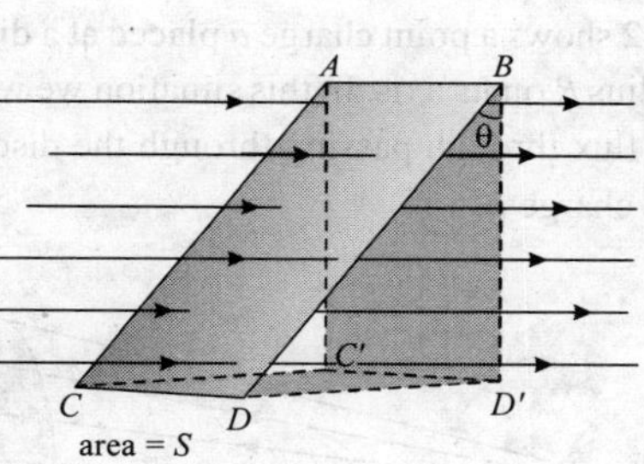

Figure 1.237

Here the electric flux passing through the given area *ABCD* is same that is passing through its normal component $S\cos\theta$, the area of surface component *ABC'D'* thus here the flux ϕ through the area can be given by equation-(1.175) as

$$\phi = ES\cos\theta \quad \ldots(1.176)$$

As we consider the direction of area vector normal to the area surface, as discussed in article-1.13.2, θ would be the angle between area vector $\vec{S}$ and $\vec{E}$ as shown in figure-1.238. Thus electric flux through the surface *ABCD* can be given in vector notations as

$$\phi = \vec{E}\cdot\vec{S} \quad \ldots(1.177)$$

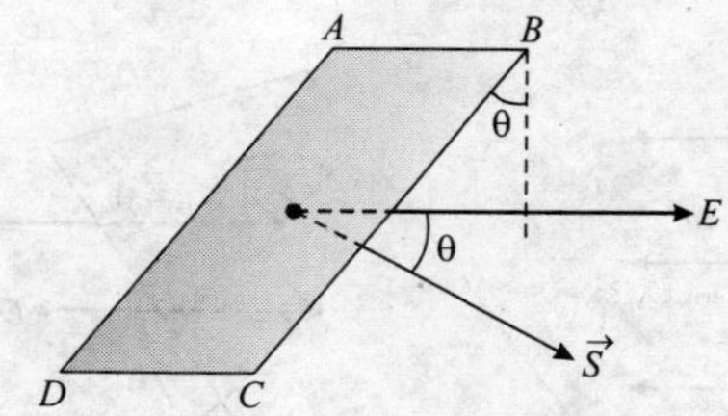

Figure 1.238

For any given surface, in uniform electric field we can calculate the electric flux by using equation-(1.177) which gives the product of electric field with the component of the surface normal to electric field. As already seen in figure-1.237 the component of the area *CC'DD'* which is along the direction of electric field, no electric flux passes through its surface. From equation-(1.177) also we can state that any surface which is parallel or oriented along the direction of electric field will have its area vector normal to electric field vector thus flux through this surface will be zero.

1.13.5 Positive and Negative Electric Flux

We've analyzed in previous article that electric flux through any surface in a uniform electric field can be calculated by the product of electric field strength and the normal component of the surface area. One important viewpoint here is about the area vector of a given surface. Every surface has two area vectors on the two sides of the surface or more clearly we can say that a plane has two surfaces one is at front and other is at back and both surfaces have their area vectors normal to the surface in opposite directions as shown in figure-1.239.

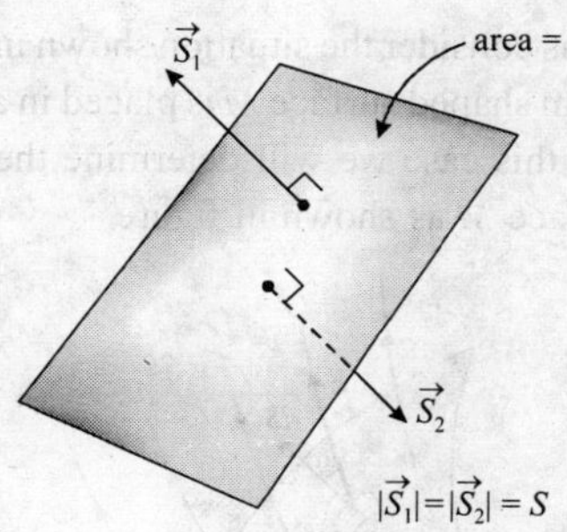

Figure 1.239

Figure-1.240 shows a rectangular plane *M* placed in a uniform electric field. This plane has two surfaces S_1 and S_2 and if we calculate electric flux passing through the plane *M* as a body, the flux can be directly given as

$$\phi_{\text{through body M}} = ES\cos\theta$$

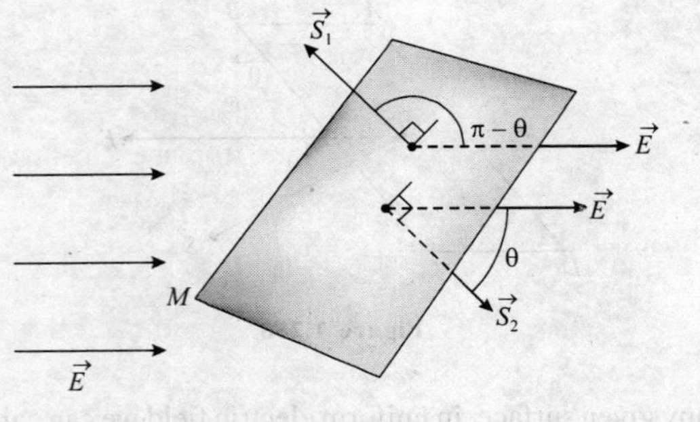

Figure 1.240

If we calculate the electric flux at surfaces S_1 and S_2 separately then by using equation-(1.177) these values are given as

$$\phi_1 = \vec{E} \cdot \vec{S}_1 = ES\cos(\pi-\theta) = -ES\cos\theta \quad \ldots(1.178)$$

$$\phi_2 = \vec{E} \cdot \vec{S}_2 = ES\cos\theta \quad \ldots(1.179)$$

In figure-1.240 and from above equations-(1.178) and (1.179) we can see that the flux is entering at surface S_1 is negative and the same flux is coming out from surface S_2 is positive. This must be remembered always that from any surface if electric flux is coming out, it is considered positive flux and if from a surface electric flux is going in then for that surface we consider it negative flux.

1.13.6 Electric Flux in Non-uniform Electric Field

In non-uniform electric field, we can calculate electric flux through a given surface by integrating the electric flux for an elemental surface area of the given surface using expression given in equation-(1.177).

To understand this consider the situation shown in figure-1.241 in which a random shaped surface M is placed in a non uniform electric field. In this case we will determine the electric flux through this surface M as shown in figure.

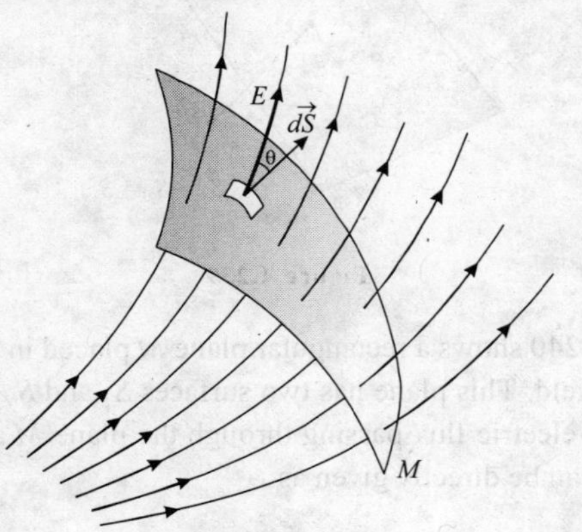

Figure 1.241

To calculate the flux we consider an elemental area dS on the surface M as shown. At the location of the area dS, if electric field strength is E then the electric flux through this elemental area dS can be given as

$$d\phi = EdS\cos\theta \quad \ldots(1.180)$$

$$\Rightarrow \quad d\phi = \vec{E}\cdot\vec{dS} \quad \ldots(1.181)$$

Total flux through the surface M can be given by integrating the expression in equation-(1.180) as

$$\phi = \int d\phi = \int_M EdS\cos\theta$$

$$\Rightarrow \quad \phi = \int \vec{E}\cdot\vec{dS} \quad \ldots(1.182)$$

Using equation-(1.182) we can calculate the electric flux through any given surface of defined shape placed in an electric field. Upcoming articles will help in understanding this calculation for some standard surfaces.

1.13.7 Electric Flux Through a Circular Disc

Figure-1.242 shows a point charge q placed at a distance l from a disc of radius R on its axis. In this situation we will determine the electric flux through passing through the disc surface due to the point charge q.

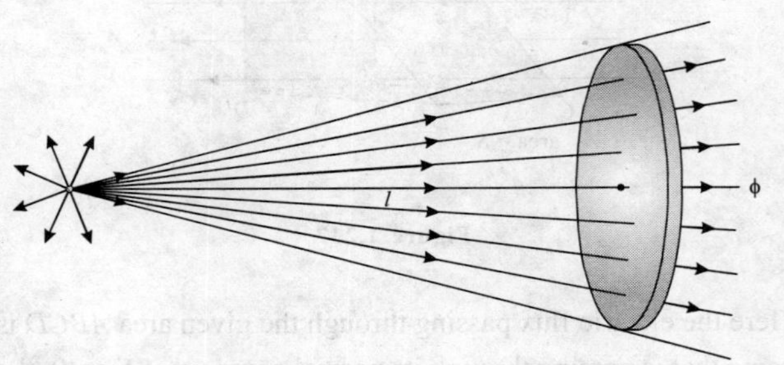

Figure 1.242

We know a point charge q originates electric flux in radially outward direction. The flux of q which is originated within the cone shown in figure passes through the disc surface. The electric field due to the point charge q at different points on the disc surface is different so we need to use the concept explained in article-1.13.6 for electric flux calculation in this case.

As shown in figure-1.243 we consider an elemental ring on disc surface of radius x and width dx as shown. The area of this elemental ring shaped strip is

$$dS = 2\pi x\,dx$$

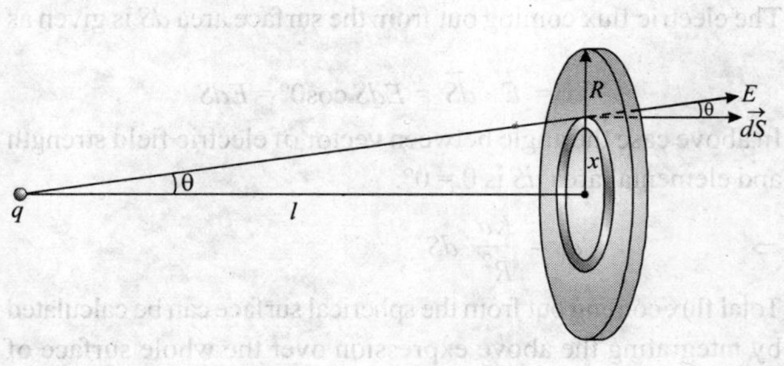

Figure 1.243

The electric field due to the point charge q at this elemental ring is given as

$$E = \frac{Kq}{(x^2 + l^2)}$$

If we consider that $d\phi$ is the electric flux passing through this elemental ring then by equation-(1.180) it is given as

$$d\phi = EdS \cos\theta$$

$$\Rightarrow \quad d\phi = \frac{Kq}{(x^2 + l^2)} \times 2\pi x\, dx \times \frac{l}{\sqrt{x^2 + l^2}}$$

$$\Rightarrow \quad d\phi = 2\pi Kql \frac{x\, dx}{(l^2 + x^2)^{3/2}}$$

The total electric flux through the disc surface can be calculated by integrating the above expression of flux through the elemental ring over the whole area of disc. Thus total flux through disc surface can be given as

$$\phi = \int d\phi = \int_0^R \frac{ql}{2\epsilon_0} \frac{x\, dx}{(l^2 + x^2)^{3/2}}$$

$$\Rightarrow \quad \phi = \frac{ql}{2\epsilon_0} \int_0^R \frac{x\, dx}{(l^2 + x^2)^{3/2}}$$

$$\Rightarrow \quad \phi = \frac{ql}{2\epsilon_0} \left[-\frac{1}{\sqrt{l^2 + x^2}} \right]_0^R$$

$$\Rightarrow \quad \phi = \frac{ql}{2\epsilon_0} \left[1 - \frac{1}{\sqrt{l^2 + x^2}} \right] \quad \ldots(1.183)$$

The above result can be used as a standard result and can be obtained in a much simpler way by using the concept of solid angle and Gauss's Law which we will discuss in upcoming articles.

1.13.8 Electric Flux Through the Lateral Surface of a Cylinder due to a Point Charge

Figure-1.244 shows a cylindrical surface of length L and radius R. On its axis at its centre a point charge q is placed. In this situation we will calculate the electric flux coming out of the lateral surface of this cylinder due to the point charge q.

For this we consider an elemental strip of width dx on the surface of cylinder as shown. The area of this strip is

$$dS = 2\pi R \cdot dx$$

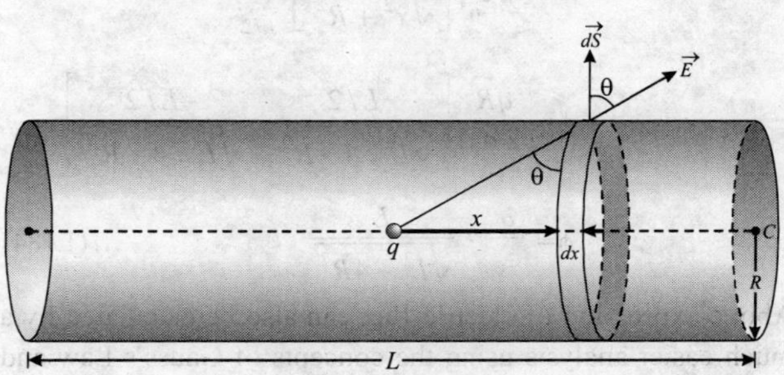

Figure 1.244

The electric field due to the point charge on the elemental strip can be given as

$$E = \frac{Kq}{(x^2 + R^2)}$$

If $d\phi$ is the electric flux through the strip, this can be given as

$$d\phi = E\, dS \cos\theta$$

$$\Rightarrow \quad d\phi = \frac{Kq}{(x^2 + R^2)} \times 2\pi R dx \times \frac{R}{\sqrt{x^2 + R^2}}$$

$$\Rightarrow \quad d\phi = 2\pi KqR^2 \times \frac{dx}{(x^2 + R^2)^{3/2}}$$

Total electric flux through the lateral surface of cylinder can be given by integrating the above expression of electric flux through the elemental strip for the complete lateral surface within limits from $-L/2$ to $+L/2$, which can be given as

$$\phi = \int d\phi = \frac{qR^2}{2\epsilon_0} \int_{-L/2}^{+L/2} \frac{dx}{(x^2 + R^2)^{3/2}}$$

To integrate we substitute

$$x = R \tan\theta$$

$$\Rightarrow \quad dx = R \sec^2\theta\, d\theta$$

$$\Rightarrow \quad \phi = \frac{qR^2}{2\epsilon_0} \int \frac{R \sec^2\theta d\theta}{(R^2 \sec^2\theta + R^2)^{3/2}}$$

$$\Rightarrow \quad \phi = \frac{qR^2}{2\epsilon_0} \int \frac{R \sec^2\theta d\theta}{R^3 \sec^3\theta}$$

$$\Rightarrow \quad \phi = \frac{qR}{2\epsilon_0}\int \cos\theta d\theta$$

$$\Rightarrow \quad \phi = \frac{qR}{2\epsilon_0}[\sin\theta]_{x=-L/2}^{x=+L/2}$$

As we have used the substitution $x = R\tan\theta$, we use

$$\sin\theta = \frac{x}{\sqrt{x^2+R^2}}$$

$$\Rightarrow \quad \phi = \frac{qR}{2\epsilon_0}\left[\frac{x}{\sqrt{x^2+R^2}}\right]_{-L/2}^{+L/2}$$

$$\Rightarrow \quad \phi = \frac{qR}{2\epsilon_0}\left[\frac{L/2}{\sqrt{L^2/4+R^2}} - \frac{-L/2}{\sqrt{L^2/4+R^2}}\right]$$

$$\Rightarrow \quad \phi = \frac{q}{\epsilon_0}\cdot\frac{L}{\sqrt{L^2+4R^2}} \qquad \ldots(1.184)$$

Above expression of electric flux can also be calculated by a much easier analysis using the concepts of Gauss's Law and solid angle, we'll discuss it in upcoming articles.

1.13.9 Electric Flux Produced by a Point Charge

The figure-1.245 shows a point charge placed at the centre of a spherical surface of radius R from which electric lines are originated and coming out of the surface of sphere. For clarity and convenience only lower half of sphere is drawn in the picture. As the charge q is inside the sphere, whatever flux it originates will come out from the spherical surface. To find the total flux from the sphere enclosing the charge we consider an elemental area dS on surface as shown. The electric field on the points on surface of sphere can be given as

$$E = \frac{Kq}{R^2}$$

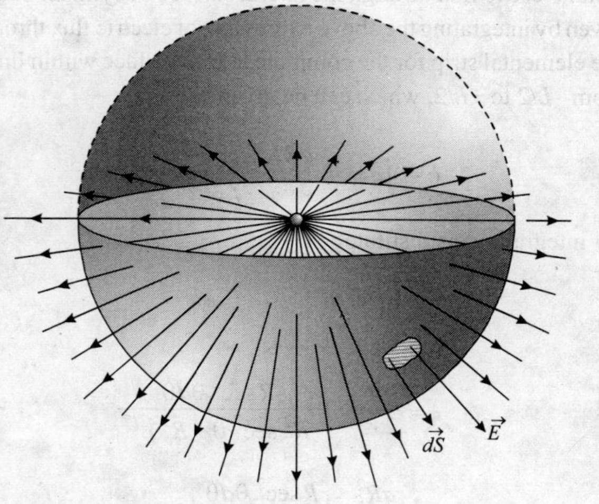

Figure 1.245

The electric flux coming out from the surface area dS is given as

$$d\phi = \vec{E}\cdot\vec{dS} = EdS\cos 0° = EdS$$

In above case the angle between vector of electric field strength and elemental area dS is $\theta = 0°$.

$$\Rightarrow \quad d\phi = \frac{Kq}{R^2}dS$$

Total flux coming out from the spherical surface can be calculated by integrating the above expression over the whole surface of sphere as

$$\phi = \int d\phi = \int \frac{Kq}{R^2}dS$$

At every point of spherical surface, magnitude of electric field remains same thus we use

$$\phi = \frac{Kq}{R^2}\int dS$$

$$\Rightarrow \quad \phi = \frac{Kq}{R^2}\times 4pR^2$$

$$\Rightarrow \quad \phi = \frac{q}{\epsilon_0} \qquad \ldots(1.185)$$

Thus total flux coming out from the spherical surface is the flux which is originated by the point charge q as it is completely enclosed by the spherical surface. Thus charge q originates total electric flux $\frac{q}{\epsilon_0}$. Similarly a charge $-q$ absorbs $\frac{q}{\epsilon_0}$ electric flux into it.

Figure-1.246 shows a charge q enclosed in a closed surface S of random shape. Here we can say that the total electric flux emerging out from the surface S is the complete flux which charge q is originating, hence flux emerging from surface is

$$\phi_S = \frac{q}{\epsilon_0}$$

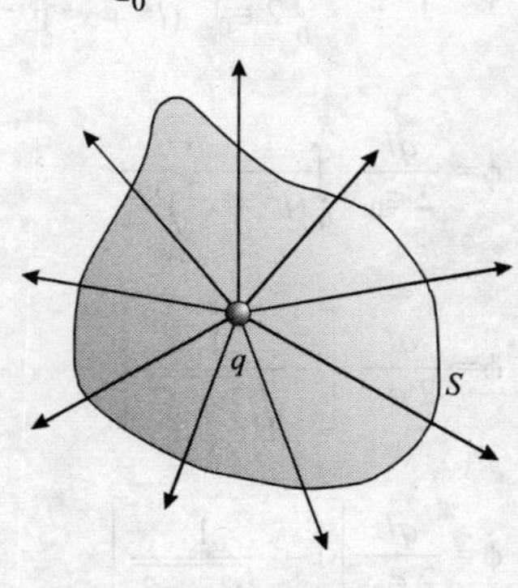

Figure 1.246

The above result is independent of the shape of surface as it only depends on the amount of charge enclosed by the surface and a charge originates or absorbs electric flux which is directly proportional to the magnitude of charge.

 # Illustrative Example 1.68

A cylinder of height H and radius R is placed in a uniform electric field as shown in figure-1.247. Find flux crossing through the cylinder.

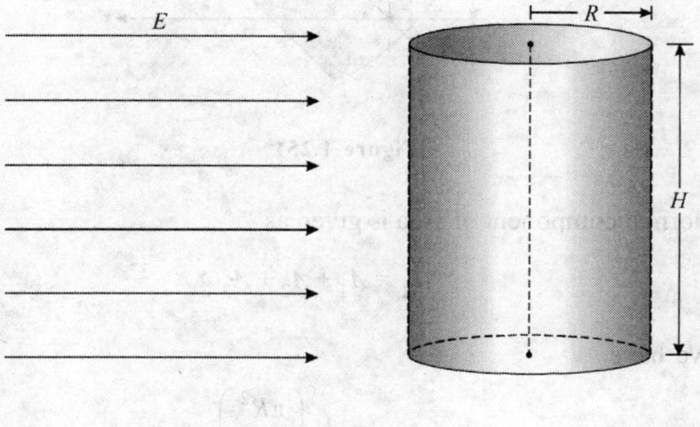

Figure 1.247

Solution

The cross sectional area perpendicular to the electric field is

$$S = 2R \times H$$

Thus electric flux crossing the cylinder is

$$\phi = ES$$

$$\Rightarrow \qquad \phi = E(2RH) = 2ERH$$

 # Illustrative Example 1.69

The electric field in a region is given by $\vec{E} = a\hat{i} + b\hat{j}$. Here a and b are constants. Find the net electric flux passing through a square area of side l parallel to YZ plane.

Solution

A square area of side l parallel to YZ plane in vector form can be written as,

$$\vec{S} = l^2\hat{i}$$

Given, $\vec{E} = a\hat{i} + b\hat{j}$

Electric flux passing through the given area is given as

$$\phi_e = \vec{E} \cdot \vec{S}$$

$$\Rightarrow \qquad \phi_e = (a\hat{i} + b\hat{j}) \cdot (l^2\hat{i})$$

$$\Rightarrow \qquad \phi_e = al^2$$

 # Illustrative Example 1.70

Two mutually perpendicular infinite wires along x-axis and y-axis carry charge densities λ_1 and λ_2 (see figure-1.248). The electric line of force at P is along the line $y = \frac{1}{\sqrt{3}}x$, where P is also a point lying on the same line, then find λ_1/λ_2.

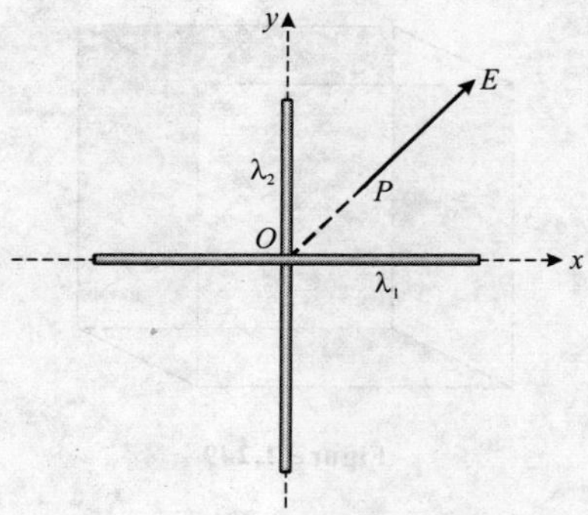

Figure 1.248

Solution

Net Electric field at point P is given as

$$\vec{E} = \vec{E_1} + \vec{E_2} \text{ due to vertical wire}$$

$$\vec{E_1} = \frac{\lambda_1}{2\pi\varepsilon_0 y} \quad \text{in } +y \text{ direction}$$

$$\vec{E_2} = \frac{\lambda_2}{2\pi\varepsilon_0 x}$$

due to vertical wire in x direction a angle of electric field with x direction

$$\tan\alpha = \frac{E_1}{E_2} = \frac{\lambda_1 / 2\pi\varepsilon_0 y}{\lambda_2 / 2\pi\varepsilon_0 x}$$

$$\Rightarrow \qquad \frac{1}{\sqrt{3}} = \frac{\lambda_1 x}{\lambda_2 y}$$

$$\Rightarrow \qquad \frac{\lambda_1}{\lambda_2} = \frac{x}{y}\sqrt{3}$$

$$\Rightarrow \qquad \frac{\lambda_1}{\lambda_2} = 3$$

 # Illustrative Example 1.71

Find the electric flux coming out from one face of a cube of edge a, centre of which a point charge q is placed.

Solution

Here the total solid angle subtended by cube surface at the point charge q is 4π. As charge q is at centre of cube, we can say the each face of cube subtend equal solid angle at the centre, thus solid angle subtended by each face at point charge is

$$\Omega_{face} = \frac{4\pi}{6} \text{ steradian}$$

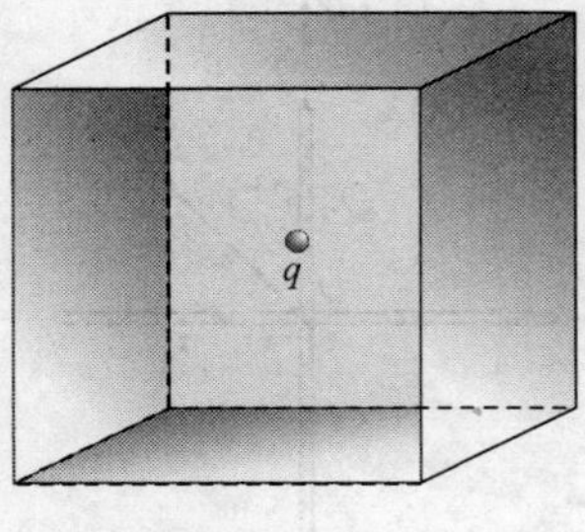

Figure 1.249

Thus electric flux through each face is

$$\phi_{face} = \frac{q/\epsilon_0}{4\pi} \times \Omega_{face}$$

$$\Rightarrow \quad \phi_{face} = \frac{q/\epsilon_0}{4\pi} \times \frac{4\pi}{6}$$

$$\Rightarrow \quad \phi_{face} = \frac{q}{6\epsilon_0}$$

 # Illustrative Example 1.72

The cylinder of previous example is now tilted by an angle θ from vertical. Find the flux crossing the cylinder.

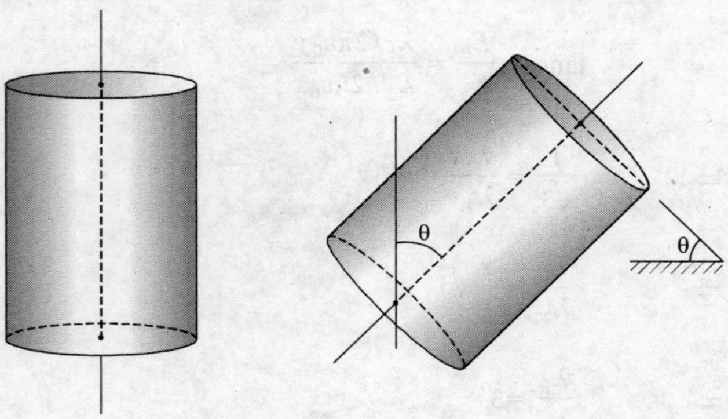

Figure 1.250

Solution

Looking at the cylinder shown in figure-1.251 along $-x$-axis it appears in the view as shown in figure-1.252

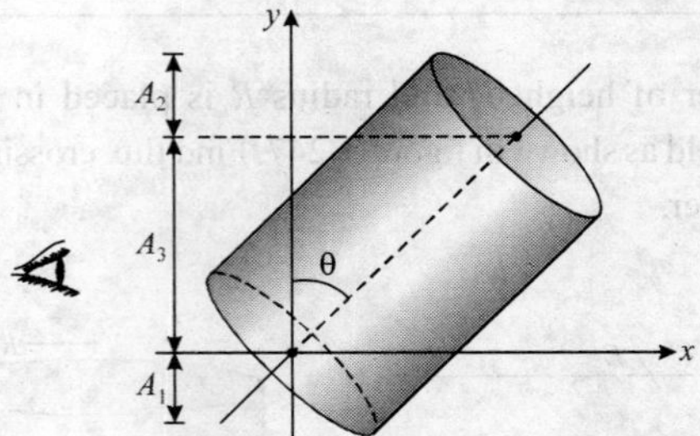

Figure 1.251

Normal component of area is given as

$$A_{\perp} = A_1 + A_2 + A_3$$

We have

$$A_1 = A_2 = \left(\frac{\pi R^2}{2}\right) \sin\theta$$

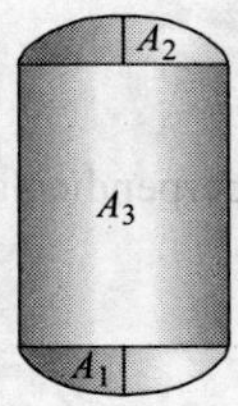

Figure 1.252

And we also have

$$A_3 = 2HR\cos\theta$$

Total normal component of area is

$$A_{\perp} = \left(\frac{\pi R^2}{2}\right) \sin\theta \times 2 + 2HR\cos\theta$$

$$\Rightarrow \quad A_{\perp} = 2RH\cos\theta + \pi R^2 \sin\theta$$

Thus flux passing through cylinder is

$$\phi = EA_{\perp}$$

$$\Rightarrow \quad \phi = E(2RH\cos\theta + \pi R^2 \sin\theta)$$

1.14 Gauss's Law

This law is the mathematical analysis of the relation between the electric flux from a closed surface and its enclosed charge.

This law states "*The total electric flux emerging out from a closed surface is equal to the product of sum of enclosed charge by the surface and the constant $1/\epsilon_0$.*"

Mathematically Gauss's Law is written as

$$\oint_M \vec{E}\cdot\overrightarrow{dS} = \frac{\Sigma q_{encl.}}{\epsilon_0} \qquad \ldots(1.186)$$

Here the sign $\oint$ represents the integration over a closed surface M which encloses a total charge Σq_{encl}

To understand Gauss's law we consider a surface M as shown in figure-1.253 which encloses three charges q_1, $-q_2$ and q_5. For the surface M if we find surface integral of electric field $\oint_M \vec{E}\cdot\overrightarrow{dS}$ for the whole surface M, it gives the total electric flux coming out from the surface which is equal to the total electric flux produced by all the charges enclosed by this surface and it can be given as

$$\oint_M \vec{E}\cdot\overrightarrow{dS} = \frac{q_1+q_5-q_3}{\epsilon_0} \qquad \ldots(1.187)$$

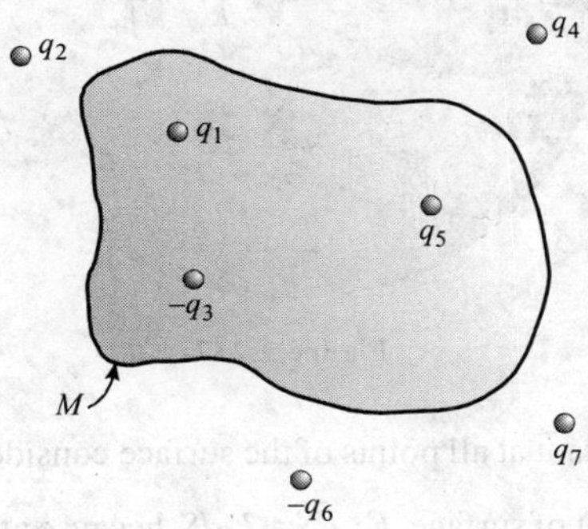

Figure 1.253

In above expression electric field $\vec{E}$ is the net electric field at the points on the surface of M. For electric flux calculation we use the net electric field of the system due to all the charges in the system but the total flux coming out from the surface is the flux originated by the charges enclosed in the closed surface only. This is because any electric line of force originated by any charge which is outside the surface will not contribute in the electric flux coming out of the surface as if we consider one or more electric lines of force due to the charge q_4 which is going into the surface M and terminate on charge q_2 inside the surface then same number of lines or same amount of electric flux which was terminating on q_2 due to other charges will come out of surface M and go to infinity and thus no effect will be there on total flux coming out from surface M due to charge q_4 or any other externally placed charges. The surface M for which the equation of Gauss's law such as equation-(1.187) is written is called '*Gaussian Surface*'.

Gauss's Law can also be used to determine electric field strength in a region due to some symmetrical distribution of charges.

1.14.1 Electric Field Strength Calculation using Gauss's Law

As already discussed in previous article that to apply Gauss's law, we need to choose a closed surface over which we apply Gauss's law which is called Gaussian surface. For a given system of charges for application of Gauss's law selection of proper Gaussian surface in the given situation is very important.

Some times if a random Gaussian surface is chosen then the integral $\oint \vec{E}\cdot\overrightarrow{dS}$ in equation-(1.186) involves complex calculations. To calculate electric field strength in a given region with proper and practical calculations and to make these calculations easier, we choose a Gaussian surface based on the points given below.

General points for selection of Gaussian surface for electric field calculation using Gauss's law are -

(i) The Gaussian surface should be chosen in such a way that at every point of surface the magnitude of electric field is either constant or zero.

(ii) The surface should be chosen in such a way that at every point of surface electric field strength is either parallel or perpendicular to the surface.

We can illustrate the applications of Gauss's Law in calculation of electric field in the surrounding of some charge configurations.

Gauss's Law is a helpful tool in calculating the electric field strength due to various distribution of charges. First to understand the application we calculate the electric field strength due to a point charge q at a distance x, using Gauss's law.

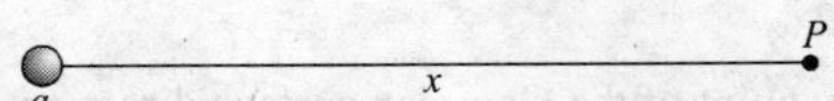

Figure 1.254

Figure-1.254 shows a point charge q and a point P located at a distance x from the charge. To calculate electric field strength at P, we need to consider a Gaussian surface so that point P will be on its surface. For this consider the two surfaces shown in figure-1.255.

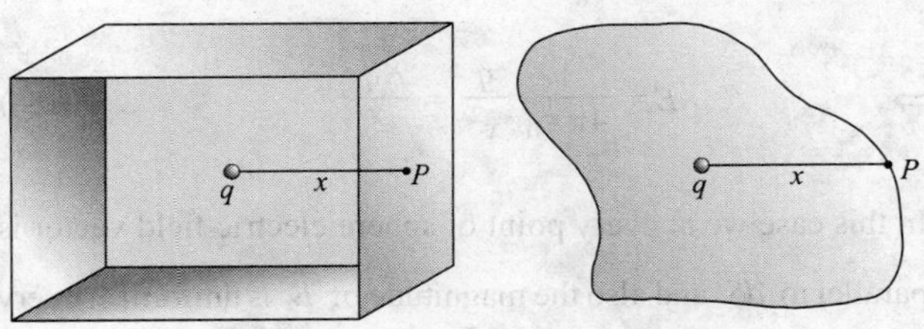

Figure 1.255

If we apply Gauss's Law to the above two Gaussian surface then it will be very difficult to carry out the calculations of integral $\oint \vec{E} \cdot \vec{dS}$ over these surfaces as at every point of the surfaces electric field strength is different due to the point charge and the angle between $\vec{E}$ and $\vec{dS}$ also changes continuously so selecting any Gaussian surface randomly is not a good option. The Gaussian surface should be chosen in such a way to minimize the calculations. Now we consider a spherical Gaussian surface as shown in figure-1.256 which is of radius x and the point charge q is considered at its center. At every point of this surface electric field due to the charge q is constant which is given as

$$E = \frac{Kq}{x^2}$$

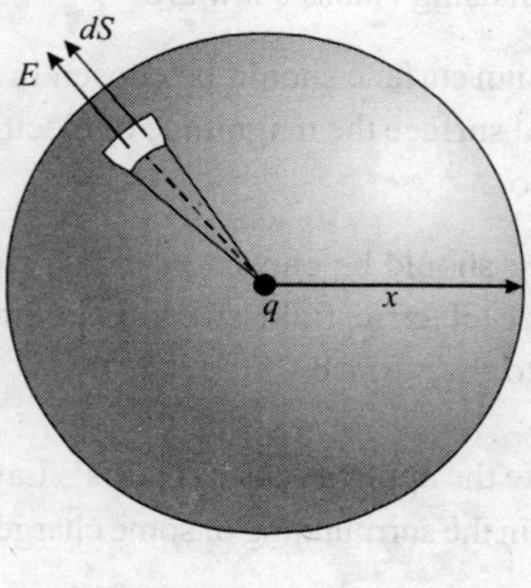

Figure 1.256

Here if apply Gauss's law for this spherical surface, we have

$$\oint \vec{E} \cdot \vec{dS} = \frac{q}{\epsilon_0}$$

As at every point of the Gaussian surface direction of electric field and elemental area vector are same and electric field is constant over the whole surface, we use

$$\Rightarrow \quad E \int dS = \frac{q}{\epsilon_0}$$

$$\Rightarrow \quad E \cdot 4\pi x^2 = \frac{q}{\epsilon_0}$$

$$\Rightarrow \quad E = \frac{1}{4\pi \epsilon_0} \frac{q}{x^2} = \frac{Kq}{x^2} \quad \ldots(1.188)$$

In this case we at every point of sphere electric field vector is parallel to $\vec{dS}$ and also the magnitude of $\vec{E}$ is uniform at every point, thus the integral $\oint \vec{E} \cdot \vec{dS}$ can be easily evaluated.

1.14.2 Electric Field Strength due to a Charged Conducting Sphere

To find electric field at an outer point at a distance x from the centre of sphere, similar to the case of a point charge in previous article, in this case also we consider a spherical Gaussian surface of radius x $(x > R)$ as shown in figure-1.257. If electric field strength at every point of this surface is E, using Gauss's Law we have

$$\oint \vec{E} \cdot \vec{dS} = \frac{q_{encl}}{\epsilon_0}$$

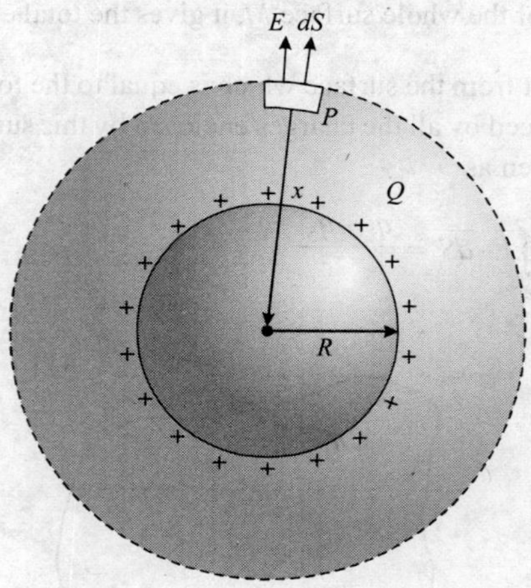

Figure 1.257

As E is constant at all points of the surface considered and also at every point of surface $\vec{E} \cdot \vec{dS} = E\,dS$, because at all points $\vec{E}$ is parallel to the surface area vector $\vec{dS}$, thus we have for the Gaussian Surface M, on applying Gauss's law we get

$$E \oint dS = \frac{Q}{\epsilon_0}$$

$$\Rightarrow \quad E \cdot 4\pi x^2 = \frac{Q}{\epsilon_0}$$

$$\Rightarrow \quad E = \frac{1}{4\pi \epsilon_0} \frac{Q}{x^2}$$

Similarly for surface points we can consider a spherical Gaussian surface of radius R which gives electric field strength on the sphere surface as

$$E_S = \frac{1}{4\pi \epsilon_0} \cdot \frac{Q}{x^2}$$

To find electric field strength at an interior point of the sphere, we consider an inner spherical Gaussian surface of radius x $(x < R)$ as shown in figure-1.258. If we apply Gauss's Law for this surface, we have

$$\oint \vec{E} \cdot \vec{dS} = \frac{q_{encl}}{\epsilon_0}$$

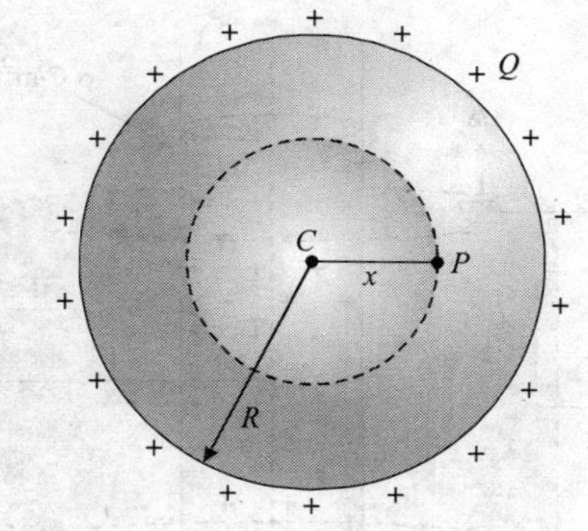

Figure 1.258

As all the charges in a conducting or a hollow uniformly charged surface is on the surface, thus $q_{encl} = 0$ and by symmetry at every point of Gaussian surface E must be constant so by symmetry we have

$$E_{in} = 0$$

All the above results of electric field strength due to the charge on a uniformly charged conducting sphere we've obtained using Gauss's law are same which we have obtained in article-1.7.4 by considering whole charge concentrated at center of the sphere by symmetry. Same results are also valid for a uniformly charged hollow non conducting sphere or any spherical uniform surface charge distribution.

1.14.3 Electric Field Strength due to a Non-conducting Uniformly Charged Sphere

In case of a uniformly charged non conducting sphere for outer and surface points the electric field strength can be calculated by using Gauss Law similar to the case of conducting sphere as discussed in previous article by considering spherical Gaussian surfaces of radius $x > R$ and $x = R$ respectively.

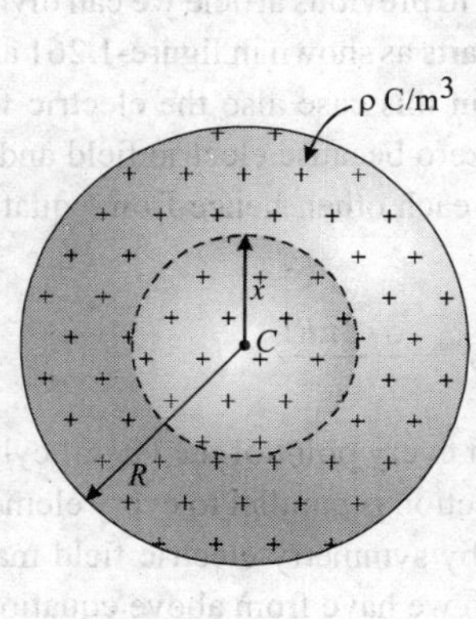

Figure 1.259

For calculation of electric field strength at interior points of sphere, we consider a spherical Gaussian surface of radius x $(x < R)$ as shown in figure-1.259 inside a uniformly charged solid non conducting sphere of radius R and volume charge density ρ C/m^3. If we apply Gauss Law for this surface, we have

$$\oint \vec{E} \cdot d\vec{S} = \frac{q_{encl}}{\epsilon_0}$$

In this case charge enclosed within the sphere of radius x is given by

$$q_{encl} = \rho \times \frac{4}{3}\pi x^3$$

$$\Rightarrow \qquad E_{in} \cdot 4\pi x^2 = \frac{\rho \times \frac{4}{3}\pi x^3}{\epsilon_0}$$

$$\Rightarrow \qquad E_{in} = \frac{\rho x}{3\epsilon_0}$$

All the above results of electric field strengths for exterior, surface and inside points of a uniformly charged non conducting sphere we've obtained using Gauss's law are same which we obtained in article-1.7.7 by considering the inner charge of the region inside any point at the center.

1.14.4 Electric Field Strength due to a Long Charged Wire

Due to a long charged wire having a linear charge density λ C/m we've calculated the electric field strength at a point located a distance x from the wire in article-1.5.2 by considering an elemental charge in the wire and then integrating the result of electric field strength due the element over the whole length of wire. We can obtain the same result by using Gauss's law without using integration as shown in figure-1.260. This figure shows a cylindrical Gaussian surface of radius x and length l considered symmetrically in surrounding of the line charge such that a point P is located on the Gaussian surface as shown.

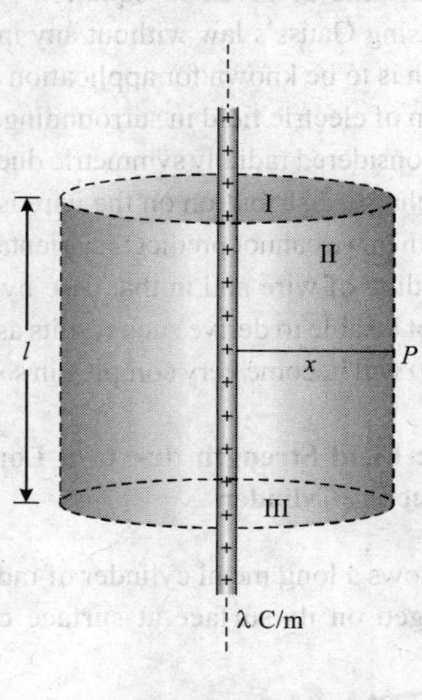

Figure 1.260

Applying Gauss's Law on this surface, we have

$$\oint \overline{E}\cdot\overline{dS} = \frac{q_{encl}}{\epsilon_0} \quad \ldots(1.189)$$

To determine the left side integral of the above equation we consider that the closed Gaussian surface is made of three parts I, II and III which are two flat circular faces and one cylindrical lateral surface respectively. Thus we split the closed surface integration in above equation-(1.189) in three parts for these three surfaces as

$$\oint \overline{E}\cdot\overline{dS} = \int_I \overline{E}\cdot\overline{dS} + \int_{II} \overline{E}\cdot\overline{dS} + \int_{III} \overline{E}\cdot\overline{dS}$$

We can see that part I and III, by symmetry electric field strength vector is perpendicular to the area vector so no flux will come out of these two circular surfaces. Thus we have

$$\int_I \overline{E}\cdot\overline{dS} = \int_{III} \overline{E}\cdot\overline{dS} = 0$$

The total charge enclosed in the Gaussian cylindrical surface is λl so from equation-(1.198) we have

$$\int_{II} \overline{E}\cdot\overline{dS} = \frac{\lambda l}{\epsilon_0}$$

For lateral surface by symmetry as direction of electric field is normal to the area of surface at every point $\overline{E}$ is parallel to $\overline{dS}$, we have

$$E\int_{II} dS = \frac{\lambda l}{\epsilon_0}$$

$$\Rightarrow \quad E\cdot 2\pi x l = \frac{\lambda l}{\epsilon_0}$$

$$\Rightarrow \quad E = \frac{\lambda}{2\pi\epsilon_0 x} = \frac{2k\lambda}{x}$$

Above result is same as given in equation-(1.42) and it is obtained here using Gauss's law without any integration. The only thing which is to be known for application of Gauss's law is the orientation of electric field in surrounding of the charged wire which we considered radially symmetric due to the uniform charges. If the charge distribution on the wire is considered to be non uniform then we cannot predict the orientation of electric field in surrounding of wire and in that case by using Gauss's law we might not be able to derive such results as the integral in equation-(1.189) will become very complex in solving.

1.14.5 Electric Field Strength due to a Long Uniformly Charged Conducting Cylinder

Figure-1.261 shows a long metal cylinder of radius R which is uniformly charged on its surface at surface charge density σ C/m^2.

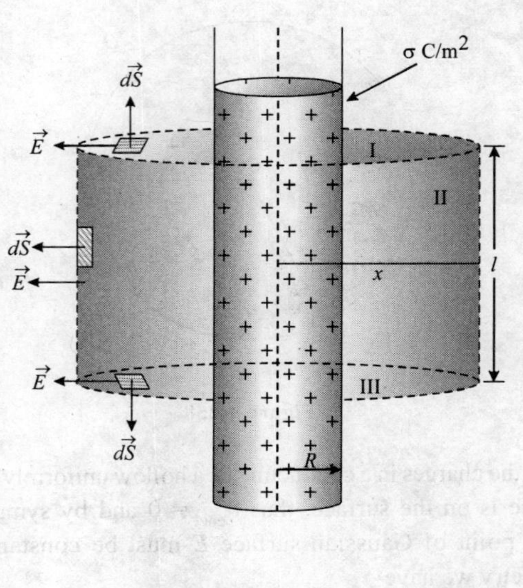

Figure 1.261

We know at interior points of a metal body electric field strength is zero. Similar to the case of a uniformly charged wire, in this case also the electric field configuration in surrounding of the charged cylinder would be in radially outward direction as charge distribution is uniform so for calculation of electric field strength at outer points at a distance x from the axis of the cylinder, we consider a cylindrical Gaussian surface of radius x and length l as shown in figure-1.261. By applying Gauss's Law on this surface we have

$$\oint \overline{E}\cdot\overline{dS} = \frac{q_{encl}}{\epsilon_0} \quad \ldots(1.190)$$

The enclosed charge in the cylindrical Gaussian surface can be given as

$$q_{encl} = \sigma\cdot 2\pi R l$$

Here also similar to previous article we can divide the Gaussian surface in three parts as shown in figure-1.261 and by symmetry we can see that in this case also the electric flux through the circular faces is zero because electric field and area vector are perpendicular to each other, hence from equation-(1.190), we have

$$\int_{II} \overline{E}\cdot\overline{dS} = \frac{\sigma\cdot 2\pi R l}{\epsilon_0} \quad \ldots(1.191)$$

For part II also at every point of the lateral cylindrical surface electric field direction is parallel to every elemental area dS on this surface and by symmetry electric field magnitude can be taken constant, so we have from above equation-(1.191)

$$E\int_{II} dS = \frac{\sigma\cdot 2\pi R l}{\epsilon_0}$$

$$\Rightarrow \qquad E \cdot 2\pi x l = \frac{\sigma \cdot 2\pi R l}{\epsilon_0}$$

$$\Rightarrow \qquad E = \frac{\sigma R}{\epsilon_0 \, x} \qquad \ldots(1.192)$$

Above expression is same as given in equation-(1.65) which we obtained in article-1.7.9 but here we've obtained it by using Gauss's law. For surface points we can consider the Gaussian surface at $x = R$ and repeat the above process to obtain the result for surface point which is given as

$$E_S = \frac{\sigma}{\epsilon_0} \qquad \ldots(1.193)$$

Being a symmetrically charged body if we consider an inner cylindrical Gaussian surface then by the same analysis we did for a conducting uniformly charged sphere, here also we can state that for uniform surface charge distribution on a cylindrical surface $E_{in} = 0$.

1.14.6 Electric Field Strength due to a Uniformly Charged Non-conducting Cylinder

Figure-1.262 shows a long cylinder of radius R, charged uniformly with volume charge density ρ C/m^3. The electric field strength at outer and surface points we can repeat the process we did in previous article as the electric field configuration in surrounding of wire is radially symmetric. To calculate electric field strength at a distance x ($x > R$) from the axis of cylinder we consider a cylindrical Gaussian surface shown in figure-1.262.

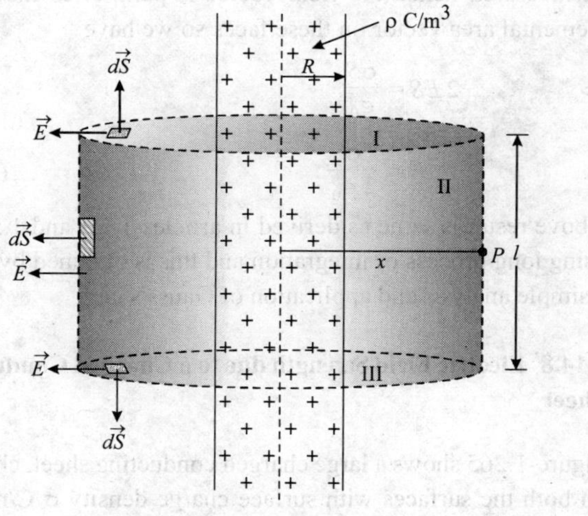

Figure 1.262

If we apply Gauss Law on this surface, we have

$$\oint \vec{E} \cdot \overrightarrow{dS} = \frac{q_{encl}}{\epsilon_0} \qquad \ldots(1.194)$$

The enclosed charge in the Gaussian surface is given as

$$q_{encl} = \rho . \pi R^2 l$$

Again we can divide the Gaussian surface in three parts as shown in figure-1.262 and by symmetry we can see that in this case also the electric flux through the circular faces is zero, hence from equation-(1.194), we have

$$\int_{II} \vec{E} \cdot \overrightarrow{dS} = \frac{\rho \cdot \pi R^2 l}{\epsilon_0}$$

For part II also at every point of the lateral cylindrical surface electric field direction is parallel to every elemental area dS on this surface and by symmetry electric field magnitude can be taken constant over this surface, so we have from above equation-(1.191)

$$\Rightarrow \qquad E \int dS = \frac{\rho \pi R^2 l}{\epsilon_0}$$

$$\Rightarrow \qquad E \cdot 2\pi x l = \frac{\rho \pi R^2 l}{\epsilon_0}$$

$$\Rightarrow \qquad E = \frac{\rho R^2}{2 \epsilon_0 \, x} \qquad \ldots(1.195)$$

Above expression is same as given in equation-(1.68) which we obtained in article-1.7.10 but here we've obtained it by using Gauss's law. For surface points we can consider the Gaussian surface at $x = R$ and repeat the above process to obtain the result for surface point which is given as

$$E_S = \frac{\rho R}{2 \epsilon_0} \qquad \ldots(1.196)$$

To calculate electric field inside the cylinder at a distance x from the axis, we consider a small cylindrical Gaussian surface of radius x and length l inside the cylinder as shown in figure-1.263. If we apply Gauss Law for this surface, we have

$$\oint \vec{E} \cdot \overrightarrow{dS} = \frac{q_{encl}}{\epsilon_0} \qquad \ldots(1.197)$$

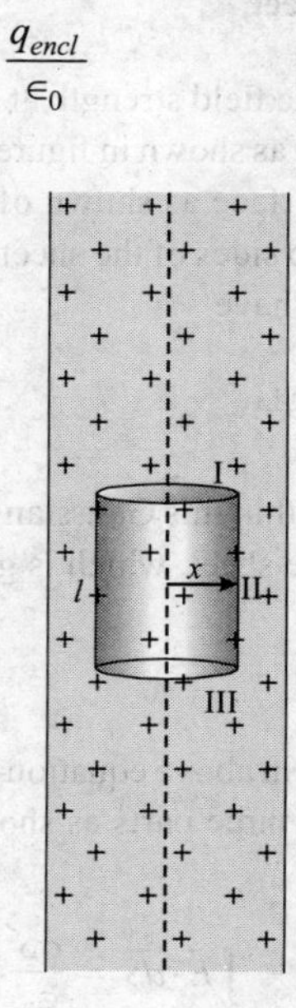

Figure 1.263

The enclosed charge in the above Gaussian surface is given as

$$q_{\text{encl}} = \rho.\pi x^2 l$$

Again we can divide the Gaussian surface in three parts as shown in figure-1.263 and by symmetry we can see that in this case also the electric flux through the circular faces is zero, hence from equation-(1.197), we have

$$\int_{II} \vec{E}\cdot \vec{dS} = \frac{\rho\cdot\pi x^2 l}{\epsilon_0} \quad \ldots(1.198)$$

For part II like previously discussed cases, at every point of the lateral cylindrical surface electric field direction is parallel to every elemental area dS on this surface and by symmetry electric field magnitude can be taken constant over this surface, so we have from above equation-(1.198), we have

$$E\int_{II} dS = \frac{\rho\pi x^2 l}{\epsilon_0}$$

$$\Rightarrow \quad E.2\pi x l = \frac{\rho\pi x^2 l}{\epsilon_0}$$

$$\Rightarrow \quad E = \frac{\rho x}{2\epsilon_0} \quad \ldots(1.199)$$

All the above results are same which we've obtained in article-1.7.10 but here we calculated these using Gauss's law. The only point where we need to be careful while applying Gauss's law is the selection of an appropriate Gaussian surface which is done based on the basic rules in cases of symmetric charge distribution as explained in article-1.14.1.

1.14.7 Electric Field Strength due to a Non-conducting Uniformly Charged Sheet

To determine the electric field strength at a point P infront of a uniformly charged sheet as shown in figure-1.264 we consider a cylindrical Gaussian surface as shown of circular face area S and length $2x$ on the two sides of the sheet. If we apply Gauss's law for this surface, we have

$$\oint \vec{E}\cdot\vec{dS} = \frac{q_{\text{encl}}}{\epsilon_0} \quad \ldots(1.200)$$

The enclosed charge within this Gaussian surface is the charge on surface area S on the sheet, which is given as

$$q_{\text{encl}} = \sigma S$$

To carry out the integral in above equation-(1.200) for the given surface, we divide it in three parts as shown in figure and we split the integral as

$$\int_I \vec{E}\cdot\vec{dS} + \int_{II} \vec{E}\cdot\vec{dS} + \int_{III} \vec{E}\cdot\vec{dS} = \frac{\sigma S}{\epsilon_0} \quad \ldots(1.201)$$

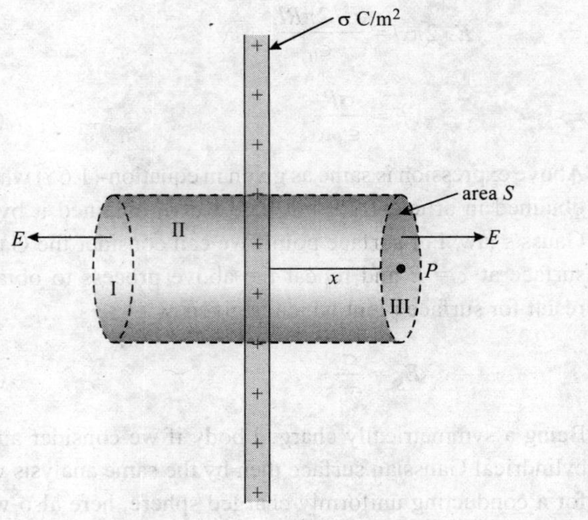

Figure 1.264

In this case we can see that for lateral part of the surface $\int_{II} \vec{E}\cdot\vec{dS} = 0$ as the direction of electric field at every point of surface is parallel to the surface, hence no flux is coming out from the lateral surface, thus from equation-(1.201) we have

$$\int_I EdS + \int_{II} EdS = \frac{\sigma S}{2\epsilon_0}$$

By symmetry for both circular faces we can consider that electric field magnitude is same at every point and it is normal to the surface area hence the field vector is parallel to the every elemental area vector on these faces so we have

$$\Rightarrow \quad 2ES = \frac{\sigma S}{\epsilon_0}$$

$$\Rightarrow \quad E = \frac{\sigma}{2\epsilon_0} \quad \ldots(1.202)$$

Above result is same as derived in articles-1.5.3 and 1.5.4 by using long process of integration and this is obtained by using a simple analysis and application of Gauss's law.

1.14.8 Electric Field Strength due to a Charged Conducting Sheet

Figure-1.265 shows a large charged conducting sheet, charged on both the surfaces with surface charge density σ C/m². As we've studied that in a metal body there is no charge within the volume of body and thus here also the electric field inside the metal sheet is zero. To find electric field strength at a point P in front of the sheet we consider a cylindrical Gaussian surface of face area S and length x which has one face at point P where electric field is to be calculated and other face of this surface is considered within the volume of sheet. If we apply Gauss's Law on this surface, we have

$$\oint \vec{E}\cdot\overline{dS} = \frac{q_{encl}}{\epsilon_0} \qquad \ldots(1.203)$$

With the similar analysis done in previous articles, we divide the Gaussian surface in three parts as shown, and the enclosed charge within this Gaussian surface is taken as σS as only one sheet surface is enclosed here, so from equation-(1.203) we have

$$\int_I \vec{E}\cdot\overline{dS} + \int_{II} \vec{E}\cdot\overline{dS} + \int_{III} \vec{E}\cdot\overline{dS} = \frac{\sigma S}{\epsilon_0} \qquad \ldots(1.204)$$

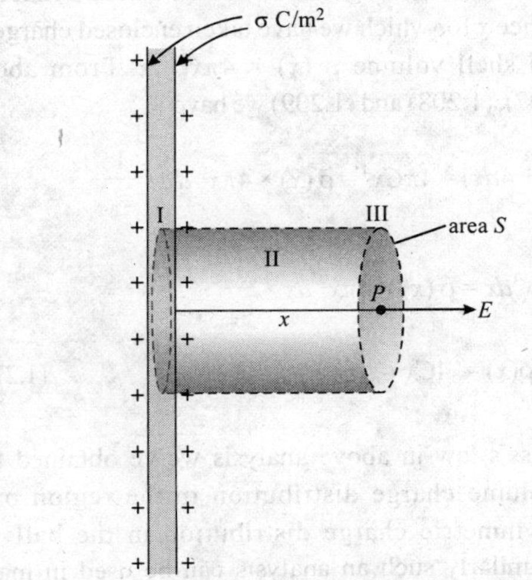

Figure 1.265

As on surface I of the Gaussian surface $E_{in} = 0$ hence $\int_I \vec{E}\cdot\overline{dS} = 0$

and for lateral surface II as electric field direction is parallel to the surface so we can use $\int_{II} \vec{E}\cdot\overline{dS} = 0$ as no electric flux is coming out from the lateral surface of cylinder. Thus from equation-(1.203) we have

$$\int_{III} \vec{E}\cdot\overline{dS} = \frac{\sigma S}{\epsilon_0}$$

$$\Rightarrow \qquad ES = \frac{\sigma S}{\epsilon_0}$$

$$\Rightarrow \qquad E = \frac{\sigma}{\epsilon_0}$$

Above result can also be obtained by considering the cylindrical Gaussian surface of length $2x$ as analyzed in previous article in which we could have doubled the enclosed charge but to gain an insight how different Gaussian surfaces can be chosen in case of metal bodies here we've chosen a different Gaussian surface.

1.14.9 Application of Gauss's Law in the Region of Non uniform Electric Field

Gauss Law is useful in the problems related to the cases where electric field varies with the distance. Figure-1.266 shows cubical surface of edge a placed in a region the electric field strength depends on x direction as

$$E = E_0x^2$$

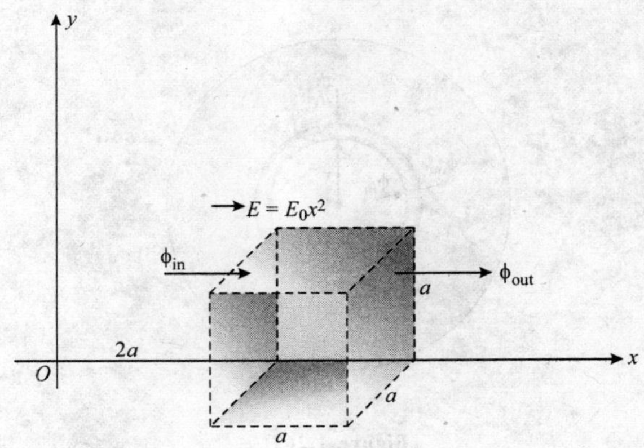

Figure 1.266

As the electric field varies with x coordinate in the region, it is uniform at every point of any yz plane. If we analyze the total electric flux going into the cube shown from the front face of the cube, this can be calculated as

$$\phi_{in} = E_A.S = E_0(2a)^2.\ a^2 = 4E_0a^4 \qquad \ldots(1.205)$$

From the other surface flux coming out can be calculated as

$$\phi_{out} = E_B.\ S = E_0\,(3a)^2.\ a^2 = 9\,E_0\,a^4 \qquad \ldots(1.206)$$

As we can see from above equations that $\phi_{out} > \phi_{in}$ for the cubical surface hence net charges enclosed in the cube are positive, we can apply Gauss's law to calculate the net charge enclosed in the cube as

$$\phi_{out} - \phi_{in} = \frac{q_{encl}}{\epsilon_0}$$

$$\Rightarrow \qquad E_0\,(9-4)a^4 = \frac{q_{encl}}{\epsilon_0}$$

$$\Rightarrow \qquad q_{encl} = 5\epsilon_0E_0a^4$$

Above example illustrates that if in a region electric field is varying in space then there can be charges distributed in space responsible for this variation in space which can be calculated in any region of space using Gauss's law.

In the above situation electric field was varying with x-coordinate. Now we consider a case when in a region electric field is varying in radial direction from a fixed point. Consider a ball of radius R shown in figure-1.267, it is non-uniformly charged with a radially symmetric distribution of charge, which varies with the distance from centre of sphere r. In this situation, inside the ball we consider that the electric field strength at a distance r from centre is given as

$$E = Cr^2 \text{ V/m}$$

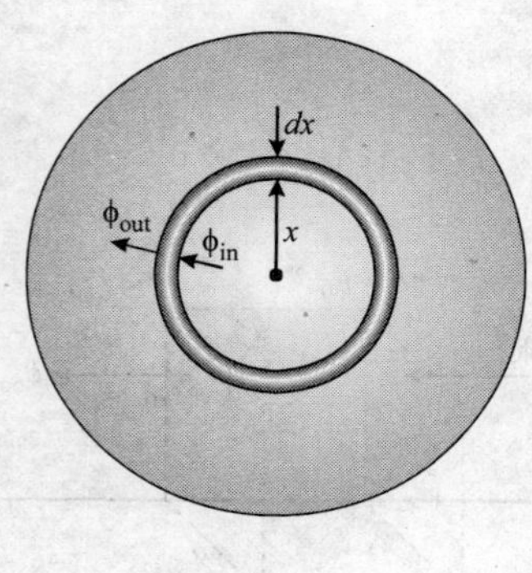

Figure 1.267

If we wish to determine the distribution of volume charge density in the ball then it can be done by using Gauss's law. For this we consider an elemental shell of radius x and width dx as shown in the figure. On the inner surface of shell as $r = x$ the electric field strength can be given as

$$E_{in} = Cx^2$$

Thus the electric flux ϕ_{in} which goes into the elemental shell from its inner surface can be given as

$$\phi_{in} = Cx^2 \times 4\pi x^2$$

$$\Rightarrow \quad \phi_{in} = 4\pi Cx^4 \qquad \ldots(1.207)$$

Similarly the electric field strength at the outer surface of the shell can be given as

$$E_{out} = C(x + dx)^2$$

$$\Rightarrow \quad E_{out} = C(x^2 + 2x\,dx)$$

In above equation as dx is very small we considered $dx^2 \to 0$. The electric flux ϕ_{out} which comes out from the elemental shell from its outer surface is given as

$$\phi_{out} = C(x^2 + 2x\,dx) \times 4\pi (x + dx)^2$$

$$\Rightarrow \quad \phi_{out} = C(x^2 + 2x\,dx) \times 4\pi (x^2 + 2x\,dx)$$

$$\Rightarrow \quad \phi_{out} = 4\pi C(x^4 + 4x^3dx)$$

$$\Rightarrow \quad \phi_{out} = 4\pi Cx^3(x + 4dx) \qquad \ldots(1.208)$$

Now we use Gauss's Law for the region of elemental shell which gives

$$\phi_{out} - \phi_{in} = \rho(x) \times 4\pi x^2\,dx \times \frac{1}{\epsilon_0} \qquad \ldots(1.209)$$

Here $\rho(x)$ is the volume charge density in the ball as a function of radial distance x for which we have taken enclosed charge in the elemental shell volume $\rho(x) \times 4\pi x^2\,dx$. From above equation-(1.207), (1.208) and (1.209) we have

$$4\pi Cx^3(x + 4dx) - 4\pi Cx^4 = \rho(x) \times 4\pi x^2\,dx \times \frac{1}{\epsilon_0}$$

$$\Rightarrow \quad 16\pi Cx^3dx = \rho(x) \times 4\pi x^2\,dx \times \frac{1}{\epsilon_0}$$

$$\Rightarrow \quad \rho(x) = 4Cx\,\epsilon_0 \qquad \ldots(1.210)$$

By using Gauss's law in above analysis we've obtained the density of volume charge distribution in the region of a spherically symmetric charge distribution in the ball we considered. Similarly such an analysis can be used in many different situations.

1.14.10 Electric Field Strength in the Vicinity of a Charged Conductor using Gauss's Law

We've already studied whenever charge is given to a conducting body, it will automatically spread on the outer surface of the conductor in such a way that its surface charge density is inversely proportional to the radius of curvature. We've also studied that inside a metal body at every interior point net electric field strength is zero and the whole metal body and its surface is equipotential hence the electric field which originates from its surface must be perpendicular to the surface at every point as shown in figure-1.268.

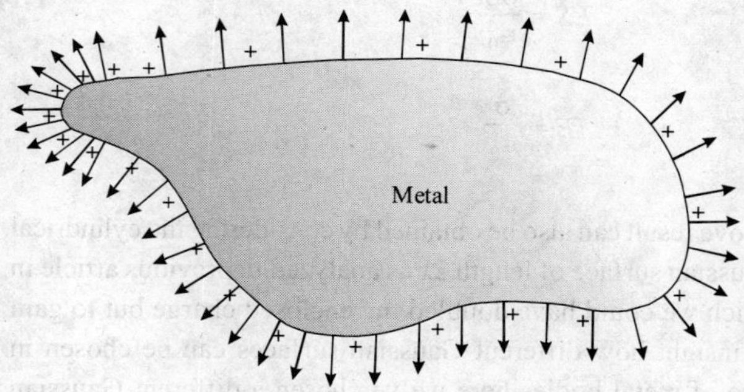

Figure 1.268

As already discussed in article-1.11.5 that at the sharp edges of the conductor surface charge density σ is high so electric lines originating at these sharp edge are more dense compared to flat parts of the body.

Now we will calculate the electric field strength at a point P just out side the surface of the conductor at a place where charge density is σ C/m^2.

For this we consider a small cylindrical Gaussian surface near to point P as shown in figure-1.269. This surface is intersecting the surface of the conductor having circular face area dS and very small length sufficient enough that its outer circular face is just outside the conductor surface and inner circular face is just inside the conducting body as shown. Here point P lies on the outer face of the cylinder. In this case the charge which is enclosed in the Gaussian surface can be given as

$$q_{\text{encl}} = \sigma\, dS$$

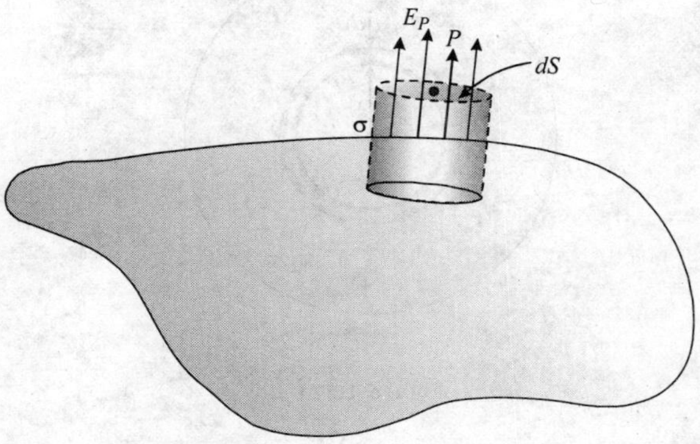

Figure 1.269

The electric flux is coming out only from the outer face of the cylinder as inside there is no electric field and outside electric field is normal to surface hence there is no flux from the lateral surface of cylinder. Thus by applying Gauss Law on this cylindrical surface, we consider only outer face for flux calculation thus we have

$$E \cdot dS = \frac{\sigma dS}{\epsilon_0}$$

$$\Rightarrow \qquad E = \frac{\sigma}{\epsilon_0} \qquad \text{... (1.211)}$$

Thus net electric field strength just outside a charged conducting surface is $\frac{\sigma}{\epsilon_0}$ normal to the surface where σ is the local surface charge density at that point of the conductor.

Here we can also note that just outside a charged metal body, electric field strength depends only on the surface charge density σ C/m^2 and at the sharp edges of conductor, electric field is more as σ is high.

Illustrative Example 1.73

The electric field in a region is given by $\vec{E} = E_0 \frac{x}{l}\hat{i}$. Find the charge contained inside a cubical volume bounded by the surfaces $x = 0, x = l, y = 0, y = l, z = 0$ and $z = l$.

Solution

Figure-1.270 shows the situation described in the question.

At $x = 0$, $E = 0$ and at $x = l$, $\vec{E} = E_0\hat{i}$

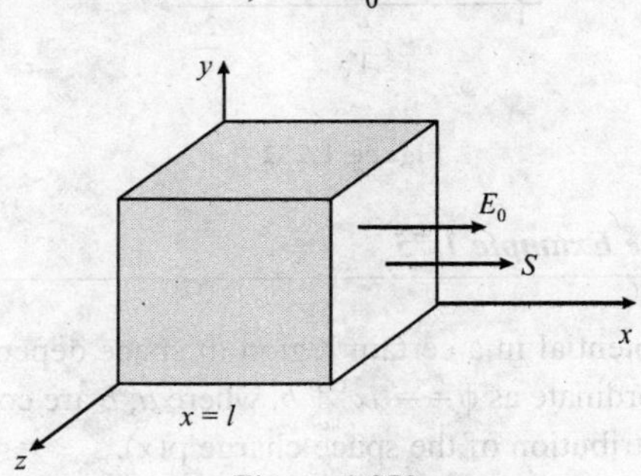

Figure 1.270

The direction of the field is along the x-axis, so it will cross the YZ face of the cube. The flux of this field through the cube is given as

$$\phi = \phi_{\text{left face}} + \phi_{\text{right face}}$$

$$\Rightarrow \qquad \phi = 0 + E_0 l^2 = E_0 l^2$$

By Gauss's law, we have

$$\phi = \frac{q}{\epsilon_0}$$

$$\Rightarrow \qquad q = \epsilon_0 \phi = \epsilon_0 E_0 l^2$$

Illustrative Example 1.74

Figure-1.271 shows an imaginary cube of side a. A uniformly charged rod of length a moves towards right at a constant speed v. At $t = 0$, the right end of the rod just touches the left face of the cube. Plot a graph between electric flux passing through the cube versus time.

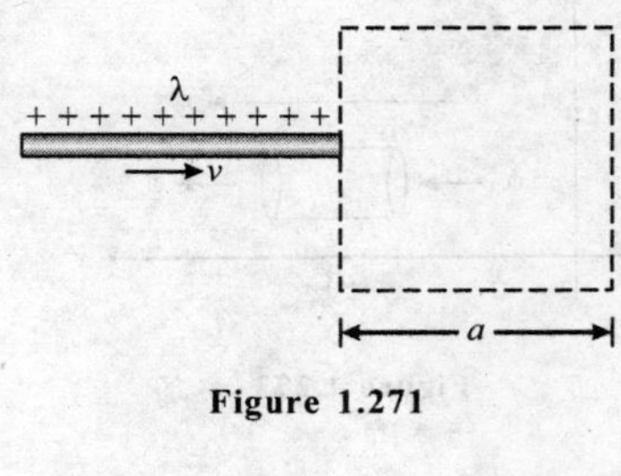

Figure 1.271

Solution

The electric flux, passing through a closed surface depends on the net charge inside the surface. Net charge in this case first increases, reaches a maximum value and finally decreases to zero. The same is the case with the electric flux. The electric flux ϕ_e versus time graph is as shown in figure-1.272 below.

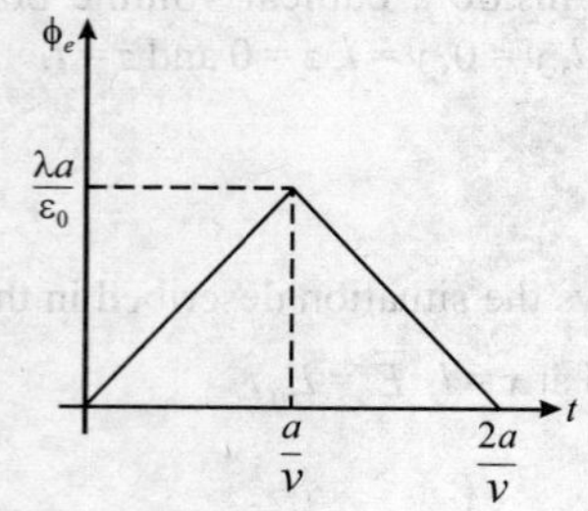

Figure 1.272

Illustrative Example 1.75

The field potential in a certain region of space depends only on the x-coordinate as $\phi = -ax^3 + b$, where a, b are constants. Find the distribution of the space charge $\rho(x)$.

Solution

We know that the field strength is given as

$$E_x = -\frac{\partial \phi}{\partial x} = 3ax^2 \qquad \ldots(1.212)$$

If we consider an elemental cylinder of length dx and cross-sectional surface area S as shown in figure-1.273. Using Gauss's law on this we have

$$\phi_{out} - \phi_{in} = \frac{q_{encl}}{\varepsilon_0}$$

$$\Rightarrow \quad 3a(x+dx)^2 . Sdx - 3ax^2 . Sdx = \frac{\rho(x).Sdx}{\epsilon_0}$$

$$\Rightarrow \quad 6ax.\, Sdx = \frac{\rho(x).Sdx}{\epsilon_0}$$

$$\Rightarrow \quad \rho(x) = 6ax\,\varepsilon_0$$

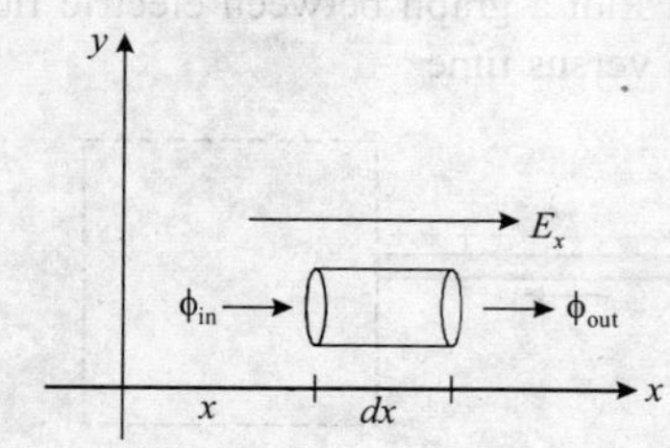

Figure 1.273

Illustrative Example 1.76

The field potential inside a charged ball depends only on the distance from its centre as $\phi = ar^2 + b$, where a and b are constants. Find the space charge distribution $\rho(r)$ inside the ball.

Solution

Inside the ball, electric field strength is given as

$$E = -\frac{d\phi}{dr} = 2ar^2 \qquad \ldots(1.213)$$

If we wish to determine the distribution of volume charge density in the ball then it can be done by using Gauss's law. For this we consider an elemental shell of radius x and width dx as shown in the figure-1.274.

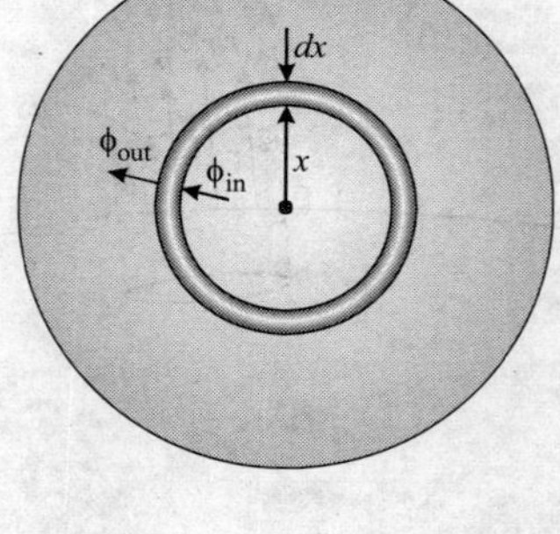

Figure 1.274

On the inner surface of shell as $r = x$ the electric field strength can be given as

$$E_{in} = 2ax$$

Thus the electric flux ϕ_{in} which goes into the elemental shell from its inner surface can be given as

$$\phi_{in} = 2ax \times 4\pi x^2$$

$$\Rightarrow \quad \phi_{in} = 8\pi a x^3 \qquad \ldots(1.214)$$

Similarly the electric field strength at the outer surface of the shell can be given as

$$E_{out} = 2a\,(x + dx)$$

In above equation as dx is very small we considered $dx^2 \to 0$. The electric flux ϕ_{out} which comes out from the elemental shell from its outer surface is given as

$$\phi_{out} = 2a\,(x + dx) \times 4\pi\,(x + dx)^2$$

$$\Rightarrow \qquad \phi_{out} = 2a\,(x+dx) \times 4\pi\,(x^2 + 2x\,dx)$$

$$\Rightarrow \qquad \phi_{out} = 8\pi a\,(x^3 + 3x^3 dx)$$

$$\Rightarrow \qquad \phi_{out} = 8\pi a\,x^2(x + 3dx) \qquad \ldots(1.215)$$

Now we use Gauss's Law for the region of elemental shell which gives

$$\phi_{out} - \phi_{in} = \rho\,(x) \times 4\pi x^2\,dx \times \frac{1}{\epsilon_0} \qquad \ldots(1.216)$$

Here $\rho(x)$ is the volume charge density in the ball as a function of radial distance x for which we have taken enclosed charge in the elemental shell volume $\rho(x) \times 4\pi x^2\,dx$. From above equation-(1.214), (1.215) and (1.216) we have

$$8\pi a\,x^2(x+3dx) - 8\pi a x^3 = \rho\,(x) \times 4\pi x^2\,dx \times \frac{1}{\epsilon_0}$$

$$\Rightarrow \qquad 24\pi a x^2 dx = \rho\,(x) \times 4\pi x^2\,dx \times \frac{1}{\epsilon_0}$$

$$\Rightarrow \qquad \rho(x) = 6a\,\epsilon_0 \qquad \ldots(1.217)$$

Thus in this case the volume charge density is constant. This can also be predicated by the expression of electric field strength which is directly proportional to the distance from center of the ball which happens in case of a sphere uniformly charged with a constant volume charge density. The expression in equation-(1.217) can be directly obtained by equating the expression of electric field strength to the equation-(1.64) in article-1.7.7.

 # Illustrative Example 1.77

The intensity of an electric field depends only on the coordinates x and y as follows,

$$\vec{E} = \frac{a(x\hat{i} + y\hat{j})}{x^2 + y^2}$$

where, a is a constant and $\hat{i}$ and $\hat{j}$ are the unit vectors of the x and y axes. Find the charge within a sphere of radius R with the centre at the origin.

Solution

At any point $P(x, y, z)$ on the sphere a unit vector perpendicular to the sphere radially outwards is,

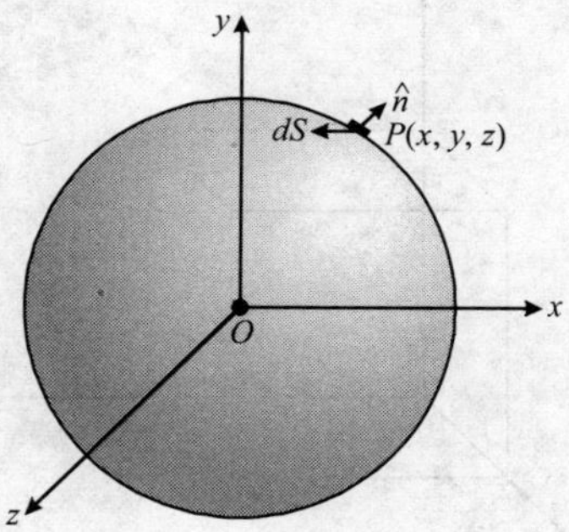

Figure 1.275

$$\hat{n} = \frac{x}{\sqrt{x^2+y^2+z^2}}\hat{i} + \frac{y}{\sqrt{x^2+y^2+z^2}}\hat{j} + \frac{z}{\sqrt{x^2+y^2+z^2}}\hat{k}$$

As $x^2 + y^2 + z^2 = R^2$, we use

$$\hat{n} = \frac{x}{R}\hat{i} + \frac{y}{R}\hat{j} + \frac{z}{R}\hat{k}$$

The electric flux passing through an elemental area dS at point P on the sphere is given as

$$d\phi_e = \vec{E}\cdot\hat{n}dS = \left\{\frac{ax^2}{R(x^2+y^2)} + \frac{ay^2}{R(x^2+y^2)}\right\}dS$$

$$\Rightarrow \qquad d\phi_e = \left(\frac{a}{R}\right)dS$$

Here we can note that $d\phi_e$ is independent of the co-ordinates x, y and z thus total electric flux passing through the sphere is given as

$$\phi_e = \int d\phi_e = \frac{a}{R}\int dS = \left(\frac{a}{R}\right)(4\pi R^2)$$

$$\Rightarrow \qquad \phi_e = 4\pi a R$$

From Gauss's law, we use

$$\phi_e = \frac{q_m}{\epsilon_0}$$

$$\Rightarrow \qquad (4\pi a R) = \frac{q_m}{\epsilon_0}$$

$$\Rightarrow \qquad q_m = 4\pi\epsilon_0 a R$$

 # Illustrative Example 1.78

Electric field in a region is given by $\vec{E} = -4x\hat{i} + 6y\hat{j}$. Find charge enclosed in the cube of side 1 m as shown in the diagram.

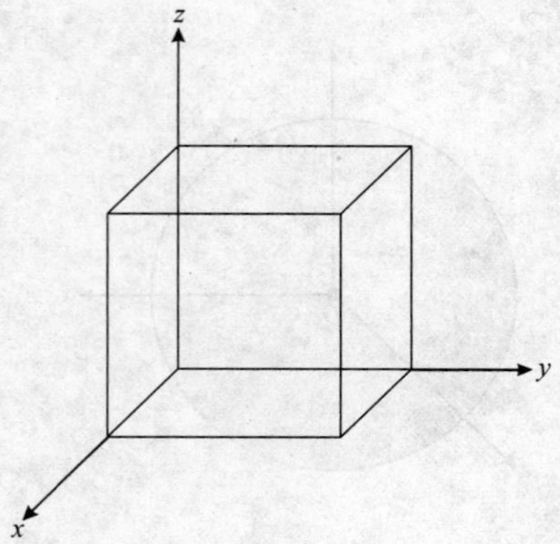

Figure 1.276

Solution

From the given function of electric field strength we can see that at plane $x = 0$ and the plane $y = 0$ $E = 0$ thus no flux will enter in the cube through these two planes but flux will come out of the cube from the planes $x = 1$ and $y = 1$ which is given as

$$\phi_{out} = [-4(1)(1)^2]_{y=1} + [6(1).(1)^2]_{x=1}$$

$$\Rightarrow \quad \phi_{out} = 2\text{V-m}$$

Using Gauss's law we can find the net enclosed charge in the cube. If q is the charge then we use for the cube surface

$$\phi_{out} = \frac{q}{\epsilon_0}$$

$$\Rightarrow \quad q = 2\epsilon_0$$

1.15 Concept of Solid Angle

Solid angle is a three dimensional angular region enclosed by the lateral surface of a cone at its vertex as shown in figure-1.277. Solid angle can also be defined as a three dimensional angle subtended by a spherical section at its centre of curvature. As shown in the figure-1.277 point A is the centre of curvature of a spherical section S of radius R which subtend a solid angle Ω (omega) at point A.

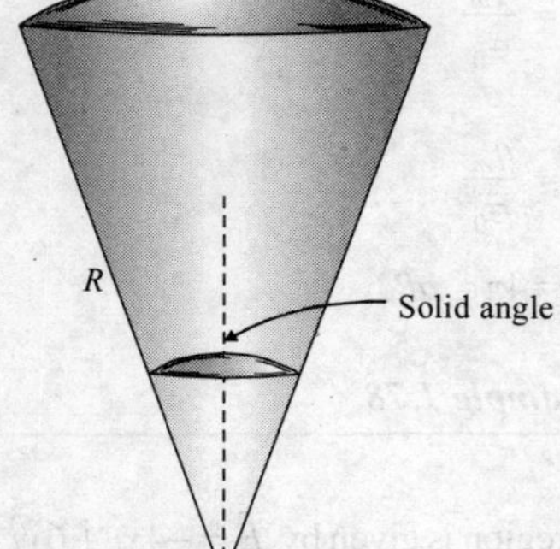

Figure 1.277

1.15.1 Calculation of Solid Angle of a Random Surface at a Given Point

Figure-1.278 shows a surface M. To find the solid angle subtended by this surface at point C, we join all the points of the periphery of the surface M to the point C by straight lines. This gives a conical surface with vertex at C.

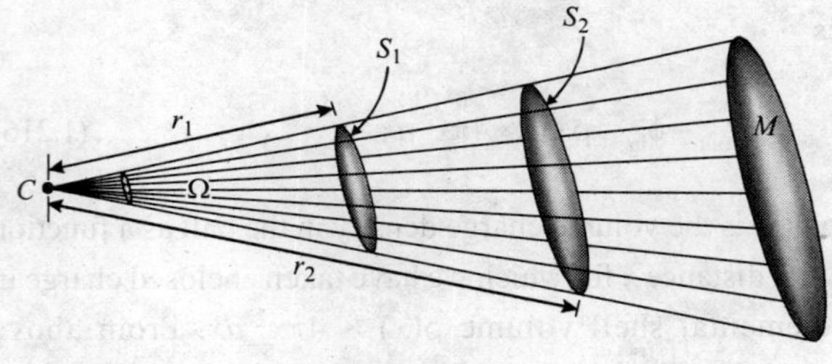

Figure 1.278

Now by taking centre at C, we draw several spherical sections on this cone of different radii as shown. The area of spherical section which is of radius r_1 is S_1 and the area of section having radius r_2 is S_2. If is found that the ratio of area of any spherical section interrupted by cone to the square of radius of that sphere is a constant and this constant is considered as solid angle. It is denoted by Greek letter Ω (omega)

In the above figure-1.278 the solid angle Ω can be given as

$$\Omega = \frac{S_1}{r_1^2} = \frac{S_2}{r_2^2}$$

Solid angle is a dimensionless physical quantity and its S.I. unit used is steradian.

One steradian is the solid angle subtended at the centre of sphere by the surface of the sphere having area equal to square of the radius of sphere.

1.15.2 Solid Angle of a Surface not Normal to Axis of Cone

Consider a small surface AB of area $\overline{dS}$ as shown in figure-1.279. Let PQ is the axis of cone formed by this surface at point P. In this case as surface AB is oriented at some tilt, PQ is not normal to the surface AB. In this situation the solid angle Ω subtended at point P can be given as

$$\Omega = \frac{dS\cos\theta}{r^2} \qquad \ldots(1.218)$$

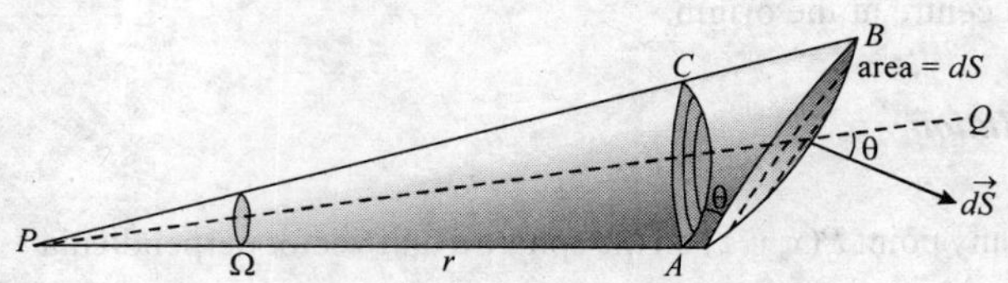

Figure 1.279

Here θ is the angle between surface area vector $\vec{S}$ and the axis of cone PQ as shown in figure-1.279. For small surfaces, solid angle can be obtained by equation-(1.218) for any point in the surrounding.

1.15.3 Relation in Half Angle of Cone and Solid Angle at Vertex

Consider a spherical section M of radius R, which subtend a half angle θ (radian) at the centre of curvature. To find the area of this section, we consider an elemental strip on this section of radius $R\sin\theta$ and angular width $d\theta$ as shown in figure-1.280. The surface area of this strip can be given as

$$dS = 2\pi R\sin\theta \times R d\theta$$

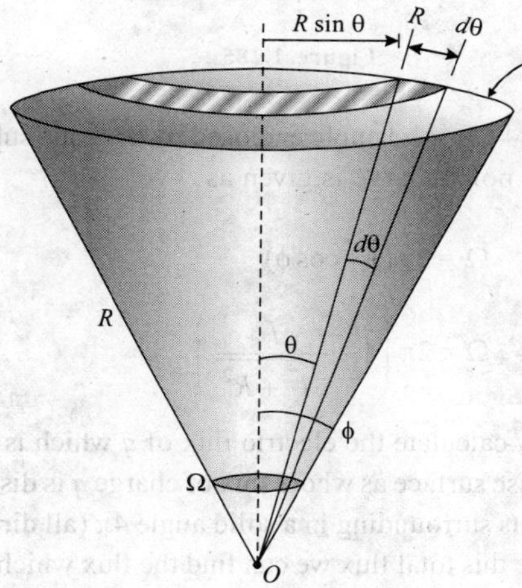

Figure 1.280

The total area of spherical section can be given by integrating the area of this elemental strip within limits from 0 to ϕ. Given as

$$S = \int dS = \int_0^{\phi} 2\pi R^2 \sin\theta \, d\theta$$

$$\Rightarrow \quad S = 2\pi R^2 [-\cos\theta]_0^{\phi}$$

$$\Rightarrow \quad S = 2\pi R^2 (1-\cos\phi) \qquad \ldots(1.219)$$

If solid angle subtended by this section at its centre O is Ω then its area can be given as

$$S = \Omega R^2$$

From equation-(1.219) we have

$$S = \Omega R^2 = 2\pi R^2 (1-\cos\phi)$$

$$\Rightarrow \quad \Omega = 2\pi(1-\cos\phi) \qquad \ldots(1.220)$$

Equation-(1.220) gives the relation in half angle of a cone ϕ and the solid angle enclosed by the lateral surface of cone at its vertex.

1.15.4 Solid Angle Enclosed by a Closed Surface

Consider the figure-1.281 shown. S is a spherical section of radius R which subtend a solid angle Ω at its centre of curvature O. The half angle of cone formed for this solid angle is ϕ.

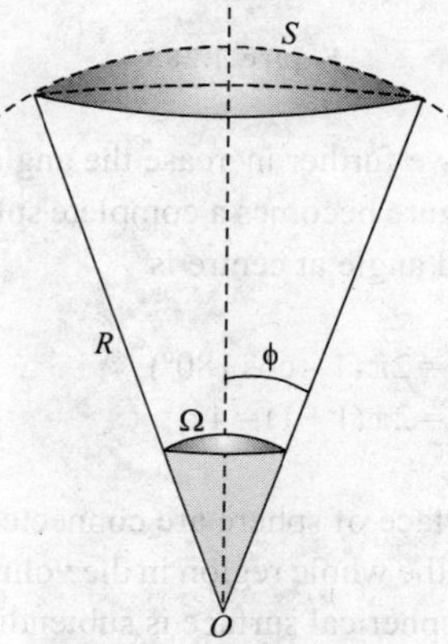

Figure 1.281

In above figure if we gradually increase the half angle of cone, size of surface S also increases. When ϕ becomes 90°, surface becomes a hemisphere as shown in figure-1.282.

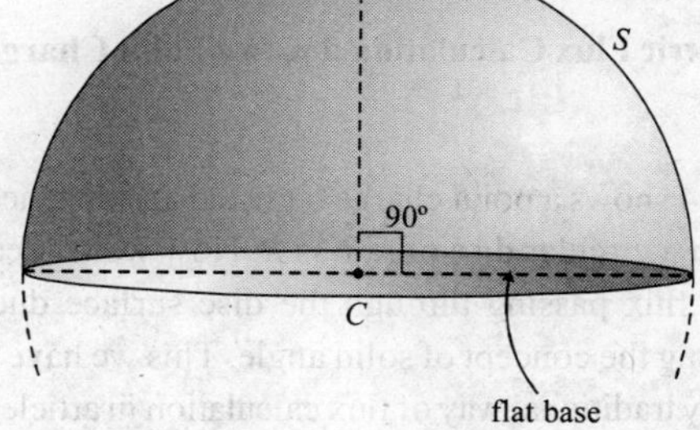

Figure 1.282

In this situation if we use equation-(1.220) to find the solid angle subtended by a hemispherical surface at its centre then it can be given as

$$\Omega = 2\pi(1-\cos 90°)$$

$$\Rightarrow \quad \Omega = 2\pi \text{ steradian}$$

Thus if we generalize our result, it can be stated that any surface having a flat base and closed on the curved side, subtend a solid angle 2π at every point of the base. In the surfaces shown in figure-1.283 we can say that the surfaces subtend a solid angle 2π at every point on their base.

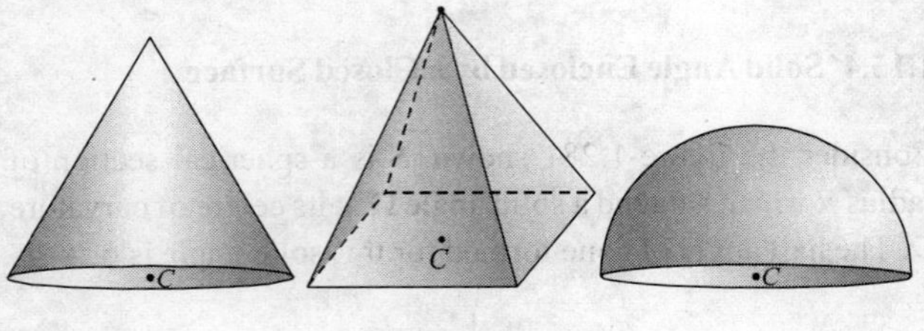

Figure 1.283

In figure-1.282 if we further increase the angle ϕ, at $\phi = 180°$, surface S in this figure becomes a complete sphere (closed). In this situation, solid angle at centre is

$$\Omega = 2\pi(1-\cos 180°)$$

$$\Rightarrow \quad \Omega = 2\pi(1+1) = 4\pi$$

If all points on surface of sphere are connected by a line at its center, it occupies the whole region in the volume of sphere for which we say the spherical surface is subtending a solid angle 4π at its center. Even the spherical surface subtend the same solid angle at every interior point inside it as the surface is completely surrounding all the interior points. Similarly to this case we can say that every closed surface subtend a solid angle 4π at every interior point.

We can also say that 4π is the solid angle of complete three dimensional surrounding space at every point in the space.

1.15.5 Electric Flux Calculation due to a Point Charge Using Solid Angle

Figure-1.284 shows a point charge q placed at a distance l from the centre of a circular disc of radius R. Now we will calculate the electric flux passing through the disc surface due to the charge q using the concept of solid angle. This we have already calculated by traditional way of flux calculation in article-1.13.7.

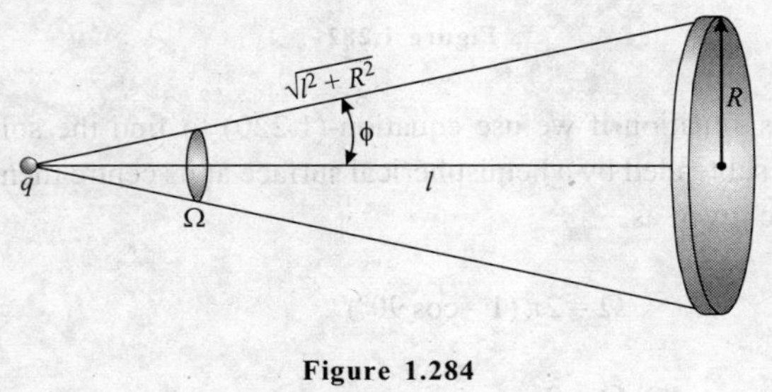

Figure 1.284

We have studied that from a point charge q total amount of electric flux originated is $\frac{q}{\epsilon_0}$ in all directions radially or we can also state that from a point charge q, $\frac{q}{\epsilon_0}$ flux is originated in 4π solid angle in surrounding of the charge q as shown in figure-1.285 below.

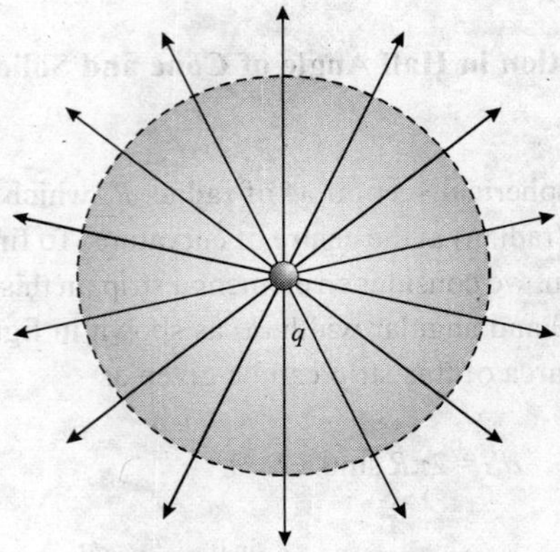

Figure 1.285

In figure-1.284 the solid angle enclosed by the cone subtended by disc at the point charge is given as

$$\Omega = 2\pi(1-\cos\phi)$$

$$\Rightarrow \quad \Omega = 2\pi\left(1-\frac{l}{\sqrt{l^2+R^2}}\right) \quad \ldots(1.221)$$

We can easily calculate the electric flux of q which is passing through the disc surface as whole flux of charge q is distributed uniformly in its surrounding in a solid angle 4π (all directions) thus out of the this total flux we can find the flux which goes in a solid angle given by the equation-(1.221) as

$$\phi_{disc} = \frac{q/\epsilon_0}{4\pi} \times \Omega$$

$$\Rightarrow \quad \phi_{disc} = \frac{q/\epsilon_0}{4\pi} \times 2\pi\left(1-\frac{l}{\sqrt{l^2+R^2}}\right)$$

$$\Rightarrow \quad \phi_{disc} = \frac{q}{2\epsilon_0}\left(1-\frac{l}{\sqrt{l^2+R^2}}\right) \quad \ldots(1.222)$$

Equation-(1.222) gives the flux of charge q which is passing through the disc as shown in figure-1.284 or it is the flux going through the conical region having solid angle Ω. This result can be used as a standard result in calculation of electric flux in many different situations due to a point charge which is being discussed in upcoming articles.

1.15.6 Electric Flux due to a Point Charge Through Random Surface

Consider the situation shown in figure-1.286. A point charge q is placed at a depth h below the centre of mouth of a vessel called "*Lota*" whose open end is circular having a radius R. We will calculate the electric flux through the lateral surface of this vessel. Using equation-(1.222) in previous article we can calculate the electric flux due to the point charge which comes out from the circular mouth of the vessel. Thus the electric flux through the lateral surface of vessel can be calculated by subtracting the flux coming out from the circular mouth of vessel from the total flux originated from the point charge q which is given as

$$\phi_{\text{lateral surface}} = \frac{q}{\epsilon_0} - \textit{flux through the mouth}$$

$$\Rightarrow \quad \phi_{\text{lateral surface}} = \frac{q}{\epsilon_0} - \frac{q}{2\epsilon_0}\left(1 - \frac{h}{\sqrt{h^2+R^2}}\right)$$

$$\Rightarrow \quad \phi_{\text{lateral surface}} = \frac{q}{2\epsilon_0}\left(1 + \frac{h}{\sqrt{h^2+R^2}}\right) \qquad \ldots(1.223)$$

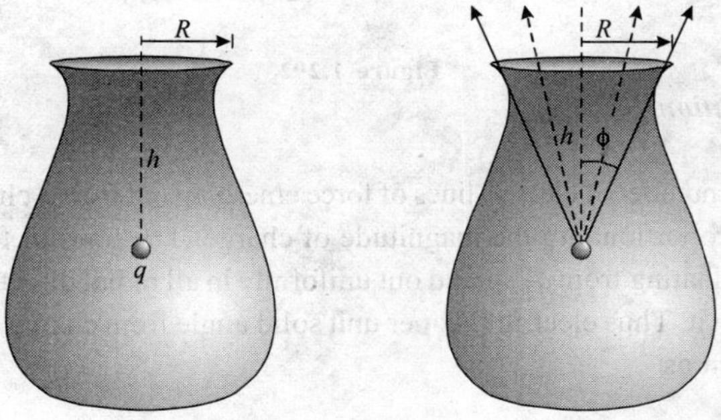

Figure 1.286

Illustrative Example 1.79

A point light source of 100 W is placed at a distance x from the centre of a hole of radius R in a sheet as shown in figure-1.287. Find the power passing through the hole in sheet.

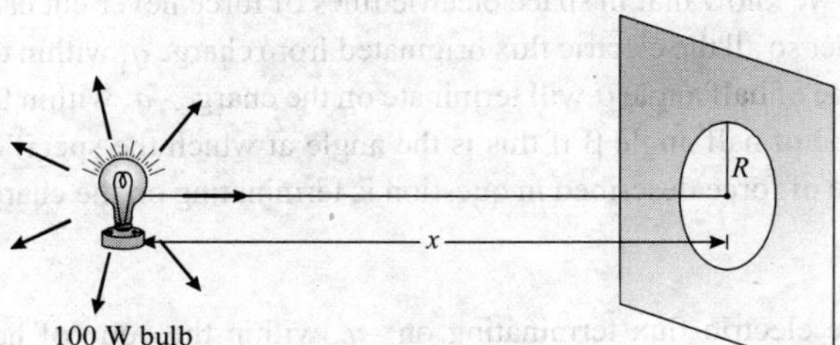

Figure 1.287

Solution

From figure, the solid angle of cone shown in figure-1.288 can be given as

$$\Omega = 2\pi(1 - \cos\theta)$$

$$\Rightarrow \quad \Omega = 2\pi\left(1 - \frac{x}{\sqrt{R^2+x^2}}\right)$$

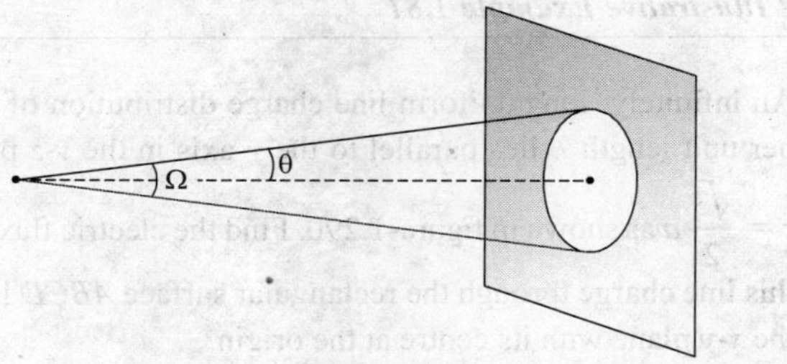

Figure 1.288

Power in hole = power given in solid angle Ω

$$P = \frac{100}{4\pi} \times \Omega$$

$$\Rightarrow \quad P = \frac{100}{4\pi} \times 2\pi\left(1 - \frac{x}{\sqrt{R^2+x^2}}\right)$$

$$\Rightarrow \quad P = 50\left(1 - \frac{x}{\sqrt{R^2+x^2}}\right) \text{ watt}$$

Illustrative Example 1.80

A point charge q is placed at the centre of the cubical box. Find, (a) total flux associated with the box (b) flux emerging through each face of the box (c) flux through shaded area of surface.

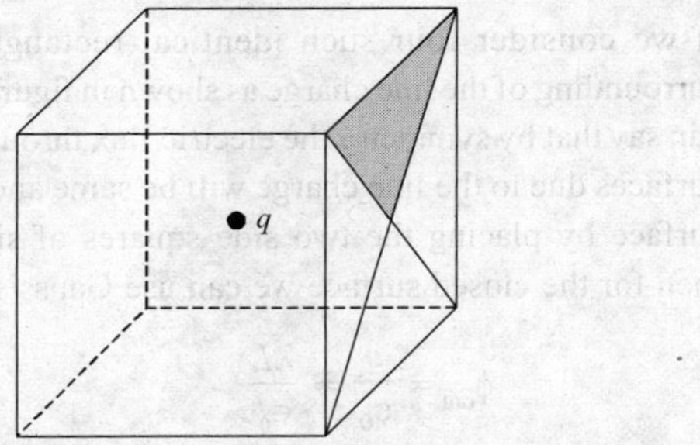

Figure 1.289

Solution

(a) Total flux coming out of the cubical box is given as

$$\phi_0 = \frac{q}{\epsilon_0}$$

(b) This total flux is emerging equally from each of the six face of the box. Thus flux through each face can be given as

$$\phi = \frac{q}{6\epsilon_0}$$

(c) The flux through shaded portion would be one fourth of the flux through each face as through all the four triangular portions flux would be same due to symmetry, thus we have

$$\phi' = \frac{\phi}{4} = \frac{q}{24\epsilon_0}.$$

Illustrative Example 1.81

An infinitely long uniform line charge distribution of charge per unit length λ lies parallel to the y-axis in the y-z plane at $z = \frac{\sqrt{3}}{2}a$ as shown in figure-1.290. Find the electric flux due to this line charge through the rectangular surface $ABCD$ lying in the x-y plane with its centre at the origin.

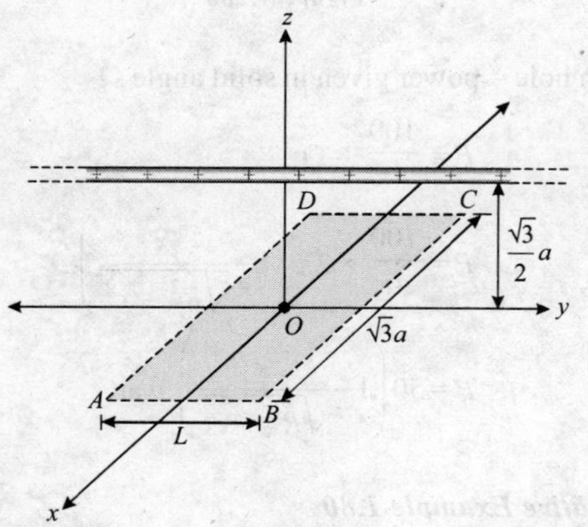

Figure 1.290

Solution

If we consider four such identical rectangular surface in surrounding of the line charge as shown in figure-1.291 then we can say that by symmetry the electric flux through all these four surfaces due to the line charge will be same and if we close the surface by placing the two side squares of side length $\sqrt{3}a$ then for the closed surface we can use Gauss's law as

$$\phi_{out} = \frac{q}{\varepsilon_0} = \frac{\lambda L}{\epsilon_0} \quad \ldots(1.224)$$

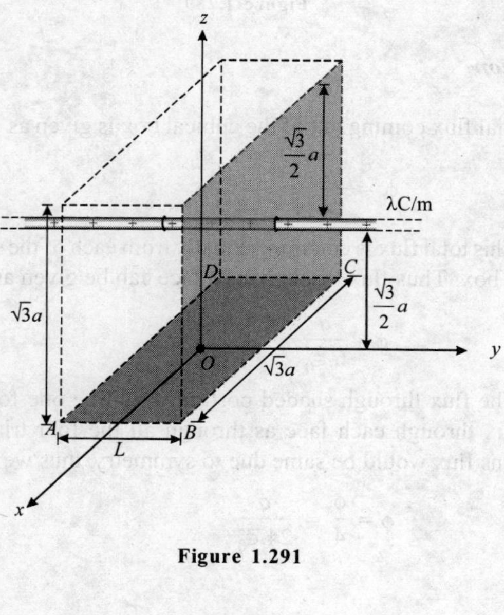

Figure 1.291

As the total flux is symmetrically coming out from the four rectangular surfaces, the flux through the surface $ABCD$ is given as

$$\phi_{ABCD} = \frac{\phi_{out}}{4} = \frac{\lambda L}{4\epsilon_0}$$

Illustrative Example 1.82

Two charges $+q_1$ and $-q_2$ are placed at points A and B respectively. A line of force originates from the charge q_1 at an angle α with the line AB. Find at what angle this line will be terminating at the charge $-q_2$?

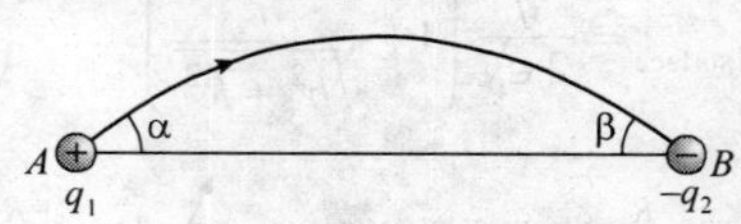

Figure 1.292

Solution

The number of electric lines of force emerging out from a charge is proportional to the magnitude of charge. The lines of force originating from q_1 spread out uniformly in all radial directions from it. Thus electric flux per unit solid angle from charge q_1 is given as

$$\phi_0 = \frac{q_1}{4\pi\epsilon_0}$$

The electric flux through cone of half angle α as shown in figure-1.293 is given as

$$\phi_\alpha = \frac{q_1}{4\pi\epsilon_0} \times 2\pi(1-\cos\alpha) \quad \ldots(1.225)$$

As we know that in space electric lines of force never cut each other so all the electric flux originated from charge q_1 within the cone of half angle α will terminate on the charge $-q_2$ within the cone of half angle β if this is the angle at which the specified line of force described in question is terminating on the charge $-q_2$.

The electric flux terminating on $-q_2$ within the cone of half angle β is given as

$$\phi_\beta = \frac{q_2}{4\pi\epsilon_0} \times 2\pi(1-\cos\beta) \quad \ldots(1.226)$$

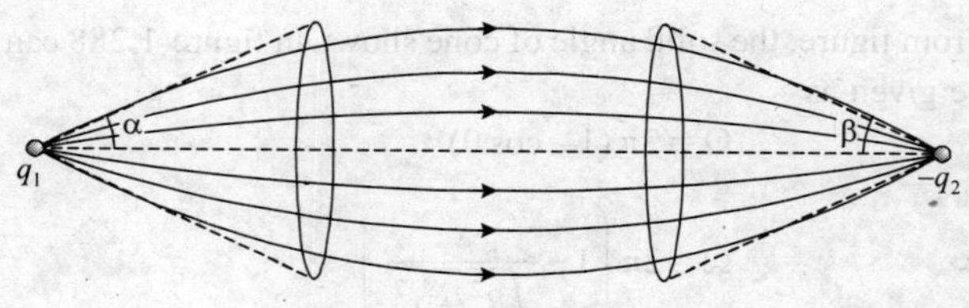

Figure 1.293

As the electric flux originating from q_1 as given in equation-(1.225) is equal to the electric flux terminating on q_2 as given by equation-(1.226), we have

$$\frac{q_1}{4\pi\epsilon_0}\times 2\pi(1-\cos\alpha)=\frac{q_2}{4\pi\epsilon_0}\times 2\pi(1-\cos\beta)$$

$$\Rightarrow \quad \frac{q_1}{2}2\sin^2\frac{\alpha}{2}=\frac{q_2}{2}2\sin^2\frac{\beta}{2}$$

$$\Rightarrow \quad \sin\frac{\beta}{2}=\sqrt{\frac{q_1}{q_2}}\sin\frac{\alpha}{2}$$

$$\Rightarrow \quad \beta=2\sin^{-1}\left[\sqrt{\frac{q_1}{q_2}}\sin\frac{\alpha}{2}\right]$$

Illustrative Example 1.83

A point charge q is placed on the top a cone of semi vertex angle θ. Show what the electric flux through the base of the cone is given as

$$\phi_{base}=\frac{q(1-\cos\theta)}{2\varepsilon_0}$$

Solution

The total flux originated from the point charge is given as

$$\phi=\frac{q}{\epsilon_0}$$

Above flux is emerged out from the point charge uniformly in the radial direction in total solid angle 4π of the space surrounding the point charge. Thus the flux emerging out per unit solid angle from the point charge is given as

$$\phi_0=\frac{q}{4\pi\epsilon_0}$$

The solid angle subtended by the base of cone at its vertex is given as

$$\Omega=2\pi(1-\cos\theta)$$

Thus the electric flux through the base of cone is given as

$$\phi_{base}=\frac{q}{4\pi\epsilon_0}\times\Omega$$

$$\Rightarrow \quad \phi_{base}=\frac{q}{4\pi\epsilon_0}\times 2\pi(1-\cos\theta)=\frac{q}{2\epsilon_0}(1-\cos\theta)$$

Web Reference at www.physicsgalaxy.com

Age Group - Grade 11 & 12 | Age 17-19 Years

Section - ELECTROSTATICS

Topic - Electric Lines & Gauss's Law

Module Number - 1 to 24

Practice Exercise 1.8

(i) Find flux through the hemispherical cup due to the charge q placed as shown in figure-1.294.

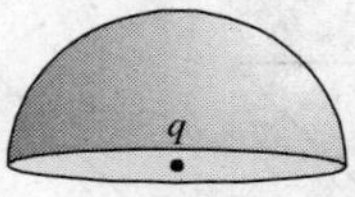

Figure 1.294

$[\frac{q}{2\epsilon_0}]$

(ii) Two point charges $+q$ and $-q$ are separated by a distance $2l$. Find the flux of the electric field strength vector across a circle of radius R located symmetrically in a plane normal to line joining the charges.

$[\frac{ql}{\epsilon_0}\left(\frac{1}{l}-\frac{1}{\sqrt{R^2+l^2}}\right)]$

(iii) A charge q_0 is distributed uniformly on a ring of radius R. A sphere of equal radius R is constructed with its centre on the circumference of the ring. Find the electric flux through the surface of the sphere.

$[\frac{q_0}{3\varepsilon_0}]$

(iv) An electric field given by $\vec{E}=4\hat{i}+3(y^2+2)\hat{j}$ pierces a gaussian cube of side 1 m placed at origin such that one of its corners is at origin and rest of sides are along positive side of coordinate axis. Find the magnitude of net charge enclosed within the cube.

$[3\epsilon_0]$

(v) A point charge q is located on the axis of a disc of radius R at a distance b from the plane of the disc as shown in figure-1.295. What should be the radius of the disc if one-fourth of the total electric flux from the charge passes through the disc.

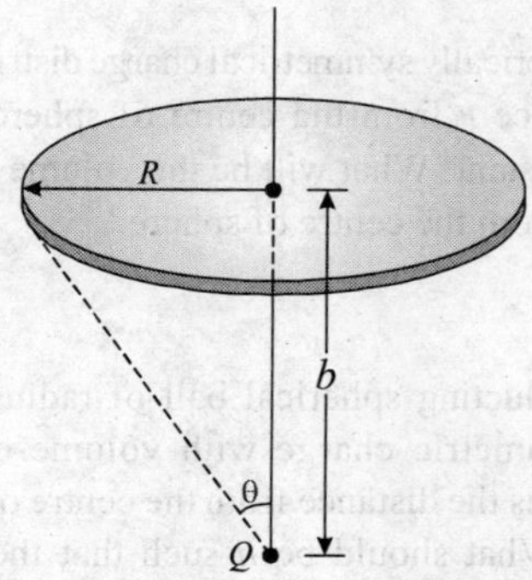

Figure 1.295

$[\sqrt{3}b]$

(vi) Find the electric flux through a cubical surface due to a point charge q placed (a) at centre of one face (b) corner of the cubical box as shown in figures-1.296 below, in case (b) find the flux through each face of the cube.

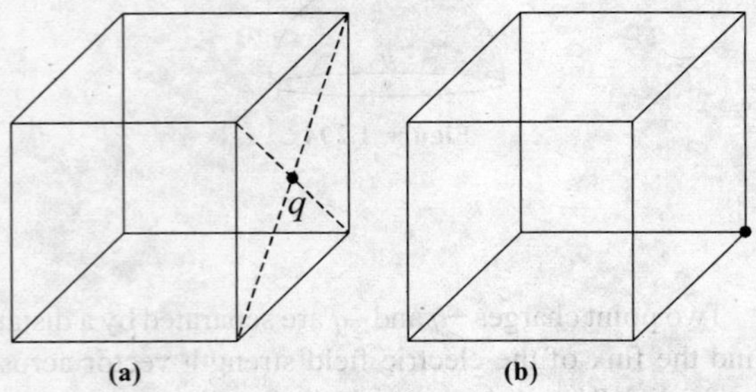

Figure 1.296

$[\frac{q}{2\epsilon_0}, \frac{q}{8\epsilon_0}, \frac{q}{24\epsilon_0}, 0]$

(vii) A cube has sides of length $L = 0.2$ m. It is placed with one corner at the origin as shown in figure-1.297. The electric field is uniform and given by $\vec{E} = (2.5\,\hat{i} - 4.2\,\hat{j})$ N/C. Find the electric flux through the entire cube.

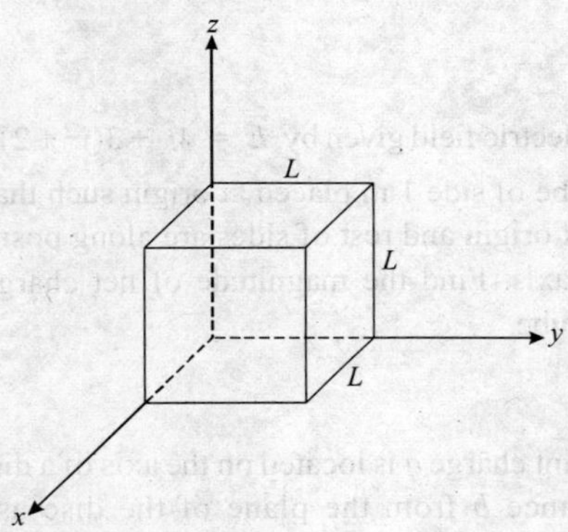

Figure 1.297

[Zero]

(viii) For a spherically symmetrical charge distribution, electric field at a distance r from the centre of sphere is $\vec{E} = kr^7\hat{r}$, where k is a constant. What will be the volume charge density at a distance r from the centre of sphere?

$[9k\varepsilon_0 r^6]$

(ix) A non-conducting spherical ball of radius R contains a spherically symmetric charge with volume charge density $\rho = kr^n$, where r is the distance from the centre of the ball and n is a constant. What should be n such that the electric field inside the ball is directly proportional to square of distance from the centre?

[1]

(x) An infinite, uniformly charged sheet with surface charge density σ cuts through a spherical Gaussian surface of radius R at a distance x from its center, as shown in the figure-1.298. The electric flux ϕ through the Gaussian surface is :

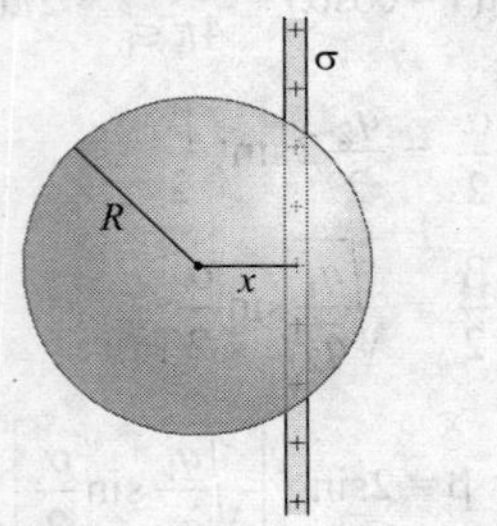

Figure 1.298

$[\frac{\pi(R^2 - x^2)\sigma}{\varepsilon_0}]$

1.16 Electric Pressure

When a charged surface is placed in an electric field then due to the electric force on the surface charges the surface experiences a pressure which we term electric pressure. If the surface is made up of a flexible material then surface may get deshaped due to electric pressure. Even in a surface charged single body surface charges on one part of body may exert electric pressure on other parts of body due to mutual repulsion.

1.16.1 Electric Pressure on in a Charged Metal body

We have already studied when some charge is given to a metal body it will spread on the outer surface of the body due to mutual repulsion in the charge. As on surface every charge experiences an outward repulsive force due to repulsion by remaining charges on other parts of body, every part of body experiences an outward pressure. We will calculate this electric pressure on surface of a charged metal body.

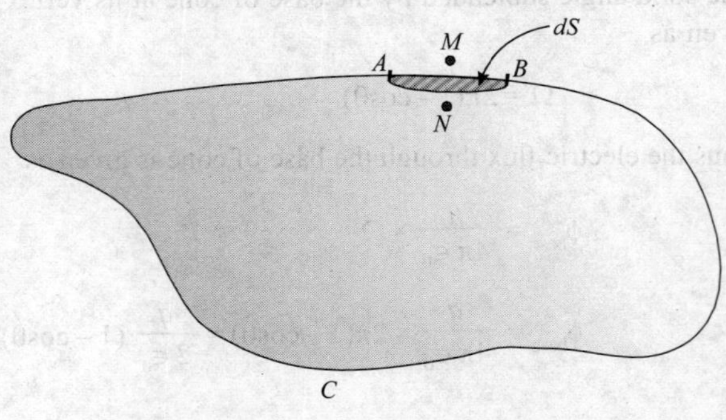

Figure 1.299

Figure-1.299 shows a charged metal body. On this body surface we consider a small segment AB of area dS as shown. If σ be the surface charge density on AB, charge on it is given as

$$dq = \sigma\, dS$$

Now we consider two points M and N just outside and inside of section AB as shown in the figure. At the two points if E_1 is the electric field strength due to charges only on section AB then directions of the electric fields at points M and N will be away from AB as charge is considered positive and this is as shown in figure-1.300(a). If we remove the charges from section AB from the metal body then due to remaining body ACB, if we consider E_2 is the electric field strength at point M and N, then the direction of E_2 will be same at M and N as both points are in close vicinity which is as shown in figure-1.300(b).

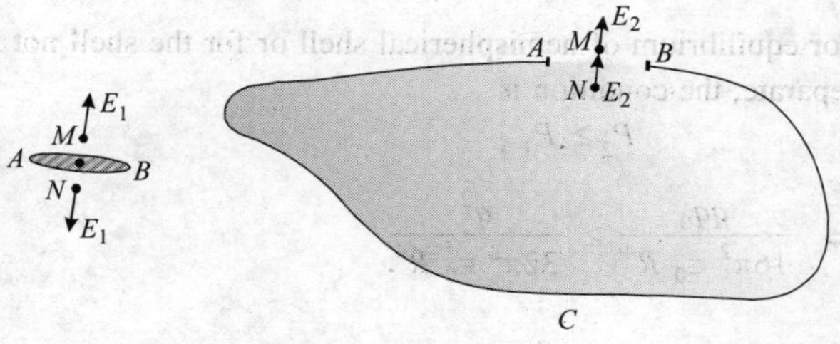

Figure 1.300

At point M, the electric field strength is given by equation-(1.211) as explained in article-1.14.10 and at point N the electric field must be zero as it is inside the metal body. The net electric field strengths at points M and N due to complete body can also be obtained by vector sum of the electric fields at these points due to both parts of body AB and ACB which are given as

$$E_M = E_1 + E_2 = \frac{\sigma}{\epsilon_0} \quad \ldots(1.227)$$

and $$E_N = E_1 - E_2 = 0 \quad \ldots(1.228)$$

Solving equations-(1.236) and (1.237) we get

$$E_1 = E_2$$

$$\Rightarrow \quad E_1 = E_2 = \frac{\sigma}{2\epsilon_0} \quad \ldots(1.229)$$

Thus electric field at the location of section AB due to remaining body ACB is $\frac{\sigma}{2\epsilon_0}$, using which we can find the outward force on section AB, due to the rest of the body ACB as

$$dF = dq\, E_2$$

$$\Rightarrow \quad dF = \sigma\, dS \times \frac{\sigma}{2\epsilon_0}$$

Thus pressure experienced by the section AB can be given as

$$P_e = \frac{dF}{dS} = \frac{\sigma^2}{2\epsilon_0} \quad \ldots(1.230)$$

As net electric field outside the surface is given as

$$E_{\text{net at } M} = \frac{\sigma}{\epsilon_0}$$

In equation-(1.230), we can substitute the value of σ which gives

$$P_e = \frac{(\epsilon_0 E_{net})^2}{2\epsilon_0}$$

$$P_e = \frac{1}{2}\epsilon_0 E_{\text{net}}^2 \quad \ldots(1.231)$$

For a charged metal body at any point of its surface the electric pressure is given by equation-(1.230) or (1.231). As discussed this pressure is due to the charges present on other parts of body. Equation-(1.230) gives the electric pressure in terms of the surface charge density of the body at the local point on surface and equation-(1.231) gives the electric pressure in terms of the net electric field just outside the surface point of the body where it is giving electric pressure.

Another important thing to be noted in above analysis is that from equation-(1.229) we can see that the electric field strength at any point just outside a charged metal body surface half is contributed by the section just below the point and remaining half is due to the rest of the body.

1.16.2 Electric Pressure on a Charged Surface due to External Electric Field

Figure-1.301 shows a surface uniformly charged with charge density σ C/m^2. If we consider a small section AB on the surface area dS, the charge on AB is given as

$$dq = \sigma\, dS$$

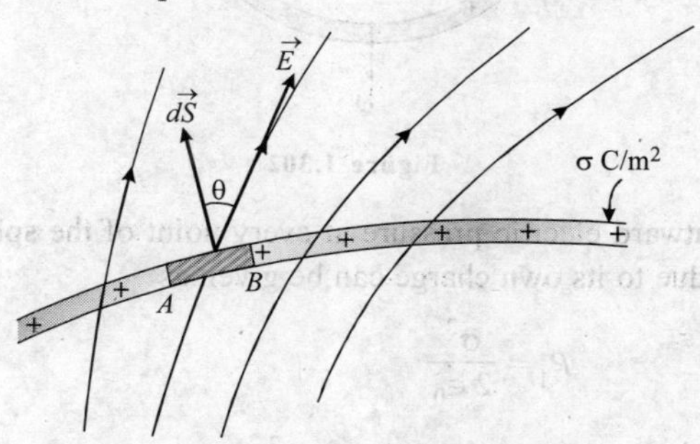

Figure 1.301

As shown in figure-1.301 we consider the strength of external electric field on the location of section AB is E. It has two components, one component parallel to the surface and other perpendicular to the surface, given as

$$E_\perp = E\cos\theta$$

$$E_\parallel = E\sin\theta$$

In this situation due to the component $E_{\parallel}$, the force on surface is tangential which stretches the surface and due to the component $E_{\perp}$, surface experiences an outward pressure. The outward force on AB due to external electric field is

$$dF = dq\, E_{\perp}$$

$$\Rightarrow \quad dF = \sigma E_{\perp}\, dS$$

Thus outward electric pressure can be given as

$$P_e = \frac{dF}{ds} = \sigma E_{\perp}$$

1.16.3 Equilibrium of Hemispherical Shells under Electric Pressure

Figure-1.302 shows a thin spherical shell of radius R having uniformly distributed charge q. At the centre of shell a negative point charge $-q_0$ is placed. If the shell is cut in two identical hemispherical portions by a diametrical section XY as shown, due to mutual repulsion the two hemispherical parts tend to move away from each other but due to the attraction of $-q_0$, they may remain in equilibrium. Let us find the condition of equilibrium of these hemispherical shells.

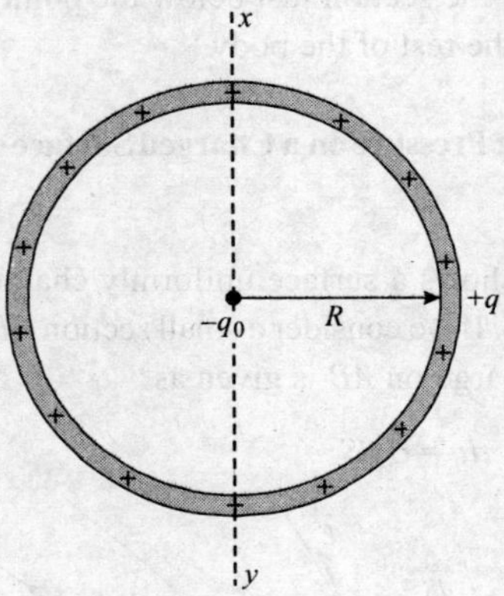

Figure 1.302

The outward electric pressure at every point of the spherical shells due to its own charge can be given as

$$P_1 = \frac{\sigma^2}{2\epsilon_0}$$

$$\Rightarrow \quad P_1 = \frac{1}{2\epsilon_0}\left(\frac{q}{4\pi R^2}\right)^2$$

$$\Rightarrow \quad P_1 = \frac{q^2}{32\pi^2 \epsilon_0 R^4}$$

Due to charge $-q_0$, the electric field on the surface of shell is given as

$$E = \frac{Kq_0}{R^2}$$

This electric field pulls every point of the shell in inward direction thus inward pressure on the surface of shell due to this negative point charge at centre is

$$P_2 = \sigma E$$

$$\Rightarrow \quad P_2 = \left(\frac{q}{4\pi R^2}\right)\left(\frac{Kq_0}{R^2}\right)$$

$$\Rightarrow \quad P_2 = \frac{qq_0}{16\pi^2 \epsilon_0 R^4}$$

For equilibrium of hemispherical shell or for the shell not to separate, the condition is

$$P_2 \geq P_1$$

$$\Rightarrow \quad \frac{qq_0}{16\pi^2 \epsilon_0 R^4} \geq \frac{q^2}{32\pi^2 \epsilon_0 R^4}$$

$$\Rightarrow \quad q_0 \geq \frac{q}{2}$$

In this case the net outward electric pressure on shells is balanced by the inward electric pressure due to the point charge situated at center is giving us the condition for shells not to separate by their mutual repulsion. Similarly there are many such situations in which the concept of electric pressure is used. In upcoming illustrations we will discuss different such situations where electric pressure is used in analysis.

 # Illustrative Example 1.84

A soap bubble of radius r is given a charge q uniformly on its surface. As a result of which the radius of soap bubble slightly increases. If surface tension of soap solution is T, find the increase in radius of bubble due to supply of charge q.

Solution

We know that the excess pressure in a soap bubble of radius r due to surface tension T is given by

$$\Delta P = \frac{4T}{r}$$

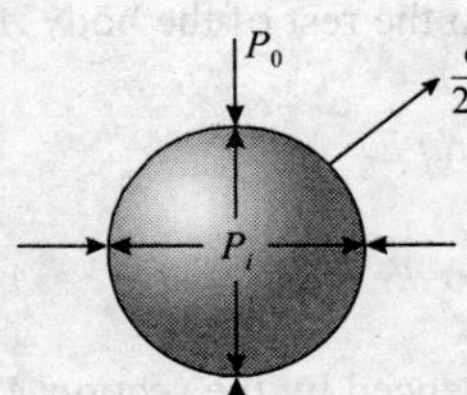

Figure 1.303

If now bubble is given a charge q, then the outward electrical pressure change due to this is given as

$$dP_e = \frac{\sigma^2}{2\epsilon_0} = \frac{1}{2\epsilon_0}\left(\frac{q}{4\pi r^2}\right)^2 = \frac{q^2}{32\pi^2\epsilon_0 r^4}$$

For the equilibrium of the bubble, we have

$$\left(P_i + \frac{\sigma^2}{2\epsilon_0}\right) - P_{atm} = \frac{4T}{r}$$

$$\Rightarrow \quad P_i - P_{atm} = \frac{4T}{r} - \frac{\sigma^2}{2\epsilon_0} = \frac{4T}{r} - \frac{q^2}{32\pi^2\epsilon_0 r^4} \quad \ldots(1.232)$$

Thus decrease in pressure due to charge on the bubble

$$dP_e = -\frac{q^2}{32\pi^2\epsilon_0 r^4} \quad \ldots(1.233)$$

At constant temperature for air inside the bubble, we can use

$$PV = \text{constant}$$

$$\Rightarrow \quad P \times \frac{4}{3}\pi r^3 = \text{constant}$$

$$\Rightarrow \quad Pr^3 = \text{constant} \quad \ldots(1.234)$$

Differentiating equation-(1.234), we get

$$\frac{dP}{P} = -\frac{3dr}{r}$$

$$\Rightarrow \quad dr = \frac{r}{3}\left(\frac{-dP}{P}\right) \quad \ldots(1.235)$$

In above expression dP is the decrease in inside pressure due to supply of charge because of which the radius of bubble increases by dr. Further we have

$$dr = \frac{r}{3} \times \left(\frac{q^2}{32\pi^2\epsilon_0 r^4}\right)\frac{1}{P}$$

$$\Rightarrow \quad dr = \frac{q^2}{96\pi^2\epsilon_0 r^3 P} \quad \ldots(1.236)$$

In above expression P is the initial pressure inside the soap bubble before supply of charge which is given as

$$P = P_i = P_{atm} + \frac{4T}{r}$$

$$\Rightarrow \quad dr = \frac{q^2}{96\pi^2\epsilon_0 r^2 (rP_{atm} + 4T)}$$

Illustrative Example 1.85

A soap bubble of radius r and surface tension T is given a potential V. Show that the new radius R of the bubble is related with the initial radius by the equation

$$P(R^3 - r^3) + 4T(R^2 - r^2) = \frac{\epsilon_0 V^2 R}{2}$$

where P is the atmospheric pressure.

Solution

If P_1 is the initial pressure inside the bubble, then for equilibrium of bubble we have

$$P_1 = P + \frac{4T}{r},$$

Initial volume of the bubble is $V_1 = \frac{4}{3}\pi r^3$

When bubble is charged, its electric field becomes $E = \frac{V}{R}$

Outward pressure due to charging is given as

$$P_e = \frac{1}{2}\epsilon_0 E^2$$

If P_2 is the final pressure inside the bubble then for equilibrium of bubble we have

$$P_2 = P + \left(\frac{4T}{R} - \frac{1}{2}\epsilon_0 E^2\right),$$

Final volume of bubble is $V_2 = \frac{4}{3}\pi R^3$

Using Boyle's law for inside air of bubble, we have

$$P_1 V_1 = P_2 V_2$$

Substituting the values in above equations, we get

$$P(R^3 - r^3) + 4t(R^2 - r^2) = \frac{\epsilon_0 V^2 R}{2}$$

Illustrative Example 1.86

The minimum strength of a uniform electric field which can tear a conducting uncharged thin-walled sphere into two parts is known to be E_0. Determine the minimum electric field strength E_1 required to tear the sphere of twice as large radius if the thickness of its walls is the same as in the former case.

Solution

If $\pm\sigma$ is the induced surface charge density on the two halves of the sphere then force on these halves in opposite directions due to the external electric field is given as

$$F \propto (\sigma \cdot \pi R^2)E \quad \ldots(1.237)$$

In above expression proportionality sign is used because induced surface charge density will not be uniform. As the surface charge density is induced due to the external electric field it will be proportional to the magnitude of electric field which will be analyzed in upcoming section of conductors. Thus from equation-(1.237) we have

$$F \propto R^2E^2$$

$$F = kR^2E^2, \quad \ldots(1.238)$$

In above equation k is a proportionality constant. If S be the rupturing stress of the material then to tear the two halves of the shell at the cross section where the two halves are attached, the stress due to the above force is given as

$$\frac{F}{2\pi Rt} \geq S$$

$$\Rightarrow \quad E^2R \geq \text{Constant}$$

For the sphere of twice the radius, we use

$$E_0^2R = E_1^2(2R),$$

$$\Rightarrow \quad E_1 = \frac{E_0}{\sqrt{2}}$$

1.17 Distribution and Induction of Charges on Cavity Surfaces in Conductors

In articles-1.6 and 1.10 we've already discussed about the charge distribution and induction of charges in metal bodies. Induction of charges take place till the whole metal body becomes equipotential and at every interior point of the body net electric field becomes zero. So always remember that there can never be any electric field inside a conductor due to static charges and after final distribution of charges on any metal body no electric line of force can enter in it.

Consider a point charge $+q$ inside a spherical cavity at centre within a metal body shown in figure-1.304. The total electric flux originated by $+q$ is $\frac{q}{\epsilon_0}$. Due to this charge at the inner surface of cavity a charge $-q$ is induced on which this complete electric flux will terminate and no electric lines of force enters into the metal body. At point A inside the metal body as shown we know that net electric field is zero thus the electric field at A due to the point charge $+q$ is nullified by the electric field due to the negative induced charges on the inner surface of cavity and the positive charge induced on outer surface is automatically distributed on the surface in such a way that it does not produce any electric field within the metal body.

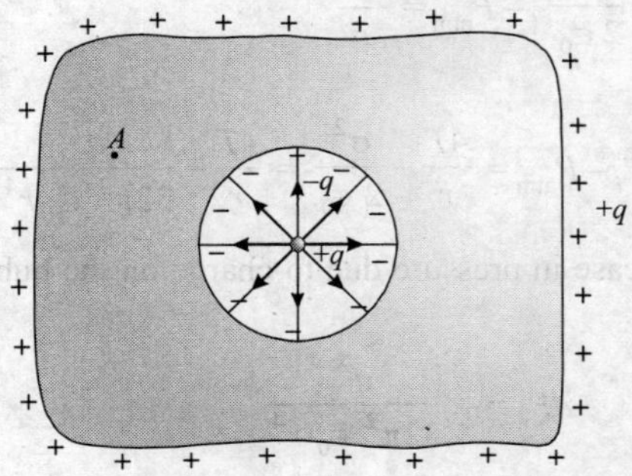

Figure 1.304

From the above analysis we can conclude some points about the induction and distribution of charges on cavity surface and that on conductor when a charge is placed inside the cavity of a metal body. Below listed points are always valid for such cases.

(i) Whenever a charge is placed inside a metal cavity, an equal and opposite charge is induced on the inner surface of cavity.

(ii) A similar charge is induced on the outer surface of body with surface charge density inversely proportional to radius of curvature of body to have electric field inside the metal body zero due to this charge on outer surface of conductor.

(iii) When the charge inside cavity is displaced, the induced charge distribution on inner surface of body changes in such a way that its centre of charge can be assumed to be at the point charge so as to nullify the electric field in region outside cavity surface.

(iv) Due to movement in the point charge inside the body. The charge distribution on outer surface of body does not change as shown in figure-1.305.

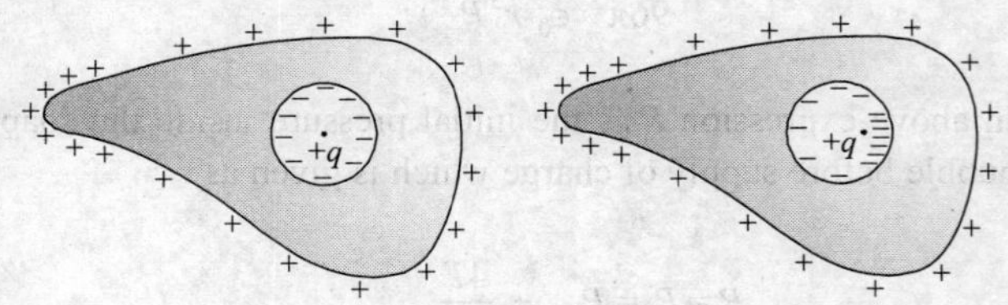

Figure 1.305

(v) If another charge is brought close to the body from outside, it will only affect the outer distribution of charges and does not produce any effect on the charge distribution inside the cavity as shown in figure-1.306. Outer charge distribution of conductor changes in such a way that inside the body of conductor at every point the electric field due to external charge is nullified by the electric field due to the outer surface charge distribution.

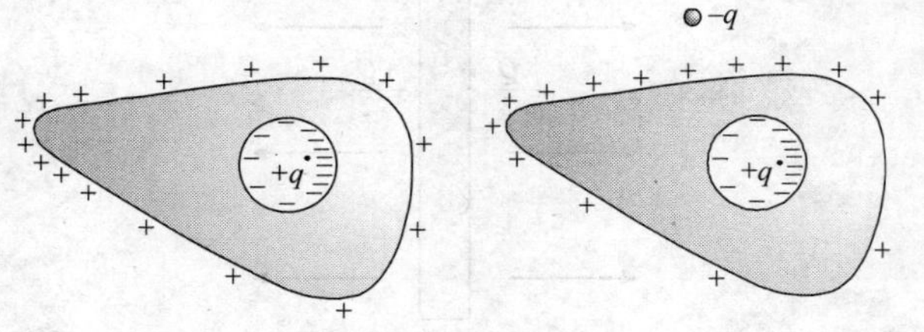

Figure 1.306

In next article we will discuss an illustration to understand this concept of charge induction and distribution on conducting surface.

1.17.1 Electric Field and Potential due to Induced Charges on a sphere

Consider the situation shown in figure-1.307. A metal sphere of radius R is placed at a distance r from the point charge $+q$. There is a point M in the sphere at a distance x from the point charge $+q$. In this situation we will calculate the electric field strength and electric potential at point M due to the induced charges on the surface of sphere.

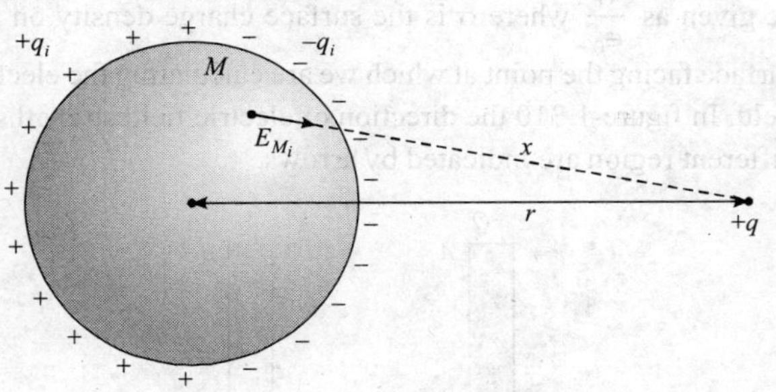

Figure 1.307

We know that inside a metal body net electric field strength is always zero. Thus at point M electric field due to induced charges balances the electric field of the point charge $+q$. The electric field strength at point M due to external point charge $+q$ is given as

$$E_M = \frac{Kq}{x^2} \quad \dots(1.239)$$

The direction of above electric field strength is directed away from the point charge $+q$. To have net zero electric field at point M as this is a point inside metal body, the electric field strength due to induced charges at M must be exactly equal to the electric field as given in equation-(1.239) and in opposite direction. Thus due to induced charges the electric field at point M is given as

$$E_{Mi} = \frac{Kq}{x^2} \quad \dots(1.240)$$

The direction of net electric field at point M due to induced charges must be directly opposite to that due to electric field at M produced by the external point charge $+q$, the direction of E_{Mi} is shown in figure-1.307.

As inside the sphere at every point $E = 0$ and due to this the whole region is equipotential. If we find potential at centre of sphere, it is only due to the charge $+q$ as due to induced charges, potential at centre it will be zero because equal positive and negative induced charges are located equidistant from the center of sphere. Thus net potential at the centre of sphere can be given as

$$V_C = \frac{Kq}{r}$$

As whole sphere is equipotential, at point M, the potential must be equal to that at point C, but at M potential due to induced charges potential will be non-zero as all induced charges are not equidistant from point M. Thus net potential at point M is the sum of potential due to point charge $+q$ and that due to induced charges which can be given as

$$V_M = \frac{Kq}{r} = \frac{Kq}{x} + V_i \quad \dots(1.241)$$

In above equation-(1.241), V_i is the potential due to induced charges at M. This gives the value of V_i as

$$V_i = \frac{Kq}{r} - \frac{Kq}{x} \quad \dots(1.242)$$

In above analysis we've calculated the electric field strength and potential inside a charged conducting body due to induced charges distribution on the outer surface of the body.

The calculation of electric field inside a conductor by induced charges can always be done by using the fact that inside a conductor due to static charges net electric field at every point is always zero. The calculation of electric potential due to induced charges is done by using the fact that whole metal body remain equipotential in state of static charges on it.

We will have another similar illustration with a cavity in a conducting sphere. Consider the situation shown in figure-1.308. Inside a conducting spherical shell of inner radius R_1 and outer radius R_2, a point charge $+q$ is placed at a distance x from the centre as shown. If we calculate the net electric potential at centre due to this system then it can be given as

$$V_C = \frac{Kq}{r} - \frac{Kq}{R_1} + \frac{Kq}{R_2} \quad \dots(1.243)$$

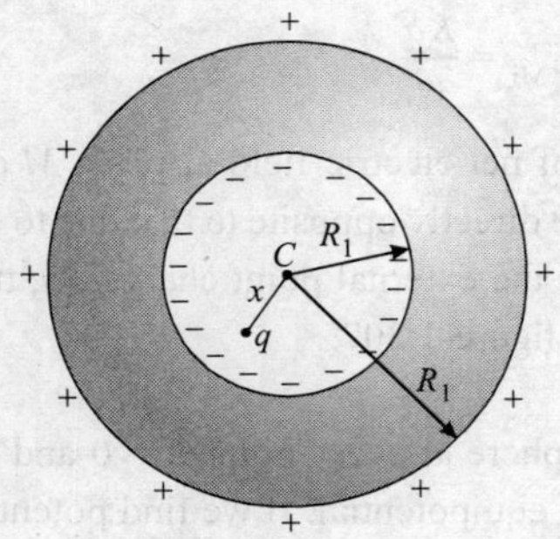

Figure 1.308

In above equation-(1.243) first term is the potential at center due to the point charge $+q$. As discussed in previous article, this charge induces equal and opposite charge on inner surface of the cavity and same charge on the outer surface of the sphere as shown. Thus second term in equation-(1.243) is the potential at C due to the charge $-q$ which is induced on the inner surface of the cavity and third term is the potential at C due to the charge $+q$ induced on the outer surface of the sphere.

If we calculate the net electric field at C then due to outer induced charges it is zero as outer surface charges $+q$ are uniformly distributed on it and due to point charge $+q$ it can be directly given by using the result of a point charge. But due to the charge $-q$ induced on the inner surface of cavity, directly the electric field strength cannot be calculated because charge distribution is not uniform so for this first we need to determine the charge distribution function on inner surface of cavity then using that we can calculate the electric field. This is a complex and long method which is not in scope here so we are not discussing in this case and this is not asked in any competitive examination at high school level.

If we calculate the electric field and potential at a distance r from the centre outside the shell, it will only be due to the charge on outer surface as induced charge on inner surface of cavity always nullify the effect of point charge inside it. Thus it can be given as

$$E_{out} = \frac{Kq}{r^2} \text{ and } V_P = \frac{Kq}{r}$$

1.17.2 Charge Distribution on a System of Parallel Plates

If a large conducting plate is given a charge $+Q$ then due to symmetry this charge is distributed equally on both of its surfaces as shown-1.309. If surface area of each face of the plate is A, charge density on surface can be given as

$$\sigma = \frac{Q}{2A}$$

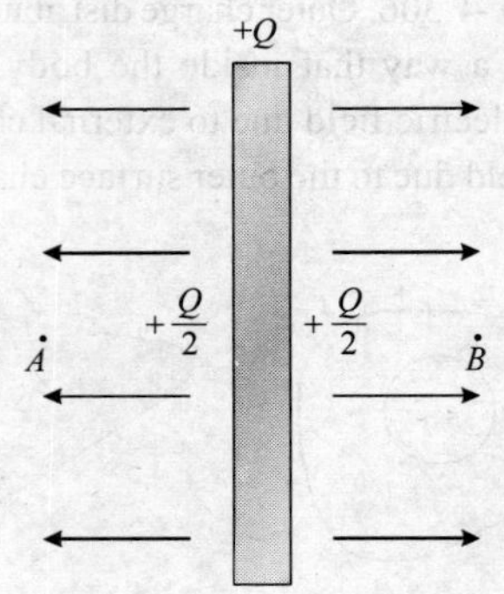

Figure 1.309

Thus electric field on both sides of the plate at points A and B can be given as

$$E_A = E_B = \frac{\sigma}{\epsilon_0} = \frac{Q}{2A\epsilon_0} \quad \ldots(1.244)$$

If another uncharged plate is placed in front of this charged sheet as shown in figure-1.310, then on the front plate of this plate an equal and opposite charge $-Q/2$ is induced as whole flux from the front face of first plate is terminating on this face of the second plate and on its back surface $+Q/2$ is induced. To calculate the electric field in surrounding region of plates, it can be given as $\frac{\sigma}{\epsilon_0}$ where σ is the surface charge density on the surface facing the point at which we are calculating the electric field. In figure-1.310 the direction of electric field strengths in different region are indicated by arrows.

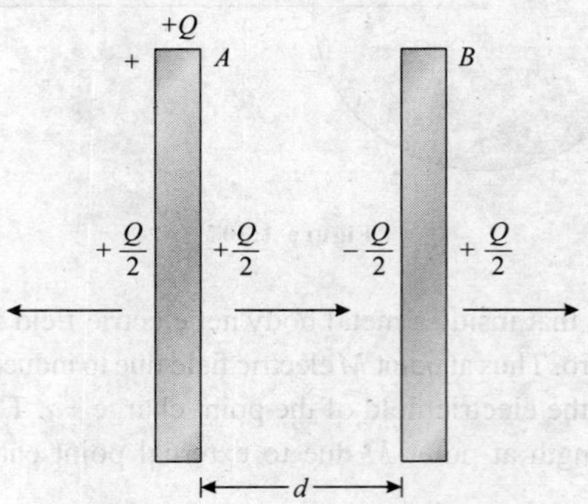

Figure 1.310

As electric field is uniform due to plates, we can calculate the potential difference between the two plates A and B as

$$V_A - V_B = \frac{\sigma}{\epsilon_0} \cdot d$$

$$\Rightarrow \quad V_A - V_B = \frac{Q}{2A\epsilon_0} d \quad \ldots(1.245)$$

We consider another illustration on the same concept to understand it better. Figure-1.311 shows a system of three parallel plates A, B and C. The plates are given charges $+Q$, $-2Q$ and $+3Q$ respectively.

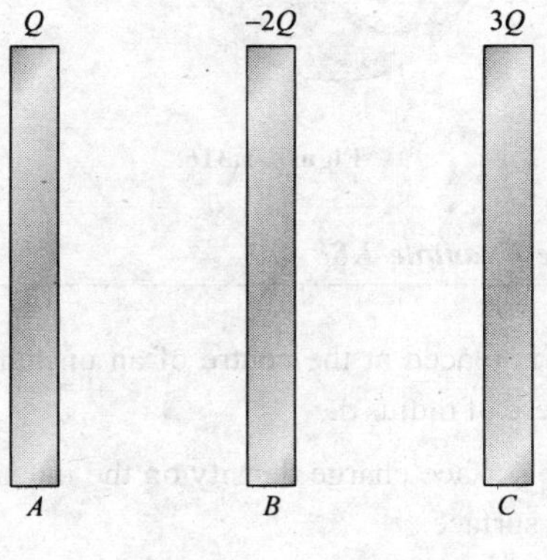

Figure 1.311

In this situation first we will calculate the charge distribution on the surfaces of these plates using the logic discussed in previous illustration of two plates. Due to the effect of charge induction on all the plates by initially present charges, these charges are redistributed on the surfaces of plates in such a way that the final electric field in the body of each plate will become zero. We assume that after final distribution of charge on the left face of plate A, if the charge is q then on right side of it remaining charge will be $(Q-q)$ as shown in figure-1.312. We have already discussed that the electric flux originating from one surface will terminate on the other facing surface and induces an equal and opposite charge on that face. This should always be remembered as

"In a system of large parallel conducting plates, the facing surfaces of plates always carry equal and opposite charges."

According to this logic we distribute the charges on the plates as shown in figure-1.312. The facing surface of plate B will have a distributed charge $-(Q-q)$ and other surface of plate B will have $[-2Q+(Q-q)]$ and so on. Now we consider a point P inside the plate A. The net electric field at point P must be zero as it is inside a conducting body. In this way we can determine the charge q and hence the complete charge distribution on all faces of the plates. We can carefully see and analyze that the electric field at point P is only due to the left face of A and right face of C as all other charges produces electric field at point P in equal and opposite direction and hence nullified.

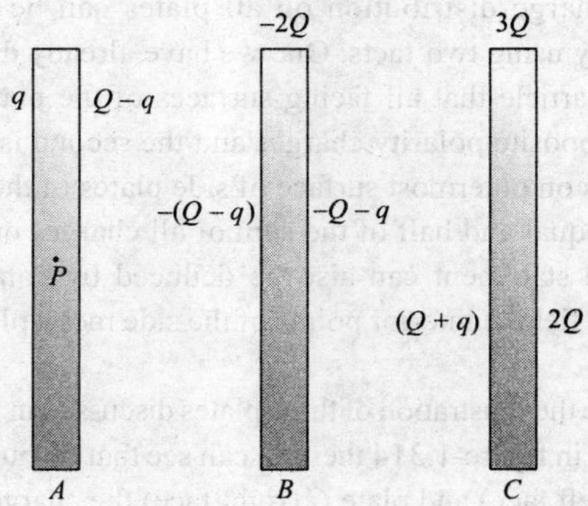

Figure 1.312

Thus the electric field strength at point P is as shown in figure-1.313.

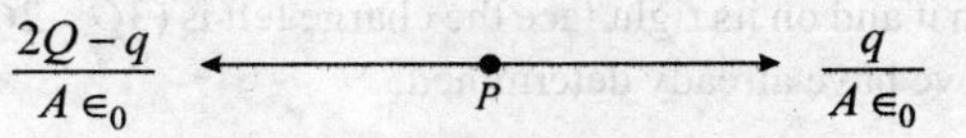

Figure 1.313

As net electric field at point P must be zero, we have

$$\frac{2Q-q}{A\epsilon_0}-\frac{q}{A\epsilon_0}=0$$

$$\Rightarrow \qquad q=Q$$

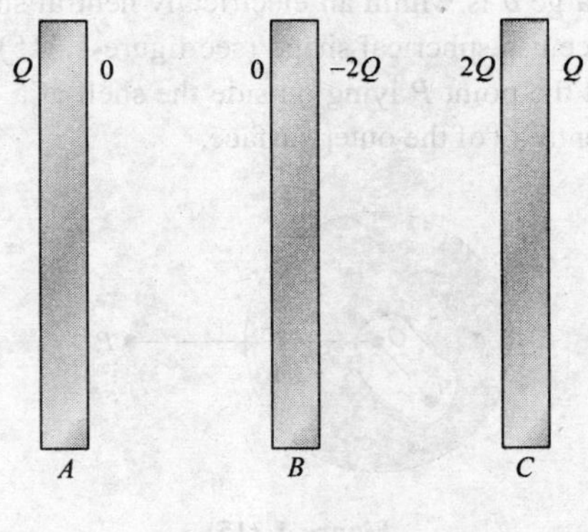

Figure 1.314

This gives us the final distribution of charges on the system of parallel plates shown in figure-1.314.

1.17.3 Alternative Method of Charge Distribution on a System of Large Parallel Metal Plates

When in a system of large isolated parallel metal plates some charges are given to one or more plates of the system then due to induction effects it is redistributed on the different faces of the plates in such a way that finally the electric field strength at all interior points of each plate net electric field becomes zero. The final charge distribution on all plates can be directly calculated by using two facts. One we have already discussed in previous article that all facing surfaces of the plates have equal and opposite polarity charges and the second is that the total charges on outermost surface of side plates of the system are always equal and half of the sum of all charges on plates. This second statement can also be deduced by considering zero electric field at interior points of the side metal plates.

If we analyze the illustration of three plates discussed in previous article again in figure-1.314 then we can see that on outer faces of plate A (left face) and plate C (right face) the charge should be half of $(Q-2Q+3Q)$ which is $+Q$. Thus on the right face of plate A total charge left is 0 as its total charge was only $+Q$. Thus the facing surface of plate B will also have 0 charge so its right face will carry its total charge $-2Q$. Similarly the left surface of plate C which is facing a charge $-2Q$ will have total charge $+2Q$ on it and on its right face the charge left is $(3Q-2Q)=+Q$ which we have already determined.

Using the above logic of charge distribution, we can calculate the charges on all faces of plates of a system of parallel plates without using any paper calculations. In solving different numerical problems this is very useful and fast analysis.

Illustrative Example 1.87

A point charge q is within an electrically neutral shell whose outer surface has spherical shape (see figure-1.315). Find the potential at the point P lying outside the shell at a distance r from the centre O of the outer surface.

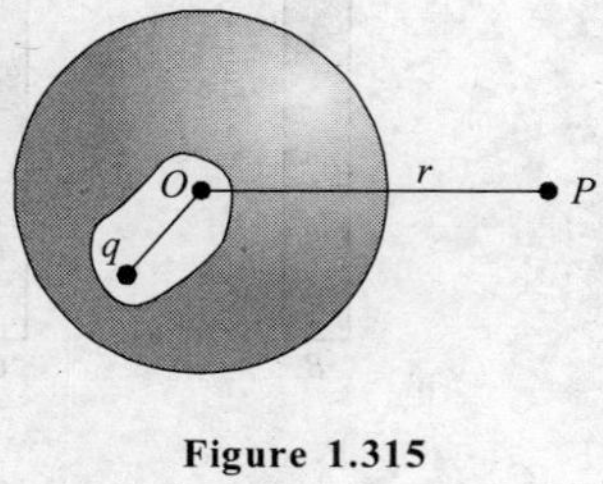

Figure 1.315

Solution

The field at the point P is determined only due to induced charges on the outer spherical surface. The field of the point charge q and of the induced charges on the inner surface of the sphere of the sphere is equal to zero everywhere outside the cavity. Also, the charge on the outer surface of the shell is distributed uniformly and hence potential at P

$$V=\frac{1}{4\pi\epsilon_0}\frac{q}{r}$$

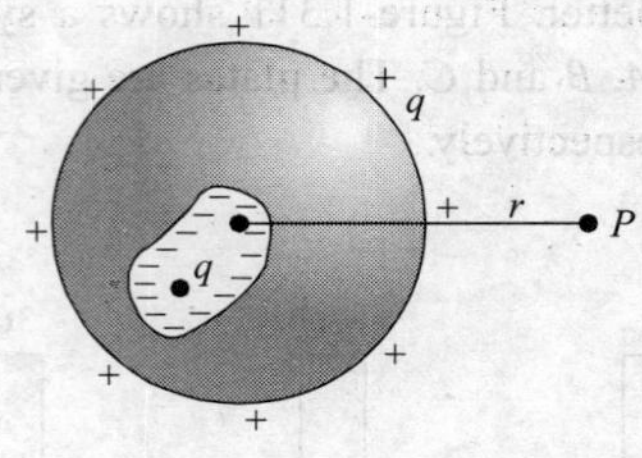

Figure 1.316

Illustrative Example 1.88

A charge Q is placed at the centre of an uncharged, hollow metallic sphere of radius a,

(a) Find the surface charge density on the inner surface and on the outer surface.

(b) If a charge q is put on the sphere, what would be the surface charge densities on the inner and the outer surfaces?

(c) Find the electric field inside the sphere at a distance x from the centre in the situations (a) and (b).

Solution

(a) Figure-1.317 shows the situation described in question. Due to the central charge induced charges appear on the inner and outer surface of the shell.

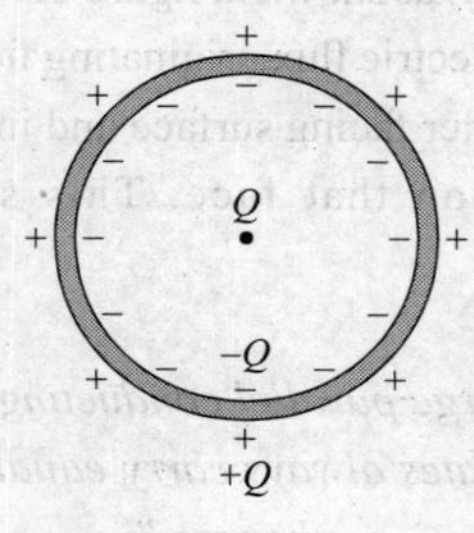

Figure 1.317

The surface charge densities on the inner and outer surfaces of the shell are given as

$$\sigma_i=\frac{-Q}{4\pi R^2} \text{ and } \sigma_0=\frac{Q}{4\pi R^2}$$

(b) Figure-1.318 shows the situation described in question. Due to the central charge induced charges appear on the inner and outer surface of the shell.

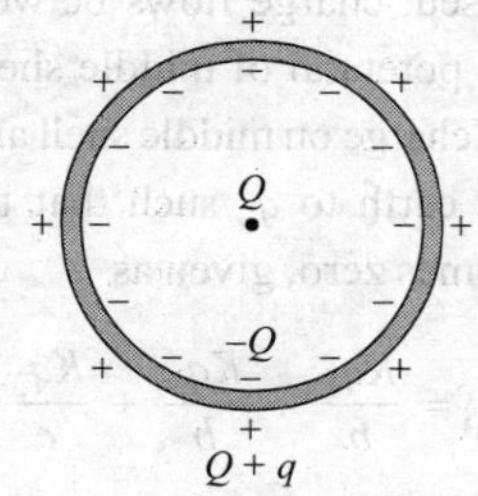

Figure 1.318

Thus the surface charge densities on inner and outer surfaces of the shell are given as

$$\sigma_i = \frac{-Q}{4\pi R^2} \text{ and } \sigma_0 = \frac{(Q+q)}{4\pi R^2}$$

(c) According to gauss theorem

$$E = \frac{1}{4\pi\varepsilon_0}\frac{q_{in}}{r^2}$$

For $x \le R$, $q_{in} = Q$

and $r = x$ both cases, we have

$$E = \frac{1}{4\pi\varepsilon_0}\frac{Q}{x^2}$$

1.18 Earthing of Charged or Uncharged Metal Bodies

In electrical analysis, earth is assumed to be a very large conducting sphere of radius 6400 km. If some charge Q is given to earth, its potential becomes

$$V_e = \frac{KQ}{R_e}$$

As R_e is very large V_e comes out to be a negligible small value. Thus for very small bodies whose dimensions are negligible compared to earth we can assume that earth is always at zero potential no matter whatever charge is given to it in practical conditions.

If we connect a small conducting body to earth, charge flow takes place between earth and the body till both will attain same potential. As potential of earth we consider to always remain zero, after connecting a metal body to earth we also consider that final potential on the body will become zero. To maintain this zero potential on body charges may flow into the earth from body or into the body from earth. This implies that if a body at some positive potential is connected to earth, earth will supply some negative charge to this body so that the final potential of body will become zero and vice versa. Figure-1.319 shows the symbol of earthing when a body is connected to earth.

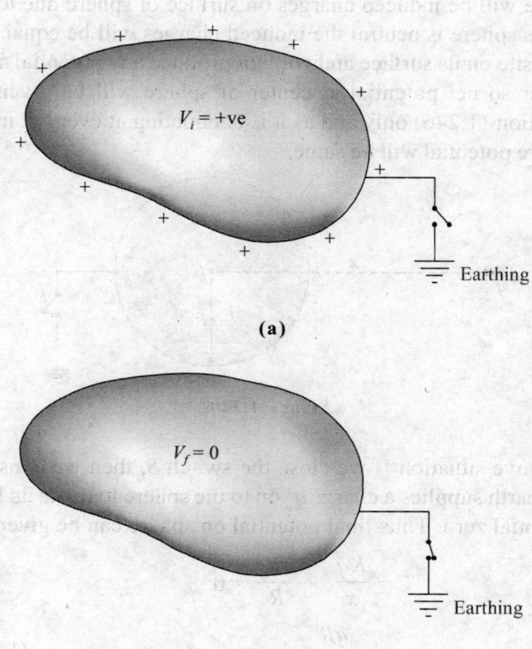

Figure 1.319

If there is an isolated metal body containing some charges then the body potential is only due to its own charges. If this body is connected to earth then all its charges flow into earth to keep it at zero potential as shown in above figure. If the body is not isolated from surrounding and it has potential due to some charges in its surrounding then after connecting such a body to earth, charges are supplied by earth to body in such a way to nullify the external potential on body due to its surrounding. In next article we will take an illustration to understand this concept in detail.

1.18.1 Earthing of a metal Sphere

Whenever an isolated charged metal sphere is connected to earth, no matter whether its charge is positive or negative whole of its charge will flow into earth as an isolated metal sphere potential is zero only when its charge is zero. In fact any isolated charged metal body when connected to earth, its complete charge flows to earth and it becomes neutral as to make its potential zero we consider that no electric field should exist in its surrounding as we consider zero potential also at infinity as a reference.

Consider a solid uncharged conducting sphere as shown in figure-1.320. A point charge $+q$ is placed in front of the sphere at a distance x from its center as shown. Due to $+q$, the potential of sphere is given as

$$V = \frac{Kq}{x} \quad \ldots(1.246)$$

There will be induced charges on surface of sphere due to $+q$ but as sphere is neutral the induced charges will be equal and opposite on its surface and will not produce any potential at its center so net potential at center of sphere will be given by equation-(1.246) only and as it is conducting at every point of sphere potential will be same.

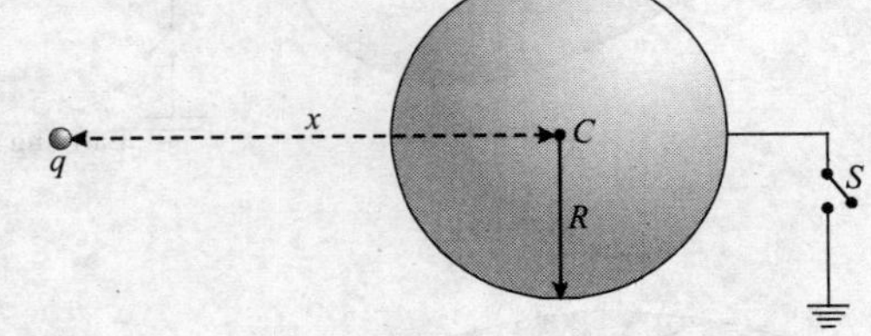

Figure 1.320

In above situation If we close the switch S, then we consider that earth supplies a charge q_e on to the sphere to make its final potential zero. Thus final potential on sphere can be given as

$$V = \frac{Kq}{x} + \frac{Kq_e}{R} = 0$$

$$\Rightarrow \quad q_e = -\frac{qR}{x} \qquad \ldots(1.247)$$

From equation-(1.247) we can see that earth has supplied a negative charge to develope a negative potential on sphere to nullify the initial positive potential on it due to q.

Always remember whenever a metal body is connected to earth, we consider that earth supplies a charge to it (say q_e) to make its final potential zero due to all the charges including the charge on body and the charges in its surrounding.

Similar to this case in next article we will discuss the case of earthing of a shell in a system of multiple concentric shells.

1.18.2 Charges on a System of Concentric Shells

Figure-1.321 shows three concentric spherical shells of radii a, b and c having charges q_1, q_2 and q_3 on these respectively. Now we'll find the final potential of the three shells if switch S is closed.

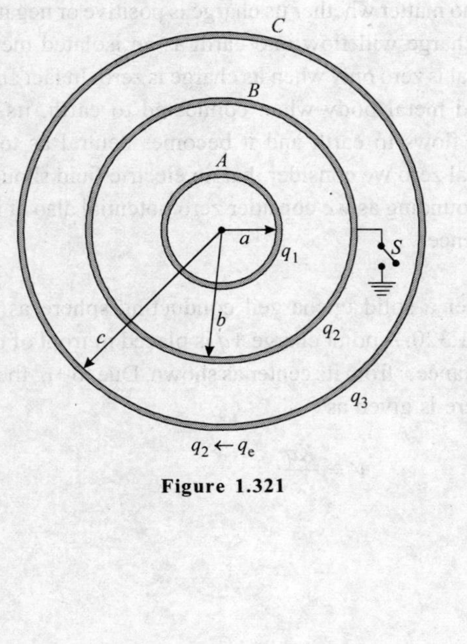

Figure 1.321

If switch S is closed, charge flows between middle shell and earth till the final potential of middle shell becomes zero. We consider that final charge on middle shell after closing the switch gets modified by earth to q_e such that the final potential of middle shell becomes zero, given as

$$V_B = \frac{Kq_1}{b} + \frac{Kq_e}{b} + \frac{Kq_3}{c} = 0 \qquad \ldots(1.248)$$

In above equation-(1.248) different potential terms are explained below

$\frac{Kq_1}{b}$ = Potential of shell B due to shell A

$\frac{Kq_e}{b}$ = Potential of shell B due to its own charge q_e

$\frac{Kq_3}{c}$ = Potential of shell B due to shell C, as B is inside C its potential is equal to that on surface of C.

On solving the above equation we get

$$q_e = -\left(q_1 + \frac{b}{c}q_3\right) \qquad \ldots(1.249)$$

Now we can write the final potentials of the three shells as

$$V_A = \frac{Kq_1}{b} + \frac{Kq_e}{b} + \frac{Kq_3}{c}$$

$$V_B = 0$$

$$V_C = \frac{K(q_1 + q_e + q_3)}{c}$$

There are cases when surrounding charges of a conductor are not at rest and in state of motion, the potential of conductor varies. If the conductor is connected to earth then continuously charges flow to or from the body to keep the instantaneous potential of conductor at zero due to which a current flows between body and earth. In next article we will consider an illustration on continuous flow of current through an earthed conductor.

1.18.3 Current flow due to Earthing

Figure-1.322 shows a metal ball connected to earth through an ammeter. If a charge $+q$ is moving toward the ball at speed v, because of which the potential of ball continuously increases. When it is at a distance x from ball, the potential of ball due to this charge can be given as

$$V = \frac{Kq}{x} \qquad \ldots(1.250)$$

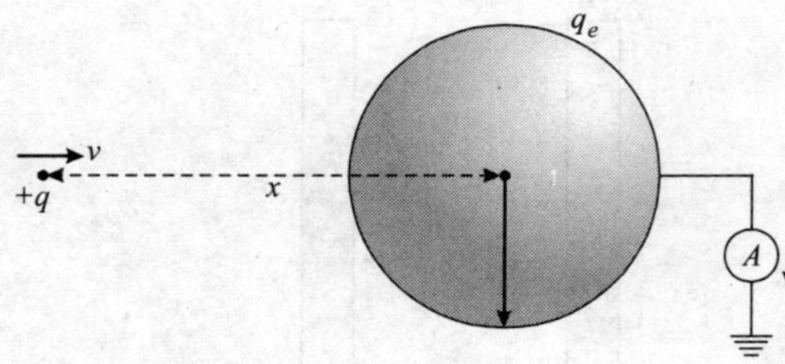

Figure 1.322

In above situation at this instant, charge on ball due to earth connection q_e can be calculated by making its potential zero which is given as

$$\frac{Kq}{x}+\frac{Kq_e}{R}=0$$

$$\Rightarrow \quad q_e=-\frac{qR}{x} \qquad \ldots(1.251)$$

As x is continuously decreasing, charge on ball must be continuously increasing hence ammeter shows a current i, which can be determined by calculating the rate of change of charge on ball, given as

$$i=\frac{dq}{dt}=\frac{qR}{x^2}\frac{dx}{dt}$$

$$\Rightarrow \quad i=\frac{qR}{x^2}v \qquad \ldots(1.252)$$

Thus we can state whenever in the surrounding of an earthed conductor one or more charges are in motion, a continuous current may flow in the wires connecting body to earth.

1.18.4 Earthing of Two or More Conductors Simultaneously

Figure-1.323 shows three conducting balls A, B and C of radii a, $2a$ and a respectively. Ball B and C are connected to earth via switches S_1 and S_2 as shown. Ball A is given a charge Q and balls B and C are uncharged. Now we'll find charges appearing on B and C if both switches S_1 and S_2 are closed. Let these charges be q_{e_1} and q_{e_2} respectively such that final potentials of balls B and C will become zero. We have

$$V_B=\frac{KQ}{5a}+\frac{Kq_{e_1}}{2a}+\frac{Kq_{e_2}}{5a}=0 \qquad \ldots(1.253)$$

and

$$V_C=\frac{KQ}{5a}+\frac{Kq_{e_1}}{5a}+\frac{Kq_{e_2}}{a}=0 \qquad \ldots(1.254)$$

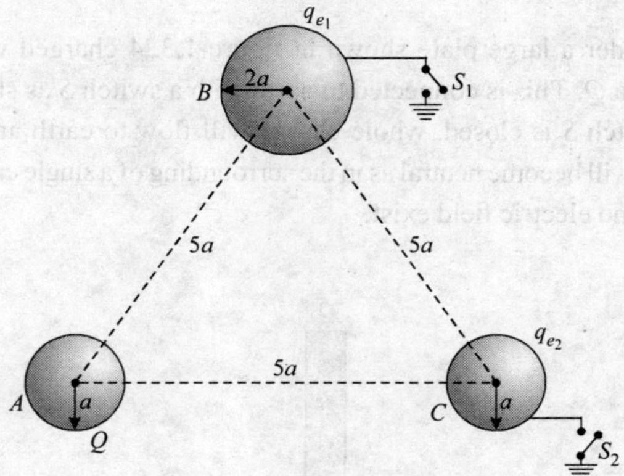

Figure 1.323

In the above equations-(1.253) and (1.254) we have considered the potential of spheres B and C due to their own charges as well as due to the charges on the other two spheres.

On solving the above two equations can calculate the values of q_{e_1} and q_{e_2}. Here we are leaving this calculation part as an exercise for students to solve and get the desired results.

One more analysis can be done in above situation. Equations-(1.253) and (1.254) are written under condition when the switches S_1 and S_2 are closed simultaneously. It could also be asked to solve the situation if initially switch S_1 is closed and opened then switch S_2 is closed then opened. In such a situation we will first write the equation of electric potential at sphere B to be equal to zero considering that earth has supplied a charge q_{e_1} to sphere B and sphere C remain neutral as switch S_2 is open. So we have

$$V_B=\frac{KQ}{5a}+\frac{Kq_{e_1}}{2a}=0 \qquad \ldots(1.255)$$

$$\Rightarrow \quad q_{e_1}=-\frac{2}{5}Q \qquad \ldots(1.256)$$

Equation-(1.256) gives the charge q_{e_1} on sphere B which remain constant as switch S_1 is opened. If now switch S_2 is closed, earth will supply a charge q_{e_2} on sphere C which makes the potential of sphere C zero, given as

$$V_C=\frac{KQ}{5a}+\frac{K\left(-\frac{2}{5}Q\right)}{5a}+\frac{Kq_{e_2}}{a}=0 \qquad \ldots(1.257)$$

$$\Rightarrow \quad V_C=-\frac{3}{25}Q \qquad \ldots(1.258)$$

1.18.5 Earthing of a System of Parallel Plates

Consider a large plate shown in figure-1.324 charged with a charge Q. This is connected to earth with a switch S as shown. If switch S is closed, whole charge will flow to earth and the plate will become neutral as in the surrounding of a single earthed body no electric field exist.

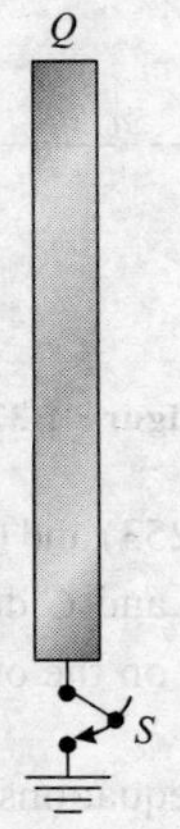

Figure 1.324

Now consider the system of two plates A and B shown here. Plate A is given a charge Q and plate B is neutral. The charge distribution on plates is as shown in figure-1.325(a). If the switch S is now closed the total charge on outer surface of the system of plates after earthing should become zero as again we consider to have no electric in surrounding of an earthed system hence whole charge on plate A will transfer to its inner surface and hence on the inner surface of plate B, an equal and opposite charge $-Q$ is induced which is supplied by earth as shown in figure-1.325(b).

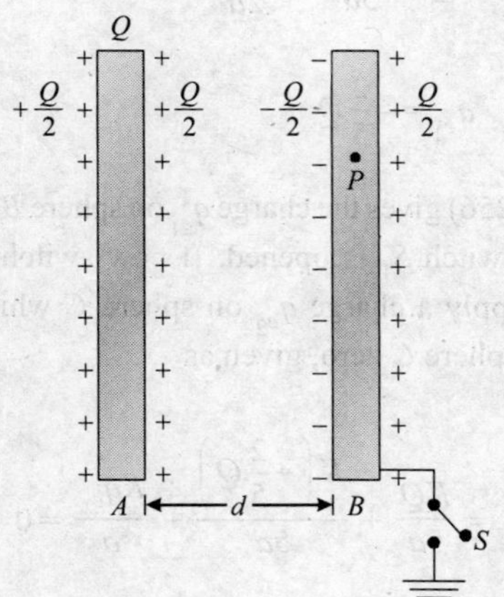

(a)

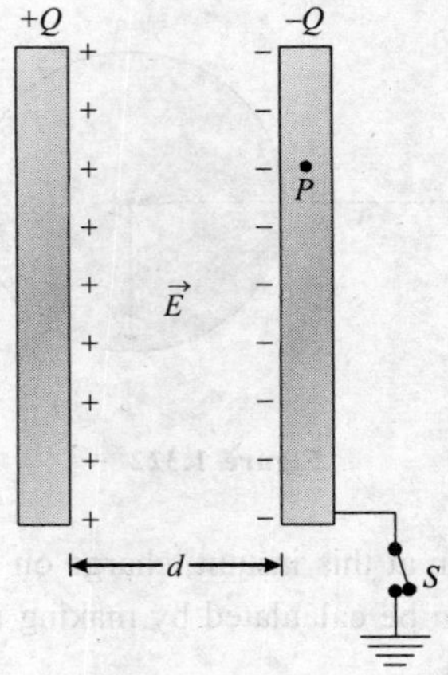

(b)

Figure 1.325

We consider area of each plate is A then the electric field between the system of plates can be given as

$$E_f = \frac{Q}{A\epsilon_0}$$

Before earthing this electric field was only due to the charge on plate A which is given as

$$E_i = \frac{Q}{2A\epsilon_0} = \frac{E_f}{2}$$

Thus just after earthing of plate B, the electric field between the plates is doubled and the potential difference between the two plates will also get doubled. As plate B is earthed, its potential is zero. The potential of plate A can be given as

$$V_A = \frac{Q}{A\epsilon_0} \cdot d$$

We can consider another example similar to the previous one as shown in figure-1.326. It shows a system of three large parallel plates A, B and C. The middle plate B is given a charge Q due to which charges are induced on plates A and C which are also shown in figure. Plates A and C are connected to earth through two switches S_1 and S_2 which are initially open.

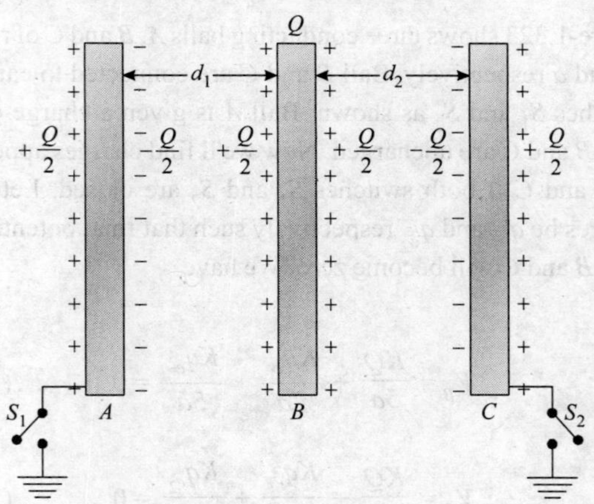

Figure 1.326

On the basis of discussion done in the previous section we can say that if switch S_1 is closed keeping S_2 open then whole charge of plate B will shift on its left surface and a charge $-Q$ is flown through S_1 from earth to plate A and final situation will be as shown in figure-1.327(a).

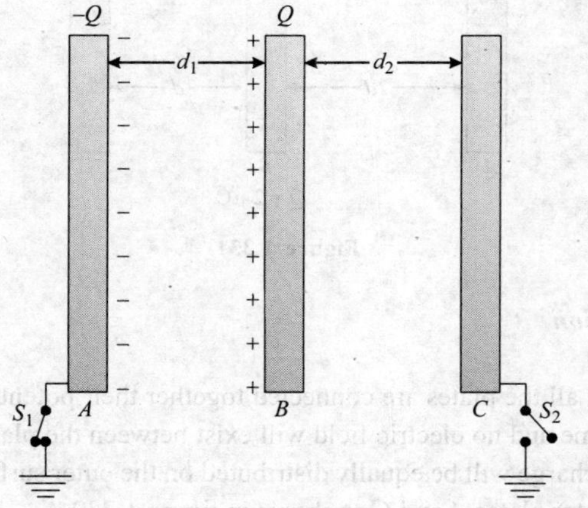

(a)

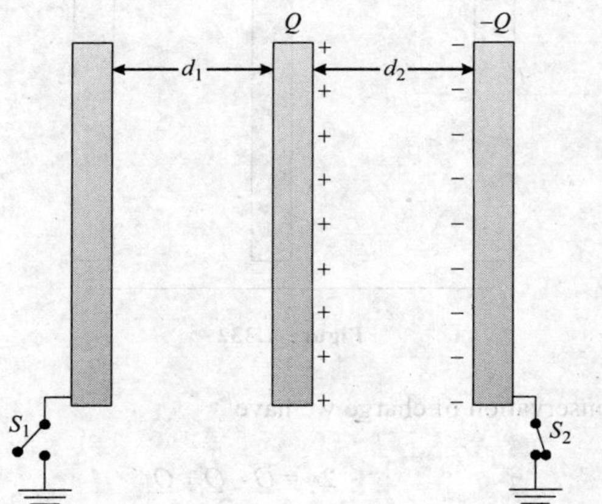

(b)

Figure 1.327

If switch S_2 is closed keeping switch S_1 open then whole charge of plate B will shift on its right surface and a charge $-Q$ flows through switch S_2 from earth to plate C as shown in figure-1.327(b).

If in above system of plates both the switches are simultaneously closed then, the charge on plate B is distributed as shown in figure-1.328. The charge on plate B is distributed on the two surface q_1 and q_2 with equal and opposite charges $-q_1$ and $-q_2$ induced on the inner surfaces of plates A and C.

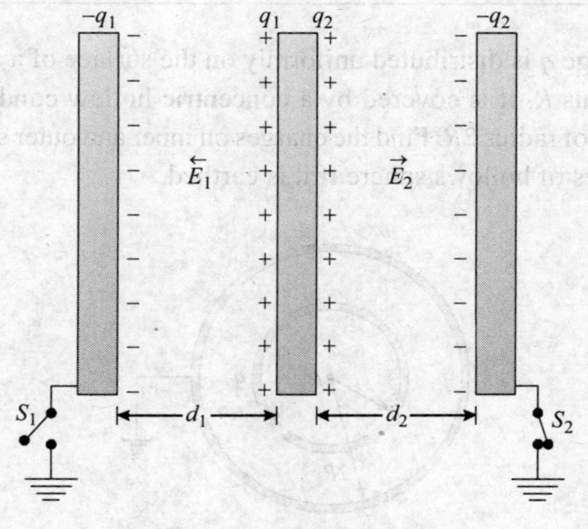

Figure 1.328

We can calculate these charges q_1 and q_2 by equating the potential difference of plates A, B and C, B as plates A and C are connected to earth and both are at same potential, so we use

$$V_B - V_A = V_B - V_C \quad \ldots(1.259)$$

The electric field between plates A and B is given as

$$E_1 = \frac{q_1}{A\epsilon_0} \quad \ldots(1.260)$$

The electric field between plates B and C is given as

$$E_2 = \frac{q_2}{A\epsilon_0} \quad \ldots(1.261)$$

From equation-(1.259), (1.260) and (1.261), we use

$$\frac{q_1}{A\epsilon_0}d_1 = \frac{q_2}{A\epsilon_0}d_2$$

$$\Rightarrow \quad q_1d_1 = q_2d_2 \quad \ldots(1.262)$$

We also have

$$q_1 + q_2 = Q \quad \ldots(1.263)$$

Solving equations-(1.262) and (1.263), we get

$$q_1 = \frac{Qd_2}{d_1 + d_2}$$

and
$$q_2 = \frac{Qd_1}{d_1 + d_2}$$

Thus if both the switches are closed simultaneously, charges $-q_1$ and $-q_2$ will flow through the switches S_1 and S_2 from earth to plates A and C.

Illustrative Example 1.89

A charge q is distributed uniformly on the surface of a sphere of radius R. It is covered by a concentric hollow conducting sphere of radius $2R$. Find the charges on inner and outer surface surfaces of hollows sphere if it is earthed.

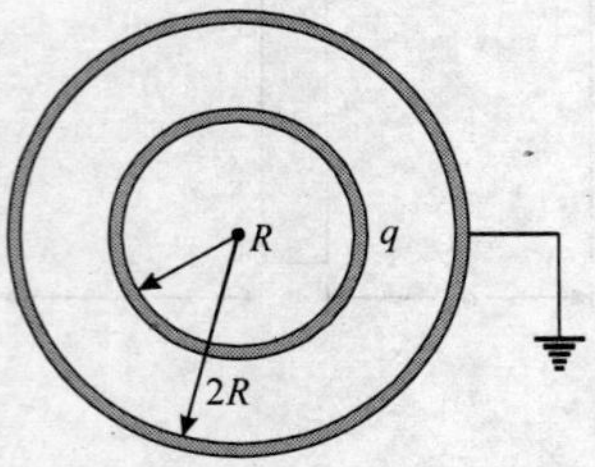

Figure 1.329

Solution

The charge on the inner surface should be $-q$, because if we draw a closed Gaussian surface through the material of the hollow sphere the total charge enclosed by this Gaussian surface should be zero. Let q' be the charge on the outer surface of the hollow sphere.

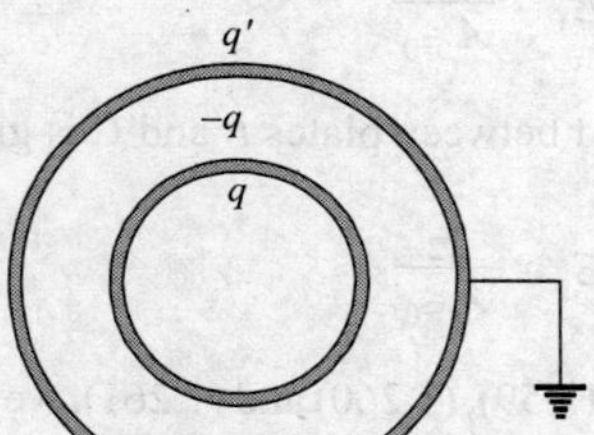

Figure 1.330

Since, the outer sphere is earthed, its potential should be zero. The potential on it is due to the charges q, $-q$ and q', Hence,

$$V = \frac{1}{4\pi\varepsilon_0}\left[\frac{q}{2R} - \frac{q}{2R} + \frac{q'}{2R}\right] = 0$$

$$\Rightarrow \qquad q' = 0$$

Thus there will be no charge on the outer surface of the hollow sphere.

Illustrative Example 1.90

Three large conducting plates are kept close to each other as shown in the figure-1.331. Now all the three plates A, B, and C are connected by a thin conducting wire. Find the charge (in μC) on left surface of plate A at electrostatic equilibrium.

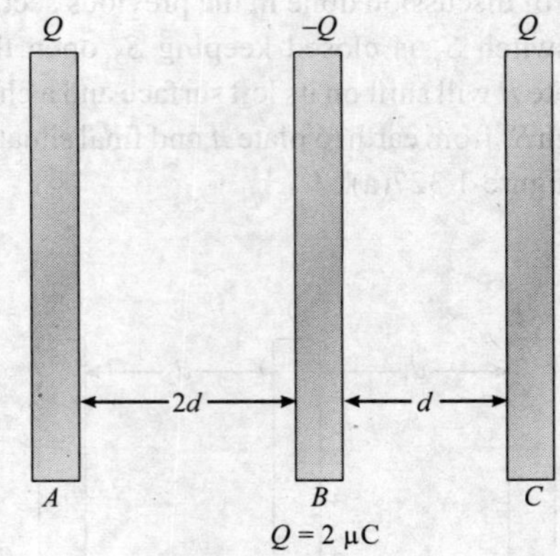

Figure 1.331

Solution

When all the plates are connected together their potential will be same and no electric field will exist between the plates and total charge will be equally distributed on the outer surfaces of the outer plates A and C as shown in figure-1.332.

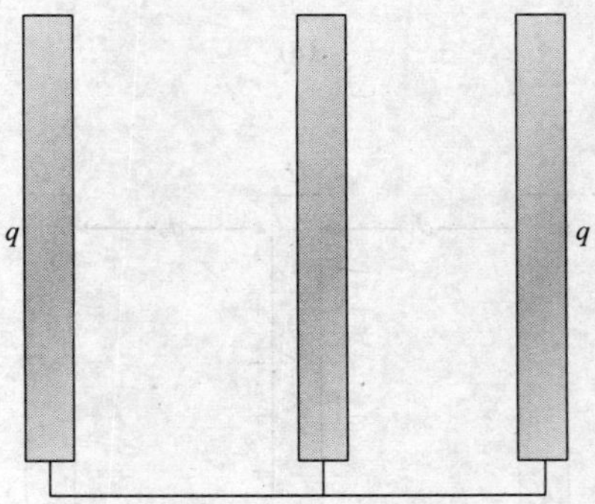

Figure 1.332

By conservation of charge we have

$$2q = Q - Q + Q$$

$$\Rightarrow \qquad q = \frac{Q}{2} = 1\,\mu C$$

Illustrative Example 1.91

There are 4 concentric shells A, B, C and D of radius a, $2a$, $3a$, $4a$ respectively. Shells B and D are given charges $+q$ and $-q$ respectively. Shell C is now earthed. Find the potential difference $V_A - V_C$.

Solution

If the shell C attains a charge q' which will be such that final potential of C is zero, we use

$$V_C = \frac{Kq}{3a} + \frac{Kq'}{3a} + \left(\frac{-Kq}{4a}\right) = 0$$

$$\Rightarrow \quad \frac{Kq}{3a} + \frac{Kq'}{3a} = \frac{Kq}{4a}$$

$$\Rightarrow \quad q' = 3q\left(\frac{1}{4} - \frac{1}{3}\right)$$

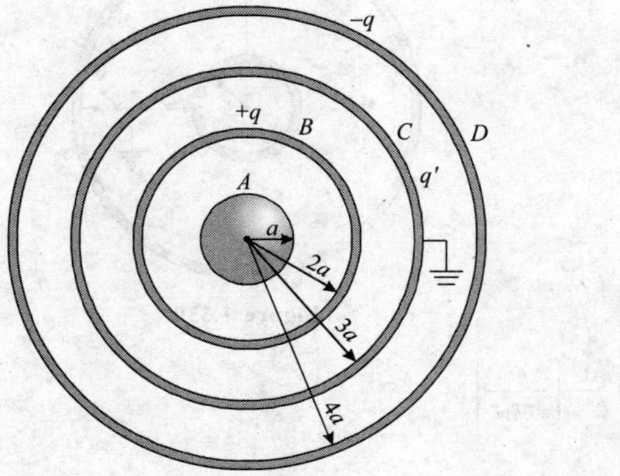

Figure 1.333

$$\Rightarrow \quad q' = -\frac{q}{4}$$

As we have

$$V_C = 0$$

$$\Rightarrow \quad V_A - V_C = V_A$$

Now calculating V_A we have

$$V_A = \frac{Kq}{2a} - \frac{K(q/4)}{3a} - \frac{Kq}{4a}$$

$$\Rightarrow \quad V_A = \frac{Kq}{6a}$$

$$\Rightarrow \quad V_A - V_C = \frac{Kq}{6a}$$

Illustrative Example 1.92

There are two uncharged identical metallic spheres of radius a, separated a distance d. A charged metallic sphere (charge q) of same radius is brought and touches sphere 1. After some time it is moved away to a far off distance. After this, the sphere 2 is earthed. Find the charge on sphere 2.

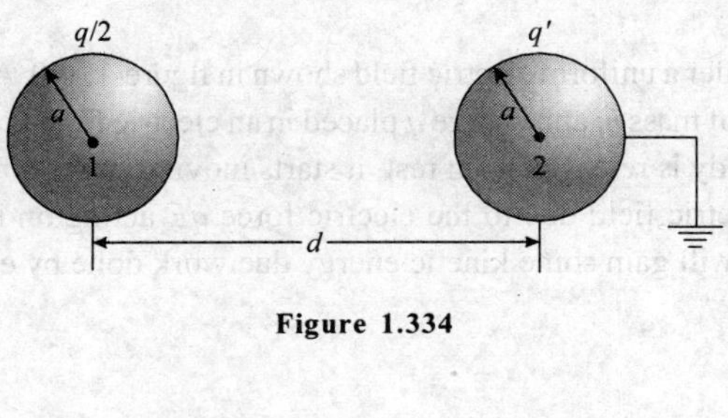

Figure 1.334

Solution

When sphere with charge q touches metallic sphere 1, the charge on 1 becomes $q/2$. The potential due to sphere 1 at the surface of 2 is given as

$$V_{21} = \frac{1}{4\pi \epsilon_0}\frac{q_1}{d} = \frac{1}{4\pi \epsilon_0}\left(\frac{q}{2d}\right)$$

When sphere 2 is earthed, its potential becomes zero. If induced charge on it is q' then we have

$$V_2 = \frac{1}{4\pi \epsilon_0}\frac{q}{2d} + \frac{1}{4\pi \epsilon_0}\frac{q'}{a} = 0$$

$$\Rightarrow \quad q' = -\frac{qa}{2d}$$

Web Reference at www.physicsgalaxy.com

Age Group - Grade 11 & 12 | Age 17-19 Years
Section - ELECTROSTATICS
Topic - Electric Potential
Module Number - 54 to 56

Web Reference at www.physicsgalaxy.com

Age Group - Grade 11 & 12 | Age 17-19 Years
Section - ELECTROSTATICS
Topic - Conductors & Dielectrics
Module Number - 1 to 22

Practice Exercise 1.9

(i) Figure-1.335 shows two conducting thin concentric shells of radii r and $3r$. The outer shell carries charge q whereas inner shell is uncharged. Find the charge that will flow from inner shell to earth after the switch S is closed.

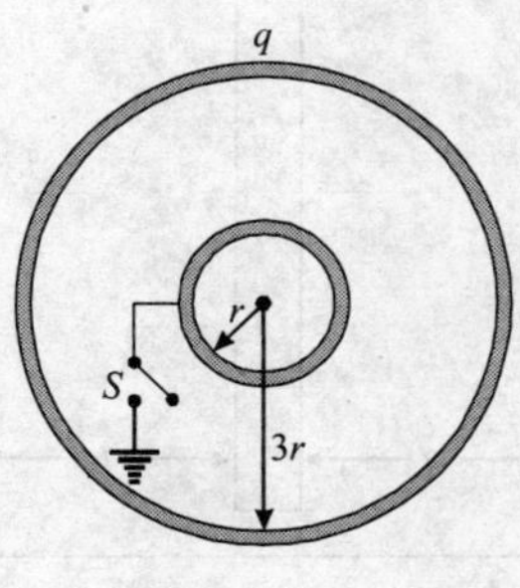

Figure 1.335

[$+\frac{q}{3}$ charge will flow from inner shell to earth]

(ii) Initially the conducting shells A and B are at potentials V_A and V_B. Find the potential of A when sphere B is earthed.

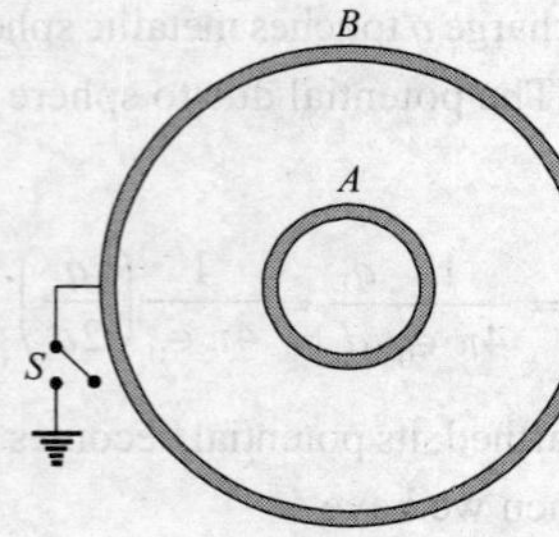

Figure 1.336

$[V_A - V_B]$

(iii) Figure shows three concentric thin conducting spherical shells A, B and C of radii R, $2R$ and $3R$. The shell B is earthed, A and C are given charges q and $2q$ respectively. Find the charges appearing on all the surface of A, B and C.

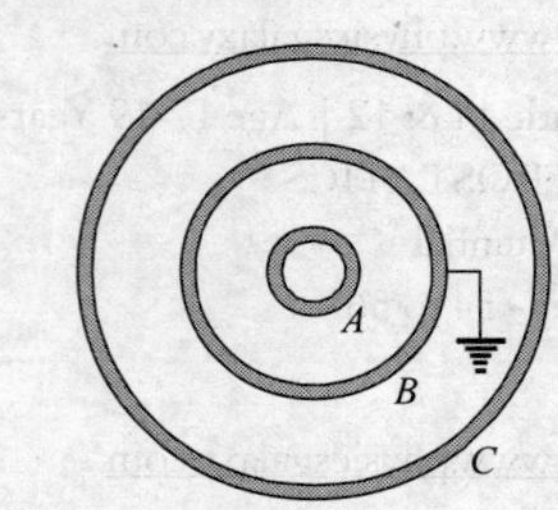

Figure 1.337

[Inner surface (A) 0, (B) $-q$, (C) $\frac{4}{3}q$

Outer surface (A) q, (B) $-\frac{4}{3}q$, (C) $\frac{2}{3}q$]

(iv) Three identical metallic plates are kept parallel to one another at a separation of a and b. The outer plates are connected by a thin conducting wire and a charge Q is placed on the central plate. Find final charges on all the surfaces of the three plates.

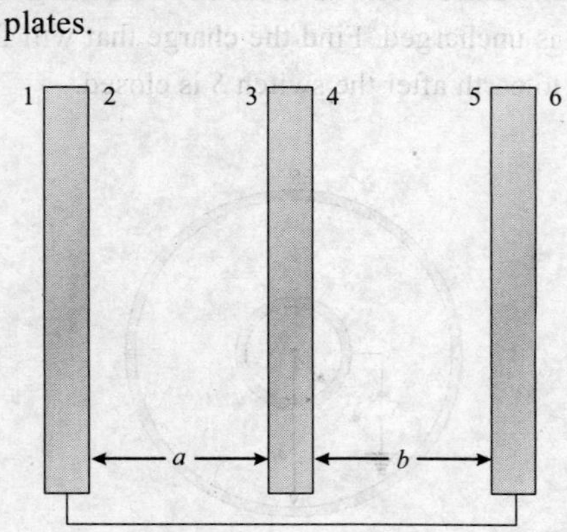

Figure 1.338

[Faces (1) $\frac{Q}{2}$, (2) $-\frac{Qb}{a+b}$, (3) $\frac{Qb}{a+b}$, (4) $\frac{Qa}{a+b}$, (5) $-\frac{Qa}{a+b}$, (6) $\frac{Q}{3}$]

(v) There are two concentric conducting spherical shells of radii r and $2r$. Initially a charge Q is given to the inner shell. Now, switch S_1 is closed and opened then S_2 is closed and opened and the process is repeated n times for both the keys alternatively. Find the final potential difference between the shells.

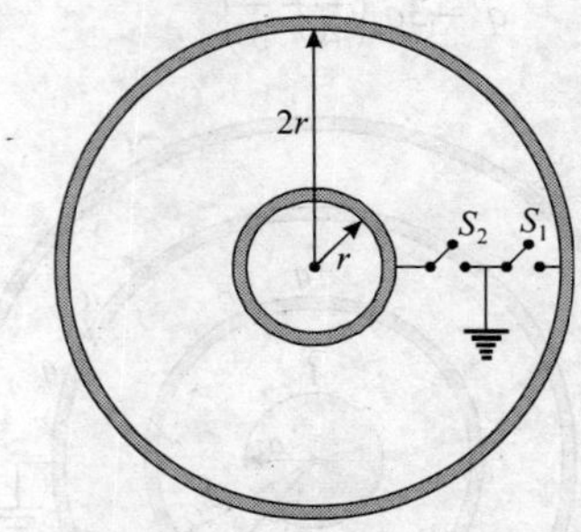

Figure 1.339

$[\frac{1}{2^{n+1}}\left[\frac{Q}{4\pi\varepsilon_0 r}\right]]$

(vi) An electrometer is charged to 3 kV. Then the electrometer is touched with a neutral metal ball, mounted on an insulating rod, and then the metal ball is taken away and earthed. The process is done for 10 times, and finally the electrometer reads 1.5 kV. After this, at least how many times must the above process be repeated in order that the electrometer reads less than 1 kV?

[6]

(vii) When an uncharged conducting ball of radius r is placed in an external uniform electric field, a surface charge density $\sigma = \sigma_0 \cos\theta$ is induced on the ball's surface where σ_0 is a constant, θ is a polar angle measured from a direction parallel to external electric field. Find the magnitude of the resultant electric force acting on an induced charge of the same sign on one half of hemisphere.

$[\frac{\pi\sigma_0^2 r^2}{4\epsilon_0}]$

(viii) Find the force with which the two halves of a uniformly charged metal spheres repel each other. Total uniformly distributed charge on surface of sphere is Q.

$[\frac{\sigma^2\pi R^2}{2\epsilon_0}]$

1.19 Field Energy of Electrostatic Field

Consider a uniform electric field shown in figure-1.340. A small body of mass m and charge q placed in an electric field E. When the body is released from rest, it starts moving in the direction of electric field due to the electric force qE acting on it. The body will gain some kinetic energy due work done by electric field.

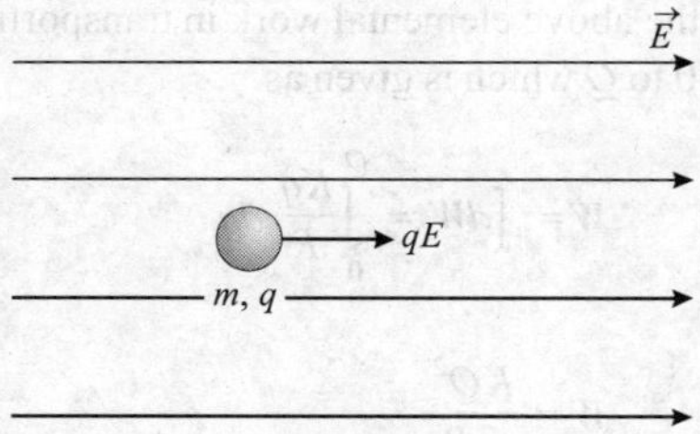

Figure 1.340

In above situation shown in figure a common question arises "*Who is giving kinetic energy to this charged particle* ?" The answer is simple - "*Electric Field*". This shows that electric field must posses some energy in the region where field exist due to which it can do work on any charged body placed in it. This energy stored in the space by which electric field can do work on any charge in it is called "*Field Energy of Electric Field*". Wherever electric field exist, field energy also exist in space. In next article we will calculate the field energy in the region electric field.

1.19.1 Field Energy Density of Electric Field

As discussed in previous article that in every region wherever electric field is present, its field energy must exist. This field energy we can calculate by considering a general illustration.

Consider a charged conducting body shown in figure-1.341. Its surface M is having a charge distributed on it. We've already studied in article-1.14.10 that the electric field just outside the surface of a conducting body at a point where surface charge density is σ, can be given as

$$E = \frac{\sigma}{\epsilon_0}$$

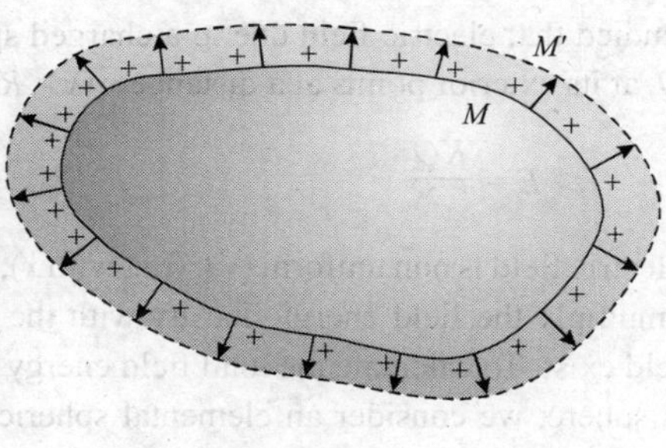

Figure 1.341

In article-1.16 we've also studied that on the surface of a charged conducting body, it experience an outward electric pressure which is given as

$$P_e = \frac{\sigma^2}{2\epsilon_0} = \frac{1}{2}\epsilon_0 E^2$$

In above case if we consider the conducting surface M is made up of a flexible material then due to electric pressure it will start expanding. We consider a very small expansion of the body to the expanded surface M' as shown in above figure. In this situation we can see that inside the conducting body there is no electric field and initially electric field was only present from surface M to infinity. Thus the field energy of electric field was also present from the surface M to infinity. After expansion the surface expands to M' then in the final stage the electric field as well as field energy exist from surface M' to infinity. In the process of expansion of surface, the field energy in the shaded volume (say dV) vanishes as before expansion there was electric field in this region and after expansion electric field becomes zero in the region.

In the above process expansion is done by electric forces in the body due electric pressure thus by conservation of energy it can be stated that the work done by electric field in process of expansion is equal to the loss in field energy in the shaded volume dV.

If P_e is the electric pressure on the body surface then in the small expansion in body volume dV, work done by electric forces can be given as

$$dW = P_e dV$$

If we consider that dU is the field energy stored in this elemental volume dV then we can use

$$dU = dW = P_e dV$$

$$\Rightarrow \quad u = \frac{dU}{dV} = P_e$$

$$\Rightarrow \quad u = \frac{\sigma^2}{2\epsilon_0} = \frac{1}{2}\epsilon_0 E^2 \text{ J/m}^3$$

In above expression $u = \frac{dU}{dV}$ is considered as the field energy stored per unit volume in the space where electric field strength is E and it is called field energy density of electric field in that region.

If in a region electric field is uniform, the total field energy stored in a given volume V of space can be given as

$$U = \frac{1}{2}\epsilon_0 E^2 \times V$$

If electric field in a region is non-uniform, the total field energy stored in a given volume of space can be calculated by integrating the field energy dU stored in an elemental volume dV of space as

$$dU = \frac{1}{2} \epsilon_0 E^2 \times dV$$

And total field energy in a given volume can be given as

$$U = \int dU = \int \frac{1}{2} \epsilon_0 E^2 dV$$

The limits of integration in above integral is substituted as per the dimensions of the region in which we will calculate the field energy. In upcoming articles applications of field energy will be understood properly.

1.19.2 Self Energy of a Charged Body

We've discussed whenever a system of charges is assembled, some work is done and this work is stored in the form of electrical potential energy of the system. Consider a metal sphere of radius R charged with a charge Q. We will discuss about the work done needed to charge this sphere or in other words we will now calculate the amount of work done in assembling the charge Q on this sphere.

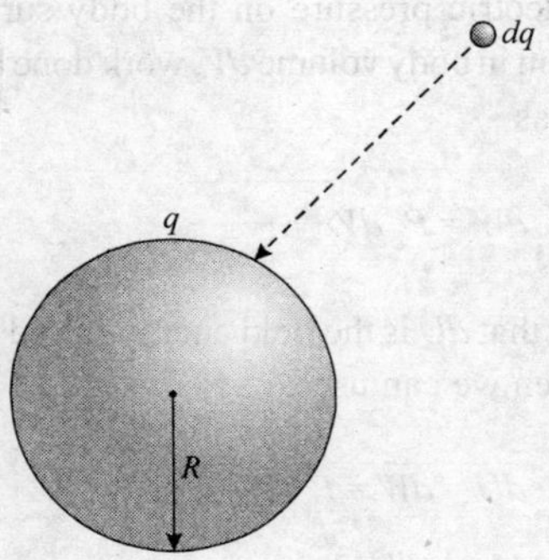

Figure 1.342

Figure-1.342 shows a conducting sphere of radius R. In the process of charging this sphere gradually we bring charge to the sphere from infinity in steps of elemental charges dq. The charge on sphere opposes the elemental charge being brought to it. At an intermediate step of charging we consider that upto this instant sphere has collected a charge q, due to which it has attained a potential given as

$$V = \frac{Kq}{R}$$

If in this state a charge dq is brought from infinity to its surface, the work done in the process can be given as

$$dW = dqV$$

$$\Rightarrow \quad dW = \frac{Kq}{R} dq$$

Total work done in charging the sphere can be given by integrating the above elemental work in transporting dq within limits from 0 to Q which is given as

$$W = \int dW = \int_0^Q \frac{Kq}{R} dq$$

$$\Rightarrow \quad W = \frac{KQ^2}{2R} \quad \quad \ldots(1.264)$$

Equation-(1.264) gives the total work done in charging the sphere of radius R with a charge Q.

We've discussed in article-1.19.1 that in space wherever electric field exist, in region field energy is stored of which energy density is given as

$$u = \frac{1}{2} \epsilon_0 E^2 \text{ J/m}^3$$

In above case we can see when the sphere was uncharged there was no electric field in its surroundings. But when it is fully charged, electric field exist in its surrounding from its surface to infinity. We can calculate the field energy associated with this charged conducting sphere in its surrounding space.

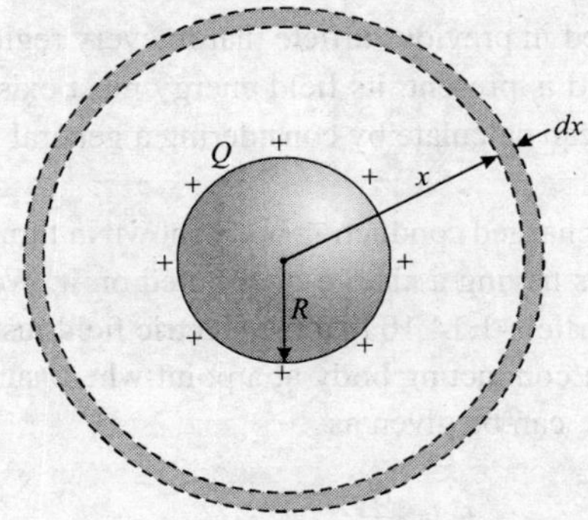

Figure 1.343

We've studied that electric field due to a charged sphere with charge Q, at its exterior points at a distance x ($x > R$) varies as

$$E = \frac{KQ}{x^2}$$

As this electric field is non uniform (varying with x), we cannot directly multiply the field energy density with the volume in which field exist. To calculate the total field energy associated with this sphere, we consider an elemental spherical shell of radius x and width dx as shown in figure-1.343. The volume of space enclosed within this shell is

$$dV = 4\pi x^2 \,.\, dx$$

Thus field energy stored within the volume of this elemental shell is given as

$$dU = \frac{1}{2} \epsilon_0 E^2 \,.\, dV$$

$$\Rightarrow \qquad dU = \frac{1}{2}\epsilon_0\left[\frac{KQ}{x^2}\right]^2 \times 4\pi x^2\, dx$$

$$\Rightarrow \qquad dU = \frac{KQ^2}{2x^2}\, dx$$

Thus total field energy associated with the sphere can be calculated by integrating the above expression from surface of sphere to infinity as electric field inside the sphere is zero. So total field energy in the surrounding space of sphere is

$$U = \int dU = \int_R^\infty \frac{KQ^2}{2x^2}\, dx$$

$$\Rightarrow \qquad U = \frac{KQ^2}{2}\left[-\frac{1}{x}\right]_R^\infty$$

$$\Rightarrow \qquad U = \frac{KQ^2}{2R} \qquad \ldots(1.265)$$

We can see that this result is same as equation-(1.264). By this analysis we can conclude that work done in charging a body is stored in its surrounding in the form of its field energy. This energy is also called "*Self Energy*" of that body. Once a body is charged in a given configuration, its self energy is considered as a constant, if the body is displaced or moved in any manner keeping its shape and charge distribution constant, its self energy does not change. As discussed above we can say that

"*Self energy of a charged body is the total field energy, associated with the electric field due to this body in its surrounding and same is the work done in charging the body in the given final charge configuration and shape.*"

1.19.3 Self Energy of a Uniformly Charged Non-conducting Sphere

We know in outside region of a non-conducting uniformly charged sphere, electric field strength at every exterior point is same as that of a conducting sphere of same radius. Thus field energy in the surrounding of this sphere from surface to infinity can be given as

$$U_{R\to\infty} = \frac{KQ^2}{2R} \qquad \ldots(1.266)$$

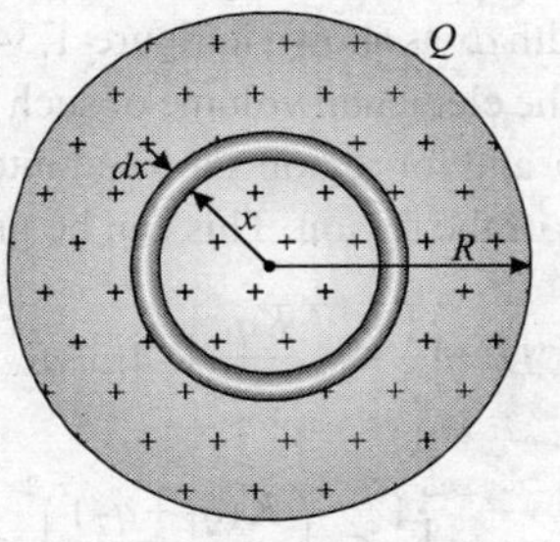

Figure 1.344

Unlike to the case of conducting sphere, in nonconducting sphere at interior points $E \neq 0$. Thus field energy also exist in the interior region. This can be calculated by considering an elemental shell inside the sphere as shown in above figure-1.344.

The field energy in the volume of this elemental shell can be given as

$$dU = \frac{1}{2}\epsilon_0\left[\frac{KQx}{R^3}\right]^2 \times 4\pi x^2\, dx$$

$$\Rightarrow \qquad dU = \frac{KQ^2}{2R^6}\, x^4 dx$$

Total field energy inside the sphere can be given by integrating the above expression within limits from 0 to R which is given as

$$U = \int dU = \frac{KQ^2}{2R^6}\int_0^R x^4 dx$$

$$\Rightarrow \qquad U = \frac{KQ^2}{2R^6}\left[\frac{x^5}{5}\right]_0^R$$

$$\Rightarrow \qquad U_{0\to R} = \frac{KQ^2}{10R} \qquad \ldots(1.267)$$

Thus total self energy of this sphere can be given by sum of inside and outside field energies as given by equation-(1.266) and (1.267) so we have

$$U_{self} = U_{0\to R} + U_{R\to\infty}$$

$$\Rightarrow \qquad U_{self} = \frac{KQ^2}{10R} + \frac{KQ^2}{2R}$$

$$\Rightarrow \qquad U_{self} = \frac{3}{5}\frac{KQ^2}{R} \qquad \ldots(1.268)$$

Equation-(1.268) gives the total field energy associated with a uniformly charged non conducting sphere. Same is the amount of work done in charging an uncharged sphere to the state of uniformly volume charged sphere. Students can calculate the work in bringing elemental charges dq from infinity to a uniformly charged non conducting sphere from 0 to Q and verify that result will be same as given in equation-(1.268).

1.19.4 Total Electrostatic Energy of a System of Charges

When a system of two or more charged bodies are brought close to a given state of charge configuration then work is done by an external agent in two ways. First is the work done in charging to bodies to their respective charges which we call self energy of objects and another work will be done bringing the bodies close to a given separation which is called interaction energy of the system. Total electrostatic potential energy a system of charges can be given by sum of the above work done given as

$$U = \sum \text{self energy of all charged bodies} + \sum \text{Interaction energy of all pairs of charged bodies.}$$

Let us consider some cases to understand this concept. Figure-1.345 shows two uniformly charged non-conducting spheres of radius R_1 and R_2 and charged with charges Q_1 and Q_2 respectively separated by a distance r. If we find the total electrostatic energy of this system, we can write as

$$U = U_{\text{Self}} + U_{\text{Interaction}}$$

$$\Rightarrow \quad U = \frac{3KQ_1^2}{5R_1} + \frac{3KQ_2^2}{5R_2} + \frac{KQ_1Q_2}{r} \qquad \ldots(1.269)$$

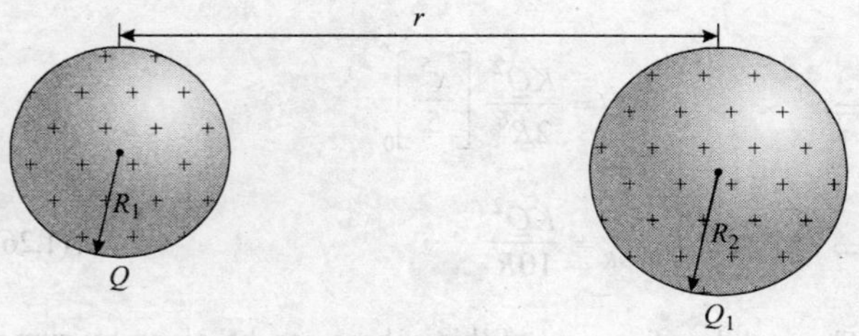

Figure 1.345

First and second terms in above equation-(1.269) are the self energies of the two spheres and third term is the interaction energy of the system of two spheres as given by equation-(1.100) in article-1.8.2. Next article will also explain this concept in more detail for understanding it better.

1.19.5 Electrostatic Energy of a System of a Conducting Sphere and a Concentric Shell

Figure-1.346 shows a solid conducting sphere and a concentric shell of radii a and b respectively charged uniformly with charges q_1 and q_2. The total energy of this system can be given as

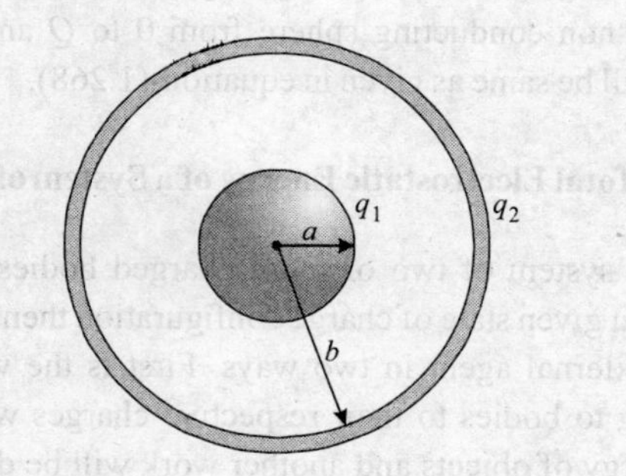

Figure 1.346

$$U_{\text{total}} = \text{Self energy of inner sphere} + \text{Self energy of outer shell} + \text{Interaction energy of the two shell}$$

$$= \frac{Kq_1^2}{2a} + \frac{Kq_2^2}{2b} + \frac{Kq_1q_2}{b} \qquad \ldots(1.270)$$

Similar to the previous article, in this case also first and second terms of the equation-(1.270) are the self energies of the inner sphere and outer shell respectively and the third term is the interaction energy of the two.

As we've already discussed that the electrostatic potential energy is always stored in a system in form of field energy so in this case we can also calculate the total energy by calculating the total field energy associated with the system.

1.19.6 Total Field Energy of a System of Conducting Sphere and a Concentric Shell

In the situation shown in Figure-1.347 we can state that the electric field inside the sphere at points $x < a$ at every point electric field is zero so no field energy exist inside this region. In the region from $x = a$ to $x = b$ the electric field exist only due to the charge on conducting sphere and in outer region where $x > b$, electric field exist due to the charges of both sphere as well as that of the shell.

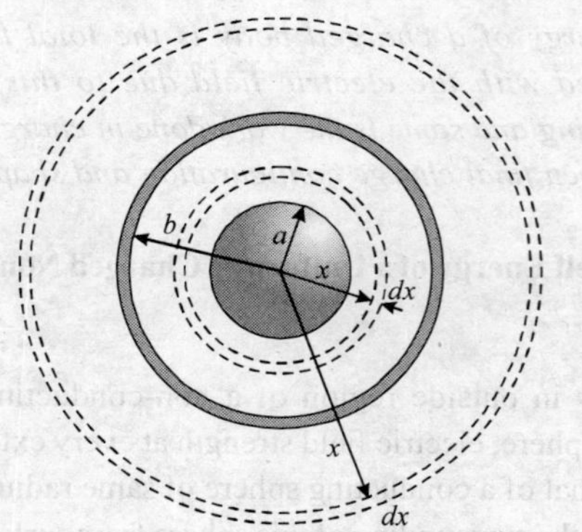

Figure 1.347

Total field energy in the electric field associated with the system can be calculated by considering elemental concentric shell of radius x and width dx as shown in figure-1.347. We can find the field energy in the elemental volume of such elemental shells in region $a < x < b$ and for region $x > b$ and integrating within the specified limits of the region. This can be given as

$$U = \int_a^b \frac{1}{2} \epsilon_0 \left(\frac{Kq_1}{x^2}\right)^2 4\pi x^2 dx + \int_b^\infty \frac{1}{2} \epsilon_0 \left(\frac{K(q_1 + q_2)}{r^2}\right)^2 4\pi r^2 dr$$

$$\Rightarrow \quad U = \frac{1}{2} K q_1^2 \left[\frac{1}{a} - \frac{1}{b}\right] + \frac{1}{2} K (q_1 + q_2)^2 \left[\frac{1}{b}\right]$$

$$\Rightarrow \quad U = \frac{1}{2} \frac{K q_1^2}{a} - \frac{K q_1^2}{2b} + \frac{K q_1^2}{b} + \frac{K q_2^2}{2b} + \frac{K q_2^2}{b}$$

$$\Rightarrow \quad U = \frac{K q_1^2}{2b} + \frac{K q_2^2}{2b} + \frac{K q_1 q_2}{b}$$

Above equation is same as equation-(1.270)

1.20 Dielectrics

Materials which do not contain any free electrons are insulating medium in which charges do not flow like a conductor. When such materials are placed in external electric field then charges in these are slightly displaced from their initial position causing polarization of material. Such materials are called '*Dielectrics*'. Dielectrics are of two types - Polar and Non Polar.

Non Polar dielectrics are made up of such atoms or molecules which do not have any dipole moment but on applying external electric field, these atoms are transformed in to dipoles with a specific dipole moment depending upon the strength of electric field applied. This can be explained with the help of figure-1.348(a) which shows an atom with its nucleus at center and spherical electron cloud in surrounding.

When an external electric field is applied then nucleus being positively charged it experiences a force in the direction of electric field and electron cloud being negatively charged, all electrons in it experience the force in direction opposite to electric field. Due to these opposite forces electron cloud gets distorted and the atom is transformed in form of a dipole with slight separation between its negative and positive centers as shown in figure-1.348(b). Such dielectrics which have initial dipole moment zero and transform into a dipole when placed in an electric field are called non polar dielectrics.

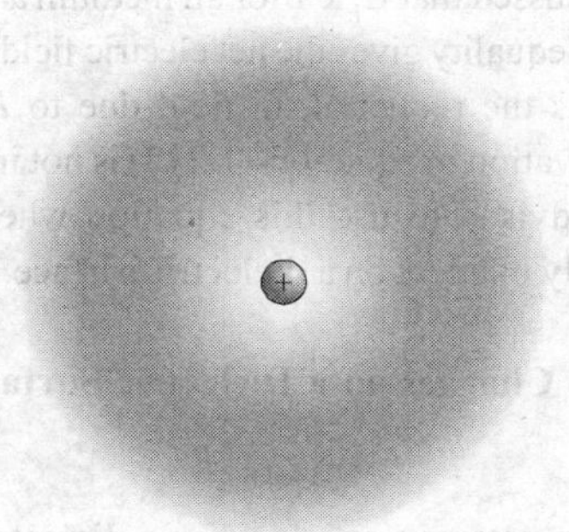

(a)

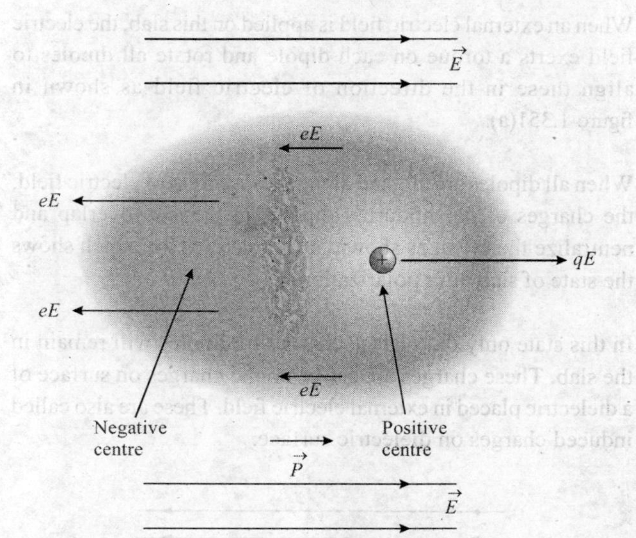

(b)

Figure 1.348

Some other insulating material which consist of molecules which have a non zero dipole moment due to ionic bonds or polar covalent bonds like HCl, NaCl and many other such substances are termed as polar dielectrics. When such material are placed in external electric field then the electric field exert a couple on the dipole as discussed in article-1.12.1 and this torque of couple the dipole rotates it and align in the direction of electric field as shown in figure-1.349.

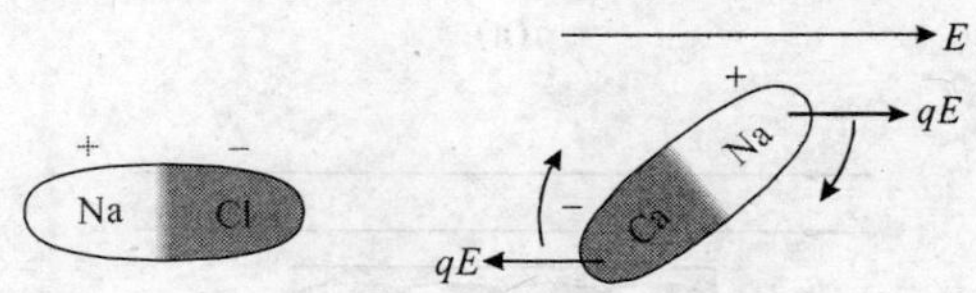

Figure 1.349

1.20.1 Polarization of Dielectrics in Electric Field

Figure-1.350 shows a polar dielectric slab at room temperature. In normal conditions the dipoles of the dielectric are randomly scattered in its volume.

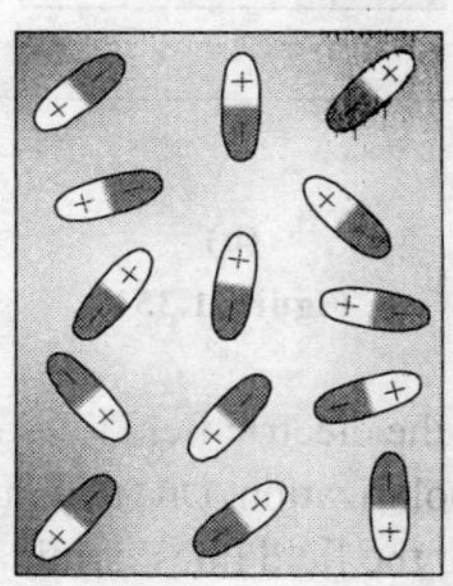

Figure 1.350

When an external electric field is applied on this slab, the electric field exerts a torque on each dipole and rotate all dipoles to align these in the direction of electric field as shown in figure-1.351(a).

When all dipoles are aligned along the direction of electric field, the charges of neighbouring dipoles in the slab overlap and neutralize the effect as shown in figure-1.351(b) which shows the state of slab after polarization.

In this state only the surface charges of dipoles will remain in the slab. These charges are called bound charges on surface of a dielectric placed in external electric field. These are also called induced charges on dielectric surface.

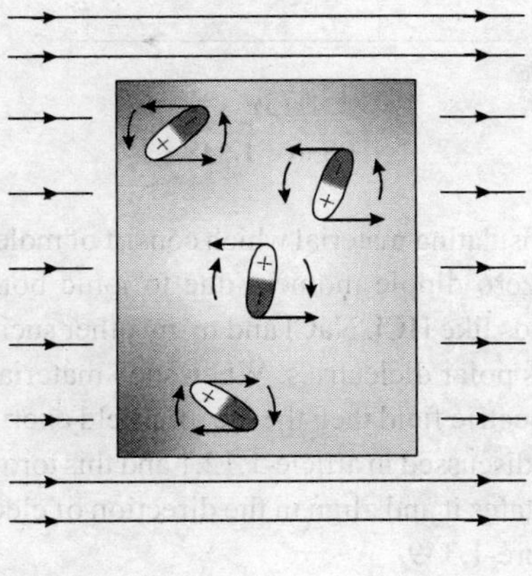

(a)

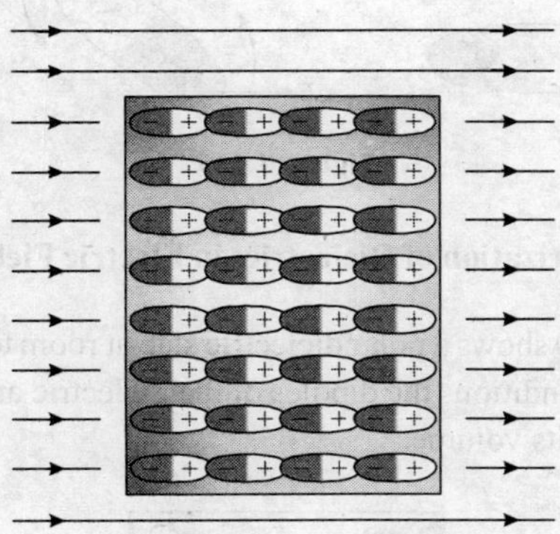

(b)

Figure 1.351

Figure-1.352 shows the electric field lines configuration in the dielectric slab after polarization. Due to induced surface charges on dielectric some of the field lines terminate on these charges due to which the flux density inside the dielectric is less than the external field.

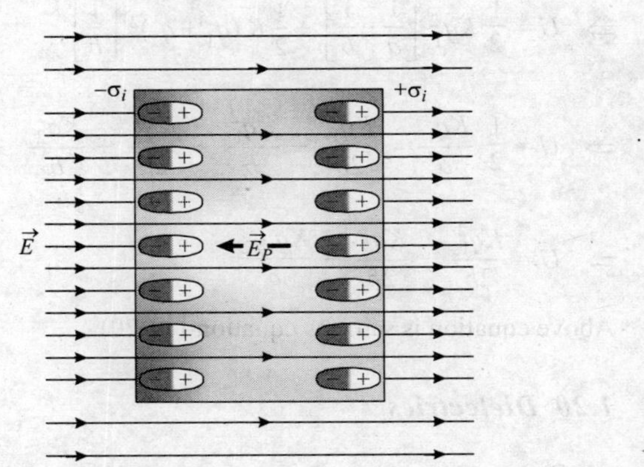

Figure 1.352

Inside the slab electric field strength is lesser because of the electric field inside the slab due to induced surface charges which exist in direction opposite to the external electric field. The net electric field strength inside the dielectric slab is given as

$$E_{net} = E - E_P \qquad \dots(1.271)$$

In above equation-(1.271) the electric field strength due to induced surface charges is E_P and E is the external applied electric field. Due to induced surface charges, always the net electric field inside a dielectric material placed in an external electric field is less than the external field. The calculation of E_P becomes complex many times in different cases so the reduction in electric field strength inside a dielectric is mathematically accounted by a constant factor called "*Dielectric Constant*" as given in equation-(1.272) below

$$E_{net} = E - E_P = \frac{E}{\epsilon_r} \qquad \dots(1.272)$$

In above equation-(1.272) ϵ_r is dielectric constant or relative permittivity of medium which is discussed briefly in article-1.2.2. As already discussed that $\epsilon_r > 1$ for all medium and the last term on right side of equality gives the net electric field in the medium which accounts the reduction in field due to E_P in opposite direction. Derivation of equation-(1.272) is not in scope now so students are advised to use this equation whenever electric field is normally incident on a dielectric surface.

1.20.2 Bound Charges on a Dielectric Surface in Electric Field

As discussed in previous article when a dielectric is placed in an external electric field, bound charges appear on the surfaces of dielectric as shown in figure-1.352. We consider that $+\sigma_i$ and

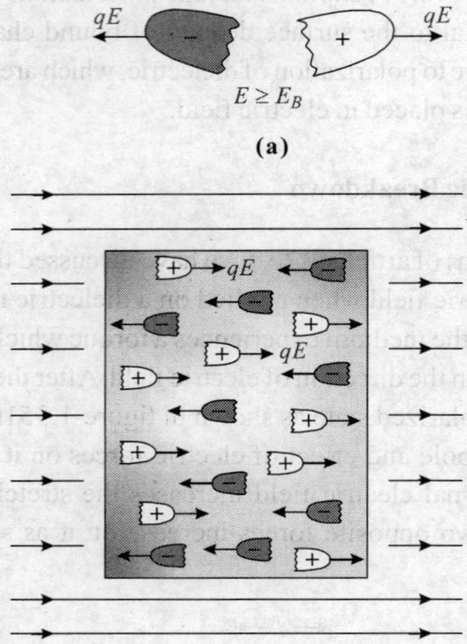

(a)

(b)

Figure 1.354

Many times the process of dielectric breakdown produces so much heat in the material that it starts melting and no longer remain in solid state.

1.20.5 Effect of Temperature on Dielectric Constant of Medium

In previous articles we've discussed as dielectric constant of a medius is a measure of the extent to which medium gets polarized when external electric field is applied onto it.

If in presence of external electric field the dipole moment of the medium particle is high then it produces more E_P and net electric field in the system will be reduced more and to account this opposite electric field due to bound charges the dielectric constant will also be higher as discussed in equation-(1.272).

If the temperature of dielectric medium is increased, it increases the thermal agitation in the medium particles. Random oscillations because of thermal energy causes particles do disalign their dipole moment from the direction of electric field. However in oscillations average dipole moment direction remain same but overall due to random oscillations the polarization of the medium will relatively less compared to the state at low temperature.

Thus we can say that at higher temperature under same value of applied electric field strength the induced electric field due to bound charges in the medium will be lesser and net electric field inside the medium will be more at higher temperature and dielectric constant is also considered to be lesser.

Thus with the above explanation we can state that on increasing temperature of a given medium its dielectric constant decreases due to thermal agitation.

Dielectric constant is also termed as relative permittivity of the medium as discussed in article-1.2.2. Here this constant also determines the amount of electric flux of an electric field which enters in to a dielectric medium.

Figure-1.355(a) shows a dielectric slab placed in an electric field. Due to induced bound charges on the surface of slab some field lines will terminate on the slab and remaining will enter in the slab and the flux density which gives the strength of net electric field is less inside the slab.

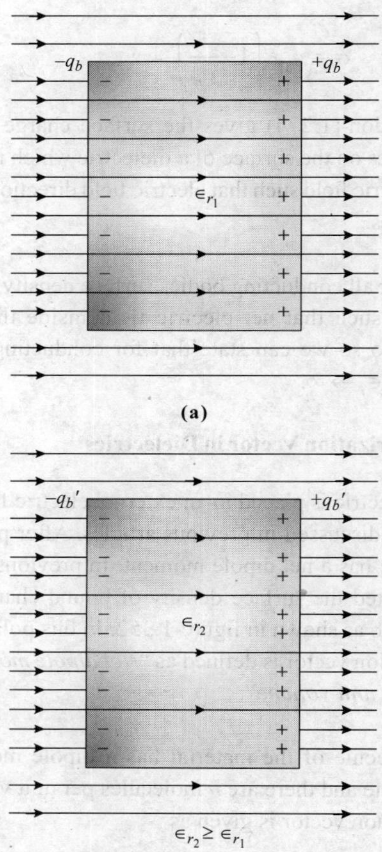

(a)

(b)

Figure 1.355

If dielectric constant is more then from equation-(1.274) we can see that surface density of induced charges will be more and more electric lines will terminate on the surface and less will enter in the slab as shown in figure-1.355(b).

For metals we can use $\in_r \to \infty$ thus all the electric lines will terminate on the surface of slab and no flux is permitted to enter in the slab. Thus indirectly we can state that the dielectric constant or relative permittivity of the medium is associated with the amount of electric flux permitted to enter in a medium. If dielectric constant of a medium is less, more flux will be allowed to enter into it and if dielectric constant of a medium is high, less flux will be allowed to enter into it.

Illustrative Example 1.93

Figure-1.356(a) shows a shell of radius R having charge q_1 uniformly distributed over it. A point charge q is placed at the centre of shell. Find amount of work required to increase the radius of shell from R to R_1 as shown in figure-1.356(b).

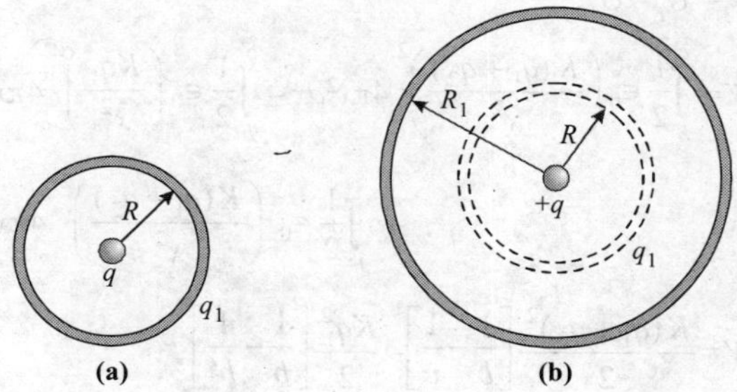

Figure 1.356

Solution

Work done required can be calculated by difference in total electrostatic energy of the shell given as

$$\text{Work} = U_f - U_i$$

Initial total electrostatic energy of the shell is given as

$$U_i = SE_q + SE_{q_1} + IE$$

$$\Rightarrow \quad U_i = SE_q + \frac{Kq_1^2}{2R} + \frac{Kq_1q_2}{R}$$

Final total electrostatic energy of the shell is given as

$$U_f = SE_q + \frac{Kq_1^2}{2R_1} + \frac{Kq_1q}{R_1}$$

Work done in the expansion process is given as

$$W = U_i - U_f$$

$$\Rightarrow \quad W = \frac{Kq_1^2}{2R_1} + \frac{Kq_1q}{R_1} - \frac{Kq_1^2}{2R} - \frac{Kq_1q}{R}$$

$$\Rightarrow \quad W = \frac{Kq_1^2}{2}\left(\frac{1}{R_1} - \frac{1}{R}\right) + Kqq_1\left(\frac{1}{R_1} - \frac{1}{R}\right)$$

$$\Rightarrow \quad W = Kq_1\left(q + \frac{q_1}{2}\right)\left(\frac{1}{R_1} - \frac{1}{R}\right)$$

Illustrative Example 1.94

Find the electrostatic energy stored in a cylindrical shell of length l, inner radius a and outer radius b, coaxial with a uniformly charged wire with linear charge density λ C/m.

Solution

For this we consider an elemental shell of radius x and width dx. The volume of this shell dV can be given as

$$dV = 2\pi xl \cdot dx$$

The electric field due to the wire at the shell is

$$E = \frac{2K\lambda}{x}$$

The electrostatic field energy stored in the volume of this shell is

$$dU = \frac{1}{2}\epsilon_0 E^2 \, dV$$

$$\Rightarrow \quad dU = \frac{1}{2}\epsilon_0\left(\frac{2K\lambda}{x}\right)^2 . \, 2\pi xl . \, dx$$

The total electrostatic energy stored in the above mentioned volume can be obtained by integrating the above expression within limits from a to b as

$$U = \int dU = \int_a^b \frac{1}{2}\epsilon_0\left(\frac{2K\lambda}{x}\right)^2 . \, 2\pi xl . \, dx$$

$$\Rightarrow \quad U = \frac{\lambda^2 l}{4\pi\epsilon_0}\int_a^b \frac{1}{x}dx$$

$$\Rightarrow \quad U = \frac{\lambda^2 l}{4\pi\epsilon_0}[\ln x]_a^b$$

$$\Rightarrow \quad U = \frac{\lambda^2 l}{4\pi\epsilon_0}\ln\left(\frac{b}{a}\right)$$

Illustrative Example 1.95

Three shells are shown carrying charge q_1, q_2 and q_3 and of radii a, b and c respectively. If the middle shell expands from radius b to b' ($b' < c$). Find the work done by electric field in process.

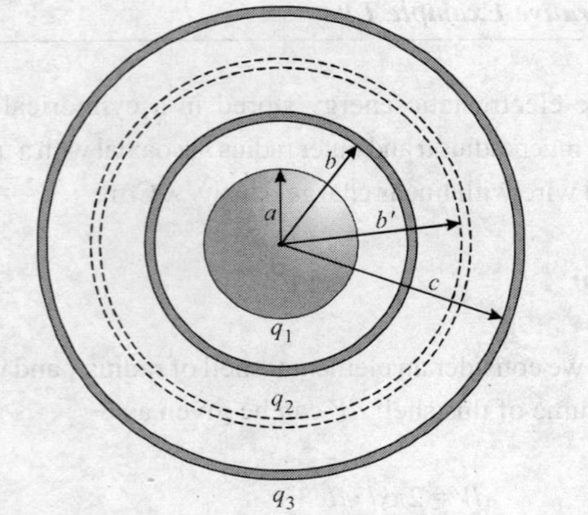

Figure 1.357

Solution

Work done by field can be given as

$$W = U_i - U_f$$

Total initial electrostatic energy of system is given as sum of all the Self Energies (SE) and Interaction Energies (IE) of all pairs of system charges which is given as

$$U_i = SE_1 + SE_2 + SE_3 + IE_{12} + IE_{13} + IE_{23}$$

$$U_i = \frac{Kq_1^2}{2a} + \frac{Kq_2^2}{2b} + \frac{Kq_3^2}{2c} + \frac{Kq_1q_3}{c} + \frac{Kq_1q_2}{b} + \frac{Kq_2q_3}{c}$$

Similarly total final electrostatic energy of system is given as

$$U_f = SE_1' + SE_2' + SE_3' + IE_{12}' + IE_{13}' + IE_{23}'$$

$$U_f = \frac{Kq_1^2}{2a} + \frac{Kq_2^2}{2b'} + \frac{Kq_3^2}{2c} + \frac{Kq_1q_3}{c} + \frac{Kq_1q_2}{b'} + \frac{Kq_2q_3}{c}$$

Work done by field in expansion process is

$$W = U_i - U_f$$

$$\Rightarrow W = \frac{Kq_2^2}{2b} - \frac{Kq_2^2}{2b'} + \frac{Kq_1q_2}{b} - \frac{Kq_1q_2}{b'}$$

$$\Rightarrow W = Kq_2\left(q_1 + \frac{q_2}{2}\right)\left(\frac{1}{b} - \frac{1}{b'}\right) \qquad \ldots(1.278)$$

Alternative Method by Field energy of the electric field

In above given situation we can calculate the total field energy of the electric field associated with the system due to all the charges by using the expression of field energy density. The total initial electrostatic energy of the system can be given as

$$U_i = \int_a^b \frac{1}{2}\epsilon_0\left(\frac{Kq_1}{x^2}\right)^2 4\pi x^2 dx + \int_b^{b'} \frac{1}{2}\epsilon_0\left(\frac{K(q_1+q_2)}{x^2}\right)^2 4\pi x^2 dx + \int_c^{\infty} \frac{1}{2}\epsilon_0\left(\frac{K(q_1+q_2+q_3)}{x^2}\right)^2 4\pi x^2 dx$$

Similarly total final electrostatic energy of the system can be given as

$$U_f = \int_a^b \frac{1}{2}\epsilon_0\left(\frac{Kq_1}{x^2}\right)^2 4\pi x^2 dx + \int_b^{b'} \frac{1}{2}\epsilon_0\left(\frac{Kq_1}{x^2}\right)^2 4\pi x^2 dx + \int_{b'}^{c} \frac{1}{2}\epsilon_0\left(\frac{K(q_1+q_2)}{x^2}\right)^2 4\pi x^2 dx + \int_c^{\infty} \frac{1}{2}\epsilon_0\left(\frac{K(q_1+q_2+q_3)}{x^2}\right)^2 4\pi x^2 dx$$

Thus work done in expansion process is given as

$$W = U_i - U_f$$

$$\Rightarrow W = \int_b^{c} \frac{1}{2}\epsilon_0\left(\frac{K(q_1+q_2)}{x^2}\right)^2 4\pi x^2 dx - \int_b^{b'} \frac{1}{2}\epsilon_0\left(\frac{Kq_1}{x^2}\right)^2 4\pi x^2 dx - \int_{b'}^{c} \frac{1}{2}\epsilon_0\left(\frac{K(q_1+q_2)}{x^2}\right)^2 4\pi x^2 dx$$

$$\Rightarrow W = \frac{K(q_1+q_2)^2}{2}\left[\frac{1}{b} - \frac{1}{c}\right] - \frac{Kq_1^2}{2}\left[\frac{1}{b} - \frac{1}{b'}\right] - \frac{K(a_1+a_2)^2}{2}\left[\frac{1}{b'} - \frac{1}{c}\right]$$

$$\Rightarrow W = \frac{K(q_1+q_2)^2}{2b} - \frac{Kq_1^2}{2b} + \frac{Kq_1^2}{2b'} - \frac{K(q_1+q_2)^2}{2b'}$$

$$\Rightarrow W = \frac{Kq_1^2}{2b} + \frac{Kq_2^2}{2b} + \frac{Kq_1q_2}{b} - \frac{Kq_1^2}{2b} + \frac{Kq_1^2}{2b'} - \frac{Kq_1^2}{2b'} - \frac{Kq_2^2}{2b'} - \frac{Kq_1q_2}{b'}$$

$$\Rightarrow W = \frac{Kq_2^2}{2b} - \frac{Kq_2^2}{2b'} + \frac{Kq_1q_2}{b} - \frac{Kq_1q_2}{b'}$$

$$\Rightarrow W = Kq_2\left(q_1 + \frac{q_2}{2}\right)\left(\frac{1}{b} - \frac{1}{b'}\right) \qquad \ldots(1.279)$$

Above equation-(1.279) is same as equation-(1.278) which was obtained by the difference of initial and final total electrostatic energies of the system calculated by sum of self and interaction energies.

 # Illustrative Example 1.96

A cable consisting of a solid conductor of 6 mm diameter is surrounded by two layers of insulating material, the inner having a thickness 3 mm and dielectric constant 7 and the other a thickness 4 mm and dielectric constant 5. Outside this is an earthed conducting sheaths. Find the ratio of falls of potential in the two insulating layers. On gradually raising the p.d. between inner conductor and earthed sheathing, which of the layers will first breakdown, assuming the dielectric strength of two materials are the same?

Solution

The intensity of the electric field due to a cylindrical conductor is given by

$$E = \frac{1}{4\pi\varepsilon_0} \times \frac{2q}{Kr}$$

where q = charge per unit length of the inner solid cylinder.

The potential difference across the inner dielectric is given by

$$V_1 = \int_{0.006}^{0.003} \frac{1}{4\pi\varepsilon_0} \times \frac{2q}{7r} dr \; (K=7)$$

$$\Rightarrow \quad V_1 = \frac{1}{4\pi\varepsilon_0} \times \frac{2q}{7} \log_e\left(\frac{6}{3}\right) \quad \ldots(1.280)$$

Similarly, the potential difference across the outer dielectric is given by

$$V_2 = \int_{0.01}^{0.006} \frac{1}{4\pi\varepsilon_0} \times \frac{2q}{5r} dr$$

$$\Rightarrow \quad V_2 = \frac{1}{4\pi\varepsilon_0} \frac{2q}{5} \log_e\left(\frac{10}{6}\right) \quad \ldots(1.281)$$

Now $$\frac{V_1}{V_2} = \frac{5}{7} \frac{\log_e(2)}{\log_e(5/3)} = 0.9693 \quad \ldots(1.282)$$

Further, $(E_{1\max})$ at $r = 3$ mm $= \frac{1}{4\pi\varepsilon_0} \times \frac{2q}{7 \times 0.003} \frac{V}{m}$

and $(E_{2\max})$ at $r = 6$ mm $= \frac{1}{4\pi\varepsilon_0} \times \frac{2q}{5 \times 0.006} \frac{V}{m}$

$$\Rightarrow \quad \frac{E_{1\max}}{E_{2\max}} = \frac{5}{7} \times \frac{0.006}{0.003} = 1.43$$

This shows that maximum intensity in the inner dielectric will always be greater than that in the outer dielectric. Given that the dielectric strength is same for both the dielectric and hence the inner dielectric will breakdown first.

 # Illustrative Example 1.97

A point charge q is isolated at the centre O of a spherical uncharged conducting layer provided with a small orifice. The inside and outside radii of the layer are equal to a and b respectively. What amount of work has to be performed to slowly transfer the charge q from the point O through the orifice and into infinity.

Solution

Figure-1.358 shows the situation described in the question.

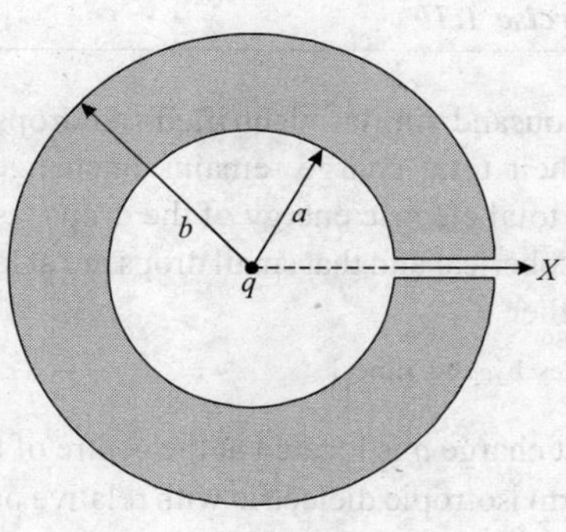

Figure 1.358

In initial state when the charge was located at the center of the shell opposite charges $-q$ and $+q$ induced on the inner and outer surface of the shell and the total electrostatic energy of the system in this state is given as

$$U_i = S_q + \frac{Kq^2}{2a} + \frac{Kq^2}{2b} + \frac{Kq^2}{b} - \frac{Kq^2}{b} - \frac{Kq^2}{a} \quad \ldots(1.283)$$

In above equation S_q is the self energy of point charge q which remain constant. When the charge q is taken to infinity then induced charges also vanish and final electrostatic energy will only be the self energy of the point charge thus we have

$$U_f = S_q$$

Total work required in the process is given as

$$W = U_f - U_i$$

$$\Rightarrow \quad W = S_q - S_q - \left(\frac{Kq^2}{2a} + \frac{Kq^2}{2b} + \frac{Kq^2}{b} - \frac{Kq^2}{b} - \frac{Kq^2}{a}\right)$$

$$\Rightarrow W = \frac{q}{8\pi\varepsilon_0}\left(\frac{1}{a} - \frac{1}{b}\right)$$

Web Reference at www.physicsgalaxy.com

Age Group - Grade 11 & 12 | Age 17-19 Years
Section - ELECTROSTATICS
Topic - Conductors & Dielectrics
Module Number - 23 to 27

Web Reference at www.physicsgalaxy.com

Age Group - Grade 11 & 12 | Age 17-19 Years
Section - ELECTROSTATICS
Topic - Electrostatic Field Energy
Module Number - 1 to 12

Practice Exercise 1.10

(i) One thousand similar electrified raindrops merge into one so that their total charge remains unchanged. Find the change in the total electric energy of the drops, assuming that the drops are spherical and that small drops are at large distance from one another.

[Energy increases by 100 times]

(ii) A point charge q is located at the centre of the spherical layer of uniform isotropic dielectric with relative permittivity k. The inside radius of the layer is equal to a and the outside radius is b. Find the electrostatic energy inside the dielectric layer.

[$\frac{q^2}{8\pi k^2 \epsilon_0}\left[\frac{1}{b}-\frac{1}{a}\right]$]

(iii) A solid conducting sphere of radius a having a charge q is surrounded by a concentric conducting spherical shell of inner radius $2a$ and outer radius $3a$ as shown in figure-1.359. Find the amount of heat produced when switch is closed.

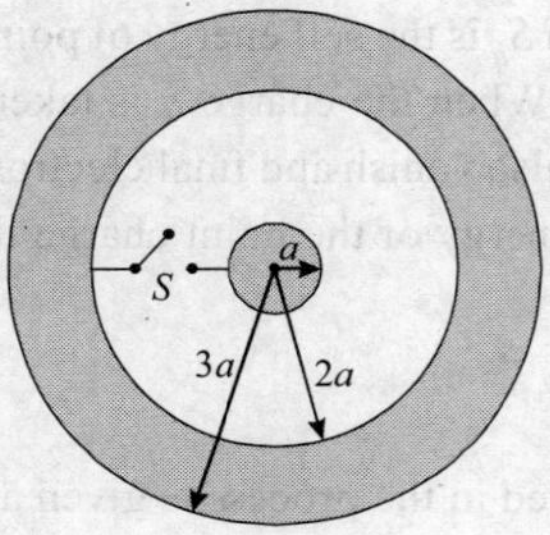

Figure 1.359

[$\frac{q^2}{16\pi \epsilon_0 a}$]

(iv) The figure-1.360 shows a conducting sphere 'A' of radius 'a' which is surrounded by a neutral conducting spherical shell B of radius 'b' ($> a$). Initially switches S_1, S_2 and S_3 are open and sphere 'A' carries a charge Q.

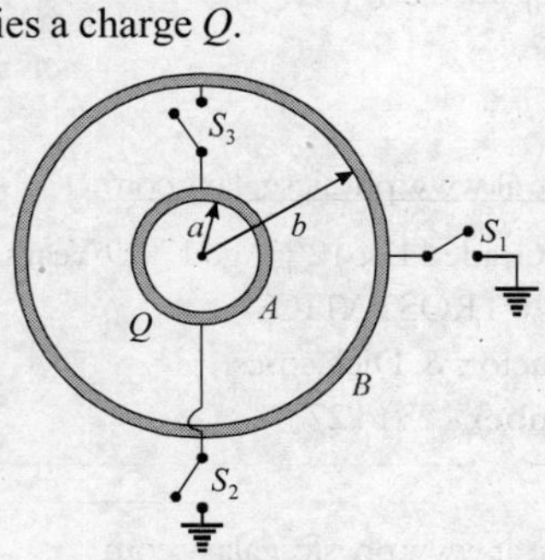

Figure 1.360

First the switch 'S_1' is closed to connect the shell B with the ground and then opened. Now the switch 'S_2' is closed so that the sphere 'A' is grounded and then S_2 is opened. Finally, the switch 'S_3' is closed to connect the spheres together. Find the heat (in Joule) which is produced after closing the switch S_3. [Consider $b = 4$ cm, $a = 2$ cm and $Q = 8$ μc]

[1.8 J]

(v) A long cylindrical shell of length l and radius a is given a uniformly distributed charge Q on its surface. If the shell is expanded uniformly to a radius b, find the work done by electrical forces in the process of expansion.

[$\frac{\lambda^2 l}{4\pi \epsilon_0}\ln\left(\frac{b}{a}\right)$]

(vi) In a system of two concentric spherical conducting shells charge q is given to both inner and outer shells as shown in figure-1.361. Inner shell is connected to earth by a switch. Find the amount of heat produced when switch is closed.

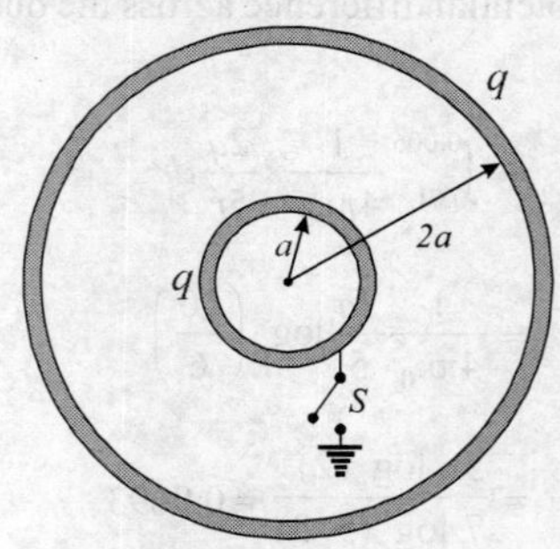

Figure 1.361

[$\frac{5Kq^2}{8a}$]

(vii) Two uniformly charged solid spheres A and B of radii a and b with charges q_1 and q_2 are kept at a separation r. Find the work done in disassembling the whole system into very small particles and displace the particles to infinite separation.

[$\frac{3}{5}\frac{Kq_1^2}{a}+\frac{3}{5}\frac{Kq_2^2}{b}+\frac{Kq_1q_2}{r}$]

(viii) Two uniformly charged concentric spherical shells are of radii a and b respectively. The charges on the two shells are q_1 and q_2. Find the work required in expanding the outer shell of radius b to increase its radius to infinity.

[$-\left(\frac{Kq_2^2}{2b}+\frac{Kq_1q_2}{b}\right)$]

Advance Illustrations Videos at www.physicsgalaxy.com
Age Group - Advance Illustrations
Section - Electrostatics
Topic - Electrostatics
Illustrations - 43 In-depth Illustrations Videos

* * * * *

$-\sigma_i$ are the surface charge densities of these bound charges on the surfaces of dielectric slab as shown. The electric field due to these bound charges exist inside the slab in direction opposite to the external electric field which can be calculated by considering the surface of dielectric to be large, given as

$$E_P = \frac{\sigma_i}{\epsilon_0} \quad \ldots(1.273)$$

From equation-(1.272) of previous article, we have

$$E_P = E\left(1 - \frac{1}{\epsilon_r}\right)$$

$$\Rightarrow \quad \frac{\sigma_i}{\epsilon_0} = E\left(1 - \frac{1}{\epsilon_r}\right)$$

$$\Rightarrow \quad \sigma_i = \epsilon_0 E\left(1 - \frac{1}{\epsilon_r}\right) \quad \ldots(1.274)$$

Above equation-(1.274) gives the surface charge density of bound charges on the surface of a dielectric which is placed in external electric field such that electric field direction is normal to its surfaces.

For metals or all conducting bodies surface density of induced charges are such that net electric field inside the material becomes zero so we can state that for conducting materials $E_P = E$ and $\epsilon_r \to \infty$.

1.20.3 Polarization Vector in Dielectrics

When a dielectric is placed in an external electric field, it gets polarized as discussed in previous articles. After polarization the dielectric has a net dipole moment. In previous article we have calculated the surface density of bound charges on the dielectric slab as shown in figure-1.352. In this polarized state the polarization vector is defined as "*Net dipole moment of the material per unit volume*".

If each molecule of the material has a dipole moment p in polarized state and there are n molecules per unit volume then the polarization vector is given as

$$\vec{P} = n\vec{p} \quad \ldots(1.275)$$

From figure-1.352 the total bound charges on the dielectric slab is given as $q_i = \sigma_i . A$ thus the magnitude of total dipole moment due to bound charges of the dielectric slab is given as

$$P_T = q_i . d = \sigma_i A\, d \quad \ldots(1.276)$$

Thus dipole moment of the whole slab per unit volume can be calculated as

$$P = \frac{P_T}{Ad} = \frac{\sigma_i Ad}{Ad} = \sigma_i \quad \ldots(1.277)$$

Above equation-(1.277) explains that the polarization vector is numerically equal to the surface density of bound charges on dielectric slab due to polarization of dielectric, which are induced when dielectric is placed in electric field.

1.20.4 Dielectric Breakdown

In figure-1.351(a) of article-1.20.1 we have discussed the effect of external electric field when applied on a dielectric medium. Every dipole of the medium experiences a torque which tend to align the dipole in the direction of electric field. After the dipoles are aligned in polarized state as shown in figure-1.351(b) if we consider one dipole and effect of electric forces on it then we can see as external electric field increases the stretch on the dipole due to two opposite forces increase on it as shown in figure-1.353.

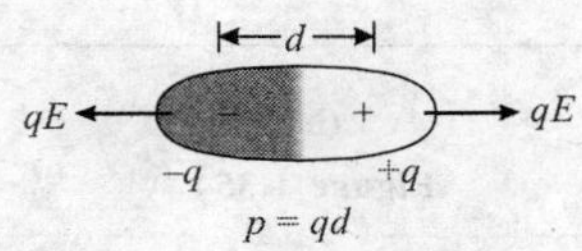

Figure 1.353

As the electric forces on dipole in polarized state are acting on the positive and negative poles of the dipole (molecule), on increasing external electric field the molecule is further stretched and effective separation between the positive and negative poles increases due to which dipole moment of each molecule increases and due to this polarization vector increases hence surface density of bound charges also increases. This is also shown by equation-(1.274) that surface density of bound charges on dielectric surface is directly proportional to the applied electric field strength.

Every molecule as a specific bond strength. If the atoms of molecules are pulled with a force more than its bond strength, the bond breaks. In figure-1.353 we can see if on increasing strength of applied electric field when the stretching electric force on the dipole increases beyond the bond strength of the dipole, it will break and its positive and negative charges will get separated. The minimum electric field strength at which the dipoles of a specific material break is call its "*Dielectric Strength*" and the phenomenon of breaking the dipoles of a dielectric medium is called "*Dielectric Breakdown*". Figure-1.354(a) shows when applied electric field strength approaches the dielectric strength E_B of the material, dipoles break and its positive and negative charges become free to move in the medium which were initially bound in form of dipoles. Figure-1.354(b) shows the dielectric medium after dielectric breakdown in which all the positive and negative charges are separated and free to move in the medium due to breakdown and the medium behave as a conductor due to freely moving charges. Thus after dielectric breakdown an insulator transforms into a conductor.

Discussion Questions

Q1-1 Two identical metallic spheres of exactly equal masses are taken. One is given a positive charge q coulombs and the other an equal negative charge. Are their masses after charging equal ?

Q1-2 It is said that the separation between the two charges forming an electric dipole should be small. Small compared to what ?

Q1-3 A point charge q is placed in a cavity in a metal block. If a charge Q is brought outside the metal, will the charge q feel an electric force ?

Q1-4 An electron and a proton are freely situated in an electric field. Will the electric forces on them be equal? Will their acceleration be equal ? Explain with reason.

Q1-5 Is there any lower limit to the electric force between two particles placed at a separation of 1 cm ?

Q1-6 Can two equipotential surfaces intersect ?

Q1-7 Why the electric field at the outer surface of a hollow charged conductor is normal to the surface ?

Q1-8 Can a gravitational field be added vectorially to an electric field to get a total field ?

Q1-9 Why does a phonograph-record attract dust particles just after it is cleaned ?

Q1-10 A spherical shell made of plastic, contains a charge Q distributed uniformly over its surface. What is the electric field inside the shell ? If the shell is hammered to deshape it without altering the charge, will the field inside be changed ? What happens if the shell is made of a metal ?

Q1-11 How can the whole charge of a conductor be transferred to another isolated conductor ?

Q1-12 Does the force on a charge due to another charge depend on the charges present nearby ?

Q1-13 A charged particle is free to move in an electric field. Will it always move along an electric lines of force ?

Q1-14 Two point charges $+q$ and $-q$ are placed at distance d apart. What are the points at which the resultant field is parallel to the line joining the two charges ?

Q1-15 A point charge is taken from a point A to a point B in an electric field. Does the work done by the electric field depend on the path of the charge ?

Q1-16 A positive charge $+q$ is located at a point. What is the work done if a unit positive charge is carried once around this charge along a circle of radius r about :

Q1-17 A rubber balloon is given a charge Q distributed uniformly over its surface. Is the field inside the balloon zero everywhere if the balloon does not have a spherical surface ?

Q1-18 Two small balls having equal positive charge q coulomb on each are suspended by two insulting strings of equal length l meter from a hook fixed to a stand. The whole set up is taken in a satellite into space where there is no gravity (state of weightlessness). What is the angle between the two strings and the tension in each string ?

Q1-19 The number of electrons in an insulator is of the same order as the number of electrons in a conductor. What is then the basic difference between a conductor and an insulator ?

Q1-20 No work is done in taking a positive charge from one point to other inside a positive charged metallic sphere, while outside the sphere work is done in taking the charge from one point to other (towards the sphere). Explain.

Q1-21 A small plane area is rotated in an electric field. In which orientation of the area is the flux of electric field through the area maximum ? In which orientation is it zero ?

Q1-22 When a charged comb is brought near a small piece of paper, it attracts the piece. Does the paper become charged when the comb is brought near it ?

Q1-23 A circular ring of radius r made of a nonconducting material is placed with its axis parallel to a uniform electric field. The ring is rotated about a diameter through 180° does the flux of electric field change ? If yes, does it decrease or increase ?

Q1-24 A charge Q is uniformly distributed on a thin spherical shell. What is the field at the centre of the shell ? If a point charge is brought close to the shell, will the field at the centre change ? Does your answer depend on whether the shell is conducting or nonconducting ?

Q-1-25 One going away from a point charge, the electric field due to the charge decreases. This is also true for a small electric-dipole. Does the electric field decreases at the same rate in both cases ?

* * * * *

Conceptual MCQs Single Option Correct

1-1 A soap bubble is given a negative charge, then its radius :
(A) Decreases
(B) Increases
(C) Remains unchanged
(D) Nothing can be predicted as information is insufficient

1-2 A given charge is situated at a certain distance from an electric dipole on its axis, experiences a force F. If the distance of the charge from dipole is doubled, the force acting on the charge will be :
(A) $2F$
(B) $F/2$
(C) $F/4$
(D) $F/8$

1-3 The electric field on two sides of a thin sheet of charge is shown in the figure-1.362 The charge density on the sheet is :

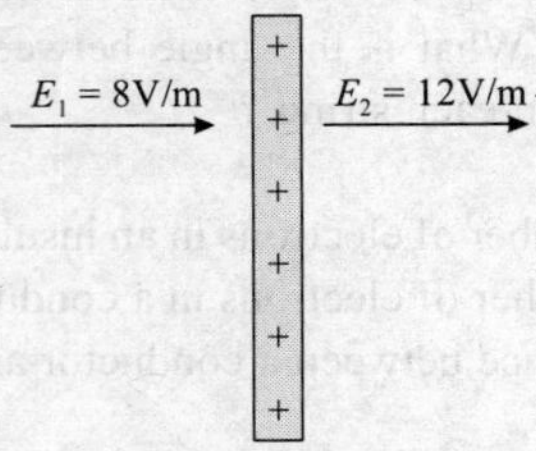

Figure 1.362

(A) $2\varepsilon_0$
(B) $4\varepsilon_0$
(C) $10\varepsilon_0$
(D) Zero

1-4 Three identical charges are placed at corners of an equilateral triangle of side l. If force between any two charges is F, the work required to double the dimensions of triangle is :
(A) $-3Fl$
(B) $3Fl$
(C) $(-3/2)Fl$
(D) $(3/2)Fl$

1-5 Three concentric conducting spherical shells carry charges $+4Q$ on the inner shell $-2Q$ on the middle shell and $+6Q$ on the outer shell. The charge on the inner surface of the outer shell is :
(A) 0
(B) $4Q$
(C) $-Q$
(D) $-2Q$

1-6 A and B are two concentric spherical shells. If A is given a charge $+q$ while B is earthed as shown in figure-1.363, then :

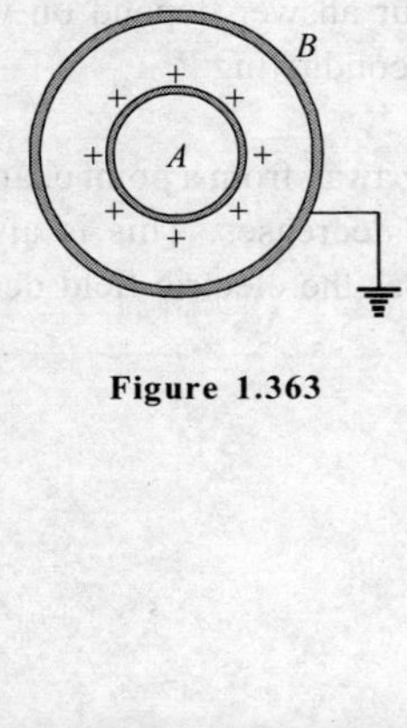

Figure 1.363

(A) Charge on the outer surface of shell B is zero
(B) The charge on B is equal and opposite to that of A
(C) The field inside A and outside B is zero
(D) All of the above

1-7 Two concentric conducting thin spherical shells A and B having radii r_A and r_B ($r_B > r_A$) are charged to Q_A and $-Q_B(|Q_B| > |Q_A|)$. The electric field strength along a line passing through the centre varies with the distance x as :

(A)
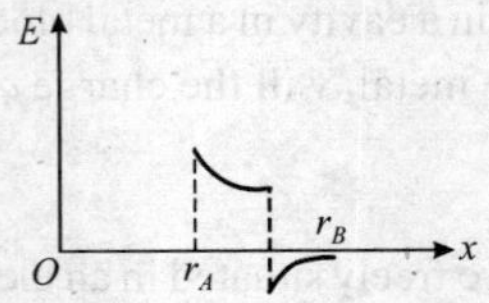

(B)
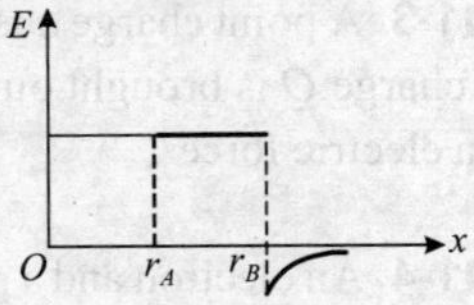

(C)
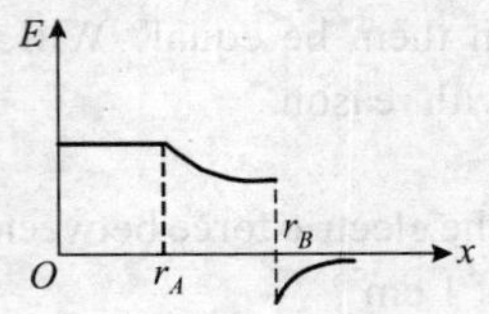

(D) None of these

1-8 Electric potential at a point P, r distance away due to a point charge located at a point A is V. If twice of this charge is distributed uniformly on the surface of a hollow sphere of radius $4r$ with centre at point A, the potential at P now is given as :
(A) V
(B) $V/2$
(C) $V/4$
(D) $V/8$

1-9 There is a point charge $+q$ inside a hollow sphere and a point charge $-q$ just outside its surface. The total flux passing through the surface of sphere is :
(A) $\frac{-q}{\epsilon_0}$
(B) $\frac{q}{\epsilon_0}$
(C) $\frac{2q}{\epsilon_0}$
(D) zero

1-10 The figure shows three non conducting rods, one circular and two straight. Each has a uniform charge of magnitude Q distributed on its one half and $-Q$ on its other half as shown in the figure-1.364. Which of these correctly represents the direction of field at point P :

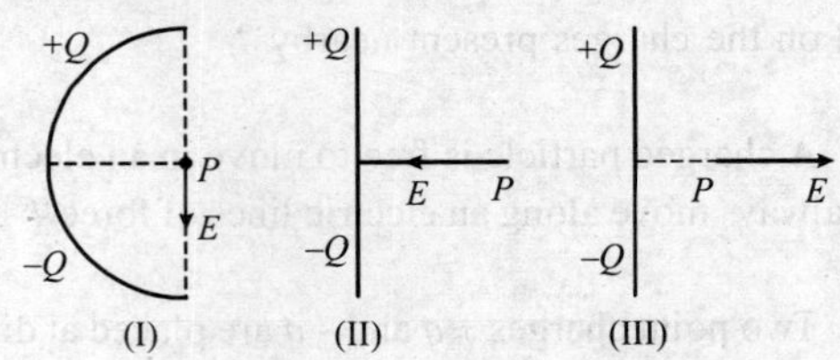

Figure 1.364

(A) I
(B) II
(C) III
(D) I and II

1-11 A conducting spherical shell having inner radius a and outer radius b carries a net charge Q. If a point charge q is placed at the centre of this shell, then the surface charge density on the outer surface of the shell is given as :

(A) $\dfrac{Q-q}{4\pi b^2}$ (B) $\dfrac{Q}{4\pi b^2}$

(C) $\dfrac{Q+q}{4\pi b^2}$ (D) zero

1-12 If a unit charge is taken from one point to another over an equipotential surface, then :

(A) Work is done on the charge
(B) Work is done by the charge
(C) Work on the charge is constant
(D) No work is done

1-13 Ten electrons are equally spaced and fixed around a circle of radius R. Relative to $V = 0$ at infinity, the electrostatic potential V and the electric field E at the centre C are :

(A) $V \neq 0$ and $\vec{E} \neq 0$ (B) $V \neq 0$ and $\vec{E} = 0$
(C) $V = 0$ and $\vec{E} = 0$ (D) $V = 0$ and $\vec{E} \neq 0$

1-14 Let $\rho(r) = \dfrac{Q}{\pi R^4} r$ be the volume charge density for a solid sphere of radius R and total charge Q. For a point 'P' inside the sphere of distance r_1 from the centre of the sphere, the magnitude of electric field is given as :

(A) $\dfrac{Q}{4\pi \epsilon_0 r_1^2}$ (B) $\dfrac{Q r_1^2}{4\pi \epsilon_0 R^4}$

(C) $\dfrac{Q r_1^2}{3\pi \epsilon_0 R^4}$ (D) 0

1-15 A hollow conducting sphere is placed in an electric field produced by a point charge placed at P as shown in figure-1.365. Let V_A, V_B, V_C be the potentials at point A, B and C respectively. Then :

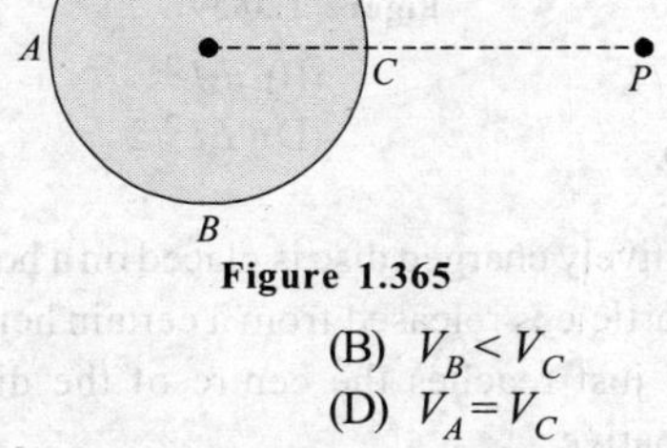

Figure 1.365

(A) $V_C > V_B$ (B) $V_B < V_C$
(C) $V_A > V_B$ (D) $V_A = V_C$

1-16 Two very large thin conducting plates having same cross-sectional area are placed as shown in figure-1.366. They are carrying charges Q and $3Q$ respectively. The variation of electric field as a function at x (for $x = 0$ to $x = 3d$) will be best represented by :

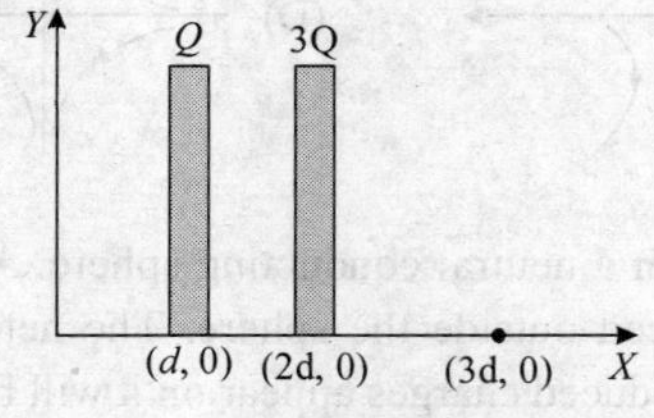

Figure 1.366

(A) 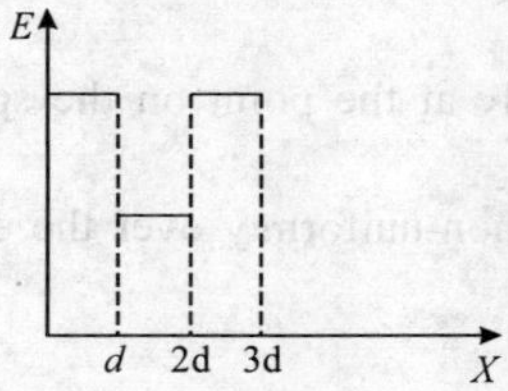

(B) 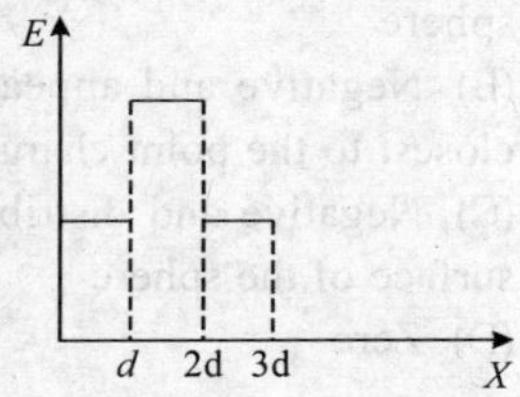

(C) 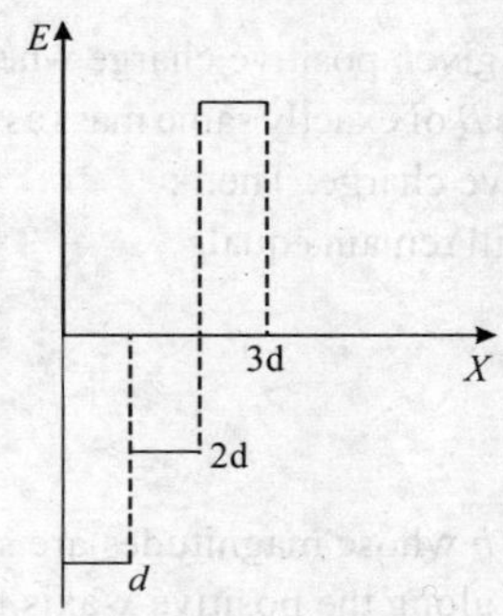

(D) 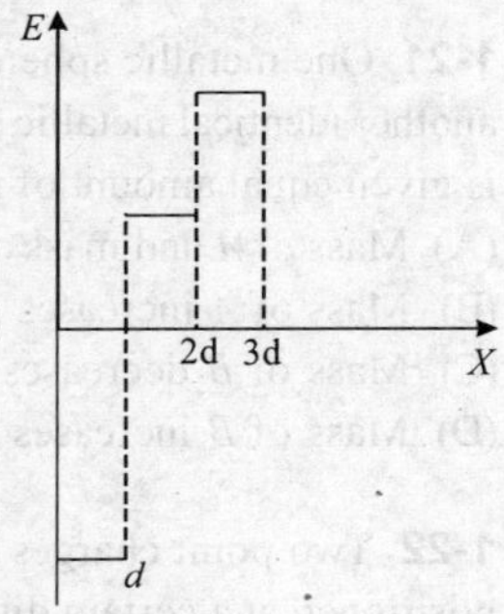

1-17 A conducting shell S_1 having a charge Q is surrounded by an uncharged concentric conducting spherical shell S_2. Let the potential difference between S_1 and that S_2 be V. If the shell S_2 is now given a charge $-3Q$, the new potential difference between the same two shells is :

(A) V (B) $2V$
(C) $4V$ (D) $-2V$

1-18 For a given surface the Gauss's law is stated as $\oint \vec{E}.d\vec{A} = 0$. From this we can conclude that

(A) E is necessarily zero on the surface
(B) E is perpendicular to the surface at every point
(C) The total flux through the surface is zero
(D) The flux is only going out of the surface

1-19 In a certain region of space, the potential field depends on x and y coordinates as $V = (x^2 - y^2)$. The corresponding electric field lines in x-y plane are correctly represented by :

(A) 

(B) 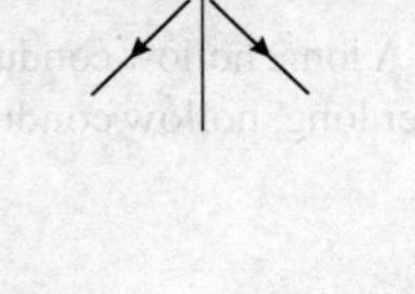

(C) 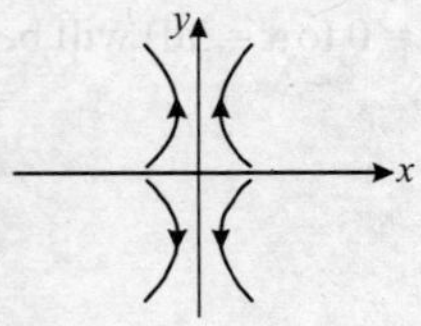 (D) 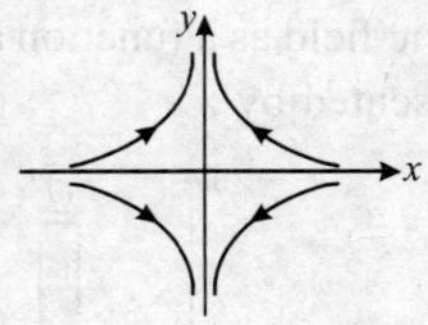

1-20 Consider a neutral conducting sphere. A positive point charge is placed outside the sphere. The net charge on the sphere after induced charges appear on it will be :
(A) Negative and distributed uniformly over the surface of the sphere
(B) Negative and appears only at the point on the sphere closest to the point charge
(C) Negative and distributed non-uniformly over the entire surface of the sphere
(D) Zero

1-21 One metallic sphere A is given positive charge whereas another identical metallic sphere B of exactly same mass as of A is given equal amount of negative charge. Then :
(A) Mass of A and mass of B still remain equal
(B) Mass of A increases
(C) Mass of B decreases
(D) Mass of B increases

1-22 Two point charges a and b whose magnitudes are same positioned at a certain distance along the positive x-axis from each other. a is at origin. Graph is drawn between electrical field strength and distance x from a. E is taken positive if it is along the line joining from a to b. From the graph it can be decided that :

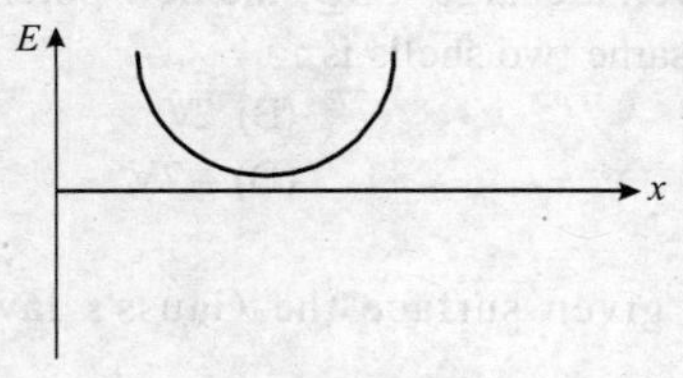

Figure 1.367

(A) a is positive, b is negative (B) a and b both are positive
(C) a and b both are negative (D) a is negative, b is positive

1-23 Two spheres A and B of radius a and b respectively are at same electric potential. The ratio of the surface charge densities of A and B is :

(A) $\frac{a}{b}$ (B) $\frac{b}{a}$

(C) $\frac{a^2}{b^2}$ (D) $\frac{b^2}{a^2}$

1-24 A long, hollow conducting cylinder is kept coaxially inside another long, hollow conducting cylinder of larger radius. Both the cylinders are initially electrically neutral. Which of the following statement is correct :
(A) A potential difference appears between the two cylinders when a charge density is given to the inner cylinder
(B) A potential difference appears between two cylinders when a charge density is given to the outer cylinder.
(C) No potential difference appears between the two cylinders when a uniform line charge is kept along the axis of the cylinders.
(D) No potential difference appears between the two cylinders when same charge density is given to both the cylinders.

1-25 The figure shows the path of a positively charged particle 1 through a rectangular region of uniform electric field as shown in the figure-1.368. What is the direction deflection of particles 1, 2, 3 and 4 ?

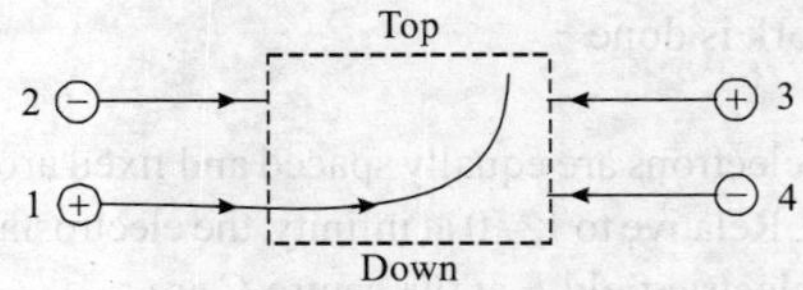

Figure 1.368

(A) Top, down, top, down (B) Top, down, down, top
(C) Down, top, top, down (D) Down, top, down, down

1-26 The force experienced by a unit positive point charge when placed in an electric field is called ?
(A) Potential of electric field at that point
(B) Moment of electric field at that point
(C) Intensity of electric field at that point
(D) Capacity of electric field at that point

1-27 A square surface of side L meters is in the plane of the paper. A uniform electric field $\vec{E}$ (in V/m), also in the plane of the paper, is limited only to the lower half of the square surface, as shown in figure-1.369. The electric flux in SI units associated with the surface is given as :

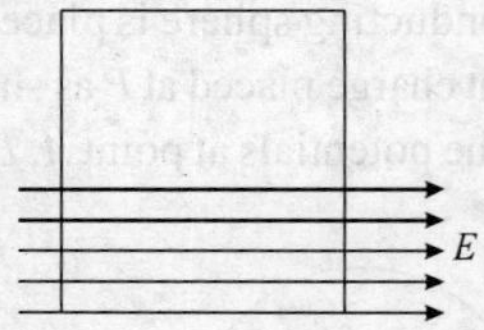

Figure 1.3639

(A) zero (B) EL^2
(C) $EL^2/2\epsilon_0$ (D) $EL^2/2$

1-28 A positively charged disc is placed on a horizontal plane. A charged particle is released from a certain height on its axis. The particle just reaches the centre of the disc. Select the correct alternative :
(A) Particle has negative charge on it
(B) Total potential energy (gravitational + electrostatic) of the particle first increases then decreases

(C) Total potential energy of the particle first decreases then increases

(D) Total potential energy of the particle continuously decreases

1-29 The electric field intensity at the centre of a uniformly charged hemispherical shell is E_0. Now, two portions of the hemisphere are cut from either side and remaining portion is shown in figure-1.370. If $\alpha = \beta = \frac{\pi}{3}$ then electric field intensity at centre due to remaining portion is given as :

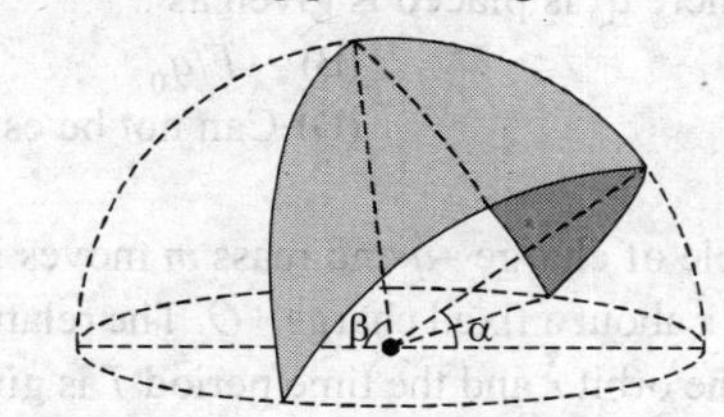

Figure 1.370

(A) $\frac{E_0}{3}$ (B) $\frac{E_0}{6}$

(C) $\frac{E_0}{2}$ (D) Information insufficient

1-30 A wooden block performs SHM on a frictionless surface with frequency v_0. The block carries a charge $+Q$ on its surface. If now a uniform electric field $\vec{E}$ is switched-on as shown, then the SHM of the block will be :

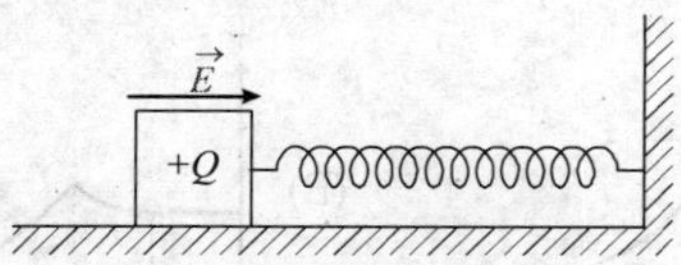

Figure 1.371

(A) Of the same frequency and with shifted mean position.

(B) Of the same frequency and with the same mean position.

(C) Of changed frequency and with shifted mean position.

(D) Of changed frequency and with the same mean position.

1-31 Two equal positive charges are kept at points A and B. The electric potential at the points between A and B (excluding these points) is studied while moving from A to B. The potential between these charges :

(A) Continuously increases (B) Continuously decreases

(C) Increases then decreases (D) Decreases then increases

1-32 Consider a system of three charges $\frac{q}{3}$, $\frac{q}{3}$ and $-\frac{2q}{3}$ placed at points A, B and C respectively which lie on a circle with O to be the center with radius R and angle $CAB = 60°$. If AB is the diameter of the circle, choose the correct statement :

(A) The electric field at point O is $\frac{q}{8\pi \epsilon_0 R^2}$ directed along the negative x-axis.

(B) The potential energy of the system is zero.

(C) The magnitude of the force between the charges at C and B is $\frac{q^2}{54\pi \epsilon_0 R^2}$

(D) The potential at point O is $\frac{q}{12\pi \epsilon_0 R}$

1-33 A solid conducting sphere having a charge Q is surrounded by an uncharged concentric conducting hollow spherical shell. Let the potential difference between the surface of the solid sphere and that of the outer surface of the hollow shell be V. If the shell is now given a charge of $-3Q$, then new potential difference between the same two surfaces is :

(A) V (B) $2V$

(C) $4V$ (D) $-2V$

1-34 Charges Q and $-2Q$ are placed at some distance. The locus of points in the plane of the charges where the potential is zero will be :

(A) A straight line (B) A circle

(C) A parabola (D) An ellipse

1-35 Three infinite long charged sheets of charge densities $-\sigma, -2\sigma$ and σ are placed parallel to xy-plane at $z = 0, z = a, z = 3a$. Electric field at point P is given as :

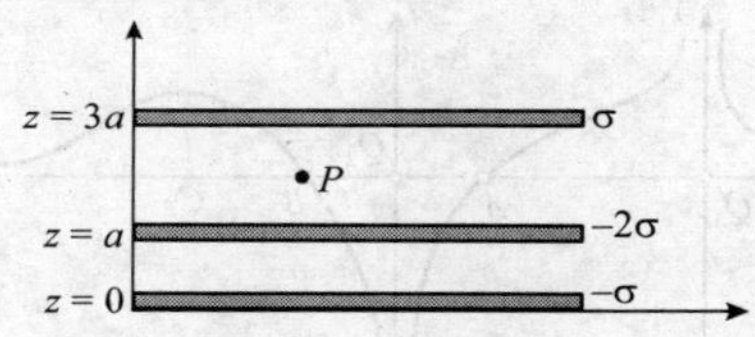

Figure 1.372

(A) $-\frac{2\sigma}{\epsilon_0}\hat{k}$ (B) $\frac{2\sigma}{\epsilon_0}\hat{k}$

(C) $\frac{-4\sigma}{\epsilon_0}\hat{k}$ (D) $\frac{4\sigma}{\epsilon_0}\hat{k}$

1-36 A spherical insulator of radius R is charged uniformly with a positive charge Q throughout its volume and contains a point positive charge of magnitude $Q/16$ located at its centre. Which of the following graphs best represent qualitatively, the variation of electric field intensity E with distance r from the centre :

(A) 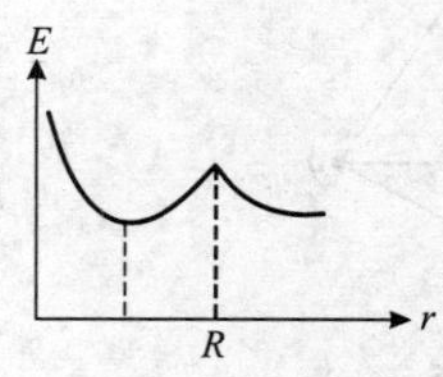

(B) 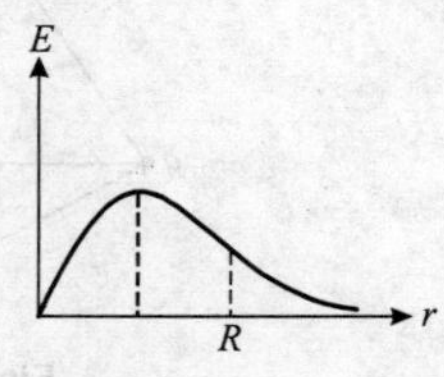

(C) 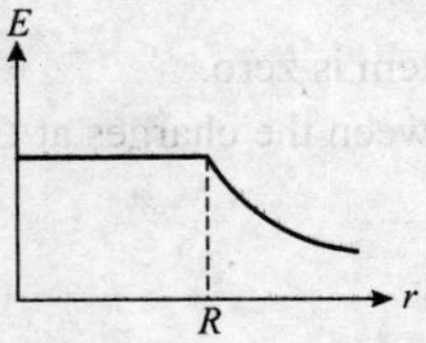

(D) 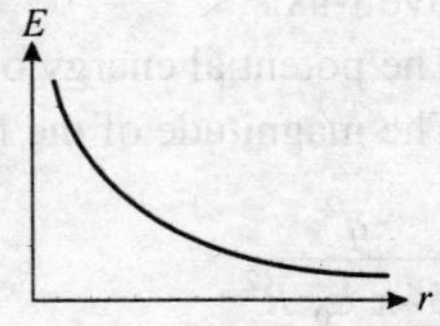

1-37 Figure shows a cubical surface of side $L/2$. A uniformly charged rod of length L moves towards left at a constant speed v. At $t = 0$, the left end just touches the centre of the face of the cube as shown in figure-1.373. Which of the graphs shown in the figure represents the electric flux through the cube as the rod passes through it :

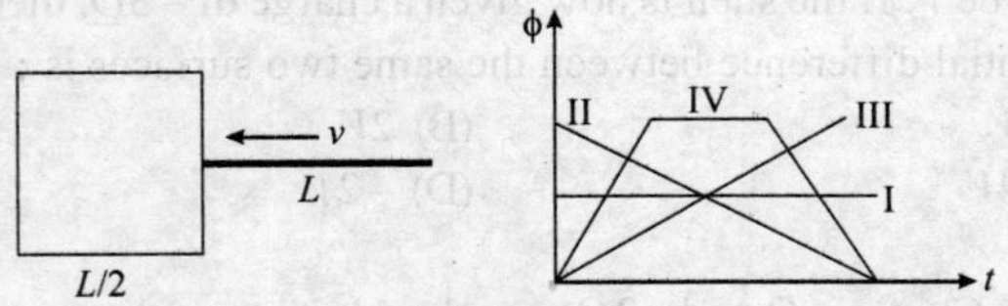

Figure 1.373

(A) I
(B) II
(C) III
(D) IV

1-38 The curve shown in figure represents the distribution of potential along the straight line joining the two charges Q_1 and Q_2 separated by a distance r then which of the following statements are correct ?

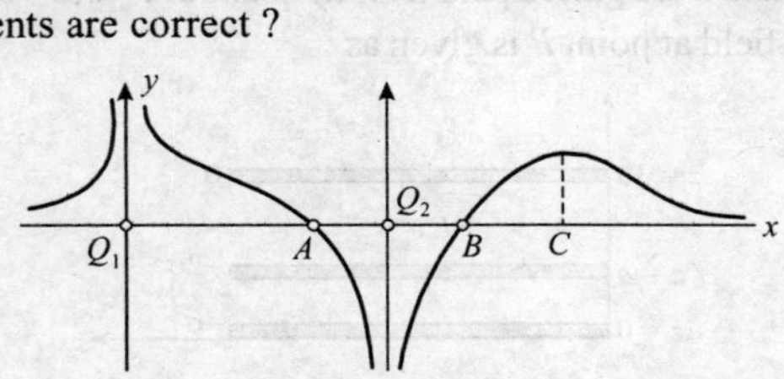

Figure 1.374

1. $|Q_1| > |Q_2|$
2. Q_1 is positive in nature
3. A and B are equilibrium points
4. C is a point of unstable equilibrium

(A) 1 and 2
(B) 1, 2 and 3
(C) 1, 2 and 4
(D) 1, 2, 3 and 4

1-39 Four similar point charges q are located at the vertices of a tetrahedron with an edge a. The energy of the interaction of charges is given as :

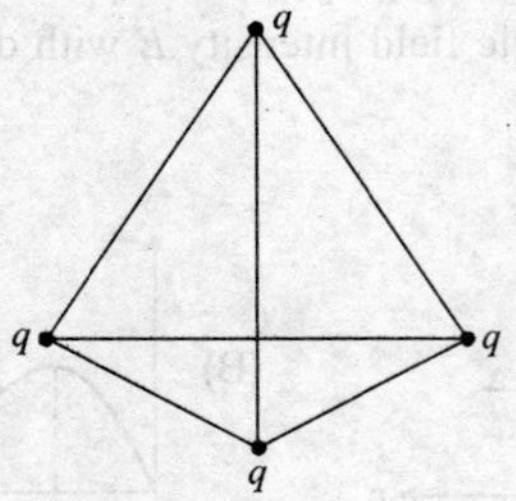

Figure 1.375

(A) $\dfrac{6q^2}{4\pi \epsilon_0 a}$
(B) $\dfrac{4q^2}{4\pi \epsilon_0 a}$
(C) $\dfrac{3q^2}{4\pi \epsilon_0 a}$
(D) $\dfrac{q^2}{4\pi \epsilon_0 a}$

1-40 A positively charged ball hangs form a silk thread. To calculate the electric field E due to ball's charge at a nearby point we put a positive charge q_0 at the point and measure F/q_0, then it can be predicted that the electric field strength E at the point where q_0 is placed is given as :

(A) $> F/q_0$
(B) $= F/q_0$
(C) $< F/q_0$
(D) Can not be estimated

1-41 A particle of charge $-q$ and mass m moves in a circular orbit of radius r about a fixed charge $+Q$. The relation between the radius of the orbit r and the time period T is given as :

(A) $r = \dfrac{Qq}{16\pi^2 \epsilon_0 m} T^2$
(B) $r^3 = \dfrac{Qq}{16\pi^3 \epsilon_0 m} T^2$
(C) $r^2 = \dfrac{Qq}{16\pi^3 \epsilon_0 m} T^3$
(D) $r^2 = \dfrac{Qq}{4\pi^3 \epsilon_0 m} T^3$

1-42 Two concentric spherical shells of radii r and R ($r < R$) have surface charge densities $-\sigma$ and $+\sigma$ respectively. The variation of electric potential V with distance x from the centre O of the shells plotted. Which of the following graphs best depict the variation qualitatively ?

(A) 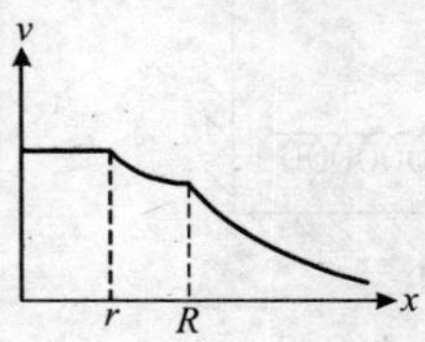

(B) 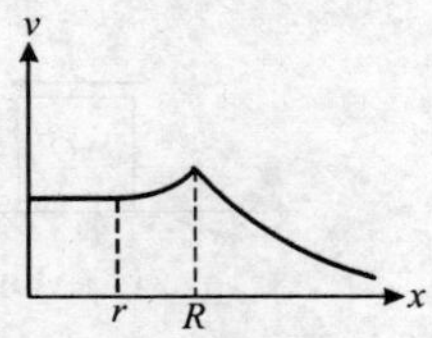

(C) 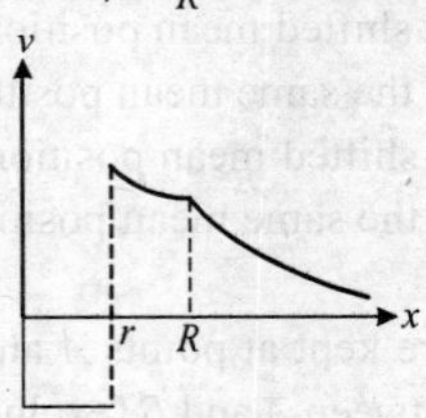

(D) 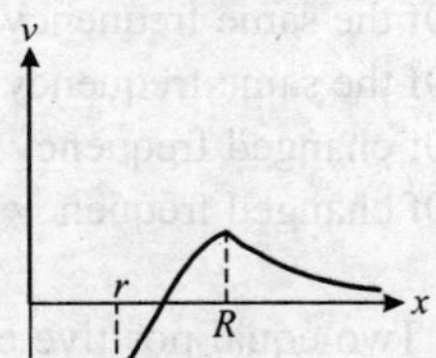

1-43 In figure $+Q$ charge is located at one of the edge of the cube as shown in figure-1.376. Then electric flux through cube due to $+Q$ charge is given as :

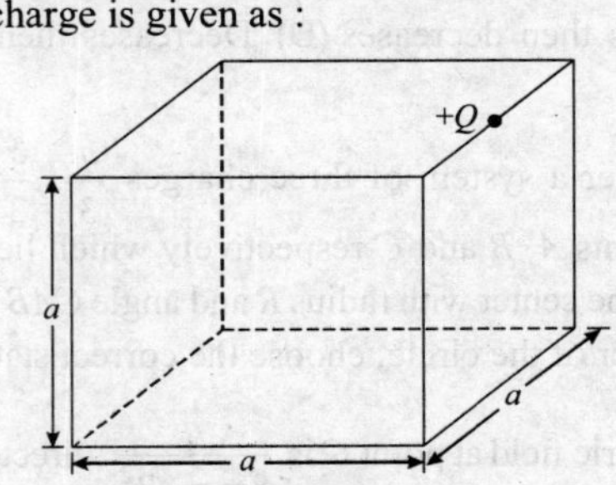

Figure 1.376

(A) $\frac{+Q}{\epsilon_0}$ (B) $\frac{+Q}{2\epsilon_0}$

(C) $\frac{+Q}{4\epsilon_0}$ (D) $\frac{+Q}{8\epsilon_0}$

1-44 Two equal negative charge $-q$ are fixed at the points $(0, a)$ and $(0, -a)$ on the Y-axis. A positive charge q is released from rest at the point $(2a, 0)$ on the X-axis. The charge q will :

(A) Execute simple harmonic motion about the origin

(B) Move to the origin and remains at rest

(C) Move to infinity

(D) Execute oscillatory but not simple harmonic motion.

1-45 The adjacent diagram shows a charge $+Q$ held on an insulating support S and enclosed by a hollow spherical conductor. O is the centre of the spherical conductor and P is a point such that $OP = x$ and $SP = r$. The electric field at point P will be given as :

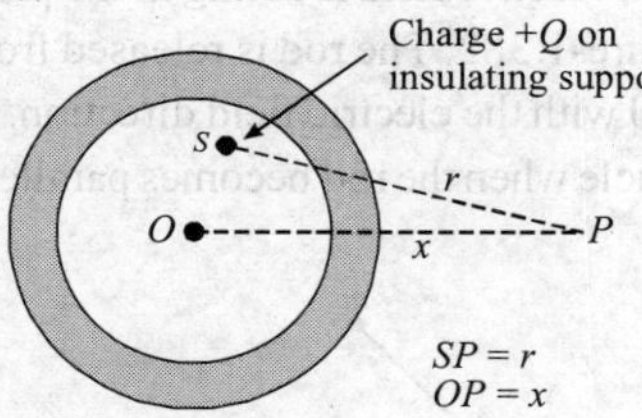

Figure 1.377

(A) $\frac{Q}{4\pi\epsilon_0 x^2}$ (B) $\frac{Q}{4\pi\epsilon_0 r^2}$

(C) 0 (D) None of the above

1-46 A charge q is placed at O in the cavity in a spherical uncharged conductor. Point S is outside the conductor. If q is displaced from O towards S slightly inside the cavity the :

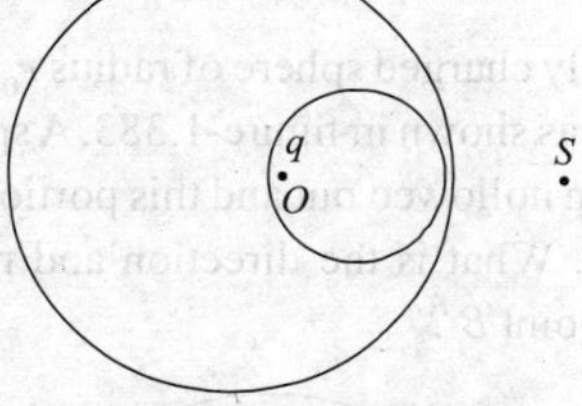

Figure 1.378

(A) Electric field at S will increase

(B) Electric field at S will decrease

(C) Electric field at S will first increase and then decrease

(D) Electric field at S will not change

1-47 Two pith balls having charge $3q$ and $2q$ are placed at distance of a from each other. For what value of charge transferred from 1st ball to 2nd ball, force between balls becomes maximum?

(A) $\frac{q}{2}$ (B) $\frac{5q}{2}$

(C) $7q$ (D) q

1-48 Two insulated charged sphere of radii R_1 and R_2 having charges Q_1 and Q_2 respectively are connected to each other. Which of the following statement is correct about the given situation :

(A) No change in the energy of the system

(B) An increase in the energy of the system

(C) Always a decrease in the energy of the system

(D) A decrease in energy of the system unless $Q_1 R_2 = Q_2 R_1$

1-49 A uniformly charged thin spherical shell of radius R carries uniform surface charge density of σ per unit area. It is made of two separate hemispherical shells, held together by pressing them with force F. This force F is proportional to :

(A) $\sigma^2 R^2$ (B) $\sigma^2 R$

(C) $\frac{\sigma^2}{R}$ (D) $\frac{\sigma^2}{R^2}$

1-50 A sphere of radius R carries charge density proportional to the square of the distance from the centre given as $\rho = Ar^2$, where A is a positive constant. At a distance of $R/2$ from the center, the magnitude of the electric field is :

(A) $A/(4\varepsilon_0)$ (B) $AR^3/(40\varepsilon_0)$

(C) $AR^3/(24\varepsilon_0)$ (D) $AR^3/(5\varepsilon_0)$

1-51 Two point charges, each with a charge of $+1\mu C$, lie at some finite distance apart. On which of the segments of an infinite line going through the charges is there a point, a finite distance away from the charges, where the electric potential is zero, assuming that it vanishes at infinity ?

(A) Between the charges only

(B) On either side outside the system

(C) Impossible to tell without knowing the distance between the charges

(D) Nowhere

1-52 In normal cases thin stream of water bends toward a negatively charged rod. When a positively charged rod is placed near the stream, it will bend in the :

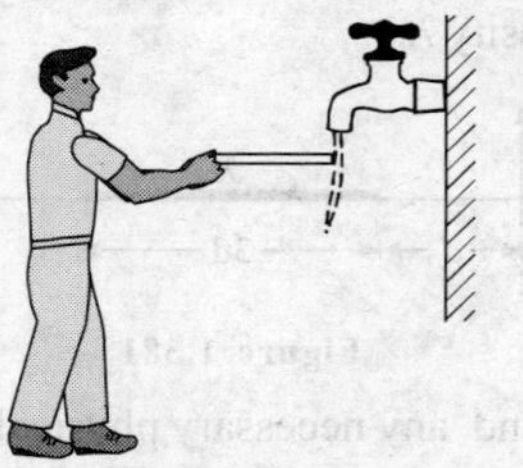

Figure 1.379

(A) Away from rod (B) Toward rod

(C) It won't bend at all (D) Can't be predicted

1-53 How does the electric field strength vary when we enter and move inside a uniformly charged spherical cloud ?

(A) Increases inversely as the square of the distance from the center.

(B) Decreases inversely as the square of the distance from the center.

(C) Increases directly as the distance from the center.

(D) Decreases directly as the distance from the centre

1-54 On an imaginary planet the acceleration due to gravity is same as that on Earth but there is also a downward electric field that is uniform close to the planet's surface. A ball of mass m carrying a charge q is thrown upward at a speed v and hits the ground after an interval t, What is the magnitude of potential difference between the starting point and top point of the trajectory ?

(A) $\frac{mv}{2q}\left(v-\frac{gt}{2}\right)$ (B) $\frac{mv}{q}\left(v-\frac{gt}{2}\right)$

(C) $\frac{mv}{2q}(v-gt)$ (D) $\frac{2mv}{q}(v-gt)$

1-55 A uniform electric field of 400 V/m is directed at 45° above the x-axis as shown in the figure-1.380. The potential difference $V_A - V_B$ is given by :

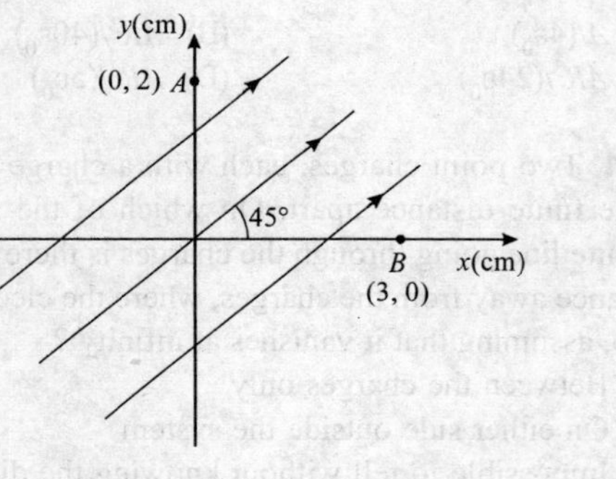

Figure 1.380

(A) 0 (B) $4V$

(C) $6.4V$ (D) $2.8V$

1-56 A continuous line of charge of length $3d$ lies along the x-axis, extending from $x=+d$ to $x=+4d$. the line carries a uniform linear charge density λ.

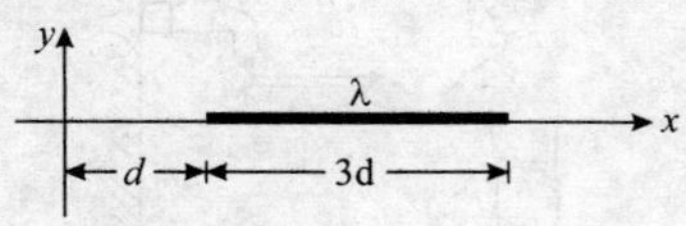

Figure 1.381

In terms of d, λ and any necessary physical constants, find the magnitude of the electric field at the origin :

(A) $\lambda/5\pi\varepsilon_0 d$ (B) $\lambda/4\pi\varepsilon_0 d$

(C) $3\lambda/16\pi\varepsilon_0 d$ (D) $3\lambda/8\pi\varepsilon_0 d$

1-57 Electric charges are distributed in a small volume. The flux of the electric field through a spherical surface of radius 1 m surrounding the total charge is 100 V-m. The flux over the concentric sphere of radius 2 m will be :

(A) 25 V-m (B) 50 V-m

(C) 100 V-m (D) 200 V-m

1-58 Three concentric spherical metallic shells A, B and C of radii a, b and c ($c > b > a$) have charge densities σ, $-\sigma$ and σ respectively. The potential of shell B is given as :

(A) $(a+b+c)\frac{\sigma}{\varepsilon_0}$ (B) $\left(\frac{a^2}{b}-b+c\right)\frac{\sigma}{\varepsilon_0}$

(C) $\left(\frac{a^2}{c}-\frac{b^2}{c}+c\right)\frac{\sigma}{\varepsilon_0}$ (D) $\frac{\sigma c}{\varepsilon_0}$

1-59 A particle of mass m and charge q is attached to a light rod of length L. The rod can rotate freely in the plane of paper about the other end, which is hinged at P, the entire assembly lies in an uniform electric field E acting in the plane of paper as shown in the figure-1.382. The rod is released from rest when it makes an angle θ with the electric field direction. Determine the speed of the particle when the rod becomes parallel to the electric field :

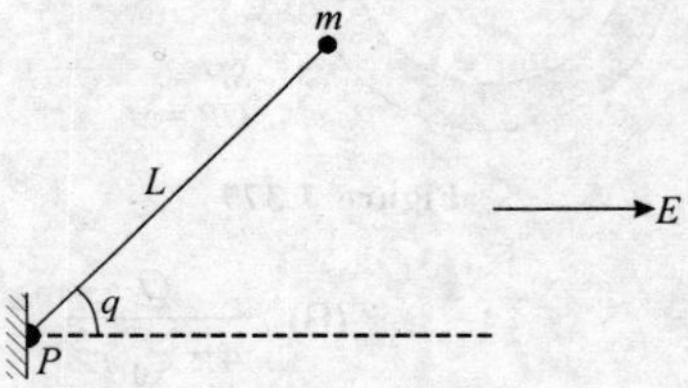

Figure 1.382

(A) $\left(\frac{2qEL(1-\cos\theta)}{m}\right)^{1/2}$ (B) $\left(\frac{2qEL(1-\sin\theta)}{m}\right)^{1/2}$

(C) $\left(\frac{qEL(1-\cos\theta)}{2m}\right)^{1/2}$ (D) $\left(\frac{2qEL\cos\theta}{m}\right)^{1/2}$

1-60 A positively charged sphere of radius r_0 carries a volume charge density ρ as shown in figure-1.383. A spherical cavity of radius $r_0/2$ is then hollowed out and this portion is left empty as cavity as shown. What is the direction and magnitude of the electric field at point B ?

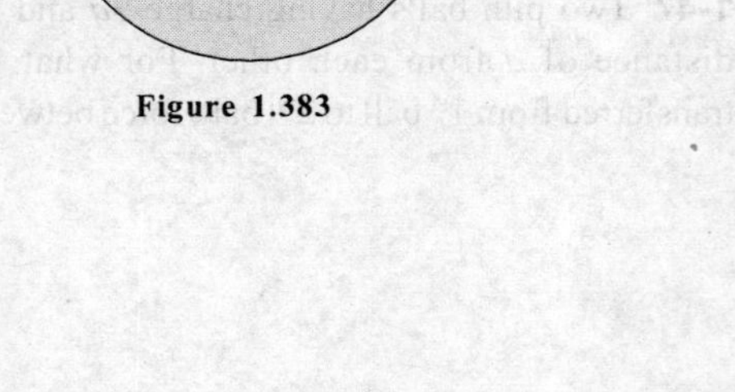

Figure 1.383

(A) $\dfrac{17\rho r_0}{54\in_0}$ left (B) $\dfrac{\rho r_0}{6\in_0}$ left

(C) $\dfrac{17\rho r_0}{54\in_0}$ right (D) $\dfrac{\rho r_0}{6\in_0}$ right

1-61 Using Thomson's model of the atom, consider an atom consisting of two electrons, each of charge $-e$, embedded in a sphere of charge $+2e$ and radius R. In equilibrium each electron is at distance d from the centre of the atom. What is equilibrium separation between electrons ?

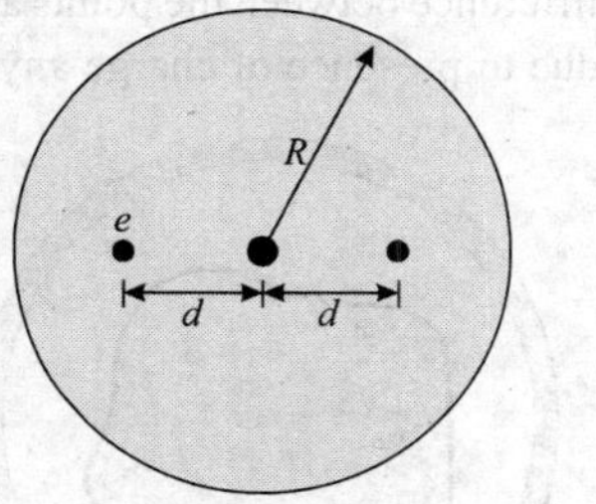

Figure 1.384

(A) R (B) $R/2$

(C) $R/3$ (D) $R/4$

1-62 If the electric potential of the inner shell is 10 V and that of the outer shell is 5 V, then the potential at the centre will be :

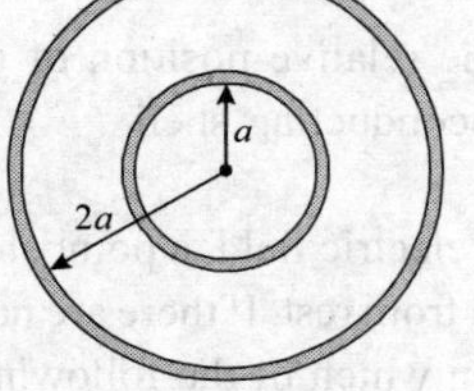

Figure 1.385

(A) 10V (B) 5V

(C) 15V (D) Zero

1-63 A nonconducting sphere with radius a is concentric with and surrounded by a conducting spherical shell with inner radius b and outer radius c. The inner sphere has a negative charge uniformly distributed throughout its volume, while the spherical shell has no net charge. The potential $V(r)$ as a function of distance from the center is given as :

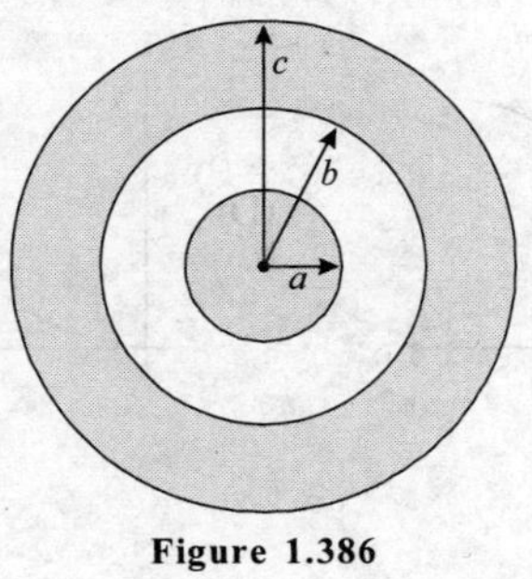

Figure 1.386

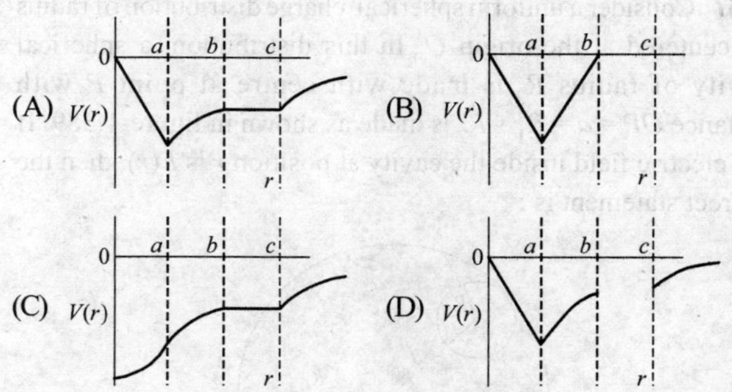

1-64 A charged particle q is shot from a large distance towards another charged particle Q which is fixed, with a speed v. It approaches Q up to a closest distance r and then returns. If q were given a speed $2v$, then distance of approach would be :

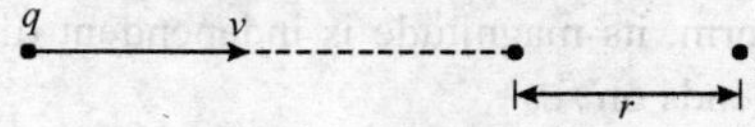

Figure 1.387

(A) r (B) $2r$

(C) $r/2$ (D) $r/4$

1-65 A sphere carrying a charge of Q having weight w falls under gravity between a pair of vertical plates at a distance d from each other. When a potential difference V is applied between the plates the acceleration of sphere changes as shown in the figure-1.388, to along line BC. The value of Q is :

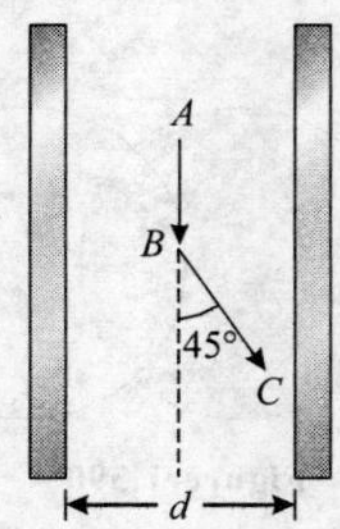

Figure 1.388

(A) $\dfrac{w}{V}$ (B) $\dfrac{w}{2V}$

(C) $\dfrac{wd}{V}$ (D) $\dfrac{\sqrt{2}wd}{V}$

1-66 Let $E_1(r)$, $E_2(r)$ and $E_3(r)$ be the respective electric fields at a distance r from a point charge Q, an infinitely long wire with constant linear charge density λ, and an infinite plane with uniform surface charge density σ. If $E_1(r_0) = E_2(r_0) = E_3(r_0)$ at a given distance r_0, then :

(A) $Q = 4\sigma\pi r_0^2$ (B) $r_0 = \dfrac{\lambda}{2\pi\sigma}$

(C) $E_1(r_0/2) = 2E_3(r_0/2)$ (D) $E_2(r_0/2) = 4E_3(r_0/2)$

1-67 Consider a uniform spherical charge distribution of radius R_1 centered at the origin O. In this distribution, a spherical cavity of radius R_2 is made with centre at point P with distance $OP = a = R_1 - R_2$ is made as shown in figure-1.389. If the electric field inside the cavity at position r is $E(r)$, then the correct statement is :

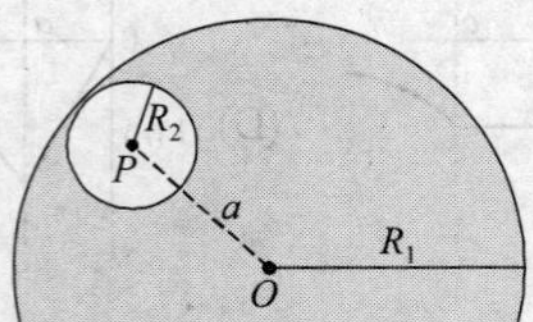

Figure 1.389

(A) E is uniform, its magnitude is independent of R_2 but its direction depends on r.

(B) E is uniform, its magnitude depends on R_2 and its direction depends on r

(C) E is uniform, its magnitude is independent of a but its direction depends on a.

(D) E is uniform and both its magnitude and direction depend on magnitude and direction of a

1-68 Figure-1.390 shows a closed dotted surface which intersects a conducting uncharged sphere. If a positive charge is placed at the point P, the flux of the electric field through the closed surface will be :

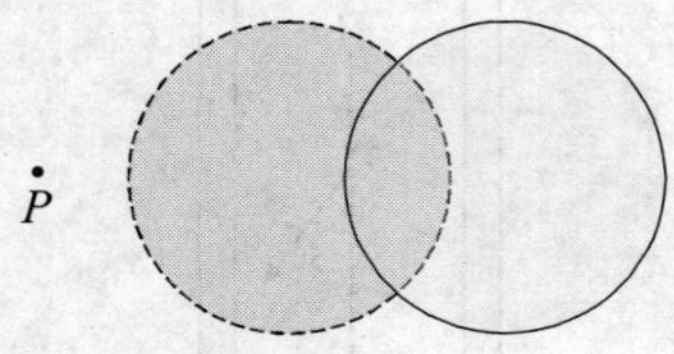

Figure 1.390

(A) Will remain zero
(B) Will become positive
(C) Will becomes negative
(D) Data insufficient

1-69 A positive point charge $+Q$ is fixed in space. A negative point charge $-q$ of mass m revolves around fixed charge in elliptical orbit. The fixed charge $+Q$ is at one focus of the ellipse. The only force acting on negative charge is the electrostatic force due to positive charge. Then which of the following statement is true :

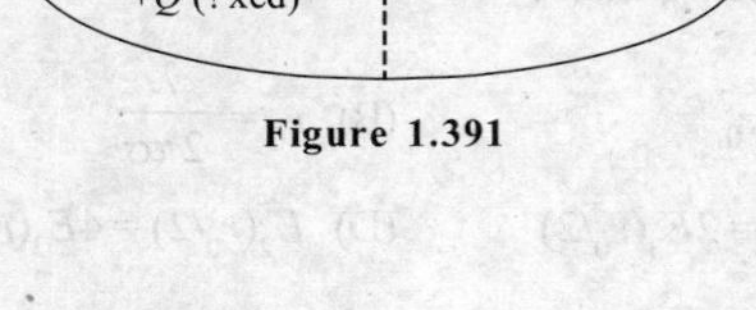

Figure 1.391

(A) Linear momentum of negative point charge is conserved

(B) Angular momentum of negative point charge about fixed positive charge is conserved

(C) Total kinetic energy of negative point charge is conserved

(D) Electrostatic potential energy of system of both point charges is conserved

1-70 An irregular shaped non conductor has some charge distribution. The potential difference between the two points A and B in it is V. If it is now enveloped in a spherical non conducting shell having uniform charge distribution in it, the new potential difference between the points any where (neglect any induction due to presence of charge any where) :

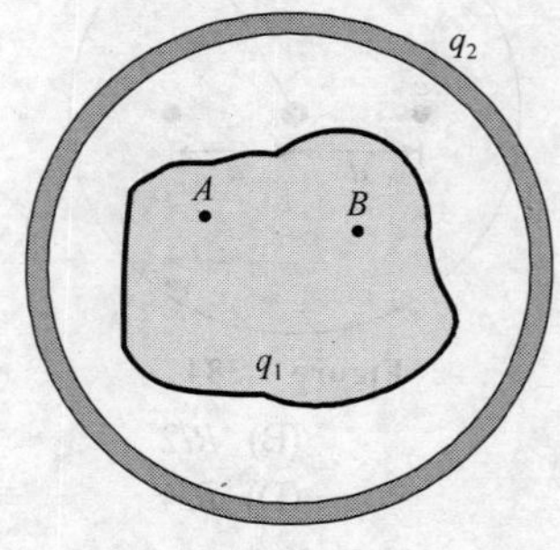

Figure 1.392

(A) Is greater than V

(B) Is less than V.

(C) Is equal to V

(D) Depends on the relative position of inner nonconductor vis-a-vis outer nonconducting shell

1-71 In a uniform electric field, a point charge of mass m and charge q is released from rest. If there are no other forces acting on the particle, then which of the following graphs, correctly show the dependence of the particles speed v on the distance x travelled by it? [Graphs are schematic and not drawn to scale]

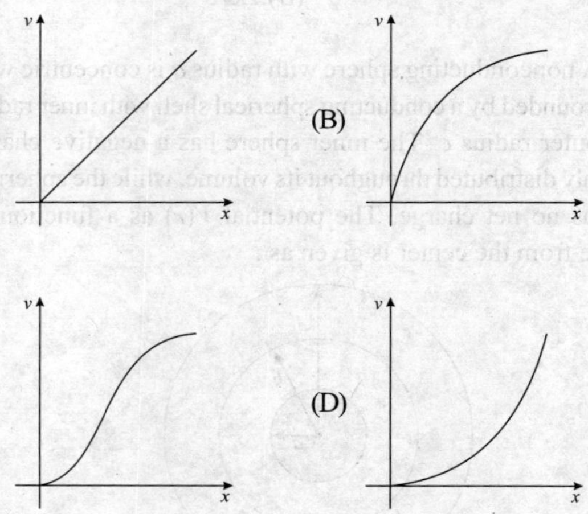

* * * * *

Numerical MCQs Single Option Correct

1-1 A particle of charge $-q$ and mass m moves in a circle of radius r around an infinitely long line charge of linear charge density $+\lambda$. Then time period will be given as :

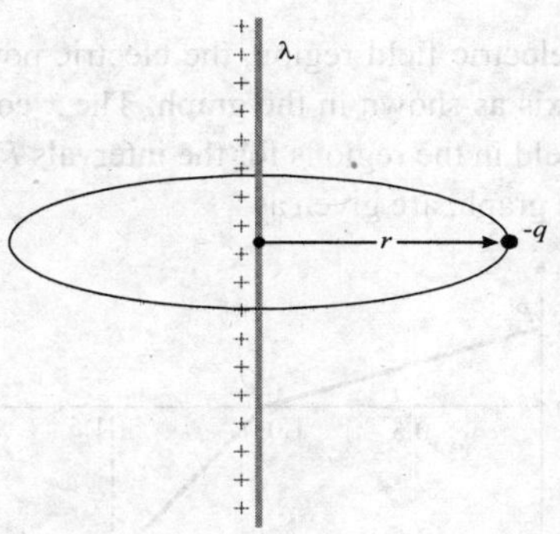

Figure 1.393

(A) $T = 2\pi r\sqrt{\dfrac{m}{2K\lambda q}}$ (B) $T^2 = \dfrac{4\pi^2 m}{2K\lambda q} r^3$

(C) $T = \dfrac{1}{2\pi r}\sqrt{\dfrac{2K\lambda q}{m}}$ (D) $T = \dfrac{1}{2\pi r}\sqrt{\dfrac{m}{2K\lambda q}}$

1-2 Electric charge is uniformly distributed along a long straight wire of radius 1 mm. The charge per cm length of the wire is Q coulomb. Another cylindrical surface of radius 50 cm and length 1 m symmetrically encloses the wire as shown in the figure-1.394. The total electric flux passing through the cylindrical surface is:

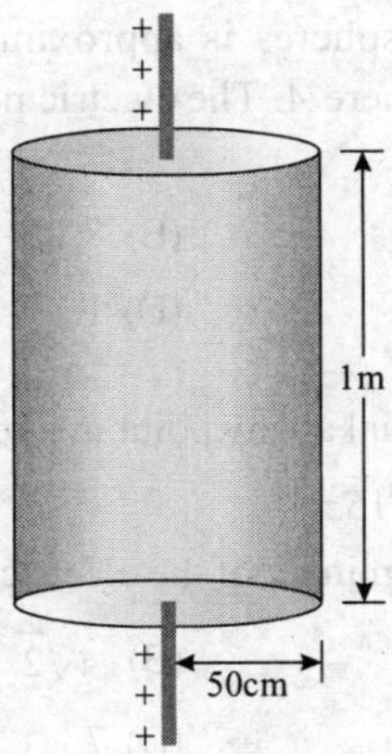

Figure 1.394

(A) $\dfrac{Q}{\varepsilon_0}$ (B) $\dfrac{100Q}{\varepsilon_0}$

(C) $\dfrac{10Q}{(\pi\varepsilon_0)}$ (D) $\dfrac{100Q}{(\pi\varepsilon_0)}$

1-3 A copper (density of $Cu = \rho_C$) ball of diameter d is immersed in oil of density ρ_0. What is the charge on the ball if, in a homogeneous electric field E directed vertically upward, it is suspended in the oil ? $\left(k \equiv \pi d^3 \dfrac{\rho_c g}{E}\right)$:

(A) $\dfrac{1}{6}k\left(1-\dfrac{\rho_0}{\rho_c}\right)$ (B) $\dfrac{1}{3}k\left(1-\dfrac{\rho_0}{\rho_c}\right)$

(C) $\dfrac{1}{2}k\left(1-\dfrac{\rho_0}{\rho_c}\right)$ (D) $k\left(1-\dfrac{\rho_0}{\rho_c}\right)$

1-4 A particle of mass m and charge q is fastened to one end of a string of length l. The other end of the string is fixed to the point O. The whole system lies on a frictionless horizontal plane. Initially, the mass is at rest at A. A uniform electric field in the direction shown in then switched on. Then :

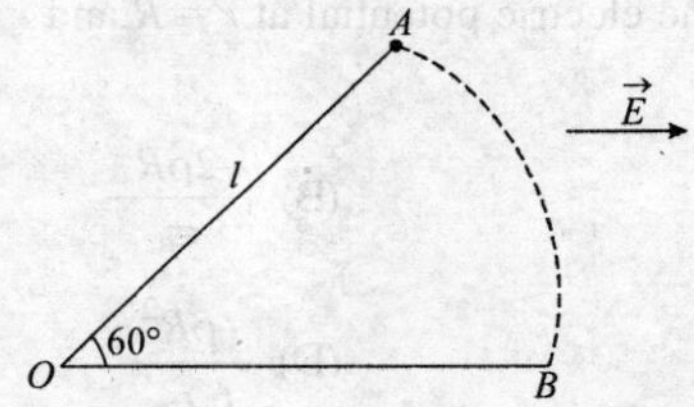

Figure 1.395

(A) The speed of the particle when it reaches B is $\sqrt{\dfrac{2qEl}{m}}$

(B) The speed of the particle when it reaches B is $\sqrt{\dfrac{qEl}{m}}$

(C) The tension in the string when the particle reaches at B is qE

(D) The tension in the string when the particle reaches at B is zero

1-5 A small ball of mass m and charge $+q$ tied with a string of length l, rotating in a vertical circle under gravity and a uniform horizontal electric field E as shown in figure-1.396. The tension in the string will be minimum at an angle :

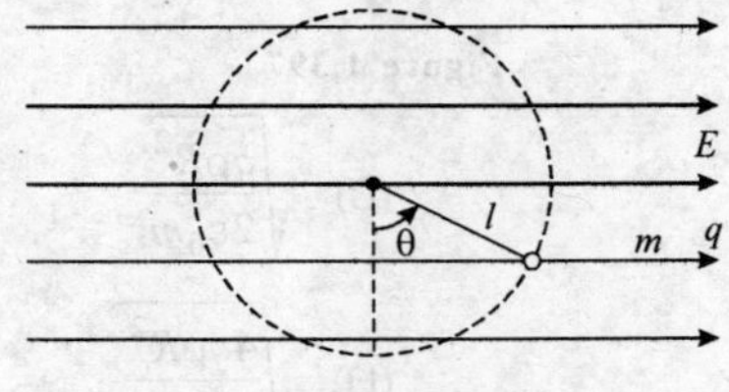

Figure 1.396

(A) $\theta = \tan^{-1}\left(\frac{qE}{mg}\right)$ (B) $\theta = \pi$

(C) $\theta = 0°$ (D) $\theta = \pi + \tan^{-1}\left(\frac{qE}{mg}\right)$

1-6 If uniform electric field $\vec{E} = E_0\hat{i} + 2E_0\hat{j}$, where E_0 is a constant, exists in a region of space and at (0, 0) the electric potential V is zero, then the potential at $(x_0, 0)$ will be :

(A) Zero (B) $-E_0x_0$

(C) $-2E_0x_0$ (D) $-\sqrt{5}E_0x_0$

1-7 Two metal pieces having a potential difference of 800 V are 0.02 m apart horizontally. A particle of mass 1.96×10^{-15} kg is suspended in equilibrium between the plates. If e is the elementary charge, then charge on the particle is :

(A) e (B) 3e

(C) 6e (D) 8e

1-8 A sphere of radius $2R$ has a uniform charge density ρ. The difference in the electric potential at $r = R$ and $r = 0$ from the centre is :

(A) $\frac{-\rho R^2}{\epsilon_0}$ (B) $\frac{-2\rho R^2}{\epsilon_0}$

(C) $\frac{\rho R^2}{3\epsilon_0}$ (D) $\frac{-\rho R^2}{6\epsilon_0}$

1-9 An infinite long cylinder of radius R has a cylindrical cavity of radius $R/2$ just touching its surface. The region inside the cylinder is filled with uniform charge density ρ except in the cavity. A charge particle of charge q and mass m is thrown from point A in the cavity. Find the minimum velocity u required at A for it to reach point B. AB is perpendicular to the diameter of the cavity passing through the axis of the cylinder :

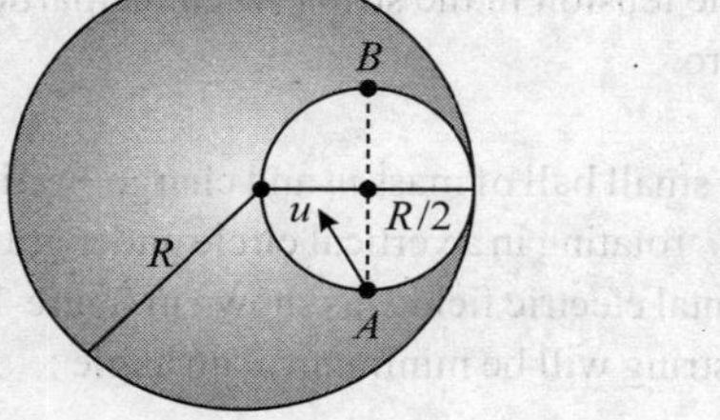

Figure 1.397

(A) $\sqrt{\frac{q\rho R^2}{4\varepsilon_0 m}}$ (B) $\sqrt{\frac{q\rho R^2}{2\varepsilon_0 m}}$

(C) $\sqrt{\frac{2q\rho R^2}{\varepsilon_0 m}}$ (D) $\sqrt{\frac{4q\rho R^2}{\varepsilon_0 m}}$

1-10 The work done in bringing a 20 C charge from point A to point B for distance 0.2 m is 2 J. The potential difference between the two points will be :

(A) 0.2 V (B) 8 V

(C) 0.1 V (D) 0.4 V

1-11. In an electric field region, the electric potential varies along the x axis as shown in the graph. The x components of the electric field in the regions for the intervals PQ and QR as marked in the graph, are given as :

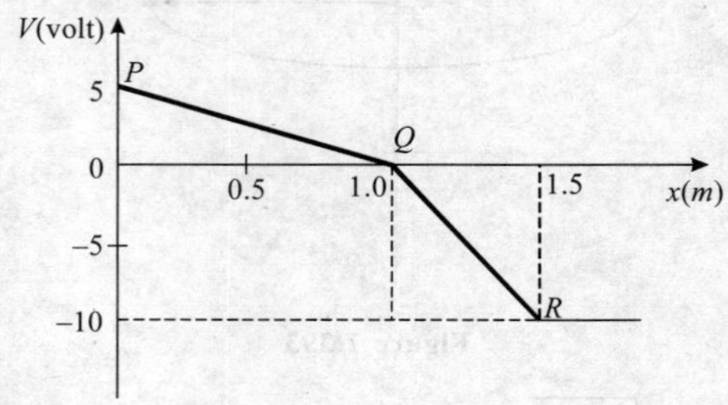

Figure 1.398

(A) 5.0 N/C along negative x-direction and 20.0 N/C along positive x-direction

(B) 5.0 N/C along positive x-direction and 20.0 N/C along negative x-direction

(C) 5.0 N/C along negative x-direction and 20.0 N/C along negative x-direction

(D) 5.0 N/C along positive x-direction and 20.0 N/C along positive x-direction

1-12 Two spheres A and B of radii 17 cm each and having charges of 1 and 2 coulombs respectively are separated by a distance of 80 cm. The electric field at a point on the line joining the centres of two spheres is approximately zero at some distance from the sphere A. The electric potential at this point is :

(A) 6.56×10^{10} V (B) 8.12×10^{7} V

(C) 2.03×10^{9} V (D) 1.2×10^{11} V

1-13 Electric potential at any point in a region is given as

$$V = -5x + 3y + \sqrt{15}z$$

In this region the magnitude of the electric field is :

(A) $3\sqrt{2}$ (B) $4\sqrt{2}$

(C) $5\sqrt{2}$ (D) 7

1-14 A charge $+Q$ is uniformly distributed in a spherical volume of radius R. A particle of charge $+q$ and mass m projected with velocity v_0 from the surface of the spherical volume to its centre inside a smooth tunnel dug across the sphere. The minimum value of v_0 such that it just reaches the centre (assume that there is no resistance on the particle except electrostatic force) of the spherical volume is :

(A) $\sqrt{\dfrac{Qq}{2\pi\varepsilon_0 mR}}$ (B) $\sqrt{\dfrac{Qq}{\pi\varepsilon_0 mR}}$

(C) $\sqrt{\dfrac{2Qq}{\pi\varepsilon_0 mR}}$ (D) $\sqrt{\dfrac{Qq}{4\pi\varepsilon_0 mR}}$

1-15 A charge $+q$ is fixed at each of the points $x = x_0$, $x = 3x_0$, $x = 5x_0$ ...upto infinite, on the x-axis and a charge $-q$ is fixed at each of the points $x = 2x_0$, $x = 4x_0$, $x = 6x_0$ ... upto infinite. Here x_0 is a positive constant. Take the electric potential at a point due to a charge Q at a distance r from it to be $Q/(4\pi\varepsilon_0 r)$. Then, the potential at the origin due to the above system of charges is :

(A) 0 (B) $\dfrac{q}{8\pi\varepsilon_0 x_0 \ln 2}$

(C) ∞ (D) $\dfrac{q \ln 2}{4\pi\varepsilon_0 x_0}$

1-16 The displacement of a charge Q in the electric field vector $\vec{E} = e_1\hat{i} + e_2\hat{j} + e_3\hat{k}$ is $\vec{r} = a\hat{i} + b\hat{j}$. The work done is :

(A) $Q(ae_1 + be_2)$ (B) $Q\sqrt{(ae_1)^2 + (be_2)^2}$

(C) $Q(e_1 + e_2)\sqrt{a^2 + b^2}$ (D) $Q\sqrt{(e_1^2 + e_2^2)}\,(a + b)$

1-17 A non-conducting ring of radius 0.5 m carries a total charge of 1.11×10^{-10} C distributed non-uniformly on its circumference producing an electric field $\vec{E}$ everywhere in space. The value of the line integral $\int_{l=\infty}^{l=0} -\vec{E}.d\vec{l}$ ($l = 0$ being centre of the ring) is

(A) +2 V (B) –1 V

(C) –2 V (D) zero

1-18. Three semi-infinite rods uniformly charged out of which one is negatively charged and other two are positively charged are kept perpendicular to plane of paper outward such that the finite ends of the rods are located at points A, B and C on a circle of radius R as shown in figure-1.399. The net electric field at centre of circle O is :

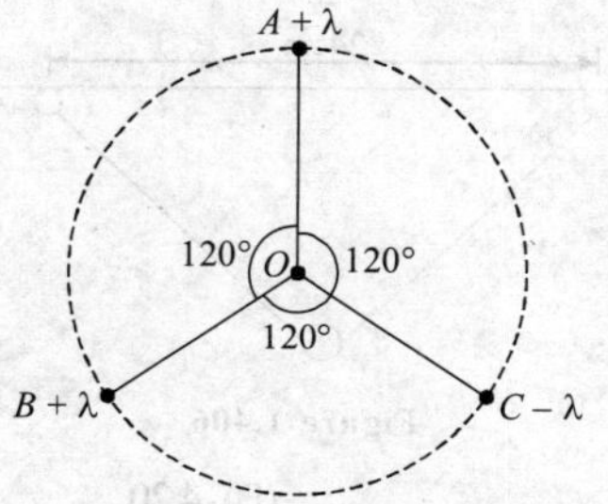

O = Centre of circle

Figure 1.399

(A) $\dfrac{2K\lambda}{R}$, along OC

(B) $\dfrac{K\lambda}{R}$, perpendicular to plane of paper and inward direction

(C) $\dfrac{\sqrt{5}K\lambda}{R}$ at an angle $\tan^{-1}\dfrac{1}{2}$ with OC

(D) $\dfrac{\sqrt{2}K\lambda}{R}$ at an angle 45° with OC

1-19 Two small balls of mass M each carrying charges $+Q$ and $-Q$, connected by a massless rigid non-conducting rod of length L lie along x-axis as shown. A uniform electric field $\vec{E} = 3\hat{k} + 3\hat{j}$ has been switched on. The angular velocity vector of the dipole when dipole moment aligns with the electric field is :

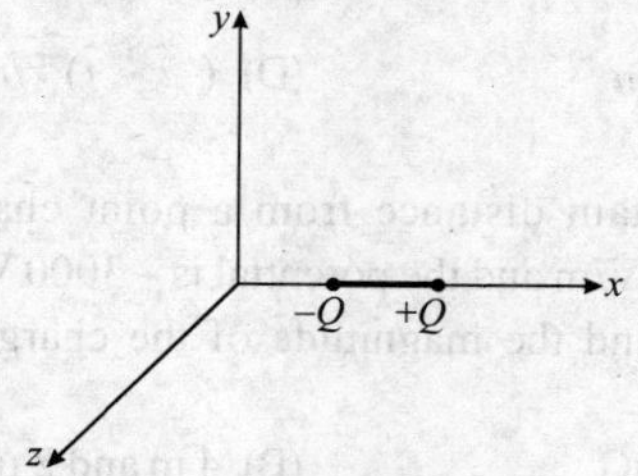

Figure 1.400

(A) $\sqrt{\dfrac{3\sqrt{2}Q}{2ML}}(-\hat{j} + \hat{k})$ (B) $\sqrt{\dfrac{6\sqrt{2}Q}{ML}}(-\hat{j} + \hat{k})$

(C) $\sqrt{\dfrac{3\sqrt{2}Q}{ML}}(-\hat{j} - \hat{k})$ (D) $\sqrt{\dfrac{3\sqrt{2}Q}{ML}}(-\hat{j} + \hat{k})$

1-20 A particle of mass m and charge $-q$ is projected from the origin with a horizontal speed v into an electric field of intensity E directed downward. Choose the wrong statement. Neglect gravity :

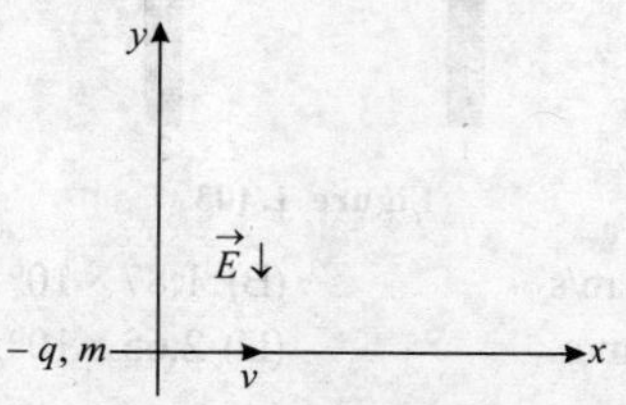

Figure 1.401

(A) The kinetic energy after a displacement y is qEy

(B) The horizontal and vertical components of acceleration are $a_x = qE/m$, $a_y = 0$

(C) The equation of trajectory is $y^2 = \dfrac{1}{2}\left(\dfrac{qEx^2}{mv^2}\right)$

(D) The horizontal and vertical displacements x and y after a time t are $x = vt^2$ and $y = \dfrac{1}{2}a_y t^2$

1-21 The grid (each square of 1 m × 1 m), represents a region in space containing a uniform electric field. If potentials at point $O, A, B, C, D, E, F, G, H$ are respectively 0, –1, –2, 1, 2, 0, –1, 1 and 0 volts. Find the electric field intensity :

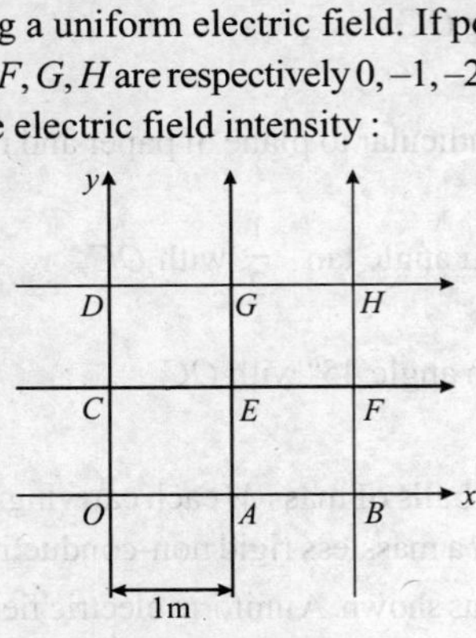

Figure 1.402

(A) $(\hat{i}+\hat{j})$ V/m (B) $(\hat{i}-\hat{j})$ V/m

(C) $(-\hat{i}+\hat{j})$ V/m (D) $(-\hat{i}-\hat{j})$ V/m

1-22 At a certain distance from a point charge, the field intensity is 500 V/m and the potential is – 3000 V. The distance to the charge and the magnitude of the charge respectively are:

(A) 6 m and 6 μC (B) 4 m and 2 μC

(C) 6 m and 4 μC (D) 6 m and 2 μC

1-23 Two large insulating plates both uniformly charged in such a way that the potential difference between them is $V_2 - V_1 = 20$ V. The plates are separated by $d = 0.1$ m. An electron is released from rest on the inner surface of plate 1. What is its speed when it hits plate 2 :

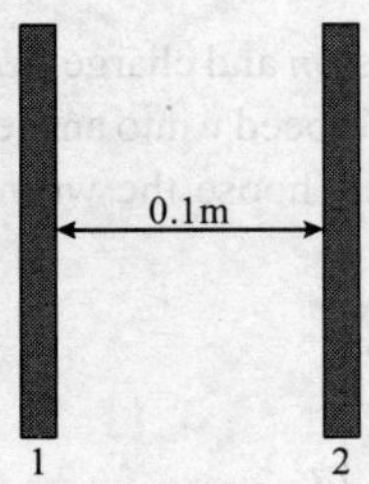

Figure 1.403

(A) 7.02×10^{12} m/s (B) 1.87×10^{6} m/s

(C) 32×10^{-19} m/s (D) 2.65×10^{6} m/s

1-24. A small ball of mass m and charge $+q$ tied with a string of length l, rotating in a vertical circle under gravity and a uniform horizontal electric field E as shown. The tension in the string will be minimum at :

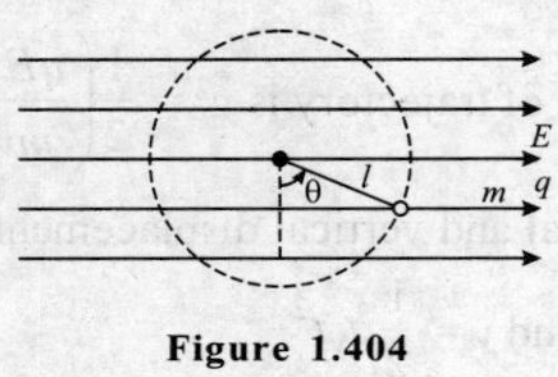

Figure 1.404

(A) $\theta = \tan^{-1}\left(\frac{qE}{mg}\right)$ (B) $\theta = \pi$

(C) $\theta = 0°$ (D) $\theta = \pi + \tan^{-1}\left(\frac{qE}{mg}\right)$

1-25 A conducting rod of length l rotates about its one end with angular velocity ω. Potential difference between A and B points of rod as shown in figure-1.405 is V_{AB}. Find V_{AB}. Take m as mass of electron and e is the charge of electron :

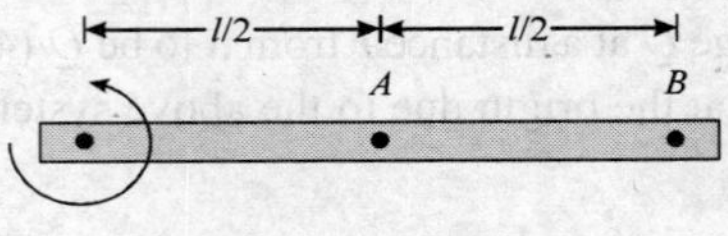

Figure 1.405

(A) $\frac{m\omega^2 l^2}{e}$ (B) $\frac{3m\omega^2 l^2}{4e}$

(C) $\frac{3m\omega^2 l^2}{8e}$ (D) Zero

1-26 A tiny spherical oil drop carrying a net charge q is balanced in still air will a vertical uniform electric field of strength $\frac{81\pi}{7} \times 10^5$ V/m. When the field is switched off, the drop is observed to fall with terminal velocity 2×10^{-3} m/s. Given $g = 9.8$ m/s², viscosity of the air = 1.8×10^{-5} Ns/m² and the density of oil = 900 kg/m³, the magnitude of q is :

(A) 1.6×10^{-19} C (B) 3.2×10^{-19} C

(C) 4.8×10^{-19} C (D) 7.8×10^{-19} C

1-27 The two ends of a rubber string of negligible mass and having unstretched length 24 cm are fixed at the same height as shown. A small object is attached to the string in its midpoint due to which the depression h of the object in equilibrium is 5 cm. Then the small object is charged and a vertical electric field E_1 is switched on in the region. The equilibrium depression of the object increases to 9 cm, now the electric field is changed to E_2 and the depression of object in equilibrium increases to 16 cm. What is the ratio of electric field in the second case to that of in the first case ?

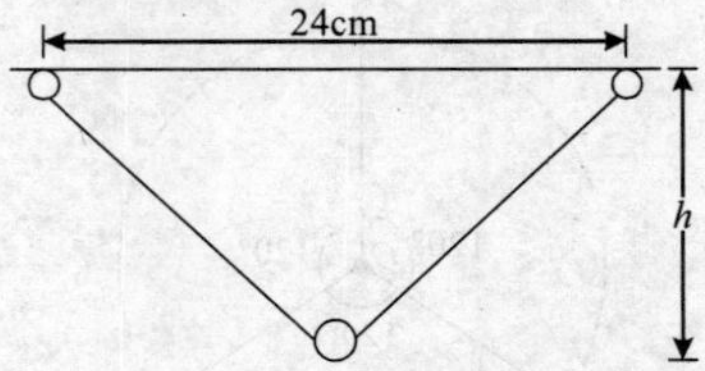

Figure 1.406

(A) 4.25 (B) 4.20

(C) 4.30 (D) 4.35

1-28 Let there be a spherically symmetric charge distribution with charge density varies with distance r from the center and given as

$$\rho(r) = \rho_0\left(\frac{5}{4} - \frac{r}{R}\right) \text{ for } r = R$$

and $\rho(r) = 0$ for $r > R$

The electric field at a distance $r(r < R)$ from the origin is given as:

(A) $\frac{\rho_0 r}{4\varepsilon_0}\left(\frac{5}{3} - \frac{r}{R}\right)$ (B) $\frac{4\pi\rho_0 r}{3\varepsilon_0}\left(\frac{5}{3} - \frac{r}{R}\right)$

(C) $\frac{4\rho_0 r}{4\varepsilon_0}\left(\frac{5}{4} - \frac{r}{R}\right)$ (D) $\frac{\rho_0 r}{3\varepsilon_0}\left(\frac{5}{4} - \frac{r}{R}\right)$

1-29 Two electrons are at a certain distance apart from one another. What is the order of magnitude of the ratio of the electric force between them to the gravitational force between them ?

(A) $10^8 : 1$ (B) $10^{28} : 1$

(C) $10^{31} : 1$ (D) $10^{42} : 1$

1-30 Two point charges q_1 and q_2 are placed at a distance of 50 m from each other in air, and interact with a certain force. The same charges are now put in oil whose relative permittivity is 5. If the interacting force between them is still the same, their separation now is :

(A) 16.6 m (B) 22.3 m

(C) 28.4 m (D) 25.0 m

1-31 The electric field in region is given by $\vec{E} = 200\,\hat{i}$ N/C for $x > 0$ and $-200\,\hat{i}$ N/C for $x < 0$. A closed cylinder of length 2 m and cross-section area 10^2 m^2 is kept in such a way that the axis of cylinder is along X-axis and its centre coincides with origin. The total charge inside the cylinder is given as.

Take the value of $\varepsilon_0 = 8.85 \times 10^{-12}$ C^{2}m^2 N :

(A) Zero (B) 1.86×10^{-5} C

(C) 1.77×10^{-11} C (D) 35.4×10^{-8} C

1-32 A solid conducting sphere of radius 5.0 cm has a charge of 0.25 nC distributed uniformly on its surface. If point A is located at the centre of the sphere and a point B is 15 cm from the center, what is the magnitude of the electric potential difference between these two points ?

(A) 23 V (B) 30 V

(C) 15 V (D) 45 V

1-33 An electric dipole is placed perpendicular to an infinite line of charge at some distance as shown in figure-1.407. Identify the correct statement :

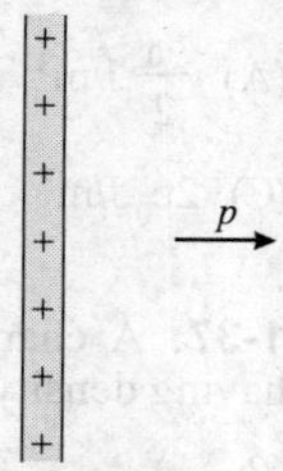

Figure 1.407

(A) The dipole is attracted towards the line charge

(B) The dipole is repelled away from the line charge

(C) The dipole does not experience a force

(D) The dipole experiences a force as well as a torque

1-34 S is a solid neutral conducting sphere. A point charge $q = 1 \times 10^{-6}$ C is placed at point A. C is the centre of sphere and AB is a tangent $BC = 3$ m and $AB = 4$ m :

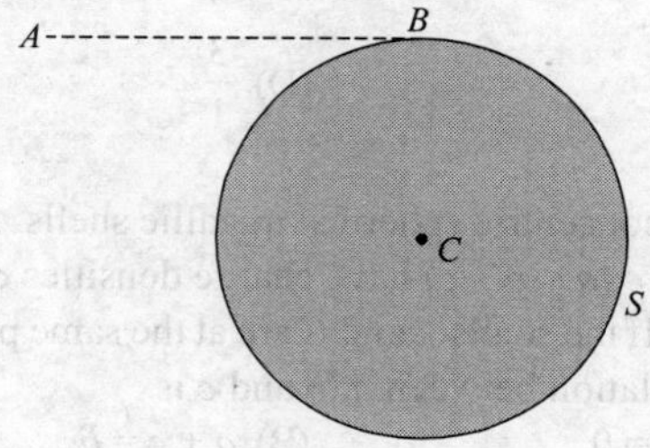

Figure 1.408

(A) The electric potential at B due to induced charge on the sphere is 1.2 kV

(B) The electric potential at B due to induced charge on the sphere is –1.2 kV

(C) The electric potential at B due to induced charge on the sphere is –0.45 kV

(D) The electric potential at B due to induced charge on the sphere is 0.45 kV

1-35 If the potential at the centre of a uniformly charged hollow sphere of radius R is V then electric field at a distance r from the centre of sphere will be $(r > R)$:

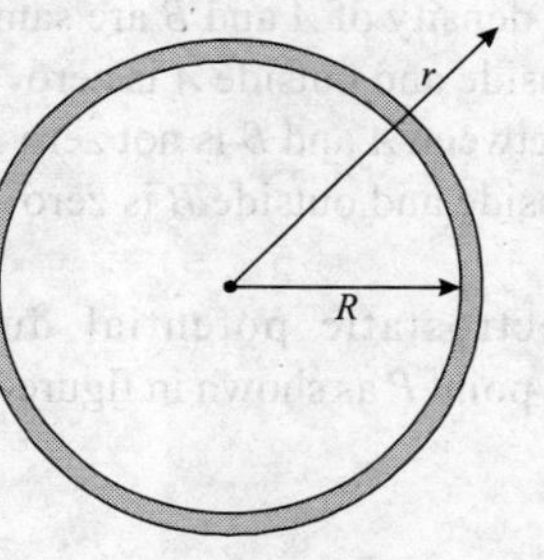

Figure 1.409

(A) $\frac{VR}{r^2}$ (B) $\frac{V_r}{R^2}$

(C) $\frac{VR}{r}$ (D) $\frac{VR}{R^2 + r^2}$

1-36 An isolated conducting sphere whose radius $R = 1$ m has a charge $q = \frac{1}{9}nC$. The energy density at the surface of the sphere is :

(A) $\frac{\varepsilon_0}{2}$ J/m^3 (B) ε_0 J/m^3

(C) $2\varepsilon_0$ J/m^3 (D) $\frac{\varepsilon_0}{3}$ J/m^3

1-37. A charged rod have continuous charge distribution having density $\lambda = 2x$ C/m. If rod is of length l then find ratio $\frac{q_1}{q_2}$. Where q_1 is charge on half of rod & q_2 is charge on 2nd half of rod :

(A) $\frac{1}{2}$ (B) $\frac{1}{4}$

(C) $\frac{1}{3}$ (D) $\frac{3}{1}$

1-38 Three concentric spherical metallic shells A, B and C of radii a, b and c ($a < b < c$) have charge densities σ, $-\sigma$ and σ, respectively. If the shells A and C are at the same potential then the correct relation between a, b and c is :

(A) $a + b + c = 0$ (B) $a + c = b$

(C) $a + b = c$ (D) $a = b + c$

1-39 A and B are two concentric spheres. If A is given a charge Q while B is earthed as shown in figure-1.410 :

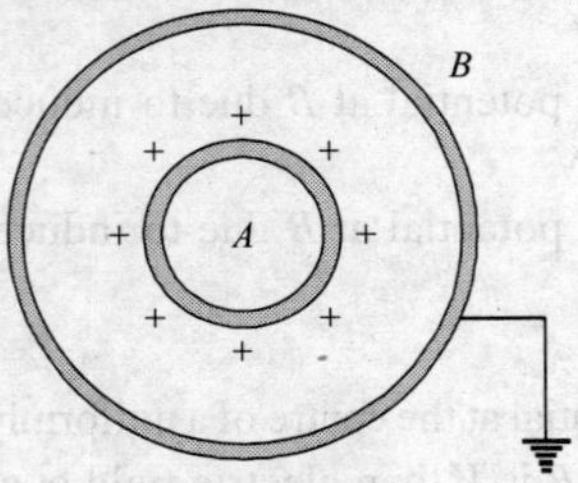

Figure 1.410

(A) The charge density of A and B are same

(B) The field inside and outside A is zero

(C) The field between A and B is not zero

(D) The field inside and outside B is zero

1-40 The electrostatic potential due to the charge configuration at point P as shown in figure-1.410 for $b << a$ is:

(A) $\frac{2q}{4\pi\varepsilon_0 a}$

(B) $\frac{2qb^2}{4\pi\varepsilon_0 a^3}$

(C) $\frac{qb^2}{4\pi\varepsilon_0 a^3}$

(D) Zero

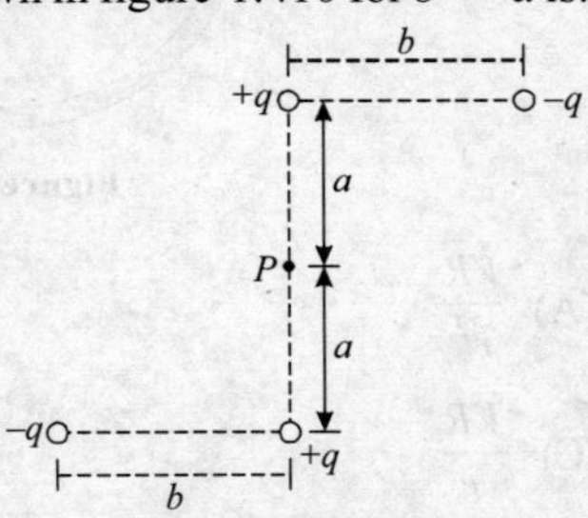

Figure 1.411

1-41 Two thin wire rings each having radius R are placed at a distance d apart with their axes coinciding. The charges on the two rings are $+Q$ and $-Q$. The potential difference between the centres of the two rings is given as :

(A) Zero (B) $\frac{Q}{4\pi\varepsilon_0}\left[\frac{1}{4} - \frac{1}{\sqrt{R^2 + d^2}}\right]$

(C) $\frac{Q}{4\pi\varepsilon_0 d^2}$ (D) $\frac{Q}{2\pi\varepsilon_0}\left[\frac{1}{R} - \frac{1}{\sqrt{R^2 + d^2}}\right]$

1-42 In a certain region of space, electric field is along the z-direction throughout. The magnitude of electric field is, however, not constant but increases uniformly along the positive z-direction, at the rate of 10^5 N/C per meter. The force experienced by a system having a total dipole moment equal to 10^{-7} cm in the negative z-direction is :

(A) 0.01 N (B) 0.02 N

(C) 0.04 N (D) Zero

1-43 There are two uncharged identical metallic spheres 1 and 2 of radius r separated by a distance $d (d >> r)$. A charged metallic sphere of same radius having charge q is touched with one of the sphere. After some time it is moved away from the system. Now the uncharged sphere is earthed. Charge on earthed sphere is :

(A) $+\frac{q}{2}$ (B) $-\frac{q}{2}$

(C) $-\frac{qr}{2d}$ (D) $-\frac{qd}{2r}$

1-44 Two small identical metal balls of radius r are at a distance a ($a >> r$) from each other and are charged, one with a potential V_1 and the other with a potential V_2. The charges on the balls are :

(A) $q_1 = V_1 a, q_2 = V_2 a$

(B) $q_1 = V_1 r, q_2 = V_2 r$

(C) $q_1 = \left(\frac{V_1 + V_2}{2}\right) a, q_2 = \left(\frac{V_1 + V_2}{2}\right) r$

(D) $q_1 = -\frac{r}{a}(rV_2 - aV_1), q_2 = -\frac{r}{a}(rV_1 - aV_2)$

1-45 In the figure-1.412 shown, the charge $+Q$ is fixed. Another charge $+2q$ and mass M is projected from a distance R from the fixed charge. Minimum separation between the two charges if the velocity becomes $\frac{1}{\sqrt{3}}$ times of the projected velocity, at this moment is given as :

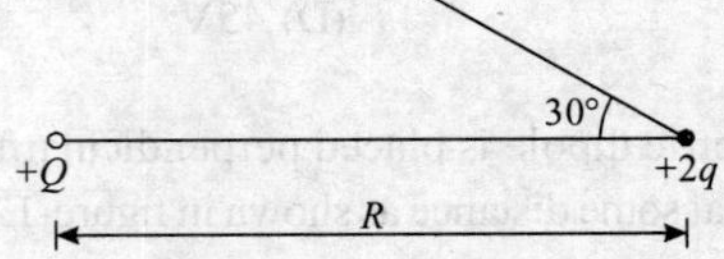

Figure 1.412

(A) $\frac{\sqrt{3}}{2}R$ (B) $\frac{1}{\sqrt{3}}R$

(C) $\frac{1}{2}R$ (D) None of these

1-46 A bullet of mass m and charge Q is fired towards a solid uniformly charged sphere of radius R and total charge Q. If it strikes the surface of sphere with speed v, the minimum speed v so that it can penetrate through the sphere is given as :

(A) $\frac{Q}{\sqrt{2\pi \epsilon_0 mR}}$ (B) $\frac{Q}{\sqrt{6\pi \epsilon_0 mR}}$

(C) $\frac{Q}{\sqrt{4\pi \epsilon_0 mR}}$ (D) $\frac{3Q}{\sqrt{4\pi \epsilon_0 mR}}$

1-47 A charged particle of mass m and charge q is released from rest in an electric field of constant magnitude E. The kinetic energy of the particle after a time t is :

(A) $\frac{2E^2t^2}{mq}$ (B) $\frac{q^2m}{2t^2}$

(C) $\frac{E^2q^2t^2}{2m}$ (D) $\frac{Eqm}{2t}$

1-48 Consider the shown uniform solid insulating sphere of mass m with a short and light electric dipole moment $p\hat{j}$ embedded at its centre placed at rest on a horizontal surface. An electric field $E\hat{i}$ is suddenly switched on in the region such that the sphere starts rolling without sliding. Speed of the sphere when the dipole becomes horizontal for the first time is given as:

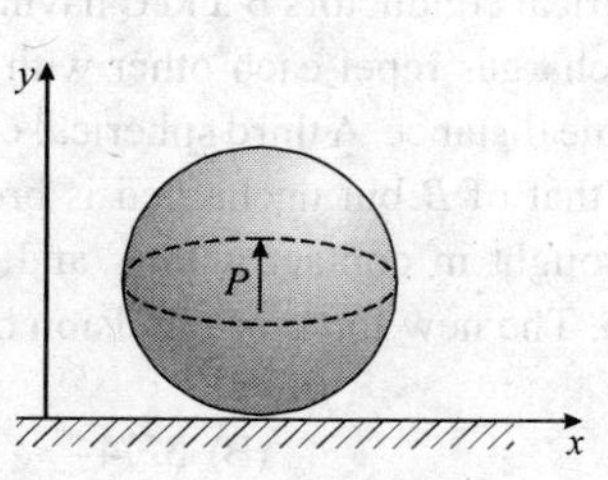

Figure 1.413

(A) $\sqrt{\frac{5pE}{m}}$ (B) $\sqrt{\frac{10pE}{7m}}$

(C) $\sqrt{\frac{5pE}{2m}}$ (D) Zero

1-49 A loop of diameter d is rotated in a uniform electric field until the position of maximum electric flux is found. The flux in this position is measured to be ϕ. What is the electric field strength ?

(A) $\frac{4\phi}{\pi d^2}$ (B) $\frac{2\phi}{\pi d^2}$

(C) $\frac{\phi}{\pi d^2}$ (D) $\frac{\pi \phi d^2}{4}$

1-50 A block of mass m and charge q is connected to a point O with help of an inextensible string. The system in on a horizontal table. An electric field is switched on in direction perpendicular to string. What will be tension in string when it become parallel to electric field ?

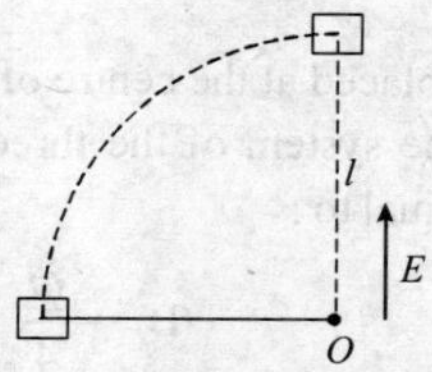

Figure 1.414

(A) $\frac{qE}{2}$ (B) $3qE$

(C) $\frac{qE}{l}$ (D) $\frac{3qE}{5}$

1-51 The electric potential V at any point O (x, y, z all in meters) in space is given by $V = 4x^2$ V. The electric field at the point (1 m, 0, 2 m) is :

(A) 8 V/m along negative x-axis

(B) 8 V/m along positive x-axis

(C) 16 V/m along negative x-axis

(D) 16 V/m along positive z-axis

1-52 A solid sphere having uniform charge density ρ and radius R is shown in figure-1.415. A spherical cavity of radius $\frac{R}{2}$ is made in it. What is the potential at point O ?

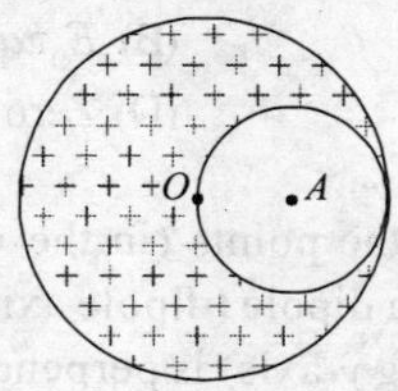

Figure 1.415

(A) $\frac{11R^2\rho}{24\varepsilon_0}$ (B) $\frac{5}{12}\frac{R^2\rho}{\varepsilon_0}$

(C) $\frac{7\rho R^2}{12\varepsilon_0}$ (D) $\frac{3}{2}\frac{R^2\rho}{\varepsilon_0}$

1-53 Initially the spheres A and B are at potential V_A and V_B respectively. Now sphere B is earthed by closing the switch. The potential of A will now become :

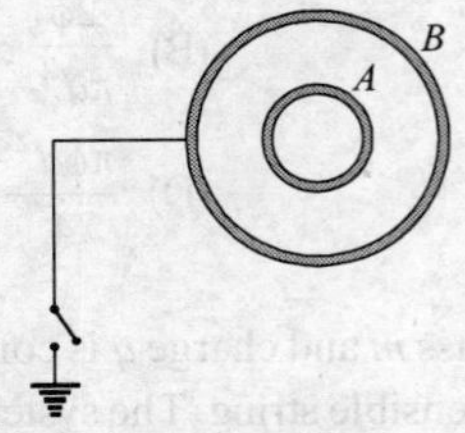

Figure 1.416

(A) 0 (B) V_A

(C) $V_A - V_B$ (D) V_B

1-54 A charge q is placed at the centre of the line joining two equal charges Q. The system of the three charges will be in equilibrium, if q is equal to :

(A) $-\frac{Q}{2}$ (B) $-\frac{Q}{4}$

(C) $+\frac{Q}{4}$ (D) $+\frac{Q}{2}$

1-55 A thin non-conducting ring or radius a has a linear charge density $\lambda = \lambda_0 \sin\phi$. A uniform electric field $E_0\hat{i} + E_0\hat{j}$ exist in the region. Net torque acting on ring is given as :

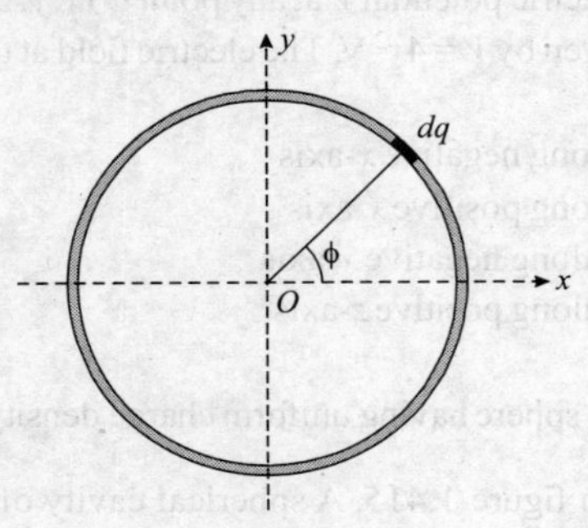

Figure 1.417

(A) $E_0\sqrt{2}\,\pi a^2\lambda_0$ (B) $E_0\pi a^2\lambda_0$

(C) $2E_0\pi a^2\lambda_0$ (D) Zero

1-56 The locus of the points (in the xy-plane) where the electric field due to a dipole (dipole axis is along x-axis and its equatorial is along y-axis) is perpendicular to its axis is :

(A) Straight line perpendicular to the axis

(B) Circle

(C) Parabola

(D) Straight line having inclination $\theta = \tan^{-1}\sqrt{2}$ with the axis

1-57 A ring of radius R having a linear charge density λ moves towards a solid imaginary sphere of radius $\frac{R}{2}$, so that the centre of ring passes through the centre of sphere. The axis of the ring is perpendicular to the line joining the centres of the ring and the sphere. The maximum flux through the sphere in this process is :

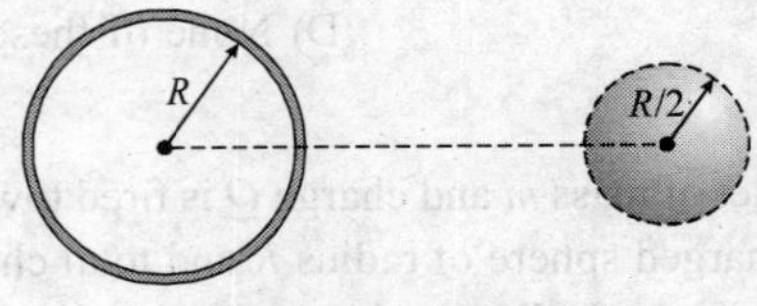

Figure 1.418

(A) $\frac{\lambda R}{\epsilon_0}$ (B) $\frac{\lambda R}{2\epsilon_0}$

(C) $\frac{\lambda \pi R}{4\epsilon_0}$ (D) $\frac{\lambda \pi R}{3\epsilon_0}$

1-58 A semi-infinite insulating rod has linear charge density λ. The electric field at the point P shown in figure-1.419 is :

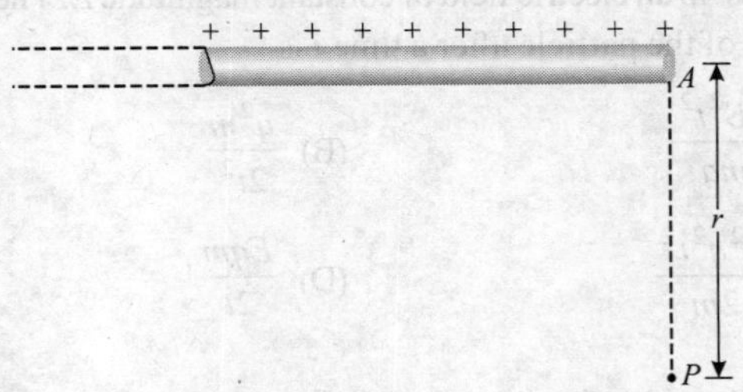

Figure 1.419

(A) $\frac{2\lambda^2}{(4\pi\varepsilon_0 r)^2}$ at 45° with AB (B) $\frac{\sqrt{2}\lambda^2}{4\pi\varepsilon_0 r^2}$ at 45° with AB

(C) $\frac{\sqrt{2}\lambda}{4\pi\varepsilon_0 r}$ at 45° with AB (D) $\frac{\sqrt{2}\lambda}{4\pi\varepsilon_0 r}$ at 135° with AB

1-59 Two spherical conductors B and C having equal radii and carrying equal charges repel each other with a force F when kept apart at some distance. A third spherical conductor having same radius as that of B but uncharged is brought in contact with B, then brought in contact with C and finally removed away from both. The new force of repulsion between B and C is :

(A) $F/4$ (B) $3F/4$

(C) $F/8$ (D) $3F/8$

1-60 Two insulated charged spheres of radii 20 cm and 25 cm respectively and having an equal charge Q are connected by a copper wire and then they are separated :

(A) Both the spheres will have the same charge

(B) Charge on the 20 cm sphere will be greater than that on the 25 cm sphere

(C) Charge on the 25 cm sphere will be greater than that on the 20 cm sphere

(D) Charge on each of the spheres will be $2Q$

1-61 A uniform electric field of strength $\vec{E}$ exists in a region. An electron enters a point A with velocity v as shown. It moves through the electric field and reaches at point B. Velocity of particle at B is $2v$ and it is moving at an angle 30° with x-axis as shown. Then which of the below options correct :

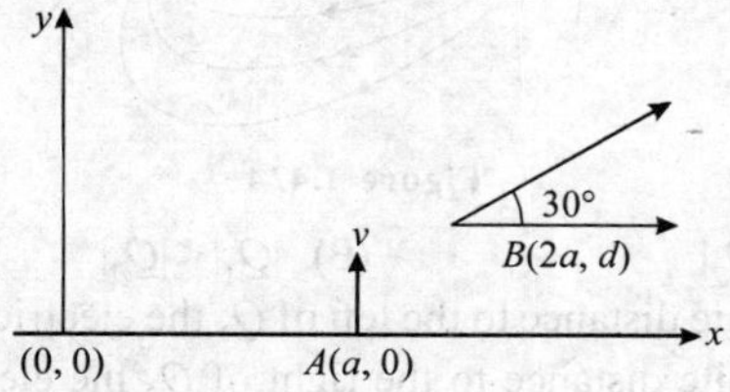

Figure 1.420

(A) Electric field $\vec{E} = -\dfrac{3mv^2}{2ea}\hat{i}$

(B) Rate of doing work done by electric field at B is $\dfrac{3mv^2}{2ea}$

(C) Both (A) and (B) are correct

(D) Both (A) and (B) are wrong

1-62 The potential at a point x (measured in μm) due to some charges situated on the x-axis is given by :

$$V(x) = \frac{20}{x^2 - 4} \text{ volts}$$

The electric field E at $x = 4$ μm is given as

(A) 5/3 V/μm and in the $-ve$ x direction

(B) 5/3 V/μm and in the $+ve$ direction

(C) 10/9 V/μm and in the $-ve$ direction

(D) 10/9 V/μm and in the $+ve$ direction

1-63 Four charges $+q$, $-q$, $+q$ and $-q$ are placed in order on the four consecutive corners of a square of side a. The work done in interchanging the positions of any two neighbouring charges of the opposite sign is :

(A) $\dfrac{q^2}{4\pi\varepsilon_0 a}(-4+\sqrt{2})$ (B) $\dfrac{q^2}{4\pi\varepsilon_0 a}(4+2\sqrt{2})$

(C) $\dfrac{q^2}{4\pi\varepsilon_0 a}(4-2\sqrt{2})$ (D) $\dfrac{q^2}{4\pi\varepsilon_0 a}(4+\sqrt{2})$

1-64 A particle of mass m and charge $+q$ approaches from a very large distance towards a uniformly charged ring of radius R and charge, mass same as that of particle, with initial velocity v_0 along the axis of the ring as shown in the figure-1.421. What is the closest distance of approach between the ring and the particle? Assume the space to be gravity free and frictionless :

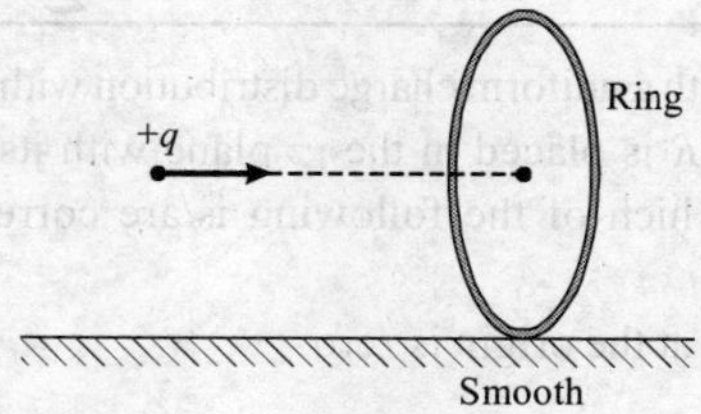

Figure 1.421

(A) $\sqrt{\dfrac{q^4}{\pi^2\varepsilon_0^2 m^2 v_0^4} - R^2}$ (B) $\sqrt{\dfrac{3q^4}{2\pi^2\varepsilon_0^2 m^2 v_0^4} + R^2}$

(C) $\sqrt{\dfrac{m^2 v_0^4}{2\pi^2 q^4 \varepsilon_0^2} - R^2}$ (D) $\sqrt{\dfrac{q^4}{4\pi^2\varepsilon_0^2 m^2 v_0^4} - R^2}$

1-65 A small positively charged ball of mass m is suspended by an insulating thread of negligible mass. Another positively charged small ball is moved very slowly from a large distance until it is in the original position of the first ball. As a result, the first ball rises by h. How much work has been done by the external agent. (Neglect the gravitational force of attraction between the balls but consideration earth Gravitation in that place the acceleration due to gravity is g).

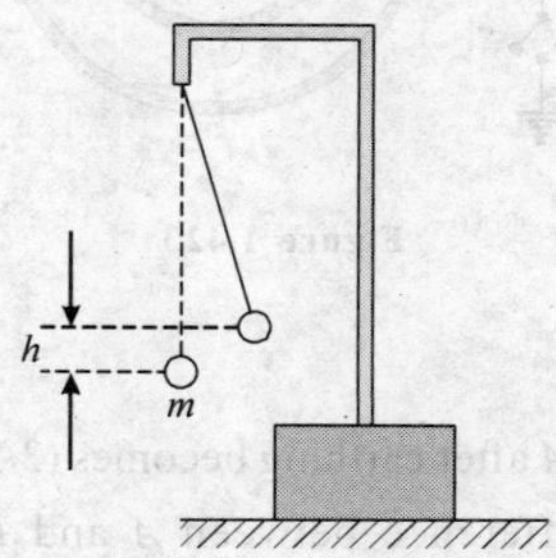

Figure 1.422

(A) $2mgh$ (B) $3mgh$

(C) $4mgh$ (D) $\dfrac{5mgh}{2}$

1-66 An electrostatic field in a region is radially outward with magnitude $E = \alpha r$, where is α constant and r is radial distance. The charge contained in a sphere of radius R in this region (centred at the origin) is :

(A) $\dfrac{2}{3}\pi\varepsilon_0 aR^3$ (B) $4\pi\varepsilon_0 aR^3$

(C) $8\pi\varepsilon_0 \alpha R^2$ (D) Zero

* * * * *

Advance MCQs with One or More Options Correct

1-1 A ring with a uniform charge distribution with a total charge Q and radius R is placed in the yz plane with its centre at the origin then which of the following is/are correct about this situation :

(A) The field at the origin is zero

(B) The potential at the origin is $\frac{1}{4\pi\varepsilon_0}\frac{Q}{R}$

(C) The field at the point $(x, 0, 0)$ is $\frac{1}{4\pi\varepsilon_0}\frac{Q}{x^2}$

(D) The field at the point $(x, 0, 0)$ is $\frac{1}{4\pi\varepsilon_0}\frac{Q}{R^2+x^2}$

1-2 Two concentric shells have radii R and $2R$ charges q_A and q_B and potentials $2V$ and $\frac{3V}{2}$ respectively. Now shell B is earthed by closing the switch S and let charges on the shells changed to q_A' and q_B'. Then we have :

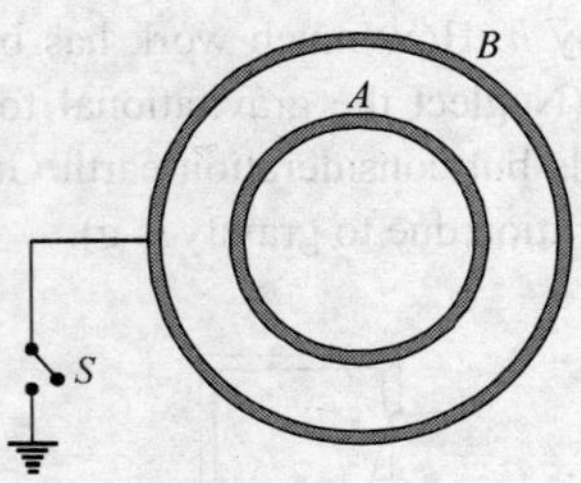

Figure 1.423

(A) $q_A/q_B = 1/2$

(B) $q_A'/q_B' = 1$

(C) Potential of A after earthing becomes $(3/2)V$

(D) Potential difference between A and B after earthing becomes $V/2$

1-3 Which of the following statement(s) is/are correct ?

(A) If the electric field due to a point charge varies as $r^{-2.5}$ instead of r^{-2}, then the Gauss law will still be valid

(B) The Gauss law can be used to calculate the field distribution around and electric dipole

(C) If the electric field between two point charges is zero somewhere, then the sign of the two charges is the same

(D) The work done by the external force in moving unit positive charge from point A at potential V_A to point B at potential V_B is $(V_B - V_A)$

1-4 A few electric field lines for a system of two charges Q_1 and Q_2 fixed at two different points on the x-axis are shown in the figure-1.424. With the figure what information about charges and electric field we are getting :

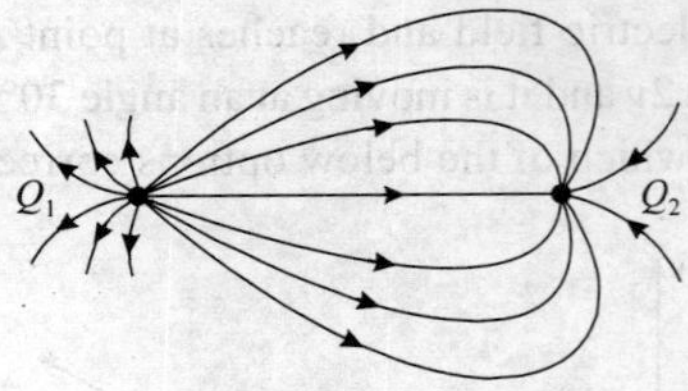

Figure 1.424

(A) $|Q_1| > |Q_2|$

(B) $|Q_1| < |Q_2|$

(C) At a finite distance to the left of Q_1 the electric field is zero

(D) At a finite distance to the right of Q_2 the electric field is zero

1-5 A spherical metal shell A of radius R_A and a solid metal sphere B of radius $R_B (< R_A)$ are kept far apart and each is given charge '$+Q/2$'. Now they are connected by a thin metal wire. Then which of the following is/are correct about this situation.

(A) Inside shell A at every point electric field is zero :

(B) After connections $Q_A > Q_B$

(C) After connections $\frac{\sigma_A}{\sigma_B} = \frac{R_B}{R_A}$

(D) After connections electric field strength on surface of A is less than that on the surface of B.

1-6 A particle of mass 2 kg and charge 1 mC is projected vertically with a velocity 10 m/s. There is a uniform horizontal electric field of 10^4 N/C :

(A) The horizontal range of the particle is 10 m

(B) The time of flight of the particle is 2 s

(C) The maximum height reached is 5 m

(D) The horizontal range of the particle is 5 m

1-7 A cubical region of side a has its centre at the origin. It encloses three fixed point charges, $-q$ at $(0, -a/4, 0)$, $+3q$ at $(0, 0, 0)$ and $-q$ at $(0, \pm a/4, 0)$. Which of the following options is/are correct :

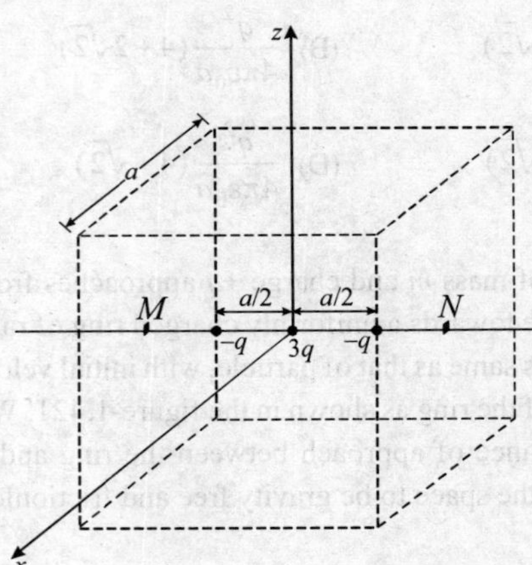

Figure 1.425

(A) The net electric flux crossing the plane $x = +a/2$ is equal to the net electric flux crossing the plane $x = -a/2$

(B) The net electric flux crossing the plane $y = +a/2$ is more than the net electric flux crossing the plane $y = -a/2$

(C) The net electric flux crossing the entire region is a/ϵ_0

(D) The net electric flux crossing the plane $z = +a/2$ is equal to the net electric flux crossing the plane $x = +a/2$

1-8 The figure-1.426 shows, two point charges $q_1 = +2Q$ and $q_2 = -Q$. The charges divide the line joining them in three parts I, II and III as shown in figure-1.424 then which of the following statements is/are correct :

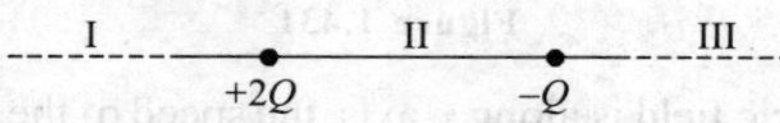

Figure 1.426

(A) Region III has a local maxima of electric field

(B) Region I has a local minima of electric field

(C) Equilibrium position for a test charge lies in region II

(D) The equilibrium for constrained motion along the line joining the charges is stable for a negative charge

1-9 At the distance of 5 cm and 10 cm from surface of a uniformly charged solid sphere, the potentials are 100 V and 75 V respectively. Then which of the following statements is/are correct about the given situation :

(A) Potential at its surface is 150 V

(B) The charge on the sphere is $\frac{50}{3} \times 10^{-10}$ C

(C) The electric field on the surface is 1500 V/m

(D) The electric potential at its centre is 250 V

1-10 Six point charges are kept at the vertices of a regular hexagon of side L and centre O, as shown in the figure-1.427. Given that $C = \frac{1}{4\pi\varepsilon_0}\frac{q}{L^2}$, which of the following statements is/are correct ?

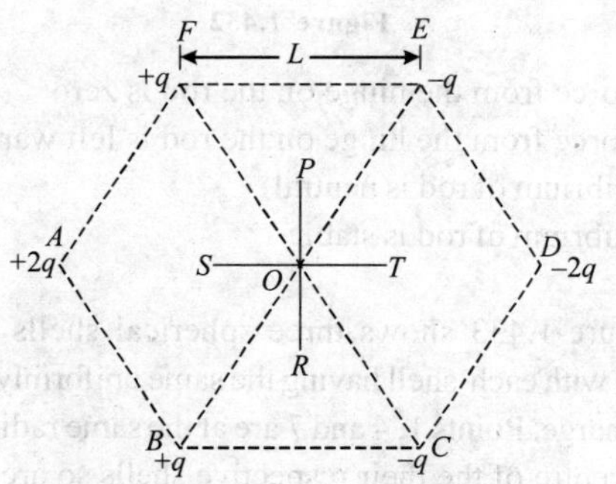

Figure 1.427

(A) The electric field at O is 6 C along OD

(B) The potential at O is zero

(C) The potential at all points on the line PR is same

(D) The potential at all points on the line ST is same

1-11 Point charges are located on the corner of a square as shown below. Find the component of electric field at any point on the z-axis which is the axis of symmetry of the square :

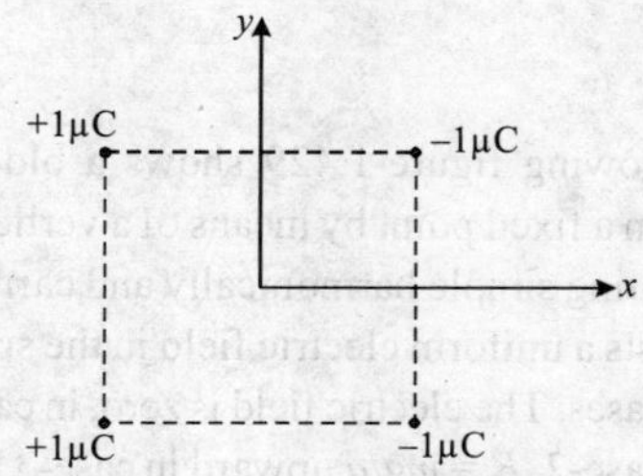

Figure 1.428

(A) $E_z = 0$ (B) $E_x = 0$

(C) $E_y = 0$ (D) None of these

1-12 Charges Q_1 and Q_2 lie inside and outside respectively of a closed surface S. Let E be the field at any point on S and ϕ be the flux of E over S :

(A) If Q_1 changes, both E and ϕ will change

(B) If Q_2 changes, E will change but ϕ will not change

(C) If $Q_1 = 0$ and $Q_2 \neq 0$ then $E \neq 0$ but $\phi = 0$

(D) If $Q_1 \neq 0$ and $Q_2 = 0$ then $E = 0$ but $\phi \neq 0$

1-13 In an uniform electric field, when we move from origin to $x = 1$ m, the potential changes by 10 V. Which of the following can be a possible magnitude of the electric field ?

(A) 10 V/m (B) 15 V/m

(C) 5 V/m (D) 20 V/m

1-14 An electric dipole is placed at the centre of a sphere. Mark the correct options :

(A) The flux of the electric field through the sphere is zero

(B) The electric field is zero at every point of the sphere

(C) The electric field is not zero at any where on the sphere

(D) The electric field is zero on a circle on the sphere

1-15 Two point charges each of magnitude Q are placed at coordinates $(0, y)$ and $(0, -y)$. A point charge q of the same polarity can move along X-axis. Then :

(A) The force on q is maximum at $x = \pm y/\sqrt{2}$

(B) The charge q is in equilibrium at the origin

(C) The charge q performs an oscillatory motion about the origin

(D) For any position of q other then origin the force is directed away from origin

1-16 Mark the correct options about electric field and Gauss's law in a region of space :

(A) Gauss's law is valid only for uniform charge distributions

(B) Gauss's law is valid only for charges placed in vacuum

(C) The electric field calculated by Gauss's law is the field due to all the charges

(D) The flux of the electric field through a closed surface due to all the charges is equal to the flux due to the charges enclosed by the surface

1-17 The following figure-1.429 shows a block of mass m suspended from a fixed point by means of a vertical spring. The block is oscillating simple harmonically and carries a charge q. There also exists a uniform electric field in the space. Consider four different cases. The electric field is zero, in case-1, $E = mg/q$ downward in case-2, $E = mg/q$ upward in case-3 and $E = 2mg/q$ downward in case-4. The speed at mean position of block is same in all cases. Select which of the following statements is/are correct :

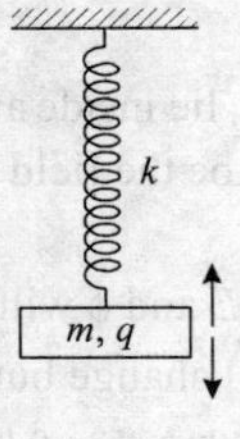

Figure 1.429

(A) Time periods of oscillation are equal in case-1 and case-3

(B) Amplitudes of displacement are same in case-2 and case-3

(C) The maximum elongation (increment in length from natural length) is maximum in case-4

(D) Time periods of oscillation are equal in case-2 and case-4

1-18 Two concentric spherical shells have charges $+q$ and $-q$ as shown in figure-1.430. Which of the statement given below is/are correct :

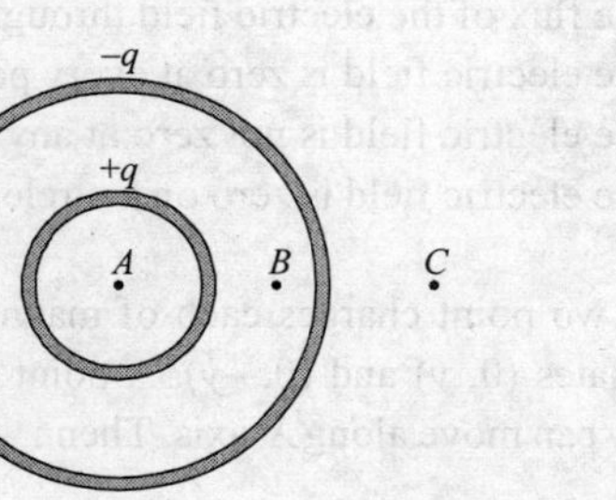

Figure 1.430

(A) At A electric field is zero, but electric potential is non-zero

(B) At B electric field and electric potential both are non-zero

(C) At C electric field is zero but electric potential is non-zero

(D) At C electric field and electric potential both are zero

1-19 An insulating rod of uniform linear charge density λ and uniform linear mass density μ lies on a smooth table whose surface is xy-plane. A uniform electric field E is switched on in the space :

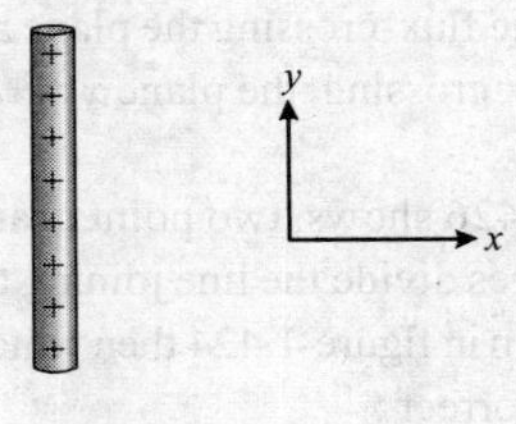

Figure 1.431

(A) If electric field is along x-axis, the speed of the rod when it has travelled a distance d is $\sqrt{\dfrac{2\lambda Ed}{\mu}}$

(B) If electric field E is at an angle θ ($< 90°$) with x-axis along the table surface then the speed of the rod when it has travelled a distance d is $\sqrt{\dfrac{2\lambda Ed\cos\theta}{\mu}}$

(C) A non zero torque acts on the rod due to the field about centre of mass in case electric field is into the plane of paper.

(D) A non zero torque acts on the rod due to the field about centre of mass in case electric field is along the surface of table.

1-20 A rod is hinged at its centre O and free to rotate about a horizontal axis of rotation as shown in figure-1.432. Two point charges $+q$ and $+q$ are fixed at the two ends of the rod. A uniform electric field E exist in the region toward right as shown. Space is gravity free. Choose the correct options :

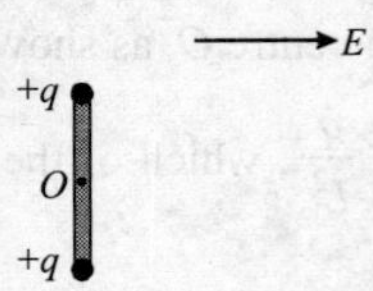

Figure 1.432

(A) Net force from the hinge on the rod is zero

(B) Net force from the hinge on the rod is left wards

(C) Equilibrium of rod is neutral

(D) Equilibrium of rod is stable

1-21 Figure-1.433 shows three spherical shells is separate situations, with each shell having the same uniformly distributed positive charge. Points 1, 4 and 7 are at the same radial distances from the centre of the their respective shells so are points 2, 5 and 8 and so are points 3, 6 and 9. With the electric potential taken equal to zero at an infinite distance, which of the following statements is/are correct :

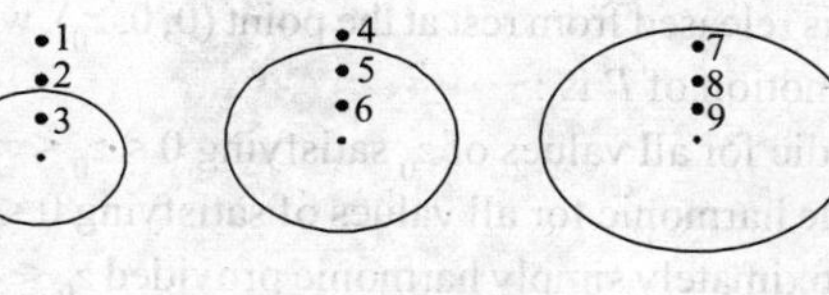

Figure 1.433

(A) Point 3 has highest potential
(B) Point 1, 4 and 7 are at same potential
(C) Point 8 has lowest potential
(D) Point 5 and 8 are at same potential

1-22 Which of the following quantities do not depend on the choice of zero potential or zero potential energy ?
(A) Potential at a point
(B) Potential difference between two points
(C) Potential energy of two-charge system
(D) Change in potential energy of a two-charge system

1-23 A charge q is revolving around another charge q as shown in a conical pendulum. The motion is in a horizontal plane. Which of the following statements is/are correct about this situation :

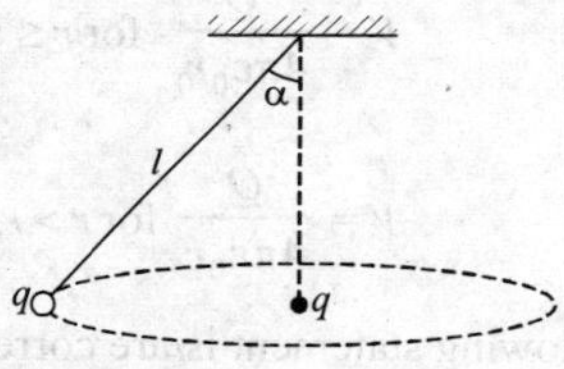

Figure 1.434

(A) Tension in the string is greater than the weight of the ball
(B) The tension in the string is greater than the electrostatic repulsive force
(C) If the charge is removed, the speed of the ball has to be increased to maintain the angle
(D) If the charge is removed, the speed of ball has to be decreased to maintain the angle

1-24 An electric dipole is placed in an electric filed generated by a point charge :
(A) The net force on the dipole never be zero.
(B) The net force on the dipole may be zero.
(C) The torque on the dipole due to the field must be zero.
(D) The torque on the dipole due to the field may be zero.

1-25 Two large thin conducting plates with small gap in between are placed in an uniform electric field E which exist in the direction as shown in figure-1.435. Area of each plate is A and charges $+Q$ and $-Q$ are given to those plates as shown in the figure. If points R, S and T are three points in space, then which of the following is/are correct :

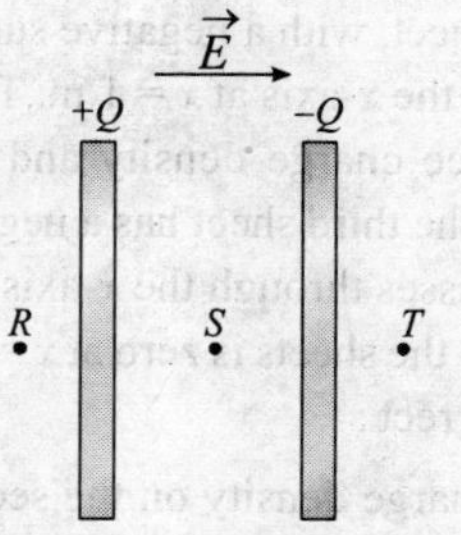

Figure 1.435

(A) field at point R is E
(B) field at point S is E
(C) field at point T is $\left(E+\frac{Q}{\epsilon_0 A}\right)$
(D) field at point S is $\left(E+\frac{Q}{A\epsilon_0}\right)$

1-26 The electric potential decreases uniformly from 100 V to 50 V as one moves on the y-axis from $y=-1$ m to $y=+1$ m. The electric field at the origin :
(A) Must be equal to 25 V/m
(B) May be equal to 25 V/m
(C) May be less than 25 V/m
(D) May be greater than 25 V/m

1-27 A large insulating thick sheet of thickness $2d$ is charged with a uniform volume charge density ρ. A particle of mass m, carrying a charge q having a sign opposite to that of the sheet, is released from the surface of the sheet. The sheet does not offer any mechanical resistance to the motion of the particle. Find the oscillation frequency ν of the particle inside the sheet :

(A) $\nu=\frac{1}{2\pi}\sqrt{\frac{q\rho}{m\varepsilon_0}}$ (B) $\nu=\frac{1}{2\pi}\sqrt{\frac{2q\rho}{m\varepsilon_0}}$

(C) $\nu=\frac{1}{4\pi}\sqrt{\frac{q\rho}{m\varepsilon_0}}$ (D) $\nu=\frac{1}{2\pi}\sqrt{\frac{q\rho}{m\varepsilon_0}}$

1-28 If the flux of electric field in a region of space through a given closed surface is zero then which of the following statements is/are correct about this situation :
(A) The electric field must be zero everywhere on the surface.
(B) The electric field may be zero everywhere on the surface.
(C) The charge inside the surface must be zero.
(D) The charge in the vicinity of the surface must be zero.

1-29 Three non-conducting infinite planar sheets are parallel to the y-z plane. Each sheet has an uniform surface charge density. The first sheet, with a negative surface charge density $-\sigma$, passes through the x-axis at $x = 1$ m. The second sheet has an unknown surface charge density and passes through the x-axis at $x = 2$ m. The third sheet has a negative surface charge density -3σ and passes through the x-axis at $x = 4$ m. The net electric field due to the sheets is zero at $x = 1.5$ m. Which of the following is/are correct :

(A) The surface charge density on the second sheet is $+2\sigma$

(B) The electric field at $x = -2$ m is $\frac{\sigma}{\epsilon_0}\hat{i}$

(C) The electric field at $x = 3$ m is $\frac{\sigma}{\epsilon_0}\hat{i}$

(D) The electric field at $x = 6$ m is $\frac{-\sigma}{\epsilon_0}\hat{i}$

1-30 An ellipsoidal cavity is carved within a perfect conductor as shown in figure-1.436. A positive charge q is placed at the centre of the cavity. The points A and B are on the cavity surface as shown in the figure-1.436. Then which of the following is/are correct :

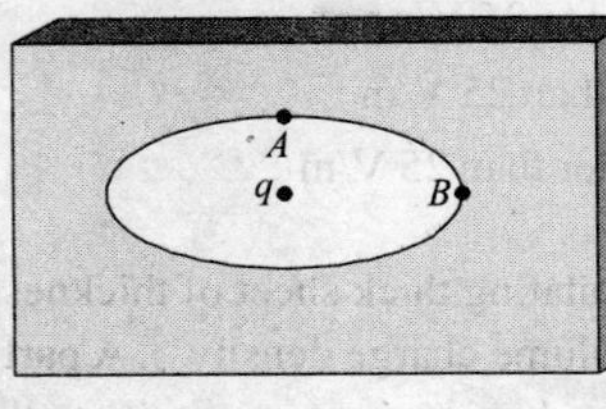

Figure 1.436

(A) Electric field near A in the cavity = Electric field near B in the cavity

(B) Charge density at A = Charge density at B

(C) Potential at A = Potential at B

(D) Total electric field flux through the surface of the cavity is q/ε_0

1-31 A positive charge q is fixed at the origin. An electric dipole withe dipole moment $\vec{p}$ is placed along the x-axis far away from the origin with $\vec{p}$ pointing along the positive x-axis and it is set free to move. The kinetic energy when it reaches a distance x from the origin is K and the magnitude of the force experienced by charge q at this moment is F. Then :

(A) K varies as $1/x$ (B) K varies as $1/x^2$

(C) F varies as $1/x^2$ (D) F varies as $1/x^3$

1-32 A positively charged thin metal ring of radius R is fixed in the xy-plane with its centre at the O. A negatively charged particle P is released from rest at the point $(0, 0, z_0)$, where $z_0 > 0$. Then the motion of P is :

(A) Periodic for all values of z_0 satisfying $0 < z_0 < \infty$

(B) Simple harmonic for all values of satisfying $0 < z_0 < R$

(C) Approximately simply harmonic provided $z_0 << R$

(D) Such that P crosses O and continues to move along the negative z-axis towards $z = -\infty$

1-33 Electric potential V due to a spherically symmetric charge distribution varies with distance r as shown in the figure-1.437.

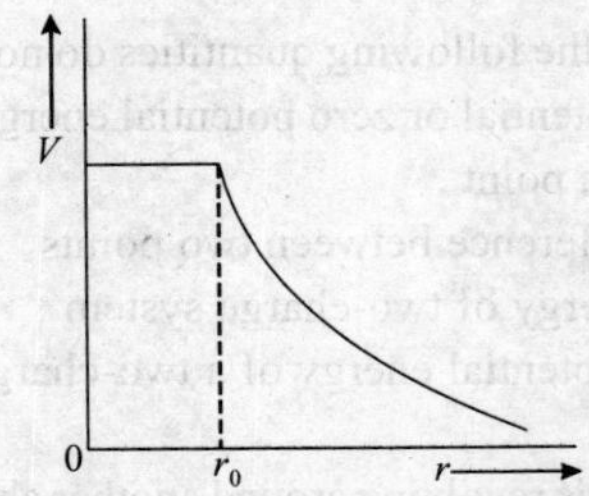

Figure 1.437

Given that potential at different positions is

$$V = \frac{Q}{4\pi\varepsilon_0 r_0} \quad \text{for } r \le r_0$$

and

$$V = \frac{Q}{4\pi\varepsilon_0 r} \quad \text{for } r > r_0$$

Which of the following statement is/are correct?

(A) Electric field due to the charge system is discontinuous at $r = r_0$

(B) The net charge enclosed in a sphere of radius $r = 2r_0$ is Q

(C) No charge exists at any point in a spherical region of radius $r < r_0$

(D) Electrostatic energy inside the sphere of radius $r = r_0$ is zero

1-34 A non conducting ring of radius R is charged as shown in figure-1.438:

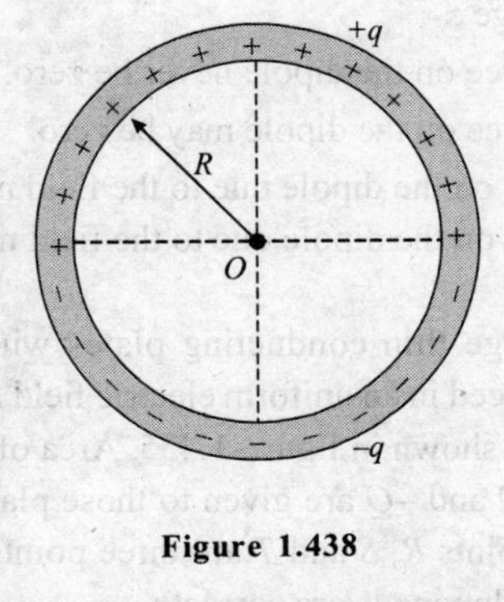

Figure 1.438

(A) The electric field is zero at the centre of the ring

(B) The electric potential is zero at centre of the ring

(C) The electric potential at the centre is, $V = \frac{2q}{4\pi \epsilon_0 R}$

(D) The electric field at the centre is, $E = \frac{q}{\pi^2 \epsilon_0 R^2}$

1-35 Under the influence of the electric field of a fixed charge $+Q$, a charge $-q$ is moving around it in an elliptical orbit. Which of the following statements is/are correct in this situation :

(A) The angular momentum of the charge $-q$ is constant

(B) The linear momentum of the charge $-q$ is constant

(C) The angular velocity of the charge $-q$ is constant

(D) The linear speed of the charge $-q$ is constant

1-36 Figure-1.439 shows a cross-section of a spherical metal shell of inner radius R and out radius $2R$. A point charge q is located at a distance $R/2$ from the centre of the shell. If the shell is electrically neutral, then which of the following statements is/are correct :

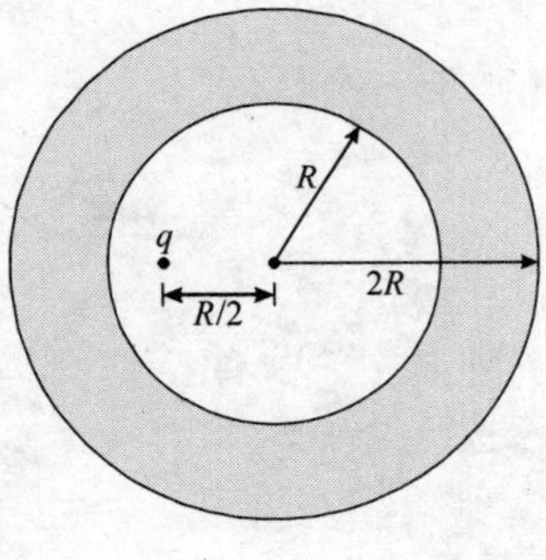

Figure 1.439

(A) The electric field at some point inside shell is zero

(B) The electric field at all the point inside shell is non-zero

(C) The electric field at the outer surface of the shell is

$$E = \frac{1}{4\pi\varepsilon_0} \frac{q}{(3R/2)^2}$$

(D) The electrical field at the outer surface is $E = \frac{1}{4\pi\varepsilon_0} \frac{q}{(2R)^2}$

1-37 Two non-conducting solid spheres of radii R and $2R$, having uniform volume charge densities ρ_1 and ρ_2 respectively are touching each other. The net electric field at a distance $2R$ from the centre of the smaller sphere, along the line joining the centres of the spheres, is zero then the ratio $\frac{\rho_1}{\rho_2}$ can be :

(A) -4 (B) $-\frac{32}{25}$

(C) $+\frac{32}{25}$ (D) 4

1-38 Two non-conducting spheres of radii R_1 and R_2 carrying uniform volume charge densities $+\rho$ and $-\rho$ respectively, are placed such that they partially overlap as shown in the figure-1.440. At all points in the overlapping region which of the statements is/are correct about the electric field and electric potential :

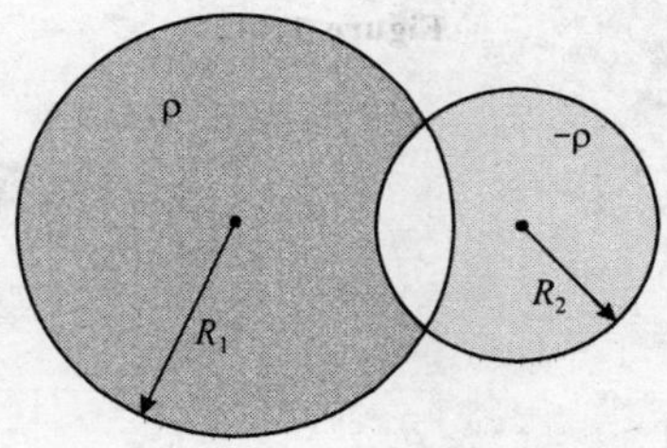

Figure 1.440

(A) The electric field is zero

(B) The electric potential is constant

(C) The electric field is constant in magnitude

(D) The electric field has same direction

1-39 X and Y are large, parallel conducting plates close to each other. Each face has an area A. Plate X is given a charge Q. Y is without any charge. Points A, B and C are as shown in the figure-1.441. Which of the following statement about electric field is correct :

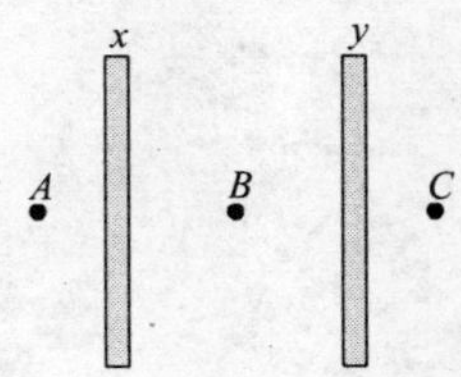

Figure 1.441

(A) The field at B is $\frac{Q}{2\varepsilon_0 A}$

(B) The field at B is $\frac{Q}{\varepsilon_0 A}$

(C) The field at A, B and C are of the same magnitude

(D) The fields at A and C are of the same magnitude, but in opposite directions

1-40 Two small balls A and B of positive charge Q each and masses m and $2m$ respectively are connected by a non conducting light rigid rod of length L. This system is released in a uniform electric field of strength E as shown. Just after the release (assume no other force acts on the system) :

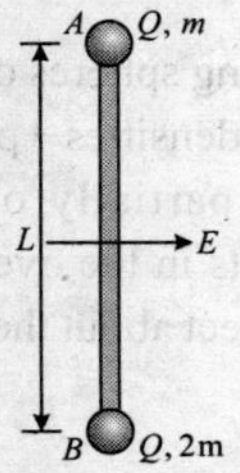

Figure 1.442

(A) Rod has zero angular acceleration

(B) Rod has angular acceleration $\dfrac{QE}{2mL}$ in anticlockwise direction

(C) Acceleration of point A is $\dfrac{2QE}{m}$ towards right

(D) Acceleration of point A is $\dfrac{QE}{m}$ towards right

* * * * *

Unsolved Numerical Problems for Preparation of NSEP, INPhO & IPhO

For detailed preparation of INPhO and IPhO students can refer advance study material on www.physicsgalaxy.com

1-1 A small sphere is charged uniformly and placed at point $A(u, v)$ so that at point $B(8, 7)$ electric field strength is $\overline{E} = (54\hat{i} + 72\hat{j})$ N/C and potential is + 900 V. Calculate :

(a) Magnitude of charge,

(b) Coordinates of point A, and

(c) If dielectric strength of air is 3×10^6 V/m, minimum possible radius of the sphere.

Ans. [(a) 1 μC; (b) (2, –1); (c) $\sqrt{3 \times 10^{-3}}$ m or 5.48 cm]

1-2 The electric intensity E at a point on the axis of a ring of radius a at a distance x from its centre is given by

$$\frac{1}{4\pi\epsilon_0}\frac{qx}{(a^2 + x^2)^{3/2}}$$

where q is charge on ring.

An electron is constrained to move along the axis of this ring. Show that the electron can perform oscillations whose frequency is given by

$$\omega = \left(\frac{eq}{4\pi\epsilon_0 ma^3}\right)^{1/3}$$

Where e is the charge on electron

1-3 Two long wires each of length l are placed on a smooth horizontal table. Wires have equal but opposite charges. Magnitude of linear charge density on each wire is λ. Calculate the work required to increase the separation between the wires from a to $2a$.

Ans. [$\frac{\lambda^2 l}{2\pi\epsilon_0}\ln(2)$]

1-4 Four charges $+50 \times 10^{-9}$ C, -12×10^{-19} C, $+36 \times 10^{-9}$ C and $+90 \times 10^{-9}$ C are placed respectively at the corners of a rectangular $ABCD$, AB being equal to 5 cm and BC being 12 cm. Find :

(a) the force on the charge at A, and

(b) the field strength at the point of intersection of the two diagonals

Ans. [(a) 4.11×10^{-3} N (b) 1.975×10^5 V/m]

1-5 A solid conducting sphere of radius R is placed in a uniform electric field E as shown in figure-1.443. Due to electric field non uniform surface charges are induced on the surface of the sphere. Consider a point A on the surface of sphere at a polar angle θ from the direction of electric field as shown in figure. Find the surface density of induced charges at point A in terms of electric field and polar angle θ.

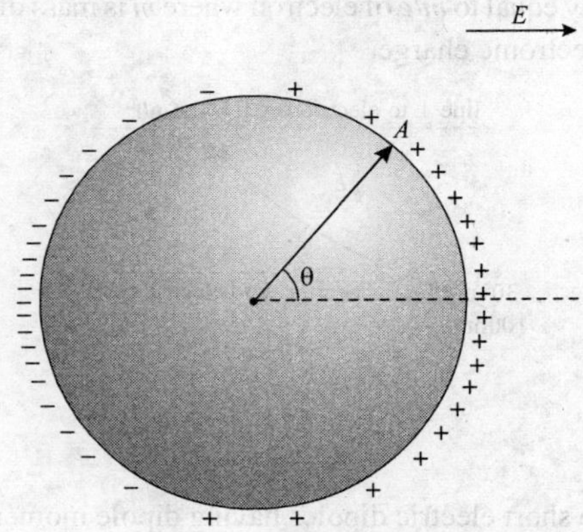

Figure 1.443

Ans. [$3\epsilon_0 E\cos\theta$]

1-6 Suppose in an insulating medium, having di-electric constant $k = 1$, volume density of positive charge varies with y-coordinate according to law $\rho = ay$. A particle of mass m having positive charge q is placed in the medium at point $A(0, y_0)$ and projected with velocity $\vec{v} = v_0\hat{i}$ as shown in figure-1.444. Neglecting gravity and frictional resistance of the medium and assuming electric field strength to be zero at $y = 0$, calculate slope of trajectory of the particle as a function of y.

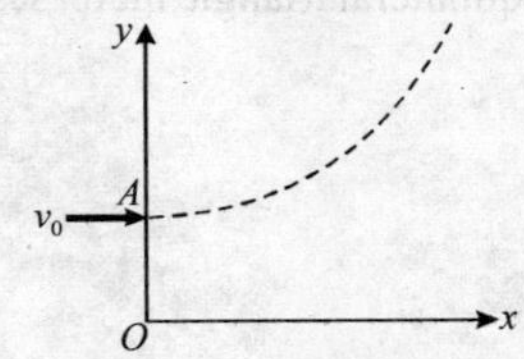

Figure 1.444

Ans. [$\sqrt{\frac{qa}{3m\epsilon_0 v_0^2}}(y^3 - y_0^3)$]

1-7 There is spherical symmetric charge distribution around origin. The electrostatic potential at a distance r from origin is given as $V = \frac{-Kr^4}{4}$ where K is a positive constant. The slope of tangent to density w.r.t r graph at $r = \frac{1}{2}m$ is $\alpha K\epsilon_0$. Then find value of α.

Ans. [5]

1-8 Two long wires have uniform charge density λ per unit length each. The wires are non-coplanar and mutually perpendicular. Shortest distance between them is d. Calculate interaction force between them.

Ans. [$\frac{\lambda^2}{2\epsilon_0}$]

1-9 Find the magnitude of uniform electric field E of which the direction is shown in figure-1.445 if an electron entering with velocity 100 m/s making 30° comes out making 60°, after a time numerically equal to m/e of electron where m is mass of electron and e is electronic charge.

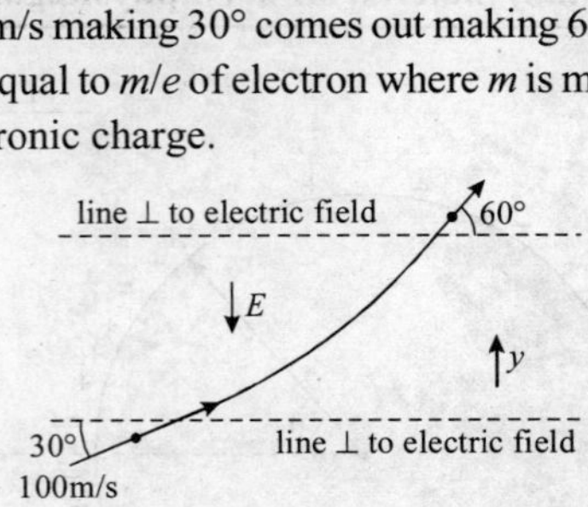

Figure 1.445

Ans. [100]

1-10 Two short electric dipoles having dipole moment p_1 and p_2 are placed co-axially and unidirectionally, at a distance r apart. Calculate nature and magnitude of force between them.

Ans. [Attraction, $\frac{1}{4\pi\varepsilon_0}\cdot\frac{6p_1p_2}{r^4}$]

1-11 Three identically charged, small spheres each of mass m are suspended from a common point by insulated light strings each of length l. The spheres are always on vertices of an equilateral triangle of length of the sides x (<< l). Calculate the rate dq/dt with which charge on each sphere increases if length of the sides of the equilateral triangle increases slowly according to law $\frac{dx}{dt} = \frac{a}{\sqrt{x}}$.

Ans. [$\sqrt{\frac{3\pi\varepsilon_0 mga^2}{l}}$]

1-12 Two plane parallel conducting plates 1.5×10^{-2} m apart are held horizontally one above the other in air. The upper plate is maintained at a positive potential of 1.5 kV while the other plate is earthed. Calculate the number of electrons which must be attached to a small oil drop of mass 4.8×10^{-15} kg between the plates to keep it in equilibrium, assuming that the density of air is negligible in comparison with that of oil. If the potential of the upper plate is suddenly changed to – 1.5 kV, what is the initial acceleration of the charged drop? Also obtain the terminal velocity of the drop if its radius is 5.9×10^{-6} m and the coefficient of viscosity of air in 1.8×10^{-5} N-s/m². Take $g = 9.8$ m/s².

Ans. [3, 20 m/s², 5.7×10^{-5} m/s]

1-13 A small cork ball A of mass m is suspended by a thread of length l. Another ball B is fixed at a distance l from point of suspension and distance $l/2$ from thread when is vertical, as shown in figure-1.446. Balls A and B have charges (+ q) each. Ball A is held by an external force such that the thread remains vertical.

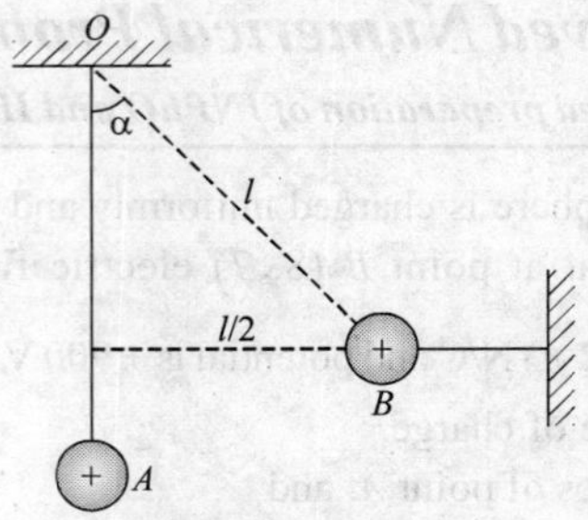

Figure 1.446

When ball A is released from rest, thread deflects through a maximum angle of $\beta = 30°$, calculate m in terms of other parameters.

Ans. [$\frac{q^2}{2\pi\varepsilon_0 gl^2}\cdot\frac{(1-\sqrt{2-\sqrt{3}})}{(2-\sqrt{3})^{3/2}}$]

1-14 A particle of mass m having negative charge q moves along an ellipse around a fixed positive charge Q so that its maximum and minimum distances from fixed charge are equal to r_1 and r_2 respectively. Calculate angular momentum L of this particle.

Ans. [$\sqrt{\frac{mr_1r_2Qq}{2\pi\varepsilon_0(r_1+r_2)}}$]

1-15 Calculate the electric field vector at centre of charged hemisphere in N/C if it has uniform surface charged density of $8\varepsilon_0$C/m². The base of hemisphere is in XZ plane with centre at the origin and the curved surface is intersecting the – Y axis.

Ans. [$-2\hat{j}$ N/C]

1-16 A charged dust particle of radius 5×10^{-7} m is located in a horizontal electric field having an intensity of 6.28×10^5 V/m. The surrounding medium is air with coefficient of viscosity $\eta = 1.6 \times 10^{-5}$ N-s/m². If this particle moves with a uniform horizontal speed 0.02 m/s, find the number of electrons on it.

Ans. [30]

1-17 2 small balls having the same mass & charge & located on the same vertical at heights h_1 & h_2 are thrown in the same direction along the horizontal at the same velocity v. The 1st ball touches the ground at a distance l from the initial vertical. At what height will the 2nd ball be at this instant? The air drag & the charges induced should be neglected.

Ans. [$H_2 = h_1 + h_2 - g\left(\frac{l}{v}\right)^2$]

1-18 What is the percentage change in distance if the force of attraction between two point charges increases to 4 times keeping magnitude of charges constant ?

Ans. [Decreased to 50% of initial value]

1-19 Two concentric rings of radii r and $2r$ are placed with centre at origin. Two charges $+q$ each are fixed at the diametrically opposite points of the rings as shown in figure-1.447. Smaller ring is now rotated by an angle 90° about Z-axis then it is again rotated by 90° about Y-axis. Find the work done by electrostatic forces in each step. If finally larger ring is rotated by 90° about X-axis, find the total work required to perform all three steps.

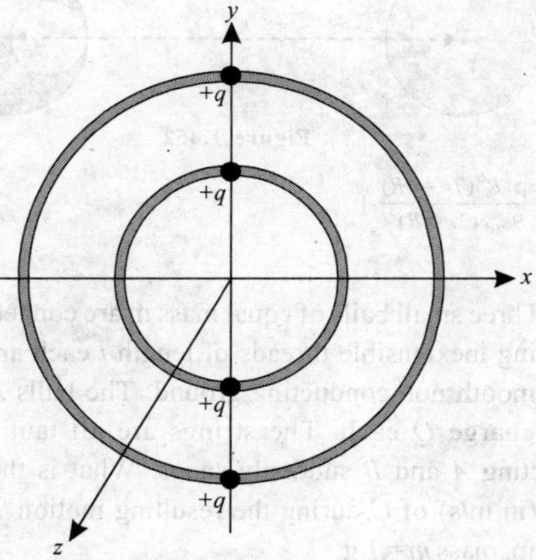

Figure 1.447

Ans. $[W_{\text{first step}} = \left(\frac{8}{3}-\frac{4}{\sqrt{5}}\right)\frac{Kq^2}{r}$, $W_{\text{second step}} = 0$, $W_{\text{total}} = 0]$

1-20 Find the electric field strength vector at the centre of a ball of radius R with volume charge density $\rho = ar$, where a is a constant vector, and r is a radius vector drawn from the ball's centre.

Ans. $[E = -1/6a\ R^2/\varepsilon_0]$

1-21 A positively charged sphere of mass $m = 5$ kg is attached by a spring of force constant $K = 10^4$ N/m. The sphere is tied with a thread so that spring is in its natural length. Another identical, negatively charged sphere is fixed with floor, vertically below the positively charged sphere as shown in figure-1.448. If initial separation between sphere is $r_0 = 50$ cm and magnitude of charge on each sphere is $q = 100\ \mu$C, calculate maximum elongation of spring when the thread is burnt. Take $g = 10$ m/s^2.

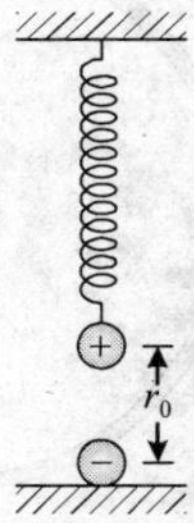

Figure 1.448

Ans. [10 cm]

1-22 The figure-1.449 shows three infinite non-conducting plates of charge perpendicular to the plane of the paper with charge per unit area $+\sigma$, $+2\sigma$ and $-\sigma$. Find the ratio of the net electric field at that point A to that at point B. The points A and B are located midway between the plates.

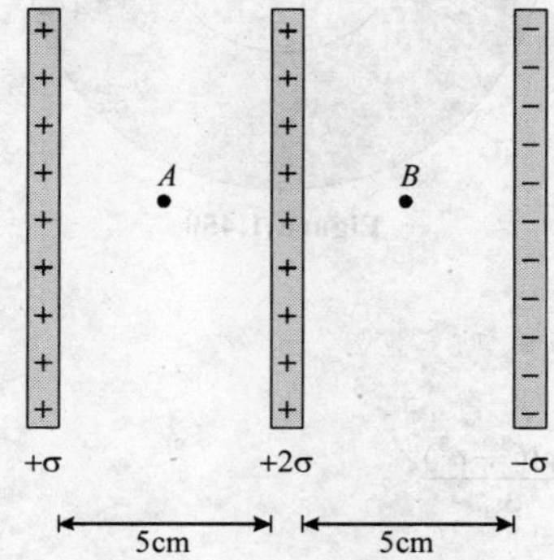

Figure 1.449

Ans. [Zero]

1-23 A ball of radius R is uniformly charged with the volume density ρ. Find the flux of the electric field strength vector across the ball's section formed by the plane located at a distance $r_0 < R$ from the centre of the ball.

Ans. $[|\phi| = 1/3\pi\rho r_0\ (R^2 - r_0^2)/\varepsilon_0]$

1-24 Small identical balls with equal charges are fixed at vertices of regular 2009-gon (A polygon with 2009 edges) with side a. At a certain instant, one of the balls is released & a sufficiently long time interval later, the ball adjacent to the first released ball is freed. The kinetic energies of the released balls are found to differ by K at a sufficiently long distance from the polygon. Determine the charge q of each part.

Ans. $[\sqrt{4\pi\epsilon_0 Ka}]$

1-25 An infinitely long cylindrical surface of circular cross. Section is uniformly charged lengthwise with the surface density $\sigma = \sigma_0 \cos\varphi$, where φ is the polar angle of the cylindrical coordinates system whose z-axis coincides with the axis of the given surface. Find the magnitude and direction of the electric field strength vector on the z-axis.

Ans. $[E = ½\ \sigma_0/\varepsilon_0$, with the direction of the vector E corresponding to the angle $\varphi = \pi$.]

1-26 A non-conducting hollow sphere having inner and outer radii a and b respectively is made of a material having dielectric constant K and has uniformly distributed charge over its entire solid volume. Volume density of charge is ρ. Calculate potential at a distance r from its centre when.

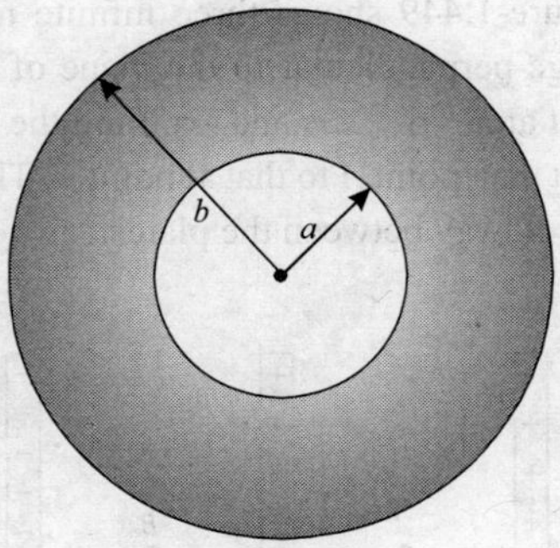

Figure 1.450

(a) $r > b$,

(b) $r < a$,

(c) $a < r < b$

Ans. [(a) $V_1 = \dfrac{\rho(b^3 - a^3)}{3\varepsilon_0 r}$;

(b) $V_i = \dfrac{\rho(b^3 - a^3)}{3\varepsilon_0 b} + \dfrac{\rho}{3\varepsilon_0 K}\left[\left(\dfrac{b^2 - a^2}{2}\right) - \dfrac{a^3(b-a)}{ab}\right]$;

(c) $V = \dfrac{\rho(b^3 - a^3)}{3\varepsilon_0 b} + \dfrac{\rho}{3\varepsilon_0 K}\left[\left(\dfrac{b^2 - a^2}{2}\right) - a^3\dfrac{(b-r)}{rb}\right]$]

1-27 Two thin parallel threads carry a uniform charge with linear densities λ and -λ. The separation between the threads is equal to *l*. Find the electric potential and electric field at a distance *r* from the central line of the threads in the plane perpendicular to the threads at an angle θ as shown in figure-1.451. Consider that the given distance $r >> l$.

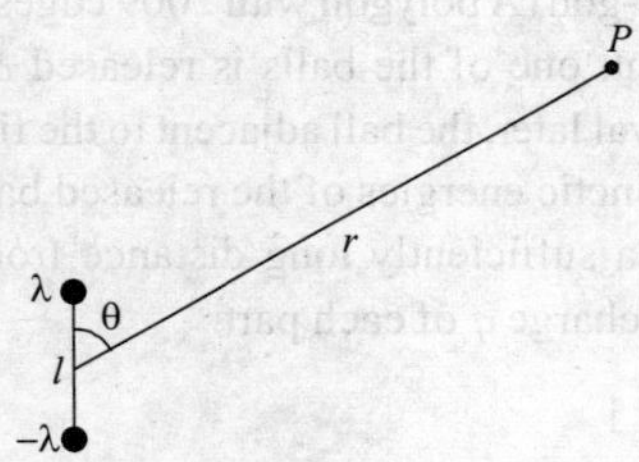

Figure 1.451

Ans. [$\dfrac{\lambda l \cos\theta}{2\pi \epsilon_0 r}$, $\dfrac{\lambda l \cos\theta}{2\pi \epsilon_0 r^2}$]

1-28 A positive charge *Q* is uniformly distributed throughout the volume of a dielectric sphere of radius *R*. A point mass having charge +*q* and mass *m* is fired towards the centre of the sphere with velocity *v* from a point at distance *x* from the centre of the sphere. Find the minimum velocity *v* so that it can penetrate *R*/2 distance of the sphere. Neglect any resistance other than electric interaction. Charge on the small mass remains constant throughout the motion.

Ans. [$\left[\dfrac{2KqQ}{mR}\left(\dfrac{r-R}{r} + \dfrac{3}{8}\right)\right]^{1/2}$]

1-29 Distance between centres of two spheres *A* and *B*, each of radius *R* is *r* as shown in figure-1.452. Sphere *B* has a spherical cavity of radius *R*/2 such that distance of centre of cavity is $(r - R/2)$ from the centre of sphere *A* and *R*/2 from the centre of sphere *B*. Dielectric constant of material of each sphere is $K = 1$ and material of each sphere has a uniform charge density ρ per unit volume. Calculate interaction energy of the two spheres.

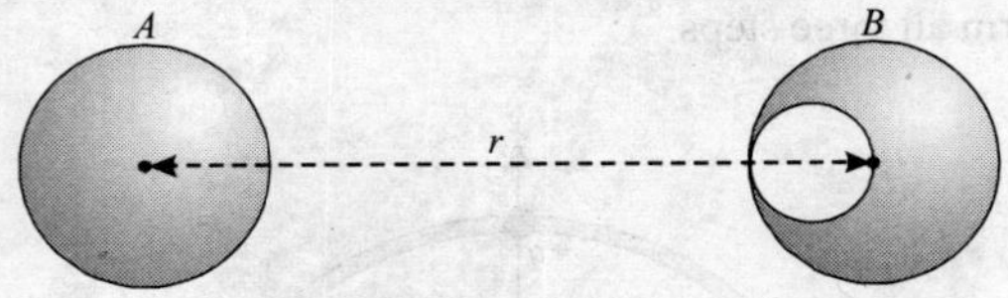

Figure 1.452

Ans. [$\dfrac{\pi\rho^2 R^6 (7r - 4R)}{9\varepsilon_0 r(2r - R)}$]

1-30 Three small balls of equal mass m are connected by light insulating inextensible threads of length *l* each and kept on a level smooth non-conducting ground. The balls *A* and *B* are given charge *Q* each. The strings are all taut. The string connecting *A* and *B* suddenly snaps. What is the maximum speed (in m/s) of *C* during the resulting motion ? $Q = 1$ μC, $l = 1.5$ m, mass $m = 1$ g.

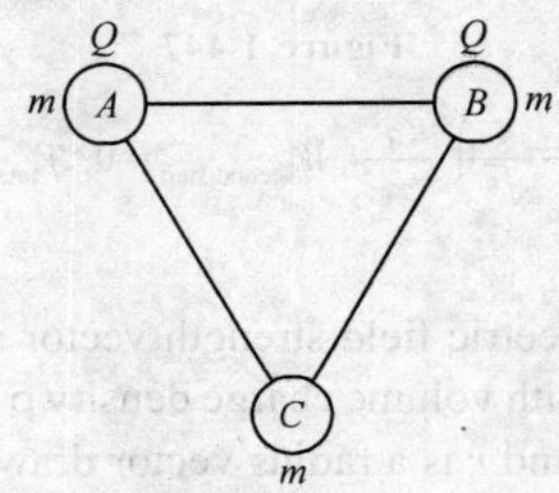

Figure 1.453

Ans. [2]

1-31 A semicircular ring of mass *m* and radius *R* with linear charge density λ, hinged at its centre is placed in a uniform electric field as shown in the figure-1.454. If the ring is slightly rotated about *O* and released find the time period (in sec) of oscillation. Take $m = 8$ kg, $\lambda = 2$ C/m and $E = 2$ N/c. Assume that coil is rotated in its own plane.

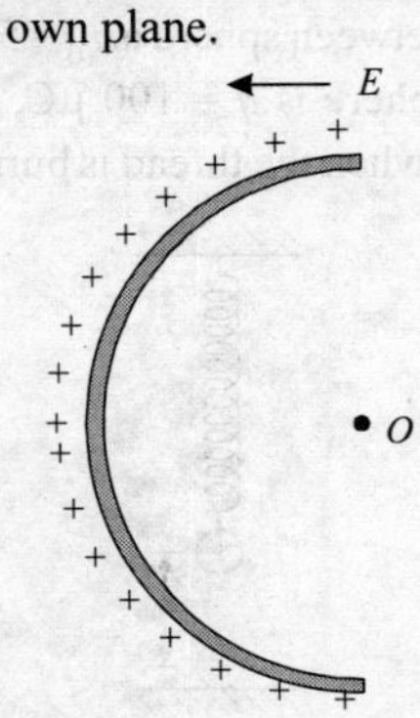

Figure 1.454

Ans. [6.28]

1-32 A charge $+10^{-9}$ C is located at the origin in free space and another charge Q at (2, 0, 0). If the X-component of the electric field at (3, 1, 1) is zero, calculate the value of Q. Is the Y-component zero at (3, 1, 1)?

Ans. [-0.46×10^{-19} C]

1-33 Two coaxial rings, each of radius R, made of thin wire are separated by a small distance l ($l << R$) and carry the charges q and $-q$. Find the electric field potential and strength at the axis of the system as a function of the x coordinate (figure-1.455) Show in the same drawing the approximate plots of the functions obtained. Investigate these functions at $|x| >> R$.

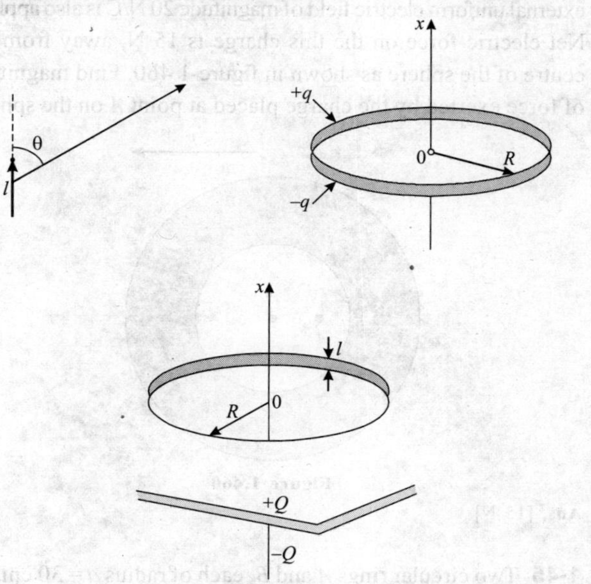

Figure 1.455

Ans. [$\phi = \frac{ql}{4\pi\varepsilon_0}\frac{x}{(R^2+x^2)^{3/2}}$, $E_x = \frac{ql}{4\pi\varepsilon_0}\frac{R^2-2x^2}{(R^2+x^2)^{5/2}}$, where E_x is the projection of the vector $\vec{E}$ on the x-axis. The functions are plotted in figure. If $|x| >> R$, then $\varphi \approx \frac{ql}{4\pi\varepsilon_0 x^2}$ and $E_x \approx \frac{ql}{2\pi\varepsilon_0 x^3}$

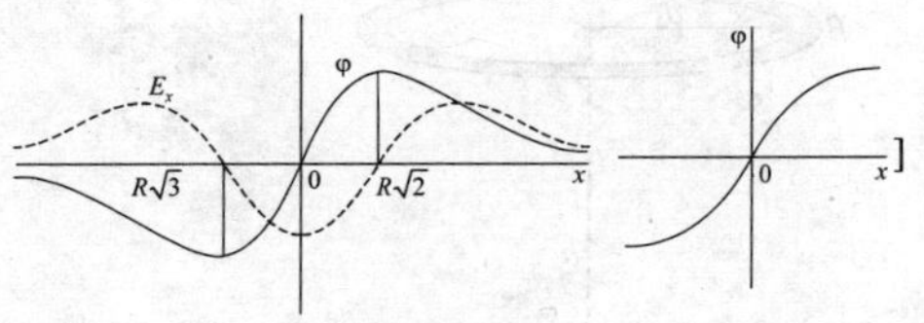

]

1-34 Two concentric rings one of radius a and the other of radius b have the charges $+q$ and $-(2/5)^{-3/2}\,q$ respectively as shown. Find the ratio b/a if a charged particle placed on the axis at $z = a$ is in equilibrium.

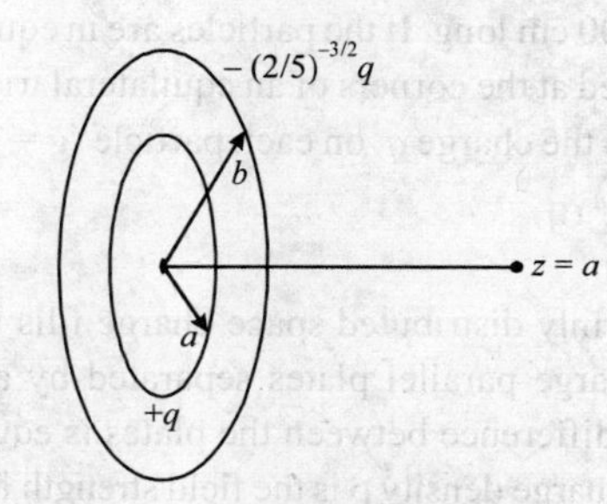

Figure 1.456

Ans. [2]

1-35 Find the interaction force between two water molecules separated by a distance l = 10 nm if their electric moments are oriented along the same straight line. The moment of each molecule equals $p = 0.62.10^{-20}$ C.m.

Ans. [$F = \frac{3p^2}{2\pi\varepsilon_0 l^4} = 2.1.10^{-16}$ N]

1-36 A non-conducting sphere of radius R = 5 cm has its centre at origin O of coordinate system, shown in figure-1.457. It has a spherical cavity of radius r = 1 cm, whose centre is at (0, 3 cm). Solid material of sphere has uniform positive charge density $\rho = \frac{10^{-6}}{\pi}$ C/m^3. Calculate potential at point P (4 cm, 0).

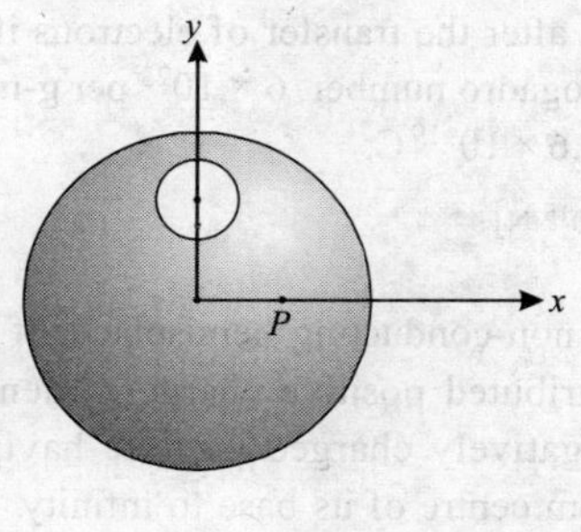

Figure 1.457

Ans. [35.16 V]

1-37 Positive and negative charges of 1 μC each are placed at two points with separation 5 cm as shown in the figure-1.458. Find the potential difference between A and B. Points A and B are located at a separation 1 cm symmetrically between the two charges.

Figure 1.458

Ans. [3000 V]

1-38 Three particles, each of mass 1 g and carrying a charge q, are suspended from a common point by insulating massless strings, each 100 cm long. If the particles are in equilibrium and these are located at the corners of an equilateral triangle of side 3 cm, calculate the charge q on each particle ($g = 10$ m/s^2).

Ans. [3.16×10^{-9} C]

1-39 A uniformly distributed space charge fills up the space between two large parallel plates separated by a distance d. The potential difference between the plates is equal to $\Delta\varphi$. At what value of charge density ρ is the field strength in the vicinity of one of the plates equal to zero? What will then be the field strength near the other plate ?

Ans. [$\rho = 2\varepsilon_0\Delta\varphi/d^2$; $E = \rho d/\varepsilon_0$]

1-40 Consider three identical metal spheres A, B and C. Spheres A carries charge $+6q$ and sphere B carries charge $-3q$. Sphere C carries no charge. Spheres A and B are touched together and then separated. Sphere C is then touched to sphere A and separated from it. Finally the sphere C is touched to sphere B and separated from it. Find the final charge on the sphere C.

Ans. [$2.25q$]

1-41 A copper atom consists of copper nucleus surrounded by 29 electrons. The atomic weight of copper is 63.5 g/mole. Let us now take two pieces of copper each weighing 10 g. Let us transfer one electron from one piece to another for every 1000 atoms in that piece. What will be the coulomb force between the two pieces after the transfer of electrons if they are 1 cm apart. Take Avogadro number 6×10^{23} per g-mole and charge on electron -1.6×10^{-19} C.

Ans. [2.057×10^{16} N]

1-42 A solid non-conducting hemisphere of radius R has a uniformly distributed positive charge of density ρ per unit volume. A negatively charged particle having charge q is transferred from centre of its base to infinity. Calculate work performed in the process. Dielectric constant of material of hemisphere is unity.

Ans. [$\dfrac{q\rho R^2}{4\varepsilon_0}$]

1-43 A small charged cork ball of mass $m = \dfrac{\sqrt{3}}{10}$ kg is suspended on a light silk string in the presence of a constant electric field given below

$$\vec{E} = 1\,\hat{i} + \sqrt{3}\,\hat{j} \text{ N/C}$$

The figure shows the situation described here. The cork ball is in equilibrium at angle $\theta = 30°$. Find the tension in the string. (Take $g = 10$ m/s^2)

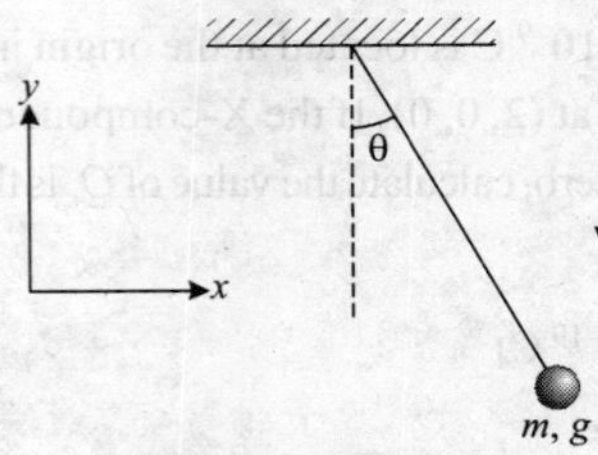

Figure 1.459

Ans. [1 N]

1-44 In a conducting hollow sphere of inner and outer radii 5 cm and 10 cm respectively, a point charge 1 μC is placed at point A, that is 3 cm from the centre C of the hollow sphere. An external uniform electric field of magnitude 20 N/C is also applied. Net electric force on the this charge is 15 N, away from the centre of the sphere as shown in figure-1.460. Find magnitude of force exerted by the charge placed at point A on the sphere.

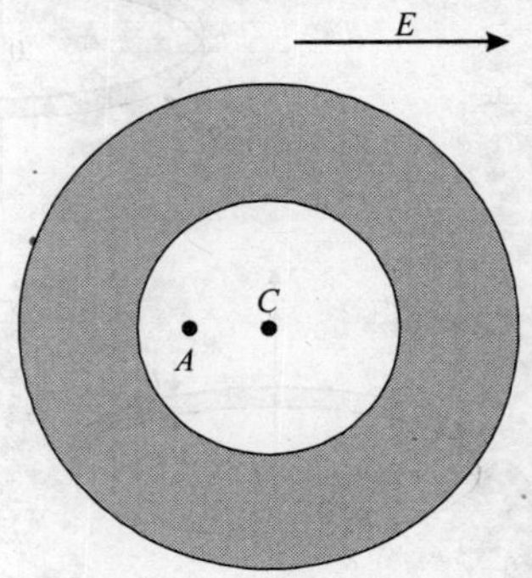

Figure 1.460

Ans. [15 N]

1-45 Two circular rings A and B, each of radius $a = 30$ cm, are placed coaxially with their axes vertical as shown in figure-1.461. Distance between centres of these rings is $h = 40$ cm. Lower ring A has a positive charge of 10 μC, while upper ring B has a negative charge of 20 μC. A particle of mass $m = 100$ gm carrying a positive charge of $q = 10$ μC is released from rest at the centre of the ring A.

(a) Calculate initial acceleration of the particle.

(b) Calculate velocity of particle when it reaches at the centre of upper ring B. ($g = 10$ ms^{-2})

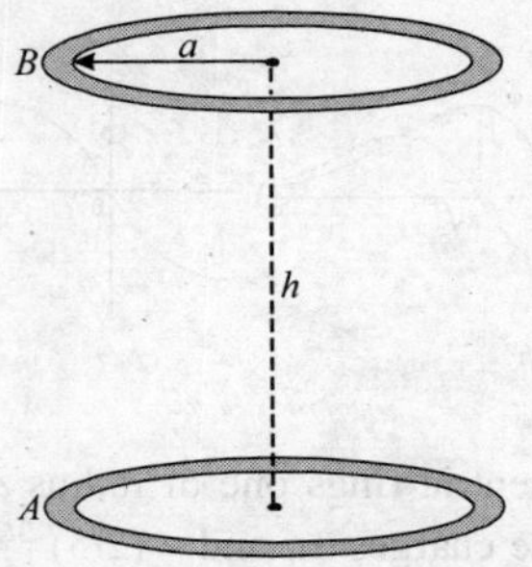

Figure 1.461

Ans. [(a) 47.6 ms^{-2}; (b) 8 ms^{-1}]

1-46 A hollow charged conductor has a tiny hole cut onto its surface. Show that the electric field in the hole is $\left(\dfrac{\sigma}{2\epsilon_0}\right)\hat{n}$, where $\hat{n}$ is the unit vector in the outward normal direction and σ is the surface charge density near the hole.

1-47 Two point charges $q_1 = 20\ \mu\text{C}$ and $q_2 = 25\ \mu\text{C}$ are placed at (–1, 1, 1) m and (3, 1, –2) m, with respect to a coordinate system. Find the magnitude and unit vector along electrostatic force on q_2 ?

Ans. [0.18 N, $\dfrac{(4\hat{i} - 3\hat{k})}{5}$]

1-48 A spherical balloon of radius R charged uniformly on its surface with surface density σ. Find work done against electric forces in expanding it upto radius $2R$.

Ans. [$\dfrac{-\pi\sigma^2 R^3}{\epsilon_0}$]

1-49 Two similar helium-filled spherical balloons tied to a 5 g weight with strings and each carrying a charge q floats in equilibrium as shown in figure-1.462. Find (a) the magnitude of q, assuming that the charge on each balloon acts as if it were concentrated at the centre and (b) the volume of each balloon. Neglect weight of the unfilled balloons and take density of air 1.29 kg/m^3 and the density of helium in the balloons 0.2 kg/m^3.

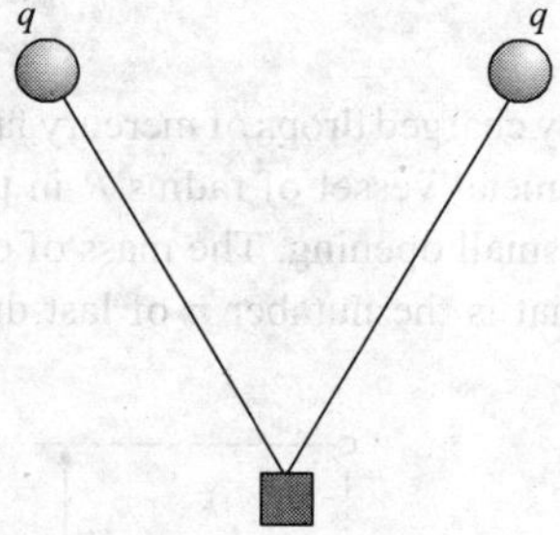

Figure 1.462

Ans. [(a) 0.555 μC, (b) 2.294 × 10^{-3} m^3]

1-50 A simple pendulum of length l and bob mass m is hanging in front of a large nonconducting sheet having surface charge density σ. If suddenly a charge $+q$ is given to the bob & it is released from the position shown in figure-1.463. Find the maximum angle through which the string is deflected from vertical.

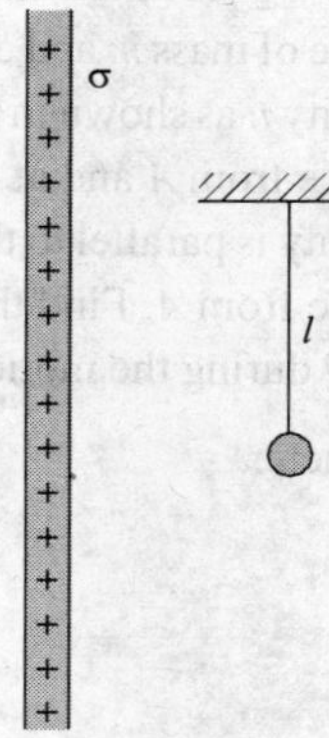

Figure 1.463

Ans. [2 tan^{-1} $\left(\dfrac{\sigma q_0}{2\epsilon_0 mg}\right)$]

1-51 The electric field in a region is given $\vec{E} = \alpha x\hat{i}$. Here α is a constant of proper dimensions. Find.

(a) The total flux passing through a cube bounded by the surface, $x = l, x = 2l, y = 0, y = l, z = 0, z = l$.

(b) The charge contained inside the above cube.

Ans. [(a) αl^3, (b) $\alpha\varepsilon_0 l^3$]

1-52 The electric field in a region is given by $\vec{E} = \dfrac{E_0 x}{l}\vec{i}$. Find the charge contained inside a cubical volume bounded by the surfaces $x = 0, x = a, y = 0, y = a, z = 0$ and $z = a$. [Take $E_0 = 5 \times 10^3$ N/C, $l = 2$ cm and $a = 1$ cm]

Ans. [2.2 × 10^{-12} C]

1-53 Suppose the surface charge density over a sphere of radius R depends on a polar angle θ as $\sigma = \sigma_0 \cos\phi$, where σ_0 is a positive constant. Show that such a charge distribution can be represented as a result of a small relative shift of two uniformly charged balls of radius R whose charges are equal in magnitude and opposite in sign. Resorting to this representation, find the electric field strength vector inside the given sphere.

Ans. [$\vec{E}$ = 1/3 $\vec{k}\ \sigma_0/\varepsilon_0$, where $\vec{k}$ is the unit vector of the z-axis with respect to which the angle θ is read off. Clearly, the field inside the given sphere is uniform.]

1-54 Two identical balls of charges q_1 & q_2 initially have equal velocity of the same magnitude and direction. After a uniform electric field is applied for some time, the direction of the velocity of the first ball changes by 60° and the magnitude is reduced by half. The direction of the velocity of the second ball changes there by 90°. In what proportion will the velocity of the second ball changes ?

Ans. [$\dfrac{v}{\sqrt{3}}$]

1-55 A positive charge $+Q$ is fixed at a point A. Another positively charged particle of mass m and charge $+q$ is projected from a point B with velocity u as shown in the figure-1.464. The point B is at large distance from A and at distance 'd' from the line AC. The initial velocity is parallel to the line AC. The point C is at very large distance from A. Find the minimum distance (in meter) of $+q$ from $+Q$ during the motion. Take $Qq = 4\pi\epsilon_0 mu^2 d$ and $d = (\sqrt{2} - 1)$ meter.

Figure 1.464

Ans. [1 m]

1-56 Figure shown a section through two long thin concentric cylinders of radii a & b with $a > b$. The cylinders have equal and opposite charges per unit length λ. Find the electric field at a distance r from the axis for (a) $r < a$, (b) $a < r < b$, (iii) $r > b$.

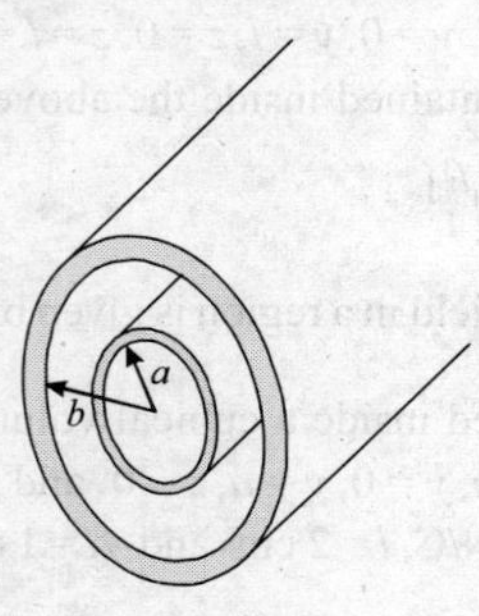

Figure 1.465

Ans. $[0, \frac{2K\lambda}{r}, 0]$

1-57 A point charge Q is located on the axis of a disc of radius R at a distance a from the plane of the disc. If one fourth of the flux from the charge passes through the disc, then find the relation between a & R.

Ans. $[a = \frac{R}{\sqrt{3}}]$

1-58 A very long uniformly charged thread oriented along the axis of a circle of radius R rests on its centre with one of the ends. The charge of the thread per unit length is equal to λ. Find the flux of the vector $\vec{E}$ across the circle area.

Ans. $[|\phi| = \frac{1}{2}\lambda R/\varepsilon_0$. The sign of Φ depends on how the direction of the normal to the circle is chosen.]

1-59 Three point charges of 1 C, 2 C and 3 C are placed at the corners of an equilateral triangle of side 1 m. Calculate the work required to move these charges to the corners of a smaller equilateral triangle of side 1.5 m.

Ans. $[99 \times 10^9$ J]

1-60 Two small metallic balls of radii R_1 & R_2 are kept in vacuum at a large distance compared to the radii. Find the ratio between the charges on the two balls at which electrostatic energy of the system is minimum. Total charge of balls is considered constant.

Ans. $[\frac{Q_1}{Q_2} = \frac{R_1}{R_2}]$

1-61 A point charge $-Q$ is placed at the centre of a uniformly charged ring of charge Q. Electric field at a point on the axis of ring at a distance x $(x >> R)$ varies as $E \alpha \frac{1}{x^n}$ find n.

Ans. [4]

1-62 A charge Q is uniformly distributed over a rod of length l. Consider a hypothetical cube of edge l with the centre of the cube at one end of the rod. Find the minimum possible flux of the electric field through the entire surface of the cube.

Ans. $[\frac{Q}{2\epsilon_0}]$

1-63 A particle having charge 8.85 μC is placed on the axis of a circular ring of radius 30 cm. Distance of the particle from centre of the ring is 40 cm. Calculate electrical flux passing through the ring.

Ans. $[10^5$ Nm^2/C]

1-64 Electrically charged drops of mercury fall from altitude h into a spherical metal vessel of radius R in the upper part of which there is a small opening. The mass of each drop is m & charge is Q. What is the number n of last drop that can still enter the sphere.

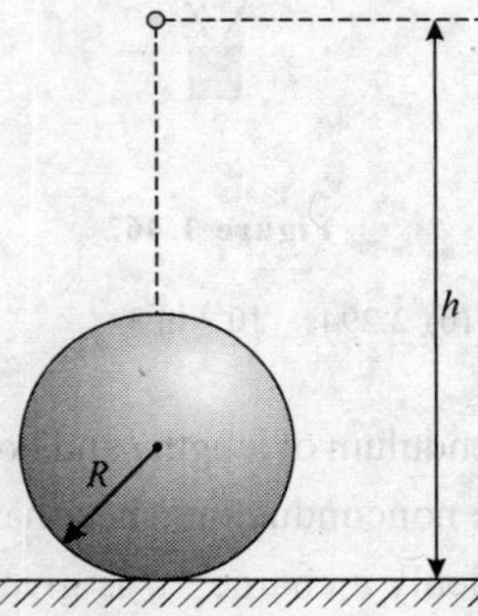

Figure 1.466

Ans. $[n = \frac{4\pi\epsilon_0 mg(h-R)R}{Q^2}]$

1-65 A non-conducting sphere of radius R has a positive charge which is distributed over its volume with density $\rho = \rho_0\left(1-\frac{x}{R}\right)$ per unit volume, where x is distance from the centre. If dielectric constant of material of the sphere is $k = 1$, calculate energy stored in surrounding space and total self energy of the sphere.

Ans. $\left[\frac{\pi\rho_0^2R^5}{72\varepsilon_0}, \frac{13\pi\rho_0^2R^5}{630\varepsilon_0}\right]$

1-66 Two identical charges 5 μC each are fixed at a distance 8 cm and between them a charged particle of mass 9×10^{-6} kg and charge – 10 μC is placed at a distance 5 cm from each of them and is released. Find the speed of the particle when it is nearest to the two charges.

Ans. [10^3 m/s]

1-67 A particle of mass m and charge $-q$ moves along a diameter of a uniformly charged sphere of radius R and carrying a total charge $+Q$. Find the frequency of oscillations of the particle if the amplitude does not exceed R.

Ans. $\left[\frac{1}{2\pi}\sqrt{\frac{qQ}{4\pi\epsilon_0 mR^3}}\right]$

1-68 Two concentric conducting thin shells of radius R and $2R$ carry charges $+Q$ and $+3Q$ respectively. The magnitude of electric field at a distance x outside and inside from the surface of outer sphere is same. It is given that $R = 30$ cm and $Q = 20$ μC. Then find the value of x in cm.

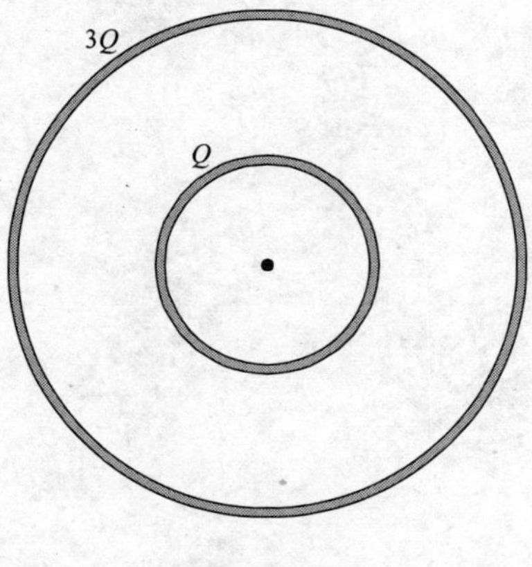

Figure 1.467

Ans. [20]

1-69 The electric field strength depends only on the x and y coordinates according to the law $E = \frac{a(x\hat{i} + y\hat{j})}{x^2 + y^2}$, where a is a constant. $\hat{i}$ and $\hat{j}$ are unit vectors of the x and y axes. Find the potential difference between $x = 1$ and $x = 5$.

Ans. [$-a$ ln(5)]

1-70 A very long charged wire (lying in the xy plane) which is having a linear charge density λ is having one of its end at a point P as shown in figure-1.468. What is electric field intensity at point Q.

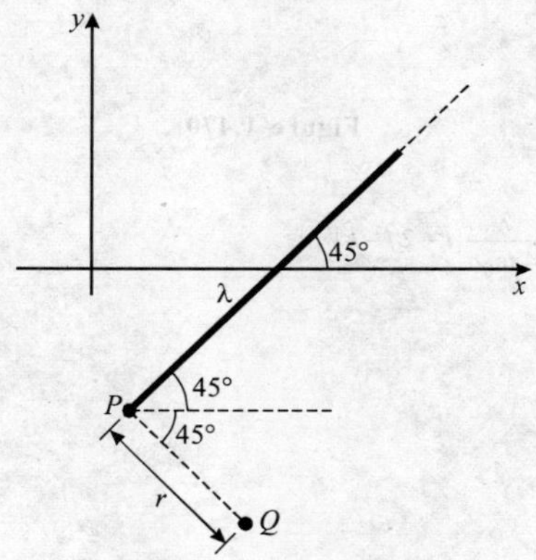

Figure 1.468

Ans. $\left[|E| = \frac{\sqrt{2}k\lambda}{r}\ \vec{E} = \frac{\sqrt{2}k\lambda}{r}(-\hat{j})\right]$

1-71 A solid sphere of radius 'R' is uniformly charged with charge density ρ in its volume. A spherical cavity of radius $\frac{R}{2}$ is made in the sphere as shown in the figure-1.469. It is given that $\frac{\rho R^2}{\epsilon_0} = 48$ V. Find the electric potential at the centre C of the sphere.

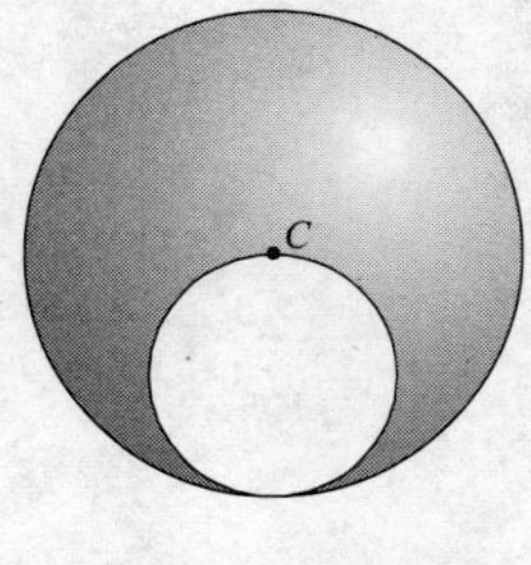

Figure 1.469

Ans. [20V]

1-72 Find the electric field at the origin due to the line charge ($ABCD$) of linear charge density λ.

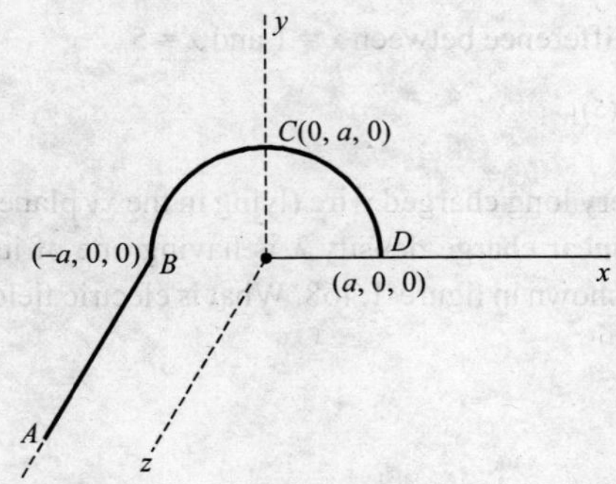

Figure 1.470

Ans. [$\vec{E}_{\text{total}} = \dfrac{\lambda}{4\pi\varepsilon_0 a}[\hat{i} - 2\hat{j} - \hat{k}]$]

1-73 A point charge $+q$ & mass 100 g experiences a force of 100 N at a point at a distance 20 cm from a long infinite uniformly charged wire. If it is released find its speed when it is at a distance 40 cm from wire.

Ans. [$20\sqrt{\ln 2}$]

* * * * *

Capacitance

2

FEW WORDS FOR STUDENTS

A charged conductor produces electric field in its surrounding and the work done in its charging process is stored in form of field energy of electric field in space surrounding the conductor. By specific methods we can use the electrical energy stored in the electric field of a charge for different purposes. The extent upto which a conductor or system of conductors can store electric energy due to charges on it is accounted in the term 'Capacitance' which is discussed in this chapter. For different applications of the stored energy in electric field we will also discuss the use of such system of conductors in electrical circuits.

CHAPTER CONTENTS

COVER APPLICATION

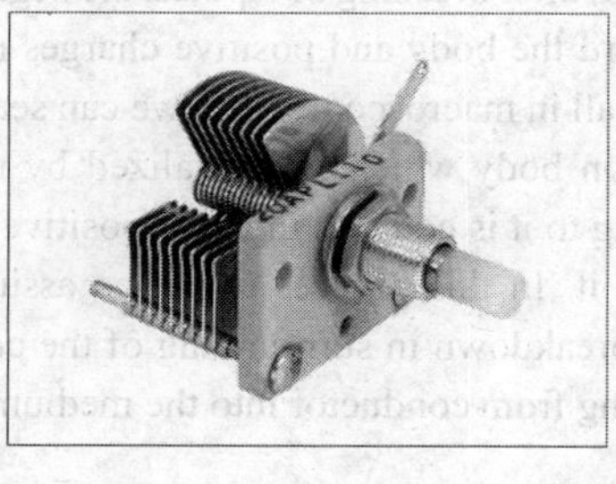

Figure (a)

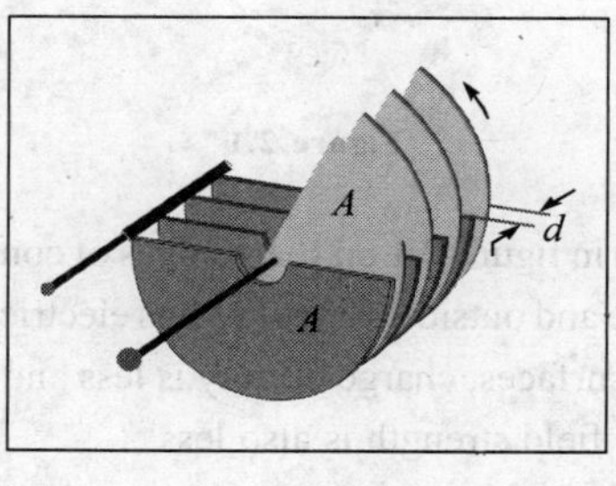

Figure (b)

Figure-(a) shows a variable capacitor used in commercial applications which has a knob to control the value of capacitance. On rotating the knob the overlapping area of the adjoining plates of the capacitor changes which effectively change the capacitance of the system. Figure-(b) shows the working of this variable capacitor which consists of several semicircular plates with alternate plates connected together and causing all capacitors thus formed in parallel combination.

Every conductor when supplied with some charge produces electric field in its surrounding and due to charge the potential of conductor increases. We've discussed in previous chapter that potential of a conductor is always proportional to the charge supplied to it. '*Capacitance*' of a conductor in qualitative terms is defined as its ability to hold charge at a given potential which depends on its size shape and the medium in which it produces electric field. A conductor of higher capacitance can hold more charge at a given potential compared to the one which has lesser capacitance.

One should not confused the term '*Capacitance*' with the maximum capacity a body can store charge. The maximum capacity to which a conductor can be charged depends upon the breakdown strength of the medium in which the conductor is placed. To analyze the maximum capacity to which a conductor can be charged see the figure-2.1. We've discussed in article-1.10.7 that an isolated conductor when supplied with some charge, it is distributed on its outer surface in which a way that the surface charge density at any point remain inversely proportional to the local radii of curvature of the surface, given as

$$\sigma \propto \frac{1}{r} \quad \ldots (2.1)$$

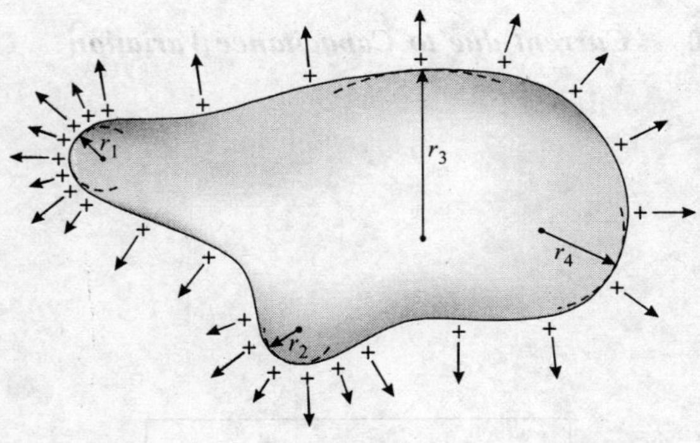

Figure 2.1

Thus as shown in figure-2.1 on sharp edges of conductor charge density is more and outside to these points electric field strength is high at flat surfaces, charge density is less and outside these points electric field strength is also less.

If the above charged body is placed in a dielectric medium then the medium dipoles get polarized in the direction of electric field produced by the conductor as shown in figure-2.2(a) due to force on poles of the medium dipoles.

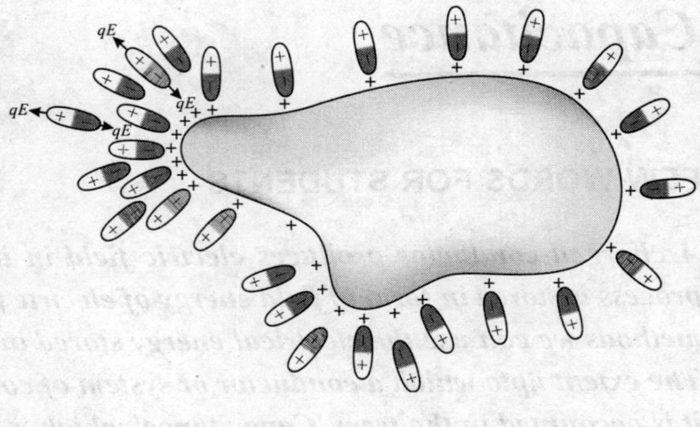

(a)

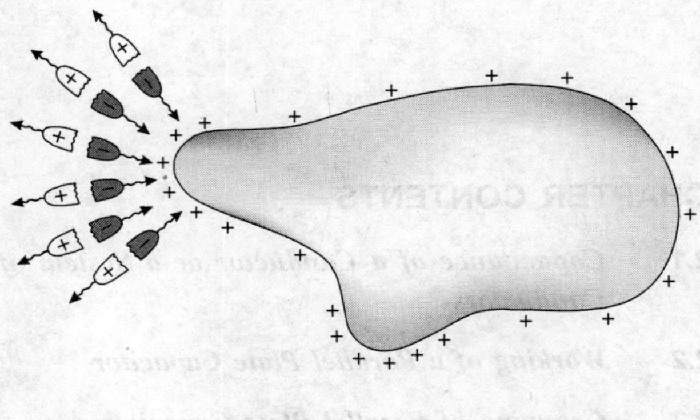

(b)

Figure 2.2

As charge of body is increased its potential an electric field strength at outside points increases which exert more stretching force on the medium dipoles. If the charge on body increases to a limit when the surrounding electric field approaches the dielectric strength of the medium then the dielectric breakdown in medium take place due to breaking of dipoles and charges in vicinity of the conductor will become free to move. As shown in figure-2.2(b) after breaking of dipoles, the negative charges will move toward the body and positive charges move away from body. Overall in macroscopic view we can see that the amount of charge on body which is neutralized by negative charges approaching to it is equal to the total positive charges flowing away from it. In this process it can be assumed that due to dielectric breakdown in surrounding of the conductor, charge starts leaking from conductor into the medium.

As electric field strength outside the sharp edges of a charged conductor is highest in surrounding so we can state that charge starts leaking from the sharp edges due as dielectric breakdown occurs first outside the sharp edges as charge of body is increased.

Thus in case of a medium with weak dipoles or which has lesser dielectric strength the conductor can store less charge compared to the medium of which dipoles are strong and it can be charged to a higher capacity. Similarly if we compare two conductors placed in same medium. One is having sharp edges and other is having relatively flat surfaces then on increasing their charge dielectric breakdown will occur more likely by the conductor which has sharp edges as electric field outside these edges will be higher so its maximum limit to which the conductor can be charged will be less compared to the one which has relatively less sharp edges.

Now we will start understanding the capacitance of a body of a system of conductors quantitatively. The maximum limit of charging a conductor placed in a medium can also be calculated by using capacitance of the conductor but students must understand that the capacitance and maximum charge the body can store are two different terms however related with each other mathematically which we will discuss in upcoming articles.

2.1 Capacitance of a Conductor or a System of Conductors

For a given conductor, its capacitance is defined as "*Charge required per unit rise in electric potential on conductor*". As when some charge is supplied to a conductor its potential increases or vice versa and the charge supplied is directly proportional to the potential of a conductor. If the potential of a conductor increases by V due to a charge q supplied to it then we use

$$q \propto V$$

$$\Rightarrow \quad q = CV \qquad \ldots(2.2)$$

In above equation-(2.2), C is a proportionality constant called '*Self Capacitance*' of the conductor and in general it is referred as '*Capacitance*' of the conductor. By rearranging the terms in equation-(2.2), the capacitance of a conductor can be given as

$$C = \frac{q}{V} \qquad \ldots(2.3)$$

The unit used for measurement of capacitance can be given by equation-(2.3) as '*coulomb per volt*' or '*C/V*' which is referred as '*farad*' or '*F*'. Farad is a practically a very large unit for measurement of capacitance as general value of capacitances are very small. So commonly we use small unit prefixes with farad such as milli(m), micro(μ) or nano(n) for capacitance measurement under practical conditions.

For finite sized conductors the potential V is considered with respect to infinity as a reference and it is calculated as

$$V = -\int_{\infty}^{P} \overline{E} \cdot \overline{dl} \qquad \ldots(2.4)$$

Where $\overline{E}$ is the electric field in surrounding of conductor and P is a point anywhere on the surface of conductor. As whole body of conductor is equipotential so point P can be considered anywhere on its body.

In above case we considered the reference as infinity with zero potential for the potential of conductor. For charging of an isolated conductor we consider that charge is brought from infinity to the conductor as shown in figure-2.3(a). In this case the electric lines of forces originating from conductor will extend upto infinity. If instead of infinity we consider another conducting body as a reference and charge is transferred to a conductor from that body as shown in figure-2.3(b) then due to the transfer of some charge from this body to the conductor the body will get negatively charged and all the electric flux originating from the conductor in this case will terminate on the reference body.

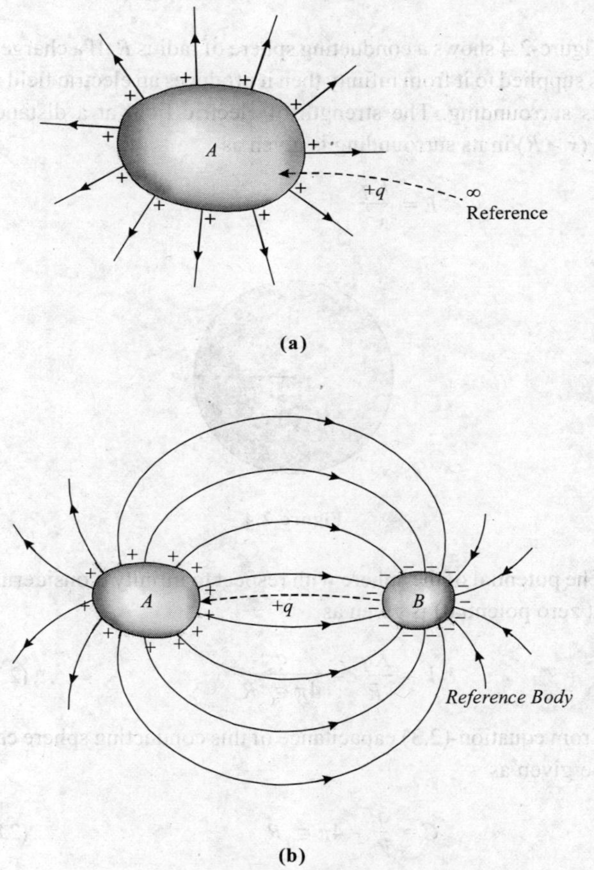

Figure 2.3

In the second case as shown in figure-2.3(b) if we consider the potential of body A with respect to body B as reference in equation-(2.3) use V as potential difference of bodies A and B then the capacitance calculated is termed as '*Mutual Capacitance*' of the system of conductors A and B and this system of two conductors is called '*Capacitor*' and in general the mutual capacitance of a system of two conductors is referred as '*Capacitance of a Capacitor*' and the term '*Mutual Capacitance*' is not a very common term used in practice.

Thus for a system of two conductors A and B, the capacitance is given as

$$C = \frac{q}{V_A - V_B} \quad \ldots(2.5)$$

In above equation the term $V_A - V_B$ can be calculated either by separately calculating the potentials of the two bodies and taking the difference of these or directly by using equation-(2.6) as explained in article-1.10.7, given as

$$V_B - V_A = -\int_A^B \vec{E} \cdot \vec{dx} \quad \ldots(2.6)$$

2.1.1 Capacitance of an Isolated Conducting Sphere

Figure-2.4 shows a conducting sphere of radius R. If a charge q is supplied to it from infinity then it produces an electric field in its surrounding. The strength of electric field at a distance x ($x > R$) in its surrounding is given as

$$E = \frac{Kq}{x^2}$$

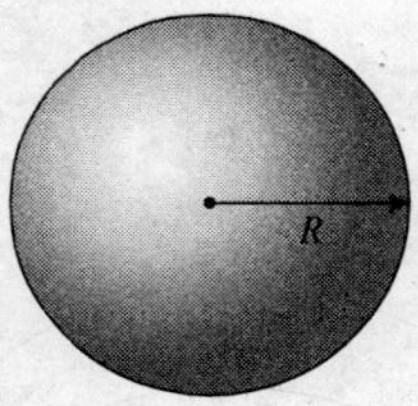

Figure 2.4

The potential of the sphere with respect to infinity (considering at zero potential) is given as

$$V = \frac{Kq}{R} = \frac{q}{4\pi \epsilon_0 R} \quad \ldots(2.7)$$

From equation-(2.3) capacitance of this conducting sphere can be given as

$$C = \frac{q}{V} = 4\pi \epsilon_0 R \quad \ldots(2.8)$$

If outer space in surrounding of the sphere is filled with a medium of dielectric constant ϵ_r then potential of sphere can be given as

$$V = \frac{Kq}{R} = \frac{q}{4\pi \epsilon_0 \epsilon_r R} \quad \ldots(2.9)$$

Thus the capacitance of the sphere in this situation is given again by equation-(2.3) as

$$C = \frac{q}{V} = 4\pi \epsilon_0 \epsilon_r R \quad \ldots(2.10)$$

Now consider the situation shown in figure-2.5 in which a conducting sphere of radius R_1 is surrounded by a dielectric layer of outer radius R_2 and inner radius R_1. We will calculate the capacitance of this conducting sphere. For this we need to calculate the potential of sphere if it is supplied with a charge q. The electric field strength at outer points of the sphere inside and outside dielectric are given as

For $R_1 < x < R_2$

$$E_1 = \frac{1}{4\pi \epsilon_0 \epsilon_r} \cdot \frac{q}{x^2} \quad \ldots(2.11)$$

For $x > R_2$

$$E_2 = \frac{1}{4\pi \epsilon_0} \cdot \frac{q}{x^2} \quad \ldots(2.12)$$

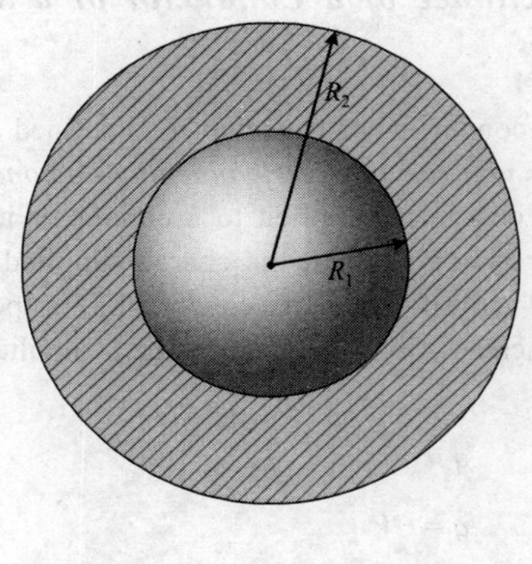

Figure 2.5

Using equations-(2.9) and (2.10) we can calculate the electric potential of sphere with respect to infinity (considering at zero potential) as

$$V = -\left[\int_{\infty}^{R_2} E_2 \cdot dx + \int_{R_2}^{R_1} E_1 \cdot dx\right]$$

$$\Rightarrow \quad V = -\int_{\infty}^{R_2} \frac{q}{4\pi \epsilon_0 x^2} \cdot dx - \int_{R_2}^{R_1} \frac{q}{4\pi \epsilon_0 \epsilon_r x^2} \cdot dx$$

$$\Rightarrow \quad V = -\frac{q}{4\pi \epsilon_0}\left[-\frac{1}{x}\right]_{\infty}^{R_2} - \frac{q}{4\pi \epsilon_0 \epsilon_r}\left[-\frac{1}{x}\right]_{R_2}^{R_1}$$

$$\Rightarrow \quad V = \frac{q}{4\pi \epsilon_0}\left[\frac{1}{R_2}\right] + \frac{q}{4\pi \epsilon_0 \epsilon_r}\left[\frac{1}{R_1} - \frac{1}{R_2}\right]$$

$$\Rightarrow\ V = \frac{q}{4\pi \epsilon_0 \epsilon_r R_1 R_2}[R_2 + R_1(\epsilon_r - 1)] \qquad \ldots(2.13)$$

Using equation-(2.3) we can calculate the capacitance of this system which is given as

$$C = \frac{q}{V} = \frac{4\pi \epsilon_0 \epsilon_r R_1 R_2}{R_2 + R_1(\epsilon_r - 1)} \qquad \ldots(2.14)$$

2.1.2 Relation in Capacitance and Maximum Capacity of Holding Charge for a Conductor

Figure-2.6 shows a conductor of capacitance C which is placed in a medium having dielectric strength E_B. For the given body we can calculate the maximum potential body can attain at which the maximum electric field at any point in its surrounding approaches to the dielectric strength of the medium. This potential we call breakdown potential of the body which is denoted as V_B. Thus the maximum charge which the body can hold is the value at which body potential rises to V_B which is given as

$$q_{max} = CV_B \qquad \ldots(2.15)$$

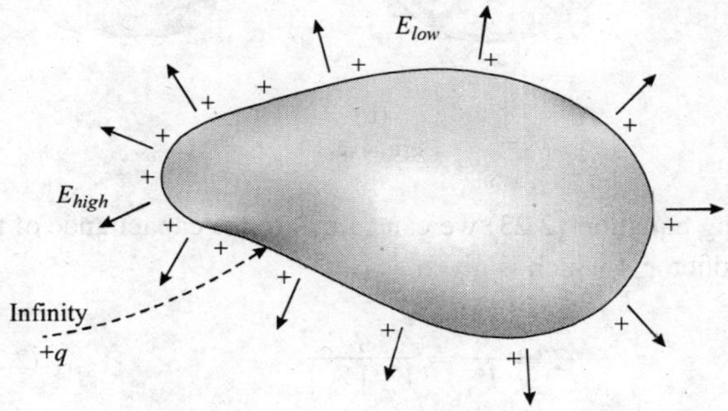

Figure 2.6

Above expression given in equation-(2.15) gives the relation in maximum charge a body can hold and the capacitance of the body. In different media as the breakdown potential changes the maximum charge upto which the body can be charged is different. As capacitance of body depends upon its shape and size also thus in same medium if the shape and size of a body is changed the maximum charge upto which it can be charged is also changed.

2.1.3 Charge Sharing between Two Isolated Conductors

Figure-2.7(a) shows two isolated conductors A and B charged with charges q_1 and q_2 at large separation. If capacitances of the two conductors are C_1 and C_2 respectively then their potentials are given as

$$V_1 = \frac{q_1}{C_1} \quad \text{and} \quad V_2 = \frac{q_2}{C_2}$$

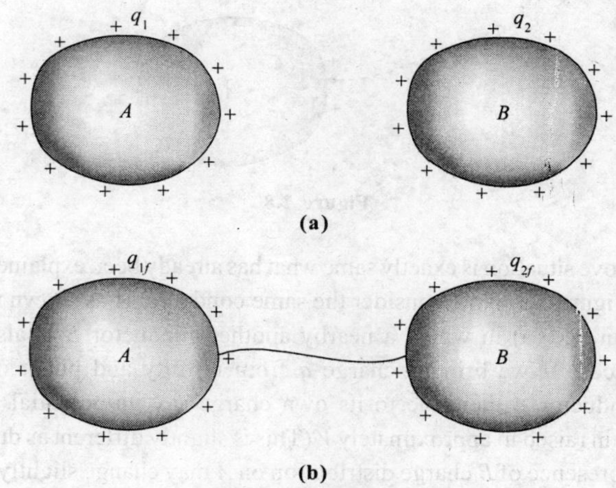

Figure 2.7

When these conductors are connected by a wire as shown in figure-2.7(b) then charge flow between the two takes place until the potential of the two conductors will become equal. If after redistribution of charges on the two conductors, final charges on these are q_{1f} and q_{2f} then we can equate their final potentials as

$$\frac{q_{1f}}{C_1} = \frac{q_{2f}}{C_2} = \frac{q_{1f} + q_{2f}}{C_1 + C_2} \qquad \ldots(2.16)$$

As the total charge of system remain conserved we can use $q_1 + q_2 = q_{1f} + q_{2f}$, thus from equation-(2.16) we have

$$q_{1f} = \frac{C_1}{C_1 + C_2}(q_1 + q_2) \qquad \ldots(2.17)$$

and $$q_{2f} = \frac{C_2}{C_1 + C_2}(q_1 + q_2) \qquad \ldots(2.18)$$

Above equations-(2.17) and (2.18) gives the final charges after redistribution between the two conductors when their potential becomes equal.

2.1.4 Effect of Placing a Conductor near other Conductors on its Capacitance

In article-2.1 we have discussed that a system of two conductors is referred as capacitor when charge is transferred from one to another instead of bringing the charge from infinity. In this system the capacitance of system increases compared to isolated conductor. We will discuss the concept of increase in capacitance for a system of two conductors step by step.

Figure-2.8 shows a single isolated conductor A. If a charge q is supplied to it and due to this if its potential is raised to V then its capacitance is given as

$$C = \frac{q}{V} \qquad \ldots(2.19)$$

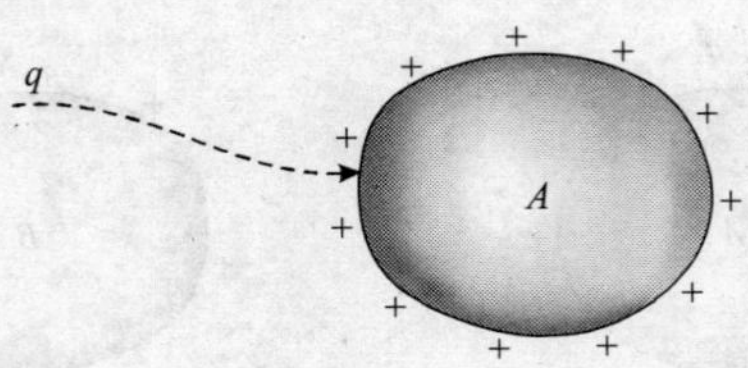

Figure 2.8

Above situation is exactly same what has already been explained in figure-2.3. Now consider the same conductor A as shown in figure-2.9(a) in which a nearby another conductor B is also placed. If we bring a charge q from infinity and put it on conductor A then due to its own charge say its potential is again raised to approximately V (This is slightly different as due to presence of B charge distribution on A may change slightly). Due to the charge on A, some charges are induced on conductor B as shown in figure-2.9(b). If due to the negative induced charges on B at its front face potential on A is V_- and due to positive induced charges on other face of B potential on A is V_+ then in presence of B, potential of A is given as

$$V_A = V - |V_-| + |V_+| \quad \ldots(2.20)$$

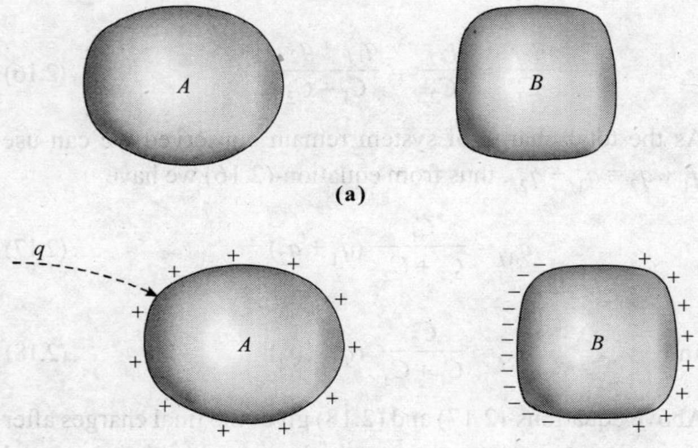

Figure 2.9

As front face of B is near to body A, the potential of A due to negative induced charges on B is higher in magnitude then the potential of A due to positive induced charges on B so we also have

$$|V_-| > |V_+| \quad \ldots(2.21)$$

From equations-(2.18) and (2.19) we can see that $V_A < V$ thus if an uncharged conducted is placed nearby to a charged conductor then its potential decreases.

In this state if we calculate the capacitance of conductor A then it can be given as

$$C' = \frac{q}{V_A} = \frac{q}{V - |V_-| + |V_+|} \quad \ldots(2.22)$$

From equation-(2.19) and (2.22) we can see that $C' > C$. Thus capacitance of a conductor increase due to presence of uncharged bodies near to a conductor. Now consider the same situation as explained in previous case but with conductor B connected to Earth as shown in figure-2.10(a). When a charge q is brought from infinity and placed on conductor A, some negative charge is supplied from earth to conductor B to keep its potential zero. If in this state potential of A due to its own charge is V and that due to the negative charges on B is V_- then the potential of A in this situation can be given as

$$V_A = V - |V_-| \quad \ldots(2.23)$$

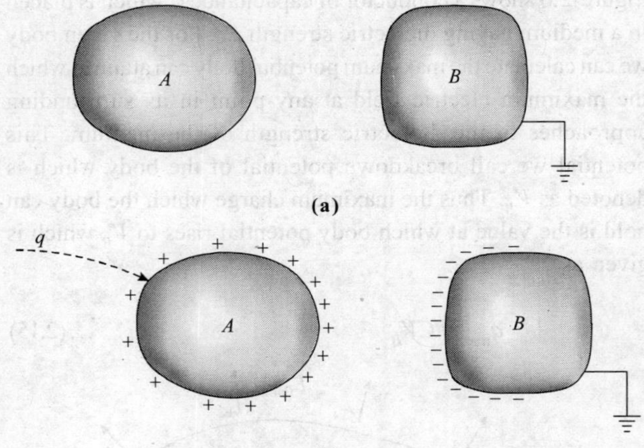

Figure 2.10

Using equation-(2.23) we can calculate the capacitance of the conductor A which is given as

$$C'' = \frac{q}{V_A} = \frac{q}{V - |V_-|} \quad \ldots(2.24)$$

From equation-(2.24) it can be seen that $C'' > C' > C$. Thus it can be stated *"When an earthed conductor is placed near to a conductor then the capacitance of the conductor is greatly increased"*.

2.1.5 Capacitance of a Capacitor

As already discussed in article-2.1 if instead of infinity we consider another conductor as a reference for a given conductor then the capacitance is termed as mutual capacitance or "*Capacitance of the Capacitor*" where the capacitor is the system of two conductors between which charge transfer takes place.

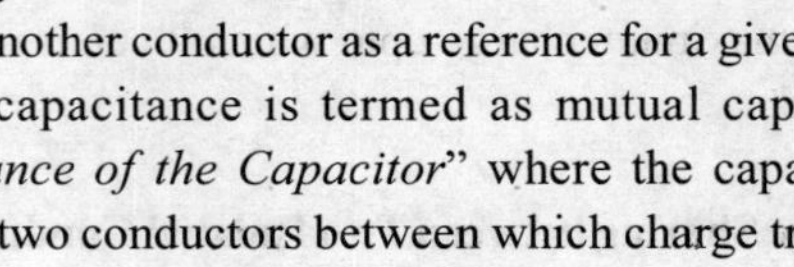

Figure 2.11

Consider two conductors A and B as shown in figure-2.11. In this situation we transfer a charge q from conductor B to conductor A because of which body B will attain a charge $-q$ and A will gain a charge $+q$ as shown. In this process if V_+ and V_- are the final potentials of conductors A and B then the potential of conductor A with respect to conductor B as a reference will be $V_+ - V_-$ and the capacitance of this system of two conductors can be given by equation-(2.5) as

$$C'' = \frac{q}{V_A - V_B} = \frac{q}{V_+ - V_-} \quad \ldots(2.25)$$

The expression in equation-(2.25) is very useful in determining the capacitance of different types of capacitors. In actual practice for different cases and in various electrical circuits also system of two conductors as a capacitor is used for storing charge and electrostatic energy because in practical applications it is difficult to use an isolated conductor with infinity as a reference. In upcoming articles we will determine capacitance of some standard and commonly used capacitors.

2.1.6 Capacitance of a Spherical Capacitor

A '*Spherical Capacitor*' is a system of two concentric shells as shown in figure-2.12(a). The radii of shells in this system are a and b respectively. To find the capacitance of this system we transfer a charge q from outer shell to inner shell as shown in figure-2.12(b) due to which inner shell will gain a charge $+q$ and outer one will have a charge $-q$ distributed on its inner surface only as the flux of inside $+q$ will terminate on the inner surface of outer shell. The potentials of inner and outer shell after this transfer of charge can be given as

$$V_A = \frac{Kq}{a} - \frac{Kq}{b} \quad \ldots(2.26)$$

and $$V_B = \frac{Kq}{b} - \frac{Kq}{b} = 0 \quad \ldots(2.27)$$

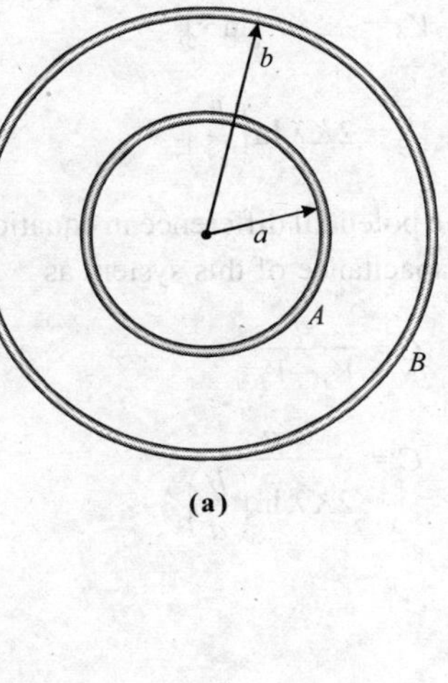

(a)

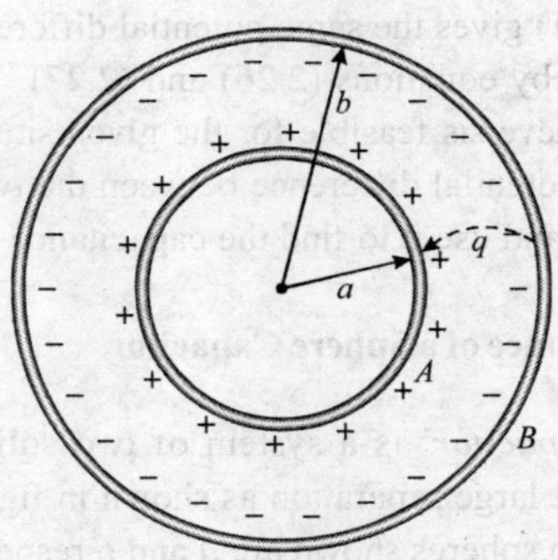

(b)

Figure 2.12

Capacitance of the spherical capacitor can be given as

$$C = \frac{q}{V_A - V_B} \quad \ldots(2.28)$$

$$\Rightarrow \quad C = \frac{q}{\left(\frac{Kq}{a} - \frac{Kq}{b}\right) - 0}$$

$$\Rightarrow \quad C = \frac{4\pi \epsilon_0 ab}{b-a} \quad \ldots(2.29)$$

Above equation-(2.29) gives the capacitance of a spherical capacitor shown in figure-2.12. If the annular region between the two shells is filled with a dielectric medium with dielectric constant ϵ_r then the capacitance of the system can be calculated by including this dielectric constant in the equation-(2.27) which is given as

$$C = \frac{4\pi \epsilon_0 \epsilon_r ab}{b-a} \quad \ldots(2.30)$$

The potentials V_A and V_B we have substituted in equation-(2.26) from equations-(2.26) and (2.27). The potential difference $V_{A|} - V_B$ can also be calculated by using equation-(2.6) as studied in article-1.10.7. The electric field strength in the annular region between the two shells at a point located a distance x from center of shells is only due to the charge of inner shell and it is given as

$$E = \frac{Kq}{x^2} \quad (b > x > a)$$

The potential difference between the two shells is given as

$$V_A - V_B = -\int_B^A \vec{E} \cdot \vec{dx}$$

$$\Rightarrow \quad V_A - V_B = -\int_b^a \frac{Kq}{x^2} dx$$

$$\Rightarrow \quad V_A - V_B = -Kq\left[-\frac{1}{x}\right]_b^a$$

$$\Rightarrow \quad V_A - V_B = Kq\left[\frac{1}{a} - \frac{1}{b}\right] \quad \ldots(2.31)$$

Equation-(2.31) gives the same potential difference which we have obtained by equations-(2.26) and (2.27). Thus in either ways or whichever is feasible for the given situation, we can calculate the potential difference between the two conductors of a capacitor and use it to find the capacitance of the system.

2.1.7 Capacitance of a Sphere Capacitor

A '*Sphere Capacitor*' is a system of two solid conducting spheres kept at large separation as shown in figure-2.13. The radii of the two spheres shown are a and b respectively and to determine the capacitance of this system we transfer a charge q from sphere B to sphere A. Being at large separation ($l >> a, b$) the effect of charge on one sphere can be neglected on the other sphere so after transfer of charge final potential of the two spheres is given as

$$V_A = \frac{Kq}{a}$$

and $$V_B = -\frac{Kq}{b}$$

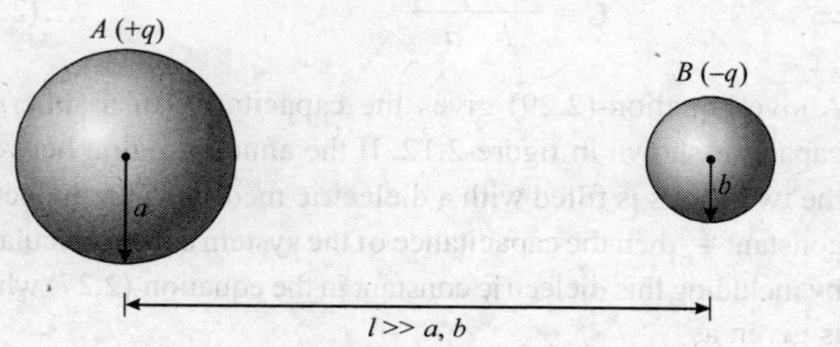

Figure 2.13

The capacitance of this system of sphere capacitor can be calculated as

$$C = \frac{q}{V_A - V_B} \qquad \ldots(2.32)$$

$$\Rightarrow \quad C = \frac{q}{\frac{Kq}{a} - \left(-\frac{Kq}{b}\right)}$$

$$\Rightarrow \quad C = \frac{4\pi \epsilon_0 ab}{a+b} \qquad \ldots(2.33)$$

Above equation-(2.33) gives the capacitance of a sphere capacitor. If this system of two spheres is submerged in a medium of dielectric constant ϵ_r then the capacitance is given by including this dielectric constant in numerator of equation-(2.33).

2.1.8 Capacitance of a Cylindrical Capacitor

Figure-2.14 shows a system of two long coaxial cylindrical shells which is called '*Cylindrical Capacitor*'. As the shells are considered to be very long in this case, we analyze the capacitance per unit length of such a capacitor. To determine the capacitance of this system we transfer a charge q from outer shell B to inner shell A due to which inner shell will gain a charge $+q$ and outer shell with a charge $-q$ which will be distributed on the inner surface of outer shell as shown in figure. In this case the electric field strength in the annular region between the two cylindrical shells is only due to the inner charge and it is in radially outward direction. The strength of electric field in this region at a distance x from the common axis is given as

$$E = \frac{2K\lambda}{x}$$

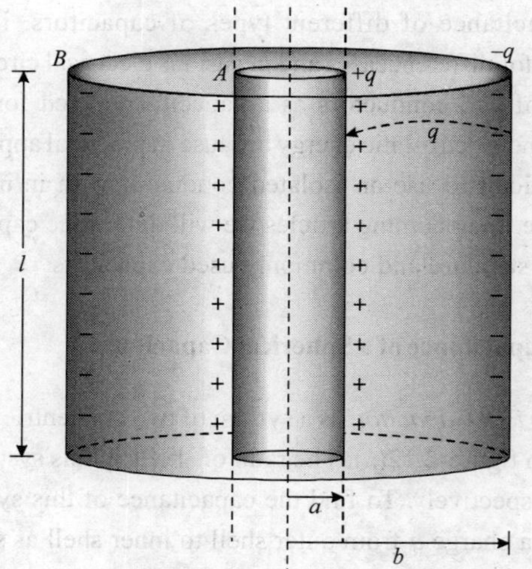

Figure 2.14

Where $\lambda = q/l$ is the linear charge density on the inner cylinder producing electric field in its surrounding. Using this electric field we can find the potential difference between the two cylindrical shells as

$$V_A - V_B = -\int_B^A \vec{E} \cdot d\vec{x}$$

$$\Rightarrow \quad V_A - V_B = -\int_b^a \frac{2K\lambda}{x} dx$$

$$\Rightarrow \quad V_A - V_B = -2K\lambda \left[\ln x\right]_b^a$$

$$\Rightarrow \quad V_A - V_B = 2K\lambda \ln\left(\frac{b}{a}\right) \qquad \ldots(2.34)$$

Using the above potential difference in equation-(2.34) we can calculate the capacitance of this system as

$$C = \frac{q}{V_A - V_B}$$

$$\Rightarrow \quad C = \frac{q}{2K\lambda \ln\left(\frac{b}{a}\right)}$$

$$\Rightarrow \quad C = \frac{2\pi \in_0 l}{\ln\left(\frac{b}{a}\right)} \quad \ldots(2.35)$$

Equation-(2.35) gives the capacitance of a cylindrical capacitor of length l but this result is approximate because in this case at the edges of the shells electric lines will have fringing in outer region also and in above calculation we considered only radial electric field thats why in central region of the shell it will be appropriate to give the capacitance per unit length of such a capacitor given as

$$C_l = \frac{C}{l} = \frac{2\pi \in_0}{\ln\left(\frac{b}{a}\right)} \quad \ldots(2.36)$$

In above equation-(2.36) we can include the dielectric constant $\in_r$ of the medium in numerator if the annular region between the shells is filled with a dielectric medium.

2.1.9 Capacitance of a Wire Capacitor

Figure-2.15 shows two long parallel wires X and Y of length l, radius r kept at a separation d ($d >> r$). This system is called '*Wire Capacitor*'. Again being long wires we will calculate the capacitance per unit length of this system to exclude the effect of fringing of electric field at the wire terminal points. If a charge q is transferred from wire Y to wire X, these will attain opposite charges as shown in figure. As $d >> r$ we can consider the two wires as line charges and due to the linear density of charge on wires which can be given as $\lambda = q/l$, we can calculate the electric field at a point P between the wires at a distance x from the wire X as shown in the figure which is given as

$$E = \frac{2K\lambda}{x} + \frac{2K\lambda}{d-x} \quad \ldots(2.37)$$

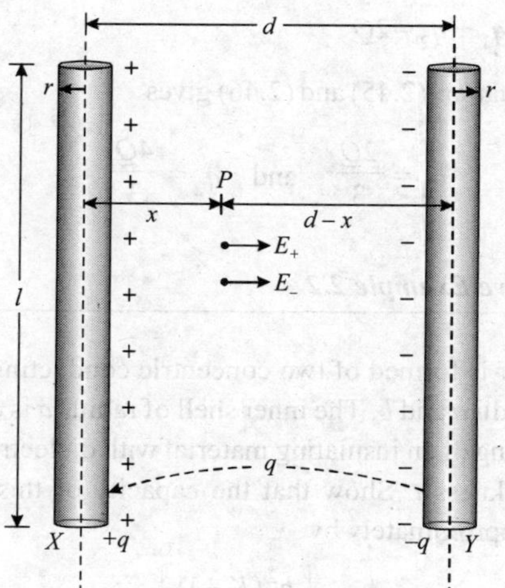

Figure 2.15

In above equation-(2.37) on right hand side first term is the electric field strength due to wire X and second term is that due to wire Y. Due to opposite charges on wires the electric field strength at P will be in same direction hence both values are added. Using this electric field we can calculate the potential difference between wires X and Y which is given as

$$V_Y - V_X = -\int_X^Y \vec{E}\cdot\vec{dx}$$

$$\Rightarrow \quad V_Y - V_X = -\int_r^{d-r} \left(\frac{2K\lambda}{x} + \frac{2K\lambda}{d-x}\right) dx$$

$$\Rightarrow \quad V_Y - V_X = -2K\lambda\left[\ln x - \ln(d-x)\right]_r^{d-r}$$

$$\Rightarrow \quad V_X - V_Y = 2K\lambda\left[\ln\left(\frac{d-r}{r}\right) - \ln\left(\frac{r}{d-r}\right)\right]$$

$$\Rightarrow \quad V_X - V_Y = 4K\lambda \ln\left(\frac{d-r}{r}\right) \quad \ldots(2.38)$$

Using the above potential difference in equaiton-(2.38) we can calculate the capacitance of this system as

$$C = \frac{q}{V_X - V_Y}$$

$$\Rightarrow \quad C = \frac{q}{4K\left(\frac{q}{l}\right)\ln\left(\frac{d-r}{r}\right)}$$

$$\Rightarrow \quad C = \frac{\pi \in_0 l}{\ln\left(\frac{d-r}{r}\right)} \approx \frac{\pi \in_0 l}{\ln\left(\frac{d}{r}\right)} \quad (\text{As } r << d) \quad \ldots(2.39)$$

Equation-(2.39) gives the capacitance of a wire capacitor of length l but this result is approximate because of fringing of electric lines at the terminal points of the wires so like we discussed in previous article of cylindrical capacitor here also it will be more appropriate to give the capacitance per unit length of such a capacitor given as

$$C_l = \frac{C}{l} = \frac{\pi \in_0}{\ln\left(\frac{d}{r}\right)} \quad \ldots(2.40)$$

In above equation-(2.40) we can include the dielectric constant $\in_r$ of the medium in numerator if the annular region between the shells is filled with a dielectric medium.

2.1.10 Capacitance of a Parallel Plate Capacitor

Figure-2.16 shows a system of two large parallel plates arranged at very close separation d. Such a system is called a '*Parallel Plate Capacitor*'. To determine the capacitance of this system, we transfer a charge q from plate Y to plate X due to which plate X will gain a charge $+q$ and plate Y will obtain a charge $-q$ as shown in figure.

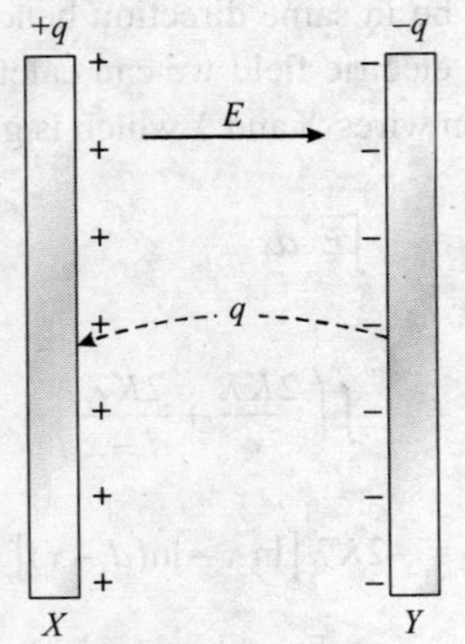

Figure 2.16

As plates are considered large, the electric field between the plates can be considered uniform. The strength of electric field between the two plates can be given as

$$E = \frac{\sigma}{\epsilon_0} = \frac{q}{A\epsilon_0} \qquad \ldots(2.41)$$

Using the above expression of electric field we can calculate the potential difference between the plates which is given as

$$V_X - V_Y = Ed$$

$$\Rightarrow \quad V_X - V_Y = \left(\frac{q}{A\epsilon_0}\right)d \qquad \ldots(2.42)$$

We can calculate the capacitance of this parallel plate capacitor using above potential difference as

$$C = \frac{q}{V_X - V_Y}$$

$$\Rightarrow \quad C = \frac{q}{\left(\frac{q}{A\epsilon_0}\right)d}$$

$$\Rightarrow \quad C = \frac{\epsilon_0 A}{d} \qquad \ldots(2.43)$$

Equation-(2.43) gives the capacitance of a parallel plate capacitor and this expression is also used as a building block of many different capacitors which can be generalized as combination of several elementary parallel plate capacitors. Such cases we will discuss in upcoming articles and illustrations.

If the region between the plates of a parallel plate capacitor is filled with a medium of dielectric constant $\epsilon_r = k$ then the capacitance can be given as

$$C' = \frac{\epsilon_0 \epsilon_r A}{d} = \frac{k\epsilon_0 A}{d} = kC \qquad \ldots(2.44)$$

As shown in equation-(2.44) and in previous cases of other capacitors also we can say that if the medium between the two conductors in a capacitor is filled with a dielectric medium then the overall capacitance of the system increases to k times the capacitance in absence of medium where k is the dielectric constant of the medium.

 # Illustrative Example 2.1

There are two conductors of capacitance C and $2C$ are charged equally with charge $+Q$ each and connected with a thin conducting wire and a switch as shown in figure-2.17. Find the final charges on the conductors after closing the switch.

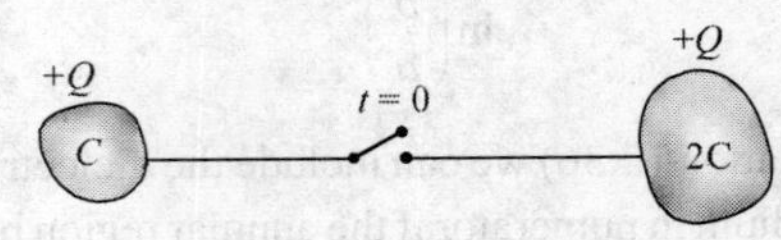

Figure 2.17

Solution

After closing the switch we consider that final charges becomes q_1 and q_2 on the two conductors as shown in figure-2.18.

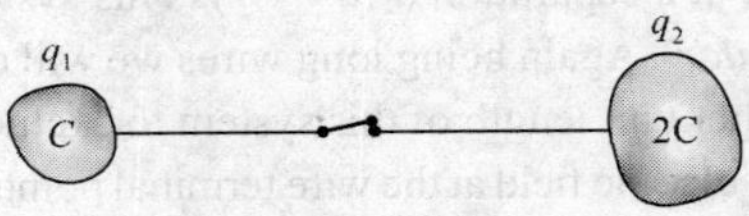

Figure 2.18

After redistribution of charges potential of both the conductors become equal so we have

$$\frac{q_1}{C} = \frac{q_2}{2C}$$

$$\Rightarrow \quad 2q_1 = q_2 \qquad \ldots(2.45)$$

We also have

$$q_1 + q_2 = 2Q \qquad \ldots(2.46)$$

Solving equation-(2.45) and (2.46) gives

$$q_1 = \frac{2Q}{3} \quad \text{and} \quad q_2 = \frac{4Q}{3}$$

 # Illustrative Example 2.2

A capacitor is formed of two concentric conducting spherical shells of radii a and b. The inner shell of radius a is covered by a thin coating of an insulating material with dielectric constant K and thickness t. Show that the capacity of this system is changed approximately by

$$4\pi\epsilon_0\left[\frac{b^2(K-1)}{K(b-1)^2}\right]t$$

Solution

We know that the capacity of a spherical capacitor without any dielectric layer is given as

$$C_0 = \frac{4\pi\varepsilon_0(ab)}{(b-a)}$$

Let the inner shell is coated with a dielectric layer of thickness t, then the potential difference between the shells can be calculated after transfer of a charge q between the shells is given as

$$V_A - V_B = \frac{Q}{4\pi\varepsilon_0}\left[\frac{1}{K}\int_a^{a+t}\frac{dr}{r^2} + \int_{a+t}^{b}\frac{dr}{r^2}\right]$$

$$\Rightarrow \quad V_A - V_B = \frac{Q}{4\pi\varepsilon_0}\left[\frac{(a+t)(b-aK)+ab(K-1)}{Kab(a+t)}\right]$$

The capacitance of the system is now given as

$$C = \frac{Q}{V_a - V_b} = \left[\frac{4\pi\varepsilon_0 Kab(a+t)}{(a+t)(b-aK)+ab(K-1)}\right]$$

The change in capacitance of the capacitor is given as

$$\Delta C = C - C_0$$

$$\Rightarrow \quad \Delta C = 4\pi\varepsilon_0\left[\frac{kab(a+t)}{(a+t)(b-aK)+ab(K-1)} - \frac{ab}{(b-a)}\right]$$

$$\Rightarrow \quad \Delta C = 4\pi\varepsilon_0\left[\frac{ab^2(K-1)t}{(b-a)\{Ka(b-a)-t(aK-b)\}}\right]$$

$$\Rightarrow \quad \Delta C \simeq 4\pi\varepsilon_0\frac{b^2(K-1)t}{K(b-a)^2}$$

Illustrative Example 2.3

Two isolated conducting solid spheres of radii R and $2R$ are charged such that both have same charge density σ. The spheres are located for away from each other. The two spheres are connected by a thin conducting wire via a switch. Find the new charge density on the bigger sphere after closing the switch using capacitor of spheres.

Solution

Initial charges on the two spheres are given as

$$q_1 = 4\sigma\pi R^2$$

and $$q_2 = 16\sigma\pi R^2 = 4q_1$$

After the two spheres are connected via a switch, their charge will be redistributed to make final potential equal on the two spheres. After connection, final common potential on the two spheres is given as

$$V_f = \frac{5q_1}{C_1 + C_2} = \frac{5q_1}{4\pi\varepsilon_0 R + 8\pi\varepsilon_0 R} = \frac{5q_1}{12\pi\varepsilon_0 R}$$

Thus final charge on bigger sphere is given as

$$q_{2f} = C_2V_f = 8\pi\varepsilon_0 R \times \frac{5q_1}{12\pi\varepsilon_0 R} = \frac{10}{3}q_1$$

Final charge density on bigger sphere is given as

$$\sigma_{2f} = \frac{q_{2f}}{4\pi(2R)^2} = \frac{10}{3}\left(\frac{q_1}{16\pi R^2}\right) = \frac{5}{6}\left(\frac{q_1}{4\pi R^2}\right) = \frac{5}{6}\sigma$$

Illustrative Example 2.4

A radioactive source is in the form of a conducting sphere of diameter 10^{-3}m which emits β particles at a constant rate of 6.25×10^{10} particles per second. If the source is electrically insulated, how long will it take for its potential to rise by 1.0 V, assuming that 80% of emitted β particles escape from the surface.

Solution

Capacitance of the conducting sphere is given as

$$C = 4\pi\varepsilon_0 R = \frac{0.5\times10^{-3}}{9\times10^{9}} = \frac{1}{18}\times10^{-12}\text{ F}$$

Rate to charging of sphere due to escape of beta particles from surface is given as

$$\frac{dq}{dt} = \frac{80}{100}\times 6.25\times10^{10}\times1.6\times10^{-19} = 8\times10^{-9}\text{ C/s}$$

Thus at any instant of time t the charge on sphere can be given as

$$q = (8\times10^{-9})\,t$$

If after time t_1 charge on sphere increases to a value such that its potential rises to 1 V then we use

$$q = CV$$

$$\Rightarrow \quad 8\times10^{-9}\times t_1 = \frac{1}{18}\times10^{-12}\times1$$

$$\Rightarrow \quad t_1 = \frac{10^{-12}}{8\times10^{-9}\times18} = \frac{10^{-3}}{144} = 6.95\ \mu\text{s}$$

Illustrative Example 2.5

A capacitor is formed of two concentric spherical conducting shells of radii a and b. If the medium between the spherical shells has a dielectric constant K_1 from radius a to r and K_2 from radius r to b, find the capacitance of such a spherical capacitor shown in figure-2.19.

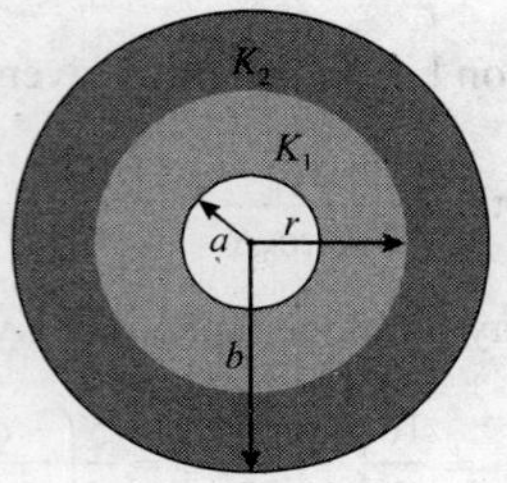

Figure 2.19

Solution

If we transfer a charge q from outer to inner shell then the potential difference between the two shells can be calculated by using the electric field strengths in the region between the shells. At a distance x from the center of the shells the electric field at points inside the two dielectrics are given as

For $a<x<r$

$$E_1 = \frac{1}{4\pi \epsilon_0 K_1} \cdot \frac{q}{x^2}$$

and for $r<x<b$

$$E_2 = \frac{1}{4\pi \epsilon_0 K_2} \cdot \frac{q}{x^2}$$

The potential difference between inner and outer shells is given by

$$V_A - V_B = -\int_b^a E \cdot dx$$

$$\Rightarrow \quad V_A - V_B = -\int_b^r E_1 dx - \int_r^a E_2 dx$$

$$\Rightarrow \quad V_A - V_B = \frac{q}{4\pi\varepsilon_0}\left[\int_a^r \frac{dx}{K_1 x^2} + \int_r^b \frac{dx}{K_2 x^2}\right]$$

$$\Rightarrow \quad V_A - V_B = \frac{Q}{4\pi\varepsilon_0}\left[\frac{1}{K_1}\left(\frac{1}{a} - \frac{1}{r}\right) + \frac{1}{K_2}\left(\frac{1}{r} - \frac{1}{b}\right)\right]$$

$$\Rightarrow \quad V_A - V_B = \frac{Q}{4\pi\varepsilon_0}\left[\frac{1}{r}\left(\frac{1}{K_2} - \frac{1}{K_1}\right) + \left(\frac{1}{K_1 a} - \frac{1}{K_2 b}\right)\right]$$

The capacitance of the given system is given as

$$C = \frac{Q}{V_a - V_b}$$

$$\Rightarrow \quad C = 4\pi\varepsilon_0\left[\left(\frac{1}{K_1 a} - \frac{1}{K_2 b}\right) + \frac{1}{r}\left(\frac{1}{K_2} - \frac{1}{K_1}\right)\right]^{-1}$$

2.2 Working of a Parallel Plate Capacitor

A parallel plate capacitor is used widely in various applications in electrical circuits and industrial applications. Figure-2.20 shows the pictures of actual parallel plate capacitors being used in industrial and research applications. Figure-2.20(a) is the picture of an electrolytic capacitor which uses a liquid dielectric in a cylindrical encloser and figure-2.20(b) shows a ceramic capacitor which uses ceramic solid medium as dielectric between the plates. Electrolytic capacitors are made of higher order of capacitances whereas ceramic capacitors are small in size and used where capacitance of lower values are required.

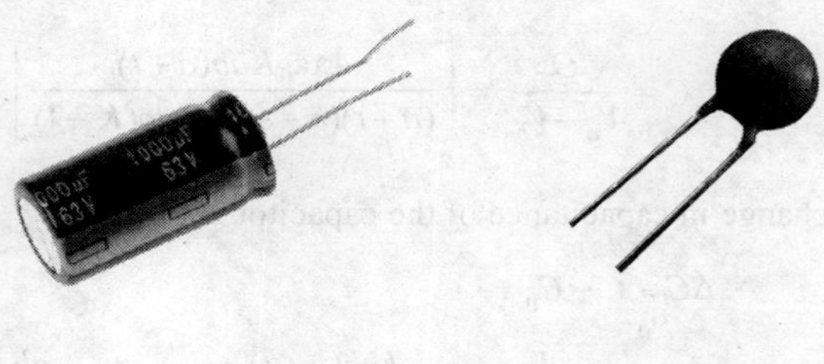

(a) **(b)**

Figure 2.20

2.2.1 Charging of a Parallel Plate Capacitor

In article-2.1.10 we've discussed that on transferring a charge q from one plate to another a potential difference is established between the two plates which can be calculated by using equation-(2.42). Figure-2.21(a) shows a parallel plate capacitor with plates X and Y of surface area A and kept at separation d which is connected across a battery along with a switch S as shown.

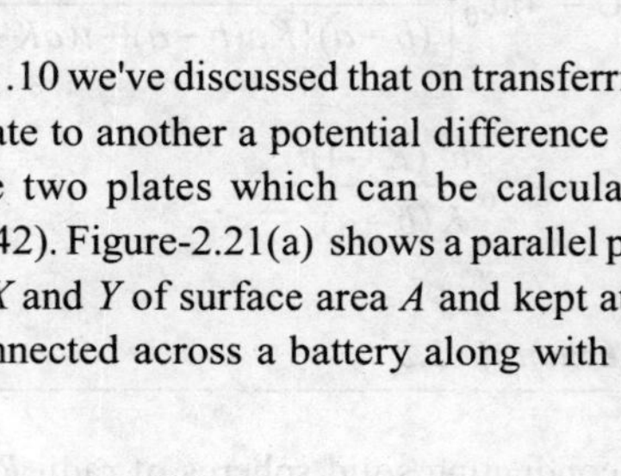

(a)

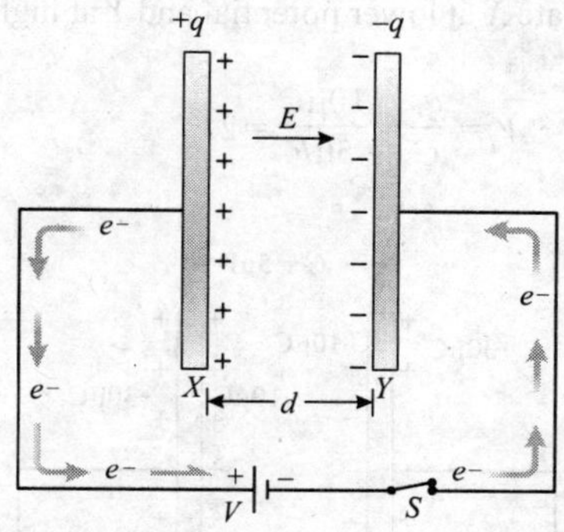

(b)
Figure 2.21

When the switch S in above circuit is closed as shown in figure-2.21(b), the positive terminal of the battery which is connected to plate X of capacitor starts pulling free electrons of the plate and pushes it toward the plate Y. As a result plate X will start getting positively charged due to loss of electrons and plate Y will receive negative charges due to gain of electrons. As on the two plates charges are equal and opposite, these charges will only reside on the inner facing surfaces of the plates and outer surfaces will remain neutral. This establishes an electric field between the plates given by equation-(2.41) as

$$E = \frac{\sigma}{\epsilon_0} = \frac{q}{A\epsilon_0} \qquad \ldots(2.47)$$

Due to this electric field the potential difference between the plates increases. Battery will continuously supply charge on the plates by transferring electrons from plate X to Y until the potential difference between the plates becomes equal to that of battery. Thus in final state when charge flow stops, the potential difference across capacitor plates will become V. This state when charge flow stops or when the potential difference across the capacitor becomes equal to that of battery terminals is called '*Steady State*' of a capacitive circuit. In steady state the final charges on capacitor plates of a capacitor of capacitance C is given as

$$q = CV \qquad \ldots(2.48)$$

In steady state the electric field between plates can be given as

$$E = \frac{\sigma}{\epsilon_0} = \frac{V}{d} \qquad \ldots(2.49)$$

In all conditions when a parallel plate capacitor of capacitance C is used in an application under an applied potential difference V then the final charge stored on inner surfaces of the plates of capacitor in steady state is given as $q = CV$ and electric field strength between the plates is $E = V/d$.

Consider the circuit shown in figure-2.22(a) which shows a capacitor having initial charge on its plates as q_0. Always remember that the charge on capacitor means its plates carry equal and opposite charges on their inner faces and that is called as charge on a parallel plate capacitor. In this state of initial charge on capacitor if switch is closed then battery will modify the charges on capacitor plates which will depend upon the initial charge on it.

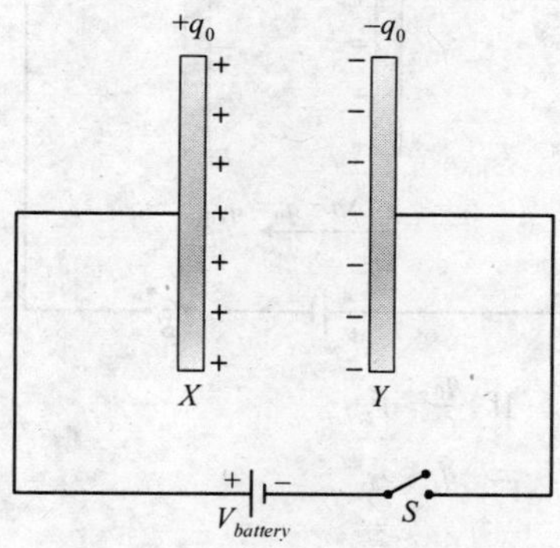

Figure 2.22

Due to initial charge on capacitor q_0 the initial potential difference of the capacitor is $V_0 = q_0/C$. If $V_0 < V_{\text{battery}}$ then on closing the switch as shown in figure-2.23, battery will supply charges to capacitor and final charge on capacitor will increase until the potential difference across capacitor becomes equal to that of battery. Thus final charge on capacitor plates will be given as

$$q_f = CV_{\text{battery}} \qquad \ldots(2.50)$$

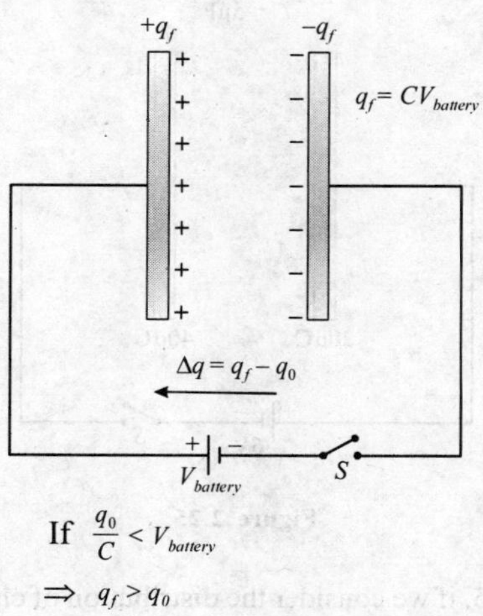

Figure 2.23

If in above case $V_0 > V_{\text{battery}}$ then on closing the switch as shown in figure-2.24, charge will flow into the battery from the capacitor and final charge on capacitor will decrease until the potential difference across capacitor decreases and becomes equal to that of the battery. The final charge on capacitor in this state will also be given by equation-(2.50).

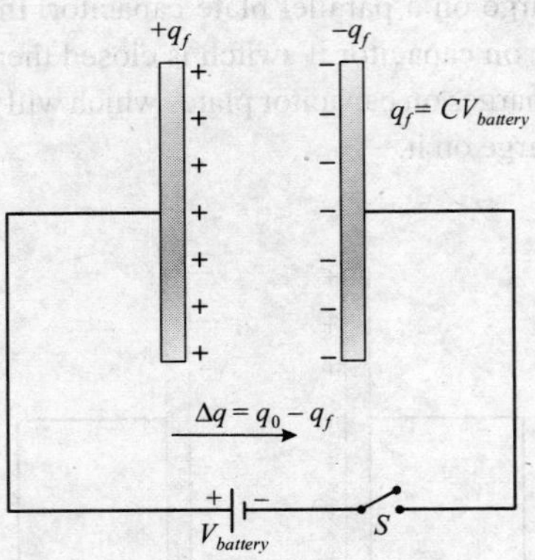

If $\frac{q_0}{C} > V_{battery}$

$\Rightarrow q_f < q_0$

Figure 2.24

2.2.2 Unequal Charges on Capacitor Plates Connected across a Battery

Figure-2.25 shows an illustration to understand distribution of charges in a capacitor. In figure a 5 μF capacitor of which the two plates *X* and *Y* are charged with 20 μC and 40 μC charges and it is connected to a 6 V battery via a switch *S*. In this circuit we are required to find the charge distribution on the surfaces of capacitor plates after closing the switch.

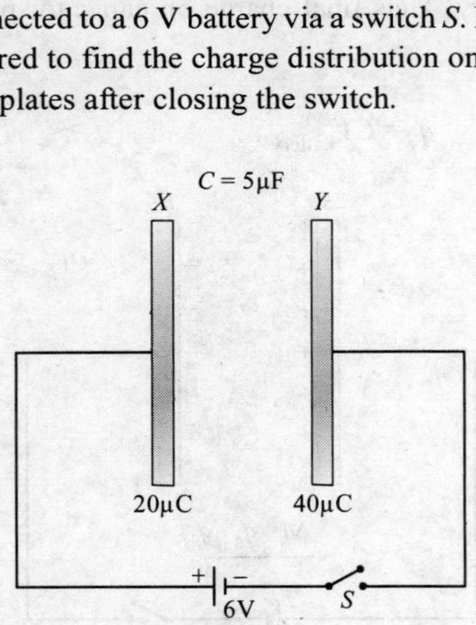

Figure 2.25

In figure-2.25, if we consider the distribution of charges on the two plates then as discussed in section-1.17.2 then we can state that the charges in open state of switch on the plates of capacitor are given as shown in figure-2.26.

In this state we can see that capacitor charge which is considered as the charge on inner faces of capacitor which is 10 μC due to which the initial potential difference between the plates is given below with plate *X* at lower potential and *Y* at higher potential.

$$V_i = \frac{q_i}{C} = \frac{10\mu C}{5\mu F} = 2V \quad \dots(2.51)$$

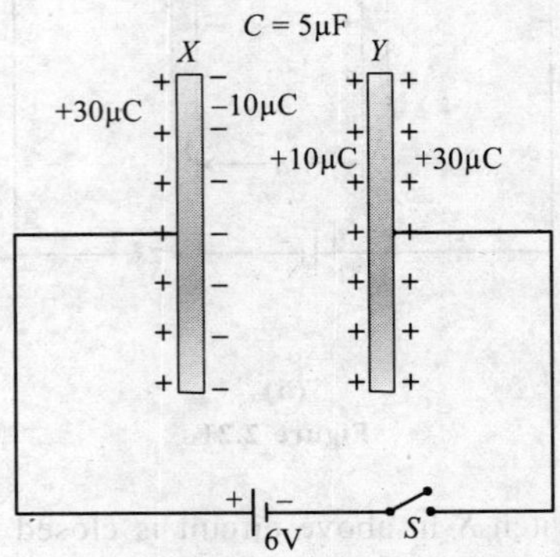

Figure 2.26

When the switch is closed in above circuit, the potential difference across plates will be equal to battery potential difference with plate *X* at higher potential as positive terminal of battery is connected to plate *X*.

Thus in steady state final charge on inner faces of capacitor plates is shown in figure-2.27 which is given as

$$q_f = CV_{\text{battery}} = 5 \times 6 = 30\ \mu C$$

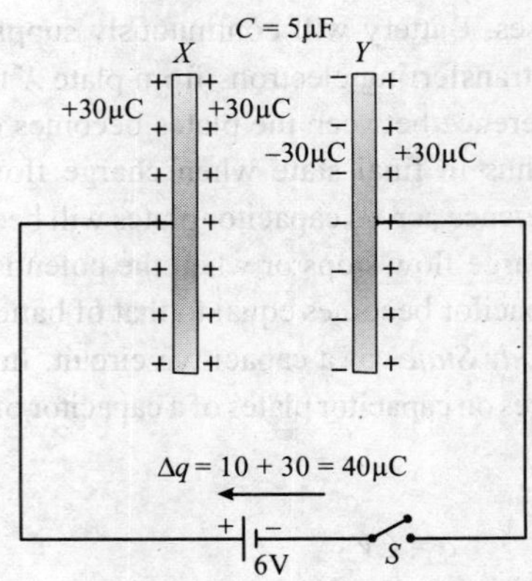

Figure 2.27

In figure-2.27 we can see that due to closing the switch the charges on outer surfaces of the plates will not be changed as battery supplies equal and opposite charges on the two plates by transferring charge from one plate to another. In above case the total charge supplied by the battery is 40 μC as after closing the switch the polarity of charges in steady state on inner faces of plates is opposite to that before closing the switch.

2.2.3 Energy Stored in a Parallel Plate Capacitor

When a capacitor is charged, it establishes an electric field due to charge on its conductors. We have already discussed in article-1.19 that field energy exist in every region of space where electric field is present thus a charged capacitor also contains field energy of electric field which can be calculated by using the field energy density of electric field as analysed and calculated in article-1.19.1 which is given as

$$u = \frac{1}{2} \epsilon_0 E^2 \qquad \ldots(2.52)$$

For a charged parallel plate capacitor as shown in figure-2.28 with a charge q on its plates, the electric field between the plates is given as

$$E = \frac{q}{A \epsilon_0} \qquad \ldots(2.53)$$

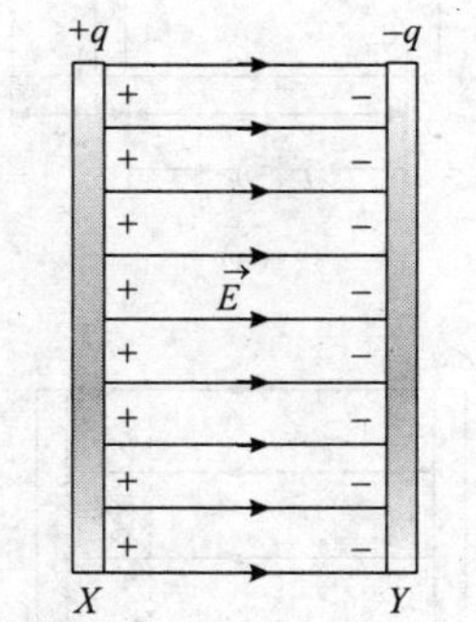

Figure 2.28

As the plates are considered large the electric field can be considered uniform between the plates and as of now we can neglect fringing effects at the edges of the plates. Thus the total energy stored in the region between the two plates of capacitor is given as

$$U = \frac{1}{2} \epsilon_0 E^2 \times Ad$$

$$\Rightarrow \quad U = \frac{1}{2} \epsilon_0 \left(\frac{q}{A \epsilon_0}\right)^2 \times Ad$$

$$\Rightarrow \quad U = \frac{q^2 d}{2A \epsilon_0}$$

$$\Rightarrow \quad U = \frac{q^2}{2C} \qquad \ldots(2.54)$$

Above equation-(2.54) gives the expression for total energy stored in a parallel plate capacitor of capacitance C charged with a charge q. This energy is stored in form of field energy of electric field in capacitor. If a capacitor is connected across a battery or having a potential difference V across its plates then in steady state its charge is given as $q = CV$ so the energy stored in capacitor can be given in terms of the potential difference as

$$U = \frac{q^2}{2C} = \frac{(CV)^2}{2C} = \frac{1}{2} CV^2 \qquad \ldots(2.55)$$

The expression of stored energy can also be expressed in terms of charge on capacitor and potential difference across plates which is given as

$$U = \frac{q^2}{2C} = \frac{q(CV)}{2C} = \frac{1}{2} qV \qquad \ldots(2.56)$$

Expressions given in equations-(2.54) and (2.55) are frequently used in different cases of numerical problems as in different situations either charge on capacitor is given or potential difference across capacitor is given whereas equation-(2.56) is rarely used for calculation of energy stored in a capacitor.

2.2.4 Heat Dissipation in Charging of a Parallel Plate Capacitor

As we've already discussed in article-2.2.1 and in figure-2.21 that on connecting a capacitor across a battery when switch is closed charges flow from one plate of capacitor to another plate due to battery and as wires are considered conducting with very low or negligible resistance, charges flow very fast and quickly capacitor plates attain the steady state charges and finally current in circuit becomes zero. In the charging process free electrons in the conducting wires gain kinetic energy while transferring and finally all charges come to rest thus the kinetic energy attained by these free electrons is finally dissipated in form of heat radiations to the surrounding. This dissipation of heat in the process of charging a capacitor can be calculated by conservation of energy.

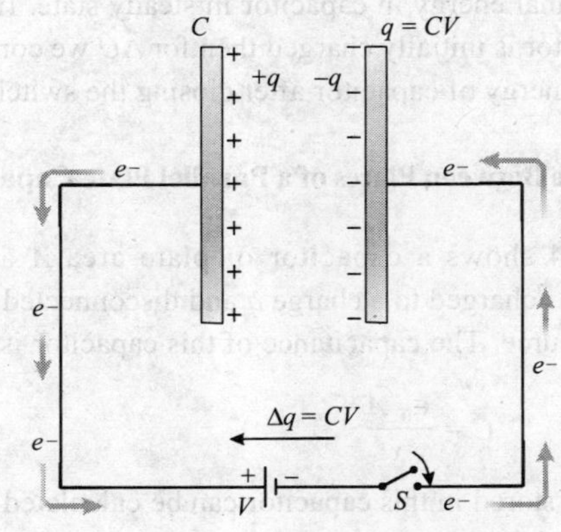

Figure 2.29

In figure-2.29 when the switch is open the initial charge on capacitor was zero and no energy was stored in capacitor. When switch is closed battery supplies a charge on capacitor plates and in steady state charge on capacitor plates becomes $q = CV$. Thus in steady state the potential difference across capacitor plates becomes V and energy stored in it is given by equation-(2.55) as

$$U = \frac{1}{2}CV^2 \quad \ldots(2.57)$$

In the process of charging of capacitor the amount of charge flowing through battery is $q = CV$ thus the work done by battery in transportation of this charge from one plate to another is given as

$$W = \Delta q V = (CV)V = CV^2 \quad \ldots(2.58)$$

Equation-(2.58) shows that in the process of charging the capacitor work done by battery is CV^2 and out of this half is stored in capacitor as field energy as expressed in equation-(2.57). Thus remaining energy which the battery supplied as work in charging is dissipated as heat which is given as

$$H = W - \Delta U \quad \ldots(2.59)$$

$$\Rightarrow \quad H = CV^2 - \frac{1}{2}CV^2$$

$$\Rightarrow \quad H = \frac{1}{2}CV^2 \quad \ldots(2.60)$$

As expressed in equation-(2.60), we can state that in process of charging an uncharged capacitor half of work done by battery in charging is stored as potential energy in capacitor and half is dissipated as heat.

The term ΔU in equation-(2.59) is the energy absorbed by capacitor or change in energy of capacitor after closing the switch. In this case as initially capacitor was uncharged so here ΔU is the final energy in capacitor in steady state. If in some case capacitor is initially charged then for ΔU we consider the change in energy of capacitor after closing the switch.

2.2.5 Force Between Plates of a Parallel Plate Capacitor

Figure-2.24 shows a capacitor of plate area A and plate separation x, charged to a charge q and disconnected from the charging source. The capacitance of this capacitor is given as

$$C = \frac{\epsilon_0 A}{x} \quad \ldots(2.61)$$

The energy stored in this capacitor can be calculated by using equation-(2.54) which is given as

$$U = \frac{q^2}{2C} = \frac{q^2}{2\left(\frac{\epsilon_0 A}{x}\right)} = \frac{q^2 x}{2\epsilon_0 A} \quad \ldots(2.62)$$

If the capacitor plates are to be pulled apart from the state shown in figure-2.30(a) then we need to apply an outward force on the plates which should be equal to the force with which the two plates are attracting each other. If the electrostatic force of attraction between the plates is F then work done in increasing the plate separation form x to $x + dx$ is given as

$$dW = F \cdot dx \quad \ldots(2.63)$$

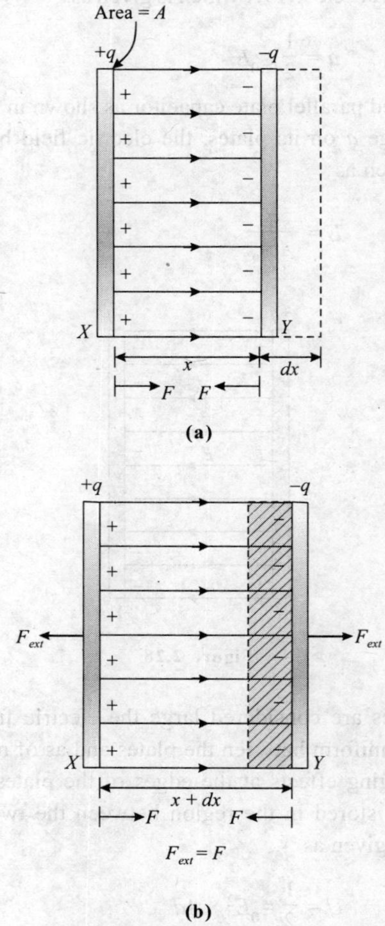

Figure 2.30

Here the work dW will be equal to the increase in energy dU due to increase in field energy in the shaded region as shown in figure-2.30(b) in which electric field is present which was not there before pulling the plates. This energy dU can also be calculated by differentiating equation-(2.62) as

$$\frac{dU}{dx} = \frac{q^2}{2\epsilon_0 A} \quad \ldots(2.64)$$

From equation-(2.63) and (2.64) we can get the force of attraction between the plates which is given as

$$F = \frac{q^2}{2\epsilon_0 A} \quad \ldots(2.65)$$

Above expression of force given in equation-(2.65) can also be obtained by using electric field strength of one plate at the location of other plate. As q is the charge on one plate then electric field strength E_1 due to this charge at the location of other plate is given as

$$E_1 = \frac{\sigma}{2\in_0} = \frac{q}{2A\in_0} \quad \ldots(2.66)$$

The force on other plate due to the electric field of one plate can be given as

$$F = qE_1 = q\left(\frac{q}{2A\in_0}\right) = \frac{q^2}{2\in_0 A} \quad \ldots(2.67)$$

Equation-(2.67) is same as that of equation-(2.65) which is obtained by work energy analysis.

In steady state we can use $q = CV$ which gives the force in terms of the applied voltage across the capacitor as

$$F = \frac{1}{2}\in_0 A\frac{V^2}{d^2} \quad \ldots(2.68)$$

 # Illustrative Example 2.6

A parallel plate capacitor is arranged horizontally in a mechanical situation with the lower plate is fixed and the other connected with a perpendicular spring as shown in figure-2.31. The area of each plate is A and in equilibrium the distance between the plates is d_0. When the capacitor is connected with a source of voltage V, a new equilibrium appears after some displacement in upper plate with the new distance between the plates d_1. Given that mass of the upper plate is m.

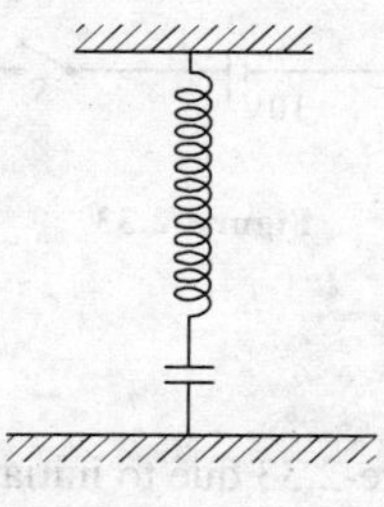

Figure 2.31

(a) Find the spring constant K.

(b) What is the maximum voltage for a given K in which an equilibrium is possible?

(c) What is the angular frequency of the oscillating system around the equilibrium value d_1. Consider that amplitude of the oscillation is less than d_1.

Solution

(a) Let l_0 be the initial extension in the spring then for equilibrium of the upper plate we have

$$Kl_0 = mg$$

After connected to a voltage source, as the plate separation changes from d_0 to d_1. The extension of the spring will be $(d_0 - d_1)$.

In new equilibrium position of upper plate we have

$$K[l_0 + (d_0 - d_1)] = mg + \frac{q^2}{2\in_0 A}$$

$$\Rightarrow \quad K(d_0 - d_1) = \frac{q^2}{2\in_0 A} \quad \ldots(2.69)$$

In final state charge on capacitor plates q can be given as

$$q = C_f V = \left(\frac{\in_0 A}{d_1}\right)V$$

Thus from equation-(2.69) we have

$$K = \frac{\varepsilon_0 A V^2}{2d_1^2(d_0 - d_1)} \quad \ldots(2.70)$$

(b) From equation-(2.70) the potential difference can be given in terms of other parameters as

$$V^2 = \frac{2Kx^2(d_0 - x)}{A\varepsilon_0} \quad \ldots(2.71)$$

In above expression we replaced d_1 with a variable x and this expression gives the potential difference in terms of the plate separation x as at different values of source voltage V the plate separation will be different.

For maximum voltage we use the concept of maxima-minima. Thus differentiating equation-(2.71) with respect to x which gives

$$2V\left(\frac{dV}{dx}\right) = \frac{2K}{A\varepsilon_0}[2x\,d_0 - 3x^2]$$

For V to be maximum, $(dV/dx) = 0$, this gives

$$x = \left(\frac{2}{3}d_0\right)$$

Thus the maximum voltage can be given by substituting the above value of x in equation-(2.71) as

$$V_{max}^2 = \frac{2K(2/3d_0)^2[d_0 - 2/3d_0]}{A\varepsilon_0}$$

$$\Rightarrow \quad V_{max} = \sqrt{\frac{K}{A\varepsilon_0}}\left(\frac{2}{3}d_0\right)^{3/2} \quad \ldots(2.72)$$

(c) Let the upper plate be displaced through a small distance x downwards from equilibrium position. Then net force on the plate is given by.

$$F = K[l_0 + (d_0 - d) + x] + mg + \frac{1}{2}\varepsilon_0 A\left[\frac{V^2}{(d_1 - x)^2}\right]$$

$$\Rightarrow \quad F = K(d_0 - d) - Kx + \frac{1}{2}\frac{\varepsilon_0 AV^2}{d_1^2}\left[1 - \frac{x}{d_1}\right]^{-2}$$

$$\Rightarrow \quad F = -K(d_0 - d) - Kx + \frac{1}{2}\frac{\varepsilon_0 AV^2}{d_1^2}\left(1 + \frac{2x}{d_1}\right)$$

$$\Rightarrow \quad F = -K(d_0 - d) - Kx + K(d_0 - d_1)\left(1 + \frac{2x}{d_1}\right)$$

$$\Rightarrow \quad F = -Kx\left[\frac{3d_1 - 2d_0}{d}\right]$$

Acceleration of upper plate is given as

$$a = \frac{F}{m} = -\frac{K}{m}\left(\frac{3d_1 - 2d_0}{d_1}\right)x \qquad \ldots(2.73)$$

As in above equation-(2.73) acceleration of the plate is directly proportional to the displacement we can infer that the plate is executing SHM so comparing above equation-(2.73) with the acceleration of SHM $a = -\omega^2 x$ we get the angular frequency of SHM of upper plate as

$$\omega = \sqrt{\left[\frac{K}{m}\left(\frac{3d_1 - 2d_0}{d_1}\right)\right]}$$

Illustrative Example 2.7

The lower plate of a parallel plate capacitor is fixed on an insulating plane as shown in figure-2.32. The upper plate is suspended from one end of a balance. Initially the capacitor is uncharged and balance is in equilibrium state. A voltage V is applied between the plates, what additional weight should be placed to maintain the balance? Consider the separation between the plates to be d and the area of each plate is A.

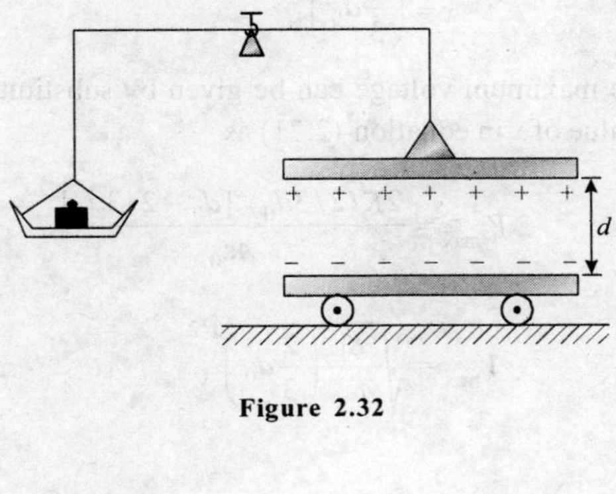

Figure 2.32

Solution

The force between the plates of capacitor is given as

$$F = \frac{1}{2}\in_0 A\frac{V^2}{d^2}$$

For the balance equilibrium we have

$$mg = F$$

$$\Rightarrow \quad mg = \frac{1}{2}\in_0 A\frac{V^2}{d^2}$$

$$\Rightarrow m = \frac{1}{2}\frac{\in_0 AV^2}{md^2}$$

Illustrative Example 2.8

A capacitor of 10 μF capacitance is having 50 μC charge. Find amount of heat produced when this capacitor is connected across a 10 V battery as shown in figure-2.33 and switch is closed.

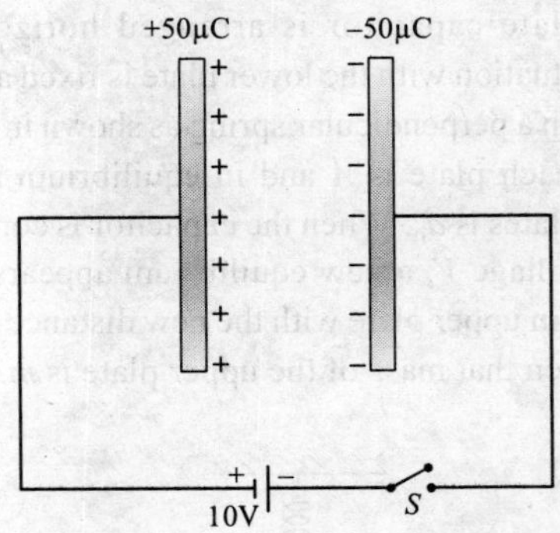

Figure 2.33

Solution

As we can see in figure-2.33 due to initial charge on capacitor its potential difference across plates is equal to $V = 50/10 = 5$V thus when switch is closed a potential difference of 10 V is applied across battery as shown in figure-2.34 which is more than initial potential difference across capacitor hence battery will supply an additional 50 μC charge to capacitor because steady state potential difference across capacitor is 10 V so final charge on it will be $10 \times 10 = 100$ μC. Thus work done in further charging the capacitor to steady state by battery is given as

$$W = \Delta q\, V = 50 \times 10 = 500\ \mu J \qquad \ldots(2.74)$$

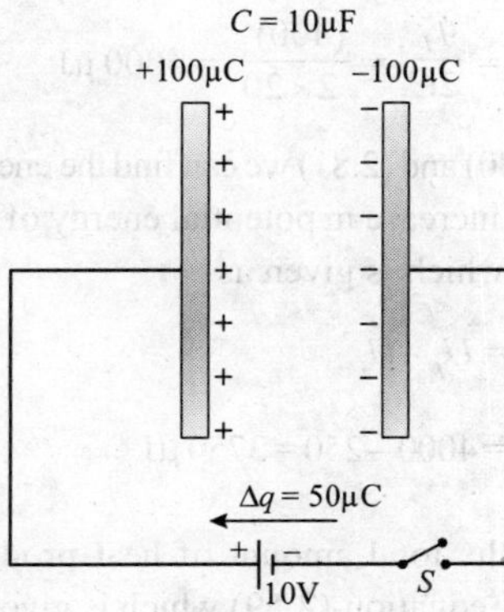

Figure 2.34

When the switch was open then the initial energy stored in capacitor is given as

$$U_i = \frac{q^2}{2c} = \frac{2500}{20} = 125\ \mu J \qquad ...(2.75)$$

After closing the switch final energy stored in capacitor is given as

$$U_f = \frac{1}{2}CV^2 = \frac{1}{2} \times 10 \times 10^{-6} \times (10)^2 = 500\ \mu J \qquad ...(2.76)$$

Thus from equations-(2.75) and (2.76) we can calculate the increase in potential energy of capacitor as

$$\Delta U = U_f - U_i$$

$$\Rightarrow \quad \Delta U = 500 - 125 = 375\ \mu J \qquad ...(2.77)$$

Now in above process we can find the total amount of heat produced by using equation-(2.59) which is given as

$$H = W - \Delta U$$

$$\Rightarrow \quad H = 500 - 375 = 125\ \mu J$$

Illustrative Example 2.9

In previous illustration if battery is connected with reverse polarity as shown in figure-2.35 then find the amount of heat produced in circuit after switch is closed.

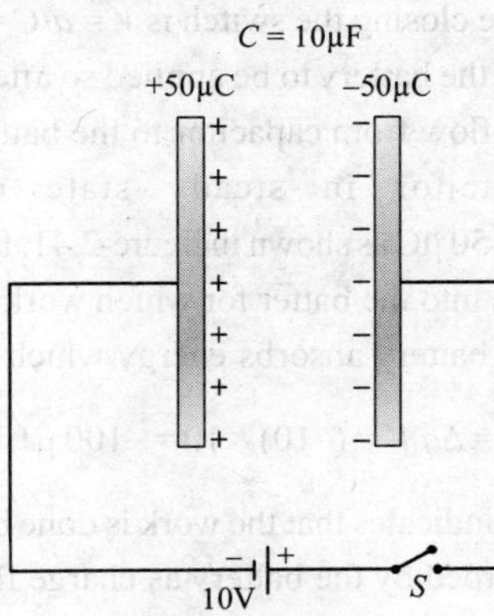

Figure 2.35

Solution

After closing the switch steady state charge on capacitor will be 100 μC but the polarity of charges gets reversed so the battery has to supply a charge of 150 μC as shown in figure-2.36. The change in energy of capacitor remain same as that of previous case which is 375 μJ as initial and final charge on capacitor are same. The work done by battery in the process can be given as

$$W = \Delta q\, V = 150 \times 10 = 1500\ \mu J \qquad ...(2.78)$$

In this case again heat produced in circuit can be calculated by using equation-(2.59) as

$$H = W - \Delta U$$

$$\Rightarrow \quad H = 1500 - 375 = 1125\ \mu J$$

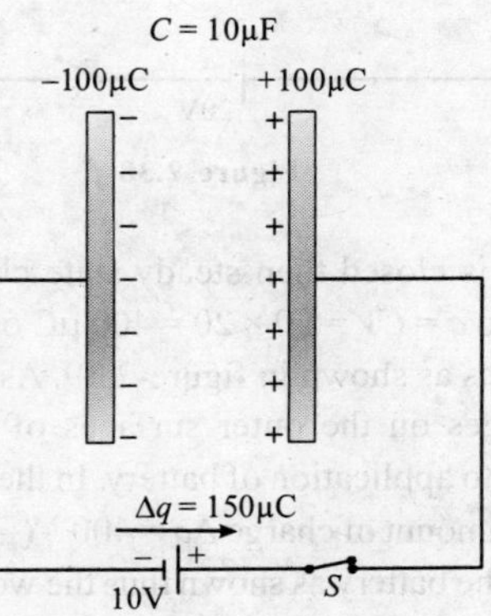

Figure 2.36

Illustrative Example 2.10

The two plates of a capacitor of capacitance 20 μF are given different charges of 100 μC and 300 μC respectively as shown in figure-2.37. Find the amount of heat produced in circuit when switch S is closed.

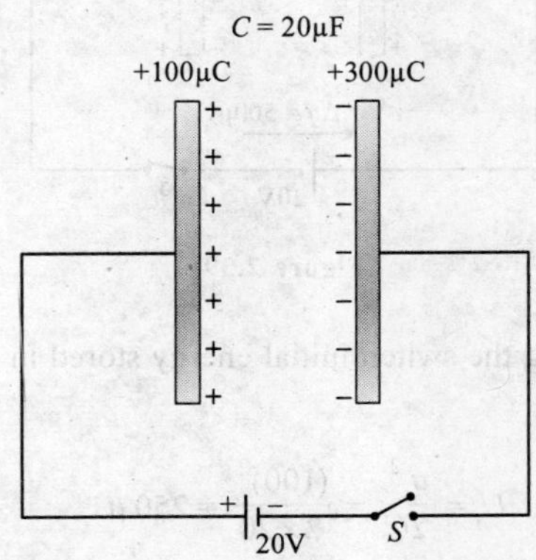

Figure 2.37

Solution

Initially the charges on capacitor plates are distributed on the surfaces of these plates as explained in article-1.17.2 and 1.17.3 and after redistribution of charges final charges on the plate surfaces are shown in figure-2.38 before closing the switch. Thus initial charge on capacitor can be considered as 100 μC and initial potential difference is $V = q/C = 100/20 = 5$ V.

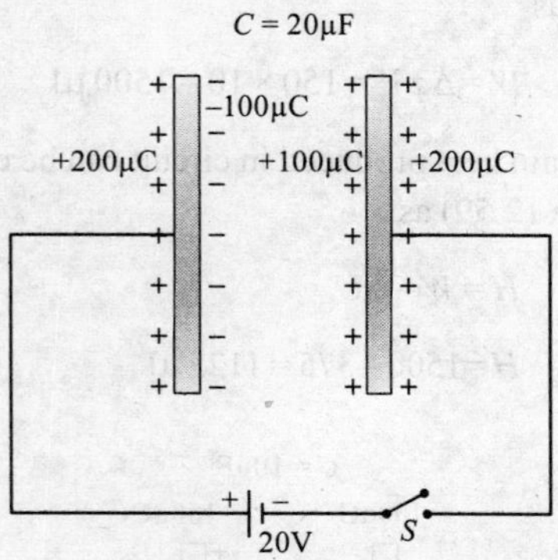

Figure 2.38

When switch is closed then steady state charge on capacitor will increase to $q = CV = 20 \times 20 = 400$ μC on inner faces of the capacitor plates as shown in figure-2.39. As already discussed that the charges on the outer surfaces of the plates remain unaltered due to application of battery. In the process of closing the switch an amount of charge $\Delta q = 400 - (-100) = 500$ μC will flow through the battery as shown thus the work done by battery in the process can be given as

$$W = \Delta q V = 500 \times 20 = 10000 \ \mu J \qquad \ldots(2.79)$$

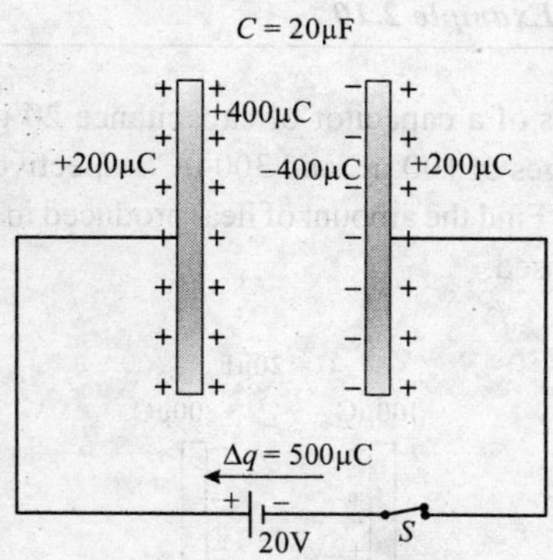

Figure 2.39

Before closing the switch initial energy stored in capacitor is given as

$$U_i = \frac{q_i^2}{2C} = \frac{(100)^2}{2 \times 20} = 250 \ \mu J \qquad \ldots(2.80)$$

After closing the switch final energy stored in capacitor is given as

$$U_f = \frac{q_f^2}{2C} = \frac{(400)^2}{2 \times 20} = 4000 \ \mu J \qquad \ldots(2.81)$$

From equations-(2.80) and (2.81) we can find the energy absorbed by the capacitor or increase in potential energy of capacitor on closing the switch which is given as

$$\Delta U = U_f - U_i$$

$$\Rightarrow \qquad \Delta U = 4000 - 250 = 3750 \ \mu J$$

Now in this case the total amount of heat produced can be calculated by using equation-(2.59) which is given as

$$H = W - \Delta U$$

$$\Rightarrow \qquad H = 10000 - 3750 = 6250 \ \mu J$$

 # Illustrative Example 2.11

A capacitor of 5 μF capacitance is charged with an initial charge 60 μC as shown in figure-2.40 and connected across a 10 V battery. Find the amount of heat produced when switch is closed.

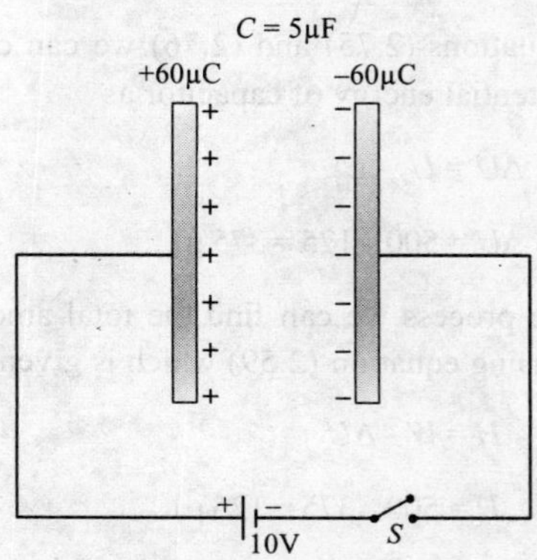

Figure 2.40

Solution

In the shown figure-2.40 the initial potential difference across the capacitor before closing the switch is $V = q/C = 60/5 = 12V$ which is more than the battery to be applied so after closing the switch charge will flow from capacitor to the battery and final charge of capacitor in steady state reduces to $q_f = CV = 5 \times 10 = 50$ μC as shown in figure-2.41. In this process 10μC charge flows into the batter for which work will be done on the battery and battery absorbs energy which is given as

$$W = \Delta q \, V = (-10) \times 10 = -100 \ \mu J \qquad \ldots(2.82)$$

Here negative sign indicates that the work is done by the battery and energy is absorbed by the battery as charge flows into the battery in direction opposite to the polarity of its terminals.

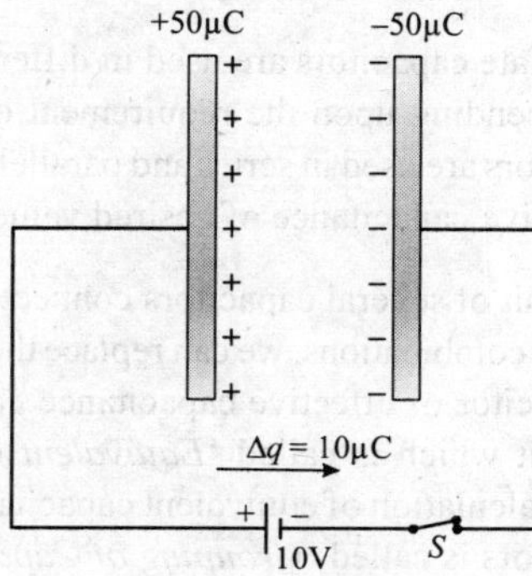

Figure 2.41

Before closing the switch initial energy stored in the capacitor is given as

$$U_i = \frac{q_i^2}{2C} = \frac{(60)^2}{2\times5} = 360\,\mu J \quad \ldots(2.83)$$

After closing the switch final energy stored in the capacitor is given as

$$U_f = \frac{q_f^2}{2C} = \frac{(50)^2}{2\times5} = 250\,\mu J \quad \ldots(2.84)$$

From equations-(2.83) and (2.84) it is clear that the energy stored in capacitor is decreased that means potential energy of capacitor is released out. We can find the energy released by the capacitor or decrease in its potential energy as

$$\Delta U = U_f - U_i$$

$$\Rightarrow \quad \Delta U = 250 - 360 = -110\,\mu J$$

Negative sign in above equation shows that potential energy of capacitor is decreased in this process. Out of the above energy released by capacitor, 100 μJ of energy is used in doing work on battery as seen by equation-(2.82) and remaining will be dissipated as heat so from equation-(2.59) we can write

$$H = W - \Delta U$$

$$\Rightarrow \quad H = (-100) - (-110) = 10\,\mu J$$

Web Reference at www.physicsgalaxy.com

Age Group - Grade 11 & 12 | Age 17-19 Years
Section - ELECTROSTATICS
Topic - Capacitance
Module Number - 1 to 16

Practice Exercise 2.1

(i) The capacitance of a parallel plate capacitor is 400 pF and its plates are separated by 2 mm of air (a) What will be the energy when it is charged to 1500 V. (b) What will be the potential difference with the same charge if plate separation is doubled? (c) How much energy is needed to double the distance between its plates ?

[(a) 4.5×10^{-4} J; (b) 3000 V; (c) 4.5×10^{-4} J]

(ii) A charge of 1 μC is given to one plate of a parallel plate capacitor of capacitance 0.1 μF and a charge of 2 μC is given to the other plate. Find the potential difference developed between the plates.

[5V]

(iii) A parallel plate capacitor of plate area 0.2 m^2 and spacing 10^{-2} m is charged to 10^3 V and is then disconnected from the battery. How much work in required if the plates are pulled apart to double the plate spacing? Calculate the final voltage on the capacitor.

[8.9×10^{-5} J, 200 V]

(iv) Two uniformly charged spherical drops at potential V coalesce to form a larger drop. If capacitance of each smaller drop is C then find capacitance and potential of larger drop.

[$2^{1/3}C$, $2^{2/3}V$]

(v) A spherical capacitor has the inner sphere of radius 2 cm and the outer one of 4 cm. If the inner sphere is earthed and the outer one is charged with a charge of 2 μC and isolated, calculate.

(a) The potential to which the outer sphere is raised

(b) The charge retained on the outer surface of the outer sphere.

[(a) 2.25×10^5 V; (b) +1 μC]

(vi) The capacitance of a variable capacitor can be changed from 50 pF to 950 pF by turning the dial from 0° to 180°. With the dial set at 180°, the capacitor is connected to a 400 V battery. After charging, the capacitor is disconnected from the battery and the dial is turned at 0°.

(a) What is the potential difference across the capacitor when the dials reads 0° ?

(b) How much work is required to turn the dial, if friction is neglected ?

[(a) 7600 V; (b) 1.368×10^{-3} J]

(vii) The stratosphere acts as a conducting layer for the earth. If the stratosphere extends beyond 50 km from the surface of earth, then calculate the capacitance of the spherical capacitor formed between stratosphere and earth's surface. Take radius of earth as 6400 km.

[0.092F]

(viii) A 40 μF capacitor in a defibrillator is charged to 3000 V. The energy stored in the capacitor is sent through the patient during a pulse of duration 2 ms. Find the average current and The power delivered to the patient will be.

[60 A, 90 kW]

(ix) The two identical parallel plates are given charges as shown in figure-2.42. If the plate area of either face of each plate is A and separation between plate is d, then find the amount of heat liberate after closing the switch.

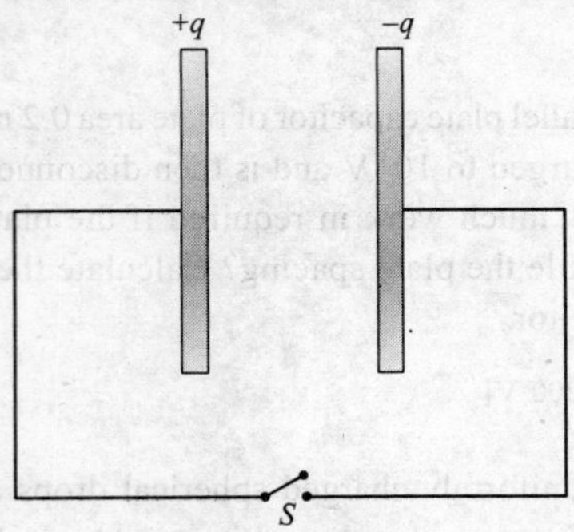

Figure 2.42

$[\frac{1}{2}\frac{q^2 d}{\epsilon_0 A}]$

(x) A capacitor has two circular plates whose radius are 8 cm each and distance between them is 1mm. When mica having dielectric constant 6 is filled between the plates, calculate the new capacitance of this capacitor and the energy stored when it is put across a potential of 150 V.

[1.068×10^{-9} F; 1.2×10^{-5} J]

(xi) If charge on 3 μF capacitor is 3 μC. Find the charge on capacitor of capacitance C in μC.

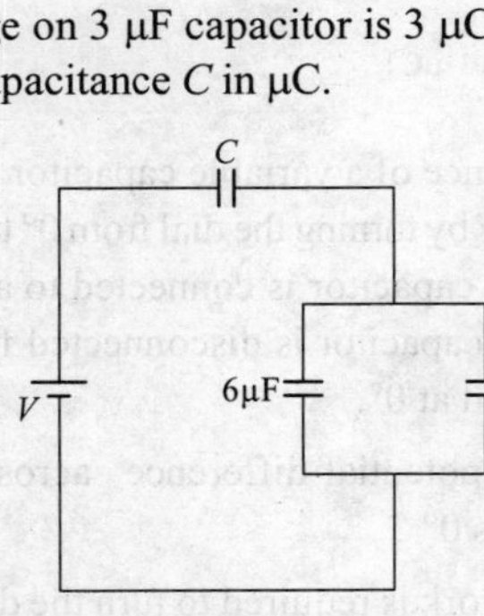

Figure 2.43

[9 μC]

(xii) An insulated conductor initially free from charge is charged by repeated contacts with a plate which after each contact is charged to Q by some mechanism. If q is charge on the conductor after the first operation, prove that the maximum charge which can be given to the conductor in this way is $Qq/(Q-q)$.

2.3 *Grouping of Parallel Plate Capacitors*

When parallel plate capacitors are used in different electronic circuits then depending upon the requirement of capacitance available capacitors are used in series and parallel combinations to achieve effective capacitance of desired value.

For a given circuit of several capacitors connected in series or parallel or mixed combinations, we can replace the whole circuit by a single capacitor of effective capacitance equal to that of the whole circuit which is called '*Equivalent Capacitance*'. The process of calculation of equivalent capacitance of a given group of capacitors is called '*Grouping of Capacitance*'.

In general there are two standard ways to connect capacitors in groups - Series Combination and Parallel Combination. These ways to connect capacitors are similar to what you have studied in your previous grades as combination of resistances. There are some specific ways to connect capacitors (and resistors also) when given capacitors are neither in series nor in parallel which are called mixed combinations. In upcoming articles, we will discuss these combinations in details and analyze how to calculate the equivalent capacitance of such combinations.

2.3.1 Equivalent Capacitance of a Group of Capacitor

Figure-2.44(a) shows a circuit in which several capacitors are connected in groups. These capacitors may be connected in series, parallel or mixed combinations and this group of capacitors across terminals A and B is connected across a battery via a switch S. When switch is closed, say a charge Δq_0 flows through the battery for charging the capacitors of the group. In this situation if the whole group of capacitors across terminals A and B is replaced by a single capacitor as shown in figure-2.44(b) such that in this situation also when the switch is closed, battery supplies the same charge Δq_0 to charge this single capacitor then the capacitance of this single capacitor is called '*Equivalent Capacitance*' of the initial group across terminals A and B of circuit. This is termed as equivalent because for battery this single capacitor is behaving identical to that of the group as on closing the switch till steady state arrives, battery does same amount of work in charging it. The capacitance of the single capacitor which replaces the group is denoted as C_{eq}.

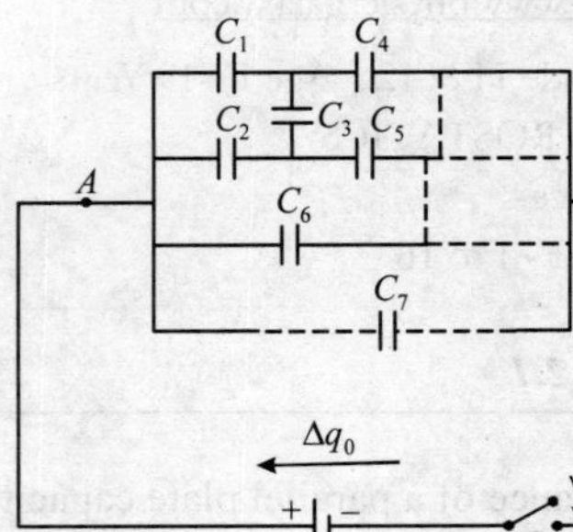

(a)

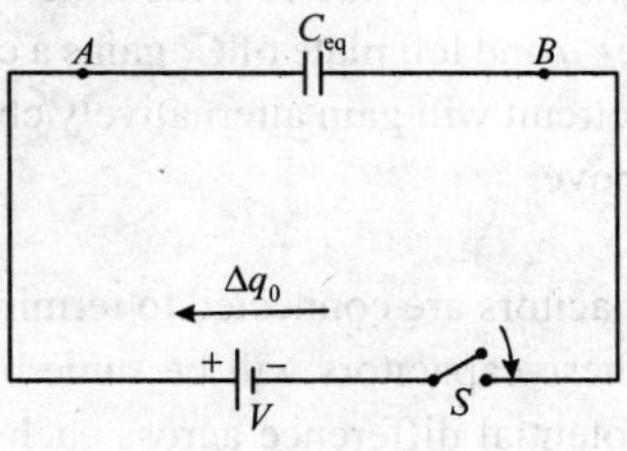

(b)
Figure 2.44

Thus the charge which flows through the battery in full charging the all the capacitors of the group can be given as

$$\Delta q_0 = C_{eq} V \quad \ldots(2.85)$$

$$\Rightarrow \quad C_{eq} = \frac{\Delta q_0}{V} \quad \ldots(2.86)$$

Thus the equivalent capacitance of any group of capacitors can be calculated by connecting a battery across the combination and taking the ratio of charge flown through battery to the battery potential difference as given in equation-(2.86).

2.3.2 Parallel Combination of Capacitors

When two or more capacitors are connected in such a way that all plates on one side of capacitors are connected together and all remaining plates of capacitors are also connected together then all such capacitors are said to be in parallel combination.

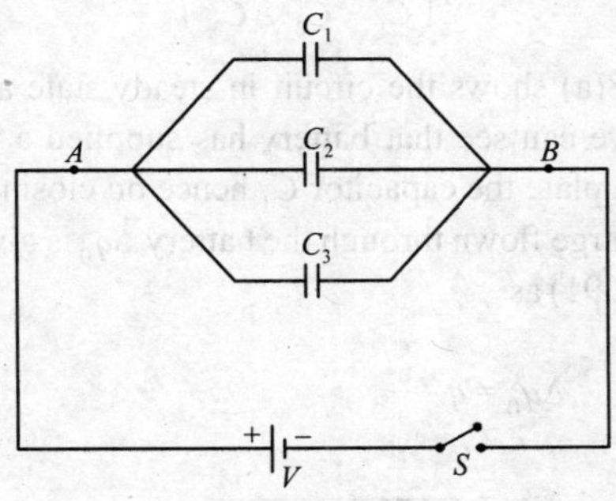

Figure 2.45

Figure-2.45 shows three parallel plate capacitors having capacitances C_1, C_2 and C_3 connected in parallel combination across terminals A and B across which a battery is connected via a switch S as shown. To calculate the equivalent capacitance of this combination across terminals A and B we close the switch S after which the potential difference across terminals A and B will be come V due to connection with battery. As all three capacitors are connected to terminals A and B, the potential difference across all these capacitors will become V and in steady state the charge on these capacitor plates will be

$$q_1 = C_1V;\ q_2 = C_2V;\ q_3 = C_3V$$

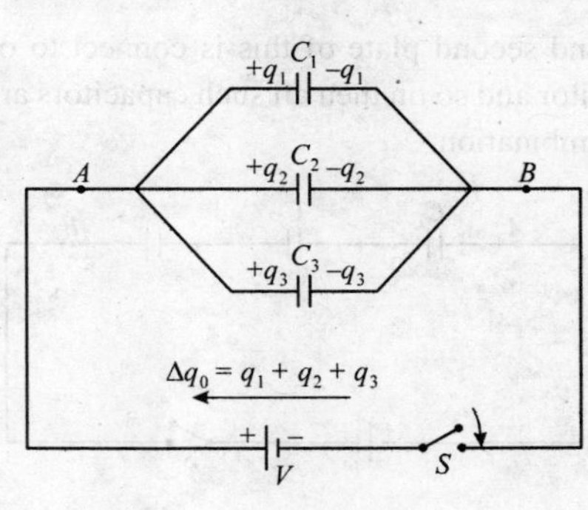

(a)

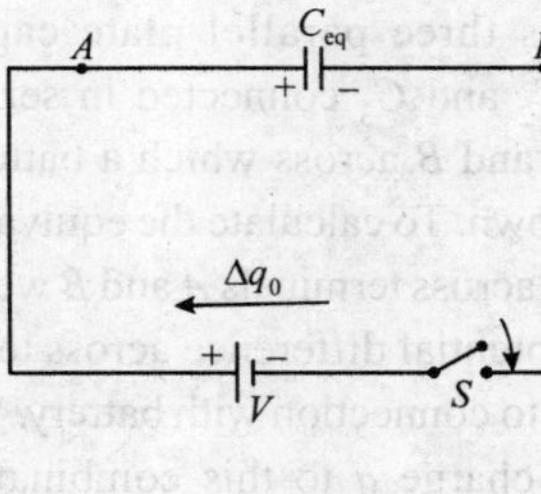

(b)
Figure 2.46

Figure-2.46(a) shows the circuit in steady state and to attain this state we can see that battery has supplied a total charge $q_1 + q_2 + q_3$ to the left plates of the three capacitors hence on closing the switch the total charge flown through the battery is given as

$$\Delta q_0 = q_1 + q_2 + q_3$$

$$\Rightarrow \quad \Delta q_0 = C_1V + C_2V + C_3V$$

$$\Rightarrow \quad \Delta q_0 = (C_1 + C_2 + C_3)\, V \quad \ldots(2.87)$$

Figure-2.46(b) shows the equivalent capacitance of 2.36(a) in which also when we close the switch battery will supply same amount of charge thus equivalent capacitance of this circuit can be given as

$$C_{eq} = \frac{\Delta q_0}{V}$$

$$\Rightarrow \quad C_{eq} = C_1 + C_2 + C_3 \quad \ldots(2.88)$$

Equation-(2.88) gives the equivalent capacitance of three capacitors connected in parallel which is the sum of capacitance of individual capacitors. This can be generalized to any number of capacitors that equivalent capacitance of all the capacitors connected in parallel combination is given by sum of capacitance of all individual capacitors.

2.3.3 Series Combination of Capacitors

When two or more capacitors are connected in such a way that one plates of a capacitor is connected to one plate of second capacitor and second plate of this is connect to one plate of third capacitor and so on then all such capacitors are said to be in series combination.

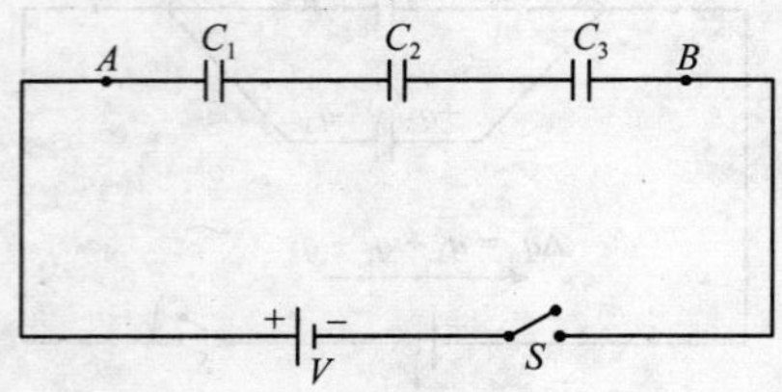

Figure 2.47

Figure-2.47 shows three parallel plate capacitors having capacitances C_1, C_2 and C_3 connected in series combination across terminals A and B across which a battery is connected via a switch S as shown. To calculate the equivalent capacitance of this combination across terminals A and B we close the switch S after which the potential difference across terminals A and B will be come V due to connection with battery. We consider that battery supplies a charge q to this combination then whole charge q will be deposited on the left plate of the capacitor C_1 due to which on other plate of C_1 a charge $-q$ is induced and as this plate is connected to one plate of C_2, it will gain an opposite charge $+q$ as the section of circuit shown in figure-2.48(a) by dotted line enclosing point M is isolated from the circuit and its total charge must be zero. Such a section in a capacitive circuit is called a '*Node*'. Due to another node of circuit at point N between capacitors C_2 and C_3, same charges $+q$ and $-q$ will appear on these plates of this second node. Thus on all the capacitors connected in series combination always in steady state charges are equal.

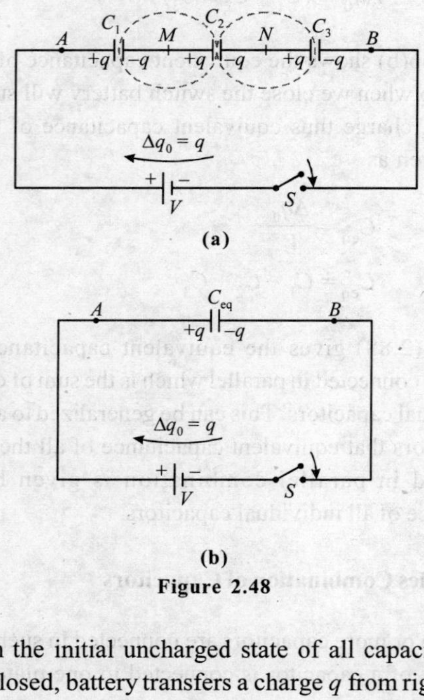

Figure 2.48

Thus from the initial uncharged state of all capacitors when switch is closed, battery transfers a charge q from right plate of C_3 to the left plate of C_1 due to which the right plate of C_3 attains a charge $-q$ and left plate of C_1 gains a charge $+q$ and all other plates in circuit will gain alternatively charges $+q$ and $-q$ as explained above.

As all three capacitors are connected to terminals A and B, the charge on all these capacitors will be same by which we can calculate the potential difference across each capacitor given as

$$V_1 = \frac{q}{C_1}\ ;\ V_2 = \frac{q}{C_2}\ ;\ V_3 = \frac{q}{C_3}$$

In above circuit shown in figure-2.48(a) we can write the following equations of potential differences

$$V_A - V_C = \frac{q}{C_1} \quad \ldots(2.89)$$

$$V_C - V_D = \frac{q}{C_2} \quad \ldots(2.90)$$

$$V_D - V_B = \frac{q}{C_3} \quad \ldots(2.91)$$

Adding the above three equations, we get

$$V_A - V_B = \frac{q}{C_1} + \frac{q}{C_2} + \frac{q}{C_3} \quad \ldots(2.92)$$

$$\Rightarrow \quad V = q\left(\frac{1}{C_1} + \frac{1}{C_2} + \frac{1}{C_3}\right) \quad \ldots(2.93)$$

Figure-2.48(a) shows the circuit in steady state and to attain this state we can see that battery has supplied a total charge q to the left plate the capacitor C_1 hence on closing the switch the total charge flown through the battery Δq_0 is given by using equation-(2.91) as

$$\Delta q_0 = q$$

$$\Rightarrow \quad \Delta q_0 = \frac{V}{\left(\frac{1}{C_1} + \frac{1}{C_2} + \frac{1}{C_3}\right)} \quad \ldots(2.94)$$

Figure-2.48(b) shows the equivalent capacitance of figure-2.48(a) in which also when we close the switch battery will supply same amount of charge thus equivalent capacitance of this circuit can be given as

$$C_{eq} = \frac{\Delta q_0}{V}$$

$$\Rightarrow \quad C_{eq} = \frac{1}{\left(\frac{1}{C_1} + \frac{1}{C_2} + \frac{1}{C_3}\right)}$$

$$\Rightarrow \qquad \frac{1}{C_{eq}} = \frac{1}{C_1} + \frac{1}{C_2} + \frac{1}{C_3} \qquad \ldots(2.95)$$

Equation-(2.95) gives the equivalent capacitance of three capacitors connected in series which is the reciprocal of sum of reciprocals of capacitance of the three individual capacitors. This can be generalized to any number of capacitors as given in equation-(2.95).

Based on the cases of series and parallel combination of parallel plate capacitors we've discussed above and on analyzing equations-(2.88) and (2.95) we can state that by connecting capacitors in parallel equivalent capacitance is more than every individual capacitance of the connected capacitors and in series combination of capacitors the equivalent capacitance is less then every individual capacitance of the connected capacitors.

2.3.4 Combination of *N* Identical Capacitors

When N identical capacitors each of capacitance C are connected in parallel as shown in figure-2.49 then by equation-(2.88) we can state that the equivalent capacitance of the combination can be given as

$$C_{eq} = NC \qquad \ldots(2.96)$$

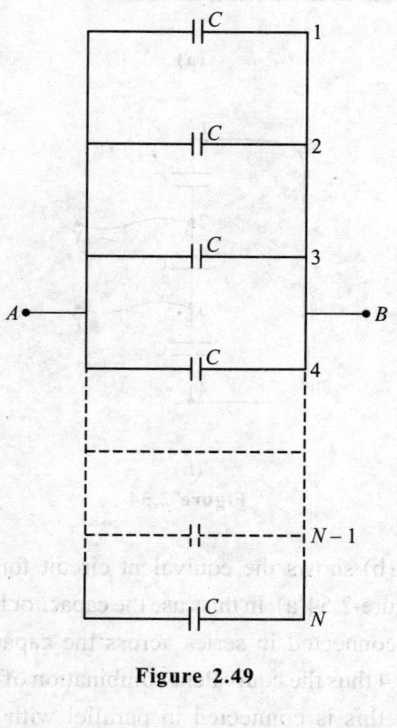

Figure 2.49

In above figure as all capacitors are connected in parallel then on applying a potential difference V across terminals A and B, potential difference across all capacitors will be same and equal to V. Steady state charge on each capacitor in this situation will be $q = CV$ and for the equivalent capacitance of above group total charge on equivalent capacitor is considered as Nq.

Similar to above when N identical capacitors are connected in series as shown in figure-2.50, then by equation-(2.88) the equivalent capacitance can be given as

$$C_{eq} = \frac{C}{N} \qquad \ldots(2.97)$$

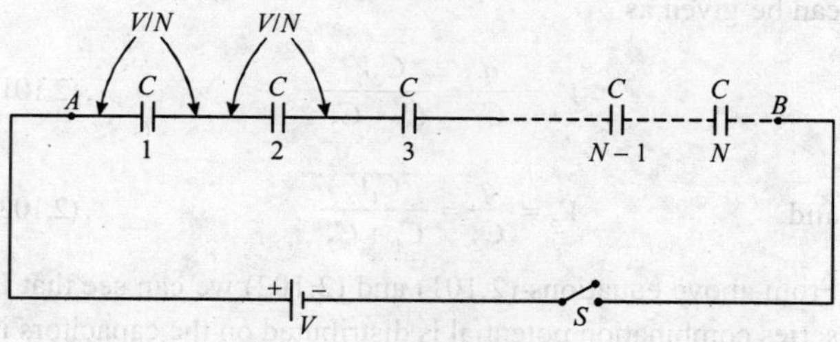

Figure 2.50

If in above case we apply a potential difference V across terminals A and B then as analyzed and discussed in article-2.3.3 all the capacitors in series will be charged to same charge q which can also be considered as the charge on equivalent capacitor and it is given as

$$q = \frac{C}{N} V \qquad \ldots(2.98)$$

Thus potential difference across each capacitor in series combination can be given as

$$V_{each} = \frac{V}{N} \qquad \ldots(2.99)$$

2.3.5 Potential Distribution in Series Combination

Figure-2.51 shows two capacitors are connected in series and connected across a battery of voltage V. In this state the equivalent capacitance across terminals A and B can be calculated using equation-(2.95) which is given as

$$C_{eq} = \frac{C_1 C_2}{C_1 + C_2}$$

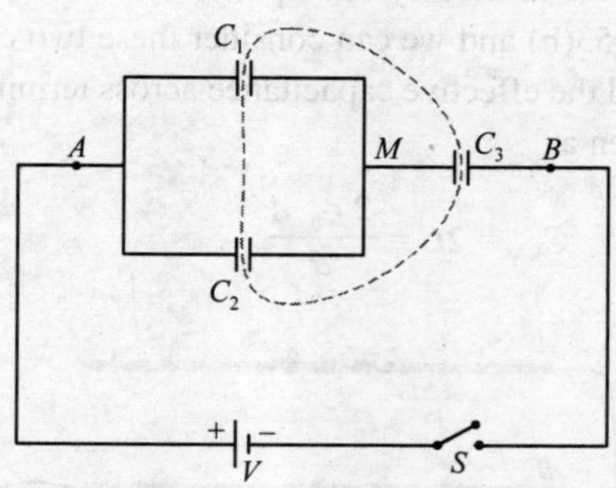

Figure 2.51

When the switch is closed in above circuit, battery supplies a charge q which is given as

$$q = C_{eq}V = \frac{C_1C_2V}{C_1 + C_2} \quad \ldots(2.100)$$

As already discussed that in series charge on both capacitors will be same and equal to that given by equation-(2.100). Thus the potential differences V_1 and V_2 across the two capacitors can be given as

$$V_1 = \frac{q}{C_1} = \frac{C_2V}{C_1 + C_2} \quad \ldots(2.101)$$

and

$$V_2 = \frac{q}{C_2} = \frac{C_1V}{C_1 + C_2} \quad \ldots(2.102)$$

From above equations-(2.101) and (2.102) we can see that in series combination potential is distributed on the capacitors in inverse ratio as $V_1/V_2 = C_2/C_1$.

2.3.6 Effective Capacitance of a System of Parallel Plates

Figure-2.52 shows three parallel plates each of area A and plate separation d. These three plates are forming two parallel plate capacitors, one between plates A and B and another between plates B and C. Capacitance of each of these capacitors is given as

$$C = \frac{\epsilon_0 A}{d}$$

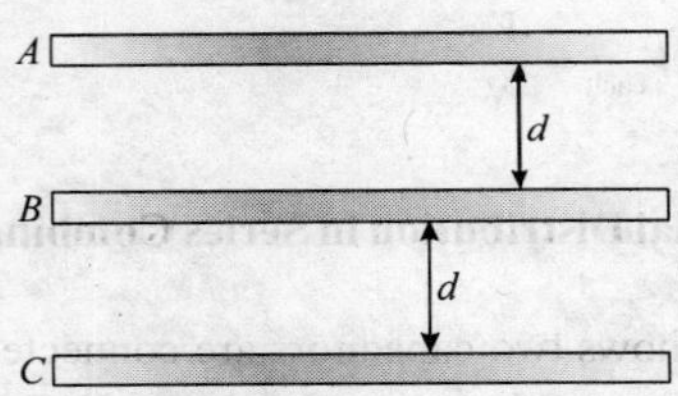

Figure 2.52

If the plates A and C are connected by a thin conducting wire as terminal X and another wire is connected to plate B as terminal Y as shown in figure-2.53(a) then the equivalent circuit of the two capacitors formed by these plates can be drawn as shown in figure-2.53(b) and we can consider these two capacitors in parallel and the effective capacitance across terminals X and Y can be given as

$$C_{XY} = 2C = \frac{2\epsilon_0 A}{d}$$

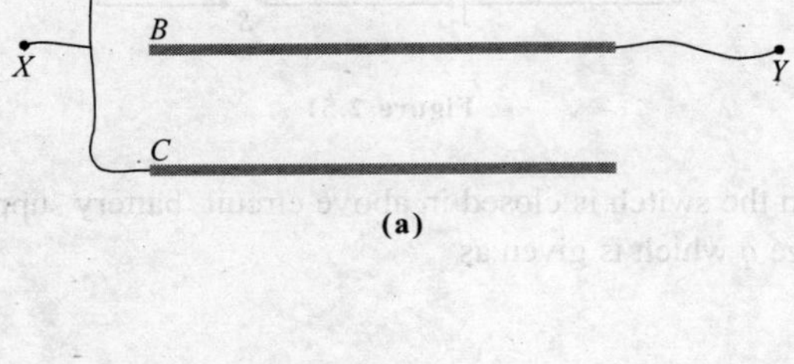

(a)

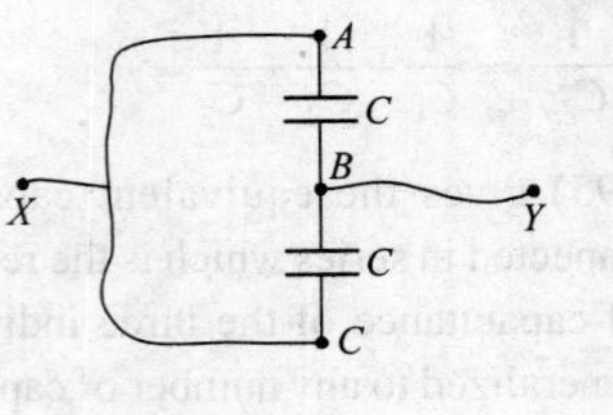

(b)

Figure 2.53

We consider another illustration to explain the same concept again. Figure-2.54(a) shows a system of four parallel plates with some connections across terminals X and Y. If capacitance between any two adjoining plates is C, here we will determine the effective capacitance of the system across terminals X and Y.

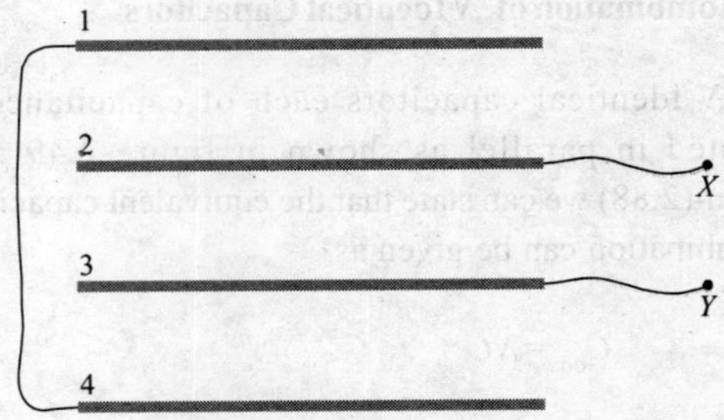

(a)

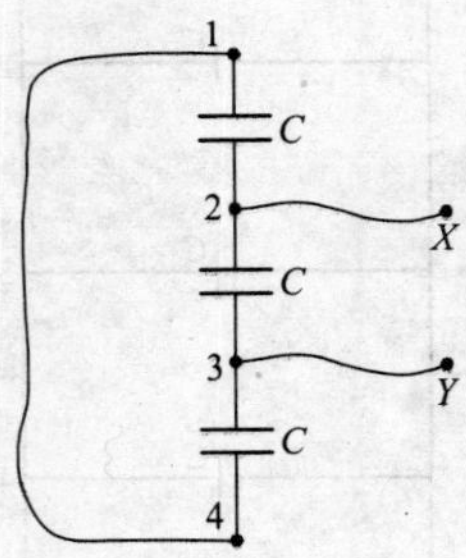

(b)

Figure 2.54

Figure-2.54(b) shows the equivalent circuit for the situation shown in figure-2.54(a). In this case the capacitor between plates 1 and 2 is connected in series across the capacitor between plates 3 and 4 thus the equivalent combination of these two will be $C/2$ and this is connected in parallel with the capacitor between plates 2 and 3 thus the overall effective capacitance across terminals X and Y is given as

$$C_{XY} = C + \frac{C}{2} = \frac{3C}{2}$$

2.3.7 Variable Capacitor

A capacitor of which capacitance can be varied as per requirement is called variable capacitor which is also termed as '*Variac*'. Figure-2.55 shows a system of N parallel plates in which every alternate plate is connected to each other on the two sides and attached to terminals X and Y as shown.

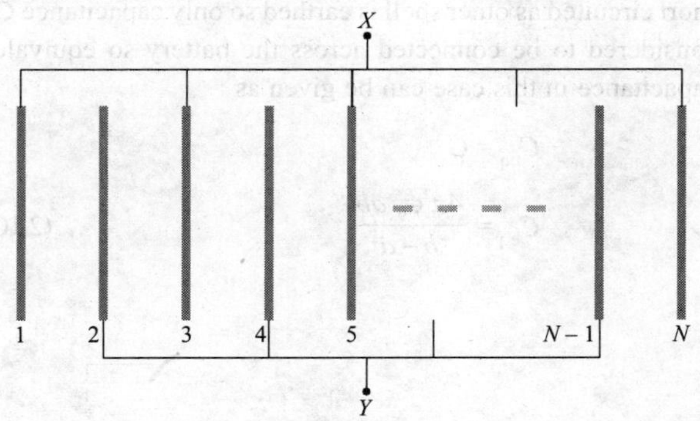

Figure 2.55

In this case if capacitance between adjoining plates is C then we can say that one plate of each of $(N-1)$ capacitors in above figure is connected to terminal X and other plate of each of the capacitors is connected to terminal Y so all can be considered in parallel combination. Thus the equivalent capacitance of this system of N parallel plates can be given as

$$C_{XY} = (N-1)C$$

Now consider a similar system shown in figure-2.56. This is made with semicircular parallel plates mounted on an axis. Alternate plates are fixed and remaining alternate plates can be rotated about the common axis of all plates. Due to rotation the overlapping area of plates will change and this changes the overall capacitance of the system. If overlapping sector area of adjoining plates in this system is A_0 then for N plates the effective capacitance of this system is given as

$$C_{XY} = \frac{(N-1)\epsilon_0 A_0}{d}$$

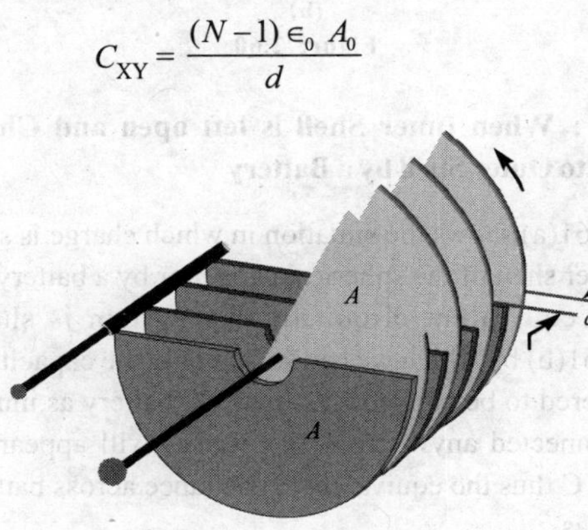

Figure 2.56

In above figure by rotating the knob K we can change the capacitance of such a capacitor as per requirement.

2.3.8 Types of Spherical Capacitors

In article-2.1.6 we've discussed about the capacitance of a spherical capacitor consisting of two concentric spherical shells which is given as

$$C = \frac{4\pi\epsilon_0 ab}{b-a} \quad \text{...(2.103)}$$

There are different ways in which such a spherical capacitor can be used in connections. Capacitance given in above equation-(2.103) gives the capacitance of the annular region between the two spherical shells. If we consider the region outside the outer shell which is extended to infinity, this has a capacitance which we've discussed in article-2.1.1. In this case it is given as

$$C' = 4\pi\epsilon_0 b$$

Figure-57 shows a spherical capacitor in which both the above capacitances are shown. C is the capacitance between inner and outer shells considered as plates of the capacitor and C' is the capacitance between the outer surface of outer shell and infinity. We can consider a spherical shell at infinity which is always at zero potential or it can be assumed to be connected to earth as shown in figure.

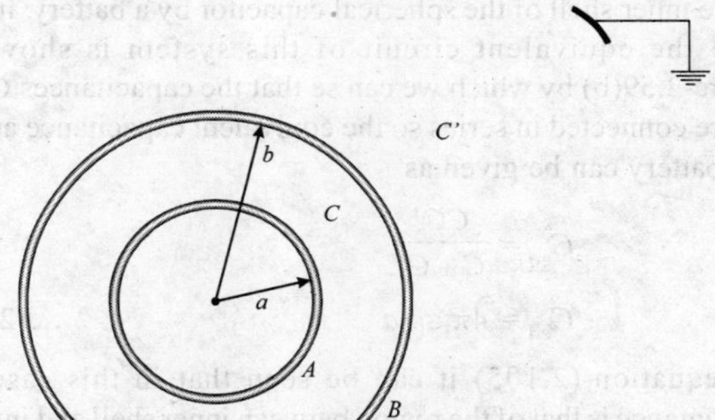

Figure 2.57

Above system of spherical shells can be used in electrical circuits in four different ways along with earth connections. These cases we will discuss one by one.

Case-I : When Inner Shell is Earthed and Charge is Supplied to Outer Shell by a Battery

Figure-58(a) shows the situation in which charge is supplied to the outer shell of the spherical capacitor by a battery. In this case the equivalent circuit of this system is shown in figure-58(b) by which we can se that the capacitances C and C' are connected in parallel so the equivalent capacitance across the battery can be given as

$$C_{eq} = C + C'$$

$$\Rightarrow \quad C_{eq} = \frac{4\pi\epsilon_0 ab}{b-a} + 4\pi\epsilon_0 b \quad \text{...(2.104)}$$

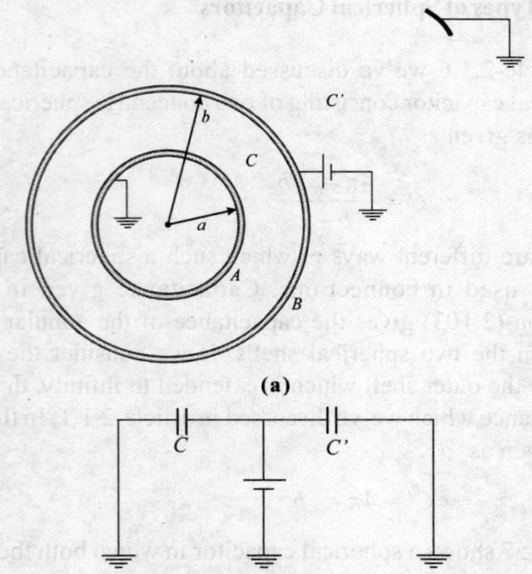

(a)

(b)

Figure 2.58

Case-II : When Outer Shell is left open and Charge is Supplied to Inner Shell by a Battery

Figure-2.59(a) shows the situation in which charge is supplied to the inner shell of the spherical capacitor by a battery. In this case the equivalent circuit of this system is shown in figure-2.59(b) by which we can se that the capacitances C and C' are connected in series so the equivalent capacitance across the battery can be given as

$$C_{eq} = \frac{CC'}{C+C'}$$

$$\Rightarrow \qquad C_{eq} = 4\pi \epsilon_0 a \qquad \ldots(2.105)$$

By equation-(2.105) it can be seen that in this case the capacitance is that of the region between inner shell and infinity so above value can directly be written as the capacitance of a sphere of radius a.

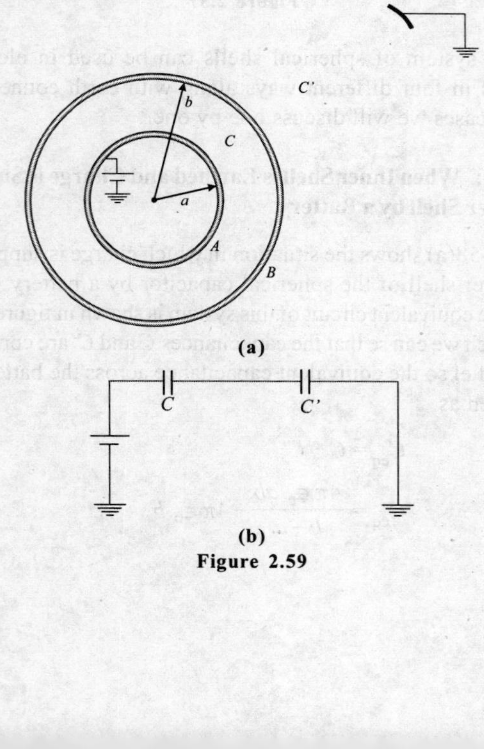

(a)

(b)

Figure 2.59

Case-III : When Outer Shell is Earthed and Charge is Supplied to Inner Shell by a Battery

Figure-2.60(a) shows the situation in which charge is supplied to the inner shell of the spherical capacitor by a battery. In this case the equivalent circuit of this system is shown in figure-2.60(b) by which we can se that the capacitances C' is short circuited as outer shell is earthed so only capacitance C is considered to be connected across the battery so equivalent capacitance in this case can be given as

$$C_{eq} = C$$

$$\Rightarrow \qquad C_{eq} = \frac{4\pi \epsilon_0 ab}{b-a} \qquad \ldots(2.106)$$

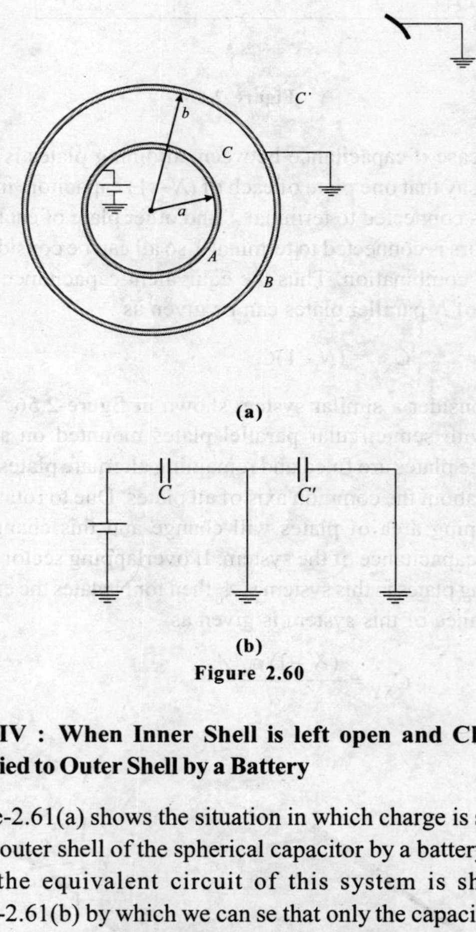

(a)

(b)

Figure 2.60

Case-IV : When Inner Shell is left open and Charge is Supplied to Outer Shell by a Battery

Figure-2.61(a) shows the situation in which charge is supplied to the outer shell of the spherical capacitor by a battery. In this case the equivalent circuit of this system is shown in figure-2.61(b) by which we can se that only the capacitance C' is considered to be connected across the battery as inner shell is not connected anywhere so no charge will appear on the capacitor C thus the equivalent capacitance across battery can be given as

$$C_{eq} = C'$$

$$\Rightarrow \qquad C_{eq} = 4\pi \epsilon_0 b \qquad \ldots(2.107)$$

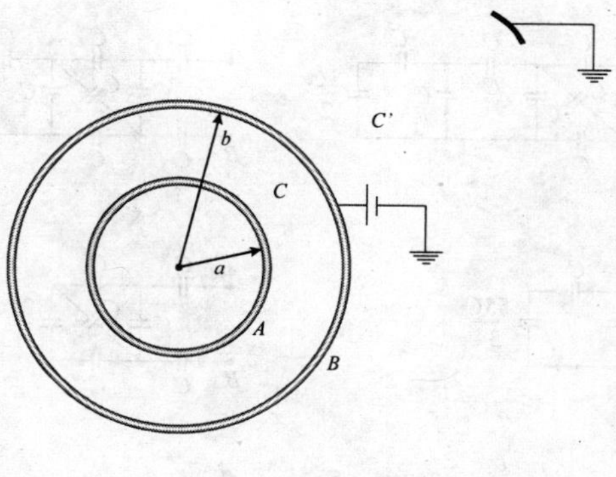

(a)

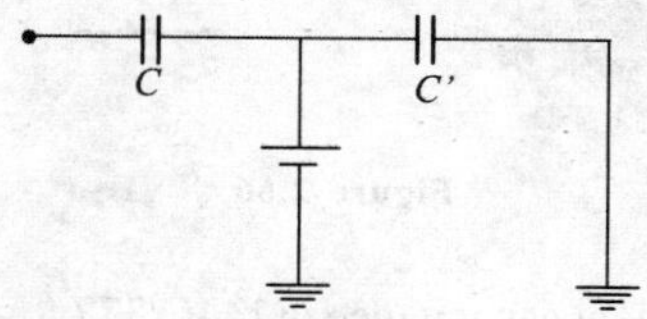

(b)

Figure 2.61

Illustrative Example 2.12

Find the capacitance C in the circuit shown in figure-2.62 if the equivalent capacitance between points A and B is 1 μF.

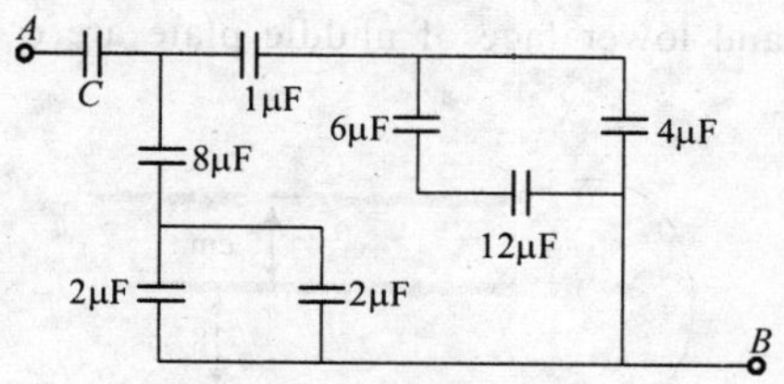

Figure 2.62

Solution

Each of the 2 μF capacitors are in parallel combination and 6 μF and 12 μF capacitors are in series combination so replacing these by their equivalent the circuit can be redrawn in figure-2.63 as

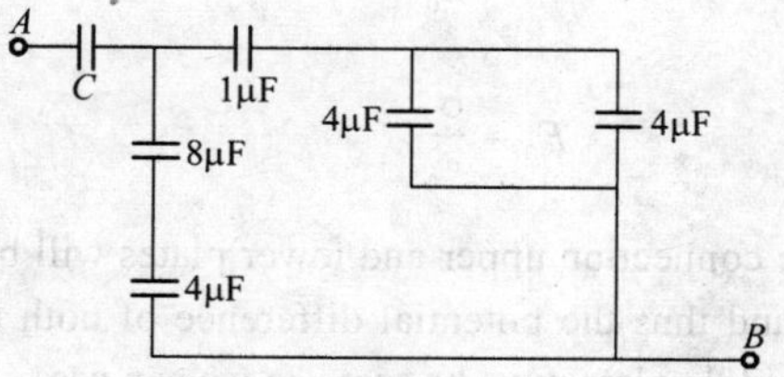

Figure 2.63

In above circuit in vertical branch 4 μF and 8 μF capacitors are in series and the two 4 μF capacitors are in parallel so replacing these by their equivalent again the respective circuit is drawn in figure-2.64(a) and further when we find the equivalent capacitance of all the capcitors except C it is 32/9 μF which is connected in series with C as shown in figure-2.64(b).

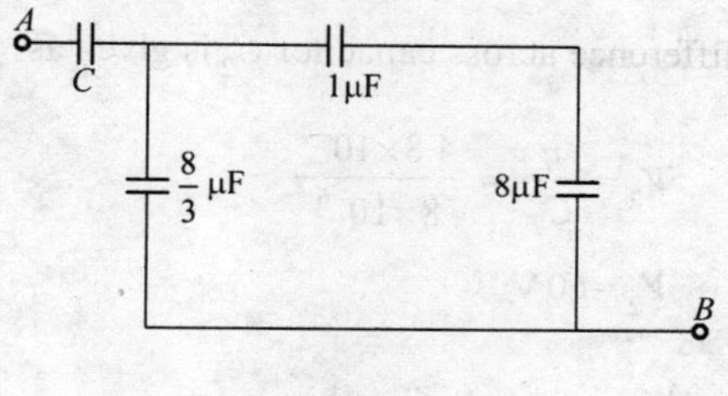

(b)

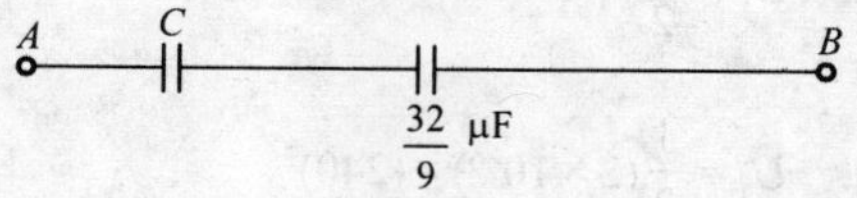

(c)

Figure 2.64

As the equivalent capacitance across terminals A and B is 1 μF, we can use

$$\frac{1}{1}=\frac{1}{C}+\frac{9}{32} \text{ or } \frac{1}{C}=\frac{23}{32}$$

$$\Rightarrow \qquad C=\frac{32}{23}\,\mu\text{F}$$

Illustrative Example 2.13

Two capacitors of capacitances C_1 = 2 μF and C_2 = 8 μF are connected in series and the resulting combination is connected across a 300 V battery. Calculate the charge, potential difference and energy stored in the capacitor separately.

Solution

Let C be the equivalent capacitance, then

$$\frac{1}{C}=\frac{1}{C_1}+\frac{1}{C_2}=\frac{1}{2}+\frac{1}{8}=\frac{5}{8}$$

$$\Rightarrow \qquad C=\frac{8}{5}=1.6\,\mu\text{F}$$

The corresponding charge on capcitors is given as

$$q=CV=(1.6\times10^{-6})\times300=4.8\times10^{-4}\,\text{C}$$

Potential difference across capacitor C_1 is given as

$$V_1 = \frac{q}{C_1} = \frac{4.8\times10^{-4}}{2\times10^{-6}}$$

$$\Rightarrow \quad V_1 = 240\,\text{V}$$

Potential difference across capacitor C_2 is given as

$$V_2 = \frac{q}{C_2} = \frac{4.8\times10^{-4}}{8\times10^{-6}}$$

$$\Rightarrow \quad V_2 = 60\,\text{V}$$

Energy stored in capacitor C_1 is given as

$$U_1 = \frac{1}{2}C_1V_1^2$$

$$\Rightarrow \quad U_1 = \frac{1}{2}(2\times10^{-6})\times(240)^2$$

$$\Rightarrow \quad U_1 = 5.76\times10^{-2}\,\text{J}$$

Energy stored in capacitor C_2 is given as

$$U_2 = \frac{1}{2}C_2V_2^2$$

$$\Rightarrow \quad U_2 = \frac{1}{2}\times(8\times10^{-6})(60)^2$$

$$\Rightarrow \quad U_2 = 1.44\times10^{-2}\,\text{J}$$

Illustrative Example 2.14

Find the equivalent capacitance of given network of capacitors between A and B. Each capacitor has capacitance $C = 1$ μF.

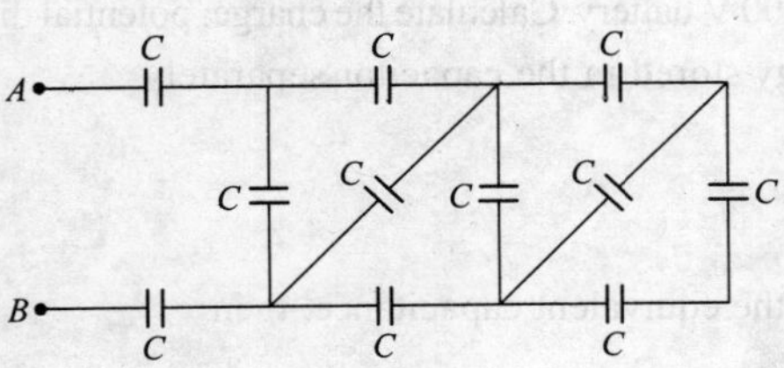

Figure 2.65

Solution

If we reduce the circuit from the right side of circuit by combining capacitors in series and parallel then sequential reduction in circuit is shown in figure-2.66

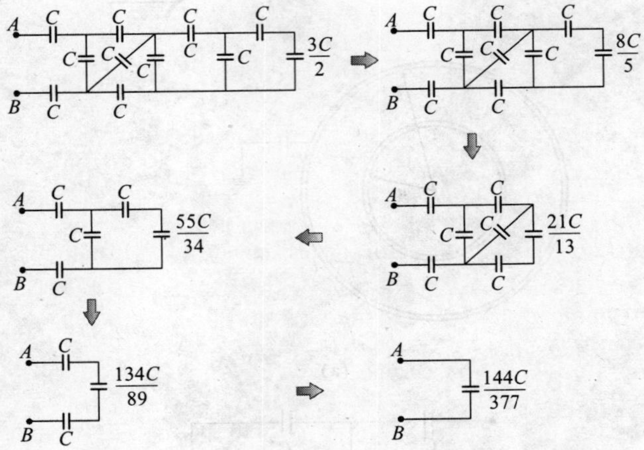

Figure 2.66

Thus the equivalent capacitance is 144C/377.

Illustrative Example 2.15

Three conducting plates are placed parallel to one another as shown in the figure-2.67. The outer plates are neutral and connected by a conducting wire. The inner plate is isolated and carries a total charge amounting to 10 μC. The charge densities on upper and lower face of middle plate are σ_1 and σ_2. Find $5\sigma_1/\sigma_2$.

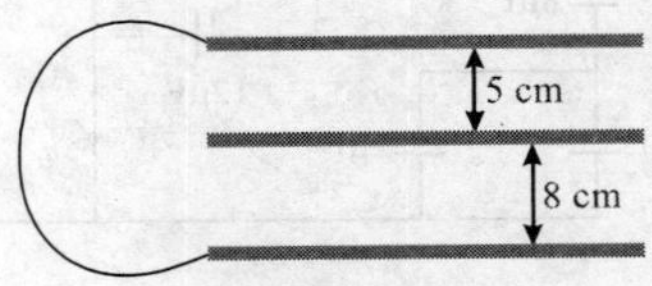

Figure 2.67

Solution

The electric field between the upper plates E_1 and between lower plates E_2 are given as

$$E_1 = \frac{\sigma_1}{\epsilon_0}$$

and

$$E_2 = \frac{\sigma_2}{\epsilon_0}$$

Due to the connection upper and lower plates will be at same potential and thus the potential difference of both the plates with the middle plate must be same so we can use

$$V_{12} = V_{23}$$

$$\Rightarrow \quad \frac{\sigma_1}{\epsilon_0} \times 5 = \frac{\sigma_2}{\epsilon_0} \times 8$$

$$\Rightarrow \quad \frac{5\sigma_1}{\sigma_2} = 8$$

Illustrative Example 2.16

Figure-2.68 shows four parallel plates kept at equal separation forming three parallel plate capacitors. The capacitance between two adjoining plates is C. Find out equivalent capacitance between A and B.

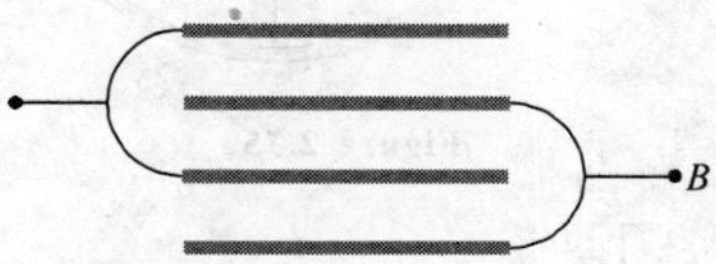

Figure 2.68

Solution

In this situation we can see that alternative plates are connected together with terminals A and B which we have discussed in article-2.3.7 that all such capacitors are considered in parallel combination thus equivalent capacitance across A and B terminals is given as

$$C_{eq} = C_1 + C_2 + C_3 = 3\,C$$

Illustrative Example 2.17

Two circular plates A and B of a parallel plate air capacitor have a diameter of 0.1 m and are 2×10^{-3} m apart. The plates C and D, of a similar capacitor have a diameter of 0.12 m and are 3×10^{-3} m apart. Plate A is earthed and plates B and D are connected together as shown in figure-2.69. Plate C is connected to the positive pole of a 120 V battery whose negative terminal is earthed. Calculate

(a) the combined capacitance of the arrangement and

(b) the energy stored in it.

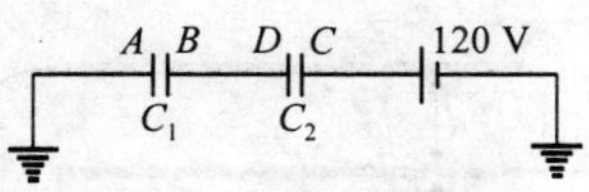

Figure 2.69

Solution

In the circuit shown in figure-2.69, the two earthed terminals can be joined together and circuit can be redrawn as shown in figure-2.70.

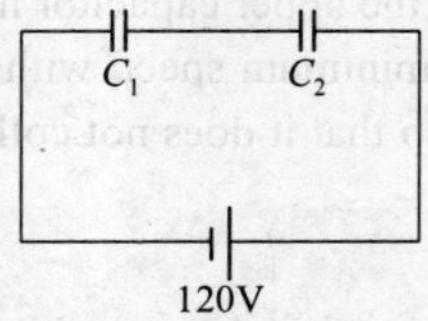

Figure 2.70

Thus the two capacitors can be considered in series across the 120V battery. The capacitances of the two parallel plate capacitors are given as

$$C_1 = \frac{\epsilon_0 A_1}{d_1} = \frac{8.85 \times 10^{-12} \times 3.14 \times (0.05)^2}{2 \times 10^{-3}} = \frac{1}{288 \times 10^8} F$$

$$\text{and } C_2 = \frac{\epsilon_0 A_2}{d_2} = \frac{8.85 \times 10^{-12} \times 3.14 \times (0.06)^2}{3 \times 10^{-3}} = \frac{1}{300 \times 10^8} F$$

(a) The equivalent capacitance is given as

$$C = \frac{C_1 C_2}{C_1 + C_2} = 17\text{ pF}$$

(b) The energy stored in capacitors is given as

$$U = \frac{1}{2} CV^2 = \frac{1}{2} \times (17 \times 10^{-12}) \times 120^2$$

$$\Rightarrow \quad U = 1.224 \times 10^{-7}\text{ J}$$

Web Reference at www.physicsgalaxy.com

Age Group - Grade 11 & 12 | Age 17-19 Years

Section - ELECTROSTATICS

Topic - Capacitance

Module Number - 17 to 20

Practice Exercise 2.2

(i) Find equivalent capacitance between points P and Q in the circuit shown in figure-2.71.

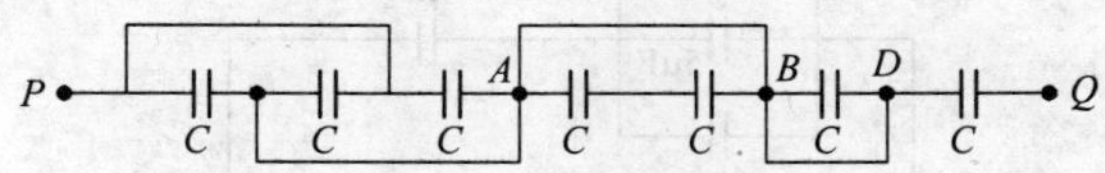

Figure 2.71

[$\frac{3C}{4}$]

(ii) The two capacitors C_1 and C_2 are made of square plates of edge length l. The separation between the plates of capacitors are d_1 and d_2 as shown in figure-2.72. A potential difference V is applied between the points a and b. An electron is projected between the plates of the upper capacitor midway between the two plates. Find the minimum speed with which the electron should be projected so that it does not collide with any plate.

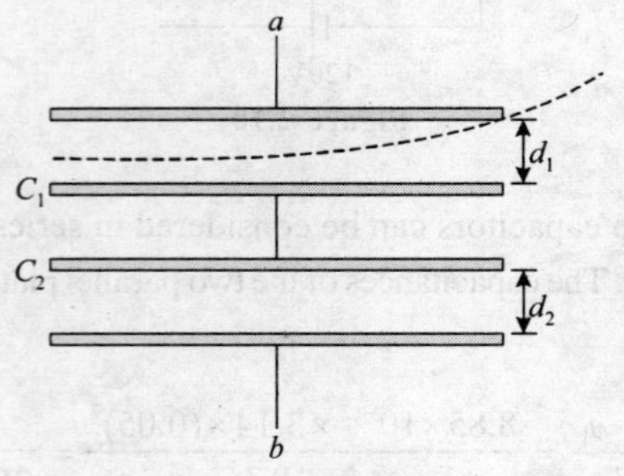

Figure 2.72

$\left[\left[\dfrac{eVl^2}{md_1(d_1+d_2)}\right]^{1/2}\right]$

(iii) Find the amount by which the total energy stored in the capacitor will increase in the circuit shown in the figure-2.73 after switch K is closed. Consider all capacitors are of capacitance 3 μF and battery voltage is 10 V.

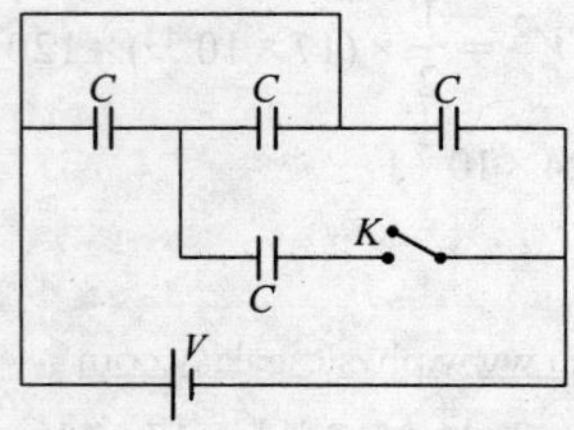

Figure 2.73

[100 μJ]

(iv) (a) In the circuit shown in figure-2.74 calculate the equivalent capacitance between terminals A and B ? (b) If the charge on the 5 μF capacitor is 120 μC, what is the potential difference between points A and C?

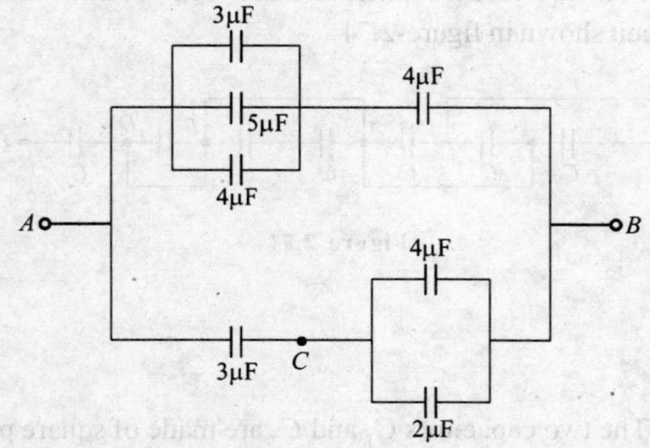

Figure 2.74

[(a) 5 μF, (b) 64 V]

(v) Three concentric thin spherical shells are of radii a, b, c $(a<b<c)$. The first and third shells are connected by a fine wire through a small hole in the second and the second is connected to earth through a small hole in the third as shown in figure-2.75. Find the capacitance of this system.

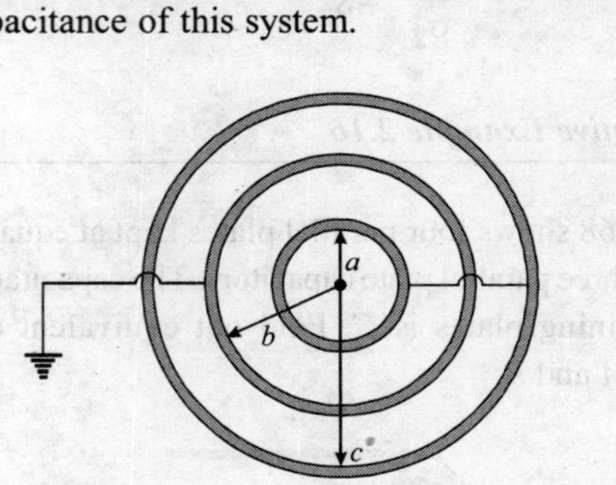

Figure 2.75

$\left[4\pi\epsilon_0\left[\dfrac{ab}{b-a}+\dfrac{c^2}{c-b}\right]\right]$

(vi) Three initially uncharged capacitors are connected in series with a battery of emf 30 V in the circuit shown in figure-2.76

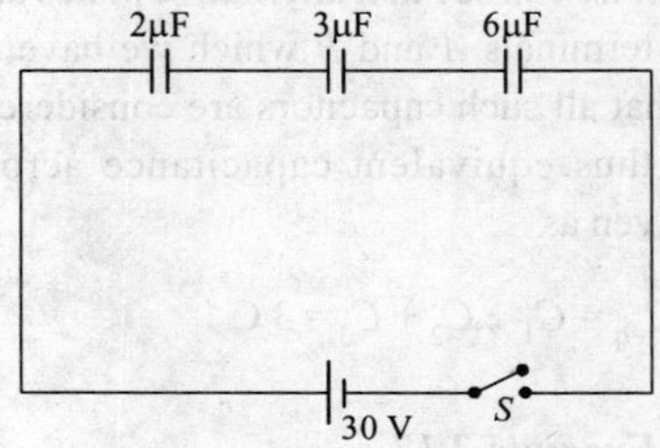

Figure 2.76

Calculate the following parameters for this circuit

(a) Charge flow through the battery

(b) Potential energy in 3μF capacitor

(c) Total energy in all capacitors

(d) Heat produced in the circuit after switch is closed

[(a) 30μC, (b) 150μJ, (c) 450 μJ, (d) 450 μJ]

(vii) In figure-2.77 find out equivalent capacitance between X and Y. Each plate is of area A.

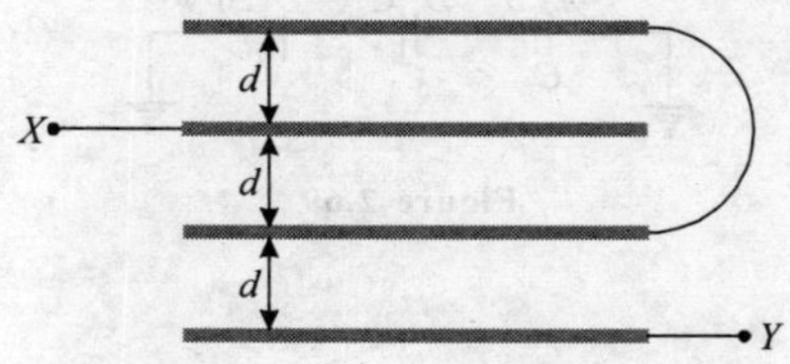

Figure 2.77

$\left[\dfrac{2\epsilon_0 A}{3d}\right]$

(viii) In figure-2.78 all the capacitors of circuit have a capacitance of 6.0 μF, and all the batteries have an emf 10 V. What is the charge on capacitor C ?

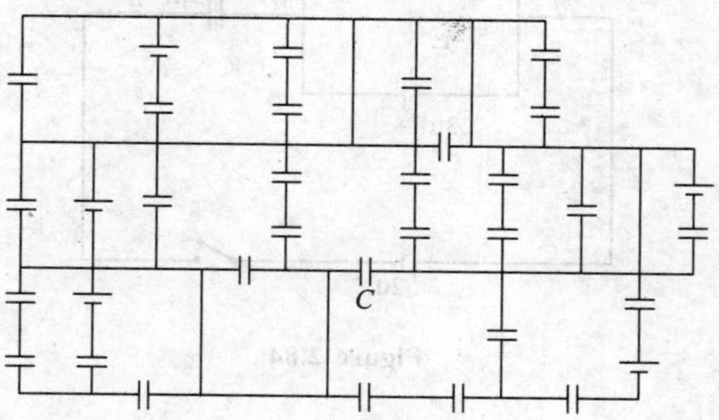

Figure 2.78

[60 μC]

(ix) Figure-2.79 shows five large parallel plates kept at equal separation d and each of plate area A with some wire connections. Find out equivalent capacitance between terminals X and Y.

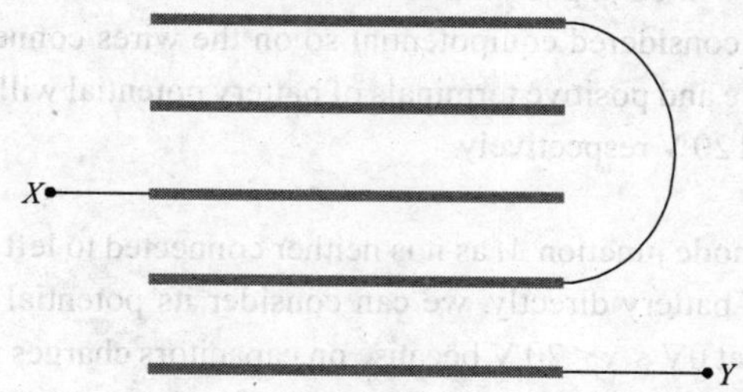

Figure 2.79

$[\frac{3\epsilon_0 A}{5d}]$

(x) X and Y are two parallel plate capacitors having the same area of plates and same separation between the plates. X has air between the plates and Y contains a dielectric medium $\varepsilon_r = 5$.

(a) Calculate the potential difference between the plates of X and Y.

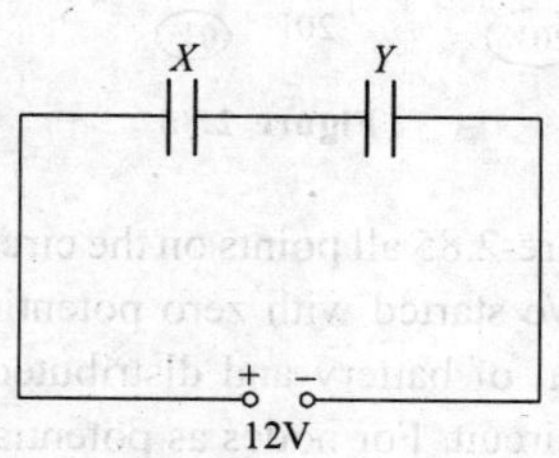

Figure 2.80

(b) What is the ratio of electrostatic energy stored in X and Y?

[(a) 10V, 2V; (b) 5]

2.4 *Nodal Analysis of Capacitive Circuits*

In previous articles we've analyzed combinations of capacitors and basic circuits containing capacitors. Most of basic circuits on capacitor groups can be handled by using the concept of series and parallel combination. As discussed earlier also that there are some cases in which capacitors are connected in such combinations which are neither series nor parallel called mixed combinations. Such cases can be easily handled by a specific method of solving capacitive circuits called '*Nodal Analysis*'. In article-2.3.3 while studying series combination of capacitors we discussed what is a '*Node*' in capacitive circuit. It is an isolated part of circuit at which two or more plates of capacitors are connected. Figure-2.81 shows a capacitive circuit in which C_1 and C_2 are connected in parallel and this group is connected in series with C_3 and connected across a battery of voltage V. In this circuit also a node is shown at junction M by closed dotted line. Before proceeding to the steps of nodal analysis it is essential to understand how to identify nodes of circuit.

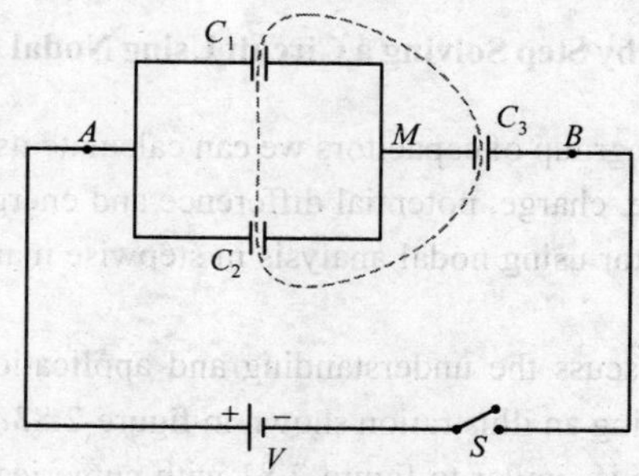

Figure 2.81

Another capacitive circuit is shown in figure-2.82 in which two nodes are shown at junctions M and N. Always remember that nodes are parts of circuit at a junction of wires which are connected to two or more plates of capacitors of circuit.

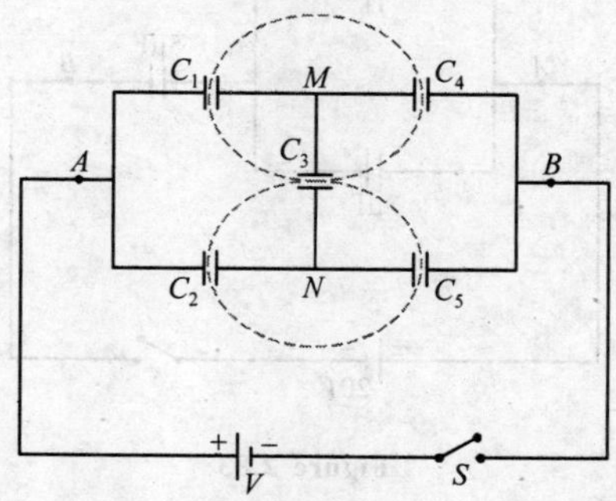

Figure 2.82

For any given circuit of capacitors if you are able to identify nodes of circuit then next step in solving the circuit is potential distribution and writing nodal equations which we will study step by step in next articles.

2.4.1 Solving Capacitive Circuits

Whenever we switch on a capacitive circuit then charges flow through the connected battery (or batteries) in the circuit and connected capacitors attain charges until steady state is arrived when charge flow stops and capacitors of circuit are said to be fully charged in the given circuit.

Analyzing the circuit for calculation of steady state charges on various capacitors of circuit, potential difference across any points of circuit, work done by batteries in charging the capacitors and energy stored in capacitors, is called '*Solving a Circuit*'. In previous article section-2.3 and Illustrations-12 to 17 we solved some circuits by using the method of series and parallel combinations. Nodal analysis is a better and fast technique to solve capacitive circuits when circuits combinations are complex. Simple circuits you can always solve by using series and parallel method.

2.4.2 Step by Step Solving a Circuit Using Nodal Analysis

For a given group of capacitors we can calculate its equivalent capacitance, charge, potential difference and energy stored in any capacitor using nodal analysis in stepwise manner.

We will discuss the understanding and application of nodal analysis using an illustration shown in figure-2.83. The circuit shown here is similar to figure-2.81 with numerical values. In this circuit we will calculate the equivalent capacitance of the circuit across terminals *AB* and steady state charge on each capacitor after closing the switch. There are three steps to be followed for solving this circuit using nodal analysis.

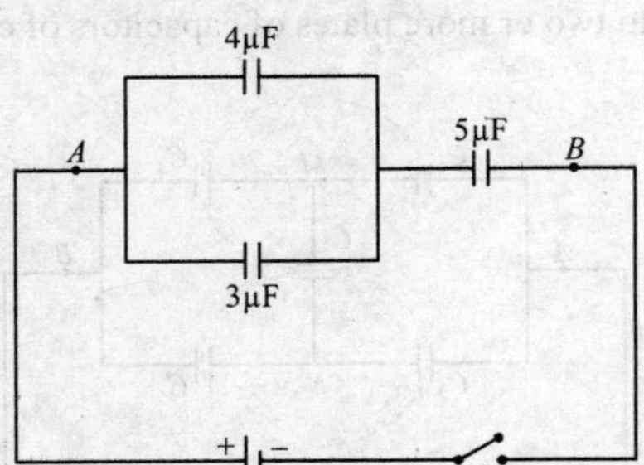

Figure 2.83

Step-I of Nodal Analysis : *Identifying the Nodes of Circuit*

As already explained in previous article about identifying the nodes of circuit, in this case we can mark the junction *M* as a node in this circuit as shown in figure-2.84.

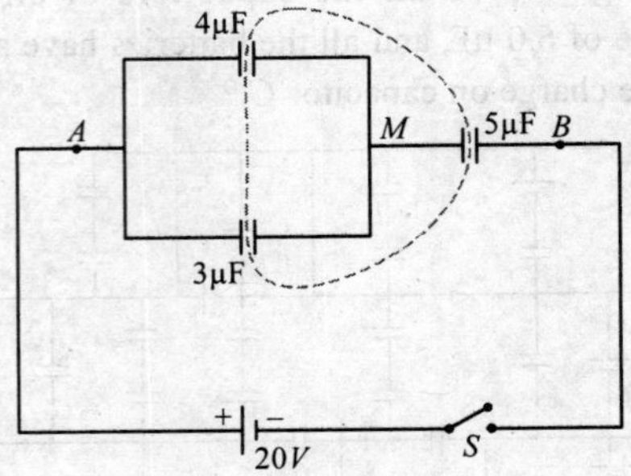

Figure 2.84

Step-II of Nodal Analysis : *Distribution of Potential in Circuit*

To proceed further we need to distribute potential at every point in the circuit. We start with the battery terminals and first consider the potential at negative terminal of the battery as zero. Battery used here is of 20 V thus positive terminal of battery will be at potential 20 V. All metallic connecting wires can be considered equipotential so on the wires connected to negative and positive terminals of battery potential will remain 0 *V* and 20 V respectively.

At the node junction *M* as it is neither connected to left or right side of battery directly, we can consider its potential to be x such that $0\text{V} < x < 20\text{ V}$ because on capacitors charges polarity is as shown in figure-2.85 and negative plate of capacitor is always at lower potential then its positive plate.

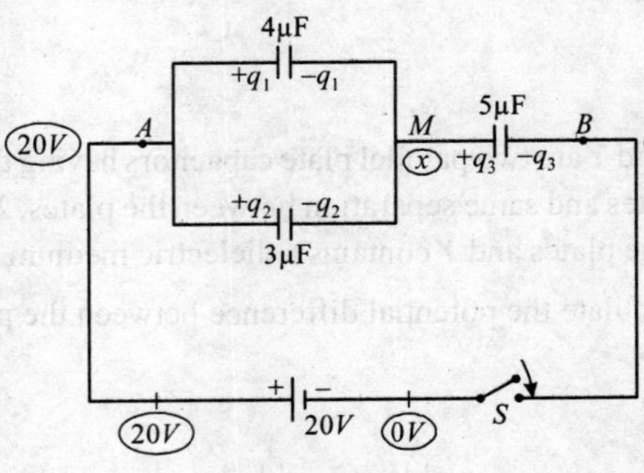

Figure 2.85

As shown in figure-2.85 all points on the circuit some potential is considered. We started with zero potential reference from negative terminal of battery and distributed potentials at all other points of circuit. For nodes as potential is unknown, we give variable potentials x, y, z.... if more than one nodes are there in a circuit.

Step-III of Nodal Analysis : *Writing Nodal Equations*

As we discussed that nodes are isolated parts of circuit so net charge on all the plates of capacitors connected to a node of circuit must be zero. On a node charges can only be induced so if capacitors are initially uncharged, net charge on a node must remain zero. So for every node of circuit we can write equation for conservation of charge as for circuit shown in figure-2.84 we can write

$$q_3 - q_1 - q_2 = 0 \qquad \text{...(2.108)}$$

As in steady state charge on a capacitor is given as $q = CV$ where V is the potential difference across the capacitor plates we can use the charge on the three capacitors as

$$q_1 = 4 \times (20 - x)\ \mu\text{C} \qquad \text{...(2.109)}$$

$$q_2 = 3 \times (20 - x)\ \mu\text{C} \qquad \text{...(2.110)}$$

and $$q_3 = 5 \times x\ \mu\text{C} \qquad \text{...(2.111)}$$

Substituting the values of charges in equation-(2.109), we get

$$5x - 4(20 - x) - 3(20 - x) = 0 \qquad \text{...(2.112)}$$

$$\Rightarrow \qquad 12x = 140$$

$$\Rightarrow \qquad x = \frac{140}{12} = \frac{35}{3}\ \text{V} \qquad \text{...(2.113)}$$

Equation-(2.112) above is called '*Nodal Equation*' used to determine the unknown potentials considered in step-II of nodal analysis. If in some circuit there are two nodes then there will be two variable potentials considered x and y in step-II and then we write two nodal equations for the two variables. Next illustration will explain such a circuit with more variables. Nodal equations are linear equations in terms of unknown potentials and solving nodal equations we can determine the values of unknown potentials considered like here we calculated the value of x given in equation-(2.113).

Once the unknown potential is obtained, we can calculate charges on all the capacitors of the circuit by using equations-(2.109), (2.110) and (2.111) which are given as

$$q_1 = 4 \times \left(20 - \frac{35}{3}\right) = \frac{100}{3}\ \mu\text{C}$$

$$q_2 = 3 \times \left(20 - \frac{35}{3}\right) = 25\ \mu\text{C}$$

and $$q_3 = 5 \times \frac{35}{3} = \frac{175}{3}\ \mu\text{C}$$

To find the equivalent capacitance of this circuit across terminals A and B we can use equation-(2.84). On closing the switch battery transfers a charge Δq_0 from right plate of 5 μF and places on the left pates of 3 μF and 4 μF capacitors thus we can write the charge flown through battery in this case is given as

$$\Delta q_0 = |q_1 + q_2| = |q_3| = \frac{175}{3}\ \mu\text{C} \qquad \text{...(2.114)}$$

Thus equivalent capacitance in this case can be given as

$$C_{eq} = \frac{\Delta q_0}{V_{battery}} = \frac{\left(\frac{175}{3}\right)}{20} = \frac{35}{12}\ \mu\text{F} \qquad \text{...(2.115)}$$

Above result of equivalent capacitance can be verified directly by using the series and parallel combination method. In the given circuit we can see the 4 μF and 3 μF capacitors are connected in parallel combination thus their equivalent can be given by sum of these two i.e. 7 μF which is connected in series with 5 μF. For two capacitors C_1 and C_2 is given as $C_1C_2/(C_1 + C_2)$ thus the overall equivalent capacitance of this circuit is given as

$$C_{eq} = \frac{7 \times 5}{7 + 5} = \frac{35}{12}\ \mu\text{F} \qquad \text{...(2.116)}$$

We can see that above result is same which is obtained in equation-(2.115) but both are entirely different methods. In this case the method of series and parallel combination seems more easier and fast, thats true but in many cases of mixed combination and complex circuits method of series and parallel combination may not work which we will analyze and discuss in upcoming illustrations.

One important point to be noted in above analysis is that the equivalent capacitance of circuit does not depend on the potential difference applied across it like if we repeat the analysis by changing the battery voltage to 50 V or 100 V instead of 20 V then also the result will remain same. So in different cases if we need to solve a capacitive circuit for its equivalent capacitance then we can connect a 100 V battery across its terminals and solve by using nodal analysis. We use 100 V to simplify the calculations otherwise any battery can be used for this purpose.

2.4.3 Alternative Way of Writing Nodal Equations

In previous article we've discussed stepwise analysis of solving a capacitive circuit using nodal analysis. In nodal analysis in last step we write nodal equations to find the unknown potentials at nodes of circuit which are the equation of conservation of charge at all the plates connected to a node junction like the equation-(2.109) we've written for the circuit shown in figure-2.84. Then we substituted the value of charges in nodal equation in terms of the unknown potential x and obtained equation-(2.112).

Equation-(2.112) can be written directly just after step-II as we distribute potentials in circuit. In figure-2.44 to add the charges on the three plates of capacitor we can directly write the plate charge as product of capacitance and difference of potential of that plate from the other plate such as

$$4(x - 20) + 3(x - 20) + 5x = 0 \qquad \text{...(2.117)}$$

In above equation-(2.117) charge on plate of 4 μF capacitor connected to M is $4(x - 20)$ μC and we don't need to bother about the sign of this charge as subtracting other plate potential from the potential of this plate will take care of the sign of charge on this plate. Similarly the charge on the plate of 3 μF capacitor connected to M is $3(x-20)$ μC and that on the plate of 5 μF capacitor connected to M is $5(x - 0)$ μC. Thus we can directly sum up these charges and equate to zero as given in equation-(2.117) which is same as equation-(2.112). This method of writing nodal equation saves time as we don't need to bother about the sign of charges on plates connected to a specific node junction.

Illustrative Example 2.18

Find the potential difference between points M and N of the circuit shown in figure-2.86. The battery voltage is equal to ξ and the capacitance ratio C_2/C_1 is equal to η.

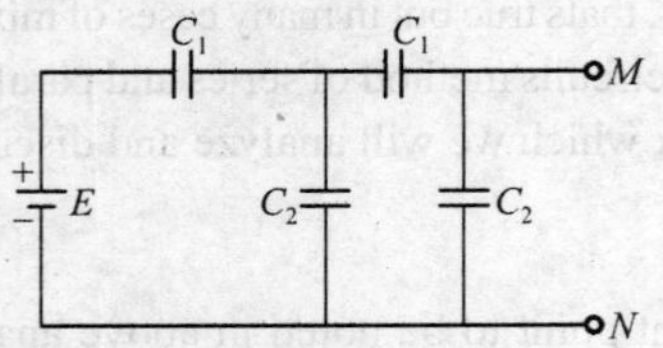

Figure 2.86

Solution

First we will calculate the equivalent capacitance of this circuit across the battery terminals. Right most capacitors C_1 and C_2 are connected in series so their equivalent capacitance is given as

$$C' = \frac{C_1C_2}{C_1+C_2}$$

$$\Rightarrow \quad C' = \frac{C_1 \cdot \eta C_1}{C_1+\eta C_1} = \frac{\eta C_1}{1+\eta}$$

Now C' is connected in parallel to the capacitor C_2 so we have their equivalent capacitance given as

$$C'' = C' + C_2 = \frac{\eta C_1}{1+\eta} + \eta\, C_1 = \frac{(\eta^2+2\eta)C_1}{1+\eta} \quad \ldots (2.118)$$

Further C'' and capacitor C_1 are in series so their equivalent capacitance C is given by

$$\frac{1}{C} = \frac{1}{C_1} + \frac{1}{C''}$$

$$\Rightarrow \quad \frac{1}{C} = \frac{1}{C_1} + \frac{(1+\eta)}{(\eta^2+2\eta)C_1}$$

$$\Rightarrow \quad \frac{1}{C} = \frac{(\eta^2+2\eta)+(1+\eta)}{(\eta^2+2\eta)C_1}$$

$$\Rightarrow \quad C = \frac{(\eta^2+2\eta)C_1}{\eta^2+3\eta+1} \quad \ldots (2.119)$$

The total charge supplied by the battery in charging the capacitors of the circuit is given as

$$q = CE = \frac{(\eta^2+2\eta)C_1E}{\eta^2+3\eta+1} \quad \ldots (2.120)$$

The voltage V across equivalent capacitor C'' is given by

$$V = \frac{q}{C''} = \frac{(\eta^2+2\eta)C_1E}{\eta^2+3\eta+1} \times \frac{(1+\eta)}{(\eta^2+2\eta)C_1}$$

$$V = \frac{(1+\eta)E}{\eta^2+3\eta+1} \quad \ldots (2.121)$$

The voltage V will be across C_2 and equivalent capacitor C' is now given as

$$q' = C'\,V = \left(\frac{\eta C_1}{1+\eta}\right)\left[\frac{(1+\eta)E}{\eta^2+3\eta+1}\right]$$

$$\Rightarrow \quad q' = \frac{\eta C_1E}{\eta^2+3\eta+1} \quad \ldots (2.122)$$

The above charge in equation-(2.122) will be distributed across C_1 and C_2 which are connected in series. The potential difference across points M and N which is the potential difference across right most capacitor C_2, is given as

$$V = \frac{q'}{C_2} = \frac{q'}{\eta C_1} = \frac{1}{\eta C_1}\left[\frac{\eta C_1E}{\eta^2+3\eta+1}\right]$$

$$\Rightarrow \quad V = \frac{E}{\eta^2+3\eta+1} \quad \ldots (2.123)$$

Above question can also be solved using nodal analysis method. Students are advised to solve this using method of nodal analysis and verify the result obtained in equation-(2.123).

Illustrative Example 2.19

In the circuit shown in figure-2.87 four capacitors are connected to a battery. Determine the potential difference $V_M - V_N$ between points M and N of the circuit. Find the conditions under which it is equal to zero.

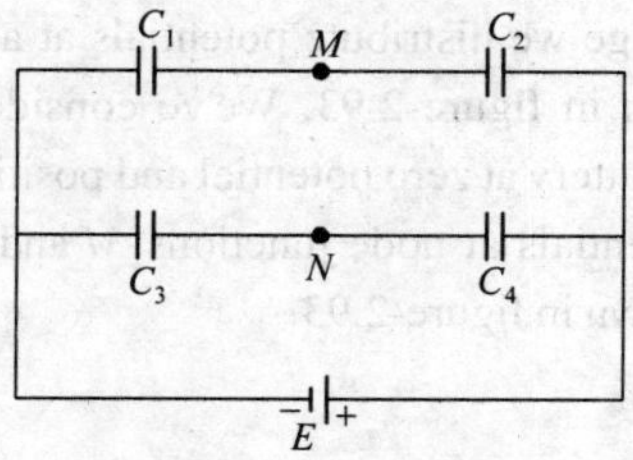

Figure 2.87

Solution

This circuit can be solved either by series and parallel analysis or by using nodal analysis. Here we will solve it using nodal analysis. As we can see in figure at junctions M and N there are two nodes in the circuit at which we can consider potentials to be x and y respectively. Figure-88 shows the potential distribution at different points of circuit.

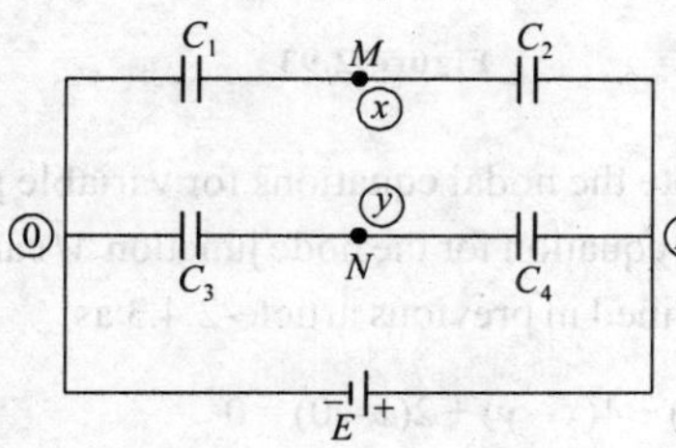

Figure 2.88

Now we can write the nodal equations for nodes M and N respectively which are written as

For node M, nodal equation is

$$C_1(x-0)+C_2(x-E)=0 \qquad \ldots(2.124)$$

Similarly for node N, nodal equation is

$$C_3(y-0)+C_4(y-E)=0 \qquad \ldots(2.125)$$

Solving equations-(2.124) and (2.125) we get the values of potentials at points M and N as

$$x=\frac{C_1E}{(C_1+C_2)}$$

$$y=\frac{C_3E}{(C_3+C_4)}$$

$$\Rightarrow \quad V_M-V_N=x-y=E\left[\frac{C_1}{(C_1+C_2)}-\frac{C_3}{(C_3+C_4)}\right]$$

$$\Rightarrow \quad V_M-V_N=E\left[\frac{C_1C_4-C_2C_3}{(C_1+C_2)(C_3+C_4)}\right] \qquad \ldots(2.126)$$

To obtain the condition under which equation-(2.126) becomes zero is given as

$$V_M-V_N=0$$

$$\Rightarrow \quad C_1C_4-C_2C_3=0$$

$$\Rightarrow \quad \frac{C_1}{C_2}=\frac{C_3}{C_4}$$

Above equation-(2.126) we obtained by using nodal analysis but students can verify the same result by using series and parallel method also. In upcoming articles we will discuss that above equation can be directly obtained by method of potential distribution.

 # Illustrative Example 2.20

In circuit shown in figure-2.89 calculate the potential difference between the points A and B and between the points B and C in the steady state.

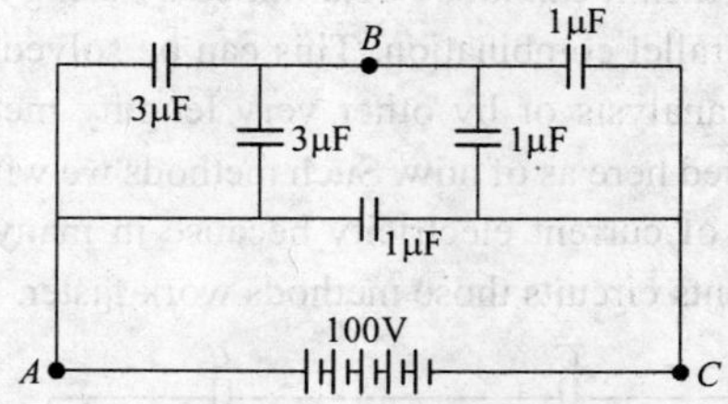

Figure 2.89

Solution

To apply nodal analysis in above circuit we distribute the potentials at different parts of circuit by considering zero reference at the negative terminal of the 100 V battery. This is shown in figure-2.90.

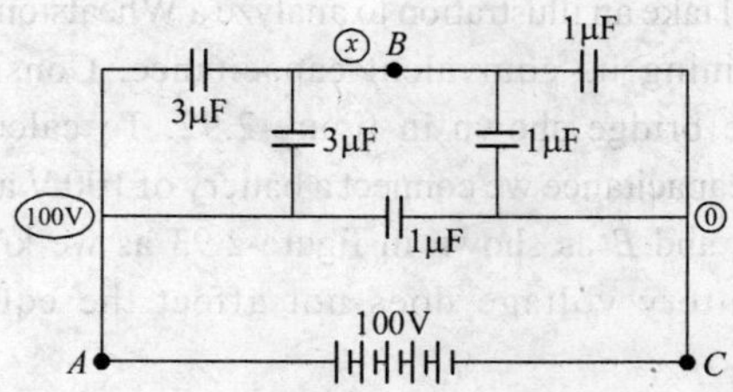

Figure 2.90

For the above node junction at point B, nodal equation is written as

$$1(x-0)+1(x-0)+3(x-100)+3(x-100)=0$$

$$\Rightarrow \quad 8x=600$$

$$\Rightarrow \quad x=75\text{ V}$$

As the potential of node B is known now, we can find the potential difference across points A and B and that across B and C, given as

$$V_{AB} = 100 - x = 100 - 75 = 25\text{ V}$$

and $$V_{BC} = x - 0 = 75 - 0 = 75\text{ V}$$

Here we can see that the required results are obtained in just two steps. For practice students are advised to solve the same circuit by using series and parallel method and see how lengthy it will be. However by using the method of potential distribution (we will study in upcoming articles) this question can be quickly solved.

2.4.4 Wheatstone Bridge and its Analysis

Figure-2.91 shows a specific combination of five capacitors in which no two capacitors are in series or in parallel connection. This specific connection is called a '*Wheatstone Bridge*'. If we wish to determine the equivalent capacitance of this combination of capacitors then it cannot be determined by using method of series and parallel combination. This can be solved either by using nodal analysis or by other very lengthy methods not being discussed here as of now. Such methods we will study in next chapter of current electricity because in many cases of electric currents circuits those methods work faster.

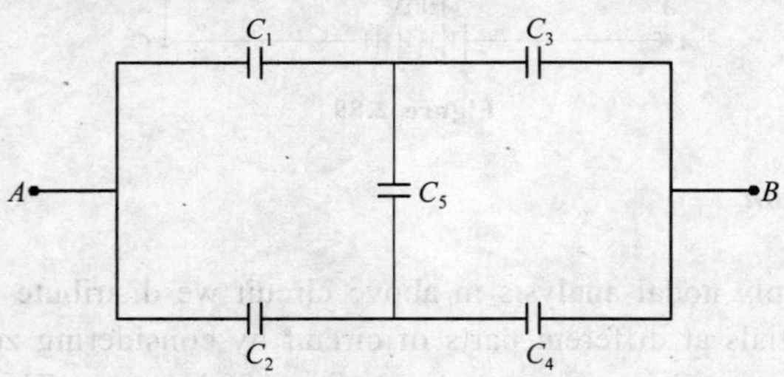

Figure 2.91

Next we will take an illustration to analyze a Wheatstone bridge for determining its equivalent capacitance. Consider the Wheatstone bridge shown in figure-2.92. To calculate its equivalent capacitance we connect a battery of 100 V across its terminals A and B as shown in figure-2.93 as we know that applied battery voltage does not affect the equivalent capacitance.

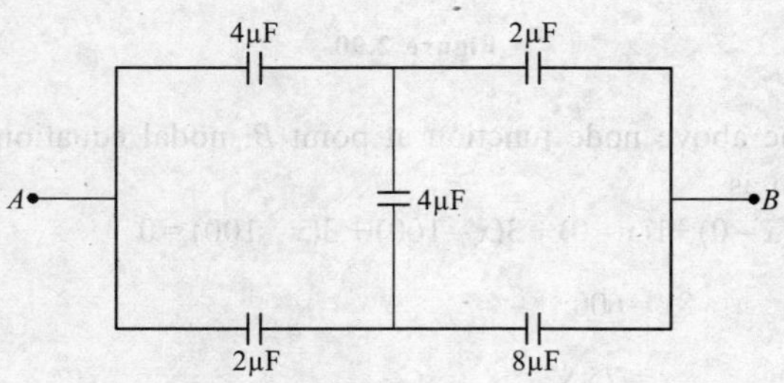

Figure 2.92

To apply nodal analysis for solving the circuit of this Wheatstone bridge we distribute potentials at all parts of the circuit as shown in figure-2.93. We've considered negative terminal of the battery at zero potential and positive terminal at 100 V with potentials at node junctions M and N at x and y respectively shown in figure-2.93.

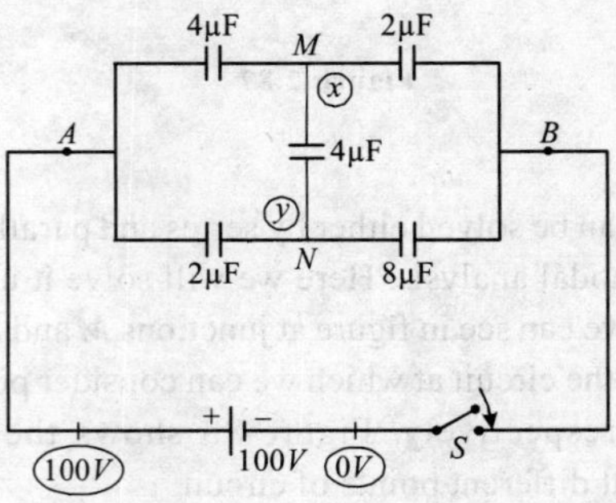

Figure 2.93

Now we can write the nodal equations for variable potentials x and y. The nodal equation for the node junction M can be written directly as explained in previous article-2.4.3 as

$$4(x - 100) + 4(x - y) + 2(x - 0) = 0 \qquad \ldots(2.127)$$

$$\Rightarrow \qquad 5x - 2y = 200 \qquad \ldots(2.128)$$

Similarly we can write the nodal equation for node junction N as

$$2(y - 100) + 4(y - x) + 8y = 0 \qquad \ldots(2.129)$$

$$\Rightarrow \qquad 7y - 2x = 100 \qquad \ldots(2.130)$$

Solving equations-(2.128) and (2.130) for variables x and y, we get

$$x = \frac{1600}{31}\, V$$

and $$y = \frac{900}{31}\, V$$

To determine equivalent capacitance across the terminals A and B we use equation-(2.86) which is given as

$$C_{eq} = \frac{\Delta q_0}{V}$$

Here Δq_0 is the charge flown through the battery in charging of the group of capacitors and V is the battery voltage. The charge flown through the battery is the sum of charges of capacitors connected to right terminal of battery of to the left terminal of the battery. Thus in above case this charge Δq_0 can be given as

$$\Delta q_0 = |2x + 8y| = |4(100 - x) + 2(100 - y)|$$

$$\Rightarrow \Delta q_0 = 2 \times \left(\frac{1600}{31}\right) + 8 \times \left(\frac{900}{31}\right) \mu C$$

$$\Rightarrow \Delta q_0 = \frac{10400}{31} \mu C$$

Thus equivalent capacitance of the Wheatstone bridge shown in figure-2.91 across terminals A and B is given as

$$C_{eq} = \frac{\left(\frac{10400}{31}\right)}{100} = \frac{104}{31} \mu F \qquad \ldots(2.131)$$

Equation-(2.131) gives the equivalent capacitance of the Wheatstone bridge which we have calculated using nodal analysis method. As already discussed that this cannot be calculated by using series and parallel method because in Wheatstone bridge capacitors are neither connected in series nor in parallel combination. There is some specific conditions for a Wheatstone bridge under which the circuit can be modified which will be discussed in next article.

2.4.5 Balancing Condition of Wheatstone Bridge

Figure-2.94 shows a Wheatstone bridge connected across a battery of voltage V. In this situation if we consider the potentials of different parts of circuit as shown in the figure and write nodal equations for node junctions M and N then these are given as

$$C_1(x - V) + C_5(x - y) + C_3(x - 0) = 0 \qquad \ldots(2.132)$$

and $$C_2(y - V) + C_5(y - x) + C_4(y - 0) = 0 \qquad \ldots(2.133)$$

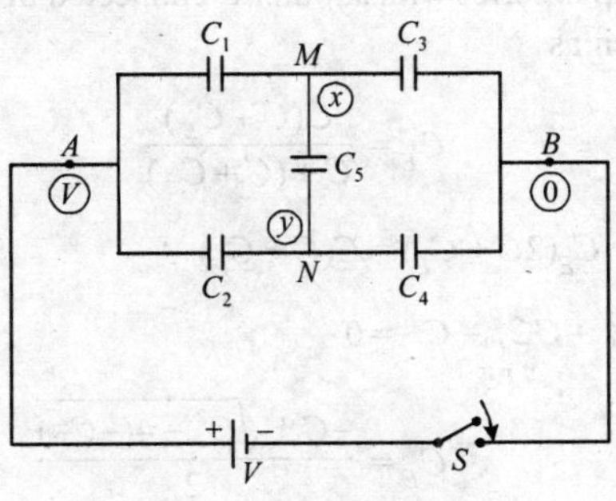

Figure 2.94

In above equations-(2.132) and (2.133) if we use $x = y$ then it gives

$$\frac{C_1}{C_2} = \frac{C_3}{C_4} \qquad \ldots(2.134)$$

From equation-(2.134) we can also say that if this ratio holds for a Wheatstone bridge then for any value of V the potential of the two junction nodes in the circuit will be equal. Thus if $x = y$ then capacitor C_5 will remain uncharged and unaffected in circuit so even if we remove this middle capacitor branch from circuit then also it will not affect the circuit. In that case figure-2.94 will reduce to the state shown in figure-2.95.

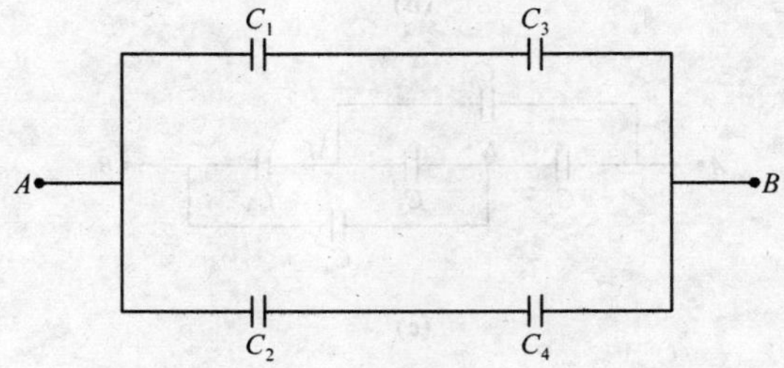

Figure 2.95

Now the equivalent capacitance of this circuit can be easily calculated by using series and parallel method. The Wheatstone bridge in which equation-(2.134) holds is called a '*Balanced Wheatstone Bridge*' and the ratio in equation-(2.1134) is called '*Balancing Condition*' of a Wheatstone bridge.

The equivalent capacitance of the balanced Wheatstone bridge after removing the middle branch as shown in figure-2.49 can be given as

$$C_{eq} = \frac{C_1C_3}{C_1 + C_3} + \frac{C_2C_4}{C_2 + C_4} \qquad \ldots(2.135)$$

2.4.6 Alternative Circuit Arrangements of Wheatstone Bridge

In previous articles we've discussed on solving a circuit of five capacitors connected in a specific fashion called Wheatstone bridge as shown in figure-2.91. The connections of capacitors in combination of Wheatstone bridge can be drawn in different ways and sometimes students get confused whether the given circuit is Wheatstone bridge is a Wheatstone bridge or not. Figure-2.96 shows different ways in which a Wheatstone bridge can be drawn as a part of capacitive circuit.

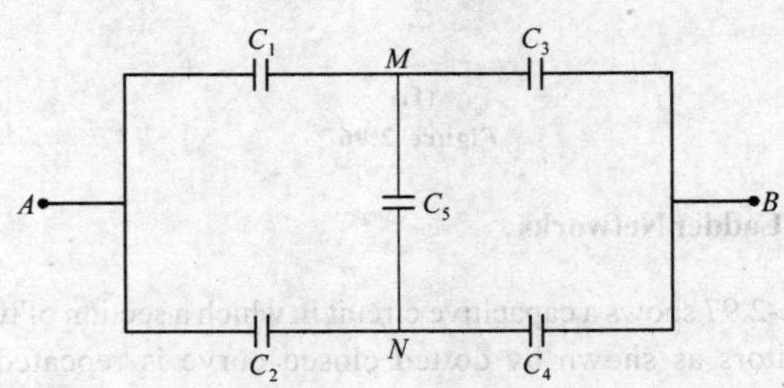

(a)

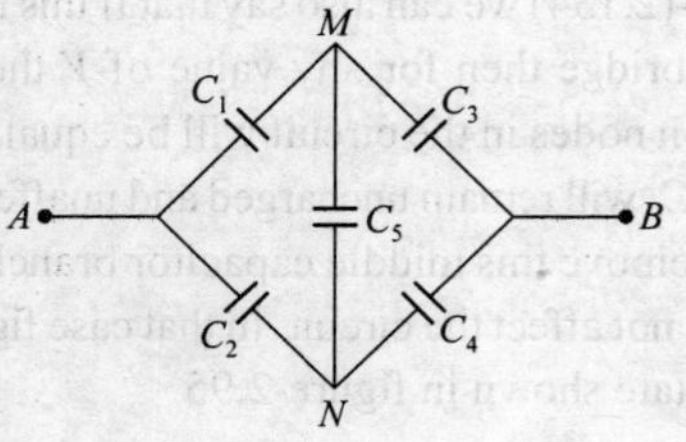

(b)

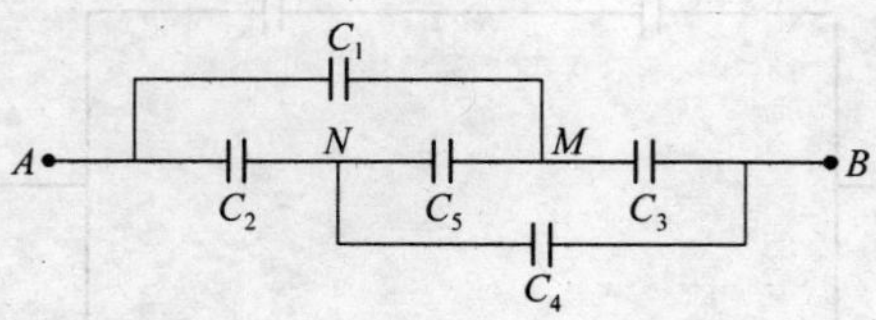

(c)

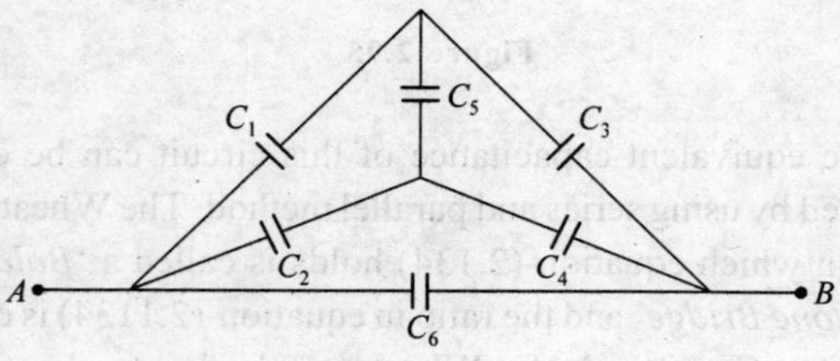

(d)

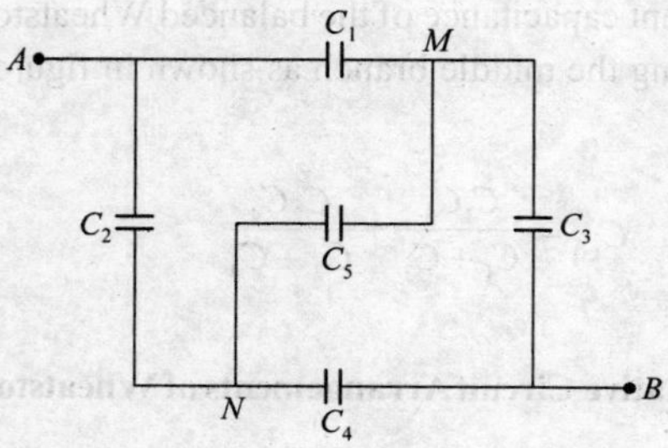

(e)

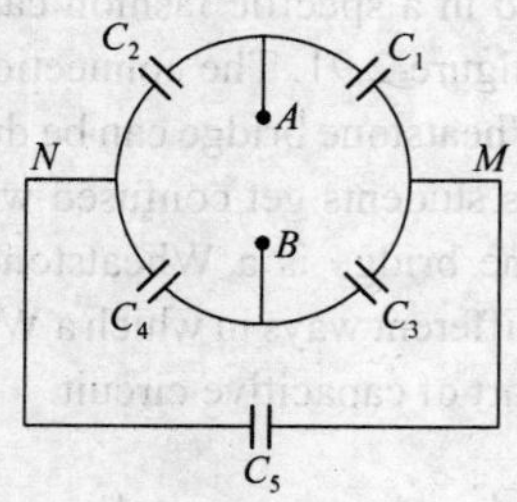

(f)

Figure 2.96

2.4.7 Ladder Networks

Figure-2.97 shows a capacitive circuit in which a section of two capacitors as shown by dotted closed curve is repeatedly connected infinitely. Such circuits are called '*Ladder Networks*' or '*Ladder Circuits*'.

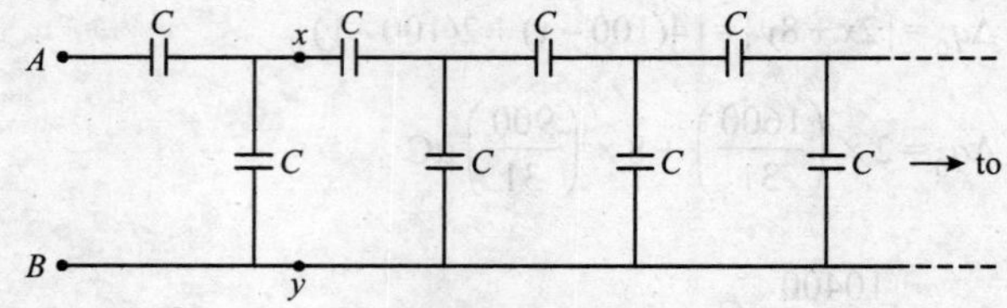

Figure 2.97

To solve such circuits for equivalent capacitance, we first consider that the equivalent capacitance of the circuit across terminals A and B in above figure is given as C_E then for infinite sections connected one after another if one section is removed then also the remaining capacitance of the circuit across terminals X and Y can also be considered as C_E as circuit across terminals X and Y as shown in figure-2.98(a) is identical to that shown in figure-2.96.

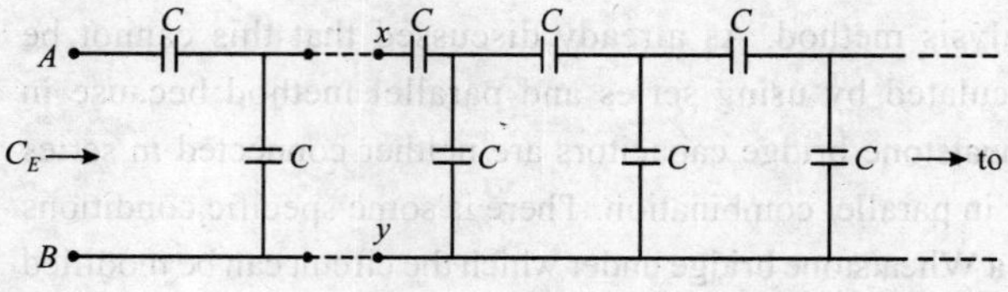

(a)

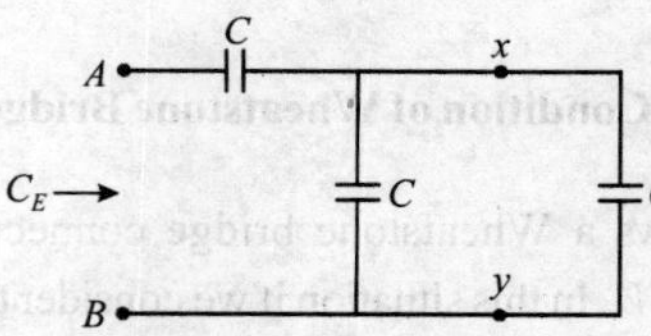

(b)

Figure 2.98

Thus the circuit after terminals XY in figure-2.97 can be replaced by a single equivalent capacitance C_E as shown in figure-2.98(b) and it can be solved using series and parallel method which gives the value of C_E by considering C_E in parallel with C and then this group in series with another C connected in top branch which is given as

$$C_E = \frac{C(C+C_E)}{C+(C+C_E)}$$

$$\Rightarrow \quad C_E(2C+C_E) = C(C+C_E)$$

$$\Rightarrow \quad C_E^2 + CC_E - C^2 = 0$$

$$\Rightarrow \quad C_E = \frac{-C \pm \sqrt{C^2 - 4(-C^2)}}{2}$$

$$\Rightarrow \quad C_E = \left(\frac{\sqrt{5}-1}{2}\right)C \qquad \ldots(2.136)$$

The expression given in equation-(2.136) is the equivalent capacitance of the ladder circuit shown in figure-2.97. Upcoming illustrations will explain the similar concepts in more details.

2.4.8 Effect of a Multiplying factor on Equivalent Capacitance

For two capacitors C_1 and C_2 in series combination the equivalent capacitance is given as

$$C_{eq} = \frac{C_1C_2}{C_1 + C_2} \quad \ldots(2.137)$$

In equation-(2.137) we can see that numerator is second order and denominator is first order. If we calculate the equivalent capacitance of three capacitors in series C_1, C_2 and C_3 then it is given as

$$C_{eq} = \frac{C_1C_2C_3}{C_1C_2 + C_2C_3 + C_1C_3} \quad \ldots(2.138)$$

In equation-(2.138) we can see that numerator is third order in unit of capacitance and denominator is second order in unit of capacitance. For any given circuit of capacitors if expression for equivalent capacitance is analyzed then always in numerator if capacitance unit order is n then in denominator it will be $n-1$ so that in this expression final unit will be of capacitance. Based on this understanding we can state "*If capacitance of all the capacitors of a circuit are made N times then equivalent capacitance of the circuit will also become N times.*"

 # Illustrative Example 2.21

Find the equivalent capacitance of the infinite ladder shown in figure-2.99 between the points A & B.

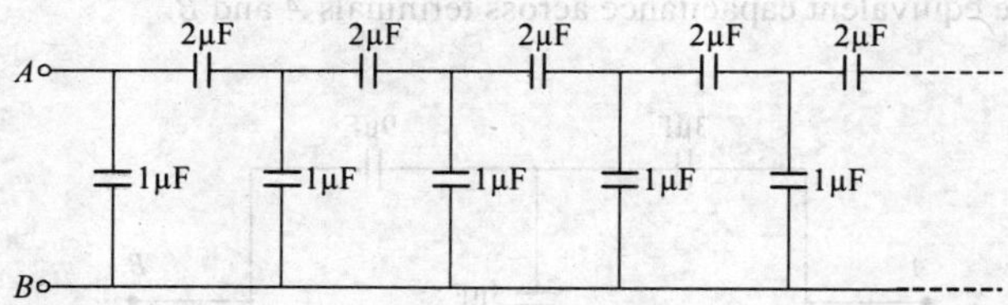

Figure 2.99

Solution

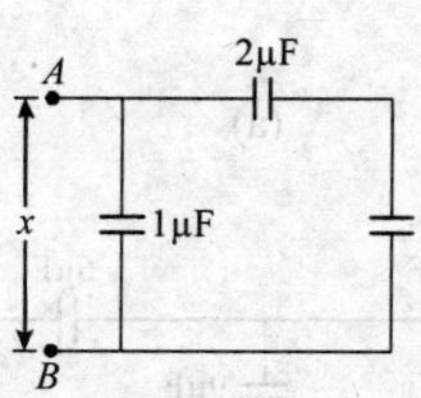

Figure 2.100

$$x = \frac{2x}{2+x} + 1$$

(Let $C_{eq} = x$)

$$x = \frac{2x+2+x}{2+x}$$

$$\Rightarrow \quad x(2+x) = 3x+2$$

$$\Rightarrow \quad 2x + x^2 = 3x + 2$$

$$\Rightarrow \quad x^2 - x - 2 = 0$$

Use $x = \frac{-b \pm \sqrt{b^2 - 4ac}}{2a} = \frac{1 \pm \sqrt{1+8}}{2} = \frac{1 \pm 3}{2} = 2$ and -1

$$x = 2, C_{eq} = 2\mu\text{F}$$

Web Reference at www.physicsgalaxy.com

Age Group - Grade 11 & 12 | Age 17-19 Years

Section - ELECTROSTATICS

Topic - Capacitance

Module Number - 21 to 29

Practice Exercise 2.3

(i) In the circuit shown in figure-2.101 find the potential at point B.

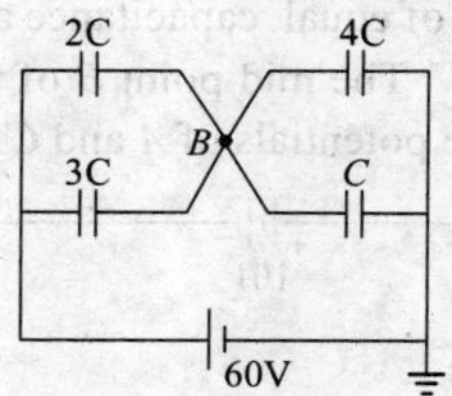

Figure 2.101

[30V]

(ii) In the ladder network shown in figure-102 find the equivalent capacitance across terminals A and B.

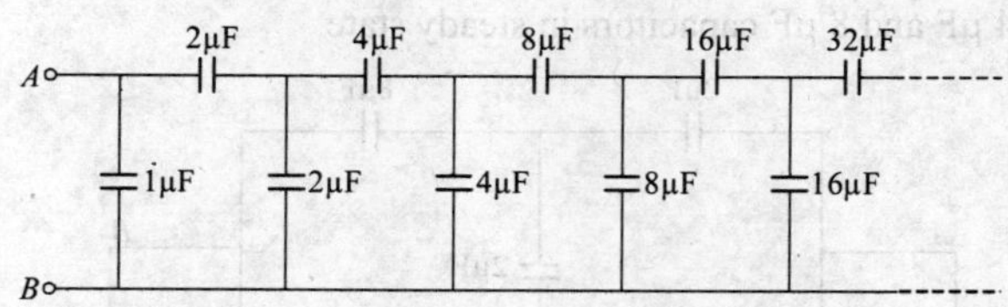

Figure 2.102

$[\frac{1+2\sqrt{2}}{2}\ \mu\text{F}]$

(iii) Infinite number of identical capacitors each of capacitance 1 μF are connected as shown in figure-2.103. Find the equivalent capacitance of system between the terminals A and B shown in figure.

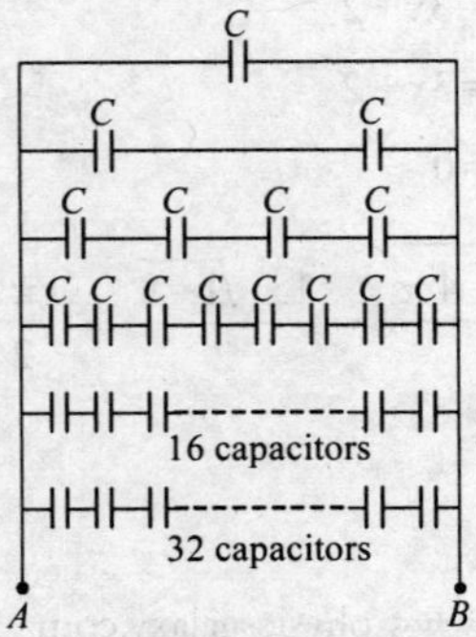

Figure 2.103

[2 μF]

(iv) A circuit has a section *MN* shown in figure-2.104. The EMF of the source is $E = 10$ V, the capacitances of capacitors are equal to $C_1 = 1$ μF and $C_2 = 2$ μF, and the potential difference $V_M - V_N = 5.0$ V. Find voltage across each capacitor.

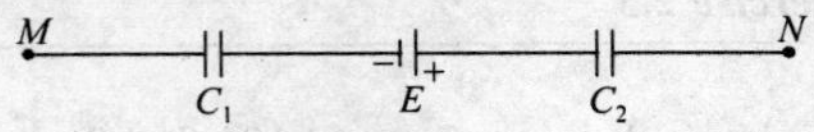

Figure 2.104

[10 V, 5 V]

(v) Four capacitors of equal capacitance are joined in series with a battery of 10 V. The mid point *B* of these capacitors is earthed. Calculate the potentials of *A* and *C*.

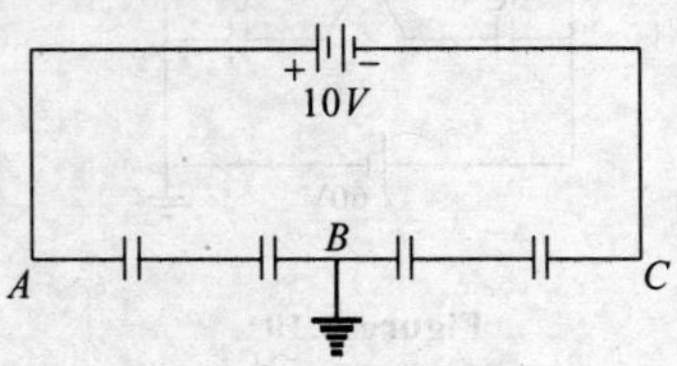

Figure 2.105

[V_A = +5 V and V_C = – 5 V]

(vi) In the circuit shown in figure-2.106 calculate the equivalent capacitance across terminals *A* and *B* and the ratio of charges on 4 μF and 8 μF capacitors in steady state.

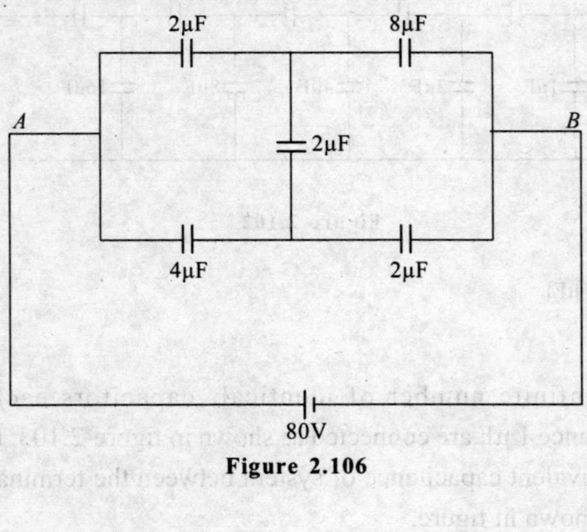

Figure 2.106

$[\frac{5}{6}]$

(vii) In the circuit shown in figure-2.107, find

(a) The equivalent capacitance of all the capacitors across the battery and

(b) The charge flown through the battery when switch is closed.

(c) Charge on capacitor C_1 in steady state.

(d) Charge on capacitor C_2 in steady state.

(e) Charge on capacitor C_3 in steady state.

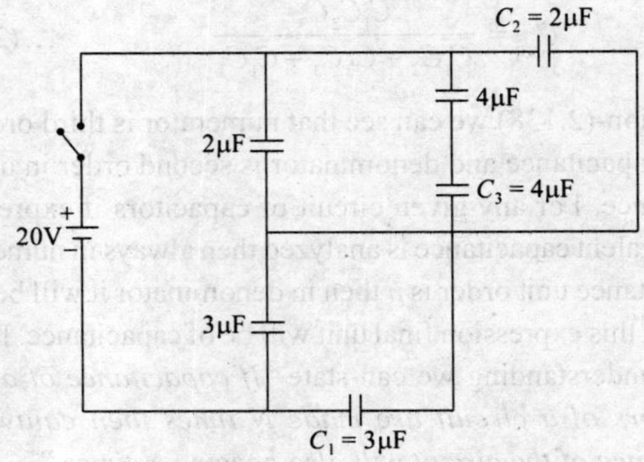

Figure 2.107

[(a) 3 μF, (b) 60 μC, (c) 30 μC, (d) 20 μC, (e) 20 μC]

(viii) In the circuit shown in figure-108(a),(b) and (c) calculate the equivalent capacitance across terminals *A* and *B*.

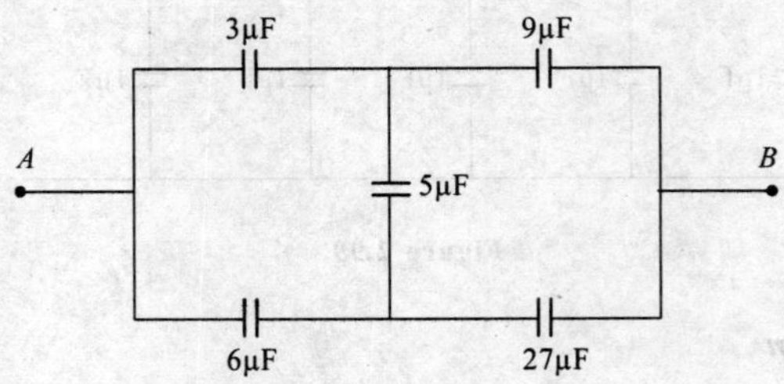

(a)

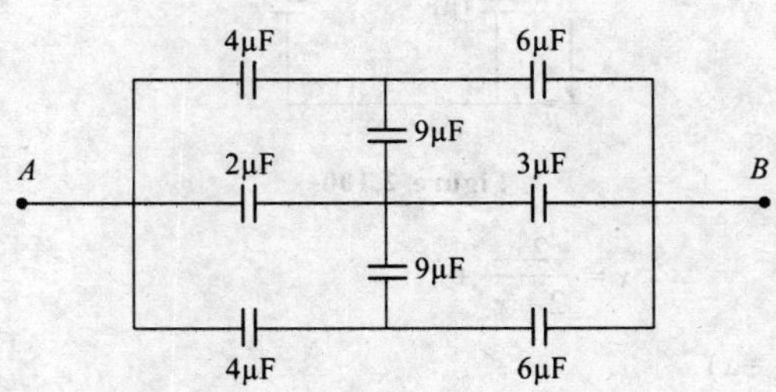

(b)

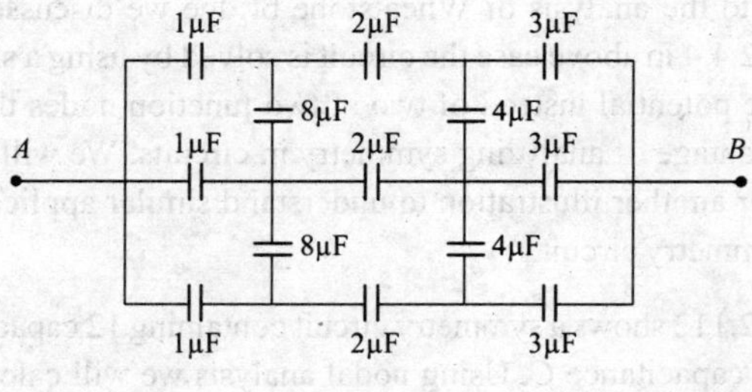

(c)
Figure 2.108

[(a) 7.16μF, (b) 6μF, (c) 3μF]

2.5 *Symmetry Circuits*

A group of capacitors which have some symmetry in connections as well as in values of capacitances used then such a circuit is called symmetry circuit. Due to symmetry in capacitances and connections by some means we can reduce the analysis of circuit while using nodal analysis or by using series and parallel method. We will discuss the analysis of symmetry circuits by using some illustrations. Figure-2.109 shows some circuits which are considered under the category of symmetry circuits. In upcoming articles we'll discuss how to solve such circuits.

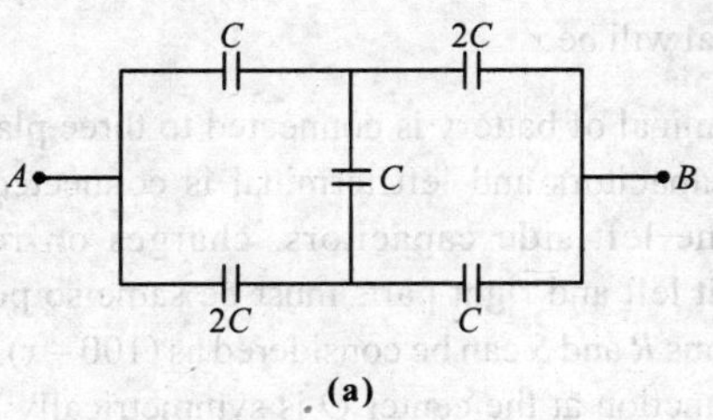

(a)

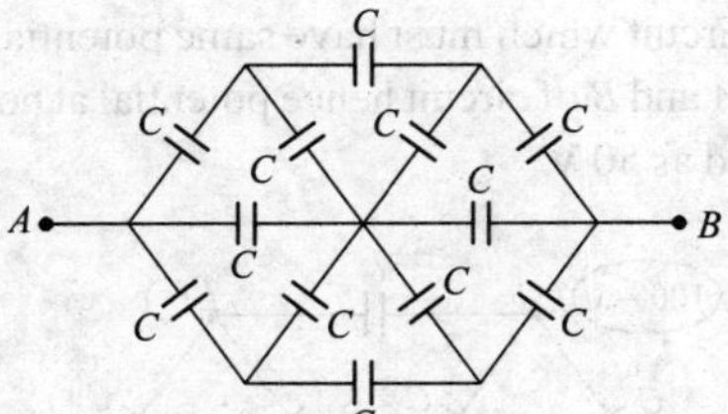

(b)

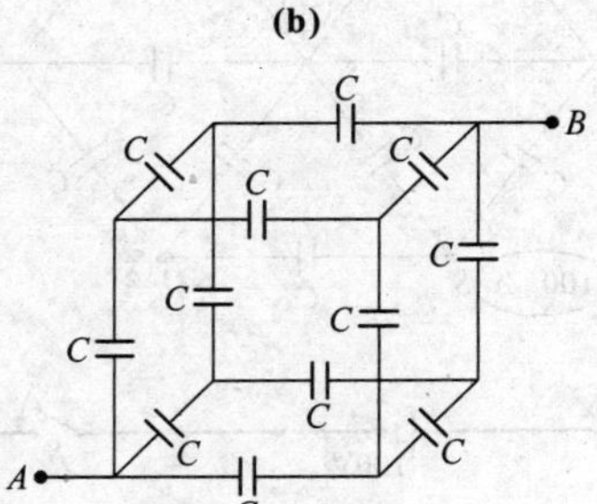

(c)

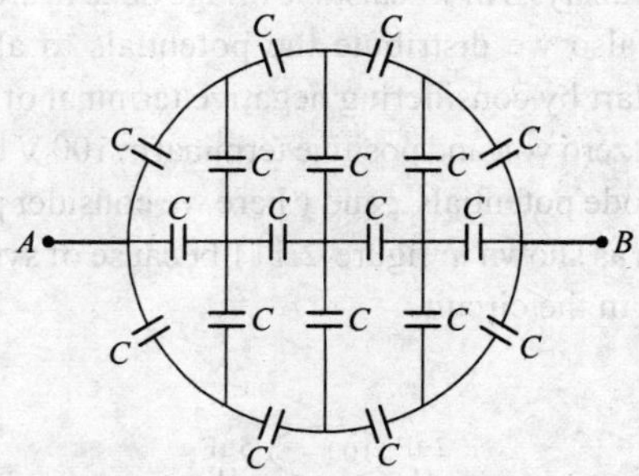

(d)

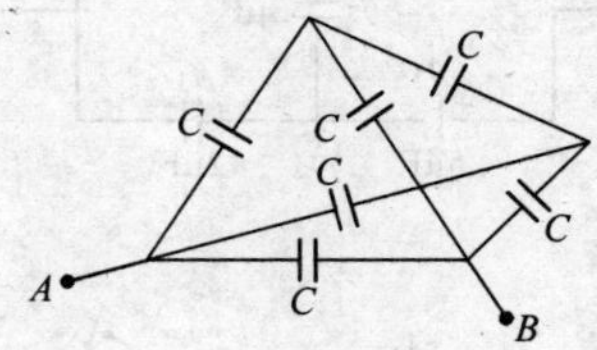

(e)

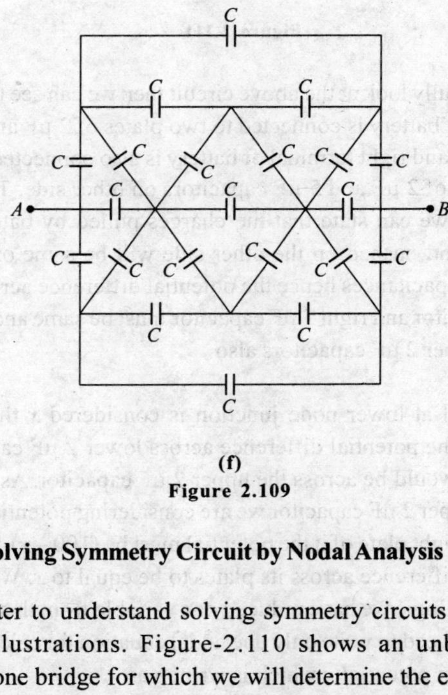

(f)
Figure 2.109

2.5.1 Solving Symmetry Circuit by Nodal Analysis

It is better to understand solving symmetry circuits by using some illustrations. Figure-2.110 shows an unbalanced wheatstone bridge for which we will determine the equivalent capacitance. To apply nodal analysis on this circuit we connect a 100 V battery across the terminals A and B as shown.

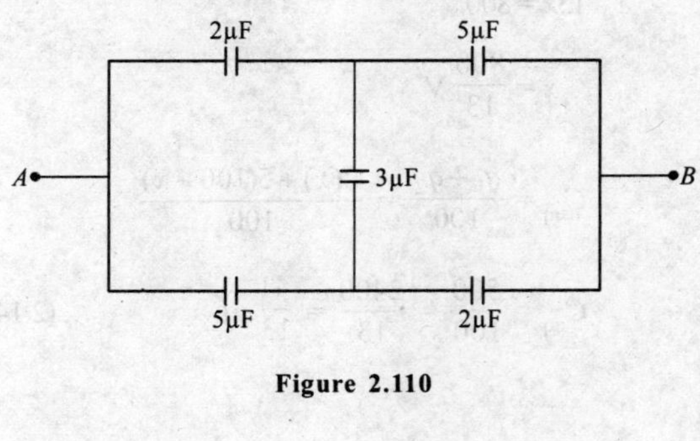

Figure 2.110

Similar to the analysis of wheatstone bridge done in article-2.4.4, in this case also we distribute the potentials to all parts of circuit. We start by considering negative terminal of battery as a reference at zero volt and positive terminal at 100 V but instead of junction node potentials x and y here we consider potential x and $(100 - x)$ as shown in figure-2.111 because of symmetry of capacitances in the circuit.

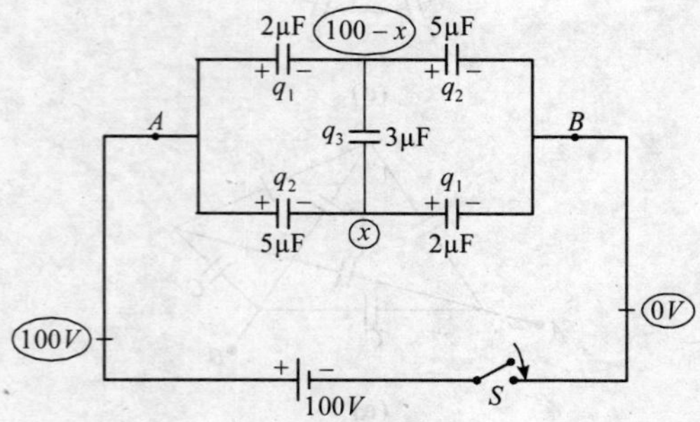

Figure 2.111

If we carefully look at the above circuit then we can see that left terminal of battery is connected to two plates of 2 μF and 5 μF capacitors and right terminal of battery is also connected to the two plates of 2 μF and 5 μF capacitors on other side. Thus by symmetry we can state that the charges pulled by battery on one side and pushed on the other side will be same on same value of capacitances hence the potential difference across left 5 μF capacitor and right 5 μF capacitor must be same and this is true for other 2 μF capacitors also.

If potential at lower node junction is considered x then this would be the potential difference across lower 2 μF capacitor and same would be across the upper 2 μF capacitor. As on left plate of upper 2 μF capacitor we are considering potential to be 100 V, on right plate of it the potential must be $(100 - x)$ to keep potential difference across its plates to be equal to x. With this qualitative logic we have reduced one variable from this circuit so now we need to write only one nodal equation for calculation of unknown potential x which is written as

$$3(2x - 100) + 5(x - 100) + 2x = 0 \qquad \ldots(2.139)$$

$$\Rightarrow \quad 13x = 800$$

$$\Rightarrow \quad x = \frac{800}{13}\,\text{V}$$

$$\Rightarrow \quad C_{eq} = \frac{q_1 + q_2}{100} = \frac{2(x) + 5(100 - x)}{100}$$

$$\Rightarrow \quad C_{eq} = \frac{500}{100} - \frac{2400}{13} = \frac{41}{13}\,\mu\text{F} \qquad \ldots(2.140)$$

Unlike to the analysis of Wheatstone bridge we discussed in article-2.4.4 in above case the circuit is solved by using a single variable potential instead of two at two junction nodes this is the advantage of analyzing symmetry in circuits. We will now consider another illustration to understand similar application on a symmetry circuit.

Figure-2.112 shows a symmetry circuit containing 12 capacitors each of capacitance C. Using nodal analysis we will calculate the equivalent capacitance of this circuit across terminals A and B.

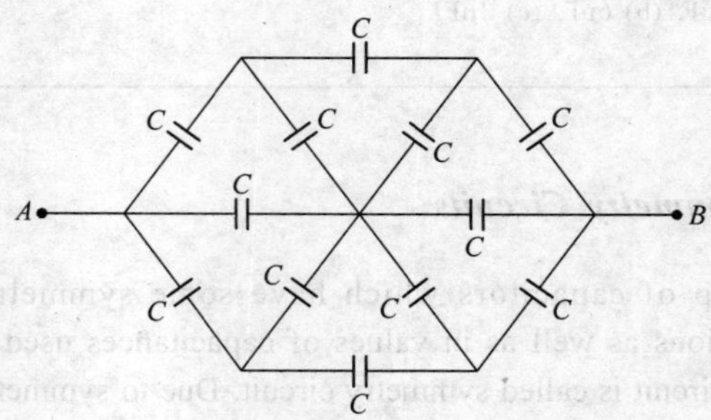

Figure 2.112

To analyze the above circuit we connect a 100V battery across the circuit as shown in figure-2.113 and distribute potentials at various parts of circuit considering zero potential reference at negative terminal of the battery. As shown in figure by symmetry if at node junction P potential is considered x then by mirror symmetry about the center line of circuit, at node junction Q also potential will be x.

As right terminal of battery is connected to three plates of the right side capacitors and left terminal is connected to three plates of the left side capacitors, charges on respective capacitors at left and right parts must be same so potential at node junctions R and S can be considered as $(100 - x)$ as shown. The node junction at the center O is symmetrically located at the center of circuit which must have same potential difference with terminal A and B of circuit hence potential at node junction O is considered as 50 V.

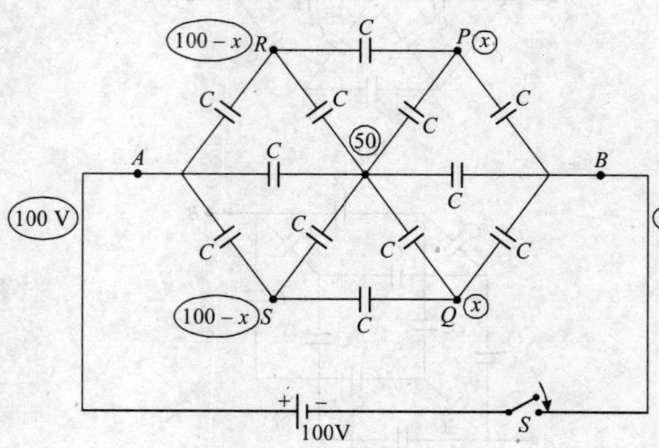

Figure 2.113

In figure-2.113, we can see that due to symmetry there is only one variable potential in this circuit and to determine the value of x, nodal equation is the sum of charges on three plates connected to node junction P which is written as

$$C[x-(100-x)]+C(x-50)+C(x-0)=0 \quad \ldots(2.141)$$

$$\Rightarrow \quad 4x=150$$

$$\Rightarrow \quad x=\frac{150}{4}=\frac{75}{2}\text{ V}$$

Now we can determine the equivalent capacitance of the given circuit by calculating the ratio of charge flown through the battery to the battery voltage as

$$C_{eq}=\frac{\Delta q_0}{V_{battery}}=\frac{C(2x)+C(50)}{100}$$

$$\Rightarrow \quad C_{eq}=\frac{(75+50)}{100}C=\frac{5}{4}C \quad \ldots(2.142)$$

Equation-(2.142) gives the capacitance of the symmetry circuit shown in figure-2.112 which is calculated by using nodal analysis. This can also be solved by using series and parallel method by joining or isolating equipotential points to modify the circuit. In next article we will discuss this method which is also very useful but still nodal analysis is a preferred method to solve most of symmetry circuit because of more organized form of solving capacitive circuits.

2.5.2 Solving Symmetry Circuits Using Circuit Modification

This method is sometimes useful but always it may not be applicable in symmetry circuits. This method is based upon the fact that on joining two junction nodes of a circuit at same potential no charge flow takes place between these two junctions and if at one junction node of the circuit we split the contacts in two junctions and if both are at same potential then also no affect will be there on the circuit and charge on all capacitors of the circuit will remain same.

To understand this method we consider the same illustration we have discussed in previous article in which 12 capacitors are connected in hexagonal form as shown in figure-2.114.

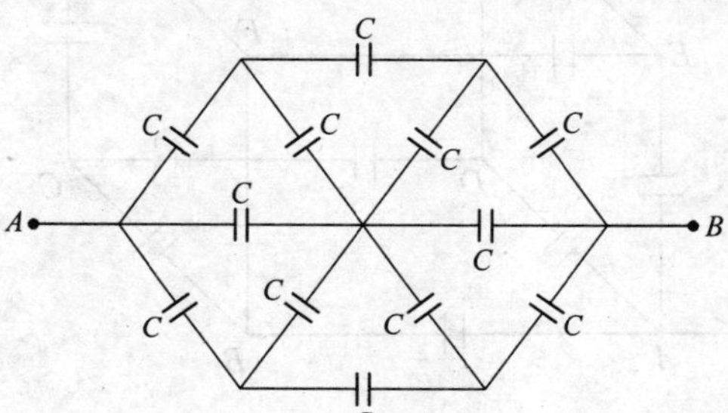

Figure 2.114

In figure-2.115(a) if node junctions P and Q are connected by a conducting wire then no charge should flow through this wire as already P and Q are at same potential. Similarly node junctions R and S can also be connected without any affect on the circuit. This is shown in figure-2.115(a) and to join node junctions P and R to node junctions S and Q, we can rotate the upper part of circuit and flip this part of circuit about the center line over the lower circuit so that P comes over Q and R comes over S. Because of this some of the capacitors will come in parallel and resulting circuit will become like as shown in figure-2.115(b).

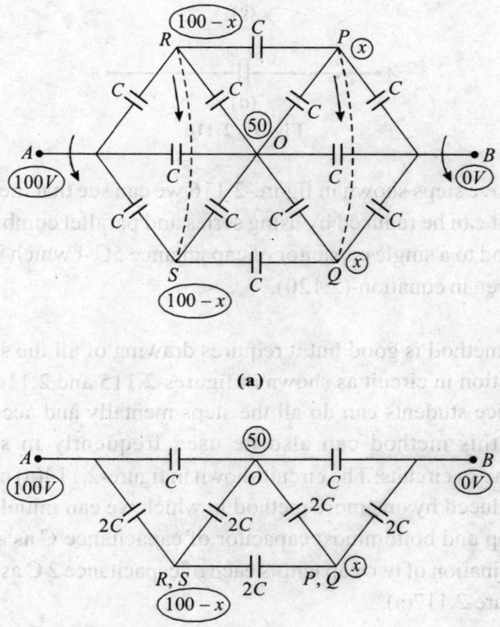

(a)

(b)

Figure 2.115

Now if the middle node junction O which is at 50 V potential split in two junctions O_1 and O_2 as shown in figure-2.116(a) then also it does not affect the circuit because due to symmetry in upper two capacitors at O_1 potential will remain 50 V and being O_2 as middle point of the lower circuit here also potential will remain 50 V. This circuit can further be reduced by series and parallel combination as shown in figure-2.116(b), (c) and (d).

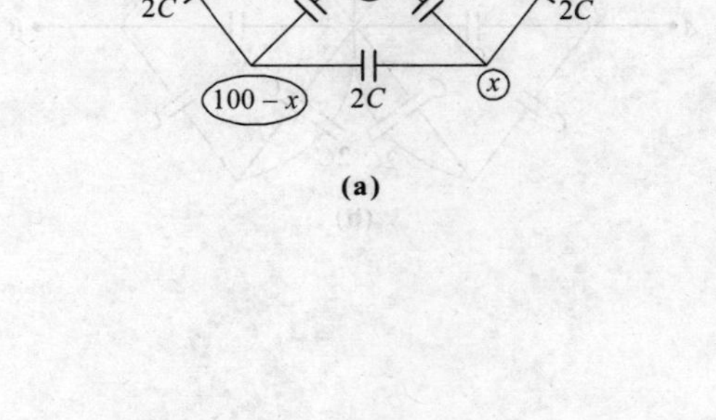

(a)

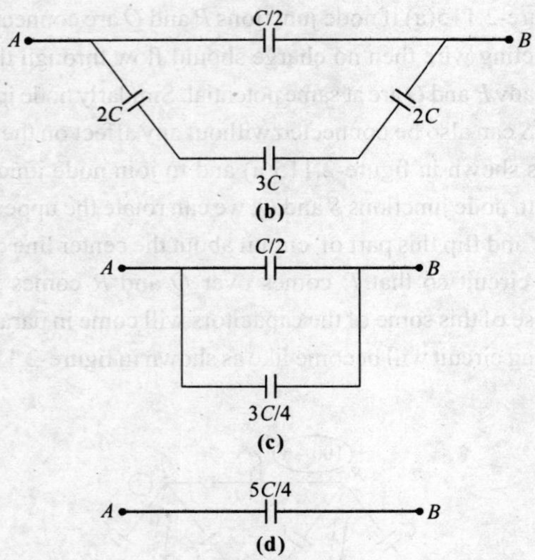

Figure 2.116

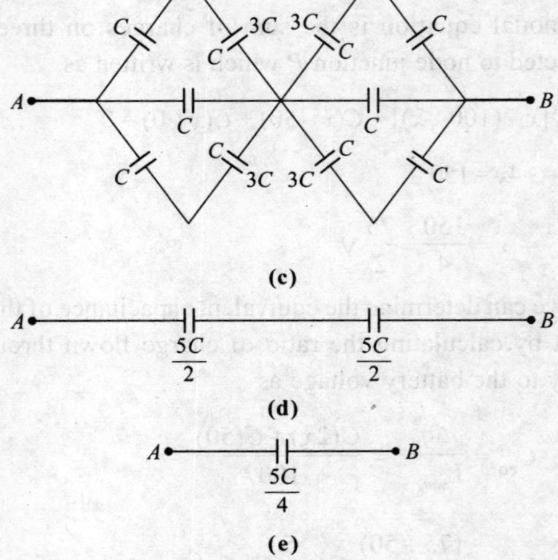

Figure 2.117

In above steps shown in figure-2.116 we can see that the whole circuit can be reduced by using series and parallel combination method to a single capacitor of capacitance 5C/4 which is same as given in equation-(2.120).

This method is good but it requires drawing of all the steps of reduction in circuit as shown in figures-2.115 and 2.116. If by practice students can do all the steps mentally and accurately then this method can also be used frequently in solving symmetry circuits. The circuit shown in figure-2.114(a) can also be reduced by one more method in which we can initially split the top and bottommost capacitor of capacitance C as a series combination of two capacitors each of capacitance 2 C as shown in figure-2.117(a).

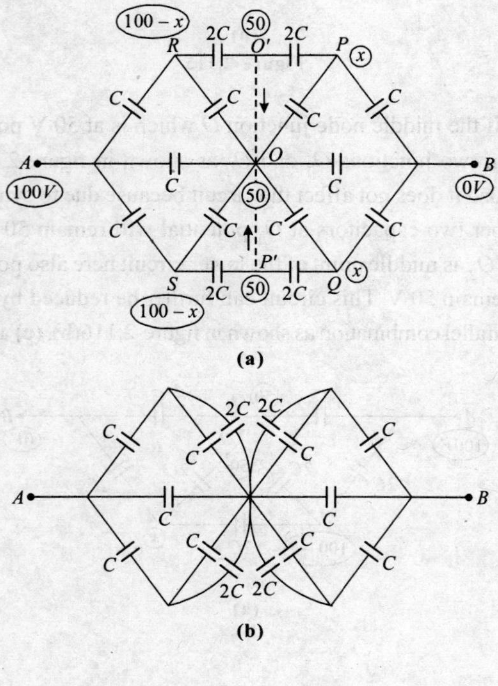

In figure-2.117 we consider a node junction O' at the mid point of the two new node junctions formed by spliting these two capacitors and being mid point of the top and bottom branch of circuit we can consider potential at O' to be 50V. As middle junctions O and O' are at same potentials these can be connected by conducting wires and circuit can now be further modified by using series and parallel method as shown in figures-2.117(b), (c), (d) and (e). Thus the circuit in this way reduces to a single capacitor of capacitance 5C/4.

We can now discuss more illustrations on symmetry circuits to understand the applications of solving such circuits.

Illustrative Example 2.22

Figure-2.118 shows a circuit of 12 capacitors each of capacitance C connected along the edges of a cubical wireframe as shown. Find the equivalent capacitance between terminals A & G.

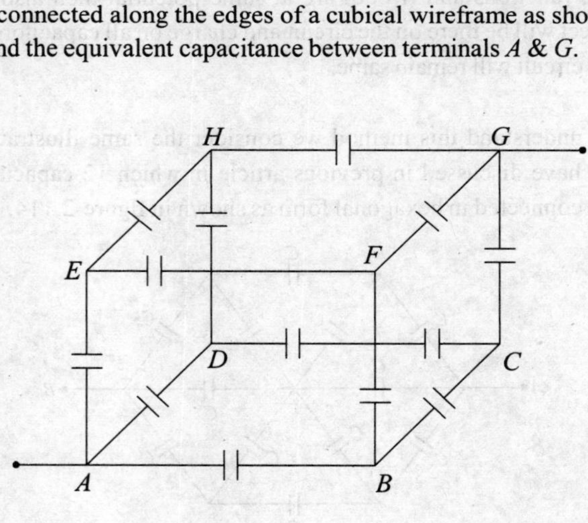

Figure 2.118

Solution

To apply nodal analysis we connect a 100 V battery across terminals A and G and distribute potentials at different nodes of circuit by using symmetry as shown in figure-2.119.

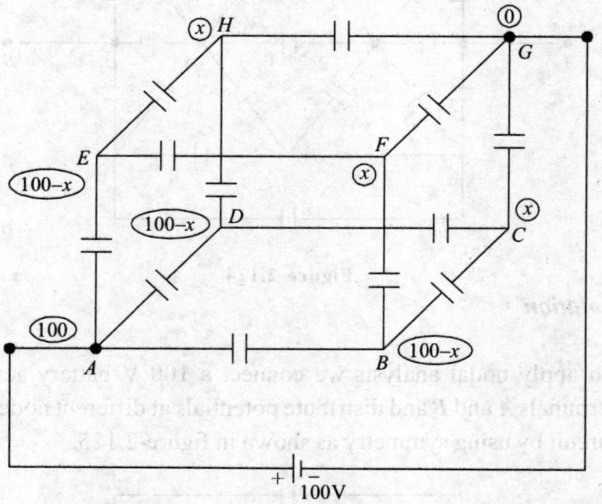

Figure 2.119

Writing nodal equation for x gives

$$Cx + C(2x - 100) + C(2x - 100) = 0$$

$$\Rightarrow \quad 5x = 200$$

$$\Rightarrow \quad x = 40\,\text{V}$$

Equivalent capacitance across terminals A and G is given as

$$C_{eq} = \frac{q_{battery}}{V_{battery}}$$

$$\Rightarrow \quad C_{eq} = \frac{3Cx}{100} = \frac{120C}{100} = \frac{6C}{5}$$

Illustrative Example 2.23

Figure-2.120 shows a circuit of 12 capacitors each of capacitance C connected along the edges of a cubical wireframe as shown. Find the equivalent capacitance between terminals A & C.

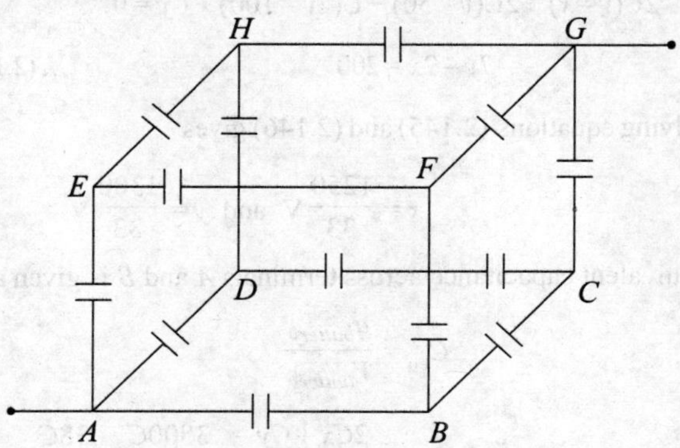

Figure 2.120

Solution

To apply nodal analysis we connect a 100 V battery across terminals A and C and distribute potentials at different nodes of circuit by using symmetry as shown in figure-2.121.

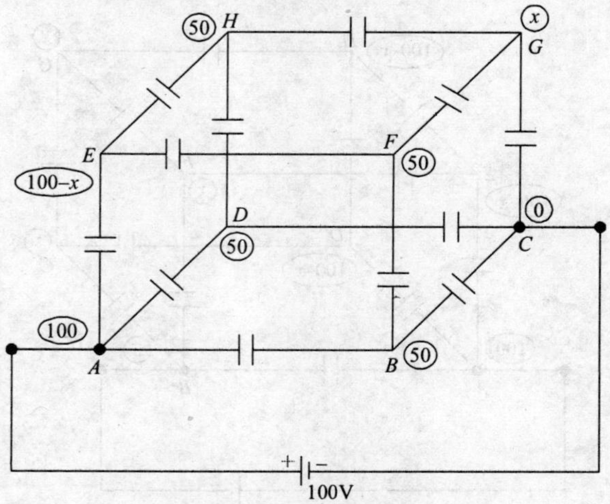

Figure 2.121

Writing nodal equation for x gives

$$Cx + C(x - 50) + C(x - 50) = 0$$

$$\Rightarrow \quad 3x = 100$$

$$\Rightarrow \quad x = \frac{100}{3}\,\text{V}$$

Equivalent capacitance across terminals A and C is given as

$$C_{eq} = \frac{q_{battery}}{V_{battery}}$$

$$\Rightarrow \quad C_{eq} = \frac{Cx + C(100)}{100} = \frac{400C}{300} = \frac{4C}{3}$$

Illustrative Example 2.24

Figure-2.122 shows a circuit of 12 capacitors each of capacitance C connected along the edges of a cubical wireframe as shown. Find the equivalent capacitance between terminals A & B.

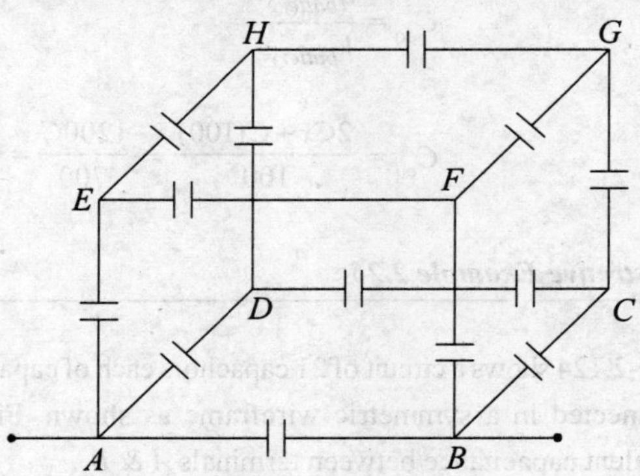

Figure 2.122

Solution

To apply nodal analysis we connect a 100 V battery across terminals A and B and distribute potentials at different nodes of circuit by using symmetry as shown in figure-123.

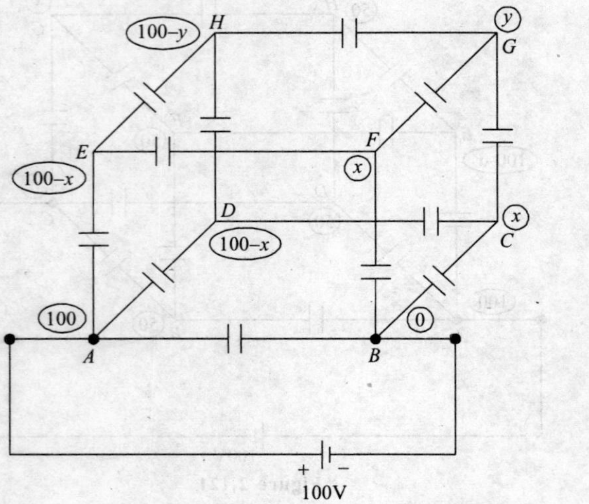

Figure 2.123

Writing nodal equation for x gives

$$Cx + C(2x - 100) + C(x - y) = 0$$

$$\Rightarrow \qquad 4x - y = 100 \qquad \ldots(2.143)$$

Writing nodal equation for y gives

$$C(y - x) + C(y - x) + C(2y - 100) = 0$$

$$\Rightarrow \qquad 4y - 2x = 100 \qquad \ldots(2.144)$$

Solving equations-(2.143) and (2.144) gives

$$x = \frac{250}{7}\text{ V}$$

Equivalent capacitance across terminals A and B is given as

$$C_{eq} = \frac{q_{battery}}{V_{battery}}$$

$$\Rightarrow \qquad C_{eq} = \frac{2Cx + C(100)}{100} = \frac{1200C}{700} = \frac{12C}{7}$$

Illustrative Example 2.25

Figure-2.124 shows a circuit of 21 capacitors each of capacitance C connected in a symmetric wireframe as shown. Find the equivalent capacitance between terminals A & B.

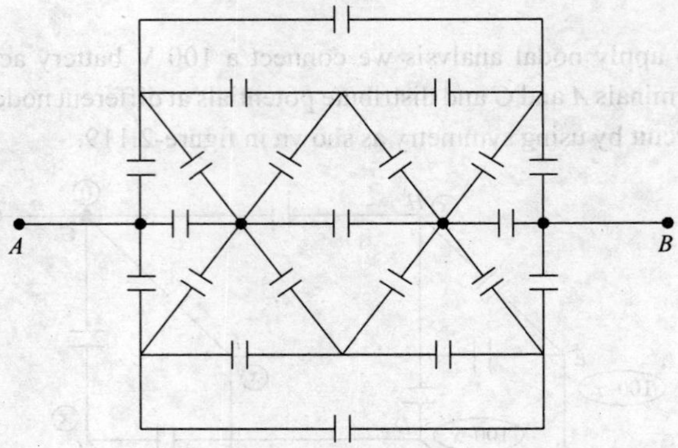

Figure 2.124

Solution

To apply nodal analysis we connect a 100 V battery across terminals A and B and distribute potentials at different nodes of circuit by using symmetry as shown in figure-2.125.

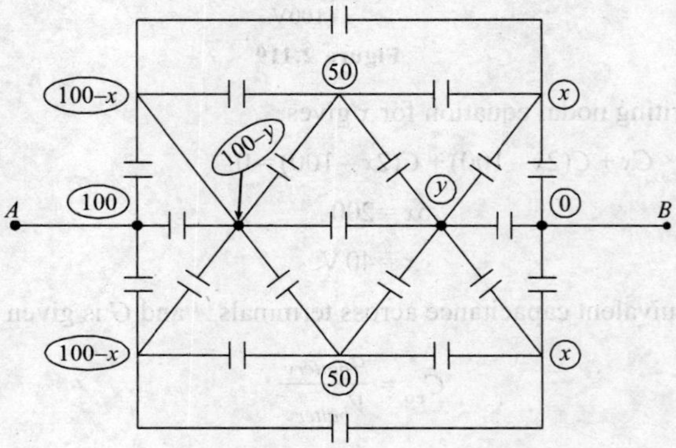

Figure 2.125

Writing nodal equation for x gives

$$Cx + C(x - 50) + C(x - y) + C(2x - 100) = 0$$

$$\Rightarrow \qquad 5x - y = 150 \qquad \ldots(2.145)$$

Writing nodal equation for y gives

$$2C(y - x) + 2C(y - 50) + C(2y - 100) + Cy = 0$$

$$\Rightarrow \qquad 7y - 2x = 200 \qquad \ldots(2.146)$$

Solving equations-(2.145) and (2.146) gives

$$x = \frac{1250}{33}\text{ V} \quad \text{and} \quad y = \frac{1300}{33}\text{ V}$$

Equivalent capacitance across terminals A and B is given as

$$C_{eq} = \frac{q_{battery}}{V_{battery}}$$

$$\Rightarrow \qquad C_{eq} = \frac{2Cx + Cy}{100} = \frac{3800C}{3300} = \frac{38C}{33}$$

Practice Exercise 2.4

Find equivalent capacitance in each of the symmetry circuits shown in figures below.

(i)

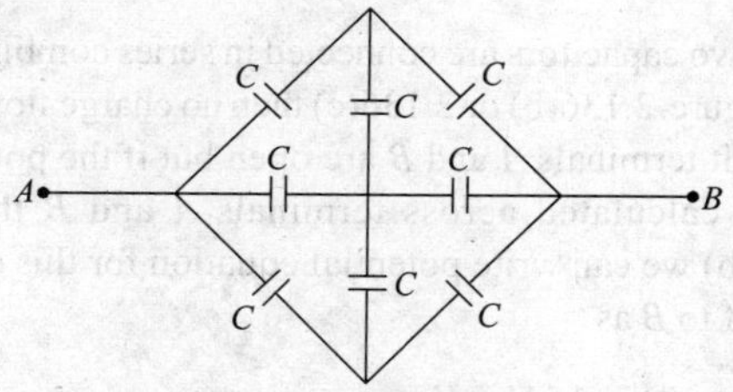

Figure 2.126

[$\frac{3C}{2}$]

(ii)

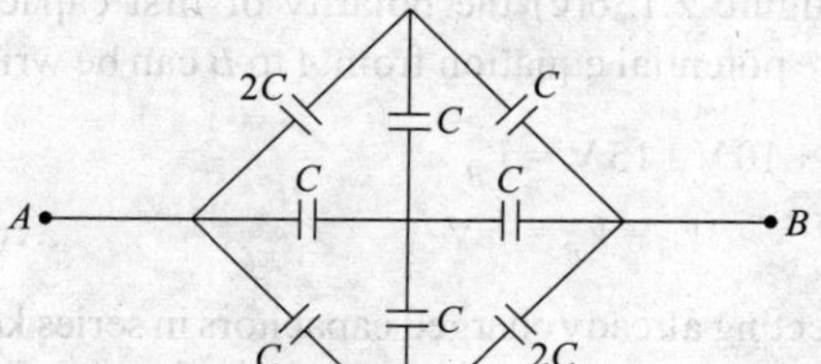

Figure 2.127

[$\frac{15C}{8}$]

(iii)

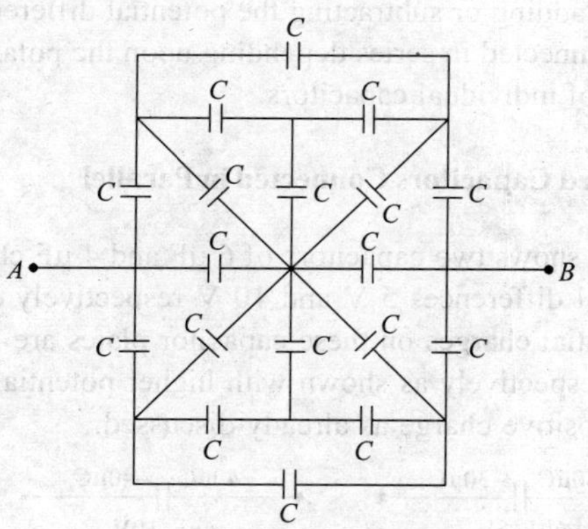

Figure 2.128

[1.3C]

(iv)

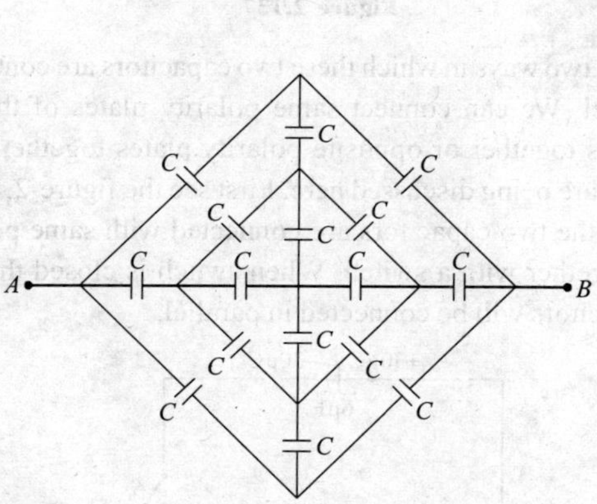

Figure 2.129

[$\frac{11C}{8}$]

(v)

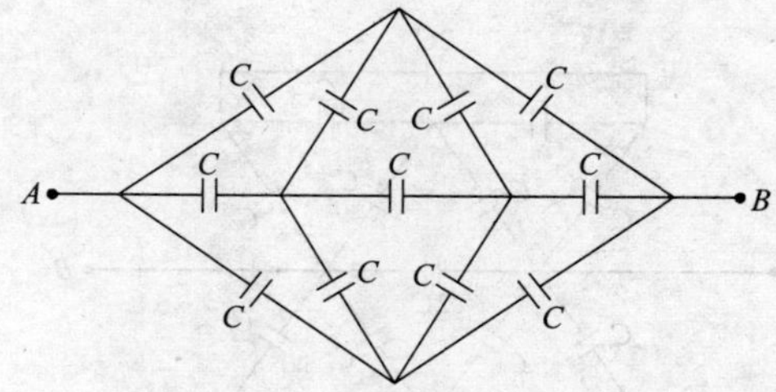

Figure 2.130

[$\frac{7C}{5}$]

(vi)

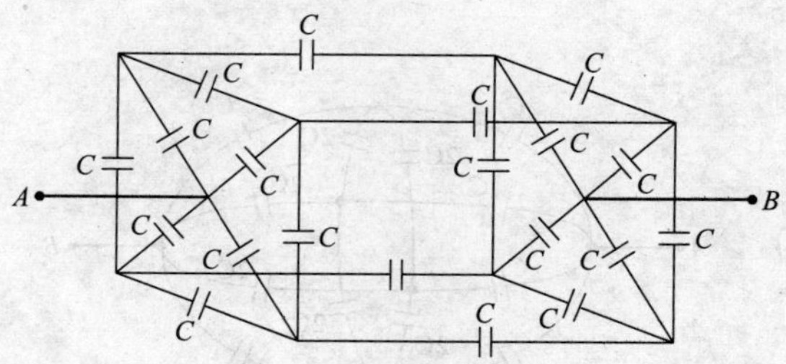

Figure 2.131

[$\frac{4C}{3}$]

(vii)

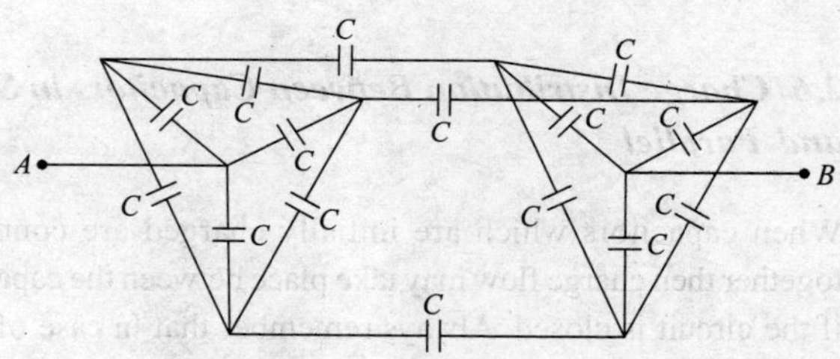

Figure 2.132

[C]

(viii)

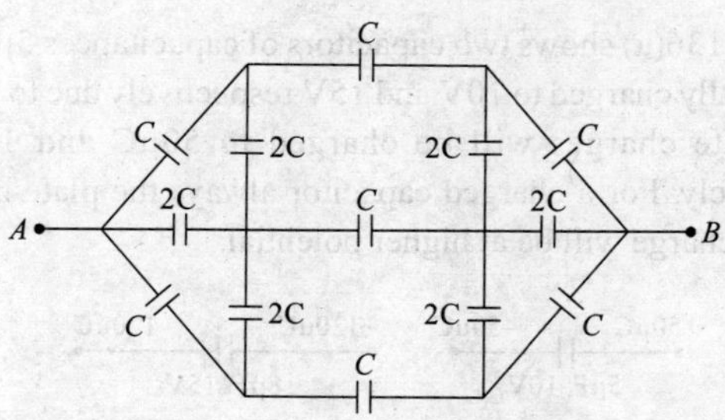

Figure 2.133

[$\frac{19C}{16}$]

(ix)

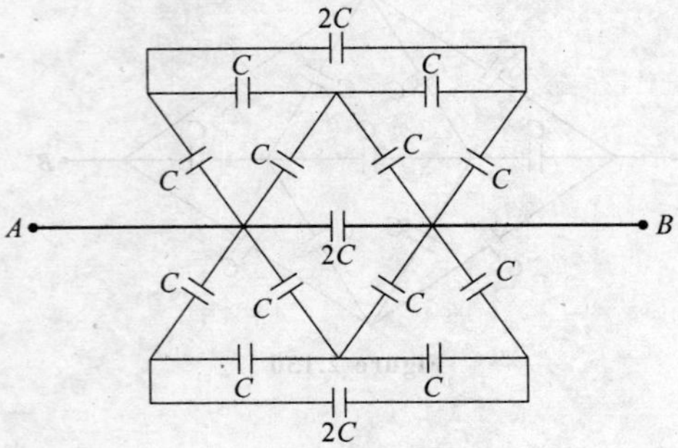

Figure 2.134

$[\frac{3C}{2}]$

(x)

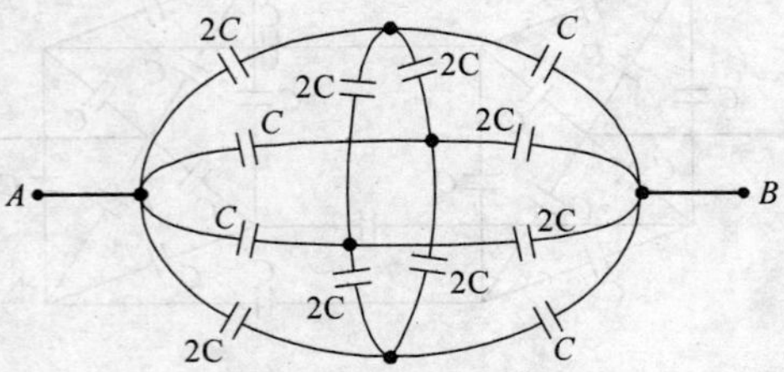

Figure 2.135

$[\frac{32C}{11}]$

2.6 Charge Distribution Between Capacitors in Series and Parallel

When capacitors which are initially charged are connected together then charge flow may take place between the capacitors if the circuit is closed. Always remember that in case of open circuit charge never flows no matter whatever potential difference exist across capacitors.

2.6.1 Charged Capacitors Connected in Series

Figure-2.136(a) shows two capacitors of capacitances 5μF and 8μF initially charged to 10V and 15V respectively due to which their plate charges will be charged to 50μC and 120μC respectively. For a charged capacitor always the plate having positive charge will be at higher potential.

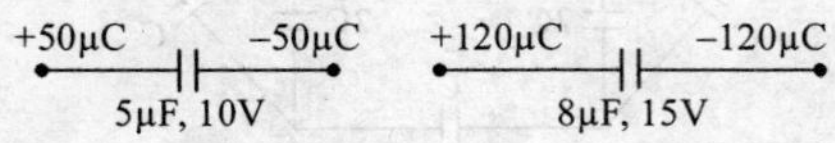

(a)

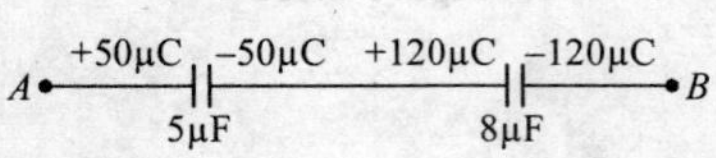

(b)

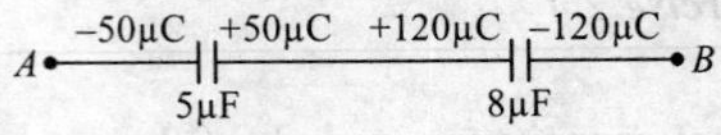

(c)

Figure 2.136

Now if these two capacitors are connected in series combination as shown in figure-2.136(b) or 2.136(c) then no charge flow take place as circuit terminals A and B are open but if the potential difference is calculated across terminals A and B then in figure-2.136(b) we can write potential equation for this circuit branch from A to B as

$$V_A - 10\,\text{V} - 15\,\text{V} = V_B$$

$$\Rightarrow \quad V_A - V_B = 25\,\text{V} \quad \ldots(2.147)$$

Similarly in figure-2.136(c) the polarity of first capacitor is reversed so the potential equation from A to B can be written as

$$V_A + 10\,\text{V} - 15\,\text{V} = V_B$$

$$\Rightarrow \quad V_A - V_B = 5\,\text{V} \quad \ldots(2.148)$$

Thus on connecting already charged capacitors in series keeping the terminals of combination open, no charge flow takes place and the final charges and energy stored in capacitor remain same and the potential difference across the combination can be calculated by writing potential equation as explained above or simply by adding or subtracting the potential difference of capacitors connected in series depending upon the polarity of connections of individual capacitors.

2.6.2 Charged Capacitors Connected in Parallel

Figure-2.137 shows two capacitors of 6 μF and 4 μF charged with potential differences 5 V and 10 V respectively due to which the initial charges on these capacitor plates are 30 μC and 40 μC respectively as shown with higher potential plate containing positive charge as already discussed.

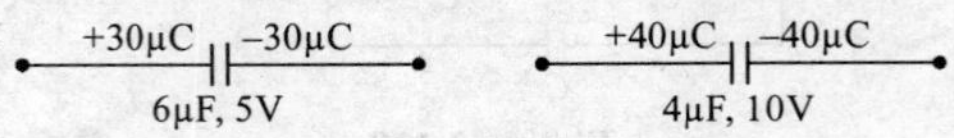

Figure 2.137

There are two ways in which these two capacitors are connected in parallel. We can connect same polarity plates of the two capacitors together or opposite polarity plates together. Both the cases are being discussed here. First see the figure-2.138(a) in which the two capacitors are connected with same polarity plates together with a switch. When switch is closed then the two capacitors will be connected in parallel.

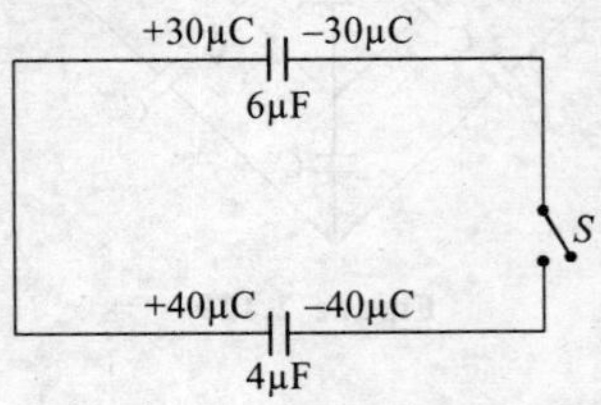

(a)

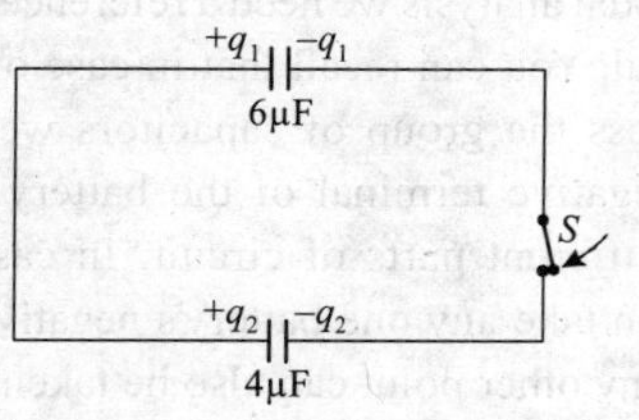

(b)

Figure 2.138

As circuit is closed charge flow takes place between the two capacitors until their potential difference becomes equal. If we consider final charges on the plates of the two capacitors becomes q_1 and q_2 in steady state after redistribution of charges as shown in figure-2.138(b) then in final state the potential difference across the two capacitors must be same and would be given as

$$V_f = \frac{q_1}{6} = \frac{q_2}{4} = \frac{q_1 + q_2}{10} = \frac{70}{10} = 7\text{V} \quad \ldots(2.149)$$

Thus final charges on the two capacitors after connecting in parallel with same polarity plates together are given as

$$q_1 = 6 \times 7 = 42\ \mu\text{C}$$

and $$q_2 = 4 \times 7 = 28\ \mu\text{C}$$

We can see that sum of final charges on capacitor plates remain 70 μC as in this case charge remain conserved and restricted to flow between these two capacitors only. Above result of final potential difference and final charges on capacitors can be directly obtained by considering the equivalent capacitance of the combination as $C_{eq} = 6 + 4 = 10$ μF and total charge on this equivalent capacitor as $q_T = 70$ μC which directly gives the final potential difference as

$$V_f = \frac{q_T}{C_{eq}} = \frac{70}{10} = 7\text{ V} \quad \ldots(2.150)$$

As the charges are flowing and quickly redistributing on the plates there may be some heat produced due to joule heating effect which is equal to loss in potential energy of the capacitors which can be calculated by difference of initial and final potential energy stored in capacitors.

Initial energy stored in the two capacitors is given as

$$U_i = \frac{1}{2}C_1V_1^2 + \frac{1}{2}C_2V_2^2$$

$$\Rightarrow \quad U_i = \frac{1}{2}(6 \times 10^{-6})(5)^2 + \frac{1}{2}(4 \times 10^{-6})(10)^2$$

$$\Rightarrow \quad U_i = (75 + 200)\ \mu\text{J} = 275\ \mu\text{J} \quad \ldots(2.151)$$

Final energy stored in the two capacitors is given as

$$U_f = \frac{1}{2}(C_1 + C_2)V_f^2$$

$$\Rightarrow \quad U_f = \frac{1}{2}(6+4) \times 10^{-6} \times (7)^2 = 245\ \mu\text{J} \quad \ldots(2.152)$$

From equations-(2.151) and (2.152) we can find out the loss in energy stored in capacitors which will be dissipated as heat after closing the switch which is given as

$$H = \Delta U = U_i - U_f$$

$$\Rightarrow \quad H = 275 - 245 = 30\ \mu\text{J}$$

Now we can consider the second way of connecting these capacitors in parallel as shown in figure-2.139(a) in which the capacitors are connected in parallel with opposite polarity plates connected together via a switch.

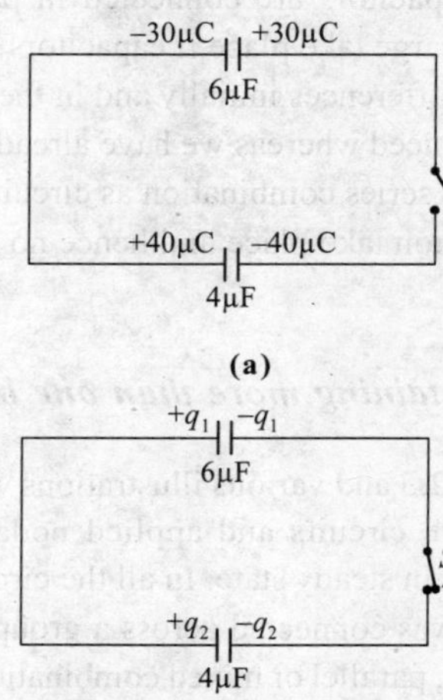

(b)

Figure 2.139

When switch is closed the two capacitors will be connected in parallel and charges will redistributed until the final potential difference of the two capacitors will be same which can be calculated by using equation-(2.150). In this case after connecting the two capacitors in parallel the equivalent capacitance will be 6 + 4 = 10 μF and total charge on the combination will be 40 – 30 = 10 μC with the left plate positive as it was having initially higher charge and will be at high potential after connection. Thus final potential of the combination is given as

$$V_f = \frac{q_T}{C_{eq}} = \frac{10}{10} = 1\text{ V} \quad \ldots(2.153)$$

Thus final charges on the two capacitors after connection can be given as

$$q_1 = 6 \times 1 = 6\ \mu\text{C}$$

and $$q_2 = 4 \times 1 = 4\ \mu\text{C}$$

As charge redistribution is taking place in this case there must be some heat produced after closing the switch which can be determined by calculating the loss in energy before and after closing the switch.

In case shown in figure-2.139, final energy stored in capacitors after closing the switch is given as

$$U_f' = \frac{1}{2}(C_1 + C_2)V_f^2$$

$$\Rightarrow \quad U_f' = \frac{1}{2}(6+4)\times 10^{-6}\times(1)^2 = 5\ \mu J \quad \ldots(2.154)$$

Thus from equations-(2.151) and (2.153) we can find out the loss in energy stored in capacitors which will be dissipated as heat after closing the switch which is given as

$$H = \Delta U = U_i - U_f'$$

$$\Rightarrow \quad H = 275 - 5 = 270\ \mu J$$

Thus whenever capacitors are connected in parallel always redistribution of charge take place if capacitors are charged at unequal potential differences initially and in the process some heat is always produced whereas we have already discussed in article-2.6.1 that in series combination as circuit remain open, no charge distribution take place and hence no loss of energy occurs.

2.7 Circuits containing more than one battery

In articles-2.4 and 2.5 and various illustrations we've analyzed different capacitive circuits and applied nodal analysis for solving the circuits in steady state. In all the circuits discussed till now a battery was connected across a group of capacitors connected in series, parallel or mixed combinations.

In this section we will discuss advanced circuits in which there may be two or more batteries are connected with some capacitors in circuits which may or may not be in any combination. Such circuits are also analyzed and solved by nodal analysis in simple ways. We will discuss and understand the method of solving such circuits with an illustration.

Figure-2.140 shows a circuit in which two batteries and three capacitors are connected with two switches which are initially open. When the switches are closed, charges will flow in the circuit and the capacitor plates will receive charges and very soon the circuit will attain steady state and current in circuit will drop to zero. To analyze the steady state charges of capacitors we use nodal analysis.

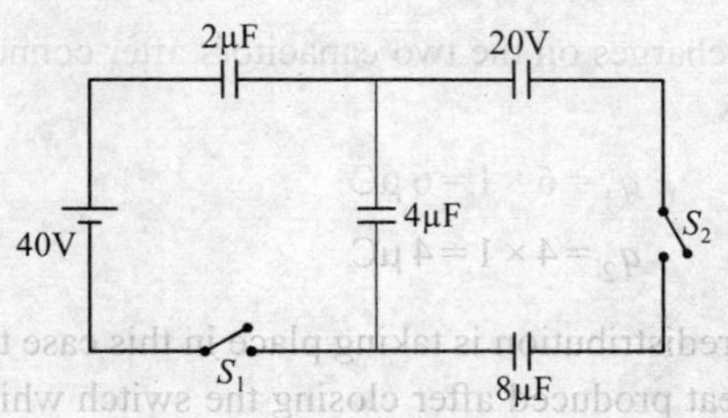

Figure 2.140

To start with nodal analysis we need a reference point in circuit at zero potential. You can recall that in case of single battery connected across the group of capacitors we consider zero potential at negative terminal of the battery and distribute potentials at different parts of circuit. In cases of multiple batteries we can take any one battery's negative terminal as a reference (or any other point can also be taken). Figure-2.141 shows the potential distribution in the circuit by considering negative terminal of 40 V battery at zero potential. Here at the node junction *M* we consider potential *x* so at the negative terminal of 20 V battery potential will be $(20 - x)$.

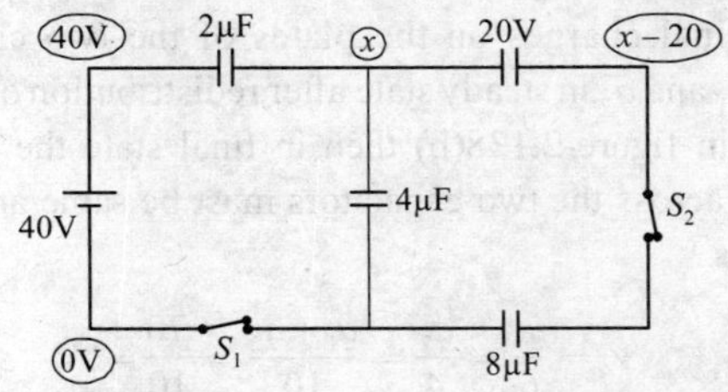

Figure 2.141

To determine unknown potential at junction *M* we write nodal equation for the node junction *M* for which we need to add charges on all the plates connected to this junction *M*. In above figure we can see that three plates are connected to junction *M* out of which plates of 2 μF and 4 μF capacitors are directly connected to *M* and one plate of 8μF is connected to *M* via 20 V battery. Thus nodal equation for node junction *M* can be written as

$$2(x-40) + 4(x-0) + 8[(x-20)-0] = 0$$

$$\Rightarrow \quad 7x = 120$$

$$\Rightarrow \quad x = \frac{120}{7}\ V$$

Thus steady state charges on the three capacitors can be given as

$$q_{2\mu F} = 2\left(40 - \frac{120}{7}\right) = \frac{320}{7}\ \mu C$$

$$q_{4\mu F} = 4\left(\frac{120}{7}\right) = \frac{480}{7}\ \mu C$$

and
$$q_{8\mu F} = 8\left(20 - \frac{120}{7}\right) = \frac{160}{7}\ \mu C$$

As charges on all capacitors are known, we can find the energy stored in all these capacitors.

In any circuit containing more than one battery we should be careful that only one point we need to consider in circuit as a zero potential reference and then distribute the potentials to all parts of circuit and write nodal equations for all the unknown potentials.

Once potential at all parts of circuit are obtained, any required parameter in the circuit can be directly calculated.

2.7.1 Branch Manipulation in Capacitive Circuits

In any capacitive circuit when several components of circuit including battery and capacitors are connected one after other in series then for solving the circuit we can change the positions or order of these components without affecting the circuit parameters. Figure-2.142(a) shows a branch of circuit in which two capacitors and a battery are connected in series. In this branch of circuit we can rearrange these components as shown in figure-2.142(b) and further we can club the two capacitors with their series equivalent as shown in figure-2.142(c). From figure-2.142(b) and 2.142(c) we can see that this process reduces one node junction in circuit so for solving the question it helps in reducing number of variable potentials in nodal analysis.

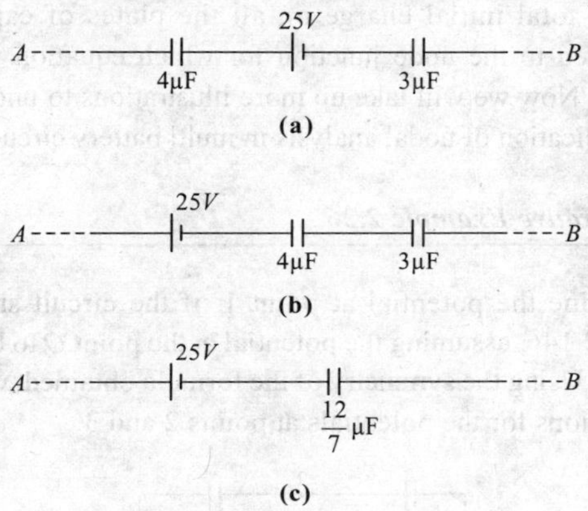

Figure 2.142

2.7.2 Circuit Analysis Using Method of Flow of Charges

In article-2.4.1 we've studied nodal analysis for solving capacitive circuits which used to be the fundamental way to solve capacitive circuit. In nodal analysis we distribute potentials at all parts of circuit and write nodal equations to find unknown potentials.

There is one more method of solving capacitive circuit which is almost opposite to nodal analysis. The method is called '*Charge Flow Method*' to solve capacitive circuits. In next chapter of electric current we will study Kirchoff's laws which is also considered same as this method for solving electrical circuits with resistances.

In charge flow method we distribute charges at various capacitors of circuit and then we write potential equation for different loops of circuit.

We will demonstrate this method by using an illustration as shown in figure-2.143 in which there are two capacitors of capacitances 4 μF and 8 μF initially charged at 20 V and 5 V respectively and connected in a single loop with two batteries of 10 V and 20 V along with a switch S. In this situation, we are required to find the steady state charges of the two capacitors when switch S is closed.

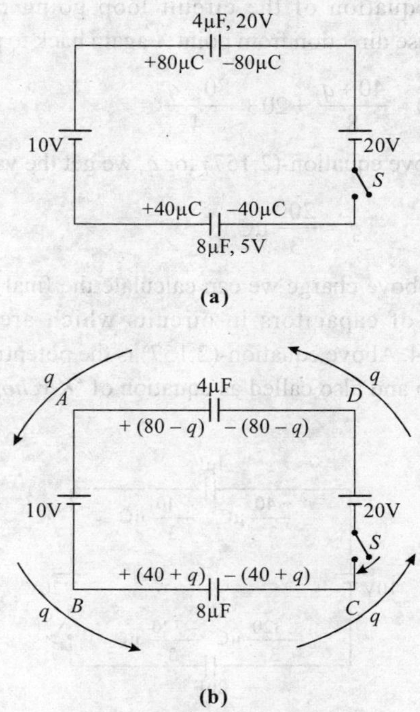

Figure 2.143

In above circuit on closing the switch S redistribution of charges will take place and here we consider that a charge q flows through the circuit in anticlockwise direction until new steady state is achieved and the final charges on capacitor plates will be as shown in figure-2.143(b).

In the state of circuit shown in 2.143(b) we can write equation of potential for the circuit loop. While writing this equation we can start from any one point in the loop move either clockwise or anticlockwise and come back to the same point as described next.

To write the potential equation of this circuit loop, if randomly we consider potential at top left corner of circuit as V_A and then we start anticlockwise then potential at bottom left corner of the circuit will be $(V_A - 10)$ then on moving further to bottom right corner the potential can be given by considering the potential difference across 8mF capacitor using relation given as

$$V_B - \frac{40+q}{8} = V_C \qquad \dots(2.155)$$

Then on moving further anticlockwise to the top right corner of the circuit the potential will be $(V_C + 20)$ and then again further upto the top left corner where we started we can use the potential difference across the 4mF capacitor given as

$$V_D + \frac{80-q}{4} = V_A \qquad \ldots(2.156)$$

Now using above equation-(2.155) and (2.156) we can write the potential equation of the circuit loop going round it in anticlockwise direction from point A again back to point A as

$$V_A - 10 - \frac{40+q}{8} + 20 + \frac{80-q}{4} = V_A \qquad \ldots(2.157)$$

Solving above equation-(2.157) for q, we get the value of q as

$$q = \frac{200}{3}\ \mu\text{C} \qquad \ldots(2.158)$$

Using the above charge we can calculate the final charges on the plates of capacitors in circuits which are shown in figure-2.144. Above equation-(2.157) is the potential equation for the loop and also called as equation of '*Kirchoff's Voltage Law*'.

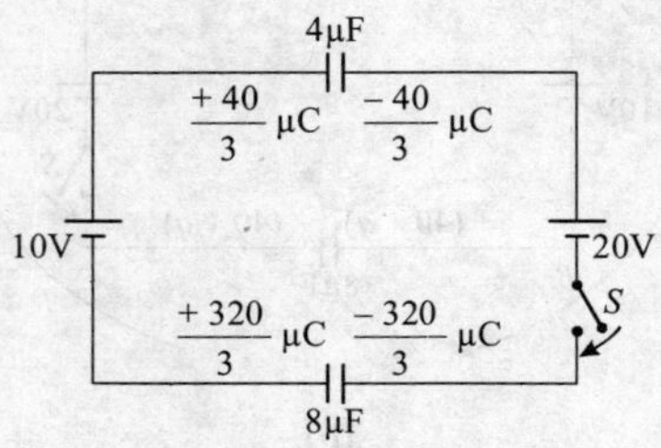

Figure 2.144

We can also solve the above illustration by using nodal analysis as shown in figure-2.145 in which we distribute the potentials in this circuit and write the nodal equation for the unknown potential x as

$$4(x+20-10)+8(x-0) = -120 \qquad \ldots(2.159)$$

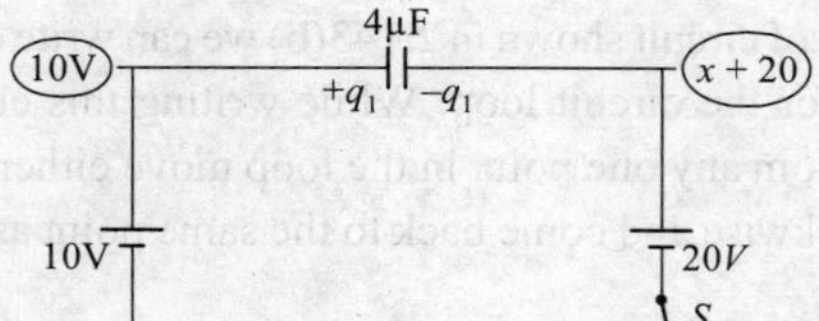

Figure 2.145

As we can see that the right plates of both the capacitors are connected to the node junction x of which the sum of charges initially is $-120\ \mu$C as capacitors are initially charged thats why unlike to the previous cases of nodal analysis when capacitors were uncharged on right hand side of nodal equation we considered zero whereas in the above nodal equation-(2.159) we used the total charge on plates connected to this node junction. Solving the above equation-(2.159) for unknown potential x, we get

$$x = -\frac{40}{3}\text{V} \qquad \ldots(2.160)$$

Thus final charges on the two capacitors can in final steady state after closing the switch S can be given as

$$q_{8\mu F} = 8x = 8 \times \frac{40}{3} = \frac{320}{3}\ \mu\text{C}$$

$$\text{and } q_{4\mu F} = 4(x+10) = 4\left(-\frac{40}{3}+10\right) = \frac{40}{3}\ \mu\text{C}$$

Above charges calculated are same as shown in figure-2.144 which were obtained by using the charge flow method.

While using nodal analysis in a capacitive circuit when one or more capacitors of circuits are initially charged then nodal equation must be very carefully written as explained in equation-(2.159) where on right hand side of equation we will use the total initial charge on all the plates of capacitors connected to the node junction for which equation is being written. Now we will take up more illustrations to understand the application of nodal analysis in multi battery circuits.

 # Illustrative Example 2.26

Determine the potential at point 1 of the circuit shown in figure-2.146, assuming the potential at the point O to be equal to zero. Using the symmetry of the formula obtained, write the expressions for the potentials at points 2 and 3.

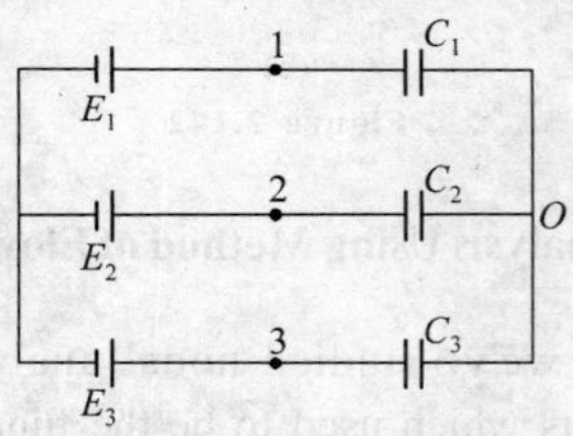

Figure 2.146

Solution

Charge distribution is shown in figure-2.147. Consider the loop $NMLKN$. Applying $-\Delta V = 0$, we have

$$-E_3 + \frac{q_1}{C_3}\left(\frac{q_1+q_2}{C_1}\right) + E_1 = 0 \qquad \ldots(2.161)$$

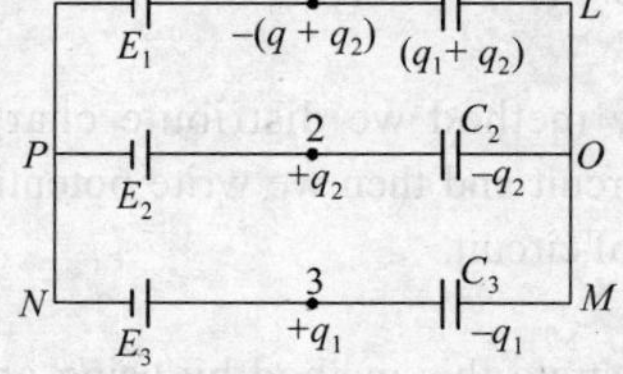

Figure 2.147

Similarly for loop *OLKPO*, we get

$$\left(\frac{q_1+q_2}{C_1}\right)+E_1-E_2+\frac{q_2}{C_2}=0 \quad \text{...(2.162)}$$

Solving these equations, we get

$$q_1=q_2=\frac{E_2C_2-E_1C_2-E_1C_3+E_3C_3}{\frac{C_3}{C_1}+\frac{C_2}{C_1}+1}$$

$$\text{Now} \quad V_1-V_0=-\frac{(q_1+q_2)}{C_1} \qquad (\because V_0=0)$$

$$\Rightarrow \quad V_1=\frac{E_1(C_2+C_3)-E_2C_2-E_3C_3}{C_1+C_2+C_3}$$

$$\text{Similarly,} \quad V_2=\frac{E_2(C_1+C_3)-E_1C_1-E_3C_3}{C_1+C_2+C_3}$$

$$\text{and} \quad V_3=\frac{E_3(C_1+C_2)-E_1C_1-E_2C_2}{C_1+C_2+C_3}$$

Students can try solving the above question using nodal analysis and verify the results obtained and compare which method is easier and quick for solving this question.

Illustrative Example 2.27

A 8 μF capacitor C_1 is charged to $V_0 = 120$ V. The charging battery is then removed and the capacitor is connected in parallel to an uncharged 4 μF capacitor C_2. (a) What is the potential difference V across the combination? (b) What is the stored energy before and after the switch S is closed?

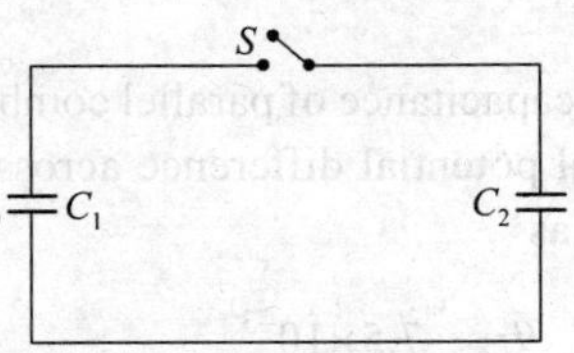

Figure 2.148

Solution

(a) Initial charges on the capacitor C_1 is

$$q_1=8\times 120=960\ \mu C$$

As discussed in article-2.6.2 the final potential difference across the combination can be given as

$$V_f=\frac{q_T}{C_1+C_2}=\frac{960}{8+4}=80\text{ V}$$

(b) Initial energy stored is only in capacitor C_1 which is given as

$$U_1=\frac{1}{2}C_1V_0^2=\frac{1}{2}(8\times 10^{-6})(120)^2$$

$$\Rightarrow \quad U_1=5.76\times 10^{-2}\text{ J}$$

Final energy stored in combination is given as

$$U_f=\frac{1}{2}C_1V_f^2+\frac{1}{2}C_2V_f^2$$

$$\Rightarrow \quad U_f=\frac{1}{2}(8\times 10^{-6})(80)^2+\frac{1}{2}(4\times 10^{-6})(80)^2$$

$$\Rightarrow \quad U_f=3.84\times 10^{-2}\text{ J}$$

Final energy is less than the initial energy thus the loss of energy is dissipated in connecting wires during redistribution of charge when switch is closed.

Illustrative Example 2.28

In the circuit shown in figure-2.149 find the charges on the three capacitors in steady state.

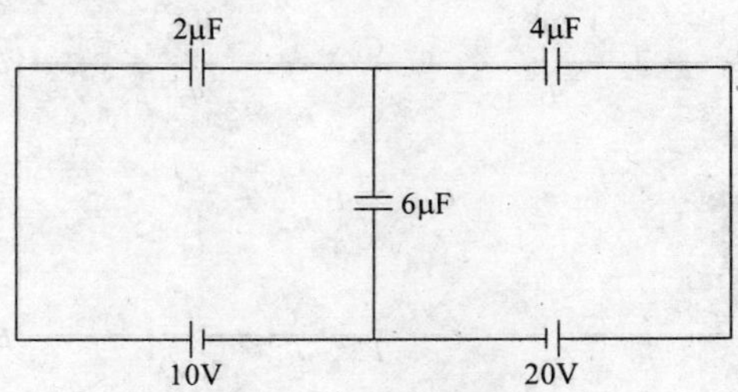

Figure 2.149

Solution

To apply nodal analysis we distribute the potentials at different parts of circuit as shown in figure-2.150.

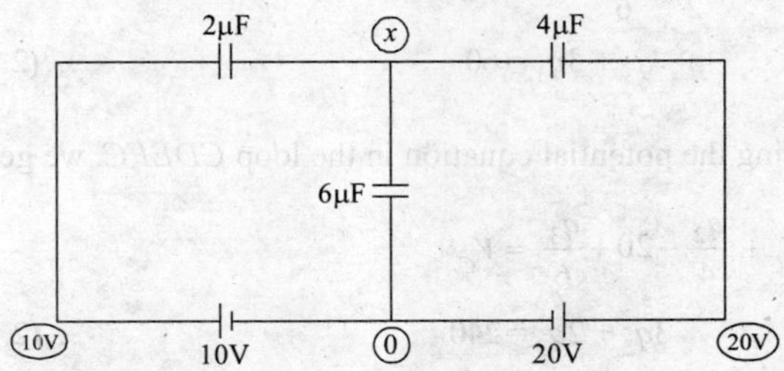

Figure 2.150

To determine the unknown potential x, we write the nodal equation for x as

$$2(x-10)+6(x-0)+4(x-20)=0$$

$$\Rightarrow \quad 6x = 50$$

$$\Rightarrow \quad x = \frac{25}{3} \text{ V}$$

As x is known we can calculate the charges on the three capacitors which are given as

$$q_{2\mu F} = 2|x-10| = 2\times\left|\frac{25}{3}-10\right| = \frac{10}{3}\ \mu C$$

$$q_{6\mu F} = 6|x-0| = 6\times\frac{25}{3} = 50\ \mu C$$

$$q_{4\mu F} = 4|x-20| = 4\times\left|\frac{25}{3}-20\right| = \frac{140}{3}\ \mu C$$

Alternative Method by Flow of Charges :

Here we can solve the same problem by the method of flow of charges. We consider charges in three capacitors after steady state as shown figure-2.151. Charge supplied by 10 V battery is q_1 and that from 20 V battery is q_2. Then for the node at point C we have

$$q_1 + q_2 = q_3 \qquad \ldots(2.163)$$

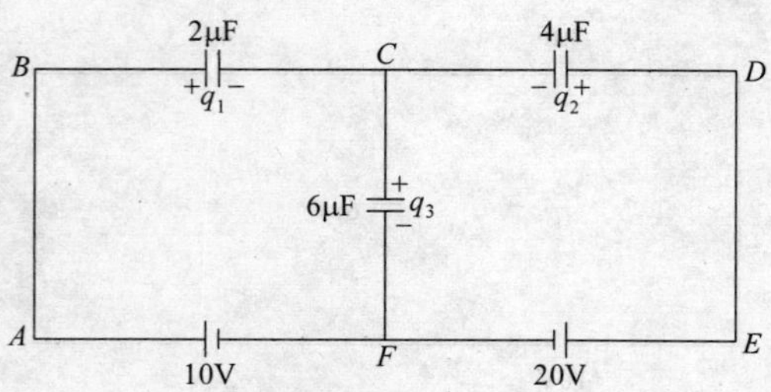

Figure 2.151

or $\quad q_3 = q_1 + q_2$

Writing the potential equation in the loop $BCFAB$, we get

$$V_B - \frac{q_1}{2} - \frac{q_3}{6} + 10 = V_B$$

$$\Rightarrow \quad q_3 + 3q_1 = 60 \qquad \ldots(2.164)$$

Writing the potential equation in the loop $CDEFC$, we get

$$V_C + \frac{q_2}{4} - 20 + \frac{q_3}{6} = V_C$$

$$\Rightarrow \quad 3q_2 + 2q_3 = 240 \qquad \ldots(2.165)$$

Solving the equation-(2.163), (2.164) and (2.165), we get

$$q_1 = \frac{10}{3}\mu C$$

$$q_2 = \frac{140}{3}\mu C$$

$$q_3 = 50\mu C$$

We can see that above charges obtained are same which we calculated by using nodal analysis by using a single variable x whereas in this method of flow of charges we solved three equations simultaneously for three variables thus in this question nodal analysis is much faster in solving. With practice students will be able to judge upon which method is to be used in which question. Specifically in single loop circuits when there are many circuit components are connected then method of flow of charges is preferred.

 # Illustrative Example 2.29

A capacitor has capacitance 10 μF and it is charged to a potential 150 V. A second capacitor has a capacitance of 20 μF and it is charged to a potential of 300 V. After charging, the two capacitors are connected in parallel with their same polarity plates together by using wires of negligible capacitance. Find how much energy is dissipated?

Solution

Charge on 10 μF capacitor is

$$q_1 = 10 \times 10^{-6} \times 150 = 1.5 \times 10^{-3}\text{ C}$$

Charge on 20μF capacitor is

$$q_2 = 20 \times 10^{-6} \times 300 = 6 \times 10^{-3}\text{ C}$$

When the two capacitors are connected in parallel, the total charge on combination is given as

$$q_T = (1.5 \times 10^{-3} + 6 \times 10^{-3}) = 7.5 \times 10^{-3}\text{ C}$$

The equivalent capacitance of parallel combination is 30 μF. If V be the final potential difference across the combination then it is given as

$$V = \frac{q_T}{C_{eq}} = \frac{7.5\times10^{-3}}{30\times10^{-6}} = 250\text{ V}$$

Total energy stored in capacitors before connection is

$$U_i = \frac{1}{2}(1.5 \times 10^{-3})\,150 + \frac{1}{2}(6 \times 10^{-3})\,300 = 1.0125\text{ J}$$

Energy after connecting capacitors in parallel is given as

$$U_f = \frac{1}{2}q_T V$$

$$\Rightarrow \quad U_f = \frac{1}{2} \times (7.5 \times 10^{-3})\,250$$

$$\Rightarrow \quad U_f = 0.9375\text{ J}$$

Energy dissipated after connecting capacitors in parallel is given as

$$\Delta U = U_i - U_f$$

$$\Rightarrow \qquad \Delta U = 1.0125 - 0.9375 = 0.075\ \text{J}$$

Illustrative Example 2.30

Figure-2.152 shows four capacitors with capacities C, 2 C, 3 C and 4 C are charged to the voltage, V, 2 V, 3 V and 4 V correspondingly. The circuit is closed by closing all the switches. Find the potential difference across all capacitors in steady state.

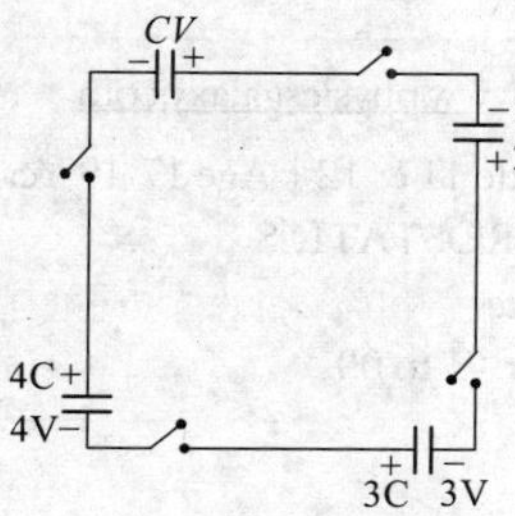

Figure 2.152

Solution

As this is a single loop circuit we prefer method of flow of charges in solving this. Here we consider a charge $+q$ circulates in the loop in clockwise direction until steady state is achieved. In steady state, the charges on the capacitors will be as shown in figure-2.153.

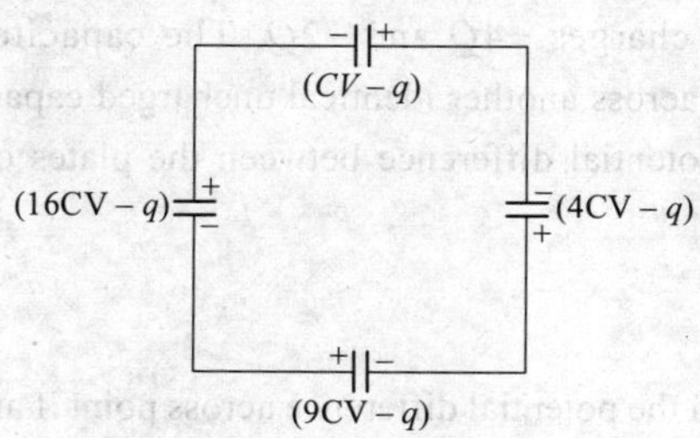

Figure 2.153

Now writing potential equation for the loop we have

$$\left(\frac{CV-q}{C}\right)+\left(\frac{4CV-q}{2C}\right)+\left(\frac{9CV-q}{3C}\right)+\left(\frac{16CV-q}{4C}\right)=0$$

$$\Rightarrow \qquad q = 4.8\,\text{CV} = \frac{24}{5}CV$$

Thus the potential difference across all the capacitors are now given as

$$V_1 = V - \frac{q}{C} = V - \frac{24}{5}V = -\frac{19}{5}V$$

$$V_2 = 2V - \frac{q}{2C} = 2V - \frac{24}{10}V = -\frac{2}{5}V$$

$$V_3 = 3V - \frac{q}{3C} = 3V - \frac{24}{15}V = \frac{7}{5}V$$

and $$V_4 = 4V - \frac{q}{4C} = 4V - \frac{6}{5}V = \frac{14}{5}V$$

Students are advised to solve this question by using nodal analysis also and verify the above results.

Illustrative Example 2.31

A battery of 10 V is connected to a capacitor of capacity 0.1 F. The battery is now removed and this capacitor is connected to a second uncharged capacitor. If the charges are distributed equally on these two capacitors, find the total energy stored in the two capacitors. Find the ratio of final energy to initial energy stored in capacitors.

Solution

As charges are equally distributed on capacitors that means the capacitors are identical so that they will have same charges at same potential difference across them and charges are distributed half and half on the two identical capacitors.

Initial energy stored in the capacitors is

$$U_i = \frac{1}{2}CV^2 + 0$$

$$\Rightarrow \qquad U_i = \frac{1}{2} \times 0.1 \times 10^2 = 5\ \text{J}$$

After connection with identical capacitor, the common potential difference across combination is given as

$$V_f = \frac{CV+0}{C+C} = \frac{V}{2} = 5\ \text{V}$$

Final energy stored in capacitors is

$$U_f = \frac{1}{2}(2C)V^2$$

$$\Rightarrow \qquad U_f = CV^2 = 0.1^2 \times 5^2$$

$$\Rightarrow \qquad U_f = 2.5\ \text{J}$$

$$\Rightarrow \qquad \frac{U_f}{U_i} = \frac{2.5}{5} = \frac{1}{2}$$

Illustrative Example 2.32

Two capacitors A and B with capacitances 3 μF and 2 μF are charged to potential difference of 100 V and 180 V respectively. The plates of the capacitors are connected as shown in figure-2.154 with one wire from each capacitor free.

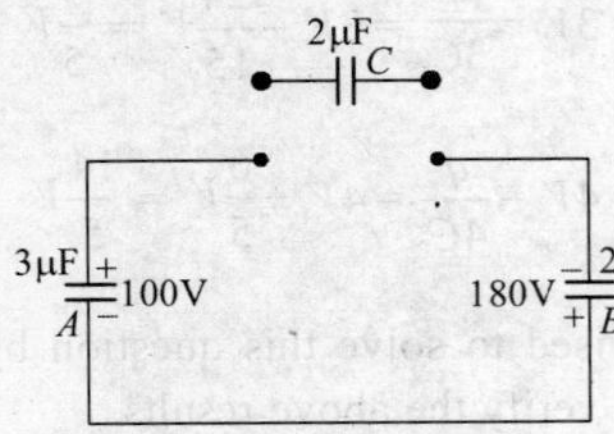

Figure 2.154

The upper plate of A is positive and that of B is negative. An uncharged 2 μF capacitor C with lead wires falls on the free ends to complete the circuit. Calculate

(i) The final charge on the three capacitors

(ii) The amount of electrostatic energy stored in the system before and after the capacitor C falls and the circuit is closed.

Solution

(i) Let q be the charge flowing in clockwise sence during redistribution of charge as shown in figure-2.155. We can write the potential equation for this loop as

$$-\frac{q}{2}+\frac{360-q}{2}+\frac{300-q}{3}=0$$

$$\Rightarrow \qquad q=210\,\mu\text{C}$$

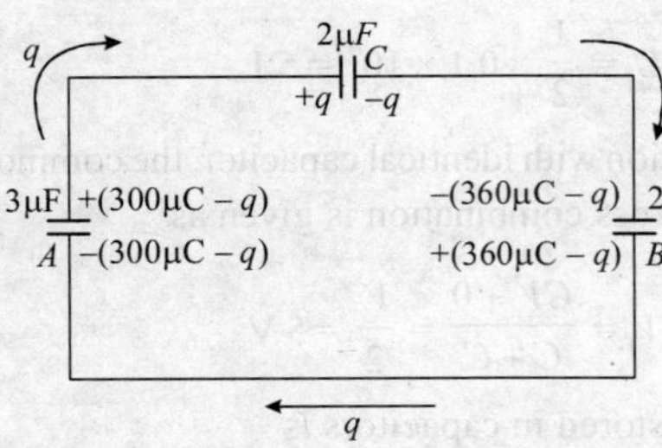

Figure 2.155

Thus final charges on the capacitors are

$$q_A=300-210=90\,\mu C$$

$$q_B=360-210=150\,\mu C$$

$$q_C=210=210\,\mu C$$

(ii) Initial electrostatic energy stored is given as

$$U_i=\frac{1}{2}\times(3\times10^{-6})(100)^2+\frac{1}{2}\times(2\times10^{-6})(180)^2$$

$$\Rightarrow \qquad U_i=4.74\times10^{-2}\,\text{J}=47.4\times10^{-3}\,\text{J}=47.4\,\text{mJ}$$

Final electrostatic energy stored is given as

$$U_f=\frac{(90\times10^{-6})^2}{2\times(3\times10^{-6})}+\frac{(150\times10^{-6})^2}{2\times(2\times10^{-6})}+\frac{(210\times10^{-6})^2}{2\times(2\times10^{-6})}$$

$$\Rightarrow \qquad U_f=1.8\times10^{-2}\,\text{J}=18\,\text{mJ}.$$

Web Reference at www.physicsgalaxy.com

Age Group - Grade 11 & 12 | Age 17-19 Years

Section - ELECTROSTATICS

Topic - Capacitance

Module Number - 1 to 00

Practice Exercise 2.5

(i) A capacitor of capacitance C_1 = 1 μF initially charged with voltage V = 300 V is connected in parallel with an uncharged capacitor C_2 = 2 μF. Find the increment of the electric energy of this system by the moment steady state is achieved.

[– 0.03 mJ]

(ii) The plates of a parallel plate capacitor of capacitance C are given charges $+4Q$ and $-2Q$. The capacitor is then connected across another identical uncharged capacitor. Find the final potential difference between the plates of the first capacitor.

[$3Q/2C$]

(iii) Find the potential difference across point A and B in the circuit shown in figure-2.156.

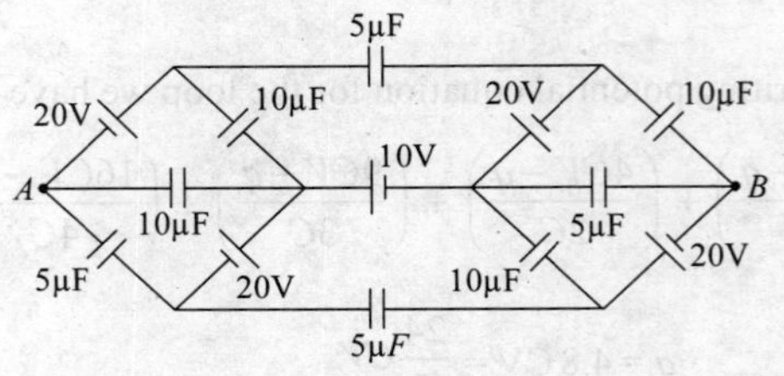

Figure 2.156

[10V]

(iv) Find the potential difference $V_a - V_b$ between the points a and b shown in figure-2.157.

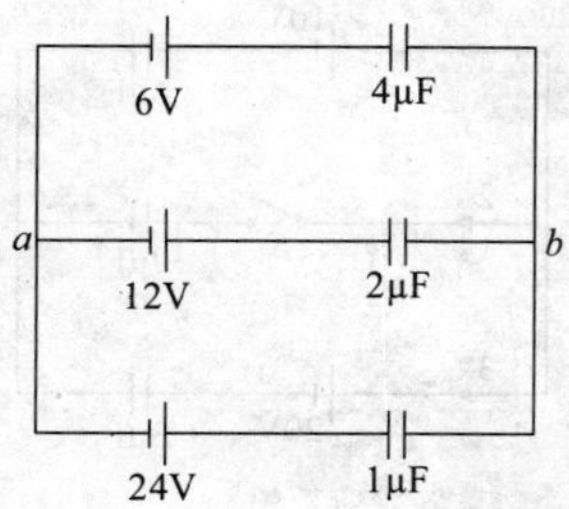

Figure 2.157

$[-\frac{72}{7}V]$

(v) In given circuit first switch S_{W_1} is closed and S_{W_2} is open. After long time S_{W_1} is opened and S_{W_2} is closed. Calculate charge on each capacitor.

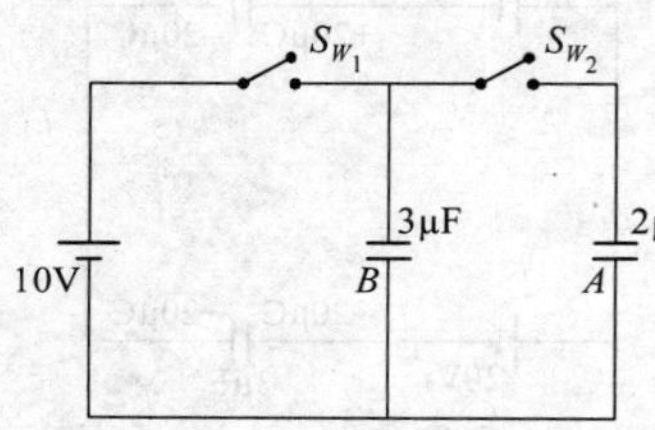

Figure 2.158

$[Q_A = 12\ \mu C;\ Q_B = 18\mu C]$

(vi) The figure-2.159 shows four identical conducting plates each of area A. The separation between the consecutive plates is equal to d. When both the switches are closed, find the charge present on the upper surface of the lowest plate from the top.

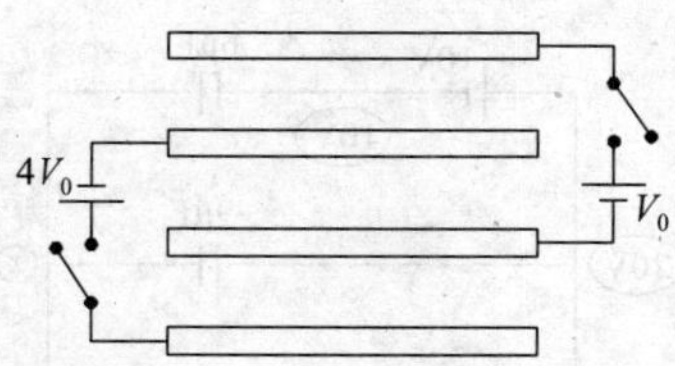

Figure 2.159

$[\frac{3\epsilon_0 AV_0}{d}]$

(vii) Two parallel plate capacitors A and B having capacitance 1 μF and 5 μF are charged separately by batteries of same voltage 100 V. Now the positive plate of A is connected to the negative plate of B and negative plate of A to the positive plate of. Find the final charge on each condenser and total loss of electrical energy in the condensers.

$[\frac{200}{3}\ \mu C,\ \frac{1000}{3}\ \mu C,\ \frac{0.05}{3}\ J]$

(viii) In the circuit shown in figure-2.160 two capacitors and two batteries are connected in a closed loop. Find the charges on capacitor C_1 and C_2 in steady state.

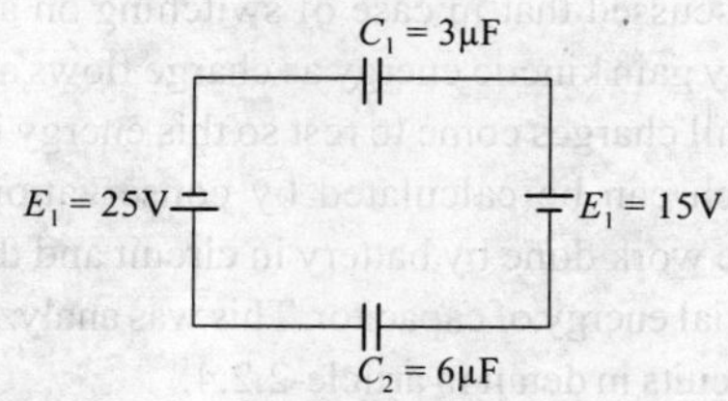

Figure 2.160

[80 μC, 80 μC]

(ix) In the circuit shown in figure-2.161 calculate the energy stored in 5μF capacitor in steady state.

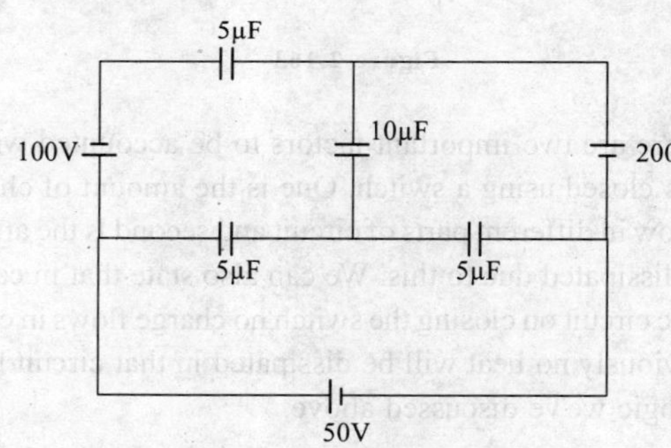

Figure 2.161

[700μC]

(x) In the circuit shown in figure-2.162 calculate the charge on 3μF capacitor in steady state.

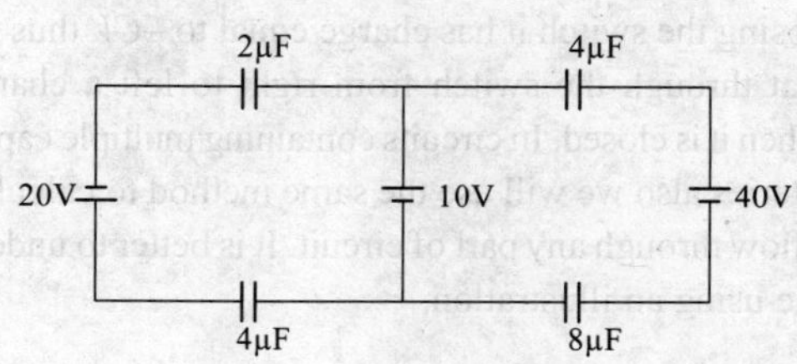

Figure 2.162

[40 μC]

2.8 *Effect of Switching in Capacitive Circuits*

Figure-2.163 shows a simple circuit containing a capacitor to a battery via a switch. We've already discussed that on closing the switch battery transfers a charge $q = CV$ from right plate of capacitor to its left plate and then current in circuit becomes zero after a short time when steady state is attained. The charging of capacitor takes place quickly because we consider connecting wires as perfect conductors due to which quickly free electrons can flow and capacitor gets fully charged to steady state. We have also discussed that in case of switching on a circuit free electrons may gain kinetic energy as charge flows and finally in steady state all charges come to rest so this energy is dissipated as heat which can be calculated by conservation of energy including the work done by battery in circuit and the change in stored potential energy of capacitor. This was analyzed for single capacitor circuits in detail in article-2.2.4.

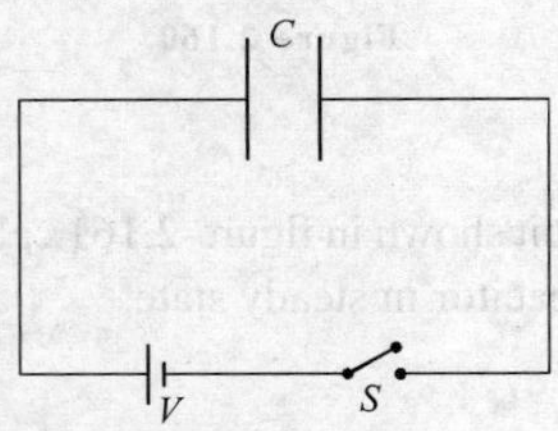

Figure 2.163

Thus there are two important factors to be accounted when a circuit is closed using a switch. One is the amount of charges which flow in different parts of circuit and second is the amount of heat dissipated due to this. We can also state that in case of a specific circuit on closing the switch no charge flows in circuit then obviously no heat will be dissipated in that circuit based on the logic we've discussed above.

2.8.1 Charge Flow in a Part of Circuit due to Switching

In the process of switching as shown in figure-2.163 if we analyze the amount of charge flown through the switch when it is closed then it can be given as the change in charges on the plate of capacitor connected to either side of the switch. In this case initially right plate of capacitor was having zero charge and after closing the switch it has charge equal to $-CV$ thus we can state that through the switch from right to left a charge CV flows when it is closed. In circuits containing multiple capacitors and batteries also we will use the same method to calculate the charge flow through any part of circuit. It is better to understand the same using an illustration.

Figure-2.164 shows a circuit containing two batteries and three capacitors along with a switch S as shown. In the circuit there are three paths shown by arrows marked 1, 2 and 3 along the three branches of the circuit. In this situation we are required to determine the charges which flows along the paths 1, 2 and 3 when the switch is closed.

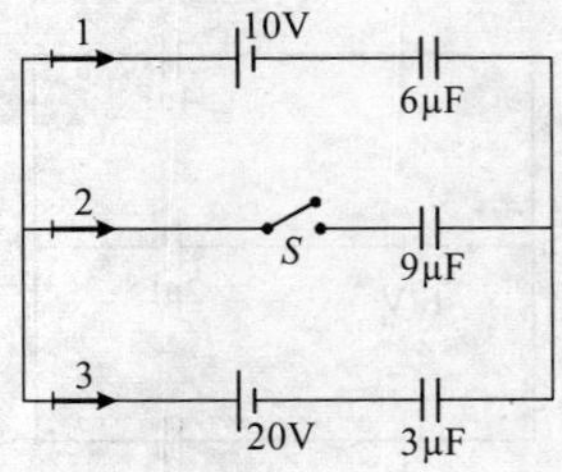

Figure 2.164

In such cases to find the charges flowing through specified paths in circuit branches we redraw the circuit and solve it twice. First before closing the switch by removing the switching branch and second after closing the switch by connecting the switching branch. In above case first we draw the circuit by removing the middle branch and solve it as shown in figure-2.165.

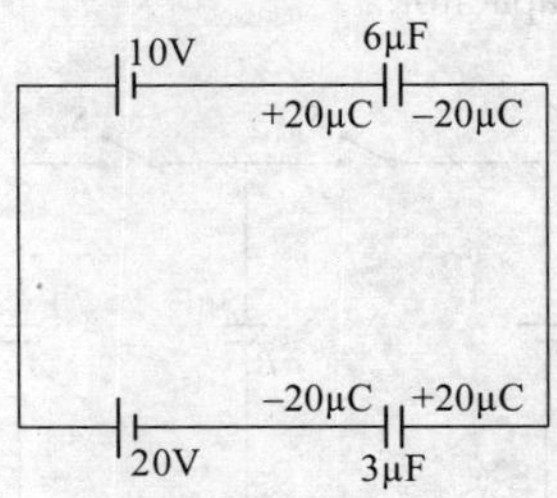

Figure 2.165

In figure-2.165 we can see that 6μF and 3μF capacitors are in series of which equivalent capacitance will be $(6 \times 3)/(6+3) = 2$ μF and connected across a potential difference of $30 - 20 = 10$ V thus charge on both capacitors will be $2 \times 10 = 20$ μC which is shown in figure-2.165 with high potential plate having positive charge. After closing the switch the middle branch will be included and the final circuit is shown in figure-166.

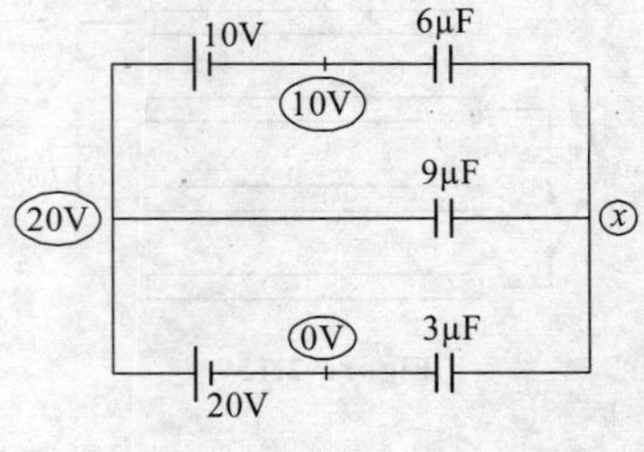

Figure-2.166

To solve this circuit we use nodal analysis for which potentials are distributed in circuit as shown in figure-2.165. If we write nodal equation for unknown potential x on the rightmost node junction then it is written as

$$3(x-0)+9(x-20)+6(x+10)=0$$

$$\Rightarrow \quad 6x=40$$

$$\Rightarrow \quad x=\frac{20}{3}\text{V}$$

Using the value of x we can calculate the final charges on the three capacitors after closing the switch which are given as

$$q_{3\mu F}=3\left(\frac{20}{3}-0\right)=20\ \mu C$$

$$q_{9\mu F}=9\left(20-\frac{20}{3}\right)=120\ \mu C$$

and $$q_{6\mu F}=6\left(\frac{20}{3}+10\right)=100\ \mu C$$

Charge on the plate of capacitor of higher potential will be positive and that at lower potential will be negative so the charges on plates of each capacitor is shown in figure-2.167.

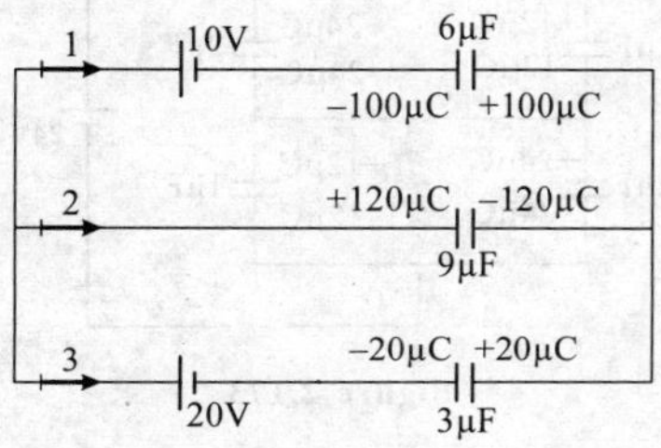

Figure 2.167

Simultaneously looking at figures-2.165 and 2.167 we can easily determine the charges flown through the paths 1, 2 and 3 by finding the difference of charges on the plates connected on either side of these paths.

For path-1 we can see that it is connected to left plate of 6 μF capacitor on which initial charges was –20 μC and after closing the switch it becomes –100 μC that means –80 μC charge is deposited on this plate through path-1. Similarly we can see the left plate of 9 μF capacitor which was uncharged before closing the switch and after switched is closed charge on this plate becomes +120 μC thus it is clear that this charge is deposited on this place through path 2. For path-3 we analyze that the initial charge on left plate of 3 μF capacitor was +20 μC and after closing the switch it becomes –20 μC thus the amount of charge flowing through path-3 is –40 μC thus we have the charges flowing through the three paths as asked in figure-2.164 which is given as

$$\Delta q_1=-80\ \mu C$$

$$\Delta q_2=+120\ \mu C$$

$$\Delta q_3=-40\ \mu C$$

Similar to above there can be many cases in which we can calculate the amount of charge flow due to switching in a circuit. Next we will understand the same concept by some illustrations.

 # Illustrative Example 2.33

What charges will flow after closing the switch S in the circuit shown in figure-2.168 through sections 1 and 2 in directions indicated by the arrows?

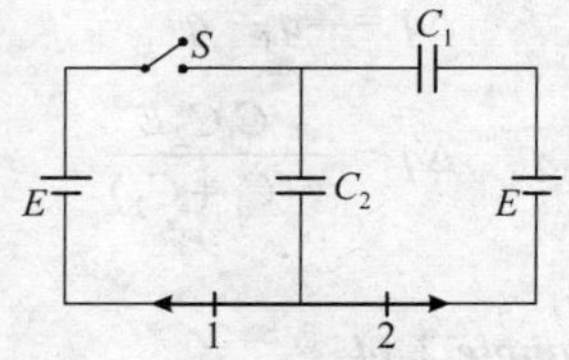

Figure 2.168

Solution

In figure-2.168, the two capacitors are connected in series when switch is open and their equivalent capacitance is given as

$$C'=\frac{C_1C_2}{C_1+C_2}$$

Charge q on both the capacitors will be due to the battery on right side which is given as

$$q=\frac{C_1C_2E}{(C_1+C_2)}$$

When the switch is closed, the charge distribution is shown in figure-2.169.

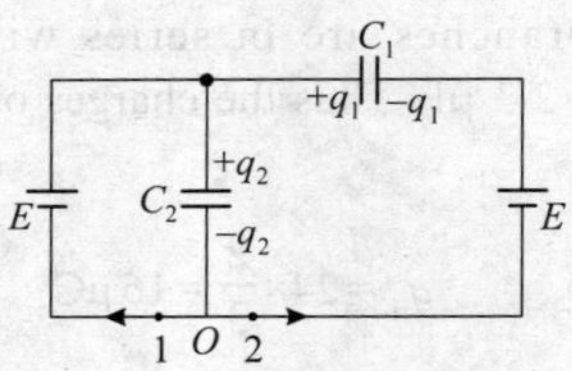

Figure 2.169

As capacitor C_2 is directly connected to left battery, its charge can be given as

$$q_2=C_2E \qquad \ldots(2.166)$$

If we carefully look at the capacitor C_1 from its left and right side potentials will be same due to the two batteries so its potential difference will be zero hence charge on it will also become zero after closing the switch.

$$q_1=0$$

Thus charge flowing through section 1 is the sum of charges on top plate of C_2 and left plate of C_1 after closing the switch because initially this sum was zero, which is now given as

$$\Delta q_1 = C_2 E$$

Charge flowing through section 2 is the difference in charges of the right plate of capacitor C_1 which is given as

$$\Delta q_2 = -q_1 - q$$

$$\Rightarrow \quad \Delta q_2 = -\frac{C_1 C_2 E}{(C_1 + C_2)}$$

Illustrative Example 2.34

Four uncharged capacitors are charged by 24 V battery as shown in the figure-2.170. How much charge flows through switch S when it is closed?

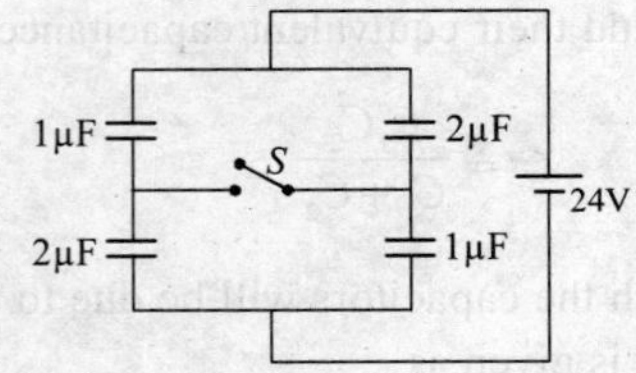

Figure 2.170

Solution

Initially when switch is open, across the terminals A and B as shown in figure-2.171 the potential difference is 24 V thus the left and right branches are in series with capacitance $(1 \times 2)/(1 + 2) = 2/3$ μF. Thus the charges on capacitors are given as

$$q_1 = 24 \times \frac{2}{3} = 16\,\mu\text{C}$$

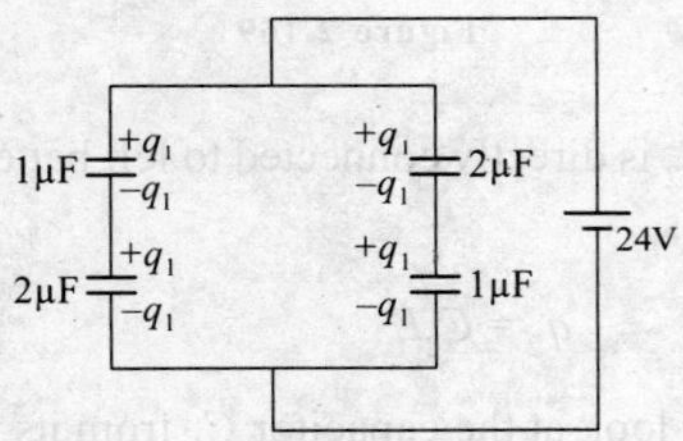

Figure 2.171

When switch is closed the circuit will be as shown in figure-2.172. To calculate the charges on capacitors in this case we apply nodal analysis and consider potentials as shown in figure.

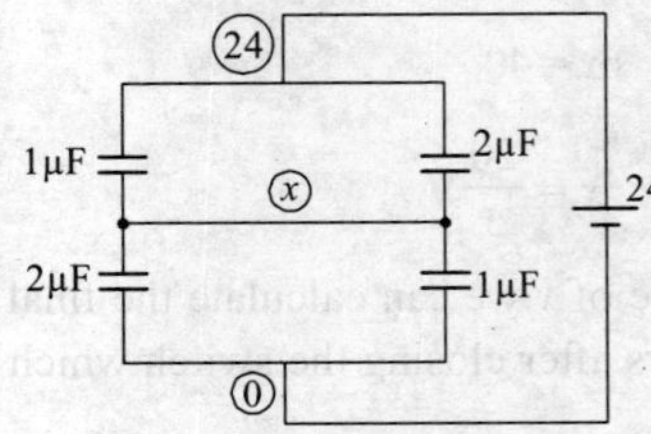

Figure 2.172

Writing nodal equation for x, we have

$$1(x - 24) + 2(x - 0) + 1(x - 0) + 2(x - 24) = 0$$

$$6x = 72$$

$$\Rightarrow \quad x = 12\,\text{V}$$

Thus final charges on the capacitor are as shown in figure-2.173

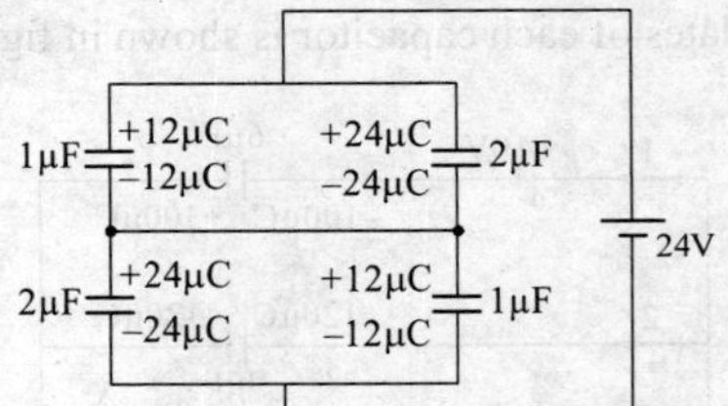

Figure 2.173

Initially on either side of the switch the sum of charges on the plates of two capacitor was zero and final sum of charges on the plates of the two capacitors on the left side is 12 μC which is flown toward left when the switch was closed thus charge flowing through switch S is 12 μC towards left.

2.8.2 Heat Produced due to Switching in a circuit

In article-2.2.4 we have discussed the amount of heat dissipated in process of charging a capacitor which was calculated by conservation of energy. In general when we close a switch in a capacitive circuit then due to redistribution of charges energy stored in capacitor changes and batteries in circuit also supply or absorb energy due to flow of charge through these batteries and we can calculate the total loss in energy as dissipation of heat in circuit.

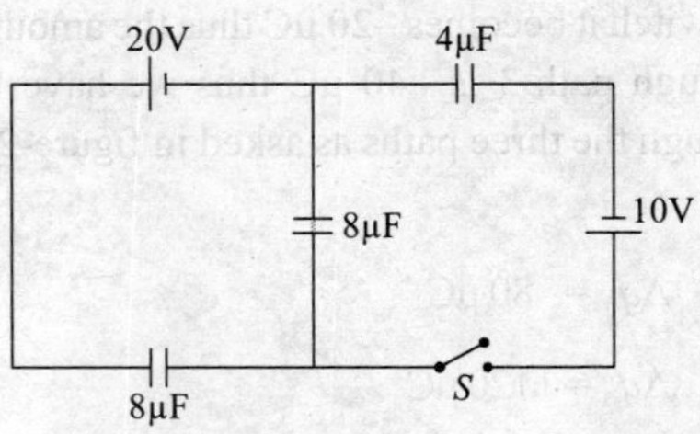

Figure 2.174

In article-2.2.4 we analyzed and calculated this for a single capacitor. Now consider a circuit shown in figure-2.174 in steady state. In this circuit we are required to calculate the amount of heat produced on closing the switch S.

To calculate the amount of charges flowing through different branches of circuit we first solve the circuit before and after closing the switch as explained in previous article. The circuit before and after closing the switch is shown in Figure-2.175(a) and (b).

In Figure-2.175(a) we can see that the two 8 μF capacitors are connected in series across 20 V battery. The equivalent capacitance of these two capacitors in series will be 4μF thus the charge on both capacitors in series will be 4 × 20 = 80 μC which is shown on plates of capacitors in figure-2.175(a).

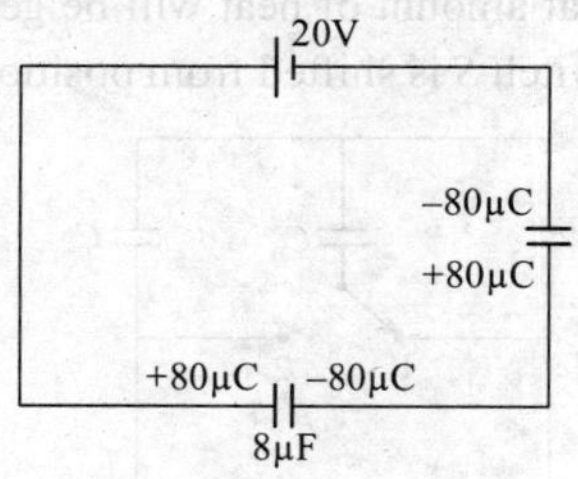

(a)

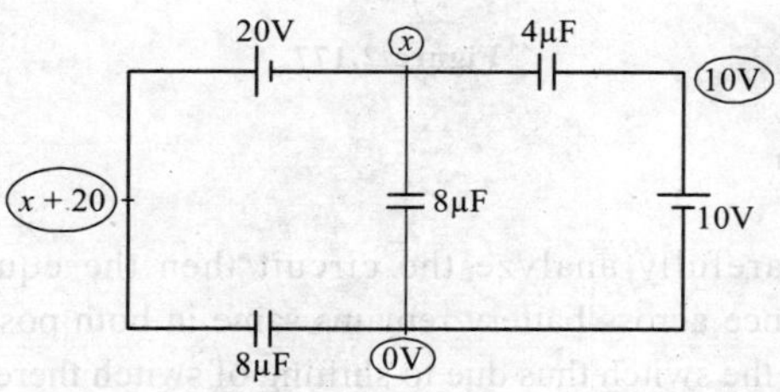

(b)

Figure 2.175

When switch S is closed then circuit is shown in figure-2.175(b). To solve the circuit we use nodal analysis and distribute the potentials at different parts of circuit as shown by considering zero potential reference at the negative terminal of the 10 V battery. In this circuit we write nodal equation for the unknown potential x as

$$8(x + 20 - 0) + 8x + 4(x - 10) = 0$$

$$\Rightarrow \quad 5x = -30$$

$$\Rightarrow \quad x = -6\text{ V}$$

As x is known we can calculate final charges on the three capacitors as

$$q_{8\mu F} = 8(20 - 6) = 112\ \mu C$$

$$q_{8\mu F} = 8 \times 6 = 48\ \mu C$$

$$q_{4\mu F} = 4 \times 16 = 64\ \mu C$$

Figure-2.176 shows the charges on the plates of the three capacitors with higher potential plate of a capacitor has positive charge.

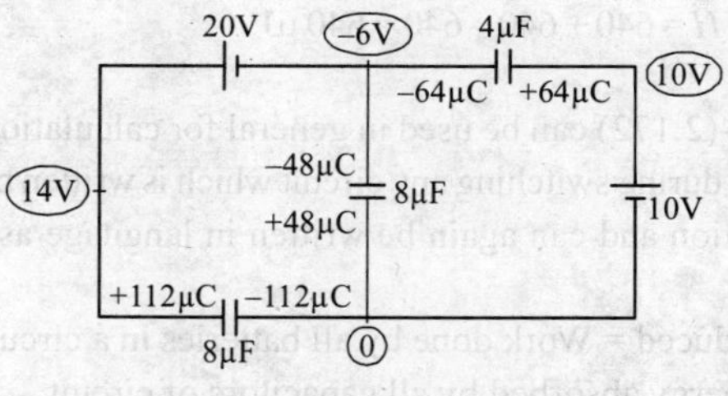

Figure 2.176

If we compare figure-2.175(a) with 2.176 we can calculate the charges which flow through batteries. On left plate of lower 8 μF capacitor initial charge was +80 μC and after closing the switch it became +112 μC that means 112 – 80 = 32 μC charge flows from right to left through 20 V battery thus work done by this battery after closing the switch is given as

$$W_{20V} = 32 \times 20 = 640\ \mu J \qquad \dots(2.167)$$

If we look at the right plate of 4 μF capacitor then initially it was uncharged and after closing the switch this plate has +64 μC charge which flows in upward direction from 10 V battery thus work done by battery after closing the switch is given as

$$W_{10V} = 64 \times 10 = 640\ \mu J \qquad \dots(2.168)$$

If we calculate the total energy stored in capacitors before closing the switch then it is given as

$$U_i = \frac{1}{2} \times 4 \times 10^{-6} \times (20)^2 = 800\ \mu J \qquad \dots(2.169)$$

After closing the switch if we calculate the total energy stored in all the capacitors then it is given as

$$U_f = \frac{1}{2} \times 8 \times 10^{-6} \times (14)^2 + \frac{1}{2} \times 8 \times 10^{-6} \times (6)^2 + \frac{1}{2} \times 4 \times 10^{-6} \times (16)^2$$

$$\Rightarrow \quad U_f = 784 + 144 + 512 = 1440\ \mu J \qquad \dots(2.170)$$

Total energy gained by capacitors due to switching can be calculated by equations-(2.169) and (2.170) which is given as

$$\Delta U = U_f - U_i$$

$$\Rightarrow \quad \Delta U = 1440 - 800 = 640\ \mu J \qquad \dots(2.171)$$

By conservation of energy as discussed in article-2.2.4 the heat produced in circuit due to switching can be given by

$$H = W_{\text{batteries}} - \Delta U_{\text{absorbed by capacitors}} \quad \ldots(2.172)$$

$$\Rightarrow \quad H = W_{20V} + W_{10V} - \Delta U$$

$$\Rightarrow \quad H = 640 + 640 - 640 = 640\ \mu\text{J} \quad \ldots(2.173)$$

Equation-(2.172) can be used in general for calculation of heat produced during switching any circuit which is written by energy conservation and can again be written in language as

Heat Produced = Work done by all batteries in a circuit – Energy absorbed by all capacitors of circuit

Both the terms on right hand side of equation-(2.172) are to be calculated separately as explained in above illustration.

There is an alternative way of calculation of total heat produced due to switching by using the change in charge on plates of each capacitor. If expressionally equation-(2.172) is solved in terms of change in charges on all capacitors then it will reduce to a form given below in equation-(2.174) which students can verify on their own and use this result directly for calculation of heat produced in a capacitive circuit. This is given as

$$H = \sum_{i=1}^{i=N} \frac{(\Delta q_i)^2}{2C_i} \quad \ldots(2.174)$$

In equation-(2.174) N are the total number of capacitors of the circuit and Δq_i is the change in charge on the plates of ith capacitor of capacitance C_i. For a given circuit containing N capacitors, above equation can be expanded as

$$H = \frac{\Delta q_1^2}{2C_1} + \frac{\Delta q_2^2}{2C_2} + \ldots\ldots + \frac{\Delta q_N^2}{2C_N} \quad \ldots(2.175)$$

Above relation given in equation-(2.175) can be directly used to calculate the amount of heat produced on switching in any capacitive circuit. We can also verify the results obtained in above illustration using this expression.

In above illustration by comparing figure-2.175(a) and 2.176 we can find the difference in charges on the plates of the three capacitors as

$$\Delta q_{8\text{mF}} = 112 - 80 = 32\ \mu\text{C}$$

$$\Delta q_{8\text{mF}} = 80 - 48 = 32\ \mu\text{C}$$

$$\Delta q_{4\text{mF}} = 64 - 0 = 64\ \mu\text{C}$$

Thus by equation-(2.175) heat produced can be calculated as

$$H = \frac{\Delta q_1^2}{2C_1} + \frac{\Delta q_2^2}{2C_2} + \frac{\Delta q_3^2}{2C_3}$$

$$\Rightarrow \quad H = \frac{(32\times10^{-6})^2}{2(8\times10^{-6})} + \frac{(32\times10^{-6})^2}{2(8\times10^{-6})} + \frac{(64\times10^{-6})^2}{2(4\times10^{-6})}$$

$$\Rightarrow \quad H = 64 + 64 + 512 = 640\ \mu\text{J} \quad \ldots(2.176)$$

Above equation-(2.176) is same as calculated in equation-(2.158). Thus the expression given in equation-(2.175) is a direct method to calculate heat produced in a capacitive circuit on switching. Students are advised to resolve all illustration on calculation of heat dissipation discussed after article-2.2.4 using equation-(2.175) and verify the results obtained.

Illustrative Example 2.35

Figure-2.177 shows a circuit with three capacitors connected with a battery. What amount of heat will be generated in the circuit when the switch S is shifted from position 1 to 2.

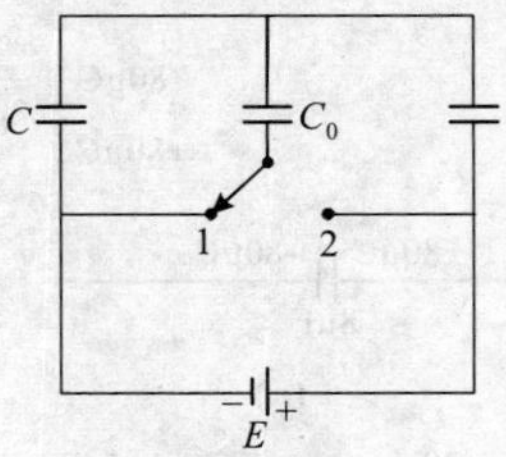

Figure 2.177

Solution

If we carefully analyze the circuit then the equivalent capacitance across battery remains same in both positions 1 and 2 of the switch thus due to shifting of switch there will be no change in total energy stored in capacitors. Thus energy absorbed by the capacitors on shifting the switch will be zero.

$$\Delta U = 0$$

The equivalent capacitance across the battery is given as

$$C_{\text{eq}} = \frac{C(C + C_0)}{C_0 + 2C}$$

Charge on bottom plate of left capacitor when switch is in position 1 is given as

$$q_1 = C_{\text{eq}} E \times \frac{C}{C + C_0} = \frac{C^2 E}{C_0 + 2C}$$

When switch is shifted to position 2, as the equivalent capacitance remain same because middle capacitor C_0 is now in parallel to the right capacitor so the charge on left capacitor after shifting the switch is given as

$$q_2 = C_{\text{eq}} E = \frac{C(C + C_0)E}{C_0 + 2C}$$

During the process of switching the charge flown through battery is given as

$$\Delta q = q_2 - q_1$$

$$\Rightarrow \quad \Delta q = \frac{C(C+C_0)E}{C_0+2C} - \frac{C^2E}{C_0+2C}$$

$$\Rightarrow \quad \Delta q = \frac{CC_0E}{C_0+2C}$$

Work done by the battery during the process of shifting of switch from position 1 to position 2 is given as

$$W = \Delta q\, E$$

$$\Rightarrow \quad W = \frac{CC_0E^2}{C_0+2C}$$

Heat dissipated can be given as

$$H = W - \Delta U$$

$$\Rightarrow \quad H = \frac{CC_0E^2}{C_0+2C} - 0 = \frac{CC_0E^2}{C_0+2C}$$

Students are advised to solve this illustration using the equation-(2.175) to understand the application of direct heat calculation.

Illustrative Example 2.36

In the circuit shown, each capacitor has a capacitance C. The cell voltage is E. Find the amount of charge flowing through the switch when it is closed and also find the heat dissipated in the circuit when the switch is closed.

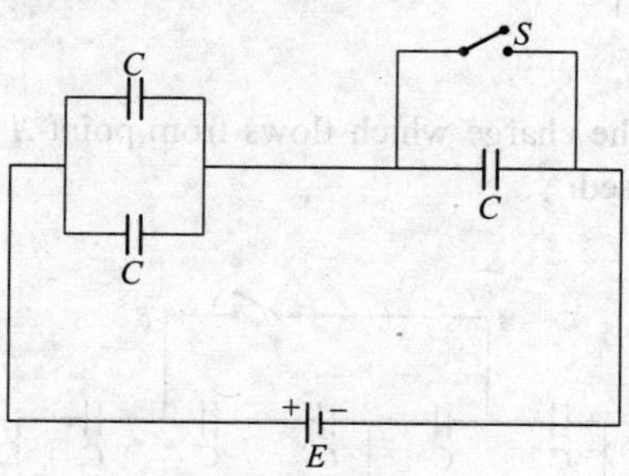

Figure 2.178

Solution

Initial capacitance of the circuit when switch was open is given as

$$C_i = \frac{(C)(2C)}{C+2C} = \frac{2}{3}C$$

Charge supplied by the battery is $q = (2C/3)E$ and the charges on capacitors in open state of switch are shown in figure-2.179.

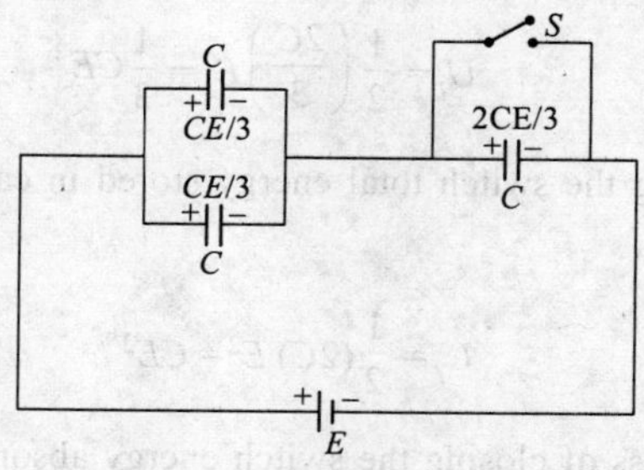

Figure 2.179

When the switch is closed, rightmost capacitor will be short circuited and no charge will reside on its plates. Final capacitance of the circuit across battery will now be given as

$$C_f = 2C$$

In this state final charges on capacitor plates are shown in figure-2.180.

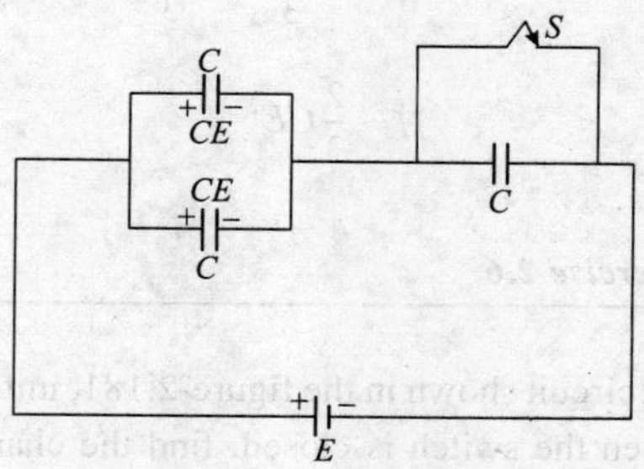

Figure 2.180

Left side of the switch is connected to the node junction M on which in its open state sum of the charges on the three plates of capacitors was 0 and in closed state it is –2 CE thus from the switch 2 CE amount of charge flows from left to right when it is closed.

On the left plates of the two capacitors which are connected to battery total charge initially before closing the switch was +2CE/3 and after closing the switch it is +2 CE thus the total charge flown through the battery is

$$\Delta q = 2CE - \frac{2CE}{3} = \frac{4CE}{3}$$

Thus in the process of closing the switch work done by the battery in redistribution of charges is given as

$$W = \Delta q\, E = \frac{4CE^2}{3} \qquad \ldots(2.177)$$

Initial energy stored in all the capacitors when switch was in open state is given as

$$U_i = \frac{1}{2}\left(\frac{2C}{3}\right)E^2 = \frac{1}{3}CE^2 \qquad \ldots(2.178)$$

After closing the switch total energy stored in capacitors is given as

$$U_f = \frac{1}{2}(2C)E^2 = CE^2 \qquad \ldots(2.179)$$

In the process of closing the switch energy absorbed by the capacitors is given as

$$\Delta U = U_f - U_i$$

$$= CE^2 - \frac{1}{3}CE^2 = \frac{2}{3}CE^2$$

By conservation of energy, heat dissipation is given as

$$H = W - \Delta U$$

$$\Rightarrow \quad H = \frac{4CE^2}{3} - \frac{2}{3}CE^2$$

$$\Rightarrow \quad H = \frac{2}{3}CE^2$$

Practice Exercise 2.6

(i) In the circuit shown in the figure-2.181, initially switch is open. When the switch is closed, find the charge passing through the switch and the direction of charge flow.

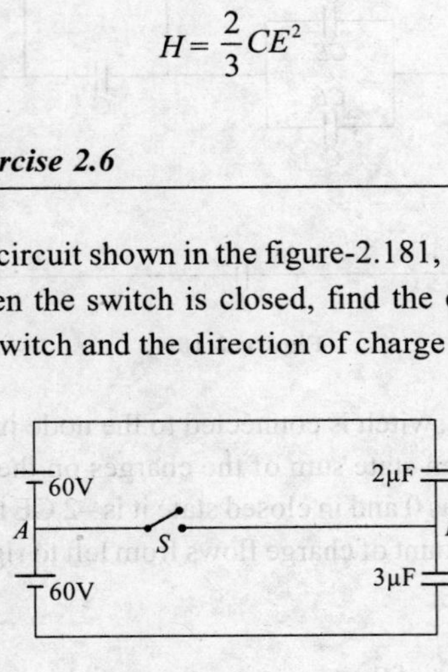

Figure 2.181

[60μC, *A* to *B*]

(ii) Three capacitor each having capacitance $C = 2\ \mu F$ are connected with a 30 V battery as shown in figure-2.182. When the switch *S* is closed. Find

(a) the amount of charge flown through the battery

(b) the heat generated in the circuit

(c) the energy supplied by the battery

(d) the amount of charge flown through the switch *S*

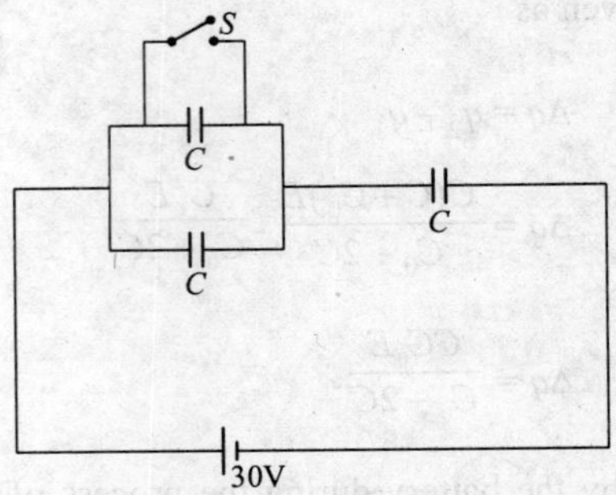

Figure 2.182

[(a) 20 μC; (b) 0.3 mJ; (c) 0.6 mJ; (d) 60 μC]

(iii) Two capacitors of capacitance 1 μF and 2 μF are charged to potential difference 20 V and 15 V as shown in figure-2.183. If now terminal *B* and *C* are connected together and terminal *A* with positive terminal of a 30 V battery and *D* with negative terminal of battery as shown in figure-2.183(b) then find the final charges on both the capacitor after closing the switch *S*.

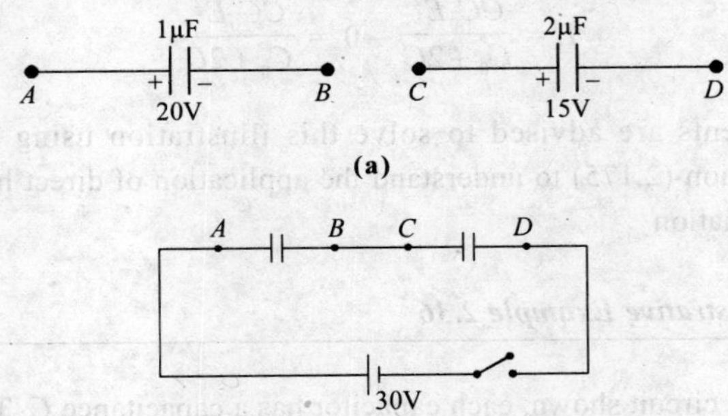

Figure 2.183

[$\frac{50}{3}$ μC, $\frac{80}{3}$ μC]

(iv) Find the charge which flows from point *A* to *B*, when switch is closed.

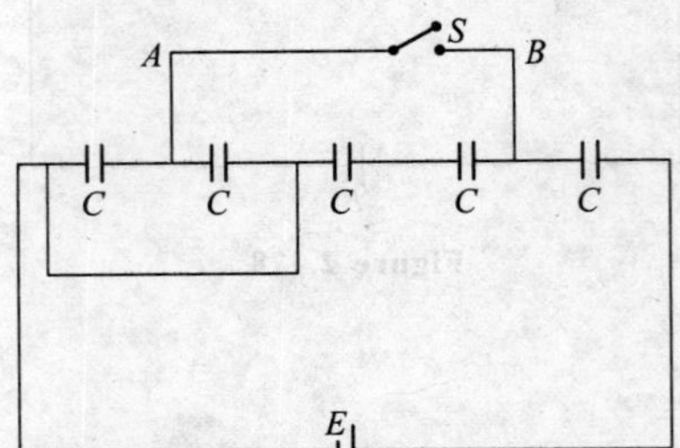

Figure 2.184

[$-\frac{4}{7}CE$]

(v) Three capacitors of 2 μF, 3 μF and 5 μF are individually charged with batteries of emf's 5 V, 20 V and 10 V respectively. After disconnecting from the voltage sources, these capacitors are connected as shown in figure-2.185 with their positive polarity plates are connected to A and negative polarity is earthed. Now a battery of 20 V and an uncharged capacitor of 4 μF capacitance are connected to the junction A as shown with a switch S. When switch is closed, find (a) the potential of the junction A. (b) final charges on all four capacitors.

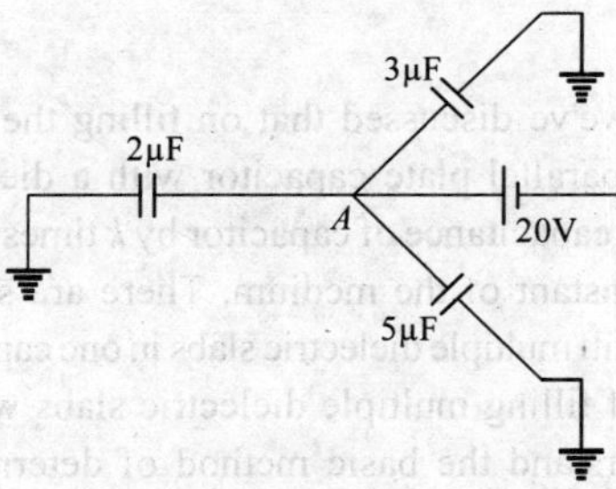

Figure 2.185

[(a) $\frac{100}{7}$ V; (b) 28.56 μC; 42.84 μC; 71.4 μC; 22.85 μC]

(vi) Find the amount of heat produced in the circuit shown in figure-2.186 when switch is closed. Capacitance of both capacitors is equal to C.

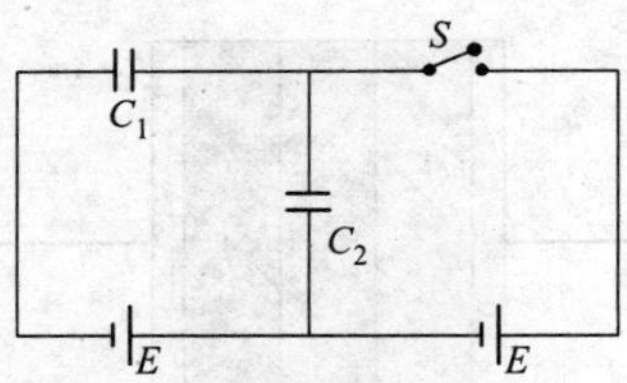

Figure 2.186

[$\frac{5}{4}CE^2$]

(vii) Find the amount of heat produced in the circuit shown in figure-2.187 when switch is closed. Each capacitor in circuit is of capacitance 2 μF.

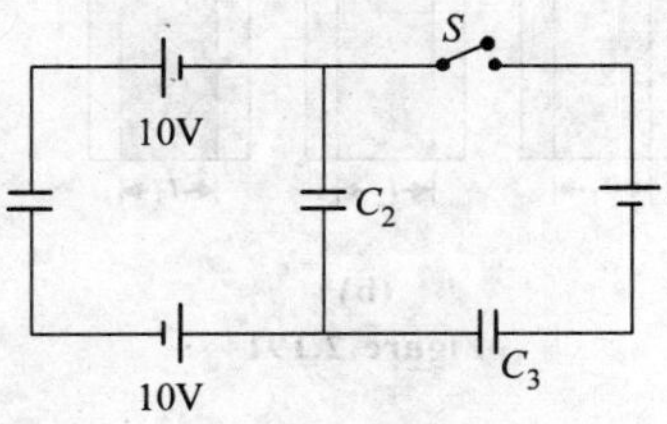

Figure 2.187

[0.3 mJ]

(viii) Find the amount of heat produced in the circuit shown in figure-2.188 when switch is closed.

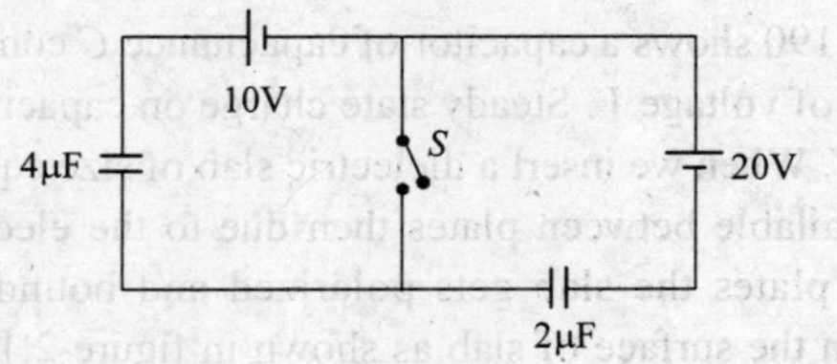

Figure 2.188

[No heat produced]

2.9 Dielectrics in Capacitors

In previous chapter we've studied that on placing a dielectric in electric field its dipoles get polarized and align along the direction of electric field. When between the plates of a parallel plate capacitor a dielectric slab of dielectric constant $\in_r = k$ is inserted to fill the space between the plates as shown in figure-2.189 then the capacitance of parallel plate capacitor is given as

$$C = \frac{\in_r \in_0 A}{d} = kC$$

Where C is the capacitance of empty capacitor. Thus on filling the space between plates of a capacitor with a dielectric medium its capacitance increases to k times where k is the dielectric constant of the medium.

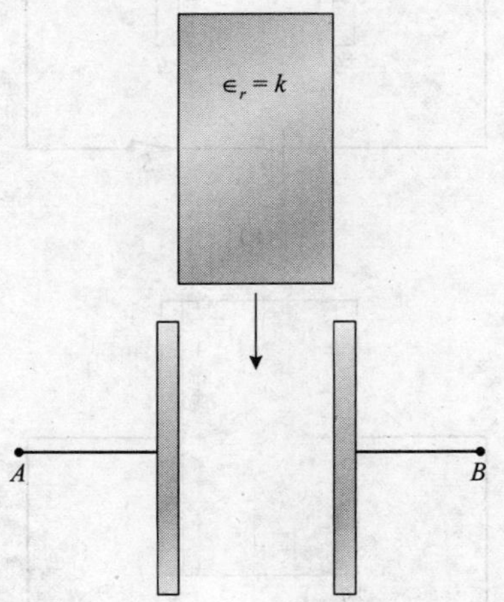

(a)

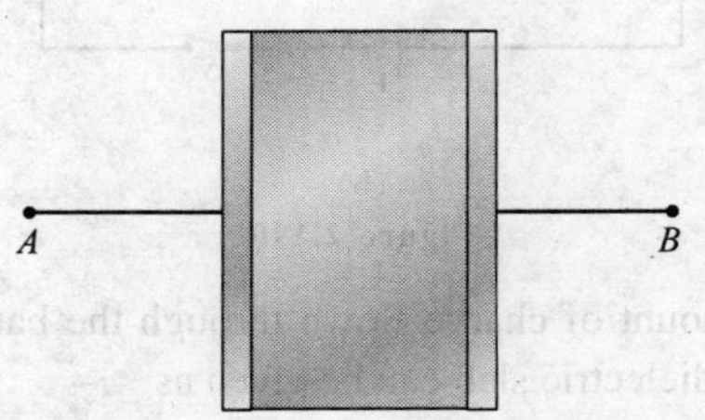

(b)

Figure 2.189

2.9.1 Dielectric Insertion in a Capacitor Connected to a Battery

Figure-2.190 shows a capacitor of capacitance C connected to a battery of voltage V. Steady state charge on capacitor plates is $q = CV$. When we insert a dielectric slab of size equal to the space available between plates then due to the electric field between plates the slab gets polarized and bound charges appear on the surface of slab as shown in figure-2.190(b). In previous article we've discussed that on insertion of dielectric slab the capacitance of capacitor increases to k times thus battery will supply more charge and new steady state charge on capacitor becomes

$$q' = kCV \qquad \text{...(2.180)}$$

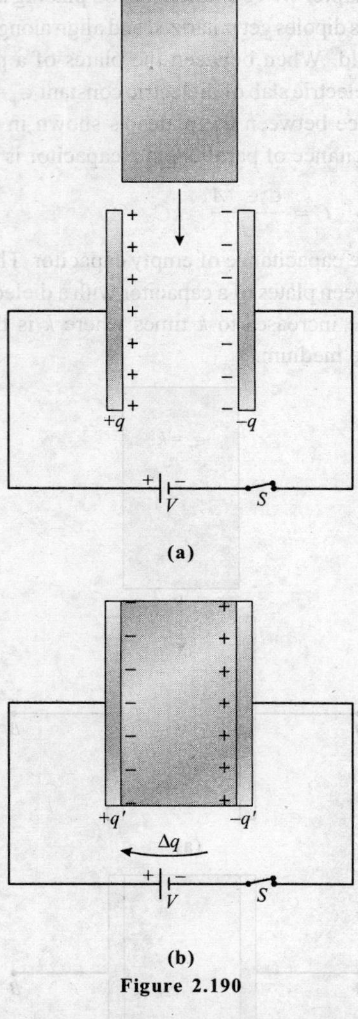

Figure 2.190

Thus the amount of charge flown through the battery due to insertion of dielectric slab can be given as

$$\Delta q = q' - q$$

$$\Rightarrow \quad \Delta q = kCV - CV$$

$$\Rightarrow \quad \Delta q = CV(k-1) \qquad \text{...(2.181)}$$

If we calculate the work done by the battery during insertion of dielectric slab in capacitor then it can be given as

$$W = \Delta q\, V = CV^2(k-1) \qquad \text{...(2.182)}$$

2.9.2 Insertion of Multiple Dielectrics in a Parallel Plate Capacitor

In previous articles we've discussed that on filling the space between plates of a parallel plate capacitor with a dielectric medium increases the capacitance of capacitor by k times where k is the dielectric constant of the medium. There are several ways in which we can fill multiple dielectric slabs in one capacitor. Two specific cases of filling multiple dielectric slabs we will discuss here to understand the basic method of determining capacitance of capacitor after filling the slabs.

Case-I : Multiple Slabs in Capacitor Parallel to Plates

Figure-2.191(a) shows a parallel plate capacitor of plate area A and plate separation d in which three dielectric slabs of dielectric constants k_1, k_2 and k_3 which are of surface area equal to that of each plate and thicknesses t_1, t_2 and t_3 are filled as shown.

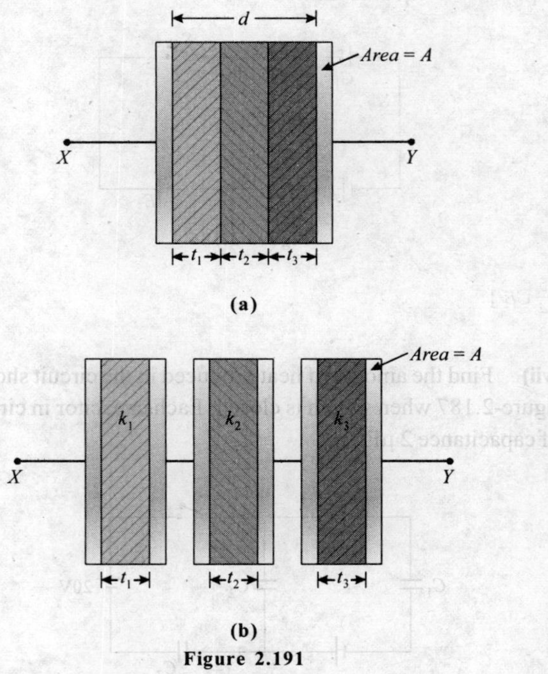

Figure 2.191

Above capacitor can be considered as a series combination of three parallel plate capacitors completely filled with these dielectrics separately as shown in figure-2.191(b).

In above figure-2.191(b) if we reduce the length of connecting wires between the three capacitors to zero then these three capacitors in series will look exactly like figure-2.191(a) and the plate thickness of these capacitors can be neglected and does not make any difference to system as these are equipotential and normal to electric field.

The capacitance of the three capacitor shown in figure-2.191 can be given as

$$C_1 = \frac{k_1 \epsilon_0 A}{t_1};\ C_2 = \frac{k_2 \epsilon_0 A}{t_2} \text{ and } C_3 = \frac{k_3 \epsilon_0 A}{t_3}$$

As these are considered in series equivalent capacitance of the capacitor can be given as

$$\frac{1}{C} = \frac{1}{C_1} + \frac{1}{C_2} + \frac{1}{C_3}$$

$$\Rightarrow \quad \frac{1}{C} = \frac{1}{\left(\frac{k_1 \epsilon_0 A}{t_1}\right)} + \frac{1}{\left(\frac{k_2 \epsilon_0 A}{t_2}\right)} + \frac{1}{\left(\frac{k_3 \epsilon_0 A}{t_3}\right)}$$

$$\Rightarrow \quad C = \frac{\epsilon_0 A}{\frac{t_1}{k_1} + \frac{t_2}{k_2} + \frac{t_3}{k_3}} \quad \text{...(2.183)}$$

For the situation shown in figure-2.191(a) the capacitance of the capacitor is given by equation-(2.183). This equation can be modified to N slabs filling the capacitor which is given as

$$C = \frac{\epsilon_0 A}{\frac{t_1}{k_1} + \frac{t_2}{k_2} + ... + \frac{t_N}{k_N}} \quad \text{...(2.184)}$$

Case-II : Multiple Slabs in Capacitor Normal to Plates

Figure-2.192(a) shows a parallel plate capacitor having rectangular plates of size ($l \times b$) of plate area $A = lb$ and plate separation d. The capacitor is filled with three dielectric slabs of dielectric constants k_1, k_2 and k_3 with equal lengths b and widths x_1, x_2 and x_3 and equal thicknesses d such that whole space between the plates is filled with these dielectrics.

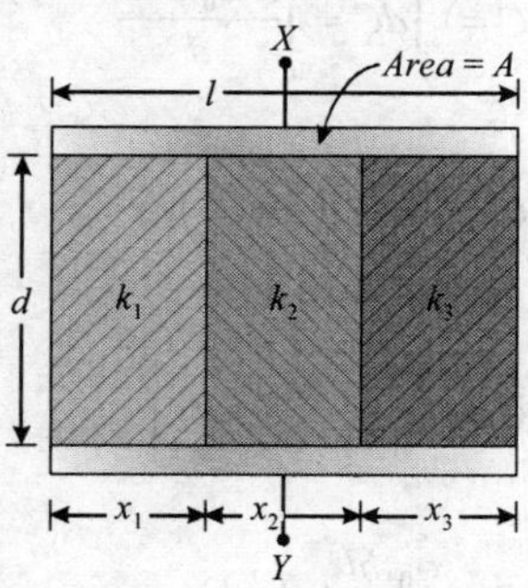

(a)

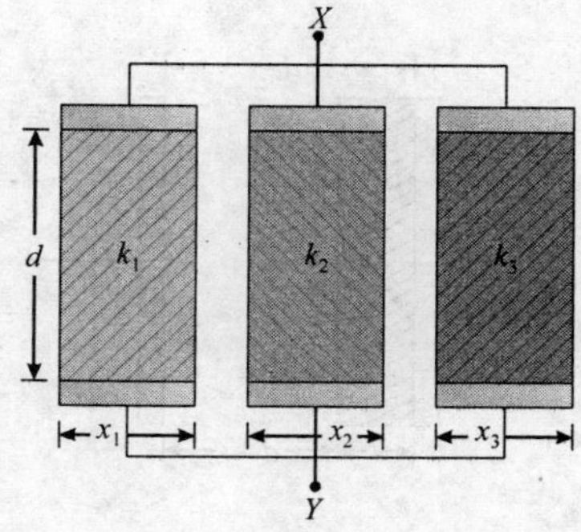

(b)

Figure 2.192

In this case we can consider that three capacitors filled with three dielectrics are connected in parallel as the top plate and bottom plate of above capacitor are common for the three dielectrics so we can split it as shown in figure-2.192(b). The capacitance of the three capacitors shown here can be given as

$$C_1 = \frac{k_1 \epsilon_0 x_1 b}{d};\ C_2 = \frac{k_2 \epsilon_0 x_2 b}{d} \text{ and } C_3 = \frac{k_3 \epsilon_0 x_3 b}{d}$$

The equivalent capacitance of above capacitor can be given by parallel combination of these three capacitors as

$$C = C_1 + C_2 + C_3$$

$$\Rightarrow \quad C = \frac{k_1 \epsilon_0 x_1 b}{d} + \frac{k_2 \epsilon_0 x_2 b}{d} + \frac{k_3 \epsilon_0 x_3 b}{d}$$

$$\Rightarrow \quad C = \frac{\epsilon_0 b}{d}(k_1 t_1 + k_2 t_2 + k_3 t_3) \quad \text{...(2.185)}$$

For the situation shown in figure-2.191(a) the capacitance of the capacitor is given by equation-(2.185). This equation can be modified to N slabs filling the capacitor which is given as

$$C = \frac{\epsilon_0 b}{d}(k_1 t_1 + k_2 t_2 + ... + k_N t_N) \quad \text{...(2.186)}$$

2.9.3 Partial Filling of a Dielectric in a Capacitor

Figure-2.193 shows a parallel plate capacitor which is partially filled with a dielectric slab of thickness $t (t < d)$ area equal to that of the plates. In this case also like previous article we can consider it as a series combination of two capacitors, one with dielectric other is without dielectric. The capacitance of this capacitor can be determined by using equation-(2.183) given as

$$C = \frac{\epsilon_0 A}{\frac{t}{k} + \frac{d-t}{1}}$$

$$\Rightarrow \quad C = \frac{\epsilon_0 A}{d - t\left(1 - \frac{1}{k}\right)} \quad \text{...(2.187)}$$

Above equation-(2.174) gives the capacitance of the capacitor shown in figure-2.195. For any capacitor of which any parameter if varies along the plate length then its capacitance can be calculated using this concept by considering an elemental section of capacitor and integrate the capacitance of the elemental capacitance as all such sections can be considered in parallel combination.

Case-II : Variation of Dielectric Constant perpendicular to Plates

Consider a dielectric filled in a parallel plate capacitor of plate area $A = lb$ and plate separation d as shown in figure-2.196(a) of which the dielectric constant varies with distance perpendicular to plates according to the below given relation.

$$k = ax + b \qquad \ldots(2.191)$$

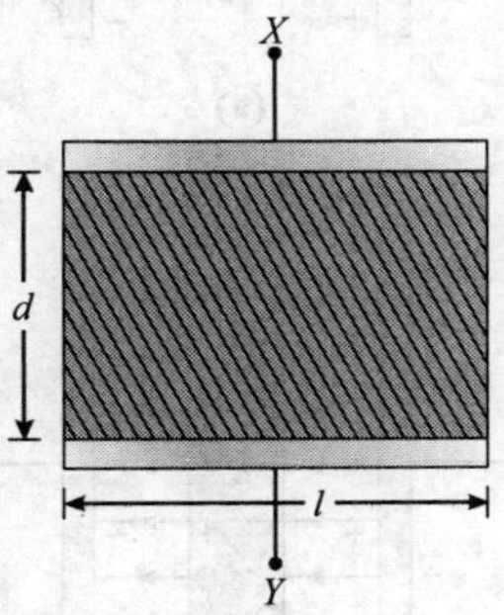

(a)

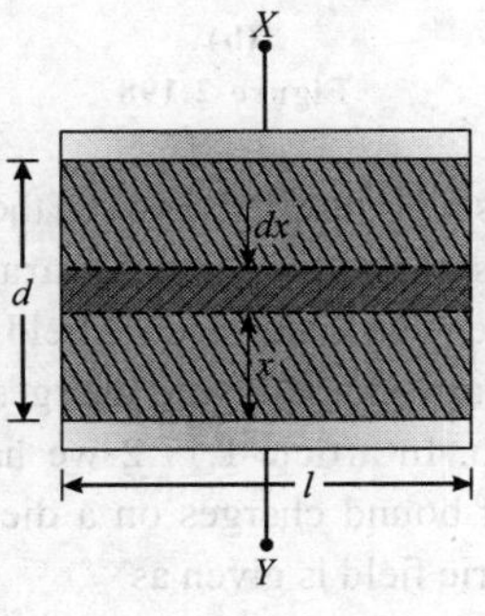

(b)

Figure 2.196

To determine the capacitance of this capacitor we consider an elemental capacitor section as shown in figure-2.196(b) of which the plate area is considered same as that of plates but having plate separation dx as shown. In such a small section of width dx we can consider that the dielectric constant does not vary and given by equation-(2.191). The capacitance of this elemental capacitor section is given as

$$dC = \frac{k \in_0 A}{dx} \qquad \ldots(2.192)$$

If we consider several such elemental capacitor sections between the two plates then all such elemental sections can be considered in series combination between the top and bottom plates of capacitor thus overall capacitance of this capacitor can be given by summing up reciprocal of capacitance of all such elemental sections which can be given as

$$\frac{1}{C} = \int \frac{1}{dC} = \int_0^d \frac{dx}{k \in_0 A}$$

$$\Rightarrow \quad \frac{1}{C} = \frac{1}{\in_0 A} \int_0^d \frac{dx}{ax+b}$$

$$\Rightarrow \quad \frac{1}{C} = \frac{1}{\in_0 Aa} \left[\ln(ax+b) \right]_0^d$$

$$\Rightarrow \quad \frac{1}{C} = \frac{1}{\in_0 Aa} \left[\ln(ad+b) - \ln b \right]$$

$$\Rightarrow \quad \frac{1}{C} = \frac{1}{\in_0 Aa} \ln\left(\frac{ad+b}{b} \right)$$

$$\Rightarrow \quad C = \frac{\in_0 Aa}{\ln\left(\frac{ad+b}{b} \right)} \qquad \ldots(2.193)$$

Equation-(2.193) gives the capacitance of the capacitor shown in figure-2.196. For any capacitor of which any parameter if varies perpendicular to the plates then its capacitance can be calculated using this concept by considering elemental sections of capacitor and integrate the reciprocal of capacitance of the elemental capacitor as all such sections can be considered in series combination.

2.9.5 Capacitance of a Spherical Capacitor by Concept of Variation of Parameters

Figure-2.197(a) shows a spherical capacitor with radii of inner and outer shell a and b respectively. If we consider the surfaces of inner and outer shells as two parallel plates of area $4\pi a^2$ and $4\pi b^2$ and plate separation $(b-a)$ then it apparently seems like a parallel plate capacitor but we cannot use the expression of capacitance of a parallel plate capacitor in this case as plate area is not same for both the plates.

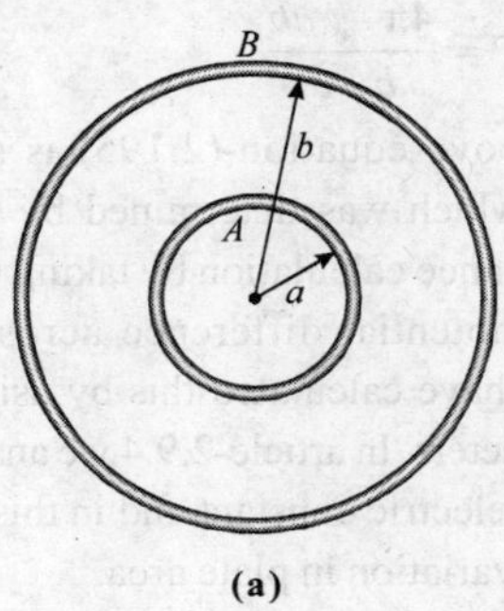

(a)

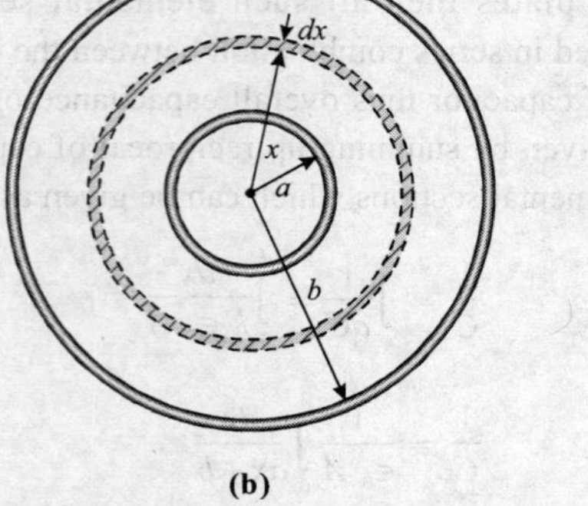

(b)

Figure 2.197

To calculate the capacitance of this spherical capacitor we consider an elemental capacitor of radius x and plate separation dx as shown in figure-2.197(b). If we carefully analize this situation then we can consider the spherical capacitor as series combination of several such elemental capacitors from radii a to b. For this elemental capacitor area of both the plates can be considered same as $4\pi x^2$ as dx tend to be negligibly small. Thus capacitance of this elemental capacitor can be given by the expression of a parallel plate capacitor which is given as

$$dC = \frac{\epsilon_0 A}{d} \equiv \frac{\epsilon_0 (4\pi x^2)}{dx} \quad \ldots (2.194)$$

The capacitance of spherical capacitor can be calculated by integrating the reciprocal of the capacitance of the elemental capacitor given in equation-(2.194) as all such elemental capacitor are considered in series from inner radius a to outer radius b, given as

$$\frac{1}{C} = \int \frac{1}{dC} = \int_a^b \frac{dx}{4\pi \epsilon_0 x^2}$$

$$\Rightarrow \quad \frac{1}{C} = \frac{1}{4\pi \epsilon_0} \int_a^b \frac{dx}{x^2}$$

$$\Rightarrow \quad \frac{1}{C} = \frac{1}{4\pi \epsilon_0} \left[-\frac{1}{x}\right]_a^b$$

$$\Rightarrow \quad \frac{1}{C} = \frac{1}{4\pi \epsilon_0} \left(\frac{1}{a} - \frac{1}{b}\right)$$

$$\Rightarrow \quad C = \frac{4\pi \epsilon_0 ab}{b-a} \quad \ldots (2.195)$$

Expression in above equation-(2.195) is same as given in equation-(2.30) which was determined by using the generic method of capacitance calculation by taking the ratio of charge supplied to the potential difference across the conductors whereas here we have calculated this by using the concept of variation of parameters. In article-2.9.4 we analyzed the concept for variation in dielectric constant and in this case we used the same method for variation in plate area.

2.9.6 Bound Charges on Dielectric Surface in a Capacitor

Figure-2.198(a) shows a parallel plate capacitor charged with a charge q and disconnected from the voltage source. This charge produces electric field between the plates which we've already studied in article-1.17.2 and it is given as

$$E = \frac{q}{A\epsilon_0} \quad \ldots (2.196)$$

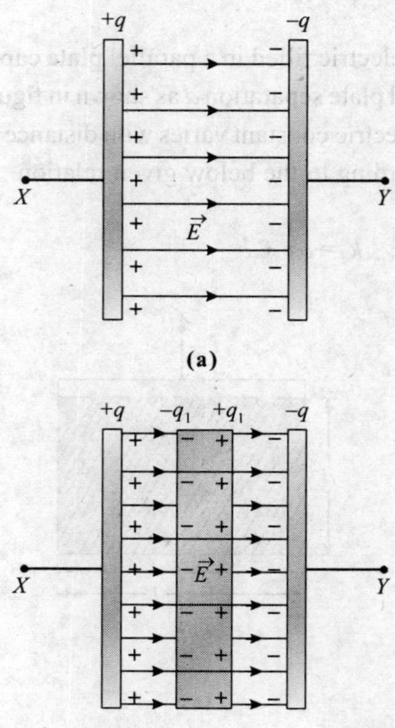

Figure 2.198

When a dielectric slab is inserted between the plates of capacitor of thickness less than the plate separation as shown in figure-2.198(b) then due to the electric field between plates this dielectric gets polarized and bound charges will appear on its surfaces as shown. In article-1.17.2 we have discussed that surface density of bound charges on a dielectric slab placed normal to an electric field is given as

$$\sigma_i = \epsilon_0 E\left(1 - \frac{1}{\epsilon_r}\right) \quad \ldots (2.197)$$

If $\pm q_i$ are the bound charges on surfaces of dielectric then we can use $\sigma_i = q_i/A$. Thus bound charges on surface of dielectric placed in a charged capacitor can be given by equation-(2.197) as

$$\frac{q_i}{A} = \epsilon_0 \left(\frac{q}{A\epsilon_0}\right)\left(1 - \frac{1}{\epsilon_r}\right)$$

$$\Rightarrow \quad q_i = q\left(1 - \frac{1}{\epsilon_r}\right) \quad \ldots (2.198)$$

2.9.7 Effect of Insertion of Dielectric Slab in a Capacitor connected to a Battery

Figure-2.199(a) shows a parallel plate capacitor of capacitance C connected to a voltage source V due to which the capacitor is charged to the steady state charge $q = CV$ and initial energy in capacitor is given as $U = 0.5CV^2$ which is stored in the electric field strength between the plates given as $E = q/A\epsilon_0$ or also given as $E = V/d$.

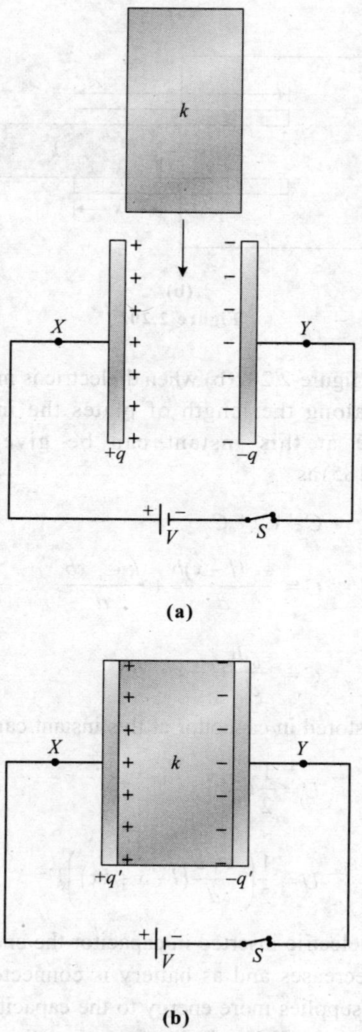

Figure 2.199

When a dielectric slab is inserted in this capacitor as shown in figure-2.199(b) which fills the space between plates then after insertion the physical quantities associated with capacitor changes as listed in table below. As battery remain connected during insertion of slab the potential difference across capacitor does not change in this case.

Table-2.1

	$C = \frac{\epsilon_0 A}{d}$	V	$E = \frac{V}{d}$	$q = CV$	$U = \frac{1}{2}CV^2$
Before Insertion	C	V	E	q	U
	↓	↓	↓	↓	↓
After Insertion	KC	V	E	kq	kU

2.9.8 Effect of Dielectric Insertion in a Charged Capacitor not connected to a Battery

Figure-2.200(a) shows a parallel plate capacitor of capacitance C which is charged to a charge q and disconnected from the voltage source. When the dielectric slab is inserted in this capacitor as shown in figure-2.200(b) which fills the space between plates then after insertion of dielectric the physical quantities associated with capacitor changes as listed in table below.

As capacitor is charged and not connected in any circuit, its charge will remain constant and does not change while insertion of dielectric slab.

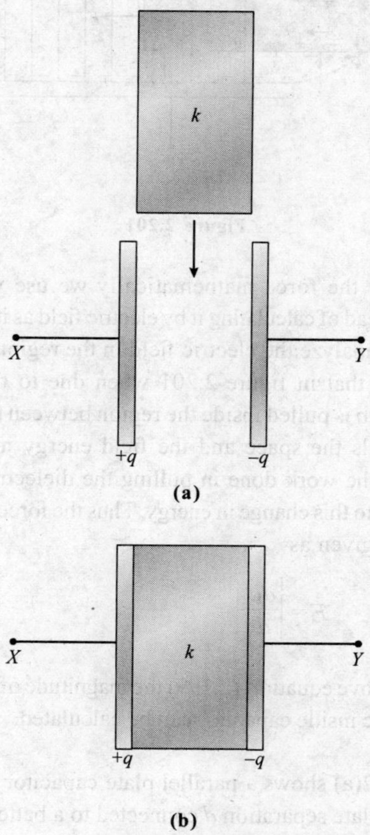

Figure 2.200

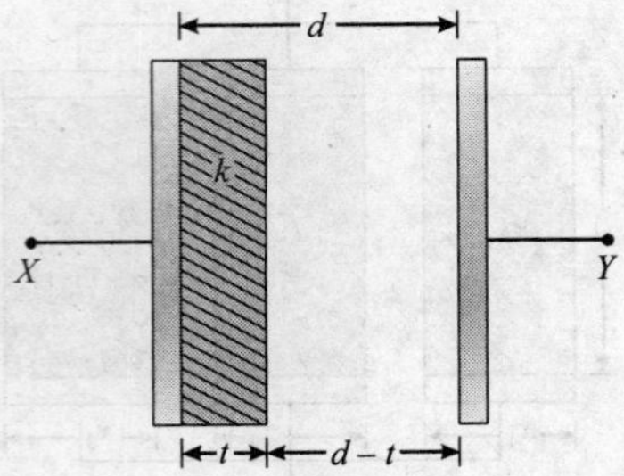

Figure 2.193

In figure-2.191 if the order of dielectric slabs is changed between the capacitor plates then by equation-(2.183) it is clear that it does not make any difference on the value of capacitance of this system. Thus in figure-2.193 also the capacitance will remain same if position of dielectric slab is changed or it is displaced anywhere between the plates as shown in figure-2.194.

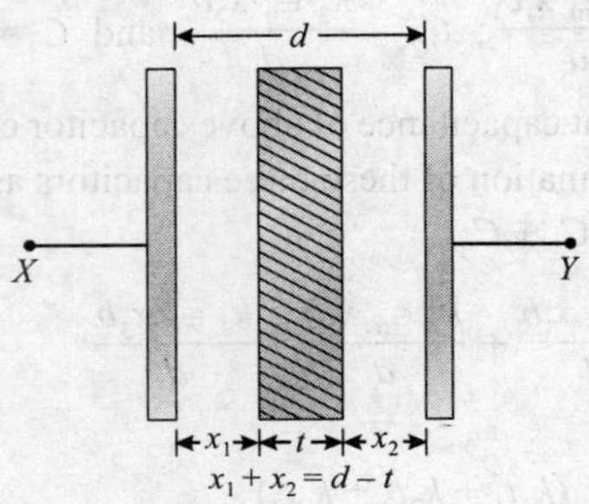

Figure 2.194

2.9.4 Capacitance Calculation by Variation of Parameters

The capacitance of a parallel plate capacitor filled with a dielectric can be directly calculated as k times the capacitance without dielectric where k is the dielectric constant of the dielectric filled in it. The cases we've considered till now are those in which k is a constant through the dielectric slab volume which may not be the case always. We consider and analyze two cases of variation of dielectric constant in a capacitor similar to the two cases discussed in article-2.9.2. These cases we will discuss with illustrations to understand the application of the concept in different situations.

Case-I : Variation of Dielectric Constant along the Plates

Consider a dielectric filled in a parallel plate capacitor of plate area $A = lb$ and plate separation d as shown in figure-2.195(a) of which the dielectric constant varies with distance along the plates according to the below given relation.

$$k = ax + b \qquad \ldots(2.188)$$

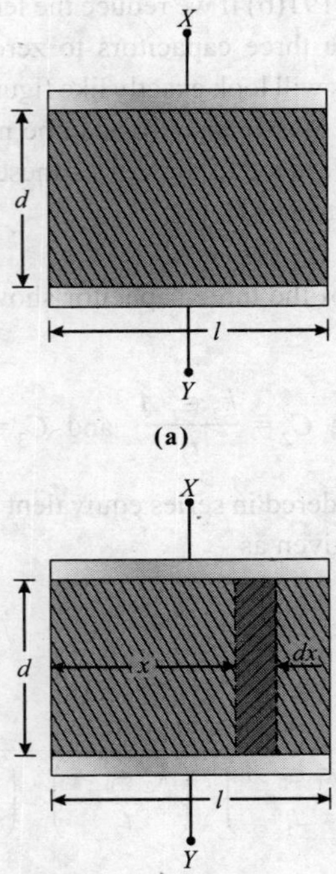

Figure 2.195

To determine the capacitance of this capacitor we consider an elemental capacitor section of width dx as shown in figure-2.195(b). In such a small section of width dx we can consider that the dielectric constant does not vary and given by equation-(2.189). The capacitance of this elemental capacitor section is given as

$$dC = \frac{k \in_0 bdx}{d} \qquad \ldots(2.189)$$

All such elemental sections have their upper and lower plate of area bdx connected together as overall top and bottom plates of the capacitor. Thus all such elemental sections can be considered in parallel combination thus overall capacitance of this capacitor can be given by summing up capacitance of all such elemental sections which can be given as

$$C = \int dC = \int_0^l \frac{k \in_0 bdx}{d}$$

$$\Rightarrow \quad C = \frac{\in_0 b}{d} \int_0^l (ax + b)\, dx$$

$$\Rightarrow \quad C = \frac{\in_0 b}{d} \left[\frac{ax^2}{2} + bx \right]_0^l$$

$$\Rightarrow \quad C = \frac{\in_0 bl}{2d}(al + b) \qquad \ldots(2.190)$$

Table-2.2

	$C=\frac{\epsilon_0 A}{d}$	$V=\frac{q}{C}$	$E=\frac{V}{d}$	$q=CV$	$U=\frac{q^2}{2C}$
Before Insertion	C	V	E	q	U
	↓	↓	↓	↓	↓
After Insertion	KC	V/k	E/k	q	U/k

2.9.9 Force on a Dielectric during Insertion in a Capacitor

When a dielectric slab is inserted in an initially charged parallel plate capacitor then due to electric field between the plates of capacitor opposite bound charges are induced on the dielectric and while insertion due to fringing of electric lines at the edges of plates, a component of electric field along the surface pulls the dielectric inside the region between the plates as shown in figure-2.201.

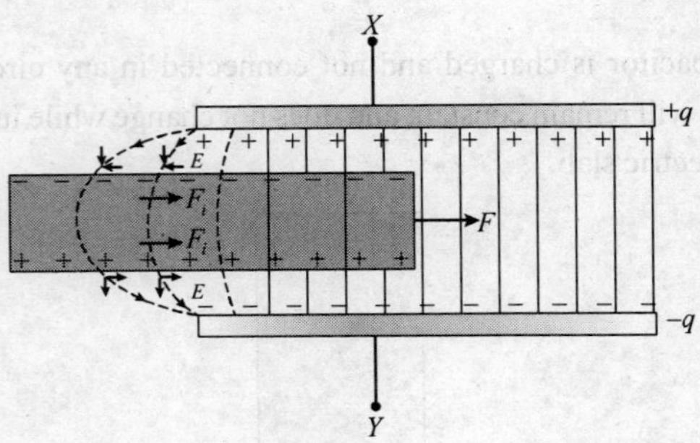

Figure 2.201

To calculate the force mathematically we use work energy theorem instead of calculating it by electric field as it will become complex to analyze the electric field in the region of fringing. We can see that in figure-2.201 when due to the force the dielectric slab is pulled inside the region between the plates the dielectric fills the space and the field energy in this region changes so the work done in pulling the dielectric inside the plates is due to this change in energy. Thus the force on dielectric slab can be given as

$$F=\left|\frac{dU}{dx}\right| \qquad \ldots(2.199)$$

Using the above equation-(2.199) the magnitude of force pulling the dielectric inside capacitor can be calculated.

Figure-2.202(a) shows a parallel plate capacitor of plate area $A = lb$ and plate separation d connected to a battery of voltage V and the capacitor is in steady state.

When a dielectric of size equal to the space between the plates is inserted from one side along the length of the plates as shown in figure-2.202(b).

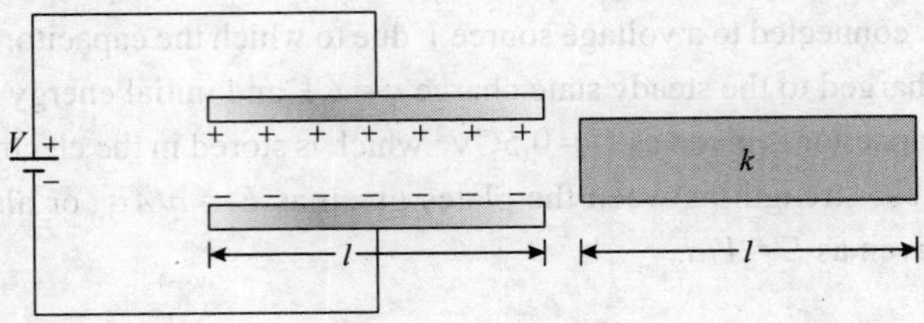

(a)

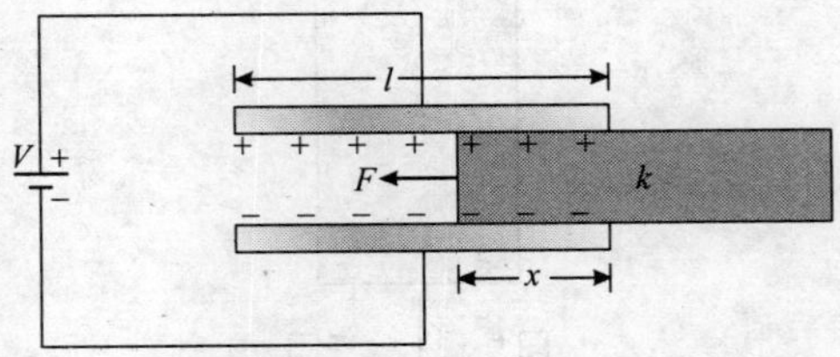

(b)

Figure 2.202

As shown in figure-2.202(b) when dielectric is inserted upto a distance x along the length of plates the instantaneous capacitance at this instant can be given by using equation-(2.185) as

$$C=C_1+C_2$$

$$\Rightarrow \qquad C=\frac{\epsilon_0 (l-x)b}{d}+\frac{k\epsilon_0 xb}{d}$$

$$\Rightarrow \qquad C=\frac{\epsilon_0 b}{d}(l-x+kx)$$

The energy stored in capacitor at this instant can be given as

$$U=\frac{1}{2}CV^2$$

$$\Rightarrow \qquad U=\frac{1}{2}\left(\frac{\epsilon_0 b}{d}(l-x+kx)\right)V^2 \qquad \ldots(2.200)$$

When the dielectric inserted in capacitor the energy stored in capacitor decreases and as battery is connected across the capacitor it supplies more energy to the capacitor. If F is the force acting on the dielectric then it can be calculated by using equation-(2.199) given as

$$F=\left|\frac{dU}{dx}\right|=\frac{\epsilon_0 bV^2}{2d}(k-1) \qquad \ldots(2.201)$$

The expression of force in above equation-(2.201) is independent of the displacement of the dielectric slab between the plate. Thus the force on dielectric slab in situation when capacitor is connected to a battery remain constant throughout.

If we consider a situation when an isolated capacitor is initially having some charge Q on its plates and then we insert a dielectric slab between its plates as shown in figure-2.203 then the energy stored in it as a function of x can be given as

$$U=\frac{Q^2}{2(C_1+C_2)}$$

$$\Rightarrow \quad U=\frac{Q^2}{2\left(\frac{\epsilon_0 b}{d}(l-x+kx)\right)} \quad \ldots(2.202)$$

Now the force on dielectric slab can be given as

$$F=\left|\frac{dU}{dx}\right|=\frac{Q^2 d(k-1)}{2\epsilon_0 b(l-x+kx)^2} \quad \ldots(2.203)$$

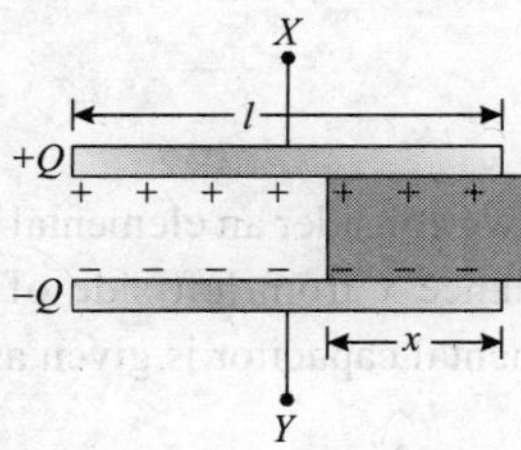

Figure 2.203

When a dielectric is inserted in a capacitor while battery remains connected as shown in figure-2.202 then for slow insertion of slab external agent has to do negative work in supporting the slab by an outward force so that it will not gain any kinetic energy. The work done in insertion of slab can be given as

$$W_{ext}=Fl$$

$$\Rightarrow \quad W_{ext}=\frac{\epsilon_0 bV^2}{2d}(k-1)\times l$$

$$\Rightarrow \quad W_{ext}=\frac{1}{2}CV^2(k-1) \quad \ldots(2.204)$$

If we calculate the difference in energy stored in capacitor before and after insertion of the dielectric slab then it is given as

$$\Delta U=U_f-U_i$$

$$\Rightarrow \quad \Delta U=\frac{1}{2}kCV^2-\frac{1}{2}CV^2$$

$$\Rightarrow \quad \Delta U=\frac{1}{2}CV^2(k-1) \quad \ldots(2.205)$$

Now we calculate the work done by battery in the process of insertion of dielectric slab in capacitor which is given as

$$W_{bat}=\Delta qV$$

$$\Rightarrow \quad W_{bat}=(kCV-CV)V$$

$$\Rightarrow \quad W_{bat}=CV^2(k-1) \quad \ldots(2.206)$$

From the above equations-(2.188), (2.189) and (2.190) by using conservation of energy we can calculate the heat produced which is given as

$$H=W_{bat}-(\Delta U+W_{ext})=0$$

Thus in slow insertion of a dielectric slab in a capacitor no heat is produced. If insertion is not slow then dielectric slab will gain some kinetic energy and it will oscillate between the plates and due to friction when oscillations will damp the kinetic energy of dielectric slab will be dissipated as heat. In this analysis we are neglecting the work done in polarization of the dielectric which is very small.

2.9.10 Dielectric Breakdown in a Capacitor

In previous chapter we've studied about dielectric breakdown in which all the dipoles of a dielectric medium breaks by the stretching force due to an external electric field applied on the medium. Breaking of dipole makes the medium behave like a conductor. Every conductor has a specific '*Dielectric Strength*' or '*Breakdown Strength*' which is the maximum electric upto which medium behave as an insulator after which it breaks down and starts conducting.

If in a capacitor a dielectric is filled in the space between plates then it is also polarized due to the electric field due to the charges on plates of capacitor. If this electric field increases beyond the breakdown strength of this dielectric then it breaks down and short circuits the two plates of capacitor after which the capacitor behaves like a conducting wire and no longer acts as a capacitor.

 # Illustrative Example 2.37

Find out capacitance between A and B if three dielectric slabs of dielectric constant K_1 of area A_1 and thickness d, K_2 of area A_2 and thickness d_1 and K_3 of area A_2 and thickness d_2 are inserted between the plates of parallel plate capacitor of plate area A as shown in figure-2.204. (Given distance between the two plates $d=d_1+d_2$)

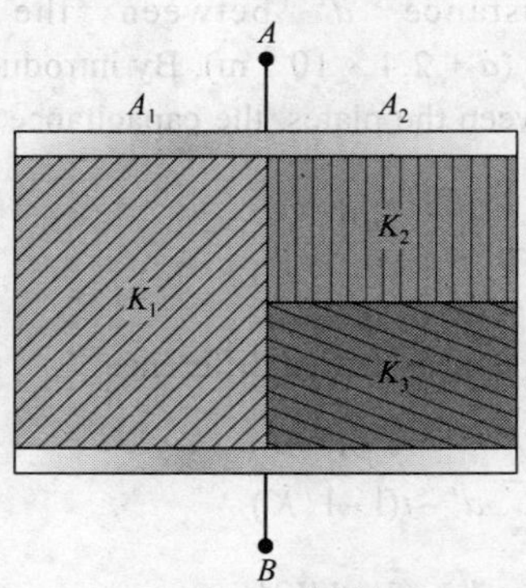

Figure 2.204

Solution

$$C_1 = \frac{A_1 \in_0 K_1}{d_1 + d_2},\ C_2 = \frac{A_2 \in_0 K_2}{d_1},\ C_3 = \frac{A_2 \in_0 K_3}{d_2}$$

$$C_{eq} = \frac{C_2 C_3}{C_2 + C_3} + C_1$$

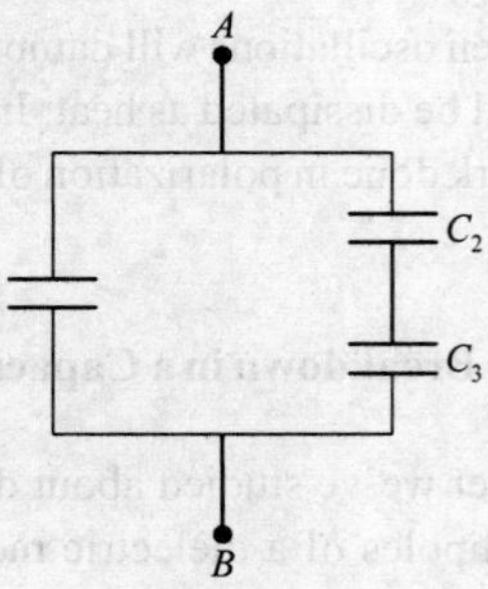

Figure 2.205

$$\Rightarrow \quad C_{eq} = \frac{A_2 K_2 K_3 \in_0}{K_2 d_2 + K_3 d_1} + \frac{A_1 K_1 \in_0}{d_1 + d_2}$$

 # Illustrative Example 2.38

A parallel plate capacitor is maintained at a certain potential difference, when a 3 mm thick slab is introduced between the plates. In order to maintain the same potential difference, the distance between the plates is increased by 2.4 mm.

Solution

The capacitance of parallel plate capacitor with air as dielectric is given by

$$C = \frac{\varepsilon_0 A}{d}$$

when the separation between the plates is increased by 2.4 mm, the new distance d' between the plates is $(d + 2.4 \text{ mm}) = (d + 2.4 \times 10^{-3} \text{ m})$. By introducing a slab of thickness t between the plates, the capacitance is given by

$$C' = \frac{\varepsilon_0 A}{d' - t(1 - 1/K)}$$

To maintain the same potential difference

$$\frac{\varepsilon_0 A}{d} = \frac{\varepsilon_0 A}{d' - t(1 - 1/K)}$$

$$\Rightarrow \quad d = d' - t(1 - 1/K)]$$

 # Illustrative Example 2.39

Figure-2.206 shows a parallel plate capacitor with its plate area $A = lb$ and plate separation d at left end of the plates. Upper plate of capacitor is slightly tilted by a very small angle θ as shown. Find the capacitance of this capacitor.

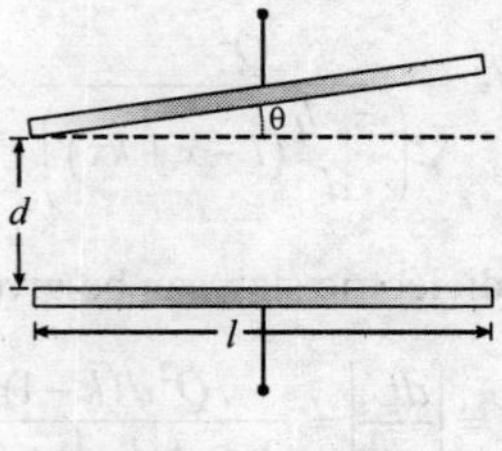

Figure-2.206

Solution

As shown in figure-207 we consider an elemental capacitor of plate area bdx at a distance x from left side of plates. The capacitance of this elemental capacitor is given as

$$dC = \frac{\in_0 bdx}{d + x\theta}$$

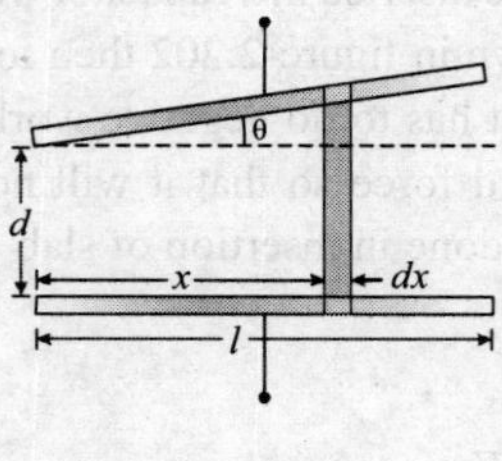

Figure-2.207

All such elemental capacitors will be considered in parallel combination between the two plates so capacitance of the given capacitor can be calculated by summing up capacitance of all such elemental capcitors given as

$$C = \int dC = \int_0^l \frac{\in_0 bdx}{d + x\theta}$$

$$\Rightarrow \quad C = \in_0 b \int_0^l \frac{dx}{d + x\theta}$$

$$\Rightarrow \quad C = \frac{\in_0 b}{d} \int_0^l \frac{1}{1 + \frac{x\theta}{d}} dx$$

$$\Rightarrow \quad C = \frac{\in_0 b}{d} \int_0^l \left(1 + \frac{x\theta}{d}\right)^{-1} dx$$

$$\Rightarrow \quad C = \frac{\epsilon_0 b}{d}\int_0^l \left(1 - \frac{x\theta}{d}\right)dx \qquad [\text{Using } (1+x)^n = 1+nx]$$

$$\Rightarrow \quad C = \frac{\epsilon_0 b}{d}\left[x - \frac{x^2\theta}{2d}\right]_0^l$$

$$\Rightarrow \quad C = \frac{\epsilon_0 b}{d}\left(l - \frac{l^2\theta}{2d}\right)$$

$$\Rightarrow \quad C = \frac{\epsilon_0 A}{d}\left(1 - \frac{l\theta}{2d}\right)$$

Illustrative Example 2.40

A parallel plate capacitor consists of two metal plates of area A and separation d. A slab of thickness t and electric constant K is inserted between the plates with its faces parallel to the plates and having the same surface area as that of the plates. Find the capacitance of the system.

If $K = 2$, for what value of t/d will the capacitance of the system be 3/2 times that of the air capacitor? Calculate the energy in the two cases and account for the energy change.

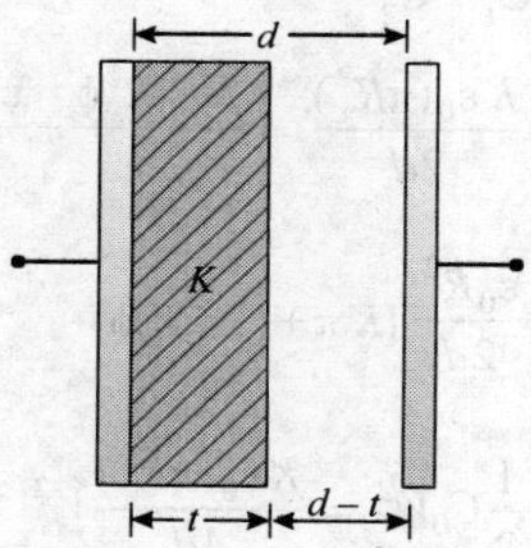

Figure 2.208

Solution

We know that the capacitance of a capacitor with a dielectric of dielectric constant K is given by $\varepsilon_0 KA/d$. Hence the capacitance C_1 of the capacitor with dielectric constant K is given by

$$C_1 = \frac{\varepsilon_0 KA}{t} \quad \text{where } t \text{ is its thickness}$$

The capacitance C_2 of remaining capacitor is

$$C_2 = \frac{\varepsilon_0 A}{(d-t)}$$

Effective capacitance C of C_1 and C_2 is given by

$$C = \frac{C_1C_2}{C_1 + C_2} = \frac{\varepsilon_0^2 A^2 K / t(d-t)}{\dfrac{\varepsilon_0 KA}{t} + \dfrac{\varepsilon_0 A}{(d-t)}}$$

On simplification, we have

$$C = \frac{\varepsilon_0 A}{d - (t/2)}$$

Now $\quad C = \frac{3}{2}C_a$

$$\Rightarrow \quad \frac{\varepsilon_0 A}{d-(t/2)} = \frac{3}{2}\frac{\varepsilon_0 A}{d}$$

Solving we have

$$\frac{t}{d} = \frac{2}{3}$$

If q is the charge on the capacitor which remain unchanged, then initial energy E_i in the air capacitor is $q^2/2\,C_a$ and final energy E_f after insertion of dielectric is $q^2/2\,C$, thus we have

$$\frac{E_i}{E_f} = \frac{3}{2}$$

When a dielectric is introduced, it decreases the potential energy of the condenser. The loss is used up to polarise the dielectric.

Illustrative Example 2.41

Two identical capacitors are connected as shown in figure-2.209. A dielectric slab is introduced between the plates of one of the capacitors so as to fill the gap, the battery remaining connected. What will be the capacitance, the charge, potential difference and stored energy for each capacitor?

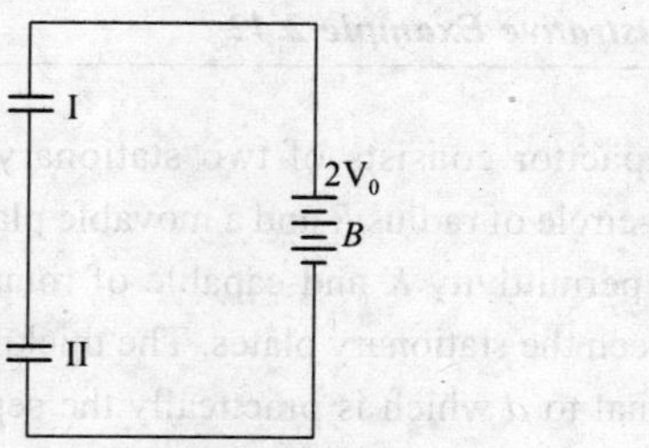

Figure 2.209

Solution

Before the introduction of dielectric, the charge on each capacitor will be the same because they are connected in series.

Initial charge on each capacitor, $q_0 = C_0 V_0$

Initial energy stored in each capacitor

$$U_0 = \frac{1}{2}C_0V_0^2$$

When dielectric is introduced, $C_1 = C_0$ and $C_2 = K\,C_0$

If C be the capacity of two condensers, then

$$C = \frac{C_1 C_2}{C_1 + C_2} = \frac{C_0 \times C_0 K}{C_0 + C_0 K} = \frac{C_0 K}{1+K}$$

charge on each capacitor is given as

$$q = C(2V_0) = \left(\frac{C_0 K}{1+K}\right) 2V_0 = \frac{2q_0}{[1+(1/K)]}$$

Potential difference across Ist, capacitor

$$V_1 = \frac{q}{C_0} = \frac{2q_0}{C_0\left[1+\frac{1}{K}\right]} = \frac{2V_0}{[1+(1/K)]}$$

Potential difference across 2nd capacitor

$$V_2 = \frac{q}{C_0 K} = \frac{2V_0}{(1+K)}$$

Potential energy stored in Ist capacitor

$$U_1 = \frac{1}{2} C_0 V_1^2 = \left(\frac{2K}{1+K}\right)^2 U_0$$

Potential energy stored in 2nd capacitor

$$U_2 = \frac{1}{2} K C_0 V_2^2 = \frac{4K}{(1+K)^2} U_0$$

Illustrative Example 2.42

A capacitor consists of two stationary plates shaped as a semi-circle of radius R and a movable plate made of dielectric with permittivity K and capable of rotating about an axis O between the stationary plates. The thickness of movable plate is equal to d which is practically the separation between the stationary plates. A potential difference V is applied to the capacitor. Find the magnitude of the moment of forces relative to the axis O acting on the movable plate in the position shown in figure-2.210.

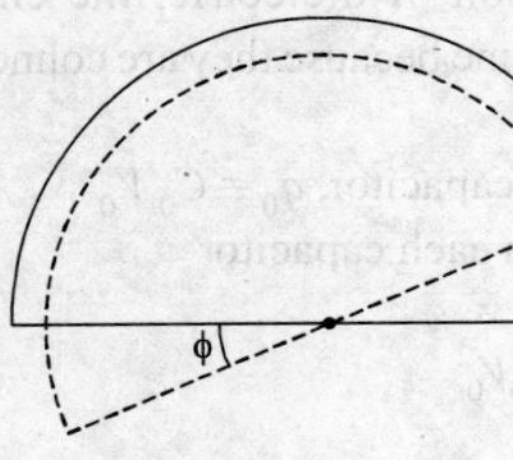

Figure 2.210

Solution

Let C_0 be the initial capacitance of the condenser. Then

$$C_0 = \frac{K\varepsilon_0(\pi R^2)}{2d}$$

In the rotated condition, let C_1 be the new capacity of inner condenser. Then

$$C_1 = \frac{K\varepsilon_0\left[\frac{\pi R^2}{3} - \frac{R^2\phi}{2}\right]}{d} \quad \ldots(2.207)$$

where outside plate area = $R^2\phi/2$, because the circumference is $R\phi$ and area is $\frac{1}{2} \times R \times (R\phi)$ i.e., $R^2\phi/2$

If C_2 be the capacity of outside condenser, then

$$C_2 = \frac{\varepsilon_0 R^2 \phi}{2d} \quad \ldots(2.208)$$

In rotated position, the arrangement in equivalent to two capacitors [of capacity C_1 and C_2] connected in parallel. Hence

$$C = C_1 + C_2$$

$$\Rightarrow \quad C = \frac{K\varepsilon_0(\pi R^2)}{2d} - \frac{K\varepsilon_0 R^2\phi}{2d} + \frac{\varepsilon_0 R^2\phi}{2d}$$

$$\Rightarrow \quad C = \frac{\varepsilon_0 R^2}{2d}[K\pi + (1-K)\phi] \quad \ldots(2.209)$$

$$\text{Initial energy } U_i = \frac{1}{2}C_0 V^2 = \frac{K\varepsilon_0(\pi R^2)}{4d}V^2 \quad \ldots(2.210)$$

$$\text{Final energy } U_f = \frac{1}{2}\cdot\frac{\varepsilon_0 R^2}{2d}[K\pi + (1-K)\phi]V^2 \quad \ldots(2.211)$$

$$\Rightarrow \quad \Delta U = U_i - U_f = \frac{\varepsilon_0 R^2}{2d}(K-1)\phi V^2 \quad \ldots(2.212)$$

If τ be the moment of force, then

$$\tau\phi = \frac{\varepsilon_0 R^2}{4d}(K-1)\phi V^2$$

$$\Rightarrow \quad \tau = \frac{\varepsilon_0 R^2}{4d}(K-1)V^2$$

Illustrative Example 2.43

The distance between the parallel plates of a charged condenser is $d = 5$ cm and the intensity of the field $e = 300$ V/cm. A slab of dielectric constant $k = 5$ and 1 cm wide is inserted parallel to the plates. Determine the potential difference between the plates before and after the slab is inserted. If the slab is replaced by a metal plates so that the final potential difference remains unchanged, what be the thickness of the plate?

Solution

Potential difference across the plates of condenser without slab

$$V = Ed = 300 \times 5 = 1500\text{ V}$$

and $$C = \frac{\epsilon_0 A}{d} = \frac{\epsilon_0 A}{0.05}$$

After the slab is inserted, the capacitance

$$C' = \frac{\epsilon_0 A}{(d-t)+\dfrac{t}{k}}$$

$$\Rightarrow \quad C' = \frac{\epsilon_0 A}{(0.05-0.01)+\dfrac{0.01}{5}} = \frac{\epsilon_0 A}{0.042}$$

If V' is the p.d. now, then for isolated condenser

$$CV = C'V'$$

$$\Rightarrow \quad V' = \frac{CV}{C'} = \frac{\left(\dfrac{\epsilon_0 A}{0.05}\right)\times 1500}{\left(\dfrac{\epsilon_0 A}{0.042}\right)}$$

$$\Rightarrow \quad V' = 1260\text{V}$$

Let x be the thickness of the metal plate. Now the capacitance

$$C'' = \frac{\epsilon_0 A}{(0.05-x)}$$

If V'' is the p.d. now, across the condenser, then

$$C''V'' = CV$$

$$\Rightarrow \quad V'' = \frac{CV}{C''} = \frac{\left(\dfrac{\epsilon_0 A}{0.05}\right)\times 1500}{\dfrac{\epsilon_0 A}{0.05-x}}$$

$$\Rightarrow \quad 1260 = \left(\frac{0.05-x}{0.05}\right)\times 1500$$

After simplifying, we get $x = 0.8$ cm

Illustrative Example 2.44

(a) A parallel plate capacitor of plate area 2 m^2 and plate separation 5 mm is charged to 10,000 V in vacuum. Compute the capacitance, charge, charge density, field intensity and the displacement in the space between the plates.

(b) The charging battery is removed and the space between the plates is filled with a material of dielectric coefficient 5. Compute the new capacitance, the potential difference and the field intensity.

(c) If now the dielectric sheet is removed and replaced by two sheets, one 2 mm thick of dielectric coefficient 5 and the other 3mm thick of dielectric coefficient 2, compute the electric field intensity in each dielectric, the potential difference across the capacitor and its capacitance.

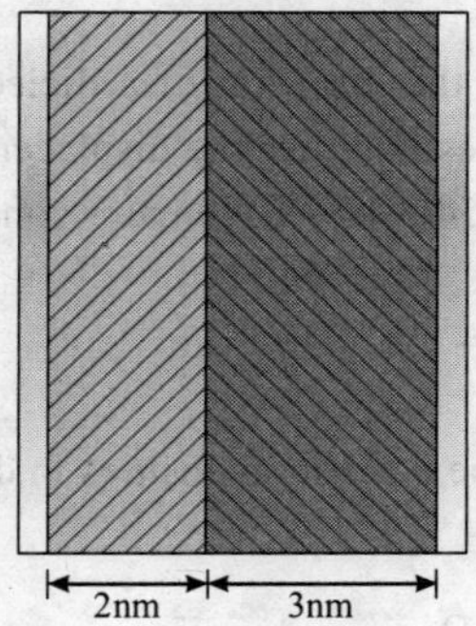

Figure 2.211

Solution

(a) The capacitance in vacuum (say C_0) is given by

$$C_0 = \frac{\varepsilon_0 A}{d} = \frac{(8.85\times10^{-12})\times(2)}{(5\times10^{-3})}$$

$$\Rightarrow \quad C_0 = 3.54\times10^{-9}\text{ F}$$

The charge q_0 on each plate is

$$q_0 = C_0V_0 = 3.54\times10^{-9}\times 10{,}000$$

$$\Rightarrow \quad q_0 = 3.54\times10^{-5}\text{ C}$$

The free charge density on each plate is given by

$$\sigma_0 = \frac{q_0}{A} = \frac{3.54\times10^{-5}}{2} = 1.77\times10^{-5}\text{ C/m}^2$$

The electric field intensity E_0 is given by

$$E_0 = \frac{V_0}{d} = \frac{10{,}000}{5\times10^{-3}} = 2\times10^6\text{ V/m}$$

The displacement D_0 is given by

$$D_0 = \varepsilon_0 E_0 = \sigma_0 = 1.77\times10^{-5}\text{ C/m}^2$$

(b) When the battery is removed, the new capacitance C is given by

$$C = \frac{K\varepsilon_0 A}{d} = K\,C_0$$

$\Rightarrow$ $$C = 5 \times (3.54 \times 10^{-9}) = 1.77 \times 10^{-8} \text{ farad}$$

The given potential difference V is given by

$$V = \frac{q_0}{C} = \frac{3.54\times10^{-5}}{1.77\times10^{-8}}$$

$\Rightarrow$ $$V = 2000 \text{ V}$$

(c) We know that the insertion of a dielectric between the capacitor plates does not alter the displacement, because the free charge ($q_0 = 3.54 \times 10^{-5}$ C) remains constant. Hence

$$D = \sigma = 1.77 \times 10^{-5} \text{ C/m}^2$$

Let E_1 and E_2 be the electric intensities in dielectric 1 and 2, then

$$E_1 = \frac{D}{K_1\varepsilon_0}$$

$\Rightarrow$ $$D = K\varepsilon_0 E_1$$

$\Rightarrow$ $$E_1 = \frac{1.77\times10^{-5}}{5(8.85\times10^{-12})} = 4 \times 10^5 \text{ V/m}$$

$$E_2 = \frac{D}{K_2\varepsilon_0} = \frac{1.77\times10^{-5}}{2(8.85\times10^{-12})}$$

$\Rightarrow$ $$E_2 = 10 \times 10^5 \text{ V/m}$$

The potential difference across the dielectrics 1 and 2 are

$$V_1 = E_1 d_1 = (4 \times 10^5 \text{ V/m}) \times (2 \times 10^{-3} \text{ m})$$

$\Rightarrow$ $$V_1 = 800 \text{ V}$$

and $$V_2 = E_2 d_2 = (10 \times 10^5 \text{ V/m}) \times (3 \times 10^{-3} \text{ m})$$

$\Rightarrow$ $$V_2 = 3000 \text{ V}$$

In the above analysis we've discussed a new characteristic property of electric field strength called '*Displacement Vector*'. This is a physical quantity which does not change with medium when electric field penetrates a medium. Numerically it measures the surface density of free charges on the surface from which electric field is originated and considered to remain constant as a source of electric field. Students can solve the above question without using displacement also.

Illustrative Example 2.45

In the arrangement shown in figure-2.212, a dielectric slab of dielectric constant K is partially inside a parallel plate capacitor. Assuming gravity to be absent, calculate the extension in the spring if the whole system is in equilibrium. If the slab is slightly displaced will it perform SHM? If the battery is disconnected and then the slab is slightly displaced, will it perform SHM? Given that l is the length of the plates, b is the breadth of plates and d is the separation between the plates.

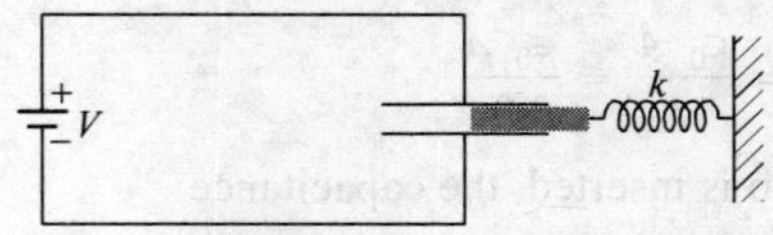

Figure 2.212

Solution

At equilibrium the force on dielectric slab is balanced by the spring force. If x is the extension in spring, we have

$$F_e = kx$$

When battery is connected across the capacitor then the force on dielectric is given by the equation-(2.200) which gives

$$\frac{1}{2}V^2\frac{\varepsilon_0 b}{d}(k-1) = kx$$

$\Rightarrow$ $$x = \frac{V^2\varepsilon_0 b(k-1)}{2kd}$$

As the force on dielectric is constant and does not depend upon x, it will not execute SHM.

When battery is disconnected after charging the capacitor the force on dielectric slab is given by the equation-(2.202) which gives

$$\frac{Q^2 d(k-1)}{2\in_0 b(l-x+kx)^2} = kx$$

Solving the above equation we can calculate the value of x. In this case force depends upon x but not a linear function so in this case also it will not execute SHM.

Illustrative Example 2.46

Figure shows two parallel plate capacitors with fixed plates and connected to two batteries. The separation between the plates is the same for the two capacitors. The plates are rectangular in shape with width b and length l_1 and l_2. The left half of the dielectric slab has a dielectric constant k_1 and the right half k_2. Neglecting any friction, find the ratio of the voltage of the left battery to that of the right battery for which the dielectric slab may remain in equilibrium.

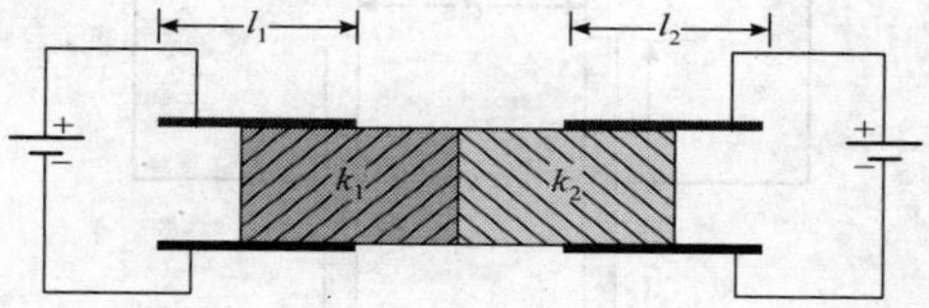

Figure 2.213

Solution

The force on a dielectric for constant potential is given by equation-(2.201) as

$$F = \frac{\epsilon_0 bV^2}{2d}(k-1)$$

For equilibrium of the slab, force by the two capacitors on dielectrics must be equal which gives

$$F_1 = F_2$$

$$\Rightarrow \quad \frac{\epsilon_0 bV_1^2(k_1-1)}{2d} = \frac{\epsilon_0 bV_2^2(k_2-1)}{2d}$$

$$\Rightarrow \quad \frac{V_1}{V_2} = \sqrt{\frac{k_2-1}{k_1-1}}$$

Illustrative Example 2.47

There is a double layer cylindrical capacitor whose parameters are shown in figure-2.214. The breakdown field strength values for these dielectrics are equal to E_1 and E_2 respectively. What is the breakdown voltage of this capacitor if $\varepsilon_1 R_1 E_1 < \varepsilon_2 R_2 E_2$?

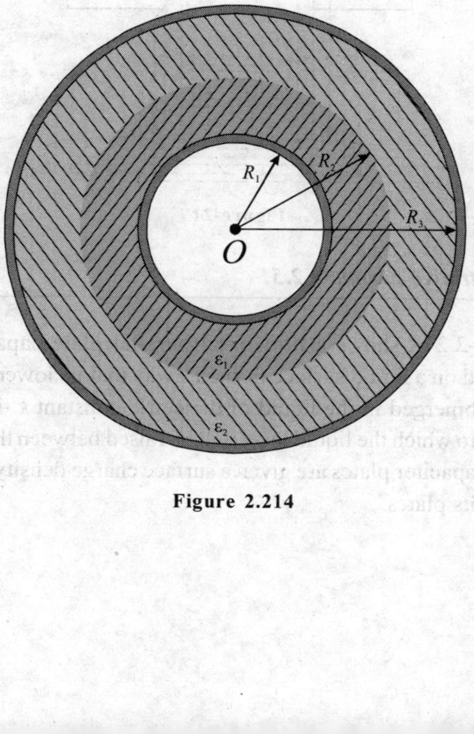

Figure 2.214

Solution

The total potential difference across the dielectric layers is

$$V = \int_{R_1}^{R_2} E_1 dr + \int_{R_2}^{R_3} E_2 dr$$

$$\Rightarrow \quad V = \frac{\lambda}{2\pi\varepsilon_0}\left[\int_{R_1}^{R_2}\frac{dr}{\varepsilon_1 r} + \int_{R_2}^{R_3}\frac{dr}{\varepsilon_2 r}\right]$$

$$\Rightarrow \quad V = \frac{\lambda}{2\pi\varepsilon_0}\left[\frac{\log_e R_2/R_1}{\varepsilon_1} + \frac{\log_e R_3/R_2}{\varepsilon_2}\right]$$

But $\varepsilon_1 R_1 < \varepsilon_2 R_2 E_2$ and for breakdown, $E_1 \varepsilon_1 R_1 = E_2 \varepsilon_2 R_2$; hence $e_1 R_1 E_1$ is the maximum value at which breakdown will occur. Hence the breakdown voltage between the plates is

$$V = E_1 \varepsilon_1 R_1\left[\frac{1}{\varepsilon_1}\log_e\frac{R_2}{R_1} + \frac{1}{\varepsilon_2}\log_e\frac{R_3}{R_2}\right]$$

$$\text{since} \quad \frac{\lambda}{2\pi\varepsilon_0} = E_1 R_1 \varepsilon_1$$

Illustrative Example 2.48

Between the plates of a parallel-plate capacitor there is a metallic plate whose thickness takes up $\eta = 0.60$ of the capacitor gap. When that plate is absent the capacitor has a capacity $C = 20$ nF. The capacitor is connected to a constant voltage source $V = 100$ V. The metallic plate is slowly extracted from the gap. Find the mechanical work performed in the process of plate extraction.

Solution

$$C_0 = \frac{\varepsilon_0 A}{d} \quad \text{without metallic slab}$$

$$C' = \frac{\varepsilon_0 A}{(0.4d)}$$

$$\Rightarrow \quad C' = 2.5\,C_0 \text{ with slab}$$

$$\Rightarrow \quad C' = 50 \text{ nF}$$

$$W_{ext} + W_{field} = 0$$

$$W_{ext} = -W_{field}$$

$$\Rightarrow \quad W_{ext} = \Delta U = \frac{1}{2}(C - C_0)V^2$$

$$\Rightarrow \quad W_{ext} = \frac{1}{2}(50-20)\times 10^{-9}\times(100)^2$$

$$\Rightarrow \quad W_{ext} = \frac{1}{2}\times 30\times 10^{-9}\times 10^4$$

$$\Rightarrow \quad W_{ext} = 15\times 10^{-5}\text{ J}$$

$$\Rightarrow \quad W_{ext} = 150\,\mu\text{J}$$

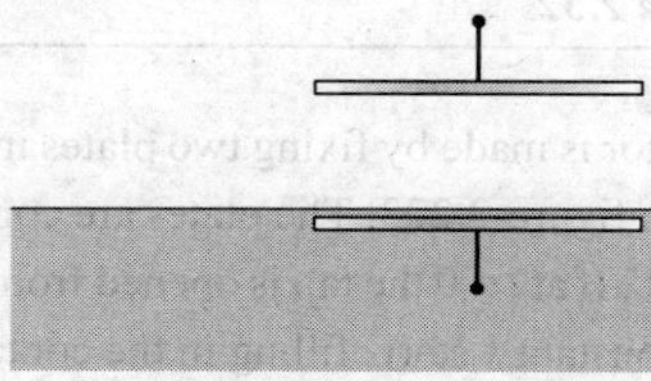

Figure-2.218

Solution

When capacitor plates are given charges then due to polarization on the liquid dielectric bound charges of surface density σ_i appear and its surface experiences an upward force due to which it is raised up to some height h as shown in figure-2.219 upto a level where the upward force on the top surface balances the weight of the liquid raised.

The electric force acts on the top surface of liquid and due to cohesive force among liquid particles whole liquid will be held stationary in equilibrium.

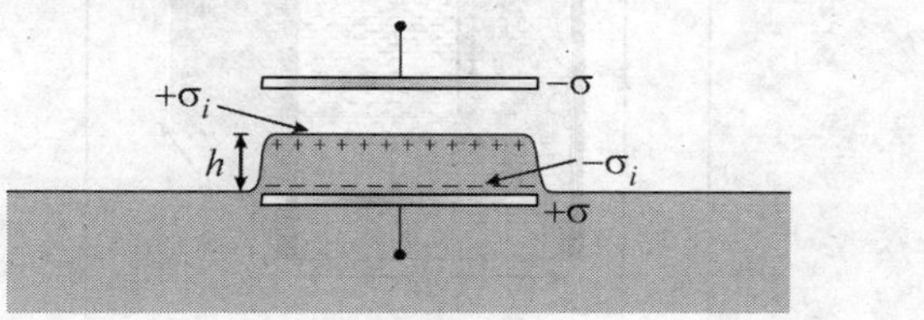

Figure-2.219

If the surface area of plates is taken as S, at equilibrium we use

$$qE = \rho hSg$$

$$\Rightarrow \quad \sigma_i S\left(\frac{\sigma}{\epsilon_0} - \frac{\sigma_i}{2\epsilon_0}\right) = \rho hSg$$

$$\Rightarrow \quad \sigma\left(1-\frac{1}{k}\right)\left(2\sigma - \sigma\left(1-\frac{1}{k}\right)\right) = 2\epsilon_0\,\rho hSg$$

$$\Rightarrow \quad h = \frac{\sigma^2(k^2-1)}{2\epsilon_0 k^2 \rho g}$$

It can also be thought to solve the above situation using conservation of energy as no battery is connected but when the liquid is raised between the plates it gains kinetic energy and oscillates about the equilibrium level and finally settles at equilibrium level after dissipating the kinetic energy gained by the liquid particles in internal friction so in such cases we cannot use conservation of energy to find the equilibrium level.

2.10 *Current in a Capacitor*

This is initially discussed when a capacitor is connected across a battery or in a circuit, current flows through the connecting wires till the potential difference across capacitor plates become equal to that of the applied battery across it and then capacitor is said to be in steady state.

Once steady state is attained capacitor is said to be fully charged and no current flows through capacitor. Before steady state potential difference across capacitor would be changing and charge on its plates would also be changing and the current through the connecting wires is given as

$$i = \frac{dq}{dt}$$

Figure-2.220 shows a capacitor in which current is flowing in opposite directions. As current denotes the flow of positive charges in figure-2.220(a) the current increases the charge on plates of capacitor and in figure-2.220(b) current decreases the charges on plates of capacitor thats why these currents are written as

$$i_1 = +\frac{dq}{dt} \quad \text{and} \quad i_2 = -\frac{dq}{dt}$$

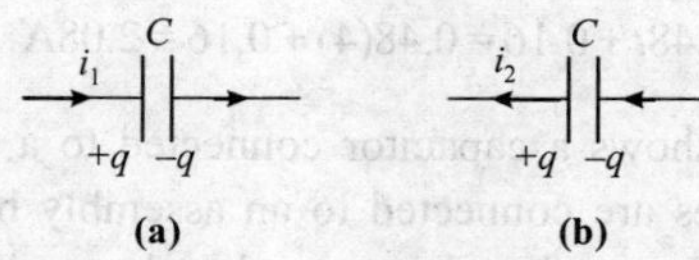

Figure-2.220

If a capacitor connected across a battery is in steady state then no current would be flowing through it and if any of its parameters starts changing with time then capacitance starts varying with time due to which charge on its plates also changes with time and it causes a continuous flow of current which is given by differentiating the instantaneous charge on plates of capacitor which is given as

$$q = CV$$

If C starts varying with time then current in connecting wires is given as

$$i = \frac{dq}{dt} = V\frac{dC}{dt} \qquad \ldots(2.213)$$

If instead of capacitance, applied voltage starts varying with time then current is given as

$$i = \frac{dq}{dt} = C\frac{dV}{dt} \qquad \ldots(2.214)$$

If both capacitance and applied voltage vary with time in a situation then current is given as

$$i = \frac{dq}{dt} = C\frac{dV}{dt} + V\frac{dC}{dt} \qquad \ldots(2.215)$$

We will discuss some illustrations to understand this better. Figure-2.221 shows a capacitor C of capacitance 4μF connected to a time varying voltage $V(t) = -0.06t^2 + 0.044t + 0.7$ volt. We will calculate the current in connecting wires at $t = 4$ s.

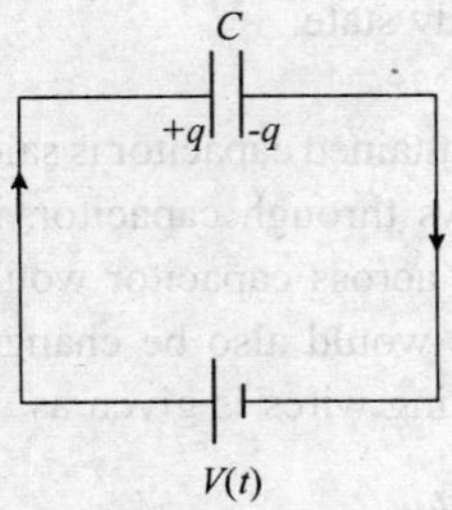

Figure-2.221

If no resistances are there in connecting wires, we can consider that steady state is achieved by the capacitor quickly and its instantaneous charge is given as

$$q = CV$$

$$\Rightarrow \quad q = 4\times(0.06t^2 + 0.04t + 0.7)$$

$$\Rightarrow \quad q = 0.24t^2 + 0.16t + 2.8$$

Current in circuit at $t = 4$ s is given as

$$i = \frac{dq}{dt} = 0.48t + 0.16 = 0.48(4) + 0.16 = 2.08\text{A}$$

Figure-2.222 shows a capacitor connected to a battery. The capacitor plates are connected to an assembly by which the separation between the plates can be changed. If at $t = 0$ capacitor plates start receding apart at speed v each then at a general time instant $t = t$ plate separation will be '$d + 2vt$' and at this instant charge on capacitor plates can be given as

$$q = \left(\frac{\epsilon_0 A}{d + 2vt}\right) V \qquad \ldots(2.216)$$

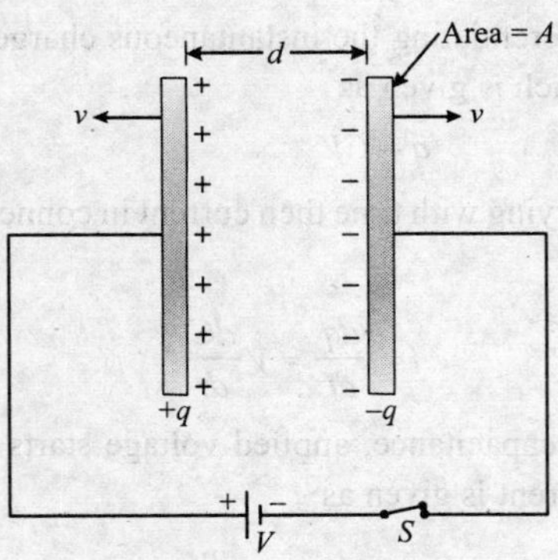

Figure 2.222

The current in connecting wires can be given as

$$i = \frac{dq}{dt} = -\frac{2v \epsilon_0 AV}{(d + 2vt)^2} \qquad \ldots(2.217)$$

Equation-(2.198) gives the current in the connecting wires as a function of time. If at any time plates stop then current also becomes zero and final charge on capacitor at that instant is given by equation-(2.197).

Illustrative Example 2.52

A parallel plate capacitor is made by fixing two plates inside of a container as shown in figure-2.223. The plates are connected to a battery of voltage V. If at $t = 0$ the tap is opened from which a liquid of dielectric constant k starts filling in the container at a constant rate of r m^3/s, find the current in connecting wires as a function of time. Neglect any resistance in connecting wires.

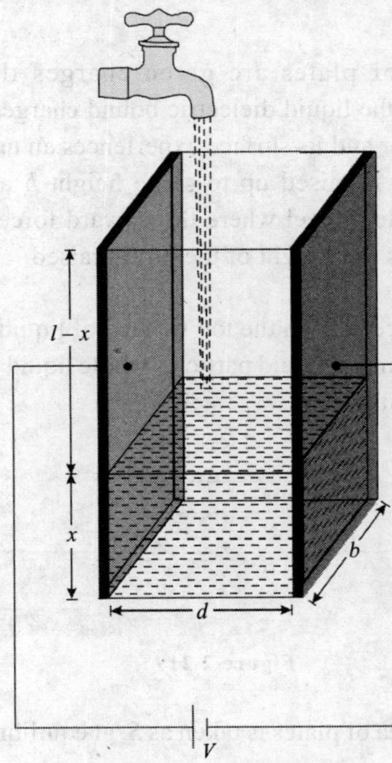

Figure-2.223

Solution

At any time height of liquid in the container is x then it is given as

$$xbd = rt$$

$$\Rightarrow \quad x = \frac{rt}{bd} \qquad \ldots(2.218)$$

At time $t = t$ the system behaves like two capacitors in parallel. One with dielectric upto height x and other with air as shown in figure-2.223. Instantaneous capacitance of this capacitor is given as

$$C = \frac{k \epsilon_0 xb}{d} + \frac{\epsilon_0 (l - x)b}{d}$$

Instaneous charge on capacitor is given as

$$q = CV$$

Current in connecting wires can be given as

$$i = \frac{dq}{dt} = V\frac{dC}{dt}$$

$$\Rightarrow \quad i = V\frac{d}{dt}\left(\frac{k \in_0 xb}{d} + \frac{\in_0 (l-x)b}{d}\right)$$

$$\Rightarrow \quad i = \frac{V \in_0 b}{d}(k-1)\frac{dx}{dt}$$

Substituting the value of x from equation-(2.218) gives

$$i = \frac{V \in_0 b}{d}(k-1) \times \frac{r}{bd} = \frac{V \in_0 r}{d^2}(k-1)$$

Web Reference at www.physicsgalaxy.com

Age Group - Grade 11 & 12 | Age 17-19 Years
Section - ELECTROSTATICS
Topic - Capacitance
Module Number - 30 to 40

Practice Exercise 2.7

(i) A parallel plate capacitor of plate area $A = 10^{-2}$ m^2 and plate separation $d = 10^{-2}$ m is charged to $V_0 = 100$ V. Then after removing the charging battery, a slab of insulating material of thickness $b = 0.5 \times 10^{-2}$ m and dielectric constant $k = 7$ is inserted between the plates. Calculate the free charge on the plates of the capacitor, electric field intensity in air, electric field intensity in the dielectric, potential difference between the plates and capacitance with dielectric present between plates.

[16 μF]

(ii) A potential difference of 100V is applied between the plates of a parallel plate capacitor, which are 1cm apart. One of the plates is in contact with a plane parallel plate of crystalline thallium bromide ($k = 173$) 9.5mm thick. After the capacitor is disconnected from the source of power, the crystalline plate is removed. What will be the potential difference between the plates after this is done?

[1802V]

(iii) A cylindrical layer of dielectric with dielectric constant k is inserted into a cylindrical capacitor to fill up all the space between the electrodes. The mean radius of the electrodes is equal to R, the gap between them is equal to d with $d << R$. A constant voltage V is applied across the electrodes of the capacitor. Find the magnitude of the electric force pulling the dielectric into the capacitor.

[$F_x = \in_0(k-1)\frac{\pi R V^2}{d}$]

(iv) Two parallel plate capacitors A and B have the same separation $d = 8.85 \times 10^{-4}$ m between the plates. The plate area of A and B are 0.04 m^2 and 0.02 m^2 respectively. A slab of dielectric constant $k = 9$ has dimensions such that it can exactly fill the space between the plates of capacitor B.

(a) The dielectric slab is placed inside A as shown in figure-2.224(a). A is then charged to a potential difference of 110V. Calculate the capacitance of A and the energy stored in it.

(b) The battery is disconnected and then the dielectric slab is removed from A. Find the work done by the external agency in removing the slab from A.

(c) The same dielectric slab is now placed inside B, filling it completely. The two capacitors A and B are then connected as shown in figure-2.224(c). Calculate the energy stored in the system.

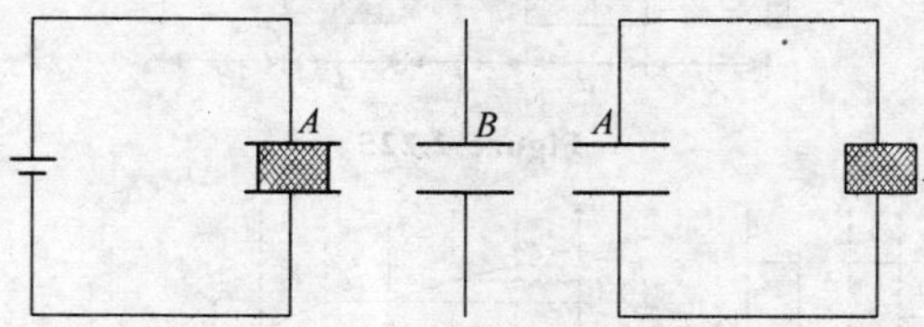

Figure 2.224

[(a) 2×10^{-9} F 1.21×10^{-5}J, (b) 4.84×10^{-5}J, (c) 1.1×10^{-5}J]

(v) Two parallel plate air filled capacitors, each of capacitance C are joined in series to a source of constant voltage V. The space between the plates of one of the capacitors is the completely filled up with a uniform dielectric having dielectric constant K.

(a) How many times the electric field strength in that capacitor decrease ?

(b) What amount of charge flows through the battery?

[(a) $\left(\frac{K+1}{2}\right)$, (b) $\frac{CV}{2}\left(\frac{K-1}{K+1}\right)$]

(vi) The gap between the plates of a parallel-plate capacitor is filled with isotropic dielectric whose relative permittivity $\in$ varies linearly from $\in_1$ to $\in_2$ ($\in_2 > \in_1$) in the direction perpendicular to the plates. The area of each plate is equal to A, the separation between the plates is equal to d. Find the capacitance of the capacitor.

[$\frac{(\in_2 - \in_1)\in_0 A}{d \ln \frac{\in_2}{\in_1}}$]

(vii) A leaky parallel capacitor is filled completely with a material having dielectric constant $K = 5$ and electrical conductivity $\sigma = 7.4 \times 10^{-12}\ \Omega^{-1}$ m^{-1}. If the charge on the plate at the instant $t = 0$ is $q = 8.85$ μC, then calculate the leakage current at the instant $t = 12$s.

[0.2μA]

Illustrative Example 2.49

Consider the situation shown in figure-2.215. The plates of the capacitor have plate area A and are clamped in the laboratory. The dielectric slab is released from rest with length a inside the capacitor. Neglecting any effect of friction or gravity, show that the slab will execute periodic motion and find its time period.

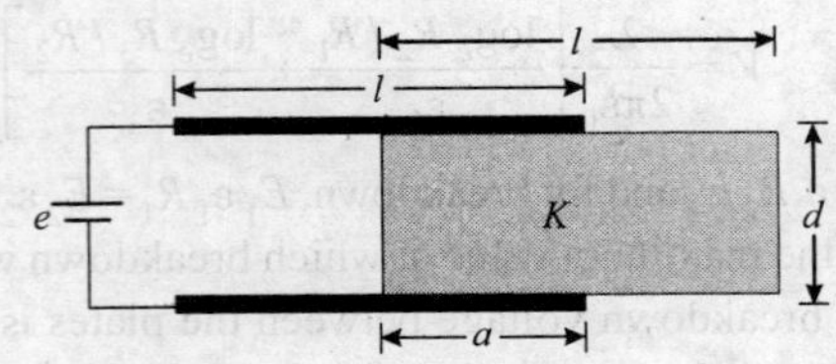

Figure 2.215

Solution

Force on dielectric slab when battery is connected is

$$F = \frac{b\varepsilon_0(-1+K)V^2}{2d}$$

Time taken by slab when it is completely inside the capacitor

is $= \frac{T}{4}$ (T = Time period)

$$S = ut + \frac{1}{2}at^2$$

$$l - a = \frac{1}{2}\left(\frac{F}{M}\right)\left(\frac{T}{4}\right)^2$$

$$\frac{T}{4} = \sqrt{\frac{2M(l-a)}{F}}$$

$$T = 8 \times \sqrt{\frac{Md(l-a)}{b\varepsilon_0(K-1)V^2}}$$

(b = width of plates, M = mass of slab)

Illustrative Example 2.50

Figure-2.216 shows a parallel plate capacitor of plate area $A = lb$ with separation d connected to a battery via a switch S. Capacitor plates are kept vertical and touched on the surface of a liquid of density ρ as shown. If S is closed find the height between plates to which the liquid level will rise.

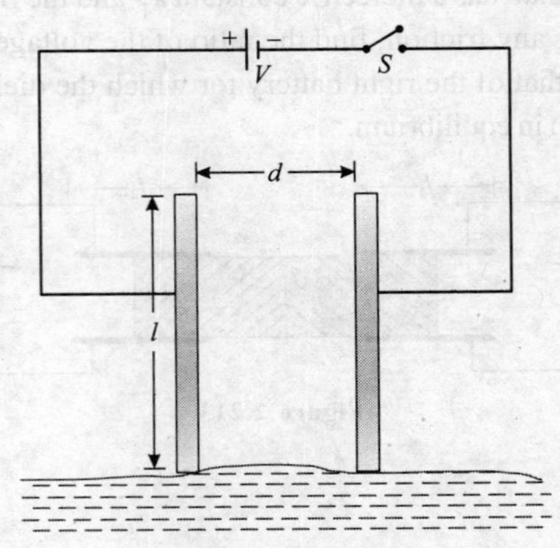

Figure-2.216

Solution

When the switch is closed due to the upward force on liquid because of polarization it starts raising up between the plates and upto a level where the upward force on liquid balances its weight. If it is raised upto a height h as shown in figure-2.217 and battery is connected to the capacitor we use equation-(2.201) for the force on dielectric liquid. At equilibrium we use

$$\frac{\epsilon_0 bV^2}{2d}(k-1) = hbd\rho g$$

$$\Rightarrow \qquad h = \frac{\epsilon_0 V^2(k-1)}{2d^2\rho g}$$

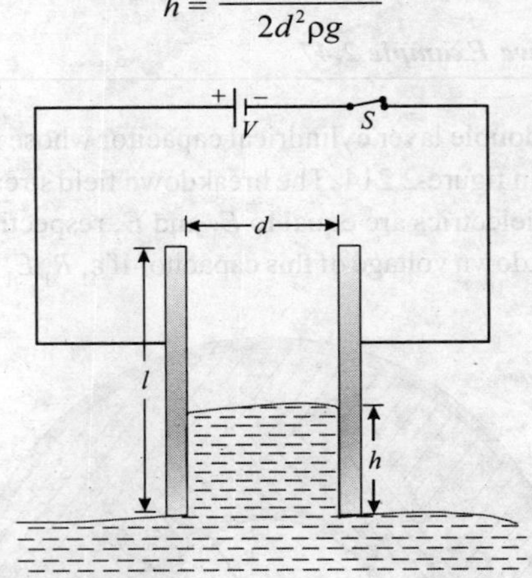

Figure-217

Illustrative Example 2.51

Figure-2.218 shows a horizontal parallel plate capacitor is lowered on a liquid surface in such a way that its lower plate is just submerged in the liquid of dielectric constant k. Find the height to which the liquid level will be raised between the plates if the capacitor plates are given a surface charge density $+\sigma$ and $-\sigma$ on its plates.

(viii) Two parallel conducting plates of area A charge $+q$ and $-q$ are as shown is figure-2.225. A dielectric slab of dielectric constant k and thickness d and a conducting plate of same thickness d is inserted between them. Taking $x = 0$ at positive plate and $x = 5d$ at negative plate, plot E-x and V-x graphs. Here E is the electric field and V the potential.

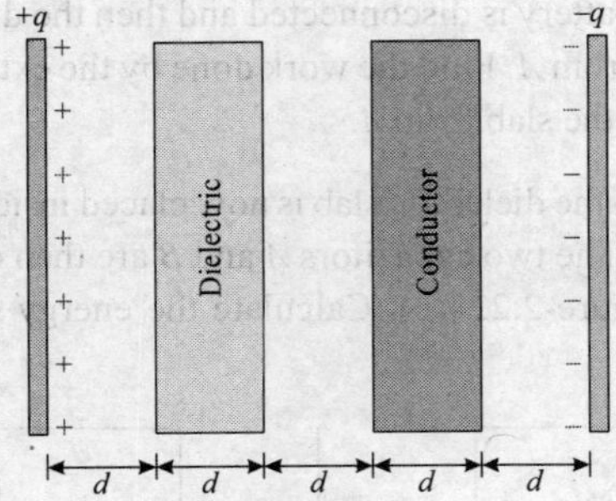

Figure 2.225

[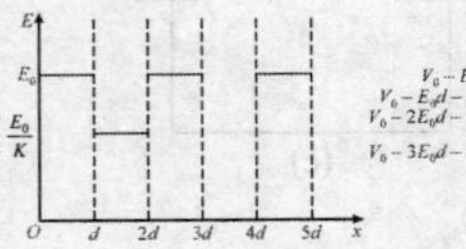 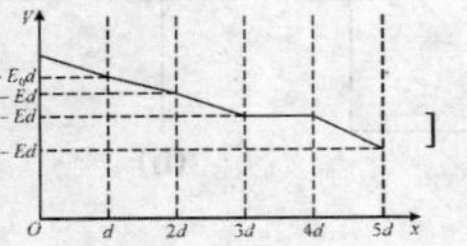]

(ix) A parallel plate capacitor is half filled with a dielectric of relative permittivity k and of mass M. Capacitor is attached with a cell of voltage E. Plates are held fixed on smooth insulating horizontal surface. A bullet of equal mass M hits the dielectric elastically and its found that dielectric just leaves out the capacitor. Find speed of bullet.

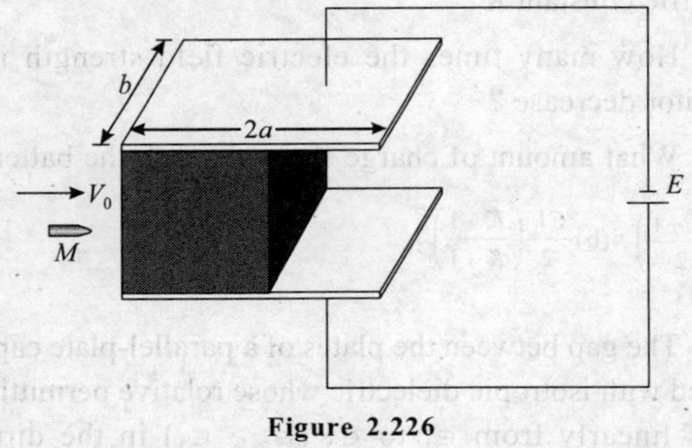

Figure 2.226

$\left[E\left[\frac{\epsilon_0 ab(K-1)}{Md}\right]^{1/2}\right]$

(x) A parallel plate capacitor is charged to a potential difference V across its plates. The capacitor is now disconnected from the battery and is placed vertically on the surface of a liquid of density ρ. If the liquid rises up to a maximum height h inside the capacitor plates, calculate the potential difference V, initially applied across the plates. Given that the plates are of area A and length l. They are separated by a distance d and the space between them is filled with a dielectric substance having dielectric constant k.

$\left[\sqrt{\frac{\rho g h d^2 (l+h(k-1))}{\epsilon_0\, l(k-1)}}\right]$

(xi) Calculate the capacitance of a parallel plate capacitor, with plate area A and distance between plates d, when filled with a dielectric whose dielectric constant varies as

$$\epsilon(x) = \epsilon_0 + \beta x \qquad 0 < x < \frac{d}{2}$$

$$\epsilon(x) = \epsilon_0 + \beta(d - x), \qquad \frac{d}{2} < x < d.$$

For what value of β would the capacitance of capacitor becomes of the capacitor twice that when it is without any dielectric?

[$\frac{2}{A\beta}\ln\left(\frac{\epsilon_0 + \beta\frac{d}{2}}{\epsilon_0}\right)$; β is given the relation $\beta d = 4\epsilon_0 \ln\left(\frac{\epsilon_0 + \beta\frac{d}{2}}{\epsilon_0}\right)$]

(xii) A parallel plate capacitor is to be designed with a voltage rating 1kV using a material of dielectric constant 10 and dielectric strength 10^6 V/m^{-1}. What minimum area of the plates is required to have a capacitance of 88.5 pF ?

[10^{-3} m^2]

(xiii) A potential difference of 300 V is applied between the plates of a plane capacitor spaced 1cm apart. A plane parallel glass plate with a thickness of 0.5 cm and a plane parallel paraffin plate with a thickness of 0.5 cm are placed in the space between the capacitor plates find (a) intensity of electric field in each layer (b) the drop of potential in each layer (c) the surface charge density of the free charge on the plates. Given that : $k_{paraffin} = 2$, $k_{glass} = 6$.

[(a) 1.55×10^4 V/m, 4.5×10^4 V/m; (b) 75 V, 225 V (c) 8×10^{-7} C/m^2]

(xiv) A parallel plate capacitor is filled by a dielectric whose relative permittivity varies with the applied voltage according to the law $\varepsilon_r = \alpha V$, where $\alpha = 1$ per volt. An other same (but containing no dielectric) capacitor charged to a voltage $V = 156$ volt is connected in parallel to the first "non–linear" uncharged capacitor. Determine the final voltage V_f across the capacitors.

[12V]

Advance Illustrations Videos at www.physicsgalaxy.com

Age Group - Advance Illustrations
Section - Electrostatics
Topic - Capacitance
Illustrations - 39 In-depth Illustrations Videos

* * * * *

Discussion Questions

Q2-1 What will happen if the plates of a charged capacitor are suddenly connected by metallic wire ?

Q2-2 Can we give any desired charge to a capacitor ?

Q2-3 The radius of the earth is 6400km, what is its capacitance?

Q2-4 Can a solid conducting sphere hold more charge than a hollow sphere of the same radius ? Give reason.

Q2-5 Why metals cannot be used as a dielectric in a capacitor?

Q2-6 A capacitor is connected to a battery. If we move its plates further apart, work will be done against the electrostatic attraction between the plates. What will happen to this work? What will be the effect on the energy of the capacitor ?

Q2-7 If the capacitor is kept connected with the battery and then the dielectric slab is inserted between the plates, then what will be the change in the charge, the capacitance the potential difference, the electric field an the stored energy ?

Q2-8 If we know the capacitance of a given conductor then can we calculate the maximum charge which it can store ?

Q2-9 A parallel plate capacitor is charged to a certain potential difference and the battery used to charged it is disconnected. Now a dielectric slab of dimensions equal to spacing between plates is introduced between the plates. What will be the changes, if any, in the charge, potential difference, capacitance, electric field strength and the energy stored in the capacitor ?

Q2-10 A capacitor of capacitance C is charged upto a potential difference V. After removing the charging battery, the capacitor is connected (i) in parallel, (ii) in series with an uncharged capacitor of the same capacitance. What will be the effect on the potential difference of the first capacitor in each case ?

Q2-11 When a dielectric slab is inserted between the plates of a capacitor which is initially charged and disconnected from the source then what can be concluded on the amount of heat dissipated during insertion ? What would be the answer if source remain connected to the capacitor while insertion of the dielectric slab ?

Q2-12 N identical capacitors are connected in parallel which are charged to a potential V. If these are separated and connected in series then what potential difference will be obtained ?

Q2-13 For a given potential difference across a parallel plate capacitor does a capacitor stores more or less charge with a dielectric than it does without a dielectric present between the plates ?

Q2-14 Why should circuits containing capacitor be handled cautiously even when there is no current.

Q2-15 When a parallel plate capacitor is charged by connecting it across a battery then battery is disconnected. If one plate of capacitor is earthed and isolated then another plate is connected to earth and then isolated. What will be the final charge on the capacitor after this operation. Will it be less than, equal to or more than the initial charge ? Explain why ?

Q2-16 A solid and a hollow metal spheres are given equal charges, which one will have higher electric potential.

Q2-17 When plastic parts are removed from the metal dies on different types of printing machines then these metal parts develop high voltage. Explain why ?

Q2-18 The distance between the plates of a parallel plate capacitor is d. A metal plate of thickness $d/2$ is placed between the plates. What will e its effect on the capacitance.

Q2-19 A parallel plate capacitor is connected to a battery and it is in steady state. Connecting wires are considered as perfect conductors. If the plates of capacitor are moved apart by some distance and then after sometime these are brought back to the same separation. Is there any heat dissipated in the circuit in above operation ? Explain why ?

Q2-20 Why do electrostatic capacitors have large capacitives?

Q2-21 Why is it that a man sitting in an insulated metal cage does not receive a shock when it is connected to a high voltage supply ?

Q2-22 As we know in steady state charge on a capacitor is given as $Q = CV$ which also implies $C = Q/V$. So can we say in steady state capacitance is proportional to the supplied charge Q.

* * * * *

Conceptual MCQs Single Option Correct

2-1 A capacitor is charged by using a battery, which is then disconnected. A dielectric slab is then inserted between the plates, which results in :

(A) Reduction of charge on the plates and in crease of potential difference across the plates

(B) Increase in the potential difference across the plates, reduction in stored energy, but no change in the charge on the plates

(C) Decrease in the potential difference across the plates, reduction in stored energy, but no change in the charge on the plates

(D) None of the above

2-2 A capacitor is composed of three parallel conducting plates. All three plates are of same area A. The first pair of plates are kept a distance d_1 apart and the space between them is filled with a medium of a dielectric ε_1. The corresponding values for the second pair of plates are d_2 and ε_2 respectively. What is the surface charge density on the middle plate ?

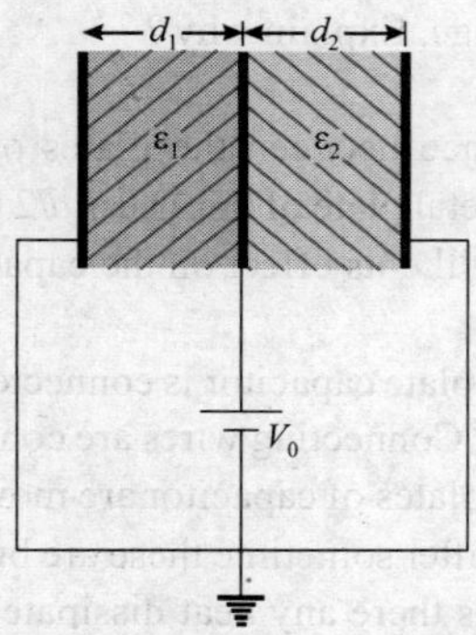

Figure 2.227

(A) $\varepsilon_0 V\left[\frac{\varepsilon_1}{d_1}+\frac{\varepsilon_2}{d_2}\right]$ (B) $-\varepsilon_0 V\left[\frac{\varepsilon_1}{d_1}+\frac{\varepsilon_2}{d_2}\right]$

(C) $2\varepsilon_0 V\left[\frac{\varepsilon_1}{d_1}+\frac{\varepsilon_2}{d_2}\right]$ (D) $-2\varepsilon_0 V\left[\frac{\varepsilon_1}{d_1}+\frac{\varepsilon_2}{d_2}\right]$

2-3 In the figure shown, the plates of a parallel plate capacitor have unequal charges. Its capacitance is C and P is a point outside the capacitor as shown in figure-2.228. The distance between the plates is d. Select the INCORRECT statement :

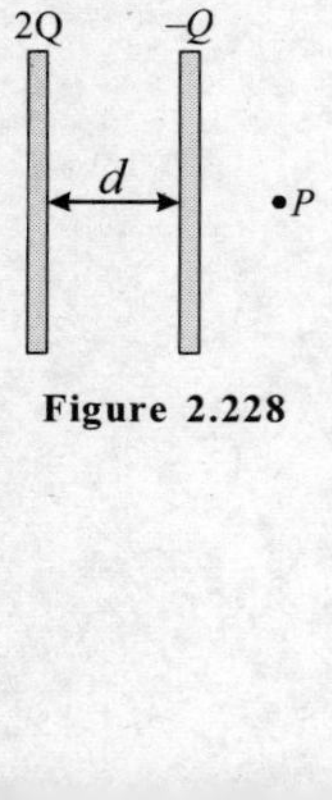

Figure 2.228

(A) A point charge at point P will experience and electric force due to capacitor

(B) The potential difference between the plates will be $3Q/2C$

(C) The energy stored in the electric field in the region between the plates is $\frac{9Q^2}{8C}$

(D) The force on one plate due to the other plate is $\frac{Q^2}{2\pi \in_0 d^2}$

2-4 You have a parallel plate capacitor, a spherical capacitor and a cylindrical capacitor. Each capacitor is charged and then removed from the same battery. Consider the following situations :

I : Separation between the plates of parallel plate capacitor is reduced

II : Radius of the outer spherical shell of the spherical capacitor is increased

III : Radius of the outer cylinder of cylindrical capacitor is increased.

Which of the following is correct ?

(A) In each of these situations I, II and III, charge on the given capacitor remains the same and potential difference across it also remains the same.

(B) In each of these situations I, II and III, charge on the given capacitor remains the same but potential difference, in situations I and III, decreases, and in situation II, increases.

(C) In each of these situations I, II and III, charge on the given capacitor remains the same but potential difference, in situations I, decreases, and in situations II and III, increases.

(D) Charge on the capacitor in each situation changes. It increases in all these situations but potential difference remains the same.

2-5 Two identical capacitors are joined in parallel and charged to a potential V. They are then disconnected from the battery and connected to each other in series. The positive plate of one being connected to the negative of the other and two outer plates terminals are left open. Which of the following statement is correct ?

(A) Charge on the plates connected to each other is reduced to zero

(B) Charge on the outer plates is doubled

(C) Potential difference between outer plates terminals is 2 V

(D) The energy stored in the system is doubled

2-6 Seven capacitors each of capacitance 2 μF are to be connected to obtain a capacitance of (10/11) μF. Which of the following combination will be used for this purpose :

(A) 5 in parallel 2 in series (B) 4 in parallel 3 in series

(C) 3 in parallel 4 series (D) 2 in parallel 5 in series

2-7 For the three circuit shown in figure-2.229 across the battery capacitors are connected in some combination. Which of the following is the correct order of combination :

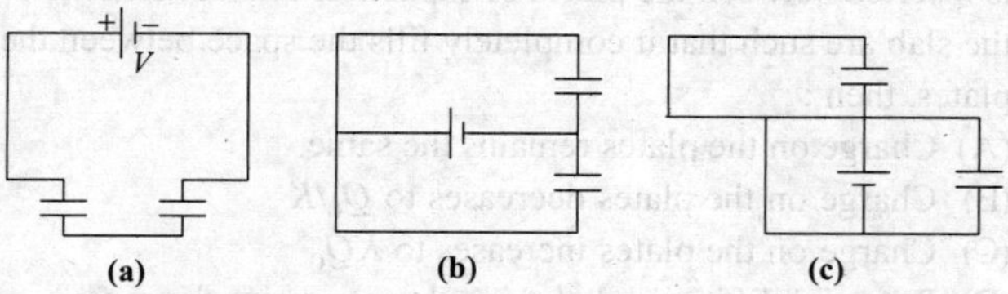

Figure 2.229

(A) Series, series, parallel (B) Series, parallel, parallel
(C) Parallel, series, parallel (D) None of these

2-8 Two identical capacitors are connected in series with a source of constant voltage V. If Q is the charge on one of the capacitors, the capacitance of each capacitor is :

(A) $Q/2V$ (B) Q/V
(C) $2Q/V$ (D) None of these

2-9 A parallel plate air capacitor is connected to a battery. After charging fully, the battery is disconnected and the plates are pulled apart to increase their separation. Which of the following statements is correct ?

(A) The electric field between the plates of capacitor decreases
(B) The electric field between the plates of capacitor increases
(C) The electric field between the plates of capacitor remains same
(D) Potential difference between the plates remains the same

2-10 A dielectric slab of thickness d is inserted in the parallel plate capacitor. The capacitor is given some charge such that it's negative plate is at $x = 0$ and positive plate is at $x = 3d$. The slab is equidistant from the plates. As one moves from $x = 0$ to $x = 3d$:

(A) Electric potential remains the same
(B) Electric potential decreases continuously
(C) Electric potential increases continuously
(D) Electric potential increases first, then decreases and again increases

2-11 Two identical capacitors A and B shown in the given circuit are joined in series with a battery. If a dielectric slab of dielectric constant K is inserted between the plates of capacitor B and battery remain connected, then the energy of capacitor A will

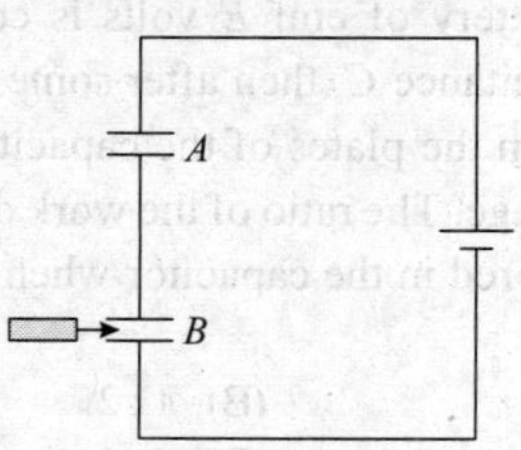

Figure 2.230

(A) Decrease (B) Increase
(C) Remain the same (D) Becomes zero

2-12 If there are n capacitors each of capacitance C in series combination connected to a V volt source, then the energy stored in each capacitor is equal to :

(A) nCV^2 (B) $\frac{1}{2}nCV^2$
(C) $\frac{CV^2}{2n}$ (D) $\frac{CV^2}{2n^2}$

2-13 The charges on two parallel copper plates separated by a small distance are $+Q$ and $-Q$. A test charge q experiences a force F when placed between these plates. Now if one of the plates is removed to infinity, then the force on the test charge will become :

(A) $F/2$ (B) F
(C) 2F (D) Zero

2-14 Two conducting shells of radius a and b are connected by conducting wire as shown in figure-2.231. The capacitance of this system is :

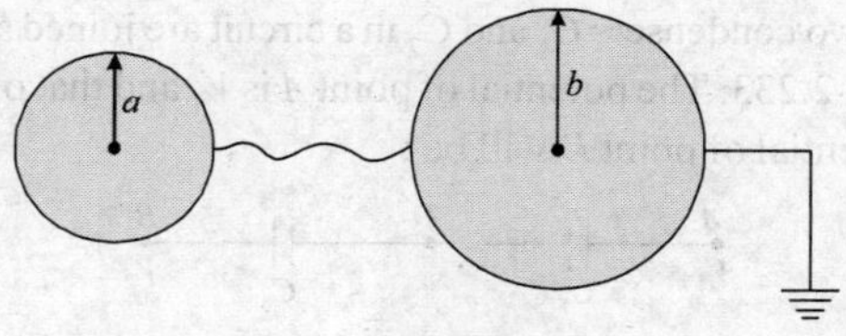

Figure 2.231

(A) $4\pi\varepsilon_0 \frac{ab}{b-a}$ (B) $4\pi\varepsilon_0(a+b)$
(C) Zero (D) Infinite

2-15 The graph given below shows the variation of electric field E (in MV/m) with time t (in μs) in a parallel plate capacitor :

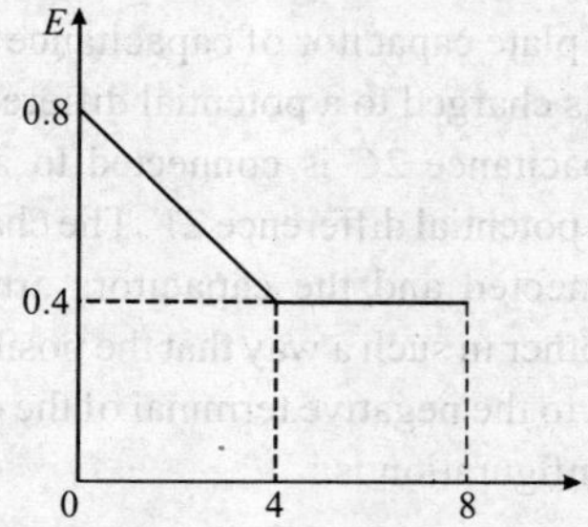

Figure 2.232

Consider the following statements :

1. The displacement current through a 1 m^2 region perpendicular to the field during the time interval $t = 0$ to $t = 4$ μs is 0.885 A (Given $\epsilon_0 = 8.85 \times 10^{-12}$ SI unit)

2. The displacement current through 1 m^2 region perpendicular to the field during the time interval $t = 4\ \mu s$ to $8\ \mu s$ is zero.

Which of the statements given above is/are correct :

(A) 1 only (B) 2 only

(C) both 1 and 2 (D) neither 1 nor 2

2-16 A parallel plate capacitor of plate area A and plate separation d is charged to potential V and then the battery is disconnected. A slab of dielectric constant k is then inserted between the plates of the capacitors so as to fill the space between the plates. If Q, E and W denote respectively, the magnitude of charge on each plate, the electric field between the plates after insertion of slab and work done on the system in the process of insertion of the slab, then which of the following relation is INCORRECT :

(A) $Q = \dfrac{\varepsilon_0 AV}{d}$ (B) $W = \dfrac{\varepsilon_0 AV^2}{2kd}$

(C) $E = \dfrac{V}{kd}$ (D) $W = \dfrac{\varepsilon_0 AV^2}{2d}\left(1 - \dfrac{1}{k}\right)$

2-17 Two condensers C_1 and C_2 in a circuit are joined as shown in figure-2.233. The potential of point A is V_1 and that of B is V_2. The potential of point D will be :

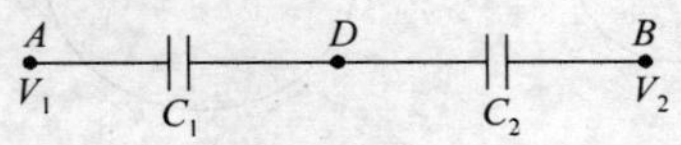

Figure 2.233

(A) $\dfrac{1}{2}(V_1 + V_2)$ (B) $\dfrac{C_2V_1 + C_1V_2}{C_1 + C_2}$

(C) $\dfrac{C_1V_1 + C_2V_2}{C_1 + C_2}$ (D) $\dfrac{C_2V_1 - C_1V_2}{C_1 + C_2}$

2-18 A parallel plate capacitor of capacitance C is connected to a battery and is charged to a potential difference V. Another capacitor of capacitance $2C$ is connected to another battery and is charged to potential difference $2V$. The charging batteries are now disconnected and the capacitors are connected in parallel to each other in such a way that the positive terminal of one is connected to the negative terminal of the other. The final energy of the configuration is :

(A) Zero (B) $\dfrac{25CV^2}{6}$

(C) $\dfrac{3CV^2}{2}$ (D) $\dfrac{9CV^2}{2}$

2-19 A parallel plate capacitor of capacitance C_0 is charged with a charge Q_0 to a potential difference V_0 and the battery is then disconnected. Now a dielectric slab of dielectric constant k is inserted between the plates of capacitor. The dimensions of the slab are such that it completely fills the space between the plates, then :

(A) Charge on the plates remains the same

(B) Charge on the plates decreases to Q_0/K

(C) Charge on the plates increases to KQ_0

(D) Potential difference between plates remains the same

2-20 n identical capacitors are connected in parallel to a potential difference V. After charging these capacitors are then disconnected reconnected in series with side terminals open. The potential difference across the side terminals of capacitors will be :

(A) Zero (B) $(n-1)V$

(C) nV (D) n^2V

2-21 Two large parallel sheets charged uniformly with surface charge density σ and – σ are located as shown in the figure-2.234. Which one of the following graphs shows the variation of electric field along a line perpendicular to the sheets :

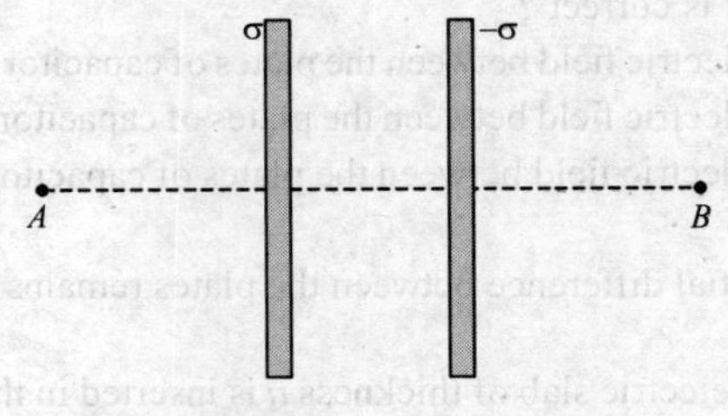

Figure 2.234

(A)
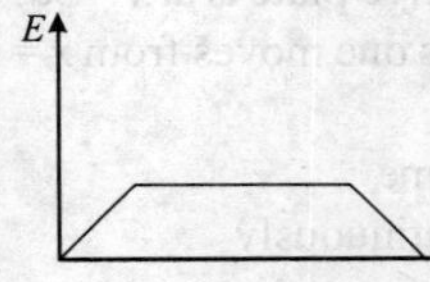

(B)
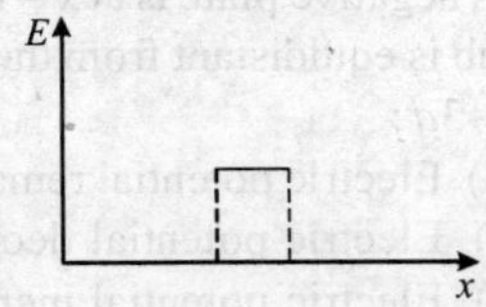

(C)
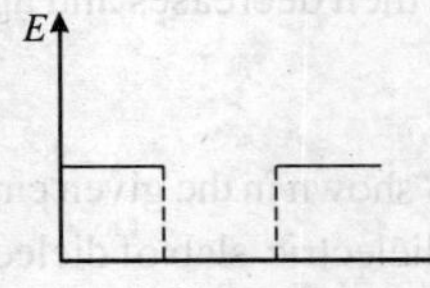

(D)
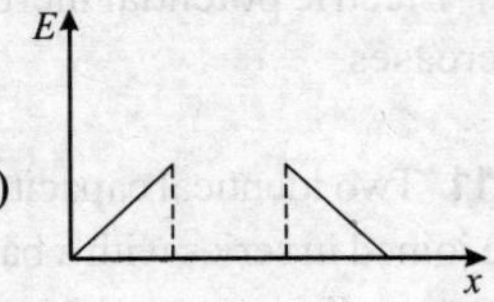

2-22 When a battery of emf E volts is connected across a capacitor of capacitance C, then after some time the potential difference between the plates of the capacitor becomes equal to the battery voltage. The ratio of the work done by the battery and the energy stored in the capacitor when it is fully charged is :

(A) 1 : 1 (B) 1 : 2

(C) 2 : 1 (D) 4 : 1

2-23 Find equivalent capacitance between points A and B. Consider each conducting plate is having same dimensions and each of area A with separation between adjoining plates as mentioned in figure and neglect the thickness of the plate. Consider $C = \frac{\varepsilon_0 A}{d} = 7\ \mu F$, where A is area of plates :

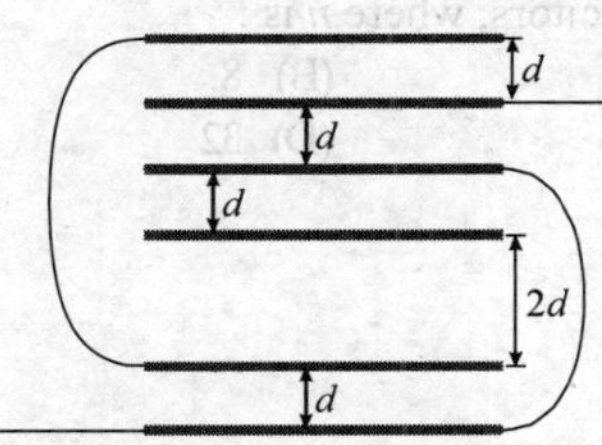

Figure 2.235

(A) 7 μF (B) 11 μF
(C) 12 μF (D) 15 μF

2-24 An uncharged capacitor having capacitance C is connected across a battery of voltage V. Now the capacitor is disconnected and then reconnected across the same battery but with reversed polarity. Then which of the statement is INCORRECT

(A) After reconnecting, heat energy produced in the circuit will be equal to two–third of the total energy supplied by battery
(B) After reconnecting, no energy is supplied by battery
(C) After reconnecting, whole of the energy supplied by the battery is converted into heat
(D) After reconnecting, thermal energy produced in the circuit will be equal to $2CV^2$

2-25 Two similar parallel plate capacitors each of capacity C_0 are connected in series. The combination is connected with a battery of voltage V_0. Now separation between the plates of one capacitor is increased by a distance d and the separation between the plates of another capacitor is decreased by the distance $d/2$. The distance between the plates of each capacitor was d before the change in separation. Then, select the correct choice :

(A) The new capacitance of the system will increase
(B) The new capacitance of the system will decrease
(C) The new capacitance of the system will remain same
(D) Data is not sufficient to arrive at a conclusion

2-26 The potential difference between points a and b of circuits shown in the figure-2.236 is :

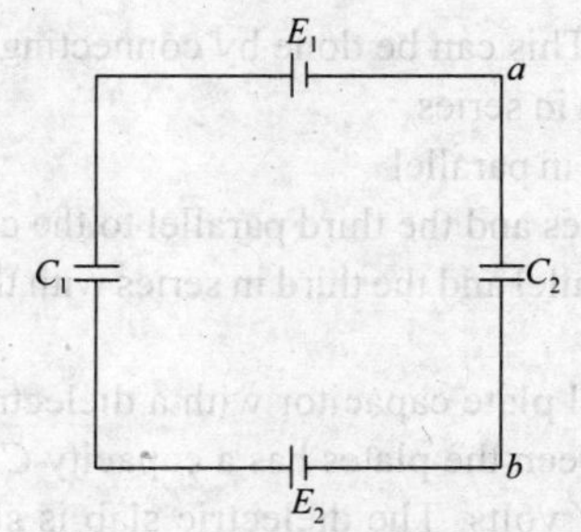

Figure 2.236

(A) $\left(\frac{E_1+E_2}{C_1+C_2}\right)C_2$ (B) $\left(\frac{E_1-E_2}{C_1+C_2}\right)C_2$

(C) $\left(\frac{E_1+E_2}{C_1+C_2}\right)C_1$ (D) $\left(\frac{E_1-E_2}{C_1+C_2}\right)C_1$

2-27 If a charged conductor is not isolated & other conducting bodies are approaching towards it then the :

(A) Capacitance of conductor will increase as potential conductor decreases due to induction phenomenon
(B) Capacitance of conductor remains constant as it is depending on shape & size of conductor
(C) Capacitance of conductor will decreases due to redistribution of charge on approaching bodies
(D) None of the above

2-28 A variable parallel plate capacitor and an electroscope are connected in parallel to a battery. The reading of the electroscope would be decreased by :

(i) Increasing the area of overlap of the plates
(ii) Placing a block of paraffin wax between the plates
(iii) Decreasing the distance between the plates
(iv) Decreasing the battery voltage

(A) Only (i), (ii) and (iii) are correct
(B) Only (i) and (ii) are correct
(C) Only (ii) and (iv) are correct
(D) Only (iv) is correct

2-29 A parallel plate capacitor with a dielectric slab with dielectric constant $k = 3$ filling the space between the plates is charged to potential V and isolated. Then the dielectric slab is drawn out and another dielectric slab of equal thickness but dielectric constant $k' = 2$ is introduced between the plates. The ratio of the energy stored in the capacitor later to that initially is :

(A) 2 : 3 (B) 3 : 2
(C) 4 : 9 (D) 9 : 4

2-30 Three capacitors each of capacitance 4 μF are to be connected in such a away that the effective capacitance becomes 6 μF. This can be done by connecting :

(A) All of them in series

(B) All of them in parallel

(C) Two in series and the third parallel to the combination

(D) Two in parallel and the third in series with the combination

2-31 A parallel plate capacitor with a dielectric of dielectric constant k between the plates has a capacity C and is charged to a potential V volts. The dielectric slab is slowly removed from between the plates and then re-inserted. The net work done by the system in this process is :

(A) $\frac{1}{2}(K-1)CV^2$ (B) $CV^2(K-1)/K$

(C) $(K-1)CV^2$ (D) Zero

2-32 To form a composite 16 μF, 1000 V capacitor from a supply of identical capacitors marked 8 μF, 250 V, we require a minimum number of n capacitors, where n is :

(A) 2 (B) 8

(C) 16 (D) 32

* * * * *

Numerical MCQs Single Option Correct

2-1 Two capacitors 3 μF and 6 μF are connected in series across a potential difference of 120 V. Then the potential difference across 3 μF capacitor is :

(A) 40 V (B) 60 V
(C) 80 V (D) 100 V

2-2 Initial charges (with proper sign) on the plates of two identical capacitors, each of 1 μF, are as shown. When both S_1 and S_2 are closed, the potential difference between A and B will finally become :

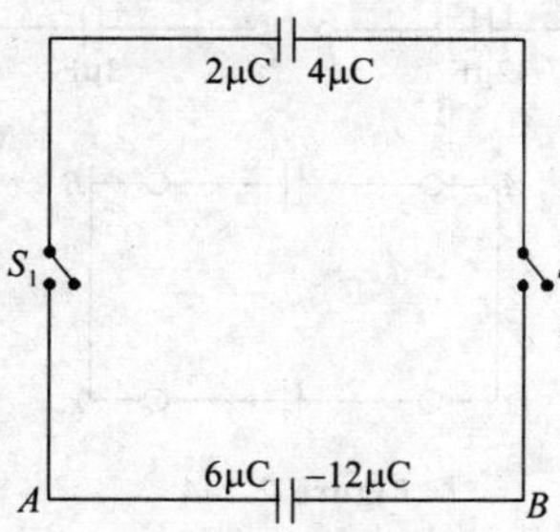

Figure 2.237

(A) 2V (B) 4V
(C) 6V (D) 0 V

2-3 Three capacitors are connected to constant voltage source of 100 V as shown in figure-2.238. If the charges accumulated on the plates of C_1, C_2 and C_3 are q_a, q_b, q_c, q_d, q_e and q_f respectively, as shown in figure-2.237 then :

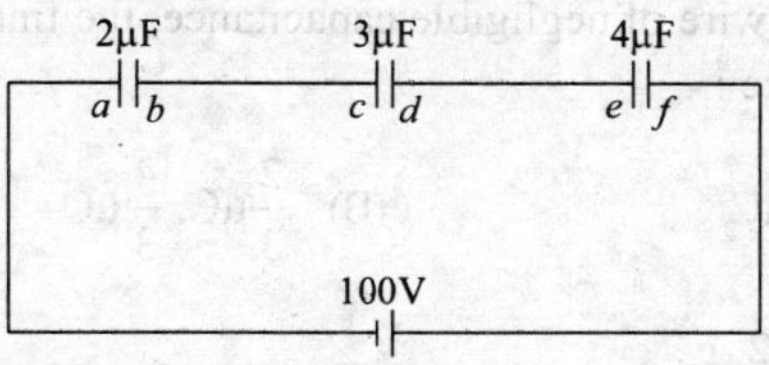

Figure 2.238

(A) $q_b + q_d + q_f = (100/9)$ C (B) $q_b + q_d + q_f = 0$
(C) $q_a + q_c + q_e = 50$ C (D) $q_b = q_d = q_f$

2-4 In the circuit shown in figure-2.239, the final voltage drop across the capacitor C is :

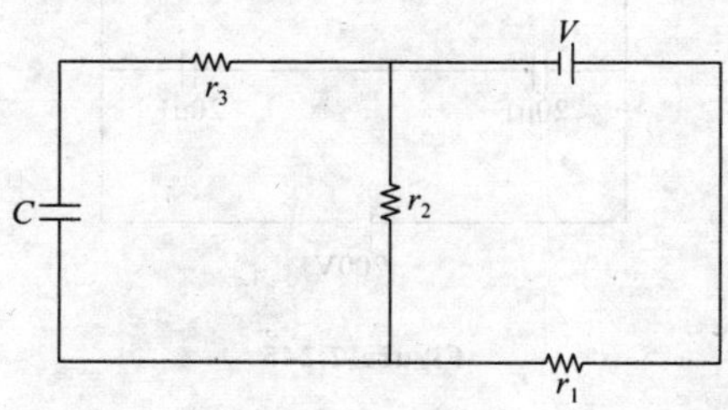

Figure 2.239

(A) $\frac{Vr_1}{r_1 + r_2}$ (B) $\frac{Vr_2}{r_1 + r_2}$

(C) $\frac{V(r_1 + r_2)}{r_2}$ (D) $\frac{V(r_2 + r_1)}{r_1 + r_2 + r_3}$

2-5 The plates of a parallel plate capacitor are charged upto 100 V and disconnected from the source. A 2 mm thick plate is inserted between the plates, then to maintain the same potential difference, the distance between the capacitor plates is increased by 1.6 mm. The dielectric constant of the plate is :

(A) 5 (B) 1.25
(C) 4 (D) 2.5

2-6 A capacitor is charged until its stored energy is 3 J and then the charging battery is removed. Now another uncharged capacitor is connected across it and it is found that charge is distributed equally in the two capacitors. The final value of total energy stored in the electric fields is :

(A) 1.5 J (B) 3 J
(C) 2.5 J (D) 2 J

2-7 Four capacitors of capacitance 10 μF and a battery of 200 V are arranged as shown. How much charge will flow through AB after the switch S is closed :

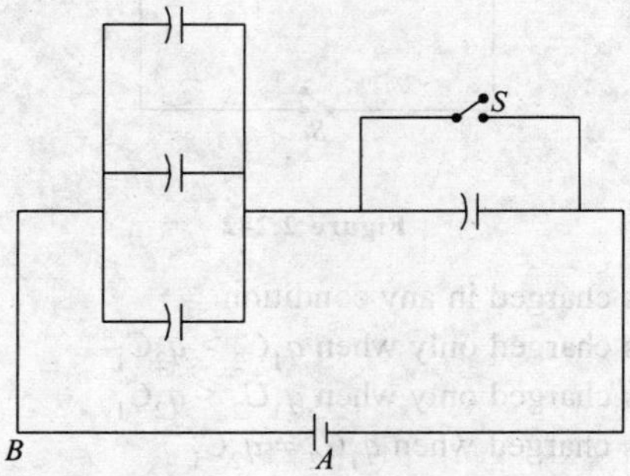

Figure 2.240

(A) 6000 μC (B) 4500 μC
(C) 3000 μC (D) 4000 μC

2-8 A capacitor of capacitance of 2 μF is charged to a potential difference of 200 V, after disconnecting from the battery, it is connected in parallel with another uncharged capacitor. The final common potential is 20 V then the capacitance of second capacitor is :

(A) 2 μF (B) 4 μF
(C) 18 μF (D) 16 μF

2-9 The equivalent capacitance between terminals A and B in the circuit shown in figure-2.241 is :

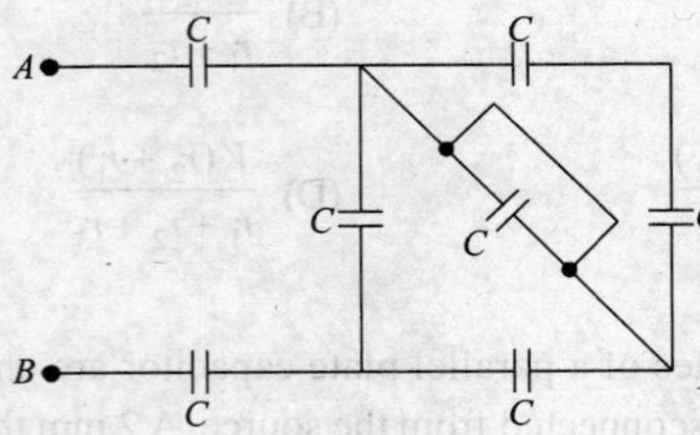

Figure 2.241

(A) $6C$ (B) $\frac{2C}{5}$

(C) $\frac{2C}{3}$ (D) None of these

2-10 Two capacitor C_1 and C_2, charged with charges q_1 and q_2 then these are connected in series with an uncharged capacitor C, as shown in figure. As the switch S is closed :

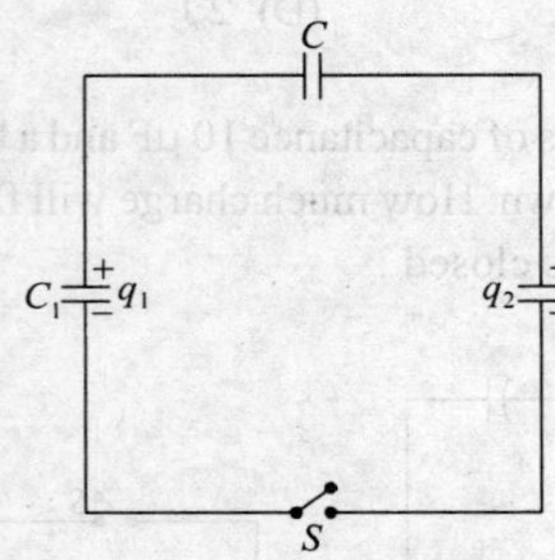

Figure 2.242

(A) C gets charged in any condition
(B) C gets charged only when $q_1C_2 > q_2C_1$
(C) C gets charged only when $q_1C_2 < q_2C_1$
(D) C gets charged when $q_1C_2 \neq q_2C_1$

2-11 The two capacitors in the circuit shown in figure-2.243 are initially uncharged and then connected as shown and switch is closed. What is the potential difference across 3 μF capacitor?

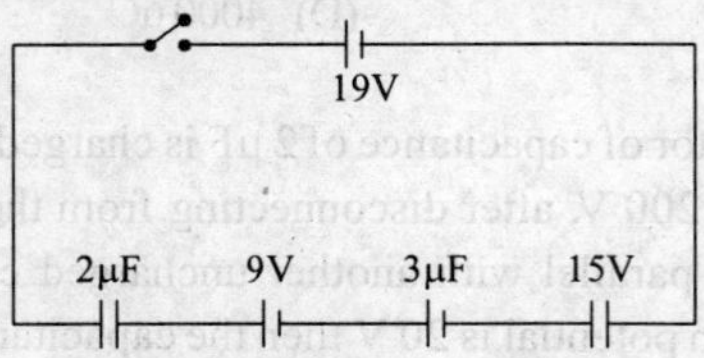

Figure 2.243

(A) 30 V (B) 10 V
(C) 25 V (D) None of these

2-12 A capacitor stores 50 μC charge when connected across a battery. When the gap between the plates is filled with a dielectric, a charge of 100 μC flows through the battery. The dielectric constant of the material is :

(A) 2.5 (B) 2
(C) 4 (D) 3

2-13 Initially two capacitors are charged to different potential differences as shown in figure-2.244 and then connected in parallel as shown. Which of the following is incorrect about this circuit?

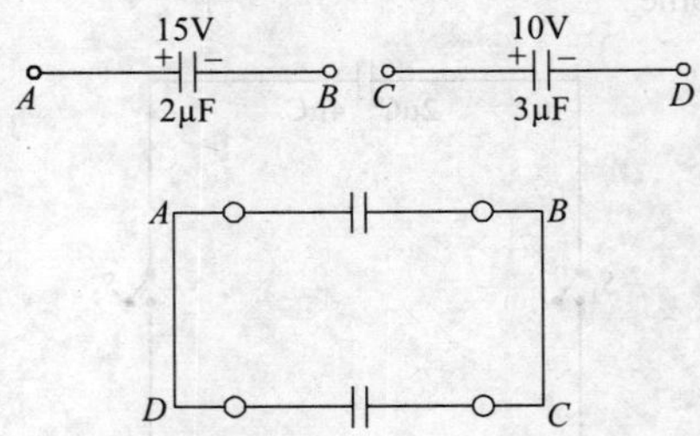

Figure 2.244

(A) Final charge on each capacitor will be zero
(B) Final total electrical energy of the capacitors will be zero
(C) Total change flown from A to D is 30 μC
(D) Total charge flown from A to D is –30 μC

2-14 The two spherical shells are at large separation, one of them has radius 10cm and 1.25 μC charge. The other is of 20 cm radius and has 0.75μC charge. If they are connected by a conducting wire of negligible capacitance, the final charge on the shells are :

(A) 1μC, 1μC (B) $\frac{2}{3}$μC, $\frac{4}{3}$μC

(C) $\frac{4}{3}$μC, $\frac{2}{3}$μC (D) 0.25 μC, 0.25 μC

2-15 In the circuit shown in figure-2.245, charge on 10μF capacitor is given as

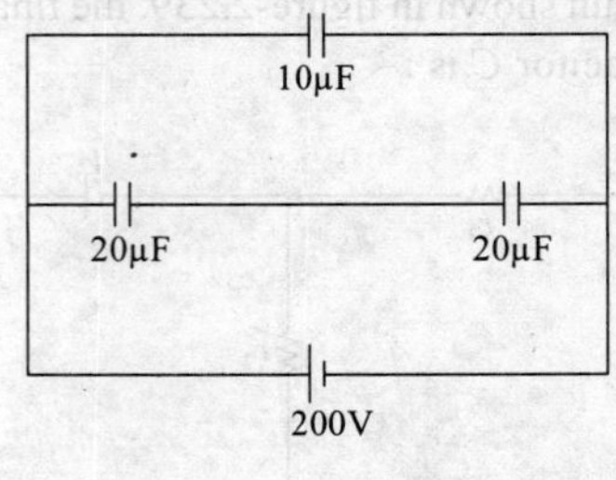

Figure 2.245

(A) 2×10^{-3} C (B) 16×10^{-4} C
(C) 4×10^{-3} C (D) 8×10^{-4} C

2-16 A capacitor consists of two parallel metal plates of area A separated by a distance d. A dielectric slab of area A, thickness b and dielectric constant k is placed inside the capacitor. If C_k is the capacitance of capacitor with dielectric, under what limits the values of k and b are to be restricted so that $C_k = 2C$, where C is capacitance without dielectric ?

(A) $k = \frac{4b}{2b-d}$ & $\frac{d}{3} < b \le d$

(B) $k = \frac{2b}{2b-d}$ & $\frac{d}{2} < b \le d$

(C) $k = \frac{2b}{2b-d}$ & $\frac{d}{2} \le b \le 2d$

(D) $k = \frac{2b}{2b-d}$ & $\frac{d}{4} \le b \le d$

2-17 The circuit shown in figure-2.246 below is in steady state. Now the switch S is closed. Calculate the charge that flows through the switch is :

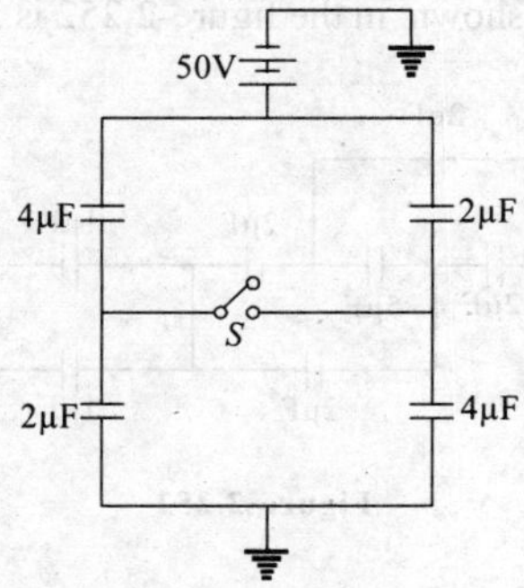

Figure 2.246

(A) $\frac{400}{3}$ μC (B) 100 μC

(C) 50 μC (D) $\frac{100}{3}$ μC

2-18 Four capacitors and two batteries are connected as shown in the figure-2.247. The potential difference between the points a and b is :

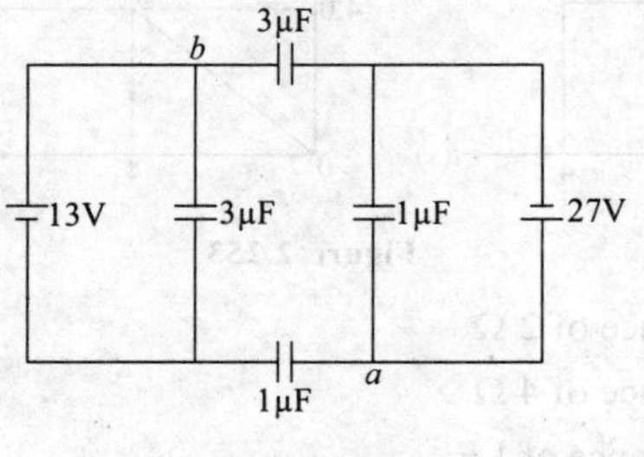

Figure 2.247

(A) 0V (B) 13V

(C) 17V (D) 27V

2-19 Two capacitors are made in series by two metal plates and one I structure as shown in figure-2.248. The area of each plate shown is A. The equivalent capacitance between top and bottom plate of this system is given as :

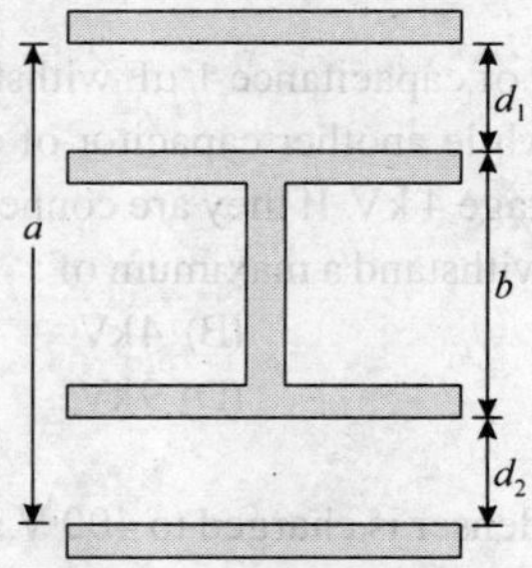

Figure 2.248

(A) $\frac{\varepsilon_0 A}{d_1 - d_2}$ (B) $\frac{\varepsilon_0 A}{a-b}$

(C) $\varepsilon_0 A\left(\frac{1}{a} - \frac{1}{b}\right)$ (D) $\varepsilon_0 A\left(\frac{1}{d_1} - \frac{1}{d_2}\right)$

2-20 A 3 μF and a 5 μF capacitor are connected in series across a 30 V battery. A 7 μF capacitor is then connected in parallel across the 3 μF capacitor. Choose the INCORRECT option :

(A) Voltage across 3 μF capacitor before connecting 7 μF capacitor is 18.75 V

(B) Charge flown through the battery after connecting 7 μF capacitor is 43.75 μC

(C) 5 μF capacitor and 7 μF capacitor can be said to be in series

(D) After connecting 7 μF capacitor, it has a charge of 70 μC

2-21 Find the capacitance between the inner and outer curved cylindrical conductor surface as shown in figure-2.249. Space between conductor surface is filled with dielectric of dielectric constant k. Consider $b << R$:

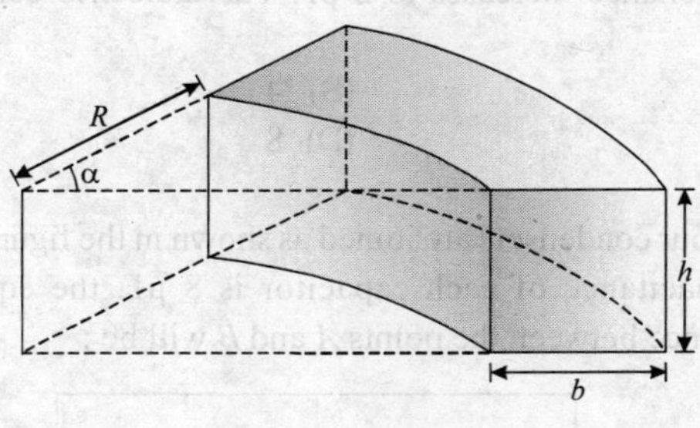

Figure 2.249

(A) $\frac{\varepsilon_0 khR\alpha}{b}$ (B) $\frac{\varepsilon_0 kbR\alpha}{h}$

(C) $\frac{\varepsilon_0 khR\alpha}{2b}$ (D) $\frac{\varepsilon_0 kbR\alpha}{2h}$

2-22 Three capacitors of capacitances 3 μF, 9 μF and 18 μF are connected once in series and another time in parallel. The ratio of equivalent capacitances in the two cases (C_S/C_P) will be :

(A) 1 : 15 (B) 15 : 1
(C) 1 : 1 (D) 1 : 3

2-23 A capacitor of capacitance 1 μF withstands a maximum voltage of 6 kV, while another capacitor of capacitance 2 μF, the maximum voltage 4 kV. If they are connected in series, the combination can withstand a maximum of :

(A) 6kV (B) 4kV
(C) 10kV (D) 9kV

2-24 A 4 μF condenser is charged to 400 V and then its plates are joined through a resistance of 1 KΩ. The heat produced in the resistance is :

(A) 0.16 J (B) 1.28 J
(C) 0.64 J (D) 0.32 J

2-25 Capacitor *A* has a capacitance 15 μF when it is filled with a medium of dielectric constant 15. Another capacitor *B* has a capacitance 1 μF with air between the plates. Both are charged separately by a battery of 100 V. After charging, both are connected in parallel without the battery and the dielectric material is removed. The common potential now is :

(A) 400 V (B) 800 V
(C) 1200 V (D) 1600 V

2-26 Two capacitors 2 μF and 4 μF are connected in parallel. A third capacitor of 6 μF is connected in series. The combination is then connected across a 12 V battery. The voltage across 2 μF capacitor is :

(A) 2V (B) 6V
(C) 8V (D) 1V

2-27 There is an air filled 1 pF parallel plate capacitor. When the plate separation is doubled and the space is filled with wax, the capacitance increases to 2 pF. The dielectric constant of wax is :

(A) 2 (B) 4
(C) 6 (D) 8

2-28 Four condensers are joined as shown in the figure-2.250. The capacitance of each capacitor is 8 μF. the equivalent capacitance between the points *A* and *B* will be :

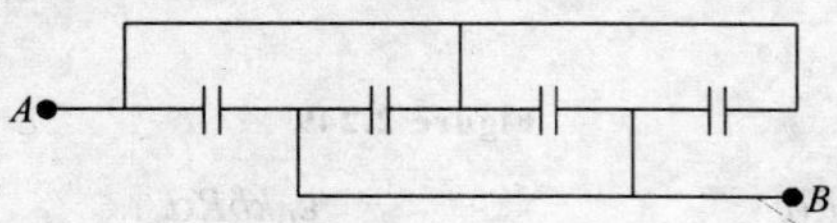

Figure 2.250

(A) 32 μF (B) 2 μF
(C) 8 μF (D) 16 μF

2-29 In the following circuit, the resultant capacitance between *A* and *B* is 1 μF. Then the value of *C* is :

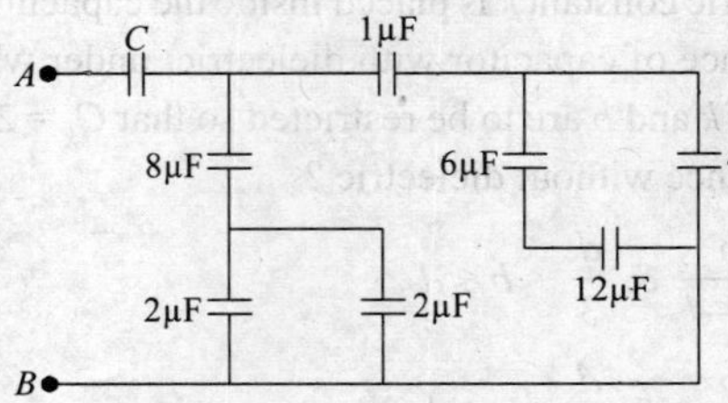

Figure 2.251

(A) $\frac{32}{11}$ μF (B) $\frac{11}{32}$ μF

(C) $\frac{23}{32}$ μF (D) $\frac{32}{23}$ μF

2-30 The effective capacitance between the points *P* and *Q* of the arrangement shown in the figure-2.252 is :

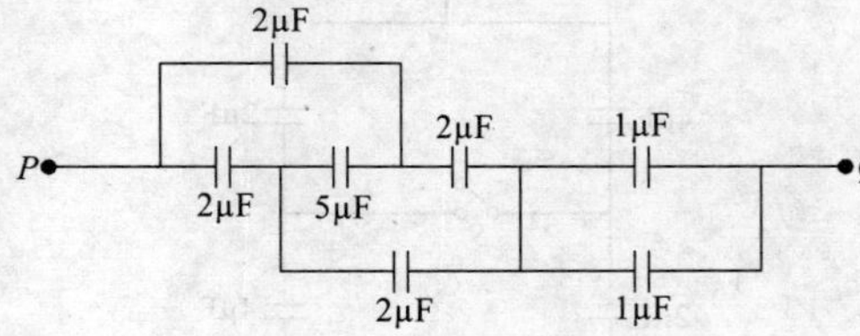

Figure 2.252

(A) $\frac{1}{2}$ μF (B) 1 μF
(C) 2 μF (D) 1.33 μF

2-31 A circuit element is placed in a black box. At $t = 0$, a switch is closed and the current flowing through the circuit element and the voltage across its terminals are recorded to have the wave shapes shown in the figure-2.253 here. The type of element and its magnitude are :

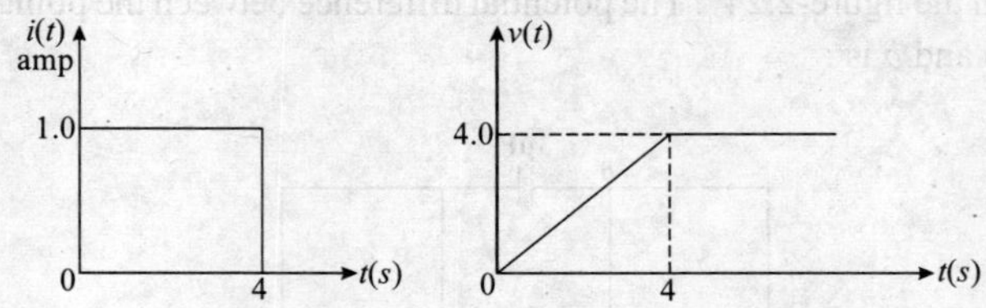

Figure 2.253

(A) resistance of 2 Ω
(B) resistance of 4 Ω
(C) capacitance of 1 F
(D) a voltage source of emf 4 V

2-32 Two parallel plate capacitor of capacitance C and $2C$ are connected in parallel and charged to a potential difference V. The battery is then disconnected and the region between the plate of the capacitor C is completely filled with a material of dielectric constant k. The potential difference across the capacitors now becomes :

(A) $\frac{2V}{k}$ (B) $\frac{3V}{k}$

(C) $\frac{3V}{k+2}$ (D) $\frac{2V}{k+3}$

2-33 In a circuit shown in the figure-2.254, what is potential of point A?

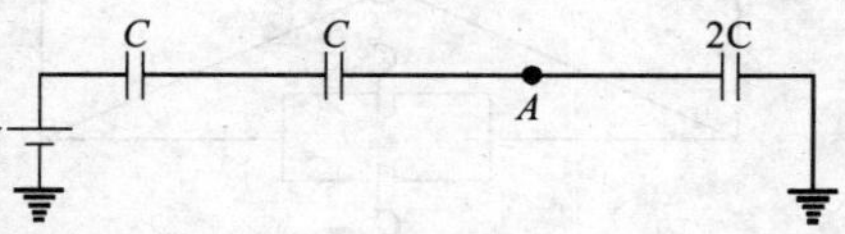

Figure 2.254

(A) 2V (B) 5V
(C) 8V (D) 4V

2-34 Two long coaxial cylindrical metal tubes stand on an insulating floor as shown in figure-2.255. A dielectric oil is filled in the annular region between the tubes. The tubes are maintained at a constant potential difference V. A small hole is opened at bottom then :

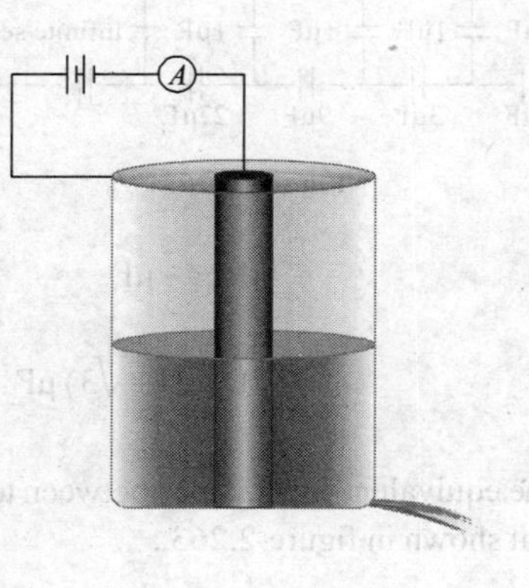

Figure 2.255

(A) Reading of ammeter remain constant
(B) Capacitance of system increases
(C) Current in circuit is dependent on area of hole
(D) Current in circuit is inversely proportional to dielectric constant

2-35 In the circuits shown in figures-2.256 (I), (II) and (III) below given $R_1 = 1\ \Omega$, $R_2 = 2\ \Omega$, $C_1 = 2\ \mu F$ and $C_2 = 4\ \mu F$. The time constant (in μs) for the circuits I, II, III are respectively :

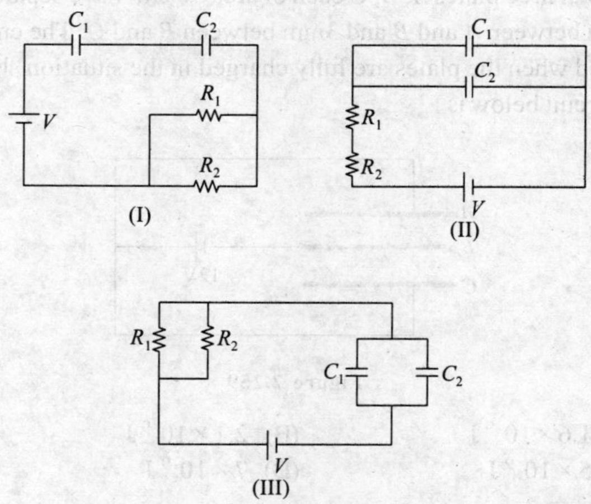

Figure 2.256

(A) 18, 8/9, 4 (B) 18, 4, 8/9
(C) 4, 8/9, 18 (D) 8/9, 18, 4

2-36 The capacitances and connection of five capacitors are shown in the figure-2.257. The potential difference between the points A and B is 60 V. Then the equivalent capacitance between A and B and the charge on 5 μF capacitance will be given as :

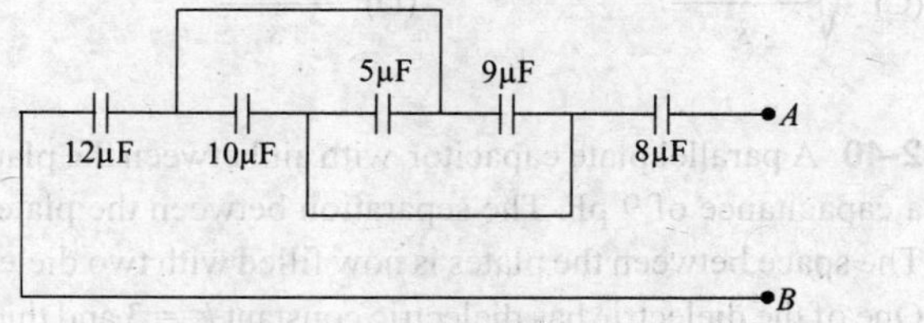

Figure 2.257

(A) 44 μF; 300 μC (B) 16 μF; 150 μC
(C) 15 μF; 200 μC (D) 4 μF; 50 μC

2-37 In the circuit shown in figure-2.258 the switch S_1 is first closed. It is then opened after a long time and then S_2 is closed. What is the final charge on C_2 :

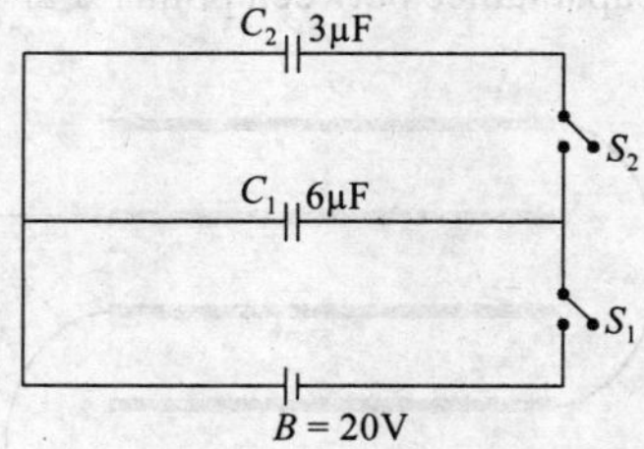

Figure 2.258

(A) 120 μC (B) 80 μC
(C) 40 μC (D) 20 μC

2-38 Three plates A, B, C each of area 50 cm^2 have separation 3mm between A and B and 3mm between B and C. The energy stored when the plates are fully charged in the situation shown in circuit below is :

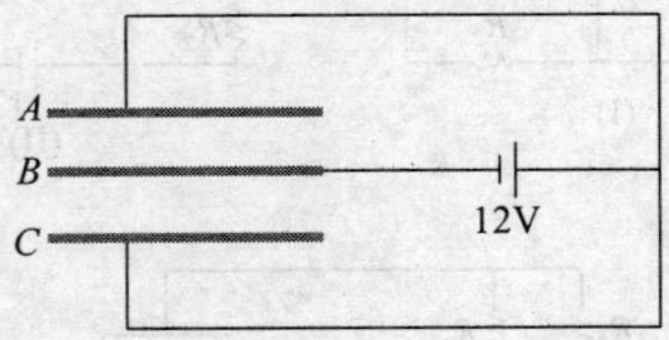

Figure 2.259

(A) 1.6×10^{-9} J (B) 2.1×10^{-9} J
(C) 5×10^{-9} J (D) 7×10^{-9} J

2-39 A fully charged capacitor has a capacitance C. It is discharged through a small coil of resistance wire embedded in a thermally insulated block of specific heat s and mass m. If the temperature of the block is raised by ΔT, the potential difference V across the capacitance is :

(A) $\frac{ms\Delta T}{C}$ (B) $\sqrt{\frac{2ms\Delta T}{C}}$

(C) $\sqrt{\frac{2mC\Delta T}{s}}$ (D) $\frac{mC\Delta T}{s}$

2-40 A parallel plate capacitor with air between the plates has a capacitance of 9 pF. The separation between the plates is d. The space between the plates is now filled with two dielectrics. One of the dielectric has dielectric constant $k_1 = 3$ and thickness $d/3$ while the other one has dielectric constant $k_2 = 6$ and thickness $2d/3$. Capacitance of the capacitor is now :

(A) 45 pF (B) 40.5 pF

(C) 20.25 pF (D) 1.8 pF

2-41 Six plates each of area A are arranged as shown in figure-2.260. The separation between adjoining plates is d. Find the equivalent capacitance between points A and B :

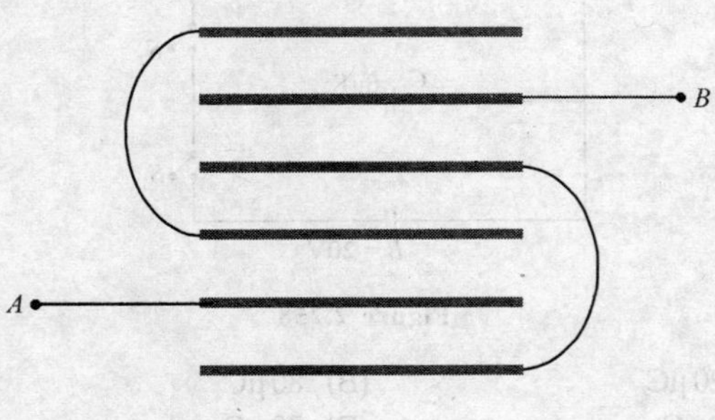

Figure 2.260

(A) $\frac{\varepsilon_0 A}{d}$ (B) $\frac{7\varepsilon_0 A}{d}$

(C) $\frac{6\varepsilon_0 A}{d}$ (D) $\frac{5\varepsilon_0 A}{d}$

2-42 Six capacitors each of capacitance of 2 μF are connected as shown in the figure-2.261. The effective capacitance between A and B is :

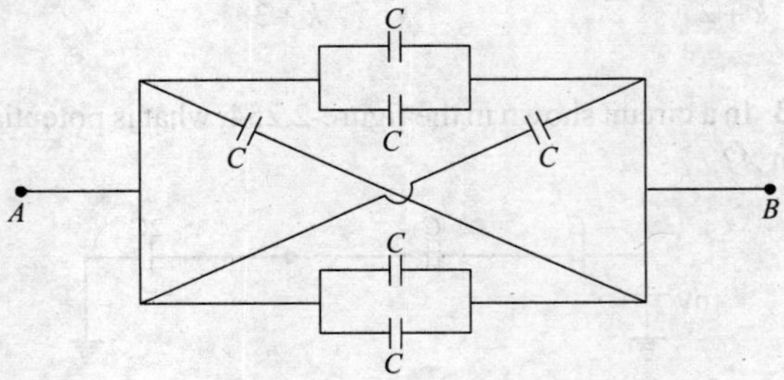

Figure 2.261

(A) 12 μF (B) 8/3 μF
(C) 3 μF (D) 6 μF

2-43 What is equivalent capacitance of ladder circuit shown in figure-2.262 between points A and B ?

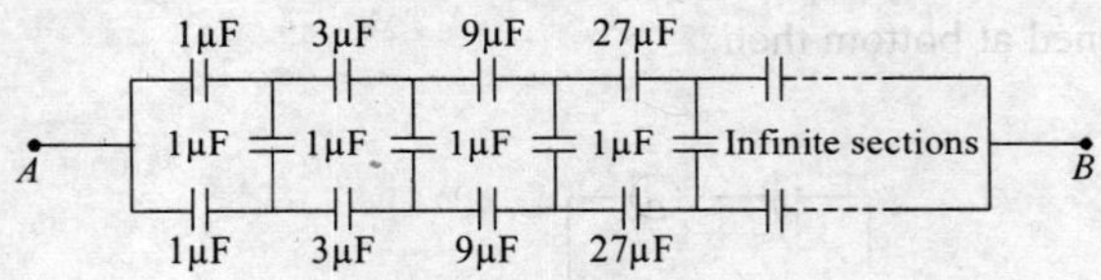

Figure 2.262

(A) $\frac{2}{3}$ μF (B) $\frac{4}{3}$ μF

(C) Infinite (D) $(1+\sqrt{3})$ μF

2-44 Find the equivalent capacitance between terminals A and B in the circuit shown in figure-2.263 :

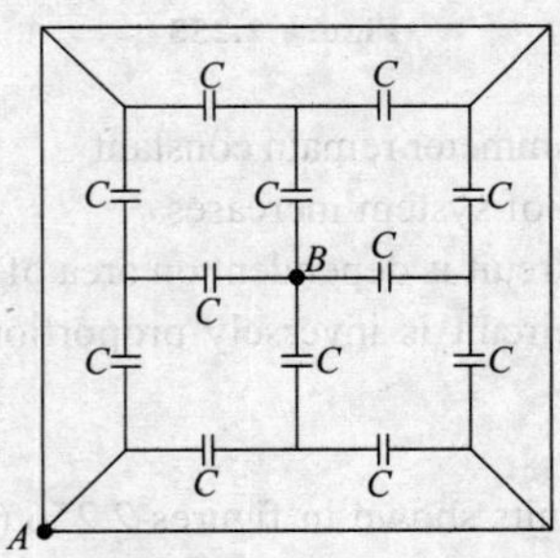

Figure 2.263

(A) $\frac{4C}{3}$ (B) $\frac{8C}{3}$

(C) $12\,C$ (D) $\frac{5C}{12}$

2-45 Circuit in figure-2.264 shows three capacitors with capacitance and their breakdown voltage. What should be maximum value of the external source voltage such that no capacitor breaks down ?

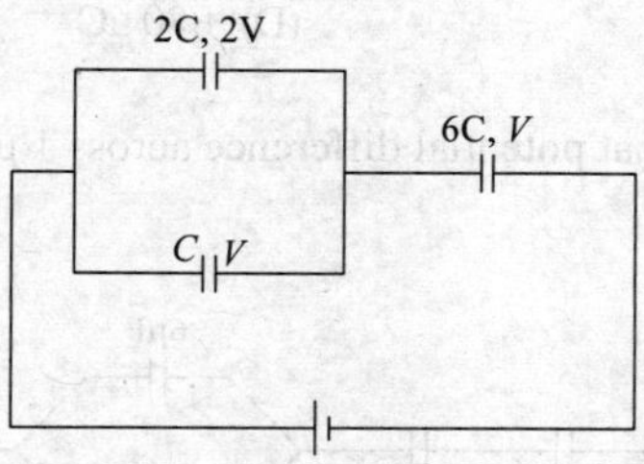

Figure 2.264

(A) 1V (B) 2V

(C) 1.5V (D) 4V

2-46 A 2 μF capacitor is charged as shown in the figure-2.265. The percentage of its stored energy dissipated after the switch *S* is shifted to position 2 is :

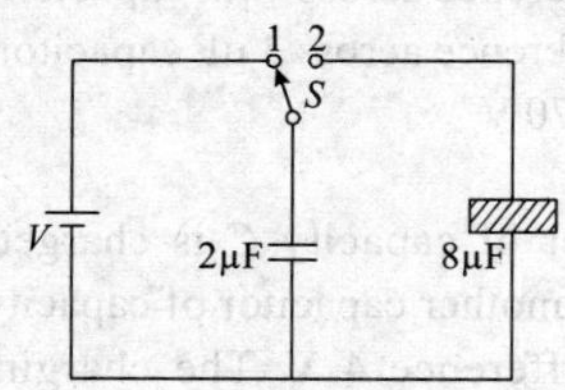

Figure 2.265

(A) 0% (B) 20%

(C) 75% (D) 80%

2-47 For the circuit shown in figure-2.266, which of the below options given is/are correct :

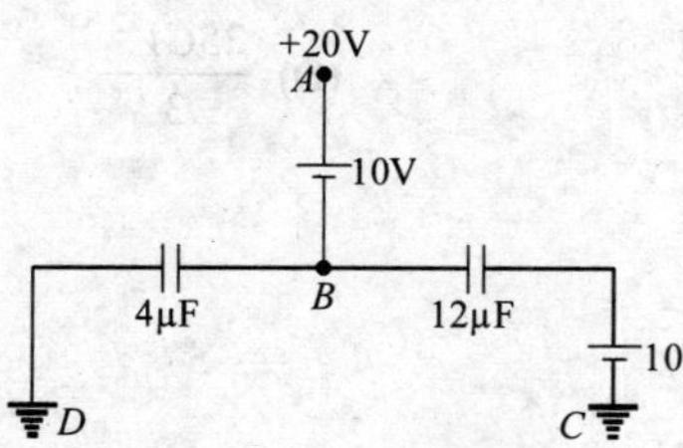

Figure 2.266

(A) The charge on the 12 μF capacitor is zero

(B) The charge on the 12 μF capacitor is 30 μC

(C) The charge on the 4 μF capacitor is 30 μC

(D) None of these

2-48 In the circuit shown a potential difference of 60 V is applied across *AB*. The potential difference between the point *M* and *N* is :

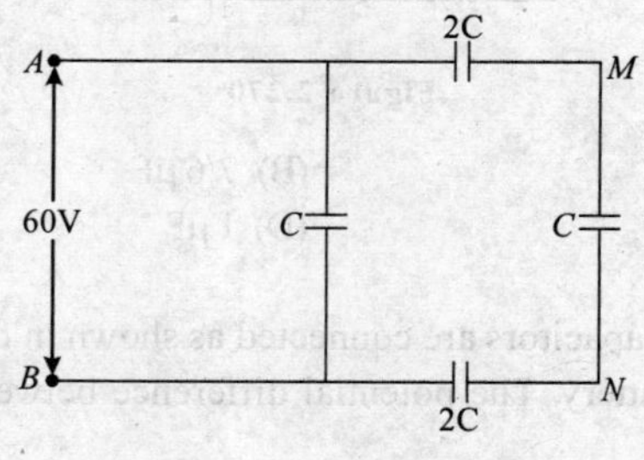

Figure 2.267

(A) 10V (B) 15V

(C) 20V (D) 30V

2-49 Four identical capacitors are connected in series with a 10 V battery as shown in the figure-2.268. The point *N* is earthed. The potentials of points *A* and *B* are :

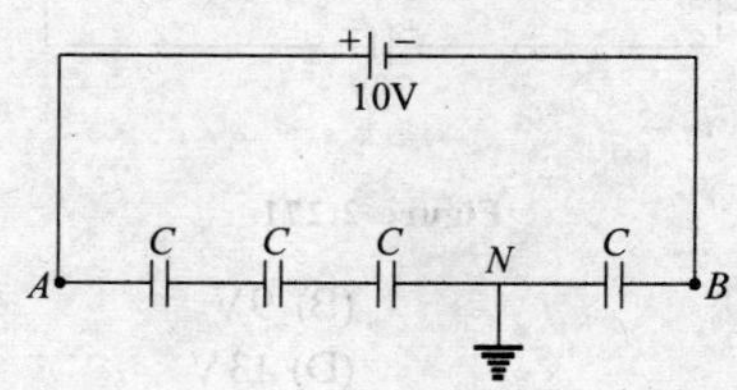

Figure 2.268

(A) 10V, 0V (B) 7.5 V, –2.5 V

(C) 5 V, –5 V (D) 7.5 V, 2.5 V

2-50 Find the equivalent capacitance across *A* and *B* for the circuit shown in figure-2.269. All the capacitors are of capacitance *C* :

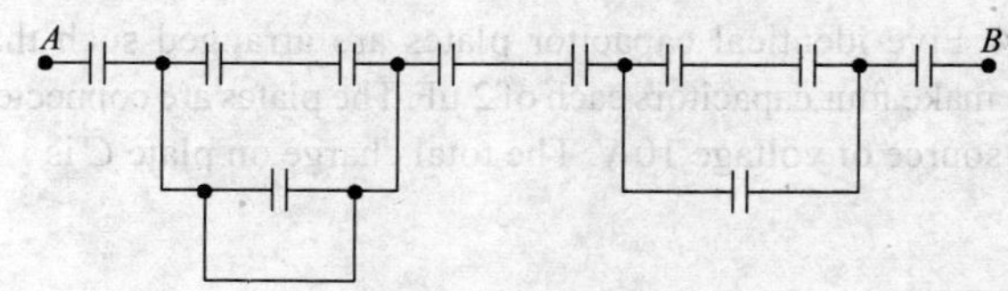

Figure 2.269

(A) $\frac{3C}{14}$ (B) $\frac{C}{8}$

(C) $\frac{3C}{16}$ (D) None of these

2-51 The equivalent capacitance between terminals x and y is:

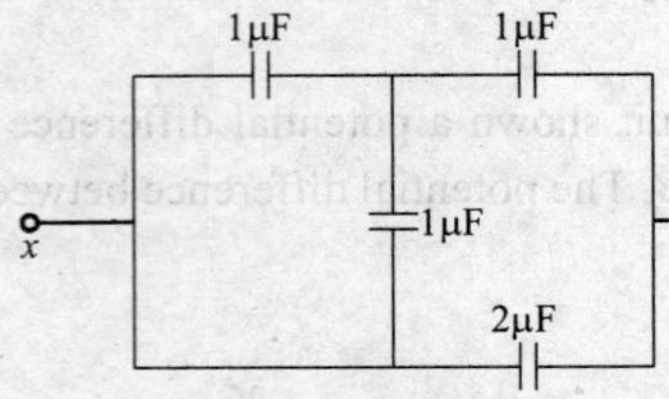

Figure 2.270

(A) 5/6 μF (B) 7/6 μF
(C) 8/3 μF (D) 1 μF

2-52 Four capacitors are connected as shown in figure-2.271 to a 30 V battery. The potential difference between points a and b is :

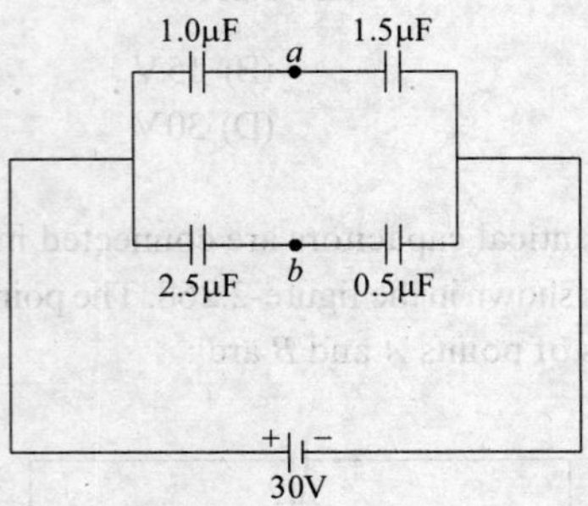

Figure 2.271

(A) 5V (B) 9V
(C) 10V (D) 13V

2-53 The distance between the plates of a charged plate capacitor disconnected from the battery is 5 cm and the intensity of the field in it is $E = 300$ V/cm. An uncharged metal bar 1cm thick is introduced into the capacitor parallel to its planes. The potential difference between the plates now is :

(A) 1500V (B) 1200V
(C) 900V (D) Zero

2-54 Five identical capacitor plates are arranged such that they make four capacitors each of 2 μF. The plates are connected to a source of voltage 10 V. The total charge on plate C is :

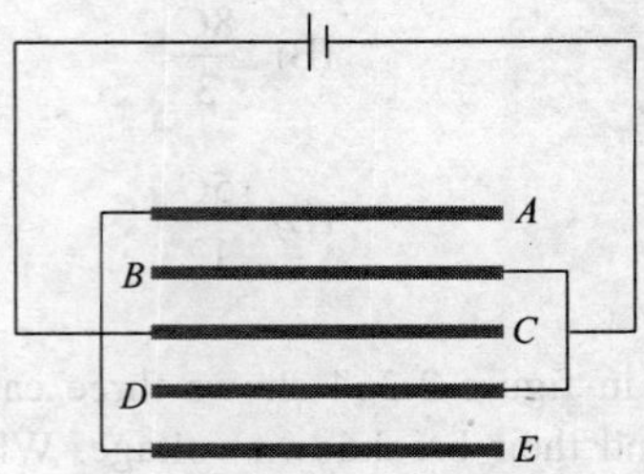

Figure 2.272

(A) +20 μC (B) +40 μC
(C) +60 μC (D) +80 μC

2-55 Given that potential difference across 1 μF capacitor is 10 V. Then :

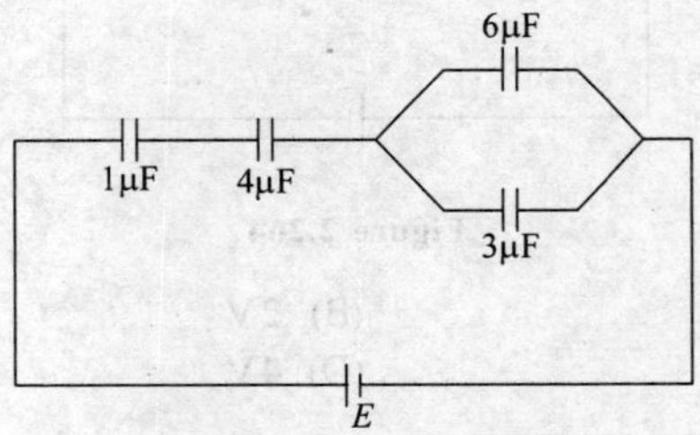

Figure 2.273

(A) Potential difference across 4 μF capacitor is 40 V
(B) Potential difference across 4 μF capacitor is 2.5 V
(C) Potential difference across 3 μF capacitor is 5 V
(D) Value of E is 70 V

2-56 A capacitor of capacity C is charged to a potential difference V and another capacitor of capacity 2 C is charged to a potential difference 4 V. The charging batteries are disconnected and the two capacitors are connected with reverse polarity to each other in parallel. The heat produced during the redistribution of charge between the capacitors will be :

(A) $\frac{125CV^2}{3}$ (B) $\frac{50CV^2}{3}$
(C) $2CV^2$ (D) $\frac{25CV^2}{3}$

* * * * *

Advance MCQs with One or More Options Correct

2-1 Two identical capacitors A and B are connected in seriesacross a battery. A dielectric slab ($k > 1$) is placed between the plates of the capacitor B and the battery remains connected. Which of the following statements is/are correct for the process of insertion of the dielectric ?

(A) The charge supplied by the battery increases.

(B) The capacitance of the system increases.

(C) The electric field in the capacitor B increases.

(D) The electrostatic potential energy of A decreases.

2-2 The figure-2.274 shows a capacitor having three dielectric layers parallel to its plates. Layer x is vacuum, y is conductor and z is a dielectric. Which of the following change(s) will result in increase in capacitance ?

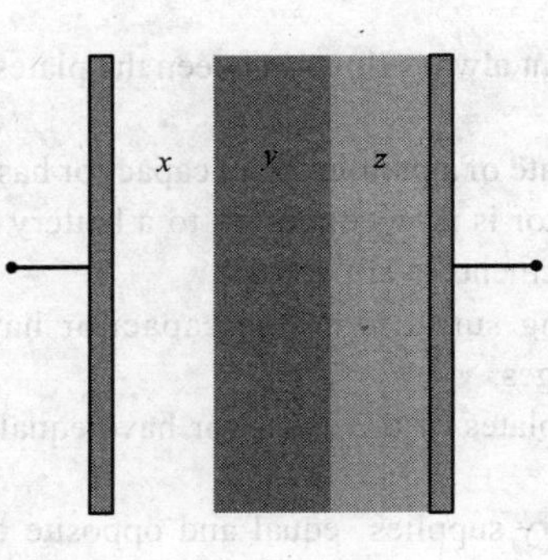

Figure 2.274

(A) Replace x by conductor

(B) Replace y by dielectric

(C) Replace z by conductor

(D) Replace x by dielectric

2-3 How does the total energy stored in the capacitors in the circuit shown in the figure-2.275 change when first switch K_1 is closed (process-1) and then switch K_2 is also closed (process-2). Assume that all capacitor were initially uncharged ?

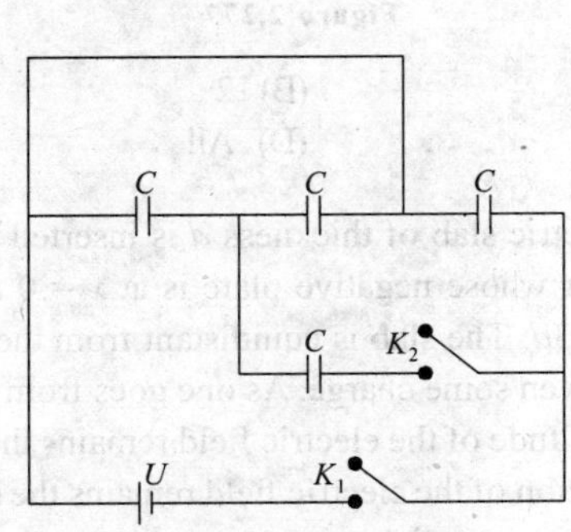

Figure 2.275

(A) Increases in process-1

(B) Increases in process-2

(C) Decreases in process-2

(D) Magnitude of change in process-2 is less than that in process -1

2-4 A parallel plate capacitor is charged and the charging battery is then disconnected. If the plates of the capacitor are moved further apart by means of insulating handles :

(A) The charge on the capacitor increases

(B) The voltage across the plate increases

(C) The capacitance increases

(D) the electrostatic energy stored in the capacitor increases

2-5 The plates of a parallel-plate capacitor are separated by a solid dielectric. This capacitor and a resistor are connected in series across the terminals of a battery. Now the plates of the capacitor are pulled slightly farther apart. After some time circuit again attains steady state.

(A) The potential difference across the plates has increased

(B) The energy stored on the capacitor has decreased

(C) The capacitance of the capacitor has increased

(D) The battery would have gained energy

2-6 For the given circuit shown in figure-2.276, which of the following statements is/are correct

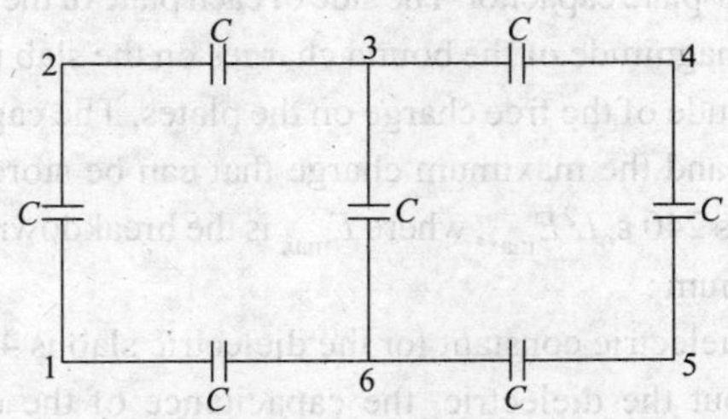

Figure 2.276

(A) The equivalent capacitance between points 1 and 2 is $\frac{15C}{11}$

(B) The equivalent capacitance between points 3 and 6 is $\frac{5C}{3}$

(C) The equivalent capacitance between points 1 and 3 is $\frac{15C}{14}$

(D) The equivalent capacitance between points 3 and 5 is $\frac{14C}{15}$

2-7 Capacitor C_1 of the capacitance 1 μF and another capacitor C_2 of capacitance 2 μF are separately charged fully by a common battery. The two capacitors are then separately allowed to discharge through equal resistors at time $t = 0$.

(A) The current in each of the two discharging circuits is zero at $t = 0$.

(B) The current in the two discharging circuits at $t = 0$ are equal but not zero

(C) The currents in the two discharging circuits at $t = 0$ are unequal

(D) Capacitor C_1 loses 50% of its initial charge sooner than C_2 loses 50% of its initial charge

2-8 A capacitor of capacity C_0 is connected to a battery of voltage V_0. When steady state is attained a dielectric slab of dielectric constant k is slowly inserted in the capacitor to fill the space between the plates completely. In final steady state which of the following statements is/are correct

(A) Magnitude of induced charge on the each surface of slab is $C_0V_0(k-1)$

(B) Electric force due to induced charges on any plate is zero

(C) Force of attraction between plates of capacitor is $\frac{k(C_0V_0)^2}{2\epsilon_0 A}$

(D) Field due to induced charges in dielectric slab is $\frac{(k-1)C_0V_0}{\epsilon_0 A}$

2-9 A dielectric slab fills the space between the square plates of a parallel-plate capacitor. The side of each plate of the capacitor is L. The magnitude of the bound charges on the slab is 75% of the magnitude of the free charge on the plates. The capacitance is 480 μF and the maximum charge that can be stored on the capacitor is $240\,\varepsilon_0 L^2 E_{max}$, where E_{max} is the breakdown strength of the medium :

(A) The dielectric constant for the dielectric slab is 4

(B) Without the dielectric, the capacitance of the capacitor would be 360 μF

(C) The plate area is 60 L^2

(D) If the dielectric slab is having the same area as that of the capacitor plate but the width is half the separation between plates of capacitor, the capacitance would be 192 μF.

2-10 In a spherical capacitor, we have two concentric spherical shells, the inner one carrying a charge Q and outer one carrying a charge of $-Q$. If the inner shell is displaced from the center without touching the outer shell :

(A) The capacitance of the capacitor will increase

(B) The capacitance of the capacitor will remain same

(C) The energy of capacitor with decrease

(D) The potential difference between inner and outershell will increase

2-11 A parallel plate air capacitor is connected to a battery. The quantities charge, voltage, electric field and energy associated with this capacitor are given by Q_0, V_0, E_0 and U_0 respectively. A dielectric slab is now inserted to fill the space between the plates with battery still in connection. The corresponding quantities now given by O, V, E and U are related of the previous one as :

(A) $Q > Q_0$ (B) $V > V_0$

(C) $E > E_0$ (D) $U > U_0$

2-12 A capacitor with no dielectric is connected to a battery at $t = 0$. Consider a point A in the connecting wires and a point B in between the plates :

(A) There is no current through A.

(B) There is displacement current through B till electric field changes between the plates.

(C) There is a current through A as long as the charging is not complete.

(D) The current always flows between the plates of capacitor.

2-13 Each plate of a parallel plate capacitor has a charge q on it. The capacitor is now connected to a battery. Which of the following statements is/are correct.

(A) The facing surfaces of the capacitor have equal and opposite charges.

(B) The two plates of the capacitor have equal and opposite charges.

(C) The battery supplies equal and opposite charges to the two plates.

(D) The outer surfaces of the plates have equal charges.

2-14 Figure-2.277 shows three circuits, each consisting of a switch and two capacitors, initially charged as indicated in the figure. In which circuit the charge on the left hand capacitor will change after the closing of the switch :

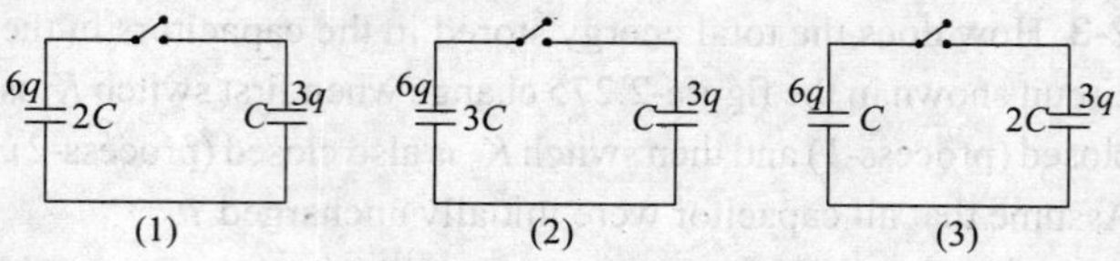

Figure 2.277

(A) 1 (B) 2

(C) 3 (D) All

2-15 A dielectric slab of thickness d is inserted in a parallel plate capacitor whose negative plate is at $x = 0$ and positive plate is at $x = 3d$. The slab is equidistant from the plates. The capacitor is given some charge. As one goes from 0 to $3d$:

(A) The magnitude of the electric field remains the same

(B) The direction of the electric field remains the same

(C) The electric potential increases continuously

(D) The electric potential increases at first, then decreases and again increases

2-16 In the circuit shown, the potential difference across the 3μF capacitor is V and the equivalent capacitance between A and B is C. Then :

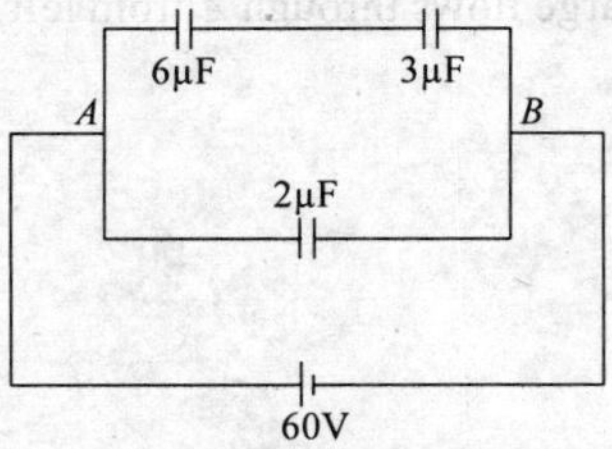

Figure 2.278

(A) $C=4\mu F$ (B) $C=11\mu F$
(C) $V=20V$ (D) $V=40V$

2-17 Two identical parallel plate capacitors of same dimensions joined in series are connected to a constant voltage source. When one of the plates of one capacitor are brought closer to the other plate :
(A) The voltage on the capacitor whose plates come closer is greater than the voltage on the capacitor whose plates are not moved
(B) The voltage on the capacitor whose plate come closer is lesser than the voltage on the capacitor whose plates are not moved
(C) The voltage on the two capacitor remain equal
(D) The applied voltage is divided among the two inversely as the capacitance

2-18 A parallel plate capacitor is first connected to a constant voltage source. It is then disconnected and then immersed in a liquid dielectric, then :
(A) The capacitance increases
(B) The liquid level between the plates increases
(C) The liquid level will remain same as that outside the plates
(D) The potential difference between the plates will decrease

2-19 In a parallel plate capacitor, the region between the plates is filled by a dielectric slab. The capacitor is connected to a cell and the slab is taken out :
(A) Some charge is drawn from the cell
(B) Some charge is returned to the cell
(C) The potential difference across the capacitor remains constant
(D) A work is done by an external agent in pulling the slab out

2-20 In a parallel plate capacitor, the region between the plates is filled by a dielectric slab. The capacitor is charged from a cell and then disconnected from it. The slab is now taken out :
(A) The potential difference across the capacitor increases
(B) The charge on the capacitor is increased
(C) The energy stored in the capacitor increases
(D) A work is done by the external agent in taking the slab out

2-21 A parallel plate capacitor is connected across a source of constant potential difference. If a dielectric slab is introduced between the two plates, then
(A) Charge on capacitor increases
(B) Some charge from the capacitor will flow back into the source
(C) He electric field between the plates will decrease
(D) The electric field between the plates will not change

2-22 Identical dielectric slabs are inserted into two identical capacitors A and B. These capacitors and a battery are connected as shown in figure-2.279. Now the slab of capacitor B is pulled out with battery remaining connected

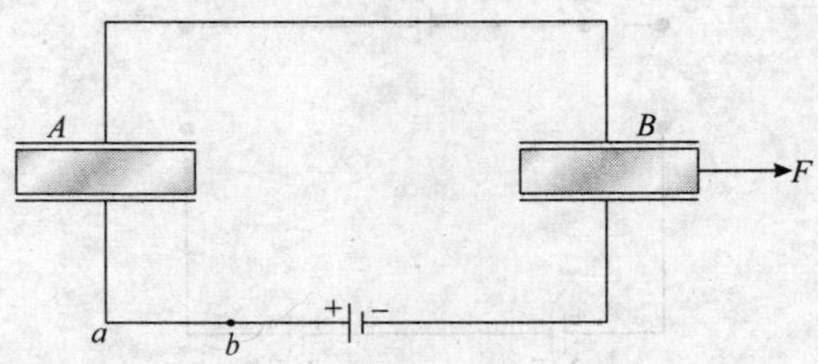

Figure 2.279

(A) During the process, charge flows from a to b
(B) Finally charge on capacitor B will be less than that on capacitor A
(C) During the process, work is done by the external force F, which appears as heat in the circuit
(D) During the process, internal energy of the battery increases

2-23 A parallel plate air capacitor is connected to a battery. If plates of the capacitor are pulled farther apart, then which of the following statements is/are correct ?
(A) Strength of electric field inside the capacitor remains unchanged, if battery is disconnected before pulling the plate
(B) During the process, work is done by external force applied to pull the plates either battery is disconnected or it remains connected
(C) Stored energy in the capacitor decreases if the battery remains connected
(D) None of these

2-24 When two identical capacitors are charged individually to different potentials & then connected in parallel, after disconnecting from the source then
(A) Net potential difference across them is equal to sum of individual potential differences
(B) Net potential difference across them is not equal to sum of individual initial potential differences
(C) Net energy stored in the two capacitors is less than the sum of individual initial energies
(D) None of these

2-25 The plates of a parallel plate capacitor are not exactly parallel. The surface charge density therefore :

(A) Is higher at the closer end

(B) The surface charge density will not be uniform

(C) Each plate will have the same potential at each point

(D) The electric field is smallest where the plates are closest

2-26 Two capacitors of 2 μF and 3 μF are charged to 150 V and 120 V respectively. The plates of capacitor are connected as shown in the figure-2.280. An uncharged capacitor of capacity 1.5 μF is connected to the free end of the wires as shown. Then:

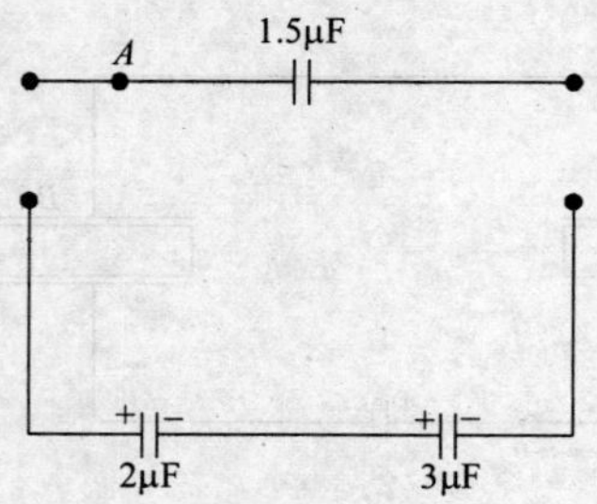

Figure 2.280

(A) Charge on 1.5 μF capacitor is 180 μC

(B) Charge on 2 μF capacitor is 120 μC

(C) Positive charge flows through *A* from right to left

(D) Positive charge flows through *A* from left to right

* * * * *

Unsolved Numerical Problems for Preparation of NSEP, INPhO & IPhO

For detailed preparation of INPhO and IPhO students can refer advance study material on www.physicsgalaxy.com

2-1 Two square metallic plates of 1m side are kept 0.01 m apart, like a parallel plate capacitor, in air in such a way that one of their edges is perpendicular to an oil surface in a tank filled with an insulating oil. The plates are connected to a battery of emf 500 V. The plates are then lowered vertically into the oil at a speed of 0.001 m/s. Calculate the current drawn from the battery during the process. Take dielectric constant of oil 11.

Ans. [4.425×10^{-9}A]

2-2 The capacitance of a parallel plate capacitor with plate area A and separation d is C. The space between the plates in filled with two wedges of dielectric constants K_1 and K_2 respectively (figure-2.281). Find the capacitance of resulting capacitor.

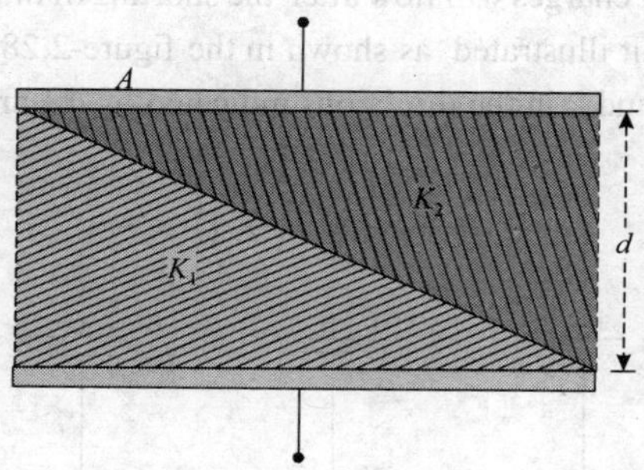

Figure 2.281

Ans. [$\frac{\varepsilon_0 A K_1 K_2}{(K_1 - K_2)d}\log\left(\frac{K_1}{K_2}\right)$]

2-3 Two conducting objects one with charge of $+Q$ and another with $-Q$ are kept on x-axis at $x = -3$ and $x = +4$ respectively. The electric field on the x-axis is given by $3Q\left(x^2 + \frac{4}{3}\right)$. What is the capacitance C of this configuration of objects?

Ans. [8.4 mF]

2-4 An air cylindrical capacitor is applied with a constant voltage $V = 200$ V across it is being submerged vertically into a vessel filled with water at a velocity $v = 5.0$ mm/s. The electrodes of the capacitor are separated by a distance $d = 2.0$ mm, the mean curvature radius of the electrodes is equal to $r = 50$ mm. Find the current flowing in this case along lead wire, if $d << r$.

Ans. [0.11 μA]

2-5 Between the plates of a parallel-plate capacitor there is a metallic plate whose thickness takes up $\eta = 0.60$ of the capacitor gap. When that plate is absent, the capacitor has a capacity $C = 20$ nF. The capacitor is connected to a *d.c.* voltage source $V = 100$ V. The metallic plate is slowly extracted from the gap. Find :

(a) The energy increment of the capacitor;

(b) The mechanical work performed in the process of plate extraction.

Ans. [(a) – 0.15 mJ (b) 0.15 mJ]

2-6 In the circuit shown in figure-2.282, each capacitor has a capacitance C and cell voltage is E. If switch S is closed, then calculate the work done by battery after closing the switch.

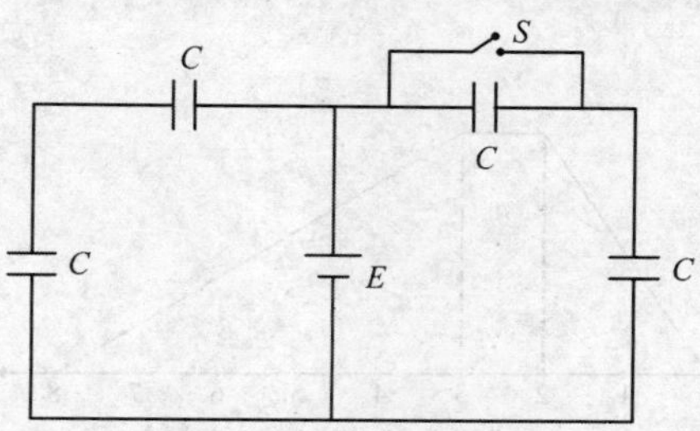

Figure 2.282

Ans. [$\frac{1}{2}CE^2$]

2-7 Find the potential difference $V_A - V_B$ between points A and B of the circuit shown in the figure-2.283.

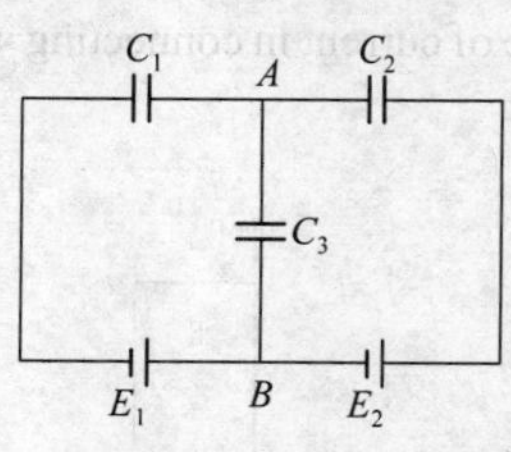

Figure 2.283

Ans. [$\frac{E_2C_2 - E_1C_1}{C_1 + C_2 + C_3}$]

2-8 (a) Find the capacitance of spherical capacitor having concentric shells of radii a and b ($b > a$). The space between the shells is completely filled by a dielectric of constant k.

(b) Find the capacitance if dielectric is filled upto an intermediate radius c ($a < c < b$) between the shells.

Ans. [(a) $C = 4\pi\varepsilon_0 k\left(\frac{ab}{b-a}\right)$; (b) $\frac{k\,abc}{ka(b-c) + b(c-a)}$]

2-9 If half the space between two concentric conducting spheres be filled with dielectric of dielectric constant k and the rest is filled with air. Show that the capacitance of the capacitor thus formed will be same as if the whole part is filled with the dielectric of dielectric constant $\frac{1}{2}(1+k)$:

2-10 Two, capacitors A and B are connected in series across a 100 V supply and it is observed that the potential difference across them are 60 V and 40 V. A capacitor of 2 μF capacitance is now connected in parallel with A and the potential difference across B raises to 90 V. Determine the capacitance of A and B :

Ans. [0.16 μF, 0.24 μF]

2-11 The voltage applied across a capacitor having a capacitance of 10 μF is varies as shown in figure-2.284:

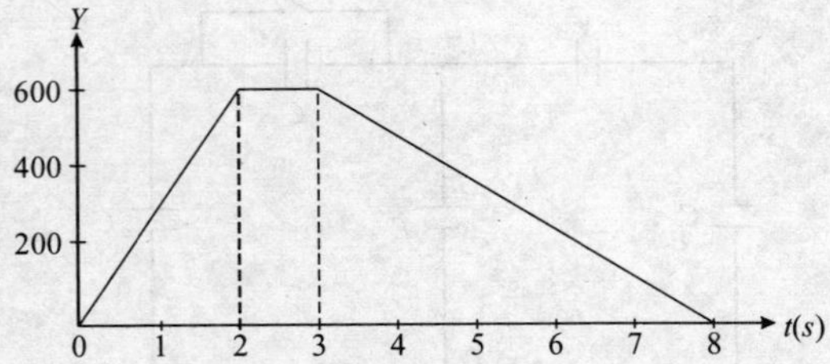

(x)

Figure 2.284

At the time instant when the terminal voltage across capacitor is 600 V calculate

(a) The charge on capacitor

(b) The energy stored in the capacitor

(c) Draw the curve of current in connecting wires as a function of time.

Ans. [(a) 6×10^{-3}C; (b) 1.8J; (c) 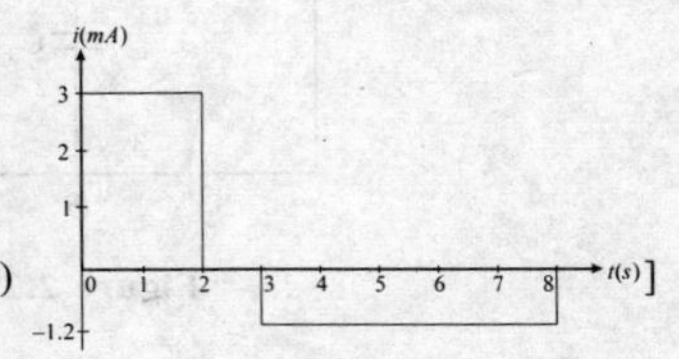]

(y)

2-12 A parallel plate capacitor of 5 μF is charged with a 12 V battery and then battery is disconnected and reconnected with its polarity reversed across the same charged capacitor. Find the amount of heat produced when battery is reconnected.

Ans. [1.44 mJ]

2-13 Find capacitance of the capacitor shown in figure-2.285 in which four same sized dielectric slabs are inserted with their dielectric constants as shown. The area and width of each slab is half of plate area of capacitor and half of the plate separation of the capacitor. Plate area of capacitor is A and plate separation is $d/2$.

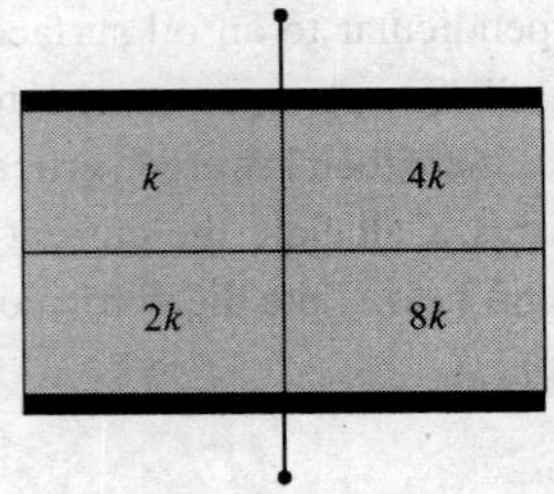

Figure 2.285

Ans. [$\frac{10k\epsilon_0 A}{3d}$]

2-14 What charges will flow after the shorting of the switch S in the circuit illustrated as shown in the figure-2.286 through sections 1 and 2 in the directions indicated by the arrows?

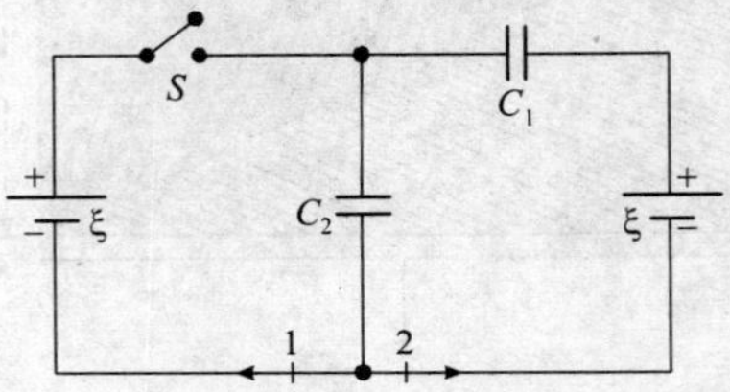

Figure 2.286

Ans. [$q_1 = \xi C_2$, $q_2 = -\frac{\xi C_1 C_2}{(C_1 + C_2)}$]

2-15 A 1 μF capacitor and a 2 μF capacitor are connected in series across a 1200 V supply line.

(a) Find the charge on each capacitor and the voltage across them.

(b) The charged capacitors are disconnected from the line and from each other and reconnected with terminals of like sign together. Find the final charge on each and the voltage across them.

Ans. [(a) 800μC, 800V, 800μC, 400V; (b) $\frac{1600}{3}$μC , $\frac{3200}{3}$μC , $\frac{1600}{3}$V]

2-16 If the total capacitance of the combination of identical capacitors shown in figure-2.287 between A and B is given by nC then find n.

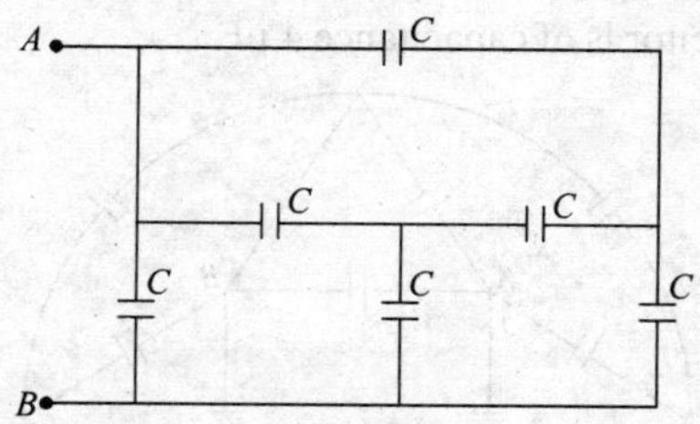

Figure 2.287

Ans. [2]

2-17 A 100 μF capacitor is charged to 100 V. After the charging, battery is disconnected. The capacitor is then connected in parallel to another capacitor. The final voltage is 20 V. Calculate the capacity of second capacitor.

Ans. [400 μF]

2-18 The dielectric to be used in a parallel-plate capacitor has a dielectric constant of 3.6 and a dielectric strength of 1.60×10^7 V/m. The capacitor is to have a capacitance of 1.25×10^{-9} F and must be able to withstand a maximum potential difference of 5500 V. What is the minimum area the plates of the capacitor may have?

Ans. [0.0135 m²]

2-19 The space between the plates of a parallel plate air capacitor is filled with an isotropic dielectric medium of which dielectric constant varies in the direction perpendicular to the plates according to the relation given as

$$k = k_1\left[1 + \sin\frac{\pi}{d}x\right]$$

Where d is the separation, between the plates and k_1 is a constant. The area of the plates is A. Determine the capacitance of the capacitor.

Ans. $[\frac{\epsilon_0 \pi k_1 A}{2d}]$

2-20 Two capacitors A and B each having slabs of dielectric constant $k = 2$ are connected in series. When they are connected across 230 V supply, potential across A is 130 V and that across B is 100 V. If the dielectric in the condenser of smaller capacitance is replaced by one for which $k = 5$, what will be the values of potential difference across them?

Ans. [78.68V, 151.32V]

2-21 A parallel plate capacitor of capacitance 0.1 μF is shown in the figure-2.288. Its two plates are given charges 2 μC and 1 μC. Find the value of heat dissipated after switch is closed :

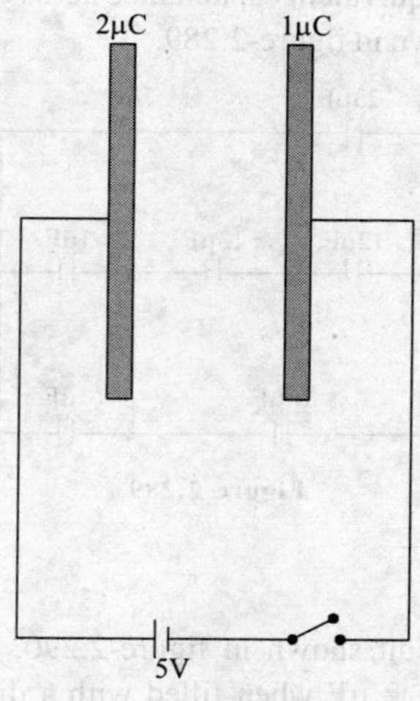

Figure 2.288

Ans. [5μJ]

2-22 Two identical planar capacitor connected in parallel and charged to a voltage $U_0 = 12$ V. When you disconnect them from the voltage source, the distance between the plates of one of the capacitors is reduced to one third of the original distance. What will be the new voltage on the capacitors ?

Ans. [6 V]

2-23 A parallel plate capacitor of plate area A and plate separation d is connected across a battery of voltage V and after charging of capacitor battery is disconnected. Now a dielectric slab of relative permittivity k is inserted between the plates to fill the complete space between the plates. Find the work done by the external agent in the process of inserting the slab into capacitor.

Ans. $[\frac{\epsilon_0 AV^2}{2d}\left(\frac{1}{k}-1\right)]$

2-24 A parallel-plate vacuum capacitor with plate area A and separation x has charges $+Q$ and $-Q$ on its plates. The capacitor is disconnected from the source of charge, so the charge on each plate remains fixed.

(a) What is the total energy stored in the capacitor?

(b) The plates are pulled apart an additional distance dx. What is the change in the stored energy?

(c) If F is the force with which the plates attract each other, then the change in the stored energy must equal the work $dW = Fdx$ done in pulling the plates apart. Find an expression for F

(d) Explain why F is not equal to QE, where E is the electric field between the plates.

Ans. [(a) $\frac{Q^2x}{2\varepsilon_0 A}$; (b) $\left(\frac{Q^2}{2\varepsilon_0 A}\right)\cdot dx$; (c) $\frac{Q^2}{2\varepsilon_0 A}$]

2-25 Find the equivalent capacitance across terminals A & B in the circuit shown in figure-2.289.

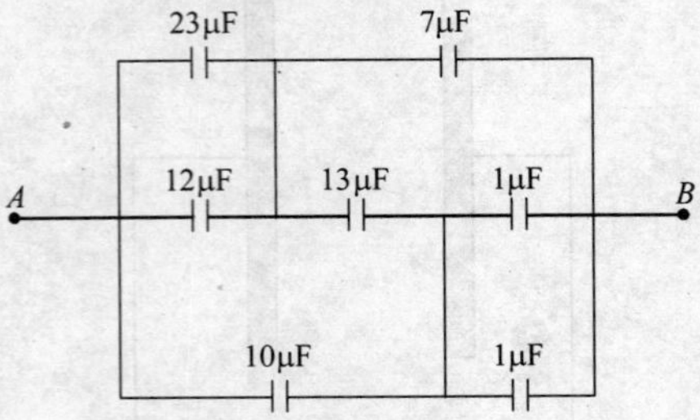

Figure 2.289

Ans. [7.5μF]

2-26 In the circuit shown in figure-2.290, capacitor A has capacitance $C_1 = 2$ μF when filled with a di-electric slab of dielectric constant $k = 2$. Capacitors B and C are air capacitors and have capacitances $C_2 = 3$ μF and $C_3 = 6$ μF, respectively. A is charged by closing switch S_1 alone.

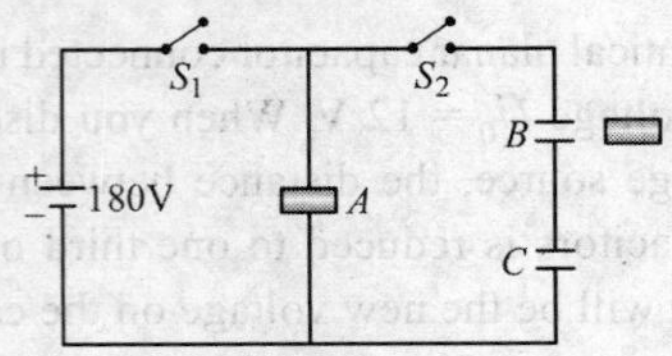

Figure 2.290

(a) Calculate energy supplied by battery during process of charging. Switch S_1 is now opened and S_2 is closed.

(b) Calculate charge on B and energy stored in the system when electrical equilibrium is attained.

Now switch S_2 is also opened, slab of A is removed. Another di-electric slab of $K = 2$, which can just fill the space in B, is inserted into it and then switch S_2 alone is closed.

(c) Calculate by how many times electric field in B is increased. Calculate also, loss of energy during redistribution of charge.

Ans. [(a) 0.0648 J, Energy stored in capacitor is $\frac{1}{2}CV^2$, but energy supplied by battery is CV^2; (b) 180 μC, 0.0162 J; (c) 0.75, 0.0054 J]

2-27 In the circuit shown in figure-2.291. $C_1 = 5$ μF, $C_2 = 29$ μF, $C_3 = 6$ μF, $C_4 = 3$ μF and $C_5 = 7$ μF. If in steady state potential difference between points A and B is 11 volt, calculate potential difference across C_5.

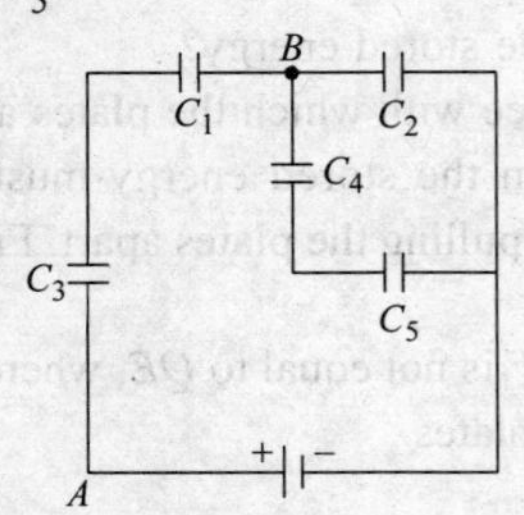

Figure 2.291

Ans. [1.8 V]

2-28 Find the equivalent capacitance between terminals A & C if each capacitor is of capacitance 4 μF.

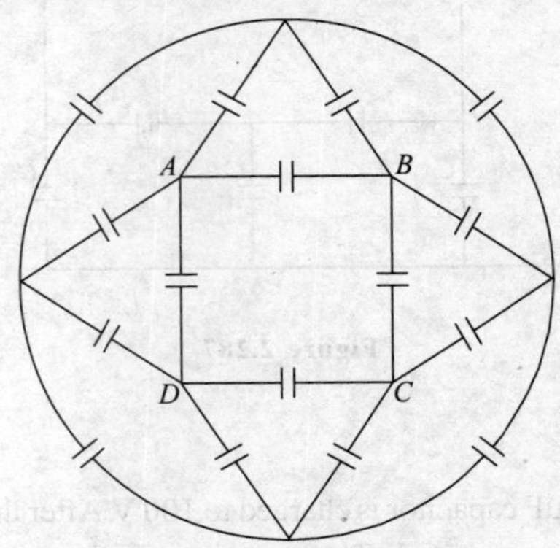

Figure 2.292

Ans. [7μF]

2-29 In the given network if potential difference between p and q is 2 V and $C_2 = 3\ C_1$, find the potential difference between a & b.

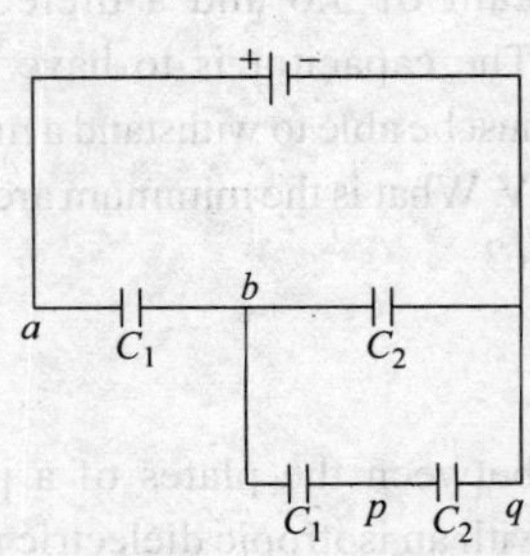

Figure 2.293

Ans. [30V]

2-30 The plates of a parallel plate capacitor are separated by a distance $d = 1$ cm. Two parallel sided dielectric slabs of thickness 0.7cm and 0.3 cm fill the space between the plates. If the dielectric constants of the two slabs are 3 and 5 respectively and a potential difference of 440 V is applied across the plates. Find

(a) The electric field intensities in each of the slabs.

(b) The ratio of electric energies stored in the first to that in the second dielectric slab.

Ans. [(a) 5×10^4 V/m, 3×10^4 V/m; (b) 35/9]

2-31 Two parallel plate capacitors of capacitance C and 2C are connected in parallel then following steps are performed.

(i) A battery of voltage V is connected across the capacitors.

(ii) A dielectric slab of relative permittivity k is slowly inserted in capacitor C.

(iii) Battery is disconnected.

(iv) Dielectric slab is slowly removed from capacitor.

Find the heat produced in (i) and work done by external agent in step (ii) & (iv).

Ans. $[\frac{3}{2}CV^2, -\frac{1}{2}(K-1)CV_0^2, \frac{1}{6}(K+2)(K-1)CV^2]$

2-32 A charge 200 mC is imparted to each of the two identical parallel plate capacitors connected in parallel. At $t = 0$, the plates of both the capacitors are 0.1 m apart. The plates of first capacitor move towards each other with velocity 0.001 m/s and plates of second capacitor move apart with the same velocity. Find the current in the circuit.

Ans. [2 μA]

2-33 A circuit is shown in figure-2.294. Find the charge on the condenser having a capacity of 5 μF in steady state.

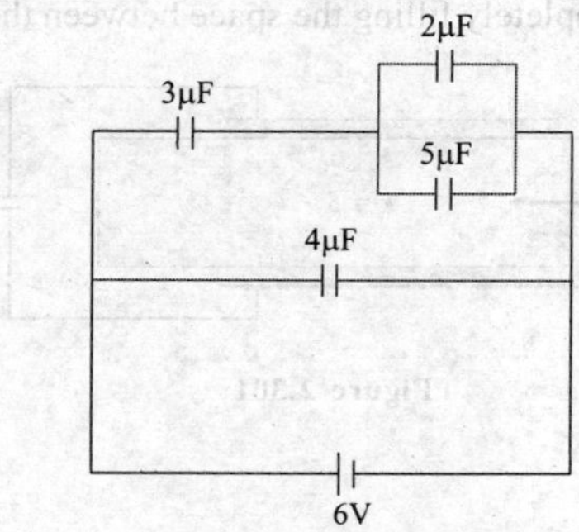

Figure 2.294

Ans. [9 μC]

2-34 A solid conducting sphere of radius 10 cm is enclosed by a thin metallic shell of radius 20 cm. A charge $q = 20$ mC is given to the inner sphere. Find the heat generated in the process, the inner sphere is connected to the shell by a conducting wire.

Ans. [9J]

2-35 In the given circuit with initially uncharged capacitors, the switch S_1 alone is closed and steady state is attained. Now S_2 is also closed. Again steady state is reached. Find the final charge on capacitor C_2. If now S_1 is opened and steady state is attained. Find final charge on C_1 and C_2 now.

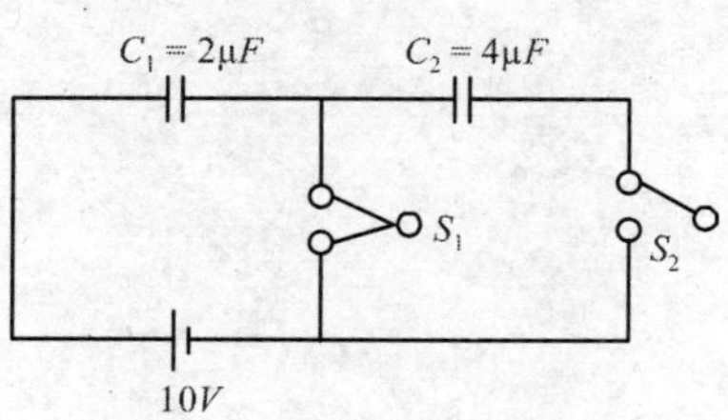

Figure 2.295

Ans. [0, 13.33 μC, 13.33 μC]

2-36 Identical parallel metal plates are mounted in air at equal distances d from one another as shown in figure below. The area of each plate is equal to A. Calcualte the capacitance of system between terminals P and Q.

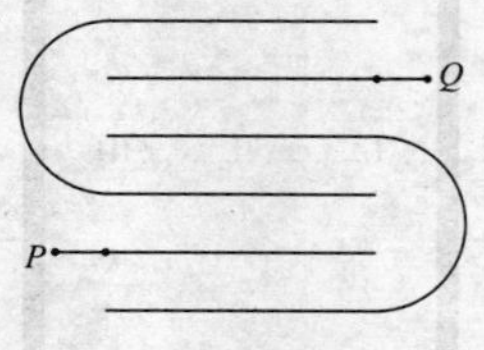

Figure 2.296

Ans. [1]

2-37 In the circuit shown in figure-2.297 find the equivalent capacitance between terminals A and B.

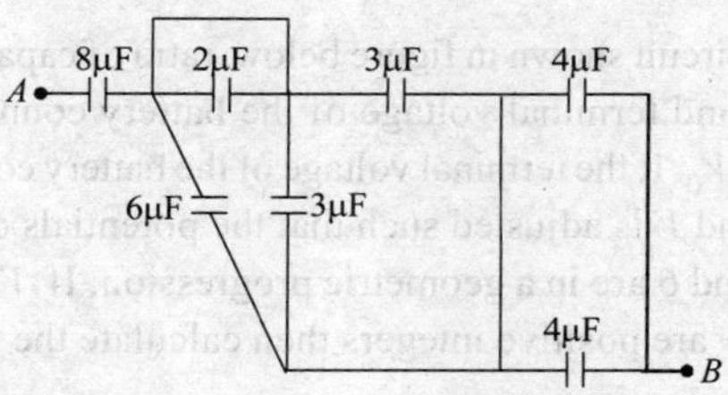

Figure 2.297

Ans. [3 μF]

2-38 A capacitor is made of a flat plate of area A and another plate is bent at four points and placed above the flat plate as shown in figure-2.298. Dimension of both the plates are shown in figure. Find the capacitance of this structure between the two plates.

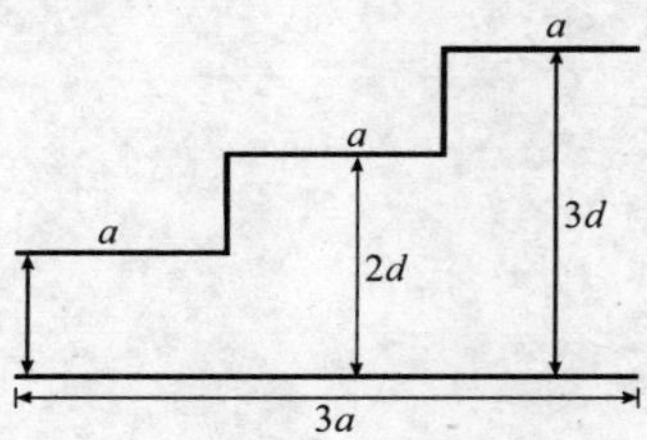

Figure 2.298

Ans. $[\frac{11\varepsilon_0 A}{18d}]$

2-39 A parallel plate capacitor with plates kept at a separation 1cm and plate area 100 cm^2 is connected across a 24 V battery. Find the force with wihch one plate will attract the other plates.

Ans. [2.5×10^{-7} N]

2-40 Figure-2.299 shows a capacitor having three layers of equal thickness and same area as that of its plates. Layer-I is free space, Layer-II is a conductor and Layer-III is a dielectric of dielectric constant k. Calculate the ratio of energy stored in region III to total energy stored in capacitor when a potential difference is applied across the plates of capacitor.

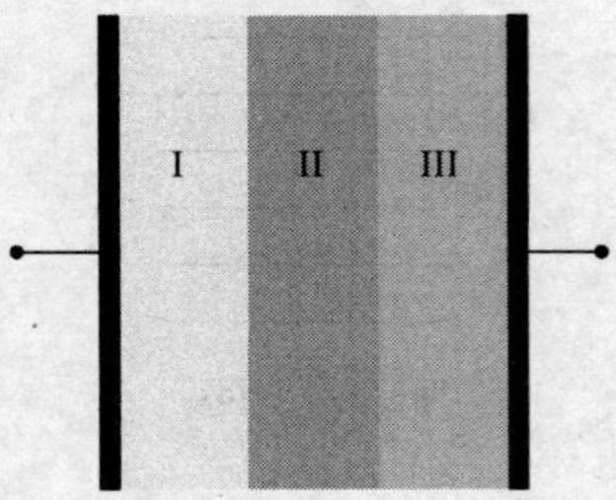

Figure 2.299

Ans. $[\frac{1}{k+1}]$

2-41 In the circuit shown in figure below, ratio of capacitors is $C_2/C_1 = 4/3$ and terminal voltage of the battery connected at the left end is V_0. If the terminal voltage of the battery connected at the right end V is adjusted such that the potentials of nodes 1, 2, 3, 4, 5 and 6 are in a geometric progression, If $V = V_0 x^y$, where x and y are positive integers then calculate the value of $x + y$.

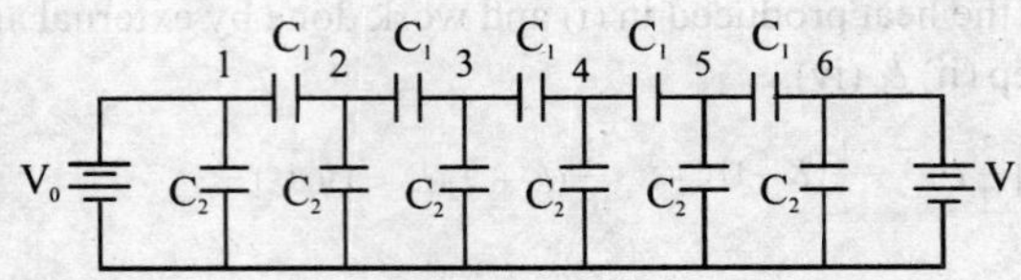

Figure 2.300

Ans. [8]

2-42 A parallel plate capacitor (square plates) has a capacitance of 1 mF. It is completely filled with a solid dielectric (constant = 5) which is performing small oscillations of SHM with amplitude 0.1% of the length of the plate with a period of 1 ms. At all times, a battery of 10 V remains connected to the capacitor. Find the amount of charge that crosses the battery when the dielectric goes from mean position to extreme position. Initially at $t = 0$ the dielectric is completely filling the space between the plates.

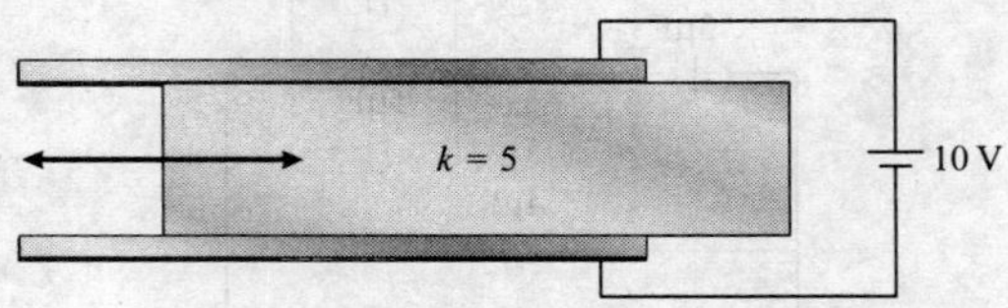

Figure 2.301

Ans. [40 μC]

* * * * *

Current Electricity 3

FEW WORDS FOR STUDENTS

Electricity is a form of energy all around us which is powering technology and many new inventions which are making our life comfortable. Electricity is generated at one point then either stored or flows from one place to another. When electrical energy is stored at a point then it is called static electricity and when it flows from one place to another then we call it current electricity. Briefly we define electricity as flow of charges but its not that simple. What causes the flow of charges and the conditions under which charges move, there are many such questions which need to be answered. In previous chapters we've broadly studied about static charges and effects associated with these. In this chapter of current electricity we will deal with all fundamentals concerned with charges in motion to enhance our knowledge for moving charges and to build a base for upcoming chapters of magnetism and electromagnetic induction.

CHAPTER CONTENTS

COVER APPLICATION

(a)

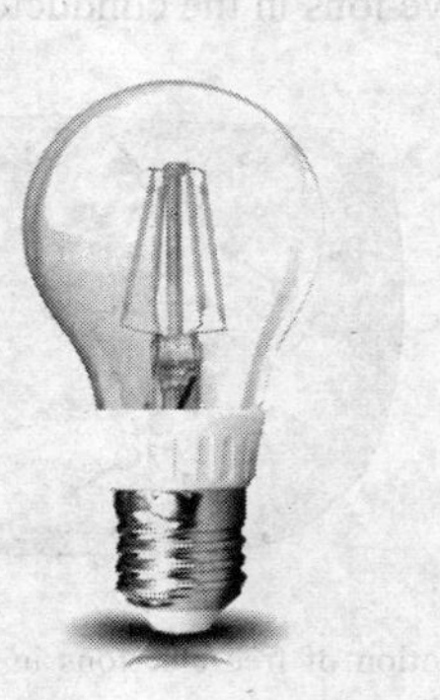

(b)

Figure-(a) shows a filament based incandescent lamp in which when current is passed due to thermal effects of current filament of the lamp heats up and starts emitting heat and visible light radiation. Figure-(b) shows a similar structure LED lamp in which semiconductor diodes are used which emits light and in these lamps heat produced is very very less compared to incandescent lamps thats why these lamps are preferred where only light application is required.

Electricity is an integral part of our day to day life. Everywhere in your surrounding you always see applications of electricity such as the sources of light we use at night, mobile phones, television remote controls, kitchen appliances and many more uses including dangerous lightning or electric sparks you might have seen from a high voltage electric pole in case of short circuits.

In all the above and many such applications of electricity the common thing is the energy in electrical form driving all the devices or phenomenon in our surrounding. In most cases the energy is delivered by electric current in wires or sometimes through air in case of lightning or sparks. Other forms of energy which we see in such applications including heat, light or sometimes mechanical energy are produced when electrical energy is converted to these forms in the device or in some phenomenon.

To understand all the phenomenon using electricity or the devices work on electrical energy we need to understand the basics of electric current and its applications.

3.1 Electric Current

As you might have studied in your previous classes that Current is the rate of flow of charges. In conductors charges can flow easily because conductors have free charge carriers which contribute in flow of current easily. These charge carriers are the free electrons inside a metal body. For an isolated metal body in it free electrons behave like gas molecules in a closed container as shown in figure-3.1. These free electrons move randomly in Brownion motion in an isolated conductor and the energy of these electrons is solely due to thermal agitation at the specific room temperature. In this random motion these electrons continuously collide with each other as well as with the fixed positive ions in the conductor lattice.

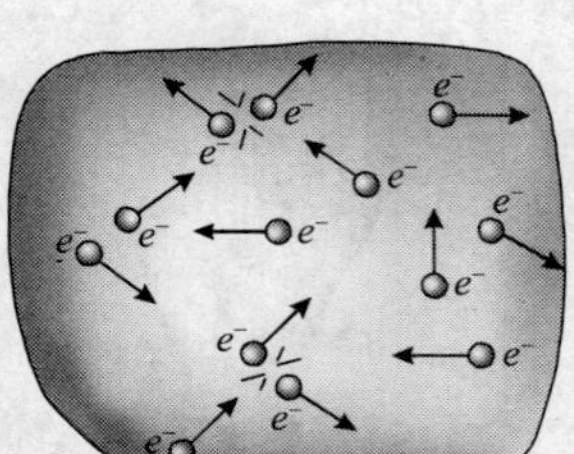

Random motion of free electrons in an isolated conductor

Figure 3.1

When a potential difference is applied across a conductor by connecting a battery as shown in figure-3.2 it sets up an electric field in the conductor from high potential to low potential side. This electric field exerts a force on free electrons due to which these electrons starts flowing in opposite direction i.e. from low potential to high potential side as shown.

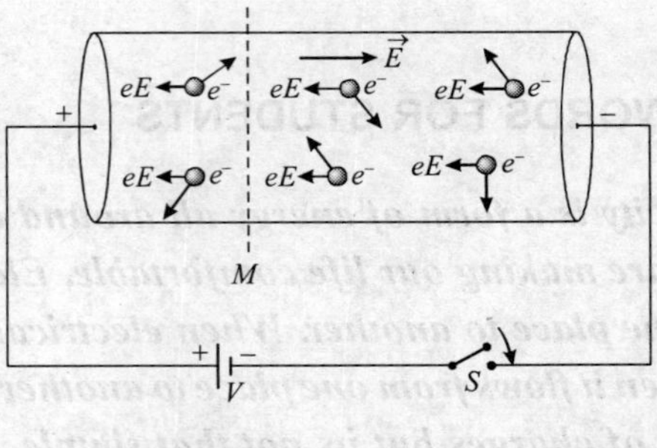

Figure 3.2

Through any cross-section of the conductor the amount of charge flowing per unit time is defined as '*Electric Current*'. If from a section M shown by dotted line in figure-3.2, Δq charge crosses in time Δt then the current in this conductor is given as

$$I = \frac{\Delta q}{\Delta t} \qquad \ldots(3.1)$$

In other way if we consider that N free electrons pass through the section M per unit time then current can also be expressed in terms of N and electron charge e as

$$I = \frac{\Delta q}{\Delta t} = Ne \qquad \ldots(3.2)$$

3.1.1 Drift Speed of Free Electrons

Consider the situation shown in figure-3.3 in which we analyze the force and motion of a free electron at microscopic level. Initially when the free electrons were in Brownoion motion as shown in figure-3.1 these were colliding randomly with other neighbouring free electrons. When a potential difference is applied across the conductor as shown in figure-3.2, the electric field exerts a force eE on each free electron as shown in figure-3.3 and it starts moving due to the force but during motion it continuously collides with the other neighbouring free electrons due to thermal agitation as these electrons have some velocity v_T in random direction due to the thermal motion and because of continuous collisions the moving electron experiences an opposition force opposite to its motion which increases as its speed increases because it collides with high momentum to other particles at higher speed, the opposing force will be higher. For simplicity we consider this force to be proportional to the velocity of the free electron hence considered as $f_{op} = kv$ if v is the average velocity of electron during drift. Here k is a proportionality constant which depends upon the nature of material and temperature. As temperature increases, thermal agitation of the conductor increases and this will lead to increase in rate of collision of free electrons and due to this opposition force will also be more, thus value of k also increases. Actually in the expression of opposition force there are other terms including higher powers of velocity but at low velocities those terms can be neglected and this proportional relation gives a fairly approximate situation.

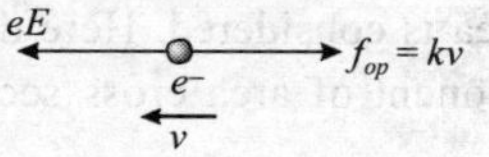

Figure 3.3

After applying potential difference across a conductor the acceleration of a free electron inside is shown in figure-3.3 which can be given as

$$a = \frac{eE - kv}{m_e} \quad \ldots (3.3)$$

From equation-(3.3) we can see that acceleration decreases as velocity of free electrons increase. After applying the potential difference in a very short interval of time velocity of all the free electrons increase till their acceleration becomes zero which is given by equation-(3.3) as

$$a = \frac{eE - kv}{m_e} = 0$$

$$\Rightarrow \quad v = \frac{eE}{k} \quad \ldots (3.4)$$

Equation-(3.4) gives the terminal velocity of the free electrons with which these free electrons will travel in a conductor and it is called '*Drift Speed*' of free electrons. In above expression e and k are constants for a specific conductor at a given temperature. Thus drift speed of electrons in a current carrying conductor is directly proportional to the electric field strength inside the conductor which is given as

$$v_d = \frac{eE}{k}$$

$$\Rightarrow \quad v_d = \mu E \quad \ldots (3.5)$$

Here μ is called '*Mobility*' of free electrons in a conductor. Mobility of a charge carrier in any medium is defined as the ease with which the charge carriers can flow in the medium and contribute in electric current.

In equation-(3.5) we can see that $\mu = e/k$ thus the mobility of free electrons in a conductor depends upon the specific material as well as temperature as electron charge is invariant.

3.1.2 Effect of Temperature on Flow of Free Electrons in a Conductor

Figure-3.4 shows the effective path of a free electron in a conductor after applying a potential difference across the conductor. Due to electric force the electrons start drifting but because of thermal agitation electrons do not follow straight line path. Continuous random collisions during drift results in a zigzag path for electrons overall drifting in the direction of the electric force as shown in figure-3.4(a). If the temperature of the conductor is decreased then due to less thermal agitation collision rate decreases and path of motion of electron will be relatively less random compared to the state of high temperature. This is shown in figure-3.4(b). Similarly figure-3.4(c) shows the path of an electron drifting in a conductor at much lower temperature.

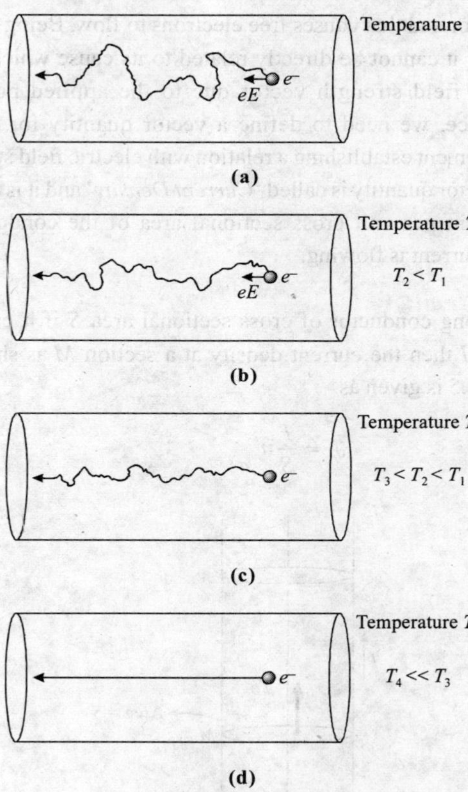

Figure 3.4

When temperature of a conductor is decreased to such a low value that its free electrons stops colliding with each other or the opposing force due to very low rate of collision can be neglected then this is the state when free electrons of conductor almost flows in a straight line path as shown in figure-3.4(d) and in this state the free electrons of conductor do not experience any opposing force while moving and will have continuous acceleration. This is the state of conductor which is called '*Zero Resistance State*' or '*Superconducting State*'.

This is the reason why resistance of a conductor increases when its temperature increases. High temperature causes more thermal agitation and random motion which causes high rate of collision and hence more opposing force to the motion of free electrons and this leads to high resistance of the conductor.

3.1.3 Current Density in a Conductor

As already discussed that current is the rate of flow of charge measured in unit of Coulomb per second or Ampere, the conventional direction of current flow is considered along the flow of positive charges or opposite to the flow of free electrons in a conductor but current itself is a scalar quantity.

In a conductor current flows when a potential difference is applied across it which establishes an electric field inside the conductor and that causes free electrons to flow. Being current a scalar, it cannot be directly related to its cause which is the electric field strength vector due to the applied potential difference, we need to define a vector quantity for current measurement establishing a relation with electric field strength. This vector quantity is called '*Current Density*' and it is defined as current per unit cross sectional area of the conductor in which current is flowing.

For a long conductor of cross sectional area S if it carries a current I then the current density at a section M as shown in figure-3.5 is given as

$$\vec{J} = \frac{I}{S}\hat{n} \qquad \ldots(3.6)$$

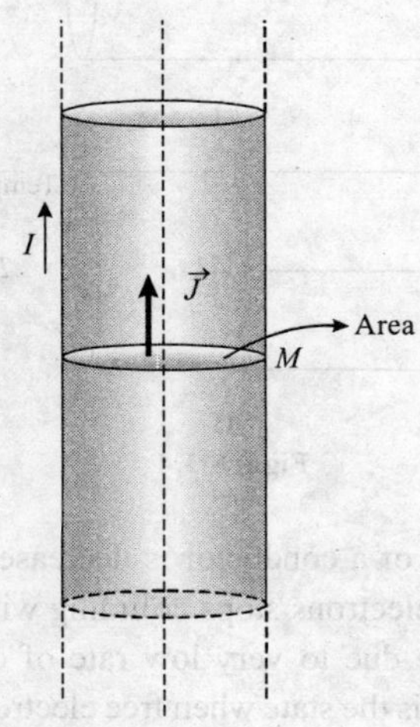

Figure 3.5

The unit used for current density is A/m^2 and the direction of current density is considered normal to the cross sectional area of the conductor through which current is flowing along the flow of positive charges or opposite to flow of free electrons in conductor. In equation-(3.6), $\hat{n}$ is the unit vector normal to the surface area S along the direction of current density.

If in a conductor across its cross sectional area current density is uniform then current through it can be directly given as

$$I = \vec{J}\cdot\vec{S} \qquad \ldots(3.7)$$

In above expression of current, dot product of current density with the given area is considered. Here dot product signifies the normal component of area cross section to the flow of current.

If current density is non uniform in cross section of a current carrying conductor then we need to consider an elemental section of area dS in the cross section of the conductor as shown in figure-3.6 and then we find the current through elemental section of the conductor as

$$dI = \vec{J}.\overrightarrow{dS} \qquad \ldots(3.8)$$

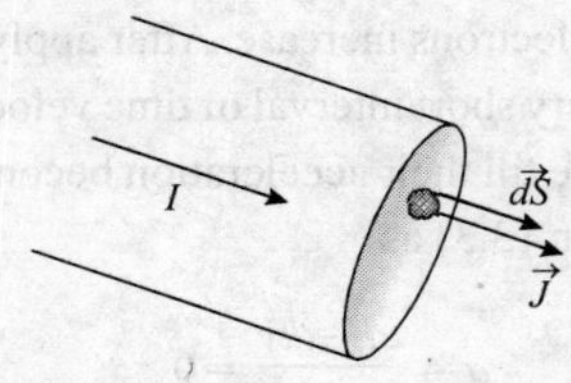

Figure 3.6

Now the total current through the given cross section of conductor can be calculated by integrating the expression of elemental current in equation-(3.8) for the whole surface of the conductor.

$$I = \int \vec{J}.\overrightarrow{dS} \qquad \ldots(3.9)$$

We will discuss above analysis with an illustration. Figure-3.7 shows a cylindrical conductor of radius R through which current is flowing of which current density is varying with distance from the axis of the conductor given as

$$J = ax^2 \qquad \ldots(3.10)$$

Above expression indicates that on outer edge of the conductor current is more and near to central axis of conductor current would be less concentrated.

To determine the current through the conductor we consider an elemental circular strip of radius x and width dx as shown in above figure. The area of this elemental strip is given as

$$dS = 2\pi x \cdot dx$$

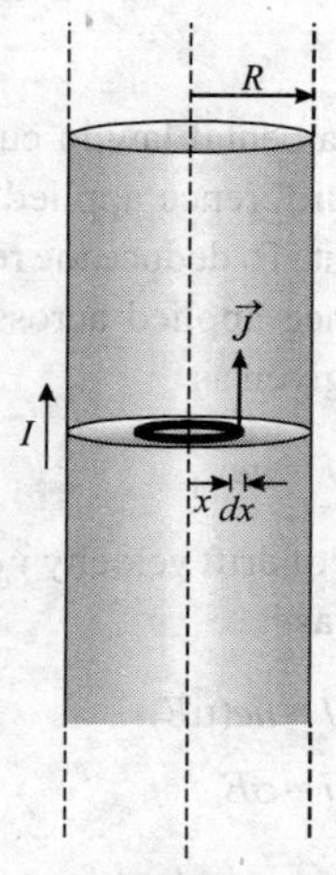

Figure 3.7

The current through this elemental cross sectional area of the conductor is given as

$$dI = \vec{J} \cdot \overline{dS}$$

Total current in conductor can be given by integrating the above expression of current through elemental cross sectional area within limits from 0 to R for the complete cross sectional area is given as

$$I = \int dI = \int \vec{J} \cdot \overline{dS}$$

$$\Rightarrow \quad I = \int_0^R (ax^2) \cdot (2\pi x \cdot dx)$$

$$\Rightarrow \quad I = 2\pi a \int_0^R x^3 \cdot dx$$

$$\Rightarrow \quad I = 2\pi a \left[\frac{x^4}{4}\right]_0^R = \frac{\pi a R^4}{2} \quad \dots (3.11)$$

3.1.4 Relation in Current Density and Drift Velocity of Electrons

Figure-3.8 shows a conductor connected across a battery of voltage V. When the switch is closed, an electric field E is established in the conductor which causes all free electrons to flow at drift velocity v_d as shown in figure.

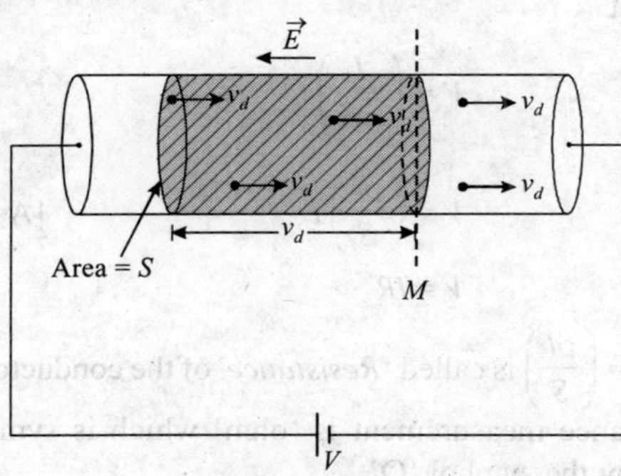

Figure 3.8

In figure-3.8 to determine the current, consider the shaded volume of length v_d and cross sectional area of the conductor as S. This shaded volume is of length v_d that means in one second all the free electrons contained in this shaded region pass through the section M of the conductor.

If n be the free electron density in the conductor material, total number of electrons passing through the section M of conductor are given as

$$N = nSv_d$$

The current through the conductor can be given as

$$I = Ne = nev_dS \quad \dots (3.12)$$

From above expression of current we can calculate the current density through the cross section of the conductor which is given as

$$J = \frac{I}{S} = nev_d \quad \dots (3.13)$$

$$\Rightarrow \quad v_d = \frac{J}{ne} \quad \dots (3.14)$$

Above expression obtained in equation-(3.13) or (3.14) is a relation between drift speed of free electrons and current density for a current carrying conductor for any cross-section.

3.1.5 Drift Velocity and Relaxation Time

In an isolated conductor free electrons behave like gas molecules which are in random motion and collide with each other. The average time between two successive collisions by an electron averaged over all the free electrons over a large period of time is called '*Relaxation Time*' in random motion of particles. It is denoted by τ. At any instant of time we can consider that different free electrons are moving at velocities $\vec{u}_i$ where $i = 1, 2, 3\ldots$ such that for random motion we know that average velocity of all the electrons (say N_0) at any instant is zero, given as

$$\sum_{i=1}^{N_0} \vec{u}_i = 0 \quad \dots (3.15)$$

When an electric field $\vec{E}$ is applied to the conductor then all the free electrons in random motion experience a force $-e\vec{E}$ and start moving in direction opposite to the direction of electric field due to the acceleration by this force. The instantaneous velocities of the free electrons at any instant of time t_i starting from their last collision can be given as

$$\vec{v}_i = \vec{u}_i + \left(-\frac{e\vec{E}}{m}\right)t_i \quad \dots (3.16)$$

In above expression $\vec{v}_i$ is the velocity of ith electron after t_i is the time from its last collision. We are taking t_i different for each free electron because at any instant of time the time lapsed from last collision of that electron would be different in random motion.

Drift velocity of free electrons is the average velocity of all the free electrons at any instant of time which can be given as

$$\vec{v}_d = \frac{\vec{v}_1 + \vec{v}_2 + \vec{v}_3 + \ldots\ldots}{N_0} = \frac{\sum_{i=1}^{N_0} \vec{v}_i}{N_0} \quad \ldots(3.17)$$

If we substitute the values of all $\vec{v}_i$ from equation-(3.16) to equation-(3.17), we will get

$$\vec{v}_d = \frac{1}{N_0}\left(\sum_{i=1}^{N_0} \vec{u}_i\right) + \left(-\frac{e\vec{E}}{m}\right)\left(\frac{t_1 + t_2 + t_3 + \ldots\ldots}{N_0}\right) \quad \ldots(3.18)$$

First term on right hand side of equation-(3.18) becomes zero as just after collision velocities of free electrons are randomly scattered in space average of which is always zero as already discussed and shown in equation-(3.15). In second term of this equation, the time durations t_1, t_2, t_3, ... are the durations between two successive collisions of each free electron some of these are more than average relaxation time and some are less than average relaxation time thus average value of all these durations is the average relaxation time given as

$$\tau = \frac{t_1 + t_2 + t_3 + \ldots.}{N_0} \quad \ldots(3.19)$$

Thus equation-(18) can now be written as

$$\vec{v}_d = -\left(\frac{e\vec{E}}{m}\right)\tau \quad \ldots(3.20)$$

The relation in magnitudes is given as

$$v_d = \left(\frac{eE}{m}\right)\tau \quad \ldots(3.21)$$

Equation-(3.20) is the relation between drift velocity of electrons, electric field inside the conductor and average relaxation time. Using this relation we can also find current in conductor in terms of relaxation time from equation-(3.12) which is given as

$$I = ne|v_d|S = neS\left(\frac{eE}{m}\right)\tau$$

$$\Rightarrow \quad I = \left(\frac{ne^2 SE}{m}\right)\tau \quad \ldots(3.22)$$

$$\Rightarrow \quad J = \frac{I}{S} = \left(\frac{ne^2 E}{m}\right)\tau \quad \ldots(3.23)$$

The expression in above equation-(3.23) gives the relation in current density and average relaxation time.

3.1.6 Ohm's Law

Ohm's Law is a fundamental law in current electricity which relates the potential difference applied across a conductor to the current flowing in it. To deduce the relation between current and potential difference applied across a conductor we start with equation-(3.13) given as

$$J = nev_d$$

Substituting the value of drift velocity v_d from equation-(3.5) in terms of electric field as

$$J = ne(\mu E)$$

$$\Rightarrow \quad J = \sigma E \quad \ldots(3.24)$$

Here $\sigma = ne\mu$ is another constant for a specific conductor at a given temperature and it is called '*Conductivity*' of the conductor. Conductivity of a conductor is a measure of how better conduction to electric current a conductor offers. Using conductivity we can compare two metals that which one is a better conductor of electric current. Reciprocal of conductivity is defined as '*Resistivity*' or '*Specific Resistance*' denoted as ρ, given as

$$\rho = \frac{1}{\sigma} \quad \ldots(3.25)$$

Using resistivity of a conductor we measure how much hinderance the conductor offers for current flow. Now equation-(3.24) can be rewritten vectorially as

$$\vec{J} = \sigma\vec{E} = \left(\frac{1}{\rho}\right)\vec{E} \quad \ldots(3.26)$$

Equation-(3.26) is called differential vector form of Ohm's Law which can be used to relate current and potential difference across a conductor. For a uniform conductor of length l and cross sectional area S we can use equation-(3.24) as

$$\left(\frac{I}{S}\right) = \sigma\left(\frac{dV}{dl}\right)$$

$$\Rightarrow \quad dV = \left(\frac{I}{\sigma S}\right) dl$$

Integrating above expression for the full length of conductor, we will get

$$V = \left(\frac{I}{\sigma S}\right) l$$

$$\Rightarrow \quad V = \left(\frac{\rho l}{S}\right) I \quad \left[\text{As } \rho = \frac{1}{\sigma}\right]$$

$$\Rightarrow \quad V = IR \quad \ldots(3.27)$$

Where $R = \left(\frac{\rho l}{S}\right)$ is called '*Resistance*' of the conductor. SI unit for resistance measurement is 'ohm' which is symbolically denoted by the symbol 'Ω'.

Resistance of a conductor is a proportionality constant in equation-(3.27) for linear relationship in current flowing and potential difference applied across a conductor and this equation-(3.27) is the '*Equation of Ohm's Law*' and Ohm's Law is stated as

"*For some conductors under constant physical conditions like temperature, mechanical strain, humidity etc. the current flowing through it is always directly proportional to the potential difference across its two ends.*"

Such conductors for which the equation-(3.27) is valid are called '*Ohmic Conductors*'. Any conductor which offers some resistance to current in a circuit is generally referred as '*Resistors*'.

3.1.7 Experimental Verification of Ohm's Law

For ohmic conductors the graph plotted for current flowing through these with potential difference across the conductors is a straight line as shown in figure-3.9(b). Figure-3.9(a) shows the circuit setup of Ohm's law verification using a variable resistance or rheostat in which we fix a value of resistance and take readings of voltmeter and ammeter by varying the voltage of the variable battery to plot the curve shown in figure-3.9(b).

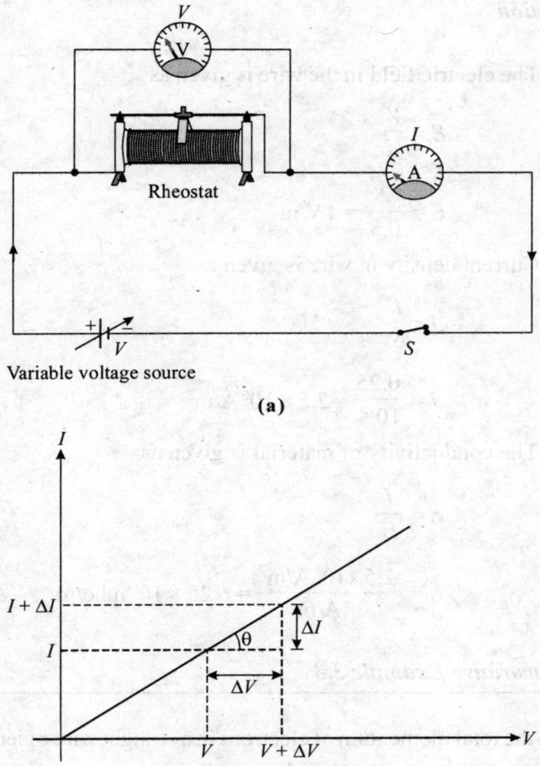

Figure 3.9

In above V-I graph of a conductor the slope of graph gives the reciprocal of resistance of conductor which is also called as '*Conductance*' of conductor, given as

$$G = \frac{1}{R} = \frac{\Delta I}{\Delta V} = \text{slope of V-I curve} \quad \ldots(3.28)$$

The SI unit used for measurement of conductance is '*mho*' which is reverse spell of '*ohm*' and symbol used to denote conductance is '*G*'. There are some conductors in which the V-I graph is not a straight line as shown in figure-3.10. Such conductors are called non-ohmic conductors. Such behaviours are due to the active nature of conductor materials in which the physical properties of material change when these are subjected to different electric fields thats why the resistance of conductor changes with different physical conditions. About some of such conductors we will study in the topic of semiconductors.

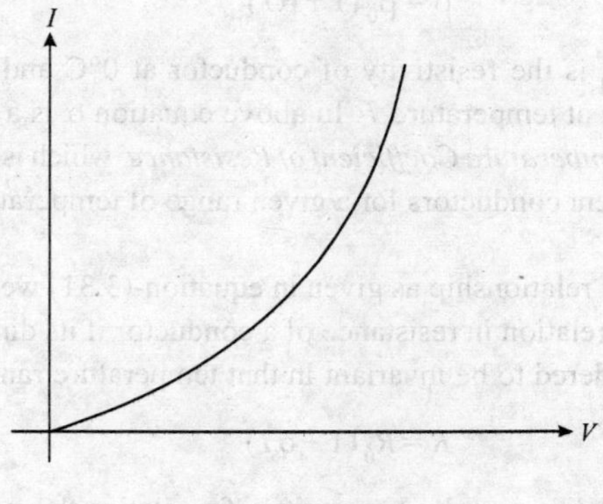

Figure 3.10

3.1.8 Temperature Dependence of Resistivity

Equation-(3.27) shows that resistance R is the proportionality constant for current voltage relationship for an ohmic conductor which is given as

$$R = \frac{\rho l}{S}$$

In above expression of resistance l and S are dimensions of the conductor and ρ is the resistivity which is a characteristic property of a conductor to measure its hinderance in flow of current through it. In previous article we've already discussed that resistivity of a current carrying conductor can be given by equation-(3.26) as

$$\rho = \frac{E}{J} \quad \ldots(3.29)$$

Substituting the value of current density from equation-(3.23) in above relation, we get

$$\rho = \frac{E}{\left(\dfrac{ne^2\tau E}{m}\right)}$$

$$\Rightarrow \quad \rho = \frac{m}{ne^2\tau} \quad \ldots(3.30)$$

In above expression resistivity depends upon average relaxation time which we know depends upon temperature. As temperature increases, it increases thermal agitation which causes rate of collision to increase due to which relaxation time decreases and hence resistivity increases. Based on article-3.1.2 also qualitatively we can state that on increasing temperature randomness of motion increases due to which flow of electrons will be more difficult hence resistivity increases.

It is observed that in general for small range of temperatures above room temperature resistivity increases linearly with temperature and temperature dependency of resistivity is given by an empirical relation which is given as

$$\rho = \rho_0(1+\alpha T) \qquad \ldots(3.31)$$

Where ρ_0 is the resistivity of conductor at 0°C and ρ is the resistivity at temperature T. In above equation α is a constant called '*Temperature Coefficient of Resistance*' which is different for different conductors for a given range of temperature.

For linear relationship as given in equation-(3.31) we can also write the relation in resistance of a conductor if its dimensions are considered to be invariant in that temperature range as

$$R = R_0(1+\alpha T) \qquad \ldots(3.32)$$

Above relation can also be rewritten for relating the resistances at two different temperatures T_1 and T_2 for small range of temperature for which α is considered constant as

$$R_{T_2} = R_{T_1}(1+\alpha\Delta T) \qquad \ldots(3.33)$$

Here $\Delta T = T_2 - T_1$ and R_{T_2} and R_{T_1} are the resistances of conductor at temperatures T_2 and T_1 respectively.

Illustrative Example 3.1

Find the velocity of charge carriers in 1 A current in a copper conductor of cross-section 1 cm^2 and length 10 km. Free electron density of copper is 8.5×10^{28} per m^3. How long will it take the charge to travel from one end of the conductor to the other ?

Solution

Drift speed of free electrons in a conductor is given as

$$v_d = \frac{i}{neA}$$

$$\Rightarrow \quad v_d = \frac{1}{(8.5\times10^{28})(1.6\times10^{-19})(10^{-4})}$$

$$\Rightarrow \quad v_d = 0.735\times10^{-6}\text{ m/s}$$

$$\Rightarrow \quad v_d = 0.735\ \mu\text{m/s}$$

Thus travel time is given as

$$t = \frac{l}{v}$$

$$\Rightarrow \quad t = \frac{10\times10^3}{0.735\times10^{-6}}$$

$$\Rightarrow \quad t = 1.36\times10^{10}\text{ s}$$

$$\Rightarrow \quad t = \frac{1.36\times10^{10}}{60\times60\times24\times365}\text{ y}$$

$$\Rightarrow \quad t = 431.4\text{ y}$$

Illustrative Example 3.2

The potential difference across a straight wire of 10^{-3} cm^2 cross sectional area and 50 cm length is 2 V, when a current of 0.25A flows in the wire. Calculate

(a) The field strength in the wire

(b) The current density, and

(c) The conductivity of the metal

Solution

(a) The electric field in the wire is given as

$$E = \frac{V}{d}$$

$$\Rightarrow \quad E = \frac{2}{0.5} = 4\text{ V/m}$$

(b) Current density in wire is given as

$$J = \frac{I}{S}$$

$$\Rightarrow \quad J = \frac{0.25}{10^{-5}} = 2.5\times10^6\text{ A/m}^2$$

(c) The conductivity of material is given as

$$\sigma = \frac{J}{E}$$

$$\Rightarrow \quad \sigma = \frac{2.5\times10^6\text{ A/m}^2}{4\text{A/m}} = 6.25\times10^5\text{ mho/m}$$

Illustrative Example 3.3

Find the total momentum of electrons in a straight wire of length 1000 m carrying a current 70 A.

Solution

The expression for the current in wire is given as

$$I = n\,e\,v_d\,S$$

Total no. of electrons in wire are given as

$$N = nAl$$

Total momentum of electrons in wire is given as

$$p = N m v_d$$

$$\Rightarrow \quad p = n S l \times m\left(\frac{I}{neS}\right) = \frac{Ilm}{e}$$

Putting of all values,

$$p = \frac{70\times1000\times9.3\times10^{-31}}{1.6\times10^{-19}}$$

$$\Rightarrow \quad p = 0.407\ \mu\text{N-s}$$

Illustrative Example 3.4

Two large parallel metal plates are located in vacuum. One of these serves as a cathode, a source of electrons with negligible initial speed. An electron flow directed toward the opposite plate produces a space charge causing the potential in the gap between the plates to vary as $V = ax^{4/3}$, where a is a positive constant, and x is the distance from the cathode. Find:

(a) The volume density of space charge as a function of x

(b) The current density.

Solution

(a) Given that the potential is given as

$$V = ax^{4/3}$$

Using above potential, the electric field in space is given as

$$E = -\frac{dV}{dx} = -\frac{4a}{3}x^{1/3} \qquad \ldots(3.34)$$

Using above electric field, volume density of space charge can be obtained by Gauss's law in the region for a small cylindrical Gaussian surface of cross section S and width dx, applied as

$$dE.S = \frac{\rho(x)Sdx}{\epsilon_0}$$

$$\Rightarrow \quad -\frac{4a}{3}\left(\frac{1}{3}x^{-2/3}dx\right)S = \frac{\rho(x)Sdx}{\epsilon_0}$$

$$\Rightarrow \quad \rho(x) = -\frac{4}{9}a\,\epsilon_0\,x^{2/3}$$

(b) Current density in the region is given as

$$J = \rho(x)\,v(x)$$

$$\Rightarrow \quad J = -\frac{4}{9}a\varepsilon_0 x^{-2/3}v(x) \qquad \ldots(3.35)$$

Due to the potential gain in kinetic energy of electrons is given as

$$\frac{1}{2}mv^2(x) = eV(x)$$

$$\Rightarrow \quad v(x) = \sqrt{\frac{2V(x)e}{m}}$$

Substituting above value of $v(x)$ in equation-(3.35) gives

$$\Rightarrow \quad J = -\frac{4}{9}\varepsilon_0 a^{3/2}\sqrt{2e/m}$$

Illustrative Example 3.5

A uniform copper wire has a square cross-section of side 6 mm. The wire is 10 m long and carries a current of 3.6 A. Free electron density in conductor is 8.5×10^{28} per m^3. Find the current density in wire and time taken for an electron to travel the length of wire.

Solution

Cross sectional area of the wire can be calculated as

$$S = a^2 = (6 \times 10^{-3})^2$$

$$\Rightarrow \quad S = 36 \times 10^{-6}\ \text{m}^2$$

Current density in wire is given as

$$J = \frac{I}{S}$$

$$\Rightarrow \quad J = \frac{3.6}{36\times10^{-6}} = 10^5\ \text{A/m}^2$$

Average time taken by *the* free electron to travel along the length of the wire is

$$t = \frac{l}{v_d}$$

$$\Rightarrow \quad t = \frac{lne}{J}$$

$$\Rightarrow \quad t = \frac{10\times8.5\times10^{28}\times1.6\times10^{-19}}{10^5}$$

$$\Rightarrow \quad t = 13.6 \times 10^5\ \text{s}$$

Illustrative Example 3.6

How many electrons per second pass through a section of resistance of 20 Ω across which a potential difference of 64 V is applied.

Solution

Current in resistance is given by Ohm's law as

$$I = \frac{V}{R} = \frac{64}{20} = 3.2\text{ A}$$

Number of electrons passing through any section of resistance per second are given as

$$N = \frac{I}{e} = \frac{3.2}{1.6\times10^{-19}}$$

$$N = 2\times10^{-19}\text{ electrons/s}$$

Illustrative Example 3.7

1 m long metallic wire is broken into two unequal parts P and Q. P part of the wire is uniformly stretched into another wire R. Length of R is double that of P. Find the ratio of the resistances of P and R and also the ratio of length of P and Q.

Solution

If we consider length of P wire is l m then length of Q wire is $(1-l)$ m and length of R wire will be $2l$ m.

For wire P and R, the volume is same so we have

$$\pi r_P^2 ld = \pi r_R^2 2ld$$

$$\Rightarrow \quad r_P = \sqrt{2}r_R$$

If ρ be the resistivity of the material of the wire, then the resistance of wires P and R are given as

$$R_P = \frac{\rho l}{\pi r_P^2} \text{ and } R_R = \frac{\rho(2l)}{\pi r_R^2}$$

$$\Rightarrow \quad R_P : R_R = 1:4$$

Given that resistance of R and Q is same which are given as

$$R_R = \frac{\rho(2l)}{\pi r_R^2} \text{ and } R_Q = \frac{\rho(1-l)}{\pi r_Q^2}$$

As we have $R_R = R_Q$ we have

$$\frac{\rho(2l)}{\pi r_R^2} = \frac{\rho(1-l)}{\pi r_P^2}$$

$$\Rightarrow \quad (2l)r_P^2 = (1-l)r_R^2$$

$$\Rightarrow \quad 2l(\sqrt{2}r_R)^2 = (1-l)r_R^2$$

$$\Rightarrow \quad l = 1/5 = 0.2\text{ m}$$

$\Rightarrow$ length of $P = 0.2$ m

and length of $Q = 0.8$ m

Illustrative Example 3.8

The area of cross-section, length and density of a piece of a metal of atomic weight 60 are 10^{-6} m^2, 1.0 m and 5×10^3 kg/m^3 respectively. Find the number of free electrons per unit volume if every atom contributes one free electron. Also find the drift velocity of electrons in the metal when the current of 16A passes through it.

Solution

Mass of the metal is given as

$$m = \rho Sl$$

$$\Rightarrow \quad m = 5\times10^3\times10^{-6}\times1 = 5\times10^{-3}\text{ kg}$$

Number of atoms in 5×10^{-3} kg of metal are given as

$$N = \frac{5\times10^{-3}\times6.023\times10^{23}}{60\times10^{-3}} = 5.02\times10^{22}\text{ per m}^3$$

Thus number of free electrons per unit volume are given as

$$n = \frac{5\times10^{22}}{10^{-6}} = 5\times10^{28}\text{ per m}^3$$

Drift velocity of free electrons v_d is given as

$$v_d = \frac{I}{neS}$$

$$\Rightarrow \quad v_d = \frac{16}{(5\times10^{28})(1.6\times10^{-19})(10^{-6})}$$

$$\Rightarrow \quad v_d = 2\times10^{-3}\text{ m/s}$$

Web Reference at www.physicsgalaxy.com
Age Group - Grade 11 & 12 | Age 17-19 Years
Section - ELECTRIC CURRENT & CIRCUITS
Topic - Current Electricity
Module Number - 1 to 17

Practice Exercise 3.1

(i) A straight copper-wire of length 100 m and cross-sectional area 1.0 mm^2 carries a current 4.5 A. Assuming that one free electron corresponds to each copper atom, find

(a) The time it takes an electron to displace from one end of the wire to the other.

(b) The sum of electric forces acting on all free electrons in the given wire. Given resistivity of copper is 1.72×10^{-8} Ω-m and density of copper is 8.96 g/cm^3.

[(a) 3.043×10^5 s (b) 10.6 N]

(ii) Two cylindrical conductors with equal cross sections and different resistivities ρ_1 and ρ_2 are put end to end as shown in figure-3.11. Find the density of surface charges at the boundary of the conductors if a current I flows from conductor 1 to conductor 2.

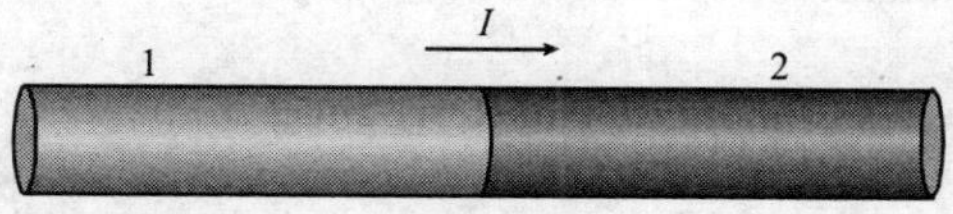

Figure 3.11

[$\epsilon_0 (\rho_2 - \rho_1) I$]

(iii) A copper wire carries a current of density 1.0 A/mm^2. Assuming that one free electron corresponds to each copper atom, evaluate the distance which will be covered by an electron during its displacement 10 mm along the wire.

[1.47×10^6 m]

(iv) In a long wire of square cross-section of side length l, current density varies with distance x from one edge of cross-section as

$$J = ae^{bx} \text{ A/m}^2$$

where a and b are positive constants. Find the current flowing in wire.

[$\frac{al}{b}[e^{bl} - 1]$]

(v) Figure-3.12 shows two plate electrodes 1 and 2 enclosed in a vacuum tube. A gas is ionised in the vicinity of the surface of the electrode 1 separated from electrode 2 by a distance l. An sinusoidal time varying voltage given as $V = V_0 \sin \omega t$ is applied to the electrodes. On decreasing the frequency ω it observed that the galvanometer G indicates a current only at $\omega < \omega_0$, where ω_0 is a certain cut-off frequency. Find the mobility of ions reaching electrode 2 under these conditions.

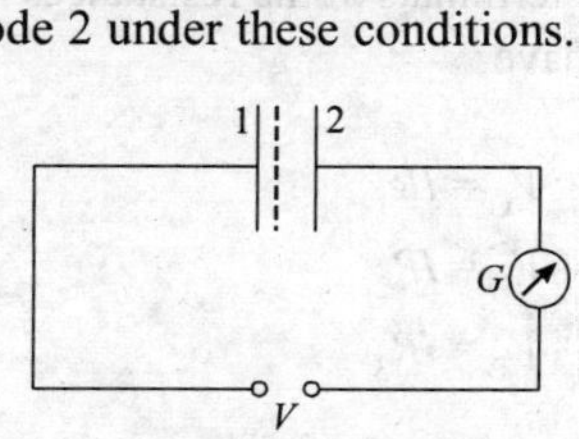

Figure 3.12

[$\frac{\omega_0 l^2}{2V_0}$]

(vi) A current of 16A is passed through a conductor in which concentration of electrons is 4×10^{28} m^{-3} and its cross-sectional area is 10^{-5} m^2. Find drift velocity of electrons in the conductor.

[2.5×10^{-4} m/s]

(vii) Consider a conductor of length 40 cm where a potential difference of 10 V is maintained between the ends of conductor. Find out mobility of electrons, if drift velocity is 5×10^{-6} m/s.

[2×10^{-7} m^2/V-s]

(viii) The air between two closely separated large plates in a sealed glass tube is uniformly ionised by ultraviolet radiation. The air volume between the plates is equal 500 cm^3, the observed saturation current is equal to 0.48 μA. Given that at saturation on an average ions take 1 s in travelling from one plate to another. Find :

(a) The equilibrium concentration of ions in saturation state.

(b) The production rate of ion pairs if the recombination coefficient for air ions is equal to $r = 1.67 \times 10^{-6}$ cm^3/s. Consider that the rate at which ion pairs recombine is given as rN^2 where N is the ion concentration.

[(a) 6×10^9 per cm^3, (b) 6.012×10^{12} per cm^3]

3.2 *Applications of Ohm's Law*

Figure-3.13 shows the circuit symbol of a resistance. If across terminals of this resistance A and B we apply a potential difference V then current flows in this resistance from high potential end to low potential end. If we consider V_A and V_B as potentials at terminals A and B then by Ohm's law we have

$$V = V_A - V_B = IR \quad \ldots(3.36)$$

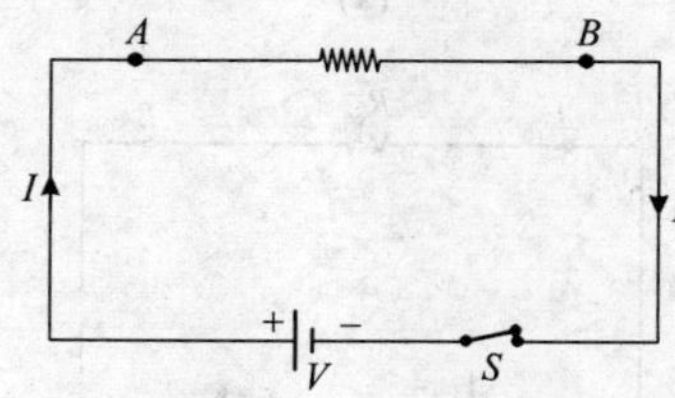

Figure 3.13

The potential difference across the resistance IR is also termed as '*Potential Drop*' across the resistance as if we move from terminal A to terminal B the potential decreases by IR. Here we generally say that along the direction of current in a circuit branch potential drops.

There are two forms in which Ohm's law is used in different ways in electrical circuits for which we rearrange equation-(3.36) as given below

$$V_A - IR = V_B \quad \ldots(3.37)$$

and
$$I = \frac{V_A - V_B}{R} \quad \ldots(3.38)$$

Above equation-(3.37) are used in a specific analysis of electrical circuits called '*Loop Analysis*' and equation-(3.38) is used in another analysis called '*Junction Analysis*' while solving electrical circuits. Above two equations are however same but still these are used in different ways of solving electrical circuits which we will understand in upcoming articles.

3.2.1 Grouping of Resistances and Equivalent Resistance

Two or more resistances can be connected in different combinations which is called '*Grouping of Resistances*'. There are several ways to connected resistances in groups but most common ways are '*Series Combination*' and '*Parallel Combination*'.

When a group of resistances is replaced by a single resistance such that all the electrical properties of the group and this single resistance are same in a circuit then this single resistance is called '*Equivalent Resistance*' of the group of resistances.

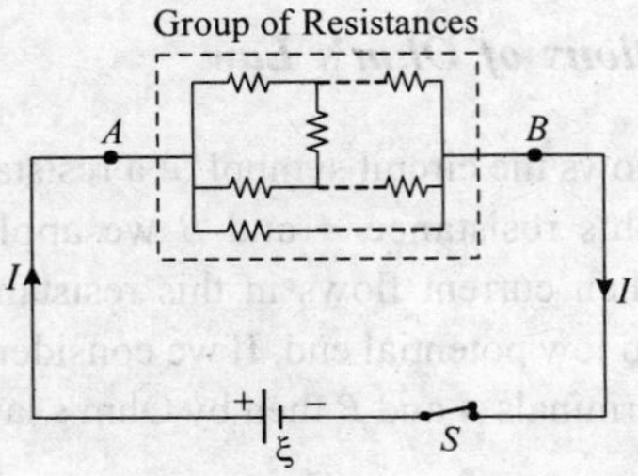

(a)

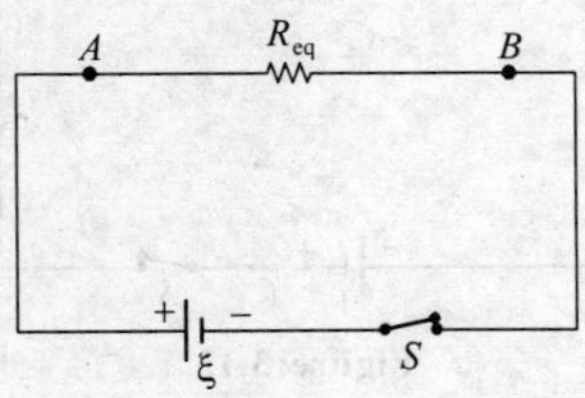

(b)

Figure 3.14

Figure-3.14(a) shows a group of resistances and the terminals of group A and B are connected to a battery of voltage ξ as shown. If the whole group is replaced by a single equivalent resistance R_{eq} as shown in figure-3.14(b) then the current through the battery can be given as

$$I = \frac{\xi}{R_{eq}}$$

$$\Rightarrow \quad R_{eq} = \frac{\xi}{I} = \frac{\text{Potential Difference across the Combination}}{\text{Current Flowing through the Combination}} \quad \ldots(3.39)$$

For any combination of resistances we can use above equation to determine the equivalent resistance of the circuit across given terminals. In upcoming illustrations we will discuss the applications of this expression. Now we will first cover the standard combination of resistors in series and parallel Combinations.

3.2.2 Series Combination of Resistances

When resistances are connected in such a manner that one terminal of one resistance kept open and other terminal of this resistance is connected to one terminal of another resistance and further any number of resistances can be connected as shown in figure-3.15. In this figure all the resistances R_1, R_2 and R_3 are considered to be connected in series combination.

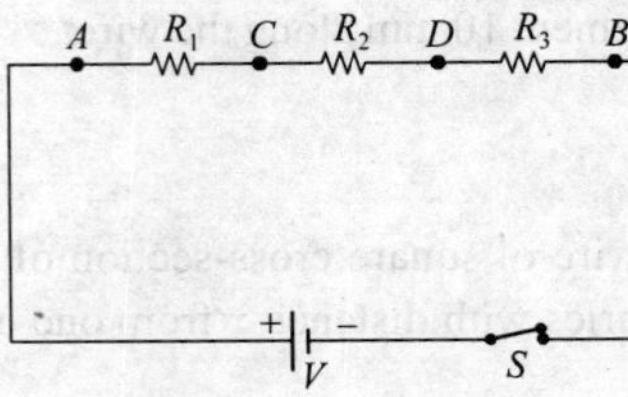

Figure 3.15

To find the equivalent resistance of series combination of these three resistances across terminals A and B, we connect a battery of voltage V across these terminals as shown in figure-3.15. Due to potential difference applied by the battery a current I flows through the circuit as shown. As the resistances are connected one after another, same current I flows through the same branch.

Here we can state that in a circuit if some resistances are connected in series combination then current through all the resistances in that branch of circuit will remain same. Using Ohm's law for the terminals of the resistances in circuit shown in figure-3.15 we have

$$V_A - V_C = IR_1 \quad \ldots(3.40)$$

$$V_C - V_D = IR_2 \quad \ldots(3.41)$$

$$V_D - V_B = IR_3 \quad \ldots(3.42)$$

Adding above three equations, we get

$$V_A - V_B = I(R_1 + R_2 + R_3) \quad \ldots(3.43)$$

If the three resistances used in circuit shown in figure-3.15 are replaced by a single equivalent resistance R_{eq} as shown in figure-3.16 then using Ohm's law for this circuit, we have

$$V_A - V_B = IR_{eq} \quad \ldots(3.44)$$

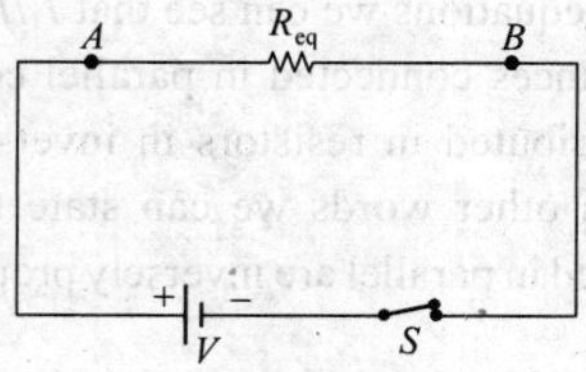

Figure 3.16

Comparing equation-(3.43) and (3.44) we get

$$R_{eq} = R_1 + R_2 + R_3 \quad \ldots(3.45)$$

Equation-(3.45) shows that the equivalent resistance of two or more resistors connected in series is given by the sum of all the resistances.

3.2.3 Parallel Combination of Resistances

Figure-3.17 shows three resistances connected in parallel combination. In parallel combination both terminals of all resistors are to be connected together as shown at terminals *A* and *B* of the group which is connected across a battery of voltage *V*.

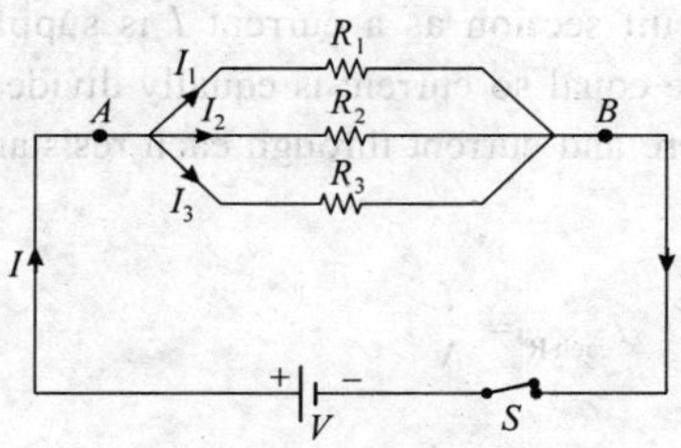

Figure 3.17

As the potential difference across terminals *A* and *B* is *V* same potential difference will be maintained across all the resistances connected in parallel across terminals *A* and *B*. In this case if I_1, I_2 and I_3 are the currents through the three resistances as shown then by Ohm's law we have

$$I_1 = \frac{V_A - V_B}{R_1} \quad \ldots(3.46)$$

$$I_2 = \frac{V_A - V_B}{R_2} \quad \ldots(3.47)$$

$$I_3 = \frac{V_A - V_B}{R_3} \quad \ldots(3.48)$$

Total current through battery can be calculated by adding the above three equations as

$$I = I_1 + I_2 + I_3$$

$$\Rightarrow \quad I = (V_A - V_B)\left(\frac{1}{R_1} + \frac{1}{R_2} + \frac{1}{R_3}\right) \quad \ldots(3.49)$$

If the group of the three resistances across *A* and *B* is replaced by a single resistance R_{eq} as shown in figure-3.18 then by Ohm's law we have

$$V_A - V_B = IR_{eq} \quad \ldots(3.50)$$

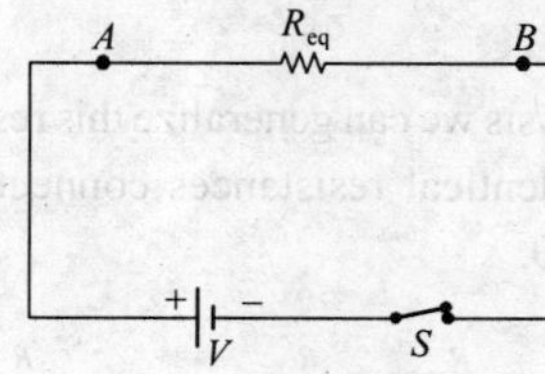

Figure 3.18

Comparing equations-(3.49) and (3.50) we get

$$\frac{1}{R_{eq}} = \frac{1}{R_1} + \frac{1}{R_2} + \frac{1}{R_3} \quad \ldots(3.51)$$

Equation-(3.51) shows that the equivalent resistance of two or more resistances connected in parallel is given by reciprocal of the sum of reciprocals of all the resistances.

3.2.4 Distribution of Potential Difference in Series Combination of Resistances

Figure-3.19 shows two resistances in series combination connected across a battery of voltage *V*. In this case the potential difference *V* is distributed across the two resistances such that sum of potential differences V_1 and V_2 across R_1 and R_2 is equal to *V*. The current through battery can be given by Ohm's law as

$$I = \frac{V}{R_{eq}} = \frac{V}{R_1 + R_2} \quad \ldots(3.52)$$

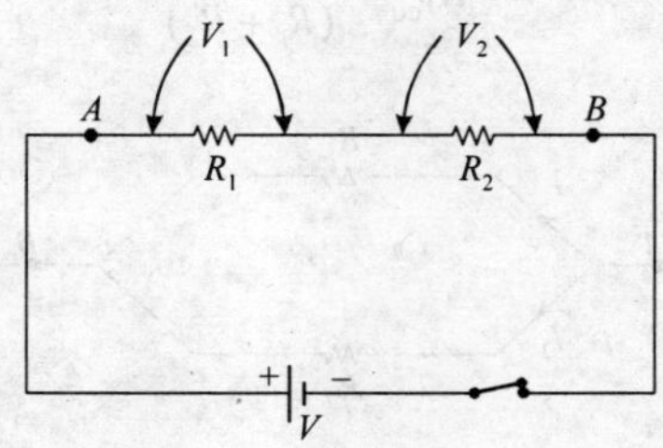

Figure 3.19

As current in the two resistances is same as they are in series the potential differences across R_1 and R_2 are given as

$$V_1 = IR_1 = \frac{VR_1}{R_1 + R_2} \quad \ldots(3.53)$$

and

$$V_2 = IR_2 = \frac{VR_2}{R_1 + R_2} \quad \ldots(3.54)$$

From above two equations we can see that $V_1/V_2 = R_1/R_2$ hence in case of resistors connected in series combination the potential differences across the resistances are distributed in same ratio of their resistances or in other words we can state that potential difference across the resistors in series are proportional to their resistances.

With the above analysis we can generalize this result for potential distribution in N identical resistances connected in series as shown in figure-3.20.

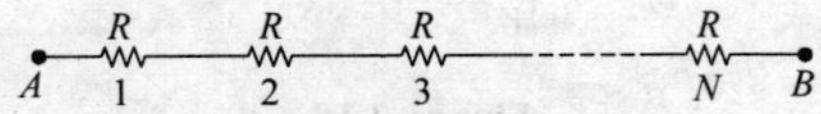

Figure 3.20

If in above circuit section, the potential difference across terminals A and B is V then we can say that potential difference across all the resistors will be same and equally distributed and will be given as

$$V_{\text{each R}} = \frac{V}{N} \qquad \ldots(3.55)$$

3.2.5 Distribution of Currents in Parallel Combination of Resistances

Figure-3.21 shows a part of circuit in which two resistances are connected in parallel combination and current flowing in this part of circuit is I. In this case the potential difference across the combination can be obtained by using the equivalent resistance of the two resistors as $R_{eq} = R_1R_2/(R_1 + R_2)$ which is given as

$$V = IR_{eq} = \frac{IR_1R_2}{(R_1 + R_2)} \qquad \ldots(3.56)$$

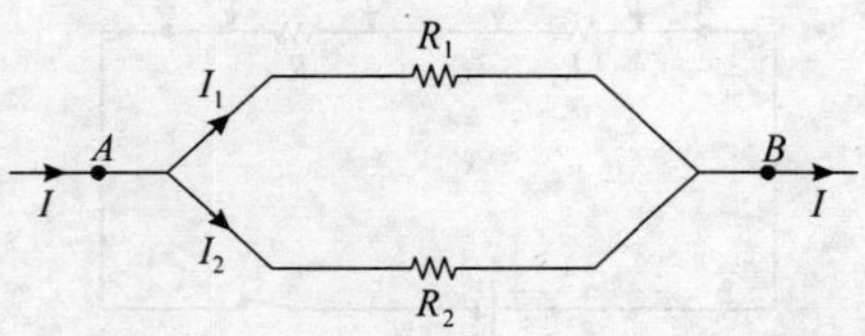

Figure 3.21

The current in main branch is divided in the two resistances which can be obtained by using same potential difference across the two resistors as

$$I_1 = \frac{V}{R_1} = \frac{IR_2}{R_1 + R_2} \qquad \ldots(3.57)$$

and

$$I_2 = \frac{V}{R_2} = \frac{IR_1}{R_1 + R_2} \qquad \ldots(3.58)$$

From above two equations we can see that $I_1/I_2 = R_2/R_1$ hence in case of resistances connected in parallel combination, the currents are distributed in resistors in inverse ratio of their resistances or in other words we can state that currents in resistors connected in parallel are inversely proportional to their resistances.

With the above analysis we can generalize the result for current distribution in N identical resistors connected in parallel as shown in figure-3.22.

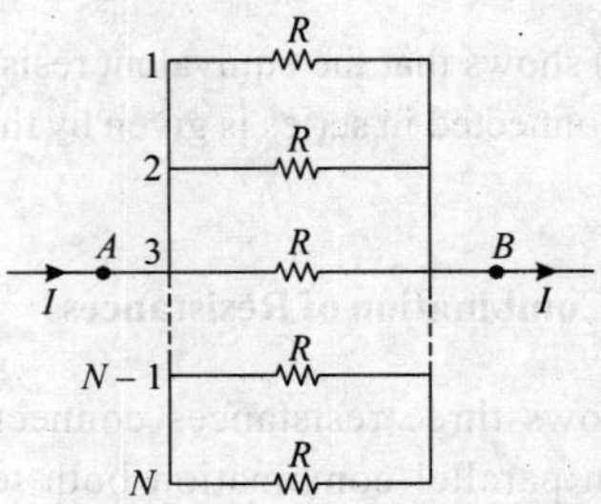

Figure 3.22

In above circuit section as a current I is supplied and all resistances are equal so current is equally divided among all resistances here and current through each resistance is given as

$$I_{\text{each R}} = \frac{I}{N} \qquad \ldots(3.59)$$

3.2.6 Solving Electrical Circuits using Series and Parallel Combination Method

Solving an electrical circuit is determining all the circuit parameters of that circuit like current in all branches, potential difference across any points of the circuit and equivalent resistance of a given group of resistances.

For a given circuit in form of group of resistances connected across a battery, we first find the equivalent resistance of the given group and then distribute currents and potential differences in parallel and series combinations like we've discussed in previous article. We can understand this with the help of an illustration.

Figure-3.23 shows a simple circuit containing three resistances connected across a battery. In this circuit we will determine the equivalent resistance across the terminals A and B, current in each branch of circuit and potential difference across each resistor of the circuit.

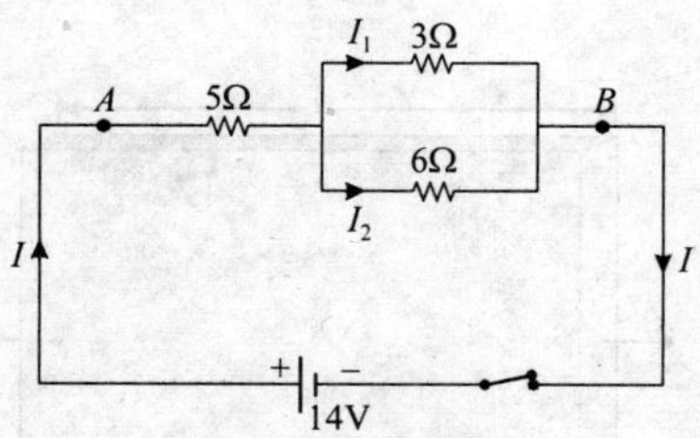

Figure 3.23

In this circuit we can see that 3 Ω and 6 Ω resistances are connected in parallel and this short group is connected in series with 5 Ω resistance. Thus equivalent resistance across terminals *A* and *B* can be given as

$$R_{AB} = \left(5 + \frac{3\times 6}{3+6}\right)\Omega$$

$$\Rightarrow \qquad R_{AB} = (5+2) = 7\Omega$$

Thus current supplied by the battery is given as

$$I = \frac{V}{R_{AB}} = \frac{14}{7} = 2\,\text{A}$$

Through the 5 Ω resistance same current 2 A will pass then it will divide in inverse ratio between 3 Ω and 6 Ω resistances which can be given by equations-(3.57) and (3.58) as

$$I_{3\Omega} = \frac{2\times 6}{3+6} = \frac{4}{3} = 1.33\,\text{A}$$

and $$I_{6\Omega} = \frac{2\times 3}{3+6} = \frac{2}{3} = 0.66\,\text{A}$$

As currents in all branches of the circuit as now known, by using Ohm's law we can calculate the potential differences. The potential difference across 5 Ω resistance is given as

$$V_{5\Omega} = IR_{5\Omega} = 2\times 5 = 10\,\text{V}$$

As 3 Ω and 6 Ω resistances are in connected in parallel their potential difference is same and it can be directly calculated as the current 2 A is flowing through their equivalent 2Ω resistance which can be given by Ohm's law as

$$V_{3\Omega} = V_{6\Omega} = IR_{3\Omega\|6\Omega} = 2\times 2 = 4\,\text{V}$$

Now for solving different types of electrical circuits using series and parallel method we will take up some illustrations to understand the analysis.

3.2.7 Resistance Calculation by Variation of Parameters

For a uniform conductor of length *l* and cross sectional area *S* with resistivity ρ, we've studied that its resistance is given as

$$R = \frac{\rho l}{S} \qquad \ldots(3.60)$$

Above expression given in equation-(3.60) is used to calculate the resistance of a uniform conductor. If any of the parameters resistivity, length of cross section varies in a conductor then this relation cannot be used. Now we consider and analyze two cases of variation of parameters in a conductor similar to the two cases we discussed in article-2.9.4 for capacitance calculations. These cases we will discuss with illustrations to understand the application of the is concept in different situations.

Case-I : Variation of parameters along the Cross Section of the Conductor

Consider a conductor in shape of a cuboid having its cross sectional area $A = bw$ and length *l* as shown in figure-3.24(a) of which the resistivity varies with distance along the cross sectional area according to the below given relation.

$$\rho = ax + c \qquad \ldots(3.61)$$

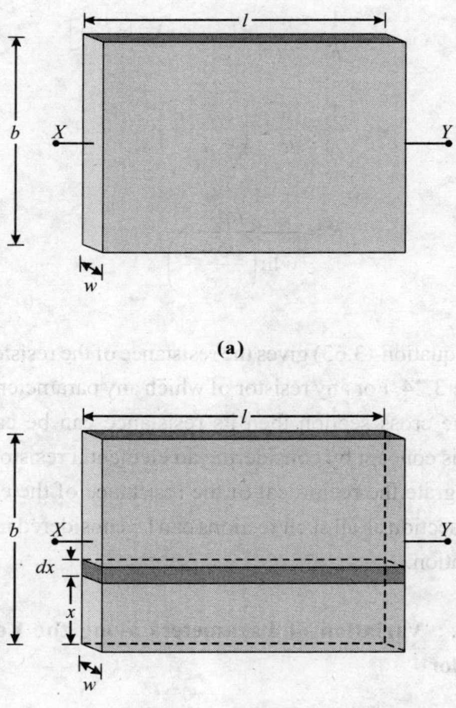

(b)

Figure 3.24

To determine the resistance of this resistor we consider an elemental resistor section of width *dx* as shown in figure-3.24(b).

In such a small section of width dx we can consider that the resistivity does not vary and given by equation-(3.61). The resistance of this elemental resistor section is given as

$$dR = \frac{\rho l}{w dx} \quad \ldots(3.62)$$

All such elemental sections connected between left and right cross sections of the conductor to terminals X and Y and we can consider all such elemental resistor sections can be considered in parallel combination thus overall resistance of this resistor can be given by reciprocal of the summing up reciprocal of all such elemental resistances which can be given as

$$\frac{1}{R} = \int \frac{1}{dR} = \int_0^b \frac{w dx}{\rho l}$$

$$\Rightarrow \quad \frac{1}{R} = \frac{w}{l} \int_0^b \frac{dx}{(ax+c)}$$

$$\Rightarrow \quad \frac{1}{R} = \frac{w}{la} \left[\ln(ax+c) \right]_0^b$$

$$\Rightarrow \quad \frac{1}{R} = \frac{w}{la} \left[\ln(ab+c) - \ln(c) \right]$$

$$\Rightarrow \quad \frac{1}{R} = \frac{w}{la} \ln\left(\frac{ab+c}{c}\right)$$

$$\Rightarrow \quad R = \frac{la}{w \ln\left(\frac{ab+c}{c}\right)} \quad \ldots(3.63)$$

Above equation-(3.63) gives the resistance of the resistor shown in figure-3.24. For any resistor of which any parameter if varies along the cross section then its resistance can be calculated using this concept by considering an elemental resistor section and integrate the reciprocal of the resistance of the elemental resistor section as all such sections can be considered in parallel combination.

Case-II : Variation of Parameters along the Length of Conductor

Consider a conductor of cross sectional area $A = wb$ and length l as shown in figure-3.25(a) of which the resistivity varies along the length of conductor according to the below given relation.

$$\rho = ax + c \quad \ldots(3.64)$$

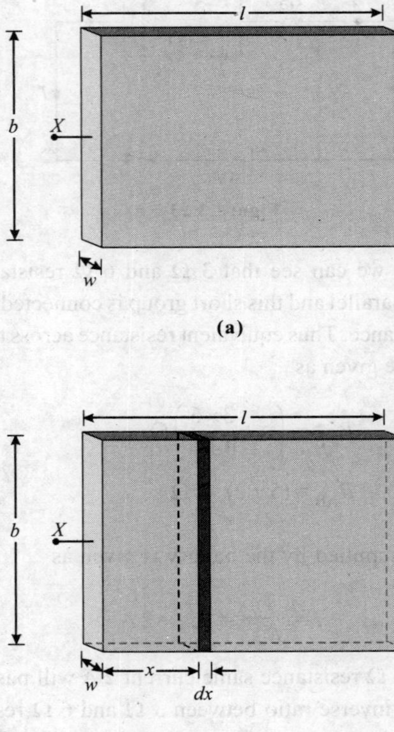

Figure 2.25

To determine the resistance of this resistor we consider an elemental resistor section as shown in figure-3.25(b) of which the cross sectional area is considered same as that of conductor but having length dx as shown. In such a small section of width dx we can consider that the resistivity does not vary and given by equation-(3.64). The resistance of this elemental resistor section is given as

$$dR = \frac{\rho dx}{A} \quad \ldots(3.65)$$

If we consider several such elemental resistor sections in between the length of conductor then all such elemental sections can be considered in series combination between the left and right sides of conductors thus overall resistance of this conductor can be given by summing up resistances of all such elemental sections which can be given as

$$R = \int dR = \int_0^l \frac{\rho dx}{A}$$

$$\Rightarrow \quad R = \frac{1}{A} \int_0^l (ax+c) dx$$

$$\Rightarrow \quad R = \frac{1}{A} \left[a\frac{x^2}{2} + cx \right]_0^l$$

$$\Rightarrow \quad R = \frac{1}{A}\left[\left(a\frac{l^2}{2} + cl\right) - (0-0)\right]$$

$$\Rightarrow \quad R = \frac{1}{A}\left(a\frac{l^2}{2} + cl\right) \quad \ldots(3.66)$$

Above equation-(3.66) gives the resistance of the resistor shown in figure-3.25. For any conductor of which any parameter if varies along the length of the plates then its resistance can be calculated using this concept by considering elemental sections of resistors and integrate the resistance of the elemental sections as all such sections can be considered in series combination.

3.2.8 Resistance of a Spherical Shell for Radial Current Flow by Concept of Variation of Parameters

Figure-3.26(a) shows a conducting spherical shell with inner and outer radii of shell a and b respectively. If we connect a battery of voltage V across inner and outer surface of this shell then a radial current flows through the cross section of the shell as shown in figure-3.26(b). In this situation the length of conductor through which current flows is $(b - a)$ but the cross section varies from inner surface of area $4\pi a^2$ to the outer surface of area $4\pi b^2$ in this case the current through battery can be given as

$$I = \frac{V}{R_{shell}} \quad \ldots(3.67)$$

In above equation R_{shell} is the resistance of the shell between inner and outer surface along for radial flow of current.

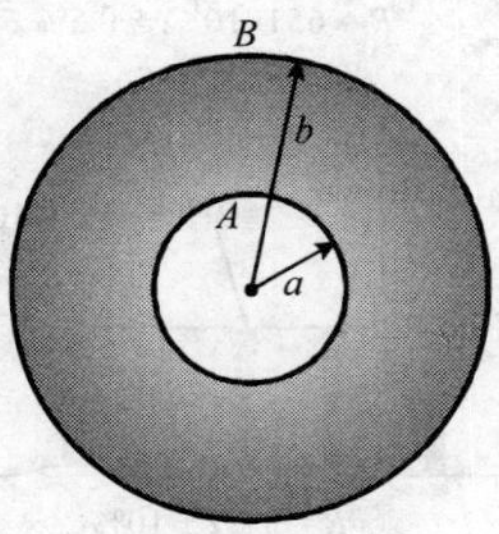

(a)

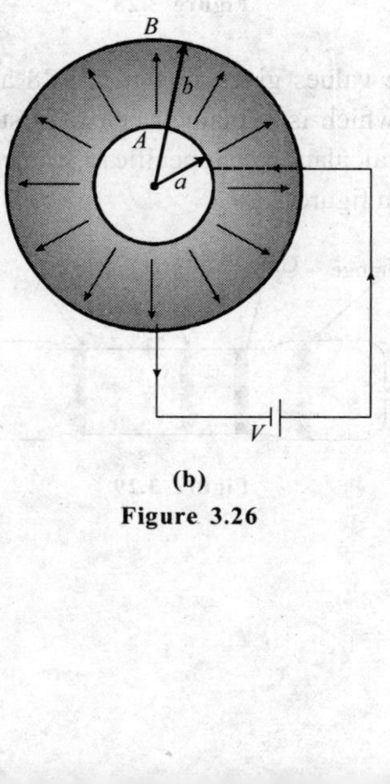

(b)

Figure 3.26

To calculate the resistance of this spherical shell along radial direction we consider an elemental resistor section of radius x and width dx as shown in figure-3.27.

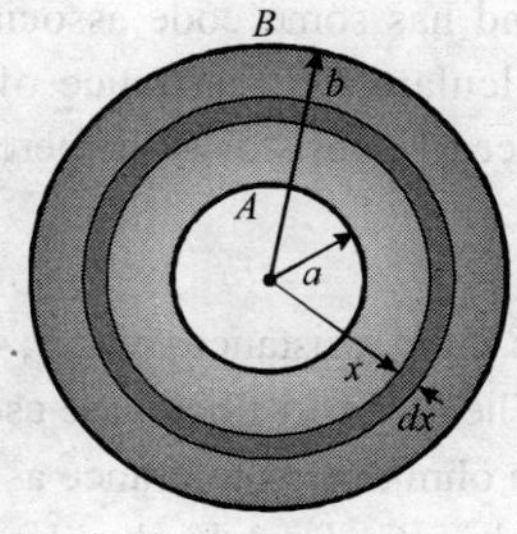

Figure 3.27

If we carefully analyse this situation then we can consider the above conducting shell as series combination of several such elemental resistor sections from radii a to b. For this elemental resistor section cross section area is $4\pi x^2$ and dx is the length through which current flows. If ρ is the resistivity of the metal of shell then the resistance of this elemental resistor section can be given as

$$dR = \frac{\rho dx}{4\pi x^2} \quad \ldots(3.68)$$

The resistance of this shell can be calculated by integrating the resistance of the elemental resistor section as given in equation-(3.68) as all such elemental resistors are considered in series from inner radius a to outer radius b which is given as

$$R = \int dR = \int_a^b \frac{\rho dx}{4\pi x^2}$$

$$\Rightarrow \quad R = \frac{\rho}{4\pi}\int_a^b \frac{dx}{x^2}$$

$$\Rightarrow \quad R = \frac{\rho}{4\pi}\left[-\frac{1}{x}\right]_a^b$$

$$\Rightarrow \quad R = \frac{\rho}{4\pi}\left[\frac{1}{b} - \frac{1}{a}\right] \quad \ldots(3.69)$$

Expression in above equation-(3.69) can be used in equation-(3.67) to determine the current flowing through the battery and along radial direction in the metal of the shell.

3.2.9 Colour Coding and Tolerances for Resistances

In different electrical and electronic circuits there are variety of resistors used having different values of resistances in different AC and DC circuit applications. Infact there are millions of different resistance values which are used in different circuit applications. When body of resistor is large then its value with tolerance can be printed over its body but with more technological advancements small sized devices are more preferred. In such case of a small sized body the resistance value and its tolerance is marked with coloured ink bands where each coloured band has some code associated with it using which we can calculate the resistance of the resistor and tolerance. Tolerance of a resistor is the percentage error in its measured value.

Figure-3.28 shows some resistances with 3,4 or 5 bands on the body of resistor. The colours of band are used to calculate the resistance value in ohm and its tolerance as well by a specific method called '*Colour Coding*'. Each color is given a specific number, a multiplier and a tolerance associated with it which are given in the table given below.

Table-3.1

	Color	Color Code	Multiplier	Tolerance (%)
B	black	0	× 1	
B	brown	1	× 10	1
R	red	2	× 100	2
O	orange	3	× 1K	
Y	yellow	4	× 10K	
G	green	5	× 100K	0.5
B	blue	6	× 1M	0.25
V	violet	7	× 10M	0.1
G	grey	8	× 100M	0.05
W	white	9	× 1G	
G	gold		× 0.1	5
S	silver		× 0.01	10
	none			20

For students its better to remember the sequence '*BBROYGBVGW*' in order of ascending color code numbers 1 to 9 which given to the colours. There are some mnemonics to remember the sequence, whichever students like they can use to remember the sequence. Some of these are -

'**BB ROY** of **G**reat **B**ritain has a **V**ery **G**ood **W**ife'

'**B**right **B**oys **R**ace **O**ver **Y**oung **G**irls **B**ut **V**iolet **G**enerally **W**ins'

'**B**etter **B**e **R**eady **O**r **Y**our **G**reat **B**ig plan **V**iolently **G**oes **W**rong'

Students can also make their own in whichever way they are able to remember the sequence easily. Next we will discuss how to use these colour codes and multipliers to calculate the resistance values.

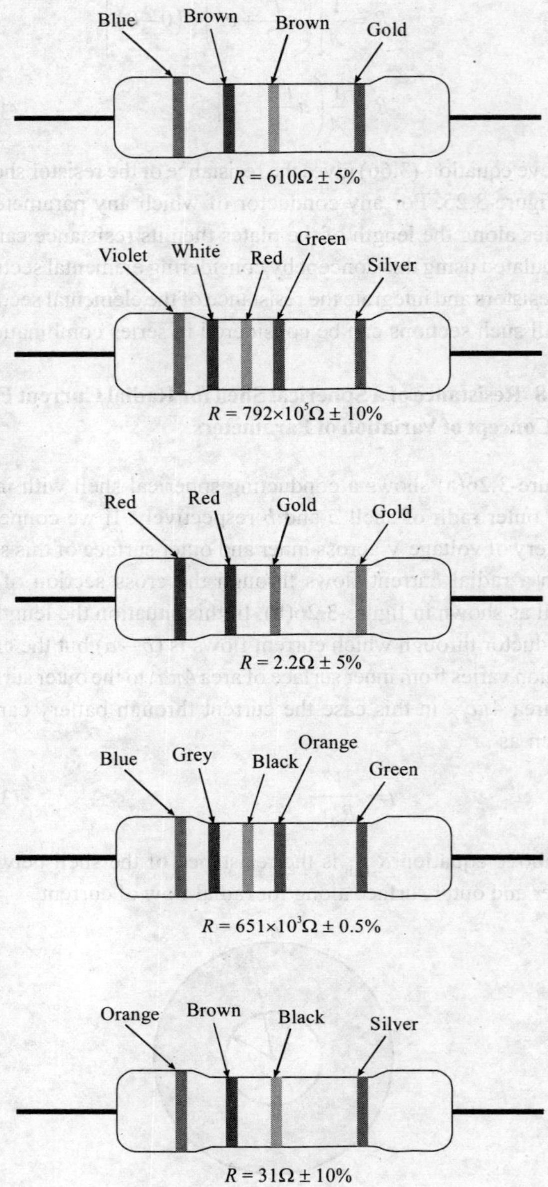

Figure 3.28

The resistance values given in figure-3.28 are calculated by color coding which is explained below in steps. We take an illustration of calculation of a specific resistance with 4 coloured bands shown in figure-3.29.

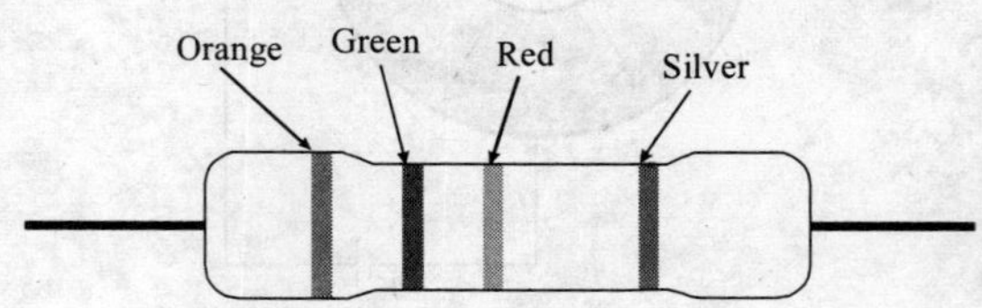

Figure 3.29

Step-I : Always place the resistor in front of you such that there is a gap between the last and second last resistor as shown in figure-3.29. In this position we start reading the resistance value from left to right. The last band indicates the tolerance of resistor as per the values given in above table-3.1. In this case it is 10%.

Step-II : Write the value of color codes from left bands with the last band before tolerance band as multiplier value as given in above table-3.1. According to the table the color codes for orange color is 3 and that for green colour is 5 and the last band before tolerance band is of red colour for which multiplier is 10^2 thus this resistance value is given as

$$R = 35 \times 10^2\,\Omega \pm 10\%$$

With the above method you can check the values of all the resistances given in figure-3.602. Only thing to be taken care while using colour coding is to identify the multiplier band which is the band immediate left to the tolerance band which is kept on right and always there is a relatively large gap between tolerance band and multiplier band.

 # Illustrative Example 3.9

Find equivalent resistance across terminals *A* and *B* in the circuit shown in figure-3.30.

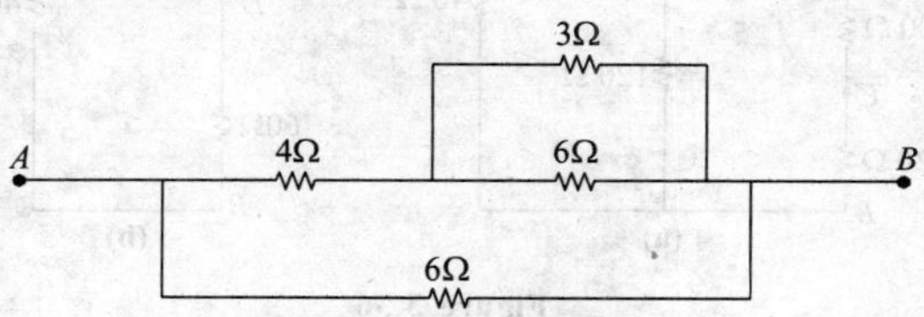

Figure 3.30

Solution

The equivalent resistance can be found by reducing the circuit by series and parallel combination of resistances step by step as shown in figure-3.31.

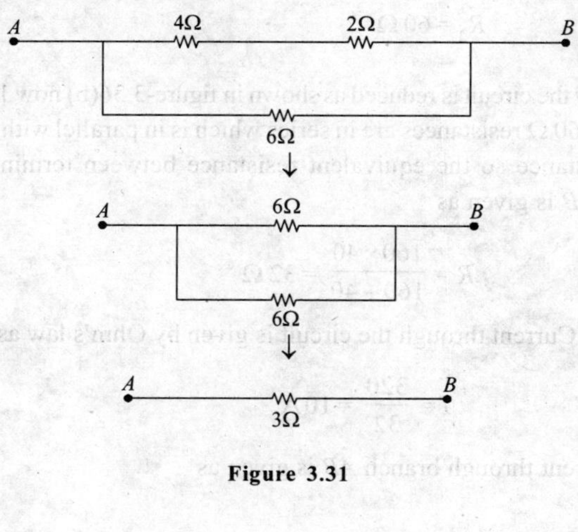

Figure 3.31

 # Illustrative Example 3.10

Find equivalent resistance of the circuit shown in figure-3.32 across terminals *A* and *B*.

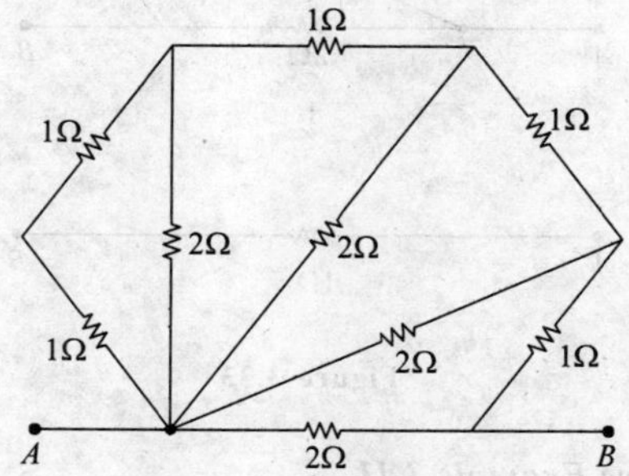

Figure 3.32

Solution

Equivalent resistance can be found by reducing the above circuit by series and parallel combinations as shown in figure-3.33 next.

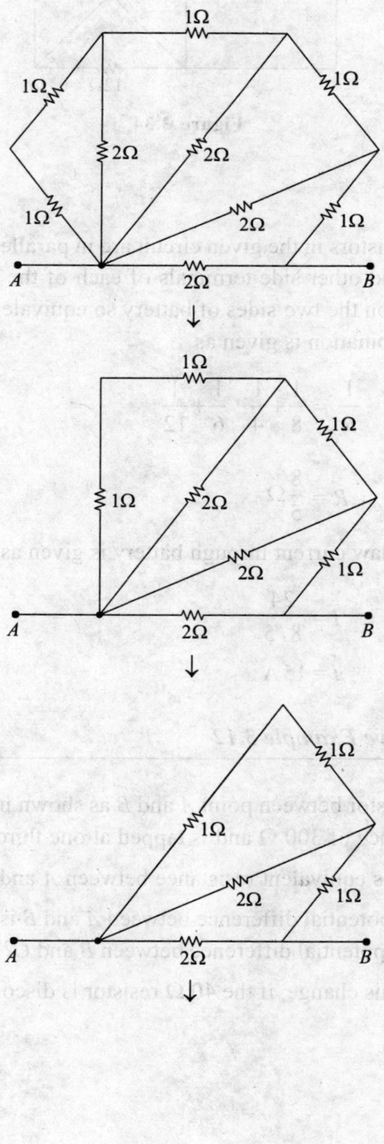

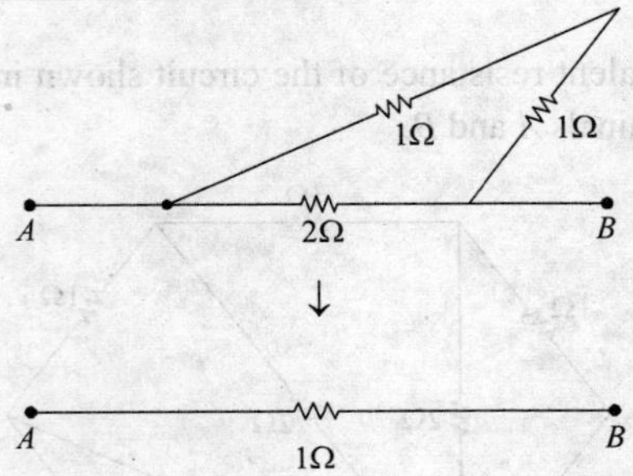

Figure 3.33

Illustrative Example 3.11

Calculate battery current and equivalent resistance of the network shown in figure-3.34.

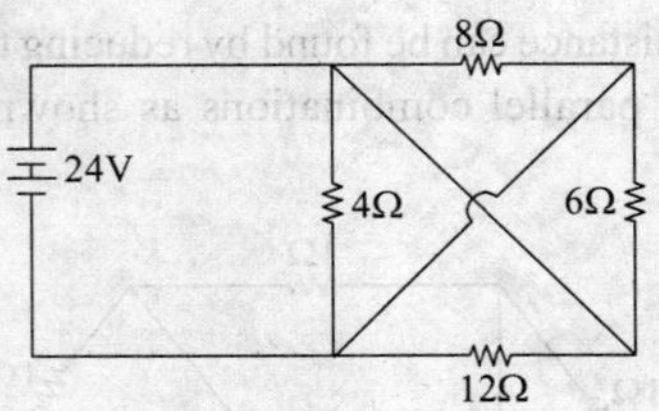

Figure 3.34

Solution

All four resistors in the given circuit are in parallel because all one side and other side terminals of each of the resistors are connected on the two sides of battery so equivalent resistance of the combination is given as

$$\frac{1}{R}=\frac{1}{8}+\frac{1}{4}+\frac{1}{6}+\frac{1}{12}$$

$$\Rightarrow \qquad R=\frac{8}{5}\Omega$$

By Ohm's law current through battery is given as

$$I=\frac{24}{8/5}$$

$$\Rightarrow \qquad I=15\,\text{A}$$

Illustrative Example 3.12

A long resistor between point A and B as shown in figure-3.35 has resistance of 300 Ω and is tapped at one third points.

(a) What is equivalent resistance between A and B

(b) If the potential difference between A and B is 320 V, what will be the potential difference between B and C?

(c) Will this change, if the 40 Ω resistor is disconnected ?

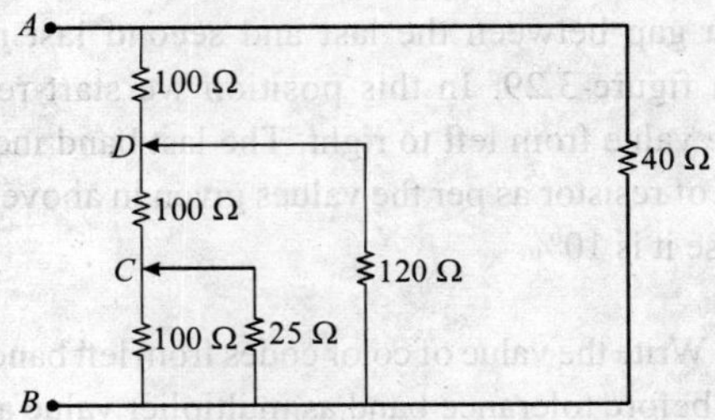

Figure 3.35

Solution

(a) In the circuit the resistance 25 Ω is in parallel to 100 Ω resistance, thus equivalent resistance of these two resistances is given as

$$\frac{1}{R_1}=\frac{1}{100}+\frac{1}{25}=\frac{1+4}{100}=\frac{5}{100}=\frac{1}{20}$$

$$\Rightarrow \qquad R_1=20\,\Omega$$

Now the circuit is reduced as shown in figure-3.36(a).

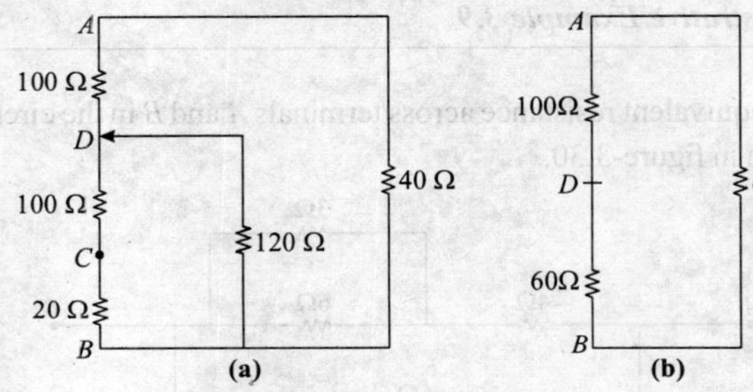

Figure 3.36

From above figure we can see that resistance 20 Ω and 100 Ω are in series and in parallel with 120 Ω. So the equivalent resistance is given as

$$\frac{1}{R_2}=\frac{1}{120}+\frac{1}{120}=\frac{2}{120}$$

$$\Rightarrow \qquad R_2=60\,\Omega$$

Now the circuit is reduced as shown in figure-3.36(b) now 100 Ω and 60 Ω resistances are in series which is in parallel with 40 Ω resistance so the equivalent resistance between terminals A and B is given as

$$R=\frac{160\times 40}{160+40}=32\,\Omega$$

(b) Current through the circuit is given by Ohm's law as

$$I=\frac{320}{32}=10\,\text{A}$$

Current through branch AB is given as

$$I_1 = \frac{40}{200} \times 10 = 2\text{ A}$$

Current through branch *DB* is given as

$$I_2 = \frac{120}{240} \times 2 = 1\text{ A}$$

Potential difference across points *BC* is given as

$$V_{BC} = 1 \times 20 = 20\text{ V}$$

(c) When 40 Ω resistor is disconnected, then equivalent resistance will be 160 Ω and current through point *A* can be given as

$$I = \frac{320}{160} = 2\text{ A}$$

Thus current through branch *DB* is 1 A

and potential difference across *BC* is given as 1 × 20 = 20 V

Illustrative Example 3.13

You need to produce a set of cylindrical copper wires 3.50 m long that will have a resistance of 0.125 Ω each. What will be the mass of each of these wires? Given that resistivity of copper is 1.72×10^{-8} Ω-m, density of copper = 8.9×10^3 kg/m³.

Solution

Resistance of conductor is given as

$$R = \frac{\rho l}{A}$$

$$\Rightarrow \quad A = \frac{\rho l}{R}$$

If *V* is the volume of conductor and *d* is its density then mass of the conductor is given as

$$m = (Vd)$$

$$\Rightarrow \quad m = (Ald)$$

$$\Rightarrow \quad m = \frac{\rho l^2}{R} d$$

$$\Rightarrow \quad m = \frac{(1.72 \times 10^{-8})(3.5)^2 (8.9 \times 10^3)}{0.125}$$

$$\Rightarrow \quad m = 15 \times 10^{-3}\text{ kg}$$

$$\Rightarrow \quad m = 15\text{ g}$$

Illustrative Example 3.14

Two resistors with temperature coefficients of resistance α_1 and α_2 have resistances R_{01} and R_{02} at 0°C. Find the temperature coefficient of the compound resistor consisting of the two resistors connected,

(a) in series and

(b) in parallel

Solution

In Series combination at a higher temperature *t*°C if the equivalent temperature coefficient of resistance is α_s then we can write

$$R_{01}(1 + \alpha_1 t) + R_{02}(1 + \alpha_2 t) = R_0(1 + \alpha_s t)$$

$$\Rightarrow \quad R_{01}(1 + \alpha_1 t) + R_{02}(1 + \alpha_2 t) = (R_{01} + R_{02})(1 + \alpha_s t)$$

$$\Rightarrow \quad R_{01} + R_{01}\alpha_1 t + R_{02} + R_{02}\alpha_2 t = R_{01} + R_{02} + (R_{01} + R_{02})\alpha_s t$$

$$\Rightarrow \quad \alpha_s = \frac{R_{01}\alpha_1 + R_{02}\alpha_2}{R_{01} + R_{02}}$$

In Parallel combination at a higher temperature *t*°C if the equivalent temperature coefficient of resistance is α_p then we can write

$$\frac{1}{R_0(1 + \alpha_p t)} = \frac{1}{R_{01}(1 + \alpha_1 t)} + \frac{1}{R_{02}(1 + \alpha_2 t)}$$

$$\Rightarrow \quad \frac{R_{01} + R_{02}}{R_{01}R_{02}(1 + \alpha_p t)} = \frac{1}{R_{01}(1 + \alpha_1 t)} + \frac{1}{R_{02}(1 + \alpha_2 t)}$$

Using the Binomial approximation, we have

$$\frac{1}{R_{02}}(1 - \alpha_p t) + \frac{1}{R_{01}}(1 - \alpha_p t) = \frac{1}{R_{01}}(1 - \alpha_1 t) + \frac{1}{R_{02}}(1 - \alpha_2 t)$$

$$\Rightarrow \quad \alpha_p t\left(\frac{1}{R_{01}} + \frac{1}{R_{02}}\right) = \frac{\alpha_1}{R_{01}} t + \frac{\alpha_2}{R_{02}} t$$

$$\Rightarrow \quad \alpha_p = \frac{\alpha_1 R_{02} + \alpha_2 R_{01}}{R_{01} + R_{02}}$$

Illustrative Example 3.15

Two resistance coils connected in series have resistance of 600 Ω and 300 Ω at 20°C and temperature co-efficient of resistances are 0.001°C⁻¹ and 0.004°C⁻¹ respectively. Find resistance of the combination at a temperature of 50°C. What is the effective temperature co-efficient of combination?

Solution

In series combination the equivalent temperature coefficient of resistance is given as

$$\alpha_{eq} = \frac{R_{01}\alpha_1 + R_{02}\alpha_2}{R_{01} + R_{02}}$$

$$\Rightarrow \qquad \alpha_{eq} = \frac{(600)(0.001)+(300)(0.004)}{600+300}$$

$$\Rightarrow \qquad \alpha_{eq} = 0.002\ °C^{-1}$$

Resistance of the combination at higher temperature can be given by using the equivalent temperature coefficient of resistance as

$$R_t = R_0[1+\alpha\Delta\theta]$$

$$\Rightarrow \qquad R_t = (600+300)[1+0.002\times 30] = 954\ \Omega$$

Illustrative Example 3.16

Figure-3.37 shows a conductor of length l carrying current I and having a circular cross-section. The radius of cross section varies linearly from a to b. Assuming that $(b-a) << l$. Calculate current density at distance x from left end.

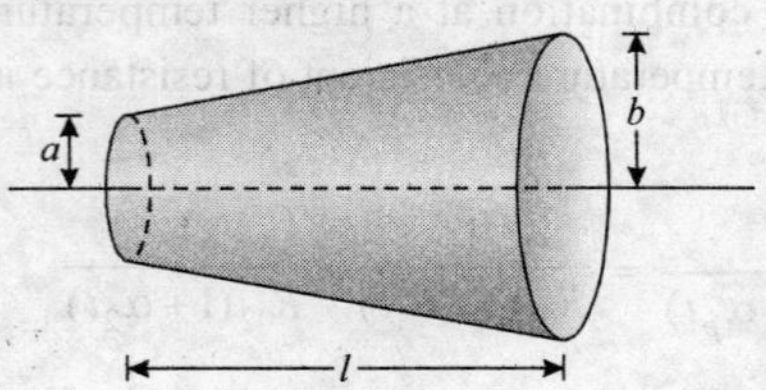

Figure 3.37

Solution

Since radius at left end is a and that of right end is b, therefore increase in radius over length l is $(b-a)$.

Hence rate of increase of radius per unit length $= \left(\frac{b-a}{l}\right)$.

Increase in radius over length $x = \left(\frac{b-a}{l}\right)x$

Since radius at left end is a so radius at distance x, $r = a + \left(\frac{b-a}{l}\right)x$

Area at this particular section $A = \pi r^2 = \pi\left[a+\left(\frac{b-a}{l}\right)x\right]^2$

Hence current density $J = \frac{I}{A} = \frac{I}{\pi r^2} = \frac{I}{\pi\left[a+\frac{x(b-a)}{l}\right]^2}$

Web Reference at www.physicsgalaxy.com

Age Group - Grade 11 & 12 | Age 17-19 Years
Section - ELECTRIC CURRENT & CIRCUITS
Topic - Current Electricity
Module Number - 21 to 27

Practice Exercise 3.2

(i) Find the equivalent resistance across terminals A and B in the circuit shown in figure-3.38.

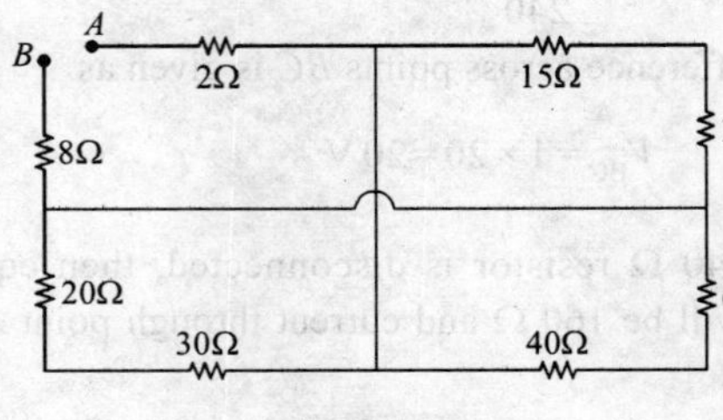

Figure 3.38

[23.33 Ω]

(ii) A uniform copper wire of mass 2.23×10^{-3} kg carries a current of 1 A when a battery of EMF 1.7V is applied across its terminals. What is the cross sectional area of the wire. If the wire is uniformly stretched to double its length, calculate the new resistance. Density of copper is 8.92×10^3 kg m^{-3} and resistivity is 1.7×10^{-8} Ωm.

[5×10^{-8} m^2, 6.8 Ω]

(iii) A rectangular block of metal of resistivity ρ has dimensions $d \times 2d \times 3d$. A potential difference V is applied between two opposite faces of the block.

(a) To which two faces of the block should the potential difference V is to be applied so that it gives maximum current density? Also find this maximum current density.

(b) To which two faces of the block should the potential difference V is to be applied so that it gives maximum current? Also find this maximum current.

[(a) $2d \times 3d, \frac{V}{\rho d}$; (b) $2d \times 3d, \frac{6Vd}{\rho}$]

(iv) At the temperature 0°C, the electric resistance of conductor 2 in η times that of conductor 1. Their temperature coefficients of resistance are equal to α_2 and α_1 respectively. Find the temperature coefficients of resistance of a circuit segment consisting of these two conductors when they are connected in (a) series (b) parallel.

[(a) $\alpha = \frac{(\alpha_1+\eta\alpha_2)}{1+\eta}$; (b) $\alpha = \frac{(\alpha_2+\eta\alpha_1)}{1+\eta}$]

(v) Find the current in 2 Ω resistance

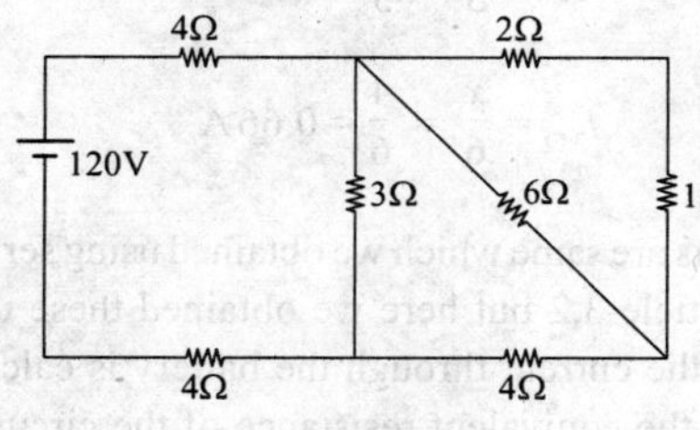

Figure 3.39

[$\frac{8}{3}$ A]

(vi) For the given carbon resistor, there are four coloured bands on it. First is yellow, second is red, third is orange and fourth is gold. What is its resistance ?

[(4.2 × 10^3 ± 5%) Ω]

(vii) An electric current of 5 A is divided in three branches of a circuit forming a parallel combination. The length of the wire in the three branches are in the ratio, 2, 3 and 4 and their diameters are in the ratio 3, 4 and 5. Find the currents in each branch if the wires are made up of the same material.

[1.40 A, 1.66 A, 1.95 A]

(viii) In the circuit shown in figure-3.40, calculate the current through 3 Ω resistor and power dissipated in the entire circuit.

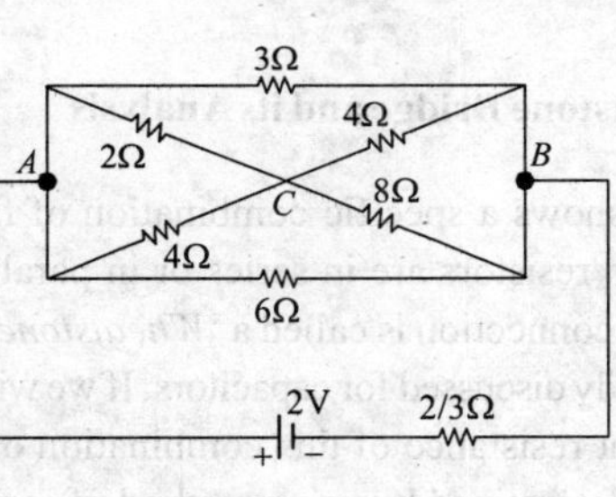

Figure 3.40

[0.44 A, 2 W]

(ix) In the circuit shown in figure-3.41, find the currents in all various parts of the circuit.

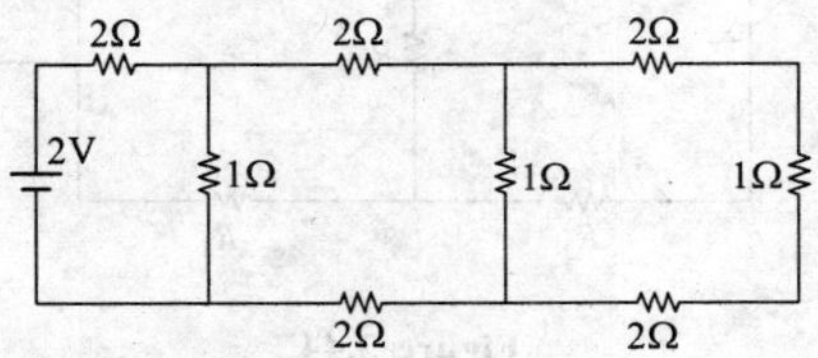

Figure 3.41

[$\frac{70}{99}$ A, $\frac{58}{99}$ A, $\frac{12}{99}$ A, $\frac{10}{99}$ A, $\frac{2}{99}$ A]

(x) An aluminium wire 7.5 m long is connected in parallel with a copper wire 6 m long. When a current of 5 A is passed through the combination, it is found that the current in the aluminium wire is 3 A. The diameter of the aluminium wire is 1mm. Determine the diameter of the copper wire. Resistivity of copper is 0.017 μΩ-m and that of the aluminium is 0.028 μΩ-m.

[0.569 mm]

3.3 Kirchhoff's Current Law(KCL)

Kirchhoff's Current Law is a fundamental law which deals with conservation of charges in electrical circuit. In a closed circuit containing one or more active sources (batteries or other current sources) current flows and at different junctions of circuit current divides in different branches of the circuit. Kirchhoff's Current Law is stated for current distribution at any junction of circuit as

"According to the principal of conservation of charge, at any junction of an electrical circuit sum of all the currents flowing into the junction must be equal to the sum of all the currents flowing out from the junction."

Figure-3.42 shows a junction at which 5 branches of a circuit are connected and currents with directions are shown in figure. For this figure according to Kirchhoff's Current Law, we have

$$I_1 + I_2 + I_3 = I_4 + I_5 \quad \ldots(3.70)$$

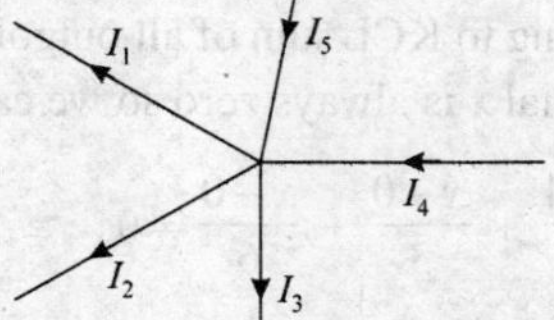

Figure 3.42

Equation-(3.70) can also be written as

$$I_1 + I_2 + I_3 - I_4 - I_5 = 0 \quad \ldots(3.71)$$

As expressed in equation-(3.71), if signs of currents in branches is considered then Kirchhoff's Current Law can also be stated as algebraic sum of all the currents in all branches meeting (outgoing or incoming) at a junction of electrical circuit is equal to zero.

3.3.1 Applications of Kirchhoff's Current Law

In article-3.2 we've discussed solving electrical circuits using method of series and parallel combinations. In many cases the analysis becomes very long if we use series and parallel method. Alternative way to solve a circuit is by using KCL. The application of KCL in electrical circuits is similar to nodal analysis we've already covered in previous chapter of capacitance which we have used in solving capacitive circuits.

In application of KCL for analyzing an electrical circuit we first distribute the potentials at different parts of circuit by considering a zero reference point which is generally negative terminal of the battery. Then for all junctions of the circuit we consider variable potentials $x, y, z\ldots$ etc. and write KCL equations to determine the values of these unknown potentials. To understand KCL analysis of electrical circuit we will solve an illustration.

Figure-3.43 shows the same electrical circuit which we solved in article-3.2.6 but here we will solve it using KCL. Figure-2.43 shows the potential distribution in circuit. At the junction of resistors we considered unknown potential x.

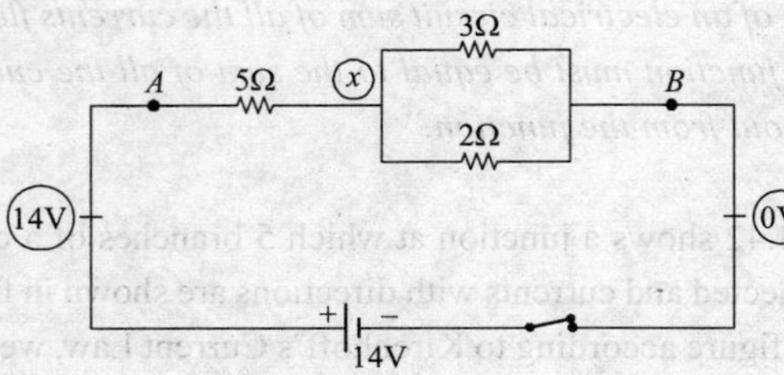

Figure 3.43

To determine the value of x we will write KCL equation at this junction. According to KCL sum of all outgoing currents from junction at potential x is always zero so we can write

$$\frac{x-14}{5}+\frac{x-0}{3}+\frac{x-0}{6}=0 \qquad \ldots(3.72)$$

The three terms in above equation are the outgoing currents from junction written by using Ohm's law. Solving this equation we will get

$$6x-84+10x+5x=0$$

$$\Rightarrow \qquad 21x=84$$

$$\Rightarrow \qquad x=4\,\text{V}$$

As the junction potential is known, we can directly write the currents in all resistances as

$$I_{5\Omega}=\frac{14-x}{5}=\frac{14-4}{5}=2\,\text{A}$$

$$I_{3\Omega}=\frac{x}{3}=\frac{4}{3}=1.33\,\text{A}$$

$$I_{3\Omega}=\frac{x}{6}=\frac{4}{6}=0.66\,\text{A}$$

Above currents are same which we obtained using series parallel analysis in article-3.2 but here we obtained these using KCL equation. As the current through the battery is calculated, we can calculate the equivalent resistance of the circuit by using equation-(3.39) as

$$R_{eq}=\frac{V_{battery}}{I_{battery}}$$

Here I_{battery} can be calculated from either side of the circuit. From left it can be given as the current through 5 Ω resistor or from right can be given as sum of currents through 3 Ω and 6 Ω resistors.

$$\Rightarrow \qquad R_{eq}=\frac{14}{\left(\frac{14-x}{5}\right)}=\frac{14}{\left(\frac{x}{3}+\frac{x}{6}\right)}$$

$$\Rightarrow \qquad R_{eq}=\frac{14}{2}=7\,\Omega$$

In upcoming articles we will take more illustrations to understand applications of KCL as in many cases when resistors are connected in mixed combination which is neither series nor parallel then this is the method which will be preferred to solve such cases.

3.3.2 Wheatstone Bridge and its Analysis

Figure-3.44 shows a specific combination of five resistors in which no two resistors are in series or in parallel connection. This specific connection is called a '*Wheatstone Bridge*' which we have already discussed for capacitors. If we wish to determine the equivalent resistance of this combination of resistors then it cannot be determined by using method of series and parallel combination. This can be solved either by using Kirchhoff's Current Law or by other methods we will discuss later.

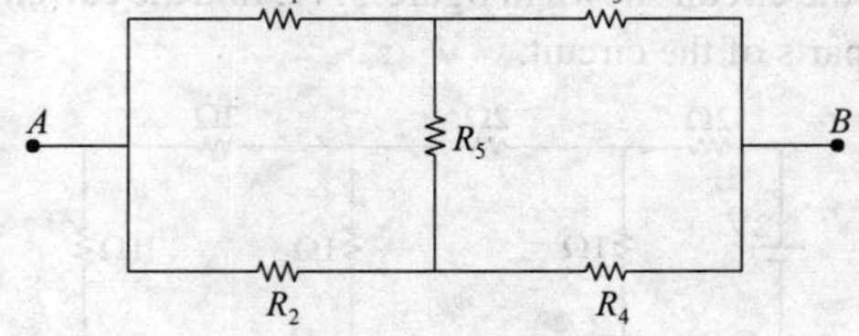

Figure 3.44

To understand the analysis of Wheatstone bridge we will take an illustration for determining its equivalent resistance. Consider the wheatstone bridge shown in figure-3.45. To calculate its equivalent resistance we connect a battery of 100 V across its terminals A and B as shown in figure-3.46 as we know that applied battery voltage does not affect the equivalent resistance.

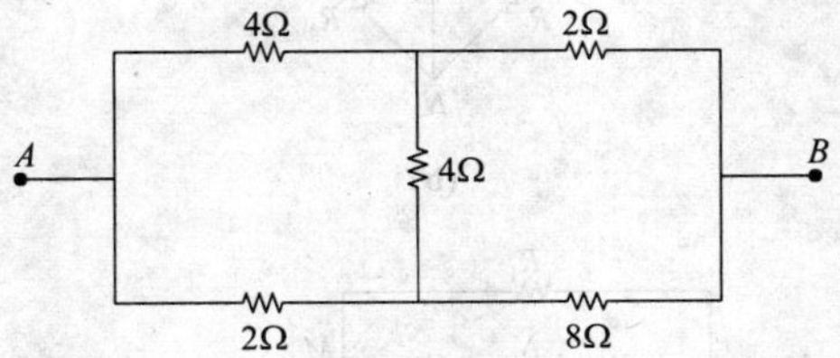

Figure 3.45

To apply Kirchhoff's Current Law for solving the circuit of this wheatstone bridge we distribute potentials at all parts of the circuit as shown in figure-3.46. We've considered negative terminal of the battery at zero potential and positive terminal at 100 V with potentials at junctions M and N at x and y respectively shown.

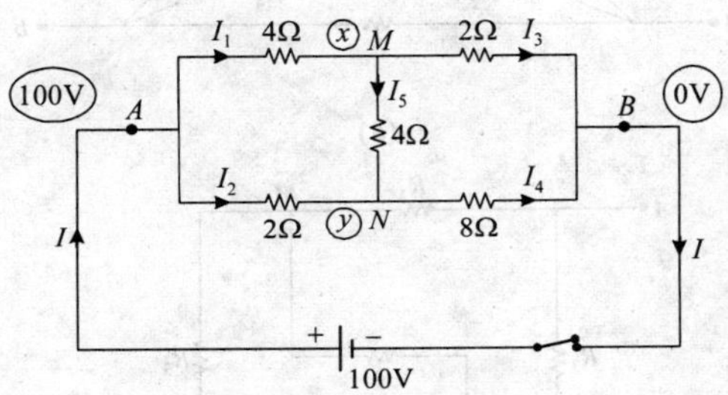

Figure 3.46

Now we can write the KCL equations for variable potentials x and y. The KCL equation for the junction M can be written directly as explained in previous article as

$$\frac{x-100}{4}+\frac{x-y}{4}+\frac{x-0}{2}=0 \qquad \dots(3.73)$$

$$\Rightarrow \qquad 4x-y=100 \qquad \dots(3.74)$$

Similarly we can write the KCL equation for junction N as

$$\frac{y-100}{2}+\frac{y-x}{4}+\frac{y-0}{8}=0 \qquad \dots(3.75)$$

$$\Rightarrow \qquad 7y-2x=400 \qquad \dots(3.76)$$

Solving equations-(3.74) and (3.76) for variables x and y, we get

$$x=\frac{550}{13}\text{ V}$$

and $$y=\frac{900}{13}\text{ V}$$

To determine equivalent resistance across the terminals A and B we use equation-(3.39) which is given as

$$R_{eq}=\frac{V_{battery}}{I_{battery}}$$

Here the current flowing through the battery is the sum of currents connected to right terminal of battery or to the left terminal of the battery. Thus in above case this current $I_{battery}$ can be given as

$$I_{battery}=\frac{x}{2}+\frac{y}{8}=\frac{100-x}{4}+\frac{100-y}{2}$$

$$\Rightarrow \qquad I_{battery}=\frac{1}{2}\times\left(\frac{550}{13}\right)+\frac{1}{8}\times\left(\frac{900}{13}\right)\text{A}$$

$$\Rightarrow \qquad I_{battery}=\frac{775}{26}\text{ A}$$

Thus equivalent resistance of the wheatstone bridge shown in figure-3.24 across terminals A and B is given as

$$R_{eq}=\frac{100}{\left(\frac{775}{26}\right)}=\frac{104}{31}\,\Omega \qquad \dots(3.77)$$

Equation-(3.77) gives the equivalent resistance of the wheatstone bridge which we have calculated using Kirchhoff's Current Law. As already discussed that this cannot be calculated by using series and parallel method because in wheatstone bridge resistors are neither connected in series nor in parallel combination. There is some specific conditions for a wheatstone bridge under which the circuit can be modified which will be discussed in next article.

3.3.3 Balancing Condition of Wheatstone Bridge

Figure shows a wheatstone bridge connected across a battery of voltage V. In this situation if we consider the potentials of different parts of circuit as shown in the figure-3.47 and write KCL equations for junctions M and N then these are written as

$$\frac{x-V}{R_1}+\frac{x-y}{R_5}+\frac{x-0}{R_3}=0 \qquad \dots(3.78)$$

and $$\frac{y-V}{R_2}+\frac{y-x}{R_5}+\frac{y-0}{R_4}=0 \qquad \dots(3.79)$$

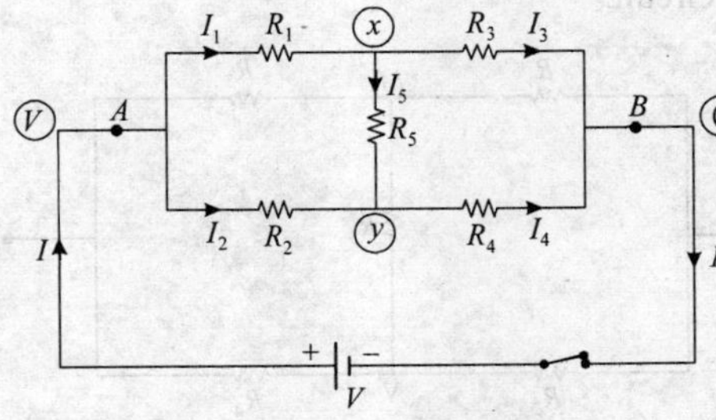

Figure 3.47

In equations-(3.78) and (3.79) if we use $x = y$ then it gives

$$\frac{R_1}{R_2} = \frac{R_3}{R_4} \qquad \ldots(3.80)$$

From equation-(3.80) we can also say that if this ratio holds for a wheatstone bridge then for any value of V the potential of the two junctions in the circuit will be equal and $I_5 = 0$. Thus if $x = y$ then no current will flow through the resistor R_5 so even if we remove this middle resistor branch from circuit then also it will not affect the circuit. In that case figure-3.47 will reduce to the state shown in figure-3.48.

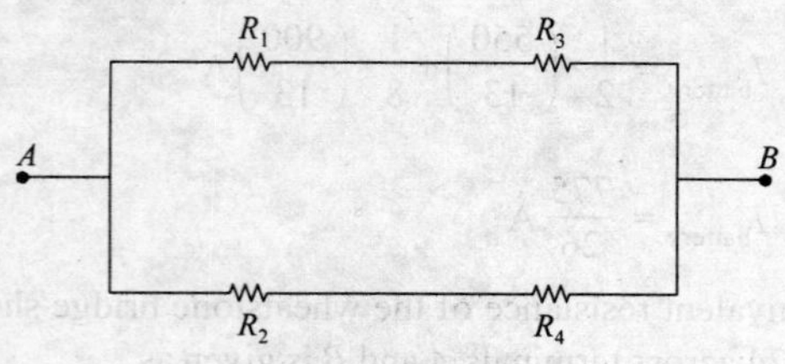

Figure 3.48

Now the equivalent resistance of this circuit can be easily calculated by using series and parallel method. The wheatstone bridge in which equation-(3.80) holds is called a '*Balanced Wheatstone Bridge*' and the ratio in equation-(3.80) is called '*Balancing Condition*' of a wheatstone bridge.

The equivalent resistance of the balanced wheatstone bridge after removing the middle branch as shown in figure-3.48 can be given as

$$R_{eq} = \frac{(R_1 + R_3)\cdot(R_2 + R_4)}{(R_1 + R_3) + (R_2 + R_4)} \qquad \ldots(3.81)$$

3.3.4 Alternative Circuit Arrangements of Wheatstone Bridge

In previous articles we've discussed solving of a circuit of five resistors connected in a specific fashion called wheatstone bridge as shown in figure-3.48. The connections of resistors in combination of wheatstone bridge can be drawn in different ways and sometimes students get confused whether the given circuit is a wheatstone bridge or not. Figure-3.49 shows different ways in which a wheatstone bridge can be drawn as a part of capacitive circuit.

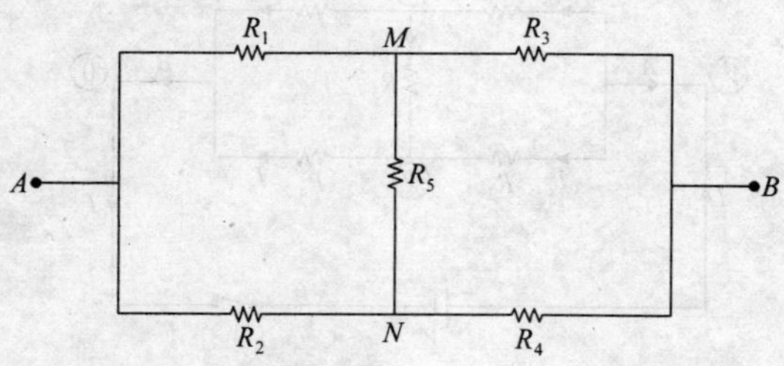

(a)

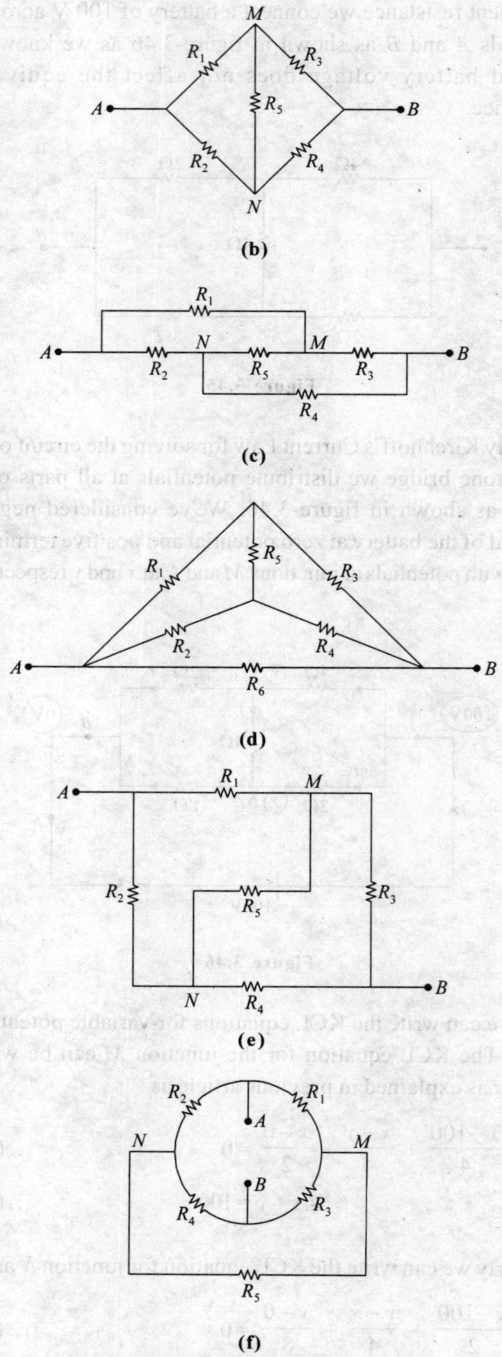

Figure 3.49

Illustrative Example 3.17

ABCD is a square where each side is a uniform wire of resistance one ohm. Find a point *E* on *CD* such that if a uniform wire of resistance 1Ω is connected across *AE* and a constant potential difference is applied across *A* and *C*, the points *B* and *E* will be equipotential.

Solution

The situation is shown in figure-3.50.

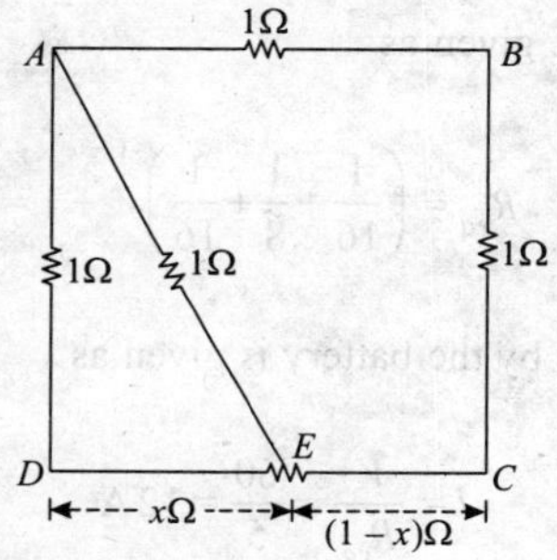

Figure 3.50

The points B and E will be equipotential, when effective resistance across AE = effective resistance across CE because resistance across AB and BC are same so it will be a balanced state of wheatstone bridge which happens when

$$\frac{(1+x)(1)}{(1+x)+(1)}=(1-x)$$

Solving we get $x=(\sqrt{2}-1)$

$$\Rightarrow \quad 1-x=1-(\sqrt{2}-1)=2-\sqrt{2}=\sqrt{2}(\sqrt{2}-1)$$

$$\Rightarrow \quad \frac{CE}{ED}=\frac{1-x}{x}=\frac{\sqrt{2}(\sqrt{2}-1)}{(\sqrt{2}-1)}=\frac{\sqrt{2}}{1}$$

Illustrative Example 3.18

A constant voltage $V = 25$ V is maintained between points A and B of the circuit as shown in figure-3.51. Find the magnitude and direction current flowing through the wire CD if the resistances are equal to $R_1 = 1\ \Omega$, $R_2 = 2\ \Omega$, $R_3 = 3\Omega$ and $R_4 = 4\ \Omega$.

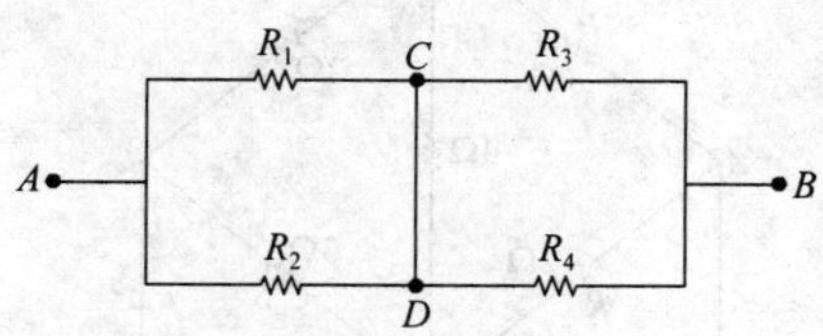

Figure 3.51

Solution

Figure-3.52 shows the potential distribution at different junctions of the circuit.

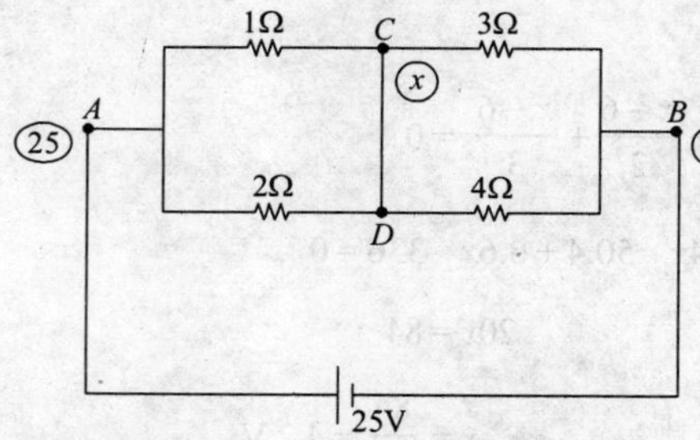

Figure 3.52

To calculate the potential x at junction CD we write KCL equation for x as

$$\frac{x-25}{1}+\frac{x-25}{2}+\frac{x-0}{3}+\frac{x-0}{4}=0$$

$$\Rightarrow \quad 12x-300+6x-150+4x+3x=0$$

$$\Rightarrow \quad 25x=450$$

$$\Rightarrow \quad x=\frac{450}{25}=18\text{ V}$$

Thus current through 1W resistance is given as

$$I_{1\Omega}=\frac{25-18}{1}=7\text{ A}$$

and $$I_{3\Omega}=\frac{18-0}{3}=6\text{ A}$$

Current in branch CD is given as

$$I_{CD}=I_{1\Omega}-I_{3\Omega}=7-6=1\text{ A}$$

Illustrative Example 3.19

Calculate the steady state current in the 2 Ω resistor shown in the circuit in figure-3.53 and steady state charge on the capacitor.

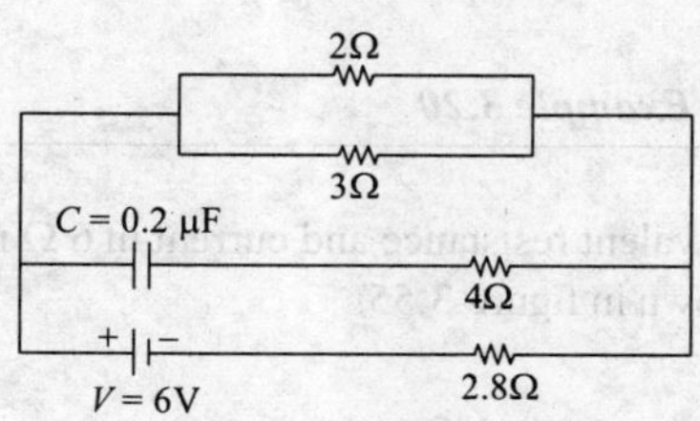

Figure 3.53

Solution

To solve the circuit we distribute potentials in circuit as shown in figure-3.54. As we know that in steady state no current flows through a capacitor thus in any circuit if we find a capacitor connect in any branch we can consider zero current in that branch in steady state after the capacitor is charged. Thus in middle branch of this circuit we consider zero potential drop across 4 Ω resistance as shown. Writing KCL equation for x gives

$$\frac{x}{2.8}+\frac{x-6}{2}+\frac{x-6}{3}=0$$

$$\Rightarrow \quad 6x+8.4x-50.4+6.6x-336=0$$

$$\Rightarrow \quad 20x=84$$

$$\Rightarrow \quad x=\frac{84}{20}=4.2\text{ V}$$

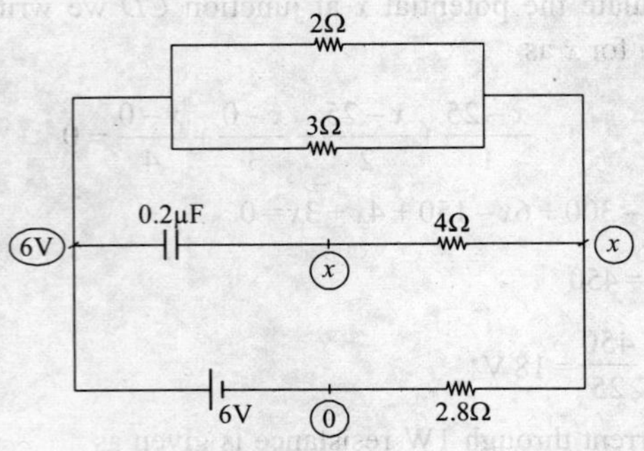

Figure 3.54

Thus current in 2 Ω resistance is

$$I_{2\Omega}=\frac{6-x}{2}=\frac{6-4.2}{2}=\frac{1.8}{2}=0.9\text{ A}$$

Steady state charge on capacitor

$$q=C(6-x)$$

$$\Rightarrow \quad q=0.2\times10^{-6}\times1.8$$

$$\Rightarrow \quad q=0.36\times10^{-6}\text{C}=0.36\ \mu\text{C}$$

Illustrative Example 3.20

Find the equivalent resistance and current in 6 Ω resistance in the circuit shown in figure-3.55.

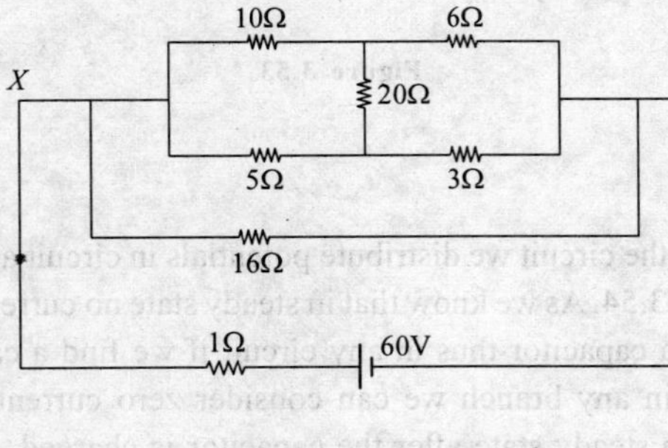

Figure 3.55

Solution

As the wheatstone bridge shown in above circuit is balanced, we can remove its middle branch. After this remaining resistances of 16 Ω, 8 Ω and 16 Ω will be in parallel for which the equivalent resistance can be given as

$$R_{eq}=\left(\frac{1}{16}+\frac{1}{8}+\frac{1}{16}\right)^{-1}+1=5\ \Omega$$

Current supplied by the battery is given as

$$I=\frac{V}{R_{eq}}=\frac{60}{5}=12\text{ A}$$

In the circuit 12 A will be distributed in the three branches in parallel. The potential drop across the three branches in parallel is given as

$$V_{XY}=IR_{XY}=12\times4=48\text{ V}$$

Thus current in top 16W resistance branch is given as

$$I_{6\Omega}=\frac{V_{XY}}{16}=\frac{48}{16}=3\text{ A}$$

We have solved this question by series and parallel analysis which is simpler here but students must also try solving this question by using KCL by distributing potential and verify the results as it is essential to understand in which case which method is to be preferred.

Illustrative Example 3.21

In a Wheatstone's bridge a battery of 2 V is used as shown in figure-3.56. Find the value of the current through the middle branch in the unbalanced condition of the bridge when $P=1\ \Omega$, $Q=2\ \Omega$, $R=2\ \Omega$ and $S=3\ \Omega$ and resistance of middle branch BD is 4 Ω.

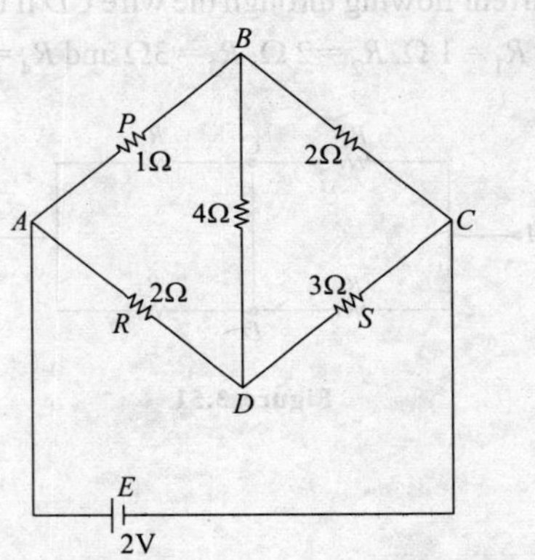

Figure 3.56

Distribute of potential is shown in figure-3.57

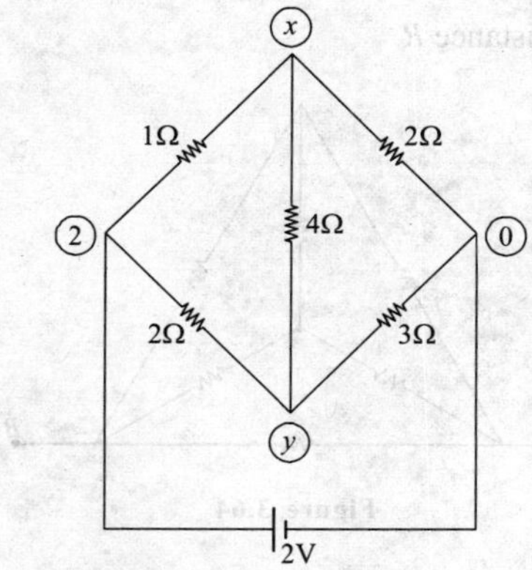

Figure 3.57

KCL equation for x and y are

$$\frac{x}{2}+\frac{x-y}{4}+\frac{x-2}{1}=0$$

$$\Rightarrow \qquad 7x-y=8 \qquad \ldots(3.82)$$

and

$$\frac{y}{3}+\frac{y-x}{4}+\frac{y-2}{2}=0$$

$$\Rightarrow \qquad 13y-3x=12 \qquad \ldots(3.83)$$

$(3.82)\times 3+(3.83)\times 7$ gives

$$88y=108$$

$$\Rightarrow \qquad y=\frac{108}{88}=\frac{27}{22}\text{ V}$$

from equation-(3.82) we have

$$x=\frac{y+8}{7}=\frac{\frac{27}{22}+8}{7}=\frac{203}{154}\text{ V}$$

Thus current in middle branch is given as

$$I_{4\Omega}=\frac{x-y}{4}=\frac{\frac{203}{154}-\frac{27}{22}}{4}$$

$$\Rightarrow \qquad I_{4\Omega}=\frac{7}{308}\text{ A}$$

Web Reference at www.physicsgalaxy.com

Age Group - Grade 11 & 12 | Age 17-19 Years
Section - ELECTRIC CURRENT & CIRCUITS
Topic - Circuit Analysis
Module Number - 1, 2, 6, 7 to 11

Practice Exercise 3.3

(i) Two points A and B are maintained at a constant potential difference of 110 V. A third point is connected to A by two resistances of 100 W and 200 W in parallel, and to B by a single resistance of 300 W as shown in figure-3.58. Find the current in each resistance and the potential difference between A and C and between C and B using Kirchhoff's Current Law.

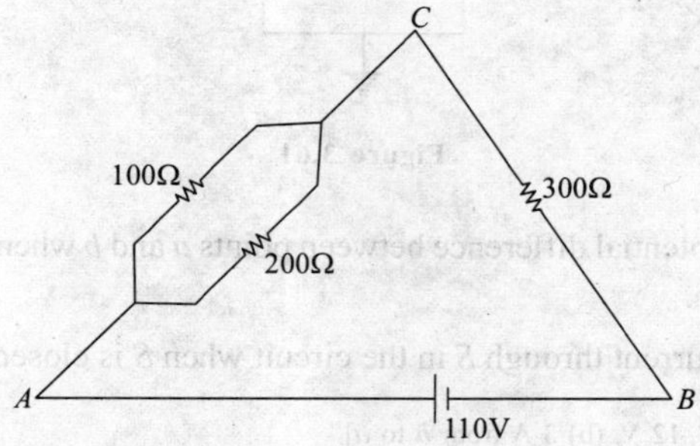

Figure 3.58

[0.33 A, 0.2 A, 0.1 A]

(ii) Find the equivalent Resistance between A and B.

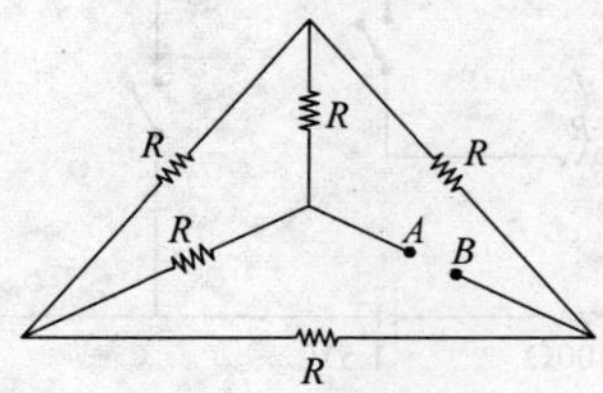

Figure 3.59

[R]

(iii) Calculate magnitude of resistance X in the circuit shown in figure-3.60 when no current flows through the 5 Ω resistor ?

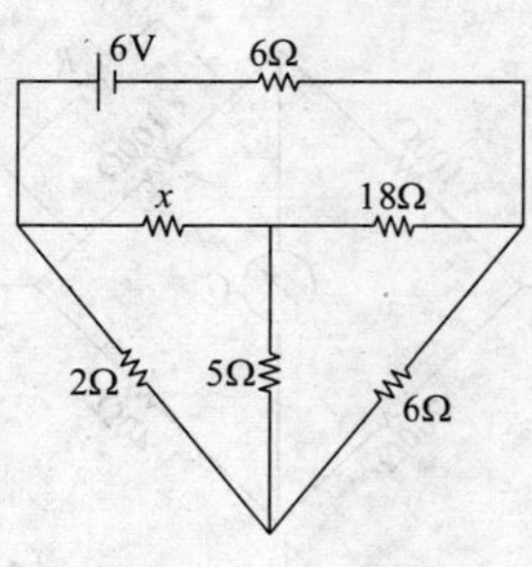

Figure 3.60

[6 Ω]

(iv) In the circuit shown in figure-3.61, calculate

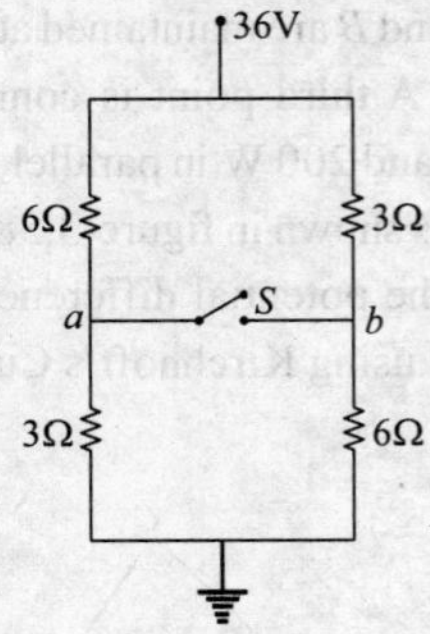

Figure 3.61

(a) Potential difference between points a and b when switch S is open.

(b) Current through S in the circuit when S is closed.

[(a) V_{ab} = –12 V, (b) 3 A from b to a]

(v) In the circuit shown in figure-3.62 the reading of ideal ammeter connected as shown is same with both switches open as with both closed. Then find the resistance R.

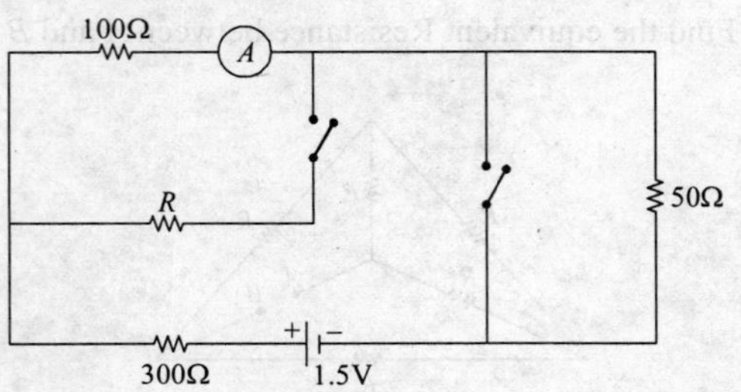

Figure 3.62

[600Ω]

(vi) For the following diagram the galvanometer shows zero deflection then what is the value of R ?

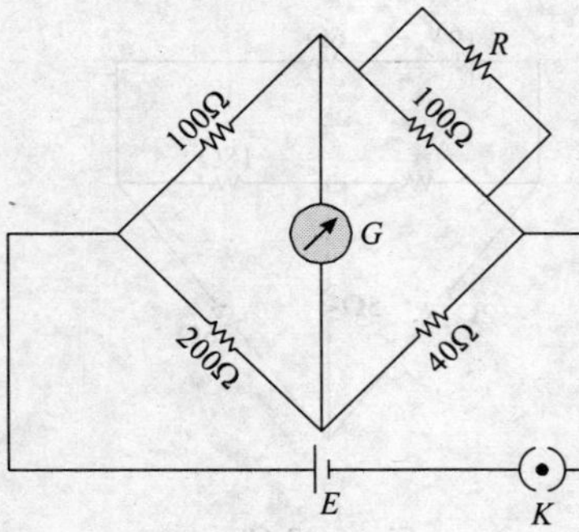

Figure 3.63

[25 Ω]

(vii) Find the equivalent resistance of the circuit shown in figure-3.64 across terminals A and B. Each resistance in this circuit is of resistance R.

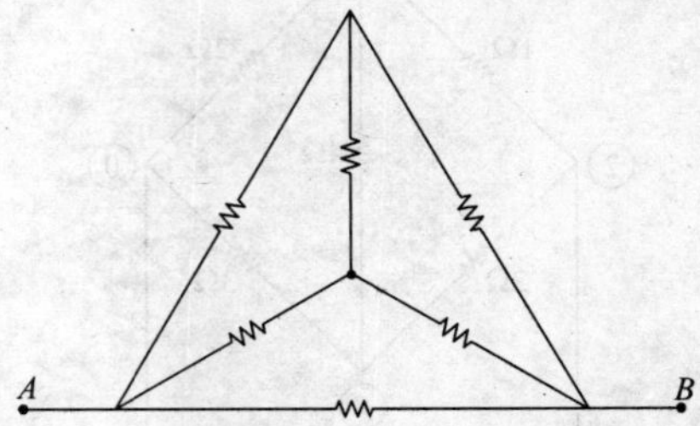

Figure 3.64

[R/2]

(viii) Find current in the branch CD of the circuit shown in figure-3.65.

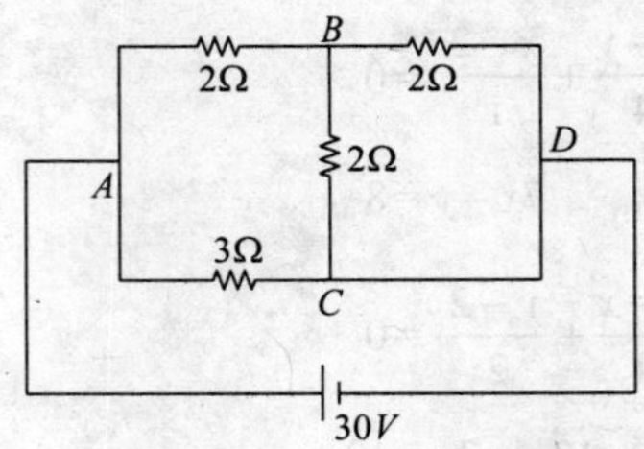

Figure 3.65

[15 A]

3.4 Symmetry Circuits

A group of resistors which have some symmetry in connections as well as in values of resistances used then such a circuit is called symmetry circuit. Due to symmetry in resistances and connections by some means we can reduce the analysis of circuit while using KCL or by using series and parallel method. The analysis is similar to what we've already discussed in symmetry circuits for capacitances studied in article-2.5. We will discuss the analysis of symmetry resistive circuits by using some illustrations. Figure-3.66 shows some circuits which are considered under the category of symmetry circuits. In upcoming articles we'll discuss how to solve such circuits.

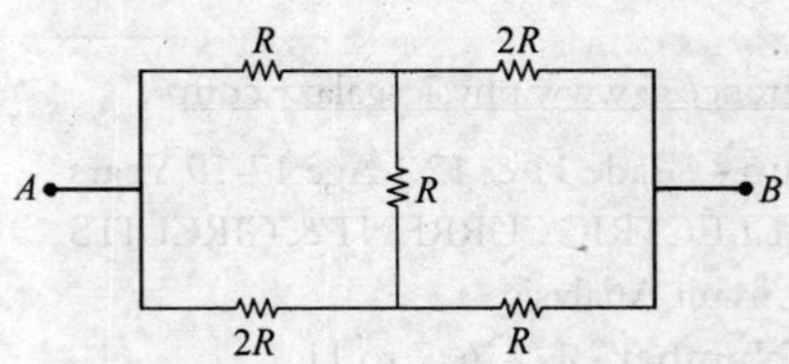

(a)

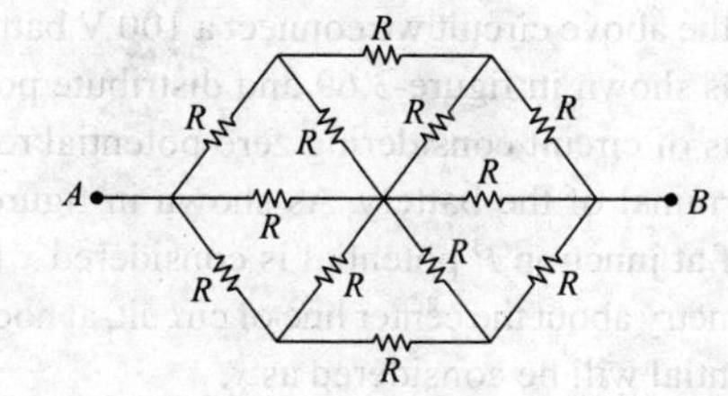

(b)

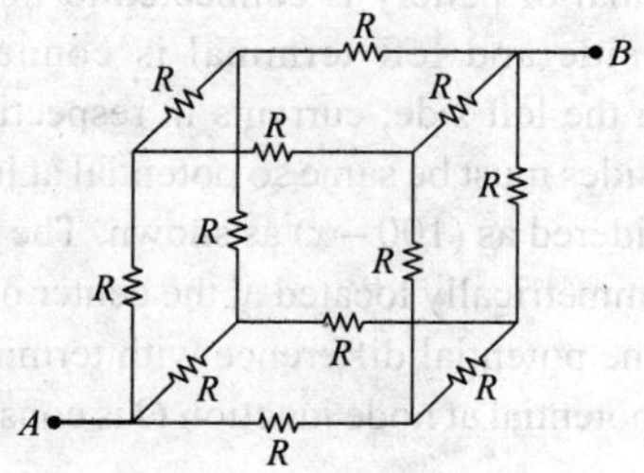

(c)

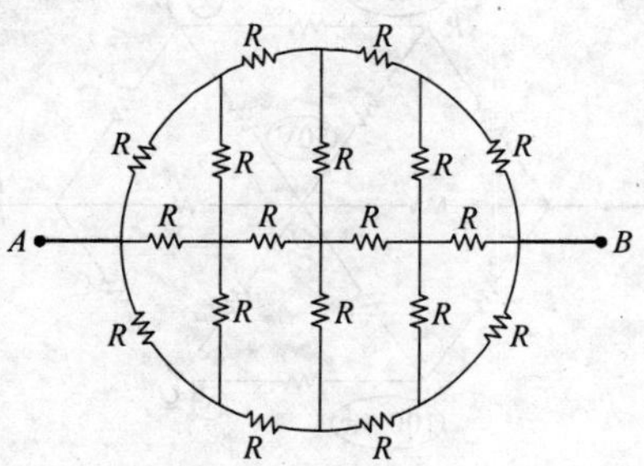

(d)

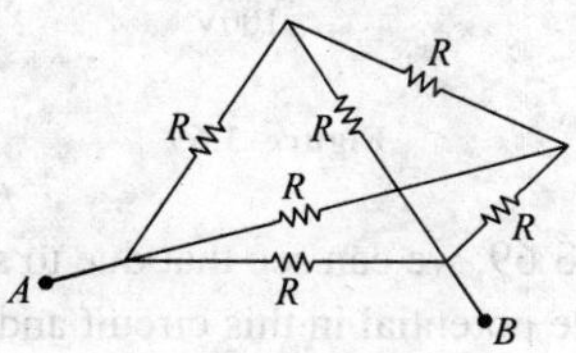

(e)

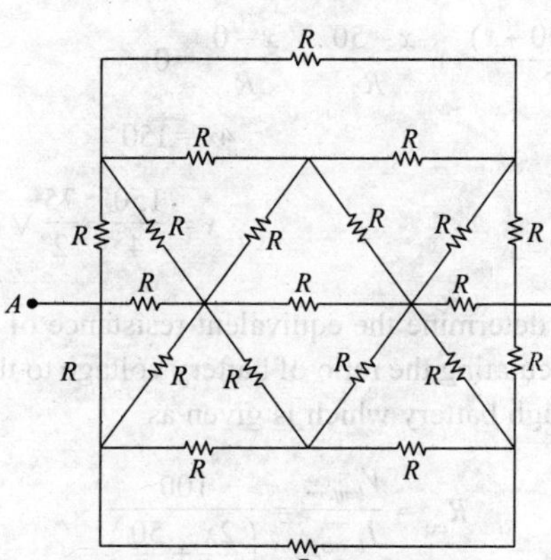

(f)

Figure 3.66

3.4.1 Solving Symmetry Circuit by using KCL

It is better to understand solving symmetry circuits by using some illustrations. Figure-3.67(a) shows an unbalanced wheatstone bridge for which we will determine the equivalent capacitance. To apply KCL on this circuit we connect a 100 V battery across the terminals *A* and *B* as shown.

Similar to the analysis of wheatstone bridge done in case of capacitive circuits, in this case also we distribute the potentials to all parts of circuit. We start by considering negative terminal of battery as a reference at zero volt and positive terminal at 100 V but instead of junction node potentials *x* and *y* here we consider potential *x* and (100 – *x*) as shown in figure-3.67(b) because of symmetry of resistances in the circuit.

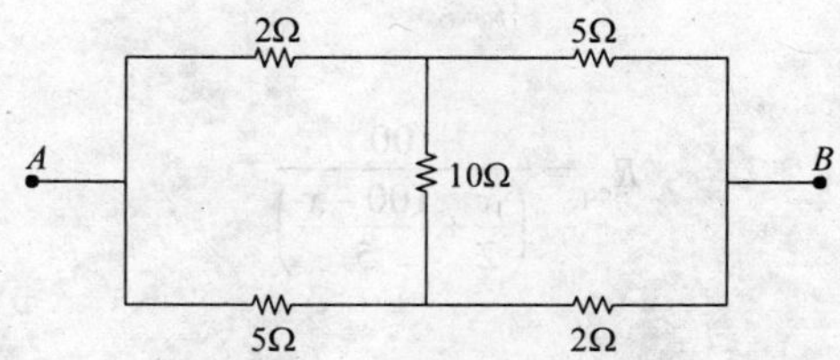

(a)

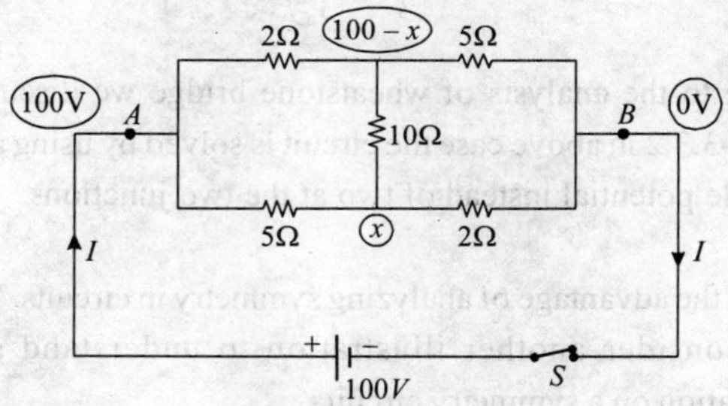

(b)

Figure 3.67

If we carefully look at the above circuit then we can see that left terminal of battery is connected to 2 Ω and 5 Ω resistors and right terminal of battery is also connected to 2 Ω and 5 Ω resistors on other side. Thus by symmetry we can state that the current supplied by battery on one side and drawn on the other side will be same on same value of resistances hence the potential difference across left 5 Ω resistor and right 5 Ω resistor must be same and this is true for other 2 Ω resistor also.

If potential at lower junction is considered *x* then this would be the potential difference across lower 2 Ω resistor and same would be across the upper 2 Ω resistor. As on left side of upper 2 Ω resistor we are considering potential to be 100 V, on right side of it the potential must be (100 – *x*) to keep potential difference across it to be equal to x. With this qualitative logic we have reduced one variable from this circuit so now we need to write only one KCL equation for calculation of unknown potential x which is written as

$$\frac{x-100}{5}+\frac{2x-100}{10}+\frac{x}{2}=0$$

$$\Rightarrow \quad 9x=300$$

$$\Rightarrow \quad x=\frac{100}{3}\text{V}$$

Now equivalent resistance of the wheatstone bridge can be calculated by using equation-(3.39) as

$$R_{eq}=\frac{V_{battery}}{I_{battery}}$$

$$\Rightarrow \quad R_{eq}=\frac{100}{\left(\frac{x}{2}+\frac{100-x}{5}\right)}$$

$$\Rightarrow \quad R_{eq}=\frac{100}{\left(\frac{50}{3}+\frac{40}{3}\right)}=\frac{10}{3}\Omega$$

Unlike to the analysis of wheatstone bridge we discussed in article-3.3.2 in above case the circuit is solved by using a single variable potential instead of two at the two junctions.

This is the advantage of analyzing symmetry in circuits. We will now consider another illustration to understand similar application on a symmetry circuit.

Figure-3.68 shows a symmetry circuit containing 12 resistances each of resistance R. Using KCL we will calculate the equivalent resistance of this circuit across terminals A and B. The analysis is somewhat similar to what we discussed for the similar capacitive circuit in article-2.5.1.

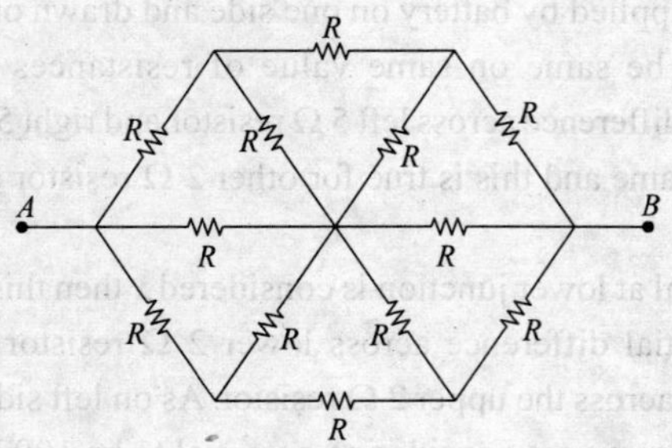

Figure 3.68

To analyze the above circuit we connect a 100 V battery across the circuit as shown in figure-3.69 and distribute potentials at various parts of circuit considering zero potential reference at negative terminal of the battery. As shown in figure-3.69, by symmetry if at junction P potential is considered x then using mirror symmetry about the center line of circuit, at node junction Q also potential will be considered as x.

As right terminal of battery is connected to three resistances on the right side and left terminal is connected to three resistances on the left side, currents in respective resistors at left and right sides must be same so potential at junctions R and S can be considered as $(100-x)$ as shown. The junction at the center O is symmetrically located at the center of circuit which must have same potential difference with terminal A and B of circuit hence potential at node junction O is considered as 50 V.

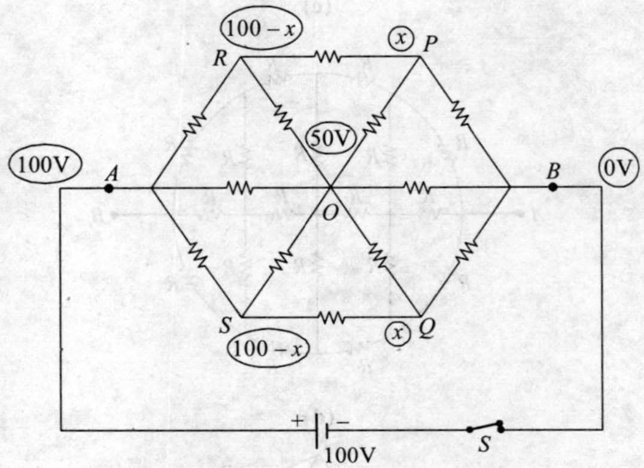

Figure 3.69

In above figure-3.69, we can see that due to symmetry there is only one variable potential in this circuit and to determine the value of x, KCL equation is written for the junction P as

$$\frac{x-(100-x)}{R}+\frac{x-50}{R}+\frac{x-0}{R}=0 \qquad \ldots(3.84)$$

$$\Rightarrow \quad 4x=150$$

$$\Rightarrow \quad x=\frac{150}{4}=\frac{75}{2}\text{V}$$

Now we can determine the equivalent resistance of the given circuit by calculating the ratio of battery voltage to the current flowing through battery which is given as

$$R_{eq}=\frac{V_{battery}}{I_{battery}}=\frac{100}{\left(\frac{2x}{R}+\frac{50}{R}\right)}$$

$$\Rightarrow \quad R_{eq}=\frac{100}{(75+50)}R=\frac{4}{5}R \qquad \ldots(3.85)$$

Equation-(3.85) gives the resistance of the symmetry circuit shown in figure-3.68 which is calculated by using KCL. This can also be solved by using series and parallel method by joining or isolating equipotential points to modify the circuit. This method we have already discussed in previous chapter of capacitance in article-2.5.2. Students are advised to solve the same circuit shown in figure-3.68 by using that method and verify the result. It has already been explained that the preferred method will always be to use KCL rather using the modification of circuit by joining or isolating equipotential points.

3.4.2 Ladder Network Circuits

Figure-3.70 shows a resistive circuit in which a section of two resistors as shown by dotted closed curve is repeatedly connected infinitely. Such circuits are called '*Ladder Networks*' or '*Ladder Circuits*'. Similar circuits we've already studied in previous chapter of capacitance in article-2.4.7.

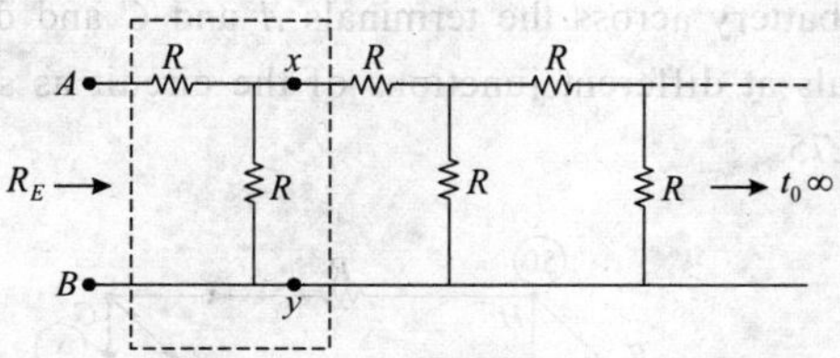

Figure 3.70

To solve such circuits for equivalent resistance, we first consider that the equivalent resistance of the circuit across terminals *A* and *B* in above figure is given as R_E then for infinite sections connected one after another, if one section is removed then also the remaining resistance of the circuit across terminals *X* and *Y* can be considered as R_E as circuit across terminals *X* and *Y* as shown in figure-3.71(a) is identical to that shown in figure-3.70.

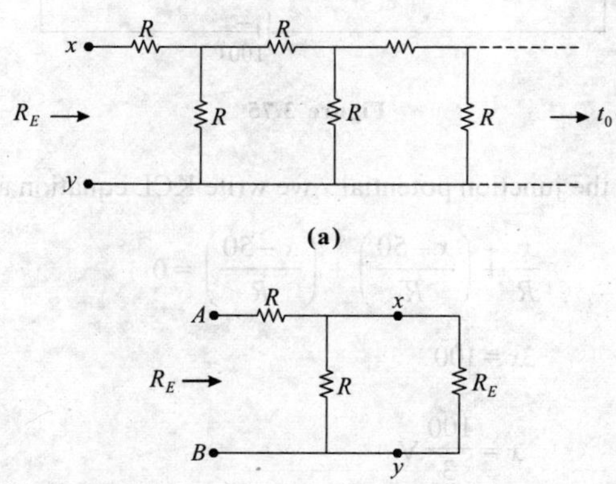

Figure 3.71

Thus the circuit after terminals *XY* in figure-3.70 can be replaced by a single equivalent resistance R_E as shown in figure-3.71(b) and it can be solved using series and parallel method which gives the value of R_E by considering R_E in parallel with *R* and then this group in series with another *R* connected in top branch which is given as

$$R_E = R + \frac{RR_E}{R + R_E}$$

$$\Rightarrow \quad R_E(R + R_E) = R(R + R_E) + RR_E$$

$$\Rightarrow \quad R_E^2 - RR_E - R^2 = 0$$

$$\Rightarrow \quad R_E = \frac{R \pm \sqrt{R^2 - 4(-R^2)}}{2}$$

$$\Rightarrow \quad R_E = \left(\frac{\sqrt{5} - 1}{2}\right) R \qquad \ldots (3.86)$$

The expression given in equation-(3.86) is the equivalent resistance of the ladder circuit shown in figure-3.70. In this expression we have discarded the root of quadratic equation with positive sign as the equivalent resistance cannot be more than twice the value of *R* as it is equivalent resistance of one *R* in series with another resistance which is having a value less than *R*. We will take more illustrations to explain the similar concepts in more details.

 # Illustrative Example 3.22

Find the equivalent resistance across the terminals *A* and *G* in the circuit shown in figure-3.72. Each resistance in circuit is *R*.

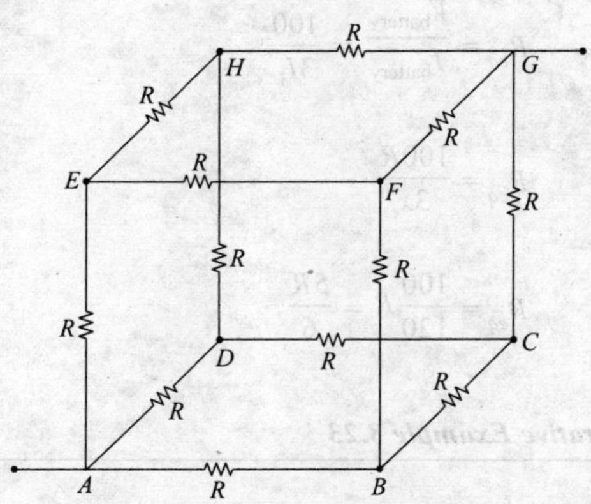

Figure 3.72

Solution

To find the equivalent resistance of the circuit, we connect a 100 V battery across the terminals A and G and distribute potentials at different junctions of the circuit as shown in figure-3.73.

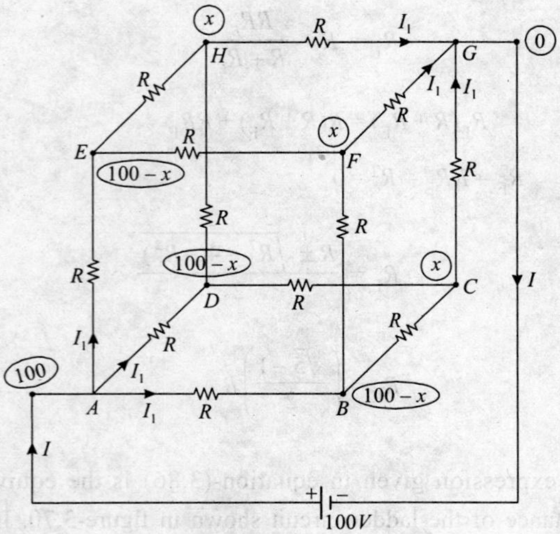

Figure 3.73

To find the junction potential x we write KCL equation as

$$\frac{x}{R} + \frac{x-(100-x)}{R} + \frac{x-(100-x)}{R} = 0$$

$$\Rightarrow \quad 5x = 200$$

$$\Rightarrow \quad x = 40\,\text{V}$$

Equivalent resistance of the circuit across points A and G is given as

$$R_{eq} = \frac{V_{\text{battery}}}{I_{\text{battery}}} = \frac{100}{3I_1}$$

$$\Rightarrow \quad R_{eq} = \frac{100R}{3x}$$

$$\Rightarrow \quad R_{eq} = \frac{100}{120}R = \frac{5R}{6}$$

 # Illustrative Example 3.23

Find the equivalent resistance across the terminals A and C in the circuit shown in figure-3.74. Each resistance in circuit is R.

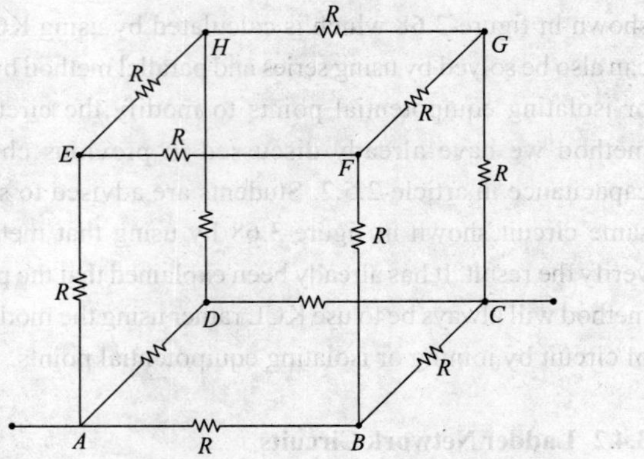

Figure 3.74

Solution

To find the equivalent resistance of the circuit, we connect a 100 V battery across the terminals A and C and distribute potentials at different junctions of the circuit as shown in figure-3.75.

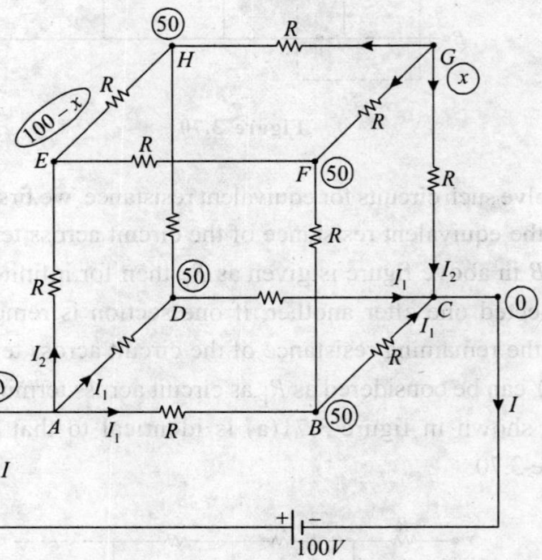

Figure 3.75

To find the junction potential x we write KCL equation as

$$\frac{x}{R} + \left(\frac{x-50}{R}\right) + \left(\frac{x-50}{R}\right) = 0$$

$$\Rightarrow \quad 3x = 100$$

$$\Rightarrow \quad x = \frac{100}{3}\,\text{V}$$

Equivalent resistance of the circuit across points A and C is given as

$$R_{eq} = \frac{V_{battery}}{I_{battery}} = \frac{100}{2I_1 + I_2}$$

$$\Rightarrow \quad R_{eq} = \frac{100}{2\left(\frac{50}{R}\right) + \frac{100}{3R}} = \frac{R}{1+1/3}$$

$$\Rightarrow \quad R_{eq} = \frac{3R}{4}$$

Illustrative Example 3.24

Find the equivalent resistance across the terminals A and B in the circuit shown in figure-3.76. Each resistance in circuit is R.

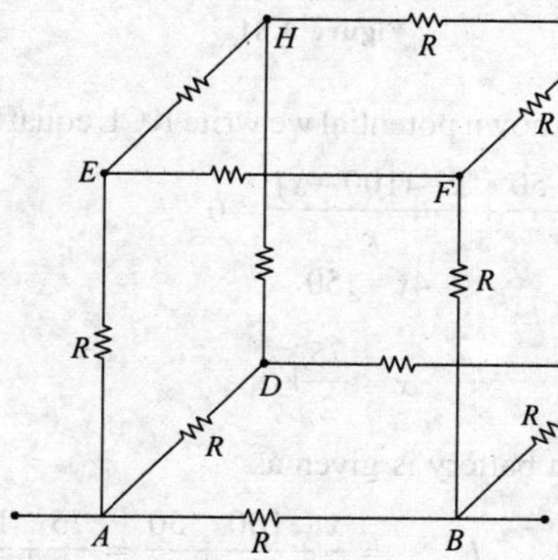

Figure 3.76

Solution

To find the equivalent resistance of the circuit, we connect a 100V battery across the terminals A and B and distribute potentials at different junctions of the circuit as shown in figure-3.77.

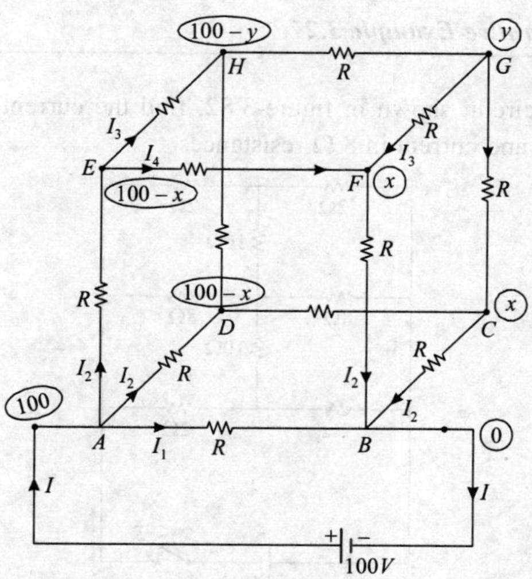

Figure 3.77

To find junction potentials we write KCL equation for x as

$$\frac{x}{R} + \frac{x-y}{R} + \frac{x-(100-x)}{R} = 0$$

$$4x - y = 100 \quad -(1) \times 4$$

To find junction potentials we write KCL equation for y as

$$\frac{y-x}{R} + \frac{y-x}{R} + \frac{y-(100-y)}{R} = 0$$

$$4y - 2x = 100 \quad -(2)$$

$$14x = 500$$

$$\Rightarrow \quad x = \frac{250}{7}\text{ V}$$

Equivalent resistance of the circuit across points A and B is given as

$$R_{eq} = \frac{V_{battery}}{I_{battery}} = \frac{100}{I_1 + 2I_2}$$

$$\Rightarrow \quad R_{eq} = \frac{100}{\frac{100}{R} + 2\times\frac{150}{7R}} = \frac{700R}{1200}$$

$$\Rightarrow \quad R_{eq} = \frac{7}{12}R$$

Illustrative Example 3.25

Find the equivalent resistance across terminals A and B as shown in figure-3.78. Each resistance in circuit is R.

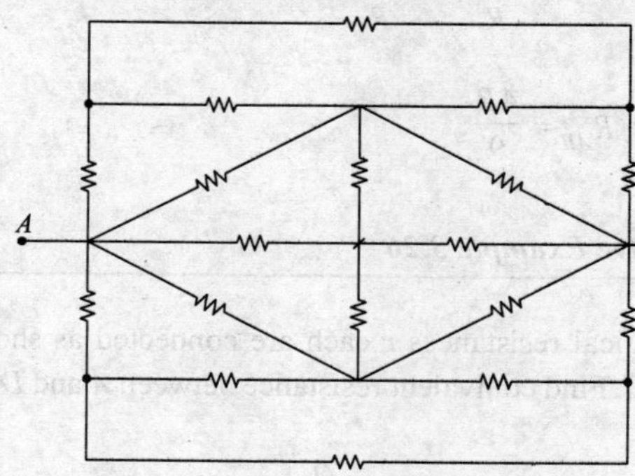

Figure 3.78

Solution

To find the equivalent resistance of the circuit, we connect a 100 V battery across the terminals A and B and distribute potentials at different junctions of the circuit as shown in figure-3.79.

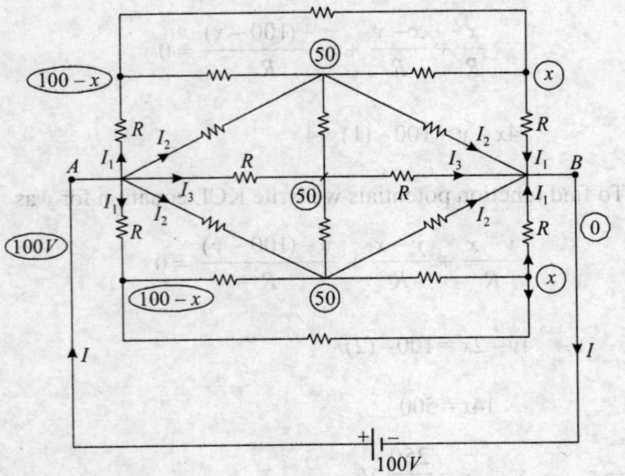

Figure 3.79

To find junction potentials we write KCL equation for x as

$$\frac{x}{R}+\frac{x-50}{R}+\frac{x-(100-x)}{R}=0$$

$$4x=150$$

$$x=\frac{75}{2}\text{V}$$

Equivalent resistance of the circuit across points A and B is given as

$$R_{eq}=\frac{V_{\text{battery}}}{I_{\text{battery}}}=\frac{100}{2I_1+2I_2+I_3}$$

$$\Rightarrow \quad R_{eq}=\frac{100}{\frac{2x}{R}+\frac{3(50-0)}{R}}=\frac{100R}{75+150}$$

$$\Rightarrow \quad R_{AB}=\frac{4R}{9}$$

Illustrative Example 3.26

Eight identical resistances r each are connected as shown in figure-3.80. Find equivalent resistance between A and D.

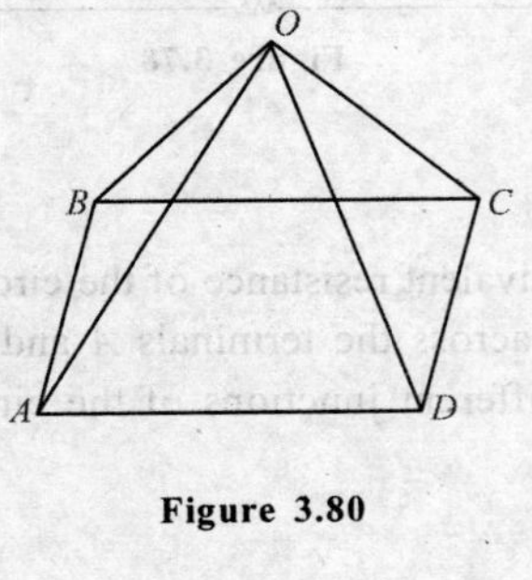

Figure 3.80

Solution

To find the equivalent resistance across A and D, we connect a 100 V battery and distribute potentials as shown in figure-3.81

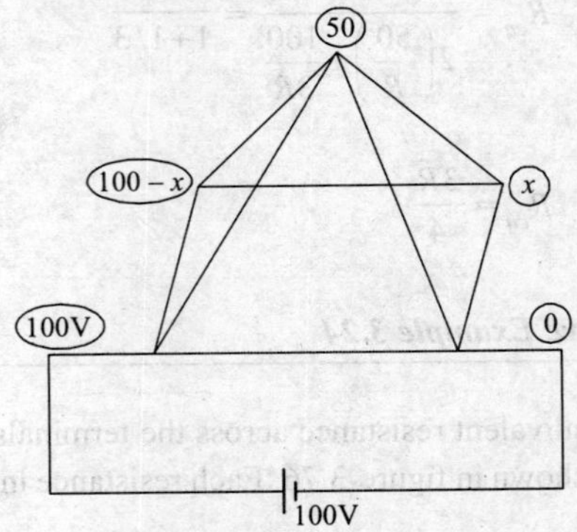

Figure 3.81

To calculate unknown potential we write KCL equation for x as

$$\frac{x-0}{r}+\frac{x-50}{r}+\frac{x-(100-x)}{r}=0$$

$$\Rightarrow \quad 4x=150$$

$$\Rightarrow \quad x=\frac{75}{2}V$$

Current through battery is given as

$$I_{\text{battery}}=\frac{x}{r}+\frac{100}{r}+\frac{50}{r}=\frac{75}{2r}+\frac{150}{r}$$

$$\Rightarrow \quad I_{\text{battery}}=\frac{375}{2r}$$

Equivalent resistance across terminals A and D is given as

$$R_{\text{eq}}=\frac{V_{\text{battery}}}{I_{\text{battery}}}=\frac{100\times 2r}{375}=\frac{8r}{15}$$

Illustrative Example 3.27

In the circuit shown in figure-3.82, find the current through battery and current in 8 Ω resistances.

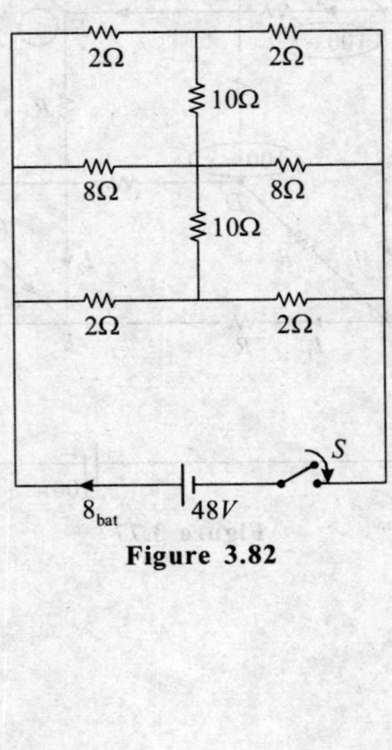

Figure 3.82

Solution

We distribute potentials in circuit as shown in figure-3.83, by symmetry we can see that no variable is used here

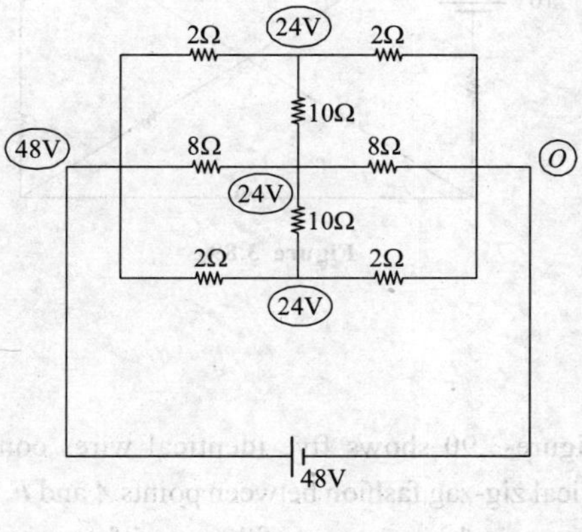

Figure 3.83

we can see that current in resistances are

$$I_{2\Omega} = \frac{24}{2} = 12\text{A}$$

$$I_{8\Omega} = \frac{24}{8} = 3\text{A}$$

Current through battery is

$$I_{\text{battery}} = 2I_{2\Omega} + I_{8\Omega} = 2 \times 12 + 3 = 27\,\text{A}$$

Illustrative Example 3.28

What is the equivalent resistance between the terminal points *A* and *B* in the circuit shown in figure-3.84.

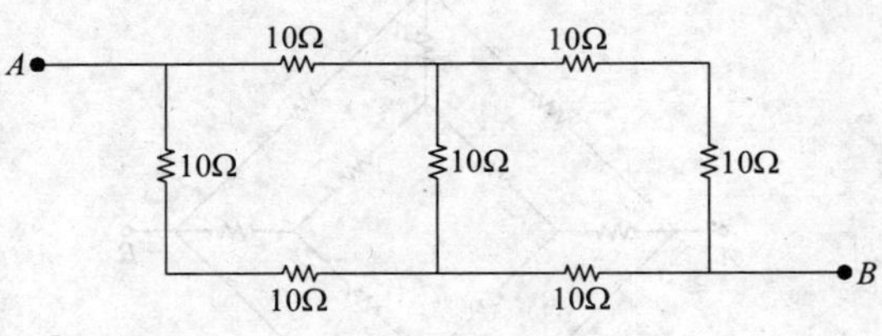

Figure 3.84

Solution

The circuit shown is an unbalanced wheatstone bridge with symmetry similar to the illustration we've solved in article-3.4.1. To analyze this circuit, we connect a 100 V battery and distribute the potentials at different junctions of the circuit as shown in figure-3.85.

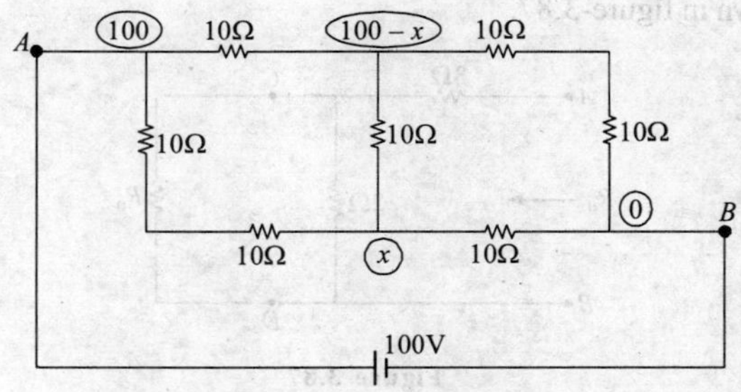

Figure 3.85

To find the unknown potential *x* we write KCL equation as

$$\frac{x-0}{10} + \frac{2x-100}{10} + \frac{x-100}{20} = 0$$

$$\Rightarrow \qquad 7x = 300$$

$$\Rightarrow \qquad x = \frac{300}{7}\,\text{V}$$

Current through the battery is given as

$$I_{\text{battery}} = \frac{x}{10} + \frac{100-x}{20}$$

$$\Rightarrow \qquad I_{\text{battery}} = \frac{300/7}{10} + \frac{400/7}{20} = \frac{50}{7}\,\text{A}$$

Equivalent resistance of the circuit is given as

$$R_{\text{eq}} = \frac{V_{\text{battery}}}{I_{\text{battery}}}$$

$$\Rightarrow \qquad R_{\text{eq}} = \frac{100}{50/7} = 14\,\Omega$$

Illustrative Example 3.29

Find the equivalent resistance of the infinite ladder circuit shown in figure-3.86 across terminals *A* and *B*.

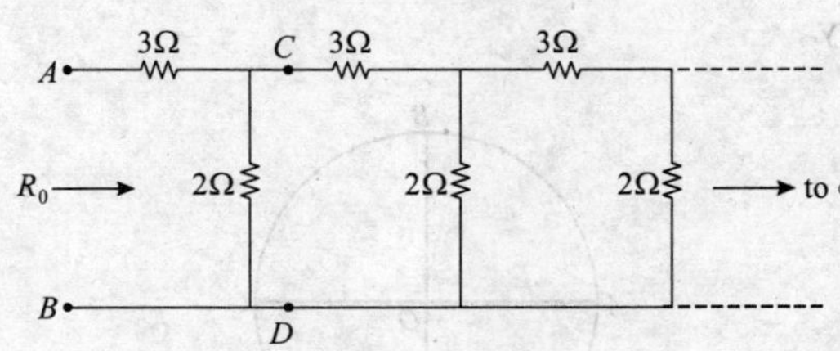

Figure 3.86

Solution

If equivalent resistance across terminals *A* and *B* is considered as R_0 then across points *C* and *D* also toward right of it the network resistance will be same so we reduce the circuit as shown in figure-3.87.

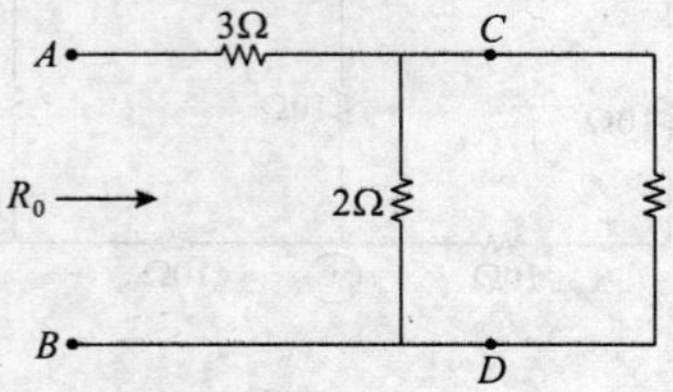

Figure 3.87

Using series and parallel combination the equivalent resistance of this circuit is given as

$$R_0 = 3 + \frac{2R_0}{2+R_0}$$

$$\Rightarrow \quad 2R_0 + R_0^2 = 6 + 5R_0$$

$$\Rightarrow \quad R_0^2 - 3R_0 - 6 = 0$$

$$\Rightarrow \quad R_0 = \frac{3 \pm \sqrt{9+24}}{2} = \frac{3+\sqrt{33}}{2}\,\Omega$$

Web Reference at www.physicsgalaxy.com

Age Group - Grade 11 & 12 | Age 17-19 Years
Section - ELECTRIC CURRENT & CIRCUITS
Topic - Circuit Analysis
Module Number - 12 to 17

Practice Exercise 3.4

(i) In the network of resistances shown in figure-3.88. *ABCDA* is a uniform circular wire of resistance 2 Ω. *AOC* and *BOD* are two wires along two perpendicular diameters of the circle, each having same resistance 1 Ω. A battery of voltage *E* is inserted in one quadrant of the network as shown in figure. Calculate the equivalent resistance of the network across the battery.

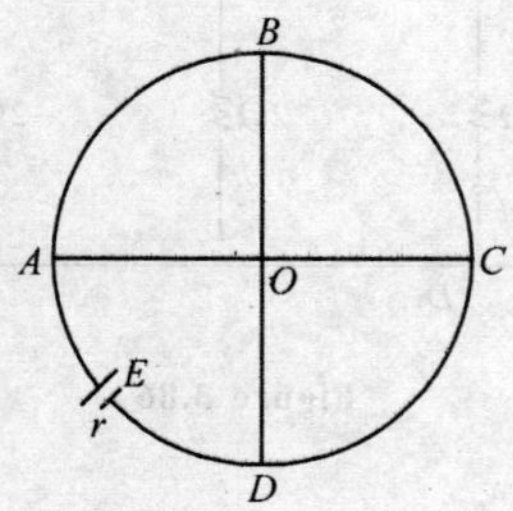

Figure 3.88

[$\frac{15}{14}$ Ω]

(ii) Determine the current *I* supplied by the battery in the circuit shown in figure-3.89, where each resistor has a resistance of 3 Ω.

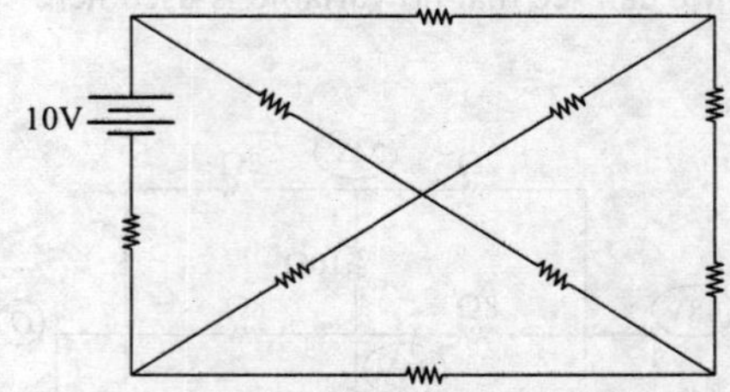

Figure 3.89

[$\frac{14}{9}$ A]

(iii) Figure-3.90 shows five identical wires connected in symmetrical zig-zag fashion between points *A* and *F*. What will be the change in the resistance of the circuit between *A* and *F* if two similar identical wires are added as shown by the dashed line in figure-3.90.

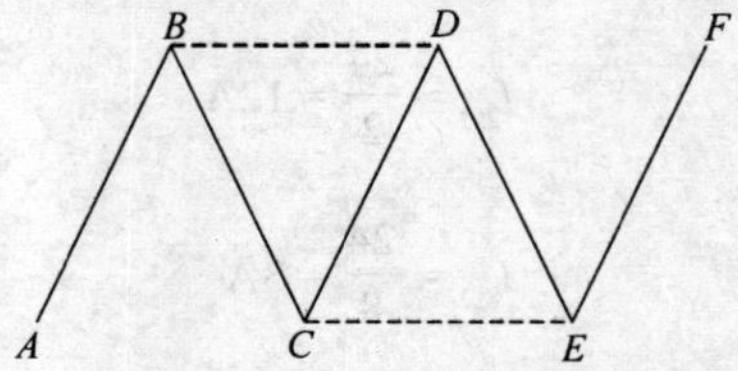

Figure 3.90

[Final Resistance becomes 0.6 times that of initial]

(iv) The figure-3.91 shows a network of resistor each heaving value 12 Ω. Find the equivalent resistance between points *A* and *B*.

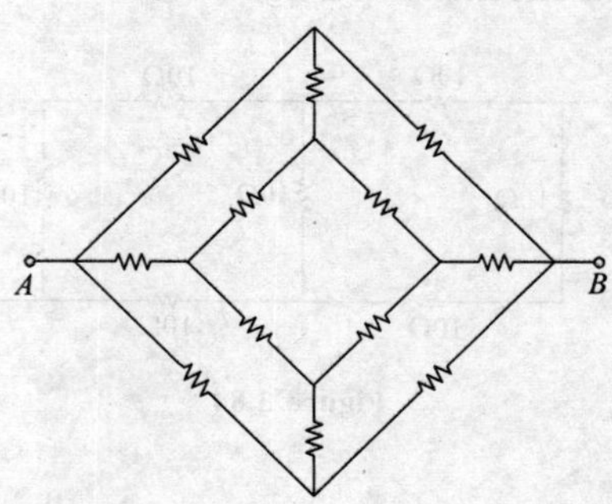

Figure 3.91

[9Ω]

(v) Nine wires each of resistance *r* are connected to make a prism as shown in figure-3.92. Find the equivalent resistance of the arrangement across terminals (a) A and D (b) A and B

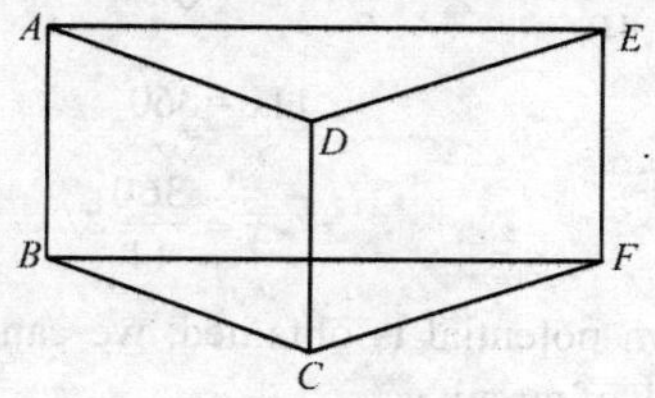

Figure 3.92

[(a) $\frac{8}{15}r$ (b) $\frac{3}{5}r$]

(vi) **An infinite ladder network of resistances constructed with 1 Ω and 2 Ω resistances as shown in figure-3.93.**

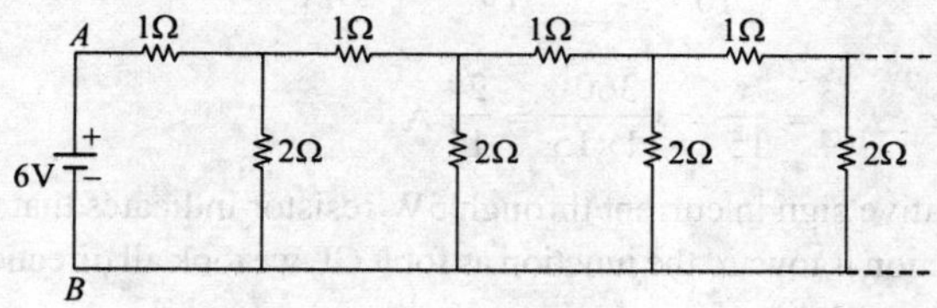

Figure 3.93

The 6V battery between A and B has negligible internal resistance.

(a) Calculate the effective resistance between points A and B.

(b) What is the current that passes through the 2 Ω resistance nearest to the battery?

[(a) 2 Ω (b) 1.5 A]

(vii) **Find the equivalent resistance of the circuit between points A and B shown in figure-3.94 is: (each branch is of resistance = 1Ω)**

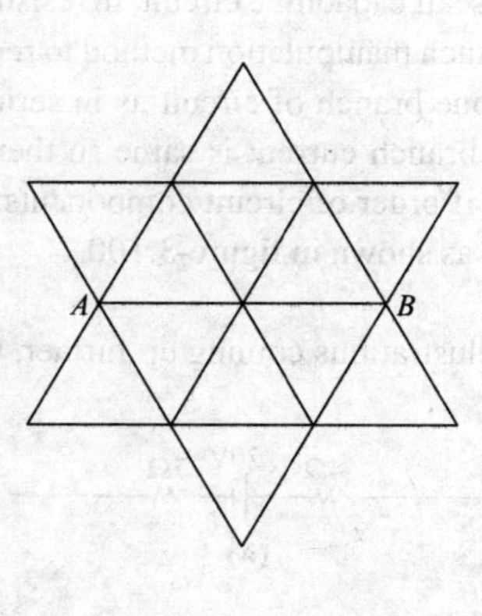

Figure 3.94

[$\frac{22}{35}$Ω]

(viii) **Find the equivalent resistance across terminals A and B in the circuit shown in figure-3.95.**

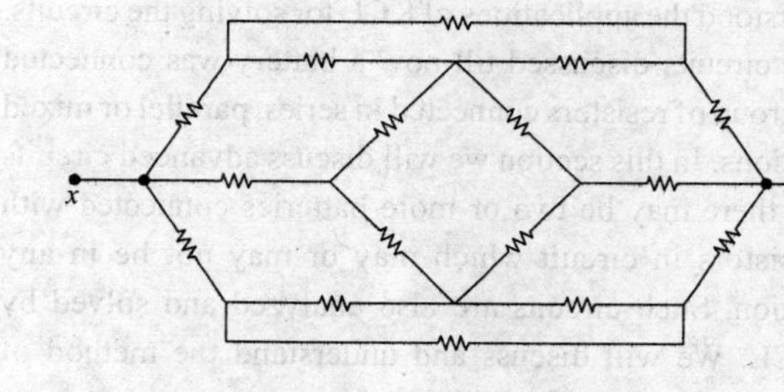

Figure 3.95

[$\frac{12R}{13}$]

(ix) **Find the equivalent resistance across terminals A and B in the circuit shown in figure-3.96.**

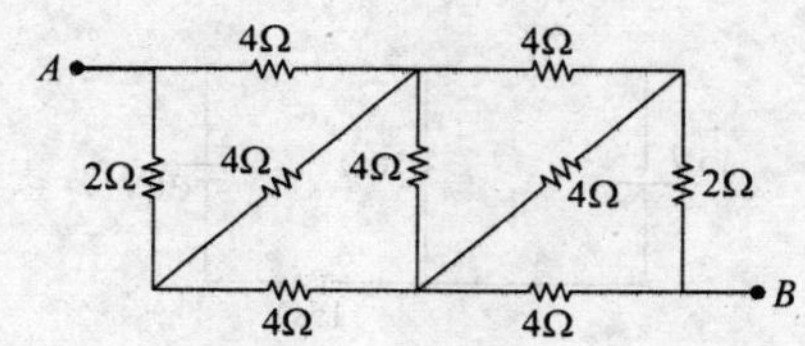

Figure 3.96

[$\frac{40}{9}$Ω]

(x) **A network of nine conductors connects six points A, B, C, D, E and F as shown in figure-3.97. The figure denotes resistances in ohms. Find the equivalents resistance between A and D.**

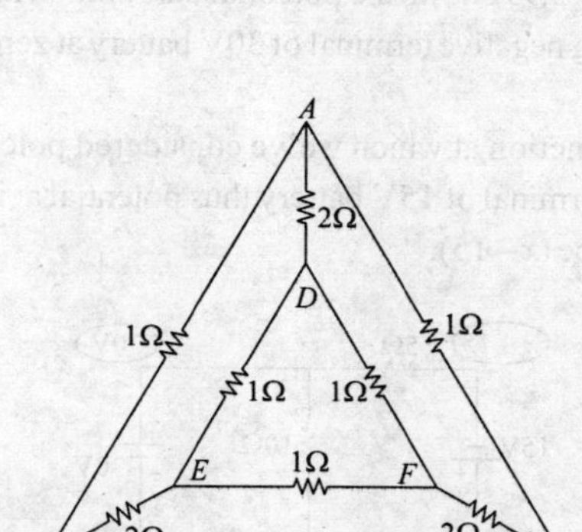

Figure 3.97

[1 Ω]

3.5 Circuits Containing More than one Battery

In previous articles we've analyzed different resistive circuits and understood the applications of KCL for solving the circuits. In all the circuits discussed till now a battery was connected across a group of resistors connected in series, parallel or mixed combinations. In this section we will discuss advanced circuits in which there may be two or more batteries connected with some resistors in circuit which may or may not be in any combination. Such circuits are also analyzed and solved by using KCL. We will discuss and understand the method of solving such circuits with an illustration.

Figure-3.98 shows a circuit in which two batteries and three resistors are connected with two switches which are initially open. When the switches are closed, current will start flowing in the circuit and these currents we will determine using Kirchhoff's Current Law as described further.

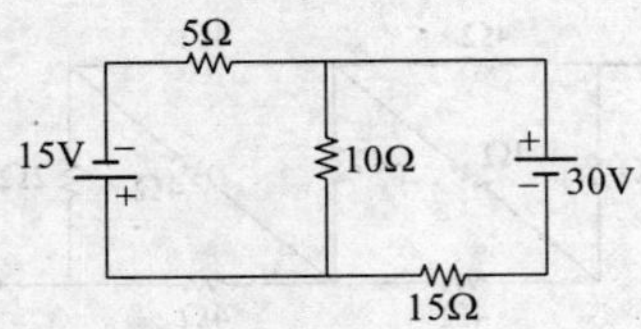

Figure 3.98

To start with KCL we need a reference point in circuit at zero potential. In case of single battery connected across the group of resistances we consider zero potential at negative terminal of the battery and distribute potentials at different parts of circuit. In cases of multiple batteries we can take any one battery's negative terminal as a reference (or any other point can also be taken). Figure-3.99 shows the potential distribution in the circuit by considering negative terminal of 30V battery at zero potential.

Here at the junction at which we've considered potential x is at the positive terminal of 15V battery thus potential at its negative terminal will be $(x-15)$.

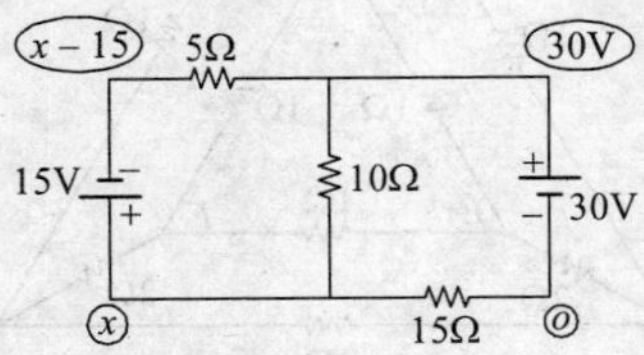

Figure 3.99

To determine the unknown potential x, we write KCL equation for the this junction at which three wires are connected and we write the sum of outgoing currents from the junction is equal to zero thus we have

$$\frac{x}{15}+\frac{x-30}{10}+\frac{x-15-30}{5}=0$$

$$\Rightarrow \qquad 11x=360$$

$$\Rightarrow \qquad x=\frac{360}{11}\text{ V}$$

As the unknown potential is obtained, we can write current from any branch of circuit as

$$I_{5\Omega}=\frac{x-45}{5}=\frac{\left(\frac{360}{11}-45\right)}{5}=-\frac{27}{11}\text{ A}$$

$$I_{10\Omega}=\frac{x-30}{10}=\frac{\left(\frac{360}{11}-30\right)}{10}=\frac{3}{11}\text{ A}$$

$$I_{15\Omega}=\frac{x}{15}=\frac{360}{11\times 15}=\frac{24}{11}\text{ A}$$

Negative sign in current through 5W resistor indicates that the direction is toward the junction as for KCL we took all directions in outward direction.

Like the application we have already discussed in nodal analysis of capacitive circuits, in case of KCL also if any circuit is containing more than one battery then we should be careful that only one point we need to consider in circuit as a zero potential reference and then distribute the potentials to all parts of circuit and write KCL equations for all the unknown potentials.

Once potential of all parts of circuit are obtained, current in any branch of the circuit can be directly calculated by using Ohm's law.

3.5.1 Branch Manipulation in Resistive Circuits

Similar to the case of capacitive circuit, in resistive circuits also we can apply branch manipulation method to reduce number of components in one branch of circuit as in series combination through out the branch current is same so there would be no effect on circuit if order of circuit components are changed in the same branch as shown in figure-3.100.

In some of the illustrations coming up further, we will see this application.

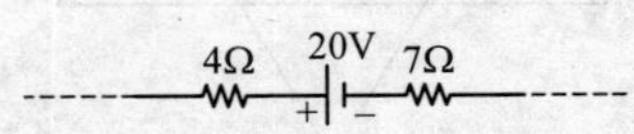

(a)

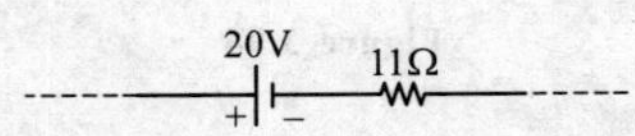

(b)

Figure 3.100

Illustrative Example 3.30

In the circuit shown in figure-3.101, find the potentials of A, B, C and D and the current through 1Ω and 2Ω resistance.

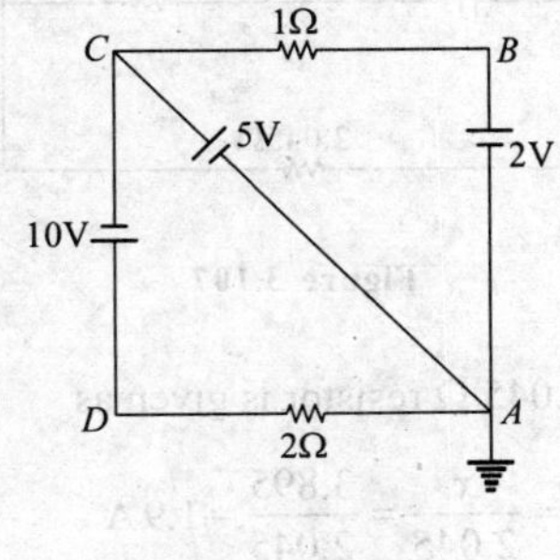

Figure 3.101

Solution

Distributing potentials as shown in figure-3.102

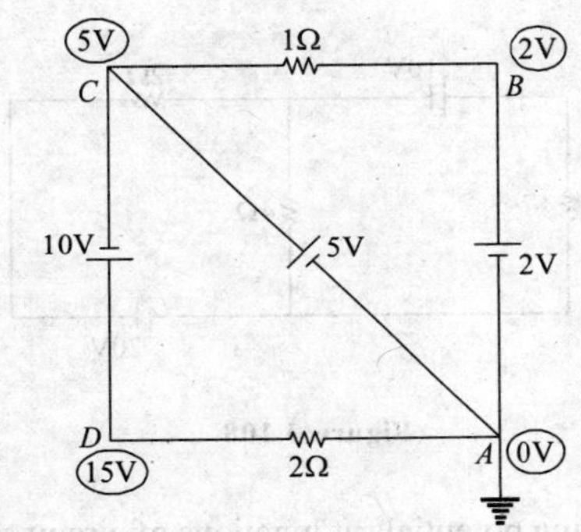

Figure 3.102

As all potentials are known currents in resistance can be given as

$$I_{1\Omega} = \frac{5-2}{1} = 3\,\text{A (left to right)}$$

and

$$I_{2\Omega} = \frac{15-0}{2} = 7.5\,\text{A (left to right)}$$

Illustrative Example 3.31

Find the current flowing through the resistance R_1 of the circuit shown in figure-3.103. The resistances are equal to $R_1 = 10\ \Omega$, $R_2 = 20\ \Omega$ and $R_3 = 30\ \Omega$ and the potentials of points 1, 2 and 3 are given as $V_1 = 10$ V, $V_2 = 6$ V and $V_3 = 5$ V.

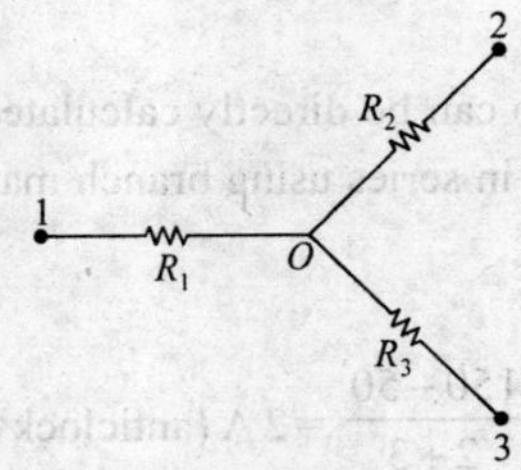

Figure 3.103

Solution

Considering potential at junction O to be equal to x as shown in figure-3.104 and writing KCL equation at this junction, we have

$$\frac{x-10}{10} + \frac{x-5}{30} + \frac{x-6}{20} = 0$$

$$\Rightarrow \quad 6x - 60 + 2x - 10 + 3x - 18 = 0$$

$$\Rightarrow \quad 11x = 88$$

$$\Rightarrow \quad x = 8\text{ V}$$

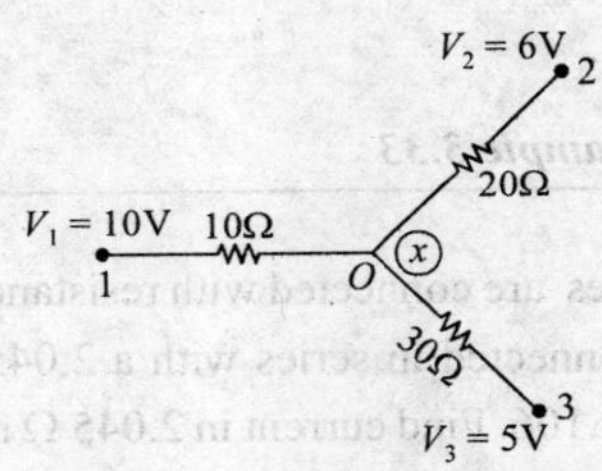

Figure 3.104

Current through R_1 is given as

$$I_1 = \frac{10-x}{R_1} = \frac{10-8}{10} = 0.2\text{ A}$$

Illustrative Example 3.32

In figure-3.105, if the potential at point P is 100 V, what is the potential at point Q ?

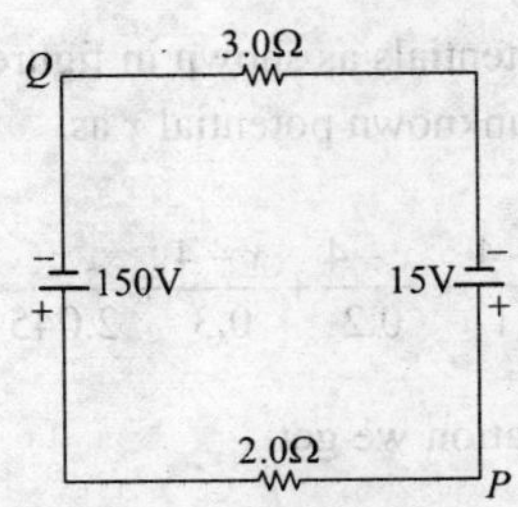

Figure 3.105

Solution

The current in loop can be directly calculated by considering the two resistances in series using branch manipulation which gives

$$I = \frac{150-50}{2+3} = 2\text{ A (anticlockwise)}$$

If potential at point Q is V_Q then potential at the bottom terminal of the 150 V battery will be $(V_Q + 150)$ and the potential drop across 2 Ω resistance is given by Ohm's law which gives the potential of point P which can be written as

$$V_Q + 150 - 20 \times 2 = V_P$$

$$\Rightarrow \quad V_Q = V_P - 110 = -10\text{ V.}$$

Above solution we analyzed by using Ohm's law and writing the equation of potential drop. Students are advised to solve this question by using KCL by considering potential x at point Q and then writing KCL equation for x and verify the result obtained.

 # Illustrative Example 3.33

Three 4 V batteries are connected with resistance 0.1 Ω, 0.2 Ω and 0.3 Ω are connected in series with a 2.045 Ω resistor as shown in figure-3.106. Find current in 2.045 Ω resistance.

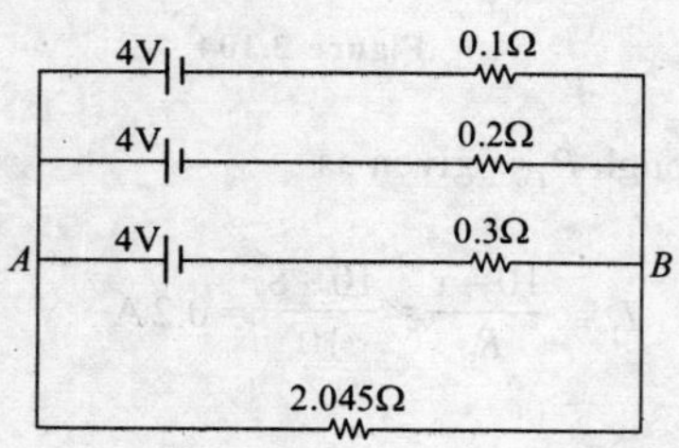

Figure 3.106

Solution

Distributing the potentials as shown in figure-3.107, we write KCL equation for unknown potential x as

$$\frac{x-4}{0.1} + \frac{x-4}{0.2} + \frac{x-4}{0.3} + \frac{x}{2.045} = 0$$

Solving above equation we get

$$x = 3.895\text{ V}$$

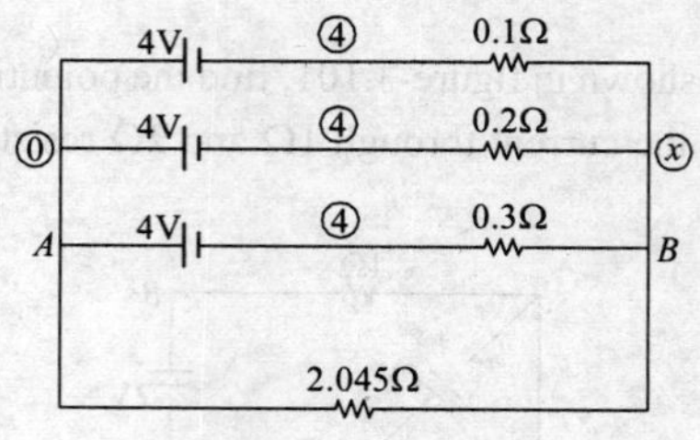

Figure 3.107

Thus current in 2.045 Ω resistor is given as

$$I = \frac{x}{2.045} = \frac{3.895}{2.045} = 1.9\text{ A}$$

Above can be directly analyzed by using the combination of cells which we will study in upcoming articles.

 # Illustrative Example 3.34

Find the current in 4 Ω resistance in circuit shown in figure-3.108.

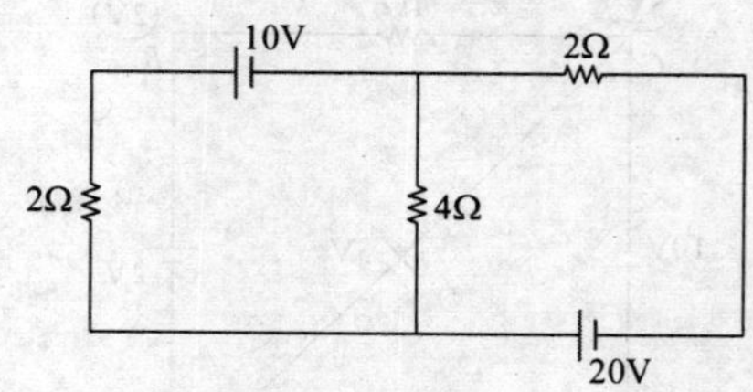

Figure 3.108

Sol. Distributing potentials at junctions of circuit as shown in figure-3.109, we write KCL equation for unknown potential x as

$$\frac{x}{4} + \frac{x-20}{2} + \frac{x-10}{2} = 0$$

$$\Rightarrow \quad x = 12\text{ V}$$

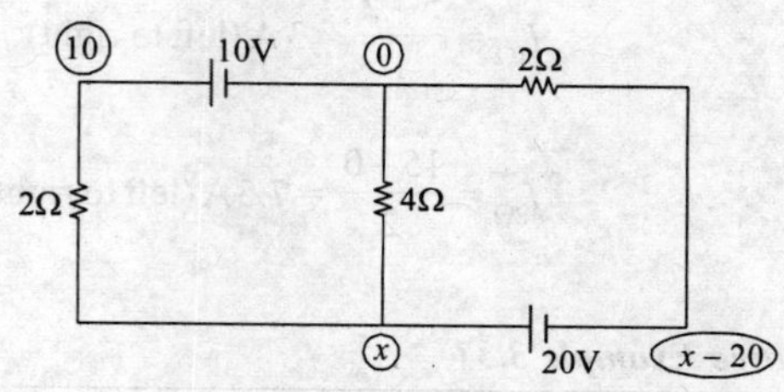

Figure 3.109

The current in 4 Ω resistance is given as

$$I = \frac{12}{4} = 3\text{ A}$$

Practice Exercise 3.5

(i) Find the current in 5 Ω resistance in circuit shown in figure-3.110

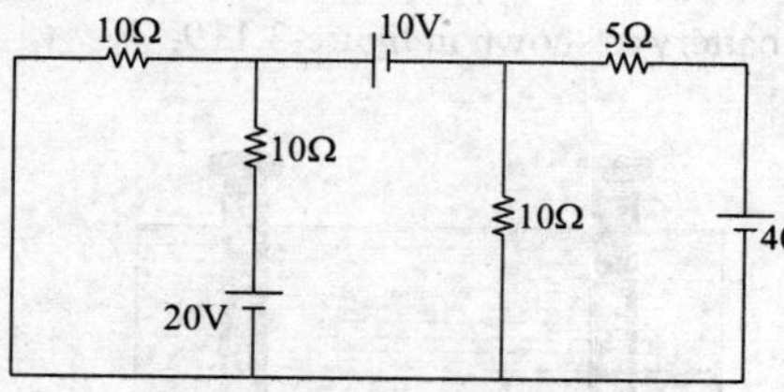

Figure 3.110

[4.8A]

(ii) For what value of battery voltage *E* the potential of *A* is equal to the potential of *B*?

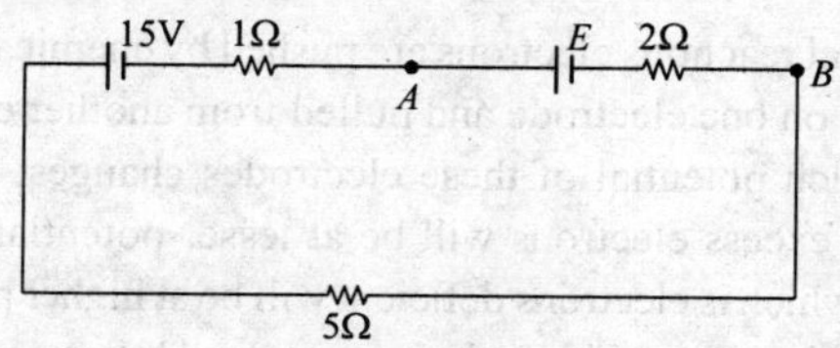

Figure 3.111

[5V]

(iii) Find current in 4 Ω resistance in circuit shown in figure-3.112

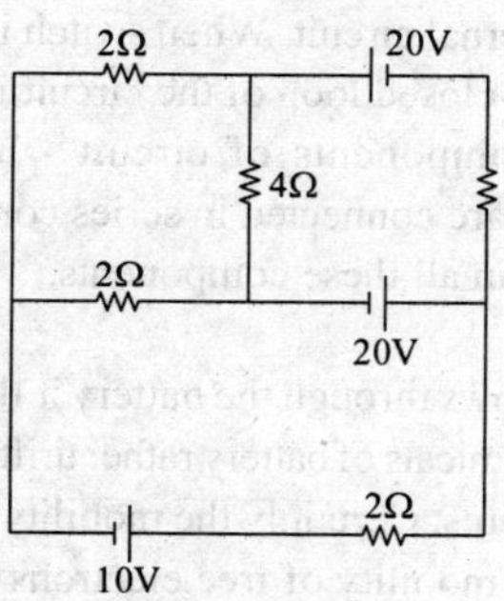

Figure 3.112

[5A]

(iv) In the circuit shown in figure-3.113 find potential difference between the point *A* and *B* and the currents through each branch.

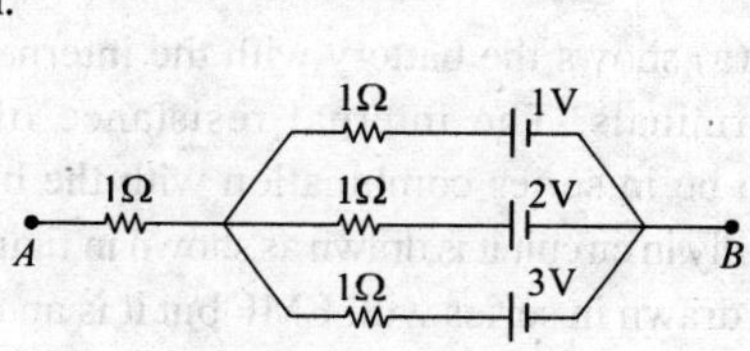

Figure 3.113

[2 V, 1 A, 0, 1 A]

(v) Find current in 10 Ω resistance in the circuit shown in figure-3.114.

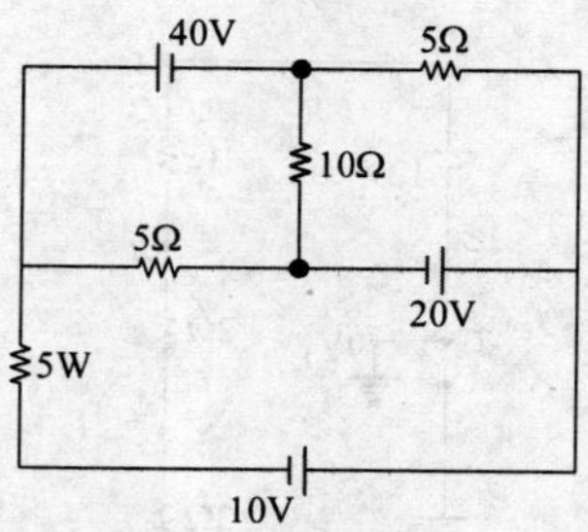

Figure 3.114

[$\frac{10}{7}$ A]

(vi) Find the currents in different resistors shown in figure-3.115.

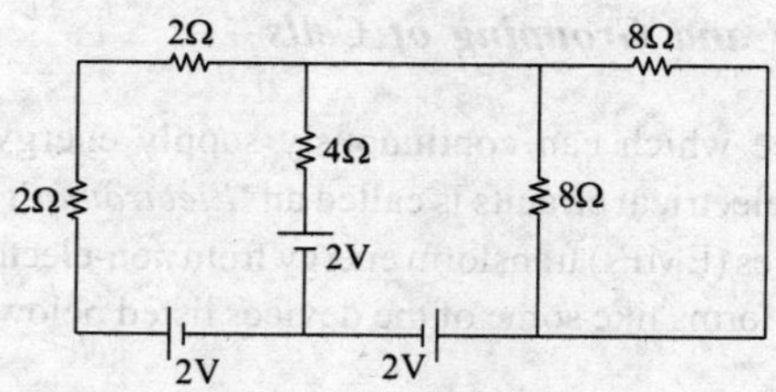

Figure 3.115

[Zero in all resistors]

(vii) In the circuit shown in figure-3.116, find :

(a) The current in the 3 Ω resistor

(b) The unknown emfs E_1 and E_2

(c) The resistance *R*

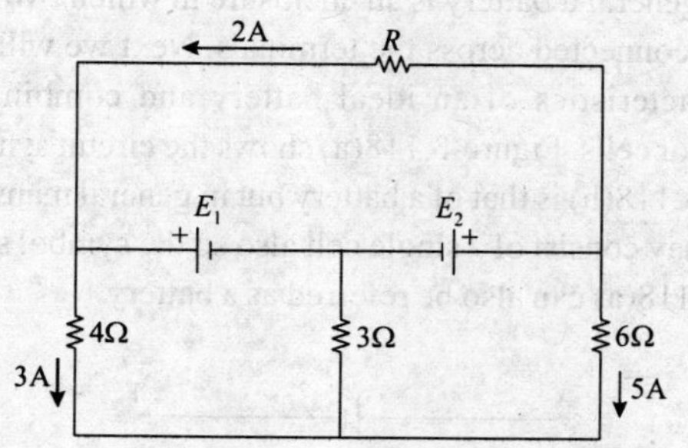

Figure 3.116

[(a) 8 A (b) 36 V, 54 V (c) 9 Ω]

(viii) Calculate the potentials of points A, B, C and D as shown in figure-3.117. What would be the new potential values if connections of 6 V battery are reversed ?

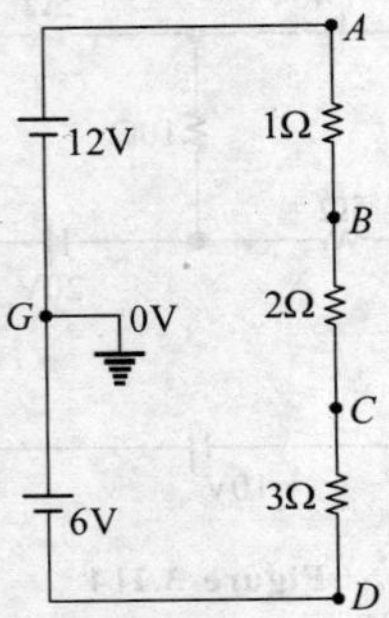

Figure 3.117

[12 V, 9 V, 3 V, –6 V and 12 V, 11 V, 9 V, 6 V]

3.6 EMF and Grouping of Cells

Any device which can continuously supply energy to flow current in electrical circuits is called an '*Electromotive Force*'. Such devices (EMFs) transform energy from non-electrical form to electric forms like some of the devices listed below.

Battery : Transforms chemical energy to electrical energy.
Generator : Transforms mechanical energy to electrical energy.
Nuclear Reactor : Transforms nuclear energy to electrical energy

The term EMF as a standard is referred to the open circuit potential difference of such devices like a battery is of EMF 5 V, 10 V, 20 V etc.

Mostly in electrical circuits at low voltages we use batteries or cells. In general a battery is an enclosure in which two or more cells are connected across the terminals. Next we will discuss the characteristics of an ideal battery and combination of batteries or cells. Figure-3.118(a) shows the circuit symbol of a cell and 3.118(b) is that of a battery but in general many times a battery may consist of a single cell also so the symbol shown in figure-3.118(a) can also be referred as a battery.

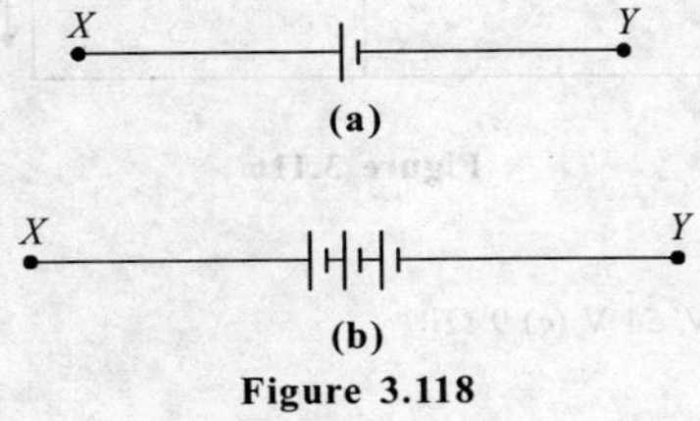

Figure 3.118

3.6.1 Internal Resistance of a Battery

As already discussed that a battery transforms chemical energy to electrical energy. Inside a battery there are some chemicals in which two electrodes are dipped or submerged which are called terminals of battery as shown in figure-3.119.

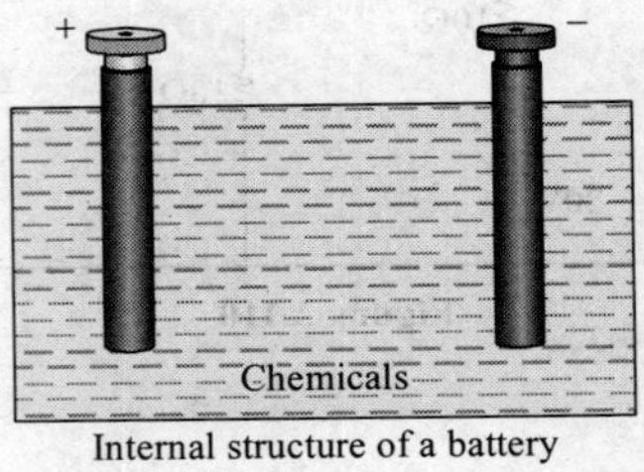

Internal structure of a battery

Figure 3.119

By chemical reactions electrons are pushed by chemicals inside the battery on one electrode and pulled from another electrode due to which potential of these electrodes changes. The one which has excess electrons will be at lesser potential and the other one which is electrons deficient will be at higher potential. When the circuit outside the battery is closed then continuous chemical reactions take place inside the battery and a continuous supply of current by the battery is maintained in circuit until whole of chemicals of battery gets exhausted.

Figure-3.120 shows a rough internal structure of a battery connected to an external circuit. When switch is closed current starts flowing in the closed loop of the circuit in which we can consider all the components of circuit - battery, switch, resistance and bulb are connected in series combination. Thus same current flows in all these components.

When the current flows through the battery it flows due to flow of ions inside the chemicals of battery rather drift of free electrons in the connecting wires. Certainly the mobility for flow of ions is less compared to mobility of free electrons in conductor so conductivity of chemicals is less compared to connecting wires hence the battery chemicals always offer some resistance to flow of current as it is connected in series. This resistance due to chemical composition of battery is called '*Internal Resistance of battery*'.

Figure-3.120(a) shows the battery with the internal resistance across its terminals. The internal resistance of battery is considered to be in series combination with the battery EMF and symbolically in circuit it is drawn as shown in figure-3.120(b). It is however drawn in series with EMF but it is an integral part of battery structure so it can never be isolated from the battery and always there will be a potential drop across this resistance when current flows through the battery.

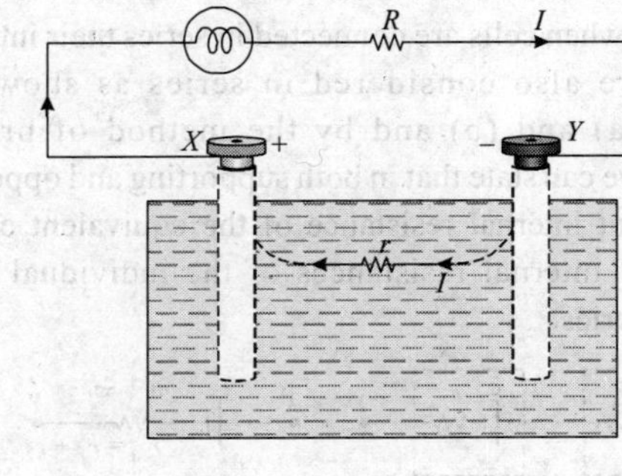

(a)

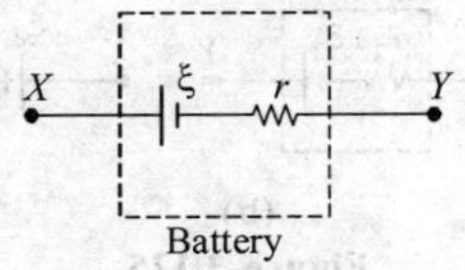

(b)

Figure 3.120

For an ideal battery its internal resistance is considered as zero and for a real battery under practical conditions as it is used its chemicals are consumed and with time its internal resistance increases and as already discussed, we can consider a real battery as a combination of an ideal battery in series with its internal resistance.

3.6.2 Terminal Potential Difference of a Battery

Under open circuit conditions as shown in figure-3.121(a) the terminal potential difference of battery is equal to its emf ξ as no current is flowing through the battery so no potential drop take place across the internal resistance of the battery thus under open circuit we have

$$V_X - V_Y = \xi \quad \ldots(3.87)$$

When a battery is supplying current in a circuit then current flows out from the positive terminal of the battery which is at higher potential as shown in figure-3.121(b). We can write the potential equation from terminal X to Y in this figure as

$$V_X - \xi + Ir = V_Y$$

$$\Rightarrow \quad V_X - V_Y = \xi - Ir \quad \ldots(3.88)$$

From equation-(3.88) we can see that under the state when a battery is supplying current in a circuit, the terminal potential difference of the battery is less than its EMF. There can be another condition in which current is supplied into the battery or the case when current enters into the positive terminal of the battery as shown in figure-3.121(c). This happens when a higher EMF battery is connected across this battery so the higher EMF battery dominates the current flow. In this state if we write potential equation from terminal X to Y then we have

$$V_X - \xi - Ir = V_Y$$

$$\Rightarrow \quad V_X - V_Y = \xi + Ir \quad \ldots(3.89)$$

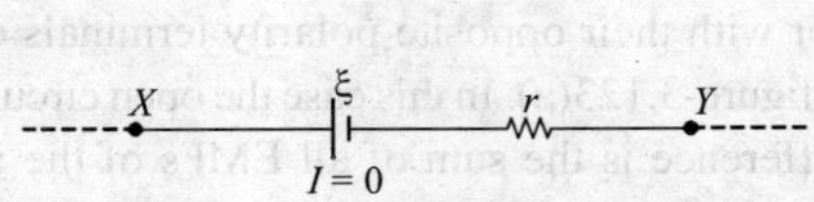

(a)

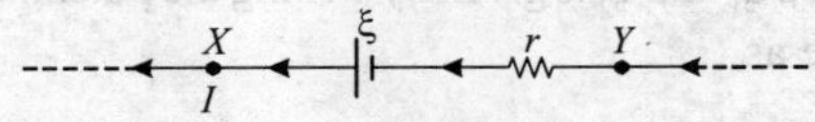

(b)

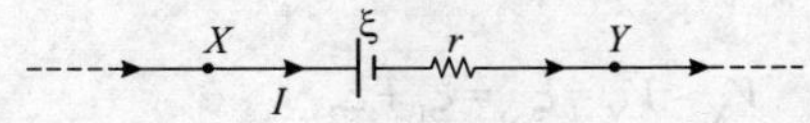

(c)

Figure 3.121

From equation-(3.89) we can see that under state when current is supplied into a battery by some other external source then terminal potential difference of the battery is more than the battery EMF.

For a real battery when it supplies current then its chemicals are used and with time its internal resistance increases and during supply of current according to equation-(3.88) its terminal potential difference decreases as r increases due to which current in circuit also drops further. For a battery its EMF always remain constant but over a period of time when it gets exhausted its internal resistance increase to a high value because of which it cannot supply current when connected in a circuit because its terminal potential difference drops to almost zero as r becomes very high. This is the state when we say that a battery is completely discharged.

3.6.3 Grouping of Cells in Series

When two or more cells are connected one after another as shown in figure-3.122(a) then these cells are said to be connected in series and for the combination we replace it with a single cell called '*Equivalent Cell*' having its '*Equivalent EMF*' and '*Equivalent Internal Resistance*' of the cell combination as shown in figure-3.122(b)

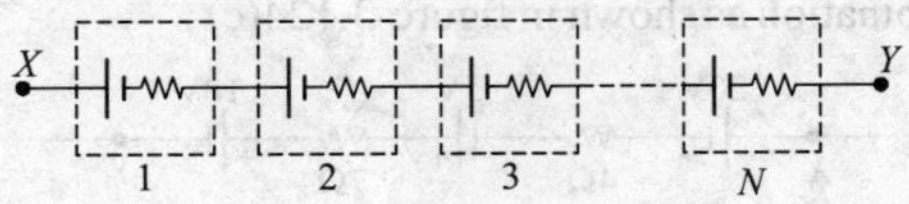

(a)

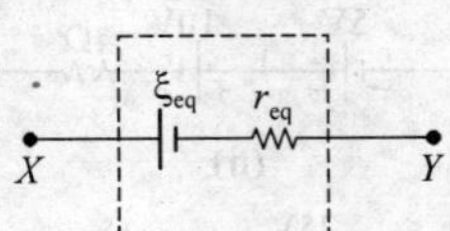

(b)

Figure 3.122

There are two ways in which cells can be connected in series combination called '*Supporting Mode*' and '*Opposing Mode*'. In supporting mode series combination cells are connected one after another with their opposite polarity terminals connected as shown in figure-3.123(a). In this case the open circuit terminal potential difference is the sum of all EMFs of the individual cells as in this case equivalent EMF of this combination of two cells of EMFs ξ_1 and ξ_2 is given by writing the potential equation for this case as

$$V_X - \xi_1 - \xi_2 = V_Y$$

$$\Rightarrow \quad V_X - V_Y = \xi_{eq} = \xi_1 + \xi_2 \quad \ldots (3.90)$$

In opposite mode series combination cells are connected one after another with their same polarity terminals connected together so that they oppose each other in supplying the current as shown in figure-3.123(b). In this case open circuit potential difference is the difference of EMFs of the individual cells. If we write the potential equation for this case, we have

$$V_X - \xi_1 + \xi_2 = V_Y$$

$$\Rightarrow \quad V_X - V_Y = \xi_{eq} = \xi_1 - \xi_2 \quad \ldots (3.91)$$

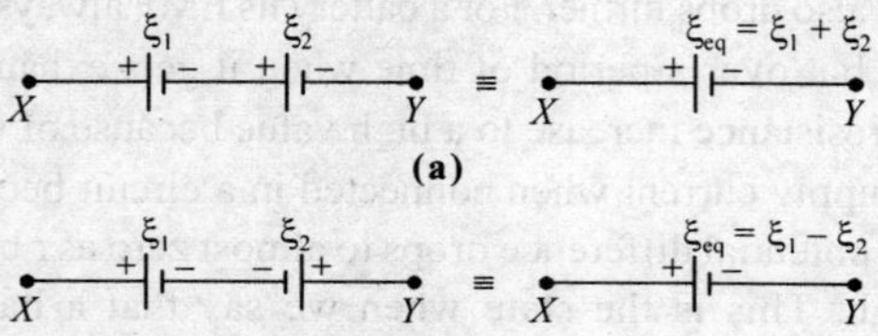

Figure 3.123

When multiple batteries are connected in series combination, we can always club the batteries using supporting and opposing mode and branch manipulation method. Figure-3.124(a) shows a branch of a circuit in which three batteries are connected with two resistances. Using branch manipulation method we can shuffle the components of this branch as shown in figure-3.124(b) and then we can reduce this branch by using cell combination as shown in figure-3.124(c)

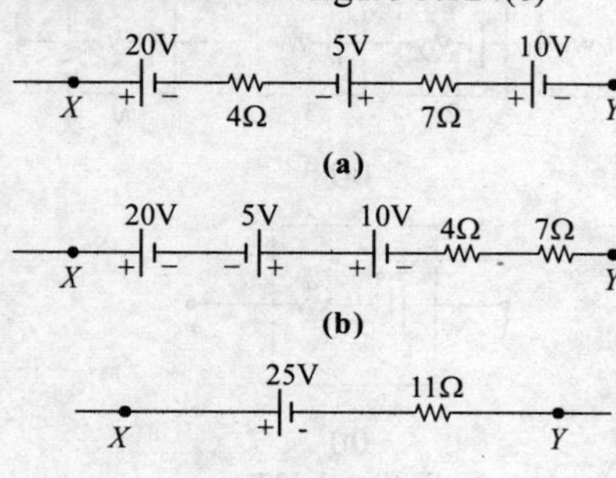

Figure 3.124

In above cases we considered ideal cells without their internal resistances but when cells are connected in series their internal resistances are also considered in series as shown in figure-3.125(a) and (b) and by the method of branch manipulation we can state that in both supporting and opposing mode equivalent internal resistance of the equivalent cell is always sum of internal resistances of the individual cells connected in series.

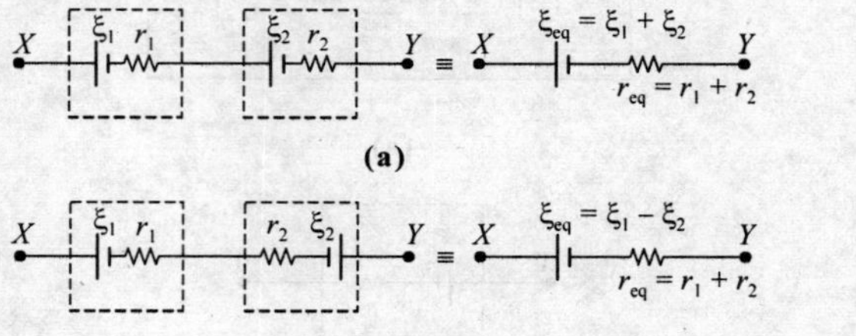

Figure 3.125

When N identical cells each of EMF ξ and internal resistance r are connected in series then from equation-(71) we can see that the equivalent EMF of the combination will be $N\xi$ and internal resistance of combination will be Nr.

3.6.4 Grouping of Cells in Parallel

Parallel combination of cells is joining both terminals of cells together with same polarity in general whereas in some cases opposite polarity terminals can also be connected. Figure-3.126(a) shows three cells connected in parallel across terminals A and B. In this state the terminals A and B are not externally connected and across the two we consider the single equivalent cell for this combination as shown in figure-3.126(b).

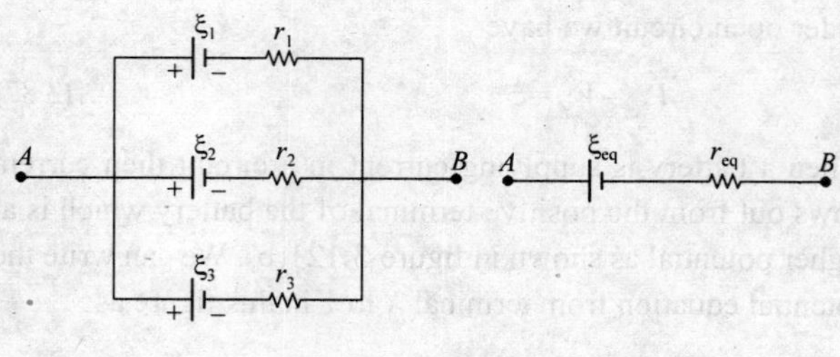

Figure 3.126

The open circuit potential difference across terminals A and B in figure-3.126(a) will be considered as equivalent EMF of the combination and as ideal battery resistance is zero across terminals A and B we can see that total resistance will be the parallel combination of the three internal resistance only, thus equivalent internal resistance is given as

$$\frac{1}{r_{eq}} = \frac{1}{r_1} + \frac{1}{r_2} + \frac{1}{r_3} \quad \ldots (3.92)$$

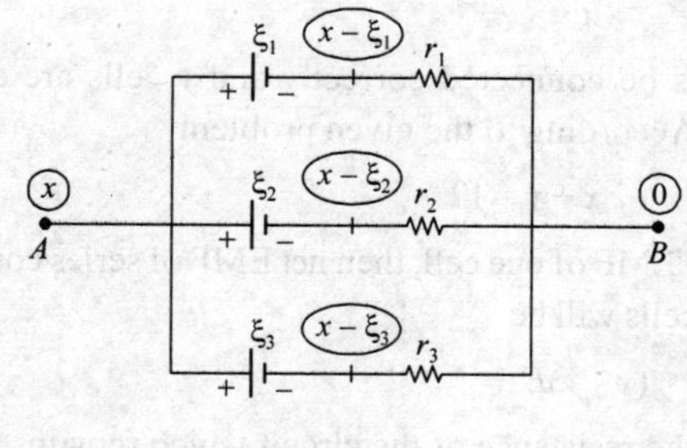

Figure 3.127

To find open circuit potential difference across terminals A and B in figure-3.126(a) we distribute potentials in this circuit as shown in figure-3.127 and write KCL equation to calculate the value of x which is written as

$$\frac{x-\xi_1}{r_1}+\frac{x-\xi_2}{r_2}+\frac{x-\xi_3}{r_3}=0$$

$$\Rightarrow \quad x=\left(\frac{\dfrac{\xi_1}{r_1}+\dfrac{\xi_2}{r_2}+\dfrac{\xi_3}{r_3}}{\dfrac{1}{r_1}+\dfrac{1}{r_2}+\dfrac{1}{r_3}}\right)=\xi_{eq} \qquad \ldots(3.93)$$

Above expression for equivalent EMF of parallel combination of cells can be generalized for N cells connected in parallel and if any cell is connected with opposite polarity then the specific term in numerator of this expression will be taken with negative sign. This we can understand with the help of an illustration shown in figure-3.128.

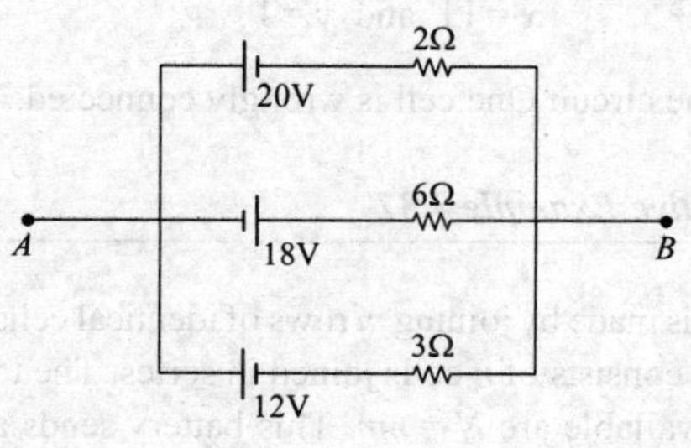

Figure 3.128

In above circuit we will calculate the equivalent EMF and equivalent internal resistance of this circuit which is a parallel combination of three cells as shown. By using equation-(3.92) we can find the equivalent internal resistance of this combination as

$$\frac{1}{r_{eq}}=\frac{1}{2}+\frac{1}{6}+\frac{1}{3}$$

$$\Rightarrow \qquad r_{eq}=1\Omega \qquad \ldots(3.94)$$

From equation-(3.93) we can find the equivalent EMF of this combination as

$$\xi_{eq}=\left(\frac{\dfrac{20}{2}-\dfrac{18}{6}+\dfrac{12}{3}}{\dfrac{1}{2}+\dfrac{1}{6}+\dfrac{1}{3}}\right)=11\text{V} \qquad \ldots(3.95)$$

Equation-(3.94) and (3.95) gives the equivalent EMF and internal resistance of the equivalent cell which can replace the circuit shown in figure-3.128 as shown in figure-3.129.

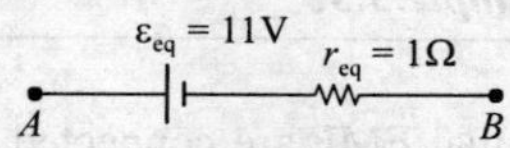

Figure 3.129

When n identical cells each of emf ξ and internal resistance r are connected in parallel then from equation-(3.93) we can see that the equivalent EMF of the combination remain same as ξ and internal resistance becomes r/n. So if in some application we need a battery with low internal resistance then we can make it by connecting the available cells in parallel without compromising on EMF.

3.6.5 Battery Grid

Battery Grid is a combination of several cells connected in series and several such series combination of cells in parallel as shown in figure-3.130.

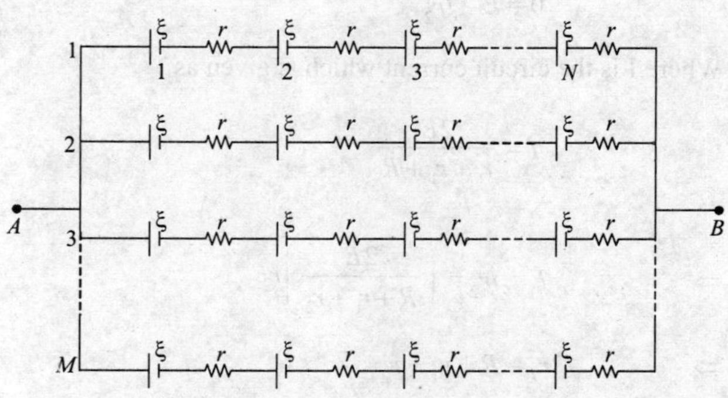

Figure 3.130

In above battery grid n identical cells each of EMF ξ and internal resistance r are connected in series in a branch and m such branches are connected in parallel. In this state equivalent EMF of each branch will be $n\xi$ and equivalent resistance nr. When such m rows are connected in parallel the equivalent EMF will remain same as in previous article we've studied that equivalent EMF doesn't change when identical cells are connected in parallel and the equivalent resistance will become nr/m. Thus the equivalent cell of above battery grid is as shown in figure-3.131.

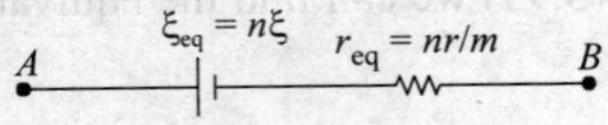

Figure 3.131

Such battery grids are made to reduce the overall internal resistance without compromising on the overall EMF to supply required power in specific applications.

Illustrative Example 3.35

Two sources of equal EMF are connected in series and have different internal resistances r_1 and $r_2(r_2 > r_1)$. Find the external resistance R at which the potential difference across the terminals of one of the sources (which one in particular) becomes equal to zero.

Solution

Terminal potential difference across a cell is given as

$$V = E - ir$$

As the sources are connected in series current for both the sources are equal so terminal potential difference will be zero for a source having higher internal resistance. Thus we can use

$$0 = E - Ir_2$$

Where I is the circuit current which is given as

$$I = \frac{2E}{r_1 + r_2 + R}$$

$$\Rightarrow \quad E = ir_2 = \left(\frac{2E}{R + r_1 + r_2}\right)r_2$$

$$\Rightarrow \quad 2r_2 = R + r_1 + r_2$$

$$\Rightarrow \quad R = r_2 - r_1$$

Illustrative Example 3.36

12 cells each having the same EMF are connected in series and are kept in a closed box. Some of the cells are wrongly connected. This battery is connected in series with an ammeter and two cells identical with the others. The current is 3 A when the cells and battery aid each other and is 2 A when the cells and battery oppose each other. How many cells in the battery are wrongly connected?

Solution

Let x cells be connected correctly and y cells are connected wrongly. According to the given problem

$$x + y = 12 \qquad \ldots(3.96)$$

If E be the EMF of one cell, then net EMF of series combination of all the cells will be

$$(x - y)E$$

Let R be the resistance of the circuit which remains constant.

(i) When the cells aid the battery, the net EMF is given as

$$E_1 = (x - y)E + 2E$$

The circuit current in this case is given as

$$I_1 = \frac{(x - y)E + 2E}{R} = 3\text{ A} \qquad \ldots(3.97)$$

(ii) When the cells oppose the battery, net EMF is given as

$$E_2 = (x - y)E - 2E$$

$$I_2 = \frac{(x - y)E - 2E}{R} = 2\text{ A} \qquad \ldots(3.98)$$

Dividing equation-(3.97) by (3.98), we get

$$\frac{(x - y)E + 2E}{(x - y)E - 2E} = \frac{3}{2}$$

$$\Rightarrow \quad \frac{(x - y) + 2}{(x - y) - 2} = \frac{3}{2}$$

Solving we get

$$x - y = 10 \qquad \ldots(3.99)$$

From equation-(3.96) and (3.99), we get

$$x = 11 \text{ and } y = 1$$

Thus in the circuit One cell is wrongly connected.

Illustrative Example 3.37

A battery is made by joining m rows of identical cells in parallel. Each row consists of n cells joined in series. The total number of cells available are $N = mn$. This battery sends a maximum current I in a given external circuit of resistance R. Now the cells are so arranged in the battery that instead of m rows, n rows are joined in parallel and each row consists of m cells joined in series. What would be the current in the external circuit now in terms of I, m and n.

Solution

Let E be the EMF of each cell. The equivalent EMF of each row will be nE and internal resistance of each row will be nr where we consider that r is the internal resistance of each cell.

Here m rows are joined in parallel. So, the total internal resistance of the circuit will be given as

$$r_{eq} = \frac{nr}{m} = \left(\frac{n^2}{N}\right)r \qquad [\text{As } mn = N]$$

Total resistance of the circuit is given as

$$R_T = R + \left(\frac{n^2}{N}\right)r$$

Current in the circuit is given as

$$I = \frac{nE}{R + \left(\frac{n^2}{N}\right)r}$$

For current to be maximum, $dI/dn = 0$ which gives

$$\frac{d}{dn}\left[\frac{nE}{R + \left(\frac{n^2}{N}\right)r}\right] = 0$$

$$\Rightarrow \frac{d}{dn}\left[nE \cdot \left\{R + \left(\frac{n^2}{N}\right)r\right\}^{-1}\right] = 0$$

$$\Rightarrow E\left\{R + \left(\frac{n^2}{N}\right)r\right\}^{-1} - \frac{nE2nr}{N}\left\{R + \left(\frac{n^2}{N}\right)r\right\}^{-2} = 0$$

$$\Rightarrow E\left\{R + \left(\frac{n^2}{N}\right)r\right\}^{-2}\left[R + \frac{n^2}{N}r - \frac{2n^2r}{N}\right] = 0$$

$$\Rightarrow R - \frac{n^2r}{N} = 0$$

$$\Rightarrow R = \frac{n^2r}{mn} = \frac{nr}{m}$$

Hence maximum current in the circuit will flow when the external resistance is equal to the internal resistance of the battery so the maximum current is given as

$$\Rightarrow \quad I = \frac{nE}{\frac{nr}{m} + \frac{nr}{m}} = \frac{mnE}{2r} \qquad \dots(3.100)$$

In second case EMF of each row is mE and internal resistance of each row is mr when n such rows are joined in parallel, the total internal resistance of battery grid will be mr/n so the total resistance of the circuit now is given as

$$R_T' = R + \frac{mr}{n} = \frac{nr}{m} + \frac{mr}{n}$$

Current in circuit in this case is given as

$$I' = \frac{mE}{\left[\left(\frac{nr}{m}\right) + \left(\frac{mr}{n}\right)\right]} = \frac{m^2nE}{r(m^2 + n^2)} \qquad \dots(3.101)$$

Dividing equation-(3.101) by (3.100) gives

$$I' = \frac{2mn}{(m^2 + n^2)} \times I$$

Illustrative Example 3.38

A galvanometer together with an unknown resistance in series is connected across two identical batteries each of 1.5 V. When the batteries are connected in series, the galvanometer records a current of 1 A, and when the batteries are in parallel the current is 0.6 A. What is the internal resistance of the battery?

Solution

The respective circuits are shown in figure-3.132(a) and (b).

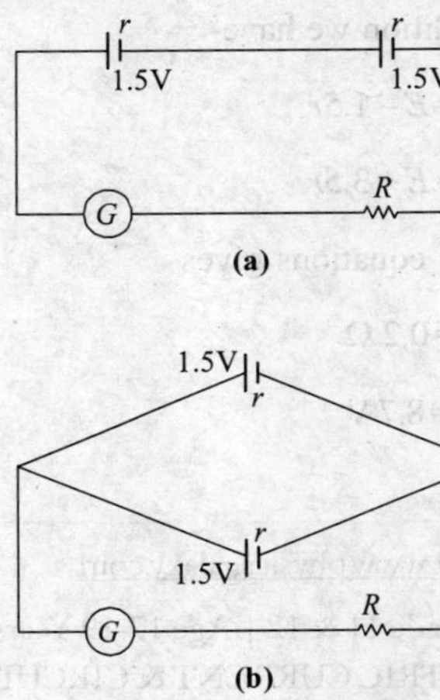

Figure 3.132

If the internal resistance of battery is r then in first case circuit current is given as

$$i = \frac{3}{R + 2r} = 1\,\text{A}$$

$$\Rightarrow \quad R + 2r = 3$$

$$\Rightarrow \quad R = (3 - 2r) \qquad \dots(3.102)$$

In second case as batteries are in parallel equivalent EMF remains same at 1.5 V and the two internal resistances are in parallel so their effective internal resistance is $r/2$ and the current in external resistance will be

$$i' = \frac{E}{R + r/2} = 0.6$$

$$\Rightarrow \quad 0.6 = \frac{E}{R + r/2}$$

From equation-(1) substituting the value of R gives

$$\Rightarrow \quad 0.6 = \frac{1.5}{(3-2r) + r/2}$$

Solving we get

$$r = \frac{1}{3}\,\Omega$$

Illustrative Example 3.39

The potential difference across the terminals of a battery is 8.4 V when there is a current of 1.5 A in the battery from the negative to the positive terminal. When the current is 3.5 A in the reverse direction, the potential difference becomes 9.4 V.

(a) What is the internal resistance of the battery?

(b) What is the emf of the battery?

Solution

As per given condition we have

$$8.4 = E - 1.5r \quad \dots(3.103)$$

$$9.4 = E + 3.5r \quad \dots(3.104)$$

Solving these two equations gives

$$r = 0.2\,\Omega$$

and $E = 8.7\,\text{V}$

Web Reference at www.physicsgalaxy.com

Age Group - Grade 11 & 12 | Age 17-19 Years

Section - ELECTRIC CURRENT & CIRCUITS

Topic - Current Electricity

Module Number - 18 to 20

3.7 *Kirchhoff's Voltage Law (KVL)*

In previous articles we've studied that Kirchhoff's Current Law is extremely useful in solving electrical circuits which is similar in application somewhat like nodal analysis for capacitive circuits. There is one more very useful law among many ways of solving electrical circuits '*Kirchhoff's Voltage Law*'. However with KCL we are able to handle any type of circuit but in some specific circuits use of KVL may reduce the length of analysis. There are some ways to judge but still its only by practicing you can get an edge of judging by looking at a circuit about which law or method is to be used to quickly solve the circuit.

Kirchhoff's Voltage Law states "*In any closed loop of an electrical circuit sum of all EMFs is equal to the sum of all potential drops across all resistances (or any other devices present) in that loop*".

With the above language it is clear that KVL is applied for a closed loop in electrical circuit. So for any circuit before applying KVL we must identify closed loop or loops such that these loops cover all the components of the circuit. To understand the above stated Kirchhoff's Voltage Law we consider an illustration on solving of a circuit shown in figure-3.133.

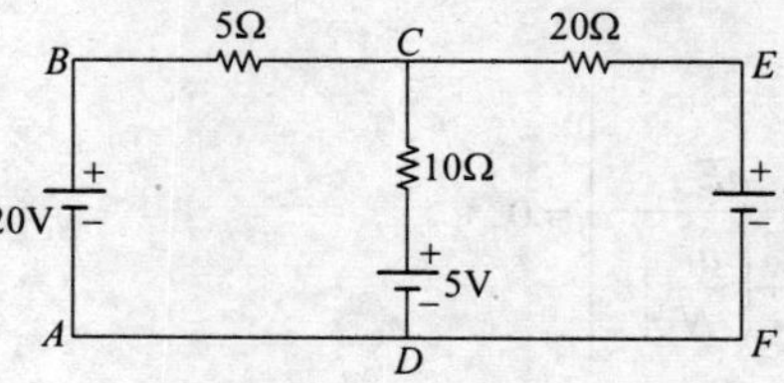

Figure 3.133

In above circuit we will calculate the current through each resistance in the circuit. To apply KVL in this circuit first we identify closed paths which cover all the components of the circuit. Simplest way to choose the paths is to select the loops which are shown in circuit in which there are no middle branch of the loop like in above case $ABCDA$ and $CEFDC$ are two loops within which there is not any branch of concern. However to apply KVL we can also choose the loops $ABCDA$ and $ABCEFDA$ and in these loops also all the components are covered in the circuit.

As next step after identifying the loops in circuit we distribute currents in these loops as shown in figure-3.134. We can consider these current either clockwise or anticlockwise in these loops like we've taken clockwise and named these I_1 and I_2. The next step is to write KVL equations for the two loops which are potential equations for going around the loop along the currents for all components in a loop of circuit.

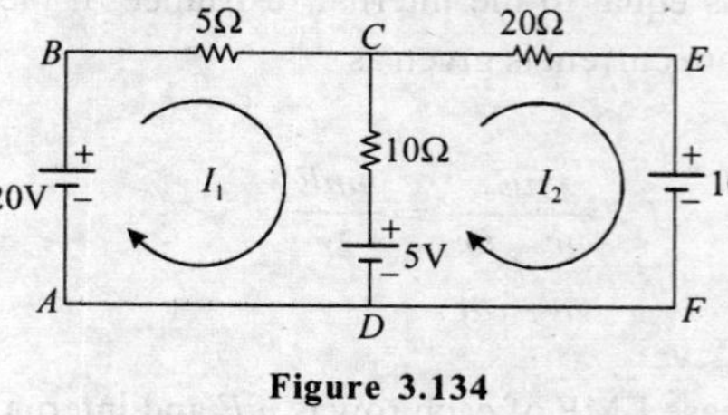

Figure 3.134

While writing KVL equations for the loop we start from any one point in loop and move along current and write potential difference for every component and come back to the same point. This is written for first loop with current I_1 starting from point A as

$$V_A + 20 - 5I_1 - 10(I_1 - I_2) - 5 = V_A \quad \ldots(3.105)$$

$$\Rightarrow \quad 15I_1 - 10I_2 = 15 \quad \ldots(3.106)$$

$$\Rightarrow \quad 3I_1 - 2I_2 = 3 \quad \ldots(3.107)$$

Simplifying equation-(3.105) we get equation-(3.106) and it can also be directly written by using definition of KVL as sum of all EMFs in a loop is equal to the sum of all the potential drops across all devices of the loop. On RHS of equation-(3.06) we can see is the sum of the two EMFs present in the loop which are of 20V and 5V batteries in opposing mode for current I_1 and on LHS of this equation is the total potential drop in this loop. But while directly writing this equation without using the potential equation students must be very careful about the sign of every term in the equation. In upcoming some of the illustrations we will write the KVL equations directly to develop a better understanding of this.

Similarly we can write the KVL equation for the second loop with current I_2 starting from point D as

$$V_D + 5 - 10(I_2 - I_1) - 20I_2 - 10 = V_D \quad \ldots(3.108)$$

$$\Rightarrow \quad 30I_2 - 10I_1 = -5 \quad \ldots(3.109)$$

$$\Rightarrow \quad 6I_2 - 2I_1 = -1 \quad \ldots(3.110)$$

Equation-(3.109) above is the KVL equation for second loop. Now after solving equations-(3.107) and (3.110) we get the values of I_1 and I_2 as

$$I_1 = \frac{8}{7}\text{A}$$

$$I_2 = \frac{3}{14}\text{A}$$

Thus looking at figure-3.134 we can now write currents in all resistors of the circuit as

$$I_{5\Omega} = I_1 = \frac{8}{7}\text{A}$$

$$I_{20\Omega} = I_2 = \frac{3}{14}\text{A}$$

$$I_{10\Omega} = I_1 - I_2 = \frac{13}{14}\text{A}$$

Above results of current in all resistances we obtained by writing KVL equations for loops in circuit and solving these equations. To verify the results students can resolve this circuit on their on by using KCL also to understand applications of both the methods. Next we will take more illustrations to understand KVL applications.

Illustrative Example 3.40

Find the current in 6 Ω resistance in the circuit shown in figure-3.135 using Kirchhoff's Voltage Law.

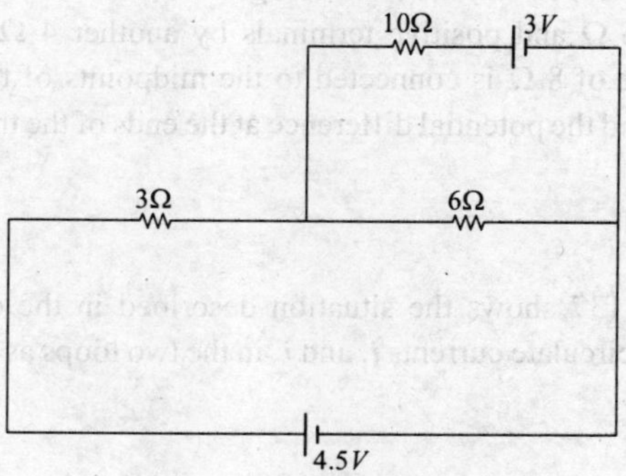

Figure 3.135

Solution

In the given circuit we circulate currents I_1 and I_2 in the two loops as shown in figure-3.136.

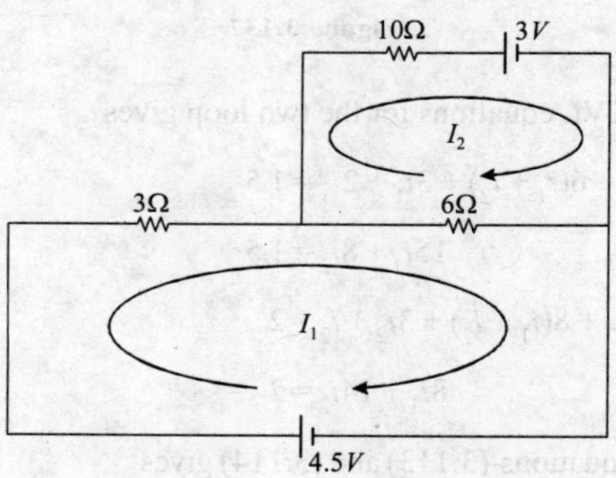

Figure 3.136

Writing KVL equation for I_1

$$+4.5 - 3I_1 - 6(I_1 - I_2) = 0$$

$$\Rightarrow \quad 9I_1 - 6I_2 = 4.5$$

$$\Rightarrow \quad 6I_1 - 4I_2 = 3 \quad \ldots(3.111)$$

Writing KVL equation for I_2

$$-6(I_2 - I_1) - 10I_2 - 3 = 0$$

$$\Rightarrow \quad 6I_1 - 16I_2 = 3 \quad \ldots(3.112)$$

Solving (3.111) – (3.112) gives

$$12I_2 = 0$$

$$\Rightarrow \quad I_2 = 0$$

From equation-(3.111) $\quad 6I_1 = 3$

$$\Rightarrow \quad I_1 = 3/6 = 0.5\text{ A}$$

Illustrative Example 3.41

Two cells of EMF 1.5 V and 2.0 V and internal resistances 2 Ω and 1 Ω respectively, have their negative terminals joined by a wire of 6 Ω and positive terminals by another 4 Ω. A third resistance of 8 Ω is connected to the midpoints of these two wires. Find the potential difference at the ends of the third wire.

Solution

Figure-3.137 shows the situation described in the question. Now we circulate currents i_1 and i_2 in the two loops as shown in figure.

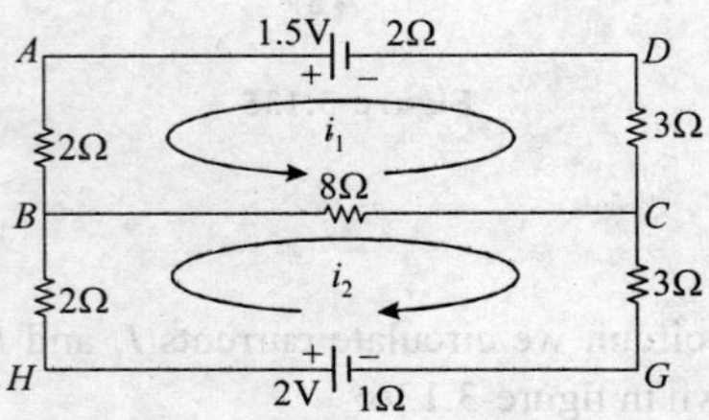

Figure 3.137

Writing KVL equations for the two loop gives

$$2i_1 + 6(i_1 + i_2) + 3i_1 + 2i_1 = 1.5$$

$$\Rightarrow \quad 15i_1 + 8i_2 = 1.5 \qquad \text{...(3.113)}$$

and $\quad 2i_2 + 8(i_1 + i_2) + 3i_2 + i_2 = 2$

$$\Rightarrow \quad 8i_1 + 14i_2 = 2 \qquad \text{...(3.114)}$$

Solving equations-(3.113) and (3.114) gives

$$i_1 = \frac{5}{146}\text{ A}$$

and $\quad i_2 = \dfrac{18}{146}\text{ A}$

$$\Rightarrow \quad i_1 + i_2 = \frac{23}{146}\text{ A}$$

Potential difference across 8 Ω resistance is given by Ohm's law as

$$V_{8\Omega} = 8(i_1 + i_2) = 8 \times (23/146) = 1.26\text{ V}$$

Illustrative Example 3.42

Find out the potential difference between points x and y in the figure shown-3.138.

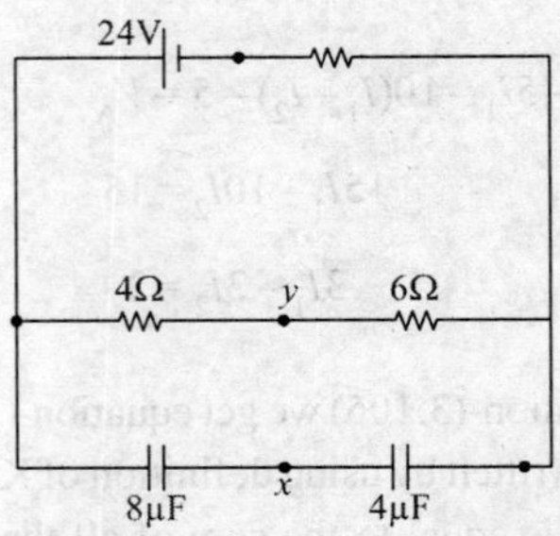

Figure 3.138

Solution

Distributing potentials in circuit as shown in the figure-3.139.

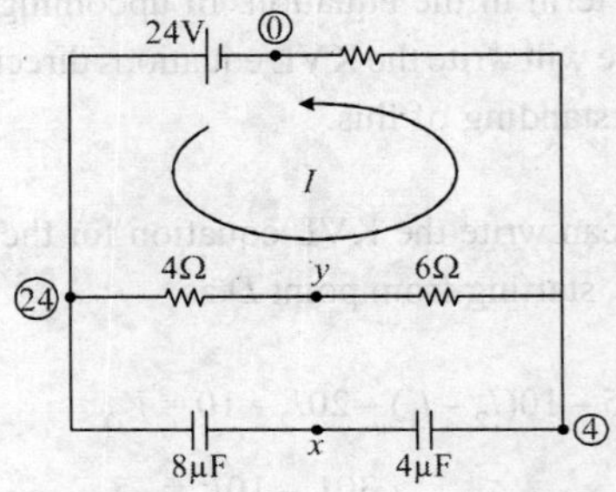

Figure 3.139

As there is a single loop in the circuit, current is given as

$$I = \frac{24}{12} = 2\text{ A}$$

By writing the equation of potential drop potential at point y can be given as

$$V_y = 24 - 4(2) = 16\text{ V}$$

For the node of two capacitors, nodal equation for potential V_x is written as

$$4(V_x - 4) + 8(V_x - 24) = 0$$

$$\Rightarrow \quad 3V_x = 52$$

$$\Rightarrow \quad V_x = \frac{52}{3}\text{ V}$$

$$\Rightarrow \quad V_x - V_y = \frac{52}{3} - 16 = \frac{4}{3}\text{ V}$$

Illustrative Example 3.43

N sources of current with different EMFs are connected as shown in figure-3.140. The EMFs of the sources are proportional to their internal resistances given as $E = \alpha R$, where α is a positive constant. Consider the resistances of connecting wires are negligible. Find

(a) The current in the circuit

(b) The potential difference between points A and B dividing the circuit in n and $N - n$ links.

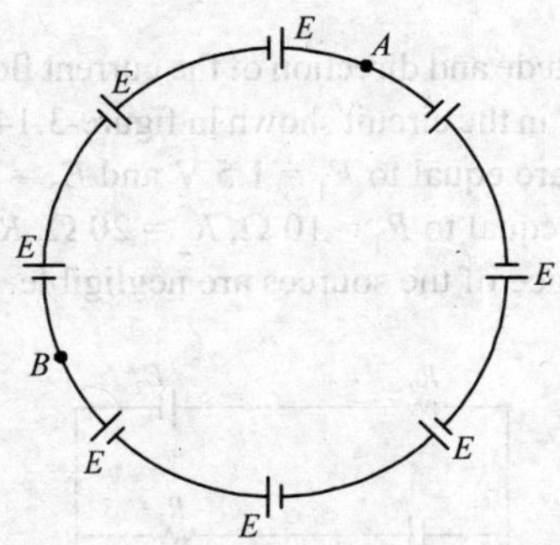

Figure 3.140

Solution

(a) The N sources are connected in series in a single loop so the current in the circuit is given as

$$i = \frac{NE}{NR} = \frac{E}{R}$$

$$\Rightarrow \quad i = \frac{\alpha R}{R} = \alpha$$

(b) Potential difference across points A and B can be given by writing the equation of potential drop from the side of n sources, we get

$$V_A - V_B = nE - n(iR)$$

$$\Rightarrow \quad V_A - V_B = n(\alpha R) - n(E/R)R$$

$$\Rightarrow \quad V_A - V_B = n(\alpha R) - n(E/R)R$$

$$\Rightarrow \quad V_A - V_B = n(\alpha R) - n\,\alpha R$$

$$\Rightarrow \quad V_A - V_B = 0$$

Illustrative Example 3.44

In the circuit shown in figure-3.141, find the energy stored in 4 μF capacitor in steady state.

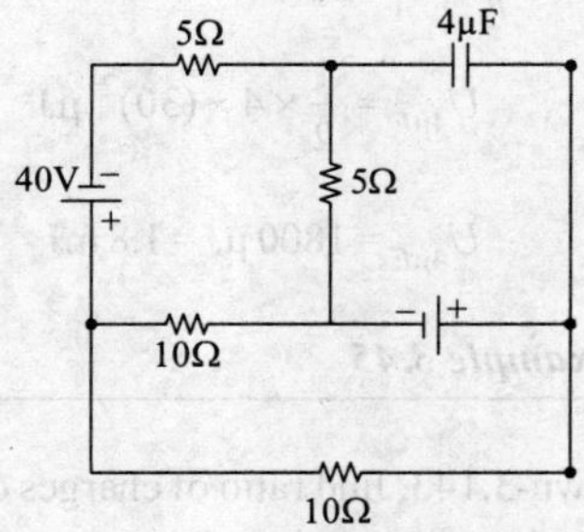

Figure 3.141

Solution

In the given circuit we circulate currents I_1 and I_2 in the two loops as shown in figure-3.142. As we know that in steady state no current flows through the branch of capacitor so we do not consider any current in this loop as shown.

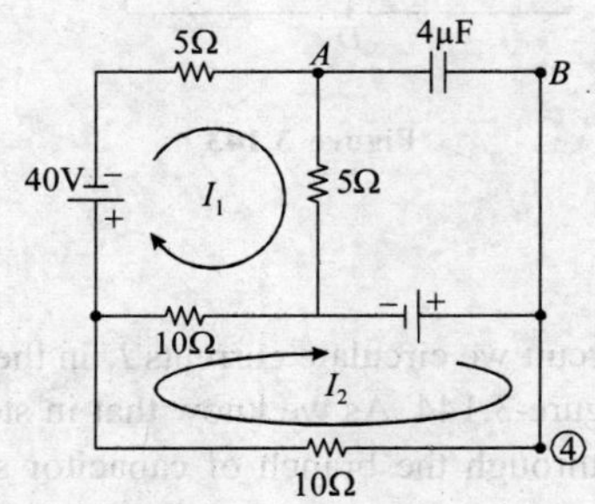

Figure 3.142

Writing KVL equation for I_1 as

$$-40 - 5I_1 - 5I_1 - 10(I_1 - I_2) = 0$$

$$\Rightarrow \quad 4I_1 - 2I_2 = -8$$

$$\Rightarrow \quad 2I_1 - I_2 = -4 \qquad \ldots(3.115)$$

Writing KVL equation for I_2 as

$$-10I_2 - 10(I_2 - I_1) + 20 = 0$$

$$\Rightarrow \quad I_1 - 2I_2 = -2 \qquad \ldots(3.116)$$

Solving equation-(3.115) and (3.116) gives

$$3I_1 = -6$$

$$\Rightarrow \quad I_1 = -2A$$

Energy stored in capacitor in steady state is given as

$$U_{4\mu F} = \frac{1}{2}CV_{AB}^2$$

Writing equation of potential drop from A to B gives

$$V_A - 5(-2) + 20 = V_B$$

$$\Rightarrow \qquad V_B - V_A = 30\,\text{V}$$

$$\Rightarrow \qquad U_{4\mu F} = \frac{1}{2} \times 4 \times (30)^2\ \mu\text{J}$$

$$\Rightarrow \qquad U_{4\mu F} = 1800\ \mu\text{J} = 1.8\ \text{mJ}$$

Illustrative Example 3.45

In the figure shown-3.143, find ratio of charges on 4μF and 2μF capacitors in steady state.

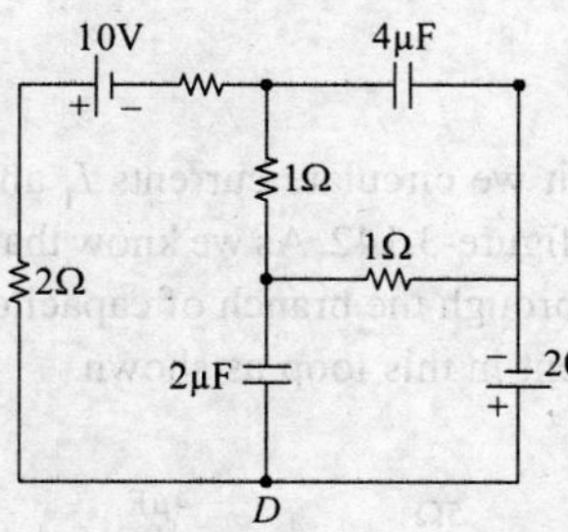

Figure 3.143

Solution

In the given circuit we circulate currents I_1 in the single loops as shown in figure-3.144. As we know that in steady state no current flows through the branch of capacitor so we do not consider any current in the branches in which capacitors are connected as shown.

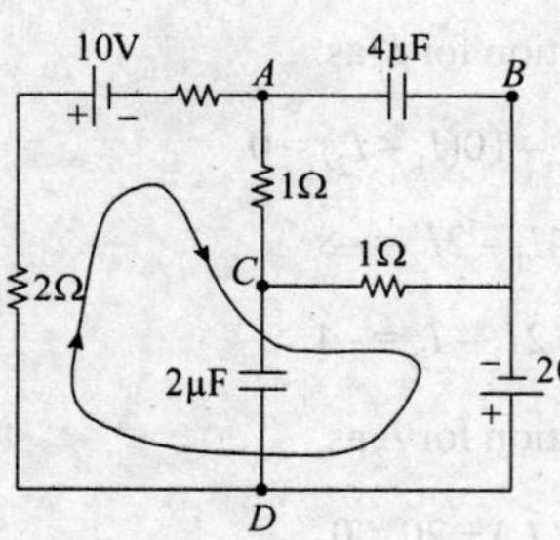

Figure 3.144

Current in the single loop can be directly given as

$$I = \frac{10}{5} = 2\,\text{A}$$

Writing potential drop equation from A to B gives

$$V_A - (2) - (2) = V_B \Rightarrow V_A - V_B = 4\,\text{V}$$

Writing potential drop equation from C to D gives

$$V_C - (2) + 20 = V_D \Rightarrow V_A - V_B = 18\,\text{V}$$

Charge on capacitors are now given as

$$q_{4\mu F} = CV_{AB}$$

$$\Rightarrow \qquad q_{4\mu F} = 4 \times 4 = 16\ \mu\text{C}$$

and $$q_{2\mu F} = CV_{CD}$$

$$\Rightarrow \qquad q_{2\mu F} = 2 \times 18 = 36\ \mu\text{C}$$

$$\Rightarrow \qquad \frac{q_{4\mu F}}{q_{2\mu F}} = \frac{16}{36} = \frac{4}{9}$$

Illustrative Example 3.46

Find the magnitude and direction of the current flowing through the resistance R in the circuit shown in figure-3.145 if the EMFs of the sources are equal to $E_1 = 1.5$ V and $E_2 = 3.7$ V and the resistances are equal to $R_1 = 10\ \Omega$, $R_2 = 20\ \Omega$, $R = 5.0\ \Omega$. The internal resistance of the sources are negligible.

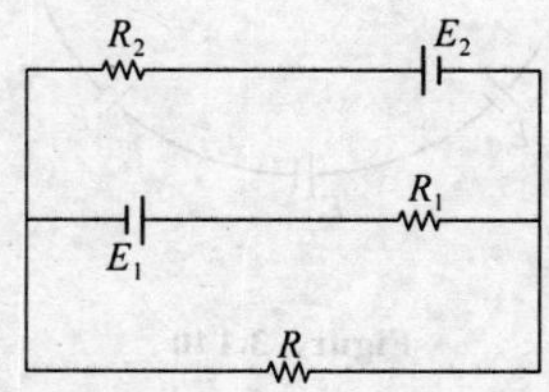

Figure 3.145

Solution

The current distribution in the circuit is shown in figure-3.146.

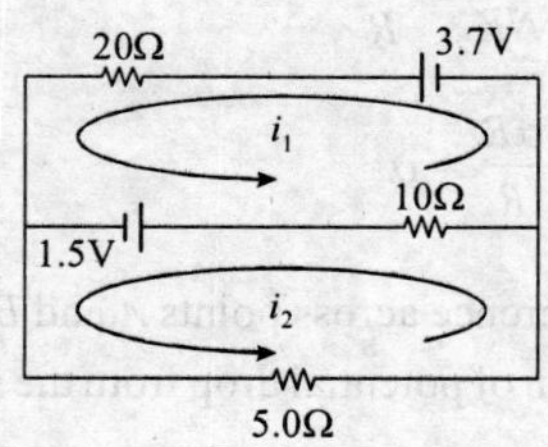

Figure 3.146

Writing KVL equation from currents i_1 and i_2 gives

$$30i_1 - 10i_2 = 5.2 \qquad \ldots(3.117)$$

and $$15i_2 - 10i_1 = -1.5 \qquad \ldots(3.118)$$

Solving (3.117) + (3.118) × 3 gives

$$35i_2 = 0.7$$

$$\Rightarrow \qquad i_2 = 0.02\ \text{A}$$

Illustrative Example 3.47

Find the current flowing through battery and charge on capacitor in steady state.

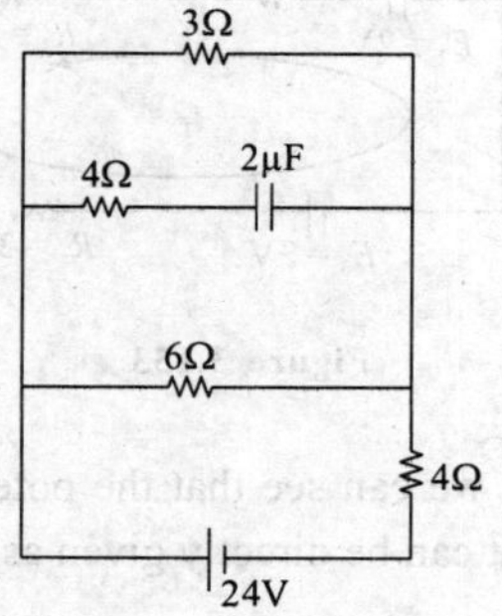

Figure 3.147

Solution

In the given circuit 3 Ω and 6 Ω resistances can be considered in parallel so the circuit can be reduced as shown in figure-3.148 in which we can find the current in the loop as shown. No current flows through capacitor in steady state.

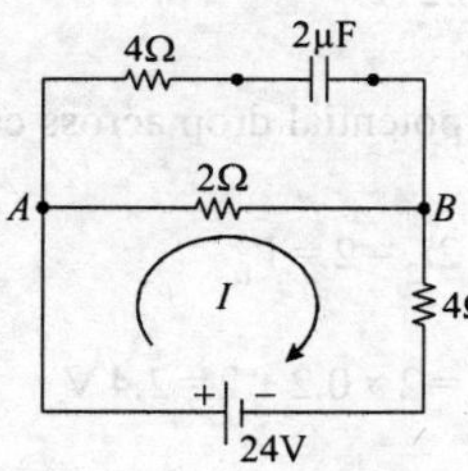

Figure 3.148

Current in the loop of circuit is given as

$$I=\frac{24}{6}=4\,\text{A}$$

The potential difference across capacitor will be same as that across terminals A and B shown in figure-3.148 because there will be zero potential drop across 4 Ω resistance as current in this branch is zero in steady state.

$$V_{AB}=2I=8\,\text{V}$$

Charge on capacitor is given as

$$q=CV_{AB}$$

$$\Rightarrow \quad q=2\,\mu\text{F}\times 8\,\text{V}$$

$$\Rightarrow \quad q=16\,\mu\text{C}$$

Illustrative Example 3.48

Figure-3.149 shows part of a circuit. Calculate the current through 3 Ω resistance and also find the potential difference $V_C - V_B$?

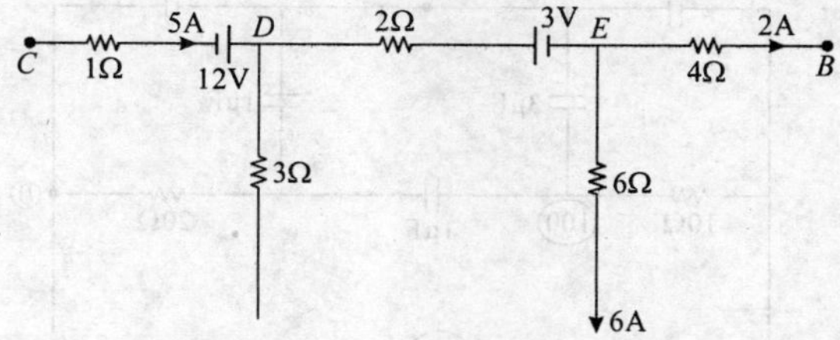

Figure 3.149

Solution

Using KCL we can see that at junction E current in wire DE is 8 A from D to E. Again using KCL at terminal D the current in 3 Ω resistance can be given as 3 A towards D.

Potential difference across points C and B can be given by writing equation of potential drop from terminal C to B which is given as

$$V_C-5\times 1+12-8\times 2-3-4\times 2=V_B$$

$$\Rightarrow \quad V_C-V_B=5-12+16+3+8$$

$$\Rightarrow \quad V_C-V_B=20\,\text{V}$$

Illustrative Example 3.49

In circuit shown in figure-3.150, find potential difference across points A and B and across B and C in steady state.

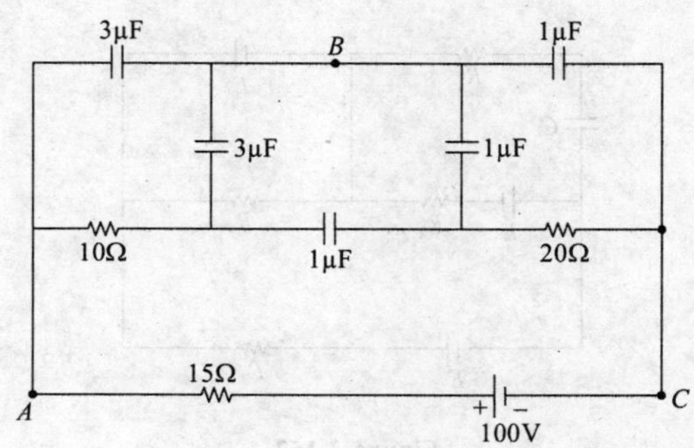

Figure 3.150

Solution

In the figure shown we can see that in steady state current through all capacitors will be zero so not even a single loop is being formed in the circuit in which current can flow so we can solve this situation by using nodal analysis for capacitors for which we distribute the potentials in circuit as shown in figure-3.151.

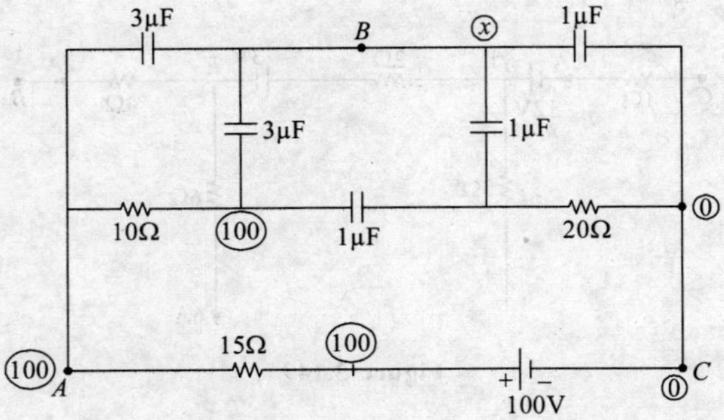

Figure 3.151

We write nodal equation for the unknown potential x as

$$3(x-100)+3(x-100)+x+x=0$$

$$\Rightarrow \qquad 8x=600$$

$$\Rightarrow \qquad x=75\text{ V}$$

The required potential differences are given as

$$V_A-V_B=100-75=25\text{ V}$$

$$V_B-V_C=75-0=75\text{ V}$$

Illustrative Example 3.50

In the given circuit as shown in figure-3.152 we use $E_1=6$ V, $E_2=2$ V, $E_3=3$ V, $R_1=6\ \Omega$, $R_2=2\ \Omega$, $R_3=4\ \Omega$, $R_4=3\ \Omega$ and $C=5\ \mu$F. Find the current in R_3 and energy stored in the capacitor in steady state.

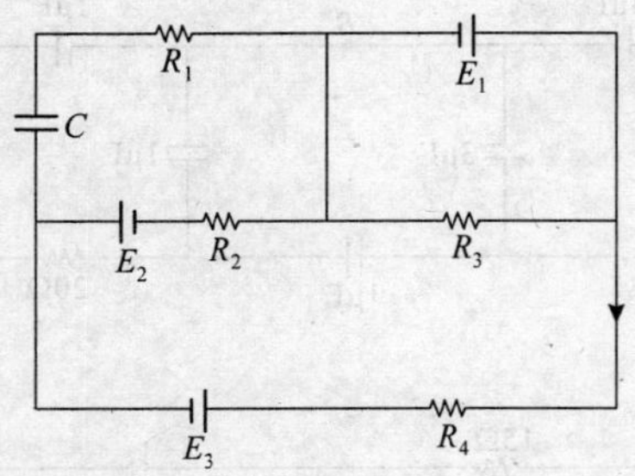

Figure 3.152

Solution

In steady state the current through the branch in which capacitor is connected is zero and in remaining loops we distribute currents as shown in figure-3.153.

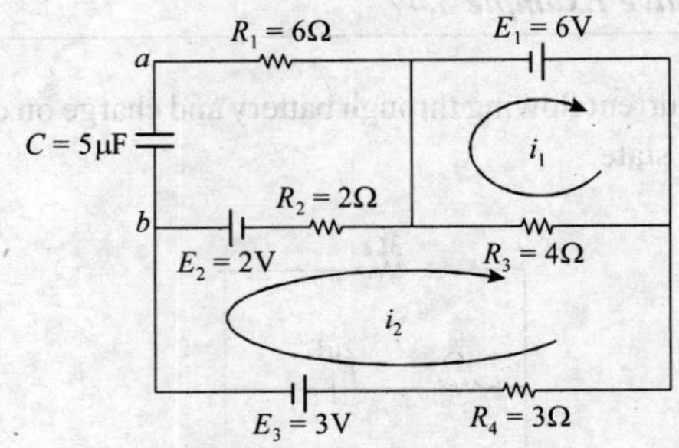

Figure 3.153

Across resistor R_3 we can see that the potential difference is 6 V thus its current can be directly given as

$$i_1-i_2=\frac{6}{4}=1.5\text{ A}$$

Now writing KVL equation for the second loop gives

$$9i_2-4i_1=5$$

$$\Rightarrow \qquad 5i_2=-5+6=1\text{ A}$$

$$\Rightarrow \qquad i_2=0.2\text{ A}$$

Writing equation of potential drop across capacitor gives

$$V_b-2i_2-2=V_a$$

$$\Rightarrow \quad V_b-V_a=2i_2+2=2\times0.2+2=2.4\text{ V}$$

Energy stored in capacitor in steady state is given as

$$U=\frac{1}{2}CV^2=\frac{1}{2}(5\times10^{-6})(2.4)^2=14.4\times10^{-6}\text{ J}$$

Illustrative Example 3.51

In the circuit shown in figure-3.154 find the potential difference V_A-V_D.

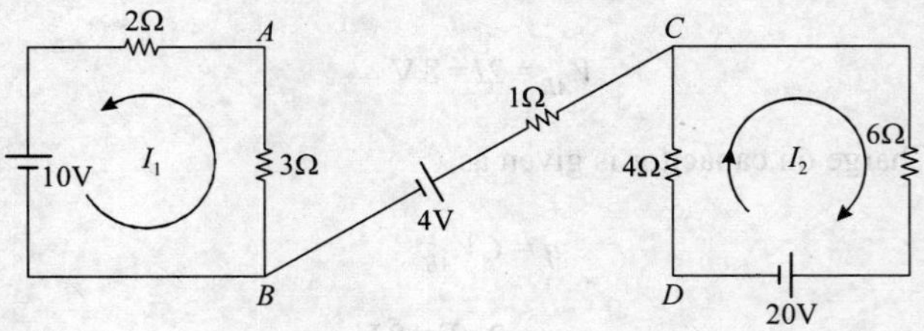

Figure 3.154

Solution

Figure-3.155 shows the current distribution in the two loops of the circuit.

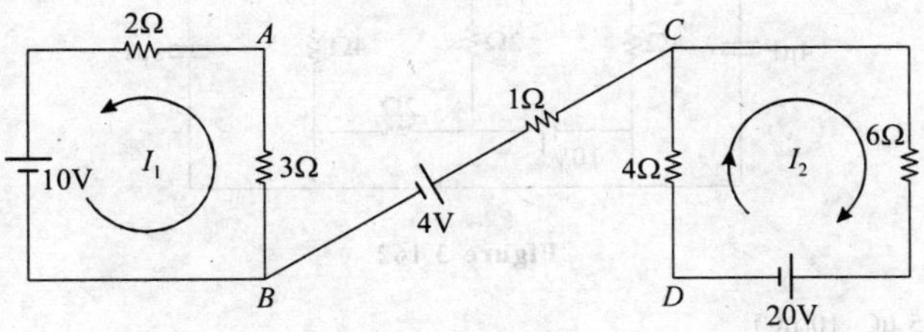

Figure 3.155

Writing KVL equation for I_1 gives

$$+10-2I_1-3I_1=0$$

$$\Rightarrow \quad I_1=\frac{10}{5}=2\text{ A}$$

Writing KVL equation for I_2 gives

$$-4I_2-6I_2-20=0$$

$$\Rightarrow \quad I_2=\frac{20}{10}=-2\text{ A}$$

Now writing equation of potential drop from point *A* to *D*, gives

$$V_A-3I_1+4+4I_2=V_D$$

$$\Rightarrow \quad V_A-V_D=3I_1-4I_2-4$$

$$\Rightarrow \quad V_A-V_D=3(2)-4(-2)-4$$

$$\Rightarrow \quad V_A-V_D=6+8-4$$

$$\Rightarrow \quad V_A-V_D=10\text{V}$$

Illustrative Example 3.52

In the circuit shown in figure-3.156 three ideal sources have EMFs E_1 = 1 V and E_2 = 2.5 V and the resistances have the values R_1 = 10 Ω and R_2 = 20 Ω. Find the potential difference $V_A - V_B$ between the plates *A* and *B* of the capacitor *C* in steady state.

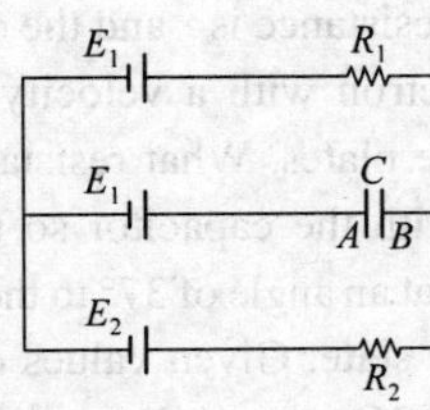

Figure 3.156

Solution

As we know that in steady state no current flows through the branch in which capacitor is connected so in above circuit current only flows in the outer loop as shown in figure-3.157.

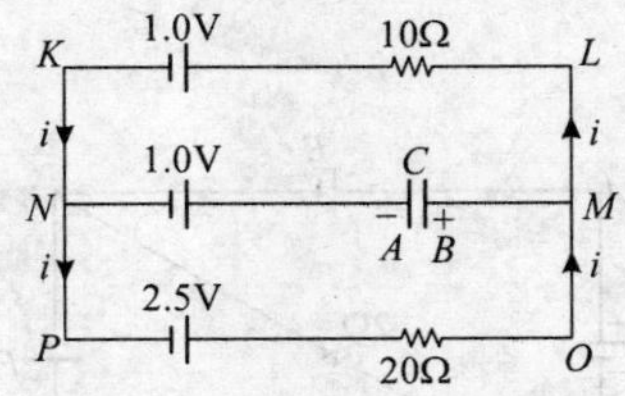

Figure 3.157

Writing KVL equation for the outer loop gives

$$20i+10i=2.5-1.0$$

$$\Rightarrow \quad 30i=1.5$$

$$\Rightarrow \quad i=\frac{1.5}{30}=0.05\text{ A}$$

Writing equation of potential drop from capacitor terminal *A* to *B* gives

$$V_B+20i-2.5+1=V_A$$

$$\Rightarrow \quad V_B-V_A=1.5-20i$$

$$\Rightarrow \quad V_B-V_A=1.5-20\times 0.05$$

$$\Rightarrow \quad V_B-V_A=0.5\text{ V}$$

> Web Reference at www.physicsgalaxy.com
>
> **Age Group** - Grade 11 & 12 | Age 17-19 Years
>
> **Section** - ELECTRIC CURRENT & CIRCUITS
>
> **Topic** - Circuit Analysis
>
> **Module Number** - 3 to 5

Practice Exercise 3.6

(i) Find the current in the circuit shown in figure-3.158

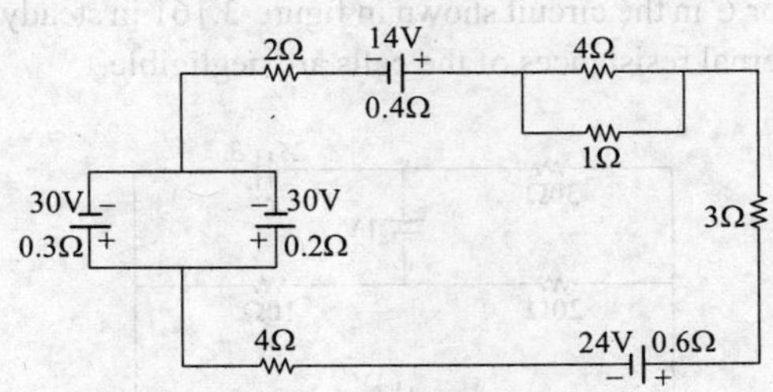

Figure 3.158

[3.92A]

(ii) In the circuit shown in figure-3.159 cells E, F, G and H are of EMF 2 V, 1 V, 3 V and 1 V respectively and their internal resistance are 2 Ω, 1 Ω, 3 Ω and 1 Ω respectively. Calculate

(a) The potential difference between points B and D

(b) The potential difference across the terminals of the cells G and H.

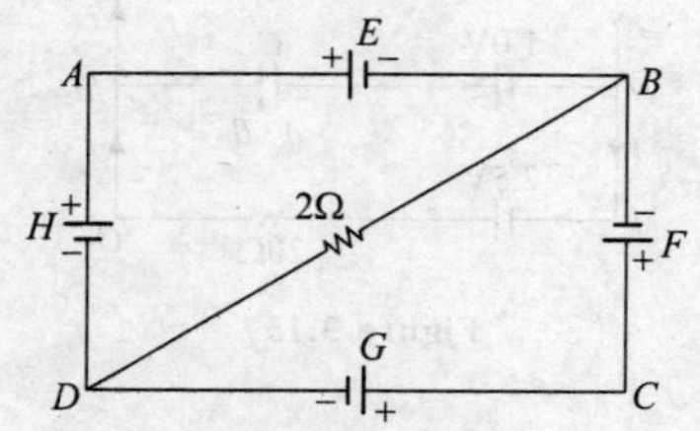

Figure 3.159

[(a) 0.154 V (b) 1.615 V, 1.384 V]

(iii) In the circuit shown-3.160, all the ammeters are of zero resistance.

(a) If the switch S is open, find the reading of all ammeters and the potential difference across the switch

(b) If the switch S is closed, find the reading of all ammeters and the also find the current through the switch.

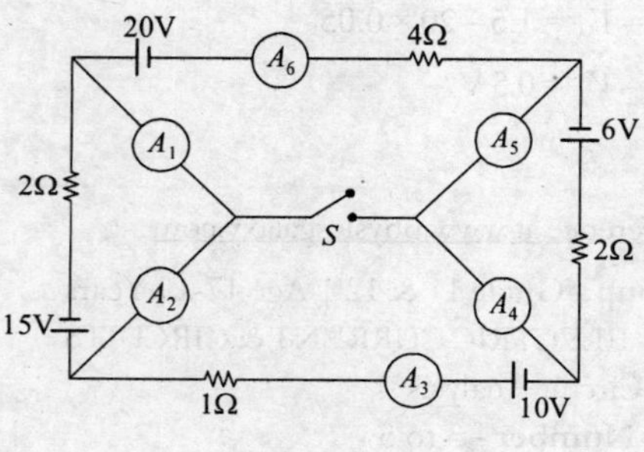

Figure 3.160

[(a) 9.5 A, 9.5 A, 2 A, 5 A, 5 A, 2 A, 12 V; (b) 12.5 A, 2.5 A, 10 A, 7 A, 8 A, 5 A, 15 A]

(iv) Find the potential difference between the plates of the capacitor C in the circuit shown in figure-3.161 in steady state. The internal resistances of the cells are negligible.

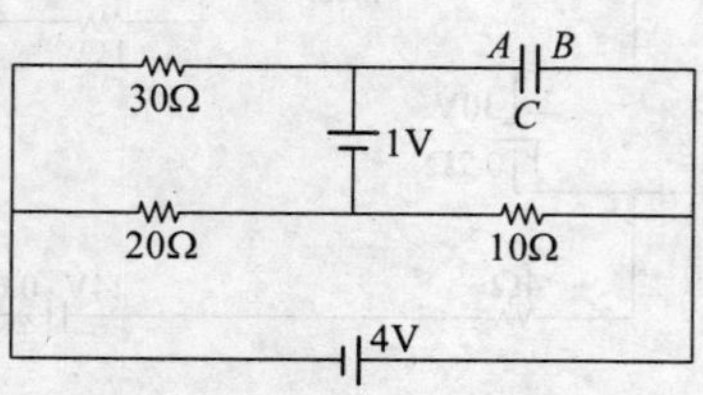

Figure 3.161

[1 V]

(v) Find the charges on 4 μF and 2 μF capacitors in steady state in the circuit shown in figure-3.162.

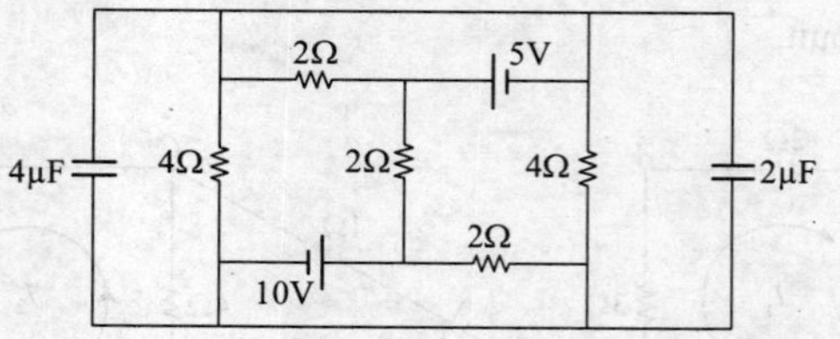

Figure 3.162

[5 μC, 10 μC]

(vi) AB, BC, CD and DA are resistors of 1 Ω, 1 Ω, 2 Ω and 2 Ω respectively connected in series forming a closed loop. Between terminals A and C a 1 V cell of internal resistance 2 Ω is connected with A being positive terminal and between terminals B and D another 2 V cell of internal resistance 1 Ω is connected with B being positive. Find the current through each resistor of the circuit.

[0.2 A, 0.6 A, 0.3 A, 0.5 A]

(vii) A part of the circuit in a steady state along with the currents flowing in the branches is shown in figure-3.163. Calculate the energy stored in capacitor C in steady state.

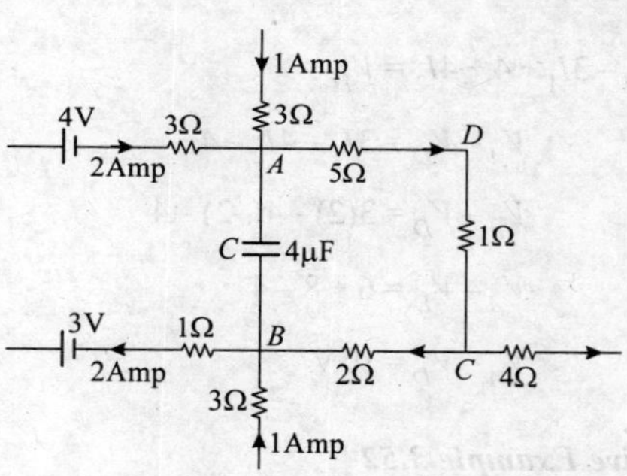

Figure 3.163

[0.8mJ]

(viii) A parallel plate capacitor with plates of length l is included in a circuit as shown in figure-3.164. The EMF of the source is ε, its internal resistance is r and the distance between the plates is d. An electron with a velocity u files into the capacitor, parallel to the plates. What resistance R should be connected in parallel with the capacitor so that the electron files out of the capacitor at an angle of 37° to the plates? Assume that circuit is in steady state. Given values of parameters as l = 91 cm, $\xi = 3V$, $r = 2\Omega$, d = (1/3) mm, $u = 4 \times 10^7$ m/s, $m_e = 9.1 \times 10^{-31}$ kg and $e = 1.6 \times 10^{-19}$ C.

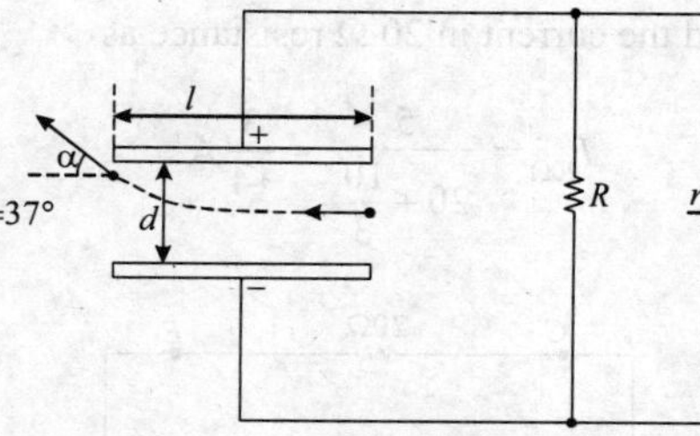

Figure 3.164

[10 Ω]

(ix) Find the current flowing through the resistance R in the circuit shown in figure-3.165. Consider all batteries are ideal.

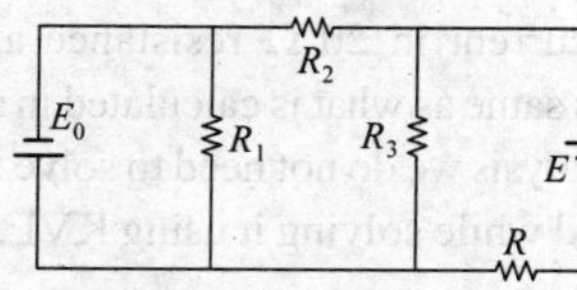

Figure 3.165

$$\left[\frac{E(R_2+R_3)+E_0R_3}{R(R_2+R_3)+R_2R_3}\right]$$

(x) In the circuit shown in figure-3.166 the cells are ideal. Calculate (a) The current in 3 Ω resistance (b) Current through the 8 V cell and (c) The steady state charge on the capacitor.

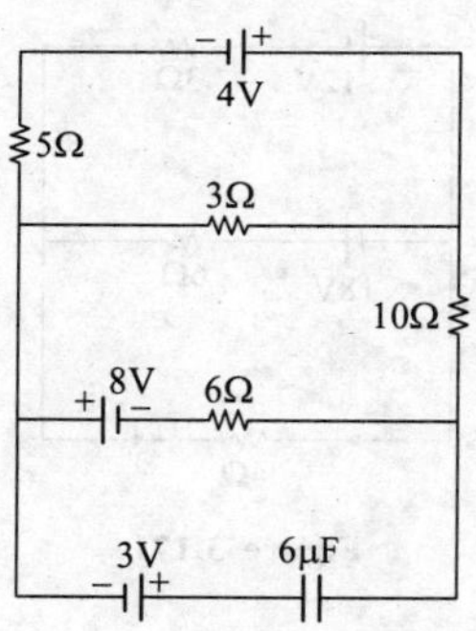

Figure 3.166

[(a) 0.168 A (b) 0.53 A (c) 46.92 μC]

3.8 *Thevenin's Analysis*

KCL and KVL studied in previous articles play an important role in solving electrical circuits. Students must try solving each circuit given in any illustration or in practice exercises by both methods and understand on your own about which method is fastest in solving which specific circuit. Mostly we prefer KVL for solving single loop circuits or multi loop circuits when number of components are large. KCL is preferred when loops are more but components are less as in such conditions number of variables in application of KCL will be less which are to be calculated. With consistent practice students can excel over these methods.

There is one more important analysis for solving electrical circuits which is sometimes more useful over KCL or KVL. This is '*Thevenin's Analysis*'. This method is useful and quick when current through a specific resistance in a circuit is to be calculated. In this analysis except the specific resistance through which we are required to calculate the current, rest of the circuit we reduce by an equivalent battery with an EMF and an internal resistance. To understand the concept superficially first, see the circuit given in figure-3.167(a) which is same circuit we considered as illustration in article-3.7. If we are required to find the current through 20 Ω resistance then rest of the circuit across terminals C and E we reduce like a single equivalent battery as shown in figure-3.167(b). Now in this state the current through 20 Ω resistance can be directly given as

$$I_{20\Omega}=\frac{\xi_{eq}}{20+r_{eq}} \quad \ldots(3.119)$$

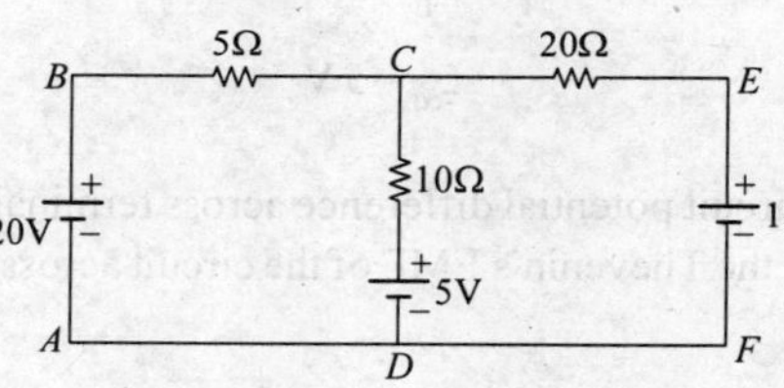

(a)

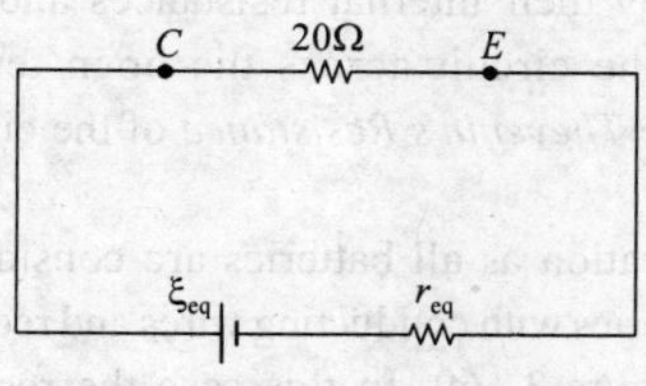

(b)

Figure 3.167

There are specific ways to determine the equivalent EMF and equivalent internal resistance of the singe equivalent battery of the circuit as shown in figure-3.167(b). This EMF of equivalent battery is called '*Thevenin's EMF*' and the internal resistance of this equivalent battery is called '*Thevenin's Resistance*' of rest of the circuit.

Calculation of Thevenin's EMF : Remove the component of the circuit across which we have to reduce rest of the circuit and calculate the open circuit potential difference across these terminals using KCL or KVL. This open circuit potential difference across the terminals is the *Thevenin's EMF* of the circuit.

Figure-3.168 shows the circuit in figure-3.167(a) after removing the 20 Ω resistance. To find the open circuit potential difference across terminals C and E we consider a current I_1 in the loop as shown in figure-3.168 as this is the only one loop left in circuit so to solve it we write KVL equation for this loop as

$$15I_1 = 15$$

$$\Rightarrow \quad I_1 = 1\text{ A}$$

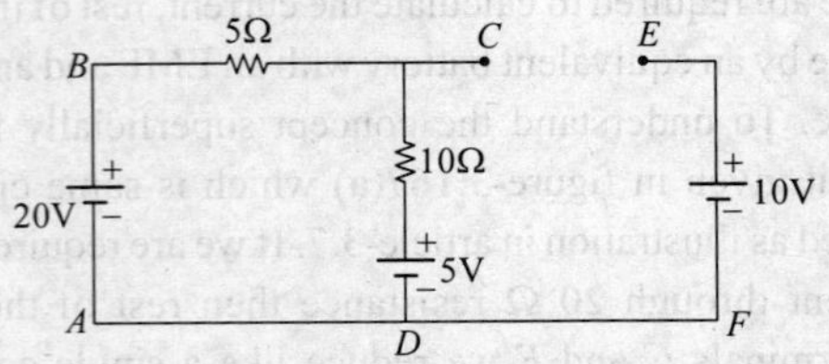

Figure 3.168

Now we can write potential equation from terminal C to E as

$$V_C - (10\times 1) - 5 + 10 = V_E$$

$$\Rightarrow \quad V_C - V_E = 5\text{ V}$$

$$\Rightarrow \quad \xi_{eq} = 5\text{ V} \qquad \ldots(3.120)$$

Thus open circuit potential difference across terminals C and E is 5 V or this the Thevenin's EMF of the circuit across terminals C and E.

Calculation of Thevenin's Resistance : Replace all the batteries of the circuit by their internal resistances and calculate the resistance of the circuit across the open terminals. This resistance is the *Thevenin's Resistance* of the circuit.

In above illustration as all batteries are considered ideal we replace the batteries with conducting wires and redraw the circuit as shown in figure-3.169. In this case the resistance inside terminals C and E is the parallel combination of 5 Ω and 10 Ω resistance which is given as

$$r_{eq} = \frac{5\times 10}{5+10} = \frac{10}{3}\,\Omega \qquad \ldots(3.121)$$

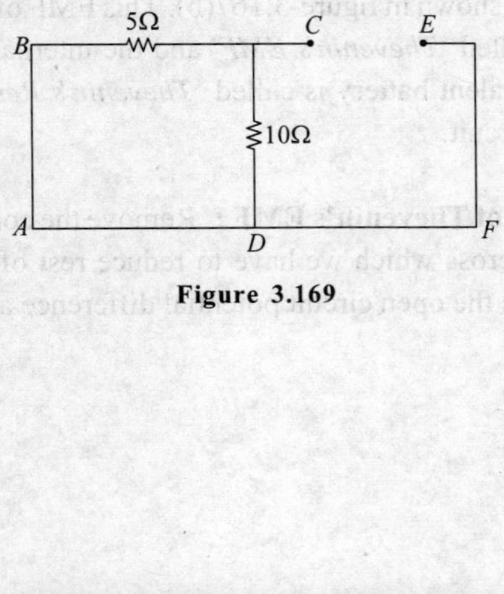

Figure 3.169

Now we can redraw the circuit in figure-3.167(b) as 3.170 given below to find the current in 20 Ω resistance as

$$I_{20\Omega} = \frac{5}{20+\dfrac{10}{3}} = \frac{3}{14}\text{ A} \qquad \ldots(3.122)$$

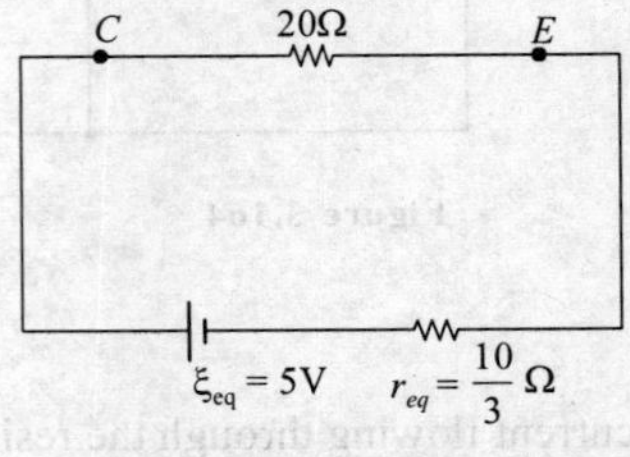

Figure 3.170

We can see that current in 20 Ω resistance as calculated in equation-(3.122) is same as what is calculated in article 3.7 using KVL and in this analysis we do not need to solve for two variable currents like we did while solving it using KVL.

We will take more illustrations on Thevenin's analysis to understand its applications better and students can also solve the illustrations taken until now by using Thevenin's analysis for practice.

Illustrative Example 3.53

In the circuit shown in figure-3.171, find current in 4 Ω resistance.

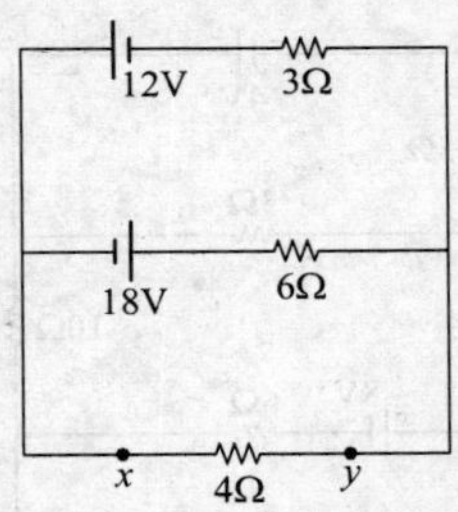

Figure 3.171

Solution

Here we can consider (12 V, 3 Ω) cell in parallel combination with (18 V, 6 Ω) cell so we can reduce the circuit by replacing the cell combination with its equivalent cell and internal resistance as shown in figure-3.172.

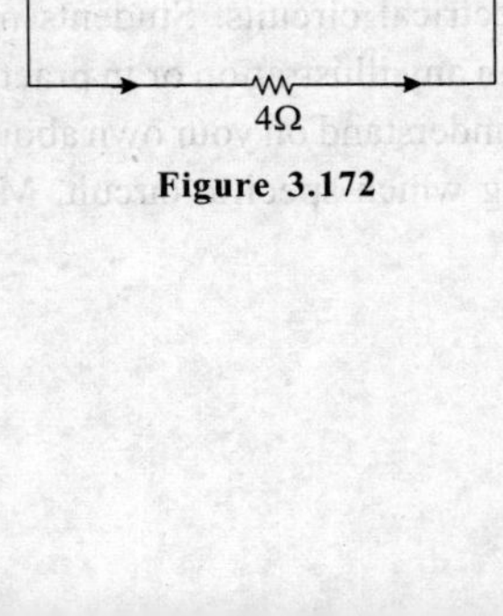

Figure 3.172

The equivalent EMF of the combination of cells is given as

$$\xi_{eq} = \frac{\xi_1/r_1 + \xi_2/r_2}{1/r_1 + 1/r_2} = \frac{\frac{12}{3} - \frac{18}{6}}{\frac{1}{5} + \frac{1}{6}} = \frac{1}{1/2} = 2\text{ V}$$

The equivalent internal resistance of the combination of cells is given as

$$r_{eq} = 3\Omega \,|P|\, 6\Omega = \frac{3\times 6}{3+6} = 2\,\Omega$$

From the above circuit shown in figure-3.172 the current in 4 Ω resistance is given as

$$I_{4\Omega} = \frac{2}{6} = \frac{1}{3}\text{ A}$$

Illustrative Example 3.54

Find current in 6 Ω resistance and potential difference across each cell in circuit shown in figure-3.173.

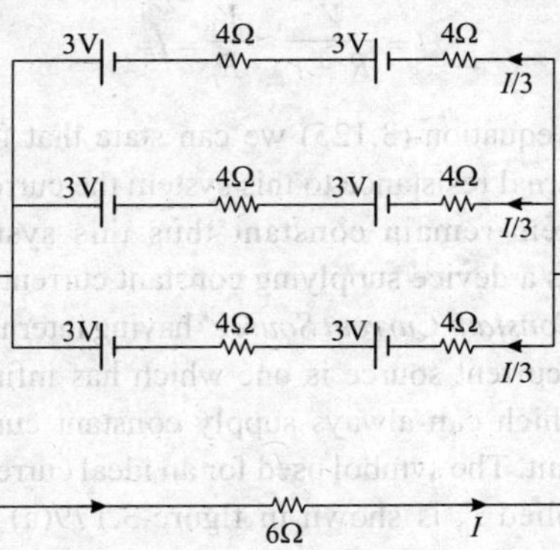

Figure 3.173

Solution

Using the concept of battery grid we can write the equivalent EMF and equivalent internal resistance of the combination of above 6 cells as

$$\xi_{eq} = N\xi = 2\times 3 = 6\text{ V}$$

and $$r_{eq} = \frac{Nr}{M} = \frac{2\times 4}{3} = \frac{8}{3}\Omega$$

Terminal potential difference across each cell is given as

$$V_{\text{cell}} = \varepsilon - ir = 3 - \frac{3}{13}\times 4 = 3 - \frac{12}{13}$$

$$V_{\text{cell}} = \frac{27}{13}\text{ V}$$

The given circuit is reduced to the circuit shown in figure-3.174 across 6 Ω resistance.

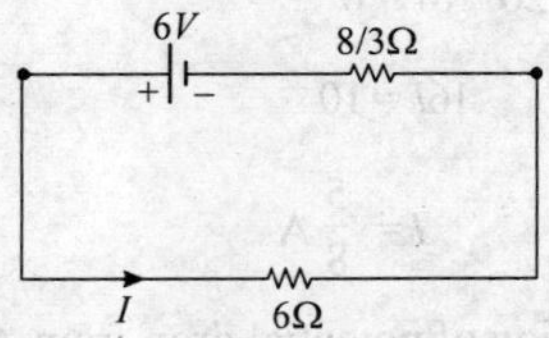

Figure 3.174

The current through 6 Ω resistance is given as

$$I_{6\Omega} = \frac{6}{6+\frac{8}{3}}$$

$$\Rightarrow \quad I_{6\Omega} = \frac{18}{20} = \frac{9}{13}\text{ A}$$

Illustrative Example 3.55

In the circuit shown in figure-3.175, find current in 4 Ω resistance by using Thevenin's Analysis.

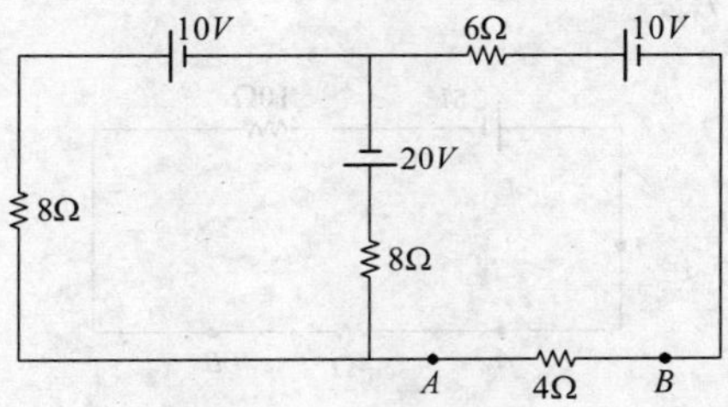

Figure 3.175

Solution

To find the current in 4 Ω resistance we will replace the whole circuit across this resistance by a single equivalent battery with equivalent internal resistance. For this we remove the 4 Ω resistance as shown in figure-3.176.

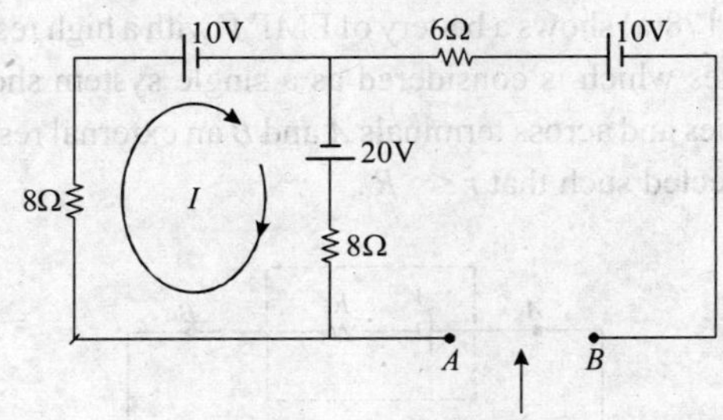

Figure 3.176

In above circuit current flows only in one loop which is given by writing its KVL equation as

$$-8I-10+20-8I=0$$

$$\Rightarrow \qquad 16I=10$$

$$\Rightarrow \qquad I=\frac{5}{8}\text{ A}$$

Writing the equation of potential drop from A to B gives

$$V_A+8\left(\frac{5}{8}\right)-20-10=V_B$$

$$\Rightarrow \qquad V_A-V_B=30-5=25\text{ V}$$

Thus 25 V is the open circuit potential difference across terminals A and B which is the equivalent EMF and equivalent internal resistance can be obtained by short circuiting all batteries of circuit and finding the resistance across terminals A and B which gives

$$r=4+6=10\,\Omega$$

Thus the given circuit will be reduced to the circuit shown in figure-3.177.

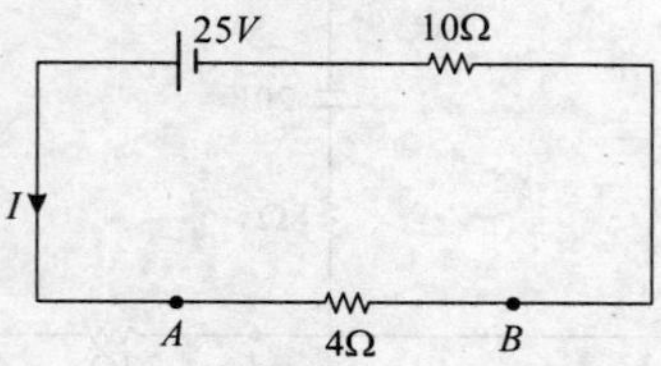

Figure 3.177

The current in 4 Ω resistance can be given as

$$I_{4\Omega}=\frac{25}{4+10}=\frac{25}{14}\text{ A}$$

3.9 Understanding Constant Current Sources

Figure-3.178(a) shows a battery of EMF V with a high resistance R_i in series which is considered as a single system shown by dotted lines and across terminals A and B an external resistance r is connected such that $r << R_i$.

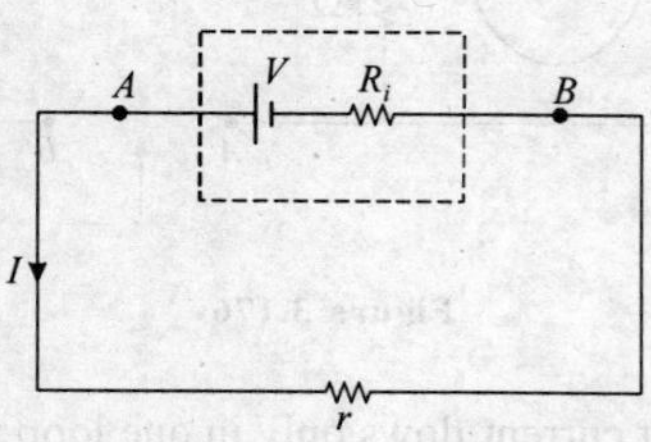

(a)

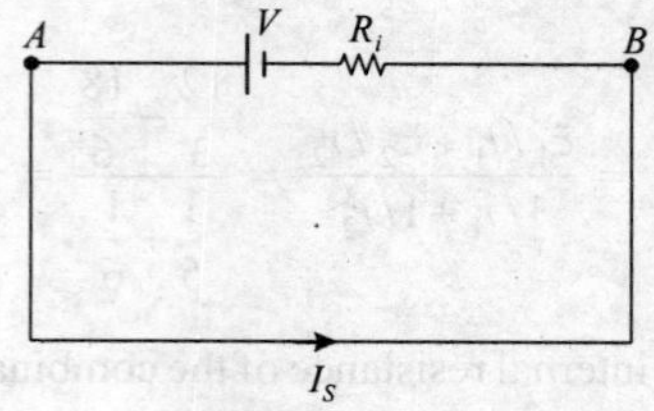

(b)

Figure 3.178

If we short circuit the terminals A and B as shown in figure-3.178(b), the current flowing out of this system is

$$I_S=\frac{V}{R_i} \qquad \ldots(3.123)$$

In figure-3.178(a) the current in external resistance is given as

$$I=\frac{V}{R_i+r} \qquad \ldots(3.124)$$

In above equation if we use $r << R_i$ then we can write

$$I=\frac{V}{R_i+r}\approx\frac{V}{R_i}=I_S \qquad \ldots(3.125)$$

From above equation-(3.125) we can state that for very low value of external resistance to this system the current supplied by this system remain constant thus this system can be considered as a device supplying constant current or it can be called as a '*Constant Current Source*' having internal resistance R. An ideal current source is one which has infinite internal resistance which can always supply constant current to any external circuit. The symbol used for an ideal current source of current supplied I_0 is shown in figure-3.179(a) and figure-3.179(b) shows a real current source in which its internal resistance is considered to be connected in parallel to an ideal current source. This is unlike to the case of a battery which is a constant voltage source and in case of a real battery we consider its internal resistance in series to an ideal EMF.

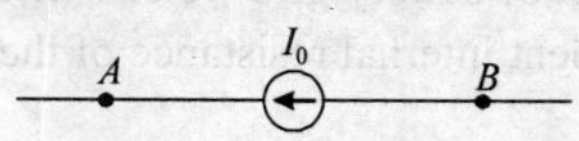

(a)

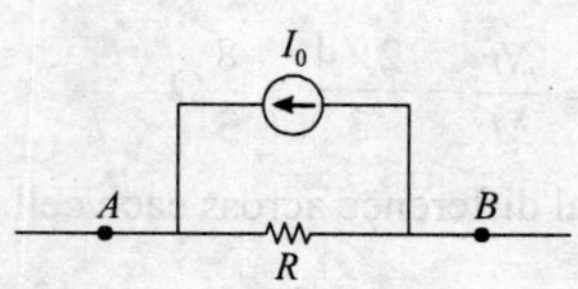

(b)

Figure 3.179

To verify and understand the internal resistance of a real current source we extend our previous discussion by redrawing the figure-3.178(b) in form of a current source as shown in figure-3.180.

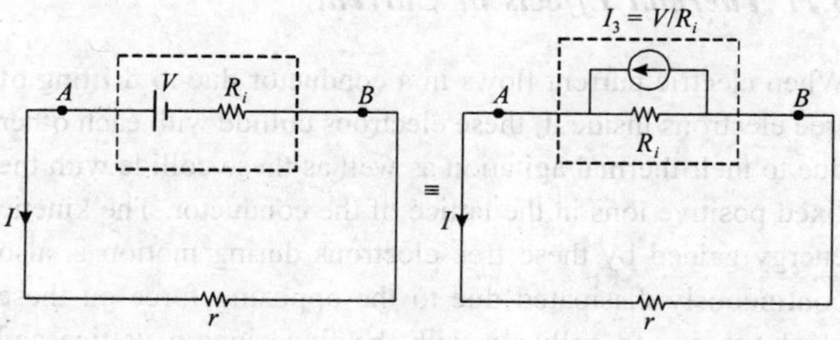

Figure 3.180

The current supplied by the source is I_S which will distribute between R_i and r which are connected in parallel and we know that for parallel combination of resistances current is divided in inverse ratio of resistances thus current through external resistance r will be given as

$$I = I_S\left(\frac{R_i}{R_i + r}\right) = \left(\frac{V}{R_i}\right)\left(\frac{R_i}{R_i + r}\right) = \frac{V}{R_i + r} \quad \ldots(3.126)$$

Above equation-(3.126) is same as equation-(3.125) which verifies the qualitative analysis we did for understanding of current sources.

Web Reference at www.physicsgalaxy.com

Age Group - Grade 11 & 12 | Age 17-19 Years
Section - ELECTRIC CURRENT & CIRCUITS
Topic - Circuit Analysis
Module Number - 22 to 25

3.10 Star-Delta (Y-Δ) *Transformation*

'*Star-Delta*' or 'Y-∇' transformation is a mathematical technique to simplify electrical circuits. Sometimes resistances are connected in mixed combinations which are neither in series nor in parallel and in such cases using this transformation we can simplify the circuit after which it can be solved by using series and parallel method. The name 'Y-Δ' or also called 'Star-Delta' comes from the shape of circuit in which resistances are connected. Figure-3.181(a) and (b) shows combination of three resistances called 'Y' or 'Δ' connections.

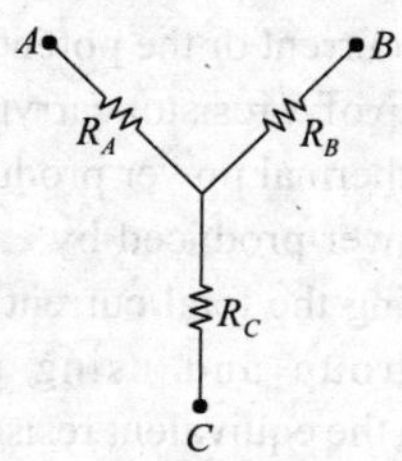

(a)

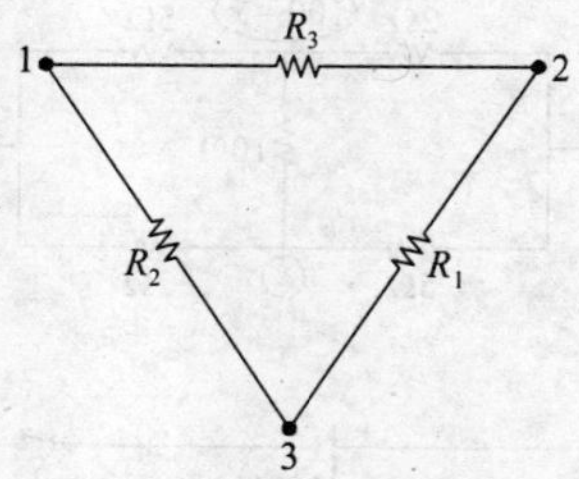

(b)

Figure 3.181

In different electrical circuits whenever resistances are connected in either 'Y' or 'Δ' fashion then these can be transformed into each other by using relation between resistances R_A, R_B, R_C and R_1, R_2, R_3.

The relations are established by considering equivalent resistances across terminals A, B, C and terminals 1, 2, 3 are all equal by taking any two terminals and keeping third terminal open.

For the above circuits transformations of 'Δ' to 'Y' we get the values of R_A, R_B and R_C in terms of R_1, R_2 and R_3 as

$$R_A = \frac{R_2 R_3}{R_1 + R_2 + R_3} \quad \ldots(3.127)$$

$$R_B = \frac{R_1 R_3}{R_1 + R_2 + R_3} \quad \ldots(3.128)$$

$$R_C = \frac{R_1 R_2}{R_1 + R_2 + R_3} \quad \ldots(3.129)$$

Rearranging above terms, we can calculate the values of R_1, R_2 and R_3 in terms of R_A, R_B and R_C for 'Y' to 'Δ' transformation.

$$R_1 = \frac{R_A R_B + R_B R_C + R_A R_C}{R_A} \quad \ldots(3.130)$$

$$R_2 = \frac{R_A R_B + R_B R_C + R_A R_C}{R_B} \quad \ldots(3.131)$$

$$R_3 = \frac{R_A R_B + R_B R_C + R_A R_C}{R_C} \quad \ldots(3.132)$$

To understand the application of this analysis we can take an illustration.

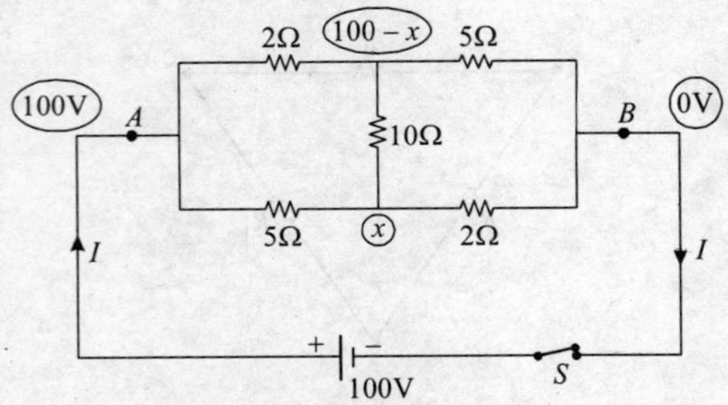

Figure 3.182

Figure-3.182 shows an unbalanced wheatstone bridge of which we will calculate the equivalent resistance using 'Δ' to 'Y' transformation without using KCL or any other analysis. In this circuit we can figure out the 'Δ' pattern by three resistances across terminals A, P and Q. If we find out the corresponding resistances to transform it to 'Y' pattern using equations-(3.127), (3.128) and (3.129) then we get

$$R_A = \frac{2\times 10}{2+5+10} = \frac{20}{17}\Omega$$

$$R_B = \frac{5\times 10}{2+5+10} = \frac{50}{17}\Omega$$

$$R_C = \frac{2\times 5}{2+5+10} = \frac{10}{17}\Omega$$

If we redraw the above circuit transforming 'Δ' to 'Y' across terminals A, P and Q then it is shown in figure-3.183 which can now be solved using series and parallel analysis.

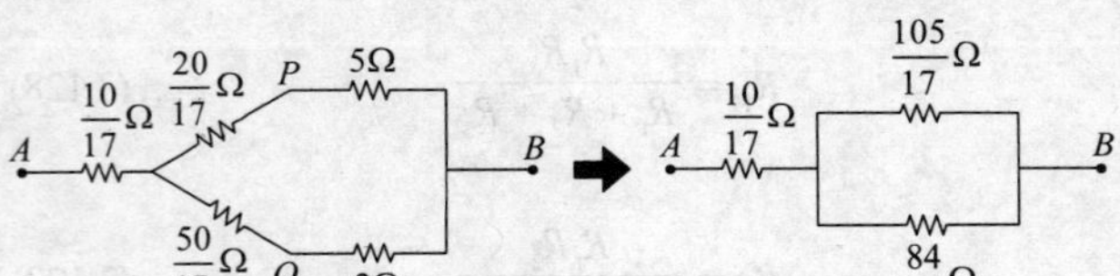

Figure 3.183

Thus equivalent resistance of this circuit across terminals A and B is given as

$$R_{eq} = \left(\frac{\frac{105}{17}\times\frac{84}{17}}{\frac{105}{17}+\frac{84}{17}}+\frac{10}{17}\right) = \frac{10}{3}\Omega \quad \ldots(3.133)$$

The equivalent resistance obtained in above equation-(3.133) is same what we've calculated using KCL in article-3.4.1. In this method the only drawback is tedious calculations of resistances used in transformation. To practice more students can try solving the above circuit using 'Y' to 'Δ' transformation using equations-(3.130), (3.131) and (3.132) across points A, B and Q and verify the same result.

3.11 Thermal Effects of Current

When electric current flows in a conductor due to drifting of free electrons inside it, these electrons collide with each other due to their thermal agitation as well as these collide with the fixed positive ions in the lattice of the conductor. The kinetic energy gained by these free electrons during motion is also continuously dissipated due to the opposing force on these electrons due to collision with the fixed ions in lattice and transformed into heat. This is called '*Joule Heating Effect*'. Whenever a current flows in a conductor heat is dissipated in conductor and conducted or radiated to surrounding.

3.11.1 Thermal Power in a Resistor

When a current I flows through a resistor of resistance R as shown in figure-3.184 the potential difference across this resistor will be $V = IR$. If we calculate the work done in transporting a charge dq from terminal A to B through the resistance, it is given as

$$dW = dq\,V$$

Due to continuous flow of current we can write $dq = Idt$ so we have

$$dW = (Idt)V = I^2R\,dt$$

This work is done by electric field in continuous flow of current through the resistor and is continuously dissipated as heat in it. The rate at which this work is done or at which heat is being dissipated in this resistor is called '*Thermal Power*' produced in resistor which is given as

$$P_{th} = \frac{dW}{dt} = I^2R = \frac{V^2}{R} \quad \ldots(3.134)$$

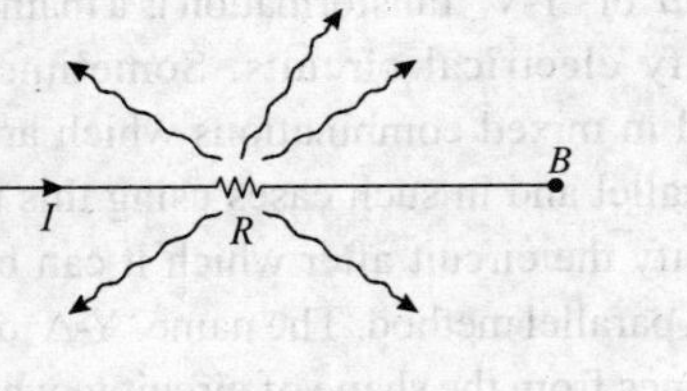

Figure 3.184

Equation-(3.134) gives the expression of rate of heat produced in resistor in terms of current or the potential difference across the resistor. For a group of N resistor carrying current $I_1, I_2, I_3\ldots$ we can find the total thermal power produced by summing all individual thermal power produced by each resistance of the group or by considering the total current I_T supplied into the terminals of the group and using the expression in equation-(3.134) with the equivalent resistance of the group as

$$P_{Total} = I_T^2R_{eq} = \sum_{i=1}^{N} I_i^2R_i \quad \ldots(3.135)$$

3.11.2 Total Heat Dissipated in Resistor in a given Time Duration

Equation-(98) gives the thermal power dissipated in a resistor through which a current I flows. If the current is constant then in time duration Δt total heat produced in resistor is given as

$$H = I^2 R \Delta t \quad \text{...(3.136)}$$

If the current which flows through the resistor is varying with time as $I = f(t)$ then for a short elemental duration 'dt' this current can be considered constant and heat produced in resistor for this duration 'dt' is given as

$$H = I^2 R\, dt \quad \text{...(3.137)}$$

To calculate the total heat produced we can integrate the above expression for the time duration in which heat is to be calculated as

$$H = \int_{t=0}^{t} I^2 R dt = \int_{t=0}^{t} [f(t)]^2 R dt \quad \text{...(3.138)}$$

3.11.3 Power Supplied or Absorbed by a Battery

When current is supplied by a battery then by chemical energy inside battery it does continuous work in flow of free electrons to maintain the current in circuit. When a charge dq is supplied by a battery of EMF ξ then work done by the battery is

$$dW = dq\xi$$

If a current I is maintained by the battery then the rate at which continuously work is done by the battery or *Power Supplied by the Battery* is given as

$$P_{\text{battery}} = \frac{dW}{dt} = \xi I \quad \text{...(3.139)}$$

In some cases when a current is supplied into the battery by some external source which dominates the EMF of the battery then the charges are pushed into the battery and work is done on the battery continuously as current flows in that case the expression in equation-(3.139) gives the '*Power Absorbed by the Battery*' which restores the chemical energy back in battery if it is chargeable otherwise it will be dissipated as heat in chemicals of the battery.

Figure-3.185 shows the two cases when a battery supplies power and it absorbs power when connected in a circuit.

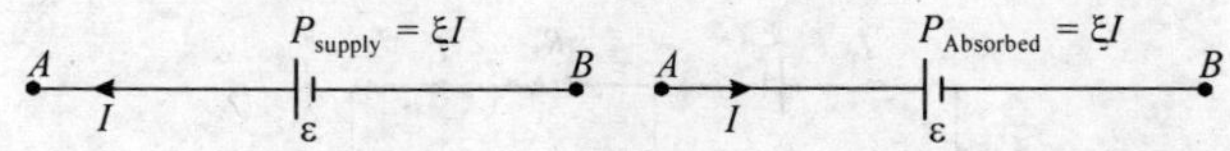

Figure 3.185

Above are the cases of power supplied or absorbed by ideal battery. Figure-3.186(a) shows a real battery of EMF ξ and internal resistance r supplying power to external circuit. In this case battery produces a power ξI and due to its internal resistance inside the battery thermal power is also produced which heats up the battery. Thus total power supplied by this battery to external circuit is given as

$$P_{\text{supply}} = \xi I - I^2 r \quad \text{...(3.140)}$$

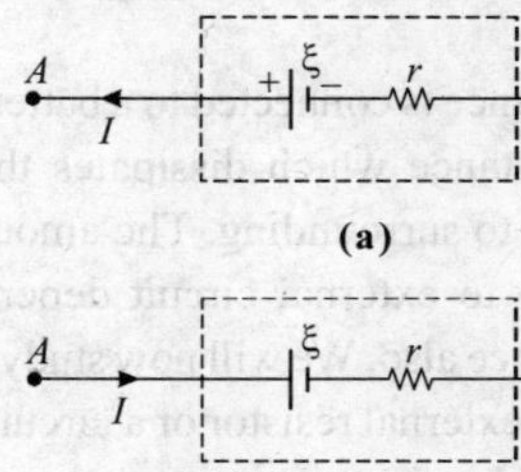

(b)

Figure 3.186

If we analyze the situation shown in figure-3.186(b) in which a current I is supplied into a real battery of EMF ξ and internal resistance r. In this case battery is absorbing power ξI and a thermal power is also being produced inside the battery due to its internal resistance. Thus total power consumed by this battery is given as

$$P_{\text{consumed}} = \xi I + I^2 r \quad \text{...(3.141)}$$

3.11.4 Total Energy Conservation in an Electrical Circuit

In an electrical circuit containing resistances and batteries, there are some batteries which supply power and there are some which absorb power. By conservation of energy we can state that in any electrical circuit total power supplied by some batteries is equal to the sum of total power absorbed by some other batteries and total thermal power produced in all resistances of the circuit including internal resistances of the batteries.

Figure-3.187 shows an electrical circuit containing four batteries and some resistors with directions of currents flowing in the resistors and batteries. We can see that batteries with EMFs ξ_1 and ξ_4 are supplying power and batteries with EMFs ξ_2 and ξ_3 are absorbing power from circuit so the power equation for this circuit can be written by conservation of energy as

$$\xi_1 I_3 + \xi_4 I_6 = \xi_2 I_2 + \xi_3 I_5 + I_1^2 R_1 + I_2^2 R_2 + I_3^2 R_3 + I_4^2 R_4 + I_6^2 R_5 \quad \text{...(3.142)}$$

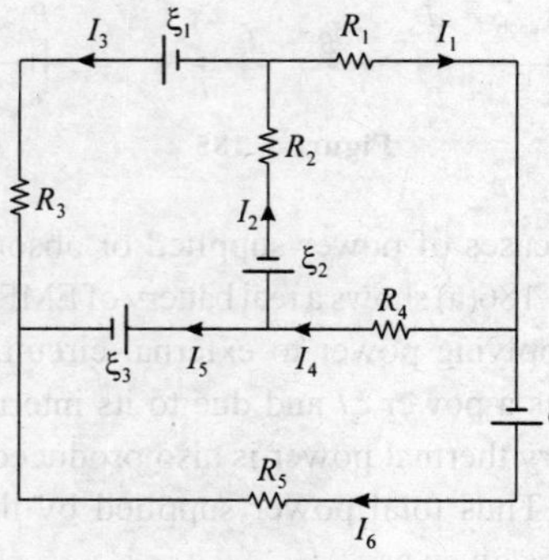

Figure 3.187

3.11.5 Maximum Power Transfer Theorem

When an external resistance is connected to a battery, it supplies power to external resistance which dissipates this energy in form of thermal energy to surrounding. The amount of energy supplied by the battery to external circuit depends upon the value of external resistance also. We will now study the variation of power supplied to an external resistor or a circuit by a battery with variation in external resistance.

Figure-3.188 shows a real battery with EMF ξ and internal resistance *r* which is connected to an external variable resistance *R*. The current supplied by the battery in this case is given as

$$I=\frac{\xi}{R+r} \quad \ldots(3.143)$$

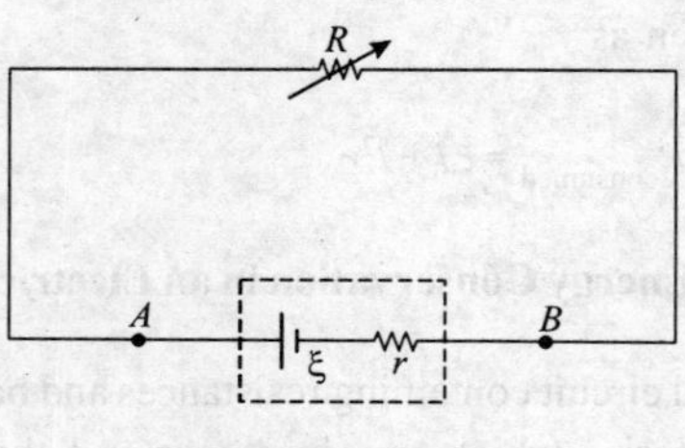

Figure 3.188

Using the current in circuit, we can calculate the power supplied to the external resistance as

$$P_R = I^2R$$

$$\Rightarrow \quad P_R=\left(\frac{\xi}{R+r}\right)^2 R=\frac{\xi^2 R}{(R+r)^2} \quad \ldots(3.144)$$

From equation-(3.144) we can see that the power supplied to external resistor varies with value of its resistance *R* which first increases with *R* then decreases. We can find out the maximum value of power supplied by using concept of maxima-minima. So the power supplied by battery is maximum when

$$\frac{dP_R}{dR}=0$$

$$\Rightarrow \quad \frac{d}{dR}\left(\frac{\xi^2 R}{(R+r)^2}\right)=0$$

$$\Rightarrow \quad \xi^2\left(\frac{(R+r)^2.1-R.2(R+r)}{(R+r)^4}\right)=0$$

$$\Rightarrow \quad R^2=r^2$$

$$\Rightarrow \quad R=r \quad \ldots(3.145)$$

From above expression in equation-(3.145) it is evident that maximum power is supplied by the battery to external resistance when external resistance value is equal to internal resistance of the battery. This is called '*Maximum Power Transfer Theorem*'.

Above relation in equation-(3.145) also indicates that above and below internal resistance of battery there can be two values of external resistance for which the power supplied by battery will be same that can be calculated by using equation-(3.144).

3.11.6 Use of Maximum Power Transfer by Thevenin's Analysis

To understand the use of maximum power transfer theorem with Thevenin's analysis we take an illustration. Figure-3.189 shows a circuit with one variable resistance *R* and some other components. In this circuit we are required to find the value of *R* for which the thermal power produced in this resistor will be maximum.

One way of solving this is to solve the circuit using KCL or KVL with *R* as variable and calculate the current through *R* in terms of R and then maximize I^2R with respect to *R* using concept of maxima-minima by equating its derivative to zero. That equation will give us the value of *R* for which maximum thermal power is produced in this resistor.

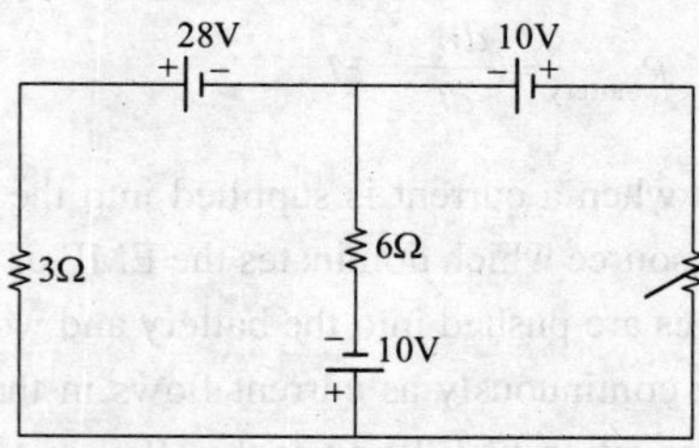

Figure 3.189

Another way to solve the circuit using Thevenin's method. For this we remove the resistance *R* and redraw the circuit as shown in figure-3.190 and calculate the current *I* in the loop by KVL equation of the loop as

$$9I = 18$$

$$\Rightarrow \qquad I = 2\text{A} \qquad \ldots(3.146)$$

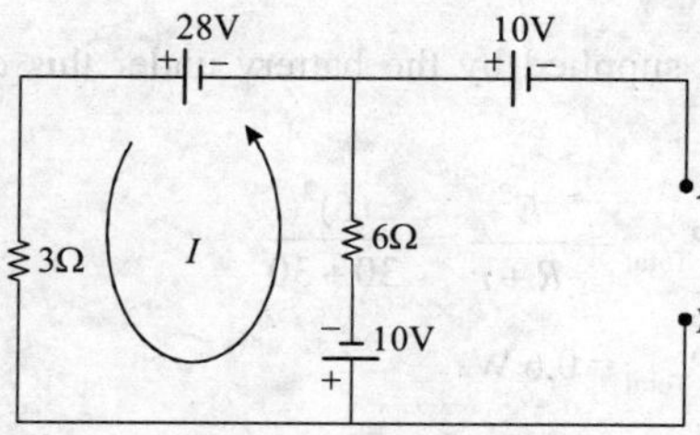

Figure 3.190

To find the open circuit potential difference across terminals *X* and *Y* we write the potential equation from *X* to *Y* as

$$-10 + 2 \times 6 + 10 = V_Y$$

$$\Rightarrow \qquad \xi_{eq} = V_Y - V_X = 12\text{ V} \qquad \ldots(3.147)$$

If we replace all batteries in circuit by straight wires as these are considered ideal, the effective resistance between the terminals *X* and *Y* for the circuit will be parallel combination of 3W and 6W resistance given as

$$r_{eq} = \frac{3 \times 6}{3+6} = 2\,\Omega \qquad \ldots(3.148)$$

From equations-(3.147) and (3.148) we can redraw the Thevenin's equivalent circuit as shown in figure-3.191.

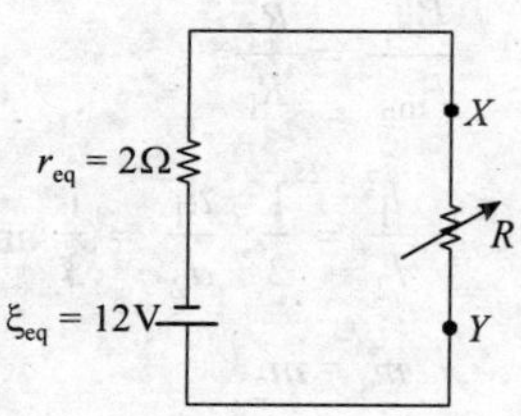

Figure 3.191

Now we can directly state by maximum power transfer theorem that maximum thermal power will be produced in *R* when *R* = 2 Ω. If we carefully see then to solve this specific question we do not need to solve for the equivalent EMF of this circuit as we only need the value of internal resistance of the equivalent battery as we've studied that for external resistance equal to the internal resistance of source the power transferred to external resistance will be maximum.

Illustrative Example 3.56

In the circuit shown in figure-3.192, find the heat developed across each resistance in 2 s.

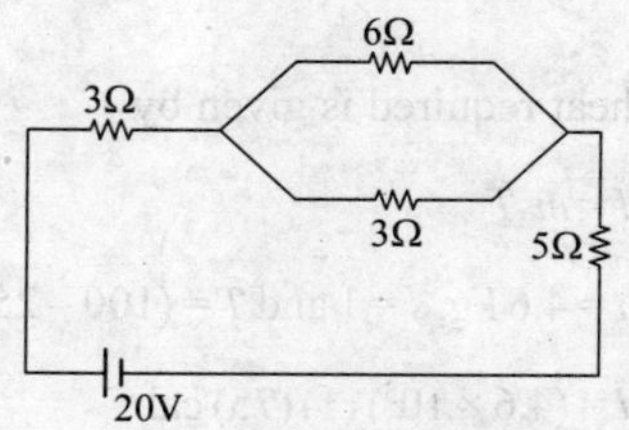

Figure 3.192

Solution

The 6 Ω and 3 Ω resistances are in parallel. So their combined resistance is given as

$$\frac{1}{R} = \frac{1}{6} + \frac{1}{3} = \frac{1}{2}$$

$$\Rightarrow \qquad R = 2\,\Omega$$

Now the circuit is reduced as shown in figure-3.193.

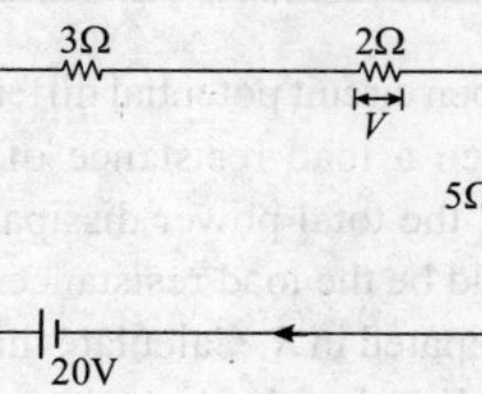

Figure 3.193

Current supplied by the battery is given as

$$i = \frac{20}{3+2+5} = 2\text{ A}$$

The potential difference across the combination of 6 Ω and 3 Ω resistance is given as

$$V = 2 \times 2 = 4\text{ V}$$

Now total heat produced across all the resistances are given as

$$H_{3\Omega} = i^2Rt = (2)^2 \times 3 \times 2 = 24\text{ J}$$

$$H_{6\Omega} = \frac{V^2}{R}t = \frac{(4)^2}{6} \times 2 = \frac{16}{3}\text{ J}$$

$$H_{3\Omega} = \frac{V^2}{R}t = \frac{(4)^2}{3} \times 2 = \frac{32}{3}\text{ J}$$

and $\qquad H_{5\Omega} = i^2 Rt = (2)^2 \times 5 \times 2 = 40\text{ J}$

Illustrative Example 3.57

Calculate the cost of heating 4.6 kg of water for 25°C to the boiling point, assuming that no energy is wasted. Electrical energy costs 25 paisa per kWh.

Solution

We know that heat required is given by

$$H = msT$$

Here we use $m = 4.6$ kg, $s = 1$ and $T = (100 - 25) = 75°C$

$$\Rightarrow \quad H = (4.6 \times 10^3)(1)(75) \text{ cal}$$

Total electrical energy supplied is given as

$$W = JH = 4.2 \times (4.6 \times 10^3)(1)(75) \text{ J}$$

$$\Rightarrow \quad W = \frac{(4.2)(4.6 \times 10^3)(75)}{60 \times 60 \times 10^3} \text{ kWh}$$

$$\Rightarrow \quad W = 0.4 \text{ kWh}$$

Total cost is given as

$$C = 0.4 \times 25 = 10 \text{ paisa}$$

 # Illustrative Example 3.58

A battery has an open circuit potential difference of 6 V between its terminals. When a load resistance of 60 Ω is connected across the battery, the total power dissipated by the battery is 0.4 W. What should be the load resistance *R*, so that maximum power will be dissipated in *R*. Calculate this power. What is the total power supplied by the battery when such a load is connected ?

Solution

Figure-3.194 shows the situation described in question. Here *r* is the internal resistance of the battery and *E* its EMF.

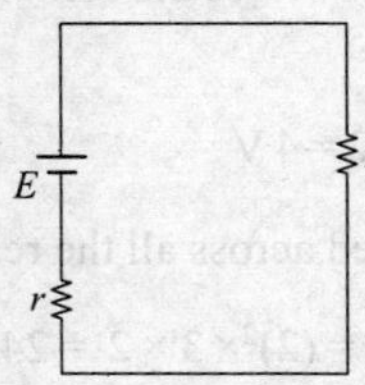

Figure 3.194

Power supplied by the battery in this case is given as

$$P = \frac{E^2}{R + r}$$

Substituting the values gives

$$0.4 = \frac{(6)^2}{60 + r}$$

$$\Rightarrow \quad r = 30\,\Omega$$

Maximum power is dissipated in the circuit when external resistance is equal to net internal resistance which gives

$$R = r$$

$$\Rightarrow \quad R = 30\,\Omega$$

Total power supplied by the battery under this condition is given as

$$P_{\text{Total}} = \frac{E^2}{R + r} = \frac{(6)^2}{30 + 30}$$

$$\Rightarrow \quad P_{\text{Total}} = 0.6 \text{ W}$$

Out of this 0.6 W half of the power is dissipated in *R* and half is dissipated in *r*. Therefore, maximum power dissipated in *R* is 0.3 W.

 # Illustrative Example 3.59

Two wires of same mass having ratio of lengths 1 : 2, density 1 : 3 and resistivity 2 : 1. These are connected one by one to the same voltage supply. The rate of heat dissipation in the first wire is found to be 10 W. Find the rate of heat dissipation in the second wire.

Solution

Across a given voltage source power dissipated in a resistance is given as

$$P_{\text{th}} = \frac{V^2}{R}$$

$$\Rightarrow \quad \frac{P_{\text{th}_1}}{P_{\text{th}_2}} = \frac{R_2}{R_1}$$

Given that $\quad \dfrac{l_1}{l_2} = \dfrac{1}{2}; \; \dfrac{d_1}{d_2} = \dfrac{1}{3}$ and $\dfrac{\rho_1}{\rho_2} = \dfrac{2}{1}$

and $\quad m_1 = m_2$

$$\Rightarrow \quad d_1 l_1 A_1 = d_2 l_2 A_2$$

$$\Rightarrow \quad \frac{A_1}{A_2} = \frac{d_2 l_2}{d_1 l_1}$$

$$\Rightarrow \quad \frac{P_{\text{th}_1}}{P_{\text{th}_2}} = \frac{\rho_2 l_2 / A_2}{\rho_1 l_1 / A_1} = \frac{\rho_2 l_2}{\rho_1 l_1} \times \frac{A_1}{A_2}$$

$$\Rightarrow \quad \frac{P_{\text{th}_1}}{P_{\text{th}_2}} = \frac{\rho_2 l_2^2 d_2}{\rho_1 l_1^2 d_1} = \left(\frac{1}{2}\right) \times \left(\frac{2}{1}\right)^2 \times \left(\frac{3}{1}\right)$$

$$\Rightarrow \quad \frac{P_{\text{th}_1}}{P_{\text{th}_2}} = 6$$

$$\Rightarrow \quad P_{\text{th}_2} = \frac{P_{\text{th}_1}}{2} = \frac{10}{6} = \frac{5}{3} \text{ W}$$

Illustrative Example 3.60

A current passing through a resistance R decreases uniformly to zero in a time internal T and a total charge q passes through resistance. Find the total heat produced in resistance in this process.

Solution

Figure-3.195 shows the variation of current falling linearly with time as described in the question. Here we consider at $t = 0$, $i = i_0$ and after time $t = T$ current in circuit becomes $i = 0$.

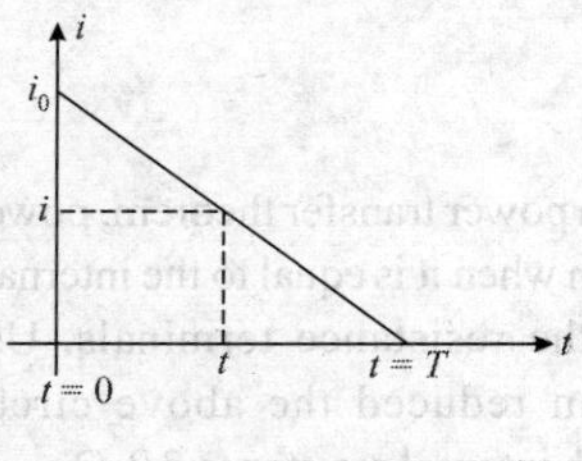

Figure 3.195

As total charge q passes through the circuit, we use

$$q = \int_0^T i\,dt = \frac{1}{2} i_0 T$$

$$\Rightarrow \quad i_0 = \frac{2q}{T}$$

Thus current in circuit as a function of time is given as

$$i = i_0 - \frac{i_0}{T}t = \frac{2q}{T}\left(1 - \frac{t}{T}\right)$$

Total heat produced from 0 to T is given as

$$H = \int_0^T i^2 R\,dt = \int_0^T \frac{4q^2R}{T^2}\left(1 - \frac{t}{T}\right)^2 dt$$

$$\Rightarrow \quad H = \frac{4q^2R}{T^2}\int_0^T \left(1 + \frac{t^2}{T^2} - \frac{2t}{T}\right) dt$$

$$\Rightarrow \quad H = \frac{4q^2R}{T^2}\left[t + \frac{t^3}{3T^2} - \frac{t^2}{T}\right]_0^T$$

$$\Rightarrow \quad H = \frac{4q^2R}{T^2}\left[T + \frac{T}{3} - T\right]$$

$$\Rightarrow \quad H = \frac{4}{3}\frac{q^2R}{T}$$

Illustrative Example 3.61

A bulb is marked 220 V, 100 W. What will be the current in the filament when connected to 200 V ?

Solution

Resistance of the given bulb can be calculated as

$$R = \frac{V^2}{P} = 484\,\Omega$$

Thus current through the bulb when it is connected across a 200 V supply is given as

$$I = \frac{200}{484} = \frac{50}{121}\text{ A}$$

Illustrative Example 3.62

A 500 W heater is designed to operate at 200 V potential difference. If it is connected across 160 V line, find the heat it will produce in 20 minute.

Solution

The resistance of heater coil is given as

$$R = \frac{V^2}{P} = \frac{(200)^2}{500} = \frac{40000}{500} = 80\,\Omega$$

When connected across 160V supply, the power consumed by heater will be given as

$$P' = \frac{V^2}{R} = \frac{(160)^2}{80} = \frac{160 \times 160}{80}$$

$$\Rightarrow \quad P' = 320\text{ W}$$

Total heat produced in 20 minute (1200s) is given as

$$H = P't$$

$$\Rightarrow \quad H = 320 \times 1200$$

$$\Rightarrow \quad H = 384000 = 384\text{ kJ}$$

Illustrative Example 3.63

In the circuit shown in figure-3.196, find the value of resistance R at which the power transferred to this resistance will be maximum.

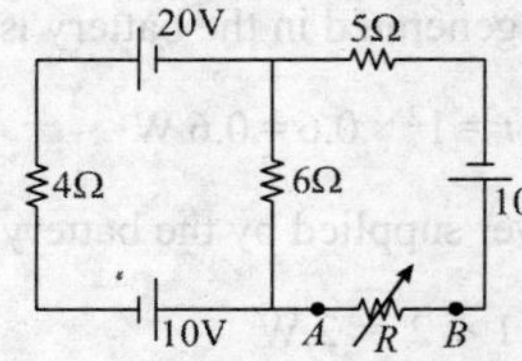

Figure 3.196

Solution

After removing the resistance R the circuit is shown in figure-3.197. The internal resistance across A and B for the circuit is given as

$$r_{AB} = \frac{4\times 6}{4+6} + 5 = 2.4 + 5 = 7.4\,\Omega$$

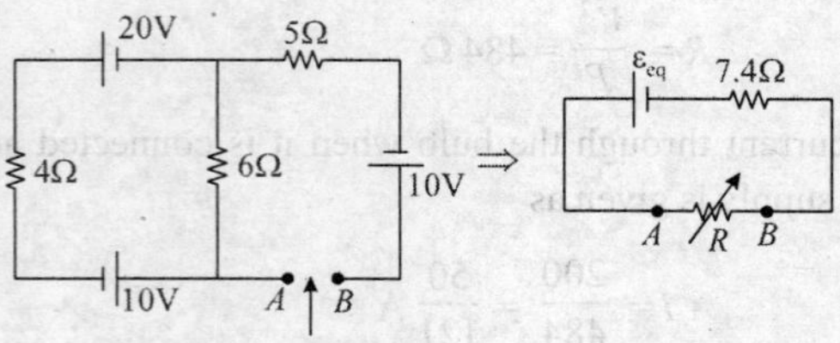

Figure 3.197

For maximum power to be transferred to R using maximum power transfer theorem, the value of R should be equal to the internal resistance of the circuit which is given as

$$R = 7.4\,\Omega$$

Illustrative Example 3.64

A storage battery with EMF $E = 2.6$ V loaded with and external resistance produces a current $I = 1.0$ A. In this case the potential difference between the terminals of the storage battery equals $V = 2.0$ V. Find the thermal power generated in the battery and the power supplied by the battery.

Solution

When a current is drawn from the battery, its potential difference across the terminals decreases which is given as

$$2.0 = 2.6 - Ir$$

$$\Rightarrow \quad r = 0.6\,\Omega$$

If external resistance is R, we use

$$R + r = \frac{2.6}{1} = 2.6\,\Omega$$

$$\Rightarrow \quad R = 2.6 - 0.6 = 2.0\,\Omega$$

The thermal power generated in the battery is given as

$$P_{th} = I^2 r = 1^2 \times 0.6 = 0.6\text{ W}$$

Total electrical power supplied by the battery is given as

$$P = 1 \times 2 = 2\text{ W}$$

Illustrative Example 3.65

In the circuit shown in figure-3.198, for what value of R the power dissipated in it will be maximum.

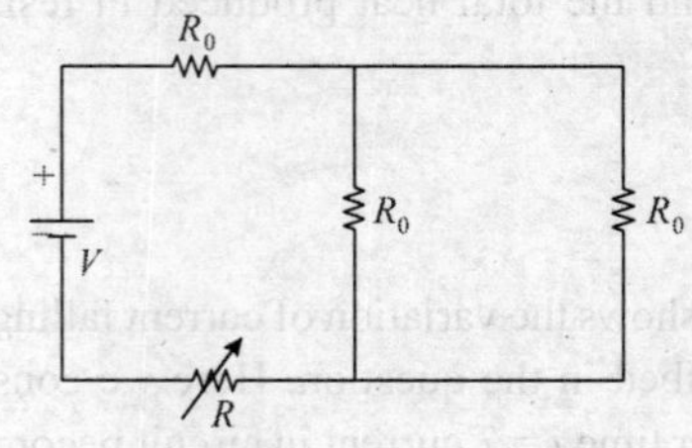

Figure 3.198

Solution

Using maximum power transfer theorem, power dissipated in R will be maximum when it is equal to the internal resistance of the circuit across the resistance terminals. Using Thevenin's analysis we can reduced the above circuit as shown in figure-3.199 with internal resistance $3R_0/2$.

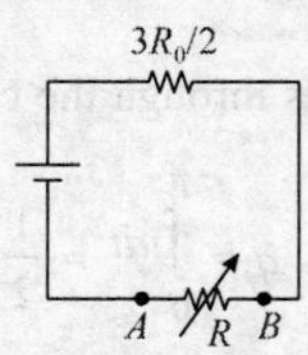

Figure 3.199

Thus maximum power will be dissipated in the resistance R when it is given as

$$R = \frac{3R_0}{2}$$

Illustrative Example 3.66

The walls of a closed cubical box of edge 60 cm are made of material of thickness 1mm and thermal conductivity 4×10^{-4} cal s^{-1}cm^{-1}°C^{-1}. The interior of the box is maintained 1000 °C above the outside temperature by a heater placed inside the box and connected across 400V DC supply. Calculate the resistance of the heater.

Solution

The amount of heat transmitted per second through the walls of closed cubical box is given by steady conduction rate which is given as

$$\frac{Q}{t} = \frac{KA(T_2 - T_1)}{d}$$

Substituting the values we have

$$\frac{Q}{t} = \frac{(4\times10^{-4})(6\times50\times50)(100)}{0.1}$$

$$\Rightarrow \quad \frac{Q}{t} = 6000\ \text{cal}$$

This heat loss must be compensated by the electric current fowling through the coil which is given as

$$H = \frac{V^2}{R\times4.2}\ \text{cal}$$

$$\Rightarrow \quad R = \frac{V^2}{H\times4.2}$$

Here we use $V=400$ V and $H=6000$ cal

$$\Rightarrow \quad R = \frac{400\times400}{6000\times4.2} = 6.35\ \Omega$$

Illustrative Example 3.67

The figure-3.200 shows a part of certain circuit, find

(a) Power dissipated in 5 Ω resistance

(b) Potential difference $V_C - V_B$

(c) Which battery is being charged

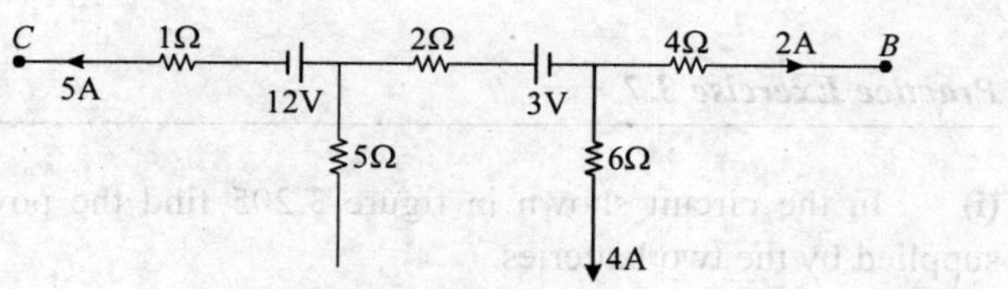

Figure 3.200

Solution

(a) By KCL at the two junctions we can see that the current flowing through resistance 5 Ω is 11A. Thus power dissipated in this is given as

$$P = i^2 R$$

$$\Rightarrow \quad P = (11)^2\times5 = 605\ \text{W}$$

(b) Writing the equation of potential drop from point C to B gives

$$V_B + 8\ \text{V} + 3\ \text{V} + 12\ \text{V} - 12\ \text{V} - 5\ \text{V} = V_C$$

$$\Rightarrow \quad V_B + 11\ \text{V} - 5\ \text{V} = V_C$$

$$\Rightarrow \quad V_C - V_B = 6\ \text{V}$$

(c) As in both batteries current is flowing into the positive terminals of the batteries thus both batteries are being charged.

Illustrative Example 3.68

Find the power supplied or supplied by each battery in the circuit shown in figure-3.201.

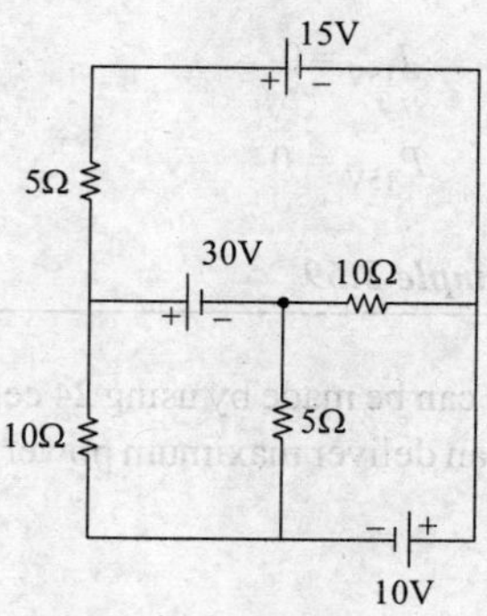

Figure 3.201

Solution

To solve the circuit we distribute potentials at different junctions of the circuit as shown in figure-3.202.

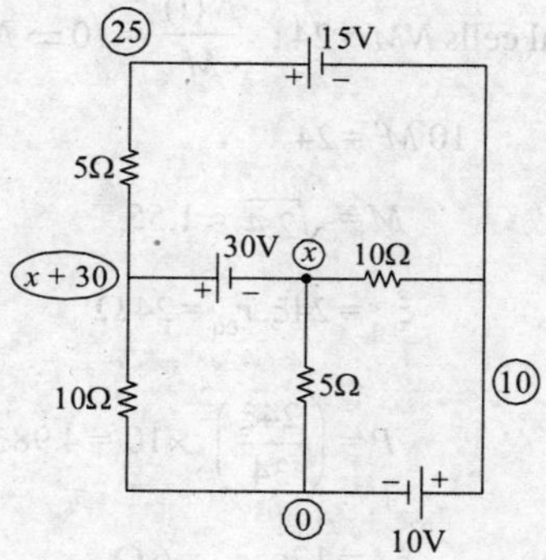

Figure 3.202

Writing KCL equation for x gives

$$\frac{x}{5} + \frac{x-10}{10} + \frac{x+30}{10} + \frac{x+5}{5} = 0$$

$$\Rightarrow \quad \frac{2x + x - 10 + x + 30 + 2x + 10}{10} = 0$$

$$\Rightarrow \quad 6x = -30$$

$$\Rightarrow \quad x = -5\text{V}$$

Current through the batteries and power supplied by batteries is given as

$$I_{10\text{V}} = \frac{x}{5} + \frac{x+30}{10} = -1 + 2.5 = 1.5\ \text{A}$$

$$P_{\text{suppied } 10\text{V}} = \varepsilon I = 10\times1.5 = 15\ \text{W}$$

and $$I_{30V} = \frac{25}{10} = 2.5A$$

$$P_{\text{suppied } 30V} = \varepsilon I = 30 \times 2.5 = 75 \text{ W}$$

$$I_{15V} = 0$$

$$P_{15V} = 0$$

Illustrative Example 3.69

How a battery grid can be made by using 24 cells of 1 Ω internal resistance which can deliver maximum power to a load of 10 Ω resistance.

Solution

In a battery grid with N cells in series and M rows in parallel the equivalent EMF and equivalent internal resistance is given as

$$\xi_{eq} = N\xi;\ r_{eq} = \frac{Nr}{M}$$

$$\text{Total cells } NM = 24;\quad \frac{N(1)}{M} = 10 \Rightarrow N = 10\,M$$

$$10\,M^2 = 24$$

$$M = \sqrt{2.4} \approx 1.55$$

If $M = 1; N = 24,$ $$\xi_{eq} = 24\xi,\ r_{eq} = 24\,\Omega$$

$$\Rightarrow \quad P = \left(\frac{24\xi}{34}\right)^2 \times 10 = 4.98\xi^2$$

If $M = 2; N = 12$ $$\xi_{eq} = 12\varepsilon,\ r_{eq} = 6\,\Omega$$

$$\Rightarrow \quad P = \left(\frac{12\xi}{16}\right)^2 \times 10 = 5.62\xi^2$$

Thus for $M = 2$ & $N = 12$, power supplied by grid will be maximum.

Illustrative Example 3.70

In the circuit shown in figure-3.203, for what value of R will the power consumed by this resistance will be maximum.

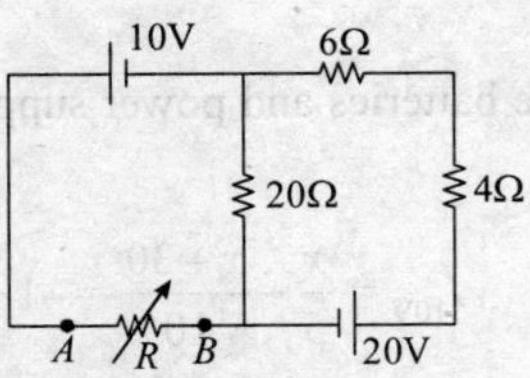

Figure 3.203

Solution

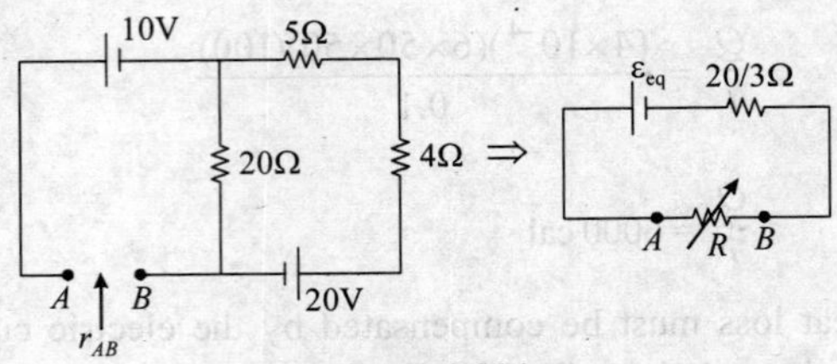

Figure 3.204

Here r_{AB} is given as

$$r_{AB} = 20\,\Omega\,|P|\,[6\,\Omega\,|S|\,4\,\Omega$$

$$\Rightarrow \quad r_{AB} = 20\,\Omega\,|P|\,10\,\Omega$$

$$\Rightarrow \quad r_{AB} = \frac{20 \times 10}{20 + 10} = \frac{20}{3}\,\Omega$$

By maximum power transfer theorem for resistance R we use

$$R = \frac{20}{3}\,\Omega$$

Web Reference at www.physicsgalaxy.com
Age Group - High School Physics | Age 17-19 Years
Section - ELECTRIC CURRENT & CIRCUITS
Topic - Thermal Effect of Current
Module Number - 1 to 5

Practice Exercise 3.7

(i) In the circuit shown in figure-3.205 find the power supplied by the two batteries.

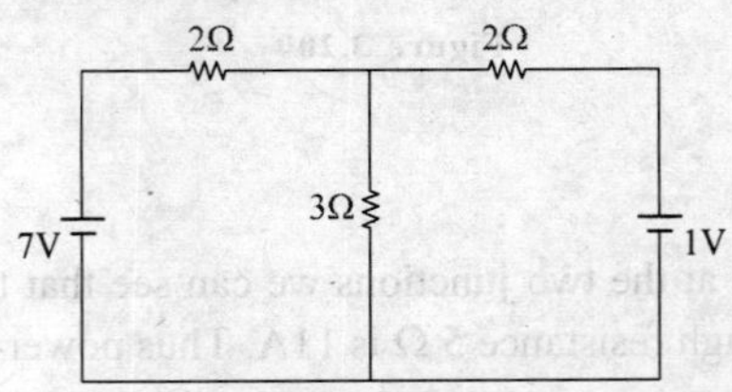

Figure 3.205

[14W, – 1W]

(ii) A 20 V battery with an internal resistance of 5 Ω is connected to a resistor of $x\Omega$. If an additional 6 Ω resistor is connected across the battery, find the value of x so that external power supplied by battery remains the same.

[x = 7.5 Ω]

(iii) Two identical batteries each of emf E = 2 V and internal resistance r = 1 Ω are available to produce heat in an external resistance by passing a current through it. What is the maximum power that can be developed across an external resistance R using these batteries.

[2W]

(iv) How would you connect 24 cells in series and/or parallel combination, each of internal resistance 1 Ω, so as to get maximum output across a load resistance of 10 Ω.

[2 rows of cells, each containing 12 cells in series must be connected in parallel.]

(v) A circuit shown in the figure-3.206 has resistances 20 Ω and 30 Ω. At what value of resistance R_x will the thermal power generated in it be practically independent of small variations of that resistance? The voltage between points A and B is supposed to be constant in this case.

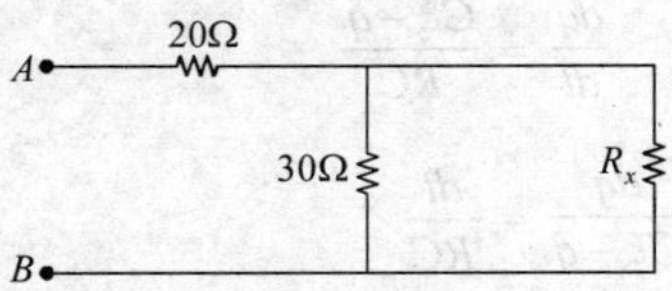

Figure 3.206

[12 Ω]

(vi) How much has a filament diameter decreased due to evaporation if the maintenance of the previous temperature required an increase of voltage by $\eta = 1.0\%$. The amount of heat transferred from the filament to surrounding space is assumed to be proportional to the filament surface area.

[2%]

(vii) An electric toaster uses nichrome for its heating element. When a negligible small current passes through it. Its resistance at room temperature 27.0°C is found to be 75.3 Ω. When the toaster is connected to a 230 V supply, the current settles, after a few seconds, to a steady value of 2.68 A. What is the steady temperature of the nichrome element? The temperature coefficient of resistance of nichrome averaged over the temperature range involved, is $1.70 \times 10^{-4}\ °C^{-1}$.

[850°C]

(viii) What amount of heat will be generated in a coil of resistance R due to a charge q passing through it if the current in coil decreases to zero halving its value every Δt seconds.

$[\frac{1}{2}\frac{q^2 R \ln(2)}{\Delta t}]$

(ix) A conductor has a temperature independent resistance R and a total heat capacity C. At the moment $t = 0$ it is connected to a DC voltage source of EMF V. Find the time dependence of the conductor's temperature T assuming the thermal power dissipated into surrounding space to vary as $q = k(T - T_0)$, where k is a constant, T_0 is the surrounding temperature which is considered to be equal to conductor's initial temperature.

$[T = T_0 + (1 - e^{-kt/C})\frac{V^2}{kR}]$

(x) A fuse of lead wire has an area of cross-section 0.2 mm². On short-circuiting, the current in the fuse wire reaches 30A. How long after the short-circuiting, will the fuse begin to melt? For lead, take its specific heat 0.032 cal g^{-1} (°C)$^{-1}$, melting point 327°C, density 11.34 g/cm³ and the resistivity = 22×10^{-6} Ω-cm. The initial temperature of wire is 20°C. Neglect heat losses.

[0.095 s]

3.12 *Transient Analysis of RC Circuits*

Figure-3.207 shows a capacitor connected across a battery via a switch. We've studied that on closing the switch for a short interval of time current flows and charge on capacitor plates increases to $q = C\xi$ and then current in circuit becomes zero. This state is called steady state of circuit. The state of circuit just after closing the switch and before it attains the steady state is called '*Transient State*' and the duration for which the current flows in the circuit until steady state is attained is called '*Transient Duration*'.

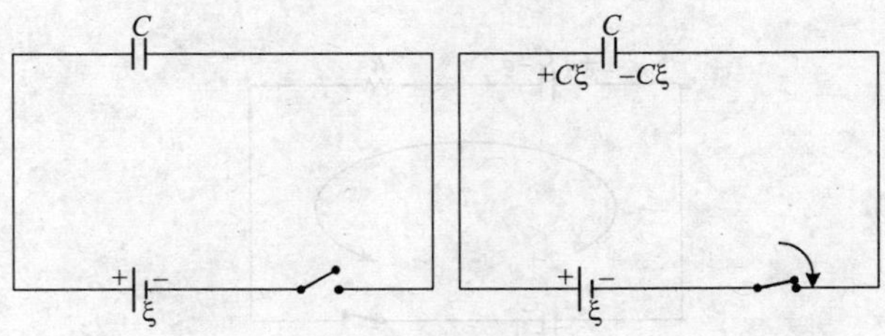

(a)

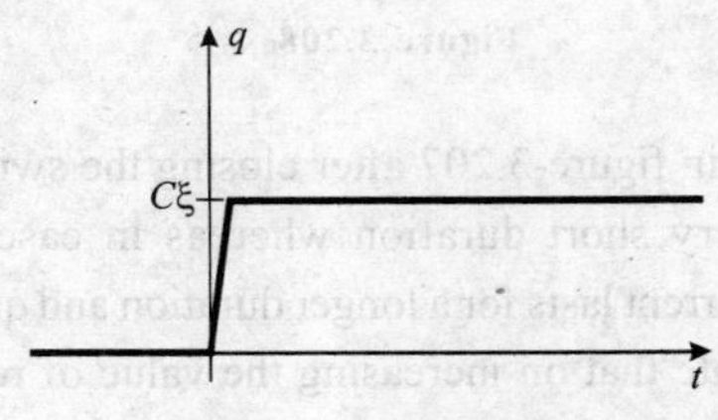

(b)

Figure 3.207

Figure-3.207(b) shows the variation of charge with time on capacitor plates after closing the switch at $t = 0$. We can see that before $t = 0$ when the switch was open charge on capacitor was zero and on closing the switch at $t = 0$ within almost no time charge suddenly rises to the steady state value $q = C\xi$.

The charging of capacitor is very quick because connecting wires are perfect conductors. Figure-3.208(a) shows a circuit in which along with a capacitor of capacitance C, a resistor of resistance R is connected in series across the battery of EMF ξ via a switch.

Now when we close the switch at $t = 0$ again a current flows in circuit which charges the capacitor but due to the presence of resistance charging is not as fast as it was in case of figure-3.208 and charge on capacitor gradually increases and finally attains the same steady state value $q = C\xi$ and current in circuit becomes zero as in steady state potential difference across capacitor becomes equal to that of battery EMF. Figure-3.208(b) shows the gradual variation in charge on capacitor plates from 0 to $C\xi$. In this figure transient period is also indicated after which circuit attains steady state.

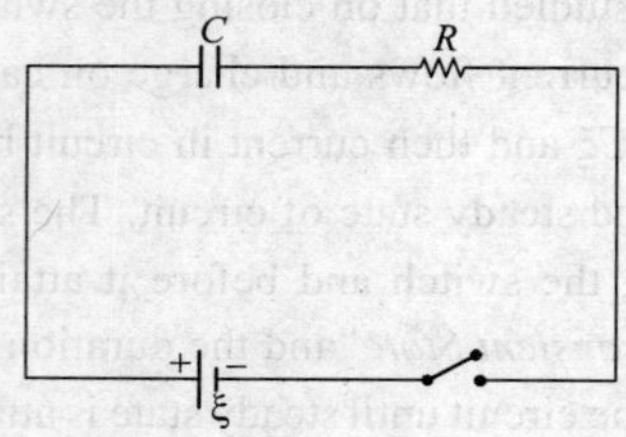

(a)

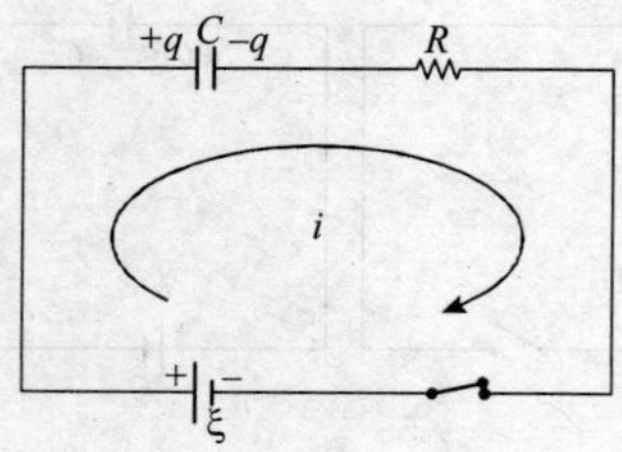

(b)

Figure 3.208

In case shown in figure-3.207 after closing the switch current flows for a very short duration whereas in case shown in figure-3.208 current lasts for a longer duration and qualitatively we can also state that on increasing the value of resistance R the transient duration in which capacitor receives its full charge increases.

3.12.1 Analysis of Charging of a Capacitor in RC circuit

When a capacitor is charged through a resistance by a battery as shown in figure-3.208(a) we can analyze the charge on capacitor and circuit current as a function of time by using KVL. When the switch is closed at $t = 0$ a current starts flowing in circuit and at any instant $t = t$ if current in circuit is i and charge on capacitor plates at this instant is q then the KVL equation for this loop of circuit is written as

$$+\xi - \frac{q}{C} - iR = 0$$

$$\Rightarrow \quad i = \frac{C\xi - q}{RC} \qquad \dots(3.149)$$

The current in circuit supplies charge on capacitor which can be written as rate of variation of charge on capacitor so we have

$$\frac{dq}{dt} = \frac{C\xi - q}{RC}$$

$$\Rightarrow \quad \frac{dq}{C\xi - q} = \frac{dt}{RC}$$

Integrating the above equation within limits of $t = 0$ to $t = t$ for charge on capacitor plate increases from $q = 0$ to $q = q$, we get

$$\int_0^q \frac{dq}{C\xi - q} = \int_0^t \frac{dt}{RC}$$

$$\Rightarrow \quad [-\ln(C\xi - q)]_0^q = \frac{1}{RC}[t]_0^t$$

$$\Rightarrow \quad [\ln(C\xi - q) - \ln(C\xi)] = -\frac{t}{RC}$$

$$\Rightarrow \quad \ln\left(\frac{C\xi - q}{C\xi}\right) = -\frac{t}{RC}$$

$$\Rightarrow \quad \left(\frac{C\xi - q}{C\xi}\right) = e^{-\frac{t}{RC}}$$

$$\Rightarrow \quad (C\xi - q) = C\xi e^{-\frac{t}{RC}}$$

$$\Rightarrow \quad q = C\xi\left(1 - e^{-\frac{t}{RC}}\right) \qquad \dots(3.150)$$

Above equation-(3.150) gives the charge on capacitor plates as a function of time during Transient state. We can see from this equation that charge increases exponentially as shown in figure-3.209 and at $t \to \infty$ charge on capacitor becomes $q = C\xi$. This indicates that transient duration is infinite and capacitor attains steady state after infinite time from the time of closing the switch. Theoretically its correct but practically it is not considered.

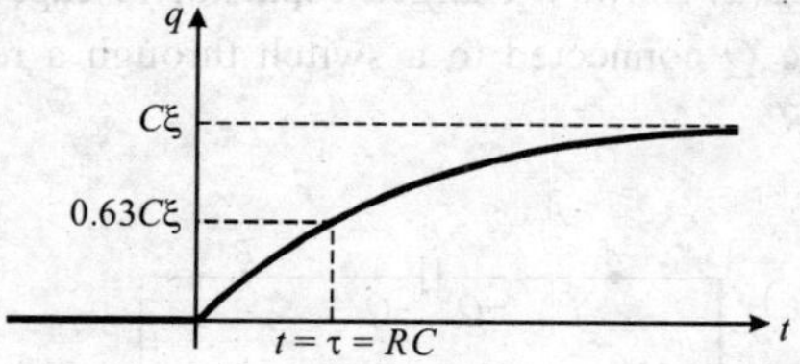

Figure 3.209

In above equation-(3.150) at time $t = RC$ if we calculate the charge on capacitor plates, it is given as

$$q_\tau = C\xi\,(1 - e^{-1})$$

$$\Rightarrow \quad q_\tau = C\xi\left(1 - \frac{1}{e}\right)$$

$$\Rightarrow \quad q_\tau = C\xi\left(1 - \frac{1}{2.718}\right)$$

$$= C\xi\,(1 - 0.37) = 0.63C\xi \quad \ldots(3.151)$$

The time duration $t = RC$ seconds is an important duration in analysis of RC circuits and it is called 'Time Constant' of a RC circuit and it is denoted by symbol 'τ'. Time constant of a given RC circuit is defined as "*The time duration in which the capacitor of RC circuit charged upto 63% of its steady state value*"

If we calculate the charge on capacitor after $t = 5\tau = 5$ RC then from equation-(3.151) we get

$$q = C\xi\,(1 - e^{-5}) = 0.99\,C\xi \quad \ldots(3.152)$$

From above equation-(3.152) it is clearly seen that in duration five times the time constant charge on capacitor rises to 99% of steady state value and theoretically remaining 1% charge it will attain in infinite duration.

So for practical purposes we can wait maximum upto five times the time constant duration and consider that steady state is almost attained so in general for practical purposes for a given RC circuit transient duration can be taken as 5 RC seconds.

When the switch is closed current flows to charge the capacitor which can be obtained by differentiating equation-(3.150) as

$$i = \frac{dq}{dt} = \frac{\xi}{R}e^{-\frac{t}{RC}} \quad \ldots(3.153)$$

Above current is also varying exponentially. Variation of current with time in charging of a capacitor in RC circuit is shown in figure-3.210.

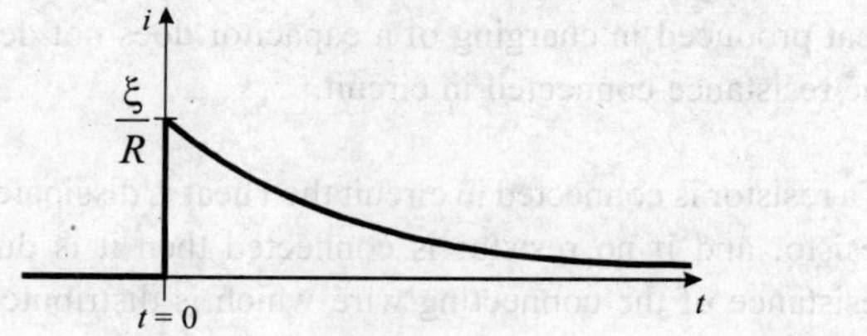

Figure 3.210

From above equation-(3.153) we can see that current just after closing the switch at $t = 0$ is given as

$$i = \frac{\xi}{R} \quad \ldots(3.154)$$

Above current is called '*Charging Current of a Capacitor in RC Circuit*'. Using this expression of current we can calculate the potential difference across resistor at any instant of time which is given as

$$V_R = iR = \xi e^{-\frac{t}{RC}} \quad \ldots(3.155)$$

3.12.2 Heat Produced in Charging of a Capacitor in RC circuit

We can also calculate the total heat dissipated in the resistor during charging of capacitor by integrating the heat produced in resistor for an elemental duration 'dt' and integrating it within limits from 0 to ∞ as theoretically charging lasts for infinite time which is given as

$$H = \int_{t=0}^{\infty} i^2 R\,dt = \int_{t=0}^{\infty}\left[\left(\frac{\xi}{R}\right)^2 e^{-\frac{2t}{RC}}\right]R\,dt$$

$$\Rightarrow \quad H = \int_{t=0}^{\infty}\frac{\xi^2}{R}e^{-\frac{2t}{RC}}dt$$

$$\Rightarrow \quad H = \frac{\xi^2}{R}\left(-\frac{RC}{2}\right)\left[e^{-\frac{2t}{RC}}\right]_0^{\infty}$$

$$\Rightarrow \quad H = -\frac{1}{2}C\xi^2\,[0-1] = \frac{1}{2}C\xi^2 \quad \ldots(3.156)$$

Total heat produced upto steady state can also be calculated by the traditional method which we have already calculated in previous chapter in article-2.2.4 as

$$H = \textit{Work done by battery} - \textit{Energy absorbed by Capacitor}$$

$$\Rightarrow \quad H = C\xi^2 - \frac{1}{2}C\xi^2 = \frac{1}{2}C\xi^2 \quad \ldots(3.157)$$

As already discussed in article-2.2.4 the result obtained for heat produced in charging of a capacitor was same as obtained in above equations-(3.156) and (3.157). This signifies that the heat produced in charging of a capacitor does not depend on the resistance connected in circuit.

If a resistor is connected in circuit then heat is dissipated in that resistor and if no resistor is connected then it is due to the resistance of the connecting wire which is distributed across the circuit.

3.12.3 Discharging of a Capacitor through a Resistor

When a capacitor is charged by a potential difference V and disconnected from the voltage source, the charge and potential difference across it is maintained until it is reconnected in some closed circuit. Figure-3.211(a) shows a charged isolated capacitor of capacitance C with charge Q of which the two terminals are connected via an open switch S.

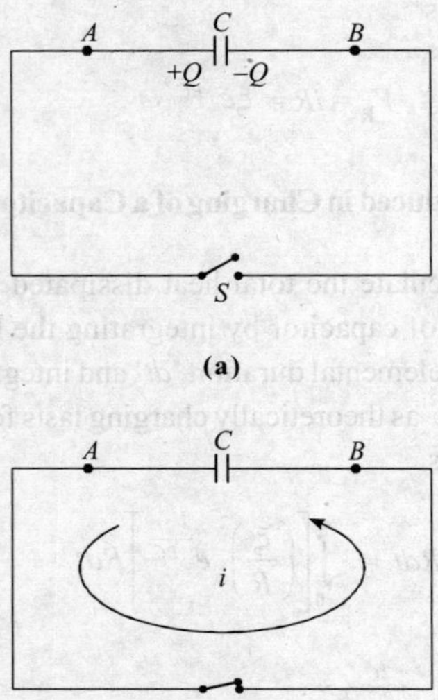

(b)
Figure 3.211

When the switch is closed as shown in figure-3.211(b), due to short circuiting the plates, the charge on one plate at high potential will flow toward the lower potential plate and capacitor will get discharged. As wires are considered perfectly conducting discharging of capacitor will be very quick. Figure-3.212 shows the time variation of the charge on capacitor as switch is closed at $t = 0$.

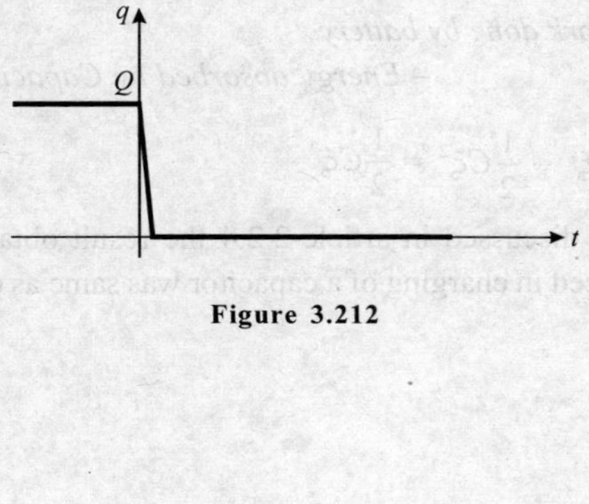

Figure 3.212

Figure-3.213(a) shows a charged capacitor of capacitance C with charge Q connected to a switch through a resistor of resistance R.

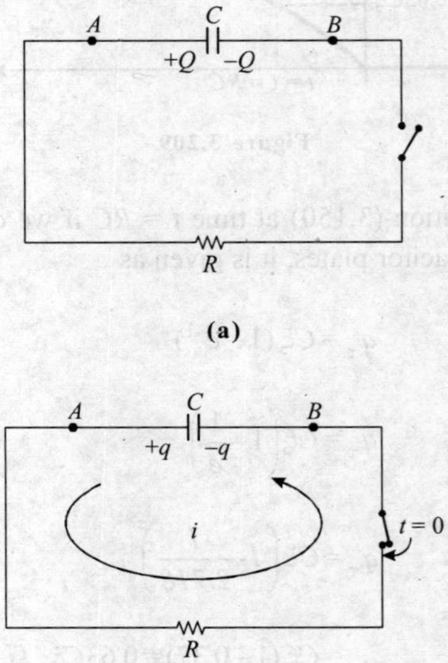

(b)
Figure 3.213

When the switch is closed the charge on capacitor plates starts discharging but at a slow pace due to presence of resistance. If we consider that switch was closed at $t = 0$ then at a general instant of time $t = t$ if current in circuit is i and charge on capacitor plates is q as shown in figure-3.213(b) then to analyze the circuit we can write the potential equation of the loop as

$$-iR + \frac{q}{C} = 0 \quad \ldots(3.158)$$

As during discharge the charge on capacitor plates decreases so the potential difference across capacitor also decreases, the current in circuit also decreases with time so we use

$$i = -\frac{dq}{dt} = \frac{q}{RC}$$

$$\Rightarrow \quad \frac{dq}{q} = -\frac{dt}{RC}$$

We can integrate above expression from the time of closing the switch $t = 0$ to an intermediate instant $t = t$ as shown in figure-3.213(b).

$$\int_{q=Q}^{q} \frac{dq}{q} = -\int_{t=0}^{t} \frac{dt}{RC}$$

$$\Rightarrow \quad [\ln(q)]_Q^q = -\frac{1}{RC}[t]_0^t$$

$$\Rightarrow \quad [\ln(q) - \ln(Q)] = -\frac{1}{RC}[t-0]$$

$$\Rightarrow \quad \ln\left(\frac{q}{Q}\right) = -\frac{t}{RC}$$

$$\Rightarrow \quad q = Qe^{-\frac{t}{RC}} \qquad \ldots(3.159)$$

Equation-(3.159) gives the charge on capacitor plates as a function of time during discharging of capacitor. The variation of charge during discharging of capacitor through a resistance is shown in figure-3.214.

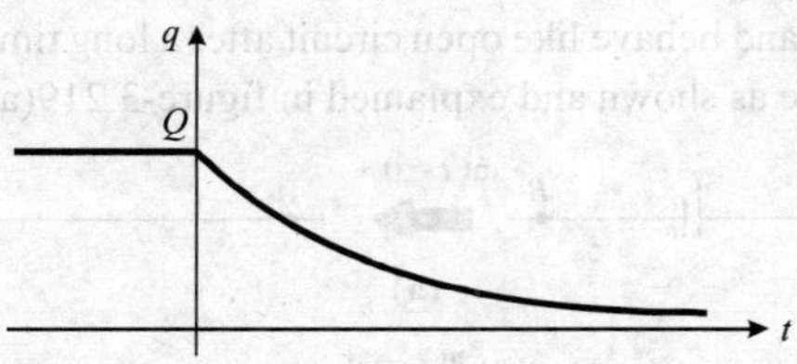

Figure 3.214

We can calculate the discharge in above RC circuit as a function of time by differentiating the equation-(3.159) which is given as

$$i = \frac{dq}{dt} = -\frac{Q}{RC}e^{-\frac{t}{RC}} \qquad \ldots(3.160)$$

The current also decays exponentially till capacitor is fully discharged. Just after closing the switch at $t = 0$ the discharge current is given by above equation as

$$i = \frac{Q}{RC} \qquad \ldots(3.161)$$

The variation of discharge current as a function of time is shown in figure-3.215.

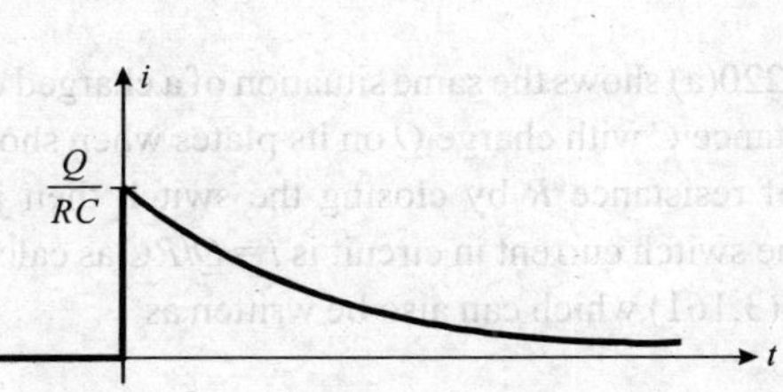

Figure 3.215

3.12.4 Initial and Steady State Behaviour of Uncharged Capacitor in RC Circuits

In previous chapter of Capacitance we have already discussed the analysis of solving capacitive circuits in steady state and in previous article we analyzed RC circuits during transient state. For many cases it is essential to understand the behaviour of capacitors in circuit just after closing the circuit and in steady state. We will discuss the same for two states of capacitor if it is initially uncharged or charged when connected in a circuit.

For a simple RC circuit shown in figure-3.216(a) we've discussed that on closing the switch at $t = 0$ the current in circuit is calculated as expressed in equation-(3.153) which is given as

$$i = \frac{dq}{dt} = \frac{\xi}{R}e^{-\frac{t}{RC}}$$

Figure-3.216(a) and (b). In above equation we've also discussed that just after closing the switch at $t = 0$ circuit current is ξ/R as if no capacitor is connect in circuit or we can consider that at $t = 0$ capacitor of the circuit is behaving like a short circuit or just a straight wire as shown in figure-3.216(b).

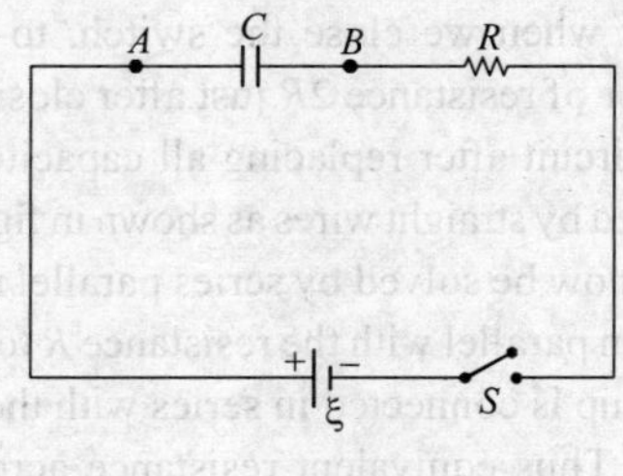

(a)

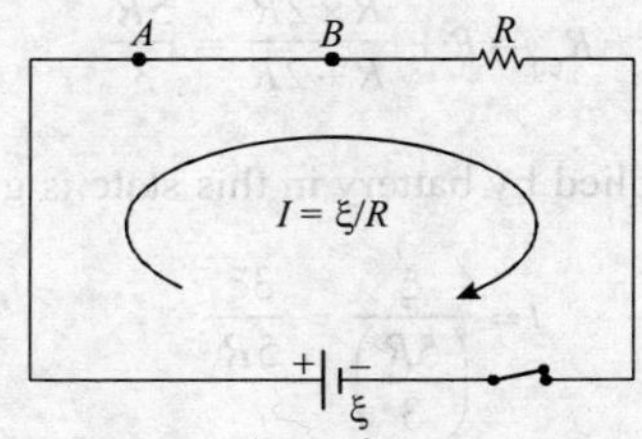

At $t = 0+$

(b)

Figure 3.216

This can be generalized for all RC circuits that just after switching on a circuit containing resistors and capacitors all the uncharged capacitors of the circuit behave like a short circuit or at an initial instant we can replace all uncharged capacitors of the circuit by a straight conducting wire and solve the circuit for any parameter of the circuit. We can understand it with the help of an illustration in better way. Figure-3.217(a) shows a circuit containing some resistors and capacitors. In this case we are required to find the current in resistor of resistance $2R$ just after closing the switch S.

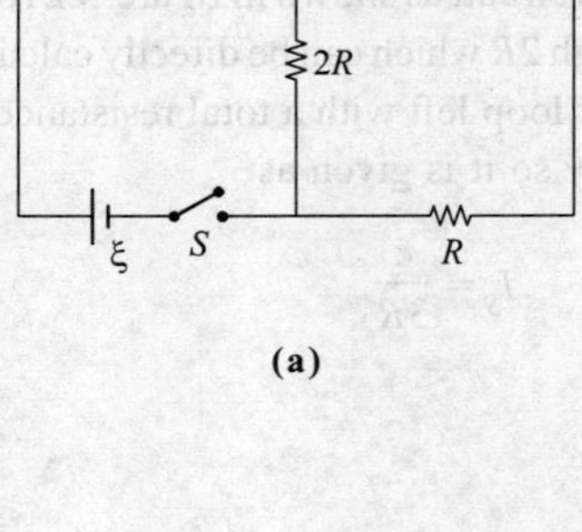

(a)

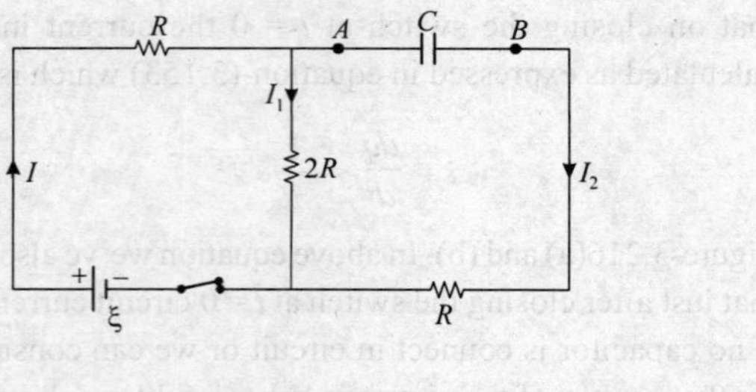

(b)

Figure 3.217

In above circuit when we close the switch, to calculate the current in resistor of resistance $2R$ just after closing the switch we redraw the circuit after replacing all capacitors which are initially uncharged by straight wires as shown in figure-3.217(b). This circuit can now be solved by series parallel method as the resistance $2R$ is in parallel with the resistance R to the right side of it and this group is connected in series with the resistance R to the left of it. Thus equivalent resistance across battery in this circuit is given as

$$R_{eq} = R + \frac{R \times 2R}{R + 2R} = \frac{5R}{3} \qquad \dots(3.162)$$

The current supplied by battery in this state is given as

$$I = \frac{\xi}{\left(\frac{5R}{3}\right)} = \frac{3\xi}{5R} \qquad \dots(3.63)$$

This current is divided in the two resistances $2R$ and R in parallel which is divided in inverse ratio as discussed in article-3.2.5. Thus current through the resistance $2R$ just after closing the switch can be given as

$$I_1 = \left(\frac{3\xi}{5R}\right) \times \frac{R}{R + 2R} = \frac{\xi}{5R} \qquad \dots(3.64)$$

Once the switch is closed capacitor starts receiving the charge and its transient period starts. After full charging of capacitor in its steady state current through the branch of circuit in which capacitor is connect becomes zero so it behaves like open circuit in steady state. There can be current in other branches of the circuit if remaining branches are forming a closed loop with a battery like in above circuit shown in figure-3.217(a) if we wish to determine the current through the same resistance $2R$ after steady state is attained then we can redraw the circuit with capacitor as open circuit as shown in figure-3.218 and calculate the current through $2R$ which can be directly calculate as current flows only in left loop left with a total resistance $R + 2R = 3R$ across the battery so it is given as

$$I_S = \frac{\xi}{3R} \qquad \dots(3.165)$$

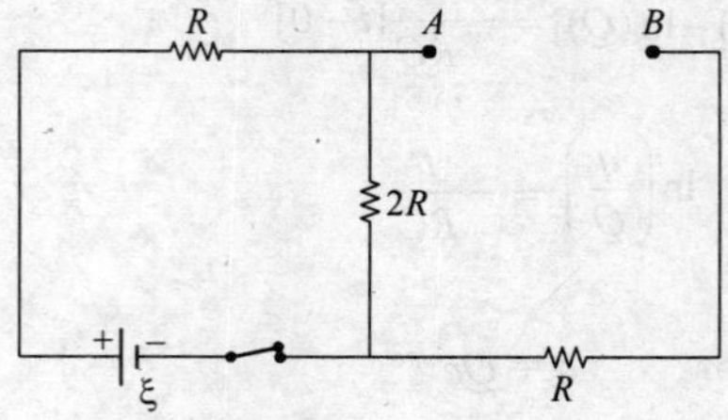

Figure 3.218

Thus as a thumb rule students can remember that in RC circuits uncharged capacitors behave like short circuit just after closing the switch and behave like open circuit after a long time in their steady state as shown and explained in figure-3.219(a) and (b)

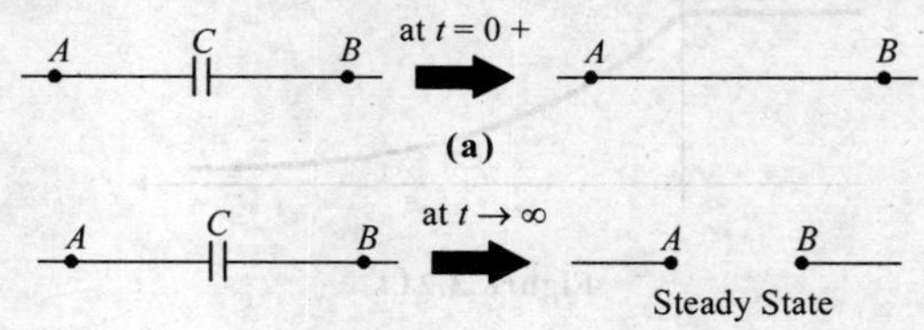

(b)

Figure 3.219

3.12.5 Initial and Steady State Behaviour of Initially Charged Capacitor in RC Circuits

In article-3.12.3 while discussing about discharging of a capacitor we've seen that for a simple RC circuit during discharge the current is calculated as expressed in equation-(3.160) which is given as

$$i = \frac{dq}{dt} = -\frac{Q}{RC} e^{-\frac{t}{RC}}$$

Figure-3.220(a) shows the same situation of a charged capacitor of capacitance C with charge Q on its plates when shorted by a resistor of resistance R by closing the switch then just after closing the switch current in circuit is $i = Q/RC$ as calculated in equation-(3.161) which can also be written as

$$i = \frac{Q}{RC} = \left(\frac{Q/C}{R}\right) = \left(\frac{E_C}{R}\right) \qquad \dots(3.166)$$

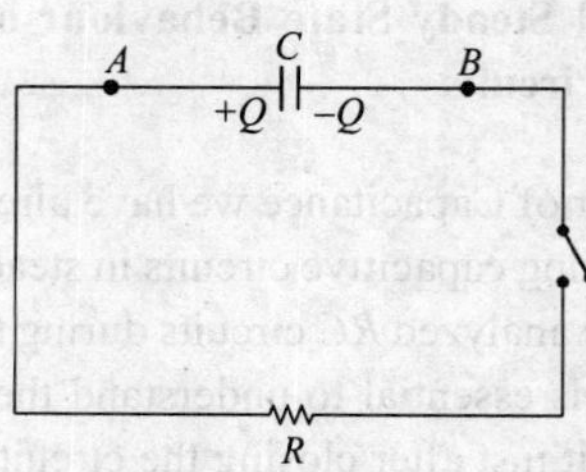

(a)

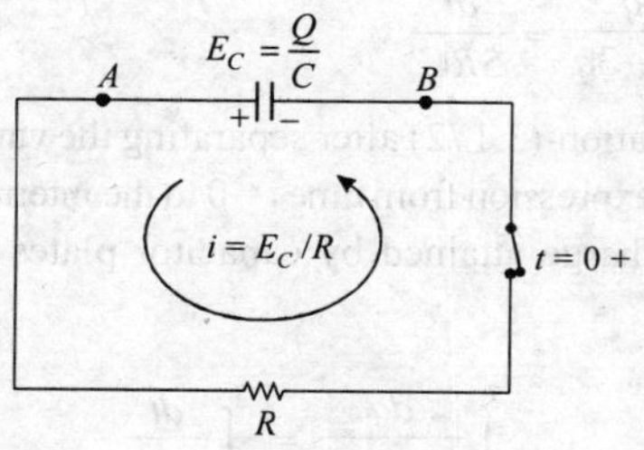

(b)

Figure 3.220

Expression in above current shows that just after closing the switch the capacitor is behaving like a battery of EMF $E_C = Q/C$ to supply a current through resistor at the initial moment only as shown in figure-3.220(b). At $t \to 0$ when circuit attains steady state we can see from above equation that current becomes zero that implies in steady state even charged capacitors also behave like open circuits.

This concept can be generalized as all charged capacitors of a given *RC* circuit can be considered as a battery of EMF equal to their initial potential difference for a moment just after closing the circuit. Figure-3.221(a) shows an illustration. In this circuit we are required to find the current in resistance 3*R* just after closing the switch and after a long time when steady state is attained.

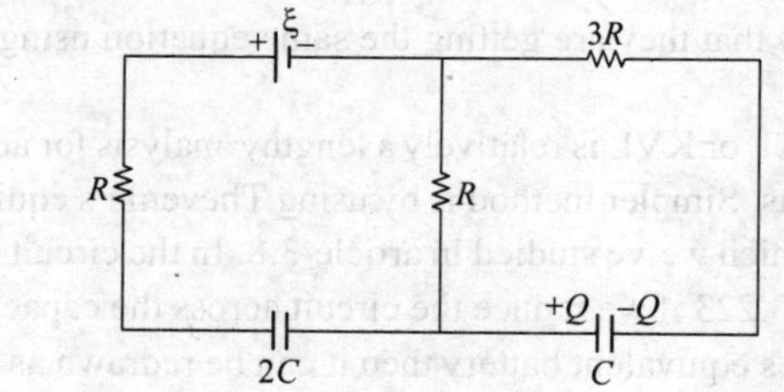

(a)

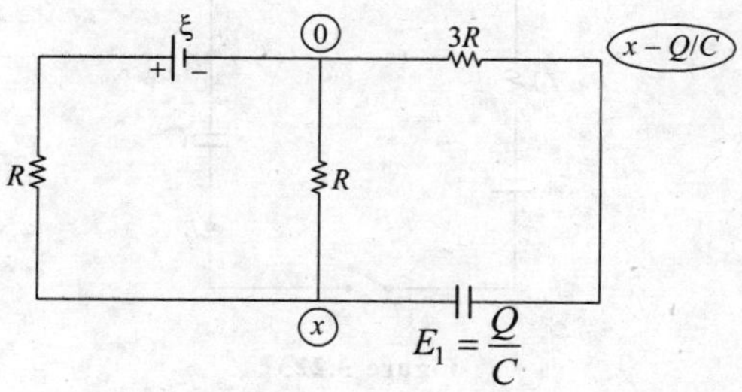

(b)

Figure 3.221

As discussed above just after closing the switch we replace the charged capacitor by a battery with EMF *Q*/*C* and short circuit the uncharged capacitor and redraw the circuit as shown in figure-3.221(b).

To solve the circuit shown in figure-3.221(b) we distribute the potentials in circuit parts as shown and write KCL equation for calculating the value of unknown potential *x* which is written as

$$\frac{x-\xi}{R} + \frac{x}{R} + \frac{x-\left(\frac{Q}{C}\right)}{3R} = 0$$

$$\Rightarrow \qquad 7x = 3\xi + \frac{Q}{C}$$

$$\Rightarrow \qquad x = \frac{3}{7}\xi + \frac{Q}{7C} \qquad \ldots(3.167)$$

Using the above value of *x* which is valid only for the moment just after closing the switch we can calculate the current in resistance 3*R* given as

$$I_{3R} = \frac{x-\left(\frac{Q}{C}\right)}{3R}$$

$$\Rightarrow \qquad I_{3R} = \frac{\left(\frac{3}{7}\xi + \frac{Q}{7C}\right) - \left(\frac{Q}{C}\right)}{3R}$$

$$\Rightarrow \qquad I_{3R} = \frac{3C\xi - 6Q}{21RC} \qquad \ldots(3.168)$$

In above circuit we can see that in steady state when both the capacitors are replaced by open circuit no closed loop is left in the circuit so no current will flow anywhere in the circuit so steady state current in resistance 3*R* will be zero.

Thus as a thumb rule students can remember that in *RC* circuits charged capacitors behave like a battery of EMF equal to initial potential difference across the capacitors just after closing the switch and behave like open circuit after a long time in their steady state as shown and explained in figure-3.222(a) and (b)

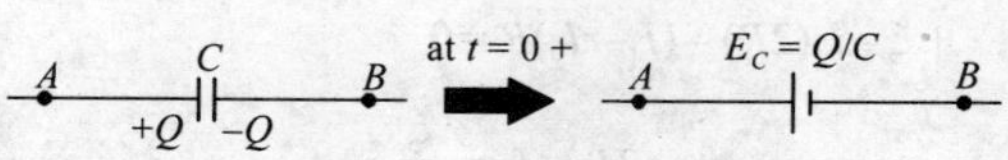

(a)

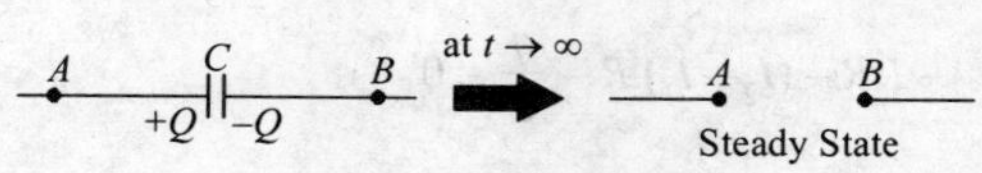

(b)

Figure 3.222

3.12.6 Analysis of Advance *RC* Circuits using Thevenin's Method

For simple *RC* circuits with one capacitor and one resistor we've analyzed charging and discharging transients in previous article. Circuits involving multiple resistors in charging and discharging of RC Circuits are called advance RC circuits. For transient analysis of such circuits either we solve the circuit using KCL or KVL for all the branches of circuit or we replace the circuit across the capacitor by Thevenin's equivalent battery. We will consider an illustration to understand both the methods for analysis of such circuits. Figure-3.223 shows a circuit in which the switch is closed at $t=0$ and we are required to determine the charge on capacitor as a function of time.

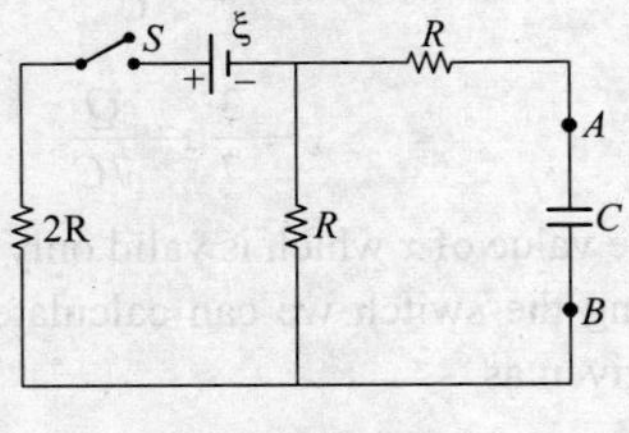

Figure 3.223

In above circuit on closing the switch at a general instant of time $t=t$ we apply KVL for which we first consider currents I_1 and I_2 in the two loops with charge on capacitor plates at this time to be q as shown in figure-3.224. The charge on capacitor is deposited by the current I_2 in this loop so we can use

$$I_2 = \frac{dq}{dt} \quad \ldots(3.169)$$

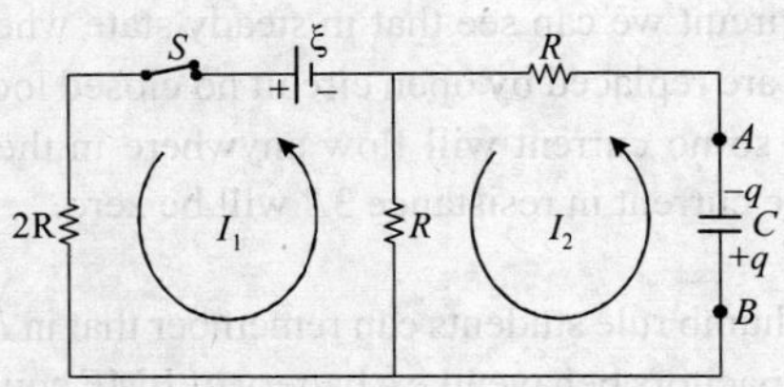

Figure 3.224

Now we can write KVL equations for the two loops as

$$+\xi - I_1(2R) - (I_1 - I_2)R = 0$$

$$\Rightarrow \quad 3I_1 - I_2 = \frac{\xi}{R} \quad \ldots(3.170)$$

and $\quad -I_2R - (I_2 - I_1)R - \frac{q}{C} = 0$

$$\Rightarrow \quad I_1 - 2I_2 = \frac{q}{RC} \quad \ldots(3.171)$$

From the above equations-(3.170) and (3.171) we eliminate current I_1 and substitute I_2 from equation-(3.169) we get

$$I_2 = \frac{C\xi - 3q}{5RC} = \frac{dq}{dt} \quad \ldots(3.172)$$

$$\frac{dq}{C\xi - 3q} = \frac{dt}{5RC}$$

In above equation-(3.172) after separating the variables we can integrate the expression from time $t=0$ to the intermediate instant $t=t$ when charge attained by capacitor plates is q which is given as

$$\int_{q=0}^{q} \frac{dq}{C\xi - 3q} = \int_{t=0}^{t} \frac{dt}{5RC}$$

$$\Rightarrow \quad \left[-\frac{1}{3}\ln(C\xi - 3q)\right]_0^q = \frac{1}{5RC}[t]_0^t$$

$$\Rightarrow \quad [\ln(C\xi - 3q) - \ln(C\xi)] = -\frac{3}{5RC}[t-0]$$

$$\Rightarrow \quad \ln\left(\frac{C\xi - 3q}{C\xi}\right) = -\frac{3t}{5RC}$$

$$\Rightarrow \quad \frac{C\xi - 3q}{C\xi} = e^{-\frac{3t}{5RC}}$$

$$\Rightarrow \quad q = \frac{1}{3}C\xi\left(1 - e^{-\frac{3t}{5RC}}\right) \quad \ldots(3.173)$$

Equation-(3.173) gives the charge on capacitor as a function of time. Same equation can also be obtained by using KCL on above circuit which students are required to solve on their own and verify that they are getting the same equation using KCL.

Use of KCL or KVL is relatively a lengthy analysis for advance RC circuits. Simpler method is by using Thevenin's equivalent battery which we've studied in article-3.8. In the circuit shown in figure-3.223 if we reduce the circuit across the capacitor by Thevenin's equivalent battery then it can be redrawn as shown in figure-3.225.

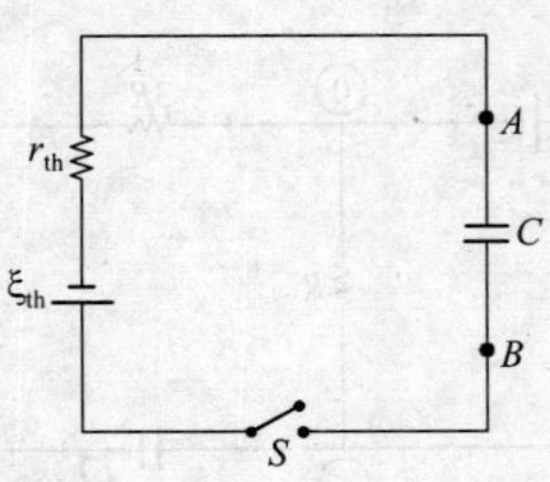

Figure 3.225

Above circuit is a simple RC circuit in which the charge as a function of time on capacitor can be directly given by equation-(3.150) written for the above circuit as

$$q = C\xi_{th}\left(1 - e^{-\frac{t}{r_{th}C}}\right) \quad \ldots(3.174)$$

To calculate equivalent Thevenin's battery EMF, we remove the capacitor from terminals A and B and redraw the circuit as shown in figure-3.226.

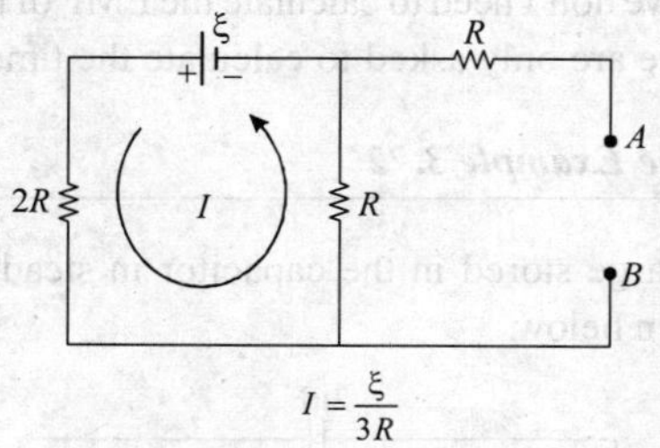

Figure 3.226

In above circuit current flows only in left loop which is $i = \xi/3R$ due to which the open circuit potential difference across the terminals A and B is given as

$$\xi_{th} = V_A - V_B = iR = \left(\frac{\xi}{3R}\right)R = \frac{\xi}{3} \quad \ldots(3.175)$$

To calculate the Thevenin's internal resistance of this circuit across terminals A and B, we replace the battery by a straight wire as it is considered as ideal battery and redraw the circuit as shown in figure-3.227 for which the resistance across A and B is calculated as

$$r_{th} = R + \frac{2R \times R}{2R + R} = \frac{5R}{3} \quad \ldots(3.176)$$

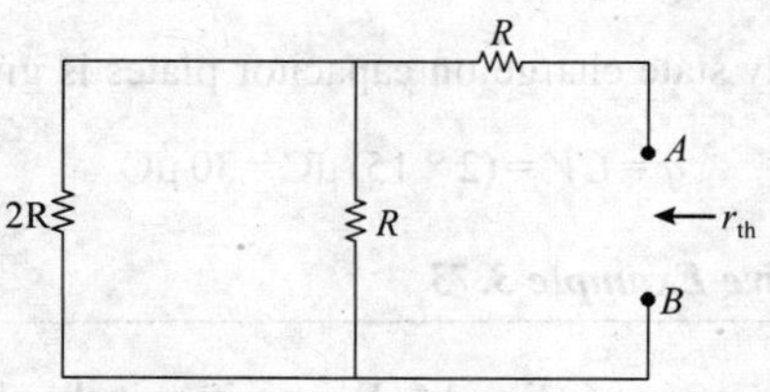

Figure 3.227

Now from equations-(3.175) and (3.176) we substitute the values of E_{th} and r_{th} in equation-(132) to get the charge as a function of time which is given as

$$q = \frac{1}{3}C\xi\left(1 - e^{-\frac{3t}{5RC}}\right) \quad \ldots(3.177)$$

Above equation-(3.177) is same as equation-(3.173) which verifies the result and the use of Thevenin's method for analysis of advance RC circuits. Further we will take more illustrations to understand the applications of different RC circuits.

3.12.7 Leaky Capacitor

When a capacitor is filled with a dielectric which has some low conductivity then such a capacitor cannot sustain charge on its plates as due to poor conductivity of the medium between the plates charge from one plate of capacitor will flow toward the other plate and gradually gets neutralised. Such a capacitor is called '*Leaky Capacitor*' and the current which flows internally in the medium between the plates of capacitor by which its charge discharges is called '*Leakage Current*'.

If a capacitor of plate area A and plate separation d is filled with a medium which has a dielectric constant k and resistivity ρ then the capacitance and resistance of such a capacitor as shown in figure-3.228 across its terminals X and Y is given as

$$C = \frac{k \in_0 A}{d} \quad \text{and} \quad R = \frac{\rho d}{A}$$

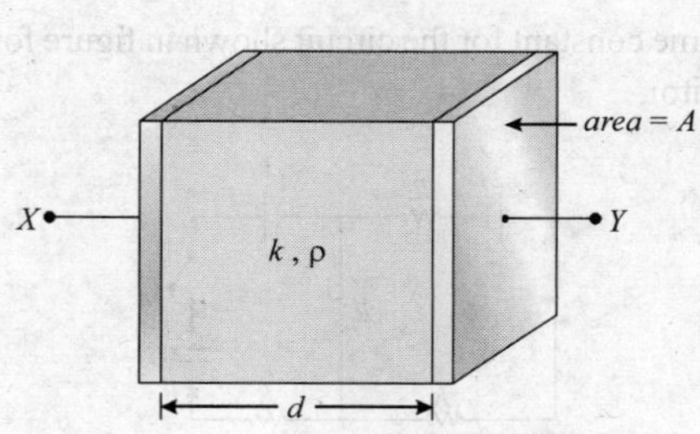

Figure 3.228

When the capacitor is connected to a battery of emf V as shown in figure then a steady current flows through the capacitor due to the resistance of the medium. This steady current is given as

$$I = \frac{V}{R} = \frac{VA}{\rho d} \quad \ldots(3.178)$$

The charge on the capacitor plates is due to the constant voltage V applied across its plates by the battery and it is given as

$$Q = CV \quad \ldots(3.179)$$

If at $t = 0$ the switch is opened then the charge of capacitor will start discharging through the medium between the plates by leakage current for which the time constant of capacitor is given as

$$\tau = RC = \frac{\rho d}{A} \times \frac{k \in_0 A}{d} = \rho k \in_0 \quad \ldots(3.180)$$

From equation-(3.180) it is clear that the time constant of a leaky capacitor does not depend on the dimensions of a capacitor. It only depends upon the nature of leakage material used in it. The leakage current as a function of time can be calculated by using equation-(3.160) which is given as

$$i = \frac{Q}{RC} e^{-\frac{t}{RC}} = \frac{Q}{\rho k \epsilon_0} e^{-\frac{t}{\rho k \epsilon_0}} \quad \ldots(3.181)$$

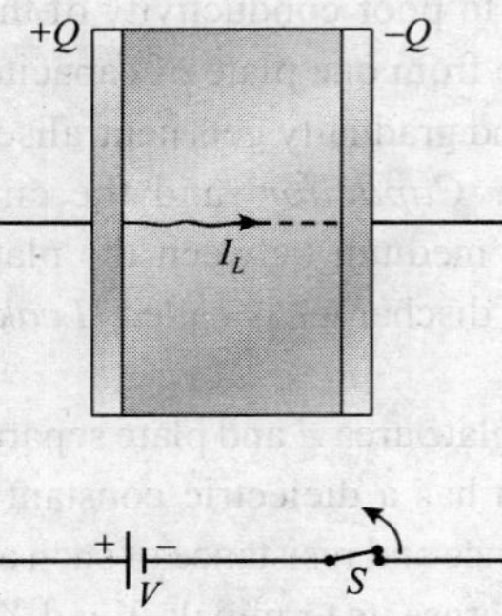

Figure 3.229

Illustrative Example 3.71

Find the time constant for the circuit shown in figure for charging the capacitor.

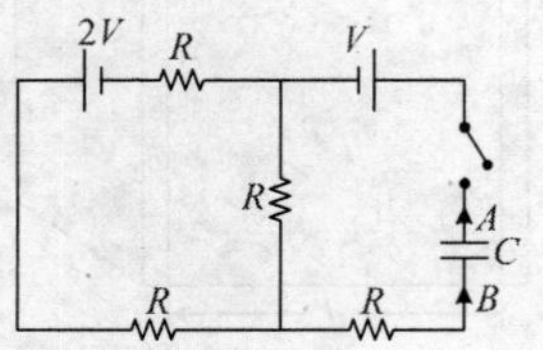

Figure 3.230

Solution

To find the time constant of the circuit we replace the circuit across the capacitor by an equivalent battery using Thevenin's analysis for which the circuit is redrawn as shown in figure-231.

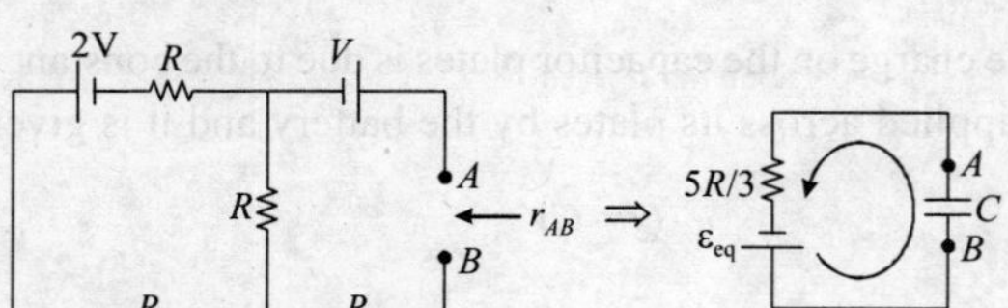

Figure 3.231

The equivalent internal resistance of the circuit can be obtained by short circuiting all the batteries and finding the resistance across terminals A and B, which is given as

$$r_{AB} = [2R \,|P|\, R] \,|S|\, R$$

$$\Rightarrow \quad r_{AB} = \frac{2R \times R}{2R + R} + R$$

$$\Rightarrow \quad r_{AB} = \frac{2R}{3} + R = \frac{5R}{3}$$

Thus time constant of this circuit is given as

$$\tau = \frac{5RC}{3}$$

In this case we don't need to calculate the EMF of the equivalent battery as we are only asked to calculate the time constant.

Illustrative Example 3.72

Find the charge stored in the capacitor in steady state in the circuit shown below.

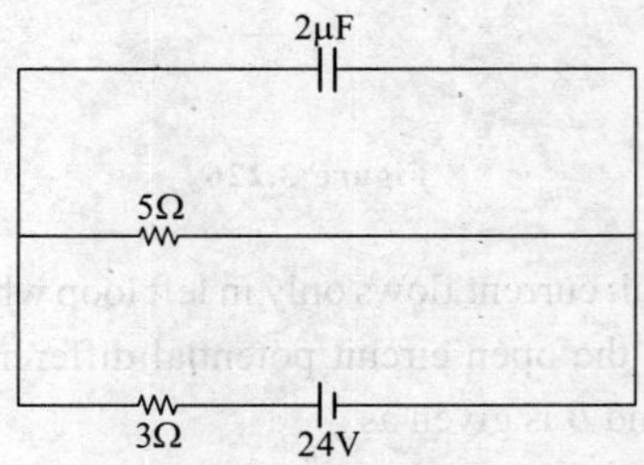

Figure 3.232

Solution

In above circuit current will only flow in the lower loop as in steady state no current will flow through capacitor so the current is given as

$$i = \frac{24}{5+3} = 3\,\text{A}$$

The potential difference across the capacitor is equal to that across the 5 Ω resistance so we use

$$V_C = iR = 3 \times 5 = 15\,\text{V}$$

Thus steady state charge on capacitor plates is given as

$$q = CV = (2 \times 15)\,\mu\text{C} = 30\,\mu\text{C}$$

Illustrative Example 3.73

Find the charges on 6μF and 4μF capacitors in the circuit shown in figure-2.233 in steady state.

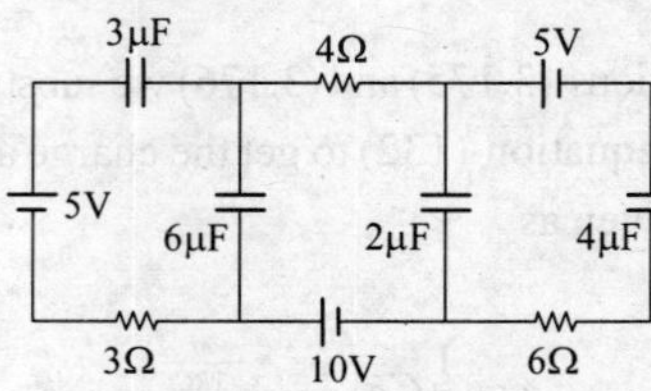

Figure 3.233

Solution

Figure-3.234 shows the potential distribution in the circuit as in steady state no current flows anywhere in the loop so consider resistances as short circuit for this case.

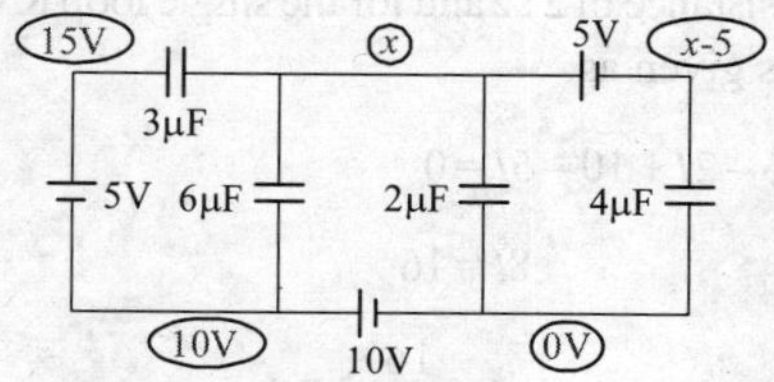

Figure 3.234

We now write nodal equation for x which gives

$$3(x-15)+6(x-10)+2x+4(x-5-0)=0 \qquad \ldots(3.182)$$

$$\Rightarrow \qquad 15x=125$$

$$\Rightarrow \qquad x=\frac{25}{3}\text{ V} \qquad \ldots(3.183)$$

Charge on 6 μF capacitor is given as

$$q_{6\mu F}=6\left(10-\frac{25}{3}\right)=10\ \mu C \qquad \ldots(3.184)$$

Charge on 4 μF capacitor is given as

$$q_{4\mu F}=4\left(\frac{25}{3}-5\right)=\frac{40}{3}\ \mu C \qquad \ldots(3.185)$$

Illustrative Example 3.74

In the circuit shown in figure-3.235, find charge on capacitor as a function of time t if at $t = 0$, switch is closed.

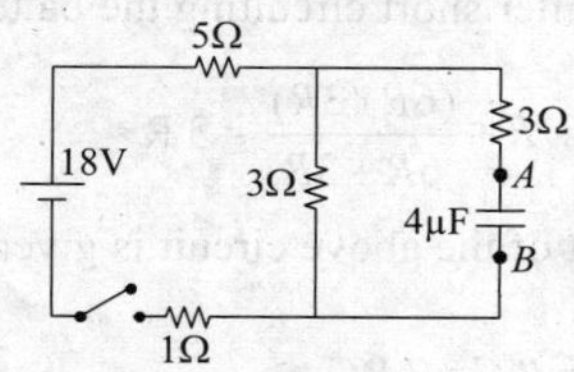

Figure 3.235

Solution

To do the transient analysis of the circuit we replace the circuit across the capacitor by an equivalent battery using Thevenin's analysis for which the circuit is redrawn as shown in figure-3.236 with internal resistance across A and B are given by replacing batteries of circuit by straight wires of zero resistance.

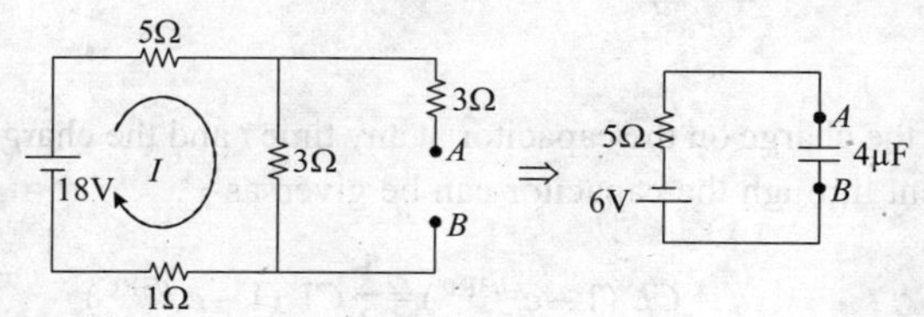

$$r_{AB}=\frac{6\times 3}{6+3}+3\Omega$$

$$r_{AB}=2\Omega+3\Omega=5\Omega$$

Figure 3.236

The current in left loop of circuit is given as

$$I=2\text{ A}$$

Open circuit potential difference across terminals A and B is given by writing equation of potential drop from A to B as

$$V_A-3\times 2=V_B$$

$$\Rightarrow \qquad V_A-V_B=6\text{V}$$

Now charge as a function of time on capacitor plates can be calculated by using equation-(110) which is given as

$$q_C=CV(1-e^{-t/RC})$$

$$\Rightarrow \qquad q_C=24(1-e^{-t/20})\ \mu C$$

Illustrative Example 3.75

(a) What is the steady state potential of point a with respect to point b in figure-3.237 when switch S is open ?

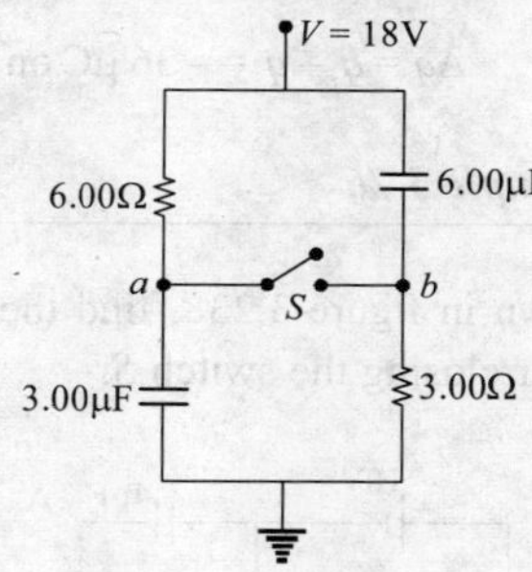

Figure 3.237

(b) Which point, a or b, is at the higher potential?

(c) What is the final potential of point b with respect to ground when switch S is closed ?

(d) How much does the charge on each capacitor change when S is closed ?

Solution

(a) When switch S is open no current would be flowing in any branch in steady state so we have $V_a = 18$ V and $V_b = 0$ as no potential drop occurs at any resistor

$$\Rightarrow \qquad V_a-V_b=18\text{ V}$$

(b) As $V_a - V_b = +ve$. Hence $V_a > V_b$

(c) When switch is closed a current flows through two resistors from the terminal at 18V to ground which is given as

$$i=\frac{18-0}{6+3}=2\text{ A}$$

Now the potential at point b can be given by Ohm's law as

$$V_b - 0 = iR = 2 \times 3$$

$$\Rightarrow \quad V_b = 6\,\text{V}$$

(d) Initially when switch is open then capacitor charges are given as

$$V_{3\mu F} = V_{6\Omega} = 18\,\text{V}$$

$$\Rightarrow \quad q_{3\mu F} = 54\,\mu\text{C}$$

$$\text{and} \quad q_{6\mu F} = 108\,\mu\text{C}$$

Finally when switch is closed capacitor charges are given as

$$V_{6\mu F} = V_{6\Omega} = iR = 2 \times 6 = 12\,\text{V}$$

$$\Rightarrow \quad q_{6\mu F} = 72\,\mu\text{C}$$

$$\text{and} \quad V_{3\mu F} = V_{3\Omega} = 6\,\text{V}$$

$$\Rightarrow \quad q_{3\mu F} = 18\,\mu\text{C}$$

Change in charges is given as

$$\Delta q = q_f - q_i = -36\,\mu\text{C on both capacitors.}$$

Illustrative Example 3.76

In the circuit shown in figure-3.238, find the current in 6 Ω resistance just after closing the switch S.

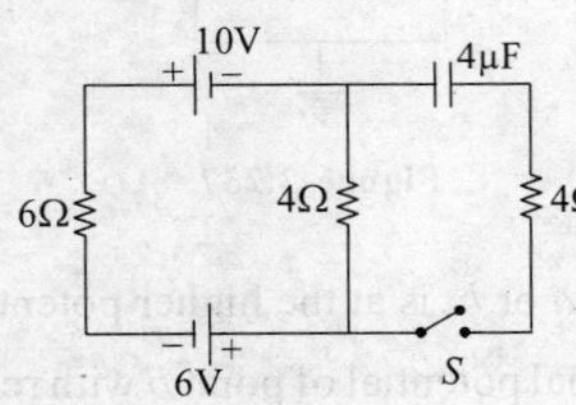

Figure 3.238

Solution

Just after closing the switch all the uncharged capacitors of the circuit behave like short circuit so the circuit can be redrawn at an instant just after closing the switch as shown in figure-3.239.

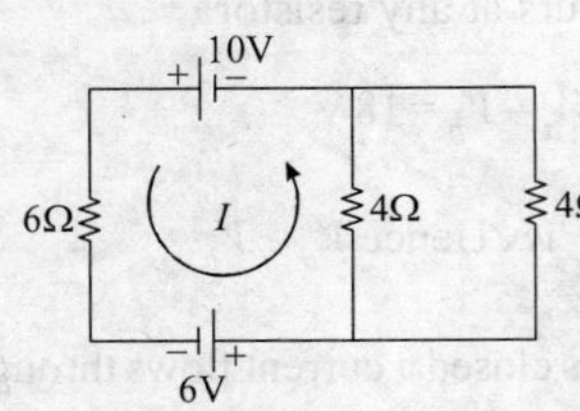

Figure 3.239

The two 4 Ω resistances are in parallel which can be considered as a single resistance of 2 Ω and for the single loop KVL equation for current is given as

$$+6 - 2I + 10 - 6I = 0$$

$$\Rightarrow \quad 8I = 16$$

$$\Rightarrow \quad I = \frac{16}{8} = 2\,\text{A}$$

Illustrative Example 3.77

In the circuit shown in figure-3.240 switch S is closed at time $t = 0$. Find the current through different wires and charge stored on the capacitor at any time t.

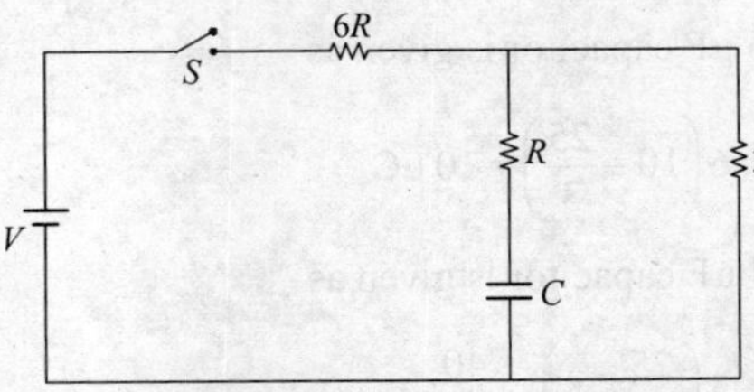

Figure 3.240

Solution

Here first we use Thevenin's analysis to find the equivalent battery across the capacitor in circuit. Equivalent resistance across capacitor after short circuiting the battery is given as

$$R_i = R + \frac{(6R)(3R)}{6R + 3R} = 3\,\text{R}$$

The time constant of the above circuit is given as

$$\tau_c = R_i C = 3\,\text{RC}$$

Open circuit potential difference across the capacitor terminals can be given as the potential difference across the resistance 3R which is given as

$$E = \left(\frac{V}{9\text{R}}\right)(3\text{R})$$

$$\Rightarrow \quad E = \frac{V}{3}$$

Now the charge on the capacitor at any time t and the charging current through the capacitor can be given as

$$q = CE\,(1 - e^{-t/3\text{RC}}) = \frac{1}{3}CV\,(1 - e^{-t/3\text{RC}})$$

$$\text{and} \quad i = \frac{dq}{dt} = \frac{V}{9R}e^{-t/3RC} \quad \ldots(3.186)$$

In the circuit loops we consider instantaneous current i_1 and i_2 as shown in figure-3.241.

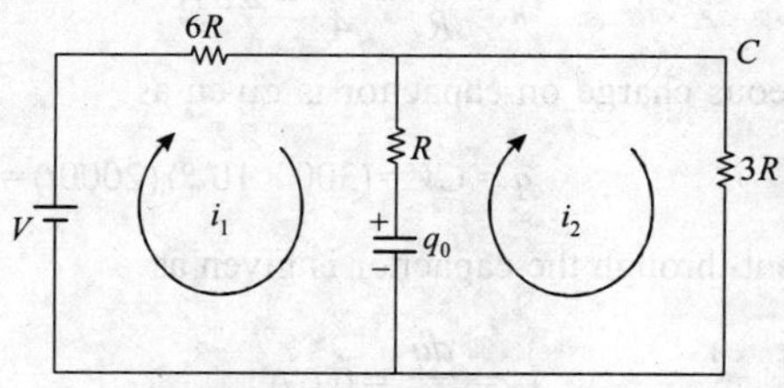

Figure 3.241

Now we write KVL equation for the outer loop of circuit as

$$-6i_1R - 3i_2R + V = 0$$

$$\Rightarrow \quad 2i_1 + i_2 = \frac{V}{3R} \quad \ldots(3.187)$$

Writing KCL equation for the current in circuit, we have

$$i = i_1 - i_2 = \frac{V}{9R}e^{-t/3RC} \quad \ldots(3.188)$$

Solving equations-(3.186), (3.187) and (3.188), we have

$$i_2 = \frac{V}{9R} - \frac{2}{3}i$$

$$i_2 = \frac{V}{9R} - \frac{2V}{27R}e^{-t/3RC}$$

and $$i = \frac{V}{9R} + \frac{V}{27R}e^{-t/3RC}$$

Illustrative Example 3.78

In the circuit shown in figure-3.242 capacitor is charged with 50 μC charge. Find the current in 4 Ω resistance just after switch S is closed.

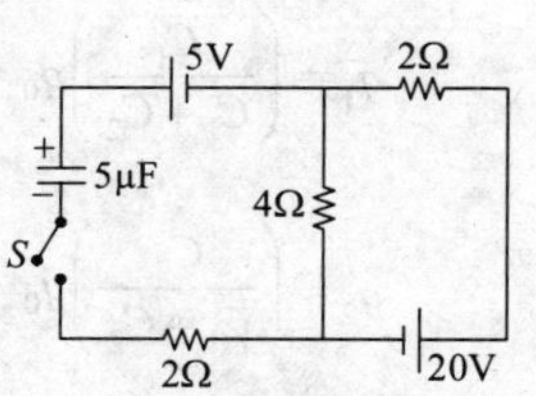

Figure 3.242

Solution

Potential difference across 5 μF capacitor initially is given as

$$V_{5\mu F} = \frac{q}{C} = \frac{50}{5} = 10\text{ V}$$

As we know that just after closing the switch all the charged capacitors of the circuit behaves like a battery of EMF equal to their initial potential difference so using this we can distribute the potentials in the above circuit as shown in figure-3.243.

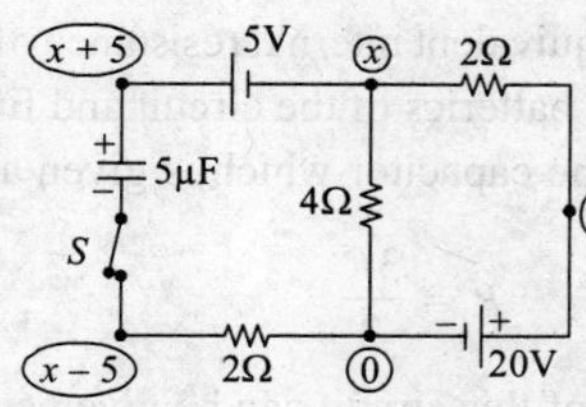

Figure 3.243

Writing KCL equation for x gives

$$\frac{x-20}{2} + \frac{x}{4} + \frac{x-5}{2} = 0$$

$$\Rightarrow \quad 2x - 40 + x + 2x - 10 = 0$$

$$\Rightarrow \quad 5x = 50$$

$$\Rightarrow \quad x = 10\text{ V}$$

Thus current through 4 W resistance is given as

$$I_{4\Omega} = \frac{x}{4} = \frac{10}{4} = 2.5\text{ A}$$

Illustrative Example 3.79

In the circuit shown in figure-3.244, the battery is an ideal one with emf V. The capacitor is initially uncharged. The switch S is closed at time $t = 0$.

(a) Find the charge Q on the capacitor at time t

(b) Find the current in branch AB at time just after closing the switch.

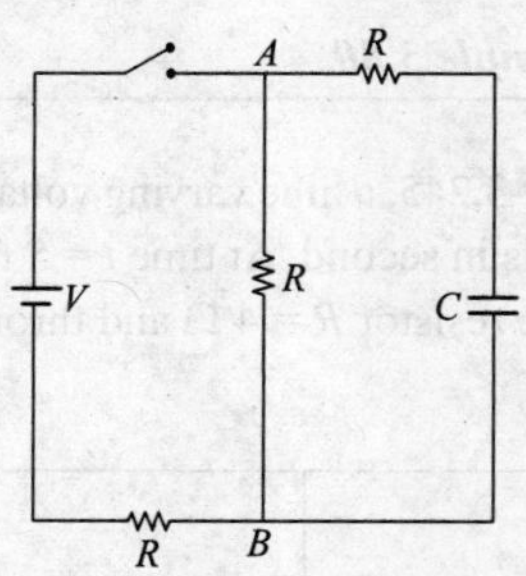

Figure 3.244

Solution

(a) In steady state potential difference across capacitor is given as

$$V_C = \frac{V}{2}$$

Above is the open circuit potential difference across capacitor which is the EMF of equivalent battery as analyzed in Thevenin's analysis.

To determine the equivalent internal resistance of the circuit we short circuit all the batteries of the circuit and find the internal resistance across the capacitor which is given as

$$R_i = \frac{3R}{2}$$

The time constant of this circuit can be given as

$$\tau = CR_{net} = \frac{3RC}{2}$$

Thus charge on capacitor as a function of time can be given as

$$q = CV_C(1 - e^{-t/\tau})$$

$$\Rightarrow \quad q = \frac{1}{2}CV\left(1 - e^{-\frac{2t}{3RC}}\right)$$

(b) At $t = 0$ capacitor behaves as a short circuit so the resistance across the battery just after closing the switch is given as

$$R_{net} = \frac{3R}{2}$$

Current supplied by the battery just after closing the switch is given as

$$i = \frac{V}{3R/2} = \frac{2V}{3R}$$

Current through the branch AB will be half of the total current given as

$$i_{AB} = \frac{1}{2}\frac{2V}{3R} = \frac{V}{3R}$$

 # Illustrative Example 3.80

In the circuit shown-3.245, a time varying voltage $V = 2000\,t$ volt is applied where t is in second. At time $t = 5$ ms, determine the current through the resistor $R = 4\ \Omega$ and through the capacitor $C = 300\ \mu F$.

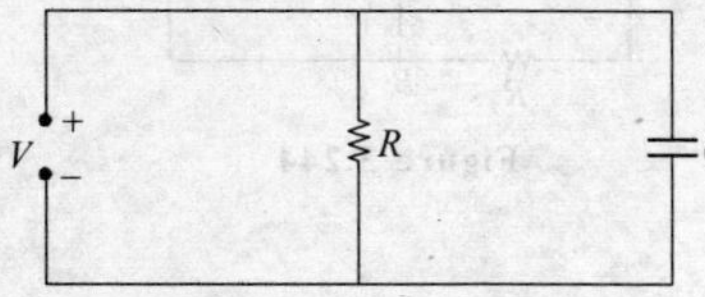

Figure 3.245

Solution

At $\quad t = 5\text{ ms}, V = 10\text{ V}$

Current through the resistor is given as

$$i_R = \frac{V}{R} = \frac{10}{4} = 2.5\text{ A}$$

Instantaneous charge on capacitor is given as

$$q = CV = (300 \times 10^{-6})(2000t) = 0.6t$$

The current through the capacitor is given as

$$i_C = \frac{dq}{dt} = 0.6\text{ A}$$

 # Illustrative Example 3.81

The capacitor C_1 in the figure-3.246 initially carries a charge q_0. When the switch S_1 and S_2 are closed, capacitor C_1 is connected to a resistor R and a second capacitor C_2, which initially does not carry any charge.

(a) Find the charges on the capacitors in steady state and the current through R just after closing the switch.

(b) What is heat lost in the resistor after a long time of closing the switch.

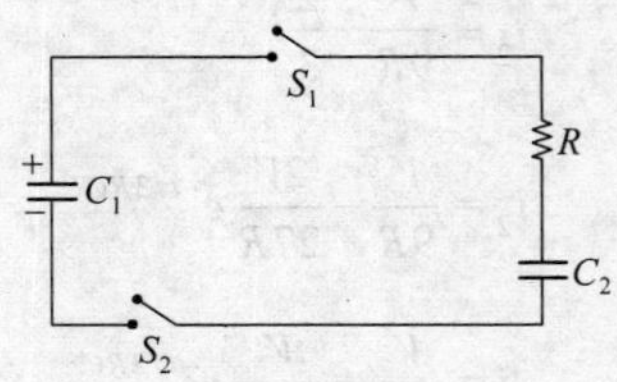

Figure 3.246

Solution

(a) In final steady state the potential difference across capacitors will be equal so after distribution of charges final charges on the two capacitors will be given as

$$q_1 = \left(\frac{C_1}{C_1 + C_2}\right)q_0$$

and $$q_2 = \left(\frac{C_2}{C_1 + C_2}\right)q_0,$$

Just after closing the switch capacitor C_2 behaves like a straight wire of zero resistance and C_1 behaves like a battery of EMF q_0/C_1 so the current in circuit at this instant is given as

$$i = \frac{q_0}{RC_1}$$

(b) Initial and final energies stored in capacitors are given as

$$U_i = \frac{1}{2}\frac{q_0^2}{C_1}$$

and $$U_f = \frac{1}{2}\frac{q_0^2}{C_1 + C_2}$$

Heat lost in the resistor is the total loss in electrostatic energy of capacitors which is given as

$$H = U_i - U_f = \frac{q_0^2}{2}\left[\frac{C_2}{C_1(C_1+C_2)}\right]$$

Illustrative Example 3.82

The charge on the capacitor in the circuit shown in figure-3.247 is initially zero. Find the charge on the capacitor as a function of time t if the switch is closed at $t = 0$. Resistance of all resistors in the circuit is R.

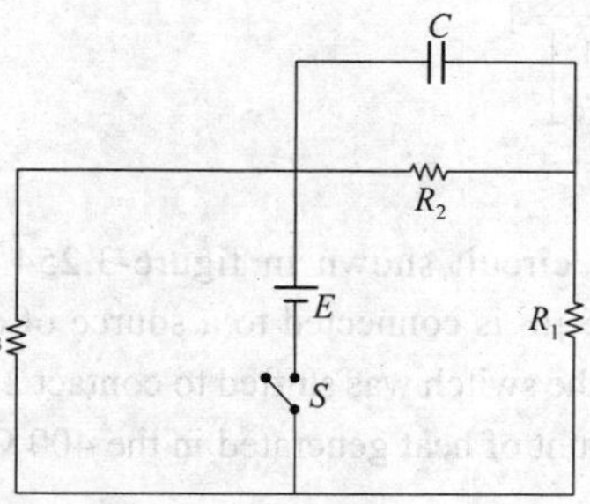

Figure 3.247

Solution

After closing the switch we analyze the circuit using Thevenin's analysis. To calculate the equivalent internal resistance across the capacitor we short circuit the battery and find that R_3 is short circuited and will be of no use now and remaining two capacitors are in parallel so equivalent internal resistance of Thevenin's battery is $R/2$.

Steady state potential difference (which is same as open circuit potential difference) across the capacitor is $E/2$ so the charge on capacitor as a function of time can be directly given as

$$q = C\left(\frac{E}{2}\right)(1 - e^{-t/\tau})$$

$$\Rightarrow \quad q = \frac{CE}{2}\left(1 - e^{-\frac{2t}{CR}}\right)$$

Illustrative Example 3.83

The capacitor shown in figure-3.248 has been charged to a potential difference of V volt, so that it carries a charge CV with both the switches S_1 and S_2 remaining open. Switch S_1 is closed at $t = 0$. At $t = R_1C$ switch S_1 is opened and S_2 is closed. Find the charge on the capacitor at $t = 2R_1C + R_2C$.

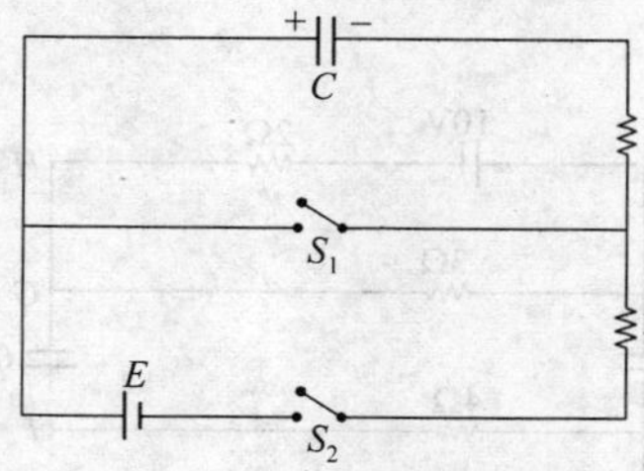

Figure 3.248

Solution

When S_1 is closed and S_2 open, capacitor will discharge through the resistance R_1. At time $t = R_1C$, one time constant, charge will remains $q_1 = CV/e$. When S_1 is open and S_2 closed, charge will increase (or may decrease also) from CV/e to CE exponentially. Time constant for this would be $(R_1C + R_2C)$. Charge as function of time would be,

$$q = q_1 + (q_f - q_i)(1 - e^{-t/\tau})$$

$$\Rightarrow \quad q = \frac{CV}{e} + \left(CE - \frac{CV}{e}\right)(1 - e^{-t/\tau})$$

After total time $2R_1C + R_2C$ or $t = R_1C + R_2C$, one time constant in above equation, charge will remain

$$q = \frac{CV}{e} + \left(CE - \frac{CV}{e}\right)\left(1 - \frac{1}{e}\right)$$

$$\Rightarrow \quad q = EC\left(1 - \frac{1}{e}\right) + \frac{VC}{e^2}$$

Web Reference at www.physicsgalaxy.com

Age Group - High School Physics | Age 17-19 Years
Section - ELECTRIC CURRENT & CIRCUITS
Topic - Thermal Effect of Current
Module Number - 16 to 33

Practice Exercise 3.8

(i) Find the steady state charge stored in the capacitor.

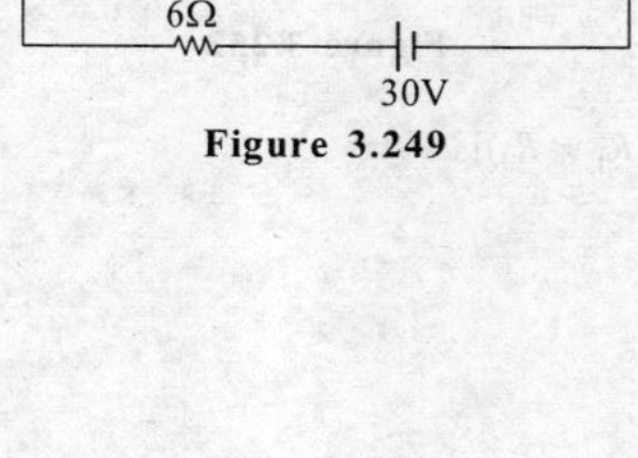

Figure 3.249

[24 μC]

(ii) In the circuit shown in figure-3.250, find the steady state charges on both the capacitors.

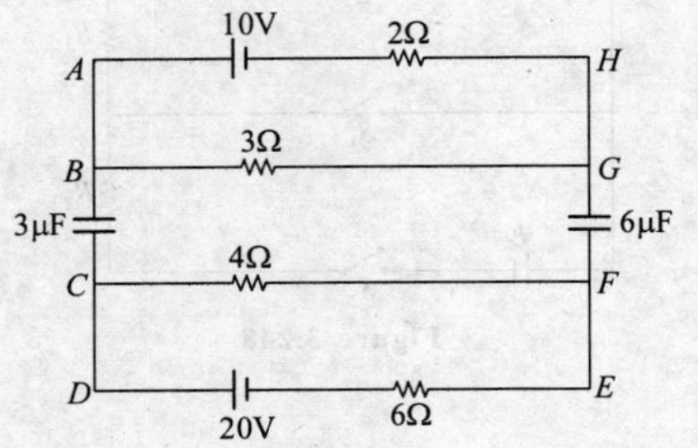

Figure 3.250

[4 μC]

(iii) Three capacitors $C_1 = 3$ μF, $C_2 = 6$ μF and $C_3 = 6$ μF have equal charge $q = 30$ μC each. C_1 and C_2 are connected in series as shown in figure-3.251. If C_3 is connected across the series combination by connecting A with C and B with D and if resistance of connecting wires is 10 Ω, calculate initial current in the circuit just after connections are made and also total amount of heat generated after connections are made.

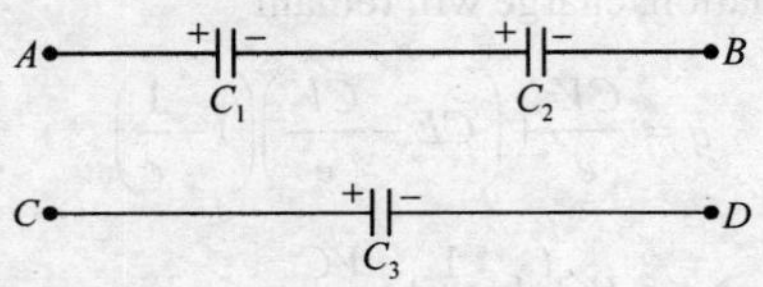

Figure 3.251

[1 A, 75 μJ]

(iv) Determine the current through the battery in the circuit shown in figure-3.252

(a) Immediately after the switch S is closed

(b) After a long time after the switch S is closed

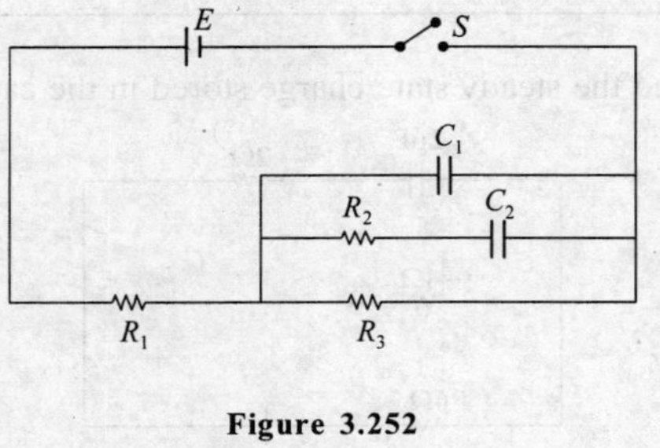

Figure 3.252

[(a) E/R_1; (b) $E/(R_1 + R_3)$]

(v) In the following R-C circuit, the capacitor is in the steady state. The initial separation of the capacitor plates is x_0. If at $t = 0$, the separation between the plates starts changing so that a constant current flows through R. Find the velocity of the moving plates as a function of time. The area of each plate of capacitor is A.

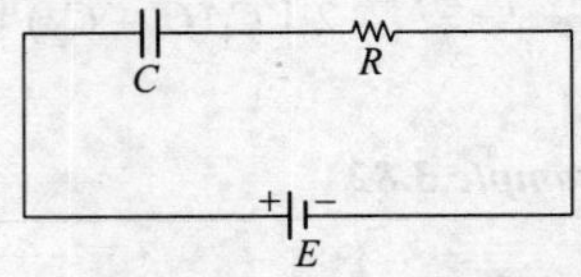

Figure 3.253

$$\left[\frac{\left(\frac{i/\varepsilon_0 A}{iR-E}\right)}{\left[\left(\frac{i/\varepsilon_0 A}{E-iR}\right)t+\frac{1}{x_0}\right]^2}\right]$$

(vi) In the circuit shown in figure-3.254 a capacitor of capacitance 5 μF is connected to a source of constant emf of 200 V. Then the switch was shifted to contact 2 from contact 1. Find the amount of heat generated in the 400 Ω resistance.

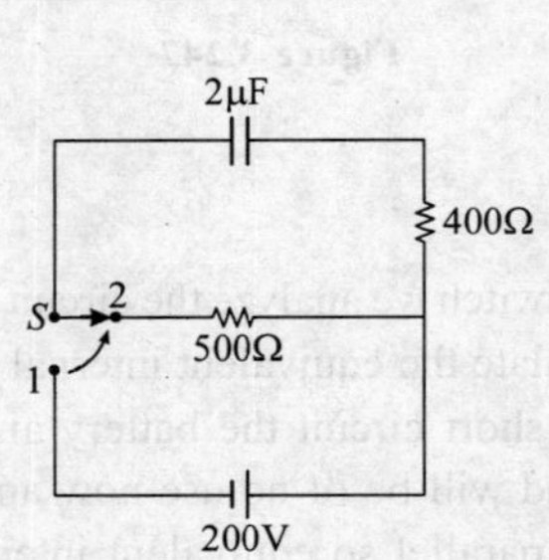

Figure 3.254

[44.4 mJ]

(vii) Calculate the charge on capacitor A in the circuit shown in figure-3.255 in steady state.

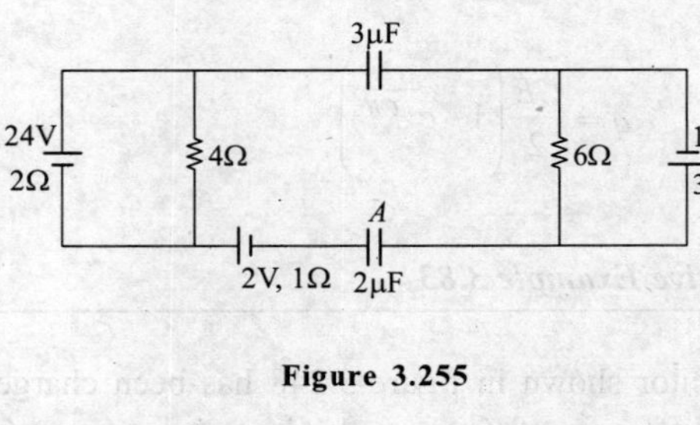

Figure 3.255

[36 μC]

(viii) In the circuit shown in figure-3.256 $E_1 = 2\ E_2 = 20$ V, $R_1 = R_2 = 10$ kΩ and $C = 1$ μF. Find the current through R_1, R_2 and C when

(a) S has been kept connected to A for a long time.

(b) The switch is suddenly shifted to B.

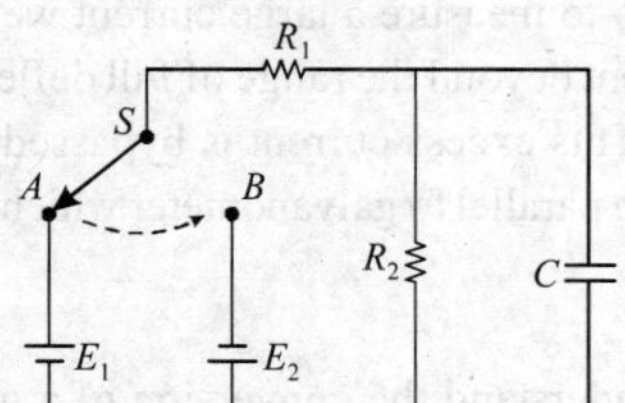

Figure 3.256

[(a) 1 mA, 1 mA, 0; (b) 2 mA, 1 mA, 3 mA]

(ix) A capacitor of capacitance $C_1 = 0.1$ F is charged by a battery of EMF $E_1 = 100$ V and internal resistance $r_1 = 1\ \Omega$ by putting switch S in position 1 as shown in figure-3.257.

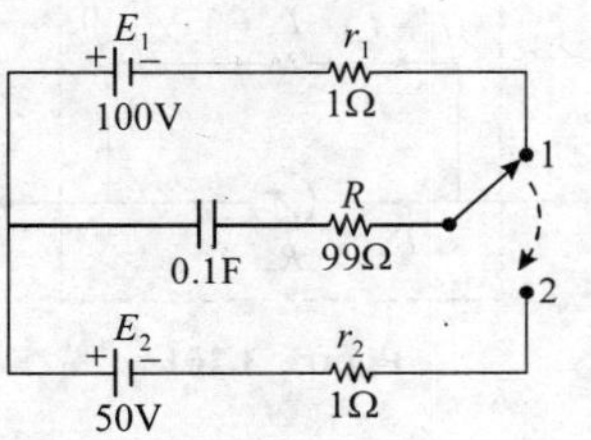

Figure 3.257

(a) Calculate heat generated across $R = 99\ \Omega$ resistor during charging of capacitor.

(b) Now the switch is thrown to position 2 at instant $t = 0$, calculate current $I(t)$ through the circuit, consisting of capacitor and battery of EMF $E_2 = 50$ V and internal resistance $r_2 = 1\ \Omega$.

(c) Calculate heat generated in 50 V battery during flow of current through this battery.

[(a) 495 J (b) $\frac{1}{2}e^{-t/10}$, (c) 1.25 J]

(x) An isolated parallel plate capacitor has circular plates of radius 4.0 cm. If the gap is filled with a partially conducting material of dielectric constant k and conductivity $5.0 \times 10^{-14}\ \Omega^{-1}\text{m}^{-1}$. When, the capacitor is charged to a surface charge density of 15 μC/cm², the initial current between the plates is 1.0 μA ?

(a) Determine the value of dielectric constant k.

(b) If the total heat produced is 7500 J, determine the separation of the capacitor plates.

[(a) 4.25 (b) 5 mm]

(xi) A circuit consists of a source of a constant EMF E and a resistance R and a capacitor with capacitance C connected in series. The internal resistance of the source is negligible. At a moment $t = 0$, the capacitance of the capacitor is abruptly decreased η-fold. Find the current flowing through the circuit as a function of time t.

[$\frac{(\eta-1)}{R}Ee^{-\eta t/RC}$]

3.13 Electrical Measurements

For practical purposes it is very important to measure parameters in branches of an electrical circuits like current, potential difference across different points, resistance, power etc. by using various equipments and gadgets. Accuracy of such devices is a critical factor in industrial applications. Many times some specific types of circuits are used in measurement of circuit parameters with good precision and accuracy. Different devices may have errors and have different accuracy for different range of measurements. In this section we will study some specific devices and set of experiments used commonly in measurement of electrical parameters.

3.13.1 Galvanometer

A galvanometer is the most common type of deflection type meter used for measuring direction and magnitude of current which gives the measurement of current by deflection of its needle connected to a specific rotary arrangement which rotates when a current is passed through it. There are two types of galvanometers - Unidirectional and Bidirectional. Figure-3.258 shows the industrial image of these galvanometers which are used in laboratories. Unidirectional galvanometer has coloured terminal with red and black colours with red indicates the high potential connection and black indicates the low potential connections and it has a unidirectional scale as shown with zero on left side and maximum current which it can read on the right side of scale like the galvanometer shown in figure-3.258(a) is a unidirectional galvanometer of range 5mA. Another type of galvanometer shown in figure-3.258(b) is a bidirectional galvanometer which has zero at center of scale and maximum current which it can read on both sides of scale. Both the terminals of a bidirectional galvanometer are identical black in colour which can be connected in either ways in a circuit as depending upon direction of current needle will deflect on that side. Thus unidirectional galvanometer can only measure the magnitude of current whereas bidirectional galvanometer can measure both magnitude and direction of current in the branch of circuit in which these are connected.

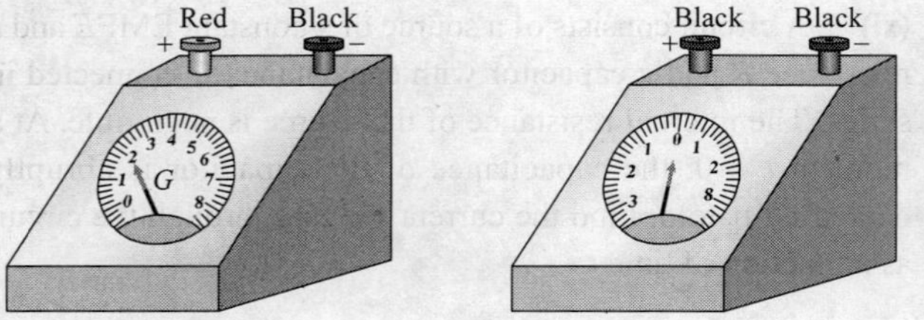

Figure 3.258

Detailed working of a galvanometer we will study in next chapter of Magnetic Field and applications. In this section we need to discuss the uses and applications of a galvanometer. There are two important characteristics of a galvanometer which are useful in its applications and uses. One is the internal resistance of galvanometer also called as its '*Coil Resistance*' which is denoted by R_g and other is the full deflection current of galvanometer also called as '*Range of Galvanometer*' which is denoted by I_g. Generally the resistance of a common galvanometer is in the range of 50 – 100 Ω and its range is in *mA*. An efficient galvanometer generally measures current at low order in *mA* on a precalibrated scale over which its needle rotates. Circuit symbol of galvanometer is shown in figure-3.259.

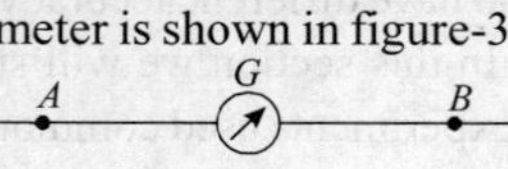

Figure 3.259

3.13.2 Ammeter

Ammeter is also a deflection type meter used to measure current in electrical circuits. Current is measured in units of Ampere and from the name of unit this name of this device is derived as *AM*pere *METER* or *'Ammeter'*. Basic difference between an ammeter and galvanometer is the range of measurement. Galvanometer is a fundamental instrument to measure current in short range of *mA* whereas ammeter is used for large range of current measurement from microampere to several ampere. Very low range ammeters are constructed specifically and not in scope now and high range ammeters are constructed by modifying a galvanometer. A common ammeter is shown in figure-3.260 which has specific terminals for connections to high and low potential ends in a circuit indicated by red and black in colour. To measure current in any branch of circuit we can cut the branch and place the ammeter in series of that branch of circuit.

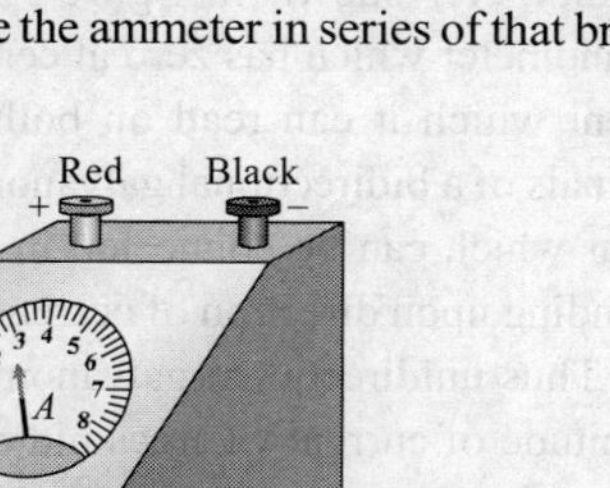

Figure 3.260

3.13.3 Conversion of a Galvanometer into an Ammeter

A galvanometer can be converted into an ammeter of desired range of current measurement by connecting a very small resistance across the terminals of galvanometer. As a galvanometer is a very small range device for current measurement so to measure a large current we need to bypass the excess current beyond the range of full deflection current of galvanometer. This excess current is bypassed through a very low resistance in parallel to galvanometer which is called '*Shunt Resistance*'.

We will now understand the conversion of a galvanometer of coil resistance R_g and full deflection current I_g to an ammeter of specified range I_R where $I_R >> I_g$. In the desired ammeter we want it to deflect full scale when a current I_R is passed through it. Actually we are using a galvanometer which deflects full scale at a current I_g so we must bypass the excess current $(I_R - I_g)$ which is done by connecting a very low resistance in parallel to the galvanometer as shown in figure-3.261.

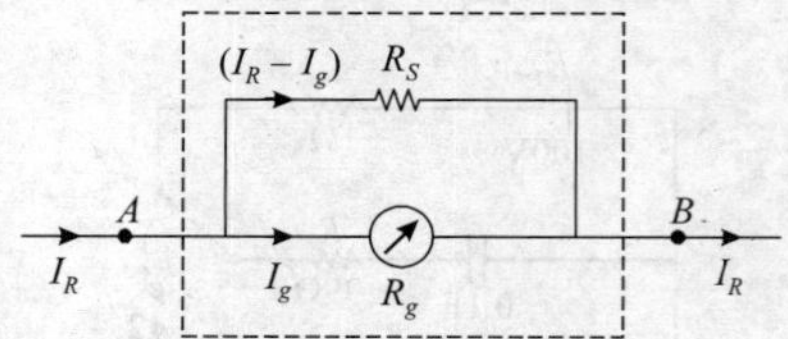

Figure 3.261

As the current is divided in inverse ratio of resistances in parallel combination we use

$$I_g = I_R\left(\frac{R_S}{R_S + R_g}\right)$$

$$\Rightarrow \qquad R_S = R_g\left(\frac{I_g}{I_R - I_g}\right) \approx R_g\left(\frac{I_g}{I_R}\right) \qquad \ldots(3.189)$$

Above equation-(3.189) gives the value of shunt resistance required to be connected across the galvanometer to convert it into an ammeter of range I_R. In figure-3.261 dotted line represent the enclosure in which the assembly of galvanometer and shunt resistance is kept and the scale behind the needle of galvanometer is changed to measure current in range from 0 to I_R. Upcoming illustrations will help in further understanding of conversion of a galvanometer into ammeter.

3.13.4 Voltmeter

Voltmeter is also a deflection type meter used to measure potential difference across two points in an electrical circuit. As potential difference is also called as voltage in commercial terms, the name of this device is derived as ***volt**age **meter*** or voltmeter. This is also constructed by modifying a galvanometer. A common voltmeter is shown in figure-3.262. It has two terminals marked in red and black in colour which are to be connected to high and low potential terminals across which potential difference is to be measured by the voltmeter.

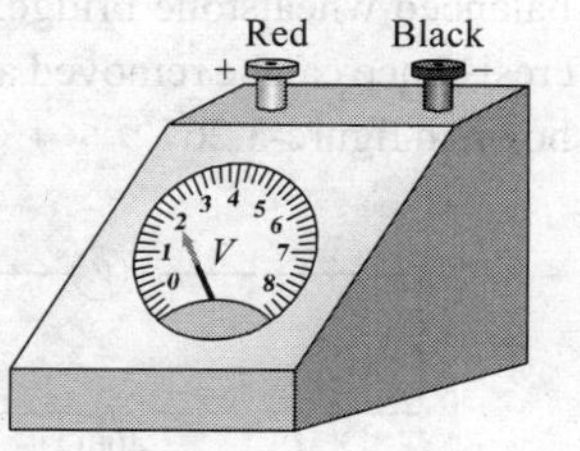

Figure 3.262

3.13.5 Conversion of a Galvanometer into a Voltmeter

A galvanometer can be converted into a voltmeter of desired range of voltage measurement by connecting a very high resistance in series with the galvanometer. As a galvanometer is a very small range device for current measurement so when a potential difference is connected across it a current flows through it because of its coil resistance R_g. The current through R_g due to potential difference is generally much higher than full deflection current of galvanometer which may damage the device. To reduce the current we connect a high resistance R_h in series with the galvanometer as shown in figure-3.263. The high resistance connected is having an appropriate value such that exactly current I_g flows through it when a potential difference V_R is connected across it. V_R is the desired range of voltmeter to be constructed.

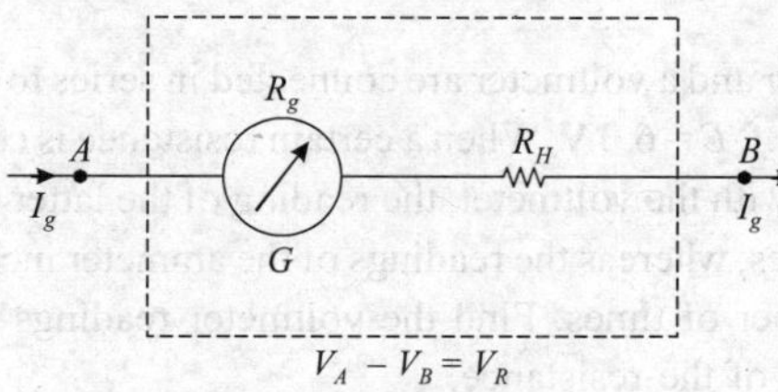

Figure 3.263

When a potential difference V_R is connected across the terminals A and B a current I_g flows through it and it deflects the needle to full scale. If the scale behind the needle is changed to one which is calibrated for measurement of voltages in volt in range from 0 to V_R then on applying potential difference V_R across terminals A and B needle shows the reading V_R by full deflection. For figure-3.263 we have by Ohm's law

$$I_g = \left(\frac{V_R}{R_g + R_h}\right)$$

$$\Rightarrow \quad R_h = \frac{V_R}{I_g} - R_g \qquad \ldots(3.190)$$

Equation-(3.190) gives the value of high resistance which is required to convert a galvanometer of coil resistance R_g and full deflection current I_g into a voltmeter of range V_R. Further illustrations will help in understanding of conversion of a galvanometer into voltmeter.

3.13.6 Errors in Deflection Type Measurement devices

Any measurement device which is deflection type whether galvanometer, ammeter or voltmeter when connected in an electrical circuit, these draw some current and power from the circuit to produce torque on the needle which is deflected. Due to drawing of some current from the circuit actual parameters of the circuit which are to be measured changes hence always there will be some error in reading of deflection type meters so these are not preferred to be used in sensitive experiment. We can understand this with an illustration shown in figure-3.264.

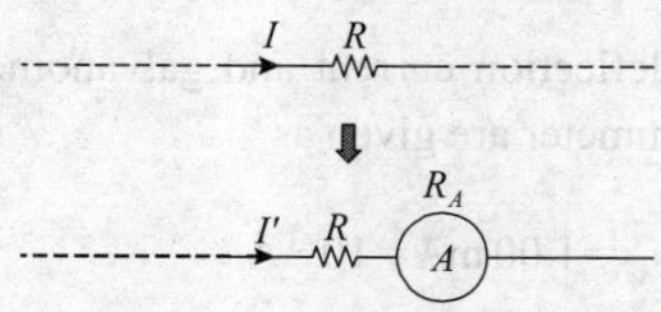

Figure 3.264

If an ammeter is inserted in a branch of circuit where current I was flowing which was to be measured then after insertion of ammeter its resistance also came in series of that branch due to which the actual current which was to be measured get altered and this new current will pass through the ammeter and measured.

Similarly see the figure-3.265 in which the potential difference across a resistance of 100 Ω through which a constant current 5 A current is flowing is to be measured by using a voltmeter of resistance 50000 Ω across it. As it is very high resistance it may not affect the overall current but the current is divided in resistance and voltmeter in inverse ratio of their resistance so now the current which will be drawn by the voltmeter will be given as

$$I_V = 5 \times \left(\frac{100}{50000 + 100}\right) \approx 0.01\,\text{A}$$

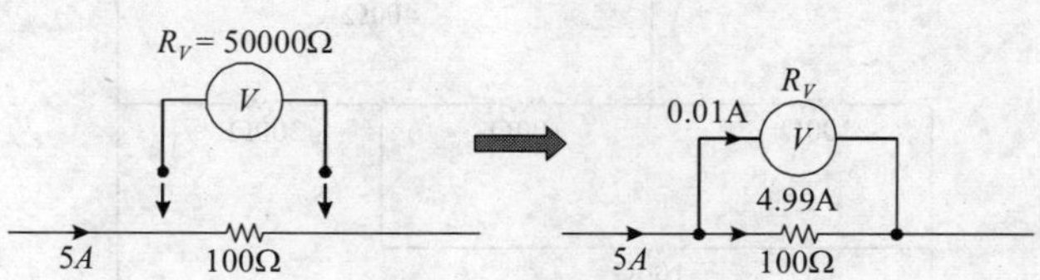

Figure 3.265

Thus the current which will flow through the 100 Ω resistance is (5 – 0.01) = 4.99 A thus the potential difference which was to be measured is changed after connection of voltmeter and the measured value will be $iR = 4.99 \times 100 = 499$ V. In this case error is small because voltmeter resistance we considered is very high. If it is less then error will be more. Thats why deflection type meters always affect the circuit and change the values of circuit parameters to be measured and always have errors in their readings. For an ideal ammeter its internal resistance is considered to be zero and for an ideal voltmeter its internal resistance is considered to be infinite for accurate measurements.

Illustrative Example 3.84

What shunt resistance is required to make the 1.00 mA, 20 Ω galvanometer into an ammeter with a range of 0 to 50.0 mA?

Solution

Here the full deflection current and galvanometer resistance and range of ammeter are given as

$$i_g = 1.00\,\text{mA} = 10^{-3}\,\text{A}$$

$$R_G = 20\,\Omega,$$

$$i_R = 50.0 \times 10^{-3}\,\text{A}$$

Substituting in equation-(136) gives

$$R_S = \left(\frac{i_g}{i - i_g}\right) R_G = \frac{(10^{-3})(20)}{(50.0 \times 10^{-3}) - (10^{-3})}$$

$$\Rightarrow \qquad R_S = 0.408\,\Omega$$

Illustrative Example 3.85

An electric circuit is shown in figure-3.266. Calculate the potential difference across the resistor of 400 Ω, as will be measured by the voltmeter V of resistance 400 Ω.

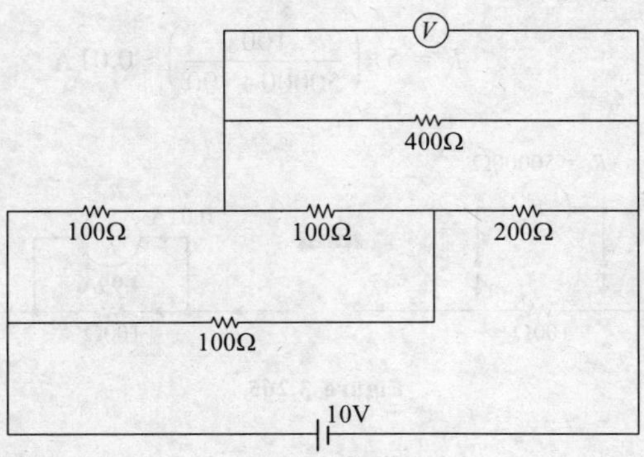

Figure 3.266

Solution

Due to resistance of voltmeter which is in parallel with 400 Ω resistance the branch resistance will be 200 Ω and this makes the circuit as a balanced wheatstone bridge. Thus the middle branch of 100 Ω resistance can be removed and the circuit will be modified as shown in figure-3.267.

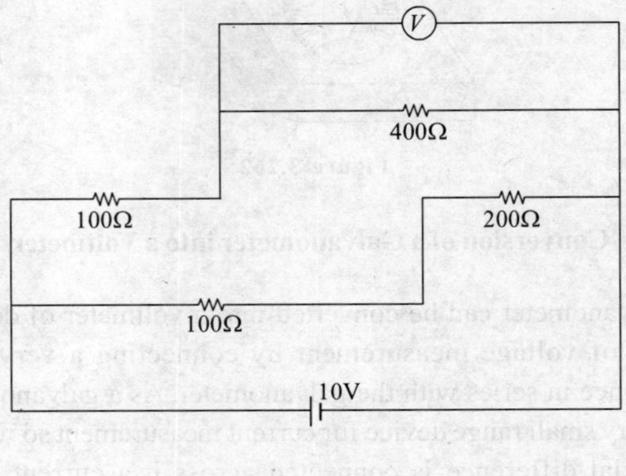

Figure 3.267

The potential difference across the 200 Ω resistance which is read by the voltmeter is given as

$$V = 10 \times \frac{200}{200 + 100} = 6.67\,\text{V}$$

Illustrative Example 3.86

An ammeter and a voltmeter are connected in series to a battery with an e.m.f. $E = 6.0$ V. When a certain resistance is connected in parallel with the voltmeter, the reading of the latter decrease $\eta = 2.0$ times, whereas the readings of the ammeter increase the same number of times. Find the voltmeter readings after the connection of the resistance.

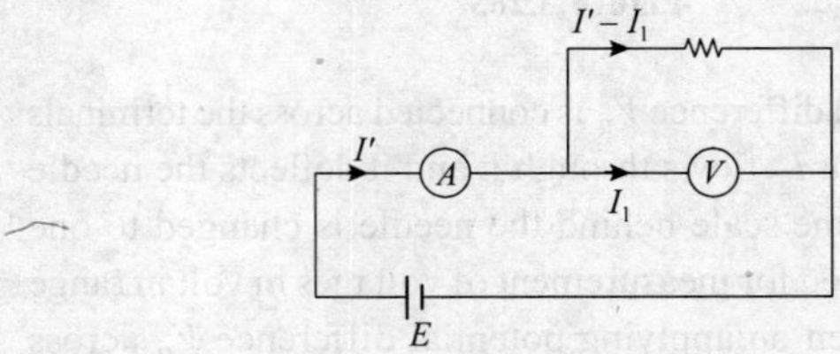

Figure 3.268

Solution

We consider that the initial readings of ammeter is I and that of voltmeter is V. When R' is connected in parallel with the voltmeter then we consider I' is the reading of ammeter and V_1'

is that of voltmeter. As it is given that $I' = \eta I$ and $V' = \frac{V}{\eta}$ if I_1 is the current entering voltmeter then we use

$$V' = (I' - I_1)R$$

For the whole circuit we can write

$$E = I'R_A + (I' - I_1)R$$

$$\Rightarrow \quad E = I'R_A + V'$$

$$\Rightarrow \quad R_A = \frac{E - V'}{I'} \qquad \ldots(3.191)$$

When no resistance is connected,

$$E = IR_A + V$$

$$\Rightarrow \quad R_A = \frac{E - V}{I} \qquad \ldots(3.192)$$

From equations-(3.193) and (3.194)

$$\frac{I}{I'} = \frac{E - V}{E - V'} \Rightarrow \frac{1}{\eta} = \frac{E - \eta V'}{E - V'}$$

$$\Rightarrow \quad E - V' = \eta E - \eta^2 V'$$

$$\Rightarrow \quad V'(\eta^2 - 1) = \eta(E - 1)$$

$$\Rightarrow \quad V' = \frac{\eta - 1}{\eta^2 - 1} E$$

Substituting the values we have

$$V' = \frac{(2-1)6.0}{2^2 - 1} = \frac{6}{3} = 2\text{ V}$$

Illustrative Example 3.87

A galvanometer having a coil resistance of 100 Ω gives a full scale deflection when a current of one milli-ampere is passed through it. What is the value of resistance which can convert this galvanometer into ammeter giving a full scale deflection for a current of 10 A? A resistance of the required value is available but it will get burnt if the energy dissipated in it is greater than one watt. Can it be used for the above described conversion of the galvanometer? When this modified galvanometer is connected across the terminals of battery, it shown a current 4 A the current drops to 1 A, when the resistance of 1.5 Ω is connected in series with modified galvanometer. Find the EMF and internal resistance of battery.

Solution

In this case a shunt resistance S should be connected in parallel with galvanometer so we have

$$\frac{S}{S + G} = \frac{10^{-3}}{10}$$

$$\Rightarrow \quad \frac{S}{S + 100} = \frac{1}{10000}$$

$$\Rightarrow \quad S = \frac{1}{99.99}\ \Omega$$

Current in the shunt resistance is given as

$$i = 10 - 0.001 = 9.999\text{ A}$$

Power dissipated in the shunt is given as

$$P = i^2 S = (9.999)^2 \times \frac{1}{99.99}$$

$$\Rightarrow \quad P = 0.9999\text{ W}$$

This is less than one watt so the above shunt can be safely used.

We consider E be the EMF and r be the internal resistance of the cell. If R be the combined resistance of shunted galvanometer, then we use

$$\frac{1}{R} = \frac{1}{100} + \frac{9999}{100}$$

$$\Rightarrow \quad R = 0.1\ \Omega$$

The current is given as

$$i = \frac{E}{R + r}$$

$$\Rightarrow \quad 4 = \frac{E}{0.01 + r} \qquad \ldots(3.193)$$

and

$$1 = \frac{E}{0.01 + r + 1.5} \qquad \ldots(3.194)$$

Solving equations-(3.193) and (3.194), we get

$$E = 2\text{ V}$$

and

$$r = 0.5\ \Omega$$

Illustrative Example 3.88

A battery of emf 1.4 V and internal resistance 2 Ω is connected to a resistance of 100 Ω resistance through an ammeter. The resistance of ammeter is 4/3 Ω. A voltmeter has also been connected to find the potential difference across the resistor.

(a) Draw the circuit diagram.

(b) The ammeter reads 0.02 A. What is the resistance of voltmeter.

(c) the voltmeter reads 1.10 V. What is the error in the reading?

Solution

(a) The circuit diagram is shown in figure-3.269

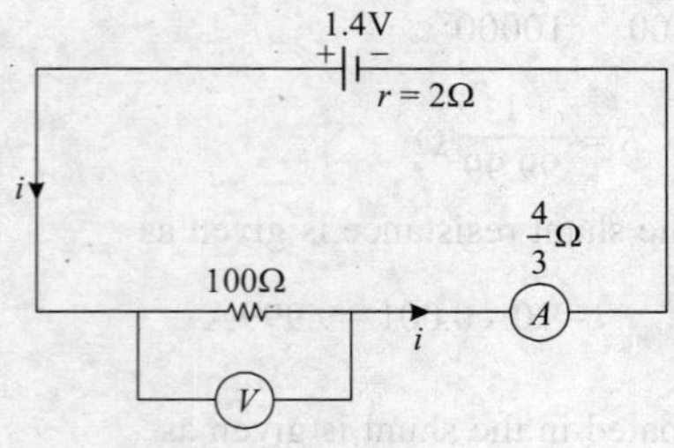

Figure 3.269

(b) Here we consider that R be the resistance of voltmeter and the voltmeter is connected in parallel with 100 Ω resistance.

The effective resistance with voltmeter will be

$$R' = 100\,R/(100 + R)$$

Total resistance of the circuit is given as

$$R_T = 2 + \frac{4}{3} + \frac{100R}{(100+R)}$$

$$\Rightarrow \quad R_T = \frac{10}{3} + \frac{100R}{(100+R)} = \frac{1000+310R}{3(100+R)}$$

Current in the circuit is given as

$$i = \frac{1.4}{\left\{\dfrac{1000+310R}{3(100+R)}\right\}}$$

$$\Rightarrow \quad 0.02 = \frac{(1.4)\{3(100+R)\}}{1000+310R}$$

$$\Rightarrow \quad R = 200\,\Omega$$

(c) Equivalent resistance R', of voltmeter ($R = 200\,\Omega$) and 100 ohm resistor is given as

$$\frac{1}{R'} = \frac{1}{100} + \frac{1}{200} = \frac{2+1}{200} = \frac{3}{200}$$

$$\Rightarrow \quad R' = \frac{200}{3}\,\Omega$$

Potential difference across voltmeter is given as

$$V' = i\,R' = 0.02 \times \frac{200}{3} = \frac{4}{3} = 1.33\text{ V}$$

Error in voltmeter reading is given as

$$\Delta V = 1.33 - 1.10 = 0.23\text{ V}$$

 # Illustrative Example 3.89

A battery of EMF 5 V and internal resistance 20 Ω is connected with a resistance R_1 = 50 Ω and a resistance R_2 = 40 Ω. A voltmeter of resistance 1000 Ω is used to measure the potential difference across R_1. What percentage error is made in the reading.

Solution

The circuit is shown in figure-3.270

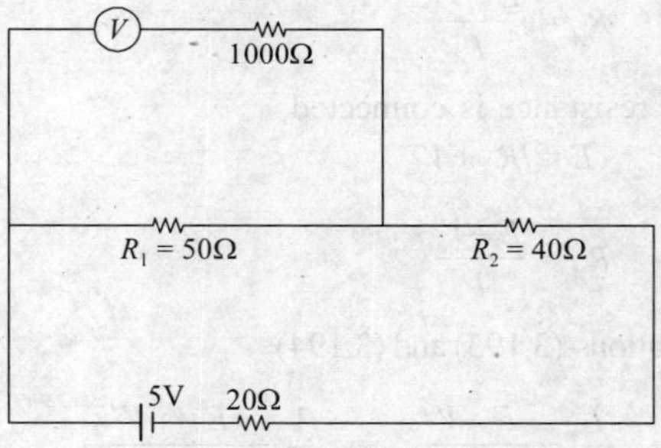

Figure 3.270

When voltameter is not connected the current in the circuit is given as

$$i = \frac{E}{r + R_1 + R_2}$$

$$\Rightarrow \quad i = \frac{5}{20+50+40} = \frac{5}{110} = \frac{1}{22}\text{ A}$$

Potential difference across resistance R_1 is given as

$$V_1 = i \times R_1$$

$$\Rightarrow \quad V_1 = \frac{1}{22} \times 50 = 2.27\text{ V}$$

When the voltmeter is connected across R_1 then the voltmeter resistance is taken in parallel with R_1 thus total resistance is of this part of circuit is given as

$$R' = \frac{1000 \times 50}{1000 + 50} = 47.62\,\Omega$$

Current in the circuit is given as

$$i' = \frac{5}{20+40+47.62} = \frac{5}{107.62}\text{ A}$$

Potential difference measured by voltmeter

$$V_2 = \frac{5}{107.62} \times 47.62 = 2.21\text{ V}$$

Percentage error in reading is given as

$$e = \frac{2.27 - 2.21}{2.27} \times 100 = 2.6\%$$

3.13.7 Multimeter

An electronic device which combines several measurement function in it is called a '*Multimeter*'. Generally as a single device multimeter can measure voltage, current and resistance and the range of measurement can also be varied by using a range knob in it. Earlier it is also called a VOM (Volt-Ohm-Milliammeter) as multimeters are directly used to measure all three circuit properties and it is a handheld device which electricians generally used for quick fault finding in an electrical or electronic circuit. Multimeters are available in analog and digital form as shown in figure-3.271(a) and (b). In most cases now a days digital multimeter is preferred but still for detection of low frequency variation of a circuit parameters still analog multimeters are preferred.

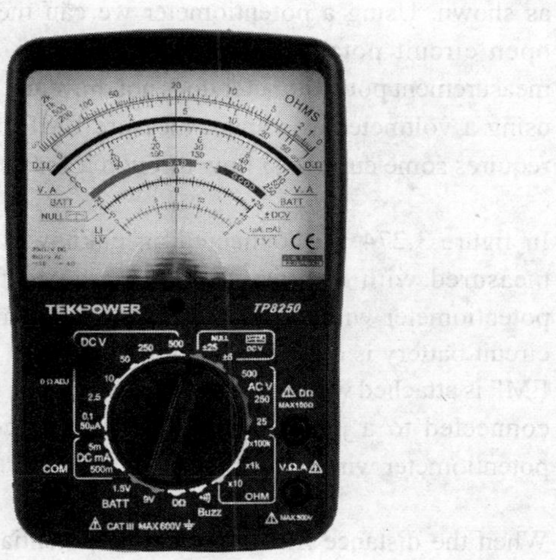

Analog Multimeter

(a)

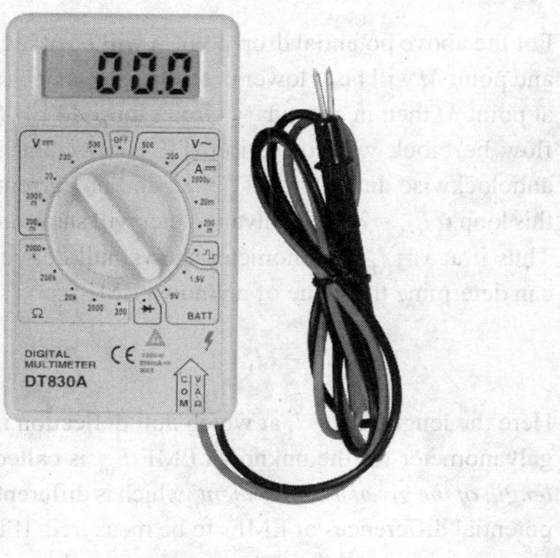

Digital Multimeter

(b)

Figure 3.271

3.13.8 Meter Bridge

Meter Bridge is an experimental setup used to measure unknown resistances. This setup is based on the concept of balancing of Wheatstone bridge. Figure-3.272 shows the setup of meter bridge. In this setup A, B and C are thick metal strips mounted on a wooden platform. Between terminals P and Q a straight resistance wire of length 1m is connected as shown parallel to which a calibrated millimeter scale is fixed. Between the gap of strips A and B a resistance box of standard resistances is connected which is denoted here by R_k and in the gap between strips B and C the unknown resistance R_{uk} which is to be measured is connected.

To the strip B one terminal of a bidirectional galvanometer is connected of which other terminal a solid metal piece called '*Jockey*' which is used to connect this terminal of galvanometer on the resistance wire PQ. Jockey makes a sliding contact on this wire at point M using which x can be varied. The whole setup is powered by a battery along with a switch across terminals P and Q as shown.

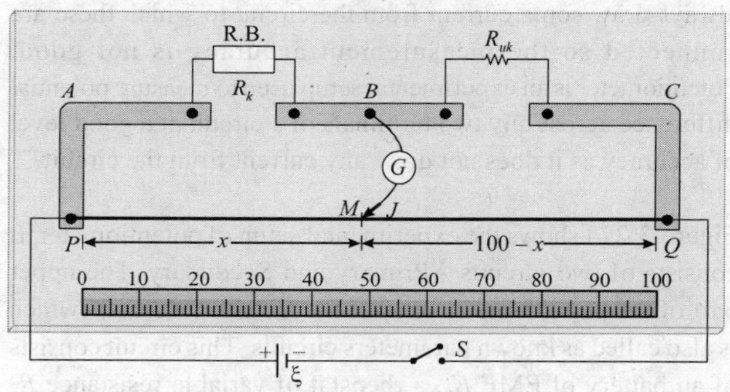

Figure 3.272

To measure the unknown resistance R_{uk} we select a standard resistance R_k in resistance box and close the switch and touch the jockey some where close to middle of the wire PQ. By this galvanometer which is acting like the middle branch of wheatstone bridge shows some deflection. In this state the equivalent circuit diagram of the above experimental setup is shown in figure-3.272. We can see if the ratio $R_k/x > R_{uk}/(100-x)$ then galvanometer shows deflection in one direction and if this ratio $R_k/x < R_{uk}/(100 - x)$ then it shows deflection in other direction. By continuously sliding the jockey on the wire PQ we can find a position M for which galvanometer shows null deflection which will happen when the bridge is balanced under the condition given as

$$\frac{R_k}{x} = \frac{R_{uk}}{(100-x)} \qquad \ldots(3.195)$$

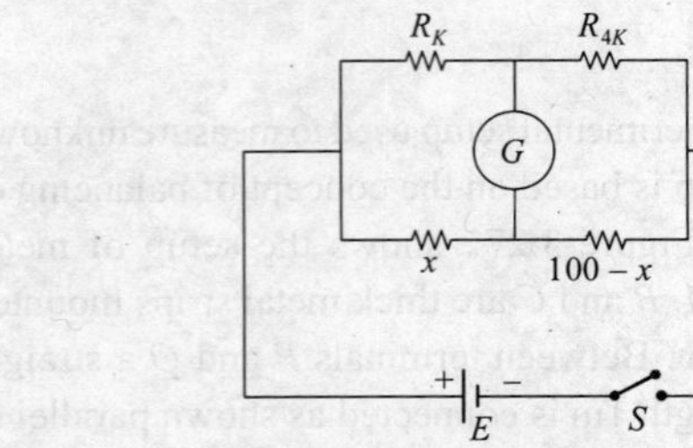

Figure 3.273

Solving equation-(3.195) we can calculate the value of unknown resistance as

$$R_{\text{uk}} = R_{\text{k}}\left(\frac{100-x}{x}\right) \quad \dots(3.196)$$

In resistance box we can change the standard resistance R_{k} and repeat the experiment and calculate the average of all the values of R_{uk} obtained in this way.

3.13.9 Potentiometer

As already discussed that deflection type measurement meters always draw some current from the circuit to which these are connected so the measurement accuracy is not good. Potentiometer is an experimental setup used to measure potential difference across any two terminals of a circuit at a good level of accuracy as it does not draw any current from the circuit.

Figure-3.274 shows the experimental setup of potentiometer. It consists of two circuits - Primary and Secondary. The upper part of the potentiometer setup is the '*Primary Circuit*' which is also called as known parameters circuits. This circuit consists of an battery of EMF E_{P}, a rheostat of variable resistance R_{h} and an ammeter connected in series with a 10m long wire called potentiometer wire *AB* of resistance R_{P}.

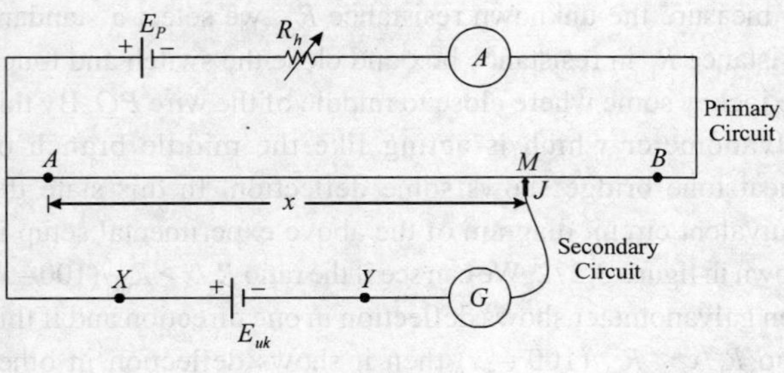

Figure 3.274

From the primary circuit we can calculate the current in potentiometer wire which is given as

$$I_{\text{P}} = \frac{E_P}{R_h + R_P} \quad \dots(197)$$

We can calculate the potential drop across the potentiometer wire *AB* using this current as

$$V_{\text{AB}} = I_{\text{P}}R_{\text{P}}$$

$$\Rightarrow \quad V_{\text{AB}} = \frac{E_P R_P}{R_h + R_P} \quad \dots(198)$$

With the above value of potential drop we can calculate the potential drop per unit length of the potentiometer wire of length *L*. This is called '*Potential Gradient*' of the potentiometer wire measured in units of 'volt/m' and it is calculated as

$$\lambda = \frac{V_{AB}}{L} = \frac{E_P R_P}{L(R_h + R_P)} \quad \dots(199)$$

In secondary circuit we connect the unknown potential difference or any EMF to be measured across terminals *X* and *Y* as shown. Using a potentiometer we can measure EMFs or open circuit potential differences also as at the point of measurement potentiometer does not draw any current whereas using a voltmeter we cannot measure EMF of a source as it requires some current to flow through it for its measurement.

In figure-3.274 we connected an unknown EMF E_{uk} to be measured with its high potential side to the left side of potentiometer wire where high potential terminal of primary circuit battery is connected. Other terminal *Y* of the unknown EMF is attached with a galvanometer of which other terminal is connected to a jockey to make a sliding contact with the potentiometer wire at point *M*.

When the distance *AM* is *x* then the potential drop form the side of primary circuit on potentiometer wire is given as

$$V_{\text{AM}} = \lambda x \quad \dots(3.200)$$

For the above potential drop point A will be at higher potential and point *M* will be at lower potential. When jockey is touched at point *M* then in secondary circuit loop *AXYMA* current will flow be clock wise direction if $E_{\text{uk}} > \lambda x$ and it will be in anticlockwise direction if $E_{\text{uk}} < \lambda x$ and no current will flow in this loop if $E_{\text{uk}} = \lambda x$ and galvanometer will show null deflection. Thus if at $x = l_1$ galvanometer shows null deflection then we can determine the value of unknown EMF as

$$E_{\text{uk}} = \lambda l_1 \quad \dots(3.201)$$

Here the length $AM = l_1$ at which null deflection is obtained in galvanometer for the unknown EMF E_{uk} is called '*Balancing length of the given measurement*' which is different for different potential differences or EMFs to be measured. If from primary circuit the potential gradient is known then any unknown potential difference can be measured on a potentiometer using equation-(3.201).

The maximum potential difference which can be measured using a potentiometer is V_{AB} beyond which unknown EMF can't be measured by the potentiometer. This is called the '*Range of Potentiometer*'.

3.13.10 Comparison of Two EMFs using Potentiometer

Figure-3.275 shows the potentiometer setup used for comparison of two EMFs. In secondary circuit we connect two EMFs with a toggle switch *T* through which either EMF can be connected to galvanometer.

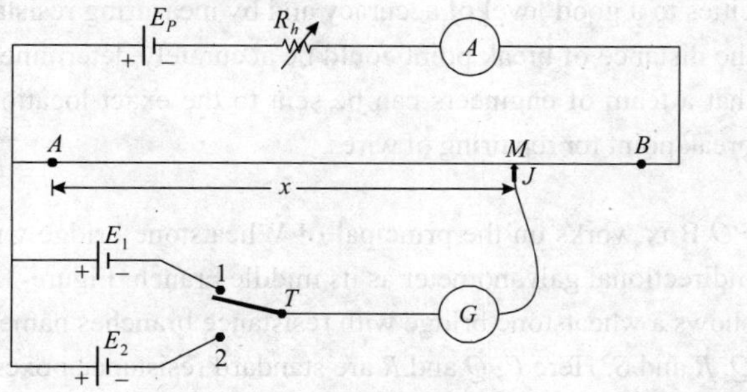

Figure 3.275

In above setup first we put the toggle switch in position 1 and find the balancing length on potentiometer wire for EMF E_1 then we put the toggle switch in position 2 and again find the balancing length for EMF E_2. If the respective lengths are l_1 and l_2 then we have

$$E_1 = \lambda l_1 \qquad \ldots(3.202)$$

$$E_2 = \lambda l_2 \qquad \ldots(3.203)$$

Dividing the above two equations-(3.202) and (3.203), we get

$$\frac{E_1}{E_2} = \frac{l_1}{l_2} \qquad \ldots(3.204)$$

Using above equation-(3.204) we can compare the two EMFs and for this relation we even don't need the value of potential gradient but we need to make sure that for the whole duration of experiment the current in primary circuit remain constant to keep potential gradient constant on potentiometer wire.

Sometimes during experiment when it takes longer duration then the cell of primary circuit gets discharged and current in primary circuit decreases. For obtaining equation-(3.204) it is essential to keep a watch on ammeter of primary circuit and if current decreases then reduce the resistance of rheostat slightly to keep the current at same value.

If one of the two cells used in secondary circuit are taken as a standard cell then by equation-(3.204) we can calculate the EMF of the other unknown cell without even knowing the potential gradient. If $E_1 = E_{std}$ and $E_2 = E_{uk}$ then we use

$$\frac{E_{std}}{E_{uk}} = \frac{l_1}{l_2}$$

$$\Rightarrow \quad E_{uk} = E_{std} \times \left(\frac{l_2}{l_1}\right) \qquad \ldots(3.205)$$

3.13.11 Measurement of Internal Resistance of a Battery using a Potentiometer

Figure-3.276 shows the potentiometer setup for measurement of internal resistance of a battery. In secondary circuit across terminals *X* and *Y* we connect the battery of EMF *E* and internal resistance *r* and across the battery we connect an external resistance *R* along with a switch *S* in open state. In this situation we find the balancing length, say it is obtained as l_1 then we have

$$E = \lambda l_1 \qquad \ldots(3.206)$$

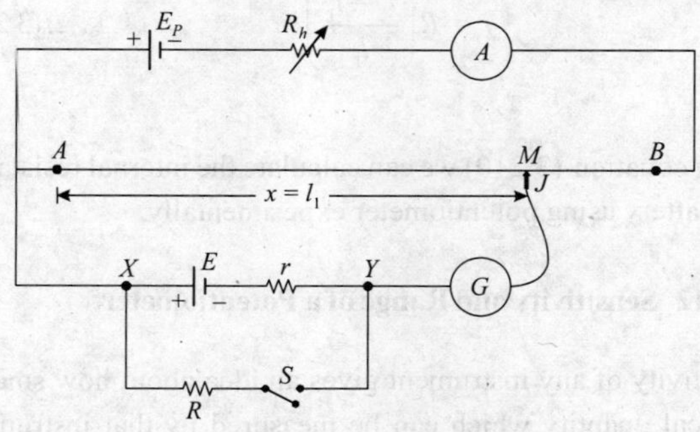

Figure 3.276

As at null deflection no current flows through the secondary circuit no potential drop occurs at internal resistance of the battery so balancing length is for the EMF of the battery. Now we close the switch *S* due to which a current flows in the loop as shown in figure-3.277. This current is given as

$$I = \frac{E}{(r+R)} \qquad \ldots(3.207)$$

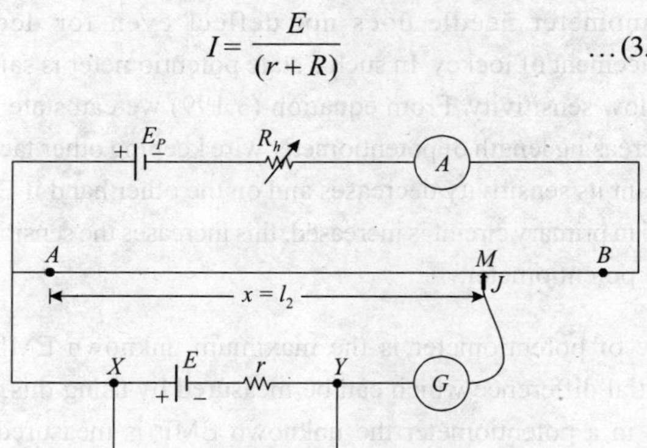

Figure 3.277

In closed state of switch S the potential difference across terminals X and Y will be IR which is given as

$$V_{XY} = IR = \frac{ER}{(r+R)} \quad \text{...(3.208)}$$

Now we calculate the balancing length of this potential difference across terminals X and Y, say this is obtained as l_2 then we have

$$\frac{ER}{(r+R)} = \lambda l_2 \quad \text{...(3.209)}$$

Dividing equations-(3.206) and (3.209), we get

$$\frac{R+r}{R} = \frac{l_2}{l_1}$$

$$\Rightarrow \quad r = R\left(\frac{l_2 - l_1}{l_1}\right) \quad \text{...(3.210)}$$

Using equation-(3.210) we can calculate the internal resistance of a battery using potentiometer experimentally.

3.13.12 Sensitivity and Range of a Potentiometer

Sensitivity of any instrument gives an idea about how small a physical quantity which can be measured by that instrument with a good level of accuracy. In a potentiometer we find the null deflection point in galvanometer by touching jockey at different points of potentiometer wire. If we displace jockey by very small displacements and by this galvanometer needle deflects significantly then we say its sensitivity is high. It happens when potential gradient of potentiometer wire is high. For very small value of potential gradient in a potentiometer the galvanometer needle does not deflect even for decent displacement of jockey. In such a state potentiometer is said to have low sensitivity. From equation-(3.199) we can state that on increasing length of potentiometer wire keeping other factors constant its sensitivity decreases and on the other hand if EMF of cell in primary circuit is increased, this increases the sensitivity of the potentiometer.

Range of potentiometer is the maximum unknown EMF or potential difference which can be measured by using this. We know in a potentiometer the unknown EMF is measured by balancing it across the potentiometer wire AB so the range of a potentiometer is the potential drop across potentiometer wire AB. Thus equation-(198) which gives the potential difference across the potentiometer wire is called range of a potentiometer. Any unknown EMF which has magnitude more than V_{AB} cannot be measured using it.

3.13.13 Post Office Box

PO Box is an experimental setup to measure unknown resistance to a good level of accuracy. It is called '*Post Office Box*' because in old times it was used to measure the resistance of telegraphic wires between city post offices to the break point of wire between cities to a good level of accuracy and by measuring resistance the distance of break point could be accurately determined so that a team of engineers can be sent to the exact location of break point for repairing of wires.

PO Box works on the principal of Wheatstone bridge with a bidirectional galvanometer as its middle branch. Figure-3.278 shows a wheatstone bridge with resistance branches named P, Q, R and S. Here P, Q and R are standard resistance boxes for which any value of resistance can be chosen for these branches and in place of S we connect the unknown resistance to be measured.

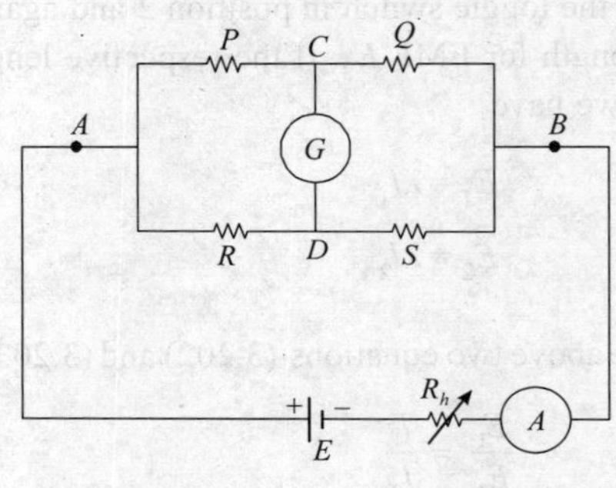

Figure 3.278

To start understanding the working of *PO* Box let us first imagine the value of unknown resistance which is to be measured. Say S is equal to 4.73 Ω and we want to determine this value by using setup of *PO* Box.

To start the experiment we setup $P = 10\ \Omega$ and $Q = 10\ \Omega$ in the resistance boxes connected in these two branches. As we've chosen $P = Q$, by balancing condition of Wheatstone bridge we know that galvanometer in above circuit will show null deflection when $R = S$ but we don't know the value of S so we start increasing the resistance step by step in the resistance box connected in branch R starting from 1 Ω with an incremental step of 1 Ω. So when we increase R as 1 Ω, 2 Ω, 3 Ω ... the needle in galvanometer will deflect toward null deflection as R

is getting closer to value of S but as the value of R is changed from 4 Ω to 5 Ω galvanometer needle will cross over the null point from one side to another. This is the point where we note down that value of S lies between 4 Ω and 5 Ω because between these two somewhere null deflection exist for value of R.

As a next step we change the resistance of branch P and make it equal to 100 Ω so that $P/Q = 10$. In this state null deflection occurs when $R = 10\,S = 47.3\ \Omega$ but while doing experiment we don't know the value of S but we know that it lies somewhere between 4 Ω and 5 Ω so for null deflection value of R must be between 40 Ω and 50 Ω. Now we start changing the value of R from 40 Ω in steps of 1 Ω. When we change R as 41 Ω, 42 Ω, 43 Ω... then needle of galvanometer crosses over the null point when R changes from 47 Ω to 48 Ω which indicates that value of S will lie somewhere between 4.7 Ω and 4.8 Ω.

In next step we change the resistance of branch P to 1000 Ω so that $P/Q = 100$ and null deflection is obtained when $R = 100$ S. We now start increasing the value of R from 470 Ω in steps of 1 Ω and now when R becomes equal to 473 Ω null deflection is obtained which indicates that value of $S = R/100 = 4.73\ \Omega$.

In above illustration we obtained the value of unknown resistance with accuracy upto to decimal places. It can be further increased but if we use P = 10000 Ω then due to such high resistance current in circuit will go down to such a level at which to detect it a highly sensitive galvanometer is required or a very high voltage source is required which sometimes make the setup impractical so in general using PO Box we calculate the unknown resistance upto two decimal places only.

Figure-3.279 shows the industrial picture of PO Box and figure-3.280 shows the arrangement of resistances in a PO Box with plug keys to select the desired resistances in branches P, Q and R. Unknown resistance is connected across terminals B and D, battery is connected across terminals A and B and galvanometer across terminals C and D as shown in figure.

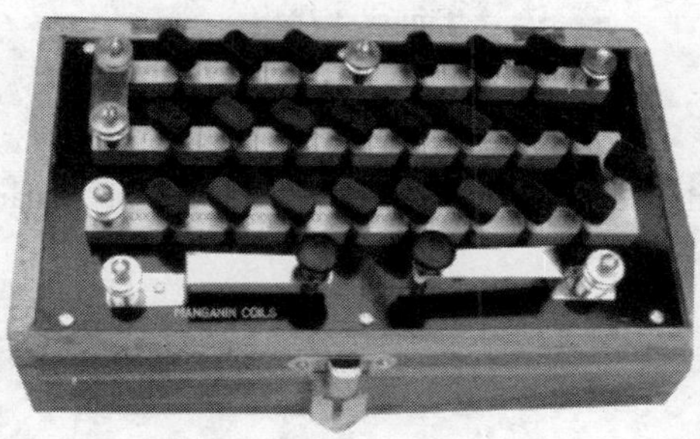

Figure 3.279

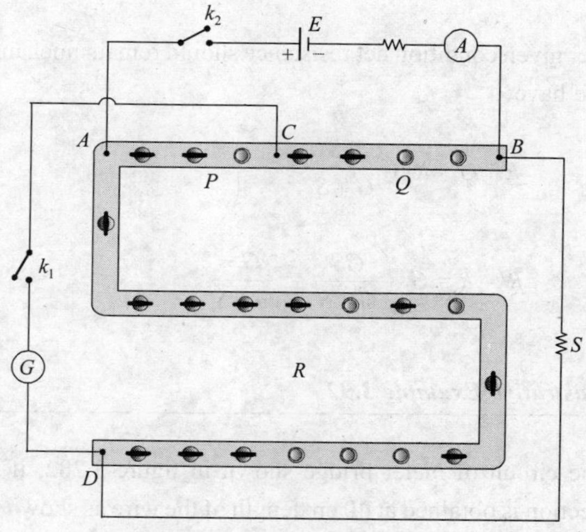

Figure 3.280

Illustrative Example 3.90

In the meter bridge circuit shown in figure-3.281 find the length AC at null deflection in galvanometer.

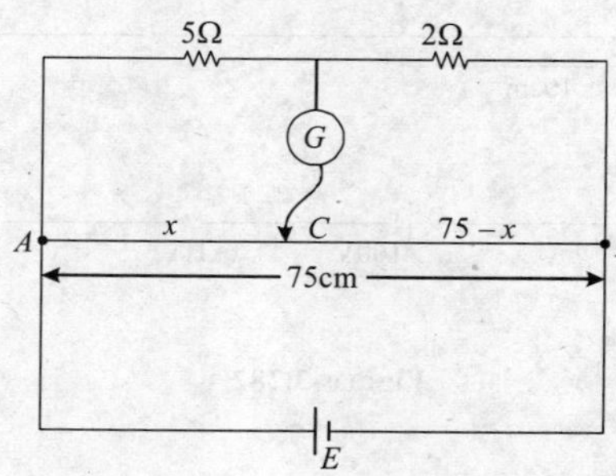

Figure 3.281

Solution

In a meter bridge null deflection occurs at balancing state of Wheatstone bridge for which we use

$$\frac{5}{x} = \frac{2}{75-x}$$

$$\Rightarrow \quad 5(75-x) = 2x$$

$$\Rightarrow \quad 7x = 5 \times 75$$

$$\Rightarrow \quad x = \frac{5\times 75}{7} = 53.57\text{ cm}$$

Illustrative Example 3.91

A resistance box, a battery and a galvanometer of resistance G are connected in series. If the galvanometer is shunted by resistance of S, find the change in resistance in the box required to maintain the current from the battery unchanged.

Solution

As per given condition net resistance should remain unchanged so we have

$$R + G = R' + \frac{GS}{G+S}$$

$$\Rightarrow \quad R' - R = G - \frac{GS}{G+S} = \frac{G^2}{G+S}$$

Illustrative Example 3.92

In the circuit of meter bridge shown in figure-3.282, if null deflection is obtained at 40 cm length of the wire as shown find the value of unknown resistance.

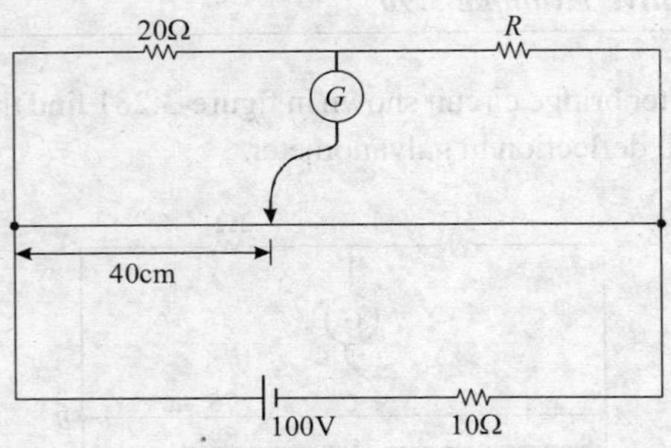

Figure 3.282

Solution

In a meter bridge null deflection occurs at balancing state of Wheatstone bridge for which we use

$$\frac{20}{40} = \frac{R}{60}$$

$$\Rightarrow \quad R = \frac{60}{2} = 30\,\Omega$$

Illustrative Example 3.93

Figure-3.283 shows a potentiometer used to determine the internal resistance of a 1.5 V cell. The balance point of the cell in open circuit 76.3 cm. When a resistor of 9.5 Ω is used in the external circuit of cell as shown, the balance point shifts to 64.8 cm. Determine the internal resistance of the cell.

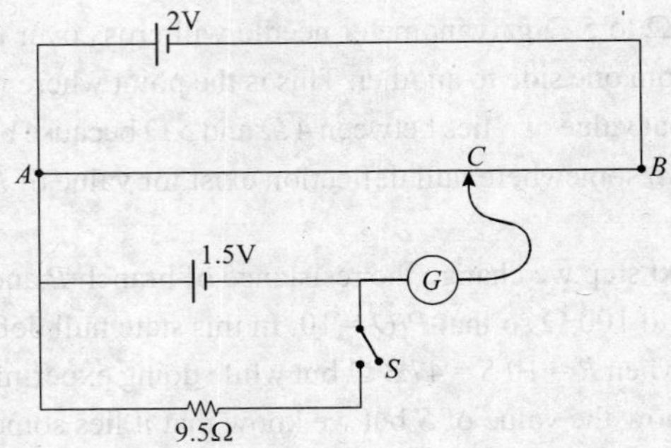

Figure 3.283

Solution

As we know the internal resistance of cell is given by the equation-(154) as

$$r = R\left(\frac{l_1 - l_2}{l_2}\right)$$

Substituting the values we have

$$r = 9.5 \times \left(\frac{76.3 - 64.8}{64.8}\right)$$

$$\Rightarrow \quad r = 1.68\,\Omega$$

Illustrative Example 3.94

The wire *AB* used in a balancing circuit shown in figure-3.284 is 40 cm long. At what distance from point *A* the free end of the galvanometer should be connected on *AB* so that the galvanometer shows zero deflection?

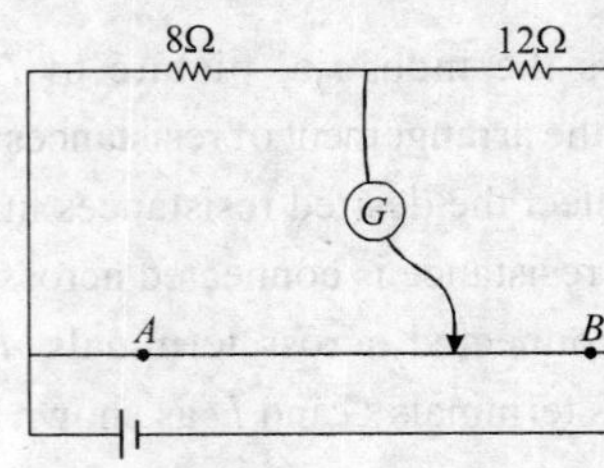

Figure 3.284

Solution

For null deflection the Wheatstone bridge must be balanced so we use

$$\frac{8}{12} = \frac{l}{40 - l}$$

$$\Rightarrow \quad l = 16\text{ cm}$$

Illustrative Example 3.95

Figure-3.285 shows a 200 cm potentiometer wire *AB* with resistance 15 Ω. Find the potential gradient of this potentiometer and also find the balancing length for a 3 V cell.

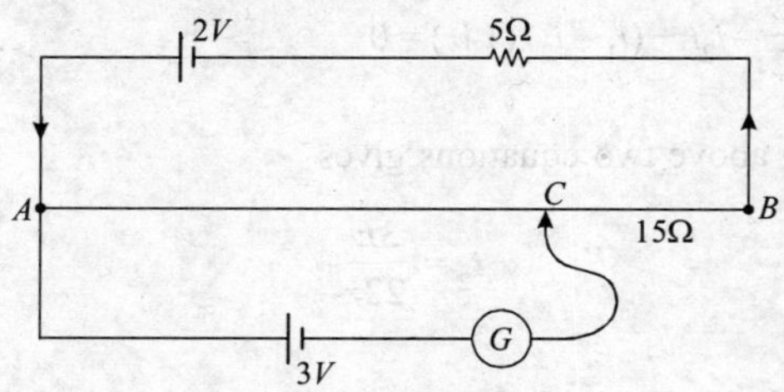

Figure 3.285

Solution

Current in primary circuit of above potentiometer is given as

$$i = \frac{20}{20} = 1\,\text{A}$$

Potential difference across wire *AB* is given as

$$V_{AB} = iR_{AB} = 15\,\text{V}$$

Potential gradient on wire is given as

$$\lambda = \frac{V_{AB}}{L} = \frac{15}{200} = 0.075\,\text{V/cm}$$

If l_1 is the balancing length we use

$$3 = \lambda l_1 \Rightarrow l_1 = \frac{3}{0.075} = 40\,\text{cm}$$

Illustrative Example 3.96

A potentiometer wire of length 100 cm has a resistance of 10 Ω. It is connected in series with a resistance and a cell of emf 2 V and of negligible internal resistance. A source of emf 10 mV is balanced against a length of 40 cm of the potentiometer wire. What is the value of external resistance?

Solution

Figure-3.286 shows the situation described in the question.

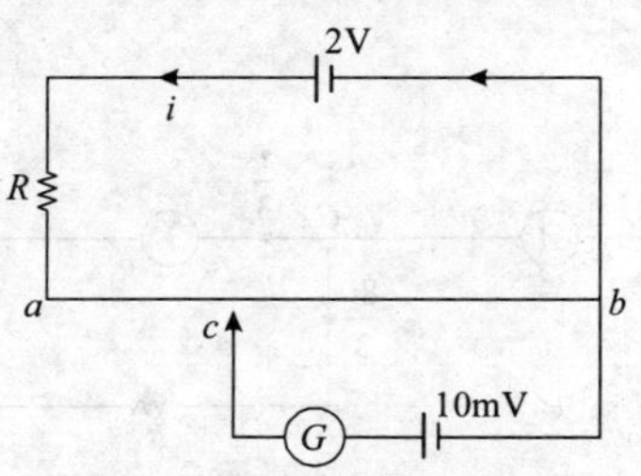

Figure 3.286

At balancing point we can write

$$\left(\frac{2}{R+10}\right)R_{cb} = 10\,\text{mV}$$

$$\Rightarrow \qquad R_{cb} = \left(\frac{40}{100}\right)\times 10 = 4\,\Omega$$

Substituting in above equation, we get

$$R = 790\,\Omega$$

Illustrative Example 3.97

Figure-3.287 shows a potentiometer with length of wire 1 m and resistance 10 Ω. In this system find length *PC* when galvanometer shows null deflection.

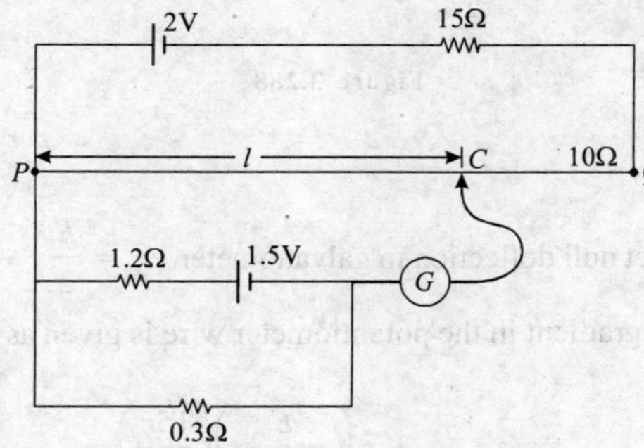

Figure 3.287

Solution

Current in primary circuit of above potentiometer is given as

$$i = \frac{2}{10+15} = \frac{2}{25}\,\text{A}$$

Potential gradient in wire is given as

$$\lambda = \frac{V_{PQ}}{100} = \frac{2/25\times 10}{100} = \frac{1}{125}\,\text{V/cm}$$

In secondary circuit potential difference across points *P* and *C* is given as

$$V_{PC} = 0.3\times 1 = 0.3\,\text{V}$$

If balancing length for V_{PC} on wire is *l* then we use

$$V_{PC} = \lambda l$$

$$\Rightarrow \qquad l = \frac{V_{PC}}{\lambda} = \frac{0.3}{1/125}$$

$$\Rightarrow \qquad V_{PC} = 125\times 0.3 = 37.5\,\text{cm}$$

Illustrative Example 3.98

The potentiometer wire AB is 600 cm long.

(a) At what distance from A should the jockey J touch the wire to get zero deflection in the galvanometer.

(b) If the jockey touches the wire at a distance 560 cm from A, what will be the current through the galvanometer.

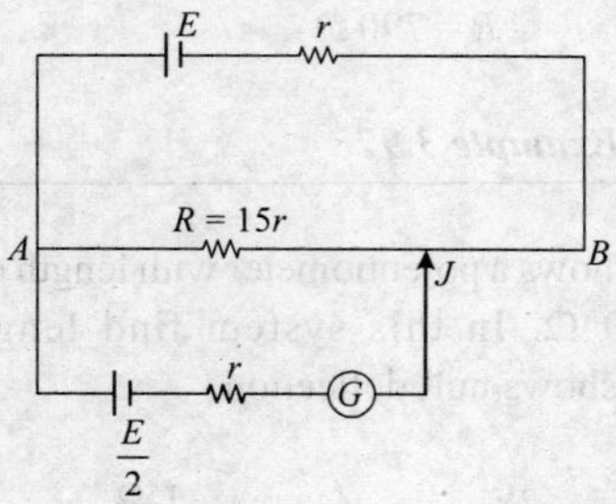

Figure 3.288

Solution

(a) To get null deflection in galvanometer $V_{AJ} = \frac{E}{2}$

Potential gradient in the potentiometer wire is given as

$$\lambda = \left(\frac{E}{15r+r}\right)\left(\frac{15r}{600}\right)$$

If balancing length for the cell of EMF E/2 is l then we have

$$\left(\frac{E}{15r+r}\right)\left(\frac{15r}{600}\right)(l) = \frac{E}{2}$$

$$\Rightarrow \qquad l = 320 \text{ cm}$$

(b) Resistance of 560 cm length of wire is

$$R' = \left(\frac{15r}{600}\right)(560)$$

Now the circuit is shown in figure-3.289

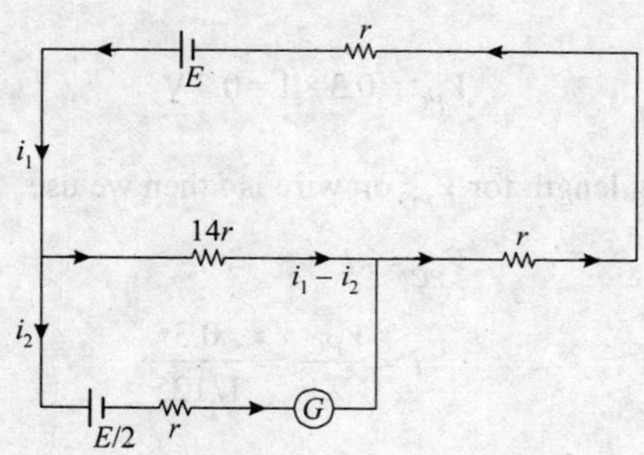

Figure 3.289

Writing KVL equation in upper loop we have

$$E - 14r(i_1 - i_2) - i_1 r - i_1 r = 0 \qquad \ldots(3.211)$$

Writing KVL equation in lower loop we have

$$-\frac{E}{2} - i_2 r + (i_1 - i_2)(14r) = 0 \qquad \ldots(3.212)$$

Solving above two equations gives

$$i_2 = \frac{3E}{22r}$$

Illustrative Example 3.99

A voltmeter of resistance R_1 and an ammeter of resistance R_2 are connected in series across a battery of negligible internal resistance. When a resistance R is connected in parallel to voltmeter, reading of ammeter increases three times while that of voltmeter reduces to one third. Find R_1 and R_2 in terms of R.

Solution

Let E be the emf of the battery and circuit is shown in figure-3.290. In the first case, let i be the current in the circuit, then

$$E = i(R_1 + R_2) \qquad \ldots(3.213)$$

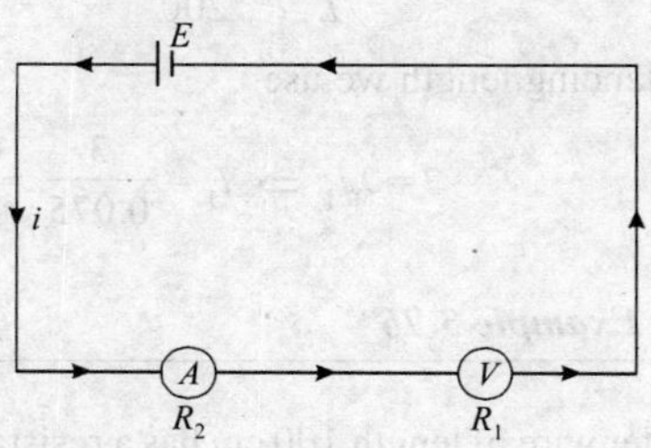

Figure 3.290

In the second, case main current increases three times while current through voltmeter will reduce to $i/3$. Hence, the remaining $3i - i/3 = 8i/3$ passes through R as shown in figure-3.291.

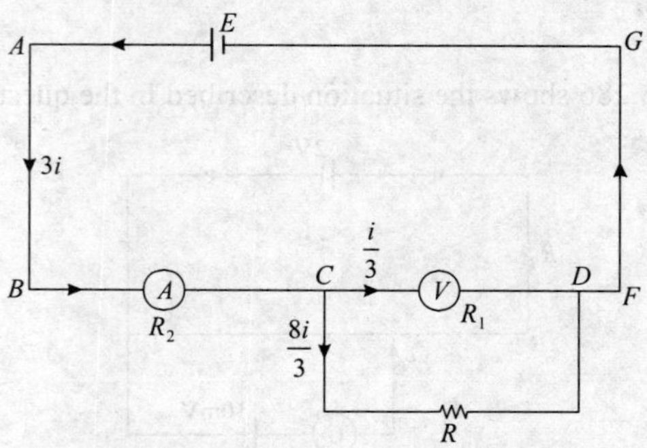

Figure 3.291

Here the potential difference across voltmeter is given as

$$V_C - V_D = \left(\frac{i}{3}\right) R_1 = \left(\frac{8i}{3}\right) R$$

$$\Rightarrow \quad R_1 = 8R$$

Using KVL in loop *ABFGA* in above circuit we have

$$E = 3i(R_2) + (i/3)(R_1) = i\left(3R_2 + \frac{R_1}{3}\right)$$

Solving above equations, we have

$$R_1 + R_2 = 3R_2 + \frac{R_1}{3}$$

$$\Rightarrow \quad 2R_2 = \frac{2R_1}{3}$$

$$\Rightarrow \quad R_2 = \frac{R_1}{3}$$

$$\Rightarrow \quad R_2 = \frac{8R}{3}$$

Web Reference at www.physicsgalaxy.com

Age Group - High School Physics | Age 17-19 Years

Section - ELECTRIC CURRENT & CIRCUITS

Topic - Electrical Measuring Instruments

Module Number - 1 to 24

Practice Exercise 3.9

(i) How can we make a galvanometer with $G = 20\ \Omega$ and $i_g = 1.0$ mA into a voltmeter with a maximum range of 10 V?

[9980 Ω]

(ii) A cell of EMF 3.4 V and internal resistance 3 Ω is connected to an ammeter having resistance 2 Ω and to an external resistance of 100 Ω. When a voltmeter is connected across the 100 Ω resistance the ammeter reading is 0.04 A. Find the voltage read by the voltmeter and its resistance. Had the voltmeter been an ideal one, what would have been its reading?

[400 Ω, 3.2 V, 3.238 V]

(iii) The resistance wire *AB* in the balancing setup shown in figure-3.292 is 10 cm long. When *AC* = 40 cm, no deflection occurs in the galvanometer. Find the unknown resistance *R*.

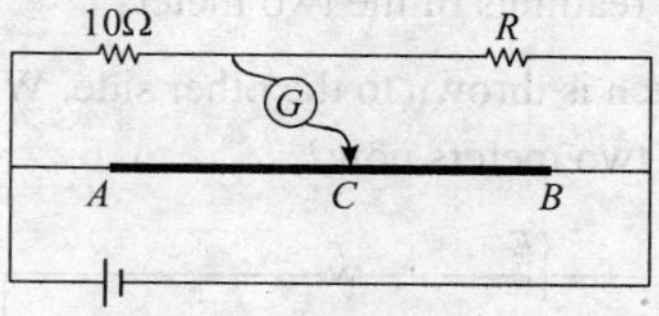

Figure 3.292

[15Ω]

(iv) A thin uniform wire *AB* of length 1m, an unknown resistance *X* and a resistance of 12 Ω are connected by thick conducting strips, as shown in the figure. A battery and a galvanometer (with a sliding jockey connected to it) are also available. Connections are to be make to measure the unknown resistance *X*. Using the principle of Wheatstone bridge answer the following questions

(a) Are there positive and negative terminals on the galvanometer?

(b) Draw the figure in and show the battery and the galvanometer (with jockey) connected at appropriate points in the circuit.

(c) After appropriate connections are made, it is found that no deflection takes place in the galvanometer when the sliding jockey touches the wire at a distance of 60 cm from *A*. Obtain the value of the resistance *X*.

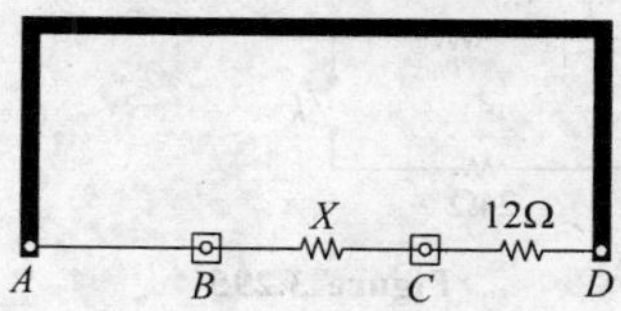

Figure 3.293

[(a) No (b)

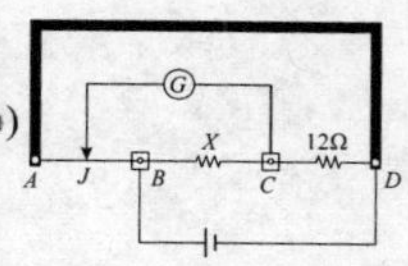

(c) 8Ω]

(v) A micrometer has a resistance of 100 Ω and full scale deflection current of 50 μA. How can it be made to work as an ammeter of range 5 mA?

[By connecting 1 Ω resistance in parallel with it]

(vi) The emf *E* and the internal resistance *r* of the battery shown in figure-3.294 are 4.3 V and 1.0 Ω respectively. The external resistance *R* is 50 Ω. The resistances of the ammeter and voltmeter are 2.0 Ω and 200 Ω respectively.

(a) Find the readings of the two meters.

(b) The switch is thrown to the other side. What will be the readings of the two meters now?

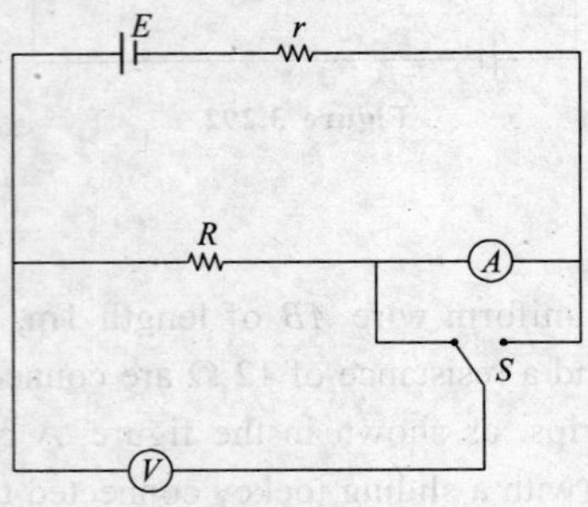

Figure 3.294

[(a) 0.1 A, 4.0 V; (b) 0.08 A, 4.2 V]

(vii) For the potentiometer setup shown in the figure below, the balance points is obtained at 75 cm from terminal A when the key k is open. Another balance point is obtained at 60 cm from A when the key k is closed. Find the internal resistance of the battery connected in secondary circuit of the setup.

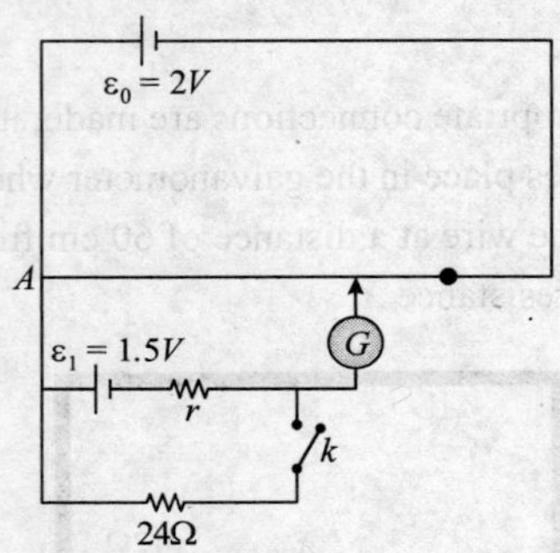

Figure 3.295

[6 Ω]

(viii) In the circuit shown in figure-3.296 V_1 and V_2 are two voltmeters of resistances 3000 Ω and 2000 Ω respectively. In addition $R_1 = 2000\ \Omega$, $R_2 = 3000\ \Omega$ and $E = 200$ V.

(a) Find the reading of voltmeters V_1 and V_2 when

(i) Switch S is open

(ii) Switch S is closed

(b) Current through S, when it is closed

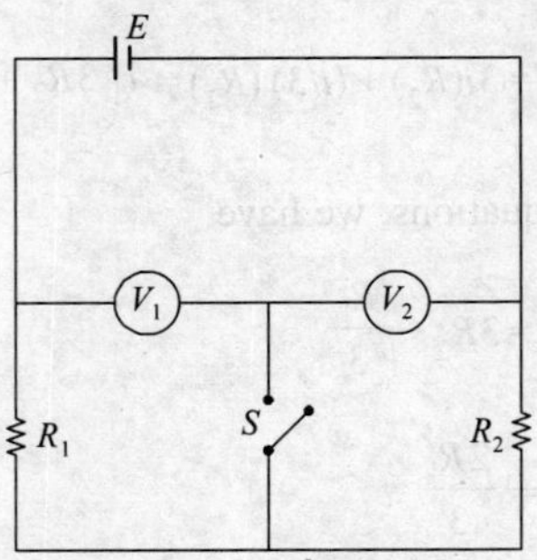

Figure 3.296

[(a) (i) 120 V, 80 V; (ii) 100 V, 100 V; (b) $\frac{1}{60}$ A]

Advance Illustrations Videos at www.physicsgalaxy.com

Age Group - Advance Illustrations
Section - Electric Current & Circuits
Topic - Current Electricity
Illustrations - 25 In-depth Illustrations Videos

* * * * *

Discussion Questions

Q3-1 A nonideal battery is connected to a resistor. Is work done by the battery equal to the thermal energy developed in the resistor ? Does your answer change if the battery is ideal ?

Q3-2 Is Ohm's law applicable to all conductors of electricity?

Q3-3 When a current is established in a wire, the free electrons drift in the direction opposite to the current. Does the number of free electrons in the wire continuously decrease ?

Q3-4 A primary and a secondary cell have the same EMF which of these will provided higher value of the maximum current that can be drawn? Explain briefly.

Q3-5 A large hollow metallic sphere *A* is charged positively to a potential of 100 volt and a small sphere *B* to a potential of 50 volt. Now *B* is placed inside *A* and they are connected by a wire. In which direction will the charge flow ?

Q3-6 A storage battery is to be charged from a D.C. supply. Should the positive or the negative terminal of the battery be connected to the positive side of the line? Explain.

Q3-7 Can Ohm's law be used to calculate currents in various parts of a complicated circuit. If not which law is then used?

Q3-8 Can the potential difference across a battery be greater than it emf ?

Q3-9 A fan with copper winding in its motor consumes less power as compared to an otherwise similar fan having aluminium winding. Explain.

Q3-10 Do the electrodes in an electrolytic cell have fixed polarity like a battery ?

Q3-11 If the current flowing in a copper wire be allowed to flow in another copper wire of double the radius, then what will be the effect on the drift velocity of the electrons? If the same current be allowed to flow in an iron wire of the same thickness, then?

Q3-12 A steady current is flowing in a cylindrical conductor. Is there any electric field within the conductor?

Q3-13 The thermal energy developed in a current-carrying resistor is given by $U = i^2 Rt$ and also by $U =$ Vit. Should we say that U is proportional to i^2 or to i ?

Q3-14 There are two wires of the same metal of same area of cross section but having lengths in the ratio 2 : 1. If same p.d. is applied across their ends, what will be the ratio of current in them?

Q3-15 When a current passes through a resistor, its temperature increases. Is it an adiabatic process ?

Q3-16 A proton beam is going from east to west. Is there an electric current ? If yes, in what direction ?

Q3-17 If a constant potential difference is applied across a bulb, the current slightly decreases as time passes and then becomes constant. Explain.

Q3-18 As temperature increases, the viscosity of liquids decreases considerably. Will this decrease the resistance of an electrolyte as the temperature increases ?

Q3-19 Does a conductor become charged when a current is passed through it ?

Q3-20 Is the formula $V = iR$ true for non-ohmic resistance also?

Q3-21 A given piece of wire of length l, cross sectional area and resistance R is stretched uniformly to a wire of length $2l$. What is the new resistance?

Q3-22 In an electrolyte, the positive ions move from left to right and the negative ions from right to left. Is there a net current ? If yes, in what direction ?

Q3-23 When the resistance connected in series with a cell is halved, the current is not exactly doubled but slightly less, why?

Q3-24 Why do the light of a car dim when the starter is operated?

Q3-25 Tthe drift speed is defined as $v_d = \Delta l/\Delta t$ where Δl is the distance drifted in a long time Δt. Why don't we define the drift speed as the limit of $\Delta l/\Delta t$ as $\Delta t \to 0$?

Q3-26 Is work done by a battery always equal to the thermal energy developed in electrical circuits ? What happens if a capacitor is connected in the circuit ?

* * * * *

Conceptual MCQs Single Option Correct

3-1 A capacitor of capacitance C is connected to two voltmeters A and B. A is ideal, having infinite resistance, while B has resistance R. The capacitor is charged and then the switch S is closed. The readings of A and B will be equal :

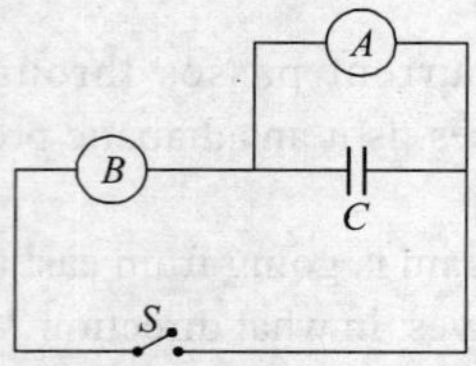

Figure 3.297

(A) at all times (B) after time RC
(C) after time $RC \ln 2$ (D) only after a very long time

3-2 In a RC circuit, the time required for the charge on a capacitor to build up to a given fraction of its steady state value, is independent of :
(A) The value of the applied EMF to the circuit
(B) The value of C
(C) The value of R
(D) None of the above

3-3 A capacitor is charged up to a potneital V_0. It is then connected to a resistance R and a battery of emf E. Two possible graphs of potential difference across capacitor with time are shown. What is the most reasonable explanation of these graphs?

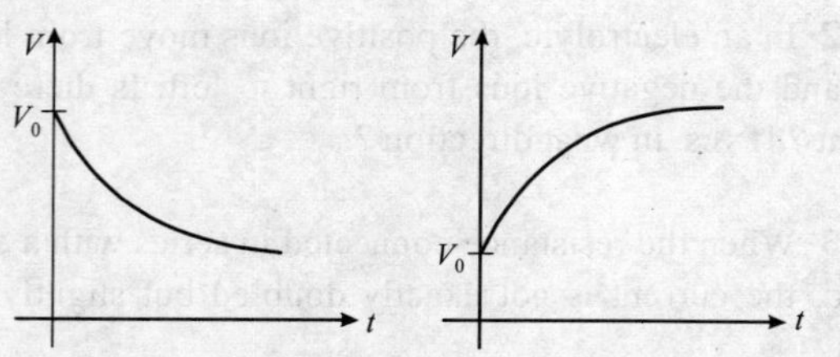

Figure 3.298

(A) The first graph shows what happens when the capacitor has potential difference less than E initially and the second shows what happens when it has potential difference greater than E initially :
(B) The first graph shows what happens when the capacitors has potential difference greater than E initially and the second shows what happens when it has a less than E potential initially.
(C) The first graph is the correct qualitative shape for any initial potential across capacitor, but the second is not possible
(D) The second graph is the correct qualitative shape for any initial potential difference across capacitor, but the first is not possible.

3-4 Through an electrolyte an electrical current is due to drift of :
(A) Free electrons
(B) Positive and negative ions
(C) Free electrons and holes
(D) Protons

3-5 An ammeter an a voltmeter are joined in series to a cell. Their readings are A and V respectively. If a resistance is now joined in parallel with the voltmeter :
(A) Both A and V will increase
(B) Both A and V will decrease
(C) A will decreaase, V will increase
(D) A will increase, V will decrease

3-6 A voltmeter and an ammeter are joined in series to an ideal cell, giving reading V and A respectively. If a resistance equal to the resistance of the ammeter is now joined in parallel to the ammeter then :
(A) V will not change
(B) V will increase
(C) A will become exactly half of its initial value
(D) A will become slightly less than double of its initial value

3-7 In the circuit shown in figure-3.299, the total resistance between points A and B is R_0. The value of resistance R is

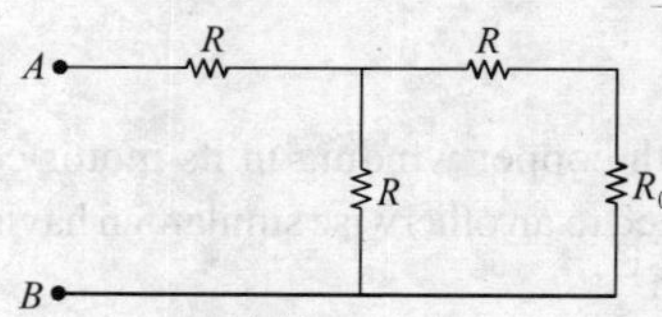

Figure 3.299

(A) R_0 (B) $\sqrt{3}R_0$
(C) $\frac{R_0}{2}$ (D) $\frac{R_0}{\sqrt{3}}$

3-8 A uniform wire of resistance 4 Ω is bent into the form of a circle of radius r. A specimen of the same wire is connected along the diameter of the circle. What is the equivalent resistance across the ends of this wire ?

(A) $\frac{4}{(4+\pi)}\Omega$ (B) $\frac{3}{(3+\pi)}\Omega$

(C) $\frac{2}{(2+\pi)}\Omega$ (D) $\frac{1}{(1+\pi)}\Omega$

3-9 All bulbs in the circuit shown in figure-3.300 are identical. Which bulb glows most brightly?

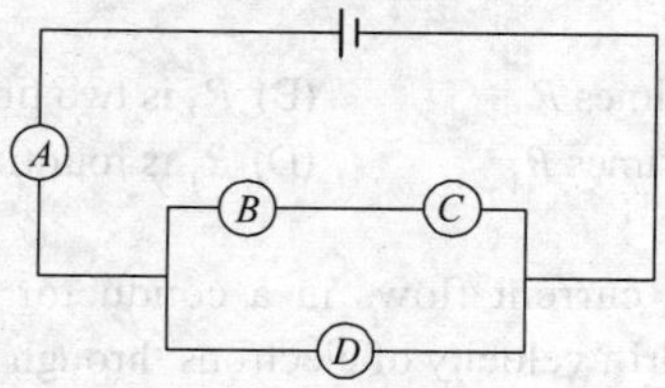

Figure 3.300

(A) *B* (B) *A*
(C) *D* (D) *C*

3-10 Switch *S* is closed at time $t = 0$. Which one of the following statements is correct ?

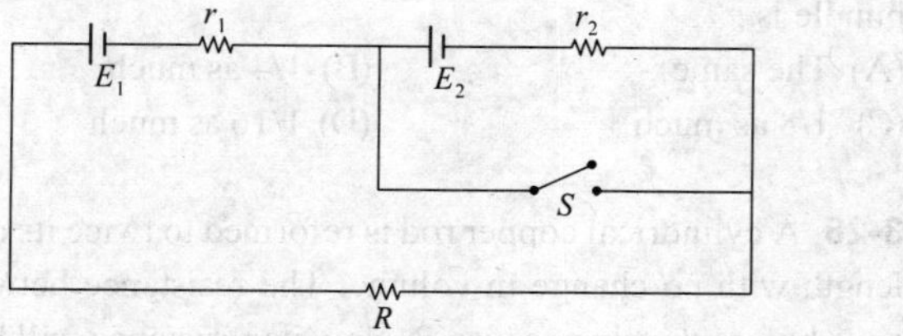

Figure 3.301

(A) Current in the resistance *R* increases if $E_1r_2 > E_2(R + r_1)$
(B) Current in the resistance *R* increases if $E_1r_2 < E_2(R + r_1)$
(C) Current in the resistance *R* decreases if $E_1r_2 > E_2(R + r_1)$
(D) Current in the resistance *R* decreases if $E_1r_2 = E_2(R + r_1)$

3-11 In the circuit here, the steady state voltage across capacitor *C* is a fraction of the battery EMF. The fraction is decided by :
(A) R_1 only
(B) R_1 and R_2 only
(C) R_1 and R_3 only
(D) R_1, R_2 and R_3

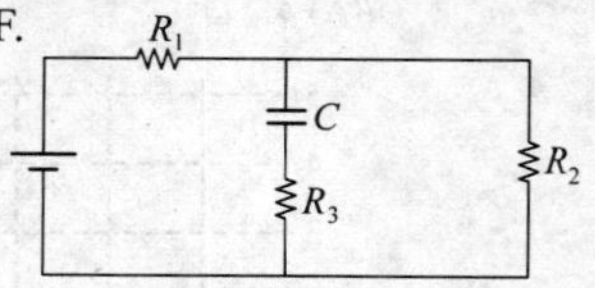

Figure 3.302

3-12 Two capacitors C_1 and $C_2 = 2C_1$ are connected in a circuit with a switch between them as shown in the figure-3.303. Initially the switch is open and C_1 holds charge *Q*. The switch is closed. In steady state, the charge on the two capacitors will be given as :

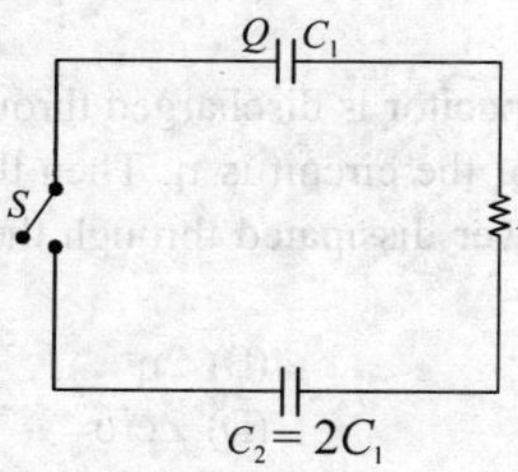

Figure 3.303

(A) $Q, 2Q$ (B) $Q/3, 2Q/3$
(C) $3Q/2, 3Q$ (D) $2Q/3, 4Q/3$

3-13 When a potential difference is applied across a conductor, the free electrons in the conductor are set into motion. Two velocities are associated with the moving electron-the drift velocity and average velocity. The fact is that the two are :
(A) Entirely different
(B) Same
(C) Same in some conductors and different in others
(D) None of the above

3-14 A metallic block has no potential difference applied across it, then the mean velocity of free electrons is :
(A) Proportional to *T*
(B) Proportional to $\sqrt{T}$
(C) Zero
(D) Finite but independent of temperature

3-15 The temperature of a metal wire rises when an electric current passes through it because :
(A) Collision of metal atoms with each other releases heat energy
(B) Collision of conduction electrons with each other releases heat energy
(C) When the conduction electrons fall from higher energy level to a lower energy level heat energy is released
(D) Collision of conduction electrons with the atoms of the metal gives them energy which appears as heat

3-16 A steady current is passing through a linear conductor of non-uniform cross-section. The net quantity of charge crossing any cross-section per second is.
(A) Independent of area of cross-section
(B) Directly proportional to the length of conductor
(C) Directly proportional to the area of cross-section
(D) Inversely proportional to the length of conductor

3-17 What is immaterial for an electric fuse :
(A) Its specific resistance (B) Its radius
(C) Its length (D) Current flowing through it

3-18 Constantain wire is used for making standard resistance because it has :
(A) Low specific resistance
(B) High specific resistance
(C) Negligible temperature coefficient of resistance
(D) High melting point

3-19 A capacitor of capacitance *C* is charged to a constant potential difference *V* and then connected in series with an open key and a pure resistor *R*. At time $t = 0$, the key is closed. If *I* is current at time $t = 0$, a plot of log *I* against *t* is shown as in the graph (1). Later one one of the parameters, i.e. *V*, *R* and *C* is changed, keeping the other two constant and graph (2) is recorded. Then

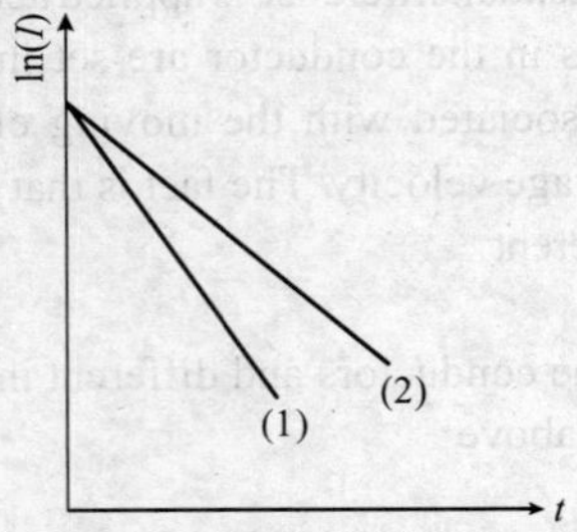

Figure 3.304

(A) C is reduced (B) C is increased
(C) R is reduced (D) R is increased

3-20 When cells are arranged in parallel
(A) The current capacity decreases
(B) The current capacity increases
(C) The equivalent EMF increases
(D) The equivalent EMF decreases

3-21 A standard 40 W tubelight is in parallel with a room heater both connected to a suitable supply line. What will happen when the light is switched of :
(A) The heater output will be larger
(B) It will be smaller
(C) It will remain the same
(D) None of the above

3-22 In a circuit containing two unequal resistors connected in parallel :
(A) The current is the same in both the resistors
(B) A large current flows through the large resistor
(C) The voltage drop across both the resistances is the same
(D) The small resistance has smaller conductance

3-23 Two wires A and B of the same material, having radii in the ratio 1 : 2 and carry currents in the ratio 4 : 1. The ratio of drift speed of electrons in A and B is :
(A) 16:1 (B) 1:16
(C) 1:4 (D) 4:1

3-24 If n, e, τ and m are representing electron density, charge relaxation time and mass of an electron respectively, then the resistance of a wire of length l and cross-sectional area A is given by
(A) $\frac{ml}{ne^2\tau A}$ (B) $\frac{m\tau A}{ne^2 l}$
(C) $\frac{ne^2\tau A}{ml}$ (D) $\frac{ne^2 A}{m\tau l}$

3-25 If R_1 and R_2 are respectively the filament resistances of a 200 W bulb and a 100 W bulb designed to operate on the same voltage.
(A) R_1 is two times R_2 (B) R_2 is two times R_1
(C) R_2 is four times R_1 (D) R_1 is four times R_2

3-26 When a current flows in a conductor, the order of magnitude of drift velocity of electrons through it is :
(A) 10^{10} cm/s (B) 10^4 cm/s
(C) 10^{-2} cm/s (D) 10^{-7} cm/s

3-27 A piece of wire is cut into four equal parts and the pieces are bundled together side by side to from a thicker wire. Compared with that of the original wire, the resistance of the bundle is :
(A) The same (B) 1/4 as much
(C) 1/8 as much (D) 1/16 as much

3-28 A cylindrical copper rod is reformed to twice its original length with no change in volume. The resistance between its ends before the change was R. Now its resistance will be :
(A) $8R$ (B) $6R$
(C) $4R$ (D) $2R$

3-29 Variation of current and voltage in a conductor has been shown in figure-3.305. The resistance of the conductor is.

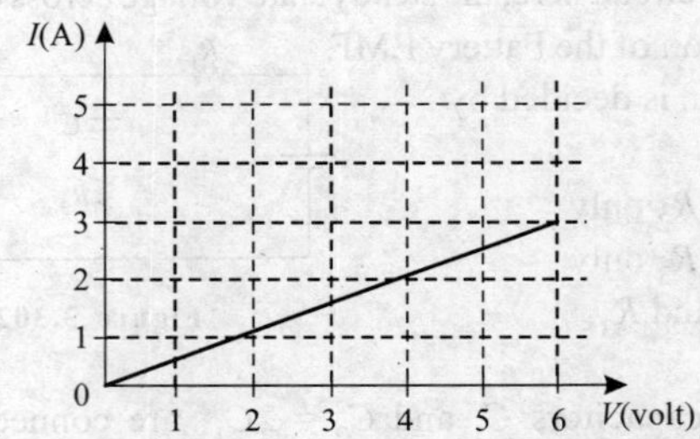

Figure 3.305

(A) 4Ω (B) 2Ω
(C) 3Ω (D) 1Ω

3-30 A charged capacitor is discharged through a resistance. The time constant of the circuit is η. Then the value of time constant for the power dissipated through the resistance will be :
(A) η (B) 2η
(C) $\eta/2$ (D) Zero

3-31 A capacitor of capacitance C is charged by a battery of EMF E and internal resistance r. A resistance $2r$ is also connected in series with the capacitor. The amount of heat liberated inside the battery by the time capacitor is charged to 50% of its steady state value is given as :

(A) $\frac{3}{8}E^2C$ (B) $\frac{E^2C}{8}$

(C) $\frac{E^2C}{12}$ (D) $\frac{E^2C}{24}$

3-32 For the circuit shown in the figure-3.306, find the charge stored on capacitor in steady state :

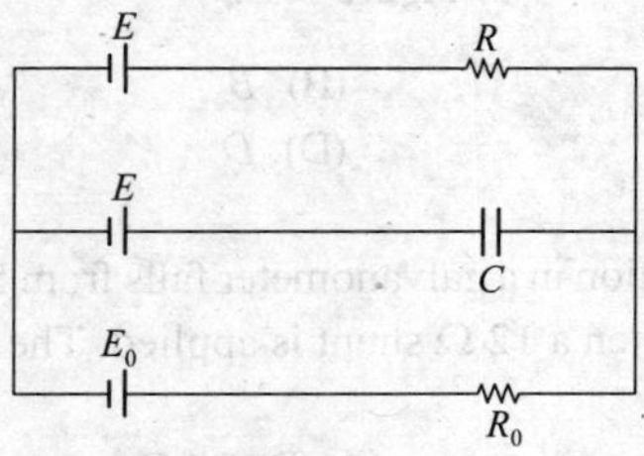

Figure 3.306

(A) $\frac{RC}{R+R_0}E$ (B) $\frac{RC}{R_0}(E-E_0)$

(C) Zero (D) $\frac{RC}{R+R_0}(E-E_0)$

3-33 The switch shown in the figure-3.307 is closed at $t = 0$. The charge on the capacitor as a function of time is given as

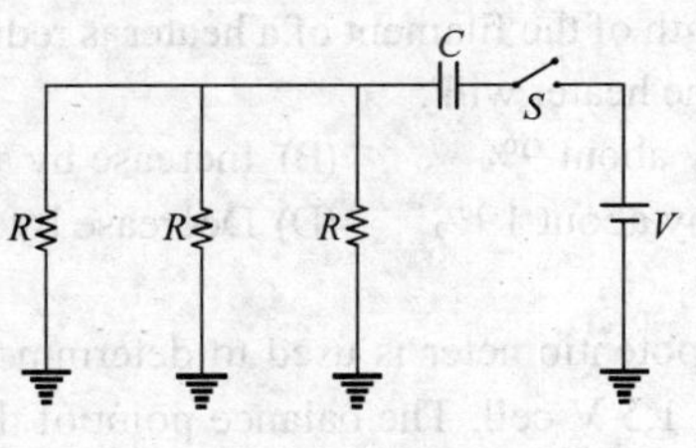

Figure 3.307

(A) $CV(1-e^{-t/RC})$ (B) $3CV(1-e^{-t/RC})$

(C) $CV(1-e^{-3t/RC})$ (D) $CV(1-e^{-t/3RC})$

3-34 A capacitor C is connected to two equal resistances as shown in the figure-3.308. Consider the following statements.

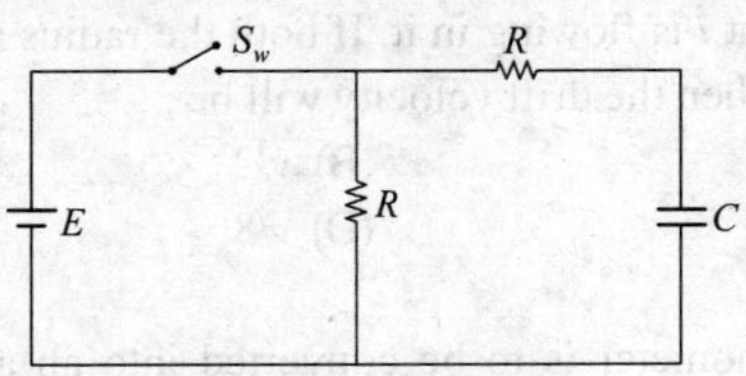

Figure 3.308

(i) At the time of charging of capacitor time constant of the circuit is $2RC$

(ii) At the time of discharging of the capacitor the time constant of the circuit is RC

(iii) At the time of discharging of the capacitor the time constant of the circuit is $2RC$

(iv) At the time of charging of capacitor the time constant of the circuit is RC

(A) Statement (i) and (ii) only are correct

(B) Statements (ii) and (iii) only are correct

(C) Statements (iii) and (iv) only are correct

(D) Statement (i) and (iii) only are correct

3-35 In the circuit diagram, the current through the battery immediately after the switch S is closed is given as :

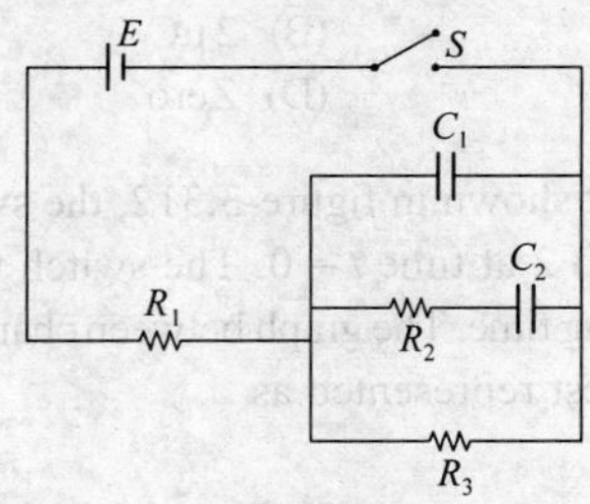

Figure 3.309

(A) Zero (B) $\frac{E}{R_1}$

(C) $\frac{E}{R_1+R_2}$ (D) $\frac{E}{R_1+\frac{R_2R_3}{R_2+R_3}}$

3-36 In the circuit shown, switch S is closed at $t = 0$. Let i_1 and i_2 be the current at any finite time t, then the ratio i_1/i_2 is

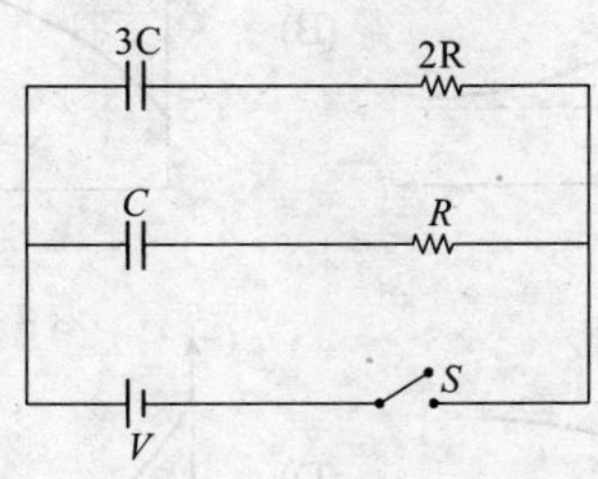

Figure 3.310

(A) Constant

(B) Increases with time

(C) Decreases with time

(D) First increases and then decreases

* * * * *

Numerical MCQs Single Option Correct

3-1 A 1 μF capacitor is connected in the circuit shown below. The EMF of the cell is 3 V and internal resistance is 0.5 Ω. The resistors R_1 and R_2 have values 4 Ω and 1 Ω respectively. The charge on the capacitor in steady state is :

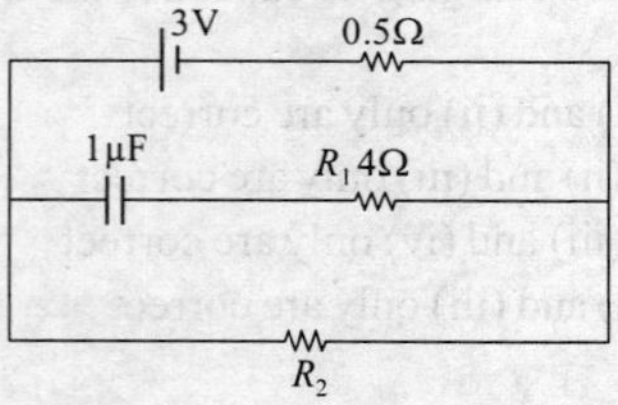

Figure 3.311

(A) 1 μC (B) 2 μC
(C) 1.33 μC (D) Zero

3-2 In the circuit shown in figure-3.312, the switch is shifted from position 1 to 2 at time $t = 0$. The switch was initially in position 1 for a long time. The graph between charge on capacitor C and time t is best represented as

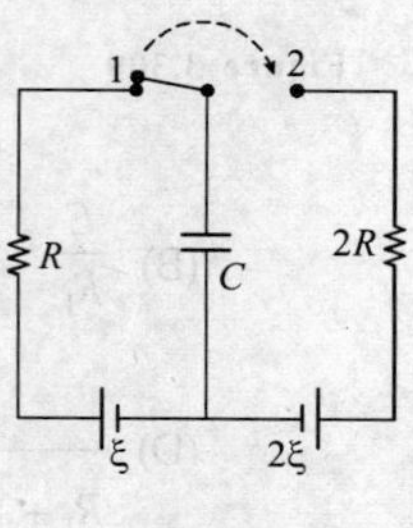

Figure 3.312

(A)
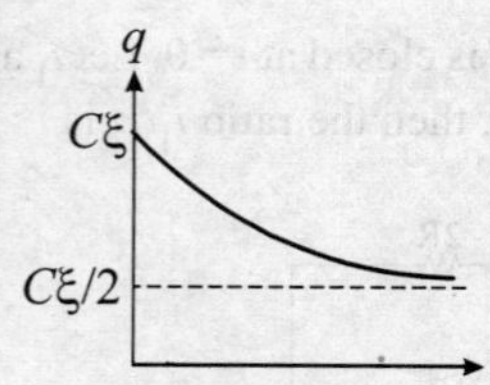

(B)
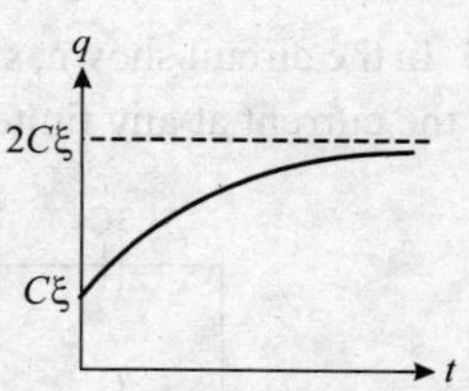

(C)
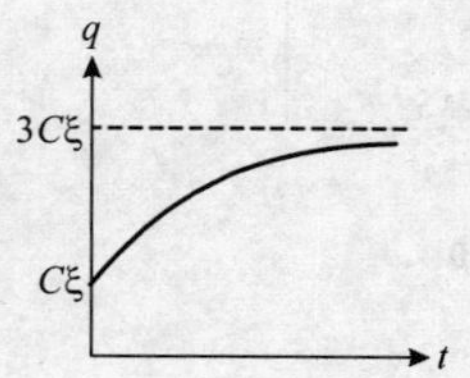

(D)
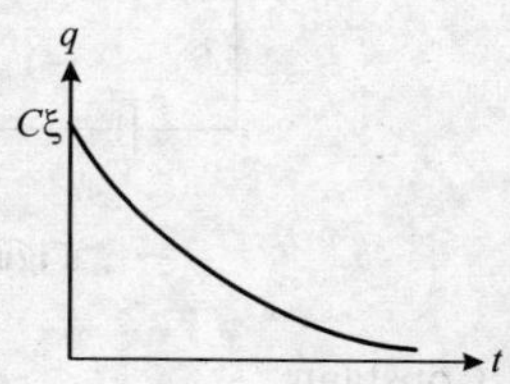

3-3 The capacitor shown in figure-3.312-(a) is charged to steady state by connecting switch S to contact a. If switch S is thrown to contact b at time $t = 0$, which of the curves in figure-3.312-(b) represents the magnitude of the current through the resistor R as a function of time?

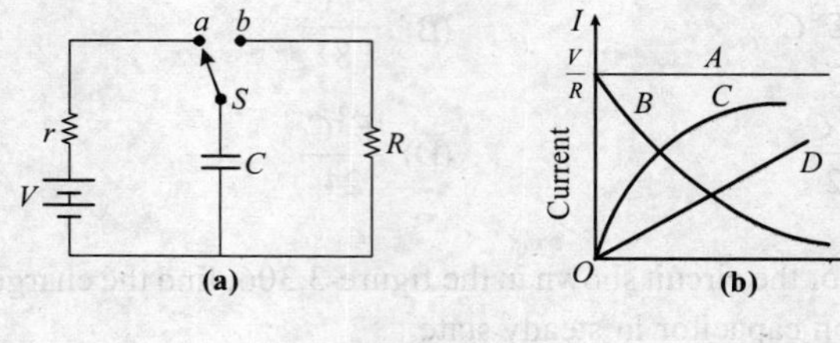

Figure 3.313

(A) A (B) B
(C) C (D) D

3-4 The deflection in a galvanometer falls from 50 divisions to 20 divisions, when a 12 Ω shunt is applied. The galvanometer resistance is

(A) 18 Ω (B) 24 Ω
(C) 30 Ω (D) 36 Ω

3-5 In conversion of a galvanometer to ammeter if 2% of the main current is to be passed through the galvanometer of resistance G, the resistance of shunt required is :

(A) $\frac{G}{49}$ (B) $\frac{G}{50}$
(C) $49G$ (D) $50G$

3-6 If the length of the filament of a heater is reduced by 10% the power of the heater will :

(A) Increse by about 9% (B) Increase by about 11%
(C) Increase by about 19% (D) Decrease by about 10%

3-7 A 2.0 V potentiometer is used to determine the internal resistance of a 1.5 V cell. The balance point of the cell in the open circuit is obtained at 75 cm. When a resistor of 10 Ω is connected across the cell, the balance point shifts to 60cm. The internal resistance of the cell is :

(A) 1.5 Ω (B) 2.5 Ω
(C) 3.5 Ω (D) 4.5 Ω

3-8 The drift velocity of free electrons in a conductor is v, when a current i is flowing in it. If both the radius and current are doubled, then the drift velocity will be :

(A) v (B) $v/2$
(C) $v/4$ (D) $v/8$

3-9 A galvanometer is to be converted into an ammeter or voltmeter. In which of the following cases the resistance of the device is greatest?

(A) An ammeter of range 10 A (B) A voltmeter of range 5 V
(C) An ammeter of range 5 A (D) A voltmeter of range 10 V

3-10 In the given circuit the current flowing through the resistance 20 Ω is 0.3 A, while the ammeter reads 0.8 A. What is the value of R_1?

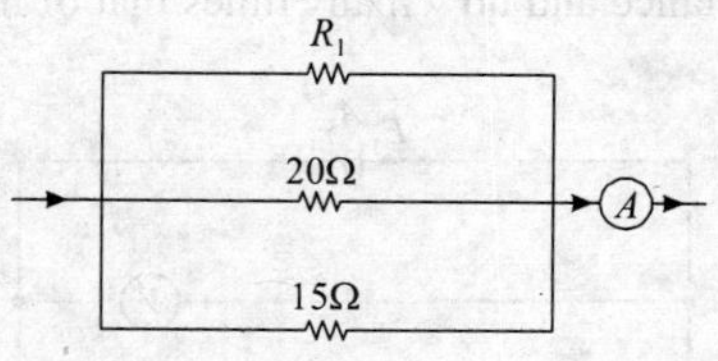

Figure 3.314

(A) 30 Ω (B) 40 Ω
(C) 50 Ω (D) 60 Ω

3-11 Two batteries one of the emf 3 V, internal resistance 1 Ω and the other of emf 15 V, internal resistance 2 Ω are connected in series with a resistance R as shown. If the potential difference between points a and b is zero, the resistance R is :

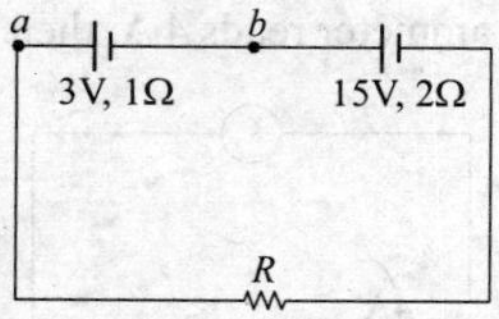

Figure 3.315

(A) 5 Ω (B) 7 Ω
(C) 3 Ω (D) 1 Ω

3-12 A part of a circuit is shown in figure-3.316. Here reading of ammeter is 5 A and voltmeter is 100 V. If voltmeter resistance is 2500 Ω, then the resistance R is approximately.

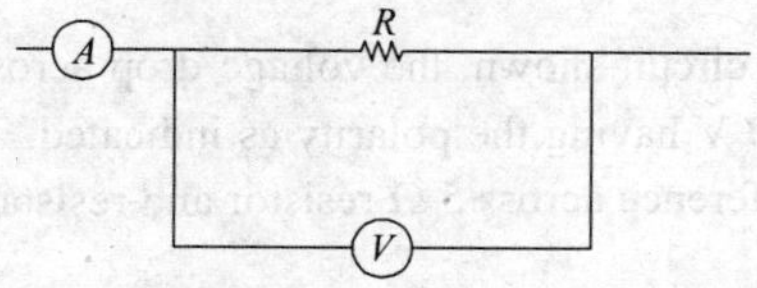

Figure 3.316

(A) 20 Ω (B) 10 Ω
(C) 100 Ω (D) 200 Ω

3-13 Two resistances are connected in two gaps of a metre bridge. The balance point is 20 cm from the zero end. A resistance of 15 Ω is connected in series with the smaller of the two. The null point shifts to 40 cm. Then value of the smaller resistance is :

(A) 3 Ω (B) 6 Ω
(C) 9 Ω (D) 12 Ω

3-14 In the given circuit, the voltmeter reads 5 V. The resistance of the voltmeter is :

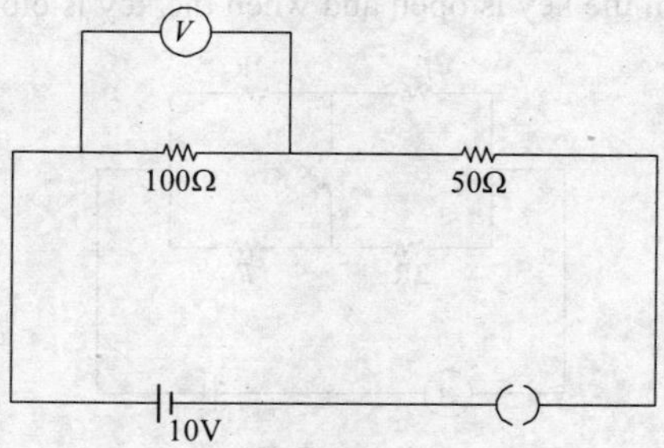

Figure 3.317

(A) 200 Ω (B) 100 Ω
(C) 10 Ω (D) 50 Ω

3-15 The wire of potentiometer has resistance 4 Ω and length 1 m. It is connected to a cell of EMF 2 V and internal resistance 1 Ω. If a cell of EMF 1.2 V is balanced by it, the balancing length will be :

(A) 90 cm (B) 60 cm
(C) 50 cm (D) 75 cm

3-16 Two identical batteries, each of EMF 2 V and internal resistance $r = 1$ Ω are connected as shown. the maximum power that can be developed across R using these batteries is :

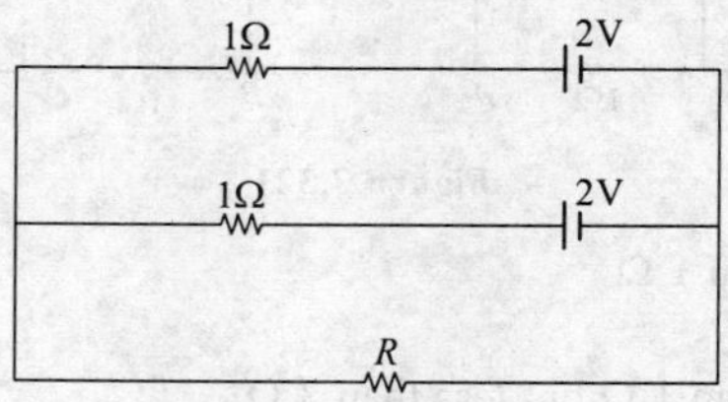

Figure 3.318

(A) 3.2 W (B) 8.2 W
(C) 2 W (D) 4 W

3-17 The potential difference between points A and B in the circuit shown in figure-3.319, will be :

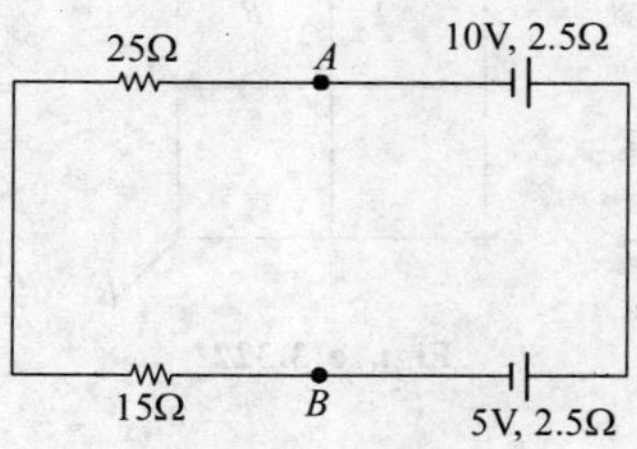

Figure 3.319

(A) 1 V (B) 2 V
(C) –3 V (D) None of these

3-18 Find the ratio of currents as measured by ammeter in two cases when the key is open and when the key is closed :

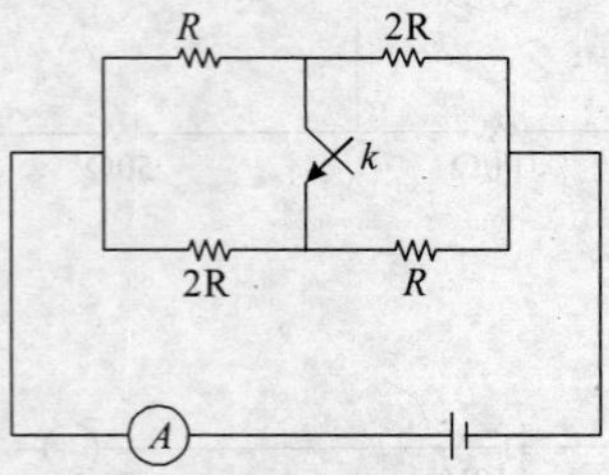

Figure 3.320

(A) 9/8 (B) 10/11
(C) 8/9 (D) None of the above

3-19 A galvanometer has a resistance of 3663 Ω. A shunt S is connected across it such that (1/34) of the total current passes through the galvanometer. Then the value of the shunt is :
(A) 222 Ω (B) 111 Ω
(C) 11 Ω (D) 22 Ω

3-20 Each resistor shown in figure-3.321 in the infinite ladder network is of resistance 1 Ω. The effective resistance in between A and B is

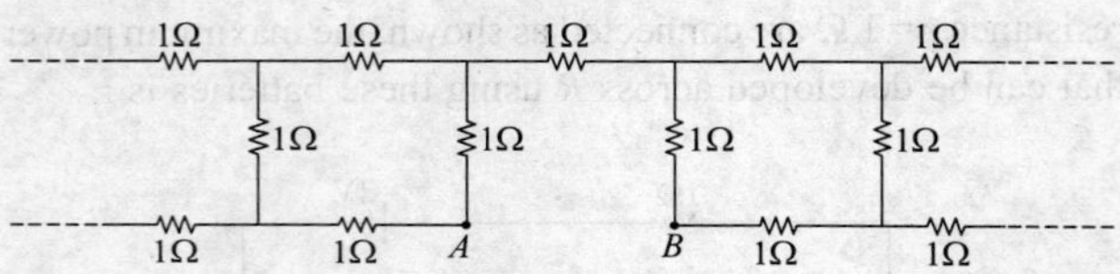

Figure 3.321

(A) Less than 1 Ω
(B) 1 Ω
(C) More than 1 Ω but less than 3 Ω
(D) 3 Ω

3-21 Each wire shown in figure-3.322 is of resistance R. The equivalent resistance between the diagonally opposite terminal point A and B is :

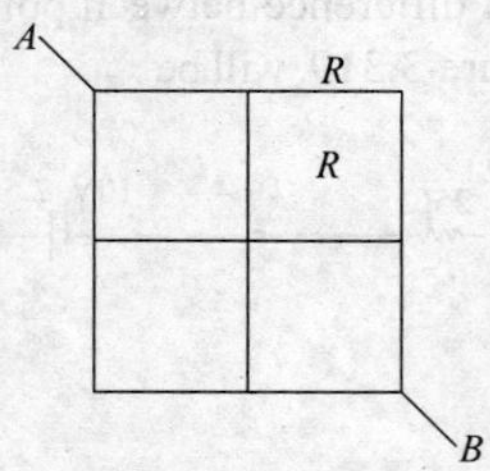

Figure 3.322

(A) R (B) $\frac{3R}{2}$

(C) $2R$ (D) $\frac{R}{2}$

3-22 Two cells A and B of EMF 1.3V and 1.5 V respectively are arranged as shown in figure-3.323. The voltmeter connected in circuit is ideal and it reads 1.45 V. Which cell has the higher internal resistance and how many times that of the other?

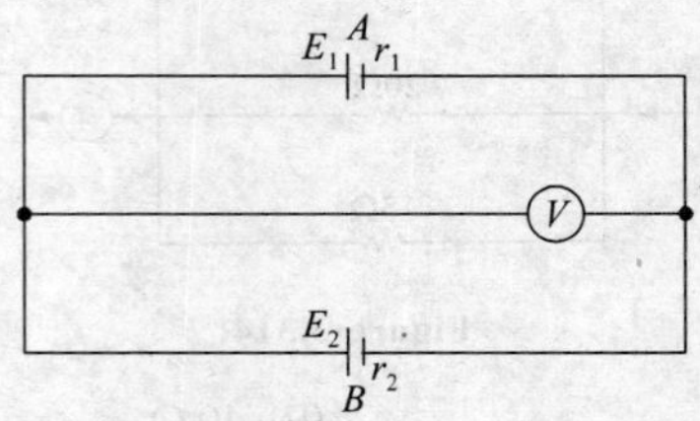

Figure 3.323

(A) $r_1 = 2r_2$ (B) $r_1 = 3r_2$
(C) $r_2 = 2r_1$ (D) $r_2 = 3r_1$

3-23 A student connects an ammeter A and a voltmeter V to measure a resistance R as shown in figure-3.324. If the voltmeter reads 20 V and the ammeter reads 4 A, then R is :

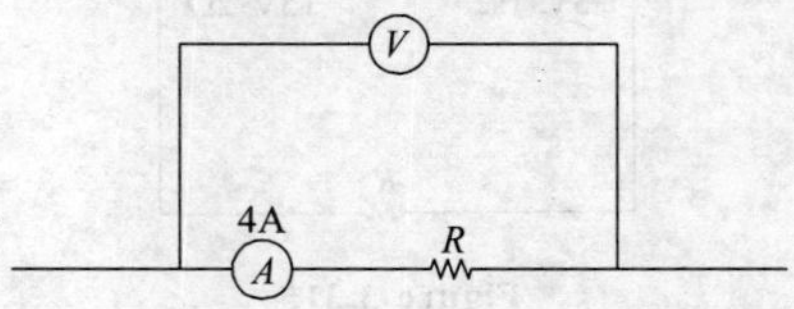

Figure 3.324

(A) Equal to 5 Ω
(B) Greater than 5 Ω
(C) Less than 5 Ω
(D) Greater or less than 5 Ω depending upon the direction of current

3-24 In the circuit shown, the voltage drop across the 15 Ω resistor is 30 V having the polarity as indicated. The ratio of potential difference across 5 Ω resistor and resistance R is :

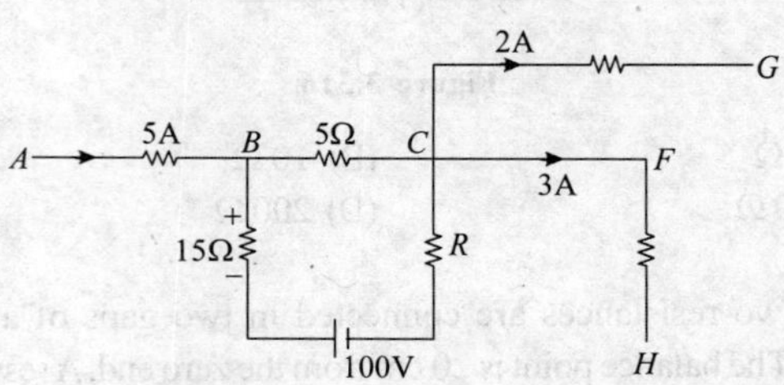

Figure 3.325

(A) 2/7 (B) 0.4
(C) 5/7 (D) 1

3-25 A source of EMF E = 10 V and having negligible internal resistance is connected to a variable resistance. The resistance varies as shown in figure-3.326. The total charge that has passed through the resistor R during the time interval from t_1 to t_2 is :

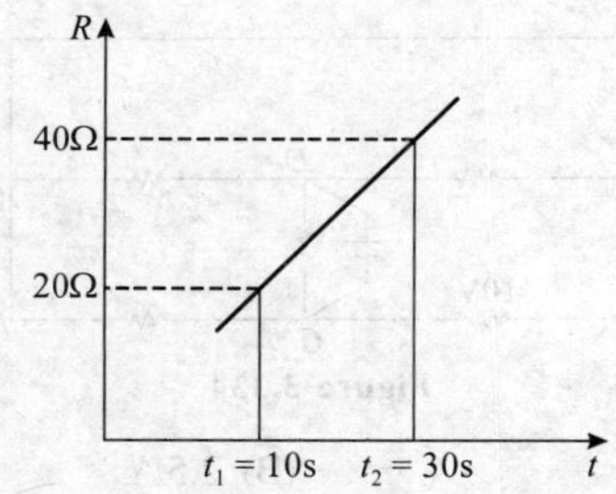

Figure 3.326

(A) 40 ln4 (B) 30 ln3
(C) 20 ln2 (D) 10 ln2

3-26 In order to increase the resistance of a given wire of uniform cross section to four times its value, a fraction of its length is stretched uniformly till the full length of the wire becomes 1.5 times the original length. What is the value of this fraction ?

(A) $\frac{1}{4}$ (B) $\frac{1}{8}$

(C) $\frac{1}{16}$ (D) $\frac{1}{6}$

3-27 The figure-3.327, shows a meter bridge circuit, with $AB = 100$ cm, $X = 12\ \Omega$ and $R = 18\ \Omega$ and the jockey J in the position of null deflection balance. If R is now changed to 8 Ω, through what distance will J have to be moved to obtain the balance again?

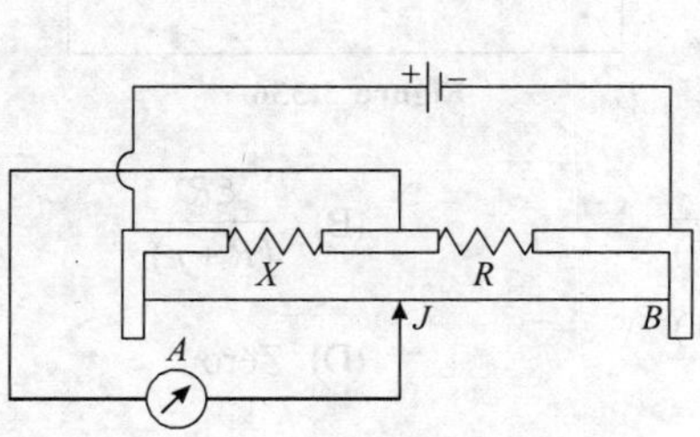

Figure 3.327

(A) 10 cm (B) 20 cm
(C) 30 cm (D) 40 cm

3-28 A milliammeter of range 10 mA and resistance 9 Ω is joined in a circuit as shown. The meter gives full-scale deflection for current I when A and B are used as its terminals with current enters at A and leaves at B and C is left open. The value of current I is :

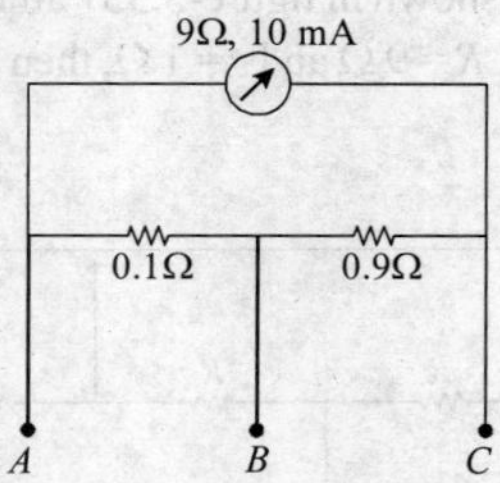

Figure 3.328

(A) 100 mA (B) 900 mA
(C) 1 A (D) 1.1 A

3-29 A battery of emf $E_0 = 12$ V is connected across a 4m long uniform wire having resistance 4 Ω/m. Two cell of small EMFs $\xi_1 = 2$ V and $\xi_2 = 4$ V having internal resistance 2 Ω and 6 Ω respectively are connected as shown in the figure-3.329. If galvanometer shows no deflection at the point N, the distance of point N from the point A is equal to :

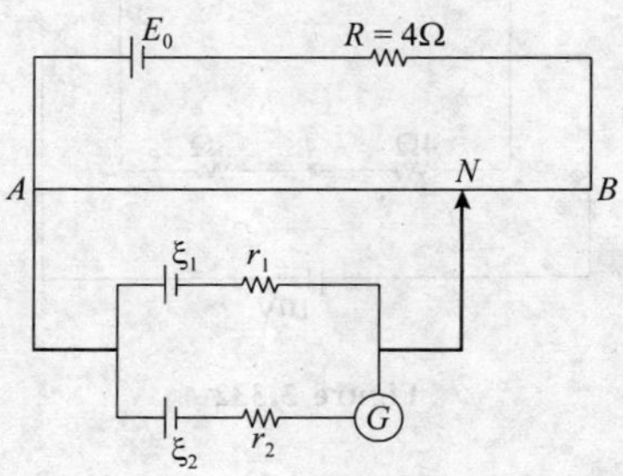

Figure 3.329

(A) $\frac{5}{3}$m (B) $\frac{4}{3}$m

(C) $\frac{3}{2}$m (D) None of these

3-30 In the circuit shown, when keys K_1 and K_2 both are closed, the ammeter reads I_0. But when K_1 is open and K_2 is closed the ammeter reads $I_0/2$. Assuming that ammeter resistance is much less than R_2, the values of r and R_1 are

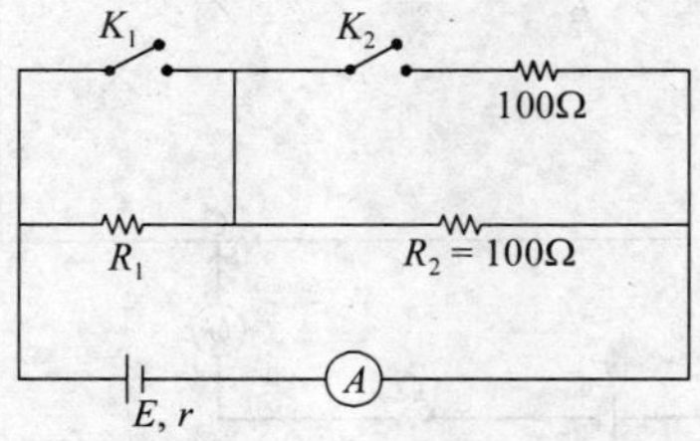

Figure 3.330

(A) 25 Ω, 50 Ω (B) 25 Ω, 100 Ω
(C) 0, 100 Ω (D) 0, 50 Ω

3-31 In the circuit shown in figure-3.331 ammeter and voltmeter are ideal. If $E = 4$ V, $R = 9\ \Omega$ and $r = 1\ \Omega$, then reading of ammeter and voltmeter are :

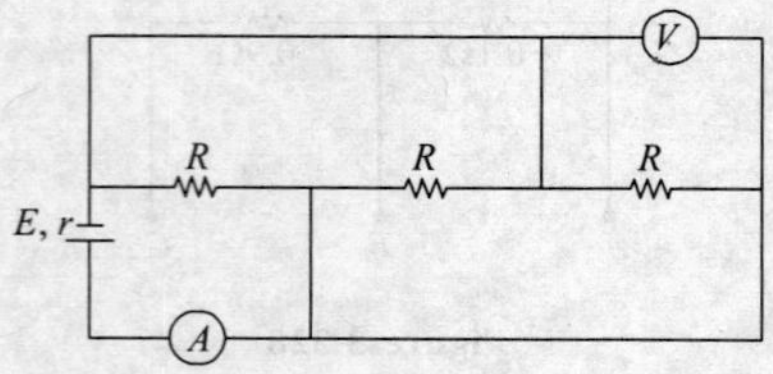

Figure 3.331

(A) 1 A, 3 V (B) 2 A, 3 V
(C) 3 A, 4 V (D) 4 A, 4 V

3-32 In the circuit shown in figure-3.332, the potential difference between points A and B is :

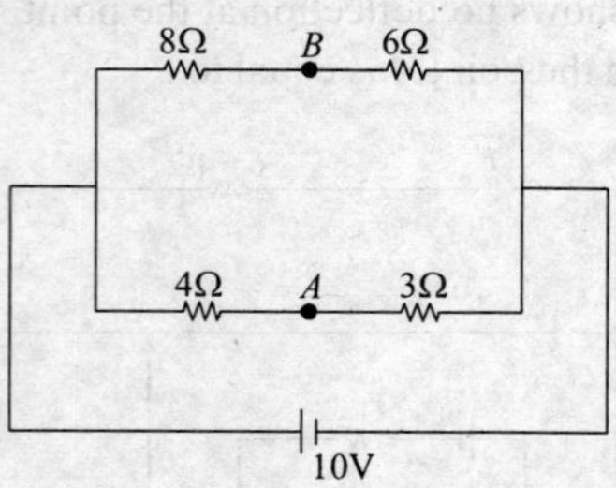

Figure 3.332

(A) $\frac{20}{7}V$ (B) $\frac{40}{7}V$

(C) $\frac{10}{7}V$ (D) Zero

3-33 figure-3.333 shows a potentiometer arrangement with $R_{AB} = 10\ \Omega$ and rheostat of variable resistance x. For $x = 0$ null deflection point is found at 20 cm from A. For unknown value of x null deflection point was at 30 cm from A, then the value of x is :

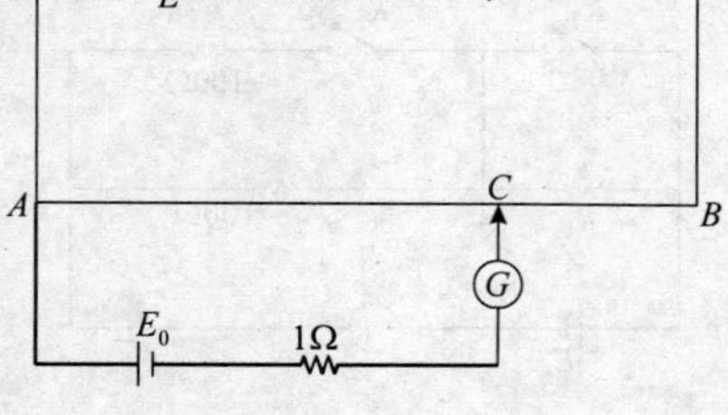

Figure 3.333

(A) 10 Ω (B) 5 Ω
(C) 2 Ω (D) 1 Ω

3-34 All resistances shown in circuit are 2 Ω each. The current in the resistance between D and E is :

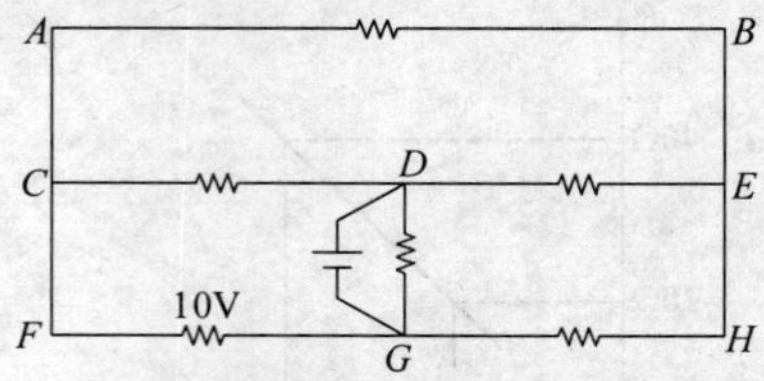

Figure 3.334

(A) 5 A (B) 2.5 A
(C) 1 A (D) 7.5 A

3-35 In the circuit shown in figure-3.335, the resistance of voltmeter is 6 kΩ. The voltmeter reading will be :

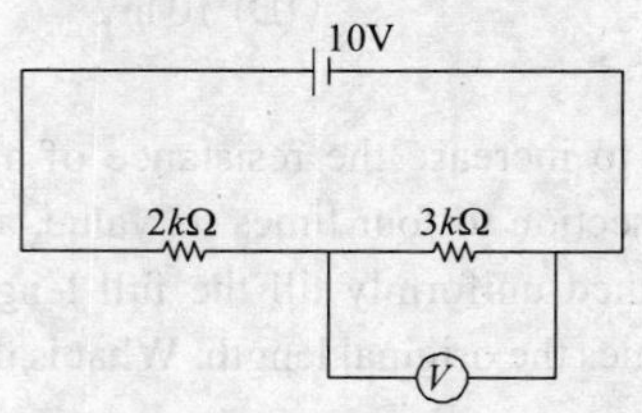

Figure 3.335

(A) 6 V (B) 5 V
(C) 4 V (D) 3 V

3-36 A circuit consists of a source of EMF ξ and internal resistance r, two capacitors each of capacitance C and two resistors, each of value R. The voltage across either capacitor is :

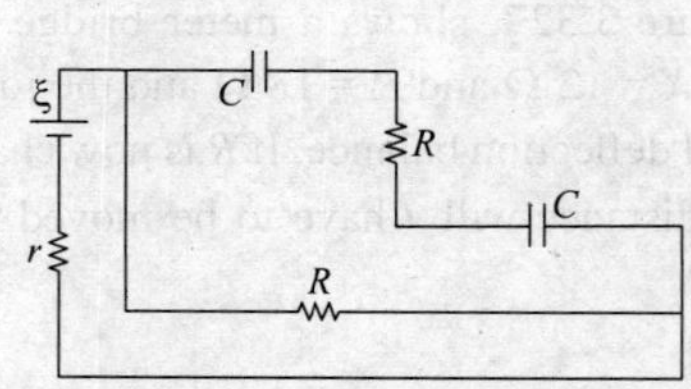

Figure 3.336

(A) $\frac{\xi R}{2(R+r)}$ (B) $\frac{\xi R}{(R+r)}$

(C) $\frac{\xi(R+r)}{2R}$ (D) Zero

3-37 The charge on a capacitor of capacitance 10 μF connected as shown in the figure-3.337 is :

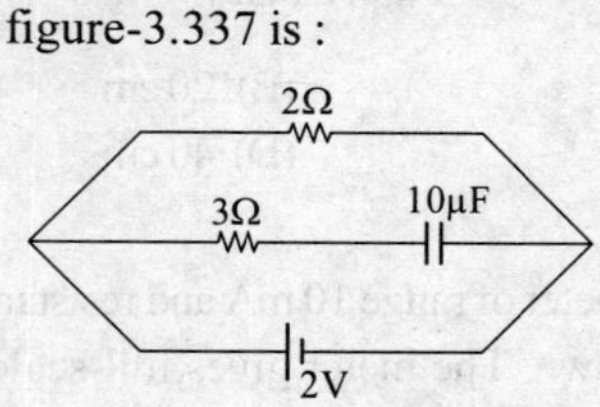

Figure 3.337

(A) 20 μC (B) 15 μC
(C) 10 μC (D) Zero

3-38 A 4 μF capacitor, a resistance of 2.5 MΩ is in series with 12V battery. Find the time after which the potential difference across the capacitor is 3 times the potential difference across the resistor :

(A) 13.86 s (B) 6.93 s
(C) 7 s (D) 14 s

3-39 In an *RC* circuit while charging, the graph of ln(*i*) versus time is as shown by the dotted line in the figure-3.338, where *i* is the current. When the value of the resistance is doubled, which of the solid curve best represents the variation of ln(*i*) versus time :

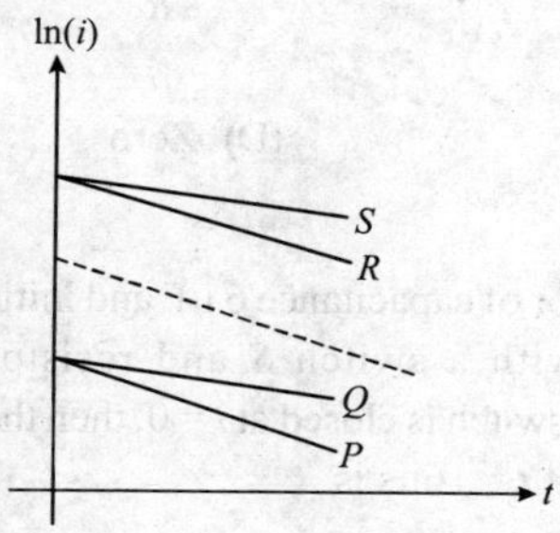

Figure 3.338

(A) *P* (B) *Q*
(C) *R* (D) *S*

3-40 A circuit is connected as shown in the figure-3.339 with the switch *S* open. When the switch is closed, the total amount of charge that flows from *y* to *x* :

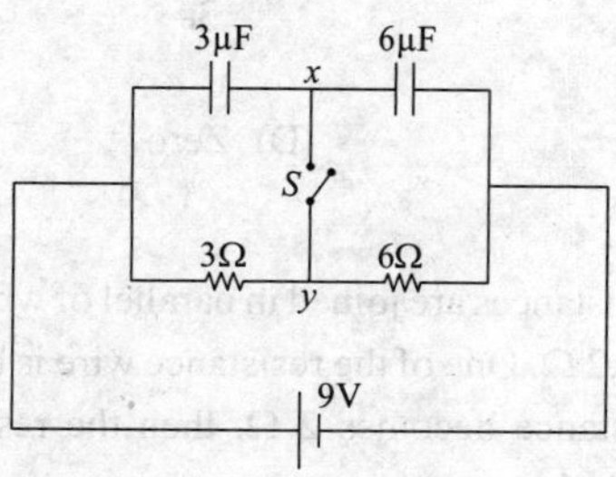

Figure 3.339

(A) 0 (B) 54 μ*C*
(C) 27 μ*C* (D) 81 μ*C*

3-41 A parallel plate capacitor *C* with plates of unit area and separation *d* is filled with a liquid of dielectric constant *k* = 2. The level of liquid is *d*/3 initially between the plates. Suppose the liquid level decreases at a constant speed *v*, the time constant of the circuit as a function of time *t* is :

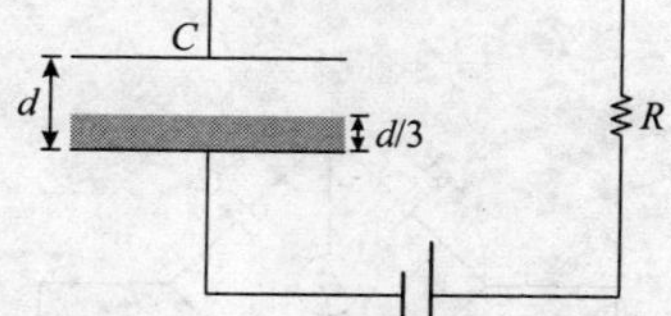

Figure 3.340

(A) $\dfrac{6 \epsilon_0 R}{5d + 3vt}$ (B) $\dfrac{(15d + 9vt) \epsilon_0 R}{2d^2 - 3dvt - 9v^2t^2}$

(C) $\dfrac{6 \epsilon_0 R}{5d - 3vt}$ (D) $\dfrac{(15d - 9vt) \epsilon_0 R}{2d^2 + 3dvt - 9v^2t^2}$

3-42 What is equivalent time constant of *RC* circuit shown in figure-3.341 ?

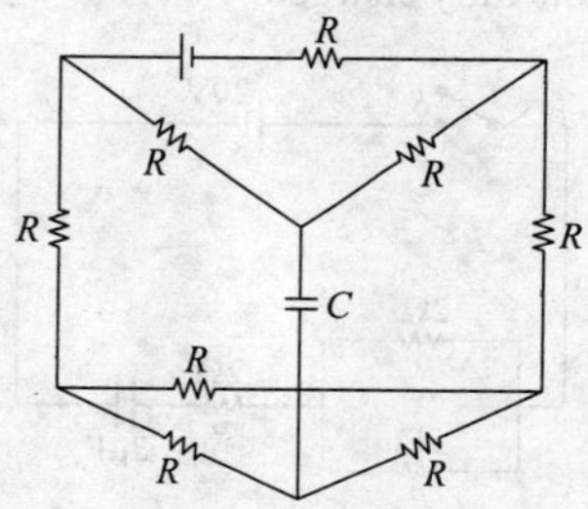

Figure 3.341

(A) 1.5 *RC* (B) 3 *RC*

(C) 2 *RC* (D) $\dfrac{RC}{2}$

3-43 In the circuit shown in figure-3.342, find the steady state charge on capacitor C_1.

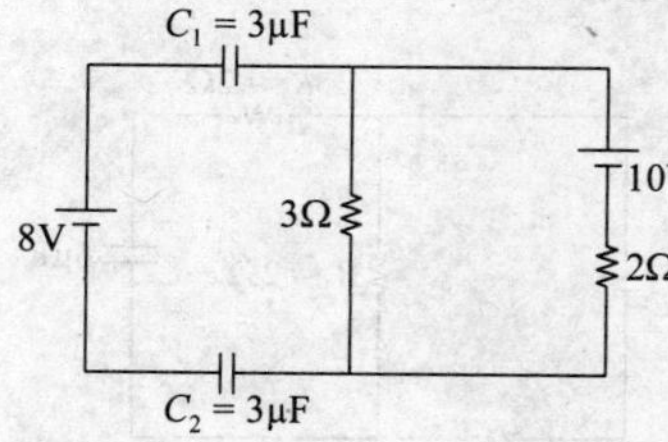

Figure 3.342

(A) 2 μC (B) 3 μC
(C) 4 μC (D) Zero

3-44 If key K_1 is closed in circuit shown in figure-3.343 and galvanometer doesn't give deflection at any time, then value of C is :

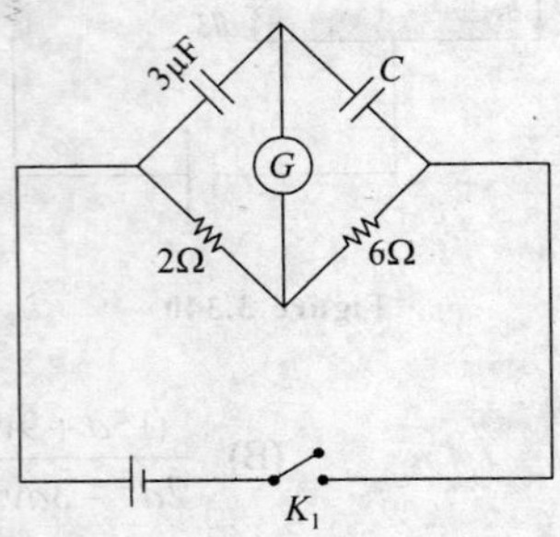

Figure 3.343

(A) 3 μF (B) 9 μF
(C) 4 μF (D) 1 μF

3-45 The circuit shown in figure-3.344 is closed at $t = 0$. Calculate the total amount of heat generated in R_2 during the time capacitor gets fully charged :

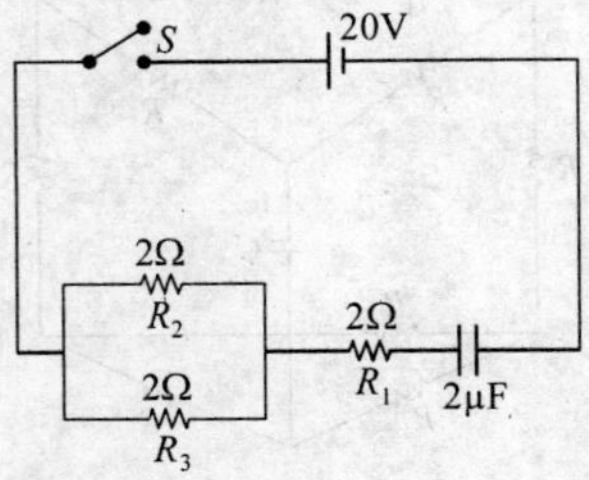

Figure 3.344

(A) $\frac{200}{3}$ μJ (B) $\frac{400}{3}$ μJ
(C) $\frac{800}{3}$ μJ (D) 400 μJ

3-46 In the circuit shown in figure-3.345 if battery is ideal, then time after which current in R_3 becomes $(1/e)$ time that of maximum current through it is :

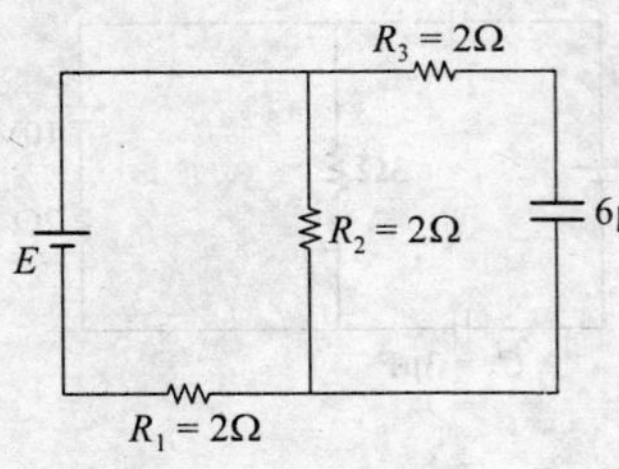

Figure 3.345

(A) 18 μs (B) 12 μs
(C) 6 μs (D) 2 μs

3-47 In the circuit shown in figure-3.346 the capacitor of capacitance C is charged to a potential difference V. The current in the circuit just after the closing of switch S is :

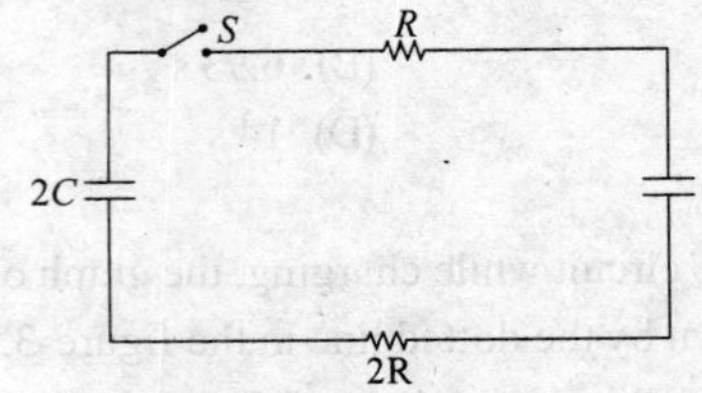

Figure 3.346

(A) $\frac{V}{3R}$ (B) $\frac{3V}{R}$
(C) $\frac{V}{2R}$ (D) Zero

3-48 A capacitor of capacitance 6 μF and initial charge 160 μC is connected with a switch S and resistors as shown in figure-3.347. If switch is closed at $t = 0$, then the current through resistor of 4 Ω at $t = 16$μs is

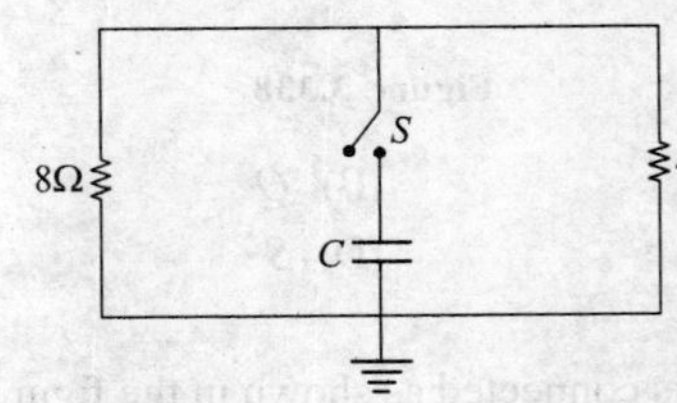

Figure 3.347

(A) $\frac{10}{e}$ A (B) $\frac{20}{3e}$ A
(C) $\frac{10}{3e}$ A (D) Zero

3-49 Two resistances are joined in parallel of which equivalent resistance is 1.2 Ω. One of the resistance wire is broken and the effective resistance becomes 2 Ω. then the resistance of the wire that got broken was :

(A) 3/5 Ω (B) 2 Ω
(C) 6/5 Ω (D) 3 Ω

3-50 A technician has only two resistance coils. By using them singly, in series or in parallel, he is able to obtain the the resistance 3 Ω, 4 Ω, 12 Ω and 16 Ω. The resistance of two coils are :

(A) 6 Ω and 10 Ω (B) 4 Ω and 12 Ω
(C) 7 Ω and 9 Ω (D) 4 Ω and 16 Ω

3-51 A 10 m long wire of resistance 20 Ω is connected in series with battery of EMF 3 V and negligible internal resistance and a resistance of 10 Ω. The potential gradient along the wire is :

(A) 0.02 V/m (B) 0.1 V/m
(C) 0.2 V/m (D) 1.2 V/m

3-52 The potential gradient along the length of a uniform wire is 10 V/m. B and C are two points at 30 cm and 60 cm point on a metre scale fitted along with the wire. The potential difference between B and C will be :

(A) 3V (B) 0.4 V
(C) 7V (D) 4V

3-53 A torch bulb rated as 4.5 W, 1.5 V is connected as shown in fig. the e.m.f. of the cell, needed to make the bulb glow at full intensity is :

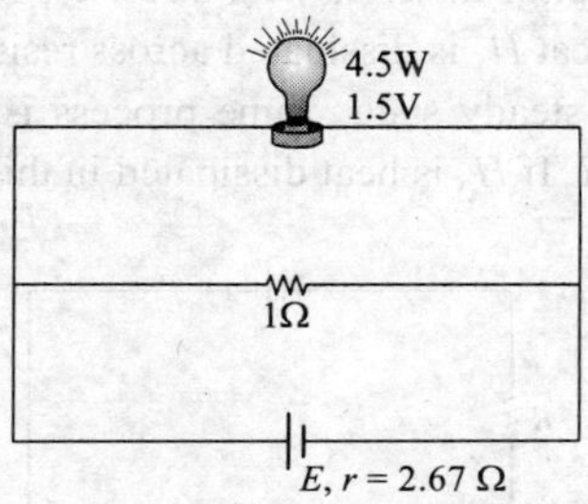

Figure 3.348

(A) 4.5 V (B) 1.5 V
(C) 2.67 V (D) 13.5 V

3-54 In the circuit shown in figure-3.349 when the switch is closed, the initial current through the 1 Ω resistor just after closing the switch is

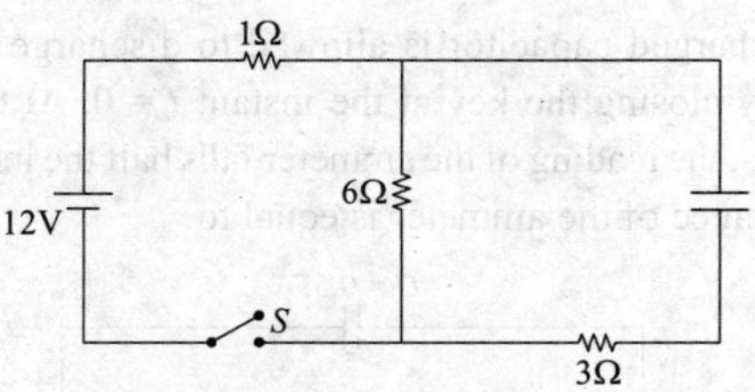

Figure 3.349

(A) 2 A (B) 4 A
(C) 3 A (D) 6 A

3-55 In the circuit shown in figure-3.350, the potential difference across the capacitor is 10 V. Each resistance is of 3 Ω. The cell is ideal. The EMF of the cell is :

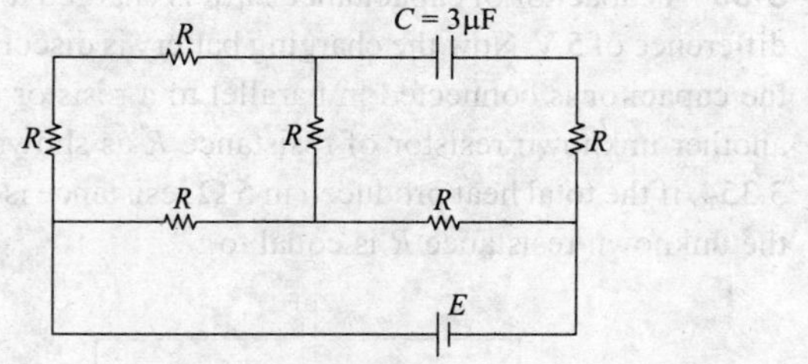

Figure 3.350

(A) 14 V (B) 16 V
(C) 18 V (D) 24 V

3-56 The potential difference $V_A - V_B$ between points A and B for the circuit segment shown in figure-3.351 at the given instant is :

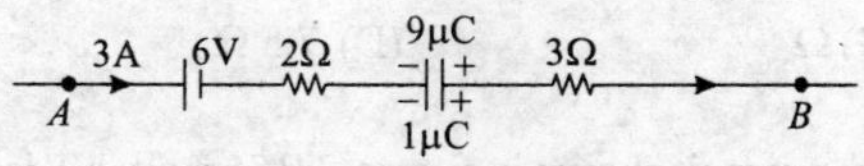

Figure 3.351

(A) 12 V (B) – 12 V
(C) 6V (D) – 6 V

3-57 In the circuit shown in figure-3.352 the capacitors are initially uncharged. The current through resistor PQ just after closing the switch is :

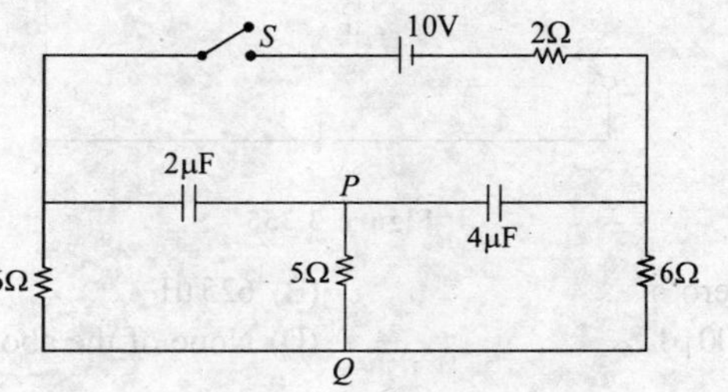

Figure 3.352

(A) 2A from P to Q (B) 2A from Q to P
(C) 6A from P to Q (D) Zero

3-58 For the circuit shown in the figure-3.353, calculate the charge on capacitor in steady state ?

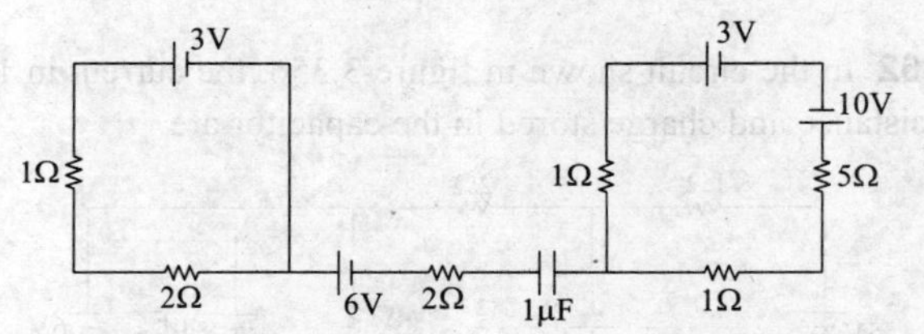

Figure 3.353

(A) 4 μC (B) 6 μC
(C) 1 μC (D) Zero

3-59 A capacitor of capacitance 2 μF is charged to a potential difference of 5 V. Now the charging battery is disconnected and the capacitor is connected in parallel to a resistor of 5 Ω and another unknown resistor of resistance R as shown in figure-3.354. if the total heat produced in 5 Ω resistance is 10 μJ, then the unknown resistance R is equal to :

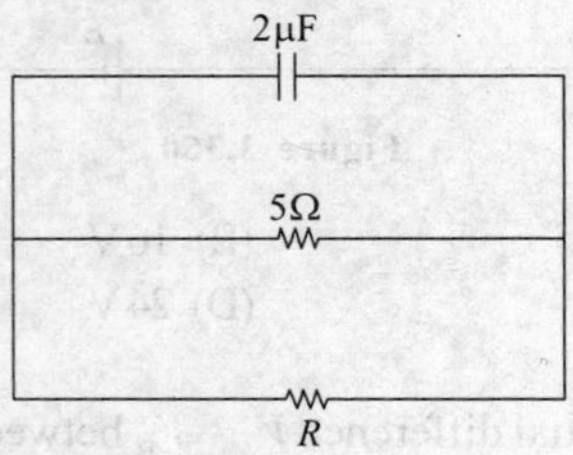

Figure 3.354

(A) 10 Ω (B) 15 Ω
(C) (10/3) Ω (D) 7.5 Ω

3-60 In the circuit shown in figure-3.355 switch S is thrown at position-1 at $t = 0$. When the current in the resistor is 1 A switch is then shifted to position-2. The total heat generated in the circuit after switch is shifted to position-2 is

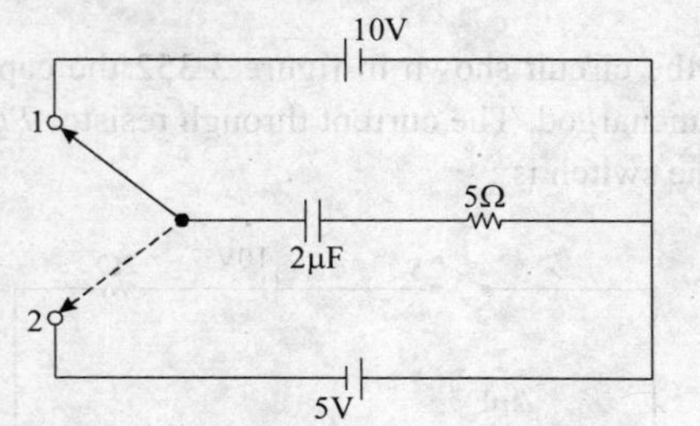

Figure 3.355

(A) Zero (B) 625 μJ
(C) 100 μJ (D) None of the above

3-61 Consider a capacitor charging circuit. Let Q_1 be the charge given to the capacitor in time interval of 20 ms and Q_2 be the charge given in the next time interval of 20 ms. Let 10 μC charge be deposited in a time interval t_1 and the next 10 μC charge is deposited in the next time interval t_2. Then :
(A) $Q_1 > Q_2, t_1 > t_2$ (B) $Q_1 > Q_2, t_1 < t_2$
(C) $Q_1 < Q_2, t_1 > t_2$ (D) $Q_1 < Q_2, t_1 < t_2$

3-62 In the circuit shown in figure-3.356, the current in 1 Ω resistance and charge stored in the capacitor are

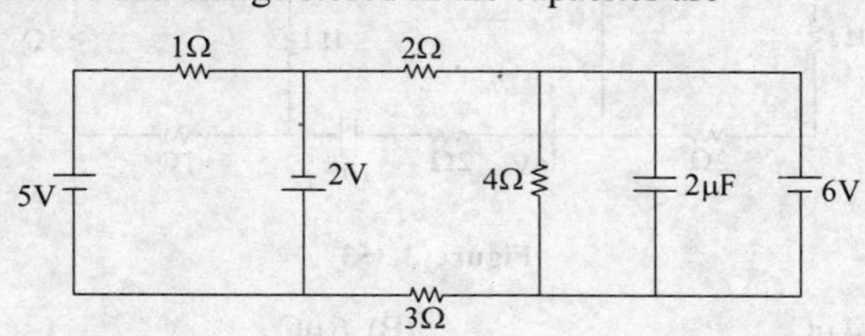

Figure 3.356

(A) 4 A, 6 μC (B) 7 A, 12 μC
(C) 4 A, 12 μC (D) 7 A, 6 μC

3-63 Two cells, two resistors and two capacitors are connected as shown in figure-3.357. The charge on 2μF capacitor is :

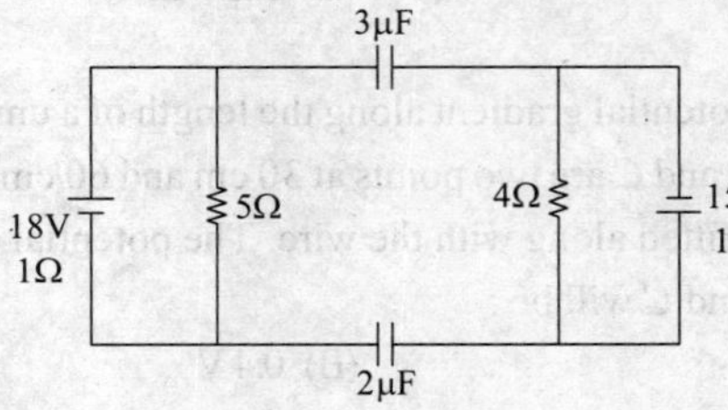

Figure 3.357

(A) 30 μC (B) 20 μC
(C) 25 μC (D) 48 μC

3-64 A capacitor C_1 is charged to a potential V and connected to another capacitor in series with a resistor R as shown. It is observed that heat H_1 is dissipated across resistance R, till the circuit reaches steady state. Same process is repeated using resistance of $2R$. If H_2 is heat dissipated in this case then,

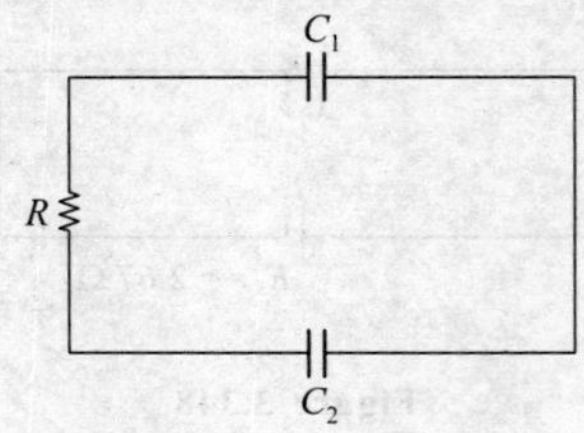

Figure 3.358

(A) $\frac{H_2}{H_1} = 1$ (B) $\frac{H_2}{H_1} = 4$

(C) $\frac{H_2}{H_1} = \frac{1}{4}$ (D) $\frac{H_2}{H_1} = 2$

3-65 A charged capacitor is allowed to discharge through a resistor by closing the key at the instant $t = 0$. At the instant $t = \ln(4)$ μs, the reading of the ammeter falls half the initial value. The resistance of the ammeter is equal to

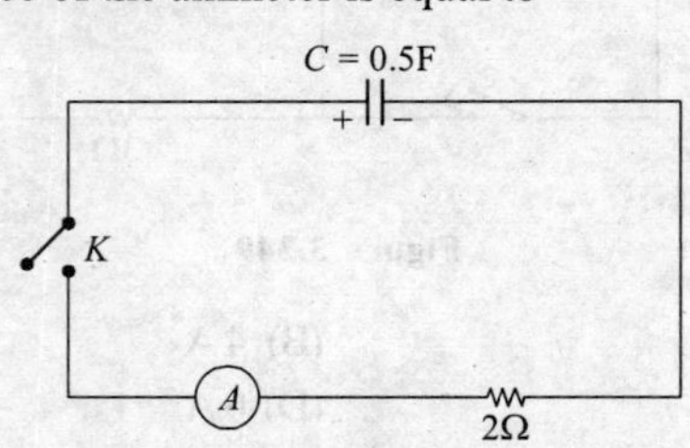

Figure 3.359

(A) 0.5 Ω (B) 1 Ω
(C) 2 Ω (D) 4 Ω

* * * * *

Advance MCQs with One or More Options Correct

3-1 In the circuit shown, which of the following statement(s) is/are correct?

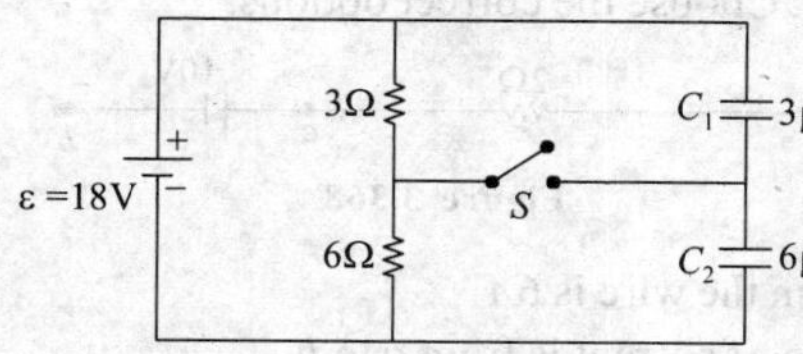

Figure 3.360

(A) When S is open, charge on C_1 is 36 μC

(B) When S is open, charge on C_2 is 36 μC

(C) When S is closed, the charges on C_1 and C_2 do not change

(D) When S is closed, charges on both C_1 and C_2 will change

3-2 In the circuit shown, capacitor is initially uncharged till the switch is turned on at time $t = 0$. Then

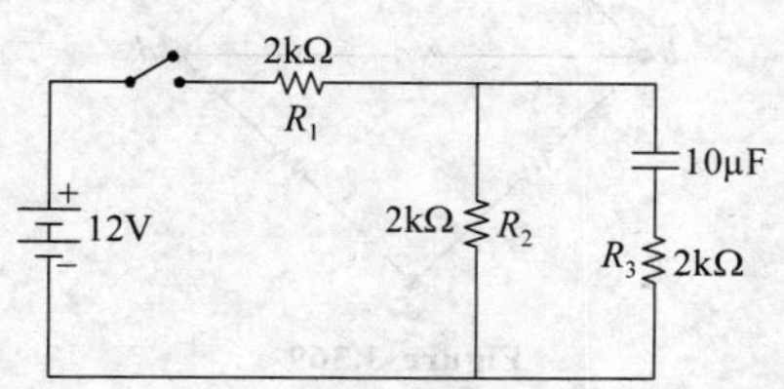

Figure 3.361

(A) at $t = 0$, current supplied by battery is 4 mA

(B) at $t = 0$, current in R_3 is 2 mA

(C) in the steady state current supplied by battery is 3 mA

(D) in the steady state current in R_3 is zero

3-3 The electric field strength in the capacitor shown in circuit below in steady state is $E = 50$ V/cm. The distance between the plates of the capacitor C is 0.5mm, square plates are of area 100 cm^2, the resistance $R = 5\ \Omega$ and the internal resistance of battery is $r = 0.1\ \Omega$.

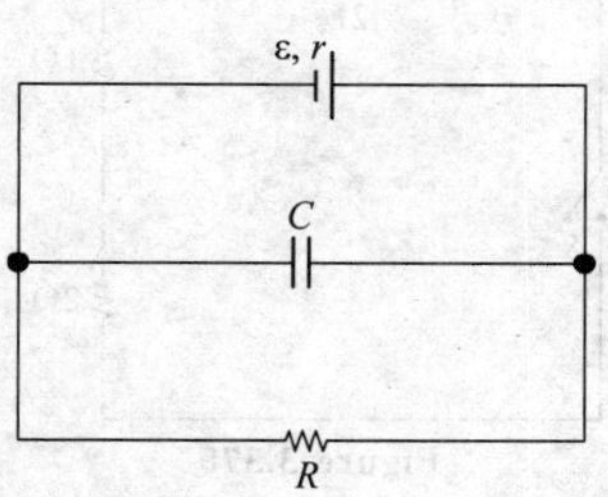

Figure 3.362

(A) the emf of the battery is 2.55 V

(B) the attractive force between the plates is 2.2×10^{-4} N (approx)

(C) the charge on the plates is 42.25×10^{-10} C

(D) the current through the battery in steady state is 0.5 A

3-4 Two heater designed for the same voltage V have different power ratings. When connected individually across a source of voltage V, they produce H amount of heat each in time t_1 and t_2 respectively. When used together across the same source, they produce H amount of heat in time t :

(A) If they are in series, $t = t_1 + t_2$

(B) If they are in series, $t = 2(t_1 + t_2)$

(C) If they are in parallel, $t = \dfrac{t_1 t_2}{(t_1 + t_2)}$

(D) If they are in paralle, $t = \dfrac{t_1 t_2}{2(t_1 + t_2)}$

3-5 Two cells of emf $E_1 = 6$ V and $E_2 = 5$ V are joined in parallel with same polarity on same side, without any external load. if their internal resistances are $r_1 = 2\ \Omega$ and $r_2 = 3\ \Omega$ respectively, then

(A) Terminal potential difference across any cell is less then 5 V

(B) Terminal potential difference across any cell is 5.6 V

(C) Current through the cells is 0.2A

(D) Current through the cells is zero if $E_1 = E_2$

3-6 Three ammeters A, B and C of resistances R_A, R_B and R_C respectively are joined as shown. When some potential difference is applied across the terminals T_1 and T_2 their readings are I_A, I_B and I_C respectively. Then :

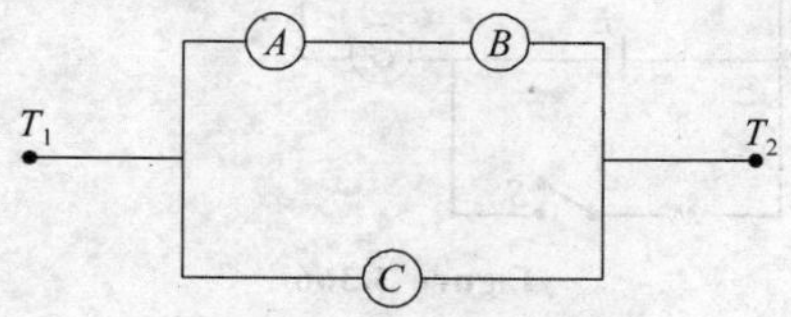

Figure 3.363

(A) $I_A = I_B$

(B) $I_A R_A + I_B R_B = I_C R_C$

(C) $\dfrac{I_A}{I_C} = \dfrac{R_C}{R_A}$

(D) $\dfrac{I_B}{I_C} = \dfrac{R_C}{R_A + R_B}$

3-7 Three voltmeters all having different resistances, are joined as shown in figure-3.364. When some potential difference is applied across A and B, their radings are V_1, V_2 and V_3. Then

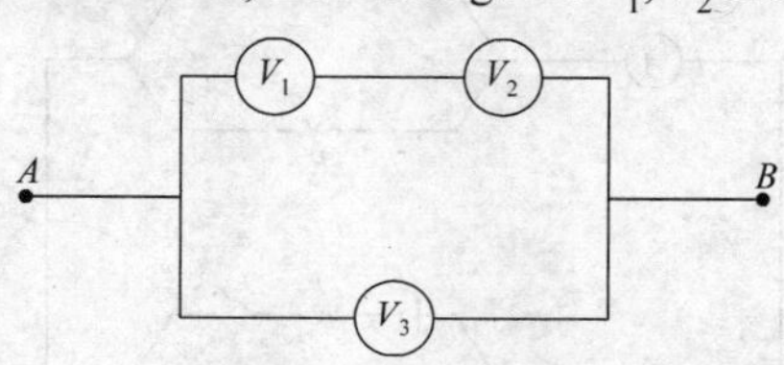

Figure 3.364

(A) $V_1 = V_2$

(B) $V_1 \neq V_2$

(C) $V_1 + V_2 = V_3$

(D) $V_1 + V_2 > V_3$

3-8 Two conductors made of the same material have length L and $2L$ but have equal resistances. The two are connected in series in a circuit in which current is flowing. Which of the following is/are correct?

(A) The potential difference across the two conductors is the same

(B) The drift speed is larger in the conductor of length L

(C) The electric field in the first conductor is twice that in the second

(D) The electric field in the second conductor is twice that in the first

3-9 In the part of circuit shown in figure-3.365

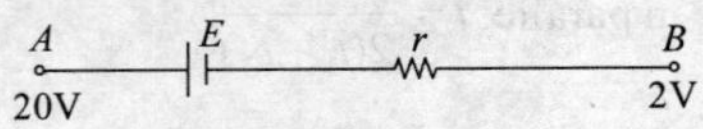

Figure 3.365

(A) Current will flow from A to B

(B) Current may flow A to B

(C) Current may flow from B to A

(D) The direction of current will depend on E

3-10 In the potentiometer experiment shown in figure-3.366, the null point length is l. Choose the correct options given below

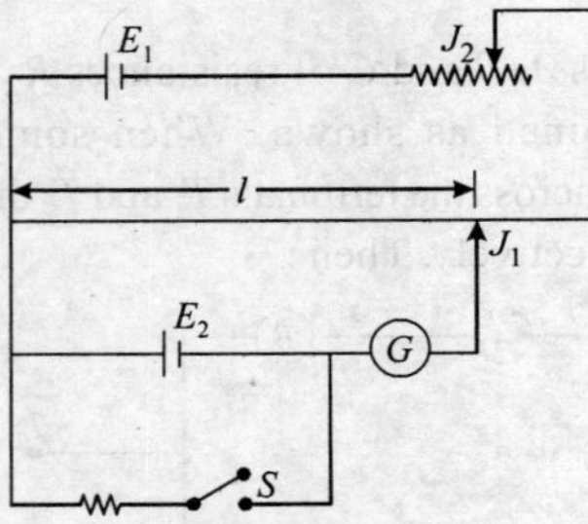

Figure 3.366

(A) If jokey J_2 is shifted towards right, l will increase

(B) if value of E_1 is increased, l is decreased

(C) If value of E_2 is increased, l is increased

(D) If switch S is closed, l will decrease

3-11 In the circuit shown in figure-3.367, reading of ammeter will

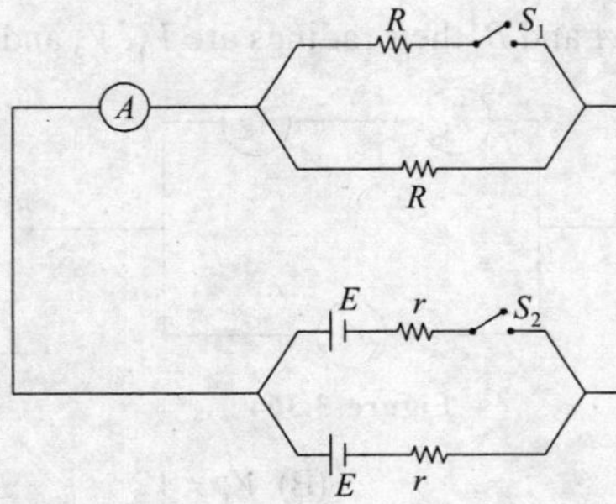

Figure 3.367

(A) Increase if S_1 is closed (B) Decrease if S_1 is closed

(C) Increases if S_2 is closed (D) Decrease if S_2 is closed

3-12 In the circuit shown in figure-3.368 it is given that $V_b - V_a = 2$ V. Choose the correct options.

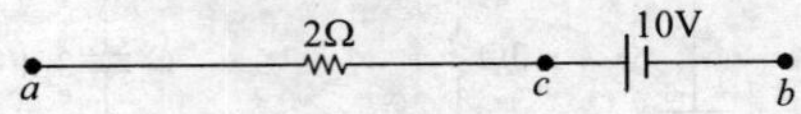

Figure 3.368

(A) Current in the wire is $6A$

(B) Direction of current is from a to b

(C) $V_a - V_c = 12$ volt

(D) $V_c - V_a = 12$ volt

3-13 Each resistance of the network shown in figure-3.369 is r. Net resistance between terminals

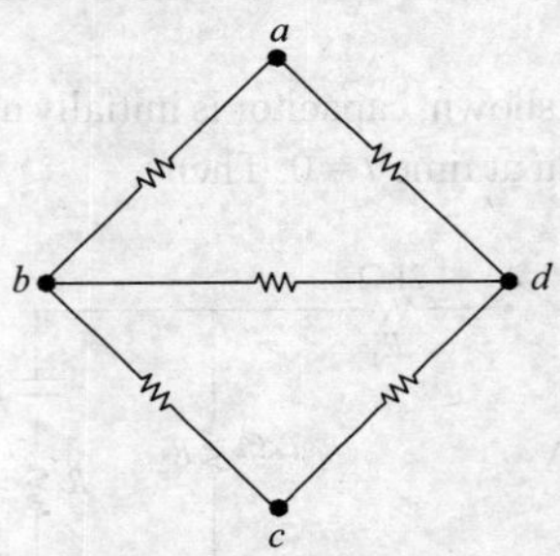

Figure 3.369

(A) a and b is $\frac{7}{3}r$ (B) a and c is r

(C) b and d is r (D) b and d is $\frac{r}{2}$

3-14 A capacitor of 2 F (theoretical value) capacitance is charged by a battery of 6 V. The charging battery is disconnected and circuit is made as shown. If the switch is closed at $t = 0$. Which of the following options is/are correct :

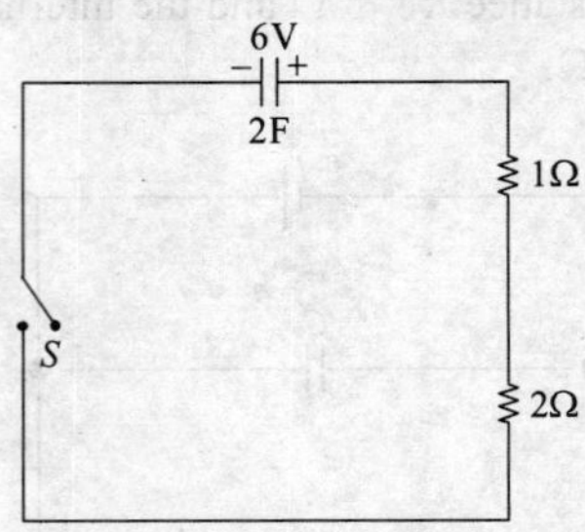

Figure 3.370

(A) At time $t = 0$ current in the circuit is 2 A

(B) At time $t = 6\ \ln(2)$ second potential difference across capacitor is 3V

(C) At time $t = 6\ \ln(2)$ second, potential difference across 1 Ω resistance is 1 V

(D) At time $t = 6\ \ln(2)$ second potential difference across 2 Ω resistance is 2 V

3-15 In the circuit shown in the figure-3.371, switch S is closed at time $t = 0$. Select the correct statements.

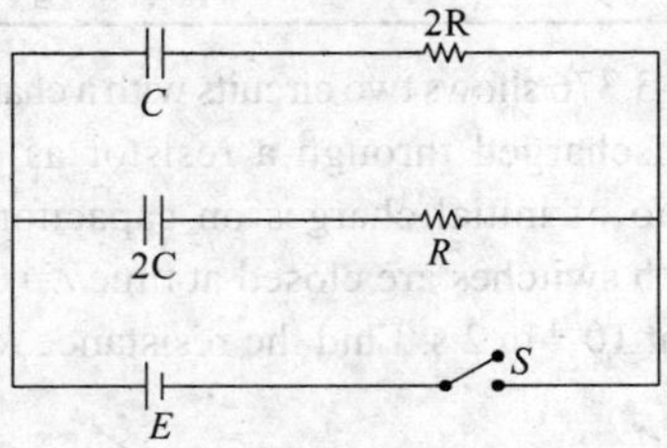

Figure 3.371

(A) Rate of increase of charge is same in both the capacitors

(B) Ratio of charge stored in capacitors C and $2C$ at any time t would be 1 : 2

(C) Time constants of both the capacitors are equal

(D) Steady state charge in capacitors C and $2C$ are in the ratio of 1 : 2

3-16 A capacitor C_1 of capacitance 1 μF and a capacitor C_2 of capacitance 2 μF are separately charged by a common battery for a long time. The two capacitors are then separately discharged through equal resistors. Both the discharge circuits are connected at $t = 0$.

(A) The current in each of the two discharging circuits is zero at $t = 0$.

(B) The currents in the two discharging circuits at $t = 0$ are equal but not zero.

(C) The current in the two discharging circuits at $t = 0$ are unequal.

(D) C_1 of losses 50% of its initial charge sooner than C_2 loses 50% of its initial charge.

3-17 An electrical circuit is shown in figure-3.372. The resistance of each voltmeter is infinite and each ammeter is 100 Ω. The charge on the capacitor of 100 μF in steady sate is 4 mC. Choose which of the following statements is/are correct regarding the given circuit :

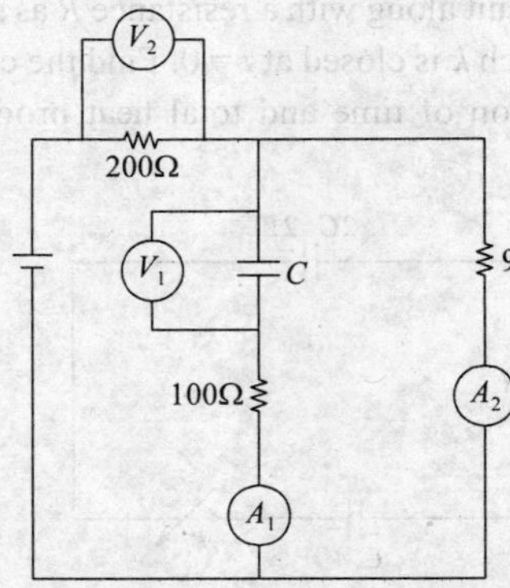

Figure 3.372

(A) Reading of voltmeter V_2 is 16 V

(B) Reading of ammeter A_1 is zero and A_2 is 1/25A

(C) Reading of voltmeter V_1 is 40 V

(D) *EMF* of the ideal cell is 48 V

* * * * *

Unsolved Numerical Problems for Preparation of NSEP, INPhO & IPhO

***For detailed preparation of INPhO and IPhO students can refer advance study material on* www.physicsgalaxy.com**

3-1 Two parallel plate capacitor of capacitance $2C$ and C are charged to the potentials $2V$ and V respectively and are connected in a circuit along with a resistance R as shown in the diagram. The switch k is closed at $t = 0$. Find the current in the circuit as a function of time and total heat produced in the circuit.

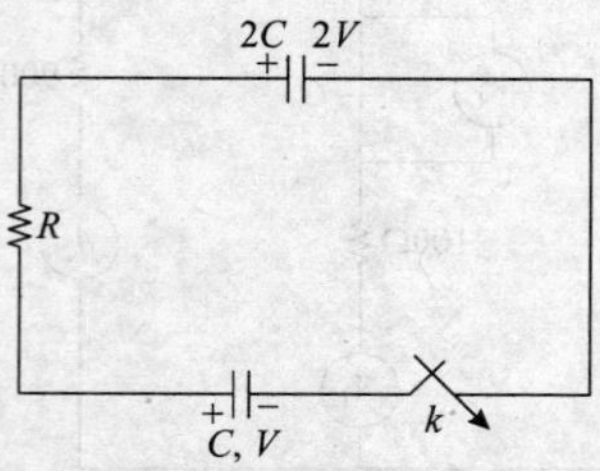

Figure 3.373

Ans. [$i = \frac{V}{R}e^{-\frac{et}{2RC}}$, $\frac{1}{3}CV^2$]

3-2 For the given circuit shown in figure-3.374 in the steady state condition charge on the capacitor is 16 μC. If the battery is removed and the junctions A and C are shorted. Find the time during which charge on the capacitor becomes 4 μC and the EMF of battery.

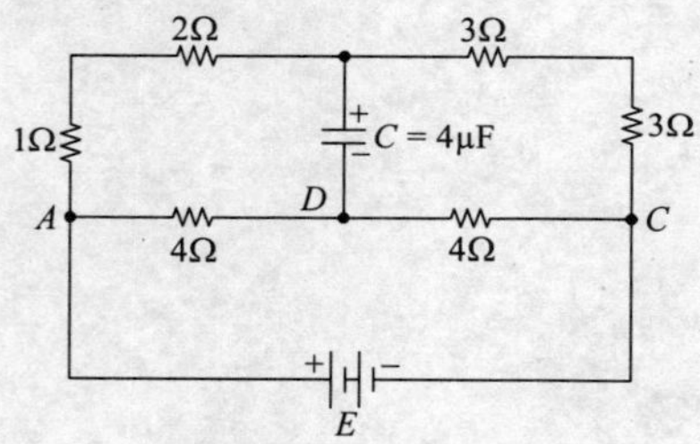

Figure 3.374

Ans. [32ln(2)μs, 24 V]

3-3 A capacitor of capacitance 5 μF is connected to a source of constant EMF of 200 V for a long time as shown in figure-3.375, then the switch was shifted to contact 1 from contact 2. Calculate the amount of heat generated in the 500 Ω resistance.

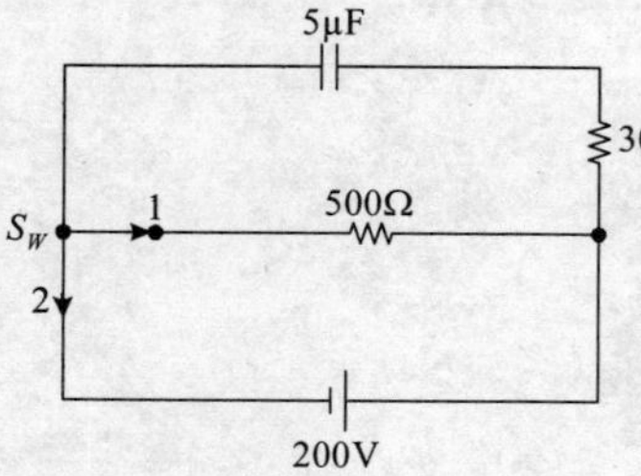

Figure 3.375

Ans. [0.0625 J]

3-4 The figure-3.376 shows two circuits with a charged capacitor that is to be discharged through a resistor as shown in the figure. The ratio of initial charges on capacitors is given as $q_2/q_1 = 2$. If both switches are closed at time $t = 0$, the charges become equal at 10^{-4} ln 2 s. Find the resistance R.

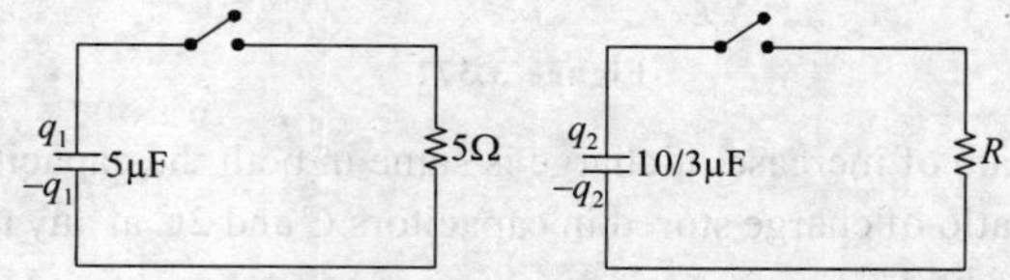

Figure 3.376

Ans. [6Ω]

3-5 In the circuit shown in figure-3.377, $E = 5$ V, $r = 1$ Ω, $R_2 = 4$ Ω, $R_3 = 3$ Ω, and $C = 3$ μF. Find the charge on the plates of capaictor A.

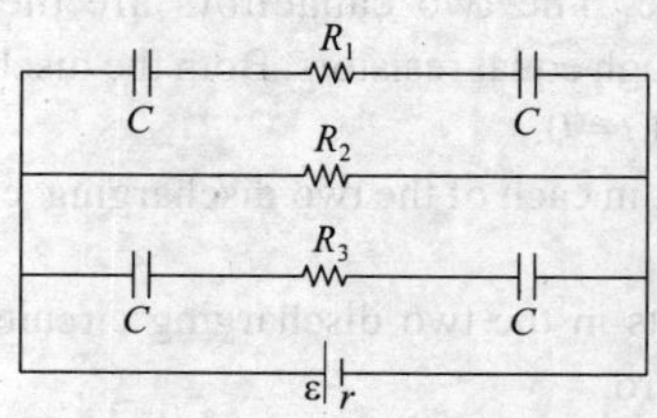

Figure 3.377

Ans. [6 μC]

3-6 A circuit shown in the figure-3.378 has resistances given as $R_1 = 20$ Ω and $R_2 = 30$ Ω. At what value of resistance R_x will the thermal power generated in it be practically independent of small variations of that resistance ? The voltage between points A and B is supposed to be constant in this case.

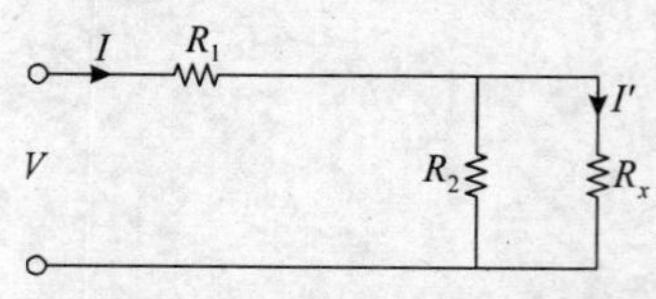

Figure 3.378

Ans. [12 Ω]

3-7 A capacitor of capacitance $C = 500$ μF is connected to a source of constant e.m.f. $E = 200$ V. Then the switch Sw was thrown over from contact 1 to contact 2. Find the amount of heat generated in a resistance $R_1 = 500$ Ω if $R_2 = 330$ Ω.

Ans. [60 mJ]

3-8 The electrodes of a capacitor of capacitance $C = 2.00$ μF carry opposite charges $q_0 = 1.00$ mC. Then the electrodes are interconnected through a resistance $R = 5.0\ M\Omega$. Find :

(a) the charge flowing through that resistance during a time interval $t' = 2$ s.

(b) the amount of heat generated in the resistance during the same interval.

Ans. [(a) 0.18 μC (b) 82 mJ]

3-9 In the circuit below, the capacitance of each capacitor is equal to C and the resistance R. One of the capacitors was connected to a voltage V_0 and then at the moment $t = 0$ was shorted by means of a switch S Find :

(a) Current in the circuit as a function of time.

(b) The amount of heat generated in the circuit.

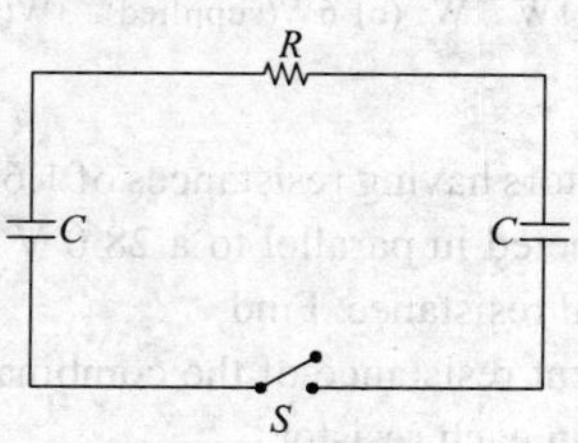

Figure 3.379

Ans. [(a) $\frac{V_0}{R}e^{-2t/RC}$, (b) $\frac{1}{4}CV_0^2$]

3-10 A coil of radius 25 cm madeup of a thin copper wire of length 500 m rotates with an angular velocity 300 rad/s about its axis. The coil is connected to a ballistic galvanometer by means of sliding contacts. The total resistance of the circuit is equal to 21 Ω. Find the specific charge of current carriers in copper if a sudden stopage of coil makes a charge 10 nC flow through the galvanometer.

Ans. [1.8×10^{11} C/kg]

3-11 Ten cells each of emf 1V and internal resistance 1Ω are connected in series. In this arrangement polarity of two cells is reversed and the system is connected to an external resistance of 2Ω. Find the current in the circuit.

Ans. [0.5A]

3-12 It is desired to make a 20.0 Ω coil of wire which has a zero thermal coefficient of resistance. To do this, a carbn resistor of resistance R_1 is placed in series with an iron resistor of resistance R_2. The proportions of iron and carbon are so chosen that $R_1 + R_2 = 20.00\ \Omega$ for all temperatures near 20°C. How large are R_1 and R_2? The temperature coefficient of resistances for carbon and iorn are $\alpha_C = -0.5 \times 10^{-3}\ K^{-1}$ and $\alpha_{Fe} = 5.0 \times 10^{-3}\ K^{-1}$.

Ans. [18.18 Ω, 1.82 Ω]

3-13 Calculate the value of current supplied by the battery in the circuit shown in figure-3.380.

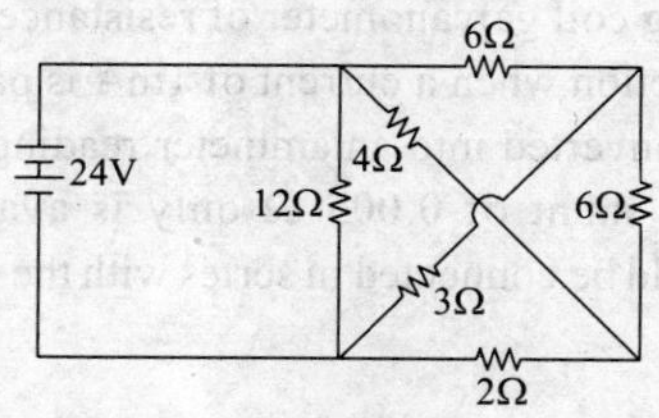

Figure 3.380

Ans. [$\frac{13}{3}$ A]

3-14 In the circuit shown in figure-3.381, battery EMFs are given as $E_1 = 12$ V and $E_2 = 8$ V.

(a) What is the direction of the current in the resistor?

(b) Which battery is doing positive work?

(c) Which point, A or B, is at the higher potential?

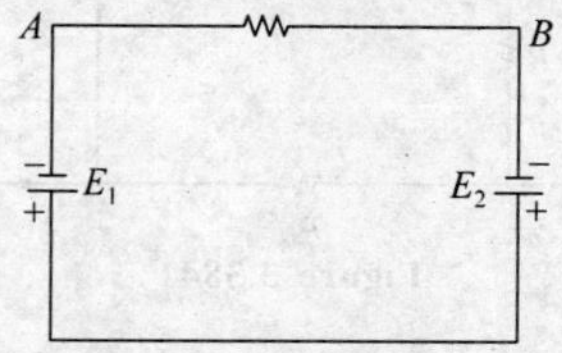

Figure 3.381

Ans. [(a) Anticlockwise; (b) E_1; (c) Point B]

3-15 Calculate the resistance r if in the part of a circuit shown in figure-3.382 an ammeter shows a current of 5A and the voltmeter reading is 100 V. The internal resistance of the voltmeter is 2.5 kΩ.

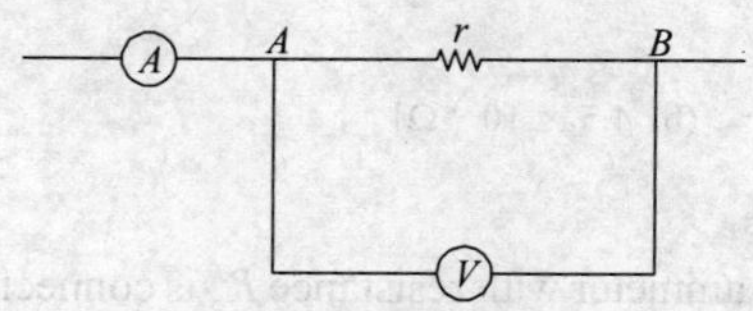

Figure 3.382

Ans [20.16Ω]

3-16 Resistances R_1 and R_2, each 60 Ω, are connected in series as shown in figure-3.383. The potential difference between points A and B is 120 V. Find the reading of voltmeter connected between points C and D if its resistance is 120 Ω.

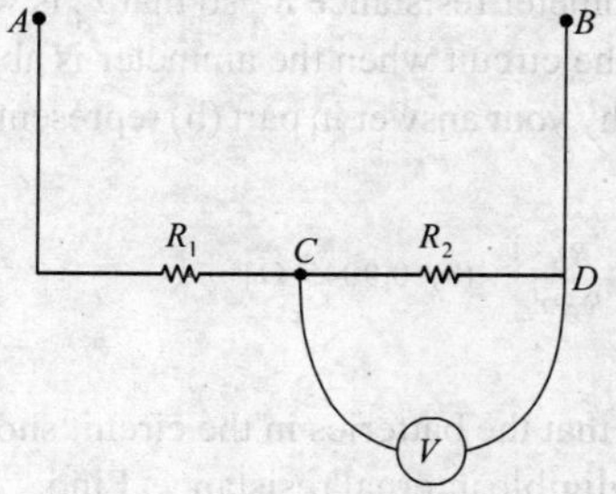

Figure 3.383

Ans. [48V]

3-17 A moving coil galvanometer of resistance 20 Ω gives a full scale deflection when a current of 1mA is passed through it. It is to be converted into an ammeter reading 20 A on full scale. But the shunt of 0.005 Ω only is available. What resistance should be connected in series with the galvanometer coil?

Ans. [79.995 Ω]

3-18 The resistance R_G of the coil of a pivoted-coil galvanometer is 9.36 Ω and a current of 0.0224 A causes it to deflected full scale. We want to convert this galvanometer to an ammeter reading 20.0 A full scale. The only shunt available has a resistance of 0.0250 Ω. What resistance R must be connected in series with the coil of galvanometer ?

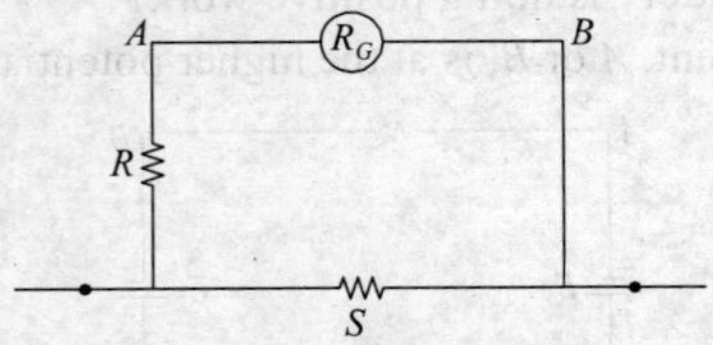

Figure 3.384

Ans. [12.9 Ω]

3-19 (a) A voltmeter with resistance R_V is connected across the terminals of a battery of emf E and internal resistance r. Find the potential difference measured by the voltmeter.
(b) If $E = 7.50$ V and $r = 0.45$ Ω, find the minimum value of the voltmeter resistance R_V so that the voltmeter reading is within 1.0% of the EMF of the battery.

Ans. [(a) $\frac{ER_V}{R_V + r}$; (b) 4.5×10^{-3} Ω]

3-20 (a) An ammeter with resistance R_A is connected in series with a resistor R and a battery of emf ε and internal resistance r. The current measured by the ammeter is I_A. Find the current through the circuit if the ammeter is removed so that the battery and the resistor form a complete circuit. Express your answer in terms of I_A, r, R_A and R. The more "ideal" the ammeter, the smaller the difference between this current and the current I_A.
(b) If $R = 3.80$ Ω, ξ = 7.50 V and $r = 0.45$ Ω, find the maximum value of the ammeter resistance R_A so that I_A is within 99% of the current in the circuit when the ammeter is absent.
(c) Explain why your answer in part (b) represents a maximum value.

Ans. [(a) $I_A\left[1+\frac{R_A}{R+r}\right]$; (b) 0.0045 Ω]

3-21 Assume that the batteries in the circuit shown in figure-3.385 have negligible internal resistance. Find
(a) The current in the circuit.
(b) The power dissipated in each resistor and
(c) The power of each battery, stating whether energy is supplied by or absorbed by it.

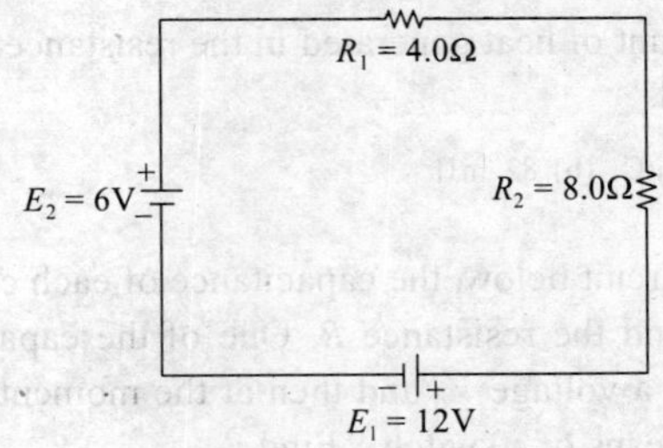

Figure 3.385

Ans. [(a) $\frac{1}{2}$A ; (b) 1W, 2W; (c) 6W(supplied), 3W(absorbed)]

3-22 Three resistors having resistances of 1.60 Ω, 2.40 Ω and 4.80 Ω are connected in parallel to a 28.0 V battery that has negligible internal resistance. Find
(a) The equivalent resistance of the combination
(b) The current in each resistor
(c) The total current through the battery
(d) The voltage across each resistor
(e) The power dissipated in each resistor
(f) Which resistor dissipates the maximum power the one with the greatest resistance or the least resistance ? Explain why this should be.

Ans. [(a) 0.80 Ω, (b) 1.60 Ω resistor 17.5A, 2.40 Ω resistor 11.7A, 4.80 Ω resistor 5.8A, (c) 35.0 A, (d) 28.0V for each, (e) 1.60 Ω resistor 490 W, 2.40 Ω resistor 327 W, 4.80 Ω resistor 163 W, (f) least resistance]

3-23 Draw the circuit for experimental verification of Ohm's law using a source of variable DC voltage, a main resistance of 100Ω, two galvanometer and two resistance of values 10^6Ω and 10^{-3}Ω respectively. Clearly show the positions of the voltmeter and the ammeter.

Ans. [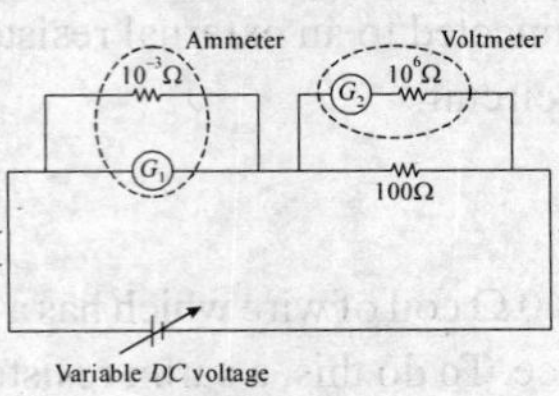

]

3-24 A galvanometer (coil resistance 99Ω) is converted into an ammeter using a shunt of 1Ω and connected as shown in figure-3.386(a). The ammeter reads 3A. The same galvanometer is converted into a voltmeter by connecting a resistance of 101Ω in series. This voltmeter is connected as shown in figure-3.386(b). its reading is found to be 4/5 of the full scale reading. Find
(a) Internal resistance r of the cell

(b) Range of the ammeter and voltmeter

(c) Full sacle deflection current of the galvanometer

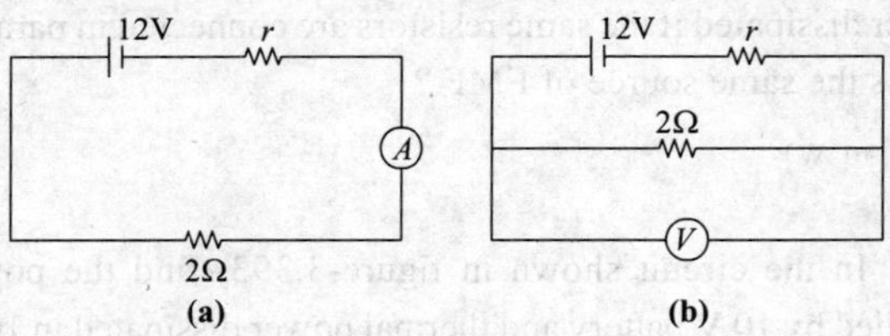

Figure 3.386

Ans. [(a) 1.01 Ω; (b) 5 A, 9.95 V; (c) 0.05 A]

3-25 (a) Two bulbs rated at 25W, 110V of 100W, 110V are connected in series to 220V electric supply. Perform the necessary calculations to find out which of the two bulbs, if any, will fuse. (b) What would happen if the two bulbs were connected in parallel to the same supply.

Ans. [(a) First bulb will fuse, (b) Both will fuse]

3-26 figure-3.387 illustrates a potentiometer circuit by means of which we can vary a voltage V applied to a certain device possessing a resistance R. The potentiometer has a length l and a resistance R_0. A voltage V_0 is applied to its terminals. Find the voltage V which is fed to the device as a function of distance x. Analyses separately the case $R >> R_0$.

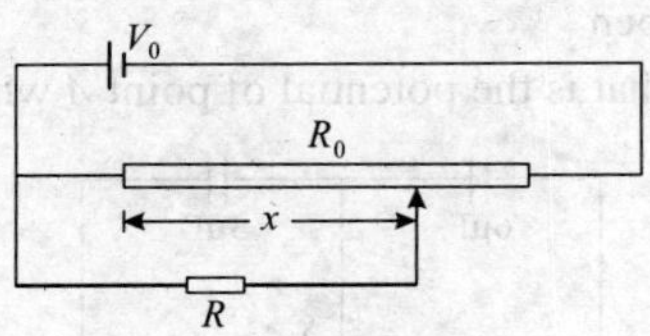

Figure 3.387

Ans. $\left[\dfrac{V_0 R x}{Rl + R_0 x\left(1-\dfrac{x}{l}\right)},\ V_0\dfrac{x}{l}\right]$

3-27 A copper coil has a resistance of 20 Ω at 0°C and a resistance of 26.4 Ω at 80°C. Find out the temperature coefficient of resistance of copper.

Ans. [4×10^{-3} °C^{-1}]

3-28 A conducting wire of resistance 120 Ω at 20°C is connected in a circuit. Due to current flow in it, its resistance increases to 240 Ω. Find the final temperature of wire. given that temperature coefficient of resistance is 2×10^{-4} °C^{-1}.

Ans. [5020°C]

3-29 A galvanometer has coil resistance of 99 Ω with its full deflection current 0.01 A. Find the value of shunt resistance required to convert it into an ammeter of range 0.1 A.

Ans. [11 Ω]

3-30 A galvanometer has coil resistance 30 Ω and full deflection current of 2 mA. What resistance is needed to convert it into a voltmeter of 0.2 V range.

Ans. [70 Ω]

3-31 In the circuit shown in figure-3.388, the voltmeter is having a resistance 4000 Ω. Find the percentage error in reading of this voltmeter.

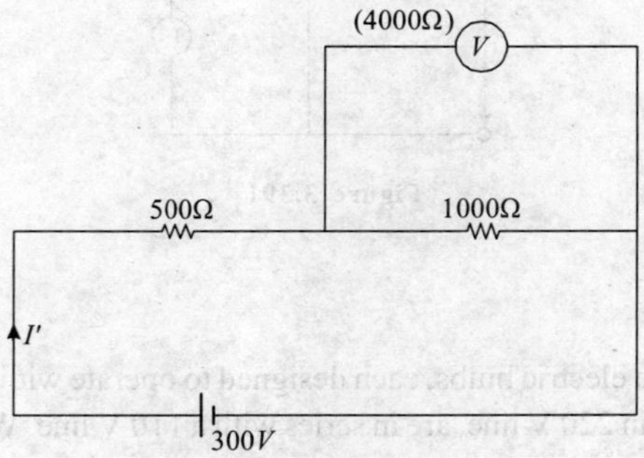

Figure 3.388

Ans. [7.69%]

3-32 In the circuit shown in figure-3.389, each ammeter has coil resistance 2 Ω, find reading of the two ammeters.

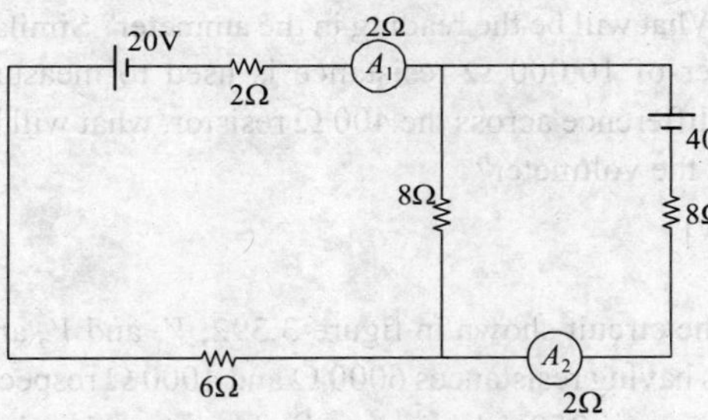

Figure 3.389

Ans. [2.13A, 2.05A]

3-33 In the circuit shown in figure-3.390, the voltmeter reads 30 V when it is connected across 400 Ω resistance. Calculate what the same voltmeter will read when it is connected across the 300 Ω resistance.

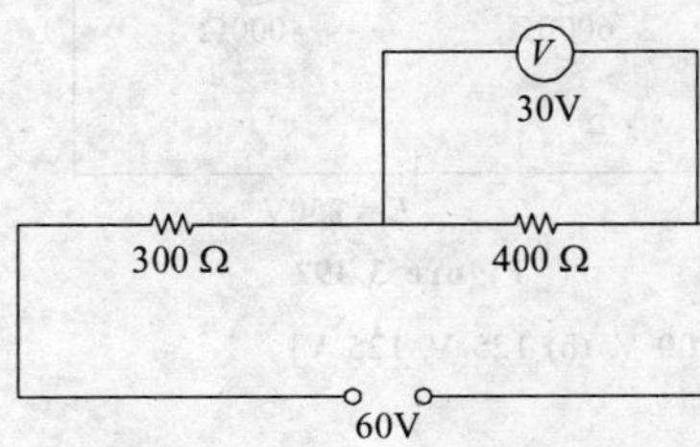

Figure 3.390

Ans. [22.5 V]

3-34 A potential difference of 220 V is maintained across a 12000 Ω rheostat as shown in figure-3.391. The voltmeter V has a resistance of 6000 Ω and point C is at one-fourth of the distance from a to b. What is the reading of voltmeter ?

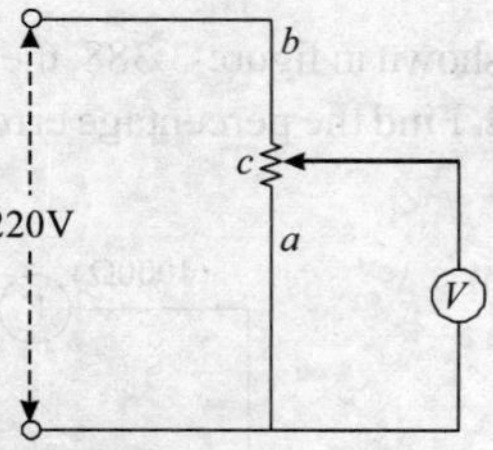

Figure 3.391

Ans. [40 V]

3-35 Two electric bulbs, each designed to operate with a power of 500 W in 220 V line, are in series with a 110 V line. What will be the power generated by each bulb?

Ans. [31.25 W]

3-36 The resistors, 400 Ω and 800 Ω are connected in series with a 6 volt battery. It is desired to measure the current in the circuit. An ammeter of 10 ohms resistance is used for this purpose. What will be the reading in the ammeter? Similarly, if a voltmeter of 10,000 Ω resistance is used to measure the potential difference across the 400 Ω resistor, what will be the reading in the voltmeter?

Ans. [1.96V]

3-37 In the circuit shown in figure-3.392, V_1 and V_2 are two voltmeters having resistances 6000 Ω and 4000 Ω respectively EMFof battery is 250V, having negligible internal resistance. Two resistances R_1 and R_2 are 4000 Ω and 6000 Ω respectively. Find the reading of the voltamter V_1 and V_2 when

(a) Switch S is open

(b) Switch S is closed

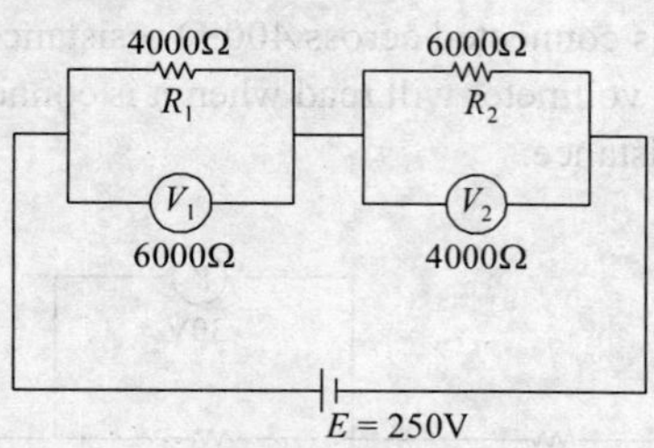

Figure 3.392

Ans. [(a) 150 V, 100 V, (b) 125 V, 125 V]

3-38 If a copper wire is stretched to make it 0.1% longer, what is the percentage change in its resistance?

Ans. [0.2%]

3-39 Three equal resistors connected in series across a source of EMF together dissipate 10 W of power. What would be the power dissipated if the same resistors are connected in parallel across the same source of EMF ?

Ans. [90 W]

3-40 In the circuit shown in figure-3.393, find the power supplied by 10 V battery and thermal power dissipated in 10 Ω resistance.

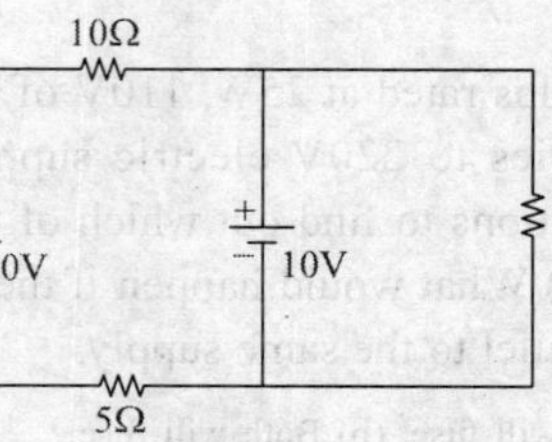

Figure 3.392

Ans. [40 W, 40 W]

3-41 Calculate the steady state charge on each capacitor in the circuits shown in figure-3.394 for the below given cases

(a) Switch S closed and

(b) Switch S open

(c) In figure what is the potential of point A when S is open?

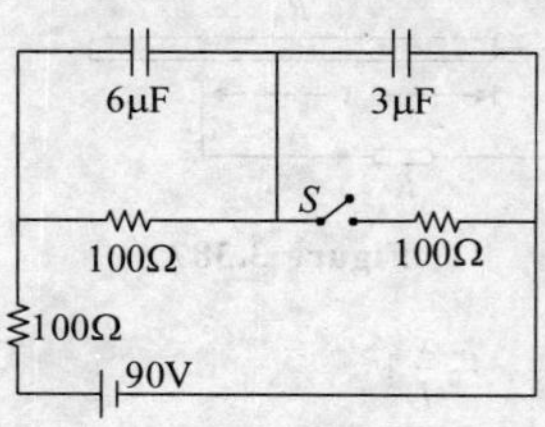

Figure 3.394

Ans. [(a) 180 μC, 90 μC (b) 0, 270 μC]

3-42 Calculate the potential of point A in the circuits shown in figure-3.395 in steady state.

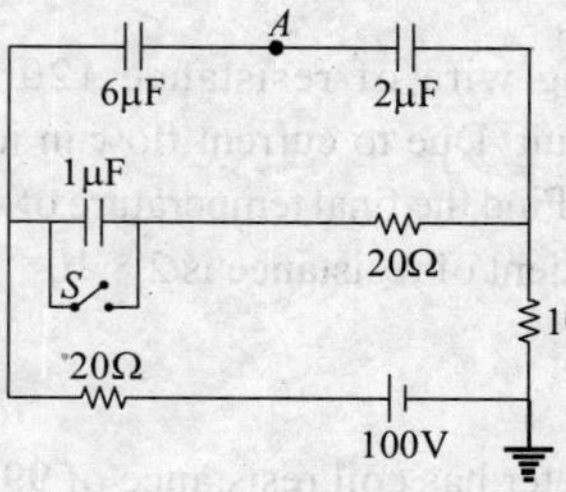

Figure 3.395

Ans. [75 V]

3-43 In the circuit shown in figure-3.396, find the charges on capacitors of capacitances 5 μF and 3 μF, in steady state.

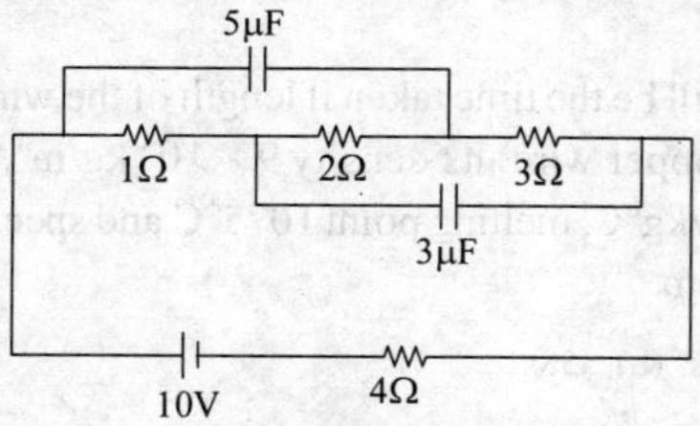

Figure 3.396

Ans. [15 μC, 15 μC]

3-44 A capacitor of capacitance C has potential difference $E/2$ and another capacitor of capacitance $2C$ is uncharged. They are joined to form a closed circuit as shown in the figure-3.397.

(a) Find the current in the circuit at $t = 0$

(b) Find the charge on C as a function of time

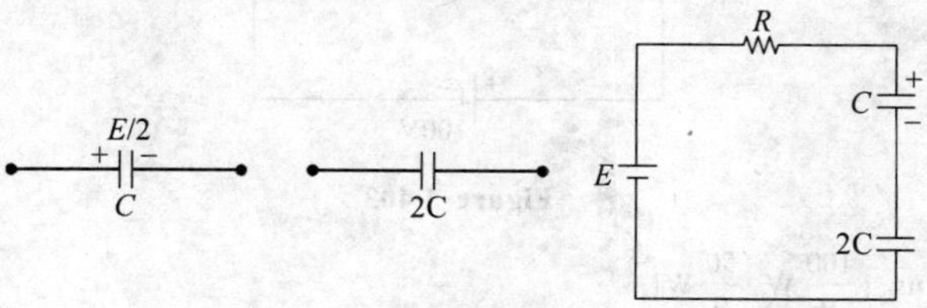

Figure 3.397

Ans. [(a) $\frac{E}{2R}$; (b) $\frac{CE}{6}(5-2e^{-3t/2RC})$]

3-45 Initially the switch is in position 1 for a long time in the circuit shown in figure-3.398. At $t = 0$, the switch is moved from 1 to 2. Obtain expressions for V_C and V_R for $t > 0$.

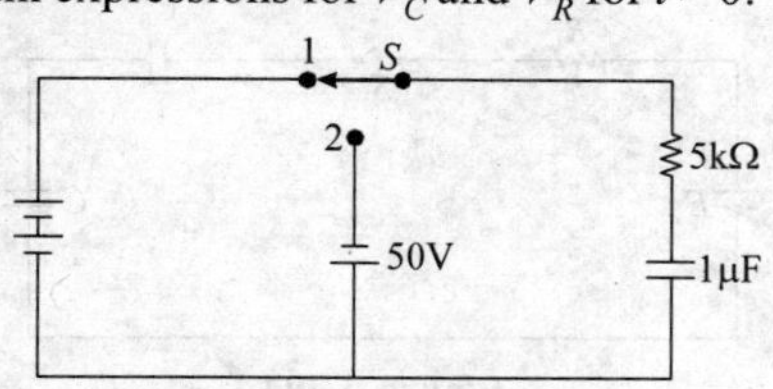

Figure 3.398

Ans. [V_C = 50 $(3e^{-200t} - 1)$, V_R = 150e^{-200t}]

3-46 A charged capacitor C_1 is discharged through a resistance R by putting switch S in position 1 of circuit shown in figure-3.399. When discharge current reduces to I_0 the switch is suddenly shifted to position 2. Calculate the amount of heat liberated in resistance R starting from this instant.

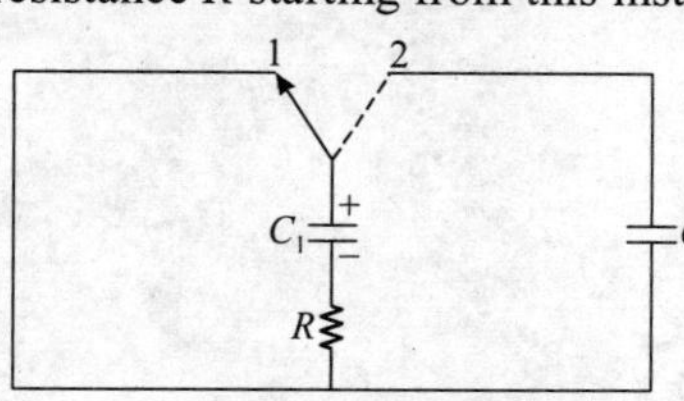

Figure 3.399

Ans. [$\frac{(I_0R)^2C_1C_2}{2(C_1+C_2)}$]

3-47 A capacitor with capacitance C = 400 pF is connected via a resistance R = 650 Ω to a source of constant voltage V_0. How soon will the voltage developed across the capacitor reach a value $V = 0.90\ V_0$?

Ans. [0.6 × 10^{-6} s]

3-48 In the circuit shown in figure-3.400 the capacitors are initially uncharged. In a certain time the capacitor of capacitance 2 μF gets a charge of 20 μC. In that time interval find the heat produced by each resistor individually.

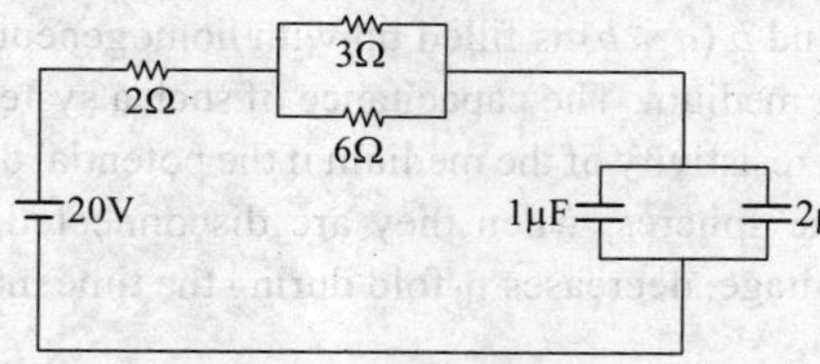

Figure 3.400

Ans. [H_2 = 0.075 mJ, H_3 = 0.05 mJ, H_6 = 0.025 mJ]

3-49 A time varying voltage is applied to the clamps A and B such that voltage across the capacitor plates is as shown in the figure-3.401. Plot the time dependence of voltage across the terminals of the resistance E and D.

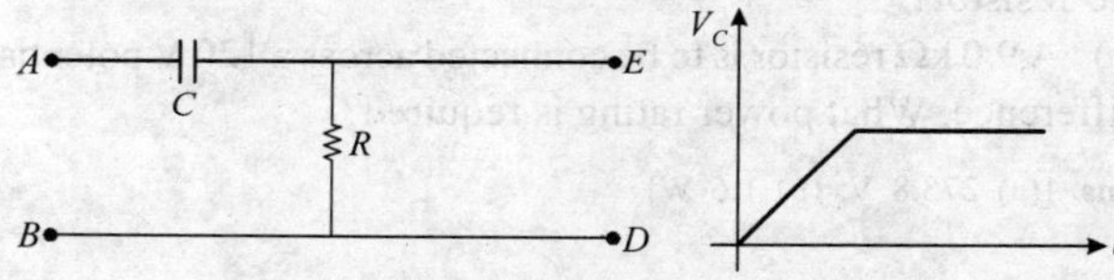

Figure 3.401

Ans. [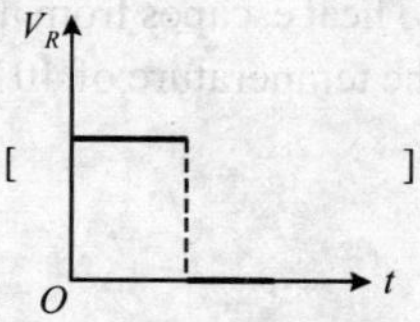

]

3-50 In the given circuit shown in figure-3.402, the switch is closed in the position 1 at t = 0 and then moved to 2 after 250 μs. Derive an expression for current as a function of time for $t > 0$. Also plot the variation of current with time.

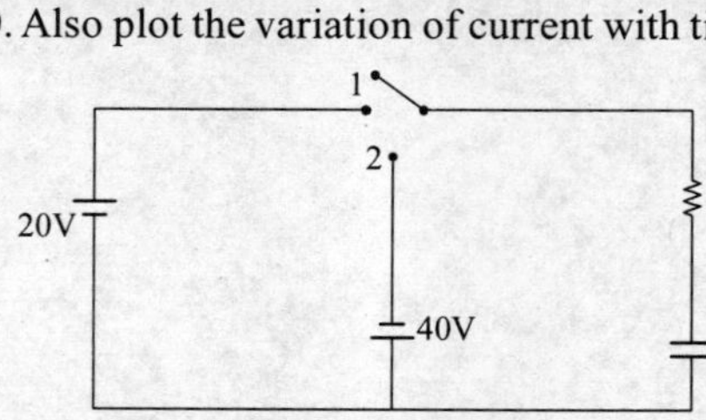

Figure 3.402

Ans. [i = $(0.04e^{-4000t})$A for $t \le 250$ μs and i = − $(0.11\ e^{-400t})$A for $t \ge 250$ μs,

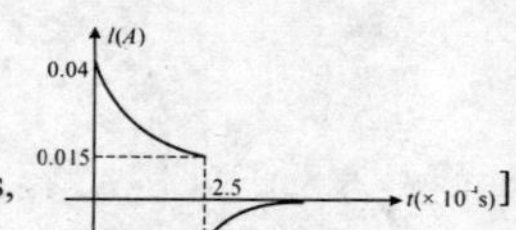

]

3-51 A metal ball of radius a is surrounded by a thin concentric metal shell of radius b. The space between these electrodes is filled up with a poorly conducting homogeneous medium of resistivity ρ. Find the resistance of the inter-electrode gap. Analyses the obtained solution at $b \to \infty$.

Ans. [$\frac{\rho}{4\pi}\left[\frac{1}{a}-\frac{1}{b}\right], \frac{\rho}{4\pi a}$]

3-52 The space between two conducting concentric spheres of radii a and b ($a < b$) is filled up with homogeneous poorly conducting medium. The capacitance of such a system equals C. Find the resistivity of the medium if the potential difference between the spheres, when they are disconnected from an external voltage, decreases η-fold during the time interval Δt.

Ans. [$\frac{\Delta t \times 4\pi ab}{C(b-a)\log_e \eta}$]

3-53 (a) The power of resistor is the maximum power the resistor can safely dissipate without too rise in temperature. The power rating of a 15 kΩ resistor is 5.0 W. What is the maximum allowable potential difference across the terminals of the resistor?

(b) A 9.0 kΩ resistor is to be connected across a 120 V potential difference. What power rating is required?

Ans. [(a) 273.8 V; (b) 1.6 W]

2-54 An electric heater has coil resistance of 12 Ω and is operated from 220 V power line. If no heat escapes from it then how much time is required to raise the temperature of 40 kg of water from 10°C to 80°C?

Ans. [2708 s]

2-55 A copper wire having cross-sectional area 0.5 mm^2 and a length 0.1 m is initially at 25°C and is thermally insulated from the surrounding. If a current of 10 A is set up in this wire,

(a) Find the time in which the wire will start melting. The change of resistance with the temperature of the wire may be neglected.

(b) What will be the time taken if length of the wire is doubled? Given for copper wire, its density 9×10^3 kg/m^3, specific heat 9×10^{-2} kcal/kg°C, melting point 1075°C and specific resistance 1.6×10^{-8} Ω-m.

Ans. [(a) 558s, (b) 558s]

2-56 figure-3.403 shows two lamps L_1 and L_2 in series and connected across 100 V battery. Find the power consumed by each lamp.

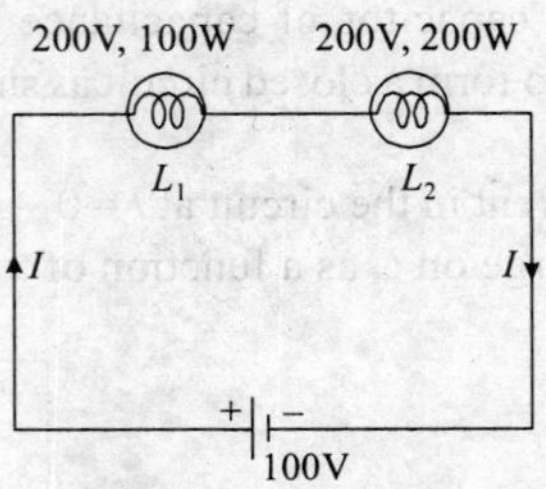

Figure 3.403

Ans. [$\frac{100}{9}$ W, $\frac{50}{9}$ W]

3-57 The switch S is closed at $t = 0$. The capacitor C is uncharged but C_0 has a charge $Q_0 = 2$ μC at $t = 0$. If $R = 100$ Ω, $C = 2$ μF, $C_0 = 2$ μF, $E = 4$ V. Calculate current in the circuit as a function of time.

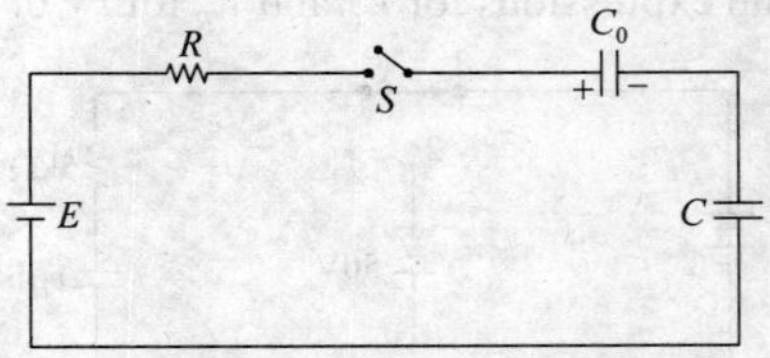

Figure 3.404

Ans. [$0.03\, e^{-10^4 t}$]

* * * * *

ANSWERS & SOLUTIONS

CONCEPTUAL MCQs Single Option Correct

1	(B)	**2**	(D)	**3**	(B)
4	(C)	**5**	(D)	**6**	(D)
7	(A)	**8**	(B)	**9**	(B)
10	(A)	**11**	(C)	**12**	(D)
13	(B)	**14**	(B)	**15**	(D)
16	(C)	**17**	(A)	**18**	(C)
19	(D)	**20**	(D)	**21**	(D)
22	(A)	**23**	(B)	**24**	(A)
25	(A)	**26**	(C)	**27**	(A)
28	(C)	**29**	(C)	**30**	(A)
31	(D)	**32**	(C)	**33**	(A)
34	(A)	**35**	(A)	**36**	(A)
37	(D)	**38**	(A)	**39**	(A)
40	(A)	**41**	(B)	**42**	(B)
43	(C)	**44**	(D)	**45**	(A)
46	(D)	**47**	(A)	**48**	(D)
49	(A)	**50**	(B)	**51**	(D)
52	(B)	**53**	(D)	**54**	(A)
55	(D)	**56**	(C)	**57**	(C)
58	(B)	**59**	(A)	**60**	(A)
61	(A)	**62**	(A)	**63**	(C)
64	(D)	**65**	(C)	**66**	(C)
67	(D)	**68**	(C)	**69**	(B)
70	(C)	**71**	(B)		

NUMERICAL MCQs Single Option Correct

1	(A)	**2**	(B)	**3**	(A)
4	(B)	**5**	(D)	**6**	(B)
7	(B)	**8**	(D)	**9**	(A)
10	(C)	**11**	(D)	**12**	(A)
13	(D)	**14**	(D)	**15**	(D)
16	(A)	**17**	(A)	**18**	(C)
19	(B)	**20**	(A)	**21**	(B)
22	(D)	**23**	(D)	**24**	(D)
25	(C)	**26**	(D)	**27**	(A)
28	(A)	**29**	(D)	**30**	(B)
31	(D)	**32**	(B)	**33**	(A)
34	(C)	**35**	(A)	**36**	(A)
37	(C)	**38**	(C)	**39**	(C)
40	(C)	**41**	(D)	**42**	(A)
43	(C)	**44**	(D)	**45**	(A)
46	(C)	**47**	(C)	**48**	(B)
49	(A)	**50**	(B)	**51**	(A)
52	(B)	**53**	(C)	**54**	(B)
55	(B)	**56**	(D)	**57**	(D)
58	(C)	**59**	(D)	**60**	(C)
61	(A)	**62**	(D)	**63**	(C)
64	(A)	**65**	(B)	**66**	(C)

ADVANCE MCQs One or More Options Correct

1	(A, B)	**2**	(A, D)	**3**	(C, D)
4	(A, D)	**5**	(A, B, C, D)	**6**	(A, B, C)
7	(A, C, D)	**8**	(A, D)	**9**	(A, B, C)
10	(A, B, C)	**11**	(A, C)	**12**	(A, B, C)
13	(A, B, D)	**14**	(A, B)	**15**	(A, B, D)
16	(C, D)	**17**	(A, B, C, D)	**18**	(A, B, D)
19	(A, D)	**20**	(B, C)	**21**	(A, C)
22	(B, D)	**23**	(A, B, C)	**24**	(A, D)
25	(A, D)	**26**	(B, D)	**27**	(A, D)
28	(B, C)	**29**	(A, B, D)	**30**	(C)
31	(B, D)	**32**	(A, C)	**33**	(A, B, C, D)
34	(B, D)	**35**	(A)	**36**	(B, D)
37	(B, D)	**38**	(C, D)	**39**	(A,C,D)
40	(D)				

Solutions of PRACTICE EXERCISE 1.1

(i) As the balls are rubbed against each other they will acquire equal and opposite charges. The *FBD* of left ball is shown in figure which shows all the forces acting on ball in equilibrium position.

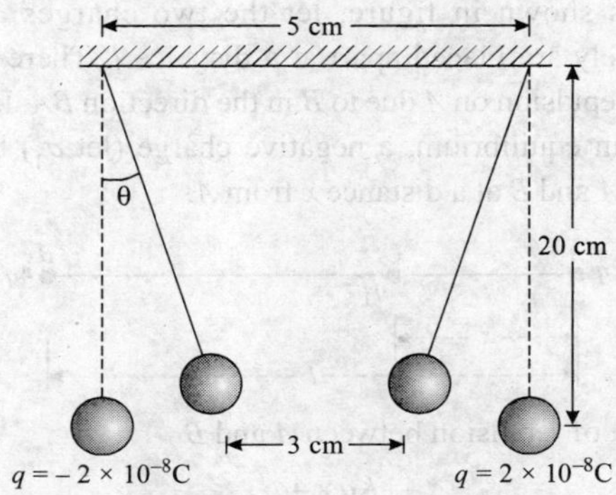

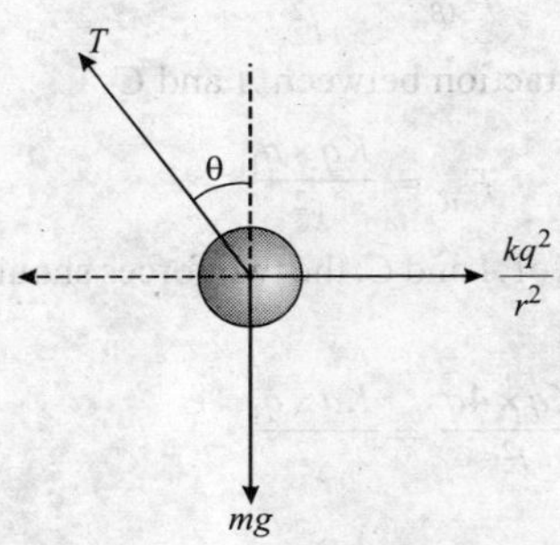

Here for equilibrium of each bob, we have

$$T \sin\theta = \frac{Kq^2}{r^2} \quad \ldots(1)$$

$$T \cos\theta = mg \quad \ldots(2)$$

$$\Rightarrow \quad \tan\theta = \frac{Kq^2}{r^2 mg}$$

$$\Rightarrow \quad \frac{1}{\sqrt{(20)^2 - 1^2}} = \frac{K(2\times10^{-8})^2}{(3\times10^{-2})^2 m\times10}$$

$$\Rightarrow \quad m = 7.96\text{ g}$$

From equation-(2) we have

$$T = \frac{mg}{\cos\theta} = \frac{7.96\times10^{-3}\times10\times20}{\sqrt{(20)^2-1}}$$

$$\Rightarrow \quad T = 7.72\times10^{-2}\text{N}$$

(ii) As the repulsive Coulombian force is equal to the weight of particles we have

$$\frac{Kq^2}{r^2} = mg$$

$$\Rightarrow \quad r = \frac{Kq^2}{mg}$$

$$\Rightarrow \quad r = g\sqrt{\frac{K}{mg}}$$

$$\Rightarrow \quad r = 1.6 \times 10^{-19} \times \left[\frac{9\times10^9}{1.7\times10^{-27}\times9.8}\right]^{1/2}$$

$$\Rightarrow \quad r = 0.117\,\text{m}$$

(iii) As shown in figure, let the two charges q and $4q$ respectively are placed apart at a distance l. There will be a force of repulsion on A due to B in the direction BA. In order to make A in equilibrium, a negative charge (let q_1) be placed between A and B at a distance x from A.

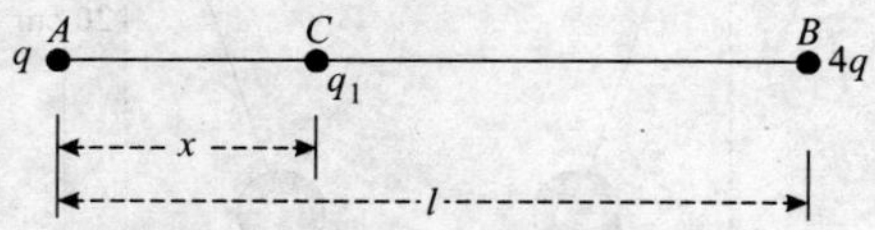

The force of repulsion between A and B

$$F_{AB} = \frac{Kq\times4q}{l^2} \qquad \ldots(1)$$

The force of attraction between A and C

$$F_{AC} = \frac{Kq\times q_1}{x^2} \qquad \ldots(2)$$

For equilibrium of A and C, the two forces should be equal, thus we have

$$\frac{Kq\times4q}{l^2} = \frac{Kq\times q_1}{x^2}$$

$$\Rightarrow \quad q_1 = \frac{4qx^2}{l^2} \qquad \ldots(3)$$

Considering the equilibrium of C, we have

$$\frac{K(q_1\times4q)}{(l-x)^2} = \frac{K(q\times q_1)}{x^2}$$

$$\Rightarrow \quad 4x^2 = (l-x)^2$$

Solving we get, $\quad x = -l \quad$ or $\quad x = -\frac{l}{3}$

As C should be between A and C, hence $x \neq -l$. This implies

$$x = \frac{l}{3} \qquad \ldots(4)$$

From equation-(3) and (4), we have

$$q_1 = \frac{4q(l/3)^2}{l^2} = \frac{4q}{9}$$

(iv) One object has a charge q and other has $(Q - q)$ as shown in figure.

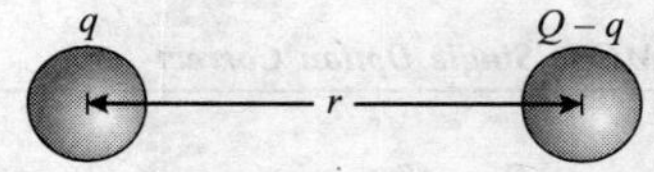

The force between the two charges is given as

$$F = \frac{Kq(Q-q)}{r^2}$$

For F to be maximum $\quad \frac{dF}{dq} = 0$

$$\frac{d}{dq}\left(\frac{KqQ}{r^2} - \frac{Kq^2}{r^2}\right) = 0$$

$$\Rightarrow \quad \frac{KQ}{r^2} - \frac{2Kq}{r^2} = 0$$

$$\Rightarrow \quad q = \frac{Q}{2}$$

Thus we have to divide charges equally on the objects for the force between then to be maximum.

(v) The force F_{12} between q_1 and q_2 is given by

$$F_{12} = \frac{Kq_1q_2}{r_{12}^2}$$

$$\Rightarrow \quad F_{12} = (9.0\times10^9)\cdot\frac{(1.0\times10^{-6})(3.0\times10^{-6})}{(15\times10^{-2})^2}$$

$$\Rightarrow \quad F_{12} = 1.2\,\text{N}$$

The force F_{13} between q_1 and q_3 is given by

$$F_{13} = \frac{Kq_1q_3}{r_{13}^2}$$

$$\Rightarrow \quad F_{13} = (9.0\times10^9)\cdot\frac{(1.0\times10^{-6})(2.0\times10^{-6})}{(10\times10^{-2})^2}$$

$$\Rightarrow \quad F_{13} = 1.8\,\text{N}$$

The x and y components of the resultant force acting on q_1 are

$$F_{1x} = (F_{12})_x + (F_{13})_x = F_{12} + F_{13}\sin\theta$$

$$\Rightarrow \quad F_{1x} = 1.2 + 1.8\sin30° = 2.1\,\text{N}$$

and $\quad F_{1y} = (F_{12})_y + (F_{13})_y$

$$\Rightarrow \quad F_{1y} = 0 + (-1.8)\cos30° = -1.6\,\text{N}$$

Net force on q_1 is given as

$$F_1 = \sqrt{F_{1x}^2 + F_{1y}^2} = \sqrt{(2.1)^2 + (1.6)^2}$$

$$\Rightarrow \quad F_1 = 2.64\,\text{N}$$

(vi) The situation is shown in figure.

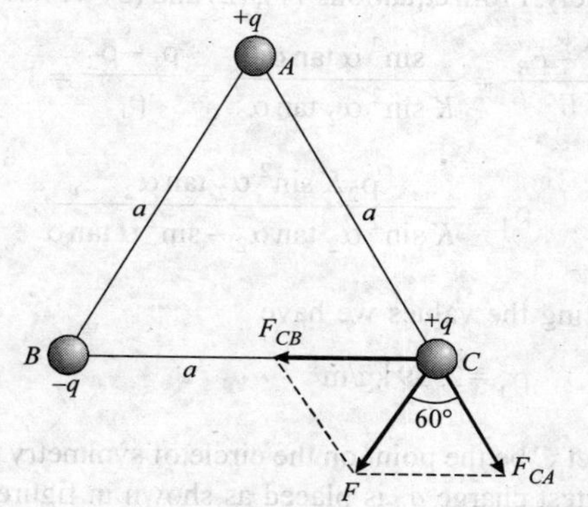

Let us consider the forces acting on C due to A and B.

The force of repulsion on C due to A is acting in direction AC is given as

$$F_{CA} = \frac{Kq \times q}{a^2}$$

The force of attraction on C due to B is acting F_{CB} in direction CB is given as

$$F_{CB} = \frac{Kq \times q}{a^2}$$

Thus the two forces are equal in magnitude. The angle between them is 120°. The resultant force F on C is given as

$$F_C = F_{CA}\cos 60° + F_{CB}\cos 60°$$

$$\Rightarrow \quad F_C = 2F\cos 60° = F$$

We used $\quad F_{CA} = F_{CB} = F = \dfrac{kq^2}{a^2}$

$$\Rightarrow \quad F_C = (9\times 10^9)\frac{(100\times 10^{-6})(100\times 10^{-6})}{(4)^2}$$

$$\Rightarrow \quad F_C = 5.625\text{ N}$$

(vii) The two negative charges A and B of unit magnitude are shown in figure. Let the positive charge q be at a distance r_A from A and at a distance r_B from B.

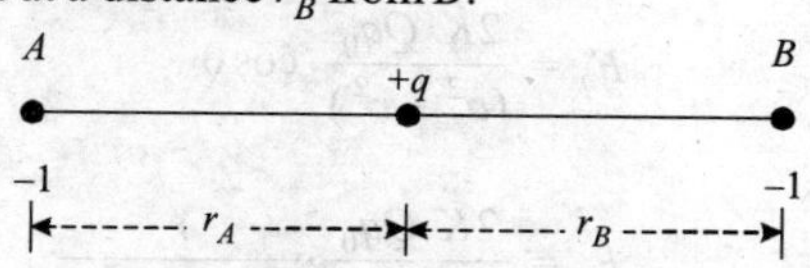

Force on q due to A is an attractive force given as

$$F_{qA} = \frac{Kq}{r_A^2}$$

Force on q due to B is an attractive force given as

$$F_{qB} = \frac{Kq}{r_B^2}$$

These two forces acting on q are opposite and collinear. For equilibrium of q, the two forces must also be equal in magnitude so we use

$$|F_{qA}| = |F_{qB}|$$

$$\Rightarrow \quad \frac{Kq}{r_A^2} = \frac{Kq}{r_B^2}$$

$$\Rightarrow \quad r_A = r_B$$

So for the equilibrium of q, it must be equidistant from A and B and placed at the mid point of AB.

Now for the equilibrium of the system, A and B must also be in equilibrium.

For the equilibrium of A, we use

Force on A by q is

$$F_{AB} = \frac{Kq}{r_A^2} \text{ towards } q$$

Force on A by B is $F_{AB} = \dfrac{K(1)(1)}{(r_A + r_B)^2}$

$$\Rightarrow \quad F_{AB} = \frac{K}{(2r_A)^2}$$

The two forces are opposite and collinear. For equilibrium of A, the forces must be equal, opposite and collinear. Hence so we use

$$\frac{Kq}{r_A^2} = \frac{K(1)}{(2r_A)^2}$$

$$\Rightarrow \quad q = \frac{1}{4}C$$

It can also be shown that for the equilibrium of B, the magnitude of q must be 1/4 of the magnitude of either charge. Here equilibrium will be unstable because we have already discussed that any equilibrium of charges only under the electrostatic forces is always unstable.

(viii) The different forces on C due to other charges are shown in figure. Let a be the side of the square. The force on due to A is given as

$$F_{AC} = \frac{KQ^2}{2a^2} \qquad \ldots(1)$$

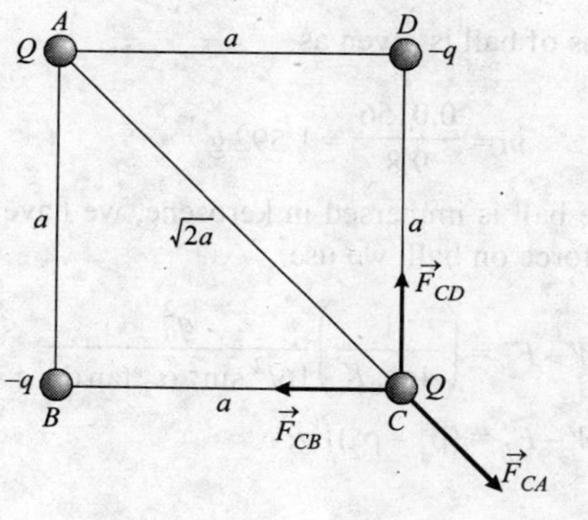

If the resultant force on C is to be zero, the force on C due to D and B must be along CD and CB respectively so charge q must be negative.

The resultant force F_{CB} and F_{CD} along CA are given as

$$F_C = \frac{KQ^2}{a^2}\cdot\frac{1}{\sqrt{2}} + \frac{KQq}{a^2}\cdot\frac{1}{\sqrt{2}}$$

$$\Rightarrow \quad F_C = \sqrt{2}\cdot\frac{KqQ}{a^2} \quad \ldots(2)$$

As resultant force on C is zero, we have from equations-(1) and (2)

$$\sqrt{2}\cdot\frac{KqQ}{a^2} = \frac{KQ^2}{2a^2}$$

$$\Rightarrow \quad Q = -2\sqrt{2}\,q$$

(ix) Let 2α be the angle between the two threads as shown in figure, F is the resultant force, W is weight of the ball and F_1 is Coulomb's force of repulsion.

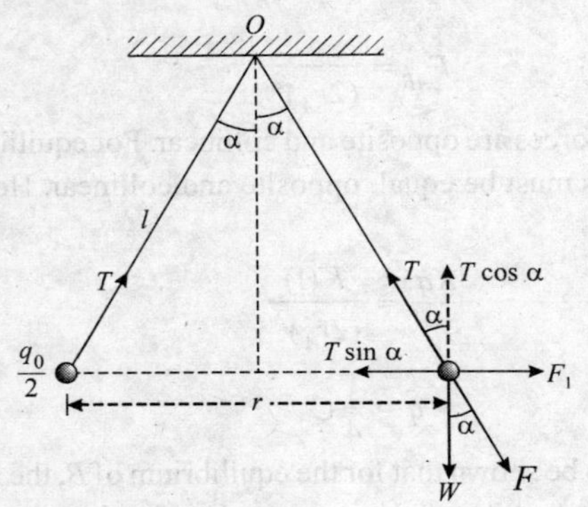

From above figure we have

$$r = 2l\sin\alpha$$

For equilibrium of ball we have

$$F_1 = W\tan\alpha = \left(\frac{1}{4\pi\varepsilon_0}\right)\frac{(q_0^2/4)}{(4l^2\sin^2\alpha)}$$

$$\Rightarrow \quad W = \left(\frac{1}{4\pi\varepsilon_0}\right)\frac{q_0^2}{16l^2\sin^2\alpha\tan\alpha} \quad \ldots(1)$$

$$\Rightarrow \quad W = 0.0156\,\text{N}$$

Thus mass of ball is given as

$$m = \frac{0.0156}{9.8} = 1.592\,\text{g}$$

When the ball is immersed in kerosene, we have if F_B is the buoyant force on ball, we use

$$W - F_B = \left(\frac{1}{4\pi\varepsilon_0 K}\right)\frac{q_0^2}{16l^2\sin^2\alpha_2\tan\alpha_2} \quad \ldots(2)$$

and $\quad W - F_B = (\rho_1 - \rho_2)Vg, \quad \ldots(3)$

Where ρ_1 and ρ_2 are the densities of ball and kerosene respectively. From equations-(1), (2) and (3) we have

$$\frac{W - F_B}{W} = \frac{\sin^2\alpha\tan\alpha}{K\sin^2\alpha_2\tan\alpha_2} = \frac{\rho_1 - \rho_2}{\rho_1} = 1 - \frac{\rho_2}{\rho_1}$$

$$\Rightarrow \quad \rho_1 = \frac{\rho_2 K\sin^2\alpha_2\tan\alpha_2}{K\sin^2\alpha_2\tan\alpha_2 - \sin^2\alpha\tan\alpha}$$

Substituting the values we have

$$\rho_1 = 2559\,\text{kg/m}^3$$

(x) Let C be the point on the circle of symmetry of radius r where a test charge q_0 is placed as shown in figure. Now the force F exerted on this test charge by either charge Q is given by

$$F = \frac{KQq_0}{(a^2 + r^2)}$$

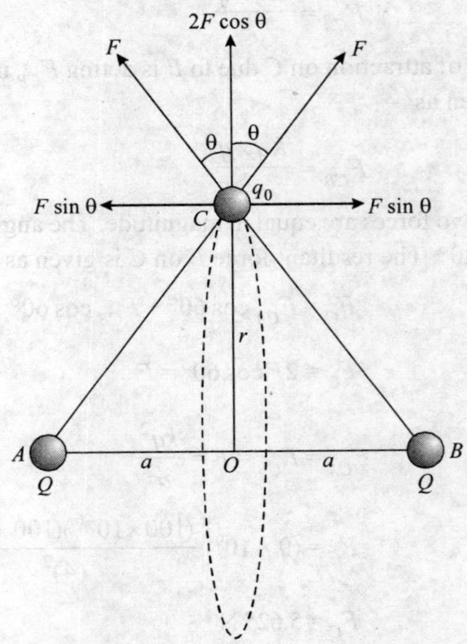

The resultant force on the test charge will be given as

$$F_R = 2F\cos\theta$$

$$\Rightarrow \quad F_R = \frac{2K\,Qq_0}{(a^2 + r^2)}\cdot\cos\theta$$

$$\Rightarrow \quad F_R = \frac{2K\,Qq_0}{(a^2 + r^2)}\cdot\frac{r}{(a^2 + r^2)^{1/2}}$$

$$\Rightarrow \quad F_R = \frac{2K\,Qq_0 r}{(a^2 + r^2)^{3/2}} \quad \ldots(1)$$

For the force to be maximum, we have

$$\frac{dF_R}{dr} = 0$$

$$\Rightarrow \quad \frac{dF_R}{dr} = 2KQq\left[\frac{(a^2+r^2)^{3/2}\cdot 1 - \frac{3}{2}(a^2+r^2)^{1/2}\cdot 2r\cdot r}{(a^2+r^2)^3}\right] = 0$$

$$\Rightarrow \quad (a^2+r^2)^{3/2} = \frac{3}{2}(a^2+r^2)^{1/2}\cdot 2r^2$$

$$\Rightarrow \quad (a^2+r^2) = 3r^2$$

$$\Rightarrow \quad a^2 = 2r^2$$

$$\Rightarrow \quad r = a/\sqrt{2}$$

As shown in figure, the force is radial and away form the centre of the circle.

(xi) Let any instant the separation between them is x. The force between them is

$$F = \frac{1}{4\pi\epsilon_0}\frac{Qq}{x^2}$$

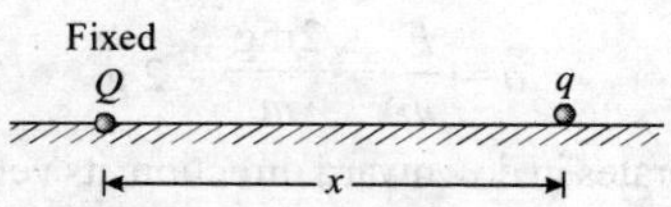

Acceleration of charge q is given as

$$a = \frac{1}{4\pi\epsilon_0}\frac{Qq}{m\,x^2}$$

$$\Rightarrow \quad \frac{vdv}{dx} = \frac{1}{4\pi\epsilon_0 m}Qqx^{-2}$$

$$\Rightarrow \quad \int_0^v vdv = \frac{1}{4\pi\epsilon_0 m}Qq\int_{x_0}^{x} x^{-2}dx$$

$$\Rightarrow \quad \frac{v^2}{2} = \frac{1}{4\pi\epsilon_0 m}Qq\left|\frac{1}{-x}\right|_{x_0}^{x}$$

$$\Rightarrow \quad v = \left[\frac{Qq}{2\pi\epsilon_0 m}\left\{\frac{1}{x_0}-\frac{1}{x}\right\}\right]^{1/2}$$

(xii) We know that electric field vector due to charge q is given as

$$\vec{E} = \frac{1}{4\pi\epsilon_0}\frac{q(\vec{r}-\vec{r}_0)}{|\vec{r}-\vec{r}_0|^3}$$

$$\Rightarrow \quad \vec{E} = 9\times 10^9 \times (50\times 10^{-6})\frac{[(8\hat{i}-5\hat{j})-(2\hat{i}+3\hat{j})]}{|(8\hat{i}-5\hat{j})-(2\hat{i}+3\hat{j})|^3}$$

$$\Rightarrow \quad \vec{E} = 9\times 10^9 \times 50\times 10^{-6}\frac{(6\hat{i}-8\hat{j})}{|(6\hat{i}-8\hat{j})|^3}$$

$$\Rightarrow \quad \vec{E} = 4.5\times 10^5\frac{(6\hat{i}-8\hat{j})}{10^3}$$

$$\Rightarrow \quad \vec{E} = 4.5\times 10^2(6\hat{i}-8\hat{j})$$

$$\Rightarrow \quad \vec{E} = 2.7\hat{i} - 3.6\hat{j}\ \text{kV/m}$$

$$\Rightarrow \quad |\vec{E}| = 4.5\,\text{kV/m}$$

(xiii)

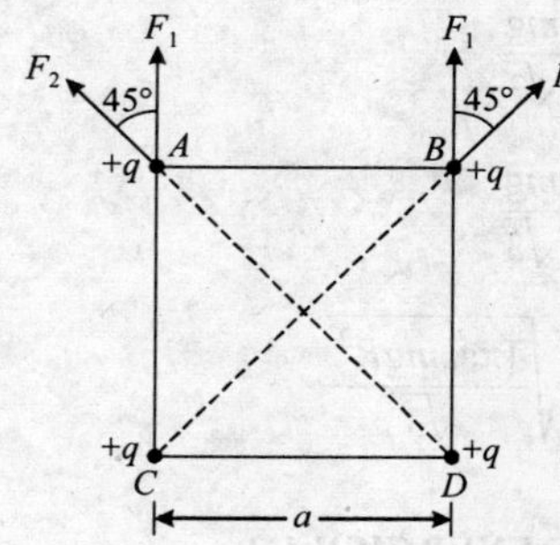

$$F_2 = \frac{q^2}{4\pi\varepsilon_0(\sqrt{2}a)^2} = \frac{q^2}{4\pi\varepsilon_0\times 2a^2}$$

Net force on side AB of the film is

$$F = 2F_1 + 2F_2\cos 45$$

$$\Rightarrow \quad F = \frac{2q^2}{4\pi\varepsilon_0 a^2} + \frac{2q^2}{4\pi\varepsilon_0 2\sqrt{2}a^2}$$

$$\Rightarrow \quad F = \frac{q^2}{4\pi\varepsilon_0 a^2}\left(2+\frac{1}{\sqrt{2}}\right)$$

Force on AB due to surface tension $= 2\sigma a$

$$\frac{q^2}{4\pi\varepsilon_0 a^2}\left(2+\frac{1}{\sqrt{2}}\right) = 2\sigma a$$

$$\Rightarrow \quad a = \left[\frac{1}{4\pi\epsilon_0}\left(1+\frac{1}{2\sqrt{2}}\right)\frac{q^2}{\sigma}\right]^{1/3} \quad \ldots(1)$$

Given that $\quad a = k\left(\frac{q^2}{\sigma}\right)^{1/N} \quad \ldots(2)$

Comparing equation (1) and (2), we have $N = 3$

and $\quad k = \left[\frac{1}{4\pi\epsilon_0}\left(1+\frac{1}{2\sqrt{2}}\right)\right]^{1/3}$

(xiv) Figure shows *FBD* of ball *B*

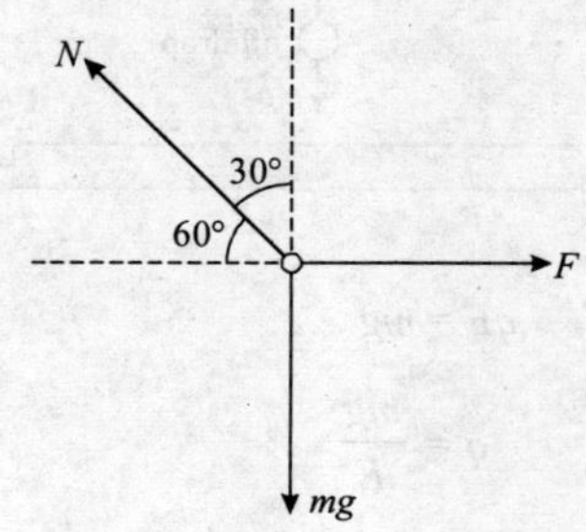

For equilibrium of ball B we use Lami's theorem which gives.

$$\frac{mg}{\sin(90+30°)} = \frac{F}{\sin(90°+60°)}$$

$$\Rightarrow \qquad F = \frac{mg}{\sqrt{3}}$$

$$\Rightarrow \qquad \frac{1}{4\pi\varepsilon_0}\frac{(q)(q)}{R^2} = \frac{mg}{\sqrt{3}}$$

$$\Rightarrow \qquad q = \sqrt{\frac{4\pi\varepsilon_0 mgR^2}{\sqrt{3}}}$$

Solutions of PRACTICE EXERCISE 1.2

(i) Here acceleration of block is given as

$$a = \frac{qE}{m}$$

Time taken by block to reach wall is given as

$$t = \sqrt{\frac{2dm}{qE}}$$

Velocity at the time of impact is

$$v = \sqrt{2ad}$$

$$\Rightarrow \qquad v = \sqrt{\frac{2qEd}{m}}$$

When the block will rebound time taken by block in coming to rest is same is the time it takes in reading the wall as accelerations and initial velocity is same. Thus time period of oscillations of block is twice the time it takes in reading the wall which is given as

$$T = 2t = 2\sqrt{\frac{2md}{qE}}$$

Since the restoring force is independent of x, the displacement from mean position, this is not a simple harmonic motion.

(ii) For the equilibrium, the drop must have negative charge q, so that its weight is balanced by the electric force given as.

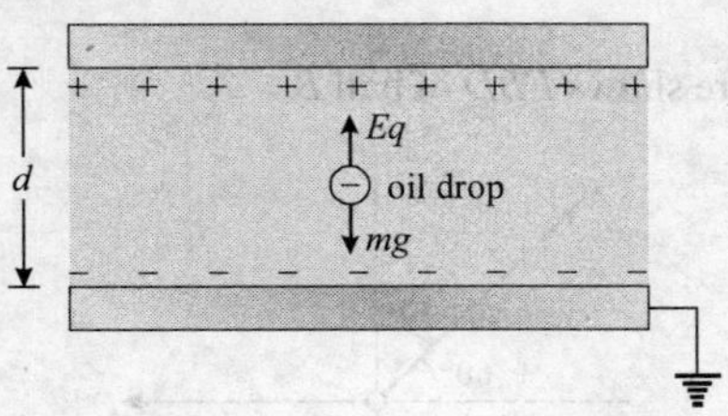

$$qE = mg \qquad \ldots(1)$$

$$\Rightarrow \qquad q = \frac{mg}{E}$$

The electric field is given as

$$E = \frac{V}{d} = \frac{1.5\times10^3}{1.5\times10^{-2}} = 10^5\text{ V/m}$$

$$\Rightarrow \qquad q = \frac{(4.9\times10^{15})\times(9.8)}{10^5}$$

$$\Rightarrow \qquad q = 4.8\times10^{-19}\text{ C}$$

If n is the number of electrons on the oil drop, then we have

$$n = \frac{q}{e} = \frac{4.8\times10^{-19}}{1.6\times10^{-19}}$$

$$\Rightarrow \qquad n = 3$$

When polarity of plates is reversed, the electric force also acts in downward direction, and so net force on drop is

$$F = mg + qE \qquad \ldots(2)$$

From equations-(1) and (2), we get

$$F = 2\text{ mg}$$

Initial acceleration of the drop

$$a = \frac{F}{m} = \frac{2\text{mg}}{m} = 2\text{ g}$$

As drop accelerates in downward direction, its velocity increases and hence viscous force increases in upward direction. At certain moment the net force on the drop becomes zero and thereafter drop will move with constant velocity. If v is the terminal velocity, then by Stoke's rule we have

$$2\text{ mg} = 6\pi\eta rv$$

$$\Rightarrow \qquad v = \frac{mg}{3\pi\eta r}$$

$$\Rightarrow \qquad v = \frac{(4.9\times10^{-15})\times9.8}{3\pi\times(1.8\times10^{-5})\times(5.0\times10^{-6})}$$

$$\Rightarrow \qquad v = 5.7\times10^{-5}\text{ m/s}$$

(iii) The situation described in question is shown in figure.

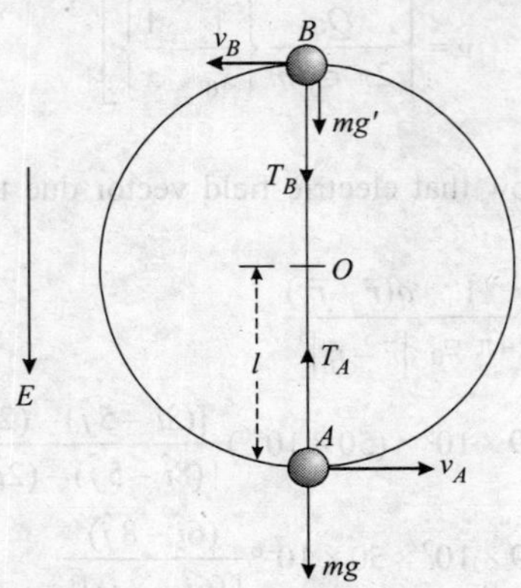

Acceleration a due to electric field is given as

$$a = \frac{qE}{m} = \frac{10^{-6}\times10^6}{0.01} = 100\text{ m/s}^2$$

Thus effective acceleration would be given as

$$g' = g + \frac{qE}{m} = 9.8 + 100 = 109.8 \text{ m/s}^2$$

The time period of particle would be given as

$$T = 2\pi\sqrt{\left(\frac{l}{g'}\right)} = 2\pi\sqrt{\left(\frac{1}{109.8}\right)}$$

$$\Rightarrow \quad T = 0.6 \text{ s}$$

From figure-127, at point A forces on particle are given as

$$\frac{mv_A^2}{l} = T_A - mg' = T_A - (qE + mg) \quad \dots (1)$$

At point B, we have

$$\frac{mv_B^2}{l} = T_B + (qE + mg)$$

With minimums speed at A, to complete the circle at point B tension T_B should be zero, thus we have

$$\frac{mv_{B\min}^2}{l} = qE + mg \quad \dots (2)$$

Using work energy theorem at points A and B, we have

$$\frac{1}{2}mv^2{}_A - 2mgl - 2gEl = \frac{1}{2}mv^2{}_B + U_B \quad \dots (3)$$

From equation-(2) and (3), we get

$$v_A^2 = \frac{5(qE + mg)l}{m} = 5g'l = 5 \times 109.8 \times 1$$

$$\Rightarrow \quad v_A = 23.42 \text{ m/s}$$

and $$T_A = (qE + mg) + \frac{mv_A^2}{l}$$

$$\Rightarrow \quad T_A = 6(qE + mg) = 6(1 + 0.098)$$

$$\Rightarrow \quad T_A = 6.588 \text{ N}$$

(iv) The drop is negatively charged and so force on it acts upward and

$$F_e = qE$$

Acceleration of ink drop upward is given as

$$a_y = \frac{F}{m} = \frac{qE}{m}$$

If t is the time taken by the drop to travel the distance L, so we use

$$L = v_x t$$

$$\Rightarrow \quad t = \frac{L}{v_x}$$

The vertical deflection of drop in this time is given as

$$y = \frac{1}{2}a_y t^2 = \frac{1}{2}\left(\frac{qE}{m}\right)\left(\frac{L}{v_x}\right)^2$$

$$\Rightarrow \quad y = \frac{qEL^2}{2mv_x^2}$$

$$\Rightarrow \quad y = \frac{(1.4\times10^6)\times(1.5\times10^{-13})\times(1.6\times10^{-2})^2}{2\times(1.3\times10^{-10})(18)^2}$$

$$\Rightarrow \quad y = 6.4 \times 10^{-4} \text{ m}$$

(v) The situation is shown in figure. We know in X-direction speed of electron remains uniform as acceleration is only in y-direction, electron velocity in x-direction is given as.

$$v_x = u$$

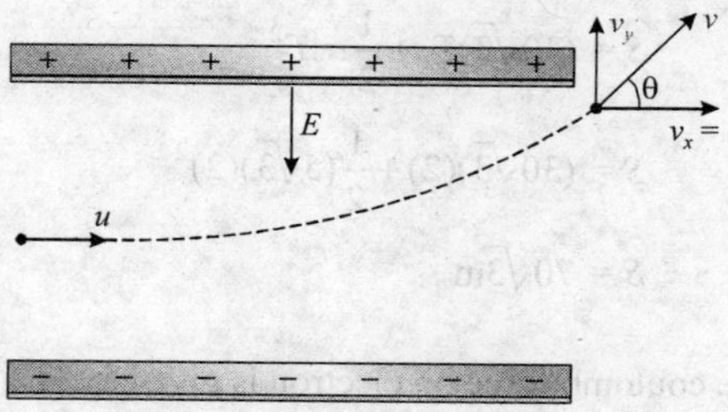

In Y direction initial velocity of electron is zero.

$$v_{Y_{\text{initial}}} = 0$$

Acceleration in y-direction of electron is

$$a = \frac{eE}{m}$$

$$\Rightarrow \quad v_{Y_{\text{final}}} = v_{Y_{\text{initial}}} + at$$

$$\Rightarrow \quad v_Y = \left(\frac{eE}{m}\right)\left(\frac{l}{u}\right)$$

$$\Rightarrow \quad \tan\theta = \frac{v_Y}{v_X} = \left(\frac{eEl/mu}{u}\right)$$

$$\Rightarrow \quad \theta = \tan^{-1}\left(\frac{eEl}{mu^2}\right)$$

(vi) Electric force on ball is

$$qE = 30 \text{ N},$$

Vertical component of electric force

$$F_y = 30 \sin 30° = 15 \text{ N}$$

Horizontal component of electric force

$$F_y = 30 \cos 30° = 15\sqrt{3} \text{ N}$$

$$\Rightarrow \quad a_y = \frac{mg - 15}{m} = \frac{30 - 15}{3} = 5 \text{ m/s}^2 \text{ (downwards)}$$

$$\Rightarrow \quad a_x = \frac{15\sqrt{3}}{3} = 5\sqrt{3} \text{ m/s}^2$$

Time of flight for first flight is given as

$$T_1 = \frac{2u_y}{a_y} = \frac{2\times 20\sin 30°}{5} = 4\text{ s}$$

Time of flight after first hit is given as

$$T_2 = eT_1 = 2\text{ s}$$

Horizontal velocity after first hit is given as

$$v_{x_1} = (20\cos 30°) + a_x T_1$$

$$\Rightarrow \quad v_{x_1} = (10\sqrt{3}) + (5\sqrt{3})4 = 30\sqrt{3}\text{ m/s}$$

Horizontal distance travelled between first hit and second hit is given as

$$S = (30\sqrt{3})T_2 + \frac{1}{2}a_x T_2^2$$

$$\Rightarrow \quad S = (30\sqrt{3})(2) + \frac{1}{2}(5\sqrt{3})(2)^2$$

$$\Rightarrow \quad S = 70\sqrt{3}\text{m}$$

(vii) The coulomb force on electron is given as,

$$F = \frac{K\, q_1 q_2}{r^2}$$

$$\Rightarrow \quad F = (9\times 10^9)\times \frac{(1.6\times 10^{-19})^2}{(0.53\times 10^{-10})^2}$$

$$\Rightarrow \quad F = 8.1\times 10^{-8}\text{ N}$$

$$a_r = \frac{F}{me} = \frac{8.1\times 10^{-8}}{9.1\times 10^{-31}} = 8.9\times 10^{22}\text{ m/s}^2$$

Radial acceleration of electron is given as during revolution electric force provides centripetal force for circular motion so we have

$$F = m\, r\, \omega^2$$

$$\Rightarrow \quad \omega = \sqrt{\frac{F}{mr}}$$

Thus angular velocity, of electrons is given as

$$\omega = \sqrt{\left(\frac{8.9\times 10^{22}}{r}\right)}\text{ s}^{-1}$$

$$\Rightarrow \quad \omega = \sqrt{\left(\frac{8.9\times 10^{22}}{0.53\times 10^{-10}}\right)}\text{ s}^{-1}$$

$$\Rightarrow \quad \omega = 4.1\times 10^{16}\text{ s}^{-1}$$

(viii) The retardation of electron is given as

$$a = \frac{F}{m} = \frac{Ee}{m} = \frac{10^3\times(1.6\times 10^{-19})}{9.1\times 10^{-31}}\text{ m/s}^2$$

$$\Rightarrow \quad a = 1.8\times 10^{14}\text{ m/s}^2$$

The distance travelled by the electron before coming to rest can be calculated by using the speed equation

$$v^2 = u^2 - 2as$$

$$\Rightarrow \quad 0 = (5\times 10^6)^2 - 2(1.8\times 10^{14})s$$

$$\Rightarrow \quad s = 0.07\text{ m}$$

The time t can be calculated by using speed equation

$$v = u - at$$

$$\Rightarrow \quad 0 = (5\times 10^6) - (1.8\times 10^{14})\,t$$

$$\Rightarrow \quad t = 2.9\times 10^{-8}\text{ s}$$

(ix) If a uniform electric field exist in vertical downward direction then positive charge feels extra acceleration in downward direction, and a negative charge will feel acceleration in upward direction. When particle is uncharged, we use

$$h = \frac{u^2}{2g} = \frac{(5\sqrt{5})^2}{2\times 10}\text{ m}$$

$$\Rightarrow \quad h = \frac{125}{20}\text{ m}$$

$$\Rightarrow \quad h = 6.25\text{ m}$$

When it is positively charged

$$g_{eff} = g + \frac{qE}{m}$$

We use $$g_{eff} = \frac{v_1^2}{2h} = \frac{(13)^2}{2\times 6.25}\text{ m/s}^2$$

$$g_{eff} = \frac{169}{12.5}\text{ m/s}^2$$

$$\Rightarrow \quad g_{eff} = 13.52\text{ m/s}^2$$

We use $$\frac{qE}{m} = 13.52 - 10\text{ m/s}^2$$

$$\Rightarrow \quad \frac{qE}{m} = 9.52\text{ m/s}^2$$

when it is negatively charged then

$$g'_{eff} = g - \frac{qE}{m} = 10 - 3.52$$

$$= 6.48\text{ m/s}^2$$

Speed required to attain same height is

$$v_2 = \sqrt{2g'_{eff}h} = \sqrt{2\times 6.48\times 6.25}$$

$$\Rightarrow \quad v_2 = 9\text{ m/s}$$

(x) At a displacement by angle θ, net restoring torque on particle is

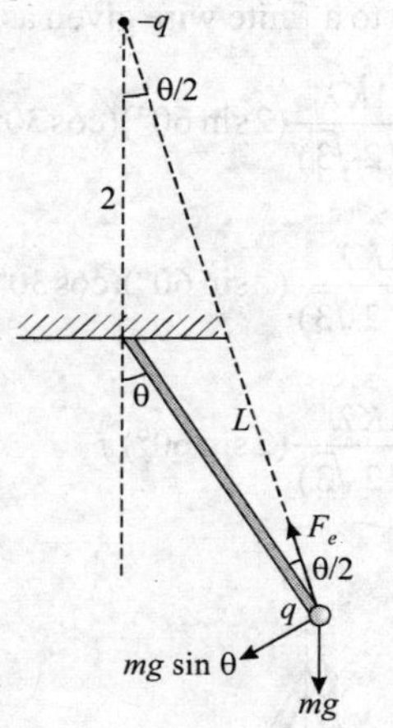

$$\tau_R = mg\sin\theta(L) - F_e\left(L\sin\frac{\theta}{2}\right) = I\alpha$$

$$\Rightarrow\quad mgL\sin\theta - \left(\frac{kq^2}{4L^2\cos^2\frac{\theta}{2}}\right)L\sin\frac{\theta}{2} = I\alpha$$

$$\Rightarrow\quad mgL\left[\sin\theta - \frac{\sin\frac{\theta}{2}}{2\cos^2\frac{\theta}{2}}\right] = mL^2 a \qquad \left[\text{as } mg = \frac{kq^2}{2L^2}\right]$$

$$\Rightarrow\quad \alpha = \frac{g}{L}\left[2\sin\frac{\theta}{2}\cos\frac{\theta}{2} - \frac{1}{2}\frac{\sin\theta/2}{\cos^2\theta/2}\right]$$

for small θ, we use

$$\sin\frac{\theta}{2} \approx \frac{\theta}{2} \text{ and } \cos\frac{\theta}{2} \approx 1$$

$$\Rightarrow\quad \alpha = \frac{g}{2}\left[2\left(\frac{\theta}{2}\right) - \frac{1}{2}\left(\frac{\theta}{2}\right)\right]$$

$$\Rightarrow\quad \alpha = \frac{3g}{4L}\theta$$

for restoring acceleration, we use

$$\alpha = -\frac{3g}{4L}\theta$$

As α is directly proportional to θ, it is SHM so comparing with angular acceleration of SHM given as $a = -\omega^2\theta$, we get

$$\omega = \sqrt{\frac{3g}{4L}}$$

$$\Rightarrow\quad T = \frac{2\pi}{\omega} = 2\pi\sqrt{\frac{4L}{3g}} = 2\sqrt{\frac{4L}{3}}$$

$$= 2\times\sqrt{\frac{4\times 3}{3}} = 4\text{ s}$$

(xi) We consider on angular element as shown in figure. Force on element is

$$dF = \lambda(R.d\theta).E_0$$

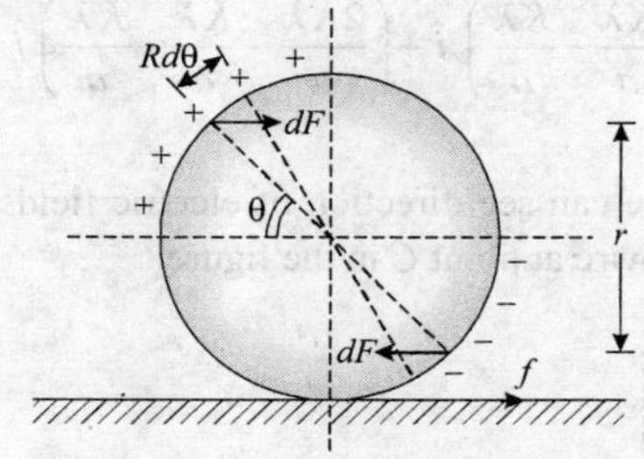

Perpendicular distance between two equal and opposite force pairs of dF will be

$$r = 2R\sin\theta$$

torque on ring is

$$d\tau = dF.r = 2\lambda R^2E_0\sin\theta.\,d\theta$$

$$\Rightarrow\quad \tau = \int_0^{\pi/2} d\tau = 2\lambda R^2E_0$$

These pair of forces will not provide net force but due to rotation tendency force of friction on ring is f in forward direction as shown.

For pure rolling to take place, we use

$$a = R\alpha$$

$$\Rightarrow\quad \frac{f}{m} = R\left[\frac{\tau - fR}{mR^2}\right]$$

$$\Rightarrow\quad f = \frac{\tau}{R} - f$$

$$\Rightarrow\quad f = \frac{\tau}{2R} = \lambda RE_0$$

Solutions of PRACTICE EXERCISE 1.3

(i) The electric fields due to the three parts of U-shaped wire are shown in figure.

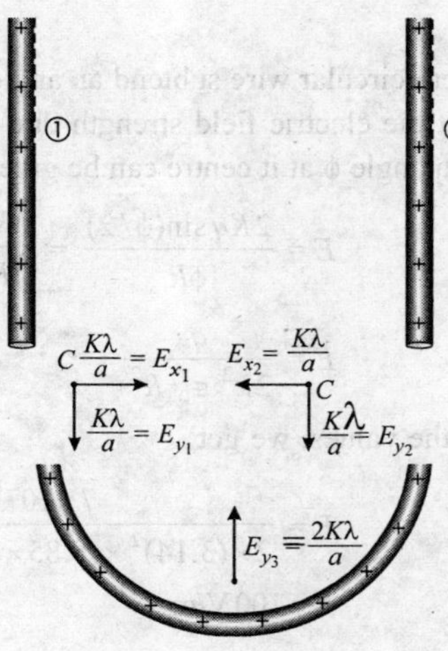

Net electric field vector at C is given as

$$\vec{E}_{net} = (E_{x_1} + E_{x_2})\,\hat{i} + (E_{y_1} + E_{y_2} + E_{y_3})\hat{j}$$

$$\vec{E}_{net} = \left(\frac{K\lambda}{a} - \frac{K\lambda}{a}\right)\hat{i} + \left(\frac{2K\lambda}{a} - \frac{K\lambda}{a} - \frac{K\lambda}{a}\right)\hat{j} = 0$$

(ii) Here we can see direction of electric fields due to the three parts of wire at point C in the figure.

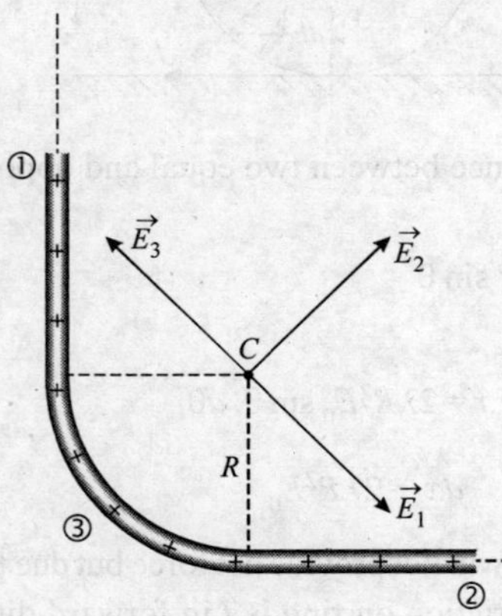

Here $\vec{E}_1$ (field due to wire (1) cancels out with $\vec{E}_3$ (field due to wire 3) and $\vec{E}_2$ (field due to wire (2) will only remain at C.

Thus net electric field is at point C given as

$$\vec{E}_{net} = \vec{E}_1 + \vec{E}_2 + \vec{E}_3$$

$$\vec{E}_{net} = \vec{E}_2 \text{ (As } \vec{E}_1 = -\vec{E}_3)$$

$$\Rightarrow \quad \vec{E}_{net} = \frac{2K\left(\lambda\dfrac{\pi R}{2}\right)\sin\left(\dfrac{\pi}{4}\right)}{\dfrac{\pi}{2}R^2}$$

$$\Rightarrow \quad \vec{E}_{net} = \frac{\lambda}{2\sqrt{2}\pi \in_0 R}$$

(iii) The semicircular wire subtend an angle π at the centre, we know that the electric field strength due to a circular arc subtending an angle ϕ at it centre can be given as

$$E = \frac{2Kq\sin(\phi/2)}{\phi R^2} = \frac{2Kq}{\pi R^2} \quad [\text{Here } \phi = \pi]$$

$$\Rightarrow \quad E = \frac{q}{2\pi^2 \in_0 R^2}$$

Substituting the values, we get

$$E = \frac{7\times10^{-10}}{2\times(3.14)^2\times(8.85\times10^{-12})\times(0.2)^2}$$

$$\Rightarrow \quad E = 100\,\text{V/m}$$

(iv) The electric field strength due to the three rods AB, BC and CA are as shown in figure which is given by the expression of electric field due to a finite wire given as

$$\vec{E}_{AC} = \frac{-1K\lambda}{(l/2\sqrt{3})}(2\sin 60^\circ)(\cos 30^\circ\,\hat{i} + \sin 30^\circ\,\hat{j})$$

$$\vec{E}_{AB} = \frac{1K\lambda}{(l/2\sqrt{3})}(2\sin 60^\circ)(\cos 30^\circ\hat{i} - \sin 30^\circ\,\hat{j})$$

$$\vec{E}_{BC} = \frac{1K\lambda}{(l/2\sqrt{3})}(2\sin 60^\circ)\,\hat{j}$$

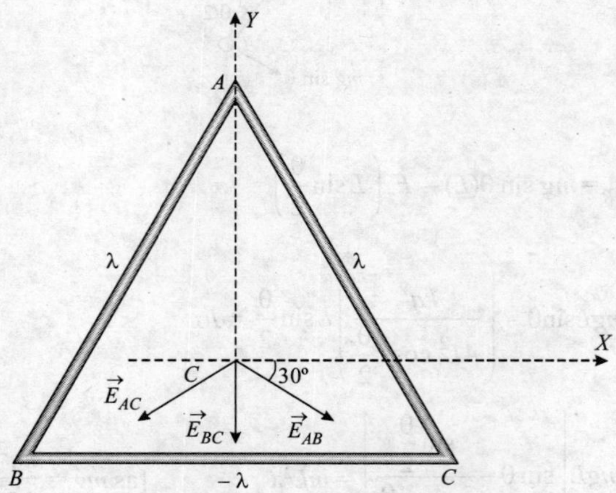

Net electric field centroid is given as

$$\vec{E}_{net} = \vec{E}_{AC} + \vec{E}_{AB} + \vec{E}_{BC}$$

$$\Rightarrow \quad \vec{E}_{net} = \frac{-\lambda}{2\pi \in_0 l}\,\hat{j}$$

(v) We know due to a ring electric field strength at a distance l from its centre on its axis can be given as

$$E = \frac{Kql}{(l^2 + r^2)^{3/2}} \quad \ldots(1)$$

For $l >> r$, we have, $E = \dfrac{1}{4\pi \in_0} \times \dfrac{q}{l^2}$

Thus the ring behaves like a point charge for far away distances

For maximum electric field we use $dE/dl = 0$

From equation-(1), we get

$$\frac{dE}{dl} = \frac{q}{4\pi \in_0}\left[\frac{(r^2+l^2)^{3/2}\cdot 1 - \frac{3}{2}(r^2+l^2)^{1/2}\times 2l}{(r^2+l^2)^3}\right] = 0$$

$$\Rightarrow \quad (r^2 + l^2)^{3/2} = 3/2\,(r^2 + l^2)^{1/2} \times 2l$$

$$\Rightarrow \quad l = r/\sqrt{2} \quad \ldots(2)$$

Substituting the value of $l = r/\sqrt{2}$ in equation-(2), we get

$$E_{\max} = \frac{1}{4\pi \epsilon_0} \times \frac{q(r\sqrt{2})}{(r^2 + r^2/2)^{3/2}} = \frac{q}{6\sqrt{3}\pi \epsilon_0 r^2}$$

(vi) The charge on the element removed is given as

$$dq = \frac{Q(dL)}{2\pi a}$$

The electric field due to the charge of the element at the centre, is given as

$$E_1 = \frac{1}{4\pi \epsilon_0} \frac{dq}{a^2} = \frac{1}{4\pi \epsilon_0}\left[\frac{QdL}{2\pi a^3}\right]$$

We know that electric field at the centre of a uniformly charged circular loop is zero. If E_2 be the electric field of the remaining wire loop, then we use

$$\vec{E} = \vec{E}_1 + \vec{E}_2 = 0$$

$$\Rightarrow \quad \vec{E}_2 = -\vec{E}_1$$

$$\Rightarrow \quad E_2 = E_1$$

$$E_2 = \frac{QdL}{8\pi^2 \epsilon_0 a^3}$$

(vii) When electron is at a distance x from the centre of the ring as shown in figure. The force on the electron is given as

$$F = -Ee$$

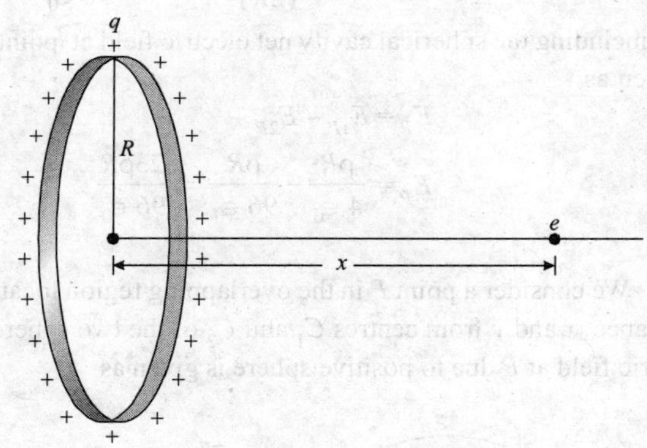

$$\Rightarrow \quad F = -\left[\frac{1}{4\pi \epsilon_0} \frac{qx}{(R^2 + x^2)^{3/2}}\right] e$$

For $x << R$, we have

$$F = -\left[\frac{1}{4\pi \epsilon_0} \frac{qe}{R^3}\right] x$$

Acceleration of electron is given as

$$a = \frac{F}{m} = \frac{1}{4\pi \epsilon_0} \frac{qe}{mR^3}(-x)$$

Compare with standard equation of SHM, $a = -\omega^2 x$, we get

$$\omega = \sqrt{\frac{qe}{4\pi \epsilon_0 mR^3}}$$

(viii) (a) Near to charge Q_2, choose field intensity is infinite along negative x-axis. Therefore Q_2 is negative.
Beyond $x > (l + a)$, field intensity is positive. Thus charge Q_1 is positive.

(b) At $x = l + a$, field intensity is zero due to the two charges so we have

$$\frac{KQ_1}{(l+a)^2} = \frac{KQ_2}{a^2}$$

$$\Rightarrow \quad \left|\frac{Q_1}{Q_2}\right| = \left(\frac{l+a}{a}\right)^2$$

(c) Intensity at distance x from charge 2 would be,

$$E = \frac{KQ_1}{(x+l)^2} - \frac{KQ_2}{x^2}$$

For E to be maximum we use

$$\frac{dE}{dx} = 0$$

$$\Rightarrow \quad -\frac{2KQ_1}{(x+l)^3} + \frac{2KQ_2}{x^3} = 0$$

$$\Rightarrow \quad \left(1 + \frac{l}{x}\right)^3 = \frac{Q_1}{Q_2} = \left(\frac{l+a}{a}\right)^2$$

$$\Rightarrow \quad 1 + \frac{l}{x} = \left(\frac{l+a}{a}\right)^{2/3}$$

$$\Rightarrow \quad x = \frac{l}{\left(\frac{l+a}{a}\right)^{2/3} - 1}$$

$$\Rightarrow \quad b = \frac{l}{\left(\frac{l+a}{a}\right)^{2/3} - 1}$$

(ix) Electric field due to rod AB at point P is given as

$$\vec{E}_{AB} = \int_{0.5}^{1.5} \frac{K\lambda dx}{x^2} = -K\lambda\left[\frac{2}{3} - 2\right] = \frac{\lambda}{3\pi \epsilon_0}$$

Electric field at P due to rod CD is given as

$$E_{CD_y} = \frac{K\lambda}{r}(\cos\theta_2 - \cos\theta_1) = \frac{\lambda}{2\pi \epsilon_0}\left(\frac{\sqrt{5}-1}{\sqrt{5}}\right)\hat{j}$$

and $E_{CD_x} = \frac{K\lambda}{r}[\sin\theta_2 + \sin\theta_1] = \frac{\lambda}{\sqrt{5}\pi\epsilon_0}(-\hat{i})$

Net electric field at point P is given as

$$\vec{E}_{net} = \vec{E}_{AB} + \vec{E}_{CD}$$

Substituting the values gives

$$\vec{E}_{net} = -839\hat{i} + 1980\hat{j}$$

Solutions of PRACTICE EXERCISE 1.4

(i) Charge enclosed in the sphere upto radius r is given as

$$q = \int_0^r kx^a 4\pi x^2 dx$$

$$\Rightarrow \quad q = 4\pi k\left[\frac{x^{3+a}}{3+a}\right]_{x=0}^{x=r} = \frac{4\pi k}{(3+a)}r^{3+a}$$

At $x = R/2$ electric field is given as

$$E_1 = \frac{kq}{(R/2)^2}$$

$$\Rightarrow \quad E_1 = \frac{1}{4\pi\epsilon_0}\frac{4\pi k}{(3+a)}\frac{(R/2)^{3+a}}{(R/2)^2}$$

$$\Rightarrow \quad E_1 = \frac{k}{\epsilon_0(3+a)}\left(\frac{R}{2}\right)^{1+a}$$

At $x = R$, electric field is given as

$$E_2 = \frac{kq}{R^2} = \frac{1}{4\pi\epsilon_0}\frac{4\pi k}{(3+a)}\frac{(R)^{3+a}}{R^2}$$

$$\Rightarrow \quad E_2 = \frac{k}{\epsilon_0(3+a)}R^{1+a}$$

Given that $\quad E_2 = \frac{E_1}{8}$

$$\Rightarrow \quad \left(\frac{R}{2}\right)^{1+a} = \frac{(R)^{1+a}}{8}$$

$$\Rightarrow \quad 1 + a = 3$$

$$\Rightarrow \quad a = 2$$

(ii) As shown in figure the electric field due to a uniformly charged sphere at a distance $2R$ from its center is given as

$$E_P = \frac{KQ}{4R^2} = \frac{K}{4R^2}\left(\rho\times\frac{4}{3}\pi R^3\right)$$

$$\Rightarrow \quad E_P = \frac{\rho R}{12\epsilon_0}$$

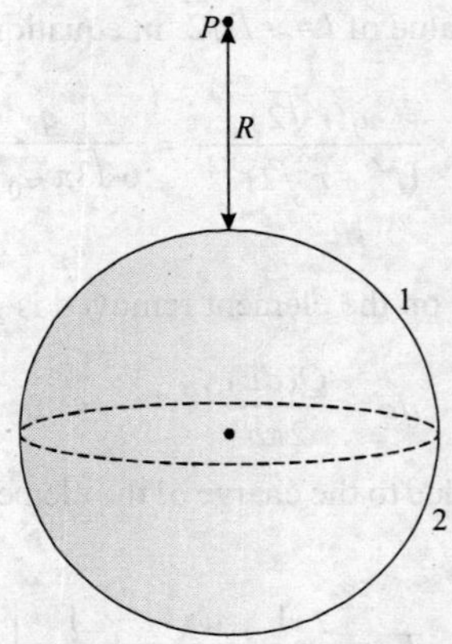

Given that due to part-2 hemisphere electric field at point P is E then due to part-1 hemisphere it is given as

$$E_1 = E_P - E_2$$

$$\Rightarrow \quad E_1 = \frac{\rho R}{12\epsilon_0} - E$$

(iii) Electric field due to the cylinder at point P is gives as

$$E_{1P} = \frac{\rho R^2}{2\epsilon_0(2R)} = \frac{\rho R^2}{4\epsilon_0 R} = \frac{\rho R}{4\epsilon_0}$$

Electric field at P due to the charge contained inside the sphere of radius $R/2$ is given as

$$E_{2P} = \frac{k\left(\rho\times\frac{4}{3}\pi\left(\frac{R}{2}\right)^3\right)}{(2R)^2} = \frac{\rho R}{96\epsilon_0}$$

Now including the spherical cavity net electric field at point P is given as

$$E_P = E_{1P} - E_{2P}$$

$$\Rightarrow \quad E_P = \frac{\rho R}{4\epsilon_0} - \frac{\rho R}{96\epsilon_0} = \frac{23\rho R}{96\epsilon_0}$$

(iv) We consider a point P in the overlapping region located a distance x and y from centres C_1 and C_2 of the two spheres. Electric field at P due to positive sphere is given as

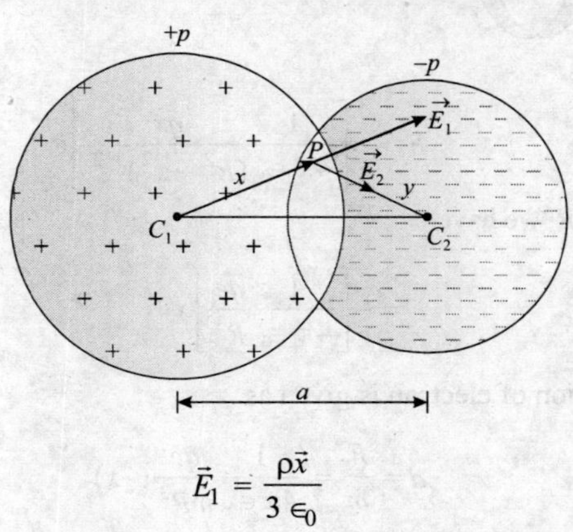

$$\vec{E}_1 = \frac{\rho\vec{x}}{3\epsilon_0}$$

Electric field at P due to negative sphere is given as

$$\vec{E}_2 = \frac{\rho\vec{y}}{3\epsilon_0}$$

Net electric field at point P is given as

$$\vec{E}_{net} = \vec{E}_1 + \vec{E}_2 = \frac{\rho}{3\epsilon_0}(\vec{x}+\vec{y}) = \frac{\rho\vec{a}}{3\epsilon_0}$$

Thus electric field in the overlapping region is uniform and given as $\frac{\rho a}{3\epsilon_0}$.

(v) As discussed in solution of the question-(iv) the electric field in the central hollow region as shown in figure is given as

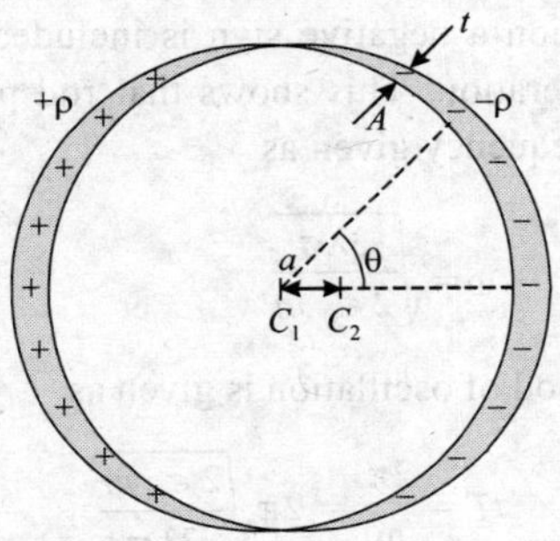

$$E = \frac{\rho a}{3\epsilon_0} \quad \text{...(1)}$$

If we consider the thickness of charged region at point A then it is given as

$$t = a\cos\theta$$

If this is system of two overlapping uniformly charged spheres at small separation a, surface charge density at point A is given as

$$\sigma = \rho t = \rho a\cos\theta = \sigma_0\cos\theta$$

Thus from equation-(1) we have

$$E = \frac{\sigma_0}{3\epsilon_0}$$

(vi) The total charge of shell from inner radius a to a radius r $(a < r < b)$ is given as

$$q_s = \int_a^r \left(\frac{A}{r}\right) 4\pi r^2 dr$$

$$\Rightarrow \quad q_s = 4\pi A\left[\frac{r^2}{2}\right]_a^r$$

$$\Rightarrow \quad q_s = 4\pi a(r^2 - a^2)$$

Electric field in the annular region of shell is given as

$$E = \frac{k(q+q_s)}{r^2}$$

$$\Rightarrow \quad E = \frac{1}{4\pi\epsilon_0 r^2}(q + 2\pi Ar^2 - 2\pi Aa^2)$$

Above electric field will be uniform only when

$$q = 2\pi Aa^2$$

$$\Rightarrow \quad A = \frac{q}{2\pi a^2}$$

(vii) Force on segments AB and CD are given as

$$F_{AB} = \frac{a}{l}(0+l)\times\lambda l = a\lambda l$$

$$F_{CD} = \frac{a}{l}(l+l)\times\lambda l = 2a\lambda l$$

Force on segments AD and BC can be given as

$$F_{AD} = F_{BC} = F$$

Where $\quad F = \int \frac{a}{l}(x+l)\lambda dx$

$$\Rightarrow \quad F = \frac{a\lambda}{l}\left[\frac{x^2}{2} + lx\right]_0^l = \frac{3}{2}a\lambda l$$

Thus total force on loop is

$$F_{net} = 6a\lambda l = 6\times 5\times 10^5\times 20\times 10^{-6}\times 0.1$$

$$F_{net} = 6\,\text{N}$$

(viii) The charge at P at $z = a$ is in equilibrium when electric field due to the two rings at point P is zero. For this we use

$$\vec{E}_P = \vec{E}_{Pa} + \vec{E}_{Pb} = \vec{0}$$

$$\Rightarrow \quad \frac{Kqa}{(a^2+a^2)^{3/2}} - \frac{Kq\left(\frac{2}{5}\right)^{-3/2} a}{(a^2+b^2)^{3/2}} = 0$$

$$\Rightarrow \quad \frac{b}{a} = 2$$

(ix) The direction of electric field inside the cavity leftward is in direction and of constant magnitude given as

$$E_{cavity} = \frac{\rho a}{3\epsilon_0}$$

For touching the sphere again, electron must move a distance $2r\cos 45°$ and time taken by electron for this is given as

$$t = \sqrt{\frac{2l}{a}}$$

$$\Rightarrow \quad t = \sqrt{\frac{2(\sqrt{2}-r)}{eE/m}}$$

$$\Rightarrow \quad t = \sqrt{\frac{6\sqrt{2}mr \in_0}{e\rho a}}$$

(x) Electric field at a distance x from the hole is given as

$$E = \frac{\sigma}{2 \in_0} - \frac{\sigma}{2 \in_0}\left(1 - \frac{x}{\sqrt{x^2 + R^2}}\right)$$

$$\Rightarrow \quad E = \frac{\sigma x}{2 \in_0 \sqrt{R^2 + x^2}}$$

Acceleration of electron at a point on axis of hole is given as

$$a = \frac{eE}{m} = \frac{e\sigma x}{2m \in_0 \sqrt{R^2 + x^2}}$$

$$\Rightarrow \quad -\int_0^v v dv = \int_{\sqrt{3}R}^0 \frac{e\sigma x}{2m \in_0 \sqrt{R^2 + x^2}} dx$$

$$\Rightarrow \quad -\frac{v^2}{2} = \frac{e\sigma}{2m \in_0}\left[\sqrt{R^2 + x^2}\right]_{\sqrt{3}R}^0$$

$$\Rightarrow \quad v^2 = \frac{e\sigma}{m \in_0}\sqrt{R^2 + 3R^2}$$

$$\Rightarrow \quad v = \sqrt{\frac{4e\sigma R}{m \in_0}}$$

$$\Rightarrow \quad v = 2\sqrt{\frac{e\sigma R}{m \in_0}}$$

(xi) Figure shows the rod when it is slightly rotated by a small angle θ.

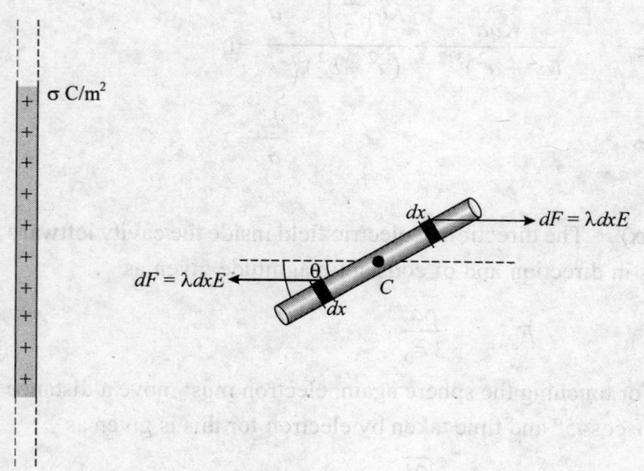

Torque on elements on rod is given as

$$d\tau = dF(2x \sin \theta)$$

$$\Rightarrow \quad \tau = \frac{\lambda\sigma \sin \theta}{\in_0}\int_0^{l/2} x dx$$

$$\Rightarrow \quad \tau = \frac{\lambda\sigma \sin \theta}{\in_0}\frac{\ell^2}{8} = \frac{\lambda\sigma\ell^2}{8 \in_0}\theta$$

[for small θ, will use sin θ ≃ θ]

$$\Rightarrow \quad I\alpha = \frac{\lambda\sigma l^2\theta}{8 \in_0}$$

$$\Rightarrow \quad \frac{Ml^2\alpha}{12} = \frac{\lambda\sigma l^2\theta}{8 \in_0}$$

$$\Rightarrow \quad \alpha = -\frac{3\lambda\sigma}{8 \in_0}\theta$$

In above equation a negative sign is included for restoring nature of acceleration. This shows that rod performs SHM with angular frequency given as

$$\omega = \sqrt{\frac{3\lambda\sigma}{2 \in_0 m}}$$

So the time period of oscillation is given as

$$T = \frac{2\pi}{\omega} = 2\pi\sqrt{\frac{2 \in_0 m}{3\lambda\sigma}}$$

Solutions of PRACTICE EXERCISE 1.5

(i) Figure below describes the situation given in question.

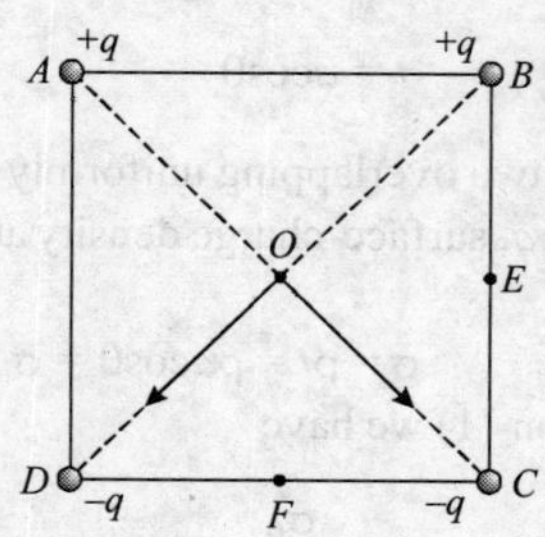

Electric field at point O is given as

$$\vec{E}_0 = \frac{2Kq}{\left(\frac{a}{\sqrt{2}}\right)^2}\widehat{OC} + \frac{2Kq}{\left(\frac{a}{\sqrt{2}}\right)^2}\widehat{OD}$$

Thus net electric field at point O is given as

$$E_{net} = \sqrt{2}\left(\frac{2Kq}{a^2/2}\right)$$

$$\Rightarrow \quad E_{net} = \frac{4\sqrt{2}Kq}{a^2}$$

Electric potential at point O is given as

$$V_0 = \frac{Kq}{a/\sqrt{2}} + \frac{Kq}{a/\sqrt{2}} - \frac{Kq}{a/\sqrt{2}} - \frac{Kq}{a/\sqrt{2}}$$

$$\Rightarrow \quad V_0 = 0$$

Electric potential of point E is given as

$$V_E = \frac{Kq}{(AE)} + \frac{Kq}{(BE)} - \frac{Kq}{(DE)} - \frac{Kq}{(CE)}$$

As $AE = DE$ and $BE = CE$

$$\Rightarrow \quad V_E = 0$$

Thus work done in carrying a charge from O to E is zero.

Electric the potential at point F is given as

$$V_F = \frac{Kq}{(AF)} + \frac{Kq}{(BF)} - \frac{Kq}{(CF)} - \frac{Kq}{(DF)}$$

We have $AF = BF = \frac{\sqrt{5}}{2} a$ and $CE = DF = \frac{a}{2}$

$$\Rightarrow \quad V_F = \frac{Kq}{a}\left[\frac{4}{\sqrt{5}} - 4\right]$$

$$\Rightarrow \quad V_F = \frac{4Kq}{a}\left(\frac{1-\sqrt{5}}{\sqrt{5}}\right)$$

Work done in shifting Q from O to F is given as

$$W = QV_F$$

$$\Rightarrow \quad W = \frac{4KQq}{a}\left(\frac{1-\sqrt{5}}{\sqrt{5}}\right)$$

(ii) (a) Electric potential at origin is given as

$$V_0 = \frac{Kq}{a} + \frac{Kq}{a} = \frac{2Kq}{a}$$

By work energy theorem we use

$$q(V_0 - V_\infty) = \frac{1}{2}mv^2$$

$$\Rightarrow \quad q_0\left(\frac{2Kq}{a}\right) = \frac{1}{2}mv^2$$

$$\Rightarrow \quad v = \sqrt{\frac{2Kqq_0}{ma}}$$

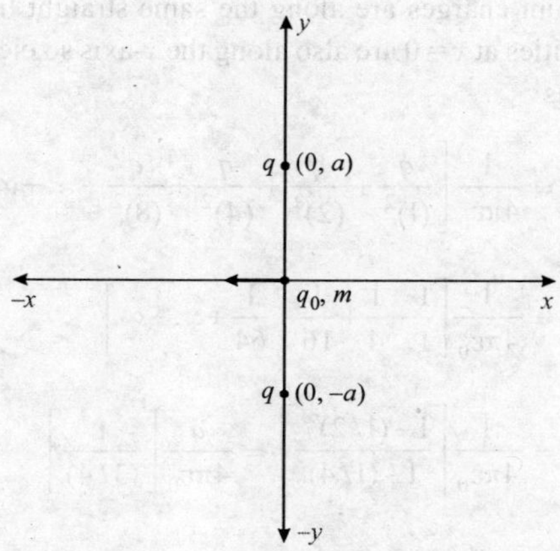

(b) Electric potential at a distance x from origin is given as

$$V_x = \frac{2Kq}{(a^2 + x^2)^{1/2}}$$

Conserving energy at the point and at the point for away of stoppage where x is the distance of stoppage point from origin, we have

$$q_0(V_x - V_\infty) = \frac{1}{2}m\left(\frac{u}{2}\right)^2$$

$$\Rightarrow \quad \frac{Kqq_0}{2a} = \frac{2Kqq_0}{(a^2 + x^2)^{1/2}}$$

$$\Rightarrow \quad (a^2 + x^2)^{1/2} = 4a$$

$$\Rightarrow \quad a^2 + x^2 = 16a^2$$

$$\Rightarrow \quad x^2 = 15a^2$$

$$\Rightarrow \quad x = \pm\sqrt{15}\, a$$

Here q_0 is coming from infinity it will stop at $(\sqrt{15}\, a, 0)$

(iii) The set of charges are shown in figure

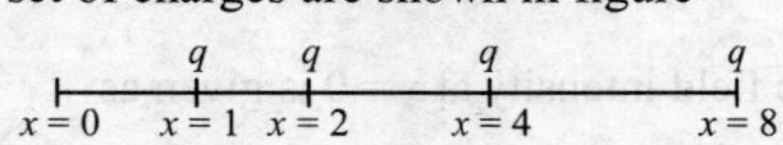

The potential at $x = 0$ due to all charges is given by

$$V = \frac{1}{4\pi\varepsilon_0}\left(\frac{q}{1} + \frac{q}{2} + \frac{q}{4} + \frac{q}{8} + \ldots + \infty\right)$$

$$\Rightarrow \quad V = \frac{q}{4\pi\varepsilon_0}\left(1 + \frac{1}{2} + \frac{1}{4} + \frac{1}{8} + \ldots + \infty\right)$$

$$\Rightarrow \quad V = \frac{q}{4\pi\varepsilon_0}\left[\frac{1 - \left(\frac{1}{2}\right)^\infty}{1 - \left(\frac{1}{2}\right)}\right] = \frac{q}{4\pi\varepsilon_0}\left[\frac{1-0}{\left(\frac{1}{2}\right)}\right]$$

$$\Rightarrow \quad V = \frac{2q}{4\pi\varepsilon_0} = \frac{q}{2\pi\epsilon_0}$$

As the point charges are along the same straight line, hence the intensities at $x = 0$ are also along the x-axis so electric field is given as

$$E = \frac{1}{4\pi\varepsilon_0}\left[\frac{q}{(1)^2} + \frac{q}{(2)^2} + \frac{q}{(4)^2} + \frac{q}{(8)^2} + \ldots + \infty\right]$$

$$\Rightarrow \quad E = \frac{1}{4\pi\varepsilon_0}\left[\frac{1}{1} + \frac{1}{4} + \frac{1}{16} + \frac{1}{64} + \ldots + \infty\right]$$

$$\Rightarrow \quad E = \frac{1}{4\pi\varepsilon_0}\left[\frac{1-(1/2)^{\infty}}{1-(1/4)}\right] = \frac{q}{4\pi\varepsilon_0}\left[\frac{1}{(3/4)}\right]$$

$$\Rightarrow \quad E = \frac{4q}{4\pi\varepsilon_0 \times 3} = \frac{q}{3\pi\varepsilon_0}$$

When the consecutive charge are negative, then we use

$$V = \frac{1}{4\pi\varepsilon_0}\left[\frac{q}{1} - \frac{q}{2} + \frac{q}{4} - \frac{q}{8} + \frac{q}{16} - \frac{q}{32} + \ldots \infty\right]$$

$$\Rightarrow \quad V = \frac{1}{4\pi\varepsilon_0}\left[\left(\frac{q}{1} + \frac{q}{4} + \frac{q}{16} + \ldots\right) - \left(\frac{q}{2} + \frac{q}{8} + \frac{q}{32} + \ldots \infty\right)\right]$$

$$\Rightarrow \quad V = \frac{1}{4\pi\varepsilon_0}\left[\left(1 + \frac{1}{4} + \frac{1}{16} + \ldots \infty\right) - \left(\frac{1}{2} + \frac{1}{8} + \frac{1}{32} + \ldots \infty\right)\right]$$

$$\Rightarrow \quad V = \frac{q}{4\pi\varepsilon_0}\left[\left(\frac{1}{1-\left(\frac{1}{4}\right)}\right) - \frac{1}{2}\left(\frac{1}{1-\left(\frac{1}{4}\right)}\right)\right]$$

$$\Rightarrow \quad V = \frac{q}{4\pi\varepsilon_0}\left[\frac{4}{3} - \frac{2}{3}\right] = \frac{2q}{4\pi\varepsilon_0 \times 3} = \frac{1}{4\pi\varepsilon_0}\left(\frac{2q}{3}\right)$$

The electric field intensity at $x = 0$ is given as

$$E = \frac{1}{4\pi\varepsilon_0}\left[\frac{q}{(1)^2} - \frac{q}{(2)^2} + \frac{q}{(4)^2} - \frac{q}{(8)^2} + \frac{q}{(16)^2} - \frac{q}{(32)^2} + \ldots \infty\right]$$

$$\Rightarrow \quad E = \frac{q}{4\pi\varepsilon_0}\left[\left(1 + \frac{1}{16} + \frac{1}{256} + \ldots\right) - \left(\frac{1}{4} + \frac{1}{64} + \frac{1}{1024} + \ldots\right)\right]$$

$$\Rightarrow \quad E = \frac{q}{4\pi\varepsilon_0}\left[\left(\frac{1}{1-(1/16)}\right) - \frac{1}{4}\left(\frac{1}{1-(1/16)}\right)\right]$$

$$\Rightarrow \quad E = \frac{q}{4\pi\varepsilon_0}\left[\frac{16}{15} - \frac{1}{4}\left(\frac{16}{15}\right)\right]$$

$$\Rightarrow \quad E = \frac{q}{4\pi\varepsilon_0}\left(\frac{4q}{5}\right)$$

(iv) The situation is shown in figure.

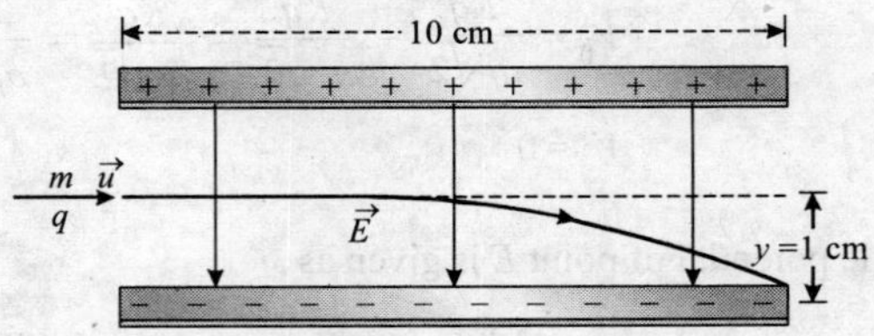

We know that the electric field between plates can be given as

$$E = \frac{V}{d}$$

$$\Rightarrow \quad E = \frac{300}{2/100} = 15000 \text{ V/m}$$

As the particle does not come out, its maximum deflection in vertical direction can be 1 cm as shown so we use

$$y = 1 \text{ cm} = 10^{-2} \text{ m}$$

We also use, $$y = \frac{1}{2} a t^2 = \frac{1}{2} \cdot \frac{qE}{m}\left(\frac{l}{u}\right)^2$$

$$\Rightarrow \quad u^2 = \frac{1}{2} \cdot \frac{qE}{my} \cdot x^2$$

$$\Rightarrow \quad u = \frac{1}{2} \frac{(1.6 \times 10^{-19})(15000)}{(12 \times 10^{-24})(10^{-2})}\left(\frac{1}{10}\right)^2 = 10^8$$

$$\Rightarrow \quad u = 10^4 \text{ m/s}$$

(v) The situation is shown in figure.

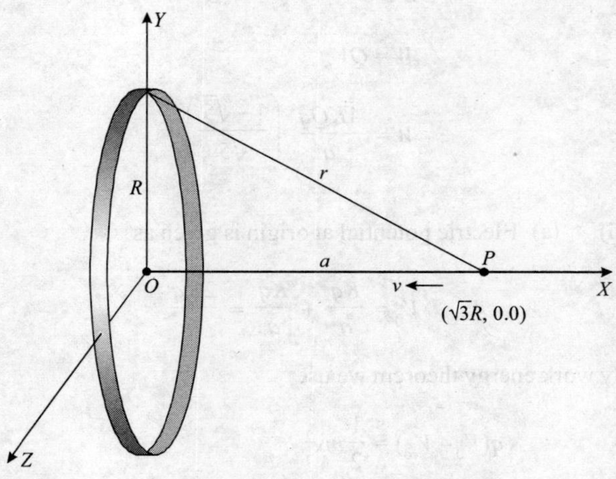

Potential at point P shown in figure is given as

$$V_P = \frac{Kq}{r} = \frac{K(\lambda \cdot 2\pi R)}{r}$$

$$\Rightarrow \quad V_P = \frac{\lambda R}{2 \in_0 \sqrt{(a^2 + R^2)}}$$

$$\Rightarrow \quad V_P = \frac{\lambda R}{2\in_0\sqrt{[(\sqrt{3}R)^2+R^2)]}} = \frac{\lambda}{4\in_0}$$

Potential energy of charge q at point P is given as

$$U_P = qV_P = \frac{q\lambda}{4\in_0}$$

Kinetic energy of particle at P is given as

$$K_P = \frac{1}{2}mv^2$$

Thus total energy at P is

$$E_P = \frac{\lambda q}{4\in_0} + \frac{1}{2}mv^2$$

When particle reaches the centre of ring its potential energy at centre is given as

$$E_C = (\lambda q/2\in_0)$$

The particle will not return to P, when it will just cross the ring centre. Thus by energy conservation we have

$$\frac{\lambda q}{4\in_0} + \frac{1}{2}mv^2 = \frac{\lambda q}{2\in_0}$$

$$\Rightarrow \quad \frac{1}{2}mv^2 = \frac{\lambda q}{2\in_0} - \frac{\lambda q}{4\in_0} = \frac{\lambda q}{4\in_0}$$

$$\Rightarrow \quad v^2 = \frac{\lambda q}{4\in_0 m}$$

$$\Rightarrow \quad v = \sqrt{\left(\frac{\lambda q}{4\in_0 m}\right)}$$

(vi) The arrangement of rings is shown in figure. The potential at the centre of ring A due to its own charge $+q$ is given as

$$V'_A = \frac{Kq}{R}$$

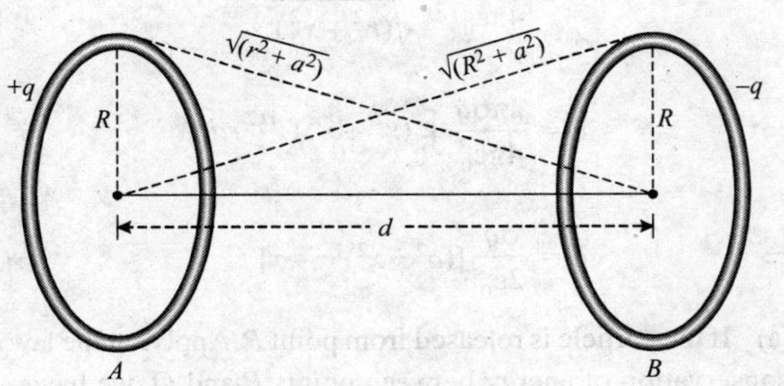

The potential at the centre of ring A due to negative charge $(-q)$ of ring B is given as

$$V''_A = \frac{K(-q)}{\sqrt{(R^2+a^2)}}$$

Net potential at centre of ring A is given as

$$V_A = V'_A + V''_A$$

$$\Rightarrow \quad V_A = \frac{Kq}{R} - \frac{Kq}{\sqrt{(R^2+a^2)}}$$

$$\Rightarrow \quad V_A = Kq\left[\frac{1}{R} - \frac{1}{\sqrt{(R^2+a^2)}}\right]$$

Similarly net potential at centre of ring B is given as

$$V_B = V'_B + V''_B$$

$$\Rightarrow \quad V_B = K\left[\frac{1}{R} - \frac{1}{\sqrt{(R^2+a^2)}} + \frac{1}{R} - \frac{1}{\sqrt{(R^2+a^2)}}\right]$$

$$\Rightarrow \quad V_B = Kq\left[-\frac{1}{R} + \frac{1}{\sqrt{(R^2+a^2)}}\right]$$

Thus potential difference is given as

$$\Delta V = V_A - V_B$$

$$\Rightarrow \quad \Delta V = Kq\left[\frac{1}{R} - \frac{1}{\sqrt{(R^2+a^2)}} + \frac{1}{R} - \frac{1}{\sqrt{(R^2+a^2)}}\right]$$

$$\Rightarrow \quad \Delta V = 2Kq\left[\frac{1}{R} - \frac{1}{R\sqrt{1+(a/R)^2}}\right]$$

$$\Rightarrow \quad \Delta V = \frac{q}{2\pi\in_0}\left[1 - \frac{1}{\sqrt{1+(a/R)^2}}\right]$$

(vii) Potentials at points P and A is figure due to sphere charge are given as

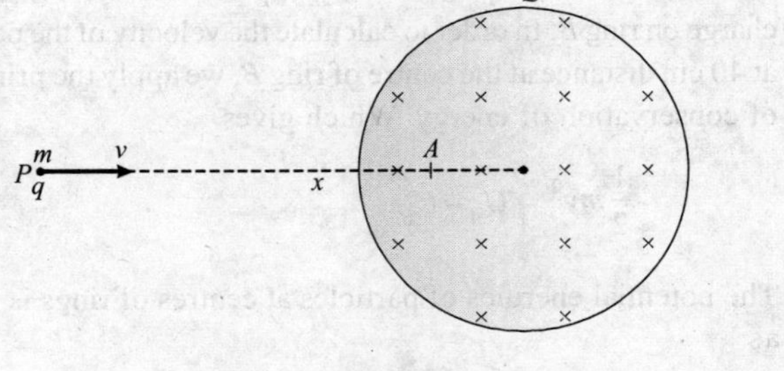

$$V_P = \frac{KQ}{x}$$

At $x = R/2$ $\quad V_A = \frac{KQ}{2R^3}\left(3R^2 - \frac{R^2}{4}\right) = \frac{11KQ}{8R}$

By energy conservation we have

$$\frac{1}{2}mv^2 + qV_P = qV_A$$

$$\Rightarrow \quad v = \sqrt{\frac{2q(V_A - V_P)}{m}}$$

$$\Rightarrow \quad v = \sqrt{\frac{2KQq}{m}\left(\frac{11}{8R} - \frac{1}{x}\right)}$$

(viii) If a point A is considered on surface of the sheet as shown in figure we have

$$V_A = V_0$$

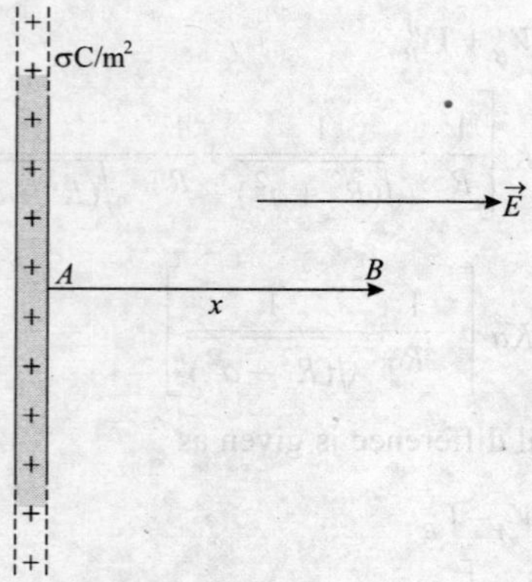

As electric field is away from sheet which is given as $E = \sigma/2\varepsilon_0$ the potential difference between points A and B is given as

$$V_A - V_B = Ex = \frac{\sigma}{2\epsilon_0}x$$

$$\Rightarrow \quad V_B = V_0 - \frac{\sigma}{2\epsilon_0}x$$

(ix) The weight of particle $W = mg = 1$ N and force due to electric field $F = qE = 1$ N. So, the weight of the particle is balanced by electric force. As the particle is at the centre of the ring and hence no force acts on the particle due to the charge on the ring A. The particle only experiences a force due to charge on ring B. In order to calculate the velocity of the particle at 40 cm distance at the centre of ring B, we apply the principle of conservation of energy. Which gives

$$\frac{1}{2}mv^2 = U_A - U_B \quad \ldots(1)$$

The potential energies of particles at centres of rings is given as

$$U_A = \frac{1}{4\pi\varepsilon_0}\frac{qq_1}{a} + \frac{1}{4\pi\varepsilon_0}\frac{q(-q_2)}{\sqrt{(a^2+h^2)}} \quad \ldots(2)$$

$$U_B = \frac{1}{4\pi\varepsilon_0}\frac{qq_1}{\sqrt{(a^2+h^2)}} + \frac{1}{4\pi\varepsilon_0}\frac{q(-q_2)}{a} \quad \ldots(3)$$

Substituting the values of U_A and U_B from equations-(2) and (3) in equation-(1) gives

$$\frac{1}{2}mv^2 = \frac{q}{4\pi\varepsilon_0}\left[q_1\left\{\frac{1}{a} - \frac{1}{\sqrt{(a^2+h^2)}}\right\} + q_2\left\{\frac{1}{a} - \frac{1}{\sqrt{a^2+h^2}}\right\}\right]$$

$$\Rightarrow \quad \frac{1}{2}mv^2 = \frac{q}{4\pi\varepsilon_0}\left[\left\{\frac{1}{a} - \frac{1}{\sqrt{(a^2+h^2)}}\right\}(q_1+q_2)\right]$$

$$\Rightarrow \quad \frac{1}{2}mv^2 = \frac{q}{4\pi\varepsilon_0}\left[\left\{\frac{\sqrt{(a^2+h^2)} - a}{a\sqrt{a^2+h^2}}\right\}(q_1+q_2)\right]$$

$$\Rightarrow \quad v = 6\sqrt{2} \text{ m/s}$$

(x) See At any instant, the charged particle q is on the axis of disc at a distance x from the centre at point P' shown in figure.

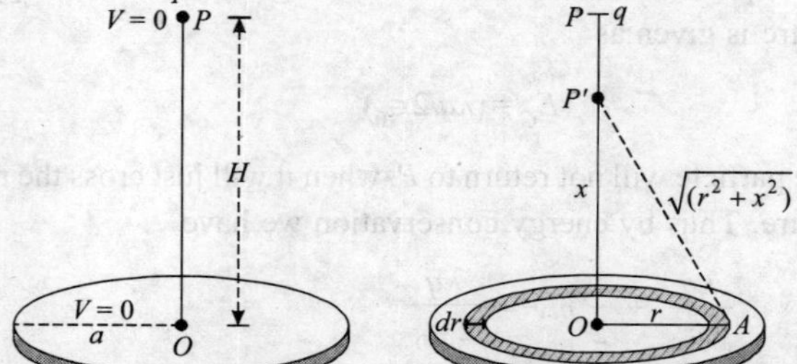

Divide the disc into large number of flat circular strips. Consider one such strip of radius r and width dr. Charge dq contained in the strip

$$dq = \sigma.\text{ (area of the strip)} = \sigma.\ (2\pi r\, dr)$$

Potential at P' due to this charge element

$$dV = \frac{1}{4\pi\varepsilon_0} \times \frac{dq}{(AP')} = \frac{1}{4\pi\varepsilon_0} \times \frac{\sigma(2\pi r dr)}{\sqrt{(r^2+x^2)}}$$

Now, electrostatic potential energy of q at P' is given as

$$U = \frac{1}{4\pi\varepsilon_0}\int_0^a \frac{2\pi r dr \sigma q}{\sqrt{(r^2+x^2)}}$$

$$\Rightarrow \quad U = \frac{2\pi\sigma q}{4\pi\varepsilon_0}\int_0^a (r^2+x^2)^{-1/2}\, r dr$$

$$\Rightarrow \quad U = \frac{\sigma q}{2\varepsilon_0}\left[(a^2+x^2)^{1/2} - x\right] \quad \ldots(1)$$

(a) If the particle is released from point P. Applying the law of conservation of energy between points P and O, we have

$$mgH + \frac{\sigma q}{2\varepsilon_0}\left[\sqrt{(a^2+H^2)} - H\right] = 0 + \frac{\sigma q}{2\varepsilon_0}\left[\sqrt{a^2+0^2} - 0\right]$$

Using $q = (4\varepsilon_0 g\, m/\sigma)$ gives

$$mgH + \frac{\sigma(4\varepsilon_0 gm/\sigma)}{2\varepsilon_0}[\sqrt{(a^2+H^2)} - H] = \frac{\sigma(4\varepsilon_0 gm/\sigma)}{2\varepsilon_0}$$

$$\Rightarrow \quad mgH + 2mg\,[\sqrt{(a^2+H^2)} - H] = 2mga$$

$$\Rightarrow \quad H + 2\sqrt{(a^2+H^2)} - 2H = 2a$$

$$\Rightarrow \quad 2\sqrt{(a^2+H^2)} = (2a+H)$$

$$\Rightarrow \quad 4(a^2+H^2) = (2a+H)^2$$

$$\Rightarrow \quad H = \frac{4a}{3}$$

(b) Total potential energy at a height x above centre is

$$U_x = \frac{\sigma q}{2\varepsilon_0}[\sqrt{(a^2+x^2)} - x] + mgx$$

Substituting the value of q, we get

$$U_x = 2mg[\sqrt{(a^2+x^2)} - x] + mgx$$

$$\Rightarrow \quad U_\alpha = mg[2\sqrt{(a^2+x^2)} - x]$$

For equilibrium position, $dU/dx = 0$

$$\Rightarrow \quad \frac{dU}{dx} = mg\left[\frac{2.2x}{2\sqrt{a^2+x^2}} - 1\right] = 0$$

$$\Rightarrow \quad \frac{2x}{\sqrt{a^2+x^2}} = 1 \text{ or } 4x^2 = (a^2+x^2)$$

$$\Rightarrow \quad x = a/\sqrt{3}$$

The variation of potential energy with x is shown in figure.

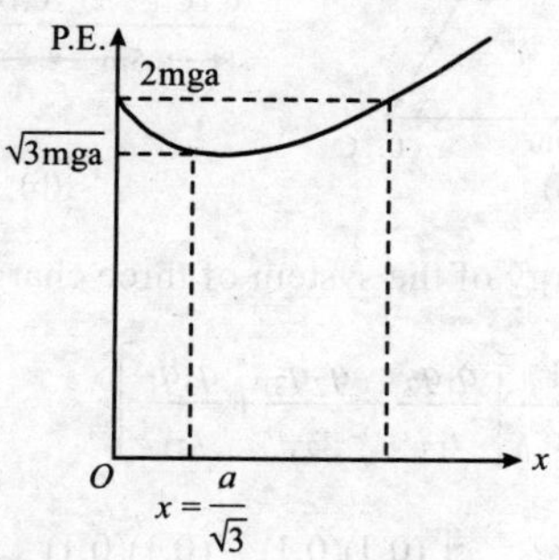

(xi) As we know

$$dV = -\vec{E}\cdot d\vec{r}$$

$$\Rightarrow \quad -dV = ay\,dx + (ax+bz)\,dy + by\,dz$$

$$-dV = a\,d(xy) + b\,d(yz)$$

Integrating, we get

$$V = -axy - byz + \text{constant}$$

$$\Rightarrow \quad V = -y(ax+bz) + \text{constant}$$

(xii) Here, the given field is uniform (constant). So using,

$$dV = -\vec{E}\cdot d\vec{r}$$

$$\Rightarrow \quad V_{ab} = V_a - V_b = \int_b^a \vec{E}\cdot d\vec{r}$$

$$\Rightarrow \quad V_{ab} = -\int_{(2,1,-2)}^{(1,-2,1)} (2\hat{i} + 3\hat{j} + 4\hat{k})\cdot(dx\hat{i} + dy\hat{j} + dz\hat{k})$$

$$\Rightarrow \quad V_{ab} = \int_{(2,1,-2)}^{(1,-2,1)} (2dx + 3dy + 4dz)$$

$$\Rightarrow \quad V_{ab} = -[2x + 3y + 4z]_{(2,1,-2)}^{(1,-2,1)}$$

$$\Rightarrow \quad V_{ab} = -1\text{ V}$$

(xiii) If we consider a point $P(x, y, z)$ on the sphere. Then from the property of the sphere, we have

$$x^2 + y^2 + z^2 = (4^2) = 16 \quad \ldots(1)$$

We have distances PA and PB gives as

$$PA = \sqrt{(x-2)^2 + y^2 + z^2} \quad \ldots(2)$$

and

$$PB = \sqrt{(x-8)^2 + y^2 + z^2} \quad \ldots(3)$$

Potential at point P is given as

$$V_P = \frac{1}{4\pi\varepsilon_0}\left[\frac{q}{PA} - \frac{2q}{PB}\right]$$

$$\Rightarrow \quad V_P = \frac{1}{4\pi\varepsilon_0}\left[\frac{q}{\sqrt{(x-2)^2+y^2+z^2}} - \frac{2q}{\sqrt{(x-8)^2+y^2+z^2}}\right]$$

$$\Rightarrow \quad V_P = \frac{1}{4\pi\varepsilon_0}\left[\frac{q}{\sqrt{x^2+y^2+z^2+4-4x}} - \frac{2q}{\sqrt{x^2+y^2+z^2+64-16x}}\right]$$

$$\Rightarrow \quad V_P = \frac{1}{4\pi\varepsilon_0}\left[\frac{q}{\sqrt{16+4-4x}} - \frac{2q}{\sqrt{16+64-16x}}\right]$$

$$\Rightarrow \quad V_P = \frac{1}{4\pi\varepsilon_0}\left[\frac{q}{\sqrt{20-4x}} - \frac{q}{\sqrt{20-4x}}\right]$$

$$\Rightarrow \quad V_P = 0$$

Proved

(xiv) (a) Electric potential at C is given as

$$V_C = \frac{Kq_{\text{net}}}{R}$$

$$\Rightarrow \quad V_C = \left(\frac{1}{4\pi\varepsilon_0}\right)\left(\frac{-5Q}{R}\right) = -\frac{5Q}{4\pi\in_0 R}$$

(b) Electric potential at point P is given as

$$V_P = \frac{Kq_{\text{net}}}{r}$$

where, r is the distance of P from any point on circumference

$$\Rightarrow \quad V_P = \left(\frac{1}{4\pi\varepsilon_0}\right)\left(\frac{-5Q}{\sqrt{R^2+x^2}}\right) = -\frac{5Q}{4\pi\in_0\sqrt{R^2+x^2}}$$

(xv)

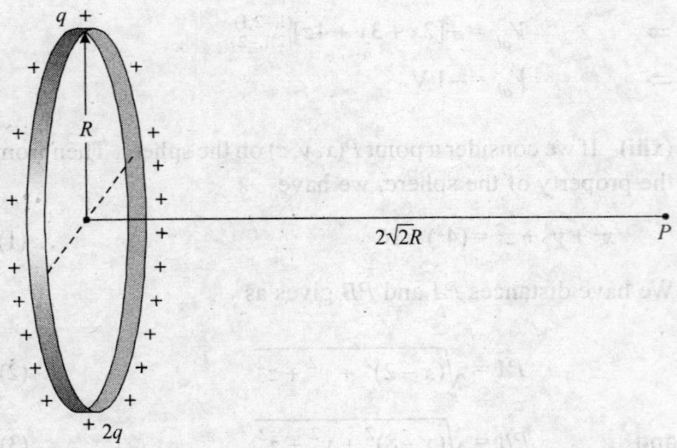

Distance of P from periphery of ring is $\sqrt{R^2+(2\sqrt{2}R)^2} = 3R$

Electric potential = Potential due to upper half + Potential due to lower half

$$V_P = \frac{Kq}{3R} + \frac{2Kq}{3R}$$

$$\Rightarrow \quad V_P = \frac{3Kq}{3R} = \frac{Kq}{R}$$

Solutions of PRACTICE EXERCISE 1.6

(i) Situation described in question is shown in figure.

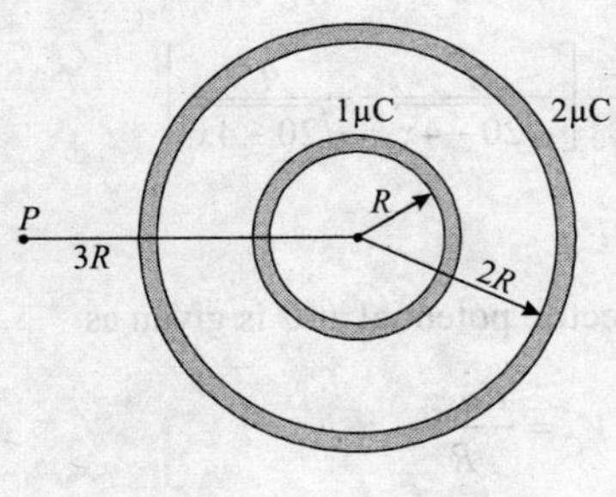

Potential at point P is given as

$$9000 = \frac{K(1\times10^{-6})}{3R} + \frac{K(2\times10^{-6})}{3R}$$

$$\Rightarrow \quad 3R = 3$$

$$\Rightarrow \quad R = 1\text{ m}$$

(ii) Charge on the oil drop is given as

$$q = \text{charge of 40 electrons}$$

$$\Rightarrow \quad q = 40\times(1.6\times10^{-19})$$

$$\Rightarrow \quad q = 64\times10^{-19}\text{ C}$$

Potential on the oil drop is given as

$$V = \frac{64\times10^{-19}}{4\pi\varepsilon_0\times r}$$

$$\Rightarrow \quad V = (9\times10^9)\frac{(64\times10^{-19})}{10^{-6}}$$

$$\Rightarrow \quad V = 9\times64\times10^{-4}\text{ V}$$

Now energy required the work done in bringing an electron from a point of zero potential to a point of potential $9\times64\times10^{-4}$ V which is given as

$$\Rightarrow \quad W = (1.6\times10^{-19})(9\times64\times10^{-4})\text{ J}$$

$$\Rightarrow \quad W = 921.6\times10^{-23}\text{ J}$$

(iii) The initial and final positions of the charges are shown in figure-(a) and (b) respectively.

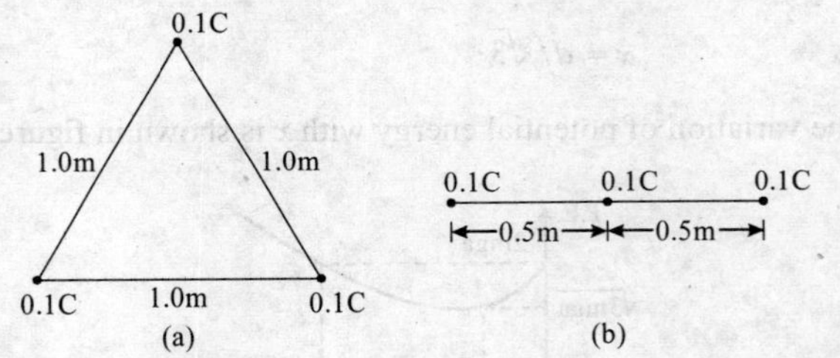

The initial energy of the system of three charges is given as

$$U_i = \frac{1}{4\pi\varepsilon_0}\left[\frac{q_1q_2}{r_{12}} + \frac{q_2q_3}{r_{23}} + \frac{q_3q_1}{r_{31}}\right]$$

$$\Rightarrow \quad U_i = (9\times10^9)\left[\frac{(0.1)(0.1)}{1.0} + \frac{(0.1)(0.1)}{1.0} + \frac{(0.1)(0.1)}{1.0}\right]$$

$$\Rightarrow \quad U_i = 0.27\times10^9\text{ J}$$

The final energy of the system is given as

$$U_f = (9\times10^9)\left[\frac{(0.1)(0.1)}{0.5} + \frac{(0.1)(0.1)}{0.5} + \frac{(0.1)(0.1)}{0.5}\right]$$

$$\Rightarrow \quad U_f = 0.45\times10^9\text{ J}$$

Increase in the energy of the system is given as

$$W = U_f - U_i = (0.45 \times 10^9) - (0.27 \times 10^9)$$

$$\Rightarrow \quad W = 0.18 \times 10^9 \text{ J}$$

If energy is being supplied at a rate of P watt, we use

$$W = Pt$$

$$\Rightarrow \quad t = \frac{W}{P}$$

$$\Rightarrow \quad t = \frac{0.18 \times 10^9}{1 \times 10^3} = 1.8 \times 10^5 \text{ s}$$

(iv) The net potential of the inner shell of charge q_1 is given as

$$V = V_1 + V_2 = \frac{1}{4\pi\varepsilon_0}\left(\frac{q_1}{a} + \frac{q_2}{b}\right)$$

As given in the question we use

$$V = 0$$

$$\Rightarrow \quad q_2 = -b/a$$

Now, the potential at an internal point of the shell is the same as on the surface of the sphere. Hence potential for $r < a$ is $V = 0$ at all points. For points $a \le r \le ab$, we have

$$V(r) = \frac{q_1}{4\pi\varepsilon_0 r} + \frac{q_2}{4\pi\varepsilon_0 b} = \frac{q_1}{4\pi\varepsilon_0}\left[\frac{1}{r} - \frac{1}{a}\right]$$

For points $r \ge b$, we have

$$V(r) = \frac{q_1}{4\pi\varepsilon_0 r} + \frac{q_2}{4\pi\varepsilon_0 r} = \frac{q_1}{4\pi\varepsilon_0 r}\left(1 - \frac{b}{a}\right)$$

Thus the corresponding plot is shown in figure below

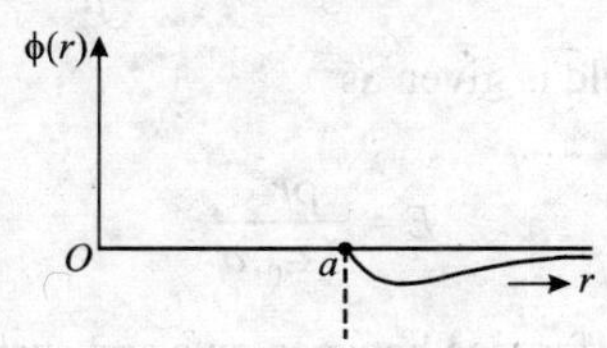

(v) At point P shown in figure distances from charges are

$$r_1 = d\cos\alpha \text{ and } r_2 = d\sin\alpha$$

So we have

$$\gamma = \frac{\sqrt{E_1^2 + E_2^2}}{V_1 + V_2} = \frac{\sqrt{\left[\frac{kq}{(d\cos\alpha)^2}\right]^2 + \left[\frac{kq}{(d\sin\alpha)^2}\right]^2}}{\frac{kq}{d\cos\alpha} + \frac{kq}{d\sin\alpha}}$$

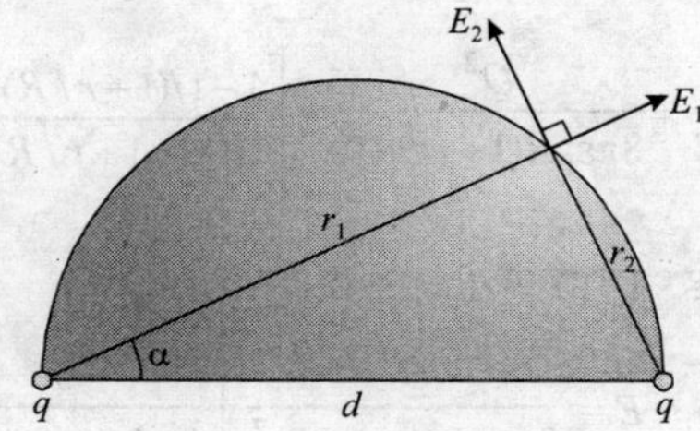

$$\Rightarrow \quad \gamma = \frac{\sqrt{\frac{\sin^4\alpha + \cos^4\alpha}{\sin^4\alpha\cos^4\alpha}}}{d\left[\frac{\sin\alpha + \cos\alpha}{\sin\alpha\cos\alpha}\right]}$$

$$\Rightarrow \quad \gamma = \frac{\sqrt{\sin^4\alpha + \cos^4\alpha}}{d[\sin\alpha + \cos\alpha]\sin\alpha\cos\alpha} = 5$$

(vi) (a) Let q_1 be the charge on sphere S_2 after S_1 is removed first. Since the potential at the surface of each sphere is the same, we have

$$\frac{q_1}{4\pi\varepsilon_0 R} = \frac{Q - q_1}{4\pi\varepsilon_0 r}$$

$$\Rightarrow \quad q_1 = \frac{Q}{1 + (r/R)} \quad \ldots(1)$$

Now S_1 is recharged such that the charge on it is again Q. Charge on S_2 is $Q/(1 + r/R)$. They are brought in contact. Total charge on S_1 and S_2 is

$$q_T = Q + \frac{Q}{1 + (r/R)}$$

When the two spheres are separated connected time. Let the charge on sphere S_2 be. q_2 so that then potentials be equal again as

$$\frac{q_2}{4\pi\varepsilon_0 R} = \frac{[Q + \{Q/(1 + r/R)\}] - q_2}{4\pi\varepsilon_0 r} \quad \ldots(2)$$

Solving for (q_2) we get

$$q_2 = \frac{Q}{\{1 + (r/R)\}} + \frac{Q}{(1 + (r/R))^2} \quad \ldots(3)$$

Similarly, we can write after connecting spheres for n times, charge on S_2 is given as

$$q_n = \frac{Q}{\{1 + (r/R)\}} + \frac{Q}{(1 + (r/R))^2} + \ldots + \frac{Q}{\{1 + (r/R)\}^n} \quad \ldots(4)$$

$$\Rightarrow \quad q_n = \frac{Q}{1 + (r/R)}\left[\frac{1 - 1/(1 + r/R)^n}{1 - 1/(1 + r/R)}\right]$$

Electrostatic energy of S_2 after n connections is given as

$$U_{S_2}=\frac{q_n^2}{8\pi\varepsilon_0 R}=\frac{Q^2}{8\pi\varepsilon_0 R(1+r/R)^2}\times\left[\frac{1-1/(1+r/R)^n}{1-1/(1+r/R)}\right]^2 \quad \ldots(5)$$

(b) Limiting energy at $n\to\infty$ is given as

$$E=\frac{Q^2}{8\pi\varepsilon_0 R(1+r/R)^2}\left[\frac{1}{1-1/(1+r/R)^2}\right]$$

$$\Rightarrow \qquad E=\frac{Q^2}{8\pi\varepsilon_0 R}\left(\frac{R}{r}\right)^2=\frac{Q^2 R}{8\pi\varepsilon_0 r^2}$$

(vii) To find potential at a point at P on edge of the disc we consider an elemental arc of radius x and width dx as shown in figure. The area of elemental arc strip is given as

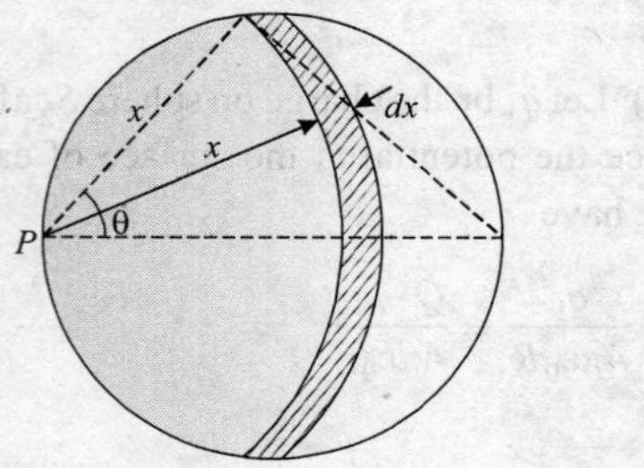

$$ds=2x\theta$$

Charge on elemental arc is given as

$$dq=\sigma ds=2\sigma x\theta$$

Potential at point P due to arc is given as

$$dV=\frac{kdq}{x}=\frac{2\sigma\theta}{4\pi\in_0}=\frac{\sigma\theta}{2\pi\in_0}$$

Total potential is given as

$$V=\int dV=\frac{\sigma}{2\pi\in_0}\int_0^{2R}\cos^{-1}\left(\frac{x}{2R}\right)$$

$$\Rightarrow \quad V=\frac{\sigma}{2\pi\in_0}\left[x\cos^{-1}\left(\frac{x}{2R}\right)+\int\frac{1}{2R}\frac{1}{\sqrt{1-(x/2R)^2}}xdx\right]$$

$$\Rightarrow \qquad V=\frac{\sigma}{2\pi\in_0}\left[x\cos^{-1}\left(\frac{x}{2R}\right)+\int\frac{xdx}{\sqrt{4R^2-x^2}}\right]$$

$$\Rightarrow \qquad V=\frac{\sigma}{2\pi\in_0}\left[x\cos^{-1}\left(\frac{x}{2R}\right)-\sqrt{4R^2-x^2}\right]_0^{2R}$$

$$\Rightarrow \qquad V=\frac{\sigma}{2\pi\in_0}[(0-0)-(0-2R)]$$

$$\Rightarrow \qquad V=\frac{\sigma R}{\pi\in_0}$$

(viii) Consider an elemental shell of radius x and thickness dx and of length l inside the cylinder a shown in figure

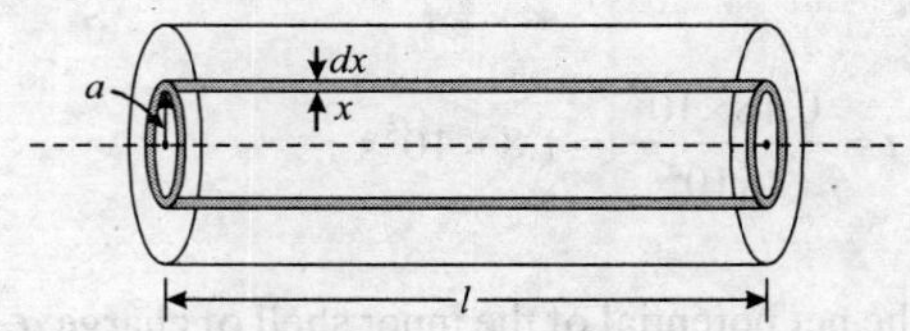

As ρ varies directly as the distance x, so here ρ can be written as $\rho = cx$, where c is a constant given by the relation

$$\rho=ca$$

$$\Rightarrow \qquad c=\frac{\rho}{a}$$

The intensity of electric field at any point P at a distance r from the axis of the cylinder can be obtained as

$$E=\frac{\lambda}{2\pi\in_0 r}$$

where $$\lambda=\int_0^r\rho(2\pi x)dx$$

$$\lambda=\int_0^r 2\pi cx^2dx$$

$$\lambda=\frac{2}{3}\pi cr^3=\frac{2\pi\rho_0}{a}r^3$$

Thus electric field is given as

$$E=\frac{\rho r^2}{3\in_0 a}$$

The potential difference between axis and surface is given as

$$V_A-V_S=\left|\int_A^B\vec{E}.d\vec{r}\right|$$

$$\Rightarrow \qquad V_{\text{axis}}-V_{\text{surface}}=\int_a^0\frac{\rho_s r^2}{3\in_0 a}dr=\frac{\rho_s}{3a\in_0}\int_a^0 r^2dr$$

$$\Rightarrow \qquad V_{\text{axis}}-V_{\text{surface}}=\frac{\rho_s a^2}{9\in_0}$$

Solutions of PRACTICE EXERCISE 1.7

(i) In figure we resolve the dipole in two components along x and y directions given as

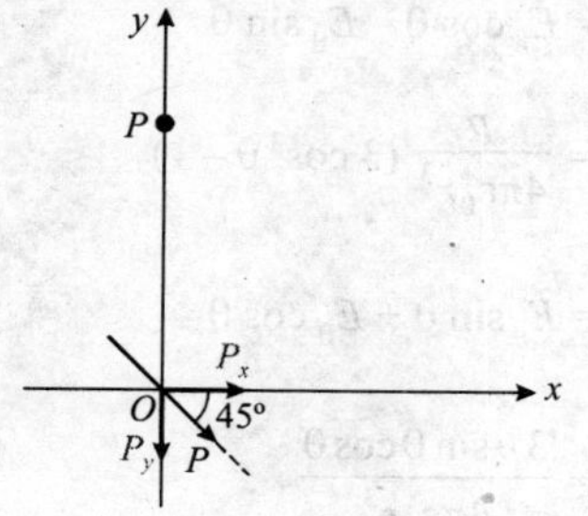

$$P_x = P\cos 45° = \frac{P}{\sqrt{2}}$$

$$P_y = P\sin 45° = \frac{P}{\sqrt{2}}$$

At point P which is located at equator of p_x and axis of p_y the electric field strength is given as

$$\vec{E}_{P_x} = -\frac{KP_x}{y^3}\hat{i} = -\frac{KP}{\sqrt{2}y^3}\hat{i}$$

and $$\vec{E}_{P_y} = -\frac{2KP_y}{y^3}\hat{j}$$

Net electric field vector at point P is given as

$$\vec{E}_P = \vec{E}_{P_x} + \vec{E}_{P_y} = \frac{Kp}{\sqrt{2}y^3}(-\hat{i} - 2\hat{j})$$

(ii) (a) Net force on dipole is given as

$$\vec{F} = p\frac{dE}{dx}\hat{i} = p\frac{d}{dx}\left(\frac{\lambda}{2\pi\epsilon_0 x}\right)\hat{i}$$

$$\Rightarrow \quad \vec{F} = -\frac{p\lambda}{2\pi\epsilon_0 x^2}\hat{i}$$

$$\Rightarrow \quad \vec{F} = -\frac{\lambda aq}{\pi\epsilon_0 x^2}\hat{i}$$

(b) Initial potential energy of dipole is given as

$$U_i = -\vec{p}.\vec{E} = -\frac{2qa\lambda}{2\pi\epsilon_0 x} = -\frac{qa\lambda}{\pi\epsilon_0 x}$$

final potential energy of dipole is given as

$$U_f = -\vec{p}.\vec{E} = -pE\cos(180°)$$

$$\Rightarrow \quad U_f = pE = \frac{qa\lambda}{\pi\epsilon_0 x}$$

work done in rotation is given as

$$W = U_f - U_i = \frac{qa\lambda}{\pi\epsilon_0 x} - \left(-\frac{qa\lambda}{\pi\epsilon_0 x}\right)$$

$$\Rightarrow \quad W = \frac{2qa\lambda}{\pi\epsilon_0 x}$$

(c) At displacement θ, torque on dipole is given as

$$\tau = \frac{\lambda a^2 q\cos\theta\sin\theta}{\pi\epsilon_0 x^2}$$

for small θ we can take $\cos\theta \approx 1$ and $\sin\theta \approx \theta$

$$\Rightarrow \quad I\alpha = -\frac{\lambda a^2 q}{\pi\epsilon_0 x^2}\theta$$

$$\Rightarrow \quad \alpha = -\frac{\lambda q}{2\pi\epsilon_0 x^2 m}\theta$$

Above negative sign is taken for restoring nature and comparing with SHM equation

$$\alpha = -\omega^2\theta \text{ gives}$$

$$\omega = \sqrt{\frac{\lambda q}{2\pi\epsilon_0 mx^2}}$$

$$\Rightarrow \quad T = \frac{2\pi}{\omega} = 2\pi\sqrt{\frac{2\pi\epsilon_0 mx^2}{\lambda q}}$$

(iii) Electric field at M due to first dipole is given as

$$\vec{E}_1 = -\frac{K(p\hat{k})}{(1)^3} = -Kp\hat{k}$$

Electric field at M due to second dipole is given as

$$\vec{E}_2 = \frac{2K\left((p/2)\hat{k}\right)}{(2)^3} = \frac{Kp}{8}\hat{k}$$

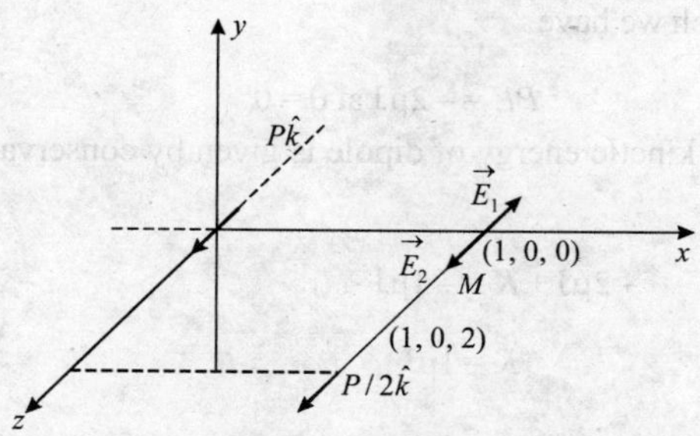

Net electric field strength at point M is given as

$$\vec{E}_M = \vec{E}_1 + \vec{E}_2$$

$$\Rightarrow \quad \vec{E}_M = -Kp\hat{k} + \frac{Kp}{8}\hat{k} = -\frac{7}{8}Kp\hat{k}$$

$$\Rightarrow \quad \vec{E}_M = -\frac{7p}{32\pi \in_0}\hat{k}$$

(iv) (a) The electric field due to a point charge can be directly given as

$$E_P = \frac{Kq}{d^2} = \frac{q}{4\pi \in_0 d^2}$$

(b) As $d >> a$ Combination of $-q$ and $+q$ can be treated as a dipole. The electric field at point P is given as

$$E_P = \frac{Kp}{r^3}\sqrt{1+3\sin^2\theta}$$

At $\theta = 0$ we have

$$E_P = \frac{Kp}{r^3} = \frac{qa}{2\pi \in_0 d^3}$$

(c) This case is the super position of above two cases which gives

$$\vec{E}_{net} = \frac{Kq}{d^2}\hat{j} + \left(-\frac{Kp}{r^3}\right)\hat{i}$$

$$\Rightarrow \quad \vec{E}_{net} = -\frac{Kp}{r^3}\hat{i} + \frac{Kq}{d^2}\hat{j}$$

$$\Rightarrow \quad E_{net} = \sqrt{\left(\frac{q}{4\pi \in_0 d^2}\right)^2 + \left(\frac{qa}{2\pi \in_0 d^3}\right)^2}$$

$$\Rightarrow \quad E_{net} = \frac{q}{4\pi \in_0 d^2}\sqrt{1+\frac{4a^2}{d^2}}$$

(v) Work done by electric field in the process is

$$PE\cos 60° = -\frac{1}{2}PE$$

From graph we have

$$PE = -2\mu J \text{ at } \theta = 0°$$

At $\theta = 0°$ kinetic energy of dipole is given by conservation of energy as

$$-2\mu J + K = -1\mu J$$

$$\Rightarrow \quad K = 1\mu J$$

(vi) In the case of a dipole, the electric field along the radius vector (i.e., the radial component) is $E_r = \dfrac{2p\cos\theta}{4\pi\varepsilon_0 r^3}$; and the transverse component

$$E_\theta = \frac{p\sin\theta}{4\pi\varepsilon_0 r^3}$$

From the figure

$$E_x = E_r\cos\theta - E_\theta\sin\theta$$

$$\Rightarrow \quad E_x = \frac{p}{4\pi\varepsilon_0 r^3}(3\cos^3\theta - 1)$$

and

$$E_y = E_r\sin\theta + E_\theta\cos\theta$$

$$\Rightarrow \quad E_y = \frac{3p\sin\theta\cos\theta}{4\pi\varepsilon_0 r^3}$$

when $\vec{E} \perp \vec{p}$, we use

$$E_z = 0$$

$$\Rightarrow \quad \cos^2\theta = 1$$

$$\Rightarrow \quad \cos\theta = \frac{1}{\sqrt{3}}$$

(vii) (a) Electric field due to ring at location of dipole is given as

$$E = \frac{KQx}{(R^2+x^2)^{3/2}},$$

We use

$$\frac{dE}{dx} = KQ\left[\frac{(R^2+x^2)^{3/2} - x\cdot\frac{3}{2}(R^2+x^2)^{1/2}(2x)}{(R^2+x^2)^3}\right]$$

$$\Rightarrow \quad \frac{dE}{dx} = KQ\left[\frac{R^2+x^2-3x^2}{(R^2+x^2)^{5/2}}\right]$$

Force on dipole is given as

$$\Rightarrow \quad F = P\frac{dE}{dx} = \frac{Qqa}{2\pi\varepsilon_0}\left[\frac{R^2-2x^2}{(R^2+x^2)^{5/2}}\right]$$

(b) Work done in rotation of dipole is given as

$$W = U_f - U_i$$

$$\Rightarrow \quad W = -PE\cos 180° + PE\cos 0°$$

$$\Rightarrow \quad W = 2PE$$

$$\Rightarrow \quad W = 2(q)(2a)\left[\frac{1}{4\pi\varepsilon_0}\frac{Qx}{(R^2+x^2)^{3/2}}\right]$$

$$\Rightarrow \quad W = \frac{aqQx}{\pi\varepsilon_0(R^2+x^2)^{3/2}}$$

(viii) (a) The electric field due to a long thread at the location of dipole is given as

$$E_r = \frac{\lambda}{2\pi\varepsilon_0 r},$$

As dipole is oriented parallel to thread equal find opposite force will act on dipole charge so net force on it will be zero

(b) $\vec{p}$ along $\vec{r}$: so force on dipole is

given as $\vec{F} = P\frac{dE}{dr}\hat{r}$

Force on dipole $\vec{F} = -\frac{\lambda p}{2\pi\varepsilon_0 r^2}\hat{r} = -\frac{\lambda\vec{p}}{2\pi\varepsilon_0 r^2}$

(c) $\vec{p}$ is oriented along transverse direction so the net force on dipole as shown in figure is given as

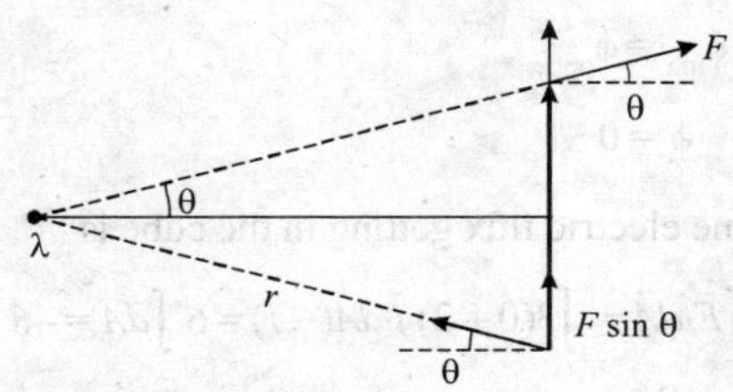

$$F_{net} = 2F\sin\theta$$

$$\Rightarrow \quad F_{net} = 2q\left(\frac{\lambda}{2\pi\epsilon_0 r}\right)\cdot\frac{a}{r}$$

$$\Rightarrow \quad F_{net} = \frac{\lambda p}{2\pi\epsilon_0 r^2}$$

(ix) Due to dipole moment $\vec{p}_1$ the radial electric field strength at the location of other dipole is given as

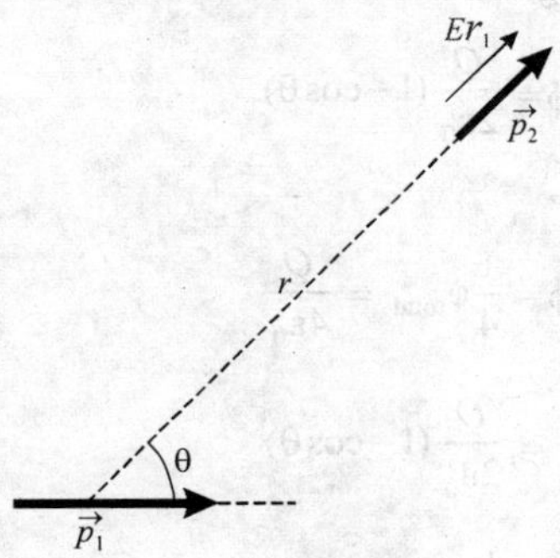

$$E_{r_1} = \frac{2Kp_1\cos\theta}{r^3}$$

Potential energy of dipole $\vec{p}_2$ with the field of first dipole is given as

$$U = -\vec{p}_2.\vec{E}_{r_1} = -\frac{2Kp_1p_2\cos\theta}{r^3}$$

Above result can also be obtained by calculating the electric field vector of dipole $\vec{p}_2$ at the location of dipole $\vec{p}_1$ and calculating potential energy of $\vec{p}_1$ in the field of $\vec{p}_2$.

(x) Net force on upper half of rod is given as

$$F = \left(\frac{\lambda l}{2}\right)\left(\frac{\sigma}{2\epsilon_0}\right)$$

Torque on upper half is given as

$$\tau = \left(\frac{\lambda l}{2}\right)\times\frac{\sigma}{2\epsilon_0}\times\frac{l}{4}$$

Same torque will be acting on lower half of rod about C. Total torque on rod out C is given as

$$\tau_T = \frac{\lambda l}{2}\times\frac{\sigma}{2\epsilon_0}\times\frac{l}{4}\times 2 = I\alpha = \frac{ml^2}{12}\alpha$$

$$\Rightarrow \quad \alpha = \frac{3\lambda\sigma}{2m\,\epsilon_0}$$

(xi) The given system of charges is equivalent to, two electric dipoles, each of the moment, $P = q\times 2l$, placed perpendicular to each other. The field of the dipole at a distance x from its centre along equatorial line is given as

$$E = \frac{KP}{x^3}$$

Thus resultant field, of the two mutually perpendicular field due to the two dipoles at point M is given as

$$E_M = \sqrt{2}\,E = \frac{\sqrt{2}KP}{x^3} = -\frac{ql}{\sqrt{2}\pi\epsilon_0 x^3}$$

Solutions of PRACTICE EXERCISE 1.8

(i) Half of the flow originated by charge q will come out of hemispherical surface of the cup.

(ii) Consider an elemental ring of thickness dr at a distance r from centre as shown. The flux through this elemental ring is given as

$$d\phi = E\times 2\pi r dr\times\cos\theta$$

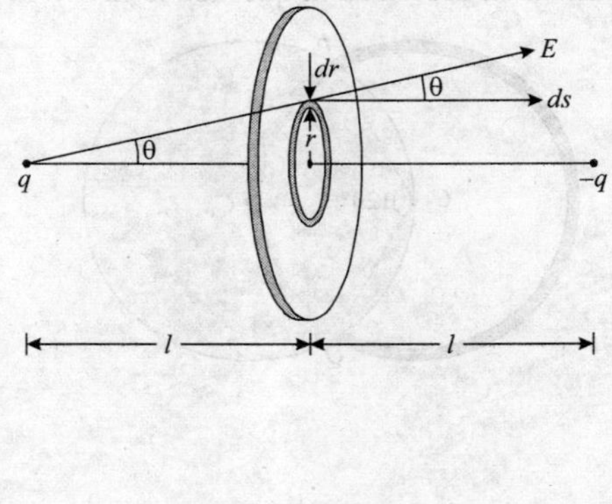

Electric field strength due to the point charges at the location of elemental ring is given as

$$E = \frac{2Kq}{(l^2 + r^2)}$$

$$\Rightarrow \qquad E\cos\theta = \frac{1}{2\pi \in_0} \cdot \frac{ql}{(l^2 + r^2)^{3/2}}$$

Total flux through circle is given as

$$\phi = \int_0^R E \times 2\pi r dr$$

$$\Rightarrow \qquad \phi = \frac{ql}{4\pi \in_0} \int_0^R \frac{2\pi r dr}{(r^2 + l^2)^{3/2}}$$

Substituting, $\quad r^2 + l^2 = z$

also $\quad 2rdr = dz$

$$\Rightarrow \qquad \phi = \frac{ql}{4 \in_0} \int_0^R z^{-3/2} dz$$

$$\Rightarrow \qquad \phi = \frac{ql}{4 \in_0} \left| \frac{z^{-1/2}}{-\frac{1}{2}} \right|_0^R$$

$$\Rightarrow \qquad \phi = \frac{-ql}{2 \in_0} \left| (r^2 + l^2)^{-1/2} \right|_0^R$$

$$\Rightarrow \qquad \phi = \frac{-ql}{2 \in_0} \left| \frac{1}{\sqrt{r^2 + l^2}} \right|_0^R$$

$$\Rightarrow \qquad \phi = \frac{-ql}{2 \in_0} \left(\frac{1}{\sqrt{R^2 + l^2}} - \frac{1}{l} \right)$$

$$\Rightarrow \qquad \phi = \frac{ql}{\in_0} \left(\frac{1}{l} - \frac{1}{\sqrt{R^2 + l^2}} \right)$$

Above result can be directly calculated by using the concept of solid angle. Students are advised to verify this result by using that method also.

(iii) The situation described in question is shown in figure.

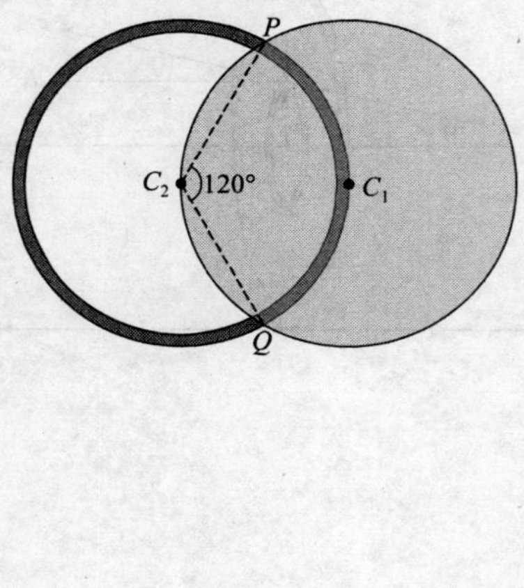

Charge on arc PQ of ring is given as

$$V_{PQ} = \frac{q_0}{3}$$

This is also the charge enclosed in the sphere so flex through surface of sphere is given as

$$\phi = \frac{q_{in}}{\varepsilon_0}$$

$$\Rightarrow \qquad \phi = \frac{(q_0/3)}{\varepsilon_0} = \frac{q_0}{3\varepsilon_0}$$

(iv) We calculate the total electric flux coming out of the cube, which is given as

Along z axis as $E_2 = 0$ no flux is these

Along x axis as E = constant

$$\Rightarrow \qquad \phi_{in\,x} = \phi_{out\,x}$$

$$\Rightarrow \qquad \phi_x = 0$$

For $y = 0$ plane electric flux getting in the cube is

$$\phi_{in} = \int \vec{E} \cdot d\vec{A} = \int 3(0 + 2)\hat{j} \cdot dA(-\hat{j}) = 6 \int dA = -6$$

For $y = 1$ plane flux coming out from the cube is

$$\phi_{out} = \int \vec{E} \cdot d\vec{A} = \int 3(1 + 2)\hat{j} \cdot dA(\hat{j}) = 9 \int dA = 9$$

$\Rightarrow$ Using Gauss's laws for cube, we have

$$\phi_{net} = \frac{q_{enclosed}}{\in_0} = 3$$

$$\Rightarrow \qquad q_{enclosed} = 3\in_0$$

(v) Using concept of solid angle the flux of Q which passes through disc is given as

$$\phi = \frac{Q}{2\varepsilon_0}(1 - \cos\theta)$$

Given that

$$\phi = \frac{1}{4}\phi_{total} = \frac{Q}{4\varepsilon_0}$$

$$\Rightarrow \qquad \frac{Q}{4\varepsilon_0} = \frac{Q}{2\varepsilon_0}(1 - \cos\theta)$$

$$\Rightarrow \qquad \cos\theta = \frac{1}{2}$$

$$\Rightarrow \qquad \theta = 60°$$

We use $\tan 60° = \dfrac{R}{b}$

$$\Rightarrow \qquad R = b \tan 60°$$

$$\Rightarrow \qquad R = \sqrt{3}b$$

(vi) If charge is kept at the centre of a face first we should enclose the charge by assuming an identical imaginary cube on other side as shown in figure below.

The total flux through both the cube surfaces is given as

$$\phi_{\text{total}} = \frac{q}{\epsilon_0}$$

Thus the flux through given cube is given as

$$\phi = \frac{q}{2\epsilon_0}$$

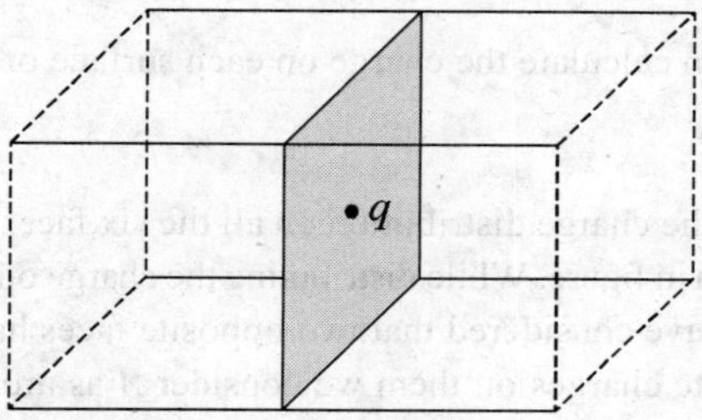

(b) If the charge is placed at the corner of a cube, seven more identical cubes are required to enclose the charge completely and symmetrically as shown in figure below.

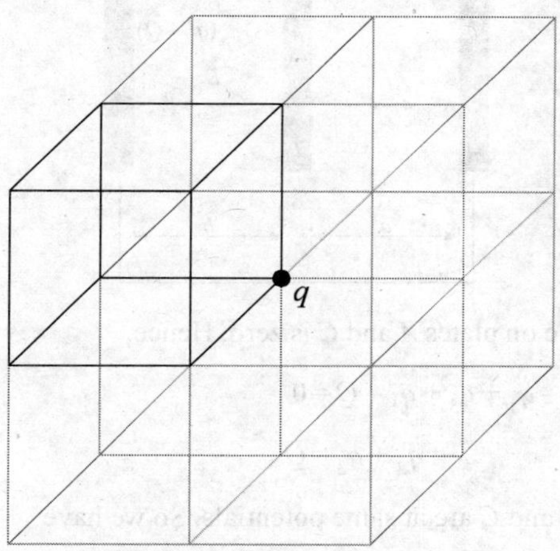

The total flux through all the faces of 8 cubes is

$$\phi_{\text{total}} = \frac{q}{\epsilon_0}$$

Flux through each cube at one corner this charge is located is given as

$$\phi = \frac{q}{8\epsilon_0}$$

This flux emerging equally through three front faces of the cube. Other three faces; junction of which charge is placed have no flux. Therefore the flux through one of the faces is given as

$$= \frac{q/8\epsilon_0}{3} = \frac{q}{24\epsilon_0}$$

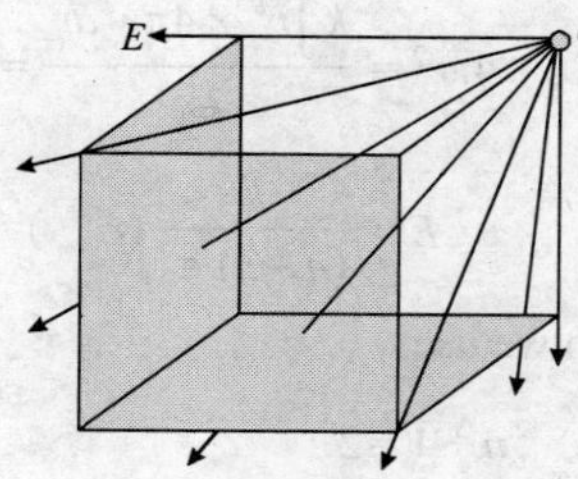

From three remaining forces no flux comes out

(vii) Given electric field is uniform in space we know that net flux from any closed surface in uniform electric field is zero.

(viii) We consider an elemental shell in the region of radius x and width dx as shown in figure.

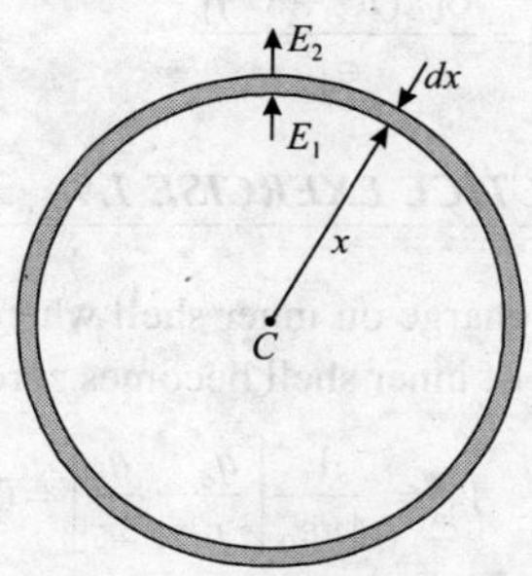

If volume charge density in the shell is $p(x)$ then we use Gauss's law for the surfaces of shell as

$$E_2(4\pi(x+dx)^2) - E_1(4\pi x^2) = \frac{\rho(x)4\pi x^2 dx}{\epsilon_0}$$

$$\Rightarrow \quad k(x+dx)^7[4p(x+dx)^2] - kx^7(4\pi x^2) = \frac{\rho(x)4\pi x^2 dx}{\epsilon_0}$$

$$\Rightarrow \quad 4\pi k[(x+dx)^9 - x^9] = \frac{\rho(x)4\pi x^2 dx}{\epsilon_0}$$

$$\Rightarrow \quad k\left[x^9\left(1+\frac{9dx}{x}\right) - x^9\right] = \frac{\rho(x)x^2 dx}{\epsilon_0}$$

$$\Rightarrow \quad 9kx^8 dx = \frac{\rho(x)x^2 dx}{\epsilon_0}$$

$$\Rightarrow \quad \rho(x) = 9k\epsilon_0 x^6$$

$$\Rightarrow \quad \rho(r) = 9k\epsilon_0 r^6$$

(ix) Using Gauss's law for a symmetric spherical surface of radius r we have

$$\oint \vec{E}\cdot d\vec{A} = \frac{\int_0^R \rho 4\pi x^2 dx}{\epsilon_0}$$

$$\Rightarrow \qquad E \times 4\pi r^2 = \frac{k\int r^n \times 4\pi r^2 dr}{\epsilon_0} = \frac{4\pi k}{\epsilon_0}\frac{r^{k+3}}{n+3}$$

$$\Rightarrow \qquad E = \frac{k}{(n+3)\,\epsilon_0}(r^{n+1})$$

Given that $E\alpha r^2$ so we use

$$n+1=2$$

$$\Rightarrow \qquad n=1$$

(x) The enclosed section of sheet within the spherical surface is a disc of radius r which in given as

$$r=\sqrt{R^2-x^2}$$

Thus flux coming out from spherical surface is given as

$$\phi = \frac{\sigma[\pi(R^2-x^2)]}{\epsilon_0}$$

Solutions of PRACTICE EXERCISE 1.9

(i) If q_e be the charge on inner shell when it is earthed so that final potential of inner shell becomes zero. This gives

$$V_{\text{in}} = \frac{1}{4\pi\varepsilon_0}\left[\frac{q_e}{r}+\frac{q}{3r}\right]=0$$

$$\Rightarrow \qquad q_e = -\frac{q}{3}$$

Thus $+\frac{q}{3}$ charge will flow from inner shell to earth.

(ii) For two concentric shells potential difference only depends upon the charge of inner shell so then potential difference will remain same when outer shell is earthed.

(iii) Since, there is no charge inside A. The whole charge q given to the shell A will appear on its outer surface. Charge on its inner surface will be zero. Moreover if a Gaussian surface is drawn on the material of shell B net charge enclosed by it should be zero. Therefore, charge on its inner surface will be $-q$. Now let q' be the charge on its outer surface, then charge on the inner surface of C will be $-q'$ and on its outer surface will be, $2q-(-q')=2q+q'$ as total charge on C is $2q$.

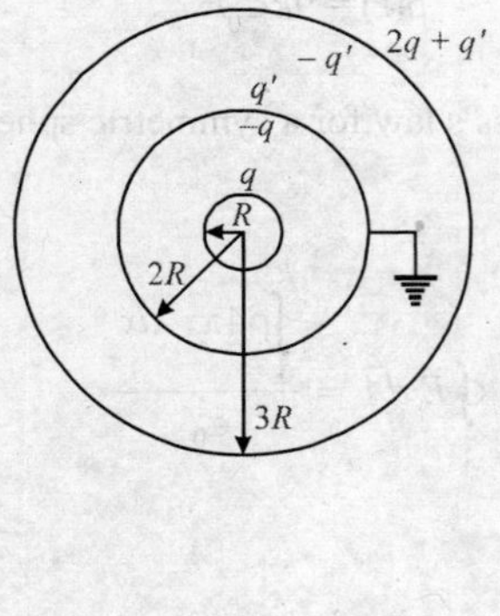

As shell B is earthed, its potential should be zero so we have

$$V_B=0$$

$$\Rightarrow \qquad \frac{1}{4\pi\varepsilon_0}\left[\frac{q}{2R}-\frac{q}{2R}+\frac{q'}{2R}-\frac{q'}{3R}+\frac{2q+q'}{3R}\right]=0$$

Solving this equation, we get

$$q' = -\frac{4}{3}q$$

Thus charge on outer surface of outer shell is given as

$$2q+q' = 2q-\frac{4}{3}q = \frac{2}{3}q$$

Now we can calculate the charge on each surface of different shells.

(iv) Let the charge distribution on all the six faces of plates be as shown in figure. While distributing the charge on different faces, we have considered that two opposite faces have equal and opposite charges on them we consider A as area of each plate.

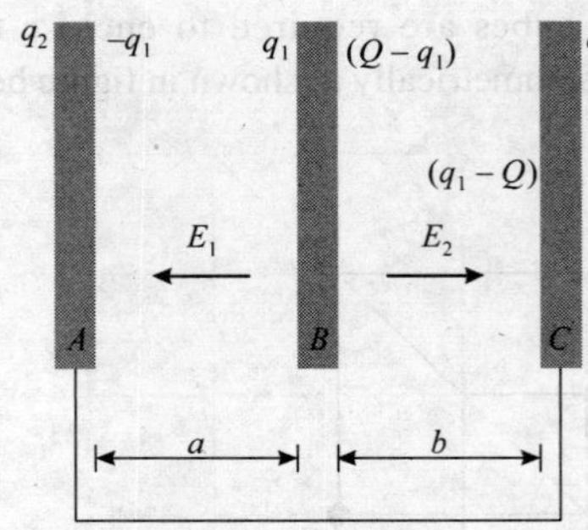

Net charge on plates A and C is zero. Hence,

$$q_2 - q_1 + q_3 + q_1 - Q = 0$$

$$\Rightarrow \qquad q_2 + q_3 = Q \qquad \ldots(1)$$

Further A and C are at same potentials. So we have

$$V_B - V_A = V_B - V_C$$

$$\Rightarrow \qquad E_1 a = E_2 b$$

$$\Rightarrow \qquad \frac{q_1}{A\varepsilon_0}.a = \frac{Q-q_1}{A\varepsilon_0}.b$$

$$\Rightarrow \qquad q_1 a = (Q-q_1)b$$

$$\Rightarrow \qquad q_1 = \frac{Qb}{a+b} \qquad \ldots(2)$$

Electric field inside any conducting plate is zero. So we use for a point inside plate C as

$$\frac{q_2}{2A\varepsilon_0} - \frac{q_1}{2A\varepsilon_0} + \frac{q_1}{2A\varepsilon_0} + \frac{Q-q_1}{2A\varepsilon_0} + \frac{q_1-Q}{2A\varepsilon_0} - \frac{q_3}{2A\varepsilon_0} = 0$$

$$\Rightarrow \qquad q_2 - q_3 = 0 \qquad \ldots(3)$$

Solving equations-(1), (2) and (3) we get

$$q_1 = \frac{Qb}{a+b},\ q_2 = q_3 = \frac{Q}{2}$$

Hence, charge on different faces are can be calculated. In above analysis, equation-(3) can be directly obtained with the fact that charges on outer plate surfaces of any system of parallel plates are equal and equal to half of the total charge of system.

(v) When S_1 is closed for first time if q_{10} is the charge comes on outer shell, we have

$$V_{\text{outer}} = K\left(\frac{Q}{2r} + \frac{q_{10}}{2r}\right)$$

$$\Rightarrow \quad q_{10} = -Q$$

then S_2 is closed for first line and a charge q_{1i} comes on inner shell, we have

$$V_{\text{inner}} = K\left(\frac{q_{10}}{2r} + \frac{q_{1i}}{r}\right) = 0$$

$$\Rightarrow \quad q_{1i} = \frac{Q_1}{2}$$

Now when S_1 is closed for the second time, if charge on outer shell is q_{2o} then we have

$$V_{\text{outer}} = K\left(\frac{q_{20}}{2r} + \frac{(Q_1/2)}{2r}\right) = 0$$

$$\Rightarrow \quad q_{20} = \frac{-Q}{2}$$

Thus with similar analysis we can state that after n times closing and opening switches S_1 and S_2 final charge on inner shell becomes

$$q_{ni} = \frac{Q}{(2)^n}$$

Thus final potential difference between shells is given as

$$V_n = K\left(\frac{q_{ni}}{r} - \frac{q_{ni}}{2r}\right) = \frac{Kq_{ni}}{2r}$$

$$\Rightarrow \quad V_n = \frac{1}{(2)^{n+1}}\left(\frac{Q}{4\pi\epsilon_0 r}\right)$$

(vi) As initial voltage of electrometer is $V_0 = 3kV$ and after 10 contacts it is reduced to half so we can use half life formula to give its potential after n contacts which is given as

$$V_n = \frac{V_0}{2^{n/10}}$$

Thus after n contacts if $v_n = 1kV$, we use

$$1 \times 10^3 = \frac{3\times 10^3}{2^{n/10}}$$

$$\Rightarrow \quad 2^{n/10} = 3$$

Taking log on both sides we have

$$\frac{n}{10}\log_{10}(2) = \log_{10}(3)$$

$$\Rightarrow \quad n = \frac{10\log_{10}(3)}{\log_{10}(2)} = \frac{10\times 0.4771}{0.301}$$

$$\Rightarrow \quad n = 15.85$$

Thus after 6 more contacts the potential of electrometer goes below 1kV.

(vii) Let the electric field be along the x-axis. The surface density of induced charge is $\sigma = \sigma_0 \cos\theta$, as shown. We now consider the force $d\vec{F}$ on the induced charge on an elemental circular strip as shown in figure. This is given as

$$dF = \frac{\sigma^2}{2\epsilon_0}\cdot ds,$$

Where $\quad ds = 2\pi r\sin\theta . r\,d\theta$

Force is only due to horizontal component of force so we use

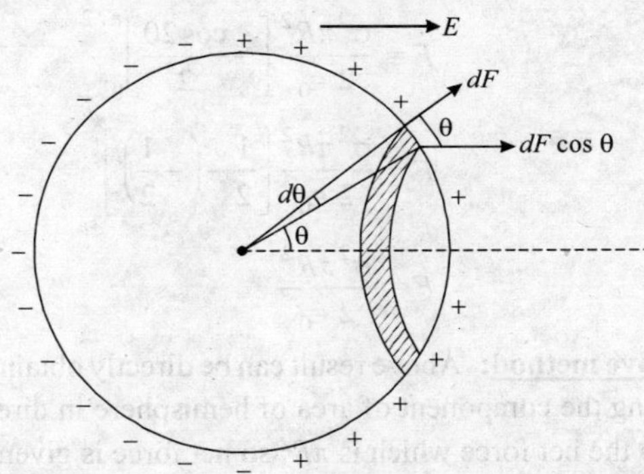

$$\Rightarrow \quad dF\cos\theta = \frac{\pi\sigma^2}{\epsilon_0} r^2 \sin\theta\cos d\theta$$

$$\Rightarrow \quad dF\cos\theta = -\frac{\pi\sigma_0^2 r^2}{\epsilon_0}\cos^3\theta\, d(\cos\theta)$$

Total force acting on the positive charge is given as

$$F_x = \int dF\cos\theta = -\int_1^0 \frac{\pi\sigma_0^2 r^2}{\epsilon_0}\cos^3\theta\, d(\cos\theta)$$

$$\Rightarrow \quad F_x = \frac{\pi\sigma_0^2 r^2}{4\epsilon_0}$$

(viii) We consider an elemental ring on sphere as shown. The force on this elemental ring is given as

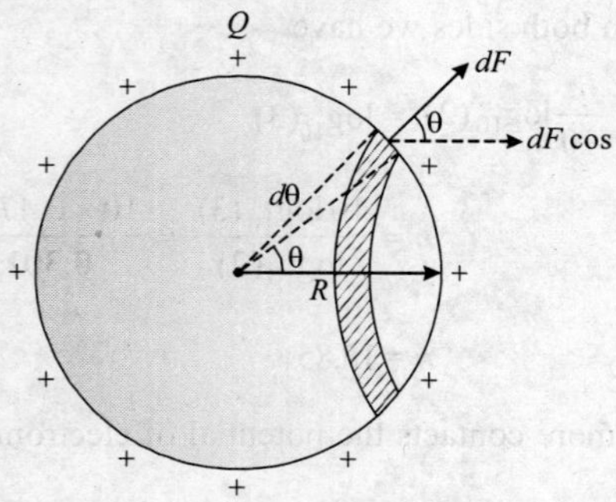

$$dF = \frac{\sigma^2}{2\epsilon_0} 2\pi R \sin\theta R d\theta$$

Net force of repulsion is away from each other in the two hemisphere so net force on half is given as

$$F = \int dF \cos\theta$$

$$F = \int_0^{\pi/2} \frac{\sigma^2}{2\epsilon_0} 2\pi R^2 \sin\theta \cos\theta d\theta$$

$$\Rightarrow \quad F = \frac{\sigma^2 \pi R^2}{2\epsilon_0} \int_0^{\pi/2} \sin 2\theta d\theta$$

$$\Rightarrow \quad F = \frac{\sigma^2 \pi R^2}{2\epsilon_0} \left[-\frac{\cos 2\theta}{2} \right]_0^{\pi/2}$$

$$\Rightarrow \quad F = \frac{\sigma^2 \pi R^2}{2\epsilon_0} \left[\frac{1}{2} - \left(-\frac{1}{2} \right) \right]$$

$$\Rightarrow \quad F = \frac{\sigma^2 \pi R^2}{2\epsilon_0}$$

Alternative method: Above result can be directly obtained by considering the component of area of hemisphere in direction normal to the net force which is πR^2 so net force is given as

$$F = P_e \times S_\perp$$

$$F = \frac{\sigma^2}{2\epsilon_0} \times \pi R^2 = \frac{\sigma^2 \pi R^2}{2\epsilon_0}$$

Solutions of PRACTICE EXERCISE 1.10

(i) If q is the charge on one drop of radius r, total electrostatic energy of all 1000 drops is given as

$$U_i = 1000\left(\frac{Kq^2}{2r}\right) \quad \ldots (1)$$

After merging drops into one, the radius of bigger drop is given as

$$\frac{4}{3}\pi R^3 = 1000 \times \frac{4}{3}\pi r^3$$

$$\Rightarrow \quad R = 10r$$

Find energy of bigger drop is given as

$$U = \frac{K(1000q)^2}{2(10r)} = 10^5 \left(\frac{Kq^2}{2r}\right) \ldots (2)$$

from equation-(1) and (2) we can see that energy increases by 100 times.

(ii) Consider a small elemental shell of radius x and thickness dx inside the given shell as shown in figure.

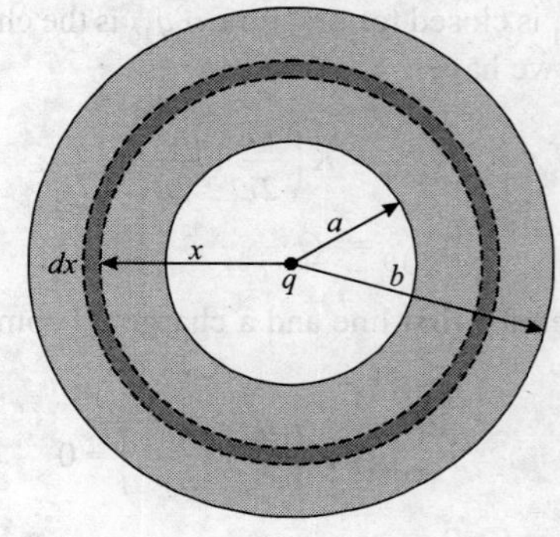

Electric field at the location of elemental shell is given as

$$E = \frac{1}{4\pi\epsilon_0 k} \frac{q}{x^2}$$

Electric energy density in the shell is given as

$$u_e = \frac{1}{2}\epsilon_0 E^2 = \frac{q^2}{32\pi^2 \epsilon_0 k^2 x^4}$$

Thus energy content in the elemental shell is given as

$$dU = \left(\frac{q^2}{32\pi^2 \epsilon_0 k^2 x^4}\right)(4\pi x^2 dx)$$

$$\Rightarrow \quad U = \int_a^b \frac{q^2}{8\pi\epsilon_0 k^2} \cdot \frac{dx}{x^2}$$

$$\Rightarrow \quad U = \frac{q^2}{8\pi\epsilon_0 k^2} \int_a^b \frac{1}{x^2} dx$$

$$\Rightarrow \quad U = \frac{q^2}{8\pi\epsilon_0 k^2}\left[\frac{1}{b} - \frac{1}{a}\right]$$

(iii) The whole charge of inner sphere transfers to outer shell on closing the switch and heat produced is due to the loss in electrostatic energy of the system. Initial energy of system as shown in below figure is given as

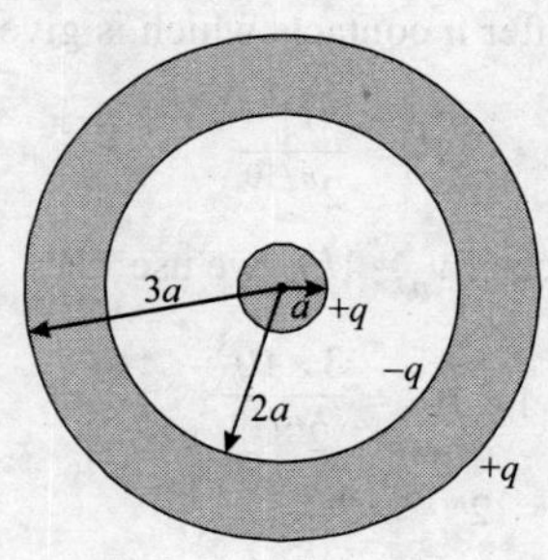

$$U_i = \frac{kq^2}{2a} + \frac{kq^2}{2a} + \frac{kq^2}{6a} - \frac{kq^2}{2a} + \frac{kq^2}{3a} - \frac{kq^2}{3a}$$

$$\Rightarrow \quad U_i = \frac{kq^2}{2a}\left(\frac{1}{2}+\frac{1}{3}\right) = \frac{5}{12}\frac{kq^2}{a}$$

$$\Rightarrow \quad U_i = \frac{5q^2}{48\pi \in_0 a}$$

Find energy of system as shown in below figure is given as

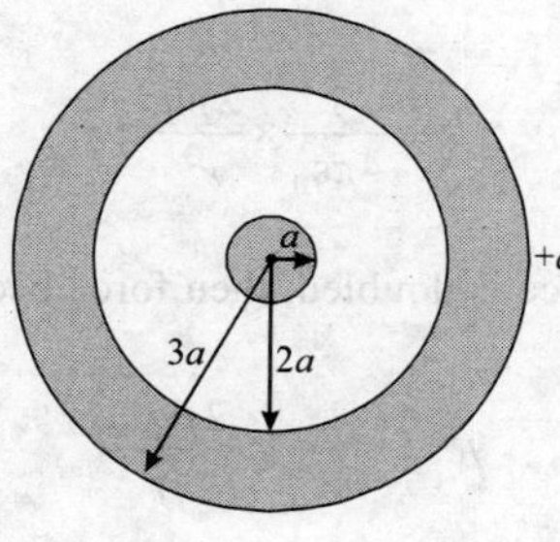

$$U_f = \frac{kq^2}{6a} = \frac{q^2}{24\pi \in_0 a}$$

Heat loss is given as

$$H = U_i - U_f = \frac{5q^2}{48\pi \in_0 a} - \frac{q^2}{24\pi \in_0 a}$$

$$\Rightarrow \quad H = \frac{q^2}{16\pi \in_0 a}$$

(iv) When outer surface is grounded, charge '$-Q$' resides on the inner surface of outer sphere 'B'

Now when sphere A is connected to Earth potential on its surface becomes zero. If charge on A is modified to q_e, we have

$$V_A = \frac{kq_e}{a} - \frac{kQ}{b} = 0$$

$$\Rightarrow \quad q_e = \frac{a}{b}Q$$

Electrostatic energy of this system is

$$V_1 = k\frac{V_e^2}{2a} + \frac{kQ^2}{2b} - \frac{kQq_e}{b}$$

$$\Rightarrow \quad V_1 = \frac{1}{8\pi\varepsilon_0 a}\left[\frac{a}{b}Q\right]^2 + \frac{Q^2}{8\pi\varepsilon_0 b} + \frac{1}{4\pi\varepsilon_0 b}\left[\frac{a}{b}Q\right](-Q)$$

When 'S_3' is closed, total charge will appear on the outer surface of shell 'B'. In this position energy stored is given as

$$E_2 = \frac{k(q_e - Q)^2}{2b}$$

$$\Rightarrow \quad V_2 = \frac{1}{8\pi\varepsilon_0 b}\left(\frac{a}{b}-1\right)^2 Q^2$$

Heat produced is given by loss in electrostatic energy of system which is given as

$$H = V_1 - V_2 = \frac{Q^2 a(b-a)}{8\pi\varepsilon_0 b^3} = 1.8\text{J}$$

(v) The linear charge density of the cylindrical shell is given as

$$\lambda = \frac{Q}{l}$$

When the shell is expanded uniformly from radius a to b then the electric field in the region between the two positions of the shell as shown in figure will become zero after expansion and the field energy which was there in this region will also become zero or we can state that this energy is used in doing work in the process of expansion of shell. To calculate this energy we consider an elemental cylindrical shell of radius x and width dx as shown in figure. The energy stored in this elemental shell volume is given as

$$dU = \frac{1}{2}\in_0 E^2 \times 2\pi x dx \times l$$

$$\Rightarrow \quad dU = \frac{1}{2}\in_0 \left(\frac{\lambda}{2\pi \in_0 x}\right)^2 \times 2\pi x dx \times l$$

$$\Rightarrow \quad dU = \frac{\lambda^2 l}{4\pi \in_0 x}dx$$

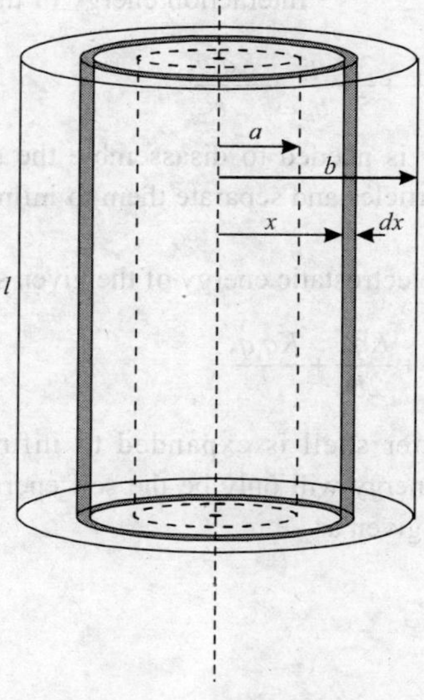

Integrating the above expression within limits from a to b gives

$$U = \int dU = \int_a^b \frac{\lambda^2 l}{4\pi \in_0 x}dx$$

$$\Rightarrow \quad U = \frac{\lambda^2 l}{4\pi \in_0}\int_a^b \frac{1}{x}dx$$

$$\Rightarrow \quad U = \frac{\lambda^2 l}{4\pi \in_0}[\ln x]_a^b$$

$$\Rightarrow \quad U=\frac{\lambda^2 l}{4\pi\epsilon_0}[\ln b-\ln a]$$

$$\Rightarrow \quad U=\frac{\lambda^2 l}{4\pi\epsilon_0}\ln\left(\frac{b}{a}\right)$$

(vi) Initial total electrostatic energy of system is given as

$$U_i=\frac{Kq^2}{2a}+\frac{Kq^2}{4a}+\frac{Kq^2}{2a}=\frac{5Kq^2}{4a}$$

After closing the switch final charge on inner shell will be changed to - $q/2$ to make final potential of inner shell to zero. Thus final electrostatic energy of the system is given as

$$U_f=\frac{K(q/2)^2}{2a}+\frac{Kq^2}{4a}+\frac{Kq(q/2)}{2a}$$

$$\Rightarrow \quad U_f=\frac{Kq^2}{8a}+\frac{Kq^2}{4a}+\frac{Kq^2}{4a}=\frac{5Kq^2}{8a}$$

Heat produced in switching is given as

$$H=U_i-U_f=\frac{5Kq^2}{4a}-\frac{5Kq^2}{8a}=\frac{5Kq^2}{8a}$$

(vii) The total electrostatic energy of the given system is
$U=$ Self energy of sphere A + Self energy of sphere B + Interaction energy of the two spheres

$$\Rightarrow \quad U=\frac{3}{5}\frac{Kq_1^2}{a}+\frac{3}{5}\frac{Kq_2^2}{b}+\frac{Kq_1q_2}{r}$$

Above energy is needed to disassemble the system into its constituent particles and separate them to infinite separation.

(viii) Initial electrostatic energy of the given system is

$$U_i=\frac{Kq_1^2}{2a}+\frac{Kq_2^2}{2b}+\frac{Kq_1q_2}{b}$$

When the outer shell is expanded to infinity then final electrostatic energy will only be the self energy of the inner shell which is given as

$$U_f=\frac{Kq_1^2}{2a}$$

Work required in expanding the outer shell to infinity is given as

$$W=U_f-U_i$$

$$\Rightarrow \quad W=\frac{Kq_1^2}{2a}-\left(\frac{Kq_1^2}{2a}+\frac{Kq_2^2}{2b}+\frac{Kq_1q_2}{b}\right)$$

$$\Rightarrow \quad W=-\left(\frac{Kq_2^2}{2b}+\frac{Kq_1q_2}{b}\right)$$

Solutions of CONCEPTUAL MCQs Single Option Correct

Sol. 1 (B) When charge is given to a soap bubble then due to outward electric pressure its radius always increases.

Sol. 2 (D) We know that at an axial point on dipole electric field is given as

$$E_{\text{end on}}=\frac{1}{4\pi\varepsilon_0}\times\frac{2p}{r^3}$$

$$\Rightarrow \quad F=\frac{1}{4\pi\varepsilon_0}\times\frac{2pq}{r^3}$$

When the distance is doubled, then force becomes

$$F'=\frac{1}{4\pi\varepsilon_0}\times\frac{2pq}{(2r)^3}$$

$$F'=\frac{1}{8}\left[\frac{1}{4\pi\varepsilon_0}\times\frac{2pq}{r^3}\right]=\frac{F}{8}$$

Sol. 3 (B) Let E be the external field toward right then on the left side of sheet we have

$$E-\frac{\sigma}{2\varepsilon_0}=8 \qquad \ldots(1)$$

On the right side of sheet we have

$$E+\frac{\sigma}{2\varepsilon_0}=12 \qquad \ldots(2)$$

Solving above equations-(1) and (2) we get $\sigma=4\varepsilon_0$

Sol. 4 (C) Work done is given as

$$W=\Delta U_i$$

$$\Rightarrow \quad W=U_f-U_i$$

$$\Rightarrow \quad W=3\left[\frac{1}{4\pi\varepsilon_0}\frac{q^2}{2l}\right]-3\left[\frac{1}{4\pi\varepsilon_0}\frac{q^2}{l}\right]$$

$$\Rightarrow \quad W=\left(-\frac{3}{2}\right)\left(\frac{1}{4\pi\varepsilon_0}\frac{q^2}{l^2}\right)l$$

$$\Rightarrow \quad W=-\frac{3}{2}Fl$$

Sol. 5 (D) Always facing surfaces carry equal and opposite charges so after distribution of charges on the surfaces of the shells from inside final distribution is shown in figure.

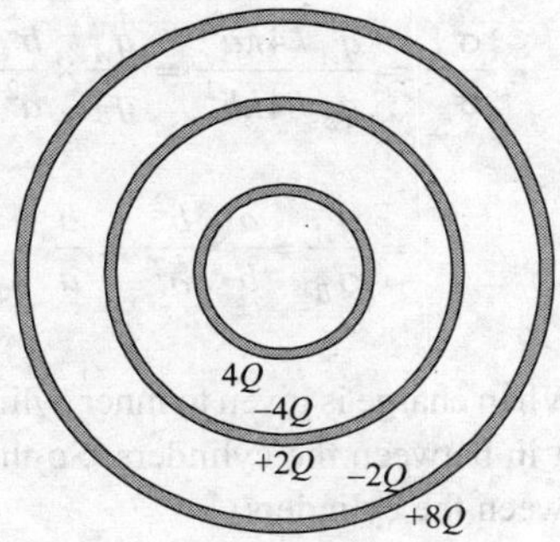

Sol. 6 (D) When shell B is earthed its final potential should be zero. If charge on B is q_B then we have

$$V_B = 0$$

$$\Rightarrow \quad \frac{Kq_A}{r_B} + \frac{Kq_B}{r_B} = 0$$

$$\Rightarrow \quad q_B = -q_A = -q$$

Final charge distribution on shells is as shown in figure below.

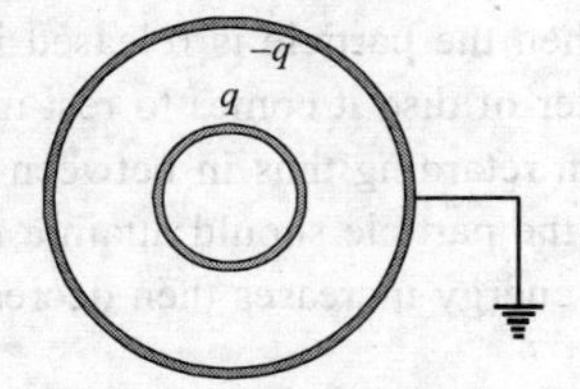

As there is no charge inside shell A electric field at all interior points is zero and outside B also as total enclosed charge is zero due to symmetry outside at every point electric field is also zero.

Sol. 7 (A) Since $|Q_B| > |Q_A|$, electric field outside sphere B is inward. From A to B enclosed charge is positive. Hence electric field is radially outwards.

Sol. 8 (B) Due to the point charge q located at A potential at a distance r from A is given as

$$V = \frac{1}{4\pi\varepsilon_0} \cdot \frac{q}{r}$$

On a hollow sphere of radius $4r$ the potential at A is same as that on the surface of this sphere as at every interior point potential is same as that of its surface which is given as

$$V' = \left(\frac{1}{4\pi\varepsilon_0}\right)\left(\frac{2q}{4r}\right) = \frac{V}{2}$$

Sol. 9 (B) The total flux passing through the sphere is only due to the enclosed charge.

Sol. 10 (A) As shown in the figure direction of electric field in case I is correctly represented. In case II and III resulting direction of electric field will be in vertically downward direction.

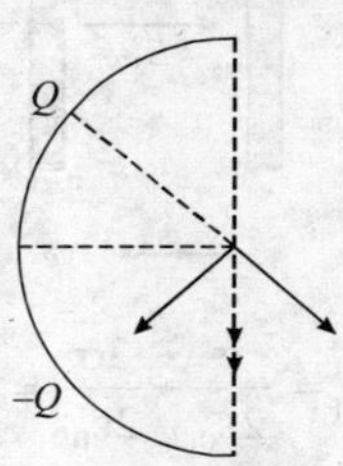

Sol. 11 (C) The total charge on the outer surface will be $Q + q$.

So charge density will be $\left[\frac{Q+q}{4\pi b^2}\right]$.

Sol. 12 (D) All the points of an equipotential surface are at same potential and work done in moving a charge from one point to another is given by the product of charge and the potential difference between the two points so in this case no work is done.

Sol. 13 (B) Due to symmetry of all the electrons net electric field strength at center of circle is zero but as all are negatively charged their potentials will be added up and will be non zero.

Sol. 14 (B) We consider a spherical shell of thickness dx and radius x. The volume of this spherical shell is $4\pi x^2 dx$. The charge enclosed within shell is given as

$$dq = \left[\frac{Qx}{\pi R^4}\right][4\pi x^2 dx] = \frac{4Q}{R^4} x^3 dx$$

The charge enclosed in the sphere of radius r_1 is given as

$$q = \frac{4Q}{R^4}\int_0^{r_1} x^3 dx = \frac{4Q}{R^4}\left[\frac{x^4}{4}\right]_0^{r_1} = \frac{Q}{R^4} r_1^4$$

The electric field at point P inside the sphere at a distance r_1 from the centre of the sphere is given as

$$E = \frac{1}{4\pi \epsilon_0} \frac{\left[\frac{Q}{R^4} r_1^4\right]}{r_1^2}$$

$$\Rightarrow \quad E = \frac{1}{4\pi \epsilon_0} \frac{Q}{R^4} r_1^2$$

Sol. 15 (D) The potential of each point on the conducting sphere will be same.

Sol. 16 (C) The direction of electric fields at different points is shown in figure below.

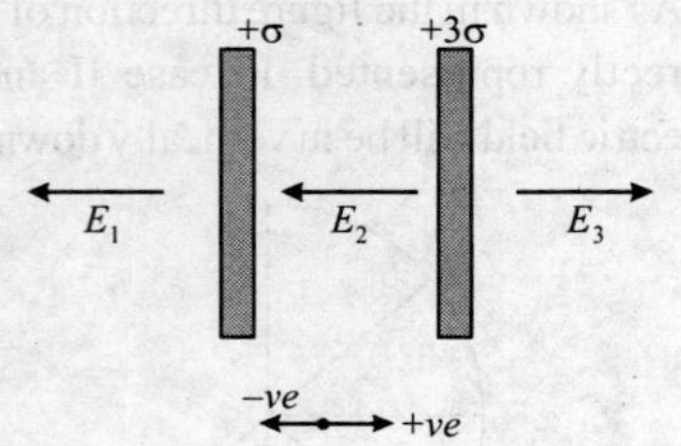

$$E_1 = \frac{\sigma}{2\varepsilon_0} + \frac{3\sigma}{2\varepsilon_0} = \frac{2\sigma}{\varepsilon_0} = E_3$$

$$E_2 = \frac{3\sigma}{2\varepsilon_0} - \frac{\sigma}{2\varepsilon_0} = \frac{\sigma}{\varepsilon_0}$$

E_1 and E_2 are in the negative direction and E_3 in positive direction

Sol. 17 (A) For two concentric metal shells their potential difference does not depend on the charge of outer shell.

Sol. 18 (C) $\oint \vec{E}.d\vec{A} = 0$, represents charge inside close surface is zero. Electric field at different points on the surface may be different in magnitude and direction to have net surface integral zero.

Sol. 19 (D) In the space electric field and potential are related as

$$\vec{E} = -\vec{\nabla} V = -\left[\frac{\partial V}{\partial x}\hat{i} + \frac{\partial V}{\partial y}\hat{i}\right]$$

$$\vec{E} = -\left[2x\hat{i} - 2y\hat{i}\right]$$

$$E = 2\sqrt{x^2 + y^2}$$

Sol. 20 (D) Equal and opposite charges will appear on the sphere. So net charge in the sphere becomes zero.

Sol. 21 (D) When negative charge is given to the sphere, electrons are put on it, and so its mass will be more.

Sol. 22 (A) Just to the right of a, electric field is along ab and tending to infinite. Similarly electric field just to the left of b electric field along ab and tending to infinite. Thus a is positive and b is negative.

Sol. 23 (B) Given that the two spheres are at same potential so we have

$$\frac{1}{4\pi \epsilon_0}.\frac{q_A}{a} = \frac{1}{4\pi \epsilon_0}.\frac{q_B}{b}$$

$$\Rightarrow \quad \frac{q_A}{q_B} = \frac{a}{b}$$

$$\Rightarrow \quad \frac{\sigma_A}{\sigma_B} = \frac{q_A / 4\pi a^2}{q_B / 4\pi b^2} = \frac{q_A}{q_B} \times \frac{b^2}{a^2}$$

$$\Rightarrow \quad \frac{\sigma_A}{\sigma_B} = \frac{a}{b} \times \frac{b^2}{a^2} = \frac{b}{a}$$

Sol. 24 (A) When charge is given to inner cylinder, an electric field will exist in between the cylinders. So there is potential difference between the cylinders.

Sol. 25 (A) From the deflection of particle 1 it is clear that the direction of electric field is toward the 'Top' side and positive charge particle deflects in the direction of field and negative charge deflects in direction opposite to the field.

Sol. 26 (C) Force per unit charge at a point in electric field gives the strength or intensity of electric field at that point.

Sol. 27 (A) As electric field is in the plane of the surface so no flux will pass through the surface due to this electric field.

Sol. 28 (C) When the particle is released it falls and till it reaches the center of disc it comes to rest means it was first accelerating then retarding thus in between there is a point, where speed of the particle should attain a maximum value. Thus its kinetic energy increases then decreases.

Sol. 29 (C) The magnitude of electric field intensity due to each part of the hemispherical surface at the centre 'O' will be same as all three parts are identical. If we suppose, It is E then the directions of E due to all three are shown in figure below.

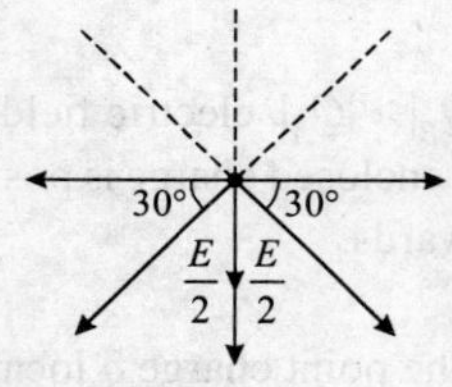

At O resulting field is given as

$$E + \frac{E}{2} + \frac{E}{2} = E_0$$

$$\Rightarrow \quad 2E = E_0$$

$$\Rightarrow \quad E = \frac{E_0}{2}$$

Sol. 30 (A) Due to any constant external force SHM frequency never changes, it can only shift the equilibrium position.

Sol. 31 (D) The variation of potential between the two charges is shown in the figure below.

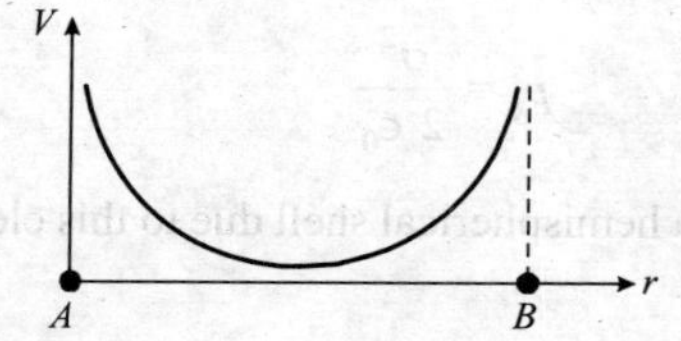

Sol. 32 (C) Electric field at the centre is due to the charge C which is given as

$$E=\frac{1}{4\pi\epsilon_0}\frac{(2q/3)}{R^2}=\frac{q}{6\pi\epsilon_0 R^2}$$

Potential energy of the system is given as

$$U=\frac{1}{4\pi\epsilon_0}\left[\frac{\frac{q}{3}\times\frac{q}{3}}{2R}+\frac{\frac{q}{3}\left(-\frac{2q}{3}\right)}{\sqrt{3}R}+\frac{\frac{q}{3}\left(-\frac{2q}{3}\right)}{R}\right]\neq 0$$

Force between charges B and C is given as

$$F_{BC}=\frac{1}{4\pi\epsilon_0}\left[\frac{\frac{q}{3}\times\left(\frac{2q}{3}\right)}{(\sqrt{3}R)^2}\right]=\frac{q^2}{54\pi\epsilon_0 R^2}$$

Sol. 33 (A) As we've studied that potential difference between two hollow concentric shells does not depend upon the charge on outer shell so the potential difference will remain the same.

Sol. 34 (A) The potential of this system of charges will be zero at any point on the line perpendicular to the line joining the charges as all points on the line are equidistant from both the charges.

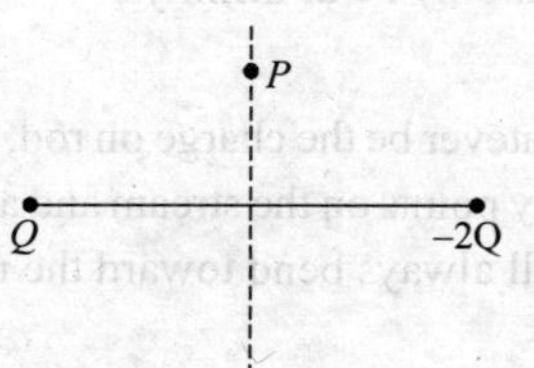

Sol. 35 (A) Electric field at point P is given as

$$\vec{E}=\left(\frac{\sigma}{2\epsilon_0}+\frac{2\sigma}{2\epsilon_0}+\frac{\sigma}{2\epsilon_0}\right)(-\hat{k})$$

$$\Rightarrow\qquad \vec{E}=-\frac{2\sigma}{\epsilon_0}\hat{k}$$

Sol. 36 (A) The electric field strength at a distance x from center is given as

$$E=\frac{Qx}{\left(\frac{4}{3}\pi R^3\right)3\varepsilon_0}+\frac{Q/16}{4\pi\varepsilon_0 x^2}$$

Electric field becomes minimum when

$$\Rightarrow\qquad \frac{dE}{dx}=0$$

$$\Rightarrow\qquad \frac{Q}{4\pi\varepsilon_0}\left(\frac{1}{R^3}-\frac{2}{16x^3}\right)=0$$

$$\Rightarrow\qquad x=\frac{R}{2}$$

Sol. 37 (D) If λ be the linear charge density of the rod, then after time t the charge enclosed in the cubical surface is given as

$$q_{in}=\lambda x=\lambda vt$$

Thus electric flux through the cubical surface is given as

$$\phi=\frac{q_{in}}{\epsilon_0}=\frac{\lambda vt}{\epsilon_0}$$

The flux of the charge increases till $vt = L/2$, when maximum electric flux passes through the cubical surface given as

$$\phi_{max}=\frac{\lambda L}{2\epsilon_0}$$

When rod comes out from left side of the cube, the flux then starts decreasing linearly the way it was increasing till this time. So option (D) is correct.

Sol. 38 (A) Over Q_1, potential is positive so Q_1 is positive. $V_A = 0$ and A point is nearer to Q_2 so Q_2 should be negative and $|Q_1| > |Q_2|$. At A and B, potential is zero, not the force so these are not equilibrium points. Equilibrium at C will depend on the nature of charge which is kept at C. so we cannot comment on the type of equilibrium at C.

Sol. 39 (A) For the six pair of charges the interaction energy is given by sum of energy of all the pair of charges given as

$$U=6\times\frac{1}{4\pi\epsilon_0}\frac{q^2}{a^2}$$

Sol. 40 (A) Due to the charge q_0 the ball will get displaced back and this decreases the electric field to be measured at this point so option (A) is correct.

Sol. 41 (B) For circular motion we use

$$\frac{1}{4\pi\epsilon_0}\frac{Qq}{r^2}=\frac{mv^2}{r}$$

$$\Rightarrow\qquad v=\sqrt{\frac{Qq}{4\pi\epsilon_0 mr}}$$

Now time period is given as

$$T=\frac{2\pi r}{v}=\frac{2\pi r}{\sqrt{\frac{Qq}{4\pi\epsilon_0 mr}}}$$

$$\Rightarrow \qquad r^3 = \left(\frac{Qq}{16\pi^3 \in_0 m}\right)T^2$$

Sol. 42 **(B)** From $x = 0$ to $x = r$ potential is constant at $\frac{\sigma}{\varepsilon_0}(R-r)$ and from $x = r$ to $x = R$ it increases we are moving opposite to field from so it decreases.

Sol. 43 **(C)** The flux of this charge will pass through such four identical cubes considered on the other sides of the charge so flux through this cube will be one fourth of the total flux due to the charge.

Sol. 44 **(D)** Due to the restoring forces charge will oscillate along the *X*- axis with mean position at origin but the motion will not be SHM as the force will not be proportional to the displacement of the charge.

Sol. 45 **(A)** As we've studied that at any point inside a metal cavity when a charge is placed equal amount of charge is induced on the outer surface of the conductor which is distributed in such a way to keep constant potential on the body of conductor. In this case for spherical shape outer charge is uniform so the electric field at point P is given as

$$E = \frac{1}{4\pi \in_0}\frac{Q}{x^2}$$

Sol. 46 **(D)** No matter wherever the charge is placed inside a metal cavity outside electric field does not change as it depends upon the distribution of charge on the outer surface of the conductor.

Sol. 47 **(A)** We have studied that the force between two small balls for constant total charge will be maximum when the charge is equally distributed on the two so half of the total charge is $5q/2$ thus a charge $q/2$ should be transferred from one ball to another to make their charges equal.

Sol. 48 **(D)** After connection charges will flow till the two spheres will attain a common potential and some energy will be dissipated as heat in case of charge flow but if initially the potentials of the two spheres are same then no charge flow will take place so the condition for no charge flow on connection is

$$\frac{KQ_1}{R_1} = \frac{KQ_2}{R_2}$$

$$\Rightarrow \qquad Q_1 R_2 = Q_2 R_1$$

Sol. 49 **(A)** The electrostatic pressure at a point on the surface of a uniformly charged sphere is given as

$$p_e = \frac{\sigma^2}{2 \in_0}$$

The force on a hemispherical shell due to this electric pressure is given as

$$F = \frac{\sigma^2}{2 \in_0} \times \pi R^2$$

Sol. 50 **(B)** Charge enclosed for sphere of radius $R/2$ is given as

$$Q = \int (4\pi r^2) dr \rho(r)$$

$$\Rightarrow \qquad Q = 4\pi A \int_0^{R/2} r^4 dr = 4\pi A\left[\frac{r^5}{5}\right]_0^{R/2}$$

$$\Rightarrow \qquad Q = \frac{4\pi A}{5 \times 32}(R^5) = \frac{\pi A}{40} R^5$$

Thus electric field at this point is given as

$$E = \frac{KQ}{(R/2)^2}$$

$$\Rightarrow \qquad E = \frac{AR^3}{40\varepsilon_0}$$

Sol. 51 **(D)** As both the charges are positive so potential cannot be zero anywhere at a point located finite distance from this system. It can only be at infinity.

Sol. 52 **(B)** Whatever be the charge on rod, it induces opposite charges at close by points on the stream and attracts the particles in stream so it will always bend toward the rod.

Sol. 53 **(D)** Inside a uniformly charged sphere electric field strength is directly proportional to the distance from center which is given as

$$E = \frac{\rho r}{3 \in_0}$$

Thus electric field decreases directly as the distance from the center.

Sol. 54 **(A)** Net downwards acceleration or effective gravity on body mass is given as

$$g_{\text{eff}} = \left(g + \frac{qE}{m}\right)$$

If it hits the ground after a time t, it is given as

$$t=\frac{2v}{\left[g+\frac{qE}{m}\right]}$$

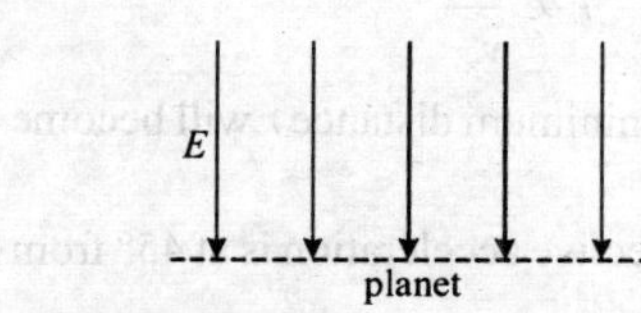

At maximum height $v_f=0$
we use

$$v^2=2\left[g+\frac{qE}{m}\right]h$$

ΔV between ground and highest point is given as

$$\Delta V=(E)h$$

$$g_{eff}=\frac{2v}{t}$$

$$\Rightarrow\quad \left(g+\frac{qE}{m}\right)=\frac{2v}{t}$$

$$\Rightarrow\quad \frac{q}{m}E=\left(\frac{2v}{t}-g\right)$$

We also have

$$h=(\text{average velocity})\times t$$

$$h=\frac{v}{2}\times t$$

$$\Rightarrow\quad \Delta V=\frac{m}{q}\left(\frac{2v}{t}-g\right)\left(\frac{v}{2}t\right)$$

$$\Rightarrow\quad \Delta V=\frac{mv}{2q}\left(v-\frac{gt}{2}\right)$$

Sol. 55 (D) The electric field strength vector in the region is given as

$$\vec{E}=400\cos 45°\,\hat{i}+400\sin 45°\,\hat{j}$$

The potential difference between points A and B can be given as

$$V_A-V_B=-\int_B^A \vec{E}\cdot\vec{dr}$$

where $\vec{dr}=dx\hat{i}+dy\hat{j}$

Sol. 56 (C) Electric field at origin can be given by integrating the electric field due to an element considered on the rod of length dx at a distance x from origin which is given as

$$E=\int_a^{4d}\frac{K\lambda dx}{x^2}$$

$$\Rightarrow\quad E=K\lambda\int_a^{4d}x^{-2}dx$$

$$\Rightarrow\quad E=\frac{\lambda}{4\pi\varepsilon_0}\int_d^{4d}\frac{dx}{x^2}$$

$$\Rightarrow\quad E=\frac{3\lambda}{16\pi\varepsilon_0 d}$$

Sol. 57 (C) Flux does not depends on the size and shape of the close surface, and so it remains same.

Sol. 58 (B) Figure below shows the charges on the three concentric shells using which we can find the potential of shell B as

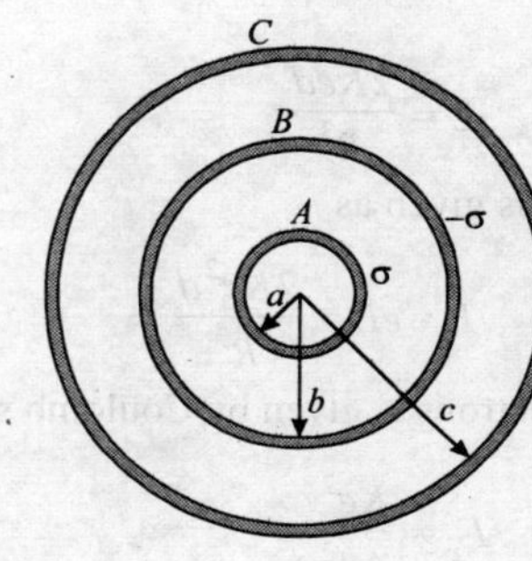

$$V_B=\frac{Kq_A}{b}+\frac{Kq_B}{b}+\frac{Kq_C}{c}$$

$$\Rightarrow\quad V_B=\left(\frac{\sigma a^2}{\varepsilon_0}\right)\left(\frac{1}{b}\right)-\left(\frac{\sigma b^2}{\varepsilon_0}\right)\left(\frac{1}{b}\right)+\left(\frac{\sigma c^2}{\varepsilon_0}\right)\left(\frac{1}{c}\right)$$

$$\Rightarrow\quad V_B=\frac{\sigma}{\varepsilon_0}\left(\frac{a^2}{b}-b+c\right)$$

Sol. 59 (A) If initial point from where the particle starts is considered as A and the point where the particle crosses the horizontal line through point P is B then the potential difference between these two points is given as

$$V_A-V_B=El(1-\cos\theta)$$

By work energy theorem we have

$$q(V_A-V_B)=\frac{1}{2}mv^2-\frac{1}{2}mv_0^2$$

$$\Rightarrow\quad qEl(1-\cos\theta)=\frac{1}{2}mv^2$$

$$\Rightarrow\quad v=\left(\frac{2qEL(1-\cos\theta)}{m}\right)^{1/2}$$

Sol. 60 (A) Electric field on surface of a uniformly charged sphere of radius R is given as

$$E_1 = \frac{Q}{4\pi\varepsilon_0 R^3} = \frac{\rho R}{3\varepsilon_0}$$

Electric field at outside point of a sphere of radius R is given as

$$E_2 = \frac{Q}{4\pi\varepsilon_0 r^2} = \frac{\rho R^3}{3\varepsilon_0 r^2}$$

The electric field at point B is given as

$$E_B = \frac{\rho r_0}{3\varepsilon_0} - \frac{\rho\left(\frac{r_0}{2}\right)^3}{3\varepsilon_0\left(\frac{3r_0}{2}\right)^2} = \frac{17\rho r_0}{54\varepsilon_0}$$

Sol. 61 (A) Field due to $+2e$ charge sphere at distance d from the centre is

$$E = \frac{2Ked}{R^3}$$

Force on electron is given as

$$F = eE = \frac{2Ke^2 d}{R^3}$$

Force between electrons is given by Coulomb's law as

$$F_c = \frac{Ke^2}{4d^2}$$

For equilibrium, we have

$$\frac{2Ke^2 d}{R^3} = \frac{Ke^2}{4d^2}$$

$$\Rightarrow \quad R^3 = 8d^3$$

$$\Rightarrow \quad R = 2d$$

Sol. 62 (A) From centre to the surface of inner shell, potential will remain constant.

Sol. 63 (C) For, $r < a$, the potential is given as

$$V = \frac{KQ(3a^2 - r^2)}{2a^3} + \frac{K(-Q)}{b} + \frac{KQ}{c}$$

for, $a < r < b$, the potential is given as

$$V = \frac{KQ}{r} + \frac{K(-Q)}{b} + \frac{KQ}{c}$$

for, $b < r < c$, the potential is given as

$$V = \frac{KQ}{r} + \frac{K(-Q)}{b} + \frac{KQ}{c} = \frac{KQ}{c}$$

for, $r > c$, the potential is given as

$$V = \frac{KQ}{r} + \frac{K(-Q)}{r} + \frac{KQ}{r} = \frac{KQ}{r}$$

Sol. 64 (D) By conservation of energy we use

$$U_i + K_i = K_f$$

$$0 + \frac{1}{2}mv^2 = \frac{1}{4\pi\varepsilon_0}\cdot\frac{Qq}{r} + 0$$

$$\Rightarrow \quad r \propto \frac{1}{v^2}$$

If v is doubled, the minimum distance r will become one fourth.

Sol. 65 (C) As effective acceleration is at 45° from the vertical direction we use

$$QE = Mg$$

$$\Rightarrow \quad \frac{QV}{d} = w$$

$$\Rightarrow \quad Q = \frac{wd}{V}$$

Sol. 66 (C) Due to a point charge electric field is given as

$$E_1(r_0) = \frac{Q}{4\pi \epsilon_0 r_0^2}$$

Due to a line charge electric field is given as

$$E_2(r_0) = \frac{\lambda}{2\pi \epsilon_0 r_0}$$

Due to a uniformly charged plane electric field is given as

$$E_3(r_0) = \frac{\sigma}{2\epsilon_0}$$

At $\quad r = \frac{r_0}{2}$ we have

$$E_1\left(\frac{r_0}{2}\right) = \frac{Q}{4\pi\epsilon_0\left(\frac{r_0}{2}\right)^2} = \frac{Q}{\pi\epsilon_0 r_0^2} = 4E_1(r_0)$$

$$E_2\left(\frac{r_0}{2}\right) = \frac{\lambda}{2\pi\epsilon_0\left(\frac{r_0}{2}\right)} = \frac{\lambda}{\pi\epsilon_0 r_0} = 2E_2(r_0)$$

$$E_3\left(\frac{r_0}{2}\right) = \frac{\sigma}{2\epsilon_0} = E_3(r_0)$$

Given $E_1(r_0) = E_2(r_0) = E_3(r_0)$. It follows from the above equations that the only option (C) can be correct.

Sol. 67 (D) The electric field inside the cavity at a position r is given by

$$E(r) = \frac{\rho a}{3\varepsilon_0}$$

where $|a| = R_1 - R_2$ and ρ is the volume charge density. Hence $E(r)$ is uniform and its magnitude as well as its direction depends on a.

Sol. 68 (C) Due to the charge negative charges are induced on the conducting sphere as shown in figure below so net flux from the closed surface will be negative.

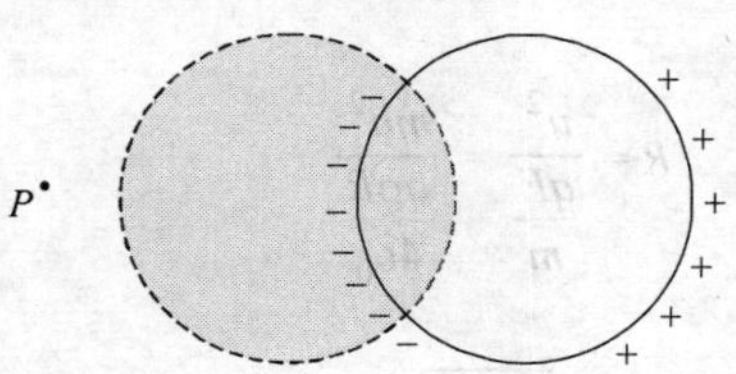

Sol. 69 (B) Since net force on negative charge is always directed towards fixed positive charge, the torque on negative charge about positive charge is zero. Therefore angular momentum of negative charge about fixed positive charge is conserved.

Sol. 70 (C) The field due to the uniformly charged shell at an inside point is zero. Hence potential difference will not change.

Sol. 71 (B) The gain in kinetic energy of charged particle is calculated by using work-energy theorem. The kinetic energy of point charge after travelling a distance x is given as

$$qEx = \frac{1}{2}mv^2$$

$$\Rightarrow \quad v^2 = \frac{2qE}{m}x$$

$$\Rightarrow \quad v = \sqrt{\frac{2qE}{m}}\sqrt{x}$$

Solutions of NUMERICAL MCQs Single Option Correct

Sol. 1 (A) For circular motion of particle we have

$$qE = \frac{mv^2}{r}$$

$$\Rightarrow \quad q\left(\frac{\lambda}{2\pi\varepsilon_0 r}\right) = \frac{mv^2}{r}$$

$$\Rightarrow \quad v = \sqrt{\frac{q\lambda}{2\pi\varepsilon_0 m}} = \sqrt{\frac{2kq\lambda}{m}}$$

Time period of circular motion is given as

$$T = \frac{2\pi r}{v}$$

$$\Rightarrow \quad T = 2\pi r\sqrt{\frac{m}{2k\lambda q}}$$

Sol. 2 (B) The charge enclosed inside the cylindrical surface is

$$q_{in} = Q \times 100$$

Electric flux is given as

$$\phi = \frac{q_{in}}{\epsilon_0}$$

$$\Rightarrow \quad \phi = \frac{100Q}{\epsilon_0}$$

Sol. 3 (A) For equilibrium of ball

$$qE = mg\left(1 - \frac{\rho_0}{\rho_c}\right)$$

[We use apparent weight of ball in oil]

$$q = \frac{4}{3}\frac{\pi d^3}{8} \times \frac{g\rho_c}{E}\left(1 - \frac{\rho_0}{\rho_c}\right)$$

$$q = \frac{1}{6}k\left(1 - \frac{\rho_0}{\rho_c}\right)$$

[As given that $k = \dfrac{\pi d^3 \rho_c g}{E}$]

Sol. 4 (B) By work energy theorem between points A and B we have

$$\frac{1}{2}mv^2 = qEl[1 - \cos 60°]$$

$$\Rightarrow \quad v = \sqrt{\frac{qEl}{m}}$$

Tension at point B is given as

$$T = qE + \frac{mv^2}{l} = 2qE$$

Sol. 5 (D) Tension will be minimum in the circle which is the point farthest away from the direction of effective gravity acting in the region as shown in figure below.

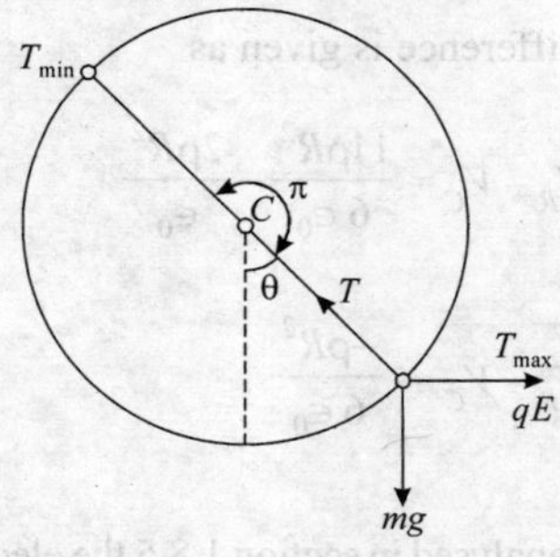

$$T\sin\theta = qE$$

$$T\cos\theta = mg$$

$$\Rightarrow \quad \theta = \tan^{-1}\left(\frac{qE}{mg}\right)$$

Minimum tension will be obtained at $\theta + \pi$

Sol. 6 **(B)** If we consider potentials V_A and V_B at (0,0) and (x_0, 0) then we use

$$\int_A^B \vec{E}\cdot\vec{dx} = V_A - V_B = O - V_B$$

$$E_0 X_0 = -V_B$$

$$V_B = -E_0 x_0$$

Sol. 7 **(B)** The electric field strength between the plates is given as

$$E = \frac{V}{d} = \frac{800}{0.02} = 40000 \text{ V/m}$$

For the equilibrium of the particle, we use

$$mg = Eq$$

$$mg = E(ne)$$

$$\Rightarrow \quad n = \frac{mg}{Ee} = \frac{1.96\times10^{-15}\times9.8}{40000\times1.6\times10^{-19}}$$

$$\Rightarrow \quad n = 3$$

Sol. 8 **(D)** The charge on the sphere is

$$Q = \pi\times\frac{4}{3}\times\pi(2R)^3 = \frac{32}{3}\pi\rho R^3$$

For a uniformly charged sphere potential at the center of sphere is given as

$$V_C = \frac{3}{2}\left(\frac{KQ}{2R}\right) = \frac{2\rho R^2}{\epsilon_0}$$

At $r = R$, potential is given as

$$V_R = KQ\left[\frac{3(2R)^2 - R^2}{2(2R)^3}\right] = \frac{11\rho R^2}{6\epsilon_0}$$

Thus potential difference is given as

$$V_R - V_C = \frac{11\rho R^2}{6\epsilon_0} - \frac{2\rho R^2}{\epsilon_0}$$

$$\Rightarrow \quad V_R - V_C = \frac{-\rho R^2}{6\epsilon_0}$$

Sol. 9 **(A)** As analysed in section 1.8.5 the electric field inside the cavity of a uniformly charged conductor is uniform and its magnitude is given as

$$E = \frac{\rho r}{2\varepsilon_0} = \frac{\rho\frac{R}{2}}{2\varepsilon_0} = \frac{\rho R}{4\varepsilon_0}$$

The direction of the field is as shown in the figure given below. For the particle projected from point A, if the particle hits at B the range of projectile at minimum speed and maximum range is given as

$$R = \frac{u^2}{\frac{qE}{m}} = \frac{mu^2}{\frac{q\rho R}{4\varepsilon_0}}$$

$$\Rightarrow \quad u = \sqrt{\frac{q\rho R^2}{4\varepsilon_0 m}}$$

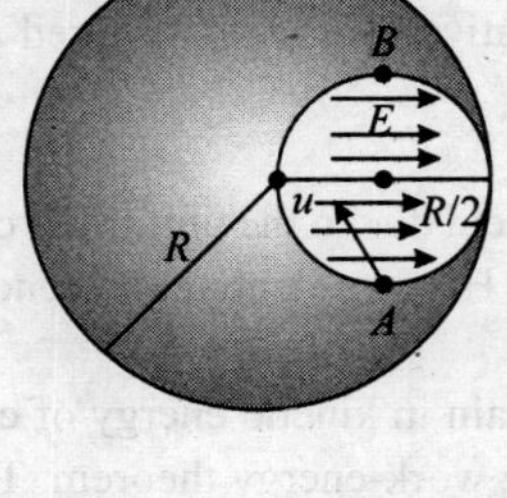

Sol. 10 **(C)** Electric potential at a point is given as

$$V = \frac{W}{q} = \frac{2}{20} = 0.1\text{V}$$

Sol. 11 **(D)** The electric field in the region is given as

$$E_{PQ} = -\frac{dV_{PQ}}{dX_{PQ}} = -\frac{(V_Q - V_P)}{X_{PQ}} = \frac{-(0-5)}{1.0} = 5 \text{ N/C}$$

and $$E_{QR} = -\frac{(-10-0)}{0.5} = 20 \text{ N/C}$$

Sol. 12 **(A)** At point P shown in figure the electric fields due to the two spheres will nullify each other so we have

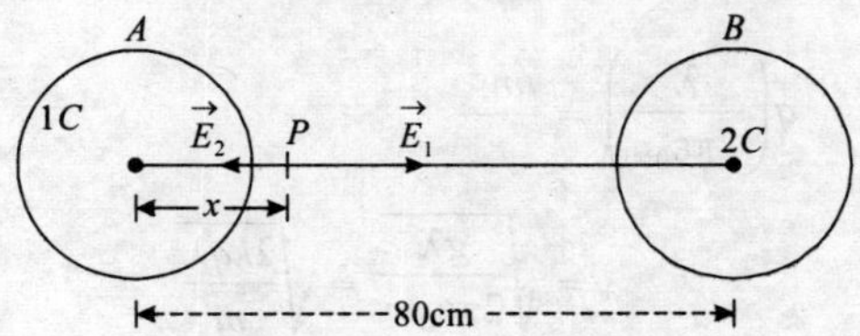

$$|\vec{E}_1| = |\vec{E}_2|$$

$$\Rightarrow \quad \frac{1}{4\pi\varepsilon_0}\times\frac{1}{x^2} = \frac{1}{4\pi\varepsilon_0}\times\frac{2}{(0.8-x)^2}$$

$$\Rightarrow \quad \frac{1}{x^2} = \frac{2}{(0.8-x)^2}$$

$$\Rightarrow \quad x \simeq 0.33 \text{ m} = 33 \text{ cm}$$

Now the potential at this point is given as

$$\Rightarrow \quad V_P = \frac{1}{4\pi\varepsilon_0}\times\frac{q_1}{x}+\frac{1}{4\pi\varepsilon_0}\times\frac{q_2}{(0.8-x)}$$

$$\Rightarrow \quad V_P = \frac{1}{4\pi\varepsilon_0}\left[\frac{q_1}{x}+\frac{q_2}{(0.8-x)}\right]$$

$$\Rightarrow \quad V_P = 9\times 10^9\left[\frac{1}{0.33}+\frac{2}{0.47}\right]$$

$$\Rightarrow \quad V_P = 6.56\times 10^{10}\,\text{V}$$

Sol. 13 (D) We calculate the potential gradient as

$$E_x = \frac{-\partial V}{\partial x} = \frac{-\partial}{\partial x}(-5x+3y+\sqrt{15}z) = 5$$

$$E_y = \frac{-\partial V}{\partial y} = -3,$$

and $$E_z = -\sqrt{15}$$

The net electric field in region is given as

$$E = \sqrt{E_x^2+E_y^2+E_z^2}$$

$$\Rightarrow \quad E = \sqrt{5^2+(-3)^2+(\sqrt{15})^2}$$

$$\Rightarrow \quad E = 7$$

Sol. 14 (D) Using energy conservation we have

$$U_i + K_i = U_f + K_f$$

$$\Rightarrow \quad qV_i + \frac{1}{2}mv_{\min}^2 = qV_f + 0$$

$$\Rightarrow \quad q\left(\frac{1}{4\pi\varepsilon_0}\right)\left(\frac{Q}{R}\right)+\frac{1}{2}mv_{\min}^2 = q\left[\frac{3}{2}\times\frac{Q}{4\pi\varepsilon_0 R}\right]$$

$$\Rightarrow \quad v_{\min} = \sqrt{\frac{Qq}{4\pi\varepsilon_0 mR}}$$

Sol. 15 (D) Potential due to the given system of charges at origin is given as

$$V = \frac{1}{4\pi\in_0}\left[\frac{q}{x_0}-\frac{q}{2x_0}+\frac{q}{3x_0}-\frac{q}{4x_0}+\ldots\infty\right]$$

$$V = \frac{q}{4\pi\in_0 x_0}\ln(1+1)$$

$$V = \frac{q\ln 2}{4\pi\in_0 x_0}$$

Sol. 16 (A) Work done is calculated as

$$W = \vec{F}.\vec{s} = Q\vec{E}.\vec{r} = Q(e_1\hat{i}+e_2\hat{j}+e_3\hat{k}).(a\hat{i}+b\hat{j})$$

Sol. 17 (A) The given line integral is the potential at center of the ring which is given as

$$\int_{l=\infty}^{l=0} -\vec{E}.dl = V = \frac{1}{4\pi\in_0 x_0}\frac{q}{R}$$

$$V = \frac{9\times 10^9\times 1.11\times 10^{-10}}{0.5} = 2\text{V}$$

Sol. 18 (C) One component of electric field at centre O is $\frac{2K\lambda}{R}$ along OC and other component is $\frac{K\lambda}{R}$ perpendicular to OC

Thus net electric field at point O is given as

$$E_{\text{net}} = \frac{K\lambda}{R}\sqrt{5}$$

Resulting electric field at O is at an angle θ from OC where we have

$$\tan\theta = \frac{K\lambda/R}{2K\lambda/R} = \frac{1}{2}$$

Sol. 19 (B) Given dipole moment is

$$\vec{P} = (QL)\hat{i}$$

The angle between $\vec{P}$ and $\vec{E}$ initially is $\theta_i = 90°$ and finally when it aligns with the direction of field vector then $\theta_f = 0$.

Using work energy theorem the angular velocity of the dipole when it is parallel to the direction of electric field is given as

$$-PE(\cos 90° - \cos 0°) = \frac{1}{2}I\omega^2$$

$$\Rightarrow \quad +PE = \frac{1}{2}\left(\frac{ML^2}{12}\right)\omega^2$$

$$\Rightarrow \quad \omega = \sqrt{\frac{12\sqrt{2}Q}{ML}}$$

Angular velocity vector,

$$\vec{\omega} = \omega(\hat{r})$$

Where $\hat{r}$ is the unit vector along the axis of rotation along which the dipole will rotate that is lying in the yz plane but perpendicular to the direction of electric field which is given as

$$\hat{r} = \frac{(-\hat{j}+\hat{k})}{\sqrt{2}}$$

Thus angular velocity vector is given as

$$\vec{\omega} = \sqrt{\frac{12\sqrt{2}Q}{ML}}\frac{(-\hat{j}+\hat{k})}{\sqrt{2}}$$

$$\Rightarrow \quad \vec{\omega} = \sqrt{\frac{6\sqrt{2}Q}{ML}}(-\hat{j}+\hat{k})$$

Sol. 20 (A) We are given

$$F_x = 0$$

$$\Rightarrow \quad a_x = 0$$

and $$F_y = qE$$

$$\Rightarrow \quad a_y = \frac{qE}{m}$$

displacement of particles along x and y direction is given as

$$x = vt$$

and $$y = \frac{1}{2}a_y t^2 = \frac{1}{2}\left(\frac{qE}{m}\right)t^2$$

Substituting $t = \frac{x}{y}$ in expression of y, we get

$$y = \frac{1}{2}\left(\frac{qEx^2}{mv^2}\right)$$

Kinetic energy of particle is given as

$$K = \frac{1}{2}m(v_x^2 + v_y^2)$$

where $v_x = v$ and $v_y = a_y t = \frac{qE}{m}t$

Sol. 21 (B) From the grid we can find the potential gradient along x and y directions separately as

$$E_x = \frac{V_O - V_A}{x} = \frac{0-(-1)}{1} = 1 \text{ V/m}$$

and $$E_y = \frac{V_O - V_B}{y} = \frac{0-1}{1} = -1 \text{ V/m}$$

Thus net electric field strength vector is given as

$$\vec{E} = E_x\hat{i} + E_y\hat{j} = (\hat{i} - \hat{j}) \text{ V/m}$$

Sol. 22 (D) The electric field and potential are given as

$$500 = \frac{k|q|}{r^2} \quad \ldots(1)$$

$$-3000 = \frac{k(-q)}{r} \quad \ldots(2)$$

Solving these two equations we get

$$r = 6 \text{ m}$$

and $$q = \frac{500r^2}{K}$$

$$\Rightarrow \quad q = \frac{(500)(6)^2}{9\times10^9}$$

$$\Rightarrow \quad q = 2\times10^{-6} \text{ C}$$

$$\Rightarrow \quad q = 2\ \mu\text{C}$$

Sol. 23 (D) By work energy theorem we have

$$e(V_2 - V_1) = \frac{1}{2}mv^2$$

Substituting the given values, we get

$$v = 2.65\times10^6 \text{ m/s}$$

Sol. 24 (D) Tension will be least when the ball is at the highest point with respect to the direction of net external force on the ball. In the given situation net force acts in the direction resultant of electric force and gravitational force, given as

$$\theta = \tan^{-1}\left(\frac{qE}{mg}\right)$$

Thus tension in string will be least at

$$\theta = \pi + \tan^{-1}\left(\frac{qE}{mg}\right)$$

Sol. 25 (C) During rotation free electrons of the rod drift outward due to centrifugal force which is balanced by the induced electric field caused by drifting of free electrons. At a distance x from the axis of rotation if induced field is E_i then we use

$$m\omega^2 x = eE_i$$

$$\Rightarrow \quad E_i = \frac{m\omega^2 x}{e}$$

The potential difference between points A and B is given as

$$V_{AB} = \int_{l/2}^{l} E\,dx = \int_{l/2}^{l} \frac{m\omega^2}{e}x.dx$$

$$\Rightarrow \quad V_{AB} = \frac{m\omega^2}{2e}\left[x^2\right]_{l/2}^{l} = \frac{m\omega^2}{2e}\left(l^2 - \frac{l^2}{4}\right) = \frac{3m\omega^2 l^2}{8e}$$

Sol. 26 (D) When the electric field is on then we use

$$qE = mg$$

$$\Rightarrow \quad qE = \frac{4}{3}\pi R^3 \rho g$$

$$\Rightarrow \quad q = \frac{4\pi R^3 \rho g}{3E} \quad \ldots(1)$$

When the electric field is switched off

$$mg = 6\pi\eta R v_t$$

$$\Rightarrow \quad \frac{4}{3}\pi R^3 \rho g = 6\pi\eta R v_t$$

$$\Rightarrow \quad R = \sqrt{\frac{9\eta v_t}{2\rho g}} \quad \ldots(2)$$

From equations-(1) and (2) we have

$$q = \frac{4}{3}\pi\left[\frac{9\eta v_t}{2\rho g}\right]^{\frac{3}{2}} \times \frac{\rho g}{E}$$

$$\Rightarrow \quad q = \frac{4}{3}\pi\left[\frac{9\times1.8\times10^{-5}\times2\times10^{-3}}{2\times900\times9.8}\right]^{\frac{3}{2}} \times \frac{900\times9.8\times7}{81\pi\times10^{5}}$$

$$\Rightarrow \quad q = 7.8\times10^{-19}\text{C}$$

Sol. 27 (A) Initially for equilibrium of mass we have

$$2T\cos\theta = mg$$

$$\Rightarrow \quad 2T\times\frac{5}{13} = mg$$

In this case the length of string is 26cm after stretching and if the force constant of spring is considered as k N/cm then tension in string can be given as $k(2)$, thus we have

$$4k\times\frac{5}{13} = mg$$

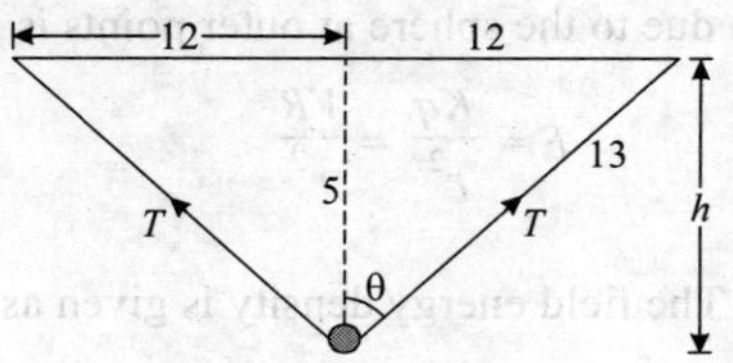

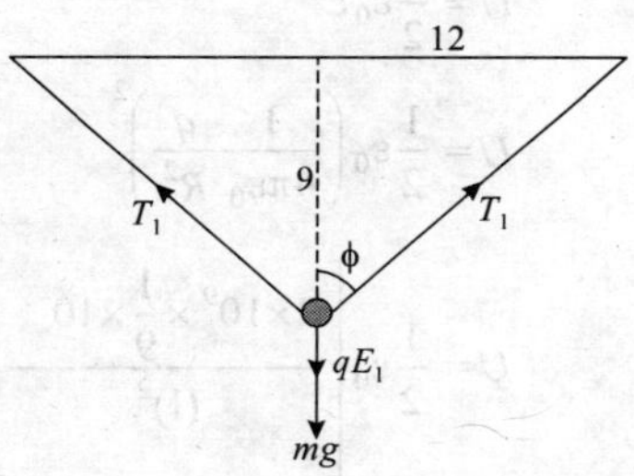

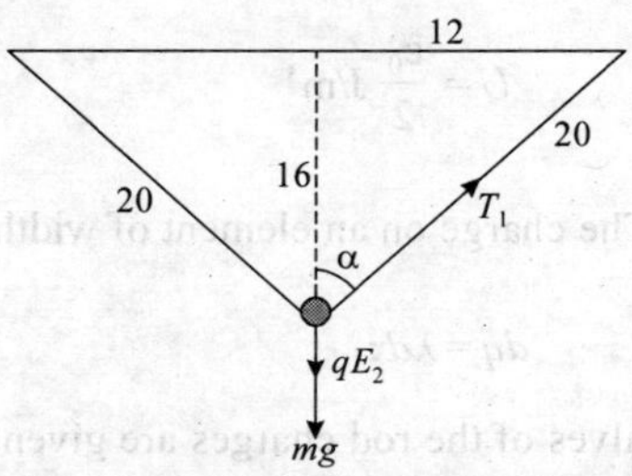

After electric field E_1 is switched on the length of string becomes 30cm as shown in above figure. Again for equilibrium of mass we use

$$T_1 = k(30-24) = 6k$$

and $\quad 2T_1\cos\phi = qE_1 + mg$

$$\Rightarrow \quad 2\times6k\times\frac{9}{15} = qE_1 + mg$$

$$\Rightarrow \quad \frac{36}{5}k - \frac{20}{13}k = qE_1$$

$$\Rightarrow \quad \frac{(468-100)k}{65} = qE_1$$

$$\Rightarrow \quad \frac{368k}{65} = qE_1$$

When electric field changes to E_2 the length of string becomes 40cm as shown in above figure and for equilibrium of mass we have

$$T_2 = k(40-24) = 16k$$

and $\quad 2\times16k\times\frac{16}{20} = qE_2 + mg$

$$\Rightarrow \quad qE_2 = \frac{128k}{5} - \frac{20k}{13} = \frac{(1664-100)k}{65}$$

$$\Rightarrow \quad qE_2 = \frac{1564}{65}k$$

$$\Rightarrow \quad \frac{E_2}{E_1} = \frac{1564}{368} = 4.25$$

Sol. 28 (A) We consider an elemental spherical shell of radius x and thickness dx as shown in figure. Charge on this elemental shell is given as

$$dq = \rho.4\pi x^2dx = \rho_0\left(\frac{5}{4}-\frac{x}{R}\right).4\pi x^2dx$$

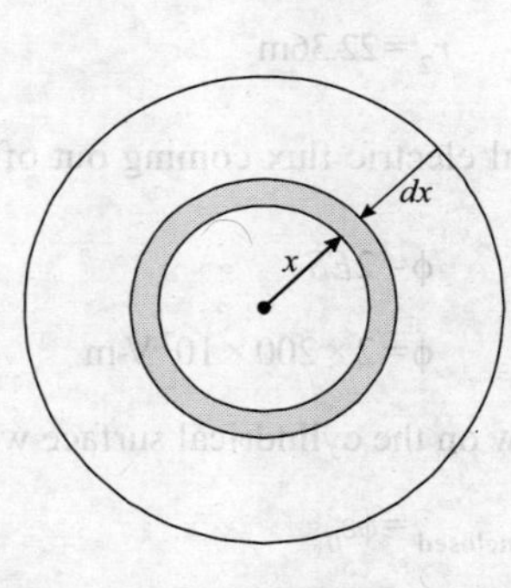

Total charge in the spherical region from centre to r $(r < R)$ is

$$q = \int dq = 4\pi\rho_0\int_0^r\left(\frac{5}{4}-\frac{x}{R}\right)x^2dx$$

$$\Rightarrow \quad q = 4\pi\rho_0\left[\frac{5}{4}\cdot\frac{r^3}{3}-\frac{1}{R}\cdot\frac{r^4}{4}\right] = \pi\rho_0 r^3\left(\frac{5}{3}-\frac{r}{R}\right)$$

Electric field at a distance r from center is given as

$$E = \frac{1}{4\pi\epsilon_0}\cdot\frac{q}{r^2}$$

$$\Rightarrow \quad E = \frac{1}{4\pi\epsilon_0}\frac{\pi\rho_0 r^3}{r^2}\left(\frac{5}{3}-\frac{r}{R}\right) = \frac{\rho_0 r}{4\epsilon_0}\left(\frac{5}{3}-\frac{r}{R}\right)$$

Sol. 29 (D) Electric force between electrons is given as

$$F_e = \frac{kq_1q_2}{r^2} = \frac{9\times10^9\times(1.6\times10^{-19})^2}{r^2}$$

$$F_e = \frac{9\times1.6\times1.6\times10^{-29}}{r^2}$$

Gravitational force between electrons is given as

$$F_g = \frac{Gm_1m_2}{r^2} = \frac{6.7\times10^{-11}\times(9.1\times10^{-31})^2}{r^2}$$

$$F_g = \frac{6.7\times9.1\times9.1\times10^{-73}}{r^2}$$

$$\Rightarrow \quad \frac{F_e}{F_g} \text{ is of the order of } 10^{42}$$

Sol. 30 (B) Given that the force of interaction between the charges in the two situations is same so we have

$$\frac{1}{4\pi\varepsilon_0}\cdot\frac{q_1q_2}{r_1^2} = \frac{1}{4\pi\varepsilon_0 K}\cdot\frac{q_1q_2}{r_2^2}$$

$$\Rightarrow \quad r_2 = \frac{r_1}{\sqrt{K}}$$

$$\Rightarrow \quad r_2 = \frac{50}{\sqrt{5}}$$

$$\Rightarrow \quad r_2 = 22.36\text{m}$$

Sol. 31 (D) Total electric flux coming out of the cylinder is given as

$$\phi = 2ES$$

$$\Rightarrow \quad \phi = 2\times200\times10^2\,\text{V-m}$$

Using Gauss's law on the cylindrical surface we have

$$q_{\text{enclosed}} = \phi\varepsilon_0$$

$$\Rightarrow \quad q_{\text{enclosed}} = 4\times10^4\times 8.85\times10^{-12} = 35.4\times10^{-8}\text{C}$$

Sol. 32 (B) Due to a solid conducting sphere potential difference between its center and an outer point is given as

$$V_A - V_B = Kq\left(\frac{1}{R}-\frac{1}{r}\right)$$

$$\Rightarrow \quad V_A - V_B = 9\times10^9\times0.25\times10^{-9}\times\left(\frac{1}{5}-\frac{1}{15}\right)\times10^2$$

$$\Rightarrow \quad V_A - V_B = 30\text{V}$$

Sol. 33 (A) Negative charge or dipole is near to positively charge line charge. Hence attraction is more.

Sol. 34 (C) The potential of a conducting sphere is constant at all points on its body so we have

$$V_B = V_C = \frac{Kq}{R}$$

At point B potential is due to the charge at A and due to the induced charges on the sphere so we have

$$V_B = V_i + \frac{Kq}{r}$$

$$\Rightarrow \quad V_i = \frac{Kq}{R} - \frac{Kq}{r}$$

$$\Rightarrow \quad V_i = -9\times10^3\left(\frac{1}{3}-\frac{1}{5}\right) = -9\times10^3\left(\frac{2}{15}\right)$$

$$= -0.45\,\text{kV}$$

Sol. 35 (A) Given that

$$V = \frac{Kq}{R}$$

$$\Rightarrow \quad Kq = VR$$

Electric field due to the sphere at outer points is given as

$$E = \frac{Kq}{r^2} = \frac{VR}{r^2}$$

Sol. 36 (A) The field energy density is given as

$$U = \frac{1}{2}\varepsilon_0 E^2$$

$$\Rightarrow \quad U = \frac{1}{2}\varepsilon_0\left(\frac{1}{4\pi\varepsilon_0}\frac{q}{R^2}\right)^2$$

$$\Rightarrow \quad U = \frac{1}{2}\varepsilon_0\left[\frac{9\times10^9\times\frac{1}{9}\times10^{-9}}{(1)^2}\right]^2$$

$$\Rightarrow \quad U = \frac{\varepsilon_0}{2}\ \text{J/m}^3$$

Sol. 37 (C) The charge on an element of width dx on rod is given as

$$dq = \lambda dx$$

For the two halves of the rod charges are given as

$$q_1 = \int_0^{l/2} 2x\,dx$$

$$\Rightarrow \quad q_1 = 2\left[\frac{x^2}{2}\right]_0^{l/2}$$

$$\Rightarrow \quad q_1 = \frac{l^2}{4}$$

and

$$q_2 = \int_{l/2}^{l} 2x\,dx$$

$$\Rightarrow \quad q_2 = 2\left[\frac{x^2}{2}\right]_{l/2}^{l}$$

$$\Rightarrow \quad q_2 = \frac{3}{4}l^2$$

Sol. 38 (C) From the solution of previous question the potential of shell A is given as

$$V_A = \frac{\sigma}{\varepsilon_0} - \frac{\sigma b}{\varepsilon_0} + \frac{\sigma c}{\varepsilon_0}$$

$$\Rightarrow \quad V_A = \frac{\sigma}{\varepsilon_0}(a - b + c)$$

The potential of shell C is given as

$$V_C = \left(\frac{\sigma a}{\varepsilon_0}\right)\left(\frac{a}{c}\right) - \left(\frac{\sigma b}{\varepsilon_0}\right)\left(\frac{b}{c}\right) + \frac{\sigma c}{\varepsilon_0}$$

$$= \frac{\sigma}{\varepsilon_0}\left(\frac{a^2}{c} - \frac{b^2}{c} + c\right)$$

Given that the potentials of shells A and C are same, we use

$$V_A = V_C$$

$$\Rightarrow \quad (a - b + c) = \left(\frac{a^2 - b^2}{c}\right) + c$$

$$\Rightarrow \quad a + b = c$$

Sol. 39 (C) Potential of B will be maintained at zero for which the charges appear on B such that

$$V_B = 0$$

$$\Rightarrow \quad \frac{Kq_A}{r_B} + \frac{Kq_B}{r_B} = 0$$

$$\Rightarrow \quad q_B = -q_A = -q$$

Charge distribution is as shown in figure below

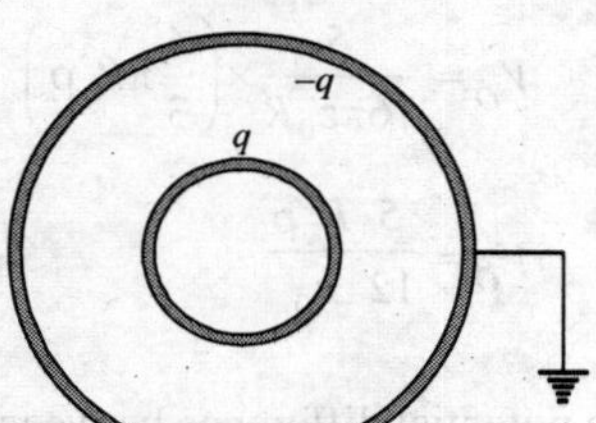

Thus electric field inside A and outside B is zero. Thus option (C) is correct.

Sol. 40 (C) Potential at point P due to the charges is given as

$$V_p = 2\left(\frac{1}{4\pi\varepsilon_0}\frac{q}{a}\right) - 2\left[\frac{1}{4\pi\varepsilon_0}\cdot\frac{q}{\sqrt{b^2 + a^2}}\right]$$

$$\Rightarrow \quad V_p = \frac{q}{4\pi\varepsilon_0 a}\left[2 - 2\left(1 + \frac{b^2}{a^2}\right)^{-1/2}\right]$$

Since $b << a$, we can apply binomial expansion.

$$\Rightarrow \quad V_p = \frac{q}{4\pi\varepsilon_0 a}\left[2 - 2\left(1 - \frac{b^2}{2a^2}\right)\right]$$

$$\Rightarrow \quad V_p = \frac{qb^2}{4\pi\varepsilon_0 a^3}$$

Sol. 41 (D) Potentials at centers of the two rings are given as

$$V_{C_1} = \frac{KQ}{R} - \frac{KQ}{\sqrt{R^2 + d^2}}$$

$$V_{C_1} = \frac{KQ}{\sqrt{R^2 + d^2}} - \frac{KQ}{R}$$

$$\Rightarrow \quad V_{C_1} - V_{C_2} = \frac{Q}{2\pi\varepsilon_0}\left[\frac{1}{R} - \frac{1}{\sqrt{R^2 + d^2}}\right]$$

Sol. 42 (A) Force on dipole is given as

$$F = P\left(\frac{dE}{dr}\right) = 10^{-7} \times 10^5 = 0.01\text{N}$$

Sol. 43 (C) On touching an identical sphere the charge is divided into half on both the spheres and the other sphere is moved away so the remaining system is shown in figure below.

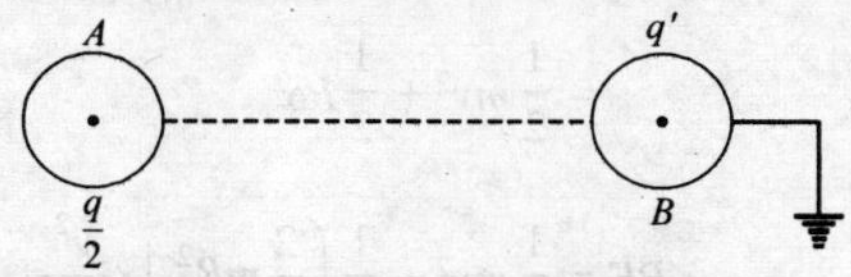

If the charge on B is q' then it is such that final potential of the sphere B should be equal to zero thus we have

$$V_B = 0$$

$$\Rightarrow \quad \frac{(K(q/2))}{d} + \frac{kq'}{r} = 0$$

$$\Rightarrow \quad q' = -\frac{qr}{2d}$$

Sol. 44 (D) Potential of the two balls are given in terms of their charges q_1 and q_2 as

$$V_1 = \frac{1}{4\pi\epsilon_0}\left[\frac{q_1}{r} + \frac{q_2}{a}\right] \text{ and } V_2 = \frac{1}{4\pi\epsilon_0}\left[\frac{q_2}{r} + \frac{q_1}{a}\right]$$

After solving above equations, and neglecting r^2 in comparison to a, we get

$$q_1 = -\frac{r}{a}(rV_2 - aV_1), \text{ and } q_2 = -\frac{r}{a}(rV_1 - aV_2)$$

Sol. 45 **(A)** We conserve angular momentum of $+2q$ charge about the fixed point charge $+Q$ which gives

$$mv_1r_1 \sin\theta_1 = mv_2 r_2 \sin\theta_2$$

$$mvR\sin 30° = m\left(\frac{v}{\sqrt{3}}\right) r_{min} \sin 90°$$

$$\Rightarrow \quad r_{min} = \frac{\sqrt{3}}{2}R$$

Sol. 46 **(C)** By energy conservation, we use

$$\frac{1}{2}mv^2 = (V_{centre} - V_{surface})Q$$

$$\frac{1}{2}mv^2 = \left(\frac{Q}{8\pi\epsilon_0 R}\right)Q$$

$$\Rightarrow \quad v = \frac{Q}{\sqrt{4\pi\epsilon_0 mR}}$$

Sol. 47 **(C)** Kinetic energy of particle is given as

$$K = qE \times \frac{1}{2}at^2 = qE \times \frac{1}{2}\left(\frac{qE}{m}\right)t^2 = \frac{q^2E^2t^2}{2m}$$

Sol. 48 **(B)** Work done by the time dipole rotates by 90° is given as

$$W = -PE(\cos 90° - \cos 0°)$$

$$= \frac{1}{2}mv^2 + \frac{1}{2}I\omega^2$$

$$\Rightarrow \quad PE = \frac{1}{2}mv^2 + \frac{1}{2}\left(\frac{2}{5}mR^2\right) \times \frac{v^2}{R^2}$$

$$\Rightarrow \quad v = \sqrt{\frac{10PE}{7m}}$$

Sol. 49 **(A)** Flux is maximum when surface area is normal to electric field so we use

$$\phi = EA\cos 0°$$

$$\phi = E \times \frac{\pi d^2}{4}$$

$$\Rightarrow \quad E = \frac{4\phi}{\pi d^2}$$

Sol. 50 **(B)** Using work energy theorem we have

$$Eql = \frac{1}{2}mv^2 - 0$$

$$\Rightarrow \quad v^2 = \frac{2Eql}{m}$$

If T is the tension in string when it becomes parallel to electric field then we have

$$T - qE = \frac{mv^2}{l}$$

$$\Rightarrow \quad T = qE + \frac{mv^2}{l}$$

$$\Rightarrow \quad T = qE + 2qE = 3qE$$

Sol. 51 **(A)** We use

$$E = -\frac{dV}{dx} = -\frac{d(4x^2)}{dx} = -8x$$

At $\quad x = 1\text{m}$

$$E = -8 \times 1 = -8 \text{ V/m}$$

Sol. 52 **(B)** Charge of the whole sphere is

$$Q = \left(\frac{4}{3}\pi R^3\right)\rho$$

Charge in the cavity region is

$$q = \frac{4}{3}\pi\left(\frac{R}{2}\right)^2 \rho = \frac{Q}{8}$$

Potential at point O is given as

$$V_O = [(V_{\text{whole sphere}})_O - (V_{\text{cavity}})_O]$$

$$\Rightarrow \quad V_O = \frac{3}{8\pi\varepsilon_0}\frac{Q}{R} - \frac{1}{4\pi\varepsilon_0}\frac{\left(\frac{Q}{8}\right)}{\frac{R}{2}}$$

$$\Rightarrow \quad V_O = \frac{5}{16\pi\varepsilon_0}\frac{Q}{R}$$

$$\Rightarrow \quad V_O = \frac{5}{16\pi\varepsilon_0 R} \times \left(\frac{4}{3}\pi R^3\rho\right)$$

$$\Rightarrow \quad V_O = \frac{5}{12}\frac{R^2\rho}{\varepsilon_0}$$

Sol. 53 **(C)** The potential difference between two concentric shells does not depend on the outer shell charge so it will remain the same.

Sol. 54 **(B)** For the equilibrium of charge Q we have

$$k\frac{Q^2}{l^2} + k\frac{qQ}{(l/2)^2} = 0$$

$$\Rightarrow \quad q = -\frac{Q}{4}$$

Sol. 55 (B) Considering elemental charge at a polar segment $d\theta$ on the ring is given as

$$dq = (\lambda_0 \sin\theta) a d\theta$$

Dipole moment due to the opposite elements on the ring is given as

$$dp = dq \times 2a$$

$$\Rightarrow \quad dp = 2a\lambda_0 \sin\theta d\theta$$

Vectorially dipole moment is written as

$$d\vec{p} = 2a\lambda_0 \sin\theta d\theta[-\cos\theta\, \hat{i} - \sin\theta\, \hat{j}]$$

The torque on ring is given as

$$\vec{\tau} = \int_0^{\pi} d\vec{p} \times \vec{E}$$

$$\Rightarrow \quad \vec{\tau} = 2\pi\lambda_0 \int_0^{\pi} (-\cos\theta \sin\theta \hat{i} - \sin^2\theta \hat{j}) \times (E_0 \hat{j} + E_0 \hat{j})$$

$$\Rightarrow \quad \tau = E_0 \pi a^2 \lambda_0 k$$

Sol. 56 (D) For the given points for the situation shown in figure, we use

$$\theta + \alpha = \pi/2$$

$$\Rightarrow \quad \alpha = \pi/2 - \theta$$

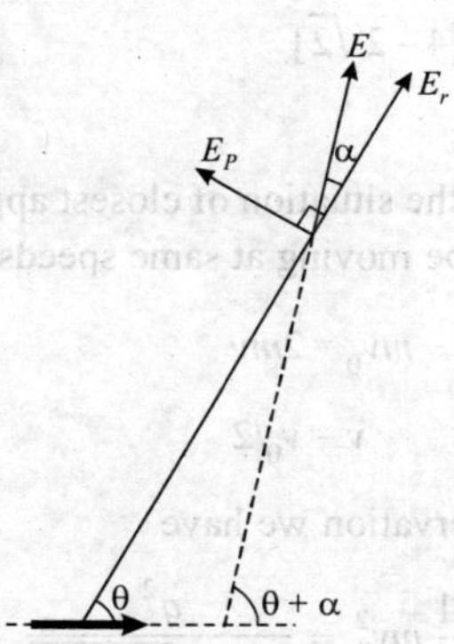

As for a dipole we know

$$\tan\alpha = \frac{\tan\theta}{2}$$

$$\Rightarrow \quad \tan\left(\frac{\pi}{2} - \theta\right) = \frac{\tan\theta}{2}$$

$$\Rightarrow \quad \tan\theta = \sqrt{2}$$

Sol. 57 (D) Electric flux will be maximum when maximum length of ring is inside the sphere.

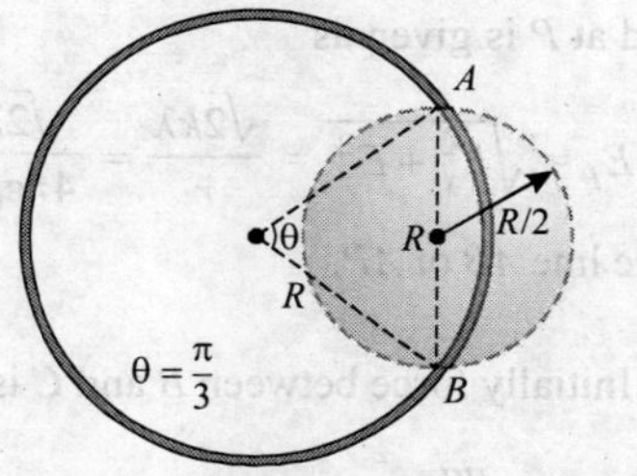

This will occur when the length of the chord AB is maximum. Now maximum length of chord AB can be the diameter of the ring. In this case the arc of ring inside the sphere subtends an angle of $\pi/3$ at the centre of ring.

Thus charge on this *arc* in this situation is given as

$$q = \frac{R\pi}{3}.\lambda$$

$$\Rightarrow \quad \phi = \frac{\frac{R\pi}{3}\lambda}{\epsilon_0} = \frac{R\pi\lambda}{3\epsilon_0}$$

Sol. 58 (C) Electric field die an element considered in rod as shown in figure at P is given as

$$dE = \frac{kdq}{(x^2 + r^2)} = \frac{k(\lambda dx)}{(x^2 + r^2)}$$

in x-direction electric field is given as

$$E_x = \int dE_x = \int_0^{\infty} dE \sin\theta$$

$$= \int_0^{\infty} \frac{k\lambda dx}{(x^2 + r^2)} \cdot \frac{x}{\sqrt{x^2 + r^2}}$$

In y-direction electric field is given as

$$E_y = \int dE_y = \int_0^{\infty} dE \cos\theta$$

$$= \int_0^{\infty} \frac{k\lambda dx}{(x^2 + r^2)} \cdot \frac{r}{\sqrt{x^2 + r^2}}$$

$$= \frac{k\lambda}{r}$$

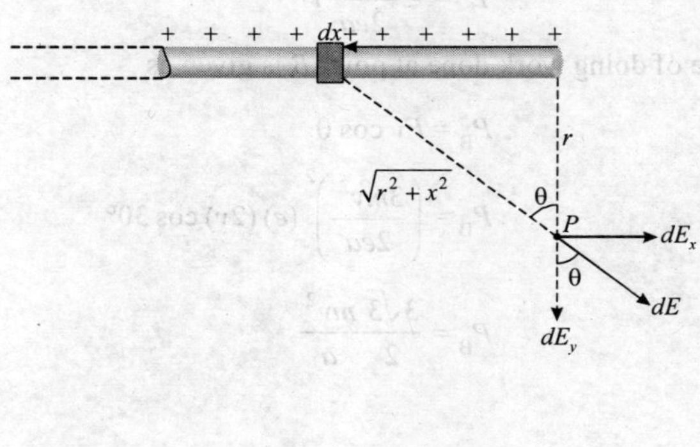

Thus net field at P is given as

$$E_P = \sqrt{E_x^2 + E_y^2} = \frac{\sqrt{2}k\lambda}{r} = \frac{\sqrt{2}\lambda}{4\pi\varepsilon_0 r}$$

at 45° with the line AB or AP.

Sol. 59 (D) Initially force between B and C is given as

$$F_{BC} = K\frac{qq}{r^2} = F$$

The charge on third conductor in after its contact with B becomes $q/2$ then after it is connected to C becomes $3q/4$. Same would be the final charges on B and C respectively as third conductor was identical in shape and size. So we have

$$q_B = \frac{q}{2} \text{ and } q_C = \frac{3q}{4}$$

Now the force between B and C is given as

$$F'_{BC} = K\frac{\left(\frac{q}{2}\right)\left(\frac{3q}{4}\right)}{r^2} = \frac{3F}{8}$$

Sol. 60 (C) The potential of the sphere of radius 20 cm will be more than the potential of the sphere of radius 25 cm. We know that charge flows from higher potential to lower potential. Hence the charge will flow from the sphere of radius 20 cm to the sphere of radius 25 cm.

Sol. 61 (A) Given that

$$v_{Ay} = v$$

$$v_{By} = 2v\sin 30° = v$$

As y-component of velocity remains unchanged we can state that electric field is along $(-\hat{i})$ direction. Work done by electrostatic force in moving from A to B is equal to the change in its kinetic energy so we use

$$(eE)(2a - a) = \frac{1}{2}m(4v^2 - v^2)$$

$$\Rightarrow \quad E = \frac{mv^2}{2ea}$$

$$\Rightarrow \quad \vec{E} = -\frac{3mv^2}{2ea}\hat{i}$$

Rate of doing work done at point B is given as

$$P_B = Fv\cos\theta$$

$$\Rightarrow \quad P_B = \left(\frac{3mv^2}{2ea}\right)^2 (e)(2v)\cos 30°$$

$$\Rightarrow \quad P_B = \frac{3\sqrt{3}}{2}\frac{mv^2}{a}$$

Sol. 62 (D) For the given potential the electric field strength in region is given as

$$E = -\frac{dV}{dx} = +20(x^2 - 4)^{-2} \times 2x$$

$$\Rightarrow \quad E = +\frac{40x}{(x^2 - 4)^2}$$

At $x = 4\mu$m electric field is given as

$$E = \frac{40 \times 4}{(4^2 - 4)^2} = \frac{10}{9}\text{ V/}\mu\text{m}$$

Sol. 63 (C) The two situations are shown in figure below

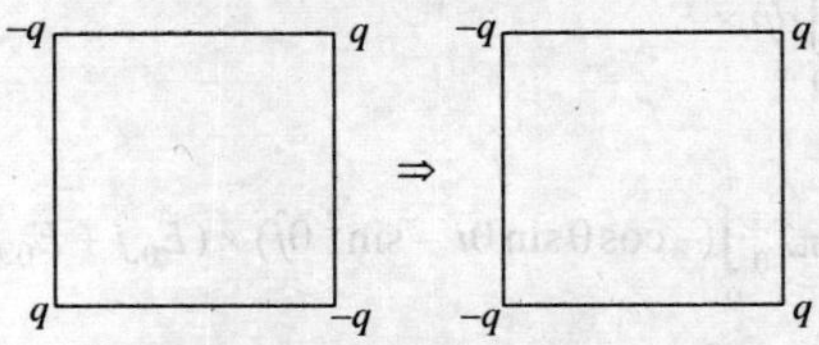

The work done will be the change in interaction energies of the two situations so we have

$$W = \frac{1}{(4\pi\varepsilon_0)}\left[\left(\frac{-q^2}{a} - \frac{q^2}{\sqrt{2}a} + \frac{q^2}{a} + \frac{q^2}{a} - \frac{q^2}{\sqrt{2}a} - \frac{q^2}{a}\right) - \left(\frac{-q^2}{a} + \frac{q^2}{\sqrt{2}a} - \frac{q^2}{a} - \frac{q^2}{a} - \frac{q^2}{\sqrt{2}a} - \frac{q^2}{a}\right)\right]$$

$$\Rightarrow \quad W = \frac{q^2}{4\pi\varepsilon_0 a}[4 - 2\sqrt{2}]$$

Sol. 64 (A) At the situation of closest approach both particle and ring would be moving at same speeds so we use

$$mv_0 = 2mv$$

$$\Rightarrow \quad v = v_0/2$$

By energy conservation we have

$$\frac{1}{2}mv_0^2 = \frac{q^2}{4\pi\varepsilon_0\sqrt{R^2 + x^2}} + 2\cdot\frac{1}{2}m\cdot\frac{v_0^2}{4}$$

$$\Rightarrow \quad \frac{1}{4}mv_0^2 = \frac{q^2}{4\pi\varepsilon_0\sqrt{R^2 + x^2}}$$

$$\Rightarrow \quad x = \sqrt{\frac{q^4}{\pi^2\varepsilon_0^2 m^2 v_0^4} - R^2}$$

Sol. 65 (B) Figure below shows the forces acting of the first ball, the equilibrium condition for this ball is given as

$$\frac{mg}{F} = \frac{l}{x},$$

Here $F = \frac{kqQ}{x^2}$ is the Coulomb force action on the first ball and x is the distance between the balls carrying charges q and Q.

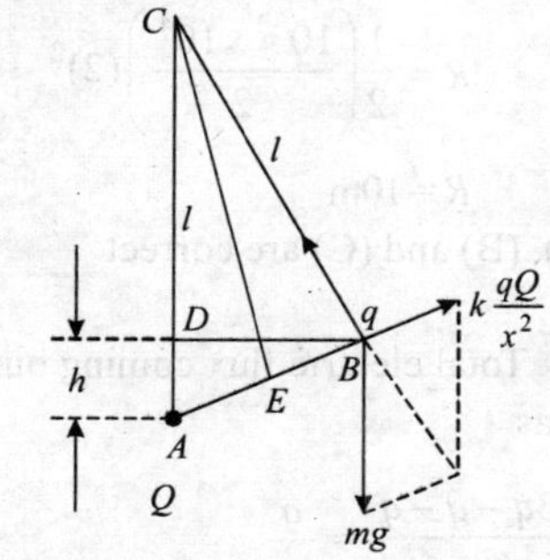

It is clear that the triangles ABD and CAE are similar and with this, we have

$$\frac{x}{2l} = \frac{h}{x}$$

From the above equations the separation of the charges and the electrostatic energy of the system can be calculated as

$$x = k\frac{qQ}{2mgh}$$

and $\quad E_{electro} = k\frac{qQ}{x} = 2mgh.$

Thus total work done by external agent is the increase in total energy of the system, given as

$$W = mgh + 2mgh = 3mgh$$

Sol. 66 (C) Consider a shell of radius r and thickness dr. Charge enclosed in this shell is given as

$$(dq)_{en} = \{4\pi(r+dr)^3\alpha - 4\pi r^3\alpha\}\varepsilon_0$$

$$\Rightarrow \quad (dq)_{en} = \{4\pi r^3\left(1+\frac{3dr}{r}\right)\alpha - 4\pi r^3\alpha\}\varepsilon_0$$

$$\Rightarrow \quad (dq)_{en} = 12\pi\alpha\varepsilon_0 r^2 dr$$

If ρ is the volume charge density at the surface of this shell within volume dV from r to $r+dr$, then we use

$$\rho.dV = 12\pi\alpha\varepsilon_0 r^2 dr$$

$$\Rightarrow \quad \rho(4\pi r^2 dr) = 12\pi\alpha\varepsilon_0 r^2 dr$$

$$\Rightarrow \quad \rho = 3\alpha\varepsilon_0$$

As volume charge density in region is constant, the charge contained within the sphere of radius R is given as

$$q = 3\alpha\varepsilon_0 \times \frac{4}{3}\pi R^3$$

$$\Rightarrow \quad q = 4\pi\varepsilon_0 R^3\alpha$$

Solutions of ADVANCE MCQs One or More Options Correct

Sol. 1 (A, B) The electric field due to a uniformly charged ring at its center is zero and potential at center is given as $V = \frac{1}{4\pi\varepsilon_0}\frac{Q}{R}$. At a distance x along the axis of the ring electric field and potential are given as

$$E = \frac{KQx}{(x^2+R^2)^{3/2}}$$

and $\quad V = \frac{KQ}{\sqrt{x^2+R^2}}$

Thus options (A) and (B) are correct.

Sol. 2 (A, D) Potentials of A and B shells are given as

$$V_A = 2V = \frac{Kq_A}{R} + \frac{Kq_B}{2R}$$

and $\quad V_B = \frac{3}{2}V = \frac{Kq_A}{2R} + \frac{Kq_B}{2R}$

Solving above two equations we get

$$\frac{q_A}{q_B} = \frac{1}{2}$$

After earthing, charge on A does not change so $q'_A = q_A$ and q'_B is such that final potential of B becomes zero so we have

$$\frac{Kq'_A}{2R} + \frac{Kq'_B}{2R} = 0$$

$$\Rightarrow \quad q'_B = 2q_A$$

$$\Rightarrow \quad \frac{q'_A}{q'_B} = -1$$

Potential difference between A and B will remain unchanged as by earthing B, charge on inner shell will not change.

Sol. 3 (C, D) Gauss's law is valid only if Coulomb's law holds that is only for the case when $E \propto 1/r^2$ otherwise the flux through a surface will depend upon the dimension of the surface instead of the enclosed charge only. Gauss's law cannot be used to calculate a non-uniform and non symmetric field distribution around an electric dipole. In an electric field the work done by external force is given as

$$W_{A\to B} = U_f - U_i$$

$$\Rightarrow \quad W_{A\to B} = q(V_B - V_A) = (V_B - V_A)$$

Thus options (C) and (D) are correct.

Sol. 4 (A, D) The electric field lines are originating from Q_1 and terminating on Q_2. Therefore Q_1 is positive and Q_2 is negative. As the number of lines associated with Q_1 is greater than that associated with Q_2 so the magnitude of Q_1 is higher. At a finite distance on the left of Q_1, the electric field intensity cannot be zero because the electric field created by Q_1 is greater than that due to Q_2 so at a finite distance to the right of Q_2, the electric field can be zero. Thus options (A) and (D) are correct.

Sol. 5 (A, B, C, D) Inside a charged metal shell always at all interior points electric field is always zero. After connecting the two spheres, we have

$$Q = Q_A + Q_B$$

and $$\frac{KQ_A}{R_A} = \frac{KQ_B}{R_B}$$

$$\Rightarrow \quad Q_A = \frac{QR_A}{R_A + R_B}$$

and $$Q_B = \frac{QR_B}{R_A + R_B}$$

As $R_A > R_B$ so $Q_A > Q_B$

If σ_A and σ_B are the surface charge densities on the spheres then

$$\frac{\sigma_A}{\sigma_B} = \frac{Q_A / 4\pi R_A^2}{Q_B / 4\pi R_B^2} = \frac{R_B}{R_A}$$

The electric field on the surface of the two spheres are

$$E_A = \frac{1}{4\pi \epsilon_0} \frac{Q_A}{R_A^2}$$

and $$E_B = \frac{1}{4\pi \epsilon_0} \frac{Q_B}{R_B^2}$$

$$\Rightarrow \quad \frac{E_A}{E_B} = \frac{Q_A}{Q_B} \times \frac{R_B^2}{R_A^2} = \frac{R_B}{R_A}$$

As $R_A > R_B$

$\Rightarrow \quad E_B > E_A$

Thus all options are correct.

Sol. 6 (A, B, C) Time of flight is given as

$$T = \frac{2u_y}{g} = \frac{2 \times 10}{10} = 2\text{s}$$

Maximum height is given as

$$H = \frac{u_y^2}{2g} = \frac{(10)^2}{20} = 5\text{m}$$

Horizontal range of particle is given as

$$R = \frac{1}{2} a_x T^2 = \frac{1}{2}\left(\frac{qE}{m}\right) T^2$$

$$R = \frac{1}{2}\left(\frac{10^{-3} \times 10^4}{2}\right)(2)^2$$

$$R = 10\text{m}$$

Thus options (A), (B) and (C) are correct

Sol. 7 (A, C, D) Total electric flux coming out of the cubical surface is given as

$$\phi = \frac{q_{net}}{\varepsilon_0} = \frac{3q - q - q}{\varepsilon_0} = \frac{q}{\varepsilon_0}$$

By symmetry, the electric flux crossing the plane $x = a/2$ and the $x = -a/2$ is same. Further, the positions of charges with respect to $x = a/2$ and $z = a/2$ are same so the flux through the planes $x = a/2$ and $z = a/2$ are also same. By symmetry the flux crossing the plane $y = a/2$ and $y = -a/2$ is also same. Thus options (A), (C) and (D) are correct.

Sol. 8 (A, D) Figure below shows the variation of electric field in the region due to the two charges and based on this options (A) and (D) are correct.

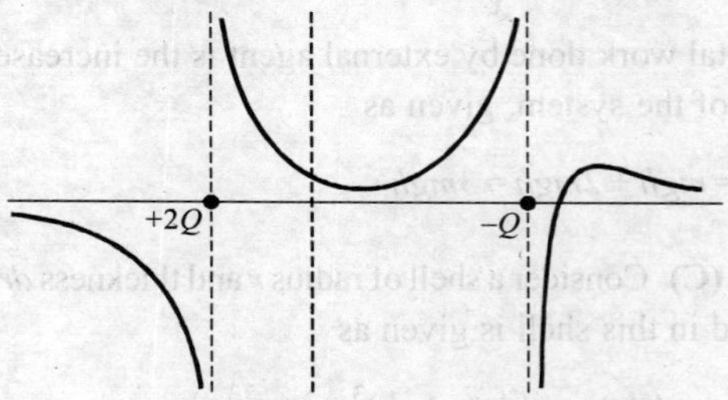

Sol. 9 (A, B, C) Potential due to a uniformly charged sphere are given as

$$100 = \frac{1}{4\pi\varepsilon_0} \cdot \frac{q}{(R + 0.05)} \quad \ldots(1)$$

and $$75 = \frac{1}{4\pi\varepsilon_0} \cdot \frac{q}{(R + 0.1)} \quad \ldots(2)$$

Solving above equations we get

$$q = \frac{5}{3} \times 10^{-9}\text{ C and } R = 0.1\text{m}$$

This gives potential at its surface is given as

$$V = \frac{1}{4\pi\varepsilon_0} \cdot \frac{q}{R} = \frac{(9 \times 10^9)\left(\frac{5}{3} \times 10^{-9}\right)}{0.1} = 150V$$

Electric field on the surface of sphere is given as

$$E=\frac{1}{4\pi\varepsilon_0}\cdot\frac{q}{R^2}=\frac{V}{R}=\frac{150}{0.1}=1500\text{V/m}$$

Electric potential at the center of sphere is given as

$$V_{\text{centre}}=1.5V_{\text{surface}}=225\text{V}$$

Sol. 10 (A, B, C)

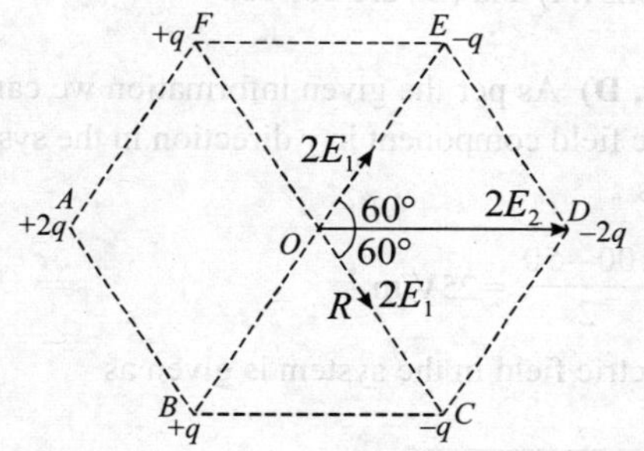

If E_1 is the electric field at O due to $-q$ at E directed from O to E and E_2 is the electric field at O due to $+2q$ at A directed from O to D then the net electric field at O is given as

$$E=2E_1\cos60°+2E_1\cos60°+2E_2$$

$$\Rightarrow \quad E=E_1+E_1+2E_2=2E_1+2E_2$$

$$\Rightarrow \quad E=\frac{1}{4\pi\varepsilon_0}\frac{2q}{L^2}+\frac{1}{4\pi\varepsilon_0}\frac{4q}{L^2}$$

$$\Rightarrow \quad E=\frac{6}{4\pi\varepsilon_0}\frac{q}{L^2}\text{ along }OD$$

If electric potential at point O is V then it is given by sum of all the potentials at O due to all individual charges given as

$$V=\frac{-q}{4\pi\varepsilon_0 L}-\frac{q}{4\pi\varepsilon_0 L}+\frac{q}{4\pi\varepsilon_0 L}+\frac{q}{4\pi\varepsilon_0 L}+\frac{2q}{4\pi\varepsilon_0 L}-\frac{2q}{4\pi\varepsilon_0 L}$$

$$=0$$

For line PR all the charges are symmetrically located at same distances from O thus potential at all points of line PR must be same. Thus options (A), (B) and (C) are correct.

Sol. 11 (A, C) Diagonally opposite charges will produce field in xy plane only, but the resulting field due to both diagonally opposite positive and negative charges will cancel in y direction so only electric field will be left in x direction.

Sol. 12 (A, B, C) Electric field at any point depends on both charges Q_1 and Q_2 but electric flux passing from any closed surface depends on the charged enclosed by that closed surface only. Thus options (A), (B) and (C) are correct.

Sol. 13 (A, B, D) With the given information we can determine the electric field component along x direction in the region which gives

$$E_x=10\text{V/m}$$

Thus in space electric field strength can be 10V/m or more than this depending upon other components of electric field. Thus options (A), (B) and (D) are correct.

Sol. 14 (A, B) Flux from any closed surface is given as

$$\phi=\frac{q_{\text{in}}}{\varepsilon_0}$$

$\Rightarrow$ As $q_{\text{in}}=0$ as net charge on a dipole is zero so flux through the sphere is zero. Due to dipole at any point in its surrounding electric field is not zero thus options (A) and (B) are correct.

Sol. 15 (A, B, D) At a point with coordinates $(x, 0)$ the force on the charge is given as

$$F=q\left(\frac{K(2Q)x}{(x^2+y^2)^{3/2}}\right)$$

Thus for F to be maximum, we solve for $dF/dx=0$ which gives

$$x\pm\frac{y}{\sqrt{2}}$$

The charge is in equilibrium at the origin where net electric field due to the two charges is zero. However, the equilibrium is not stable since the force is repulsive along x direction and it will not be able to restore the charge at the origin. The charge therefore cannot perform oscillatory motion. Thus options (A), (B) and (D) are correct.

Sol. 16 (C, D) Gauss's law is valid for all types of charge distributions in any region as it relates the electric flux through a given closed surface which is due to the electric field of all the charges in the region with the enclosed charge by the surface. Thus options (C) and (D) are correct.

Sol. 17 (A, B, C, D) By an external force in case of SHM only equilibrium position changes. Time period remains same. As speed of block at mean position is same amplitude will be same in all cases. In case - 4 equilibrium position $x_0=3mg/k$ which is maximum among all cases. Thus all the given options are correct.

Sol. 18 (A, B, D) Point A is inside the inner sphere where at every point electric field is zero but electric potential due to the two shells are not equal in magnitude so it is non zero. At point B electric field will be only due to the inner charge so it is non zero and electric potentials due to the two shells are unequal in magnitude so it is also non zero. At the outer point C as net enclosed charge is spherically symmetric and zero thus both electric field and potential at C is zero.

Sol. 19 (A, D) The force on the rod is qE, irrespective of orientation the force on the rod is distributed uniformly over the entire rod, so torque about centre of mass is always zero and the displacement of rod can be calculated by the uniform acceleration of the rod $\lambda E/\mu$. Thus only option (A) is correct.

Sol. 20 (B, C) As net force by electric field on the two charges are equal and toward right to keep the rod at rest hinge will exert an equal force on rod leftward. Now if we slightly rotate the rod, the torque on rod due to electric forces on charges are opposite and in magnitude $\tau_1 = \tau_2$ or $\tau_{net} = 0$ in displaced position too so equilibrium is neutral. Thus options (B) and (C) are correct.

Sol. 21 (A, C) Potential inside a shell is same as that of its surface so for first shell as the radius is minimum its potential will be highest among the three shells and the third shell will be at lowest potential. Thus options (A) and (C) are correct.

Sol. 22 (B, D) Potential at a point in a system or potential energy of a system of charges is defined with respect to a reference which is generally taken as infinity for a given system. As in a given system reference is considered same, potential difference and change in potential energy of a system of charges does not depend upon the reference chosen so options (B) and (D) are correct.

Sol. 23 (A, B, C) For the revolving charge we have

$$T\cos\alpha = mg$$

$$T\sin\alpha = \frac{Kq^2}{r^2} + m\omega^2 r$$

$$\Rightarrow T > mg \text{ as well as } T > \frac{Kq^2}{r^2}$$

If no charge is there on the revolving ball, we use

$$T\sin\alpha = \frac{mv^2}{r}$$

Thus to maintain the angle v must be increased as earlier electrostatic force was present which is now no longer present. Thus options (A), (B) and (C) are correct.

Sol. 24 (A, D) The electric field of point charge is non-uniform and so net force on the dipole for any orientation is non zero. The torque on the dipole may be zero, if it is placed parallel to an electric line of force in the field.

Sol. 25 (A, D) At every point in space electric field is the vector sum of the external electric field and that due to the two plates so we have electric field

At point R is given as

$$E_R = E + \frac{Q}{2A\epsilon_0} - \frac{Q}{2A\epsilon_0} = E$$

At point S is given as

$$E_S = E + \frac{Q}{2A\epsilon_0} + \frac{Q}{2A\epsilon_0} = E + \frac{Q}{A\epsilon_0}$$

At point T is given as

$$E_T = E + \frac{Q}{2A\epsilon_0} - \frac{Q}{2A\epsilon_0} = E$$

Thus options (A) and (D) are correct.

Sol. 26 (B, D) As per the given information we can calculate the electric field component in y direction in the system which is given as

$$E_y = \frac{100-50}{2} = 25\text{V/m}$$

As net electric field in the system is given as

$$E = \sqrt{E_x^2 + E_y^2 + E_z^2}$$

So net electric field in the region may be greater than 25V/m or equal to 25V/m if other components are zero.

Sol. 27 (A, D) The electric field inside a thick sheet at a distance x from its central plane is given as

$$E = \frac{\rho x}{\varepsilon_0}$$

Restoring force on the charge particle is given as

$$F = -qE = -\frac{q\rho}{\varepsilon_0}x$$

Acceleration of the particle is given as

$$a = -\frac{q\rho}{m\varepsilon_0}x$$

As the acceleration is directly proportional to distance from central plane, the charge particle is executing SHM so comparing above acceleration with standard equation of SHM $a = -\omega^2 x$ gives

$$\omega = \sqrt{\frac{q\rho}{m\varepsilon_0}}$$

$$\Rightarrow \qquad v = \frac{1}{2\pi}\sqrt{\frac{q\rho}{m\varepsilon_0}}$$

Sol. 28 (B, C) As the electric flux through a closed surface in a region of electric field is given as

$$\phi = \oint \vec{E}.\vec{dS} = \frac{q_{inside}}{\epsilon_0} = 0$$

So for zero flux through a closed surface electric field may be either zero at each point of the surface or at every point of the surface electric field vector is normal to the surface area vector at that point or at different points electric field is such that total flux going into the surface is equal to the electric flux going out from the surface for which $q_{\text{inside}} = 0$. For any case if flux is zero then enclosed charge within the closed surface must be zero. Thus options (B) and (C) are correct.

Sol. 29 (A, B, D) As electric field between sheet 2 and 3 is zero we have

$$-\frac{\sigma}{2\epsilon_0}-\frac{\sigma'}{2\epsilon_0}+\frac{3\sigma}{2\epsilon_0}=0$$

$$\Rightarrow \quad \sigma' = +2\sigma$$

The electric field strengths at all other points can be given by the vector sum of the electric fields due to individual sheets. Thus options (A), (B) and (D) are correct.

Sol. 30 (C) Electric field at each point of the cavity is normal to its surface but not necessarily equal and being a conductor at every point of conductor potential is same. An electric line of force does not penetrate a metal surface hence total flux through the cavity surface is always zero. Thus only option (C) is correct.

Sol. 31 (B, D) Potential energy of system at position x is given as

$$U = -pE$$

$$\Rightarrow \quad U = -\frac{1}{4\pi\varepsilon_0}\frac{qp}{x^2}$$

When the dipole is far away, $U = 0$ so by using energy conservation the kinetic energy is given as

$$K = 0 - \left[-\frac{1}{4\pi\varepsilon_0}\frac{qp}{x^2}\right]$$

$$K = \frac{1}{4\pi\varepsilon_0}\frac{qp}{x^2}$$

Force on the dipole at a distance x is given as

$$F = \frac{dU}{dx} = -\frac{2qp}{4\pi\epsilon_0 x^3}$$

Thus options (B) and (D) are correct.

Sol. 32 (A, C) $F = -Eq = -\dfrac{1}{4\pi\epsilon_0}\dfrac{Qzq}{(R^2+z^2)^{3/2}}$

For $z << R$, $R^2 + z^2 = R^2$, and so

$$F \propto (-z)$$

So the motion represents SHM only if $z << R$ otherwise the motion remain periodic. Thus options (A) and (C) are correct.

Sol. 33 (A, B, C, D) Electric field in the region $r > r_0$ is given by

$$E = -\frac{dV}{dr} = -\frac{d}{dr}\left(\frac{Q}{4\pi\varepsilon_0 r}\right)$$

For $r \le r_0$ $\quad E = -\dfrac{d}{dr}\left(\dfrac{Q}{4\pi\varepsilon_0 r_0}\right) = 0$

So the electric field is discontinuous at $r = r_0$. For $r < r_0$ inside the surface $r = r_0$ we have $E = 0$. So the charges resides only on the spherical surface of radius $r = r_0$

The electric energy density in region is given as

$$u = \frac{1}{2}\varepsilon_0 E^2$$

As for $r < r_0$, $E = 0$ thus $u = 0$ for $r < r_0$

As charge is only residing on the surface of spherical surface of radius $r = r_0$ so for any spherical surface outside $Q' = Q$, which is independent of r as long as r is greater than r_0. Thus all options are correct.

Sol. 34 (B, D) As net charge on right is zero thus electric potential at the center of ring will also be zero. Electric field due to the two halves at center will be added up which is given as

$$E = 2\times\frac{1}{4\pi\epsilon_0}\frac{q}{R^2}\left(\frac{\sin\pi/2}{\pi/2}\right) = \frac{q}{\pi^2\epsilon_0 R^2}$$

Thus options (B) and (D) are correct.

Sol. 35 (A) For the elliptical motion the electric force on $-q$ passes through the location of fixed charge so torque of electric force is zero thus angular momentum of revolving charge about fixed charge will remain conserved. In elliptical motion linear momentum, angular velocity and linear speed continuously vary so will not remain constant. Thus only option (A) is correct.

Sol. 36 (B, D) The electric field at any point inside the shell due to the point charge can be calculated by standard relation but that due to induced charges cannot be calculated. The electric field at points outside the outer surface is only due to the charge distribution on the outer surface of the shell so on outer surface it is given as

$$E = \frac{1}{4\pi\epsilon_0}\frac{q}{(2R)^2}$$

Thus options (B) and (D) are correct.

Sol. 37 (B, D) Let P and Q be the two points at a distance $2R$ on the line joining the centres O_1 and O_2 of the spheres as shown in figure.

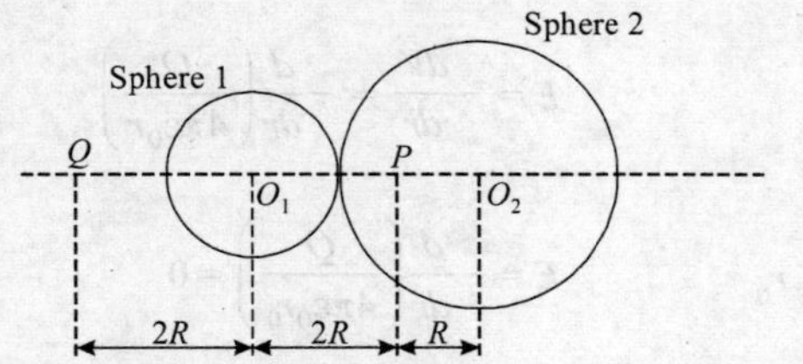

The charge on spheres 1 and 2 are given as

$$Q_1 = \frac{4\pi}{3}R^3\rho_1 \text{ and } Q_2 = \frac{4\pi}{3}(2R)^3\rho_2$$

Electric field at P will be zero if

$$\frac{Q_1}{4\pi\varepsilon_0(O_1P)^2} = \frac{\rho_2 R}{3\varepsilon_0}$$

$$\Rightarrow \quad \frac{\frac{4\pi}{3}R^3\rho_1}{4\pi\varepsilon_0\times(2R)^2} = \frac{\rho_2 R}{3\varepsilon_0} \Rightarrow \frac{\rho_1}{\rho_2} = 4$$

Electric field at Q will be zero if

$$\frac{Q_1}{4\pi\varepsilon_0(O_1Q)^2} + \frac{Q_2}{4\pi\varepsilon_0(O_2Q)^2} = 0$$

$$\Rightarrow \quad \frac{\frac{4\pi}{3}R^3\rho_1}{4\pi\varepsilon_0(2R)^2} + \frac{\frac{4\pi}{3}(2R)^3\rho_2}{4\pi\varepsilon_0(5R)^2} = 0$$

$$\Rightarrow \quad \frac{\rho_1}{\rho_2} = -\frac{32}{25}$$

Sol. 38 (C, D) As we have already discussed that in the overlapping region electric field is uniform and its direction is along the line joining the two centers. Thus options (C) and (D) are correct.

Sol. 39 (A, C, D) Below figure shows the charge distribution on the surfaces of the metal plates.

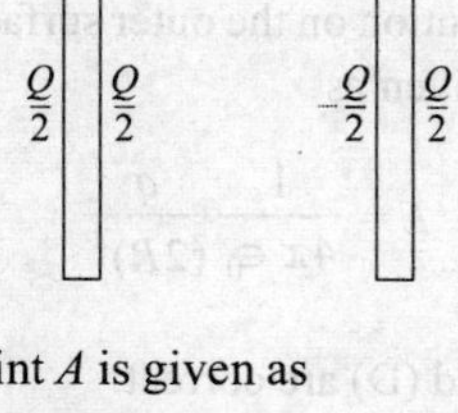

Electric field at point A is given as

$$E_A = \frac{Q}{2A\varepsilon_0} \text{ toward left}$$

Electric field at point B is given as

$$E_B = \frac{Q}{2A\varepsilon_0} \text{ toward right}$$

Electric field at point C is given as

$$E_C = \frac{Q}{2A\varepsilon_0} \text{ toward right}$$

Thus options (A), (C) and (D) are correct.

Sol. 40 (D) Figure below shows the forces acting on the balls attached to rod. The acceleration of centre of mass of the system just after release is given as

$$a_C = \frac{F_{ext}}{3m}$$

$$\Rightarrow \quad a_C = \frac{2QE}{3m}$$

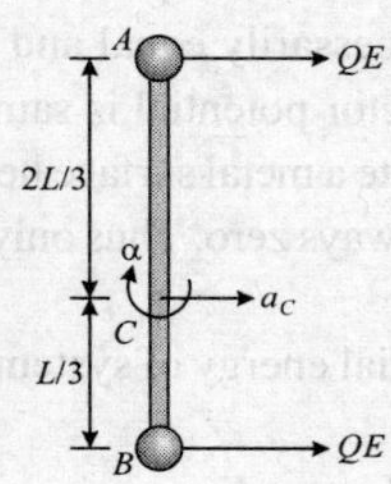

As rod is freely movable as no other external force is acting on it and if α be the angular acceleration of rod just after release, it will rotate about the common centre of mass C as shown in figure above. This angular acceleration is given as

$$\tau = I\alpha$$

$$\Rightarrow \quad QE\left(\frac{3L}{3}\right) - QE\left(\frac{L}{3}\right) = \left(m\times\frac{4L^2}{9} + 2m\times\frac{L^2}{9}\right)\alpha$$

$$\Rightarrow \quad \frac{QEL}{3} = \frac{3mL^2}{3}\alpha$$

$$\Rightarrow \quad \alpha = \frac{QE}{2mL}$$

As shown in figure the angular acceleration is in clockwise manner. The linear acceleration of the balls A is given as

$$a_A = a_C + \alpha\left(\frac{2L}{3}\right)$$

$$\Rightarrow \quad a_A = \frac{2QE}{3m} + \frac{QE}{2mL}\left(\frac{2L}{3}\right) = \frac{QE}{m}$$

* * * * *

ANSWERS & SOLUTIONS

CONCEPTUAL MCQs Single Option Correct

1	(C)	2	(A)	3	(D)
4	(C)	5	(C)	6	(A)
7	(B)	8	(C)	9	(C)
10	(C)	11	(B)	12	(D)
13	(A)	14	(D)	15	(C)
16	(B)	17	(C)	18	(C)
19	(A)	20	(C)	21	(B)
22	(C)	23	(B)	24	(B)
25	(B)	26	(C)	27	(A)
28	(D)	29	(B)	30	(C)
31	(D)	32	(D)		

NUMERICAL MCQs Single Option Correct

1	(C)	2	(B)	3	(D)
4	(B)	5	(A)	6	(A)
7	(B)	8	(C)	9	(B)
10	(D)	11	(B)	12	(D)
13	(D)	14	(B)	15	(A)
16	(B)	17	(C)	18	(C)
19	(B)	20	(C)	21	(A)
22	(A)	23	(D)	24	(D)
25	(B)	26	(B)	27	(B)
28	(A)	29	(D)	30	(B)
31	(C)	32	(C)	33	(A)
34	(C)	35	(D)	36	(D)
37	(C)	38	(B)	39	(B)
40	(B)	41	(A)	42	(A)
43	(B)	44	(B)	45	(C)
46	(D)	47	(A)	48	(D)
49	(B)	50	(A)	51	(C)
52	(D)	53	(B)	54	(B)
55	(B)	56	(D)		

ADVANCE MCQs One or More Options Correct

1	(A, B)	2	(A, C, D)	3	(A, B, D)
4	(B, D)	5	(B, D)	6	(A, B, C)
7	(B, D)	8	(A, B, D)	9	(A, C, D)
10	(A, C)	11	(A, D)	12	(B, C)
13	(A, C, D)	14	(B, C)	15	(B, C)
16	(A, D)	17	(B, D)	18	(A, B, D)
19	(B, C, D)	20	(A, C, D)	21	(A, D)
22	(A, D)	23	(A, B, C)	24	(B, C)
25	(A, B, C)	26	(A, B, D)		

Solutions of PRACTICE EXERCISE 2.1

(i) (a) The capacitor is charged to a potential $V = 1500$ V. The energy U of the capacitor is given by

$$U = \frac{1}{2}CV^2 = \frac{1}{2} \times (400 \times 10^{-12})(1500)^2$$

$$\Rightarrow \quad U = 4.5 \times 10^{-4}\,\text{J}$$

(b) We know that the capacitance of parallel plate capacitor is $C = \varepsilon_0\, A/d$. When d is doubled, the new capacitance C' is halved

$$C' = \frac{1}{2}C = \frac{1}{2} \times 400 \times 10^{-12}\,\text{F} = 200 \times 10^{-12}\,\text{F}$$

Charge on the capacitor is given as

$$q = CV = 400 \times 10^{-12} \times 1500 = 6 \times 10^{-7}\,\text{C}$$

If the new potential difference be V', then for the same charge q, we have

$$q = C'V' = 6 \times 10^{-7}$$

$$\Rightarrow \quad 200 \times 10^{-12}\, V' = V' = 6 \times 10^{-7}$$

$$\Rightarrow \quad V' = 3000\,\text{V}$$

(c) The energy required to double the distance between the plates is given as

$$\Delta U = \text{Final energy} - \text{Initial energy}$$

$$\Rightarrow \quad \Delta U = \frac{1}{2}C'V'^2 - \frac{1}{2}CV^2$$

$$\Rightarrow \quad \Delta U = \frac{1}{2}(200 \times 10^{-12})(3000)^2 - (4.5 \times 10^{-4})$$

$$\Rightarrow \quad \Delta U = 9 \times 10^{-4} - 4.5 \times 10^{-4} = 4.5 \times 10^{-4}\,\text{J}$$

(ii) Figure below shows the charge distribution on plates.

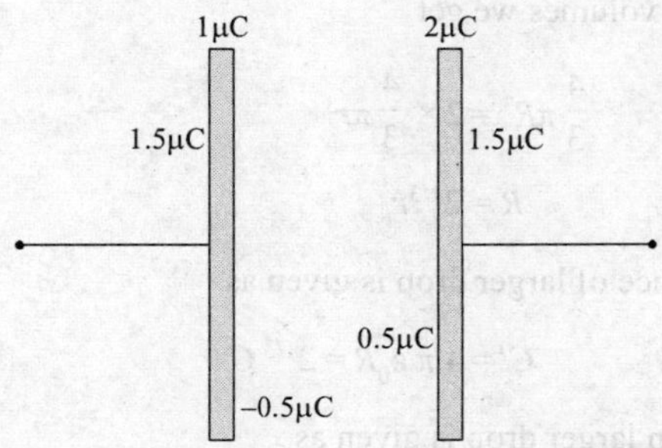

The potential difference is given as

$$V = \frac{q}{C} = \frac{0.5 \times 10^{-6}}{0.1 \times 10^{-6}} = 5\,\text{V}$$

(iii) The capacitance of a parallel plate capacitor is given by

$$C = \frac{\varepsilon_0 A}{d}$$

When the spacing d is doubled, the new capacitance C' becomes $C/2$.

We know that $U = \frac{1}{2}\frac{Q^2}{C}$

When spacing is doubled, we have

$$U' = \frac{1}{2}\frac{Q^2}{C'} = \frac{Q^2}{C}$$

If ΔW be the work required to pulle the plates to double the plate spacing, then we have

$$\Delta W = W' - W = \frac{Q^2}{C} - \frac{1}{2}\frac{Q^2}{C} = \frac{1}{2}\frac{Q^2}{C} = \frac{1}{2}CV^2$$

Substituting the value of C, we have

$$\Delta W = \frac{1}{2}\left(\frac{\varepsilon_0 A}{d}\right)V^2$$

$$\Rightarrow \quad \Delta W = \frac{1}{2}\left(\frac{8.9\times10^{-12}\times0.2}{0.01}\right)10^6$$

$$\Rightarrow \quad \Delta W = 8.9\times10^{-5}\text{ J}$$

As Q is kept constant, we use

$$CV = C'V'$$

$$\Rightarrow \quad V' = \frac{C'V}{C} = \frac{2CV}{C} = 2V = 2\times10^3\text{ V}$$

$$\Rightarrow \quad V' = 200\text{ V}$$

(iv) When drops coalesce to form a larger drop then total charge and volume remains conserved. If r is radius and q is charge on smaller drop then $C = 4\pi\varepsilon_0 r$ and $q = CV$ Equating volumes we get

$$\frac{4}{3}\pi R^3 = 2\times\frac{4}{3}\pi r^3$$

$$\Rightarrow \quad R = 2^{1/3}r$$

Capacitance of larger drop is given as

$$C' = 4\pi\varepsilon_0 R = 2^{1/3}C$$

Charge on larger drop is given as

$$Q = 2q = 2CV$$

Potential of larger drop is given as

$$V' = \frac{Q}{C'} = \frac{2CV}{2^{1/3}C} = 2^{2/3}V$$

(v) (a) Let q be the charge on smaller sphere supplied by earth. Then, we have

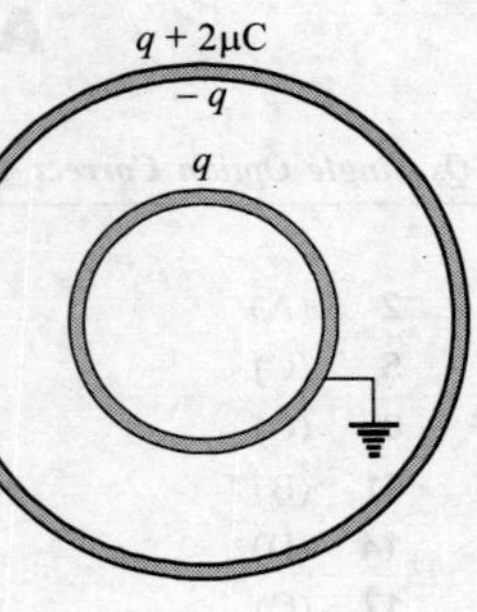

$$V_{inner} = 0$$

$$\Rightarrow \quad \frac{Kq^2}{2} + \frac{K(2)}{4} = 0$$

$$\Rightarrow \quad q = -1\text{ μC}$$

Potential of outer sphere is given as

$$V_{outer} = \frac{K(2-1)\times10^{-6}}{4\times10^{-2}}$$

$$\Rightarrow \quad V_{outer} = \frac{9\times10^9\times10^{-6}}{4\times10^{-2}}$$

$$\Rightarrow \quad V_{outer} = 2.25\times10^5\text{ V}$$

(b) Charge distribution is as shown in above figure.

(vi) With the dial at 180°, the capacitance $C = 950$ pF

The corresponding charge at 400 V is

$$q = CV$$

$$\Rightarrow \quad q = 950\times10^{-12}\times400\text{ C}$$

$$\Rightarrow \quad q = 0.38\times10^{-6}\text{C}$$

(a) For the dial at 0°, capacitance is given as

$$C' = 50\times10^{-12}\text{ F}$$

The corresponding potential difference across capacitor is

$$V' = \frac{q}{C'} = \frac{0.38\times10^{-6}}{50\times10^{-12}}$$

$$\Rightarrow \quad V' = 7600\text{ V}$$

(b) Work needed to turn the dial is

$$W = \frac{1}{2}C'V'^2 - \frac{1}{2}CV^2$$

$$\Rightarrow \quad W = \frac{1}{2}\times50\times10^{-12}\times7600^2 - \frac{1}{2}\times950\times10^{-12}\times400^2$$

$$\Rightarrow \quad W = 1.368\times10^{-3}\text{ J}$$

(vii) The capacitance of a spherical capacitor is

$$C = 4\pi\varepsilon_0\left(\frac{ab}{b-a}\right)$$

b = radius of the top of stratosphere layer

$= 6400\text{ km} + 50\text{ km} = 6450\text{ km} = 6.45 \times 10^6\text{ m}$

a = radius of earth = 6400 km = 6.4×10^6 m

capacitance of spherical capacitor is given as

$$C = \frac{4\pi \epsilon_0 ab}{b-a}$$

$$\Rightarrow \quad C = \frac{1}{9\times10^9} \times \frac{6.45\times10^6 \times 6.4\times10^6}{6.45\times10^6 - 6.4\times10^6} = 0.092\text{ F}$$

(viii) Charge on capacitor is

$$q = CV$$

$$\Rightarrow \quad q = 40 \times 10^{-6} \times 300$$

$$\Rightarrow \quad q = 0.12\text{ C}$$

$$i_{avg} = \frac{q}{\Delta t} = \frac{0.12}{2\times10^{-3}} = 60\text{ A}$$

Energy stored in capacitor is

$$U = \frac{1}{2}CV^2$$

$$\Rightarrow \quad U = \frac{1}{2} \times 40 \times 10^{-6} \times (3\times10^3)^2$$

$$\Rightarrow \quad U = 180\text{ J}$$

Powr delivered during the pulse is

$$P = \frac{U}{\Delta t} = \frac{180}{2\times10^{-3}} = 90\text{ kW}$$

(ix) Capacitance of given capacitor is

$$C = \frac{\epsilon_0 A}{d}$$

Energy stored in capacitor is

$$U = \frac{q^2}{2C} = \frac{q^2 d}{2\epsilon_0 A}$$

When switch is closed the capacitor is discharged and its stored energy is liberated as heat.

(x) Area of plate is given as

$$A = \pi r^2 = \pi \times (8 \times 10^{-2})^2 = 0.0201\text{ m}^2$$

and $\quad d = 1\text{ mm} = 1 \times 10^{-3}\text{ m}$

Capacitance of capacitor is given as

$$C = \frac{\varepsilon_0\varepsilon_r A}{d}$$

$$\Rightarrow \quad C = \frac{8.85\times10^{-12} \times 6\times0.0201}{1\times10^{-3}}$$

$$\Rightarrow \quad C = 1.068 \times 10^{-9}\text{ F}$$

Potential difference

$$V = 150\text{ V}$$

Energy stored in capacitor is given as

$$U = \frac{1}{2}CV^2 = \frac{1}{2} \times (1.068 \times 10^{-9} \times (150)^2 = 1.2 \times 10^{-5}\text{ J}$$

(xi) Potential difference across 3μF = P.D. across 6 μF = 1 V

⇒ Charge on 6 μF = 6 μC

⇒ Total charge on combination of 6 μF and 3 μF = 9 μC

Therefore charge on C = 9 μC

(xii) If we consider capacitance of conductor and plate are C_1 and C_2 then after first contact we have

$$\frac{q}{C_1} = \frac{Q-q}{C_2}$$

$$\Rightarrow \quad q = \frac{QC_1}{C_1 + C_2}$$

$$\Rightarrow \quad \frac{C_2}{C_1} = \frac{Q-q}{q}$$

After several contacts when no more charge transfers to conductor we use

$$\frac{q_{max}}{C_1} = \frac{Q}{C_2}$$

$$\Rightarrow \quad q_{max} = \frac{QC_1}{C_2} = \frac{qQ}{Q-q}$$

Solutions of PRACTICE EXERCISE 2.2

(i) The equivalent diagram of the given circuit across points P and Q is given as shown below which is reduced to the find capacitance.

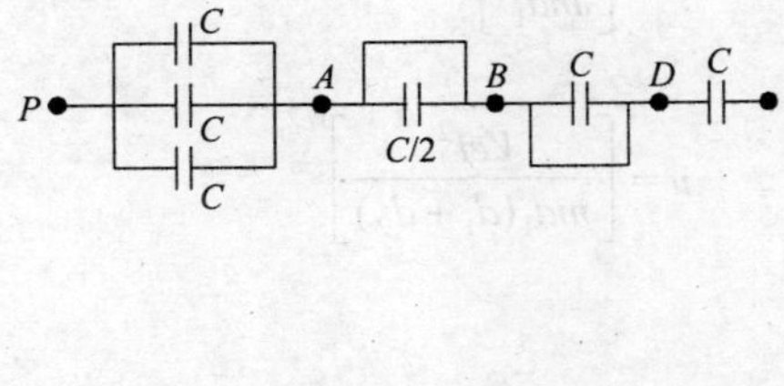

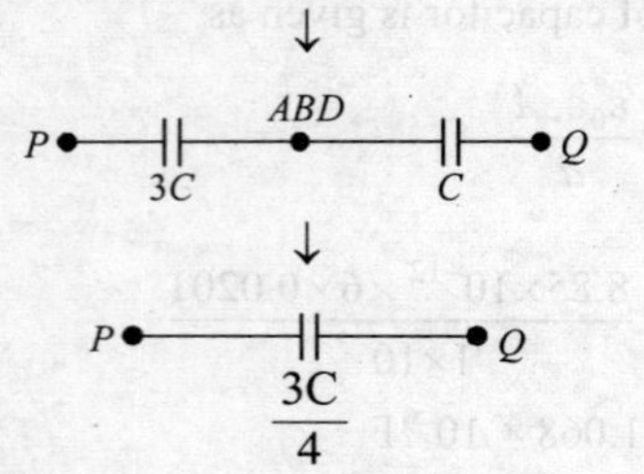

(ii) The capacitances of the two capacitors are given as

$$C_1 = \frac{\epsilon_0 A}{d_1}, \text{ and } C_2 = \frac{\epsilon_0 A}{d_2}$$

If V_1 and V_2 be the potential drop across C_1 and C_2, then we have

$$V_1 + V_2 = V \qquad \ldots(1)$$

and $$C_1V_1 = C_2V_2$$

$$\Rightarrow \quad V_1 = \frac{C_2V}{C_1 + C_2} = \frac{\epsilon_0 A}{d^2}V\left[\frac{1}{\frac{\epsilon_0 A}{d_1} + \frac{\epsilon_0 A}{d_2}}\right]$$

$$\Rightarrow \quad V_1 = V\left[\frac{d_1}{d_1 + d_2}\right]$$

The electric field between the plates of capacitor 1, is given as

$$E = \frac{V_1}{d_1} = \left[\frac{V}{d_1 + d_2}\right]$$

If u is the speed of projection, then the time to cross the plate is

$$t = \frac{l}{u}$$

For not to collide with the plate, displacement of electron in normal direction is

$$\frac{d_1}{2} = \frac{1}{2}at^2$$

$$\Rightarrow \quad \frac{d_1}{2} = \frac{1}{2}\left(\frac{Ee}{m}\right)t^2$$

$$\Rightarrow \quad \frac{d_1}{2} = \frac{1}{2}\left(\frac{Ee}{m}\right)\left(\frac{l}{u}\right)^2$$

$$\Rightarrow \quad u = \left[\frac{Eel^2}{md_1}\right]^{1/2}$$

$$\Rightarrow \quad u = \left[\frac{Vel^2}{md_1(d_1 + d_2)}\right]^{1/2}$$

(iii) We can redraw the circuit with K is open and when K is closed as shown in figures below

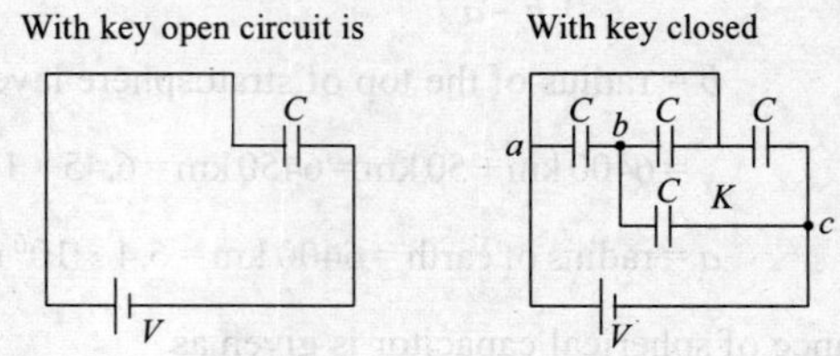

↓

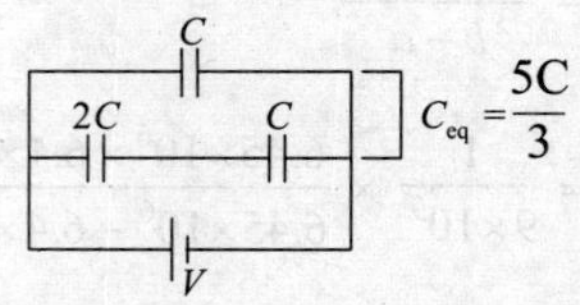

Initial and final energies stored in capacitors are

$$U_i = \frac{1}{2}CV^2$$

$$U_f = \frac{1}{2}\left(\frac{5}{3}C\right)V^2$$

Change in stored energy is given as

$$\Delta U = U_f - U_i = \frac{1}{2}\left(\frac{5C}{3} - C\right)V^2$$

$$\Rightarrow \quad \Delta U = \frac{1}{2}\left(\frac{2C}{3}\right)V^2 = \frac{1}{3}CV^2$$

$$\Rightarrow \quad \Delta U = \frac{1}{3} \times 3 \times 10^{-6} \times 10^2 = 100\ \mu\text{J}$$

(iv) (a) The equivalent capacity C_1 of the capacitors 3, 5 and 4μF in parallel is given by

$$C_1 = 3 + 5 + 4 = 12\ \mu\text{F}$$

Similarly, the equivalent capacity C_3 of the capacitors 4 and 2μF in parallel is givenby

$$C_2 = 4 + 2 = 6\ \mu\text{F}$$

Now C_1 and 4μF are in series. The equivalent capacitance C' of this is given by

$$\frac{1}{C'} = \frac{1}{C_1} + \frac{1}{4} = \frac{1}{12} + \frac{1}{4} = \frac{1}{3}$$

$$\Rightarrow \quad C' = 3\mu\text{F}$$

Again C_2 and 3 μF are in series. The equivalent capacitance C'' of this is given by

$$\frac{1}{C''} = \frac{1}{C_3} + \frac{1}{3} = \frac{1}{6} + \frac{1}{3} = \frac{1}{2}$$

$$\Rightarrow \quad C'' = 2\ \mu\text{F}$$

The equivalent capacitance C between A and B is given by

$$C = C' + C'' = 3\ \mu F + 2\ \mu F = 5\ \mu F$$

(b) The charge on 5μF capacitor

$$q = 120\ \mu C = 120 \times 10^{-6} C$$

Potential difference across 5μF capacitor is given as

$$V = \frac{120 \times 10^{-6}}{5 \times 10^{-6}} = 24\ V$$

As the three capacitors of capacities, 3 μF, 5 μF and 4 μF are in parallel, the potential difference across each capacitor will be V, we have

Charge on 3 μF capacitor

$$q_{3\mu F} = 3 \times 10^{-6} \times 24$$

$$\Rightarrow \quad q_{3\mu F} = 72 \times 10^{-6} C$$

Charge on 4 μF capacitor

$$q_{4\mu F} = 4 \times 10^{-6} \times 24$$

$$\Rightarrow \quad q_{4\mu F} = 96 \times 10^{-6} C$$

Total charge flowing through C_1 and 4μF is

$$q = (72 + 120 + 96) \times 10^{-6} = 288 \times 10^{-6} C$$

Potential difference across 4 μF is

$$V_{4\mu F} = \frac{288 \times 10^{-6}}{4 \times 10^{-6}}$$

$$\Rightarrow \quad V_{4\mu F} = 72\ V$$

Now net potential difference between A and B is given as

$$V_{AB} = 24 + 72 = 96\ V$$

The equivalent capacitance of C_2 and 3 μF is 2 μF, the charge flowing through these is 3 μF

$$q_{3\mu F} = 96 \times 2 \times 10^{-6} C = 192 \times 10^{-6} C$$

Potential difference between A and C is given as

$$V_{AC} = \frac{192 \times 10^{-6}}{3 \times 10^{-6}} = 64\ V$$

(v) In this case there are three capacitors present in this situation which are shown in figure below.

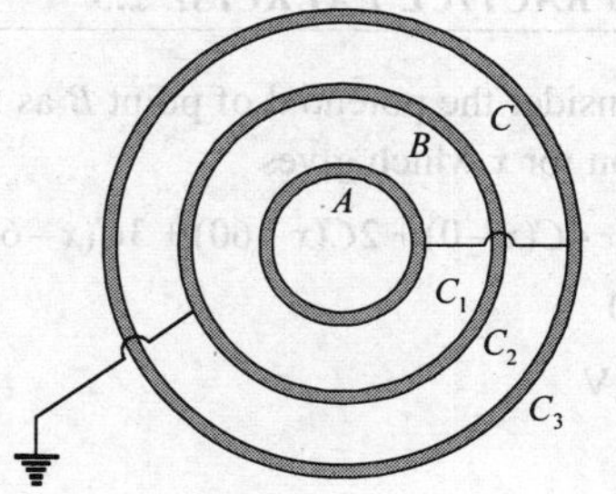

C_1 has one plate connected at A and other at B which is at zero potential, C_2 has one plate at C (which is connected to A) and other at B which is alos at zero potential. C_3 has one plate at C (which is connected at A) and other at ∞ which is at zero potential thus we can state that all three capacitances are in parallel so their equivalent capacitance is given as

$$C = C_1 + C_2 + C_3$$

$$\Rightarrow \quad C = \frac{4\pi \epsilon_0 ab}{b-a} + \frac{4\pi \epsilon_0 bc}{c-b} + 4\pi\epsilon_0 c$$

$$\Rightarrow \quad C = 4\pi \epsilon_0 \left(\frac{ab}{b-a} + \frac{c^2}{c-b} \right)$$

(vi) Equivalent capacitance is given as

$$\frac{1}{C_{eq}} = \frac{1}{2} + \frac{1}{3} + \frac{1}{6} = \frac{3+2+1}{6} = 1$$

$$C_{eq} = 1\ \mu F$$

(a) Charge flown through battery is

$$Q = C_{eq} V = 30\ \mu C$$

(b) Charge on 3 μF capacitor is alos 30 μC as all capacitors are in series. Energy stored in 3 μF capacitor is given as

$$U = \frac{Q^2}{2C} = \frac{30 \times 30}{2 \times 3} = 150\ \mu J$$

(c) Total energy in all the capacitors is

$$U_{total} = \frac{1}{2} C_{eq} V^2$$

$$\Rightarrow \quad U_{total} = \frac{30 \times 30}{2}\ \mu J = 450\ \mu J$$

(d) Heat produced on switching is given as

$$H = qV - \frac{1}{2} C_{eq} V^2$$

$$\Rightarrow \quad H = 30 \times 30 - 450\ \mu J$$

$$\Rightarrow \quad H = 450\ \mu J$$

(vii) Capacitance of each capacitor between adjoining plates is given as

$$C = \frac{\epsilon_0 A}{d}$$

If plates are numbered as 1, 2, 3 and 4 as shown in below figure the equivalent circuit of three capacitors is given as shown below and its further reduction.

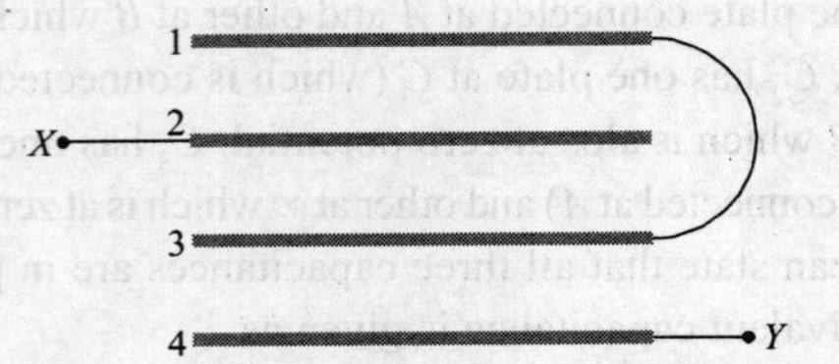

Equivalent circuit of above system of plates is shown below.

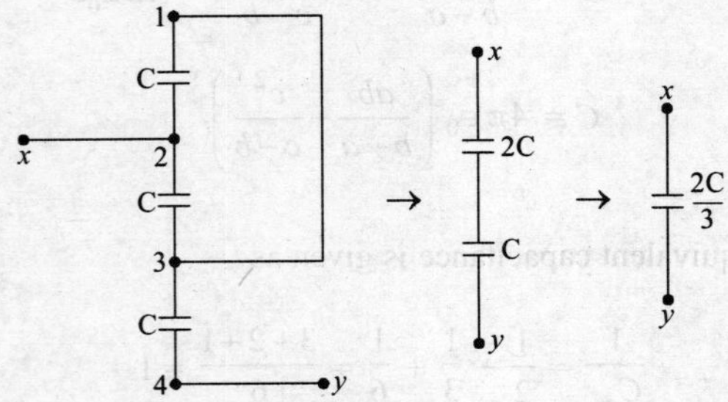

(viii) Suppose Q is the charge on the capacitor. Choose a close loop *abcdefghijklmna*, as shown below and we can see potential difference applied across is E due to the battery B, as shown in figure below.

This charge on capacitor is given as

$$q = CE = 6 \times 10^{-6} \times 10$$

$$\Rightarrow \quad q = 60\,\mu\text{C}$$

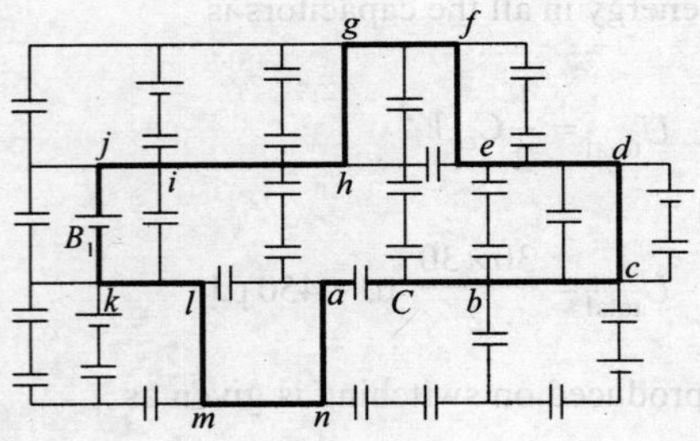

(ix) Considering numbers of plates from top to bottom and drawing the equivalent circuit as shown below

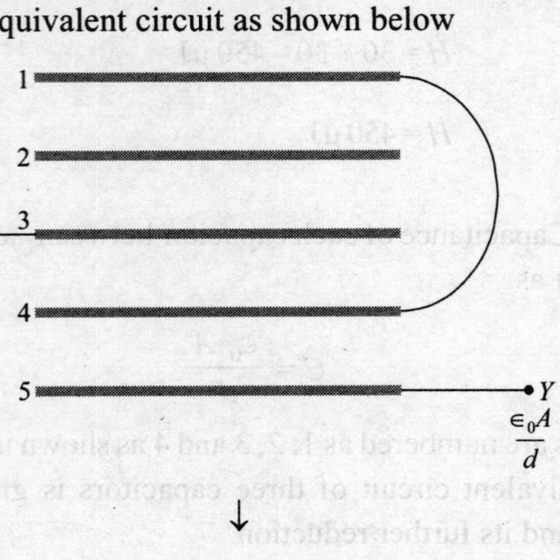

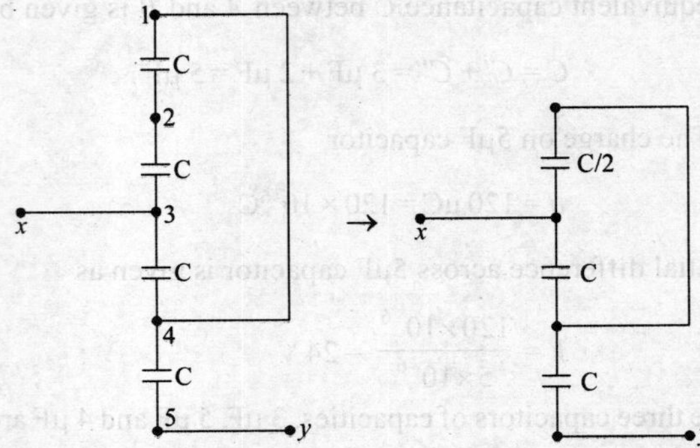

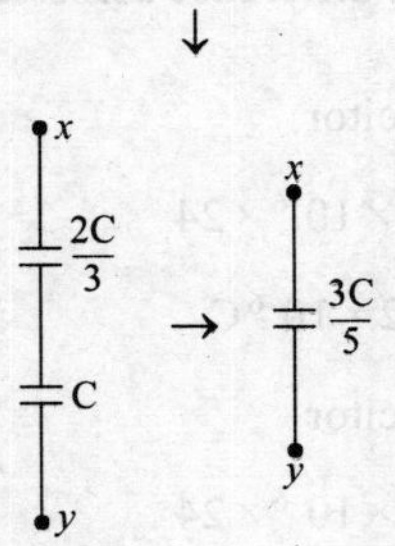

(x) Capacitances of X and Y are given as

$$C_X = \frac{\varepsilon_0 A}{d}, C_Y = \frac{5\varepsilon_0 A}{d}$$

$$\Rightarrow \quad C_Y = 5C_X$$

(a) As C_X and C_Y are in series, so potential difference across X and Y are given as

$$V_X = \frac{C_Y V}{C_X + C_Y} = \frac{5}{6} \times 12 = 10\text{V}$$

and

$$V_Y = \frac{C_X V}{C_X + C_Y} = \frac{1}{6} \times 12 = 2\text{V}$$

(b) Energy stored in capacitors X and Y are given as

$$U = \frac{q^2}{2C}$$

$$\Rightarrow \quad \frac{U_X}{U_Y} = \left(\frac{q^2}{2C_X}\right)\left(\frac{2C_Y}{q^2}\right) = \frac{C_Y}{C_X} = 5$$

Solutions of PRACTICE EXERCISE 2.3

(i) We consider the potential of point B as x and write the nodal equation for x which gives

$$C(x-0) + 4C(x-0) + 2C(x-60) + 3C(x-60) = 0$$

$$\Rightarrow \quad 10x = 300$$

$$\Rightarrow \quad x = 30\text{ V}$$

(ii) If equivalent capacitance across terminals A and B is x then after first two capacitors if the circuit is broken then the equivalent capacitance of the remaining ladder will be $2x$ as all the capacitors of the ladder after first two capacitors is twice that of the original ladder as shown in figure so the effective circuit of the given ladder can be drawan as

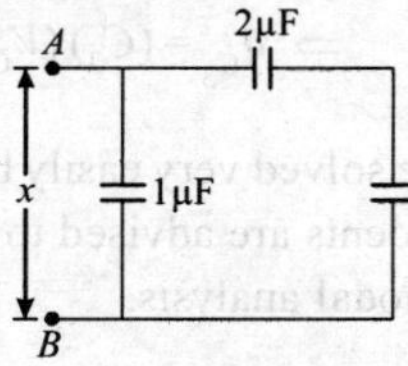

$$x = \frac{4x}{2+2x} + 1$$

$$x = \frac{4x+2+2x}{2+2x}$$

$$\Rightarrow \quad x(2+2x) = 6x+2$$

$$\Rightarrow \quad 2x + 2x^2 = 6x + 2 \quad \Rightarrow \quad x^2 - 2x - 1 = 0$$

Use $x = \dfrac{-b \pm \sqrt{b^2 - 4ac}}{2a} = \dfrac{2 \pm \sqrt{4+4}}{2} = \dfrac{1 \pm 2\sqrt{2}}{2}$

As equivalent capacitance cannot be negative the capacitance across terminals A and B is given as

$$C_{AB} = \frac{1+2\sqrt{2}}{2}\ \mu\text{F}$$

(iii) The equivalent system of capacitors is reduced as shown in figure below.

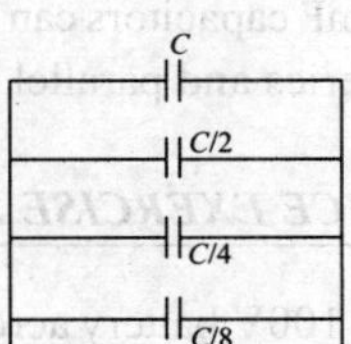

The equivalent capacitance, across A and B is given as

$$C_{eq} = C + \frac{C}{2} + \frac{C}{4} + \frac{C}{8} + \ldots\ldots$$

$$\Rightarrow \quad C_{eq} = C\left[\frac{1}{1-\frac{1}{2}}\right] = 2C = 2\ \mu\text{F}$$

(iv) Distributing potentials as shown in circuit below

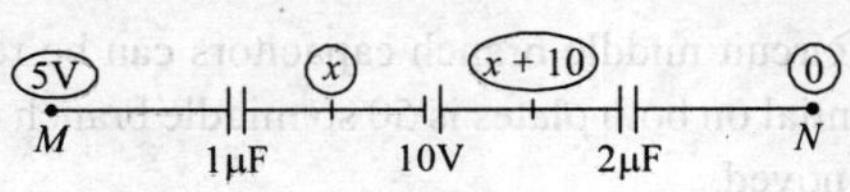

Writing nodal equation for x gives

$$1(x-5) + 2(x+10) = 0$$

$$\Rightarrow \quad 3x = -15$$

$$\Rightarrow \quad x = -5\ \text{V}$$

Thus we have

$$V_{1\mu F} = 5 - (-5) = 10\ \text{V}$$

and $$V_{2\mu F} = 5 - 0 = 5\ \text{V}$$

(v) Distributing potentials as shown in circuit below

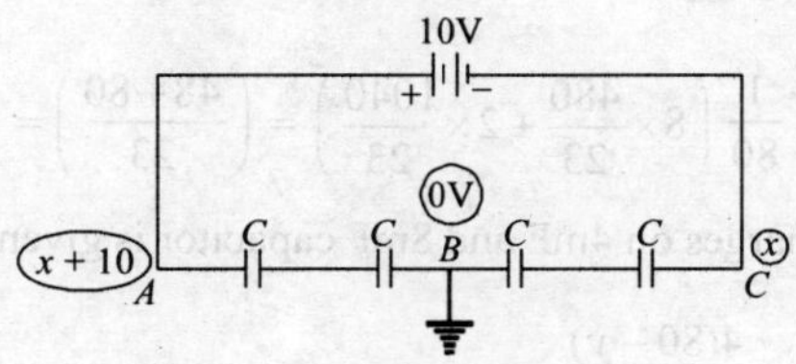

Writing nodal equation at point B gives

$$\frac{C}{2}(0-x) + \frac{C}{2}(0-x-10) = 0$$

$$\Rightarrow \quad 2x = -10$$

$$\Rightarrow \quad x = -5\text{V}$$

Thus we have

$$V_C = -5\ \text{V}$$

$$V_A = -5 + 10 = +5\ \text{V}$$

(vi) The circuit shows an unbalanced wheatstone bridge in which to apply nodal analysis we distribute the potentials as shown in figure below.

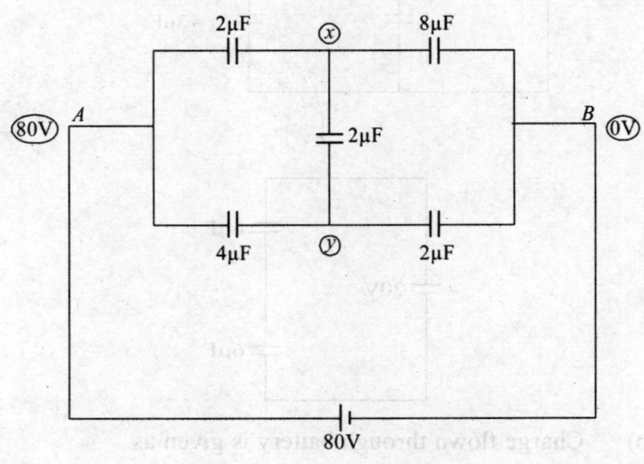

Writing nodal equations for variables x and y gives

$$8x + 2(x-y) + 2(x-80) = 0$$

$$\Rightarrow \quad 6x - y = 80 \quad \ldots(1)$$

and $2y-2(y-x)+4(y-80)=0$

$$\Rightarrow \quad 4y-x=160 \quad \ldots(2)$$

Solving equations-(1) and (2) gives

$$x=\frac{480}{23}\text{V} \quad \text{and} \quad y=\frac{1040}{23}\text{V}$$

In above circuit equivalanet capacitance is given as

$$C_{AB}=\frac{q_{battery}}{V_{battery}}$$

$$\Rightarrow C_{AB}=\frac{8x+2y}{80}$$

$$\Rightarrow C_{AB}=\frac{1}{80}\left(8\times\frac{480}{23}+2\times\frac{1040}{23}\right)=\left(\frac{48+80}{23}\right)=\frac{128}{23}\,\mu\text{F}$$

Ratio of charges on 4mF and 8mF capacitor is given as

$$\frac{q_{4\mu F}}{q_{8\mu F}}=\frac{4(80-y)}{8x}$$

$$\frac{q_{4\mu F}}{q_{8\mu F}}=\frac{4\left(80-\frac{1040}{23}\right)}{8\times\frac{480}{23}}=\frac{5}{6}$$

(vii) (a) Simple circuit is as shown below

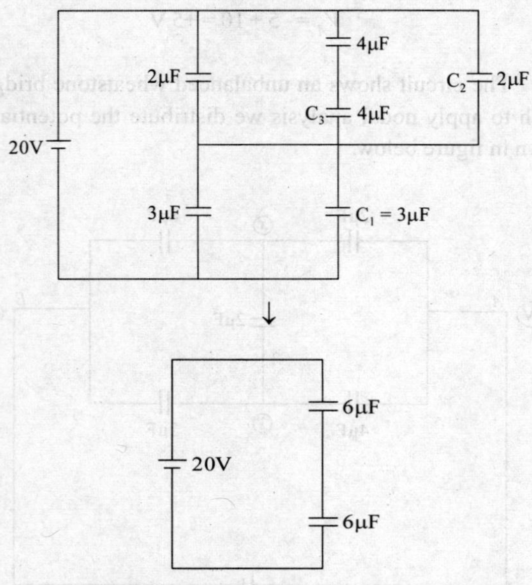

(b) Charge flown through battery is given as

$$q_{net}=(C_{net})V=(34\,\mu\text{F})\,(20\text{ V})=60\,\mu\text{C}$$

(c) In above figure shown potential difference across each 6 μF is

$$V_1=V_2=\frac{20}{2}=10\text{ V}$$

As $V_{C_1}=10\text{ V}$, $\Rightarrow q_{C_1}=(C_1)(V_{C_1})=30\,\mu\text{C}$

(d) As $V_{C_2}=10\text{ V}$, $\Rightarrow q_{C_2}=(C_2)(V_{C_2})=20\,\mu\text{C}$

(e) As $V_{C_3}=5\text{ V}$, $\Rightarrow q_{C_3}=(C_3)(V_{C_3})=20\,\mu\text{C}$

Above question can be solved very easily by using the method of nodal analysis. Students are advised to solve this question using the method of nodal analysis.

(viii) (a) The given circuit is a balanced wheatstone bridge in which we can remove the middle branch in which 5mF capacitor is connecteed after which we can solve the circuit by using series and parallel analysis or solve by nodal analysis by connecting a 100V battery. Students should try this by both methods.

(b) In this circuit also for left and right side of capacitances the ratio of capacitances on top branch and middle branch are same and similarly the bottom and middle branch are same so the circuit is similar to the balanced wheatstone bridge in which the potentials at all three middle junctions will be same so the middle 9mF capacitors can be removed and circuit can be solved using series and parallel analysis. Students can also solve it by considering different potentials *x*, *y* and *z* at the middle junction and connecting a 100V battery across terminals *A* and *B* and applying nodal analysis and verify the the result obtained.

(c) With the same concept explained in part-(b) in this circuit also all the 4mF and 8mF capacitors can be removed and circuit can be solved using series and parallel analysis.

Solutions of PRACTICE EXERCISE 2.4

(i) If we connect a 100V battery across *A* and *B* potential is distributed as shown in figure below.

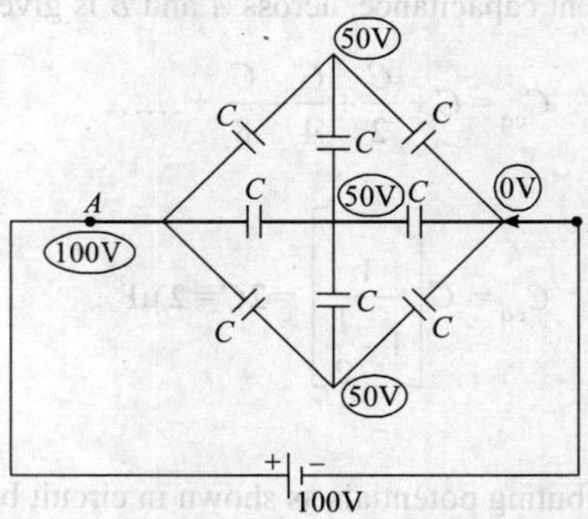

In above circuit middle branch capacitors can be renewed as their potential on both plates is 50 so middle branch capacitors can be removed.

(ii) Applying a 100 V battery and distributing potentials as shown in figure below

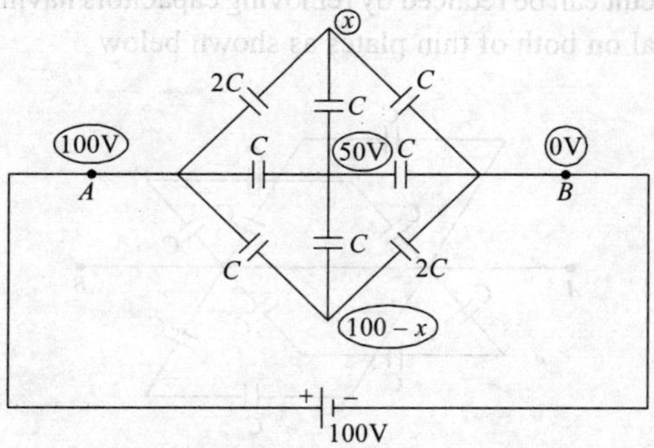

Writing nodal equation for x gives

$$C(x-0)+C(x-50)+2C(x-100)=0$$

$$\Rightarrow \quad 4x=250$$

$$\Rightarrow \quad x=\frac{125}{2}\text{V}$$

C_{eq} across A and B is given as

$$C_{eq}=\frac{q_{battery}}{V_{battery}}$$

$$\Rightarrow \quad C_{eq}=\frac{Cx+C(50)+2C(100-x)}{100}$$

$$\Rightarrow \quad C_{eq}=\frac{C}{100}\left(\frac{125}{2}+50+200-125\right)$$

$$\Rightarrow \quad C_{eq}=\frac{375}{200}\text{C}=\frac{15C}{8}$$

(iii) Applying a 100 V battery and distributing potentials as shown in figure below

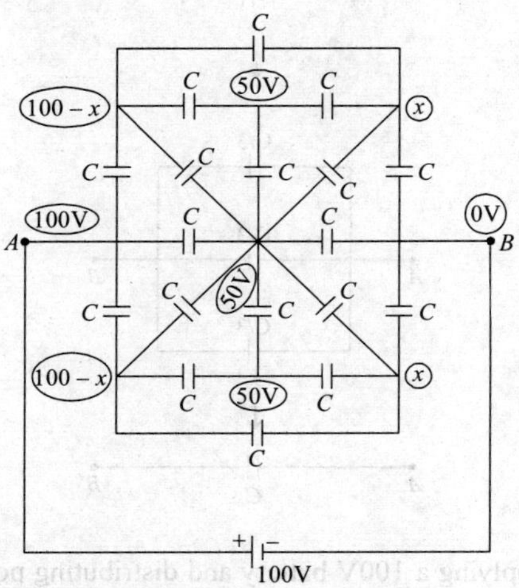

Writing nodal equation for x gives

$$C(x)+C(x-50)+C(x-50)+C(2x-100)=0$$

$$\Rightarrow \quad 5x=200$$

$$\Rightarrow \quad x=40\text{ V}$$

C_{eq} across A and B is given as

$$C_{eq}=\frac{q_{battery}}{V_{battery}}=\frac{2C(x)+C(50)}{100}$$

$$\Rightarrow \quad C_{eq}=\frac{130}{100}\text{C}=1.3\text{ C}$$

(iv) Applying a 100V battery and distributing potentials as shown in figure below

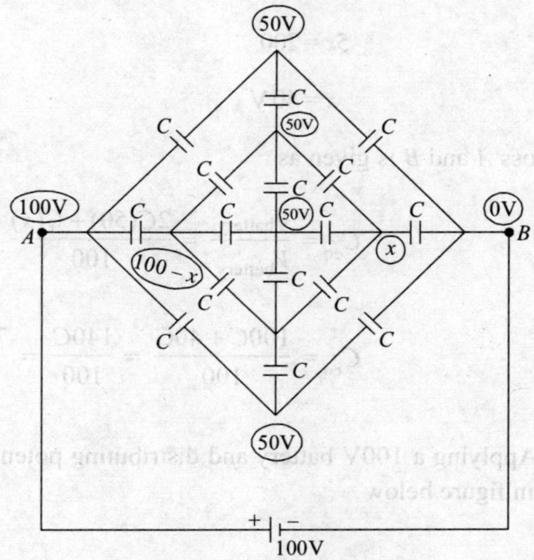

Writing nodal equation for x gives

$$C(x-0)+C(x-50)+C(x-50)+C(x-50)=0$$

$$\Rightarrow \quad 4x=150$$

$$\Rightarrow \quad x=\frac{150}{4}=\frac{75}{2}\text{V}$$

C_{eq} across A and B is given as

$$C_{eq}=\frac{q_{battery}}{V_{battery}}=\frac{2C(50)+C(x)}{100}$$

$$\Rightarrow \quad C_{eq}=\frac{100C+\frac{75}{2}C}{100}=\frac{275}{200}\text{C}=\frac{11}{8}\text{ C}$$

Students can also try solving this circuit by removing capacitors in middle branch and reducing the circuit.

(v) Applying a 100 V battery and distributing potentials as shown in figure below

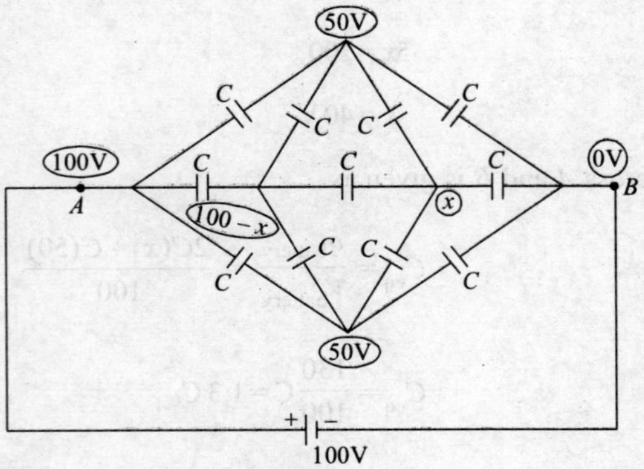

Writing nodal equation for x gives

$$C(x-0)+C(x-50)+C(x-50)+C(2x-100)=0$$

$$\Rightarrow \quad 5x=200$$

$$\Rightarrow \quad x=40\,\text{V}$$

C_{eq} across A and B is given as

$$C_{eq}=\frac{q_{\text{battery}}}{V_{\text{battery}}}=\frac{2C(50)+C(x)}{100}$$

$$\Rightarrow \quad C_{eq}=\frac{100C+40C}{100}=\frac{140C}{100}=\frac{7C}{5}$$

(vi) Applying a 100V battery and distributing potentials as shown in figure below

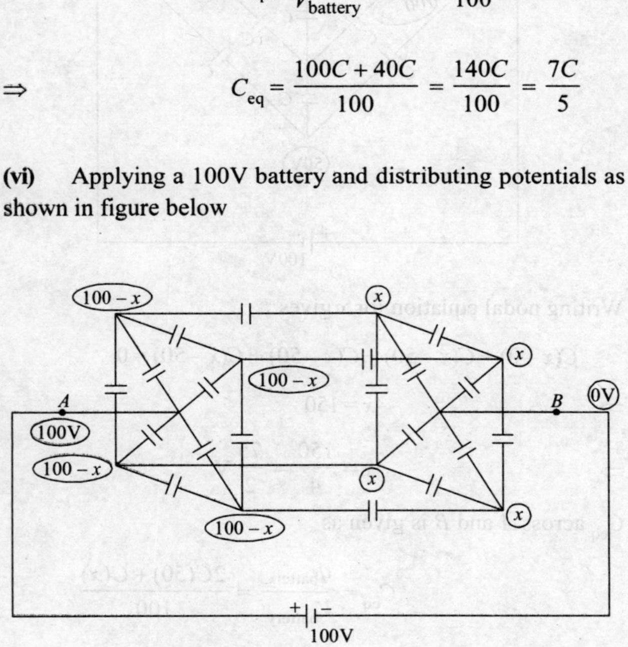

Writing nodal equation for x gives

$$C(x-0)+C(2x-100)=0$$

C_{eq} across A and B is given as

$$C_{eq}=\frac{q_{\text{battery}}}{V_{\text{battery}}}=\frac{4Cx}{100}=\frac{4C}{3}$$

Alternative method :

The circuit can be reduced by removing capacitors having same potential on both of thin plates as shown below

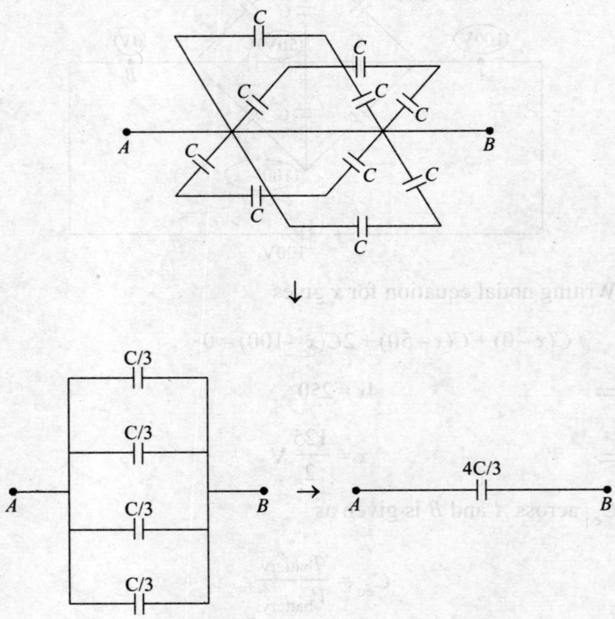

(vii) Just like previous question the circuit can be reduced as shown below.

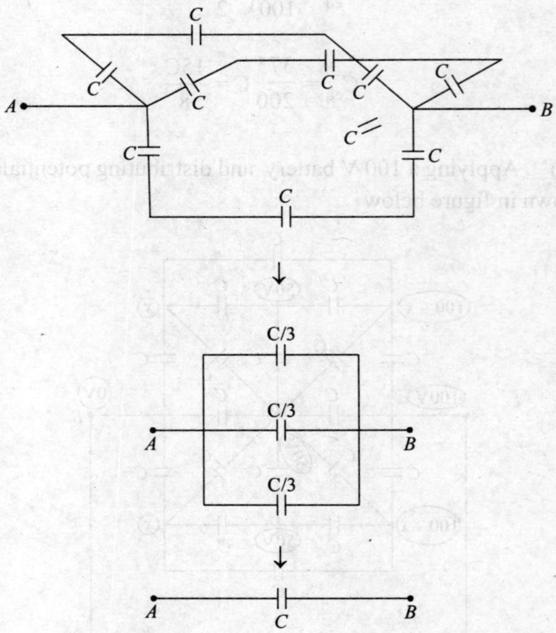

(viii) Applying a 100V battery and distributing potentials as shown in figure below

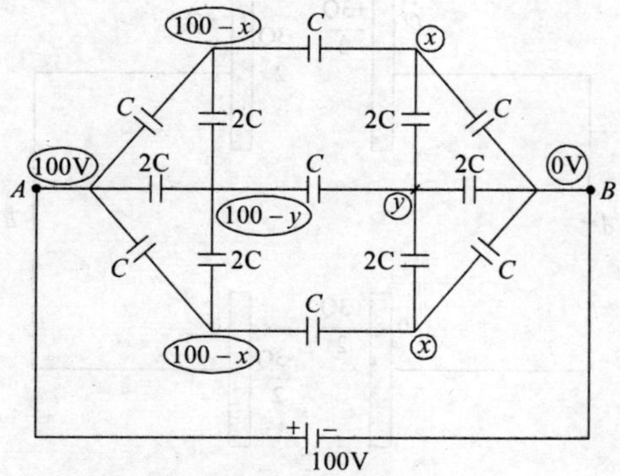

Writing nodal equation for x and y gives

$$C(x-0)+2C(x-y)+C(2x-100)=0$$

$$\Rightarrow \quad 5x+2y=100$$

and $2C(y-0)+2C(y-x)+2C(y-x)+C(2y-100)=0$

$$8y-4x=100$$

Solving we get $\quad x=\dfrac{125}{4}\text{ V and } y=\dfrac{225}{8}\text{ V}$

C_{eq} across A and B is given as

$$C_{eq}=\frac{q_{battery}}{V_{battery}}=\frac{2Cx+Cy}{100}$$

$$\Rightarrow \quad C_{eq}=\frac{475}{400}\text{C}=\frac{19}{16}\text{C}$$

(ix) Applying a 100 V battery and distributing potentials as shown in figure below

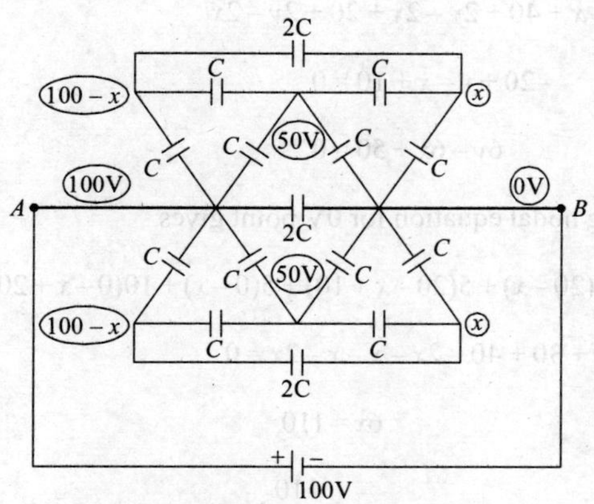

Writing nodal equation for x gives

$$C(x-0)+C(x-50)+2C(2x-100)=0$$

$$\Rightarrow \quad 6x=250$$

$$\Rightarrow \quad x=\frac{125}{3}\text{ V}$$

C_{eq} across A and B is given as

$$C_{eq}=\frac{q_{battery}}{V_{battery}}$$

$$\Rightarrow \quad C_{eq}=\frac{2Cx+2C(50)+2C(2x-100)}{100}$$

$$\Rightarrow \quad C_{eq}=\frac{C}{50}\left(\frac{125}{3}+50+\frac{250}{3}-100\right)$$

$$\Rightarrow \quad C_{eq}=\frac{C}{50}\left(\frac{375}{3}-50\right)=\frac{225}{150}\text{C}=\frac{3}{2}\text{C}$$

(x) Applying a 100 V battery and distributing potentials as shown in figure below

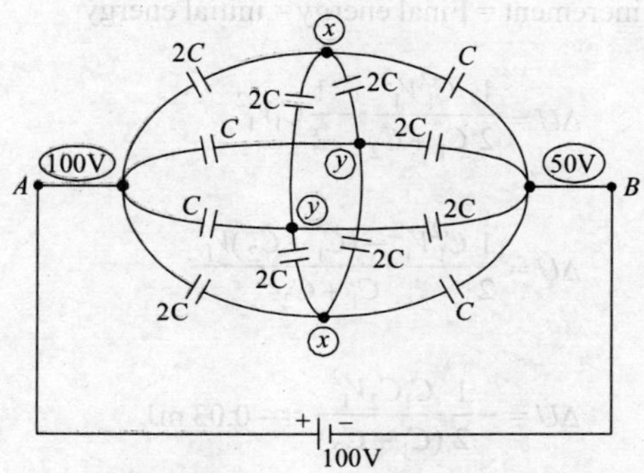

Writing nodal equation for x and y gives

$$C(x-0)+2C(x-y)+2C(x-y)+2C(x-100)=0$$

$$7x-4y=200 \qquad \ldots(1)$$

$$2C(y-0)+2C(y-x)+2C(y-x)+C(y-100)=0$$

$$7y-4x=100 \qquad \ldots(2)$$

Solving equations-(1) and (2) gives

$$x=\frac{600}{11}\text{ V and } y=\frac{500}{11}\text{ V}$$

C_{eq} across A and B is given as

$$C_{eq}=\frac{q_{battery}}{V_{battery}}=\frac{2Cx+4Cy}{100}$$

$$\Rightarrow \quad C_{eq}=\frac{C}{100}\left[2\left(\frac{600}{11}\right)+4\left(\frac{500}{11}\right)\right]$$

$$\Rightarrow \quad C_{eq}=\frac{32}{11}\text{C}$$

Solutions of PRACTICE EXERCISE 2.5

(i) Initial electrical energy is given as

$$U_i = \frac{1}{2} C_1 V_1^2$$

After the capacitors are connected in parallel, the equivalent capacitance is $C_1 + C_2$. Let V be the common potential then it is given as

$$V = \frac{q}{C_{eq}} = \frac{C_1 V_1}{C_1 + C_2}$$

Final energy is given as

$$U_f = \frac{1}{2} \frac{C_1^2 V_1^2}{C_1 + C_2}$$

Energy increment = Final energy – initial energy

$$\Delta U = \frac{1}{2} \frac{C_1^2 V_1^2}{C_1 + C_2} - \frac{1}{2} C_1 V_1^2$$

$$\Rightarrow \quad \Delta U = \frac{1}{2} \frac{C_1^2 V_1^2 - (C_1 + C_2) V_1^2}{C_1 + C_2}$$

$$\Rightarrow \quad \Delta U = -\frac{1}{2} \frac{C_1 C_2 V_1^2}{(C_1 + C_2)} = -0.03 \text{ mJ}$$

The negative sign shows that some energy is dissipated as heat when rearrangement of charges takes place.

(ii) Figure shows the initial charge distribution on capacitor plates

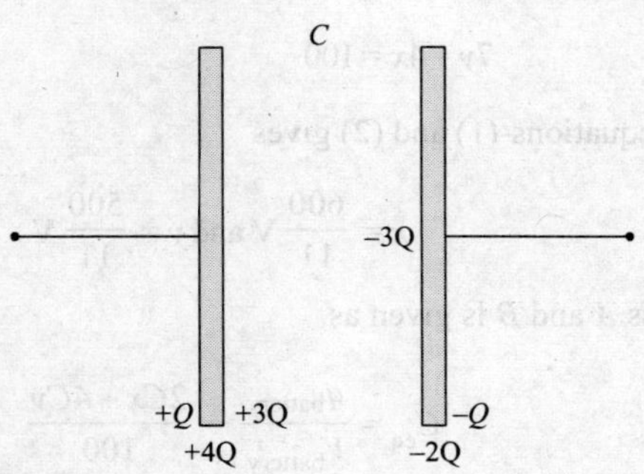

When above capcitor is connected in parallel with identical capacitor, inner plate charges will be equally distributed as shown in figure below

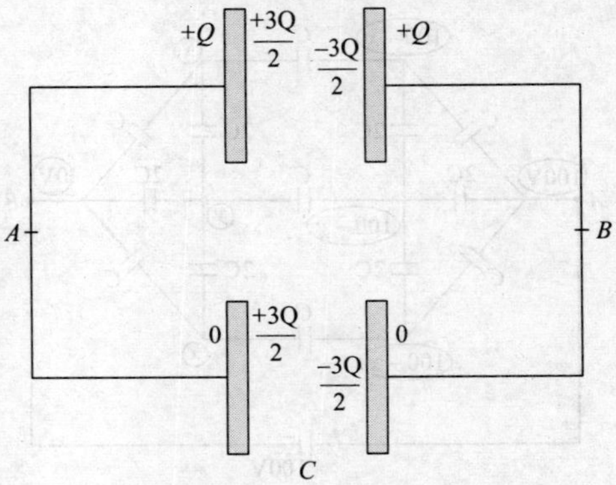

Final potential difference is

$$V_{AB} = \frac{3Q}{2C}$$

(iii) Total charge coming out of battery = 0

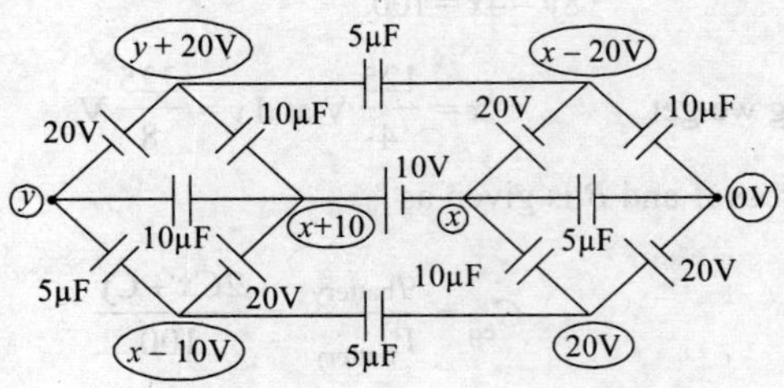

Writing nodal equation for y gives

$$5[y + 20 - (x - 20)] + 10[y + 20 - (x + 10)]$$
$$+ 10[y - (x + 10)] + 5[y - (x - 10)] = 0$$

$$\Rightarrow \quad y - x + 40 + 2y - 2x + 20 + 2y - 2x$$
$$-20 + y - x + 10 = 0$$

$$\Rightarrow \quad 6y - 6x + 50 = 0 \quad \ldots(1)$$

Writing nodal equation for 0V point gives

$$10(20 - x) + 5(20 - x + 10) + 5(0 - x) + 10(0 - x + 20) = 0$$

$$\Rightarrow \quad 40 + 30 + 40 - 2x - x - x - 2x = 0$$

$$\Rightarrow \quad 6x = 110 \quad \ldots(2)$$

$$\Rightarrow \quad x = \frac{110}{6} \text{ V}$$

from equtaion-(1)

$$y = \frac{6x - 50}{6} = \frac{60}{6} = 10 \text{ V}$$

(iv) Distributing potentials as shown in circuit below

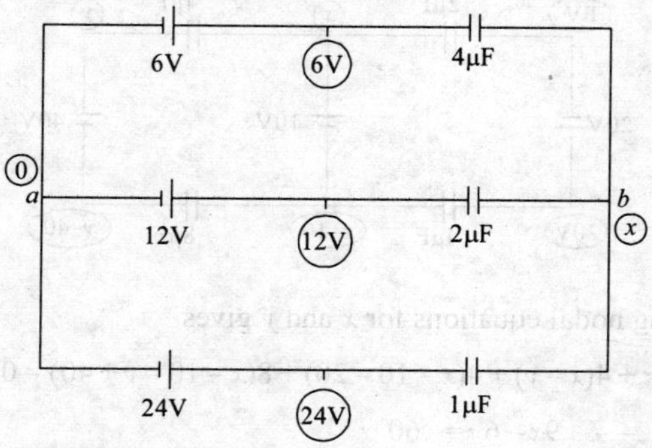

Writing nodal equation for x gives

$$4(x-6)+2(x-12)+1(x-24)=0$$

$$\Rightarrow \quad 7x=72$$

$$\Rightarrow \quad x=\frac{72}{7}\text{ V}$$

$$\Rightarrow \quad V_a-V_b=-x=-\frac{72}{7}\text{ V}$$

(v) When S_{W_1} is closed and S_{W_2} is open then capacitor B is charged upto 10 V so its find charge will be $3\times 10=30\ \mu C$

Now S_{W_1} is open and S_{W_2} is closed then find common potential difference of the two capacitors in parallel be comes

Thus find charges on capacitor are

$$V_C=\frac{30}{3+2}=6\text{ V}$$

$$Q_A=2\times 10^{-6}V_{cm}=12\ \mu C$$

$$Q_B=3\times 10^{-6}V_{cm}=18\ \mu C$$

(vi) If we number plates as 1, 2, 3 and 4 from top the equivalent circuit is shown in figure below and capacitance between two plates is given as

$$C=\frac{\epsilon_0 A}{d}$$

we distribute the potentials in the circuit shown

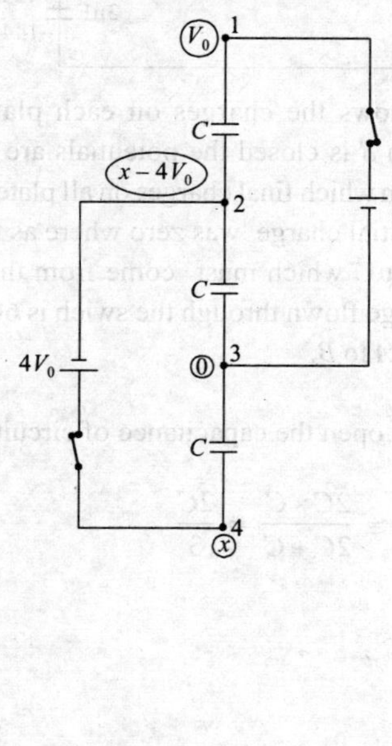

Writing nodal equation for x gives

$$C(x-0)+C(x-4V_0-0)+C(x-4V_0-V_0)=0$$

$$\Rightarrow \quad 3x=9V_0$$

$$\Rightarrow \quad x=3V_0$$

charge on lowest plate of capacitor between plates 3 and 4 is given as

$$q=C(x-0)=3CV_0=\frac{3\epsilon_0 AV_0}{d}$$

(vii) Figure shows the initial charges on capacitors A and B

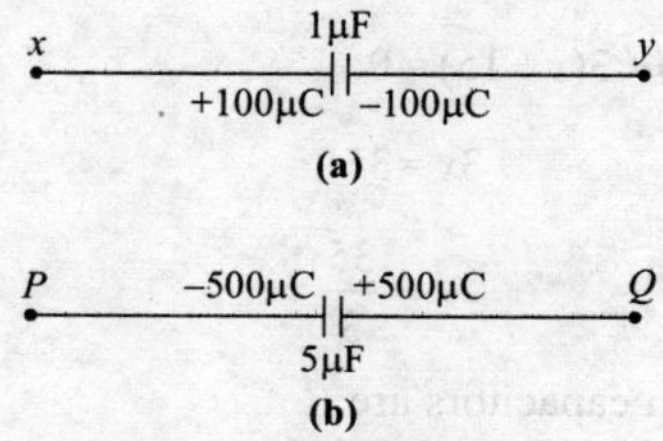

Initial energy of the two capacitors is

$$U_i=\frac{1}{2}\times 1\times(100)^2+\frac{1}{2}\times 5\times(100)^2$$

$$=3\times 10^4\ \mu J=0.03\text{ J}$$

After connection as shown in figure below final common potential difference of capacitor is given as

$$V_C=\frac{500-100}{1+5}=\frac{400}{6}=\frac{200}{3}\text{ V}$$

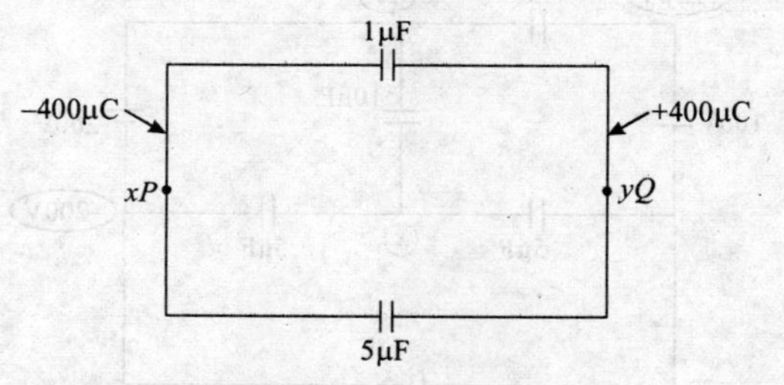

final charges on capacitor are given as

$$q_{1\mu F}=1\times\frac{200}{3}=\frac{200}{3}\ \mu C$$

$$q_{5\mu F}=5\times\frac{200}{3}=\frac{1000}{3}\ \mu C$$

Final energy stored in capacitors is given as

$$U_f=\frac{1}{2}\times 6\times 10^{-6}\times\left(\frac{200}{3}\right)^2$$

$$=\frac{4}{3}\times 10^{-2}=0.0133\text{ J}$$

Loss in energy $\quad \Delta U=U_i-U_f=0.03-0.0133=0.0167\text{ J}$

(viii) Distributing potentials as shown in figure

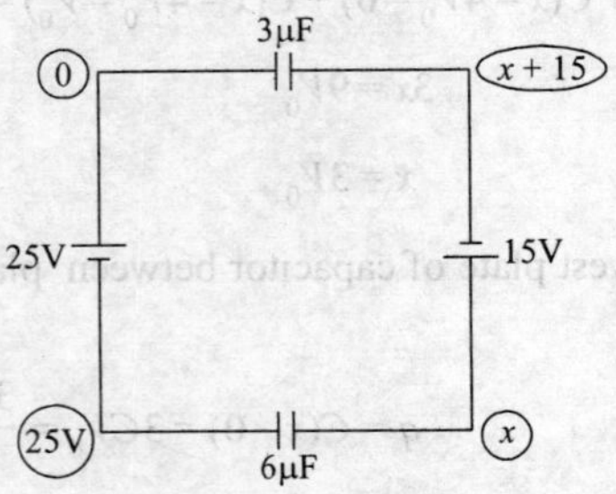

Writing nodal equation for x gives

$$6(x-25)+3(x+15)=0$$

$$\Rightarrow \quad 3x=35$$

$$\Rightarrow \quad x=\frac{35}{3}$$

Thus charge on capacitors are

$$q_{6\mu F}=6|(x-25)|=6\left|\left(\frac{35}{3}-25\right)\right|=80\ \mu C$$

and $$q_{3\mu F}=3|x+15|=3\left|\frac{35}{3}+15\right|=80\ \mu C$$

(ix) We distribute the potentials in the circuit shown in figure below

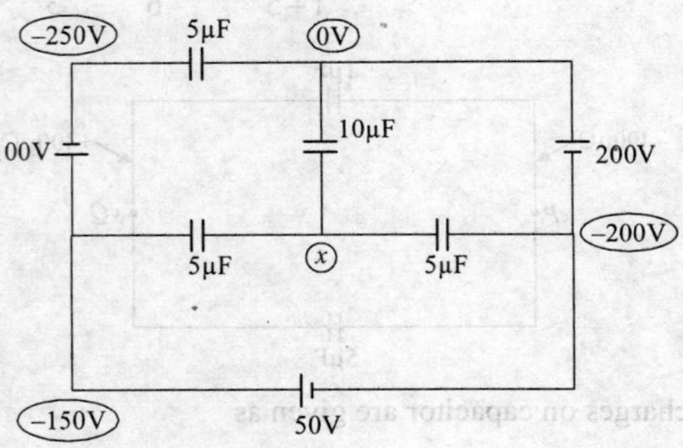

Writing nodal equation for x gives

$$10x+5(x+200)+5(x+150)=0$$

$$\Rightarrow \quad 4x=-350$$

$$\Rightarrow \quad x=-70\text{ V}$$

Thus charge on 10mF capacitor is given as

$$q_{10\mu F}=10\times 70=700\ \mu C$$

(x) In the circuit we distribute the potentials as shown in figure below with reference to a zero potential considered at negative terminal of 20V battery.

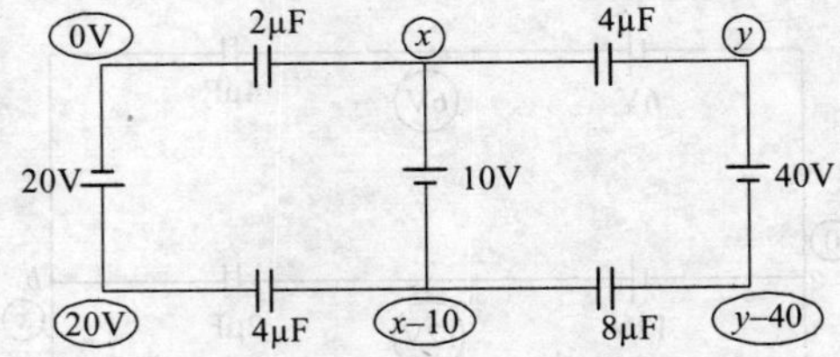

Writing nodal equations for x and y gives

$$2x+4(x-y)+4(x-10-20)+8(x-10-y+40)=0$$

$$\Rightarrow \quad 9x-6y=-60$$

$$\Rightarrow \quad 3x-2y=-20 \quad \ldots(1)$$

and $4(y-x)+8(y-40-x+10)=0$

$$\Rightarrow \quad 3y-3x=60$$

$$\Rightarrow \quad y-x=20 \quad \ldots(2)$$

Solving equaitons-(1) and (2) gives

$$x=20\text{ V}$$

This gives charge on 2mF capacitor as

$$q_{2\mu F}=2x=2\times 20=40\ \mu C$$

Solutions of PRACTICE EXERCISE 2.6

(i) When switch is open equivalent circuit is shown in figure and equivalent capacitance is given as

$$C_{eq}=\frac{3\times 2}{3+2}=\frac{6}{5}=1.2\ \mu F$$

Charge on each capacitor in series is

$$q=C_{eq}V_{total}=1.2\times 120$$

$$\Rightarrow \quad q=144\ \mu C$$

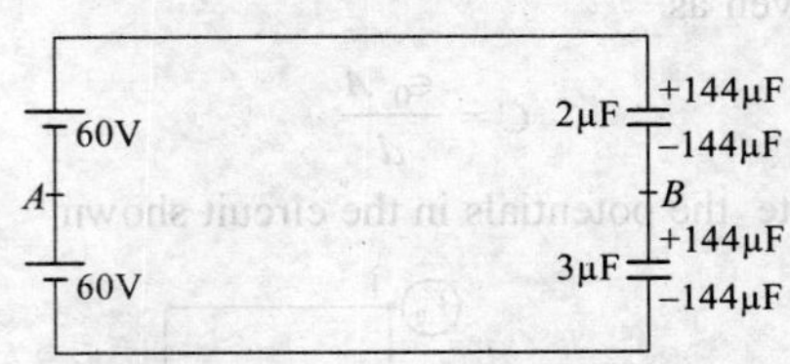

Above figure shows the charges on each plate of the two capacitors. When S is closed the potentials are distributed in circuit below from which final charges on all plates are obtained At terminal B initial charge was zero where as final charge is 180 – 120 = 60 μC which must come from the switch after closing thus charge flown through the swich is 60 μC from left to right i.e from. A to B.

(ii) When S is open the capacitance of circuit is

$$C_{initial}=\frac{2C\times C}{2C+C}=\frac{2C}{3}$$

After closing the switch final capacitance of circuit is

$$C_{\text{final}} = C$$

(a) Charge flown through battery is

$$\Delta Q = \Delta C \times V$$

$$\Rightarrow \quad \Delta Q = \left(C - \frac{2C}{3}\right)V = \frac{CV}{3} = \frac{2\times 30}{3} = 20\ \mu C$$

(b) Heat produced is

$$H = W_B - \Delta U = \Delta QV - \left(\frac{1}{2}CV^2 - \frac{1}{2}\frac{2CV^2}{3}\right)$$

$$\Rightarrow \quad H = 600 - (900 - 600) = 300\ \mu J = 0.3\ \text{mJ}$$

(c) Energy supplied by the battery is

$$W = \Delta QV = 600\ \mu J = 0.6\ \text{mJ}$$

(d) Initial charge on all capacitor plates connected to right side of switch is zero and finally after closing the switch final charge on right side of switch is the charge on right capacitor as both the left capacitors are short circuited. The charge on right capacitor after closing the switch is

$$q_f = 60\ \mu C$$

Thus total charge flown through switch is 60μC.

(iii) Initial charges on capacitors are

$$q_{1\mu F} = 1 \times 20 = 20\ \mu C$$

$$q_{2\mu F} = 2 \times 15 = 30\ \mu C$$

Distributing potentials in circuit shown

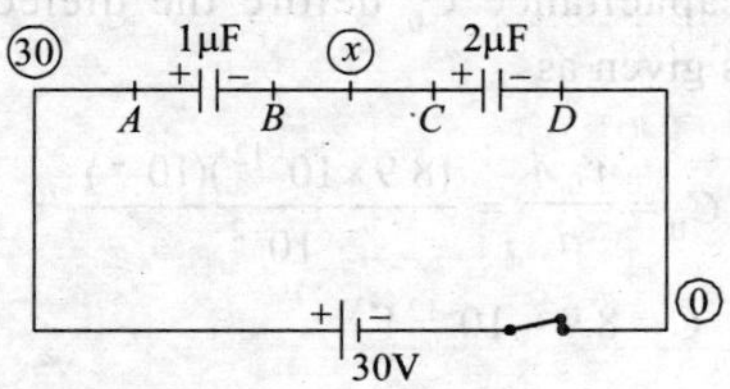

Writing nodal equation for x gives

$$2x + 1(x - 30) = 10$$

$$\Rightarrow \quad 3x = 40$$

$$\Rightarrow \quad x = \frac{40}{3}\ \text{V}$$

Thus final charges on capacitors are

$$q_{1\mu F} = 1 \times \left(30 - \frac{40}{3}\right) = \frac{50}{3}\ \mu C$$

$$\Rightarrow \quad q_{2\mu F} = 2 \times \frac{40}{3} = \frac{80}{3}\ \mu C$$

Students can also try and verify the results by solving above equation using method of flow of charges.

(iv) When S is open circuit is shown in figure below with left two capacitors are short circuited.

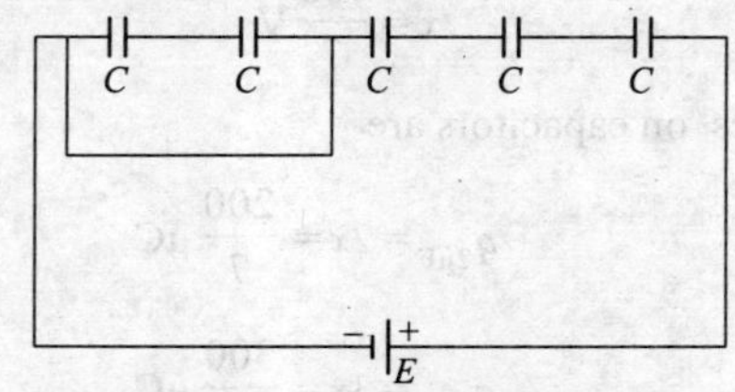

Thus charge on thre three remaining capacitors are

$$q = \left(\frac{C}{3}\right)E = \frac{CE}{3}$$

After closing the switch circuit becomes as shown in figure below in which the potentials can be calculated by series parallel or nodal analysis as mentioned in the figure.

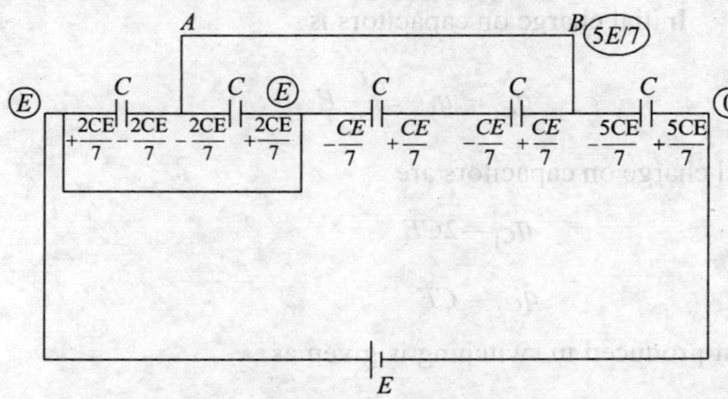

Now equivalent capacitance becomes

$$C_{eq} = \frac{\frac{5C}{2} \times C}{\frac{5C}{2} + C} = \frac{5C}{7}$$

Thus final charges on plates are shown in figure. Initial charge on terminal B wa zero and final is

$$-\frac{5CE}{7} + \frac{CE}{7} = -\frac{4CE}{7}$$

Thus charge flown from B to A through the switch is $\frac{4CE}{7}$.

(v) Distributing potenital in circuit shown below after closing the switch

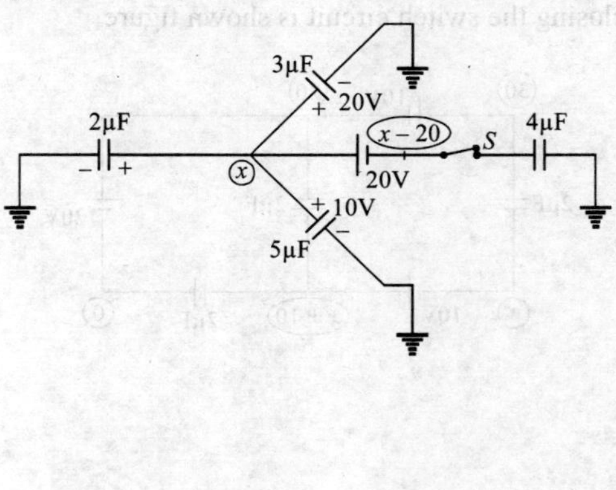

Writing nodal equation for x gives

$$2x+3x+5x+4(x-20)=120$$

$$\Rightarrow \quad 14x=200$$

$$\Rightarrow \quad x=\frac{100}{7}\text{ V}$$

Final charges on capacitors are

$$q_{2\mu F}=2x=\frac{200}{7}\ \mu C$$

$$q_{3\mu F}=3x=\frac{300}{7}\ \mu C$$

$$q_{5\mu F}=5x=\frac{500}{7}\ \mu C$$

$$q_{4\mu F}=4|(x-20)|=\frac{160}{7}\ \mu C$$

(vi) Initial charge on capacitors is

$$q_{C_1}=q_{C_2}=\frac{C}{2}E$$

final charge on capacitors are

$$q_{C_1}=2CE$$

$$q_{C_2}=CE$$

Heat produced in switching is given as

$$H=\frac{\Delta q_{C_1}^2}{2C_1}+\frac{\Delta q_{C_2}^2}{2C_2}$$

$$\Rightarrow \quad H=\frac{\left(\frac{3}{2}CE\right)^2}{2C}+\frac{\left(\frac{1}{2}CE\right)^2}{2C}$$

$$\Rightarrow \quad H=\frac{9}{8}CE^2+\frac{1}{8}CE^2=\frac{5}{4}CE^2$$

(vii) When switch is open charge on capacitors are

$$q_{C_1}=q_{C_2}=1\times 20=20\ \mu C$$

$$q_{C_3}=0$$

After closing the switch circuit is shown figure

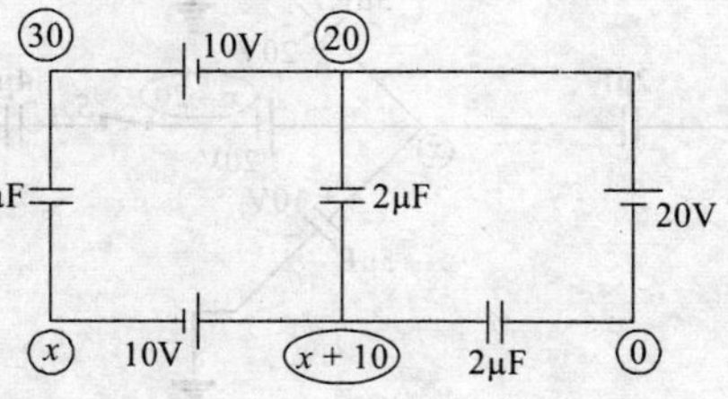

Writing nodal equation for x gives

$$2(x+10)+2(x+10-20)+2(x-30)=0$$

$$3x=30$$

$$x=10\text{ V}$$

Thus find charge on capacitors is

$$q_{C_1}=2\times 20=40\ \mu C$$

$$q_{C_2}=0$$

$$q_{C_3}=2\times 20=20\ \mu C$$

Thus heat produced on closing the switch is

$$H=\frac{\Delta q_1^2}{2C_1}+\frac{\Delta q_2^2}{2C_2}+\frac{\Delta q_3^2}{2C_3}=300\ \mu J=0.3\text{ mJ}$$

(viii) Initial charge on capacitors is

$$q_{4\mu F}=q_{2\mu F}=\frac{4}{3}\times 30=40\ \mu C$$

After closing the switch charge on capacitors are

$$q_{4\mu F}=4\times 10=40\ \mu C$$

$$q_{2\mu F}=2\times 20=40\ \mu C$$

As there is no change in charges on capacitors so no heat will be produced.

Solutions of PRACTICE EXERCISE 2.7

(i) The capacitance C_0 before the dielectric slab is introduced is given as

$$C_0=\frac{\varepsilon_0 A}{d}=\frac{(8.9\times 10^{-12})(10^{-2})}{10^{-2}}$$

$$C=8.9\times 10^{-12}\text{ F}$$

Free charge on plates is given as

$$q=C_0V_0=(8.9\times 10^{-12})\times 100$$

$$\Rightarrow \quad q=8.9\times 10^{-10}\text{ C}$$

Now, Electric field intensity between plates is

$$E_0=\frac{V_0}{d}=\frac{100}{10^{-2}}=1.0\times 10^4\text{ V/m}$$

As battery is removed plate charge will remain constant and electric field intensity in dielectric is given as

$$E=\frac{E_0}{k}=\frac{1.0\times 10^4}{7}=1.43\times 10^3\text{ V/m}$$

Potential difference between the plates with dielectric present is given by

$$V = E_0(d-b) + E\,b$$

$$\Rightarrow \quad V = (1.0\times10^4)(10^{-2} - 0.5\times10^{-2}) + (1.43\times10^3)(0.5\times10^{-2})$$

$$\Rightarrow \quad V = 57\,\text{V}$$

The free charge on the plate will remain the same as before. The capacitance with dielectric present is given as

$$C = \frac{q}{V} = \frac{839\times10^{-10}}{57}$$

$$C = 16\times10^{-12}\,\text{F} = 16\,\mu\text{F}$$

(ii) Initially, the capacitor is equivalent to two capacitors C_1 and C_2 in series which is given as

$$\frac{1}{C} = \frac{1}{C_1} + \frac{1}{C_2}$$

where $C_1 = \dfrac{\varepsilon_0 A}{0.5\times10^{-3}}$ and $C_2 = \dfrac{K\varepsilon_0 A}{9.5\times10^{-3}}$

$$\Rightarrow \quad C = 1802\,\varepsilon_0 A$$

charge on plates is given as

$$q = CV = 1802\,\varepsilon_0 A\times100 = 180200\,\varepsilon_0 A$$

The capacitance after the removal of crystalline plate is given as

$$C' = \frac{\varepsilon_0 A}{d} = \frac{\varepsilon_0 A}{1\times10^{-2}} = 100\,\varepsilon_0 A$$

If the new potential difference be V', then we use

$$q = CV = C'V'$$

$$\Rightarrow \quad 1802\times100\times\varepsilon_0 A = 100\,\varepsilon_0 A\,V'$$

$$\Rightarrow \quad V' = 1802\,\text{V}$$

(iii) For the given situation as $d << R$ we can consider the given cylindrical capacitor as a parallel plate capacitor so the capacitance when dielectric is filled upto a distance x into capacitor is given as

$$C = \frac{k\,\epsilon_0\,(2\pi Rx)}{d} + \frac{\epsilon_0\,(2\pi R(l-x)}{d}$$

$$\Rightarrow \quad C = \frac{2\pi R\,\epsilon_0}{d}(l - x + kx)$$

Energy stored in capacitor is

$$U = \frac{1}{2}CV^2 = \frac{\pi R\,\epsilon_0\,V^2}{d}(l - x + kx)$$

Force on dielectric is given is

$$F = \left|\frac{dU}{dx}\right| = \frac{\pi R\,\epsilon_0\,V^2}{d}(k-1)$$

(iv) (a) The capacitor of A without dielectric is given as half capacitor

$$C_1 = \frac{\varepsilon_0 A}{d} = \frac{(8.85\times10^{-12})(0.02)}{8.85\times10^{-4}}$$

$$\Rightarrow \quad C_1 = 0.2\times10^{-9}\,\text{F}$$

If the capacitor with dielectric be C_2 for half of A we have then

$$C_2 = \frac{k\varepsilon_0 A}{d} = \frac{(8.85\times10^{-12})(0.02)}{8.85\times10^{-4}}\times9$$

$$\Rightarrow \quad C_2 = 1.8\times10^{-9}\,\text{F}$$

Total capacitance of capacitor A with half filled dielectric is

$$C = C_1 + C_2 = 2\times10^{-9}\,\text{F}$$

Energy stored $U = \dfrac{1}{2}CV^2$

$$\Rightarrow \quad U = \frac{1}{2}\times(2\times10^{-9})\times(110)^2$$

$$\Rightarrow \quad U = 1.21\times10^{-5}\,\text{J}$$

(b) When the slab is removed, the find in capacitor will be energy $Q^2/2C$

$$Q = C_A V = 2\times10^{-9}\times110$$

$$Q = 220\times10^{-9}\,\text{C}$$

Find capacitance of empty capacitor A is

$$C_A = \frac{\varepsilon_0 A}{d} = \frac{8.85\times10^{-12}\times0.04}{8.85\times10^{-4}}$$

$$C_A = 0.4\times10^{-9}\,\text{F}$$

Find energy is given as

$$U_f = \frac{Q^2}{2C} = \frac{(220\times10^{-9})(220\times10^{-9})}{2\times0.4\times10^{-9}}$$

$$\Rightarrow \quad U_f = 6.05\times10^{-5}\,\text{J}$$

Workdone by external agency is given as

$$W = U_f - U_i = 6.05\times10^{-5} - 1.21\times10^{-5}$$

$$= 4.84\times10^{-5}\,\text{J}$$

(c) Capacitance capacitor A is given as

$$C_A = \frac{\varepsilon_0 A}{d}$$

$$C_A = 0.4\times10^{-9}\,\text{F}$$

Capacitance capacitor B with dielectric is given as

$$C_B = \frac{(8.85\times10^{-12})(0.02)}{8.85\times10^{-4}}\times 9 = 1.8\times10^{-9}\,\text{F}$$

The charge is shared by both. So find common potential difference across capacitors is given as
Common potential = charge/total capacity

$$V_C = \frac{220\times10^{-9}}{2.2\times10^{-9}} = 100\,V$$

Capcitance system in

$$C = (1.8+0.4)\mu\text{F}$$

Energy stored in system is

$$U = \frac{1}{2}CV^2 = \frac{1}{2}\times(2.2\times10^{-9})\times(100)^2$$

$$\Rightarrow \quad U = 1.1\times10^{-5}\,\text{J}$$

(v) (a) Before filling the dielectric, the equivalent capacitance of system is

$$C_1 = \frac{C\times C}{C+C} = \frac{C}{2}$$

Charge on plates of each capacitor is

$$q_0 = \frac{C}{2}\times V$$

After introducing the dielectric, the equivalent capacitance is given as

$$C_2 = \frac{C\times(KC)}{C+(KC)} = \frac{KC}{(1+K)}$$

New charge on plates of each capacitor is

$$q_2 = \frac{KC}{(1+K)}\times V$$

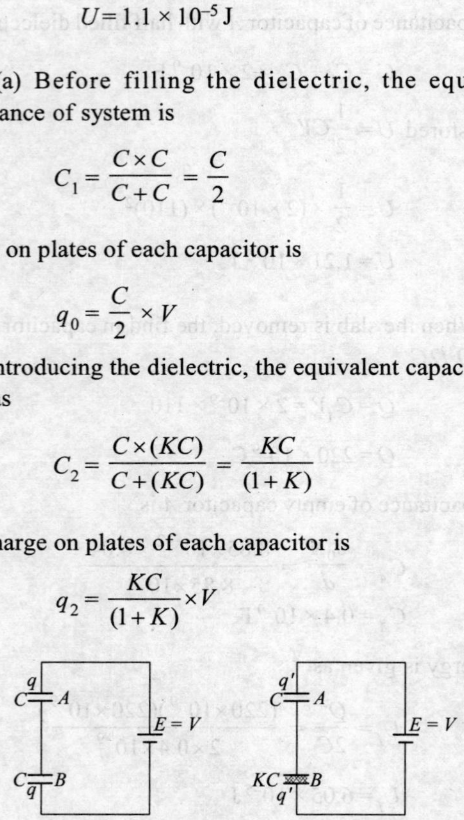

(a) (b)

Electric field strength before introducing dielectric is each capacitor is

$$E_1 = \frac{V/2}{d} = \frac{V}{2d}$$

Electric field strength after introducing dielectric is given as

$$E_2 = \frac{V_f}{d} = \frac{q_2/KC}{d} = \frac{V}{(1+K)d}$$

$$\Rightarrow \quad \frac{E_1}{E_2} = \frac{(V/2d)}{V/((1+K)f)} = \left(\frac{K+1}{2}\right)$$

(b) Charge flown through battery is

$$\Delta q = q_2 - q_1 = \frac{KC}{(1+K)}V - \frac{CV}{2} = \frac{CV}{2}\left(\frac{K-1}{K+1}\right).$$

(vi) The relative permittivity at a distance x from left plate in dielectric is given as

$$\in(x) = \in_1 + \left(\frac{\in_2 - \in_1}{d}\right)x$$

we consider an elemental capacitor as shown in figure of which capacitance is given as

$$dC = \frac{\in(x)\in_0 A}{dx}$$

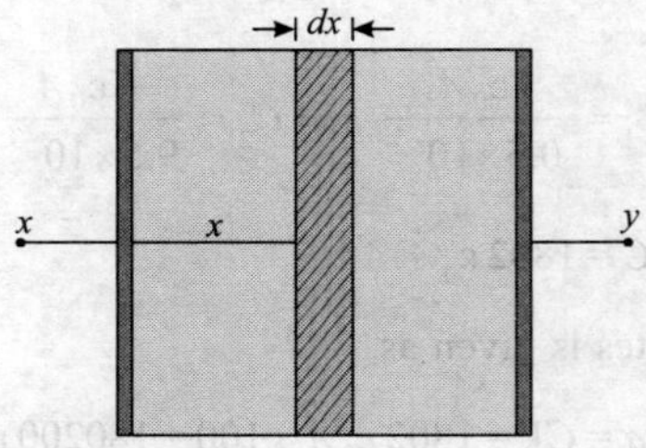

As all such elemental capacitors are in series we use

$$\frac{1}{C_{xy}} = \int\frac{1}{dC} = \int_0^d \frac{dx}{\in_0 A\left[\in_1 + \left(\frac{\in_2 - \in_1}{d}\right)x\right]}$$

$$\Rightarrow \quad \frac{1}{C_{xy}} = \frac{d}{\in_0 A(\in_2 - \in_1)}\left[\ln[\in_1 d + (\in_2 - \in_1)x]\right]_0^d$$

$$\Rightarrow \quad \frac{1}{C_{xy}} = \frac{d}{\in_0 A(\in_2 - \in_1)}\ln\left(\frac{\in_2}{\in_1}\right)$$

$$\Rightarrow \quad C_{xy} = \frac{\in_0 A(\in_2 - \in_1)}{d\ln\left(\frac{\in_2}{\in_1}\right)}$$

(vii) Leakage current in a leaky capacitor is given as

$$i = \frac{q_0}{RC}e^{-t/RC} = \frac{q}{\rho k\in_0}e^{-t/\rho k\in_0}$$

$$\Rightarrow \quad i = \frac{q_0\sigma}{k\in_0}e^{-\frac{\sigma t}{k\in_0}}$$

At $t = 12$s current is given as

$$i = \frac{8.85\times10^{-6}\times7.4\times10^{-12}}{5\times8.85\times10^{-12}}e^{-\frac{7.4\times10^{-12}\times12}{5\times8.85\times10^{-12}}}$$

$$\Rightarrow \quad i = 1.48\times10^{-6}(2.718)^{-2} = 0.2\times10^{-6}$$

$$\Rightarrow \quad i = 0.2\ \mu\text{A}$$

(viii) In air electric field is given as

$$E_0 = \frac{\sigma}{\varepsilon_0} = \frac{q}{A\varepsilon_0}$$

In dielectric, field is given as

$$E = \frac{E_0}{k}$$

and in conductor field is zero. Hence, the E-x graph is as shown in figure.

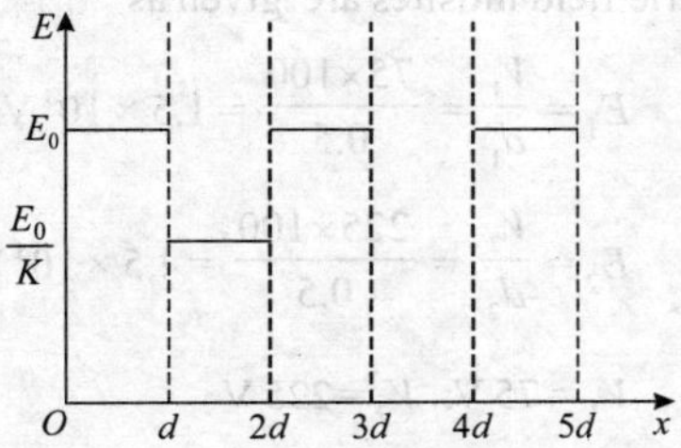

Using $V = Ed$ (in uniform field) and assuming the potential at positive plate as V_0, the V-x graph is as shown.

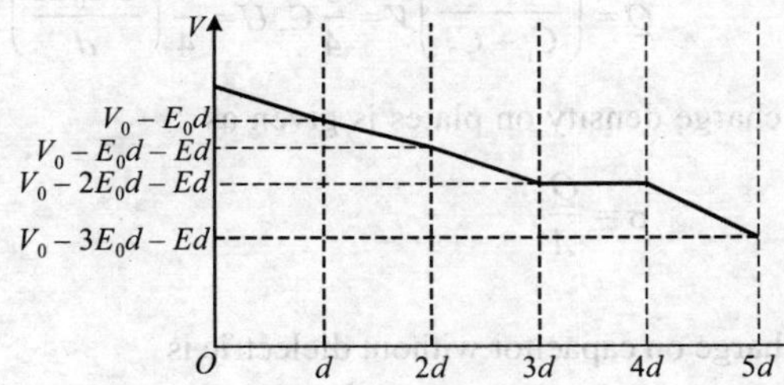

(ix) Since collision is elastic the velocity of dielectric after collision is v_0.

Dielectric will move and when it is coming out of capacitor a force is exterted on it by the capacitor in inward direction which is given as

$$F = \frac{E^2\varepsilon_0 b(K-1)}{2d}$$

Which decreases its speed to zero, till it comes out it travels a distance a so we use

$$\frac{1}{2}Mv_0^2 = \frac{E^2\varepsilon_0 b(K-1)a}{2d}$$

$$\Rightarrow \quad v_0 = E\left[\frac{\varepsilon_0 ab(K-1)}{Md}\right]^{1/2}$$

(x) If liquid is rising upto a maximum height h is capacitor plates we use

$$\frac{q^2}{2C_1} = \frac{q^2}{2C_2} + mg\frac{h}{2} \quad \ldots(1)$$

where $\quad C_1 = \frac{\epsilon_0 A}{d}$

$$\Rightarrow \quad q = C_1V = \frac{\epsilon_0 AV}{d}$$

and $\quad C_2 = \frac{k\epsilon_0 h(A/l)}{d} + \frac{\epsilon_0(l-h)(A/l)}{d}$

$$\Rightarrow \quad C_2 = \frac{\epsilon_0 A}{ld}(l-h+kh)$$

Thus we have from equation-(1)

$$\frac{1}{2}\frac{\epsilon_0 AV^2}{d} = \frac{\epsilon_0^2 A^2V^2}{2d^2}\,\frac{dl}{\epsilon_0 A(l-h+kh)} + \rho hd(A/l)g\frac{h}{2}$$

$$\Rightarrow \quad \frac{\epsilon_0 AV^2}{2d}\left(1-\frac{l}{l-h+kh}\right) = \frac{\rho gdAh^2}{2l}$$

$$\Rightarrow \quad \frac{\epsilon_0 AV^2}{d}\left[\frac{R(k-1)}{l+h(k-1)}\right] = \frac{\rho gdAh^2}{l}$$

$$\Rightarrow \quad V = \sqrt{\frac{\rho ghd^2(l+h(k-1))}{\epsilon_0 l(k-1)}}$$

(xi) We consider an elemental capacitance of with dx as shown in figure between plates of which capacitance is given as

$$dC = \frac{(\epsilon_0 + \beta x)A}{dx} \qquad \text{for } x < \frac{d}{2}$$

and $\quad dC' = \frac{[\epsilon_0 + \beta(d-x)]A}{dx} \qquad \text{for } x > \frac{d}{2}$

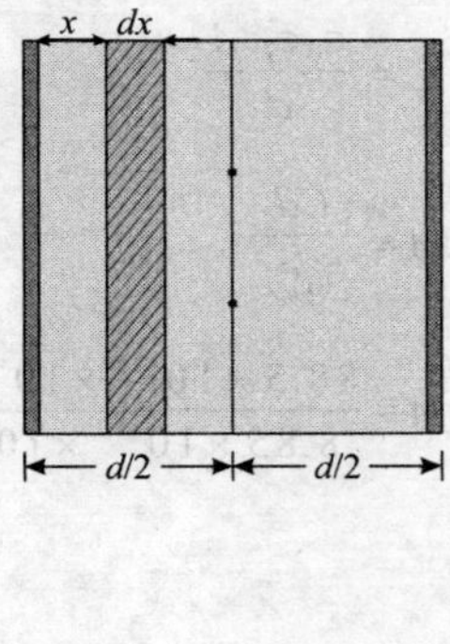

Solutions of CONCEPTUAL MCQs Single Option Correct

Sol. 1 (C) As the charging battery is disconnected, charge on plates of capacitor will remain constant and on inserting the dielectric slab capacitance increases so potential difference decreases and stored energy also decreases. Thus option (C) is correct.

Sol. 2 (A) From the given circuit we can see that there are two capacitors formed which are connected in parallel across the battery so total charge supplied by the battery to the middle plate is sum of the charges on the two capacitors which is given as

$$q=(C_1+C_2)V=\left[\frac{\varepsilon_1\varepsilon_0 A}{d_1}+\frac{\varepsilon_2\varepsilon_0 A}{d_2}\right]V$$

Surface charge density is given as

$$\sigma=\frac{q}{A}=\varepsilon_0 V\left[\frac{\varepsilon_1}{d_1}+\frac{\varepsilon_2}{d_2}\right]$$

Sol. 3 (D) The electric field between the plates of capacitor is given as

$$E=\frac{2Q}{2A\varepsilon_0}+\frac{Q}{2A\varepsilon_0}$$

$$\Rightarrow \quad E=\frac{3Q}{2A\varepsilon_0}=\frac{3}{2}\frac{Q}{Cd}$$

$$\Rightarrow \quad Ed=\frac{3Q}{2C}=V$$

The force between the two plates is given as

$$F=QE$$

$$F=Q\left(\frac{2Q}{2A\varepsilon_0}\right)$$

$$F=\frac{Q^2}{A\varepsilon_0}$$

Energy stored betwen pltes is given as

$$U=\frac{1}{2}\varepsilon_0 E^2 Ad$$

$$U=\frac{1}{2}\varepsilon_0\left(\frac{3Q}{2Cd}\right)^2 Ad$$

$$U=\frac{9}{8}\frac{Q^2}{C}$$

Thus option (D) is INCORRECT.

Sol. 4 (C) Each capacitor is charged and then removed from the battery. Changing the plate separation in a parallel plate capacitor or the radius of any shell or cylinder in the spherical or the cylindrical capacitors will not change the charge on any capacitor. Each capacitor, in the disconnected state, is an isolated system.

In situation I, as $C=\frac{\varepsilon_0 A}{d}$, capacitance will increase as d is reduced. $V=\frac{Q}{C}$ decreases as Q being the same.

In situation II, as $C=4\pi\varepsilon_0\frac{ab}{b-a}=4\pi\varepsilon_0\frac{a}{1-a/b}$, a and b are the radii of the inner and the outer spherical shells, respectively.

As b is increased, capacity will reduce and $V=\frac{Q}{C}$ increases as Q being the same.

In situation III, as $C=2\pi\varepsilon_0\frac{L}{\ln(b/a)}$, L is the length of cylinders, a and b are the radii of inner and outer cylinders, respectively.

As b is increased, capacity will decrease and $V=\frac{Q}{C}$ increases as Q being the same.

Sol. 5 (C) As outer plate terminals are open no charge flow will take place anywhere. The capacitance is halved as the two capacitors are connected in series so, the potential difference is now doubled acorss the outer plate terminals.

Sol. 6 (A) Five capacitors in parallel gives $5\times 2\mu F=10\mu F$ capacitance and two capacitors in series gives a capacity $1\mu F$. When the two combinations are connected in series, the resultant capacitance will be $(10\times 1)/(10+1)=(10/11)\mu F$.

Sol. 7 (B) In circuit (a) one plate of one capcitor is connect directly to another capacitor so these are in series. In circuit (b) and (c) both the two plates of each capacitor is connected across the battery so both the capcitors are connected in parallel across the battery in both the circuits. Thus option (B) is correct.

Sol. 8 (C) The potential difference across each capacitor in series across a voltage V is equally divided so we have

$$V_C=\frac{V}{2}$$

Capacitance of capacitor is given as

$$C=\frac{Q}{V/2}=\frac{2Q}{V}$$

Thus option (C) is correct.

Sol. 9 (C) For an isolated capacitor, charge on it remains same so electric field between the plates remains constant.

Sol. 10 (C) In the direction of electric field potential continuously decreases as inside or outside the slab electric field direciton is same from left to right.

Sol. 11 (B) As capacitance of B increases due to insertion of dielectric the potential difference across B decreases as in series combination potential difference is distributed in inverse ratio of capacitances. Thus potential difference across A increases so energy stored in capacitor A will increase. Thus opiton (B) is correct.

Sol. 12 (D) The voltage across each capacitor will be V/n. Thus energy stored in each capacitor will be given as

$$U=\frac{1}{2}C\left(\frac{V}{n}\right)^2=\frac{CV^2}{2n^2}$$

Sol. 13 (A) Electric field between the two plates is given as

$$E=\frac{\sigma}{\epsilon_0}$$

Half of above electric field is contributed by one plate and remaining half is contributed by other plate. The electric field on the charge is given as

$$F=qE$$

$$F=q\frac{\sigma}{\epsilon_0}$$

If one plate is removed then electric field on the charge will be only due to the remaining plate which is half of the initial field so new force will beclome

$$F'=q\frac{\sigma}{2\epsilon_0}=\frac{F}{2}$$

Sol. 14 (D) As system is connected to earth, system potential will be maintained to zero so its capacitance will be infinite.

Sol. 15 (C) Displacement current through the capcitor is given as

$$i_d=\epsilon_0 A\left(\frac{dE}{dt}\right)$$

From $t=0$ to $4\ \mu s$,

$$i_d=8.85\times10^{-12}\times1\times\frac{0.4\times10^6}{y\times10^{-6}}=0.885\text{A}$$

From $t=4\mu s$ to $8\mu s$,

$$i_d=8.85\times10^{-12}\times1\times0=0$$

Sol. 16 (B) As battery is disconnected after charging then charge on capacitor will remain constant and it is given as

$$Q=CV=\frac{\epsilon_0 AV}{d}$$

After insertion of slab capacitance becomes

$$C'=kC=\frac{\epsilon_0 kA}{d}$$

The potential difference across the plates and electric field between the plates will now be

$$V'=\frac{V}{k}$$

and

$$E'=\frac{E}{k}=\frac{V}{kd}$$

Work done in insertion of slab is given as

$$W=U_f-U_i=\frac{\epsilon_0 AV^2}{2d}\left(1-\frac{1}{k}\right)$$

Thus option (B) above is INCORRECT.

Sol. 17 (C) If the potential at point D is considered as x then writing nodal equation at node D gives

$$\frac{x-V_1}{C_1}+\frac{x-V_2}{C_2}=0$$

Solving above equations, we get

$$x=\left[\frac{C_1V_1+C_2V_2}{C_1+C_2}\right]$$

Sol. 18 (C) The common potential after connections is given as

$$V'=\frac{2C\times2V-CV}{C+2C}=V$$

Final energy of the system of capacitor is given as

$$U=\frac{1}{2}(C+2C)V^2$$

$$\Rightarrow\qquad U=\frac{3}{2}CV^2$$

Thus option (C) is correct.

Sol. 19 (A) As battery is disconnected from the capacitor its charge will remain constant.

Sol. 20 (C) The potential difference across each capacitor is V so when these are connected in series the terminal potential difference will become nV.

equivalent capacitance is the series combination of all dC's so we use

$$\frac{1}{C_{eq}} = \int\left(\frac{1}{dC}+\frac{1}{dC'}\right)$$

$$\Rightarrow \quad \frac{1}{C_{eq}} = \int_0^{d/2}\frac{dx}{(\epsilon_0+\beta x)A} + \int_{d/2}^{d}\frac{dx}{[(\epsilon_0+\beta(d-x)]A}$$

$$\Rightarrow \quad \frac{1}{C_{eq}} = \frac{2}{A\beta}\left[\ln\left(\frac{\epsilon_0+\beta\frac{d}{2}}{\epsilon_0}\right)\right]$$

$$\Rightarrow \quad C_{eq} = \frac{A\beta}{2\ln\left(\frac{\epsilon_0+\beta\frac{d}{2}}{\epsilon_0}\right)}$$

Without dielectric capacitance is

$$C_{eq} = 2C$$

$$\Rightarrow \quad \frac{A\beta}{2\ln\left(\frac{\epsilon_0+\beta\frac{d}{2}}{\epsilon_0}\right)} = \frac{2\epsilon_0 A}{d}$$

$$\Rightarrow \quad \beta d = 4\epsilon_0 \ln\left(\frac{\epsilon_0+\beta\frac{d}{2}}{\epsilon_0}\right) \quad \ldots(1)$$

For all values of β satisfying equation-(1) we have $C_{eq} = 2C$.

(xii) For dielectirc strength maximum potential difference which can be applied across capacitor is related as

$$E_B = \frac{V}{d}$$

$$\Rightarrow \quad d = \frac{V}{E} = \frac{10^3}{10^6} = 10^{-3}\text{ m}$$

We use capacitance of capacitor

$$C = \frac{\epsilon_0\epsilon_r A}{d}$$

$$\Rightarrow \quad A = \frac{Cd}{\epsilon_0\epsilon_r}$$

$$\Rightarrow \quad A = \frac{88.5\times10^{-12}\times10^{-3}}{8.85\times10^{-12}\times10} = 10^{-3}\text{ m}^2$$

(xiii) We can consider the given capacitor as series combination of two capacitors, one field with glass and other filled with paraffin. if capacitance of glass ($k_p = 2$) filled capacitor is C than that of paraffin ($k_2 = 6$) filled capacitor will be 3 C. if potential differences across those are V_1 and V_2 we have

$$CV_1 = 3CV_2 \quad \ldots(1)$$

$$V_1 + V_2 = 300 \quad \ldots(2)$$

$$\Rightarrow \quad V_1 = 75\text{V and}$$

$$V_2 = 225\text{ V}$$

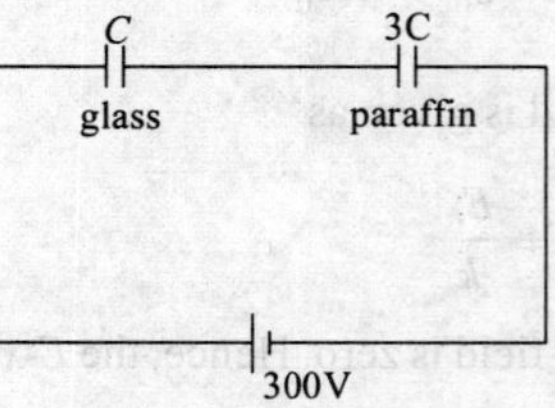

(a) Eelectric field intisites are given as

$$E_1 = \frac{V_1}{d_1} = \frac{75\times100}{0.5} = 1.5\times10^4\text{ V/m}$$

and $$E_2 = \frac{V_2}{d_2} = \frac{225\times100}{0.5} = 4.5\times10^4\text{ V/m}$$

(b) $V_1 = 75\text{ V};\ V_2 = 225\text{ V}$

(c) Free charge on plates in given as

$$Q = \left(\frac{C_1C_2}{C_1+C_2}\right)V = \frac{3}{4}C,\ U = \frac{3}{4}\left(\frac{2\epsilon_0 A}{d}\right)300$$

Surface charge density on plates is given as

$$\sigma = \frac{Q}{A}$$

(xiv) Charge on capacitor without dielectric is

$$q_0 = CV_0$$

when it is connected with another capacitor $C' = kC$ in parallel then final common potential difference is given as

$$V_C = \frac{q_0}{C+kC}$$

$$\Rightarrow \quad V_C = \frac{CV_0}{C(1+k)}$$

$$\Rightarrow \quad V_C(1+V_C) = V_0 \quad [\text{As } k = V_C]$$

$$V_C^2 + V_C - 156 = 0$$

$$\Rightarrow \quad (V_C+13)(V_C-12) = 0$$

$$\Rightarrow \quad V_C = 12\text{ V}$$

Sol. 21 (B) In the given system of sheets electric field only exist between the plates which is given as

$$E = \frac{\sigma}{\varepsilon_0} = \text{Constant}$$

Due to opposite polarity of charges on sheets in outside region at all points electric field will get cancelled out.

Sol. 22 (C) When a capacitor is charged by a battery then a charge equal to CV flows through the battery for which battery does a work equal to CV^2 and out of this amount $(1/2)CV^2$ is stored in the capacitor which is half of the total work done by battery. Remaining half is dissipated as heat in the circuit so we have

$$\frac{W_{Battery}}{E_{Stored}} = \frac{2}{1}$$

Sol. 23 (B) Figure below shows the respective capacitances between adjoining plates numbered 1 to 6.

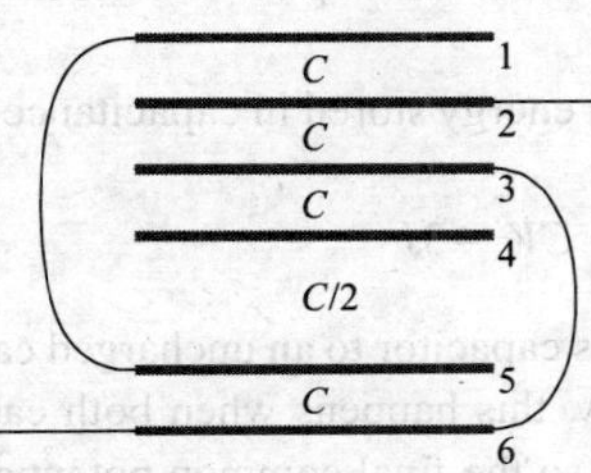

The equivalent circuit of the above system is as shown in figure below.

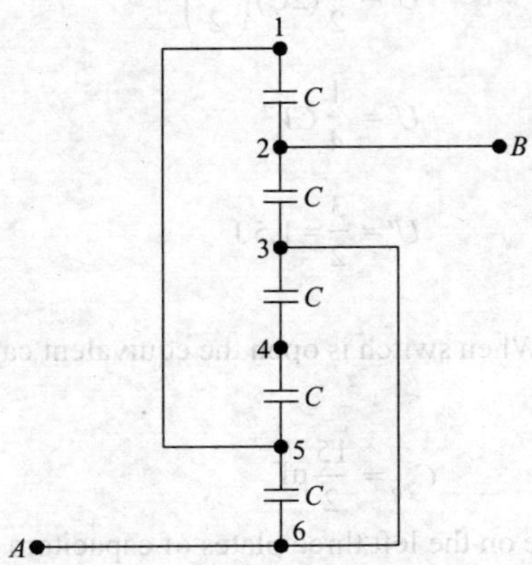

Above circuit can be redrawn as shown below.

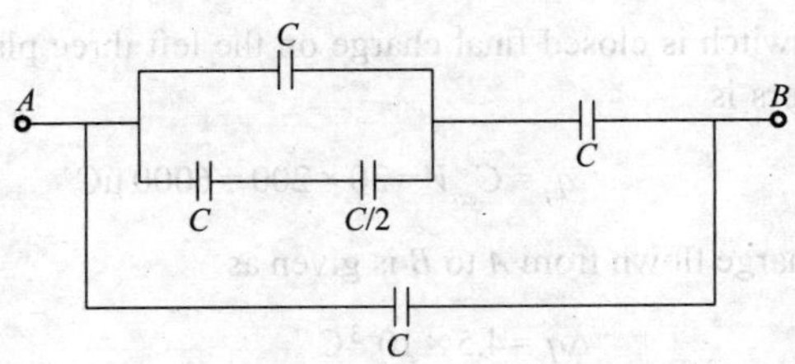

Thus across terminals AB equivalent capacitance is given as

$$C_{AB} = \frac{11}{7}C = \frac{11}{7}(7\mu F)$$

$$C_{AB} = 11\mu F$$

Sol. 24 (B) After reconnecting energy is supplied by the battery as charges will flow and capacitor is first discharged and then recharged to the same level by reverse polarity so incorrect statement is (B).

Sol. 25 (B) Initially capacitance is given as

$$C_{net} = \frac{(C_0)(C_0)}{C_0 + C_0} = \frac{C_0}{2} = 0.5C_0$$

Finally capacitance is given as

$$C_{net} = \frac{(C_0/2)(2C_0)}{(C_0/2) + 2C_0} = 0.4C_0$$

Sol. 26 (C) By branch manipulation we can consider that the two capacitors are connected in series across the series combination of the two cells in series so charge on each capacitor is given as

$$q = (E_1 + E_2)C_{net}$$

$$\Rightarrow \quad q = (E_1 + E_2)\frac{C_1C_2}{C_1 + C_2}$$

So the potential difference across the capacitor C_2 is given as

$$V_{ab} = \frac{q}{C_2} = \left(\frac{E_1 + E_2}{C_1 + C_2}\right)C_1$$

Sol. 27 (A) For a conductor if other conducting bodies approach it then due to induction potential of conductor decreases while charge remains constant so $C = \frac{Q}{V}$ increases. For all learners, it is important here to note that capacitance of an isolated conductor is not affected by changing its charge or potential but in present case this is not isolated.

Sol. 28 (D) Electroscopoe in the above case will read the battery voltage asit is connected in parallel so its reading will decrease only if battery voltage is decreased.

Sol. 29 (B) Initial charge on the capacitor is CV and energy stored is given as

$$U_i = \frac{1}{2}CV^2$$

After replacing the dielectric slab capacitance becomes $2C/3$

and charge will remain same as battery was disconnected so final energy in capacitor is given as

$$U_f = \frac{q^2}{2C'} = \frac{(CV)^2}{2(2C/3)} = \frac{3}{4}CV^2$$

Thus the ratio of energy stored is given as 3 : 2.

Sol. 30 (C) Figure below shows the connection for the desired capacitance.

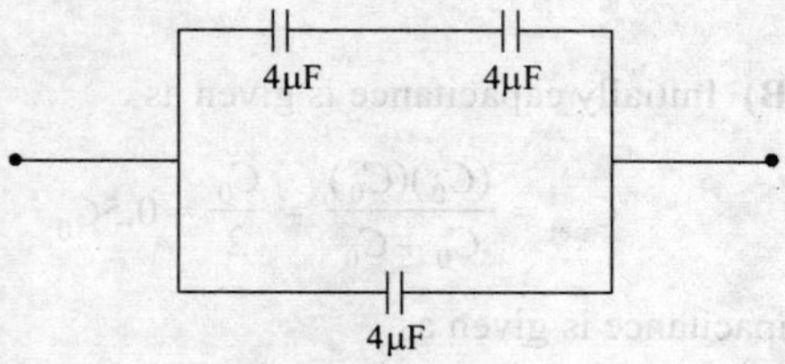

Sol. 31 (D) Net work done by the system in the process is zero, as in removing the dielectric, work done is equal and opposite to the work done in re-inserting the dielectric.

Sol. 32 (D) To get 1000 V from 250 V capacitor, we need four capacitors in series. Their capacitance becomes 2 μF. To get 16 μF, we have to connect 8 series, each of 4 capacitors in parallel. So total number of capacitors is 8 × 4 = 32.

Solutions of NUMERICAL MCQs Single Option Correct

Sol. 1 (C) The potential difference is divided in inverse ratio of capacitances in series combination so we use

$$V_{3\mu F} = \frac{6\times 120}{3+6} = 80\text{ V}$$

Sol. 2 (B) We can distribute the charges on plates on their inner and outer surfaces of the plates which gives the charges on capacitors to be 9 μC and 1 μC on the inner facing plates of the capacitors with their opposite polarity plates connected together. If the final potential difference across the capacitors is V then it is given as

$$V = \frac{9-1}{1+1} = 4\text{ V}$$

Sol. 3 (D) Equivalent capacitance of the series combination is given as

$$\frac{1}{C} = \frac{1}{2} + \frac{1}{3} + \frac{1}{4} = 1$$

$$\Rightarrow \quad C = 1\ \mu\text{F}$$

Steady state charge on all capacitors in series is given as

$$q = CV = 100\ \mu\text{C}$$

Sol. 4 (B) In steady state, the capacitor branch acts like an open circuit. So the potential difference across C is the same which is there across resistance r_2, given as

$$V_{r2} = Vr_2/(r_1 + r_2)$$

Sol. 5 (A) Potential difference between plates remains the same. Decrease in potential difference is compensated by potential difference due to the extra distance. As charge is same on plates electric field also remain constant. Thus we use

$$t\left(E - \frac{E}{k}\right) = Ed$$

$$\Rightarrow \quad t\left(1 - \frac{1}{k}\right) = d$$

$$\Rightarrow \quad k = \frac{t}{t-d} = 5$$

Here E is initial electric field between the plates, k dielectric constant of plate, t thickness of plate and d is the extra distance.

Sol. 6 (A) Initial energy stored in capacitance is

$$\frac{1}{2}CV^2 = 3\text{J}$$

On connecting this capacitor to an uncharged capacitor charge distributes equally, this happens when both capacitors are of same capacitance so the final common potential of the two in parallel will be V/2. So final energy stored in two capacitors is

$$U' = \frac{1}{2}(2C)\left(\frac{V}{2}\right)^2$$

$$U' = \frac{1}{4}CV^2$$

$$U' = \frac{3}{2} = 1.5\text{ J}$$

Sol. 7 (B) When switch is open the equivalent capacitance is given as

$$C_{eq} = \frac{15}{2}\mu\text{F}$$

Initial charge on the left three plates of capacitors is

$$q_i = C_{eq}V = \frac{15}{2} \times 200 = 1500\ \mu\text{C}$$

When switch is closed final charge on the left three plates of capacitors is

$$q_f = C_{eq}V = 30 \times 200 = 6000\ \mu\text{C}$$

Thus charge flown from A to B is given as

$$\Delta q = 4.5 \times 10^{-3}\text{ C}$$

Sol. 8 (C) Final common potential of the capacitors in parallel is given as

$$V' = \frac{CV}{C + C'}$$

$$\Rightarrow \quad 20 = \frac{200 \times 2}{2 + C}$$

$$\Rightarrow \quad C = 18\,\mu\text{F}$$

Sol. 9 (B) Reducing the circuit as shown below gives

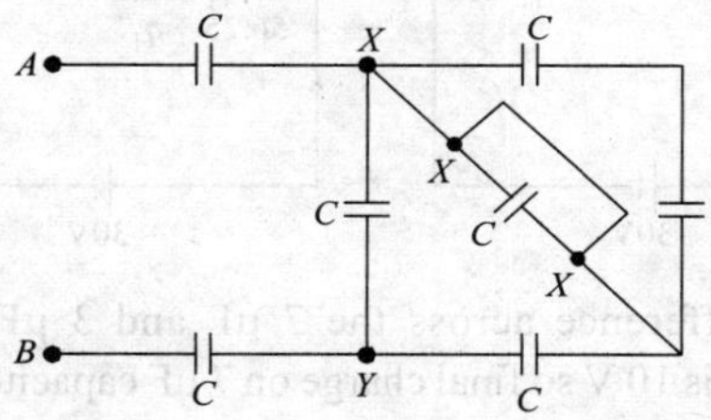

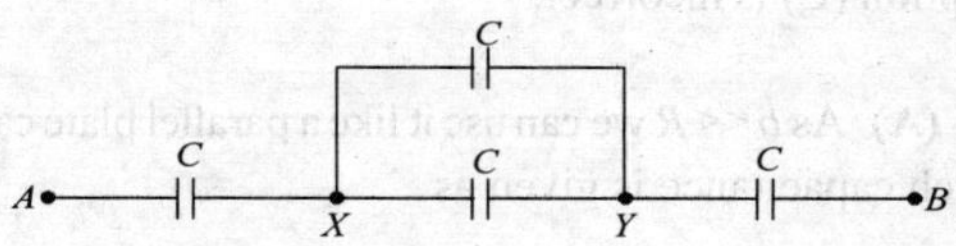

$$\frac{1}{C_{eq}} = \frac{1}{C} + \frac{1}{2C} + \frac{1}{C}$$

$$\Rightarrow \quad C_{eq} = \frac{2C}{5}$$

Sol. 10 (D) Charge in the circuit flows only when potential difference across C_1 is either greater or less than that across C_2 Thus charge flows when

$$\frac{q_1}{C_1} \neq \frac{q_2}{C_2}$$

$$\Rightarrow \quad q_1 C_2 \neq q_2 C_1$$

Sol. 11 (B) We can solve this by using method of flow of charges. If q charge flow through the circuit then writing the equation of potential drop across the loop of circuit, we have

$$19 + 15 + \frac{q}{3} - 9 + \frac{q}{2} = 0$$

$$\Rightarrow \quad 25 + \frac{5q}{6} = 0 \Rightarrow q = 30\,\mu\text{C}$$

Thus potential difference across 3 μF capacitor is given as

$$V = \frac{30\mu\text{C}}{3\mu\text{F}} = 10\,\text{V}$$

Above situation can also be easily solved by using branch manipulation or by using nodal analysis. Students can try using both the methods which are relatively shorter.

Sol. 12 (D) The charge on the capacitor before and after insertion of dielectric is given as

$$Q_1 = C_1 V$$

$$Q_2 = C_2 V$$

$$\Rightarrow \quad \frac{50}{150} = \frac{1}{k}$$

$$\Rightarrow \quad k = 3$$

Sol. 13 (D) After connections final common potential difference of the combination is given as

$$V = \frac{Q_1 + Q_2}{C_1 + C_2} = 0$$

Thus final charge on capacitors also become zero. Initial charge on capacitors is 30μC each which will discharge from D to A.

Sol. 14 (B) Total charge on the two shells is $1.25\,\mu\text{C} + 0.75\,\mu\text{C} = 2\,\mu\text{C}$.

Final charges q_1' and q_2' on shells are divided in same ratio of capacitances of shells so we have

$$q_1' : q_2' = R_1 : R_2 = 1 : 2$$

$$\Rightarrow \quad q_1' = \frac{1}{3} \times 2 = \frac{2}{3}\,\mu\text{C}$$

$$\Rightarrow \quad q_2' = \frac{2}{3} \times 2 = \frac{4}{3}\,\mu\text{C}$$

Sol. 15 (A) As 10 mF capacitor is connected directly across 200 V battery so the charge on capacitor is given as

$$Q = CV = (10 \times 10^{-6})(200) = 2 \times 10^{-3}\,\text{C}$$

Sol. 16 (B) The capacitance with dielectric inserted between the plate

$$C_k = \frac{\varepsilon_0 A}{d - b + \frac{b}{K}}$$

If $C_K = 2C$, then we use

$$\frac{\varepsilon_0 A}{d - b + \frac{b}{k}} = \frac{2\varepsilon_0 A}{d}$$

$$\Rightarrow \quad k = \frac{2b}{2b - d}$$

Thus for $k > 0$ and $b \leq d$

$$\Rightarrow \quad k = \frac{2b}{2b - d} \text{ and } 2b - d > 0$$

$$\Rightarrow \quad \frac{d}{2} < b \leq d$$

$$\Rightarrow \quad b > \frac{d}{2}$$

Sol. 17 (C) Initially on the left side of switch total charge is zero. After closing the switch circuit capacitance becomes 3 μF and final charge on the capacitors will be

$$q_1' = 25(4) = 100\,\mu\text{C}$$

$$q_2' = 25(2) = 50\,\mu\text{C}$$

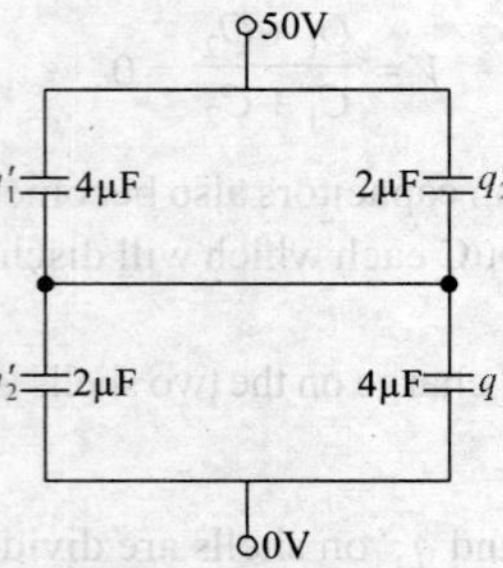

The total charge on left side of switch is given as

$$q = -q_1' + q_2'$$

$$\Rightarrow \quad q = -100 + 50 = -50\,\mu\text{C}$$

Thus the charge which flows from left to right through the switch is 50 μC.

Sol. 18 (C) Distributing potentials in circuit as shown below and writing nodal equation for x gives

$$(x+13) \times 3 = (27-x) \times 1$$

$$\Rightarrow \quad 3x + 39 = -x + 27$$

$$\Rightarrow \quad x = -3\text{ V}$$

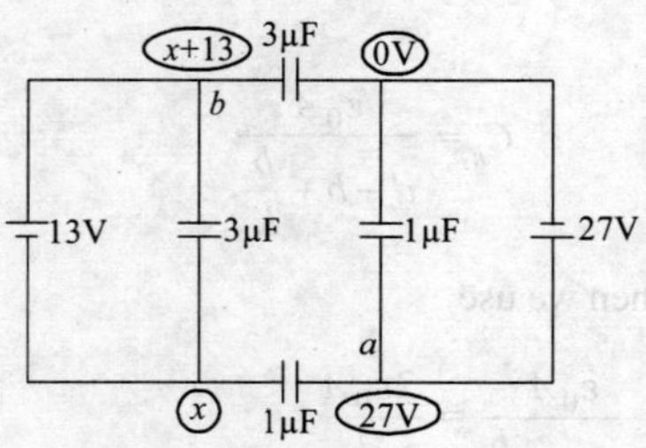

$$\Rightarrow \quad V_a - V_b = 27 - (x+13) = 17\text{ V}$$

Sol. 19 (B) When two capacitors are in series we use

$$\frac{1}{C_{eq}} = \frac{d_1}{\epsilon_0 A} + \frac{d_2}{\epsilon_0 A} = \frac{d_1 + d_2}{\epsilon_0 A}$$

$$\Rightarrow \quad C_{eq} = \frac{\epsilon_0 A}{d_1 + d_2} = \frac{\epsilon_0 A}{a - b}$$

Sol. 20 (C) Initially voltage across 3 mF capacitor is given as

$$V_1 = \frac{5 \times 30}{5+3} = 18.75\text{ V}$$

$$\Delta q = \Delta CV = \left(\frac{5 \times 10}{5+10} - \frac{5 \times 3}{5+3}\right) \times 30 = 43.75\,\mu\text{C}$$

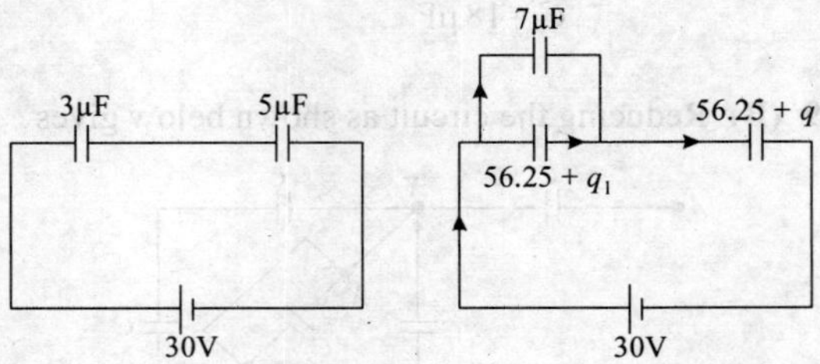

Potential difference across the 7 μF and 3 μF capacitor combination is 10 V so final charge on 7 μF capacitor is 70 μC. Thus option (C) is incorrect.

Sol. 21 (A) As $b \ll R$ we can use it like a parallel plate capacitor for which capacitance is given as

$$C = \frac{\varepsilon_0 kA}{d} = \frac{\varepsilon_0 khR\alpha}{b}$$

Sol. 22 (A) Capacitance for parallel combination is given as

$$C_P = 3 + 9 + 18 = 30\,\mu\text{F}$$

For series combination capacitance is given as

$$\frac{1}{C_S} = \frac{1}{3} + \frac{1}{9} + \frac{1}{18} = \frac{9}{18} = \frac{1}{2}$$

$$\Rightarrow \quad C_S = 2\,\mu\text{F}$$

$$\Rightarrow \quad \frac{C_S}{C_P} = \frac{2\mu F}{30\mu F} = \frac{1}{15}$$

Sol. 23 (D) When the two capacitors are connected in series, the equivalent capacitance is given as

$$C = \frac{2 \times 1}{2+1} = \frac{2}{3}\,\mu\text{F}$$

If the voltage applied across the combination is E then charge on each capacitor will be

$$Q = \frac{2}{3}E$$

The potential of condenser C_1 is given as

$$V_1 = \frac{Q}{C_1} = \frac{2}{3}E < 6\text{ kV} \Rightarrow E < 9\text{ kV}$$

The potential of condenser C_2 is given as

$$V_2 = \frac{Q}{C_2} = \frac{1}{3}E < 4\,\text{kV} \Rightarrow E < 12\,\text{kV}$$

Thus the maximum voltage which can be applied across the combination is 9kV.

Sol. 24 (D) Energy stored in the capacitor appears as heat in the resistor.

Energy stored in capacitor is given as

$$U = \frac{1}{2}CV^2$$

$$\Rightarrow \quad U = \frac{1}{2} \times (4 \times 10^{-6}) \times (400)^2 = 0.32\,\text{J}$$

Sol. 25 (B) Charge on capacitor *A* is given as

$$q_1 = C_1 \times V$$

$$\Rightarrow \quad q_1 = (15 \times 10^{-6})(100) = 15 \times 10^{-4}\,\text{C}$$

Charge on capacitor *B* is given as

$$q_2 = C_2 \times V$$

$$\Rightarrow \quad q_2 = (1 \times 10^{-6})(100) = 10^{-4}\,\text{C}$$

Capacitance of capacitor *A* after removing dielectric is given as

$$C' = (C_1/k) = (15 \times 10^{-6}/15) = 1\,\mu\text{F}$$

When both capacitors are connected in parallel their capacitance will be given as

$$1\mu\text{F} + 1\mu\text{F} = 2\mu\text{F}$$

Common potential of the combination is

$$V = \frac{q}{C}$$

$$\Rightarrow \quad V = \frac{(15\times10^{-4})+(1\times10^{-4})}{2\times10^{-6}} = 800\text{V}$$

Sol. 26 (B) Equivalent capacitance of capacitors 2 μF and 4 μF when connected in parallel is 6 μF and it is in series with another 6 μF in serie. The equivalent capacitance *C* of this circuit is 3 μF. As voltage is divided equally among the two 6 μF capacitors, voltage across each is 6 V.

Sol. 27 (B) Initial capacitance of the capacitor is

$$C = \frac{\epsilon_0 A}{d} = 1\,\text{pF}$$

New capacitance is given as

$$C' = \frac{\epsilon_0 kA}{(2d)} = 2\,\text{pF}$$

$$\Rightarrow \quad k = 4$$

Sol. 28 (A) In the given circuit all the capacitors are in parallel, and so $C = 4 \times 8 = 32\,\mu\text{F}$

Sol. 29 (D) The equivalent circuit can be reduced as shown in figure.

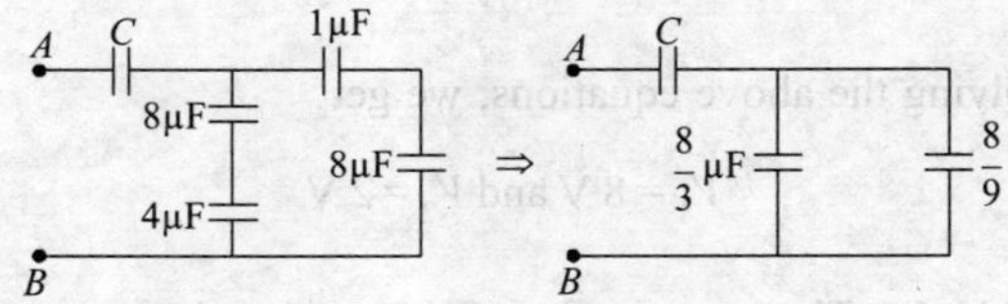

So the equivalent capacitance is given as

$$\frac{C \times \frac{32}{9}}{C + \frac{32}{9}} = 1$$

$$\Rightarrow \quad C = \frac{32}{23}\,\mu\text{F}$$

Sol. 30 (B) Left portion of the circuit is a balanced wheatstoen bridge so the 5μF capacitor remain uncharged and it can be removed so the circuit will be reduced as shown in figure below and its equivalent capacitance is given as

$$C_{PQ} = 1\mu\text{F}$$

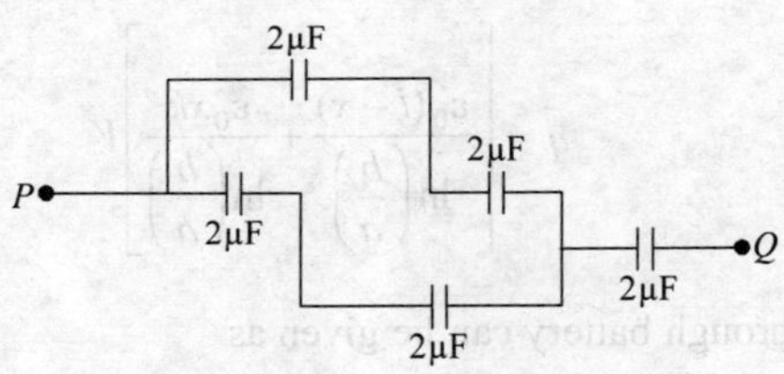

Sol. 31 (C) $\quad q = it = 1 \times 4 = 4\,\text{C}$

So, $\quad C = \frac{q}{V} = \frac{4}{4} = 1\,\text{F}$

Sol. 32 (C) The common potential is given as

$$V' = \frac{CV + 2CV}{kC + 2C} = \left(\frac{3V}{k+2}\right)$$

Sol. 33 (A) Figure below shows the equivalent circuit of the given diagram and if V_1 and V_2 are the potential differences across the capacitors *C*/2 and 2 C then we have

$$V_1 + V_2 = 10$$

and $\quad \frac{C}{2}V_1 = 2\text{CV}_2$

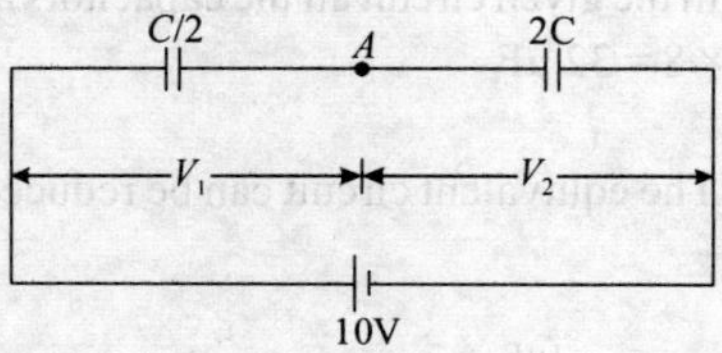

On solving the above equations, we get

$$V_1 = 8\text{ V and } V_2 = 2\text{ V}$$

Sol. 34 (C) The capacitance of the system decreases as oil flows out so the charge on the tubes will also decrease with time and a current flows through the battery.

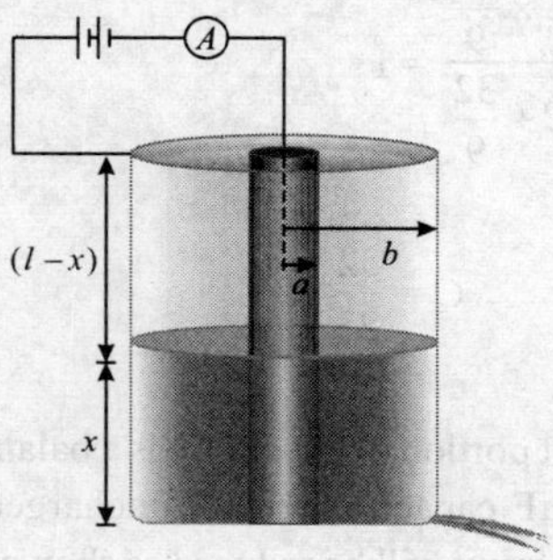

Instantaneous charge on tubes is given as

$$q = CV$$

$$\Rightarrow \quad q = \left[\frac{\varepsilon_0 (l-x)}{\ln\left(\frac{b}{a}\right)} + \frac{\varepsilon_0 xk}{\ln\left(\frac{b}{a}\right)}\right] V$$

Current through battery can be given as

$$i = \frac{dq}{dt}$$

$$\Rightarrow \quad i = \frac{\varepsilon_0}{\ln\left(\frac{b}{a}\right)}(k-1)\left(\frac{dx}{dt}\right) V$$

As $\frac{dx}{dt}$ depends on the area of the hole, so i in the circuit depends on area of the hole.

Sol. 35 (D) Circuit-I

$$C = \frac{2\times 4}{2+4} = \frac{4}{3}\,\mu\text{F and } R = \frac{1\times 2}{1+2} = \frac{2}{3}\,\Omega$$

$$\Rightarrow \quad \tau_1 = CR = \frac{4}{3}\times\frac{2}{3} = \frac{8}{9}\,\mu\text{s}$$

Circuit-II

$$C = 2 + 4 = 6\,\mu\text{F and } R = 1 + 2 = 3\,\Omega.$$

$$\Rightarrow \quad \tau_2 = CR = 6 \times 3 = 18\,\mu\text{s}$$

Circuit-III

$$C = 2 + 4 = 6\,\mu\text{F and } R = \frac{1\times 2}{1+2} = \frac{2}{3}\,\Omega$$

$$\Rightarrow \quad \tau_3 = CR = 6 \times \frac{2}{3} = 4\,\mu\text{s}$$

Sol. 36 (D) The equivalent circuit is shown in figure below

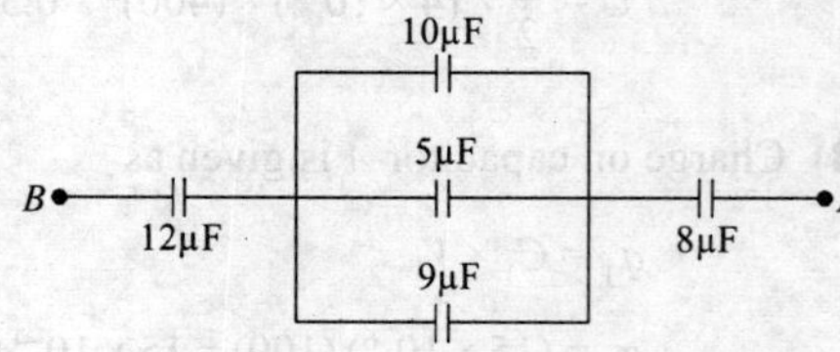

Equivalent capacitance is given as

$$\frac{1}{C_{AB}} = \frac{1}{12} + \frac{1}{24} + \frac{1}{8}$$

$$\Rightarrow \quad C_{AB} = 4\,\mu\text{F}$$

We use $\quad V_1 + V_2 + V_3 = 60$

and $\quad 12\,V_1 = 24\,V_2 = 8\,V_3$

$$\Rightarrow \quad V_2 = 10\text{ V}$$

and $\quad q = 5 \times 10 = 50\,\mu\text{C}$

Sol. 37 (C) Charge stored on capacitor C_1 is given as

$$q_1 = C_1 V = 6 \times 20 = 120\,\mu\text{C}$$

Now after opening S_1 and closing S_2 common potential of the two capacitors is given as

$$V = \left[\frac{120+0}{6+3}\right] = \frac{120}{9}\text{ V}$$

Now, charge on C_2 is given as

$$q_2 = C_2 V = 3 \times \frac{120}{9} = 40\,\mu\text{C}$$

Sol. 38 (B) The equivalent capacitance of the system shown in figure is given as

$$C_{eq} = 2C = 2\frac{\epsilon_0 A}{d}$$

$$\Rightarrow \quad C_{eq} = \frac{2\times 8.85\times 10^{-12}\times 50\times 10^{-4}}{3\times 10^{-3}}$$

$$\Rightarrow \quad C_{eq} = 2.95\times 10^{-11}\,F$$

The energy stored between plates is given as

$$U = \frac{1}{2}C_{eq}V^2$$

$$\Rightarrow \quad U = \frac{1}{2}\times 2.95\times 10^{-11}\times 12^2\,J$$

$$\Rightarrow \quad U = 2.1\times 10^{-9}\,J$$

Sol. 39 (B) The energy stored in capacitor is dissipated as heat which is used to raise the temperature of the block so we use

$$\frac{1}{2}CV^2 = ms\Delta T$$

$$\Rightarrow \quad V = \sqrt{\frac{2ms\Delta t}{C}}$$

Sol. 40 (B) Given that initial capacitance of the capacitor is

$$C = \frac{\varepsilon_0 A}{d} = 9\,pF$$

For two dielectric slabs filled in the capacitor its capacitance is given as

$$C' = \frac{\varepsilon_0 A}{\frac{t_1}{k_1} + \frac{t_2}{k_2}}$$

Substituting values in above expression gives

$$C' = 40.5\,pF$$

Sol. 41 (A) The equivalent circuit is shown in figure below.

Thus $\quad C_{ab} = C = \dfrac{\varepsilon_0 A}{d}$

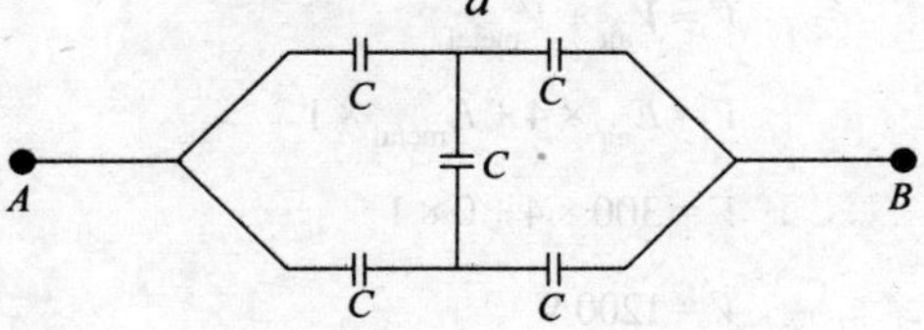

Sol. 42 (A) The equivalent circuit is shown in figure for which equivalent capacitance is given as

$$C_{AB} = 6C = 6\times 2 = 12\,\mu F$$

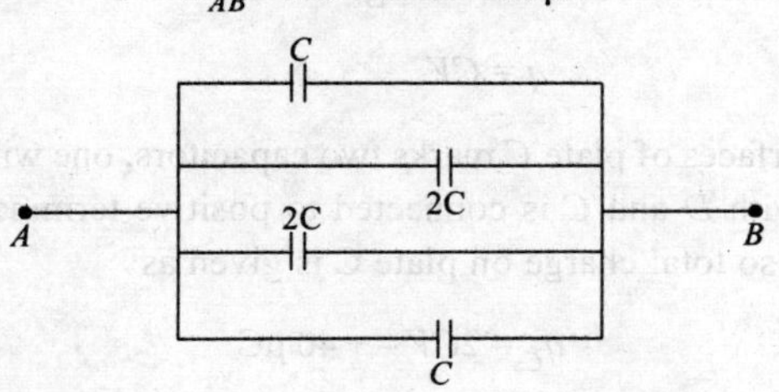

Sol. 43 (B) Because of symmetry we can state that the potentials at all upper and corresponding lower nodes of the circuit will be equal so vertical 1 μF capacitors will not receive any charge and thus these can be removed.

The capacitance of upper series of capacitors in series can be given as

$$\frac{1}{C} = \frac{1}{1} + \frac{1}{3} + \frac{1}{9} + \frac{1}{27} + \ldots \infty$$

$$\Rightarrow \quad C = \frac{2}{3}\,\mu C$$

Equivalent capacitance between terminals A and B can be given as

$$C_{AB} = 2C = \frac{4}{3}\,\mu F$$

Sol. 44 (B) We connect a battery of 100V across terminals A and B then disributing the potentials in circuit as shown in figure below.

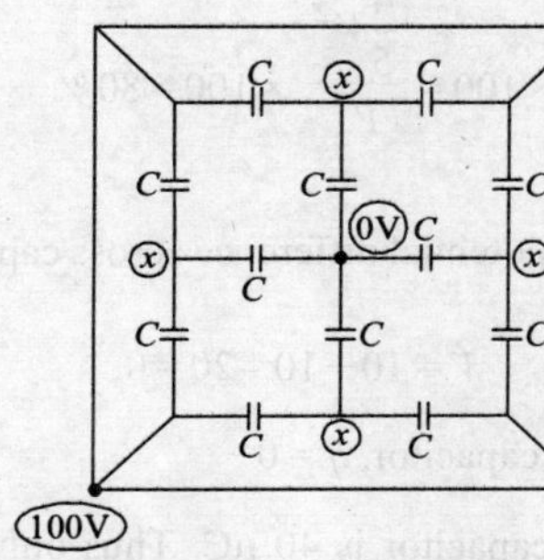

Writing nodal equation for x gives

$$C(x-100) + C(x-100) + Cx = 0$$

$$\Rightarrow \quad x = \frac{200}{3}\,V$$

Equivalent capacitance across A and B is given as

$$C_{eq} = \frac{q_{battery}}{V_{battery}} = \frac{4Cx}{100} = \frac{8C}{3}$$

Sol. 45 (C) The maximum charge which can be supplied to the circuit is given by the two left capacitors which is given as

$$q = CV + 2\,CV = 3\,CV$$

The equivalent capacitance of system is

$$C' = \left[\frac{3C\times 6C}{3C + 6C}\right] = 2\,C$$

The maximum external voltage for this case can be given as

$$V = \frac{q}{C'} = \frac{3CV}{2C} = 1.5\,V$$

Sol. 46 (D) When S is at position 1, 2 μF capacitor is charged. The potential difference across its plates will be V. The potential energy stored in 2 μF capacitor in this state is given as

$$U_i = \frac{1}{2}CV^2 = \frac{1}{2} \times 2 \times V^2 = V^2$$

When S is shifted to position 2, the 8 μF capacitor is connected in parallel with 2μF capacitor. Final common potential difference of the two capacitors is

$$V' = \frac{2V}{10} = 0.2\text{ V}$$

Final energy stored in capacitors is given as

$$U_f = \frac{1}{2} \times 10 \times (0.2V)^2 = 0.2V^2$$

Energy dissipated is given as

$$\Delta U = U_f - U_i = V^2 - 0.2V^2 = 0.8V^2$$

The percentage of the energy dissipated is given as

$$\frac{\Delta U}{U_i} \times 100 = \frac{\frac{4}{5}V^2}{V^2} \times 100 = 80\,\%$$

Sol. 47 (A) The potential difference across capacitor of 12 μF is

$$V = 10 + 10 - 20 = 0$$

So charge on this capacitor, $q = 0$

Charge on 4 μF capacitor is 40 μC. Thus only option (A) is correct.

Sol. 48 (D) Figure below shows the distribution of potentials across different capacitors.

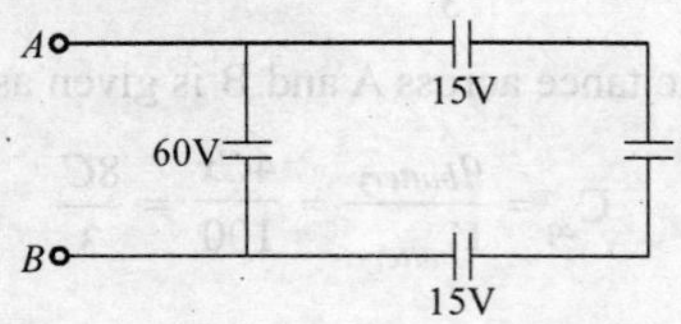

Sol. 49 (B) All capacitors have equal capacitance. Thus equal potential difference will be there will be there across all capacitors so we have

$$V_N - V_B = 2.5\text{ V}$$

$$0 - V_B = 2.5\text{ V}$$

$$\Rightarrow \quad V_B = -2.5\text{ V}$$

$$\Rightarrow \quad V_A - V_N = 3(2.5) = 7.5\text{ V}$$

$$\Rightarrow \quad V_A = +7.5\text{ V}$$

Sol. 50 (A) Three capacitors on the left side are short circuited so will be removed from the circuit and this will be a series combination of C, C, C, 3C/2 and C.

Sol. 51 (C) The equivalent circuit is as shown below.

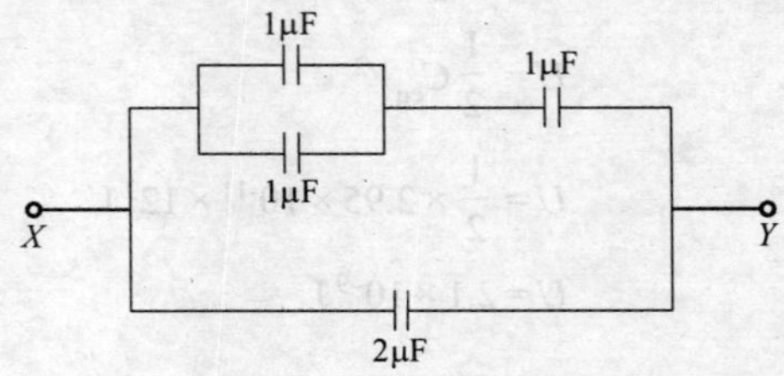

Sol. 52 (D) For the series combination of the top branch we have

$$\frac{V_{1\mu F}}{V_{1.5\mu F}} = \frac{1.5}{1}$$

$$\Rightarrow \quad V_{1\mu\text{F}} = \left(\frac{1.5}{1.5+1}\right)(30) = 18\text{ V}$$

For the series combination of the lower branch we have

$$\frac{V_{2.5\mu F}}{V_{0.5\mu F}} = \frac{0.5}{2.5} = \frac{1}{5}$$

$$\Rightarrow \quad V_{2.5\mu\text{F}} = \left(\frac{1}{1+5}\right)(30) = 5\text{ V}$$

$$\Rightarrow \quad |V_{ab}| = V_{1\mu\text{F}} - V_{2.5\mu\text{F}} = 13\text{ V}$$

Above circuit can also be easily solved by using nodal analysis. Sutdents are advised to verify the above results using nodal analysis also.

Sol. 53 (B) We use

$$V = V_{\text{air}} + V_{\text{metal}}$$

$$\Rightarrow \quad V = E_{\text{air}} \times 4 + E_{\text{metal}} \times 1$$

$$\Rightarrow \quad V = 300 \times 4 + 0 \times 1$$

$$\Rightarrow \quad V = 1200\text{ V}$$

Sol. 54 (B) As alternative plates are connected to the left and right side of the battery, four capacitors are connected in parallel combination and charge across each is

$$q = CV$$

Two surfaces of plate C marks two capacitors, one with B and other with D and C is connected to positive terminal of the battery so total charge on plate C is given as

$$q_C = 2CV = +40\text{ μC}$$

Sol. 55 (B) The circuit above can be reduced as drawn in figure below.

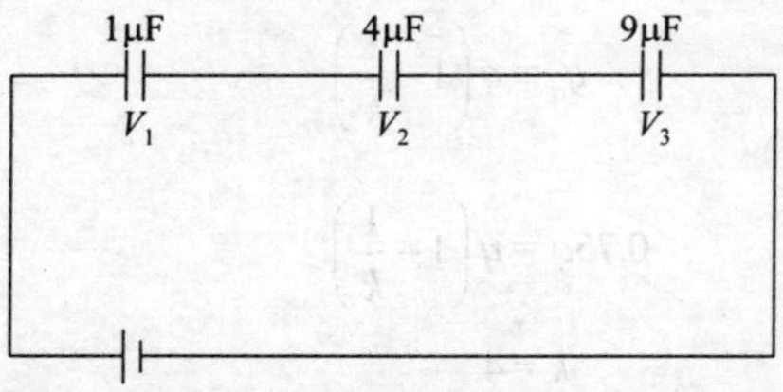

In series combination potential is divided in inverse ratio of capacitances so we use the ratio of potential differences across first and second capacitor is

$$\frac{V_2}{V_1}=\frac{1}{4}$$

$$\Rightarrow \quad V_2=\frac{V_1}{4}=\frac{10}{4}=2.5V$$

Similarly we use

$$\frac{V_3}{V_1}=\frac{1}{9}$$

$$\Rightarrow \quad V_3=\frac{V_1}{9}=\frac{10}{9}V$$

$$\Rightarrow \quad E=\left(10+2.5+\frac{10}{9}\right)V$$

Sol. 56 (D) Total charge on the two capacitor combination is

$$q=(2C)(4V)-CV=7CV$$

Common potential difference after they are connected in parallel is given as

$$V_C=\frac{7CV}{2C+C}=\frac{7}{3}V$$

Heat produced in circuit is the loss in total energy stored in capacitors which is given as

$$\Delta U=U_i-U_f$$

$$\Rightarrow \quad \Delta U=\frac{1}{2}CV^2+\frac{1}{2}(2C)(4V)^2-\frac{1}{2}\times 3C\times\left(\frac{7}{3}V\right)^2$$

$$\Rightarrow \quad \Delta U=\frac{25}{3}CV^2$$

Solutions of ADVANCE MCQs One or More Options Correct

Sol. 1 (A, B) Due to insertion of dielectric overall capacitance increases so battery supplies more charge. As capacitance of B increases so potential difference across B decreases as in series combination potential is divided in inverse ratio of capacitances so electric field in B also decreases. The potential difference across A increases so its potential energy increases. Thus options (A) and (B) are correct.

Sol. 2 (A, C, D) When x or z is replaced by a conductor, the effective separation between the capacitor plates decreases so its capacitance increases. If we replace y by a dielectric then it will act as another capacitor in series so overall capacitance will decrease. If x is replaced by a dielectric then also the capacitance of this section increases which will result in overall increase of capacitance. Thus options (A), (C) and (D) are correct.

Sol. 3 (A, B, D) In process-1, rightmost capacitor C gets connected across the battery so its energy increases. In process-2 the potential difference across the right most capacitor is not changing but charges will appear on other capacitors so overall energy further increases but the equivalent capacitance of the left three capacitors across the battery is less than C so energy increment in process-2 is less compared to process-1. Thus options (A), (B) and (D) are correct.

Sol. 4 (B, D) As chargeing battery is disconnected charge on capacitor becomes constant so on increasing the separation between plates capacitance decreases thus options (B) and (D) are correct.

Sol. 5 (B, D) In steady state the potential difference across the capacitor is same and equal to the battery voltage. As in second case capacitance is less the energy stored in capacitor is also less. As the charges of capacitor will reverse flow through the battery that means battery has absorbed some energy. Thus options (B) and (D) are correct.

Sol. 6 (A, B, C) Across points 1 and 2 equivalent capacitance can be calculated as

$$C_{12}=C\,|P|\,(C/2\,|S|\,4C/3)=\frac{15C}{11}$$

Where $|P|$ and $|S|$ stands for parallel and series combinations respectively. Across points 3 and 6 equivalent capacitance can be calculated as

$$C_{36}=C/3\,|P|\,C/3\,|P|\,C=\frac{5C}{3}$$

Across points 1 and 3 equivalent capacitance can be calculated as

$$C_{12}=C/2\,|P|\,(C\,|S|\,4C/3)=\frac{4C}{15}$$

Across points 3 and 5 equivalent capacitance can be calculated as

$$C_{35}=C/2\,|P|\,(C\,|S|\,4C/3)=\frac{4C}{15}$$

Thus options (A), (B) and (C) are correct.

and inner surfaces will have equal and opposite polarity charges supplied by the battery. Thus options (A), (C) and (D) are correct.

Sol. 14 (B, C) In circuit-(1), the potential differences of the left and right capacitors are

$$V_L = \frac{6q}{2C} = \frac{3q}{C} \text{ and } V_R = \frac{3q}{C}$$

As $V_L = V_R$ so there is no flow of charge in between the capacitors.

In circuit-(2), the potential differences of the left and right capacitors are

$$V_L = \frac{6q}{3C} = \frac{2q}{C} \text{ and } V_R = \frac{3q}{C}$$

As $V_R > V_L$, and so charge will flow towards left capacitor.

In circuit-(3), the potential differences of the left and right capacitors are

$$V_L = \frac{6q}{C} \text{ and } V_R = \frac{3q}{2C}$$

As $V_R < V_L$, and so charge will flow towards right capacitor. Thus options (B) and (C) are correct.

Sol. 15 (B, C) As positive plate is on right and negative plate is onleft, the direction of electric field is from right to left throughout the region between the plates and as we move in the direction opposite to electric field, continuously electric potential increases. Thus options (B) and (C) are correct.

Sol. 16 (A, D) The equivalent capacitance of the circuit is given as

$$C = \frac{6 \times 3}{6+3} + 2 = 4\ \mu\text{F}$$

If V_1 and V_2 are the potential differences across 6mF and 3mF capacitors then we use

$$V_1 + V_2 = 60$$

and $$6V_1 = 3V_2$$

Solving above equations, we get

$$V_1 = 20\text{ V} \text{ and } V_2 = 40\text{ V}$$

Thus options (A) and (D) are correct.

Sol. 17 (B, D) Let V be the applied potential to two capacitors and each has a capacitance C. The voltage across each will be the same and $C_{eff} = C/2$. The voltage across each capacitor is $V_C = V/2$. When the plate of one capacitor are brought closer, its capacitance increases while the other remains the same. As the applied voltage is divided in the inverse ratio of capacitances so finally voltage across the capacitor whose plates are brought closer will be less than $V/2$. Thus options (B) and (D) are correct.

Sol. 18 (A, B, D) After immersing in the liquid, the capacitance of the capacitor increases due to liquid dielectric between the plates. Its energy is decreased as $U = q^2/2C$. Due to decrease in energy, the liquid level between the plates rise. This compensate the loss in electric potential energy by increasing the gravitational potential energy. As q is constant and C is increased, the potential difference between the plates is decreased. Thus options (A), (B) and (D) are correct.

Sol. 19 (B, C, D) When slab is taken out the capacitance of the capacitor decreases so the charge on capacitor also decreases which flows through the cell in opposite direction and cell maintains the constant potential difference across the capacitor. Due to polarization of the slab capacitor attracts the slab inside so external agent has to do some work in pulling the slab out. Thus options (B), (C) and (D) are correct.

Sol. 20 (A, C, D) As before removal of the dielectric slab battery is disconnected from the capacitor, its charge will remain constant and due to removal of slab capacitance decreases so the potential difference across the capacitor increases as $V = q/C$ and the energy stored in capacitor also increases as $U = q^2/2C$. Due to polarization the dielectric slab is attracted inside the capacitor so external agent has to do work in removing the slab. Thus options (A), (C) and (D) are correct.

Sol. 21 (A, D) When dielectric slab is inserted into the capacitor that time battery is connected to it which maintains the constant potential difference across the plate as well as electric field between the plates. Due to dielectric capacitance of capacitor increases and it increases the charge of capacitor also. Thus options (A) and (D) are correct.

Sol. 22 (A, D) When slab is removed capacitance of B decreases due to which overall capaictance decreases and steady state charge flows into the battery and work is done on the battery. As capacitors A and B are in series and charge in series capacitors is always equal. In the process of removal of slab external agent will do some work but it will not appear as heat as in slow removal or insertion of dielectric slab no heat is produced. Thus options (A) and (D) are correct.

Sol. 23 (A, B, C) When plates of a capacitor connected to a battery are pulled apart it decreases the capacitance of capacitor and stored energy in the capacitor also decreases and the electric field between the plates decreases but if battery is disconnected then the electric field between the plates is maintained as charge on plates remain constant. Due to opposite charges on plates always in pulling apart work has to be done by external agent in the process. Thus options (A), (B) and (C) are correct.

Sol. 24 (B, C) The common potential difference across the capacitors when these are connected in parallel is given as

$$V_C = \frac{CV_1 + CV_2}{2C} = \frac{V_1 + V_2}{2}$$

Whenn the two capacitors are connected, some redistribution of charges take place in which some joule heating is produced so final stored energy in capacitors will be less than initial energy stored. Thus options (B) and (C) are correct.

Sol. 25 (A, B, C) The end of plates where the plates are closer the electric field will be higher as conducting plates are at same potential difference between all their points. So the metal surface out of which electric field is higher surface charge density is also higher. Thus options (A), (B) and (C) are correct.

Sol. 26 (A, B, D) We solve this question by using method of flow of charges. If a charge q flows in the closed loop in clockwise direction. Then final charges on different capacitors are as shown in figure below.

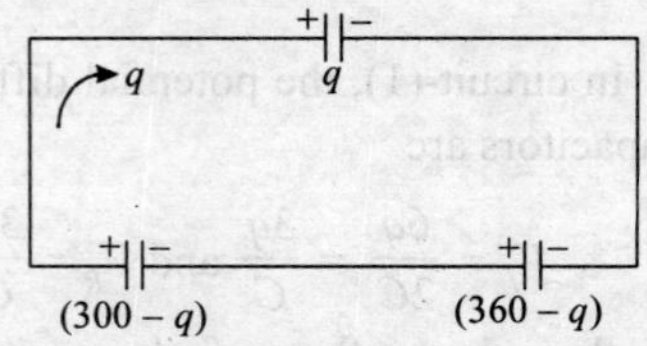

Writing the equation of potential drop in the loop we have

$$\frac{360 - q}{3} + \frac{300 - q}{2} - \frac{q}{1.5} = 0$$

Solving the above equation, we get

$$q = 180\ \mu C$$

This question can also be easily solved by using nodal anlalysis. Students are advised to verify above results by using nodal analysis also.

* * * * *

ANSWERS & SOLUTIONS

CONCEPTUAL MCQs Single Option Correct

1	(A)	**2**	(A)	**3**	(B)
4	(B)	**5**	(D)	**6**	(B)
7	(D)	**8**	(A)	**9**	(B)
10	(B)	**11**	(B)	**12**	(B)
13	(A)	**14**	(C)	**15**	(D)
16	(A)	**17**	(C)	**18**	(C)
19	(B)	**20**	(B)	**21**	(C)
22	(C)	**23**	(A)	**24**	(A)
25	(B)	**26**	(C)	**27**	(D)
28	(C)	**29**	(B)	**30**	(C)
31	(B)	**32**	(D)	**33**	(C)
34	(C)	**35**	(B)	**36**	(B)

NUMERICAL MCQs Single Option Correct

1	(B)	**2**	(B)	**3**	(B)
4	(A)	**5**	(A)	**6**	(B)
7	(B)	**8**	(B)	**9**	(D)
10	(D)	**11**	(C)	**12**	(A)
13	(C)	**14**	(B)	**15**	(D)
16	(C)	**17**	(D)	**18**	(C)
19	(B)	**20**	(C)	**21**	(B)
22	(B)	**23**	(C)	**24**	(D)
25	(D)	**26**	(B)	**27**	(B)
28	(C)	**29**	(D)	**30**	(D)
31	(A)	**32**	(D)	**33**	(B)
34	(B)	**35**	(B)	**36**	(C)
37	(A)	**38**	(A)	**39**	(B)
40	(C)	**41**	(A)	**42**	(A)
43	(C)	**44**	(D)	**45**	(A)
46	(A)	**47**	(A)	**48**	(B)
49	(D)	**50**	(B)	**51**	(C)
52	(A)	**53**	(D)	**54**	(B)
55	(A)	**56**	(A)	**57**	(D)
58	(D)	**59**	(C)	**60**	(C)
61	(B)	**62**	(B)	**63**	(A)
64	(A)	**65**	(C)		

ADVANCE MCQs One or More Options Correct

1	(A, B, D)	**2**	(All)	**3**	(A, D)
4	(A, C)	**5**	(B, C, D)	**6**	(A, B, D)
7	(B, C)	**8**	(A, B C)	**9**	(B, C, D)
10	(All)	**11**	(A, C)	**12**	(A, D)
13	(B, D)	**14**	(All)	**15**	(B, C, D)
16	(B, D)	**17**	(B, C, D)		

Solutions of PRACTICE EXERCISE 3.1

(i) **(a)** As per the condition given, free electron density of copper is equal to the number of copper atoms per m^3 thus it is given as

$$n = \frac{8.96\times10^3\times6.023\times10^{23}}{63\times10^{-3}} = 8.56\times10^{28} \text{ per m}^3$$

Current in wire is given as

$$I = JS = n\,e\,v_d\,S$$

$$\Rightarrow \quad v_d = \frac{I}{neS}$$

Time taken by a free electron to travel along the length of wire is given as

$$t = \frac{l}{v_d}$$

$$\Rightarrow \quad t = \frac{l\,neS}{I}$$

$$\Rightarrow \quad t = \frac{100\times8.56\times10^{28}\times1.6\times10^{-19}\times1\times10^{-6}}{4.5}$$

$$\Rightarrow \quad t = 3.043\times10^5\,\text{s}$$

(b) On a single electron, the electric force is eE so on N electrons, this force will be given as

$$F = (n\,A\,l)\times eE$$

Also se use $E = \frac{V}{l}$ and $V = IR$ thus electric field is given as

$$E = \frac{IR}{l}$$

$$\Rightarrow \quad F = nAle\left(\frac{IR}{l}\right) = nAeI\left(\frac{\rho l}{A}\right) = neI\rho l$$

$$\Rightarrow \quad F = 8.56\times10^{28}\times1.6\times10^{-19}\times4.5\times1.72\times10^{-8}\times100$$

$$\Rightarrow \quad F = 10.6\,\text{N}$$

(ii) The electric field in a conductor of resistivity ρ is given by

$$E = \rho J = \rho\frac{I}{A}$$

where A is the area of cross-section of each conductor. We consider a cylindrical gaussian surface surrounding the interface at the boundary as shown in figure and we now apply Gauss's law on this surface which gives

$$-\frac{\rho_1 I}{A}\cdot A + \frac{\rho_2 I}{A}\cdot A = \frac{\sigma_B A}{\epsilon_0}$$

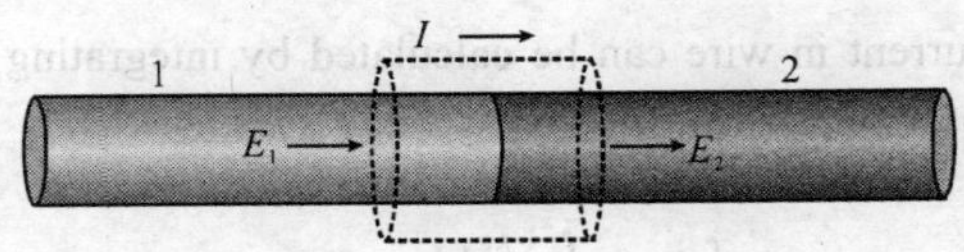

Where σ_B is the surface charge density on the boundary. Solving above equation gives

$$\sigma_B = \epsilon_0\,(\rho_2 - \rho_1)I$$

Sol. 7 (B, D) When discharging starts then discharging current is given as

$$i = \frac{V}{R}e^{-\frac{t}{RC}}$$

At $t = 0$, discharging current is given as

$$i = \frac{V}{R}$$

Given that V and R are same for both capacitors, so the initial current in both capacitors is same but not zero.

During discharge, the instantaneous charge q at time t is given as

$$q = q_0 e^{-t/RC}$$

If $\quad q = q_0/2$ at $t = t_1$,

$$\Rightarrow \quad \frac{q_0}{2} = q_0 e^{-t1/RC}$$

$$\Rightarrow \quad t_1 = RC\ln(2)$$

If t_1 and t_1' be the times in which the two capacitors lose 50% of their charge, then we have

$$\frac{t_1}{t_1'} = \frac{RC_1\ln(2)}{RC_2\ln(2)} = \frac{C_1}{C_2} = \frac{1}{2}$$

$$t_1 = t_1'/2$$

This shows that C_1 loses 50% charge sooner than C_2 because it takes time t, which is half of t_1'. Thus options (B) and (D) are correct.

Sol. 8 (A, B, D) The final charge on capacitor paltes is kC_0V_0 thus the induced charges on the dielectric slab surface are given as

$$q_i = q\left(1 - \frac{1}{k}\right) = C_0V_0(k-1)$$

As induced charges on the two surfaces of dielectric are equal and opposite net force due to these induced charges on any plate is zero. Force of attraction between the plates of capacitor is given as

$$F = \frac{q^2}{2\epsilon_0 A} = \frac{k^2C_0^2V_0^2}{2\epsilon_0 A}$$

Electric field due to induced charges inside the dielectric slab is given as

$$E_i = \frac{\sigma_i}{\epsilon_0} = \frac{(k-1)C_0V_0}{\epsilon_o A}$$

Thus options (A), (B) and (D) are correct.

Sol. 9 (A, C, D) The bound charges on dielectric slab is given as

$$q_i = q\left(1 - \frac{1}{k}\right)$$

$$\Rightarrow \quad 0.75q = q\left(1 - \frac{1}{k}\right)$$

$$\Rightarrow \quad k = 4$$

Without the dielectric capacitance will be C/k = 120μF. The maximum voltage that can be applied across the capacitor can be given as

$$V_{max} = E_{max}d$$

Thus the maximum charge that can be stored on capacitor can be given as

$$q_{max} = CV_{max} = \frac{k\epsilon_0 L^2}{d}V_{max} = 240\varepsilon_0 L^2 E_{max}$$

$$\Rightarrow \quad A = 60L^2$$

If dielectric is half filled in the space between the plates the capacitance is given as

$$C = \frac{60\epsilon_0 L^2}{\frac{d}{2} + \frac{d}{8}} = \frac{8}{5}\left(\frac{60\epsilon_0 L^2}{d}\right) = 192\mu F$$

Sol. 10 (A, C) If the inner shell is displaced by some distance the charges on the inner and outer both shell surfaces will get change and due to this some energy is dissipated so final energy will be less. As the total charge is constant on the two plates of the capacitor and energy is reduced that implies capaictance of the system increases.

Sol. 11 (A, D) As battery is connected while insertion of dielectric slab the voltage across capacitor will remain constant due to which electric field also remain constant but capacitance increases due to which charge also increase and stored energy increases. Thus options (A) and (D) are correct.

Sol. 12 (B, C) There is a current between the plates of capacitor due to change in electric field between them,

$$i_d = \epsilon_0 A\frac{dE}{dt}$$

This current exist between the plates of capacitor as well as in the conducting wires till the capacitor attains the steady state. Thus options (B) and (C) are correct.

Sol. 13 (A, C, D) Initial charge on the capacitor plates will be distributed equally half on the two outer surfaces of the plates

(iii) Current in circuit is given as

$$I = neSv_d$$

$$\Rightarrow \quad J = \frac{I}{S} = nev_d$$

We use $\quad v_d = \frac{l}{t}$

$$\Rightarrow \quad J = \frac{nel}{t}$$

If the mean thermal velocity is $\bar{v}$, the distances travelled by a free electron is given as

$$s = \bar{v}t$$

Where mean thermal speed of free electron can be given as

$$\bar{v} = \sqrt{\frac{8kT}{\pi m_e}} = \sqrt{\frac{8\times1.38\times10^{-23}\times300}{3.14\times9.1\times10^{-31}}} = 10.76\times10^4 \text{ m/s}$$

$$\Rightarrow \quad s = \bar{v}\cdot\frac{nel}{J}$$

$$\Rightarrow \quad s = 10.76\times10^4\times\left(\frac{8.5\times10^{28}\times1.6\times10^{-19}\times10\times10^{-3}}{1\times10^6}\right)$$

$$\Rightarrow \quad s = 1.47\times10^6 \text{ m}$$

(iv) Figure shows the cross-section of the wire in which we consider an elemental strip of width dx at a distance x from one side. Current in this elemental strip is given as

$$dI = JdS = J.\,ldx$$

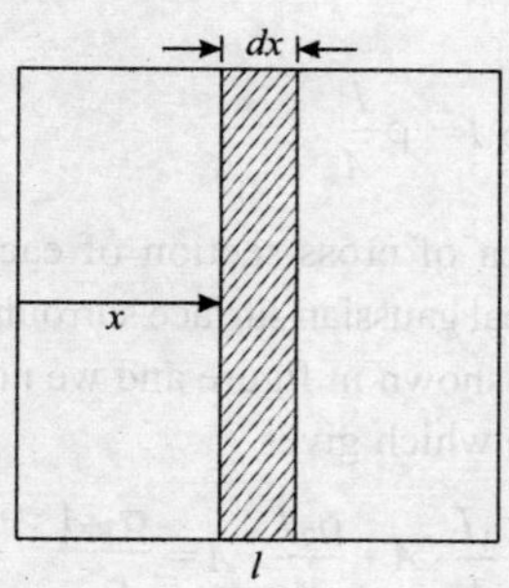

Total current in wire can be calculated by integrating above expression as

$$I = \int dI = \int_0^l ae^{bx}\,ldx$$

$$I = al\int_0^l e^{bx}dx = al\left[\frac{e^{bx}}{b}\right]_0^l = \frac{al}{b}[e^{bl}-1]$$

(v) As we know ion speed can be related to the applied electric field E as

$$v = \mu E$$

$$\Rightarrow \quad v = \mu\left(\frac{V_0\sin\omega t}{l}\right)$$

The maximum displacement of ions in one direction

$$s = \int_0^{\pi/\omega}\mu\left(\frac{V_0\sin\omega t}{l}\right)dt = \frac{2\mu V_0}{l\omega}$$

This must be equal to the distance between the plates if any current is to be registered in the galvanometer, thus we have

$$\frac{2\mu V_0}{l\omega_0} = l$$

$$\Rightarrow \quad \mu = \frac{\omega_0 l^2}{2V_0}$$

(vi) The drift velocity of free electrons in a current carrying conductor is given as

$$v_d = \frac{J}{ne}$$

$$\Rightarrow \quad v_d = \frac{I}{neS}$$

$$\Rightarrow \quad v_d = \frac{16}{4\times10^{28}\times1.6\times10^{-19}\times10^{-5}}$$

$$\Rightarrow \quad v_d = 2.5\times10^{-4} \text{ m/s}$$

(vii) **Sol.** Electric field in the conductor is

$$E = \frac{V}{l} = \frac{10}{0.4} = 25 \text{ V/m}$$

Drift velocity of free electrons is given as

$$v_d = \mu E$$

$$\Rightarrow \quad \mu = \frac{v_d}{E} = \frac{5\times10^{-6}}{25} = 2\times10^{-7} \text{ m}^2\text{/V-s}$$

(viii) **(a)** Under saturation condition, the if N is the ion concentration then saturation current is given as

$$I_{sat} = N\,e\,v_d\,S = N\,e\,V$$

Where V is the volume between plates given as

V = area of the plate × length covered by ions in one second

$$\Rightarrow \quad N = \frac{I_{sat}}{eV}$$

$$\Rightarrow \quad N = \frac{0.48\times10^{-6}}{1.6\times10^{-19}\times500}$$

$$\Rightarrow \quad N = 6\times10^{9} \text{ per cm}^3$$

(b) If N_P is the production rate of ions in air then the rate of accumulation of ions is given as

$$\frac{dN}{dt} = N_P - rN^2$$

At equilibrium the accumulation rate is zero so we have

$$\frac{dN}{dt} = 0$$

$$\Rightarrow \quad N_P = rN^2$$

$$\Rightarrow \quad N_P = 1.67\times10^{-6}\times(6\times10^{9})^2$$

$$\Rightarrow \quad N_P = 6.012\times10^{12} \text{ per cm}^3$$

Solutions of PRACTICE EXERCISE 3.2

(i) We can reduce the above circuit as shown in figure below and equivalent resistance is the series combination of the three final resistances which is given as

$$R_{AB} = 2 + 13.33 + 8 = 23.33\Omega$$

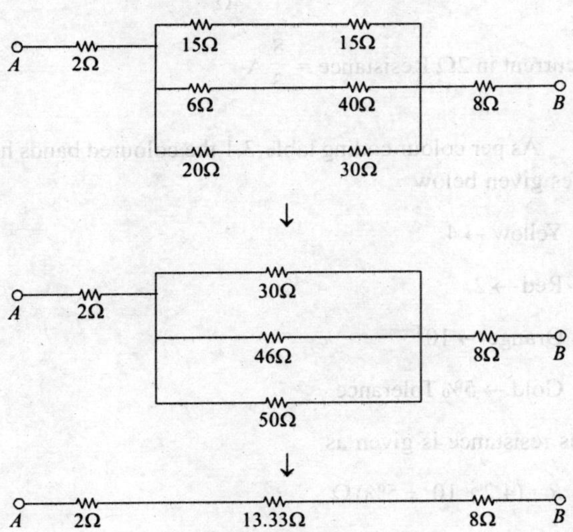

(ii) The resistance R of the copper wire is given by

$$R = \frac{V}{I} = \frac{1.7}{1} = 1.7\,\Omega$$

If ρ be the resistivity of copper wire, then we have

$$R = \rho\frac{l}{A}$$

$$\Rightarrow \quad \frac{l}{A} = \frac{R}{\rho}$$

$$\Rightarrow \quad \frac{l}{A} = \frac{1.7}{1.7\times10^{-8}} = 10^{8}$$

$$\Rightarrow \quad A = 10^{-8}\,l \qquad \ldots(1)$$

Volume of copper wire is given as

$$V_0 = lA = \frac{m}{d} = \frac{2.23\times10^{-3}}{8920}\text{ m}^3$$

$$\Rightarrow \quad lA = 2.5\times10^{-7}\text{ m}^3 \qquad \ldots(2)$$

Solving equations-(1) and (2), we get

$$l = 5\text{m and } A = 5\times10^{-8}\text{ m}^2$$

When the wire is stretched to double its length then the new length and area of cross-section becomes l' and A'. As volume of conductor material remains constant during stretching we use

$$l'A' = lA$$

In above equation using $l' = 2l$ gives $A' = A/2$

The new resistance R' of wire is given as

$$R' = \rho\frac{l'}{A'} = \rho\left\{\frac{2l}{(A/2)}\right\} = 4\left(\frac{\rho l}{A}\right) = 4R = 6.8\,\Omega$$

(iii) **(a)** Current density in the conductor is given as

$$J = \frac{I}{A} = \frac{V}{RA} = \frac{V}{\left(\frac{\rho l}{A}\right)A}$$

$$\Rightarrow \quad J = \frac{V}{\rho l} \qquad \ldots(1)$$

$$\Rightarrow \quad J \propto \frac{1}{l}$$

Thus for maximum current density separation between faces must be minimum and here $l_{min} = d$. Thus J is maximum when potential difference is applied across the face with dimensions $2d\times3d$. This maximum current density is given by equation-(1) as

$$J_{max} = \frac{V}{\rho d}$$

(b) Current in conductor is given as

$$I = \frac{V}{R} = \frac{V}{(\rho l / A)} = \frac{VA}{\rho l}$$

$$\Rightarrow \quad I \propto \frac{A}{l}$$

Across the face with dimensions $2d \times 3d$, area of cross section is maximum and l is minimum thus in this case when potential difference is applied current will be maximum which is given as

$$I_{max} = \frac{V(2d \times 3d)}{\rho(d)}$$

$$\Rightarrow \quad I_{max} = \frac{6Vd}{\rho}$$

(iv) At 0°C if R_0 is the resistance of the conductor 1 then resistance of conductor 2 is ηR_0. Resistances of these conductors at temperature t°C are given as

$$R_{1t} = R_0(1 + \alpha_1 t)$$

and $\quad R_{2t} = \eta R_0(1 + \alpha_2 t)$

Let R_t be the resistance at t°C when they are connected in series then we have

$$R_t = R_{1t} + R_{2t} = R_0(1 + \eta) + R_0(\alpha_1 + \eta\alpha_2)t$$

$$\Rightarrow \quad R_t = R_0(1 + \eta)\left[1 + \frac{(\alpha_1 + \eta\alpha_2)}{(1 + \eta)}t\right] \quad \ldots(1)$$

At 0°C if the equivalent resistance of series combination is R_0' then we have

$$R_0' = R_{10} + R_{20} = R_0 + \eta R_0 = R_0(1 + \eta)$$

Thus from equation-(1) we have

$$R_t = R_0(1 + \eta)\left[1 + \frac{(\alpha_1 + \eta\alpha_2)}{(1 + \eta)}t\right]$$

If α_s is the equivalent temperature coefficient of resistance then we use

$$R_t = R_0'(1 + \alpha_s t)$$

$$\Rightarrow \quad \alpha_s = \frac{R_t - R_0'}{R_0'(t - 0)} = \frac{(\alpha_1 + \eta\alpha_2)}{1 + \eta}$$

In parallel combination we use

$$R_t = \frac{R_0(1 + \alpha_1 t) \times R_0\eta(1 + \alpha_2 t)}{R_0(1 + \alpha_1 t) + \eta R_0(1 + \alpha_2 t)} \quad \ldots(2)$$

and $\quad \frac{1}{R_0'} = \frac{1}{R_0} + \frac{1}{\eta R_0} = \left(\frac{1 + \eta}{\eta R_0}\right)$

$$\Rightarrow \quad R_0' = \frac{\eta R_0}{1 + \eta}$$

$$\Rightarrow \quad R_t = R_0'(1 + \alpha_p t) \quad \ldots(3)$$

Comparing equation-(2) and (3) and solving the equation gives

$$\alpha_p = \frac{(\eta\alpha_1 + \alpha_2)}{1 + \eta}$$

Above results of α_s and α_p can also be directly obtained by the formulas derived in Illustration-3.6.

(v) $2\,\Omega$, $1\,\Omega$ in series $= 3\,\Omega$

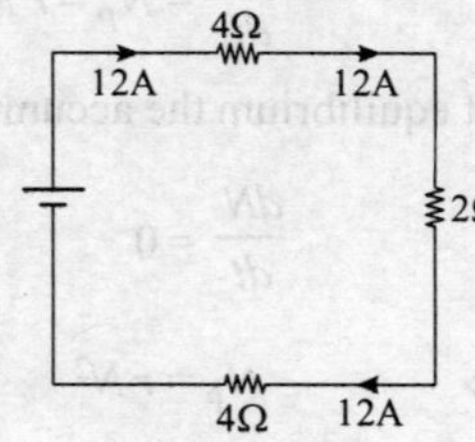

$3\,\Omega$, $6\,\Omega$ in parallel $= \frac{18}{9} = 2\,\Omega$

$2\,\Omega$, $4\,\Omega$ in series $= 6\,\Omega$

$6\,\Omega$, $3\,\Omega$ in parallel $= 2\,\Omega$

$$R_{eq} = 4 + 4 + 2 = 10\,\Omega$$

$$i = \frac{120}{10} = 12A$$

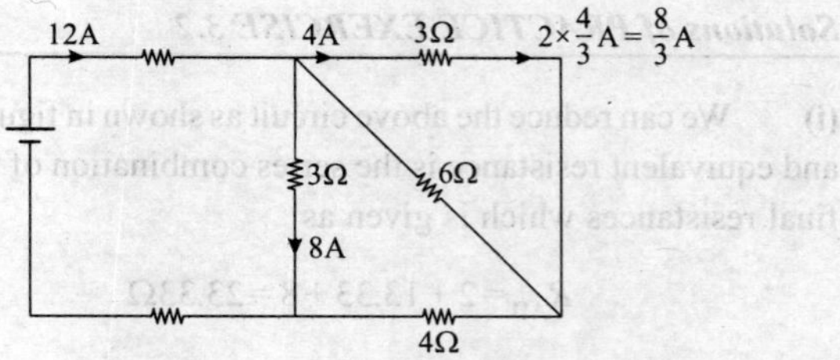

So current in 2Ω Resistance $= \frac{8}{3}$ A

(vi) As per colour coding table-3.1 the coloured bands have codes given below

Yellow → 4

Red → 2

Orange → 10^3

Gold → 5% Tolerance

Thus resistance is given as

$$R = (4.2 \times 10^3 \pm 5\%)\,\Omega$$

(vii) Let the length of three wires be $2l$, $3l$ and $4l$ respectively and their radii be $3r$, $4r$ and $5r$. If ρ be the specific resistance of the material of wires then we have their resistances given as

$$R_1 = \rho\frac{2l}{\pi(3r)^2}$$

$$R_2 = \rho\frac{3l}{\pi(4r)^2}$$

and $$R_3 = \rho \frac{4l}{\pi(5r)^2}$$

$$\Rightarrow \quad R_1 : R_2 : R_3 = \frac{2}{9} : \frac{3}{16} : \frac{4}{25}$$

The ratio of their currents must be in inverse ratio of resistances in parallel combination so we have

$$i_1 : i_2 : i_3 = \frac{9}{2} : \frac{16}{3} : \frac{25}{4}$$

$$\Rightarrow \quad i_1 : i_2 : i_3 = 54 : 64 : 75$$

Thus the currents in three branches are given as

$$i_1 = \frac{5 \times 54}{193} = 1.40\,\text{A}$$

$$i_2 = \frac{5 \times 64}{193} = 1.66\,\text{A}$$

and $$i_3 = \frac{3 \times 75}{193} = 1.94\,\text{A}$$

(viii) The diagram can be redrawn as shown in figure

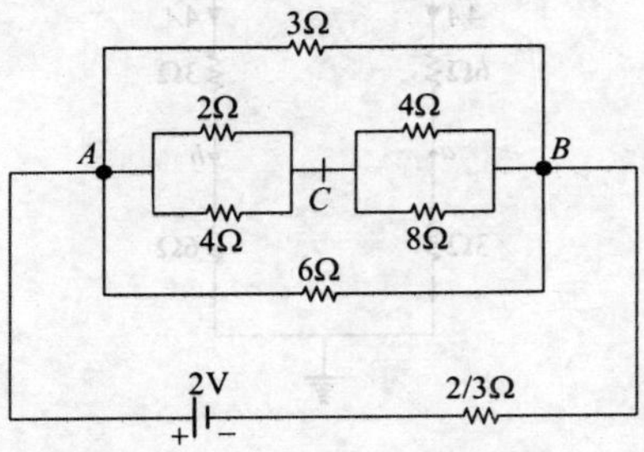

The effective resistance R_{AC} between A and C

$$\frac{1}{R_{AC}} = \frac{1}{2} + \frac{1}{4} = \frac{3}{4}$$

$$\Rightarrow \quad R_{AC} = \frac{4}{3}\,\Omega$$

The effective resistance R_{CB} between C and B.

$$\frac{1}{R_{CB}} = \frac{1}{4} + \frac{1}{8} = \frac{3}{8}$$

$$\Rightarrow \quad R_{CB} = \frac{8}{3}\,\Omega$$

The resistance of middle branch is given as

$$R_{ACB} = R_{AC} + R_{CB} = \frac{4}{3} + \frac{8}{3}\,\Omega$$

Corresponding to points X and Y, the resistances 3 Ω, 4 Ω and 6 Ω are in parallel, hence effective resistance R_{XY} is given

$$\frac{1}{R_{XY}} = \frac{1}{3} + \frac{1}{4} + \frac{1}{6} = \frac{3+3+2}{12} = \frac{9}{12}$$

$$\Rightarrow \quad R_{XY} = \frac{12}{9} = \frac{4}{3}\,\Omega$$

Total resistance of the circuit can be given as

$$R = \frac{4}{3} + \frac{2}{3} = 2\,\Omega$$

Current in the circuit is given as

$$I = \frac{V}{R} = \frac{2}{2} = 1\,\text{A}$$

In earlier grades students have already studied that in any circuit power dissipated is given as

$$P = I^2 R = 1 \times 2 = 2\,\Omega$$

Potential difference between A and B

$$V_{AB} = IR_{AB} = 1 \times \frac{4}{3} = \frac{4}{3}\,\text{V}$$

Same will be the potential difference across 3 Ω resistor using which we can calculate the current in it which is given as

$$I_{3\Omega} = \frac{4/3}{3} = \frac{4}{9} = 0.44\,\text{A}$$

(ix) The equivalent resistance by series and parallel combination can be calculated as

$$R = \frac{99}{35}\,\Omega$$

Total current supplied by the battery is

$$I = \frac{V}{R} = \frac{2 \times 35}{99} = \frac{70}{99}\,\text{A}$$

Thus current through left most part of circuit is 70/99 A. After this the current is divided among 1 Ω and 29/6 Ω resistances in parallel which are given as

$$I_{1\Omega} = \frac{70}{99} \times \left(\frac{\frac{29}{6}}{\frac{29}{6} + 1} \right) = \frac{58}{99}\,\text{A}$$

and $$I_{29/6\,\Omega} = \frac{70}{99} - \frac{58}{99} = \frac{12}{99}\,\text{A}$$

Further the current 12/99A is divided among 1 Ω and 5 Ω resistances which are given as

$$I_{1\Omega} = \frac{12}{99} \times \left(\frac{5}{1+5} \right) = \frac{10}{99}\,\text{A}$$

and $$I_{5\Omega} = \frac{12}{99} - \frac{10}{99} = \frac{2}{99}\,\text{A}$$

(x) In parallel combination current distributes in inverse ratio of resistance thus we have

$$\frac{R_1}{R_2} = \frac{i_2}{i_1}$$

$$\Rightarrow \quad \frac{\rho_1 l_1 / A_1}{\rho_2 l_2 / A_2} = \frac{2}{3}$$

$$\Rightarrow \quad \frac{\rho_1 l_1 d_2^2}{\rho_2 l_2 d_1^2} = \frac{2}{3}$$

$$\Rightarrow \quad d_2 = \left(\sqrt{\frac{2\rho_2 l_2}{3\rho_1 l_1}}\right) d_1$$

$$\Rightarrow \quad d_2 = \left(\sqrt{\frac{2\times 0.017\times 6}{3\times 0.028\times 7.5}}\right)\times 1\text{ mm} = 0.569\text{ mm}$$

Solutions of PRACTICE EXERCISE 3.3

(i) Potential is distributed in circuit as shown in figure.

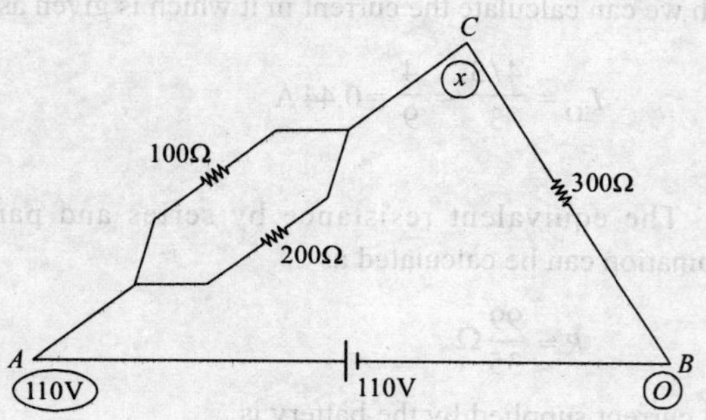

Writing KCL equation for x, we have

$$\frac{x}{300} + \frac{x-110}{100} + \frac{x-110}{200} = 0$$

$$\Rightarrow \quad 11x = 990$$

$$\Rightarrow \quad x = 90\text{V}$$

$$V_{BC} = 90\text{V}$$

$$V_{AC} = 20\text{V}$$

$$I_{300\Omega} = \frac{90}{300} = \frac{1}{3}A$$

$$I_{100\Omega} = \frac{20}{100} = \frac{1}{5}A$$

$$I_{200\Omega} = \frac{20}{200} = \frac{1}{10}A$$

(ii) Above given circuit is a balanced Wheatstone bridge in which the middle branch can be removed after which circuit will be reduced to the circuit shown in figure.

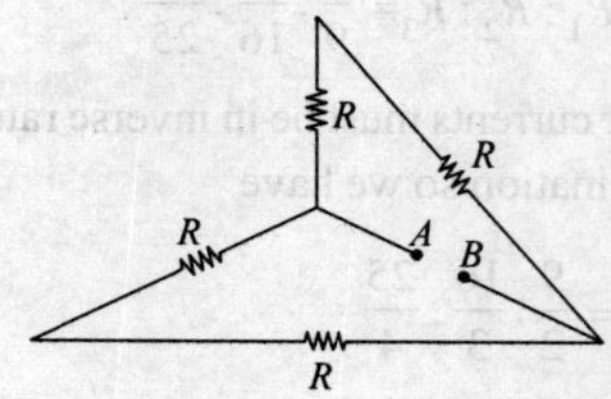

Thus the equivalent resistance of the above circuit across terminals A and B is equal to R.

(iii) Since Wheatstone bridge is balanced so we use

$$\frac{x}{18} = \frac{2}{6} \text{ or } x = \frac{18\times 2}{6} = 6\,\Omega$$

(iv) **(a)** When switch S is open

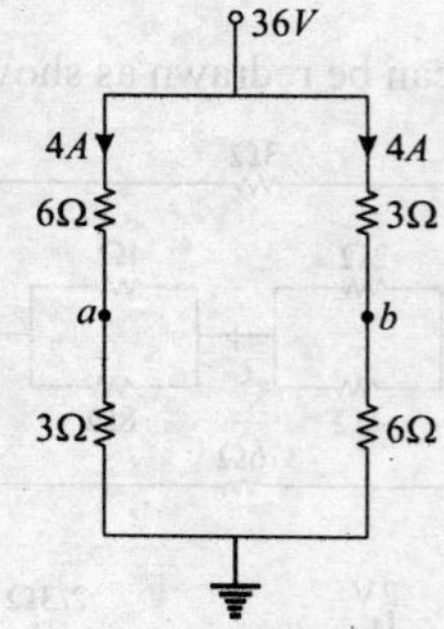

$$V_a - V_b = (36 - 6\times 4) - (36 - 3\times 4) = -12\text{ V}$$

(b) Total current through circuit $= \dfrac{36\text{V}}{4\Omega} = 9\text{ A}$

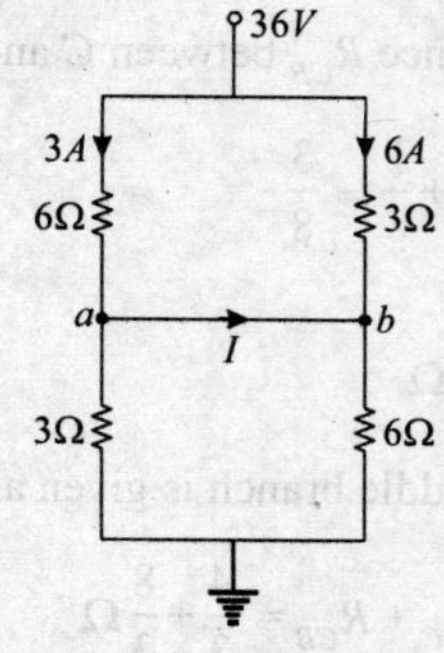

Therefore $I = 3$ A

(v) Current with both switches opened is

$$\frac{V}{R_{eq}} = \frac{1.5}{450} = \frac{1}{300} = i$$

After closing the switch, if V_1 and V_2 are potential differences as shown in figure then we have

$$V_1 + V_2 = V$$

$$\frac{1}{3} + V_2 = \frac{3}{2}$$

$$V_2 = \frac{9-2}{6} = \frac{7}{6}\text{V}$$

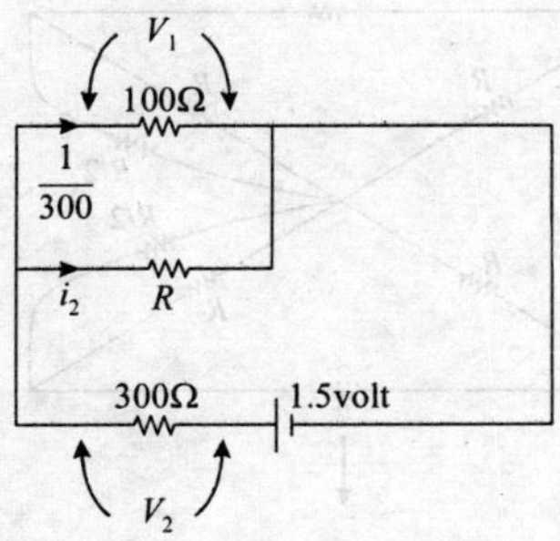

Current through battery is

$$i = \frac{7}{6} \times \frac{1}{300} = \frac{7}{1800}\text{A}$$

By KCL, we have

$$i_2 = \frac{7}{1800} - \frac{1}{300} = \frac{1}{1800}; \; i_2 R = i_1 R_1$$

$$R = 1800\left(\frac{1}{3}\right) = 600\,\Omega$$

(vi) For balanced Wheat stone bridge $\dfrac{100}{\dfrac{100R}{(100+R)}} = \dfrac{200}{40}$

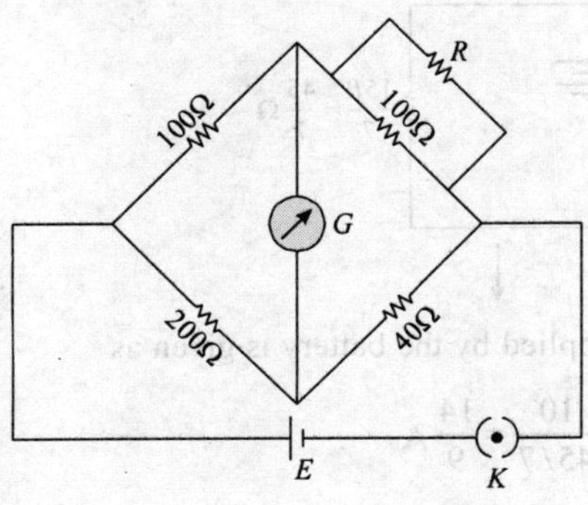

$$\Rightarrow \quad \frac{100+R}{R} = 5$$

$$\Rightarrow \quad 100 + R = 5\text{R}$$

$$\Rightarrow \quad R = \frac{100}{4} = 25\,\Omega$$

(vii) Being a balanced Wheatstone bridge its middle branch can be removed and circuit can be reduced by using series and parallel analysis as shown in figure.

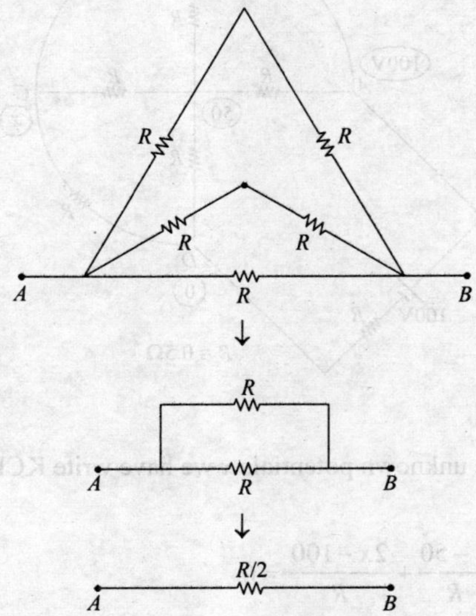

$$R_{AB} = R/2$$

(viii) Circuit can be redrawn as shown in figure below

The equivalent resistance across the battery is given as

$$R_{eq} = \frac{3}{2}\Omega$$

$$\Rightarrow \quad I = \frac{V}{R_{eq}} = 20\,\text{A}$$

Current In $\quad I_{CD} = I_{AC} + I_B$

$$\Rightarrow \quad I_{CD} = 15\,\text{A}$$

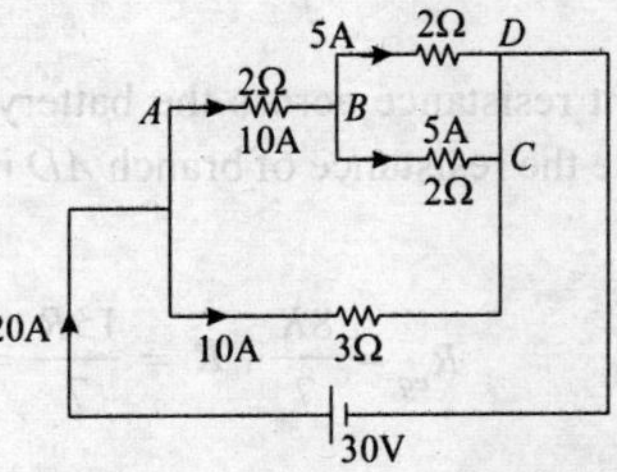

Students can also try solving above circuit using nodal analysis and verify.

Solutions of PRACTICE EXERCISE 3.4

(i) To solve the network we disconnect the branch AD and insert a 100 V battery across points A and D as shown in figure and distribute potentials at different junctions of the circuit as shown

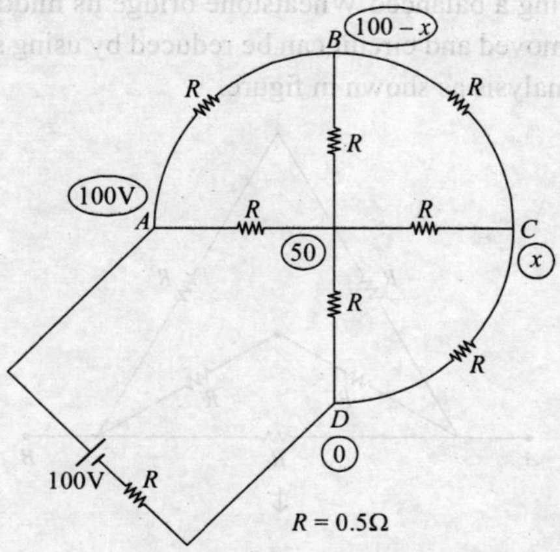

To find the unknown potentials x we have write KCL equation as

$$\frac{x}{R}+\frac{x-50}{R}+\frac{2x-100}{R}=0$$

$$\Rightarrow \quad 4x=150$$

$$\Rightarrow \quad x=\frac{150}{4}=\frac{75}{2}\Omega$$

Equivalent resistance across terminals A and D is given as

$$R_{AD}=\frac{V_{\text{battery}}}{I_{\text{battery}}}=\frac{100}{\dfrac{x}{R}+\dfrac{50}{R}}$$

$$\Rightarrow \quad R_{AD}=\frac{100}{\dfrac{75}{2R}+\dfrac{50}{R}}=\frac{200R}{175}$$

$$\Rightarrow \quad R_{AD}=\frac{8R}{7}$$

Total equivalent resistance across the battery given in figure will also include the resistance of branch AD in series which is given as

$$R_{eq}=\frac{8R}{7}+R=\frac{15R}{7}=\frac{15\times 0.5}{7}$$

$$\Rightarrow \quad R_{eq}=\frac{15}{14}\Omega$$

(ii) Here we use the method of joining equipotential points in symmetry circuits as shown in figure

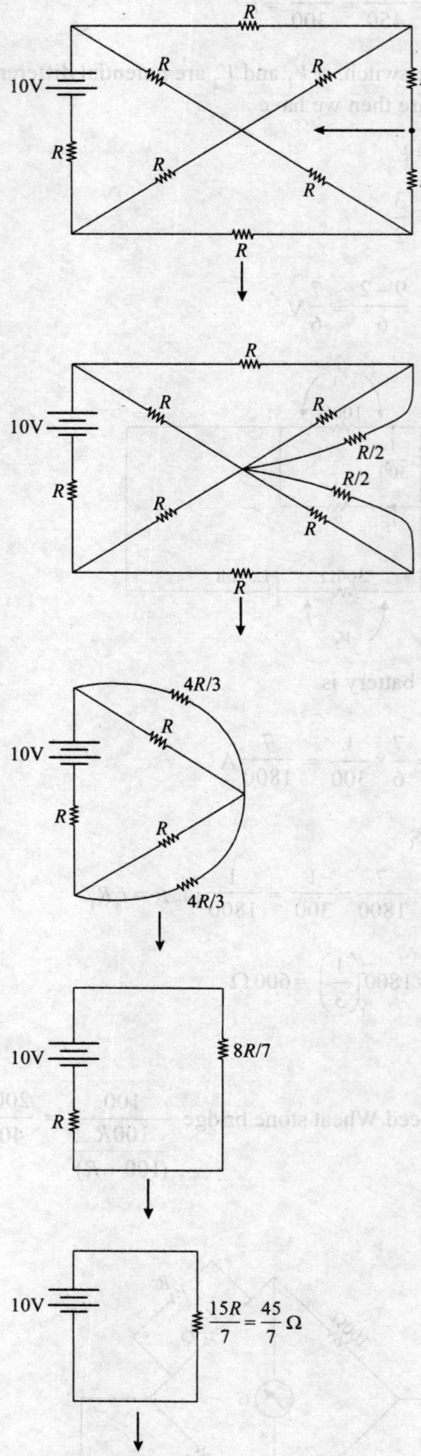

Current supplied by the battery is given as

$$I=\frac{10}{45/7}=\frac{14}{9}\text{ A}$$

(iii) If each wire is considered to be of resistance R then initial resistance across points A and F is 5 R. After adding dashed wires to calculate the equivalent resistance we can remove the wire CD as between points B and E it becomes a balanced Wheatstone bridge so the equivalent resistance becomes 3R. Thus the final resistance becomes 0.6 times that of the initial resistance after adding dashed wires.

(iv) By applying perpendicular axis symmetry. Points lying on the line 'XY' will have same potential therefore Resistance connected along line XY can be removed after which we can use series and parallel combination of resistances which gives $R_{AB} = 9\,\Omega$.

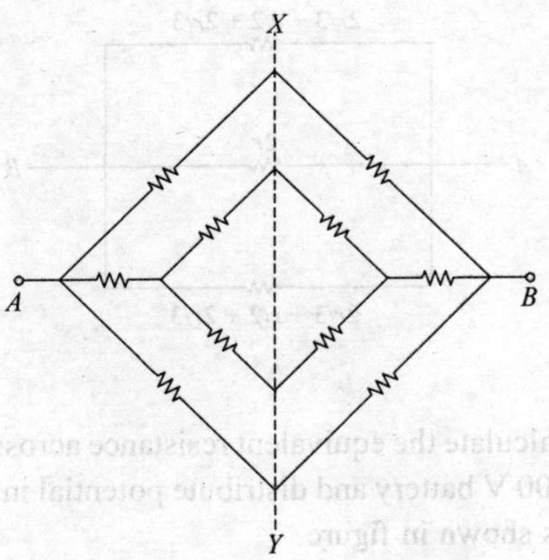

(v) **(a)** To calculate equivalent resistance across terminals A and D we connect a 100 V battery across these points and distribute potentials as shown in figure.

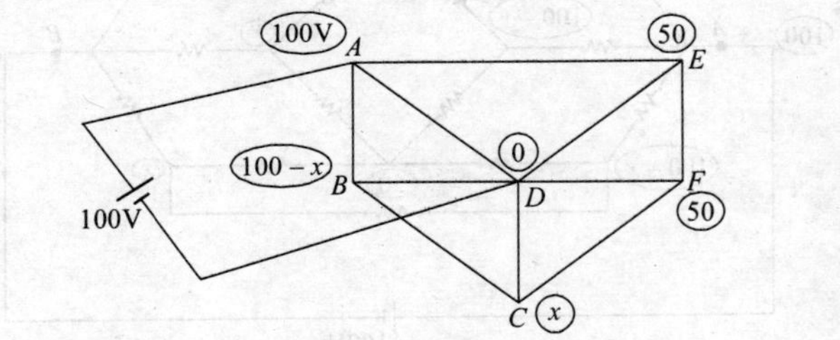

Writing KCL equation for x gives

$$\frac{x-50}{r}+\frac{x}{r}+\frac{2x-100}{r}=0$$

$$\Rightarrow \quad 4x = 150$$

$$\Rightarrow \quad x = \frac{75}{2}V$$

Current through battery is given as

$$I_{\text{battery}} = \frac{x}{r}+\frac{50}{r}+\frac{100}{r} = \frac{375}{2r}$$

equivalent resistance is given as

$$R_{\text{eq}} = \frac{V_{\text{battery}}}{I_{\text{battery}}} = \frac{100\times 2r}{375} = \frac{8r}{15}$$

(b) To calculate equivalent resistance across terminals A and B we cannot a 100 V battery across these points and distribute potentials as shown in figure

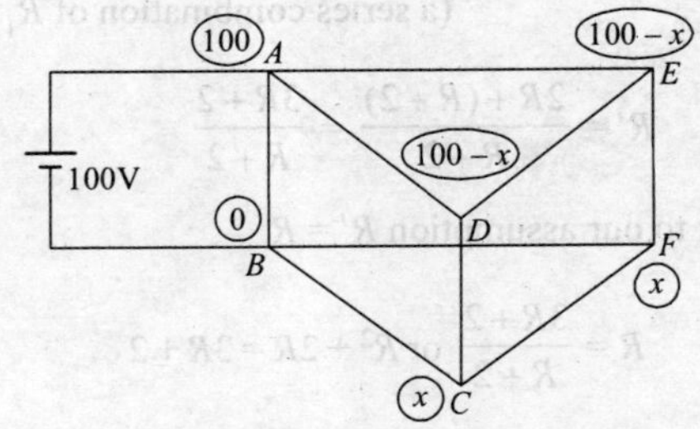

Writing KCL equation for x gives

$$\frac{x}{r}+\frac{2x-100}{r}=0$$

$$\Rightarrow \quad 3x = 100$$

$$\Rightarrow \quad x = \frac{100}{3}V$$

Current through battery is given as

$$I_{\text{battery}} = \frac{x}{r}+\frac{x}{r}+\frac{100}{r} = \frac{500}{3r}$$

Equivalent resistance is given as

$$R_{\text{eq}} = \frac{V_{\text{battery}}}{I_{\text{battery}}} = \frac{100\times 3r}{500} = \frac{3}{5}r$$

(vi) **(a)** Let R be the equivalent resistance between points A and B. Here we assume that one more set of resistances is connected between A and B as shown in figure. The assumption will not affect the resistance R because there are infinite number of such sets connected between A and B. Let R' be the new resistance between A' and B'. Now resistance R_1 between A and B is given by

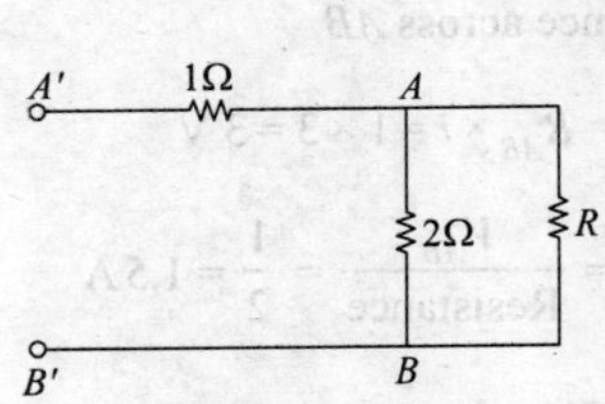

$$R_1 = \frac{R\times 2}{R+2}$$

(a parallel combination of R and $2\,\Omega$)

$$\Rightarrow \quad R_1 = \frac{2R}{R+2}\Omega$$

Resistance between A' and B'

$$R' = \frac{2R}{R+2} + 1$$

(a series combination of R_1 and 1 Ω)

$$\Rightarrow \quad R' = \frac{2R + (R+2)}{R+2} = \frac{3R+2}{R+2}$$

According to our assumption $R' = R$

$$\Rightarrow \quad R = \frac{3R+2}{R+2} \text{ or } R^2 + 2R = 3R + 2$$

$$\Rightarrow \quad R^2 - R - 2 = 0$$

$$\Rightarrow \quad R = \frac{+1 \pm \sqrt{(1+8)}}{2} = \frac{+1 \pm 3}{2} = -1 \text{ or } 2$$

$$\Rightarrow \quad R = 2\ \Omega \text{ as -1 } \Omega \text{ is not possible}$$

(b) The connection of battery and current distribution is shown in figure

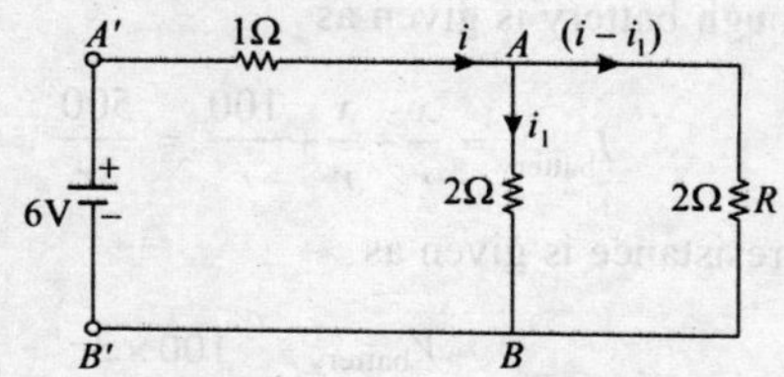

Resistance between A and $B = \frac{2 \times 2}{2+2} = 1\ \Omega$

Resistance between A' and $B' = 2\ \Omega$

Current in 1 Ω resistance is given as

$$i = \frac{6}{2} = 3\text{A}$$

Potential difference across AB

$$A_{AB} = R_{AB} \times i = 1 \times 3 = 3\text{ V}$$

$$\Rightarrow \quad i = \frac{V_{AB}}{\text{Resistance}} = \frac{1}{2} = 1.5\text{ A}$$

(vii) By perpendicular Axis symmetry all points 1, 2, 3 are at same potential therefore junction on this line can be redrawn and reduced as shown in figure below which gives the equivalent resistance by using series and parallel combination as $R_{AB} = \frac{22}{35}R$.

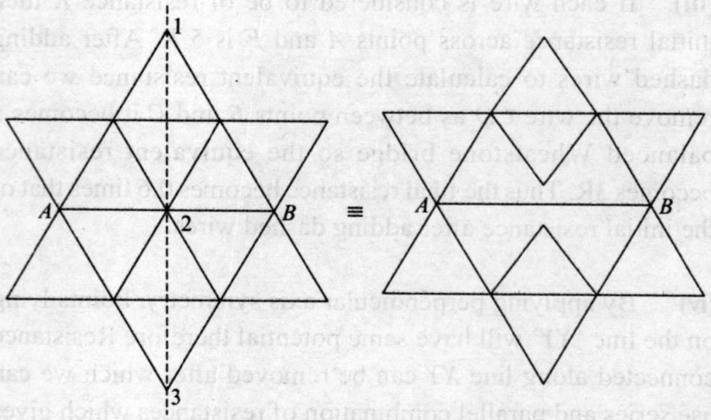

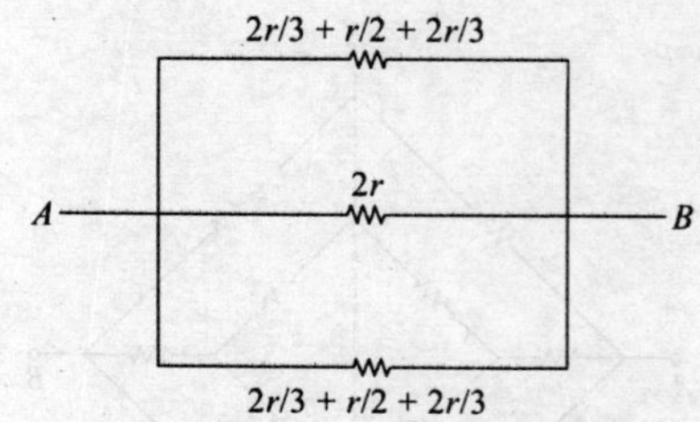

(viii) To calculate the equivalent resistance across A and B we connect a 100 V battery and distribute potential in circuit at all junctions as shown in figure.

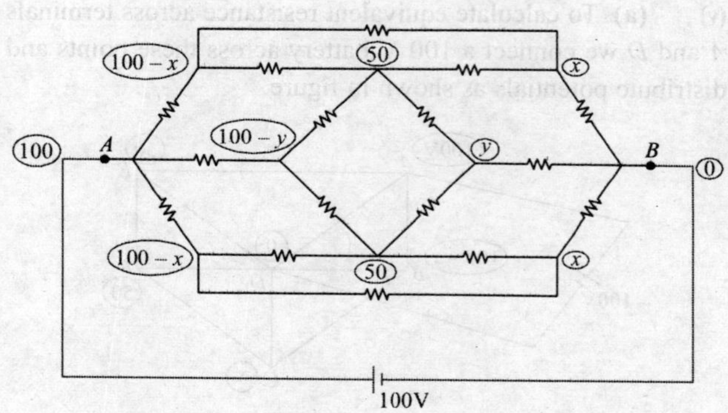

Writing KCL equations for x and y gives

$$\frac{x}{R} + \frac{x-50}{R} + \frac{2x-100}{R} = 0$$

$$\Rightarrow \quad x = \frac{75}{2}\text{V}$$

$$\text{and} \quad \frac{y}{R} + \frac{y-50}{R} + \frac{y-50}{R} = 0$$

$$\Rightarrow \quad y = \frac{100}{3}\text{V}$$

Equivalent resistance is given as

$$R_{eq} = \frac{V_{battery}}{I_{battery}} = \frac{100}{\frac{2x}{R} + \frac{y}{R}} = \frac{100R}{75 + \frac{100}{3}} = \frac{300R}{325} = \frac{12R}{13}$$

(ix) To calculate the equivalent resistance across A and B we connect a 100 V battery and distribute potential in circuit at all junctions as shown in figure.

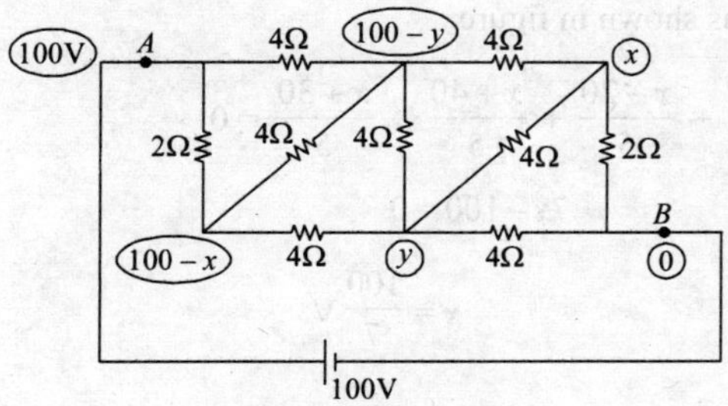

Writing KVL equations for x and y gives

$$\frac{x}{R} + \frac{x-y}{4} + \frac{x-100+y}{4} = 0$$

$$\Rightarrow \quad 4x = 100$$

$$\Rightarrow \quad x = 25\text{V}$$

and $$\frac{y}{R} + \frac{y-x}{4} + \frac{2y-100}{4} + \frac{y-100+x}{4} = 0$$

$$\Rightarrow \quad 5y = 200$$

$$\Rightarrow \quad y = 40\text{ V}$$

Equivalent resistance across A and B is given as

$$R_{eq} = \frac{V_{battery}}{I_{battery}} = \frac{100}{\frac{x}{2} + \frac{y}{4}}$$

$$\Rightarrow \quad R_{eq} = \frac{100}{\frac{25}{2} + \frac{40}{4}}$$

$$\Rightarrow \quad R_{eq} = \frac{40}{9}\,\Omega$$

(x) By symmetry we can see that in circuit points E, F and B, C are equipotential so we can remove the resistances between these terminals and using series and parallel analysis we get

$$R_{AD} = 1\,\Omega$$

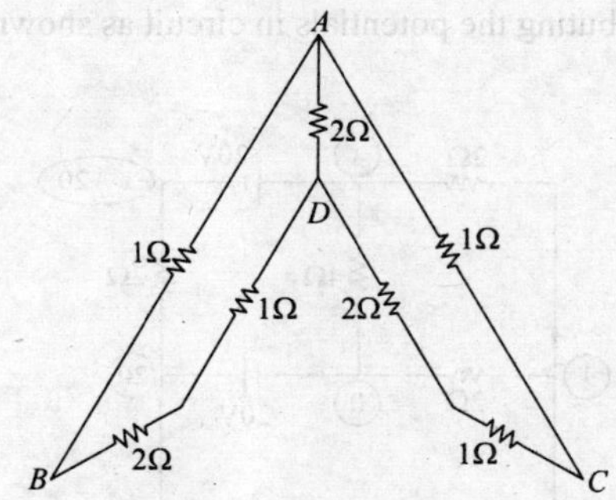

Solutions of PRACTICE EXERCISE 3.5

(i) Distributing potentials in circuit as shown in figure. Writing KCL equation for x, as

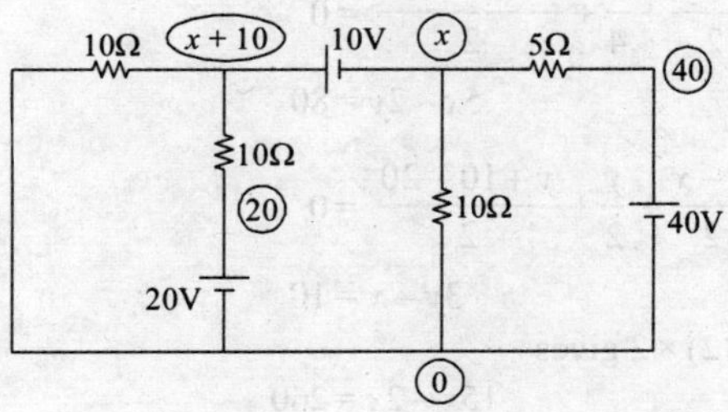

$$\frac{x-40}{5} + \frac{x}{10} + \frac{x+10-20}{10} = 0$$

$$5x = 80$$

$$\Rightarrow \quad x = 16\text{ V}$$

Current in 5 Ω resistance is given as

$$I_{5\Omega} = \frac{40-x}{5} = \frac{40-16}{5} = \frac{24}{5} = 4.8\text{ A}$$

(ii) Given that $V_A = V_B$ and if I is the current in the circuit we use

$$I = \frac{15+E}{8}$$

and $$E - Ir = 0$$

$$\Rightarrow \quad E - \left(\frac{15+E}{8}\right)(2) = 0$$

Solving this equation we get

$$E = 5\text{ V}$$

(iii) Distributing the potentials in circuit as shown in figure.

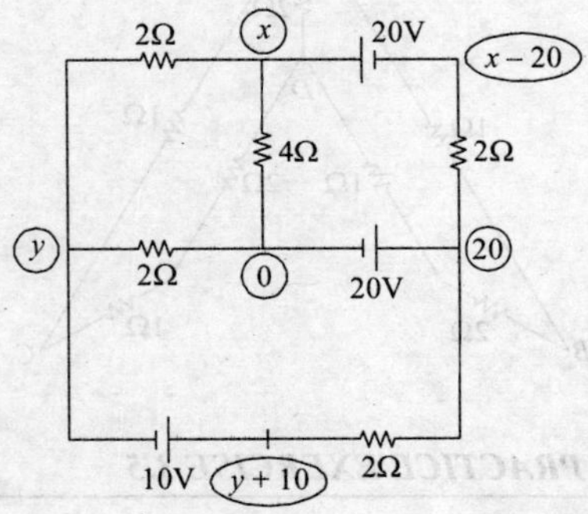

writing KCL equation for x and y, we have

$$\frac{x-y}{2}+\frac{x}{4}+\frac{x-20-20}{2}=0$$

$$5x-2y=80 \quad \ldots(1)$$

and
$$\frac{y-x}{2}+\frac{y}{2}+\frac{y+10-20}{2}=0$$

$$3y-x=10 \quad \ldots(2)$$

$(1)\times 3+(2)\times 2$ gives

$$15x-2x=260$$

$$\Rightarrow \quad x=\frac{260}{13}=20\text{ V}$$

Current in 4Ω resistance is given as

$$I_{4\Omega}=\frac{x}{4}=\frac{20}{4}=5\text{ A}$$

(iv) Distributing potentials at junctions of circuit as shown in figure

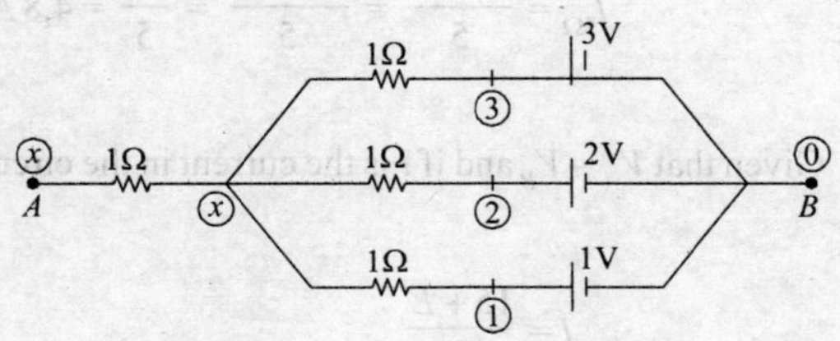

As terminal A and B are open, no current flows through R so writing KCL equation for x we have

$$x-3+x-2+x-1=0$$

$$\Rightarrow \quad x=\frac{6}{3}=2\text{ V}$$

$$\Rightarrow \quad V_A-V_B=2\text{ V}$$

Now the currents through the resistors are given as

$$I_R=0$$

$$I_{r_1}=\frac{x-3}{1}=-1\text{A}$$

$$I_{r_2}=\frac{x-2}{1}=0$$

$$I_{r_3}=\frac{x-1}{1}=1\text{A}$$

(v) Distributing the potentials at different junctions of the circuit as shown in figure.

$$\frac{x}{10}+\frac{x-20}{5}+\frac{x+40}{5}+\frac{x+30}{5}=0$$

$$\Rightarrow \quad 7x-100=0$$

$$\Rightarrow \quad x=\frac{100}{7}\text{V}$$

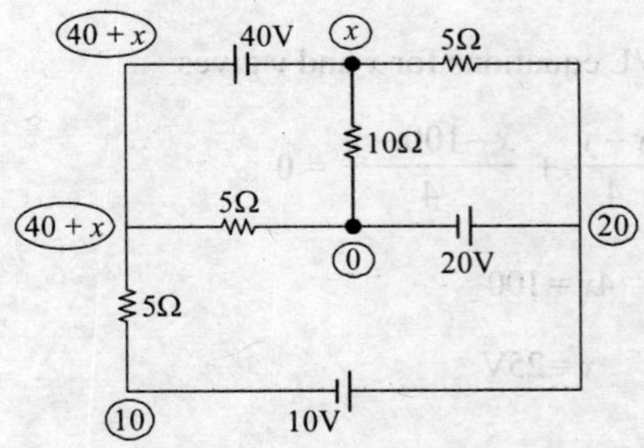

Current through 10Ω resistance is given as

$$I=\frac{x}{10}=\frac{10}{7}\text{A}$$

(vi) Distributing potentials in circuit as shown in figure and writing KCL equation for x, we have

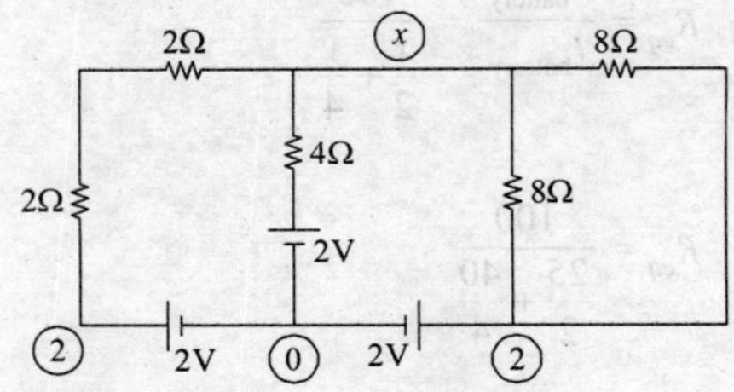

$$\frac{x-2}{4}+\frac{x-2}{4}+\frac{x-2}{4}=0$$

$$\Rightarrow \quad x=2\text{V}$$

As $x=2$ V current in all resistors of circuit is zero.

(vii) (a) Distributing potentials and currents in circuit as shown in figure. The current in 3 Ω resistance is 8 A.

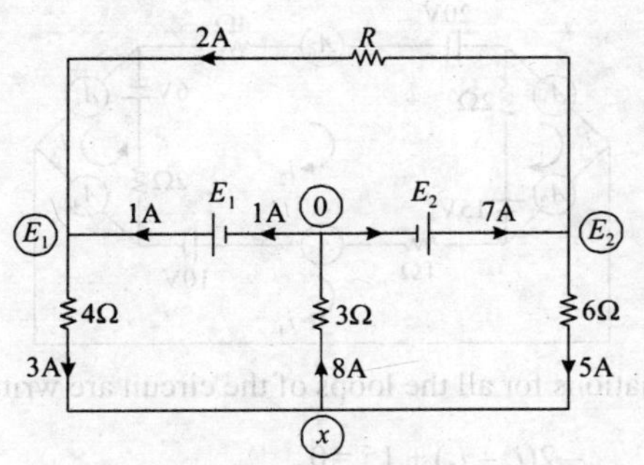

(b), (c) Using Ohm's law for resistances, we have

$$\frac{x}{3}=8$$

$$x=24$$

using $$\frac{E_1-24}{4}=3 \Rightarrow E_1=36\text{ V}$$

and $$\frac{E_2-24}{6}=5 \Rightarrow E_2=54\text{ V}$$

and $$\frac{54-36}{R}=2 \Rightarrow R=9\,\Omega$$

(viii) The current in circuit is given as

$$I=\frac{12+6}{1+2+3}=3\text{ A}$$

Now distributing potentials at circuit junctions we get the potentials of different points as shown in figure

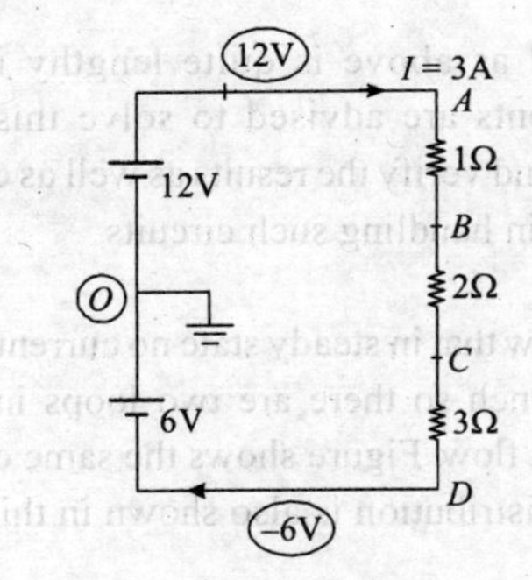

$$V_A=12\text{ V}$$

$$V_B=V_A-3\times 1=12-3=9\text{ V}$$

$$V_C=V_B-2\times 3=9-6=3\text{ V}$$

$$V_D=-6\text{ V}$$

If 6 V battery is reversed circuit current becomes

$$I=\frac{12-6}{1+2+3}=1\text{ A}$$

Now the potentials will be

$$V_A=12\text{ V}$$

$$V_B=V_A-1\times 1=11\text{ V}$$

$$V_C=V_B-2\times 1=11-2=9\text{ V}$$

$$V_D=6\text{ V}$$

Solutions of PRACTICE EXERCISE 3.6

(i) In the given circuit the two 30 V batteries can be replaced by their equivalent battery of same EMF 30 V (as EMF of both batteries are equal) and with internal resistance 0.12 Ω and the resistances 4 Ω and 1 Ω are also taken in parallel of value given as 4 × 1/(4 + 1) = 0.8 Ω. Now the whole circuit will reduce to a single loop circuit in which by the polarity of batteries we can state that current is in anticlockwise direction, which is given as

$$I=\frac{24+30-14}{0.8+3+0.6+4+0.12+2+0.4}=\frac{40}{10.2}=3.92\text{ A}$$

(ii) Figure shows the current distribution in the circuit.

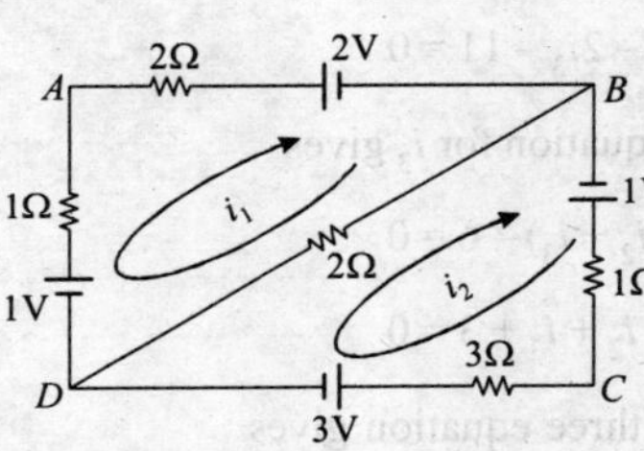

Writing KVL equation for i_1 gives

$$5i_1-2i_2=-1 \quad \ldots(1)$$

Writing KVL equation for i_2 gives

$$6i_2-2i_1=-2 \quad \ldots(2)$$

Solving equations-(1) and (2) gives

$$i_1=-\frac{5}{13}\text{ A}$$

and $$i_2=-\frac{6}{13}\text{ A}$$

(a) Potential difference between B and D is given as

$$V_B-V_D=2(i_1-i_2)=2\left(\frac{1}{13}\right)=\frac{2}{13}=0.154\text{ V}$$

(b) Potential difference across terminals of cell G is given as

$$V_G = E_G + i_2 R = 3 - \frac{6\times 3}{13} = 1.615\text{ V}$$

Potential difference across terminals of cell H is given as

$$V_H = E_F - i_1 R = 1 - \left(\frac{-5}{13}\right)(1) = 1.384\text{ V}$$

(iii) Figure shows the current distribution in circuit.

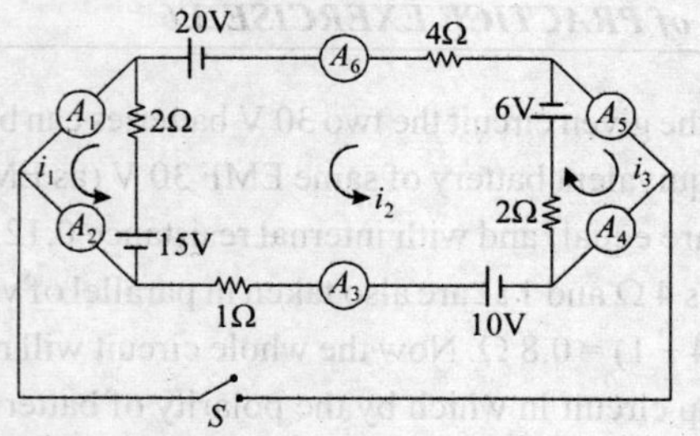

(a) Writing KVL equation for i_1 gives

$$-2(i_1 - i_2) + 15 = 0 \quad \ldots(1)$$

Writing KVL equation for i_2 gives

$$-4i_2 + 20 - 2(i_2 - i_1) - 15 - i_2$$
$$-10 - 2(i_2 + i_3) - 6 = 0$$

$$\Rightarrow \quad 2i_1 - 9i_2 - 2i_3 - 11 = 0 \quad \ldots(2)$$

Writing KVL equation for i_3 gives

$$-2(i_2 + i_3) - 6 = 0$$

$$\Rightarrow \quad i_2 + i_3 + 3 = 0 \quad \ldots(3)$$

Solving above three equation gives

$$i_1 = 9.5\text{ A}$$
$$i_2 = 2\text{ A}$$
and $$i_3 = -5\text{ A}$$

Using the above currents we can list up the reading of all the ammeters in the table below.

Ammeter	A_1	A_2	A_3	A_4	A_5	A_6
Reading (amp)	9.5	9.5	2	5	5	2

To find the potential difference across switch we write the equation of potential drop from point B to A as

$$V_B + 10 + 1\times 2 = V_A$$

$$\Rightarrow \quad V_A - V_B = 12\text{ V}$$

(b) After closing the switch S circuit is redrawn as shown in figure and the currents are distributed in all loops of circuit as shown.

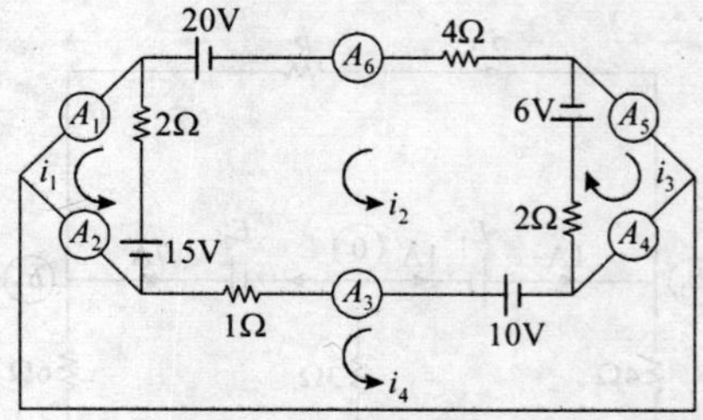

KVL equations for all the loops of the circuit are written as

$$-2(i_1 - i_2) + 15 = 0 \quad \ldots(1)$$

$$2i_1 - 9i_2 - 2i_3 - 11 + i_4 = 0 \quad \ldots(2)$$

$$i_2 + i_3 + 3 = 0 \quad \ldots(3)$$

$$10 - (i_4 - i_2) = 0 \quad \ldots(4)$$

Solving these four equation, we get

$$i_1 = 12.5\text{ A}$$
$$i_2 = 5.0\text{ A}$$
$$i_3 = -8.0\text{ A}$$
$$i_4 = 15\text{ A}$$

Using the above currents we can list up the reading of all the ammeters in the table below.

Ammeter	A_1	A_2	A_3	A_4	A_5	A_6
Reading (amp)	12.5	2.5	10	7	8	5

And the current through switch is 15 A.

Analysis we did as above is quite lengthy in solving the equations. Students are advised to solve this circuit using method of KCL and verify the results as well as compare which method is better in handling such circuits.

(iv) As we know that in steady state no current flows through the capacitor branch so there are two loops in the circuit in which the current flow. Figure shows the same circuit redrawn and the current distribution is also shown in this figure.

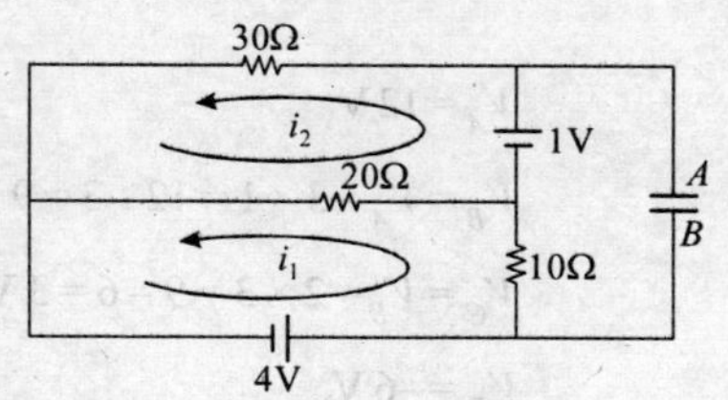

Writing KVL equations for currents i_1 and i_2 gives

$$30i_1 - 20i_2 = 4 \quad \ldots(1)$$

and $$50i_2 - 20i_1 = 1 \quad \ldots(2)$$

Solving equations-(1) and (2) gives

$$i_1 = 0.2\,\text{A}$$

and $$i_2 = 0.1\,\text{A}$$

To find the potential difference across the plates of capacitor we write equation of potential drop from point A to B as

$$V_A - 1 + 10i_1 = V_B$$

$$\Rightarrow \quad V_A - V_B = 2 - 1 = 1\,\text{V}$$

(v) The circuit given in the question is reduced and redrawn as shown in figure below. At last step we found the equivalent battery of the middle branch across terminals A and B. Calculation of equivalent battery for any circuit is taken up under article-3.8 of Thevenin's Analysis.

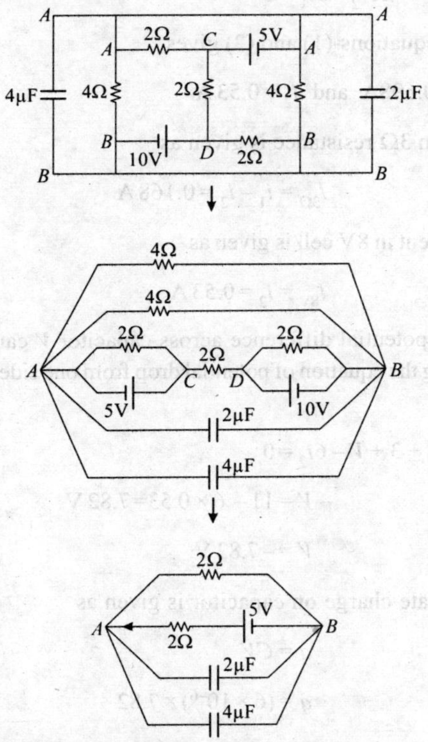

The current through the battery is given as

$$i = \frac{5}{4}\,\text{A}$$

The potential difference across terminals A and B is given as

$$V_B + 5 - \frac{5}{4} \times 2 = V_A$$

$$V_A - V_B = \frac{5}{2}\,V$$

The charges on capacitors are given as

$$q_{2\mu F} = 2 \times \frac{5}{2} = 5\,\mu\text{C}$$

and $$q_{4\mu F} = 4 \times \frac{5}{2} = 10\,\mu\text{C}$$

(vi) The circuit arrangement as described in the question and the current distribution is shown in figure.

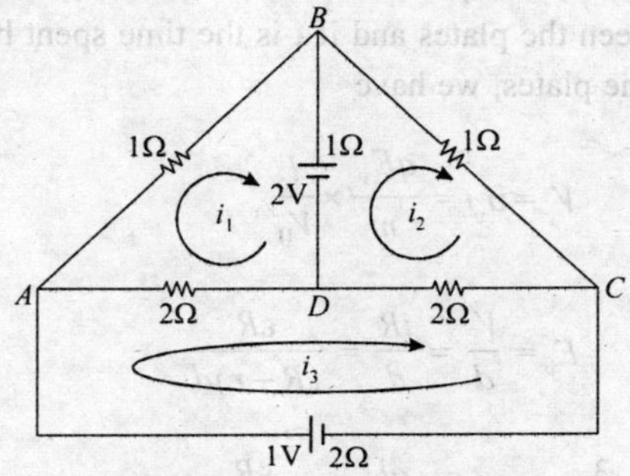

Writing KVL equations for currents i_1, i_2 and i_3 gives

$$4i_1 - i_2 - 2i_3 = -2 \quad \ldots(1)$$

and $$4i_2 - i_1 - 2i_3 = 2 \quad \ldots(2)$$

and $$6i_3 - 2i_2 - = 1 \quad \ldots(3)$$

Solving equations-(1), (2) and (3) gives

$$i_1 = -0.2\,\text{A}$$

and $$i_2 = 0.6\,\text{A}$$

and $$i_3 = 0.3\,\text{A}$$

The currents in different resistances are given as

$$I_{AB} = 0.2\,\text{A}$$

$$I_{BC} = 0.6\,\text{A}$$

$$I_{CD} = 0.3\,\text{A}$$

$$I_{AD} = 0.5\,\text{A}$$

(vii) Applying KCL at junction A, we get the current in AD branch as 3 A.

Now using KCL at junction B, we get the current in CB branch as 1 A.

To find the potential difference across the capacitor we write equation of potential drop from A to B as

$$V_A - 5 \times 3 - 1 \times 3 - 2 \times 1 = V_B$$

$$\Rightarrow \quad V_A - V_B = 20\,\text{V}$$

The energy stored in the capacitor in steady state is given as

$$U = \frac{1}{2}CV^2 = \frac{1}{2} \times (4 \times 10^{-6})(20)^2$$

$$\Rightarrow \quad U = 0.8 \times 10^{-3}\,\text{J}$$

(viii) Considering velocity components of the electron coming out, we use

$$\tan 37° = \frac{V_y}{V_x} = \frac{V_y}{V_0}$$

Where velocity component v_y is obtained due to the electric field between the plates and if t is the time spent by electron between the plates, we have

$$V_y = a_y t = \frac{qE_y}{m} \times \frac{l}{V_0}$$

$$\Rightarrow \quad E_y = \frac{V}{d} = \frac{iR}{d} = \frac{\varepsilon R}{(R+r)d}$$

$$\Rightarrow \quad \frac{3}{4}V_0 = V_y = \frac{ql}{mV_0} \times \frac{\varepsilon R}{(R+r)d}$$

$$\Rightarrow \quad \frac{3}{4}V_0^2 = \frac{16}{91} \times 10^{12} \times \frac{3 \times R}{(R+2)10^{-3}} \times 3 \times 91 \times 10^{-2}$$

$$\Rightarrow \quad 2.5R + 5 = 3R$$

$$\Rightarrow \quad 5 = 0.5R$$

$$\Rightarrow \quad R = 10\,\Omega$$

(ix) The current distribution in the above circuit is shown in figure.

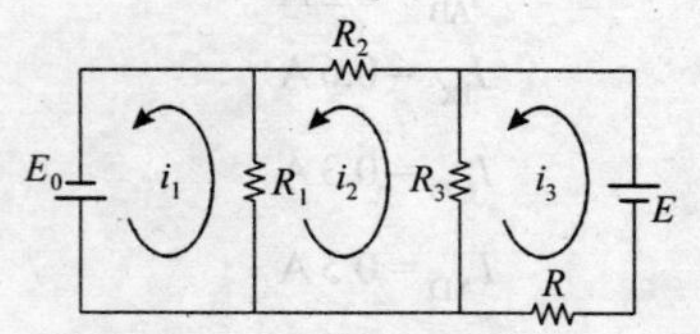

Writing KVL equations for the currents i_1, i_2 and i_3 gives

$$i_1R_1 - i_2R_1 = E_0 \quad \ldots(1)$$

and $$i_2(R_1 + R_2 + R_3) - i_1R_1 - i_3R_3 = 0 \quad \ldots(2)$$

and $$i_3(R + R_3) - i_2R_3 = E \quad \ldots(3)$$

Solving above equations-(1), (2) and (3) for i_3 gives

$$i_3 = \frac{E(R_2 + R_3) + E_0R_3}{R(R_2 + R_3) + R_2R_3}$$

(x) **(a)** In steady state no current flows through the capacitor branch so distributing currents in the two loops of circuit as shown in figure.

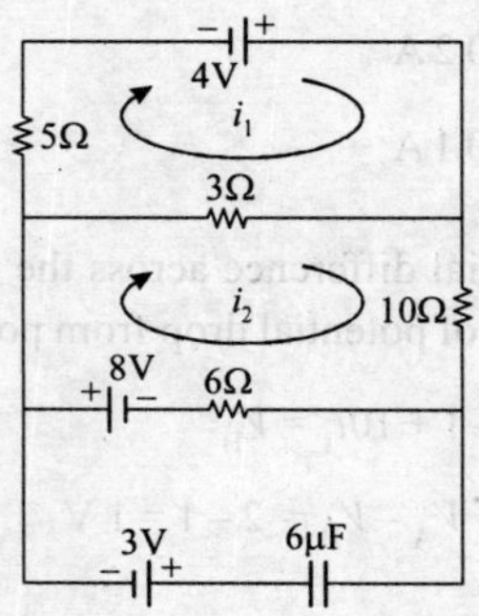

Writing KVL equations for i_1 and i_2 gives

$$8i_1 - 3i_2 = 4 \quad \ldots(1)$$

and $$19i_2 - 3i_1 = 8 \quad \ldots(2)$$

Solving equations-(1) and (2) gives

$$i_1 = 0.698\text{A} \text{ and } i_2 = 0.53\text{ A}$$

Current in 3Ω resistance is given as

$$I_{3\Omega} = i_1 - i_2 = 0.168\text{ A}$$

(b) Current in 8V cell is given as

$$I_{8V} = i_2 = 0.53\text{ A}$$

(c) The potential difference across capacitor V can be given by writing the equation of potential drop from one side to another as

$$8 + 3 + V - 6i_2 = 0$$

$$\Rightarrow \quad -V = 11 - 6 \times 0.53 = 7.82\text{ V}$$

$$\Rightarrow \quad V = -7.82\text{ V}$$

Steady state charge on capacitor is given as

$$q = CV$$

$$\Rightarrow \quad q = (6 \times 10^{-6}) \times 7.82$$

$$q = 46.92 \times 10^{-6}\text{ C}$$

Solutions of PRACTICE EXERCISE 3.7

(i) Figure shows the current distribution in the circuit.

Writing KVL equation for i_1 gives

$$+7-2i_1-3(i_1-i_2)=0 \quad \ldots(1)$$

Writing KVL equation for i_1 gives

$$-1+3(i_1-i_2)-2i_2=0 \quad \ldots(2)$$

Solving equations-(1) and (2) gives

$$i_1 = 2\text{A and } i_2 = 1\text{ A}$$

Power supplied by battery of EMF E_1 is given as

$$P_1 = E_1 i_1 = 14\text{ W}$$

But supplied by battery of EMF E_2 is given as

$$P_2 = E_2 i_2 = -1\text{ W}$$

Second battery will consume power as current i_2 is going into its positive terminal.

(ii) Current in first case is given as

$$i = \frac{E}{5+x} = \frac{50}{5+x}$$

Power supplied to the resistance is given as

$$P = i^2 R = \frac{400}{(5+x)^2} \times x$$

In second case, current is given as

$$i' = \frac{E}{\left[5+\left(\frac{6x}{x+6}\right)\right]}$$

Power supplied by the battery now is given as

$$P' = i'^2 R' = \frac{400}{\left[5+\left(\frac{6x}{6+x}\right)\right]^2} \frac{6x}{(6+x)}$$

Power supplied in two cases are equal so we use

$$\frac{400x}{(5+x)^2} = \frac{400}{\left[5+\frac{6x}{(6+x)}\right]} \times \frac{6x}{(6+x)}$$

$$\Rightarrow \quad x = 7.5\ \Omega$$

(iii) As discussed in maximum power transfer theorem the maximum power which can be transferred is given as

$$P_{max} = \frac{E^2}{4r}$$

Here E and r are the equivalent EMF and internal resistance of the equivalent battery when the given batteries are connected in series as in that case EMF will be maximum which gives

$$P_{max} = \frac{(4)^2}{4\times 2} = 2\text{ W}$$

(iv) For power supplied to be maximum, the current in the external circuit should be maximum. In mixed grouping, the condition for maximum current is to have external resistance equal to internal resistance. Let m rows, each of n cells in series be connected in parallel like a battery grid then the internal resistance of battery grid is given as

$$R_{int} = \frac{nr}{m}$$

As $R = 10\Omega$, and $r = 1\Omega$, we have

$$10 = n/m$$

As total 24 cells are there we use $mn = 24$

$$\Rightarrow \quad n = \sqrt{(240)} \text{ and } m = \sqrt{(2.4)} = 1.2$$

Thus m should lie between 1 and 2. The value of m can not be in fraction so if we use $m = 1$, then $n = 24$ and the current in external circuit is given as

$$i = \frac{nE}{R+\frac{nr}{m}} = \frac{24E}{10+24} = 0.7E$$

If we consider $m = 2$ and $n = 12$ then current in external circuit is given as

$$i = \frac{nE}{R+\frac{nr}{m}} = \frac{12E}{10+6} = 0.75E$$

Thus current in second case in more than the current in first case so to get maximum output, 2 rows each of 12 cells in series must be connected in parallel.

(v) Figure below shows the circuit and when maximum power is transferred to R_x then near to maximum value power remain constant for small variation in resistance. It happens when R_x is equal to the internal resistance of the circuit which is 20 Ω in parallel with 30 Ω as battery is considered to be idea.

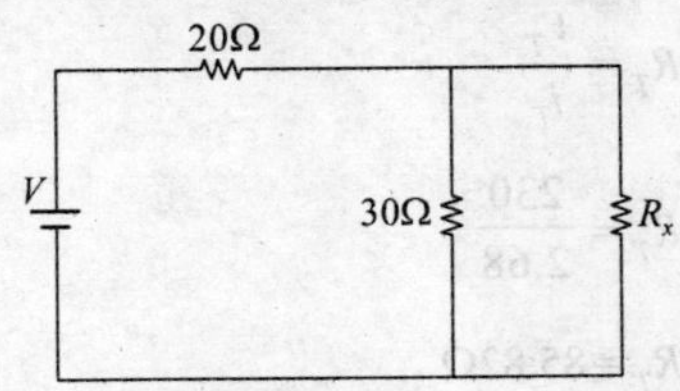

Thus for maximum power R_x is given as

$$R_x = \frac{20\times 30}{20+30} = 12\ \Omega$$

(vi) From a filament heat generated and transferred to surrounding is always proportional to the exposed surface area of the filament thus we have

$$Q \propto A,$$

If we consider l as filament length and r is its radius then its surface area is given as

$$A = 2\pi rl$$

Power developed in the filament is given by thermal power in it

$$P = \frac{V^2}{R}$$

For constant temperature of the filament in steady state we use power developed is equal to power radiated to surrounding, so we have

$$P = \frac{V^2}{R} = K.\,2\pi rl$$

K is a proportionality constant here and R is the resistance of the filament which is given as

$$R = \frac{\rho l}{a} = \frac{\rho l}{\pi r^2} = \frac{4\rho l}{\pi D^2}$$

$$\Rightarrow \quad V^2 = 2\pi K.\frac{D}{2}\cdot l.\frac{4\rho l}{\pi D^2} = \frac{4K\rho l^2}{D}$$

Taking natural log (ln) on both sides of above equation gives

$$\ln (V)^2 = \ln\left(\frac{4K\rho l^2}{D}\right)$$

Differentiating the above equation gives

$$2\frac{dV}{V} = -\frac{dD}{D}$$

$$\Rightarrow \quad \frac{dD}{D}\% = -2\frac{dV}{V}\%$$

$$\Rightarrow \quad \eta\% = -2\%$$

(vii) Given that at $T_0 = 27°C$ and $R_0 = 75.3\ \Omega$

At temperature T we use

$$R_T = \frac{V_T}{i_T}$$

$$\Rightarrow \quad R_T = \frac{230}{2.68}$$

$$\Rightarrow \quad R_T = 85.82\Omega$$

Using the equation $R_T = R_0[1 + \alpha(T - T_0)]$, we have

$$85.82 = 75.3[1 + (1.70 \times 10^{-4})(T-27)]$$

Solving above equation, gives

$$T = 850°C$$

Thus, the steady temperature of the Nichrome element is 850°C

(viii) **(a)** Since the current decreases to zero uniformly in a time interval Δt, the time function of current can be given as

$$i = i_0\left(1 - \frac{t}{\Delta t}\right)$$

Where we consider i_0 as the initial current

As total charge q is passed in time Δt, we use

$$q = \int_0^{\Delta t} i\Delta t = \int_0^{\Delta t} i_0\left(1 - \frac{t}{\Delta t}\right) = \frac{i_0 \Delta t}{2}$$

$$\Rightarrow \quad i_0 = \frac{2q}{\Delta t}$$

Thus time function of current is given as

$$i = \frac{2q}{\Delta t}\left(1 - \frac{t}{\Delta t}\right)$$

Heat generated in this time is calculated as

$$Q = \int_0^{\Delta t} i^2 R\Delta t = \int_0^{\Delta t} \frac{2q}{\Delta t}\left(1 - \frac{t}{\Delta t}\right)^2 R\Delta t$$

$$\Rightarrow \quad Q = -\frac{4}{3}\frac{q^2 R}{\Delta t}\left[\left(1 - \frac{t}{\Delta t}\right)^3\right]_0^{\Delta t} = \frac{4q^2 R}{3\Delta t}$$

(b) In this case time function of current can be written as

$$i = i_0\left(\frac{1}{2}\right)^{t/\Delta t}$$

Above function becomes zero at infinite time so total charge q passing can be given as

$$q = \int_0^{\infty} idt = \int_0^{\infty} i_0 2^{-t/\Delta t} dt = \frac{i_0 \Delta t}{\ln(2)}$$

$$\Rightarrow \quad i_0 = \frac{q\ln(2)}{\Delta t}$$

Heat generated by this current can be given as

$$H = \int_0^{\infty} i^2 Rdt = \int_0^{\infty}\left[\frac{q\ln(2)}{\Delta t}2^{-t/\Delta t}\right]^2 Rdt$$

$$\Rightarrow \quad H = \frac{1}{2}\frac{q^2 R\ln(2)}{\Delta t}$$

(ix) As per the given condition, we use

$$\frac{V^2}{R} = k(T - T_0) + C\left(\frac{dT}{dt}\right)$$

$$\Rightarrow \qquad \frac{dT}{\dfrac{V^2}{R} - k(T - T_0)} = \frac{dt}{C}$$

$$\Rightarrow \qquad \int_{T_0}^{T} \frac{dT}{\dfrac{V^2}{R} - k(T - T_0)} = \int_0^t \frac{dt}{C}$$

$$\Rightarrow \quad T = T_0 + \frac{V^2}{kR}(1 - e^{-kt/C})$$

(x) Let l be the length of the fuse wire then its resistance R is given as

$$R = \frac{\rho l}{A}$$

$$\Rightarrow \qquad R = \frac{22 \times 10^{-6} l}{0.2 \times 10^{-2}} \qquad \ldots(1)$$

Let t seconds be the time taken for melting the fuse wire, then Heat produced is given as

$$H = \frac{i^2 R t}{4.2} \text{ cal}$$

Here $I = 30$A so we have

$$H = \frac{(30)^2 \times 22 \times 10^{-6} \times l \times t}{4.2 \times 0.2 \times 10^{-2}} \text{ cal} \qquad \ldots(2)$$

We can also use

$$H = m\,s\,T$$

Where mass of fuse wire is given as

$$m = \text{volume} \times \text{density} = A \times l \times \text{density}$$

$$\Rightarrow \qquad m = (0.2 \times 10^{-2}) \times l \times 11.34$$

$$\Rightarrow \qquad H = (0.2 \times 10^{-2})\, l \times 11.34 \times 0.032 \times (327 - 20) \qquad \ldots(3)$$

From equation (2) and (3) we have

$$(0.2 \times 10^{-2})\, l \times 11.34 \times 0.034 \times 0.032 \times 307$$

$$= \frac{(30)^2 \times 22 \times 10^{-6} \times l \times t}{4.2 \times 0.2 \times 10^{-2}}$$

Solving above equation gives

$$t = 0.095 \text{ s}$$

Solutions of PRACTICE EXERCISE 3.8

(i) In steady state current flows only in lower loop of the circuit which is given as

$$i = \frac{30}{6+4} = 3\text{A}$$

Potential difference across capacitor is same as potential difference across 4Ω resistance.

$$V_C = iR$$

$$\Rightarrow \qquad V_C = 3 \times 4 = 12\text{V}$$

Charge stored on capacitor in steady state is

$$q = CV = 2 \times 12 = 24\mu\text{C}$$

(ii) In steady state current flows in upper and lower loops of the circuit which are i_1 and i_2 respectively then we have

$$i_1 = \frac{10}{3+2} = 2\text{A}$$

and
$$i_2 = \frac{20}{4+6} = 2\text{A}$$

Potential differences across points BG and CF are given as

$$V_{BG} = V_B - V_G = 3i_1 = 3 \times 2 = 6\text{V}$$

and
$$V_{CF} = V_C - V_F = 4i_2 = 4 \times 2 = 8\text{V}$$

Charge on both the capacitors will be same as sum of charges on top and bottom plates of both the capacitors must be zero as initially these are uncharged. If charge on capacitors is q then we write the equation of potential drop in loop BGFC as

$$-6 - \frac{q}{6 \times 10^{-6}} + 8 - \frac{q}{3 \times 10^{-6}} = 0$$

$$\Rightarrow \qquad \frac{(10^6)q}{2} = 2$$

$$\Rightarrow \qquad q = 4 \times 10^{-6}\text{C}$$

$$\Rightarrow \qquad q = 4\mu\text{C}$$

(iii) At the initial moment, the circuit arrangement is shown in figure.

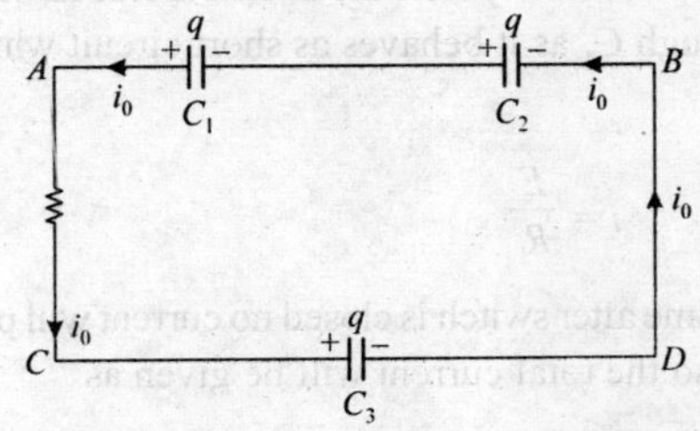

Writing KVL equation for the loop just after making the connections, we have

$$\frac{q}{C_1}+\frac{q}{C_2}-\frac{q}{C_3}-i_0 R=0$$

$$\Rightarrow \quad \frac{30}{3}+\frac{30}{6}-\frac{30}{6}-i_0\times 10=0$$

$$\Rightarrow \quad i_0 = 1\text{A}$$

Initially, the energy stored in the capacitors is given as

$$U_1=\frac{q^2}{2C_1}+\frac{q^2}{2C_2}+\frac{q^2}{2C_3}$$

$$\Rightarrow \quad U_1=\frac{900}{2\times 3}+\frac{900}{2\times 6}+\frac{900}{2\times 6}=150+75+75$$

$$\Rightarrow \quad U_1=300\ \mu\text{J}$$

Let charge δq flows rough the circuit till a steady state is reached. Then the charges on C_1, C_2 and C_3 will be

$$q_1=(q-\delta q),\ q_2=(q-\delta d)\text{ and } q_3=q+\delta q$$

Again writing KVL equation for the loop in steady state gives

$$\frac{q-\delta q}{C_1}+\frac{q-\delta q}{C_2}-\frac{q+\delta q}{C_3}=0$$

$$\Rightarrow \quad \delta q=15\mu\text{C}$$

Now, final energy stored in capacitors is given as

$$U_2=\frac{(q-\delta q)^2}{2C_1}+\frac{(q-\delta q)^2}{2C_2}+\frac{(q+\delta q)^2}{2C_3}$$

$$\Rightarrow \quad U_2=\frac{(15)^2}{2\times 3}+\frac{(15)^2}{2\times 6}+\frac{(45)^2}{2\times 6}$$

$$\Rightarrow \quad U_2=225\ \mu\text{J}$$

Thus total amount of heat generated is given by loss in total electrostatic energy of all capacitors which is given as

$$H=U_1-U_2=300-225=75\ \mu\text{J}$$

(iv) **(a)** Immediately after the switch is closed whole current passes through C_1 as it behaves as short circuit which is given as

$$i=\frac{E}{R_1}$$

(b) Long time after switch is closed no current will pass through C_1 and C_2 so the total current will be given as

$$i=\frac{E}{R_1+R_3}$$

(v) Let q be the instantaneous charge on the capacitor when a steady current i flows through the circuit. From the circuit, we can write KVL equation as

$$E=\frac{q}{C}+iR$$

$$\Rightarrow \quad E=\frac{qx}{\varepsilon_0 A}+iR \qquad \ldots(1)$$

When separation between the plates of the capacitor is x, then we use its instantaneous capacitance to be $C=\varepsilon_0 A/x$

Differentiating equation-(1), with respect to time, we get

$$0=\frac{q}{\varepsilon_0 A}\left(\frac{dx}{dt}\right)+\frac{ix}{\varepsilon_0 A}$$

$$\Rightarrow \quad q=-\frac{ix}{(dx/dt)} \qquad \ldots(2)$$

From equation-(2), substituting the value of q in equation-(1) gives

$$E=-\frac{ix^2}{\varepsilon_0 A(dx/dt)}+iR$$

$$\Rightarrow \quad \frac{dx}{dt}=v=\left(\frac{-i/\varepsilon_0 A}{E-iR}\right)x^2$$

$$\Rightarrow \quad -\frac{dx}{x^2}=\left(\frac{i/\varepsilon_0 A}{E-iR}\right)dt \qquad \ldots(3)$$

Integrating the above expression with respect to time, gives

$$\frac{1}{x}-\frac{1}{x_0}=\left[\frac{i/\varepsilon_0 A}{E-iR}\right]t \qquad \ldots(4)$$

Again differentiating with respect to time, gives

$$-\frac{1}{x^2}\frac{dx}{dt}=\frac{i/\varepsilon_0 A}{E-iR}$$

$$\Rightarrow \quad v=\left(\frac{dx}{dt}\right)=\left(\frac{i/\varepsilon_0 A}{iR-E}\right)x^2 \qquad \ldots(5)$$

From equations-(4) and (5), we have

$$v=\frac{\left(\dfrac{i/\varepsilon_0 A}{iR-E}\right)}{\left[\left(\dfrac{i/\varepsilon_0 A}{E-iR}\right)t+\dfrac{1}{x_0}\right]^2}$$

(vi) Initial potential energy stored in the capacitor,

$$U = \frac{1}{2}CV^2$$

$$\Rightarrow \quad U = \frac{1}{2} \times 5 \times 10^{-6} \times (200)^2 = 0.1\text{ J}$$

When the switch is shifted from contact 1 to 2 capacitor starts discharging and during discharging this 0.1 J, will distribute in direct ratio of resistance thus heat dissipated in 400 Ω resistance is given as

$$H_{400\Omega} = \frac{400}{400+500} \times 0.1$$

$$\Rightarrow \quad H_{400\Omega} = 44.4 \times 10^{-3}\text{ J}$$

$$\Rightarrow \quad H_{400\Omega} = 44.4\text{ mJ}$$

(vii) The current distribution is shown in figure. As we know that in steady state no current will flow in the two branches consisting of capacitors.

From figure the currents in the two loops are given as

$$i_1 = \frac{24}{4+2} = 4\text{ A}$$

and $$i_2 = \frac{18}{3+6} = 2\text{ A}$$

In the figure we consider a potential x at the right plate of the 2 μF capacitor and zero at the left plate of this capacitor and find the potentials at the plates of other capacitor as shown in figure.

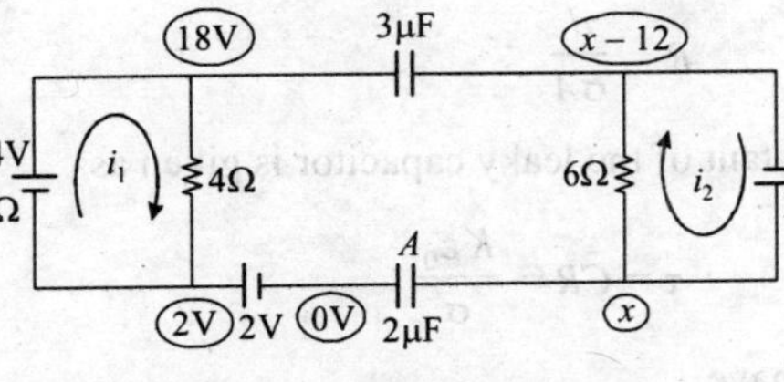

Now writing nodal equation for unknown potential x, we have

$$2x + 3(x - 12 - 18) = 0$$

$$\Rightarrow \quad 5x = 90$$

$$\Rightarrow \quad x = 18\text{ V}$$

Charge on 2 μF capacitor is given as

$$q_{2\mu F} = 2 \times 18 = 36\ \mu C$$

Charge on 3 μF capacitor is given as

$$q_{3\mu F} = 3 \times (18 - 6) = 36\ \mu C$$

(viii) **(a)** After long time in steady state capacitor gets fully charged by EMF E_1 then current through capacitor will be zero thus we have

$$i_C = 0$$

and $$i_{R_1} = i_{R_2} = \frac{E_1}{R_1 + R_2} = \frac{20}{20 \times 10^3}$$

$$i_{R_1} = i_{R_2} = 10^{-3}\ A = 1\text{ mA}$$

(b) In steady state with EMF E_1

$$V_C = V_{R_2} = V_{R_1} = \frac{E_1}{2} = 10\text{ V}$$

Now when the switch is shifted to position B, just after shifting capacitor behaves like a battery of 10 V. The currents in this situation can be calculated from the circuit shown in figure in which we distribute the potentials at different junctions of the circuit as shown.

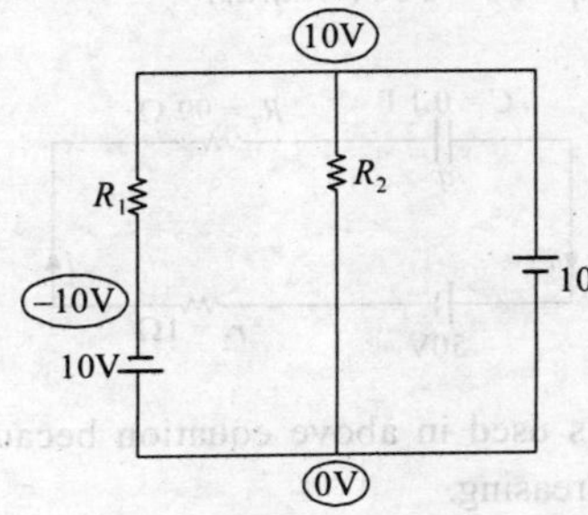

$$i_{R_1} = \frac{20}{10 \times 10^3} = 2\text{ mA}$$

and $$i_{R_2} = \frac{10}{10 \times 10^3} = 1\text{ mA}$$

By using KCL at top junction of circuit we can get the current through capacitor which is given as

$$i_C = 3\text{ mA}$$

(ix) **(a)** Initially the capacitor is uncharged. When the switch is put on position 1, the capacitor starts charging. After some time, the steady state is reached and the change on the capacitor is given as

$$q_0 = CE_1 = 0.1 \times 100 = 10\text{C}$$

Work done by the battery in charging is given as

$$W_1 = q_0 E_1 = 1000\text{ J}$$

Energy stored in the capacitor till steady state is given as

$$U_1 = \frac{q_0^2}{2C} = 500\text{ J}$$

Heat generated during flow of charge q_0 is

$$H_1 = W_1 - U_1 = 500\text{ J}$$

During charging process, the resistances r_1 and R are in series so heat is distributed in same ratio of resistance values thus heat generated across 99Ω is given by

$$H_{99\Omega} = \frac{R}{(r_1 + R)} \times H_1 = \frac{99}{100} \times 500 = 495 \text{ J} \quad \ldots(1)$$

(b) When the switch is thrown to position 2, the circuit arrangement is shown in figure. In this position, the charge on capacitor q decreases because it is connected to a battery of EMF 50V. If at any time instant t, the charge on capacitor is equal to q and suppose the current flowing in the circuit be i then using KCL in this loop gives

$$\frac{q}{C} - iR - ir_2 = E_2$$

$$\Rightarrow \quad 10q - 50 = 100\, i$$

$$\Rightarrow \quad 10q - 50 = 100\,(-dq/dt)$$

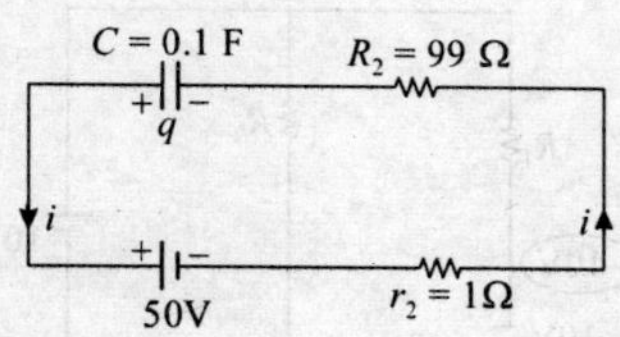

Negative sign is used in above equation because charge on capacitor is decreasing.

$$\Rightarrow \quad q - 5 = (-qd/dt)$$

$$\Rightarrow \quad \frac{10dq}{q-5} = -dt$$

$$\Rightarrow \quad \int_{q_0}^{q} \frac{10dq}{q-5} = -\int_0^t dt$$

$$\Rightarrow \quad 10\ln\left(\frac{q-5}{q_0-5}\right) = -t$$

$$\Rightarrow \quad q = 5(1 + e^{-t/10}) \quad \ldots(2)$$

The current in circuit is given as

$$i = -\frac{dq}{dt} = \frac{1}{2} e^{-t/10} \text{ A} \quad \ldots(3)$$

(c) From equation-(2) steady state charge on capacitor is given as

$$q = 5\,(1 + e^{-\infty/10})$$

$$\Rightarrow \quad q = 5 \text{ C}$$

Final energy stored in capacitor is given as

$$U_2 = \frac{q^2}{2C} = \frac{(5)^2}{2 \times 0.1} = 125 \text{ J}$$

Energy supplied to battery E_2 is given by

$$W_2 = E_2(q_0 - q)$$

$$\Rightarrow \quad W_2 = 50(10 - 5) = 250 \text{ J}$$

Heat generated during this process is given as

$$H_2 = U_1 - (U_2 + W_2) = 500 - (125 + 250)$$

$$\Rightarrow \quad H_2 = 125 \text{ J}$$

Heat generated across r_2 is given by

$$H_{r2} = \frac{r_2}{R_2 + r_2} \times H_2$$

$$\Rightarrow \quad H_{r2} = \frac{1}{100} \times 125 = 1.25 \text{ J}$$

(x) **(a)** The given capacitor is a leaky capacitor which is discharging through its medium between the plates. In this case charge at any time t is given as

$$q = q_0 e^{-t/\tau}$$

Discharging current in the circuit is given as

$$i = \left(\frac{-dq}{dt}\right) = \frac{q_0}{\tau} . e^{-t/\tau} = i_0 e^{-t/\tau}$$

Here we have

$$i_0 = \frac{q_0}{\tau_c} = \frac{q_0}{CR}$$

Capacitance and resistance between the plates are given as

$$C = \frac{K\varepsilon_0 A}{d}$$

and $$R = \frac{d}{\sigma A}$$

Time constant of the leaky capacitor is given as

$$\tau = CR = \frac{K\varepsilon_0}{\sigma}$$

Thus we have

$$i_0 = \frac{q_0}{\frac{K\varepsilon_0}{\sigma}} = \frac{\sigma q_0}{K\varepsilon_0}$$

$$\Rightarrow \quad K = \frac{\sigma q_0}{i_0 \varepsilon_0}$$

Substituting the values gives

$$K = \frac{(5.0 \times 10^{-14})(\pi)(4.0)^2(15 \times 10^{-6})}{(1.0 \times 10^{-6})(8.86 \times 10^{-12})}$$

$$\Rightarrow \quad K = 4.25$$

(b) Initial energy stored in capacitor which is dissipated as heat is given as

$$U = \frac{1}{2}\frac{q_0^2}{C} = \frac{1}{2}\frac{q_0^2}{\frac{K\varepsilon_0 A}{d}}$$

$$\Rightarrow \quad d = \frac{2K\varepsilon_0 AU}{q_0^2}$$

$$\Rightarrow \quad d = \frac{2\times 4.25\times 8.86\times 10^{-12}\times\pi\times(4.0\times 10^{-2})^2\times 7500}{(1.0\times 10^{-6})(8.86\times 10^{-12})}$$

$$\Rightarrow \quad d = 5.0\times 10^{-3}\,\text{m} = 5.0\,\text{mm}$$

(xi) From Kirchoff's Law

$$IR + q/c - E = 0$$

$$\Rightarrow \quad R\frac{dq}{dt} + \frac{q}{C} = E$$

$$\Rightarrow \quad RC\frac{dq}{dt} = CE - q$$

Integrating, $\quad q = q_0(e^{-t/RC}),\ q_0 = CE$

If the capacitance is decreased η-fold, as $t = 0$, then initial charge $q_0' = +\frac{CE}{\eta}$. Hence the charge available for flow is

$$q_0 - q_0' = (\eta - 1)\frac{CE}{\eta}$$

After this instant ($t > 0$), charge q changes according to the equation,

$$q = (\eta - 1)\frac{CE}{\eta}(1 - e^{-t\eta/RC})$$

Current through the capacitor is given as

$$I = \frac{dq}{dt} = \frac{\eta - 1}{\eta}EC\frac{\eta}{RC}e^{-t\eta/RC}$$

$$\Rightarrow \quad I = \frac{(\eta - 1)}{R}Ee^{-t\eta/RC}$$

Solutions of PRACTICE EXERCISE 3.9

(i) Using $\quad R = \frac{V}{i_g} - G$

$$\Rightarrow \quad R = \frac{10}{10^{-3}} - 20$$

$$\Rightarrow \quad R = 9980\,\Omega$$

Thus, a resistance of 9980 Ω is to be connected in series with the galvanometer to convert it into the voltmeter of desired range.

(ii) The situation described in question is shown in figure.

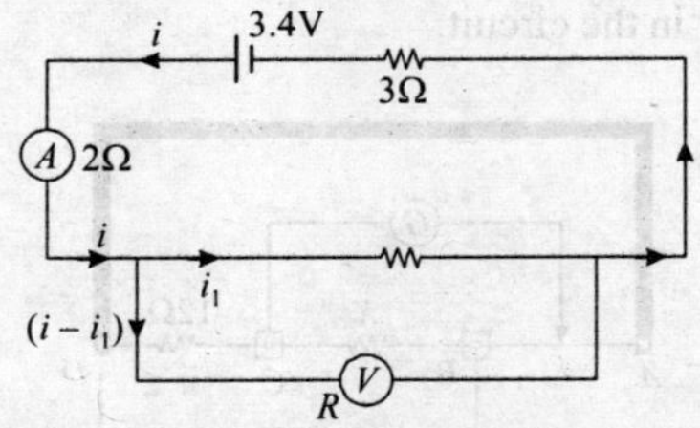

Equivalent resistance of voltmeter and 100 Ω resistance

$$R' = \frac{100R}{100 + R}\,\Omega$$

Current supplied by cell is given as

$$i = \frac{3.4}{(3 + 2 + R')}$$

$$\Rightarrow \quad 0.04 = \left(\frac{3.4}{5 + R'}\right) = \frac{3.4}{5 + (100R/100 + R)}$$

Solving we get

$$R = 400\,\Omega$$

From the above circuit current is divided in resistance and voltmeter which are in parallel connection, for which we can write

$$i_1\times 100 = (i - i_1)R = (0.04 - i_1)\times 400$$

$$\Rightarrow \quad i_1 = 0.032\,\text{A}$$

$$V_{100\Omega} = 0.032\times 100 = 3.2\,\text{V}$$

For ideal voltmeter $R = \infty$

In this case current is given as

$$i = \frac{3.4}{3 + 2 + 100} = 0.03238\,\text{A}$$

Potential difference across 100Ω resistance is given as

$$V_{100} = 0.03238\times 100 = 3.238\,\text{V}$$

(iii) In a meter bridge null deflection occurs at balancing state of Wheatstone bridge for which we use

$$\frac{10}{R} = \frac{AC}{CB}$$

$$\Rightarrow \quad R = 10\left(\frac{CB}{AC}\right) = (10)\left(\frac{100 - 40}{40}\right) = 10\left(\frac{60}{40}\right)$$

$$\Rightarrow \quad R = 15\,\Omega$$

(iv) **(a)** There are no positive and negative terminals on the galvanometer because null deflection in needed so this must be a bidirectional galvanometer.

(b) Figure shows the connections of battery and the galvanometer in the circuit.

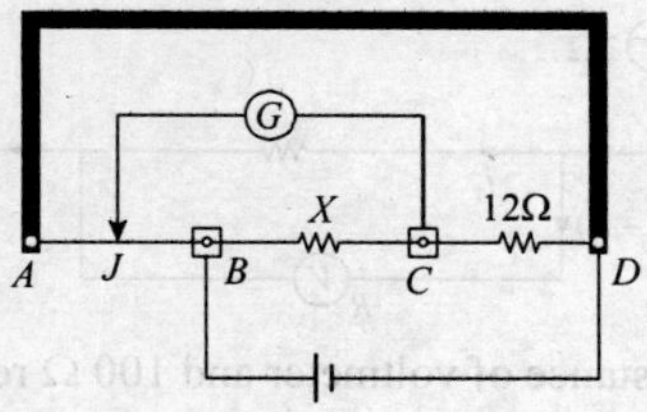

(c) Given that at null deflection distances are

$$AJ = 60\text{ cm}$$

and $$BJ = 40\text{ cm}$$

At null deflection the Wheatstone bridge is balanced so we use

$$\frac{X}{12} = \frac{R_{BJ}}{R_{AJ}}$$

$$\Rightarrow \quad \frac{X}{12} = \frac{40}{60} = \frac{2}{3}$$

$$\Rightarrow \quad X = 8\,\Omega$$

(v) Shunt resistance S can be calculated by using equation-(136) as

$$\frac{i_g}{i - i_g} = \frac{S}{G}$$

$$\Rightarrow \quad S = \left(\frac{i_g}{i - i_g}\right) G$$

$$\Rightarrow \quad S = \left[\frac{(50 \times 10^{-6})}{(5 \times 10^{-3} - 50 \times 10^{-6})}\right](100) = 1.0\,\Omega$$

(vi) **(a)** In initial state the voltmeter is connected across resistance R so the circuit is shown in figure in which we have considered the voltmeter and ammeter as their internal resistances.

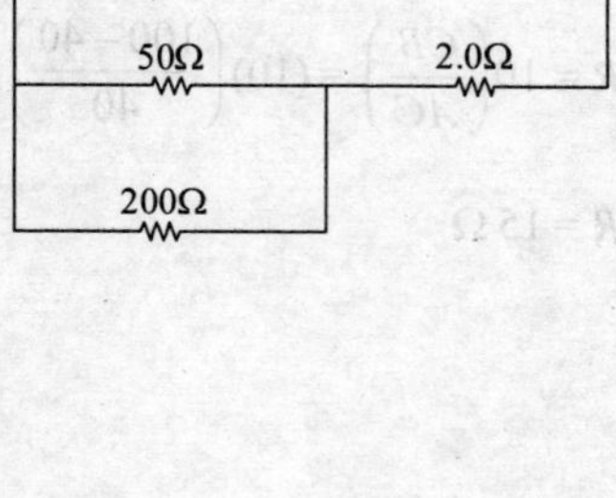

Effective resistance of the circuit in this case is given as

$$R_{net} = 1.0 + 2.0 + \frac{50 \times 200}{50 + 200}$$

$$\Rightarrow \quad R_{net} = 43\,\Omega$$

Current in circuit which will be the reading of ammeter is given as

$$i = \frac{4.3}{43} = 0.1\text{ A}$$

Reading of voltmeter is given as

$$V = i \times \text{effective resistance of } 50\,\Omega \text{ and } 200\,\Omega$$

$$\Rightarrow \quad V = (0.1)\left(\frac{50 \times 200}{50 + 200}\right)$$

$$\Rightarrow \quad V = 4\text{ V}$$

(b) After the switch is thrown on the other side the circuit is now shown in figure.

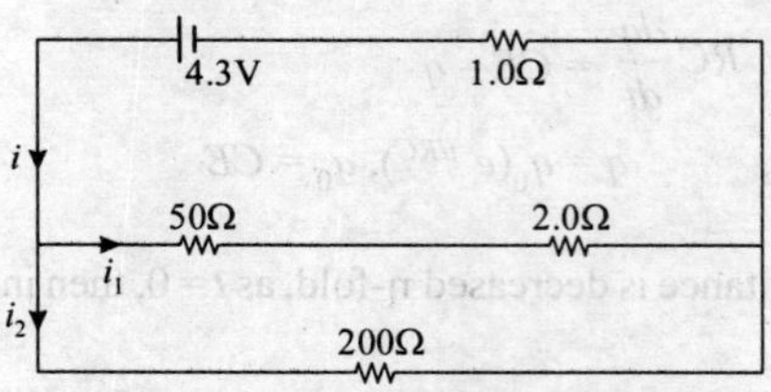

Effective resistance of the circuit across battery is given as

$$R_{net} = 1.0 + \frac{52 \times 200}{52 + 200}$$

$$\Rightarrow \quad R_{net} = 42.27\,\Omega$$

Current supplied by the battery now is given as

$$i = \frac{4.3}{42.27} = 0.1\text{ A}$$

In the above circuit the current is divided in inverse ratio of resistances in parallel combination as

$$\frac{i_1}{i_2} = \frac{200}{52}$$

Ammeter reading is given as

$$i_1 = \left(\frac{200}{252}\right)(0.1)$$

$$\Rightarrow \quad i_1 = 0.08\text{ A}$$

Reading to voltmeter is given as

$$V = \text{Potential difference across } (50 + 2.0)\,\Omega$$

$$\Rightarrow \quad V = 0.08 \times 52$$

$$\Rightarrow \quad V = 4.2\text{ V}$$

(vii) If we consider ρ as the resistance per unit length of wire AB. Initially when k is in open state we for balance point, we use

$$I(\rho x_1) = \varepsilon_1 \quad \ldots(1)$$

When the key k is closed, we use

$$I(\rho x_2) = \varepsilon_1 - ir \quad \ldots(2)$$

Current in secondary circuit is calculated as

$$i = \frac{\varepsilon_1}{R+r} \quad \ldots(3)$$

$$\Rightarrow \quad r = \left(\frac{x_1}{x_2} - 1\right)R = \left(\frac{0.75}{0.60} - 1\right)24$$

$$\Rightarrow \quad r = 6\,\Omega$$

(viii) (a) When switch S is open, V_1 and V_2 are in series, connected to 200V battery. Potential will drop in direct ratio of their resistors so we use

$$V_1 : V_2 = R_{V_1} : R_{V_2} = 3000 : 2000$$

$$\Rightarrow \quad V_1 : V_2 = 3 : 2$$

(i) Voltmeter readings are given as

$$V_1 = \frac{3}{5} \times 200 = 120\text{ V}$$

and $\quad V_2 = \frac{2}{5} \times 200 = 80\text{ V}$

(ii) When S is closed then V_1 and R_1 are in parallel. Similarly V_2 and R_2 are also in parallel. Now they are in series and these are having equal effective resistances so 200 V will be equally distribute between them thus final voltmeter readings are

$$V_1 = V_2 = \frac{200}{2} = 100\text{V}$$

(b) Figure shows the current distribution after switch is closed. The currents are given as

$$i_2 = \frac{100}{2000} = \frac{1}{20}A$$

$$i_4 = \frac{100}{3000} = \frac{1}{30}A$$

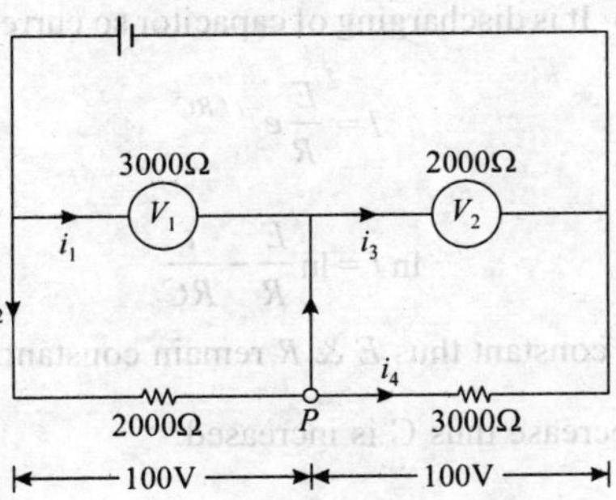

Using KCL at junction P, the current through switch is given as

$$i_S = i_2 - i_4 = \frac{1}{60}A \text{ in upward direction.}$$

Solutions of CONCEPTUAL MCQs Single Option Correct

Sol. 1 (A) A will read the potential difference across the capacitor and B will real P.D. across its own resistance which is in parallel across the capacitor so reading of both voltmeters will always be same.

Sol. 2 (A) The charge on capacitor as a function of time is given as

$$q = CVe^{-t/RC}$$

Here $CV = q_0$ is termed as steady state charge or equilibrium charge so if we use $q = fq_0$ then from above relation we get time taken for charge to grow upto f fraction of its steady state value which is given as $t = RC\ln(1/f)$ which is independent of applied EMF.

Sol. 3 (B) If initial potential difference across capacitor is less than battery EMF then battery will supply more charge to the capacitor and its potential difference increases and if initial potential difference across capacitor is greater than battery EMF then charge from capacitor flows into the battery and its potential difference decreases.

Sol. 4 (B) In an electrolyte there are positive and negative ions which drifts inside the electrolyte chemical when an electric field is applied onto it by some external potential difference.

Sol. 5 (D) As a voltmeter resistance is in general is very high so initially very low current flows in circuit and potential difference across voltmeter is almost same as that cell voltage and current reading of ammeter would be very low. When a resistance is connected in parallel to a the voltmeter then overall resistance of circuit decreases which causes current to increase and the potential difference across voltmeter will decrease.

Sol. 6 (B) Net resistance will decrease by increasing the parallel resistance in the circuit. Thus circuit current will increase. Reading of voltmeter is the potential drop across the resistance of voltmeter and as circuit current is increasing, so reading of voltmeter will increase.

Sol. 7 (D) Here we use

$$R_0 = R + \frac{(R+R_0)R}{(R+R_0)+R}$$

Solving the above quadratic equation we get $R = \frac{R_0}{\sqrt{3}}$.

Sol. 8 (A) Figure below shows the situation described in the question.

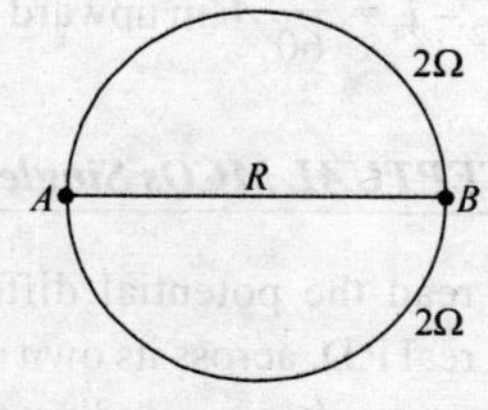

The resistance of the wire along diameter is given as

$$R = \left(\frac{4}{2\pi r}\right)(2r) = \frac{4}{\pi}$$

Here we will now consider 2 Ω, 2 Ω and *R* in parallel combination.

Sol. 9 (B) In above circuit brightness will be proportional to the current through the bulb as power dissipated is $i^2 R$. In this case maximum current will pass through *A*.

Sol. 10 (B) Initial current in circuit is given as

$$i_1 = \frac{E_1 + E_2}{R + r_1 + r_2}$$

Final current, when second battery is short circuited is given as

$$i_2 = \frac{E_1}{R + r_1}$$

We can check that $i_2 > i_1$ if

$$\frac{E_1}{R + r_1} > \frac{E_1 + E_2}{R + r_1 + r_2}$$

$$\Rightarrow \quad E_1R + E_1r_1 + E_1r_2 > E_1R + E_1r_1 + E_2R + E_2r_1$$

$$\Rightarrow \quad E_1r_2 > E_2(R + r_1)$$

Sol. 11 (B) The current in R_2 is given as

$$i = \left[\frac{V}{R_1 + R_2}\right]$$

We can see in circuit that potential difference across capacitor is same as that across R_2 which is given as

$$V_C = iR_2 = \left[\frac{VR_2}{R_1 + R_2}\right]$$

Sol. 12 (B) After closing the switch common potential across the two capacitors will be given as

$$V = \frac{Q}{C_1 + 2C_1} = \frac{Q}{3C_1}$$

Charge on the capacitors is given as

$$Q_1 = C_1 V = \frac{Q}{3}$$

and $$Q_2 = C_2 V = \frac{2Q}{3}$$

Sol. 13 (A) Drift velocity of electrons is the terminal velocity of electrons motion in presence of external electric field force which is balanced by the opposing force on electrons due to their thermal agitation where as average velocity of electrons in a conductor is defined only by their thermal motion like gas molecules in a gas in their random motion.

Sol. 14 (C) At any time inside a metal body velocities of free electrons are randomly distributed in different directions average of which is zero.

Sol. 15 (D) In a current carrying wire due to external electric field when free electrons of a metal body drifts their rate of collision increases with neighbouring electrons compared to the case when there is no electric current due to which heat is dissipated and temperature of metal wire rises.

Sol. 16 (A) The current is steady that means the total amount of charge flowing through all the cross sections of the wire are same.

Sol. 17 (C) A fuse wire melts when its temperature rises to its melting point. If a fuse wire of length *l*, cross sectional radius *r*, density ρ is heated due to passage of a current *i* through it then its equilibrium temperature is one when rate of heat produced in it due to Joule heating is equal to the rate at which heat is radiated to its surrounding which is given as

$$i^2R = \sigma(2\pi rl)(T^4 - T_s^4)$$

$$\Rightarrow \quad i^2\left(\frac{\rho l}{\pi r^2}\right) = \sigma(2\pi rl)(T^4 - T_s^4)$$

$$\Rightarrow \quad T = \left(\frac{i^2\rho}{2\sigma\pi^2 r^3} + T_s^4\right)^{1/4}$$

Thus the equilibrium temperature of a fuse wire does not depend on its length.

Sol. 18 (C) Due to high resistivity of constantine it is used to make variety of resistances within practical dimensions.

Sol. 19 (B) It is discharging of capacitor so current is given as

$$I = \frac{E}{R}e^{-t/RC}$$

$$\ln I = \ln\frac{E}{R} - \frac{t}{RC}$$

Intercept is constant thus *E* & *R* remain constant

As slope decrease thus C is increased.

Sol. 20 (B) When cells are arranged in parallel the current is divided in all the cell branches so current capacity of the equivalent cell increases.

Sol. 21 (C) As the two devices are in parallel, voltage across both will be same so if one is switched off nothing will happen to the other. It continues to work in the same way.

Sol. 22 (C) In parallel combination voltage across all resistors is equal and current is divided in inverse ratio of the resistance.

Sol. 23 (A) Drift speed of free electrons in a current carrying conductor is given as

$$v_d = J/ne$$

For the two conductors of same material we use

$$\frac{v_{dA}}{v_{dB}} = \frac{J_A}{J_B} = \frac{I_A(\pi r_B^2)}{I_B(\pi r_A^2)}$$

$$\Rightarrow \quad \frac{v_{dA}}{v_{dB}} = \left(\frac{I_A}{I_B}\right)\left(\frac{r_B}{r_A}\right)^2 = \left(\frac{4}{1}\right)\times\left(\frac{2}{1}\right)^2 = \frac{16}{1}$$

Sol. 24 (A) As we know conductivity of a material is given as

$$\sigma = \frac{ne^2\tau}{m}$$

Resistance of a conductor is given as

$$R = \frac{\rho l}{A} = \frac{l}{\sigma A} = \frac{ml}{ne^2\tau A}$$

Sol. 25 (B) If V is the voltage rating of the two bulbs then their resistances are given as

$$R = \frac{V^2}{P_2} = \frac{V^2}{200}$$

and $$R_2 = \frac{V^2}{P_1} = \frac{V^2}{100}$$

$$\Rightarrow \quad R_2 = 2R_1$$

Sol. 26 (C) If in general we consider in a copper wire of cross sectional area 1mm^2 carrying a current of 1A, the drift velocity is given as

$$v_d = \frac{J}{ne} = \frac{1/10^{-6}}{8.5\times10^{28}\times1.6\times10^{-19}} \approx 10^{-4}\text{ m/s} = 10^{-2}\text{ cm/s}$$

Sol. 27 (D) If the original wire is of length l and cross sectional area S, its resistance is given as

$$R = \frac{\rho l}{S}$$

For the bundle with four parts of this wire the length will become $l/4$ and cross sectional area will be $4S$ so its resistance is given as

$$R' = \frac{\rho(l/4)}{4S} = \frac{1}{16}R$$

Sol. 28 (C) As length is increased to double that means for the constant volume its cross sectional area will decrease to half so its resistance will become four times.

Sol. 29 (B) Resistance of a conductor is given by reciprocal of the slope of I-V curve. This graph shown in figure has a slope 1/2 so the resistance of conductor is 2Ω.

Sol. 30 (C) Power dissipated in the resistance for charging of a conductor is given as

$$P = i^2R$$

$$\Rightarrow \quad P = (i_0e^{-t/\eta})^2 R$$

$$\Rightarrow \quad P = (i_0^2R)\, e^{-2t/\eta}$$

$$\Rightarrow \quad P = P_0e^{-t/(\eta/2)}$$

From above equation we can see that the time constant for power variation is $\eta/2$.

Sol. 31 (B) During charging of a capacitorupto 50% of the steady state value i.e. upto the charge CE/2, the energy stored in capacitor is given as

$$U = \frac{1}{2}\frac{q^2}{C} = \frac{1}{2}\frac{(EC/2)^2}{C} = \frac{E^2C}{8}$$

Upto this instant work done by battery in charging capacitor is given as

$$W_{bat} = qE = \left(\frac{CE}{2}\right)E = \frac{E^2C}{2}$$

Total energy dissipated or lost upto this instant is given as

$$H = W_{bat} - U = \frac{E^2C}{2} - \frac{E^2C}{8} = \frac{3}{8}E^2C$$

This energy is divided in the two resistances in same ratio of resistances so heat dissipated inside the battery is given as

$$H_{\text{battery}} = \frac{3}{8}E^2C\times\frac{r}{r+2r} = \frac{1}{8}E^2C$$

Sol. 32 (D) In steady state current only flows through the outer loop which is given as

$$i = \frac{[E - E_0]}{R + R_0}$$

Writing the equation of potential drop from left side of capacitor to right side of it from the lower branch containing R_0 gives

$$V_a - E + E_0 + iR_0 = V_b$$

In above equation we considered left plate of capacitor is a and right one is b

$$\Rightarrow \quad V_a - V_b = (E - E_0) - iR_0$$

$$\Rightarrow \quad V_a - V_b = (E - E_0)\left[1 - \frac{R_0}{R + R_0}\right]$$

$$\Rightarrow \quad V_a - V_b = \frac{R(E - E)}{R + R_0}$$

Thus steady state charge on capacitor is given as

$$q = C(V_a - V_b) = \frac{CR(E - E_0)}{R + R_0}$$

Sol. 33 (C) The equivalent circuit of the circuit shown in figure is shown below.

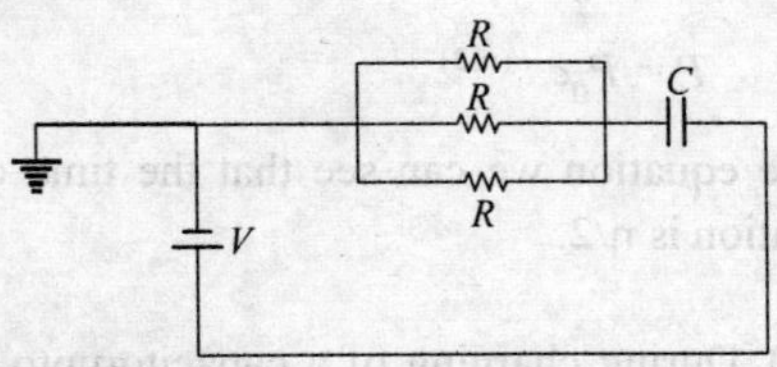

The time constant of this circuit is given as

$$\tau_C = CR_{\text{net}} = \frac{CR}{3}$$

$$\Rightarrow \quad q = q_0(1 - e^{-t/\tau_C})$$

Where $q_0 = CV$ is the steady state charge on capacitor.

Sol. 34 (C) During charging capacitor and resistance of its wire are independently connected with the battery so the time constant of the circuit is given as

$$\tau_C = RC$$

During discharging capacitor is discharged through both resistors in series so the time constant for discharging of capacitor is given as

$$\tau_C = (2R)C = 2RC$$

Sol. 35 (B) Just after the switch is closed C_1 is short circuited and current passes through R_1 and C_1 only so it is given as E/R_1.

Sol. 36 (B) The two branches in circuit are connected to the battery of voltage V which maintains the potential difference across the two branches so current in each branch can be given by the transient analysis of charging of capacitors as

$$i_1 = \left(\frac{V}{2R}\right)e^{-\frac{t}{6CR}}$$

$$\text{and} \quad i_2 = \left(\frac{V}{R}\right)e^{-\frac{t}{CR}}$$

$$\Rightarrow \quad \frac{i_1}{i_2} = \frac{e^{\frac{5t}{6CR}}}{2}$$

Above ratio is increasing with time.

Solutions of NUMERICAL MCQs Single Option Correct

Sol. 1 (B) In steady state current in the branch containing the capacitor is zero so current flows in outer loop and it gives the potential difference across capacitor which is same as potential difference across R_2 given as

$$\frac{ER_2}{R_2 + r} = 2\text{V}$$

$$\Rightarrow \quad q = CV = 2\mu\text{C}$$

Sol. 2 (B) When the switch is shifted from position 1 to 2 due to higher voltage of battery further current starts flowing as shown in figure below.

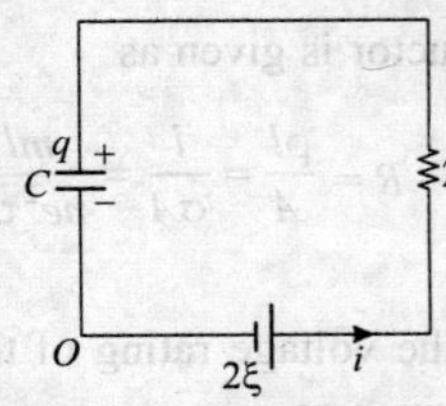

Writing KVL equation for the loop gives

$$V_0 + 2\xi - 2iR - \frac{q}{C} = V_0$$

$$\text{and} \quad i = \frac{\xi}{R} - \frac{q}{2RC}$$

We use current in circuit as

$$i = \frac{dq}{dt}$$

$$\Rightarrow \quad \int_{C\xi}^{q} \frac{dq}{\left(\frac{\xi}{R} - \frac{q}{2RC}\right)} = \int_0^t dt$$

$$\frac{\ln\left(\frac{\xi}{R} - \frac{q}{2RC}\right)\Big|_{C\xi}^{q}}{\left(-\frac{1}{2RC}\right)} = t$$

$$\ln\left(\frac{2\xi C - q}{\xi C}\right) = -\frac{t}{2RC}$$

$$q = 2\xi C - \xi C e^{-t/2RC}$$

$$q = \xi C(2 - e^{-t/2RC})$$

Sol. 3 (B) When switch is shifted to position b discharging will take place

and $$q = q_0 e^{-t/RC}$$

$$\Rightarrow \quad q = CVe^{-t/RC}$$

and $$i = -\frac{dq}{dt} = \frac{CV}{RC}e^{-t/RC}$$

$$\Rightarrow \quad i = \frac{V}{R}e^{-t/RC}$$

at $t = 0$ circuit current is given as

$$i = \frac{V}{R}$$

Sol. 4 (A) In parallel current distributes in ratio of resistance so we use

$$\frac{I_G}{I_S} = \frac{S}{G}$$

$$\Rightarrow \quad G = \left(\frac{I_S}{I_G}\right)(S)$$

$$\Rightarrow \quad G = \left(\frac{50-20}{20}\right)(12)$$

$$\Rightarrow \quad G = 18\,\Omega$$

Sol. 5 (A) For the currents through galvanometer and shunt resistance we have

$$\frac{I_G}{I_S} = \frac{S}{G}$$

$$\Rightarrow \quad S = \left(\frac{I_G}{I_S}\right)G$$

$$\Rightarrow \quad S = \left(\frac{2}{98}\right)G = \frac{G}{49}$$

Sol. 6 (B) Power of a heater is given as

$$P = \frac{V^2}{R}$$

$$\Rightarrow \quad P \propto \frac{1}{R}$$

$$\Rightarrow \quad \frac{P_2}{P_1} = \frac{R_1}{R_2} = \frac{l_1}{l_2}$$

$$\Rightarrow \quad P_2 = \left(\frac{l_1}{l_2}\right)P_1 = \left(\frac{l}{0.9l}\right)P_1 = 1.11P_1$$

So, power will increase by 11%.

Sol. 7 (B) In a potentiometer internal resistance of cell is given as

$$r = R\left(\frac{l_1}{l_2} - 1\right) = 10\left(\frac{75}{60} - 1\right) = 2.5\,\Omega$$

Sol. 8 (B) Drift speed of free electrons in a conductor carrying a current i and cross sectional area A is given as

$$v_d = \frac{i}{neA} = \frac{i}{ne(\pi r^2)}$$

$$\Rightarrow \quad v_d \propto \frac{i}{r^2}$$

Thus drift velocity will reduce to half.

Sol. 9 (D) For making voltmeter of higher range, high resistance is required.

Sol. 10 (D) Potential difference across the three resistance in parallel is given as

$$V_{20\Omega} = 20 \times 0.3 = R \times 0.8$$

$$\Rightarrow \quad R = \frac{30}{4}\Omega$$

$$\Rightarrow \quad \frac{4}{30} = \frac{1}{R_1} + \frac{1}{20} + \frac{1}{15}$$

Solving we get $\quad R_1 = 60\,\Omega$

Sol. 11 (C) We use for 3V battery

$$E - ir = 0$$

$$\Rightarrow \quad 3 - \left(\frac{3+15}{1+2+R}\right)(1) = 0$$

Solving this equation we get,

$$R = 3\,\Omega$$

Sol. 12 (A) We use Ohm's law for the given part of circuit as

$$100 = (5)\left[\frac{(2500R)}{2500+R}\right]$$

Solving this equation we get

$$R = 20\,\Omega$$

Sol. 13 (C) If the unknown resistances are P and Q, then for first case we have at null point 20 cm

$$\frac{P}{Q} = \frac{20}{100-20} \text{ or } Q = 4P \qquad \ldots(1)$$

$$\Rightarrow \quad P < Q$$

In second case we have null point at 40cm

$$\frac{P+15}{Q} = \frac{40}{100-40}$$

$$\Rightarrow \quad \frac{P+15}{Q} = \frac{2}{3} \quad \ldots(2)$$

Solving above equations we get,

$$P = 9\,\Omega$$

Sol. 14 (B) Total EMF of battery 10V is equally divided between 50Ω and other parallel combination of 100Ω and voltmeter. If R is the resistance of voltmeter then their net resistance should be same so we have

$$\frac{100\times R}{100+R} = 50$$

$$\Rightarrow \quad R = 100\,\Omega$$

Sol. 15 (D) In the figure shown below at null deflection we have $V_{AC} = V_{DE}$

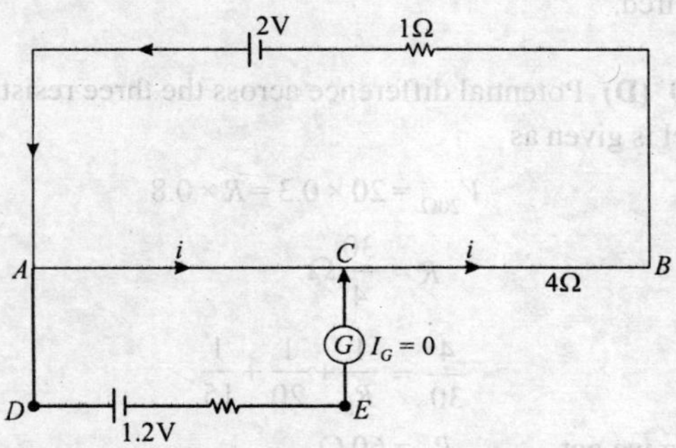

$$\Rightarrow \quad i(R_{AC}) = E = 1.2$$

$$\Rightarrow \quad \left(\frac{2}{4+1}\right)\left(\frac{4}{100}\times l\right) = 1.2$$

$$\Rightarrow \quad l = 75\text{cm}$$

Sol. 16 (C) Considering the two batteries in parallel equivalent circuit is shown in figure below

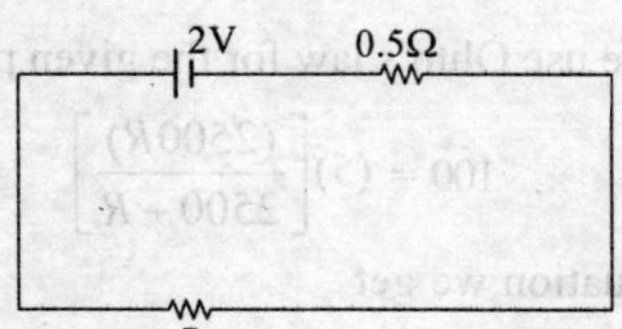

Maximum power across R is obtained when $R = r = 0.5\,\Omega$

Maximum current in circuit is given as

$$i = \frac{2}{R+r} = 2\text{ A}$$

$$\Rightarrow \quad P_{max} = i^2 R = (2)^2(0.5) = 2\text{ W}$$

Sol. 17 (D) Circuit current flows in clockwise and it is given as

$$i = \frac{10-5}{2.5+2.5+40} = \frac{1}{9}\text{A}$$

Writing equation of potential drops from B to A gives

$$V_B - 15i - 25i = V_A$$

$$\Rightarrow \quad V_A - V_B - 40i = -\frac{40}{9}\text{V}$$

Sol. 18 (C) When K is open equivalent resistance of the circuit is given as

$$R_{eq1} = 3R/2$$

$$\Rightarrow \quad i_1 = E/(3R/2) = \frac{2E}{3R}$$

When K is closed equivalent resistance of the circuit is given as

$$R_{eq2} = 2\left[\frac{R\times 2R}{R+2R}\right] = \frac{4}{3}R$$

$$\Rightarrow \quad i_2 = E/(4R/3) = \frac{3E}{4R}$$

$$\Rightarrow \quad \frac{i_1}{i_2} = \frac{8}{9}$$

Sol. 19 (B) For the current distribution between galvanometer and shunt resistance we use

$$\frac{I_G}{I_S} = \frac{S}{G}$$

$$\Rightarrow \quad S = \left(\frac{I_G}{I_S}\right)G$$

$$\Rightarrow \quad S = \frac{(1/34)}{(33/34)} \times 3663 = 111\,\Omega$$

Sol. 20 (C) In the given circuit we can see that the equivalent resistance across AB is given as

$$R_{AB} = 2(\text{Equivalent resistance of infinite series}) + 1\,\Omega$$

In parallel net resistance is always less than the 1 Ω. Thus equivalent resistance of infinite series is less than 3 Ω thus we have

$$1\,\Omega < R_{AB} < 3\,\Omega$$

Sol. 21 (B) By symmetry we can open the middle junction of the circuit due to which the circuit is reduced as shown below

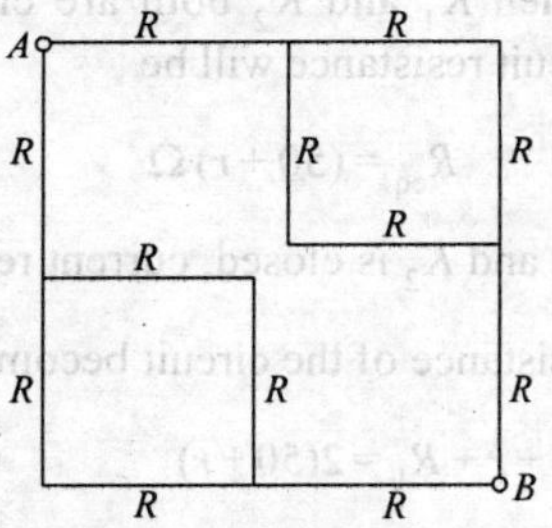

Now using series and parallel combination we can calculate that the net resistance across A and B terminals is 3R/2 because the resistance of both the branches across A and B is $3R$ which are in parallel.

Sol. 22 (B) As voltmeter is ideal no current will flow through voltmeter so current through two batteries in the circuit is given as

$$i = \frac{1.5 - 1.3}{r_1 + r_2} = \frac{0.2}{r_1 + r_2}$$

Voltmeter reading is given as

$$V = E_2 - ir_2$$

$$\Rightarrow \quad 1.45 = 1.5 - \left(\frac{0.2}{r_1 + r_2}\right)(r_2)$$

Solving this equation, we get

$$r_1 = 3r_2$$

Sol. 23 (C) As the given ammeter and voltmeter are not considered ideal, we use

$$4(R + R_A) = 20\text{V}$$

$$\Rightarrow \quad R = 5 - R_A$$

Where R_A is the resistance of ammeter

Sol. 24 (D) In the circuit shown below all the currents are indicated which can be obtained by KCl at all junctions.

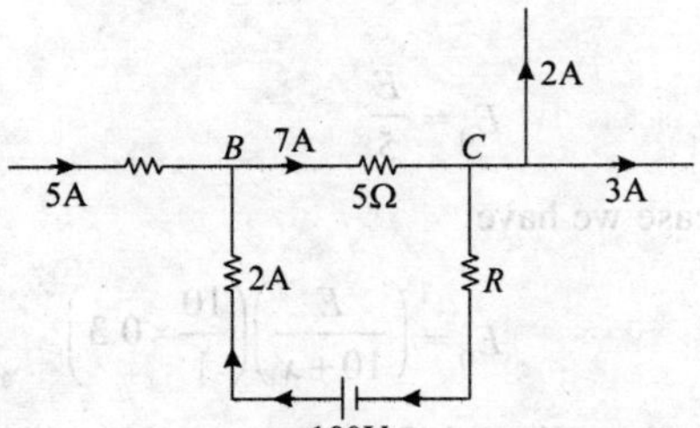

Writing KVL equation in closed loop we have

$$+100 - 30 - 35 - 2R = 0$$

$$\Rightarrow \quad 2R = 35\text{V} = V_R$$

$$\Rightarrow \quad V_{5\Omega} = 7 \times 5 = 35\text{V}$$

$$\Rightarrow \quad \frac{V_{5\Omega}}{V_R} = 1$$

Sol. 25 (D) As resistance varies linearly with time, its variation function of time is given as

$$R = at + b$$

From the graph at $t = 10$s, $R = 20\Omega$

$$\Rightarrow \quad 20 = 10a + b \quad \ldots(1)$$

From the graph at $t = 30$s, $R = 40\Omega$

$$40 = 30a + b \quad \ldots(2)$$

Solving above two equations we get

$$a = 1\Omega/\text{s}$$

and

$$b = 10\Omega$$

$$\Rightarrow \quad R = (t + 10)$$

Current in circuit is given as

$$i = \frac{E}{R} = \frac{10}{t + 10}$$

Charge flow is given as

$$\Delta q = \int_{10}^{30} i\,dt$$

$$\Delta q = \int_{10}^{30}\left(\frac{10}{t + 10}\right)dt$$

$$\Delta q = 10\ln(2)$$

Sol. 26 (B) Suppose n (< 1) fraction of the length of resistance is stretched to m-times. Then its new length is given as

$$(1 - n)l + (nl)\,m = 1.5l$$

$$\Rightarrow \quad nm - n = 0.5 \quad \ldots(1)$$

Resistance is given as

$$R = \frac{\rho l}{A}$$

$$R = \frac{\rho l}{(V/l)} \quad \text{[V is the volume of wire]}$$

$$R = \frac{\rho l^2}{V}$$

$$\Rightarrow \quad R \propto l^2 \quad \text{[As } V \text{ remain constant]}$$

The final resistance becomes four times so we use

$$(1 - n)R + (nR)m^3 = 4R$$

$$\Rightarrow \quad nm^2 - n = 3 \quad \ldots(2)$$

Solving above two equations we get

$$n = \frac{1}{8}$$

Sol. 27 (B) Initially if l_1 is the balancing length then we have

$$\frac{l_1}{100-l_1}=\frac{X}{R}=\frac{2}{3}$$

$$\Rightarrow \quad l_1=\frac{2}{5}\times 100$$

$$\Rightarrow \quad l_1=40\text{ cm}$$

If the new balancing length is l_2 then we have

$$\frac{l_2}{100-l_2}=\frac{X}{R'}=\frac{12}{8}=\frac{3}{2}$$

$$\Rightarrow \quad l_2=\frac{3}{5}\times 100$$

$$\Rightarrow \quad l_2=60\text{ cm}$$

Thus J is displaced by

$$l_2-l_1=20\text{ cm}$$

Sol. 28 (C) In parallel combination current is divided in inverse ratio of resistances so we have

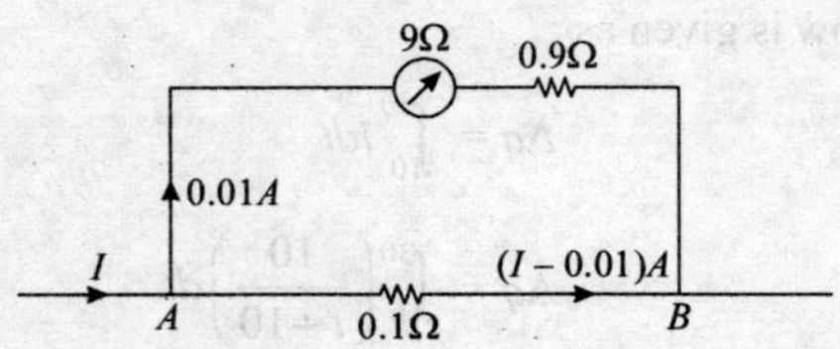

$$\frac{0.01}{I-0.01}=\frac{0.1}{9+0.9}$$

$$\Rightarrow \quad I=1\text{ A}$$

Sol. 29 (D) Equivalent EMF of the two batteries ξ_1 and ξ_2 in parallel combination is given as

$$\xi=\frac{\xi_1/r_1+\xi_2/r_2}{1/r_1+1/r_2}$$

$$\Rightarrow \quad \xi=\frac{(2/2)+(4/6)}{(1/2)+(1/6)}$$

$$\Rightarrow \quad \xi=2.5\text{ V}$$

At balancing length we have

$$V_{AN}=\xi$$

$$\Rightarrow \quad I_{AN}(R_{AN})=\xi$$

$$\Rightarrow \quad \left(\frac{12}{4+4\times 4}\right)(4)(l)=2.5$$

$$\Rightarrow \quad l=\frac{25}{24}\text{ m}$$

Sol. 30 (D) When K_1 and K_2 both are closed R_1 is short circuited and circuit resistance will be

$$R_{eq}=(50+r)\,\Omega$$

When K_1 is open and K_2 is closed, current remains half.

Therefore net resistance of the circuit becomes two times.

$$50+r+R_1=2(50+r)$$

For the given options in questions, above equation is satisfied for

$$r=0 \text{ and } R_1=50\,\Omega$$

Sol. 31 (A) All these resistors are in parallel combination across the battery so equivalent resistance is given as

$$R_{eq}=\frac{R}{3}+r=4\,\Omega$$

So circuit current is given as

$$i=\frac{E}{R_{eq}}=1\text{A}$$

Current through either of the resistance is

$$i_R=\frac{i}{3}=\frac{1}{3}\text{A}$$

Thus voltmeter reading is given as

$$V=iR=\left(\frac{1}{3}\right)(9)=3\text{V}$$

Sol. 32 (D) As the given circuit is a balanced Wheatstone bridge, the potentials of points A and B would be equal.

Sol. 33 (B) At null deflection in galvanometer we have

$$E_0=V_{AC}=i_{AC}R_{AC}$$

$$\Rightarrow \quad E_0=\left(\frac{E}{10}\right)\left(\frac{10}{1}\times 0.2\right)$$

$$\Rightarrow \quad E_0=\frac{E}{5} \quad \ldots(1)$$

In second case we have

$$E_0=\left(\frac{E}{10+x}\right)\left(\frac{10}{1}\times 0.3\right) \quad \ldots(2)$$

Solving equations-(1) and (2) we get,

$$x=5\,\Omega$$

Sol. 34 (B) Resistance between A and B can be removed as resistances between points CEHF are acting as a balanced

Wheatstone bridge. R_{DE} and R_{GH} are in series and they are connected in parallel with 10 V battery so the current in DE is given as

$$I_{DE} = \frac{10}{R_{DE} + R_{HG}} = \frac{10}{2+2}$$

$$\Rightarrow \quad I_{DE} = 2.5\text{A}$$

Sol. 35 (B) Effective resistance of 3 kΩ and voltmeter in parallel is 2 kΩ which is in series with another equal resistance. The applied 10 V is equally distributed between 2 kΩ and 2 kΩ so reading of voltmeter is given as 5 V.

Sol. 36 (C) The current in the circuit flows only in one loop which is given as

$$i = \frac{\xi}{(R+r)}$$

The potential difference across resistance R is given as

$$V = iR = \left[\frac{\xi R}{R+r}\right]$$

This potential difference will be equally divided across the two capacitors so potential difference across each capacitor is given as

$$V = \frac{\xi R}{2(R+r)}$$

Sol. 37 (A) The current in 2 Ω resistor is given as

$$i = \frac{2}{2} = 1\text{ A}$$

Potential difference across 2 Ω resistor is given as

$$V = 2 \times 1 = 2\text{ V}$$

Charge on the capacitor is given as

$$q = 10 \times 2 = 20\ \mu\text{C}$$

Sol. 38 (A) At an instant when

$$V_C = 3V_R$$

We also have $\quad V_C + V_R = 12$

which gives $V_C = 9$ V and $V_R = 3$ V

Time constant of the circuit is

$$\tau = RC$$

$$\tau = 4 \times 10^{-6} \times 2.5 \times 10^{6} = 10\text{ s}$$

The potential difference across capacitor is given as

$$V = V_0(1 - e^{-t/\tau})$$

$$\Rightarrow \quad 9 = 12(1 - e^{-t/10})$$

$$\Rightarrow \quad e^{t/10} = 4$$

$$\Rightarrow \quad \frac{t}{10} = \ln 4$$

$$\Rightarrow \quad t = 10 \times 2\ln 2$$

$$\Rightarrow \quad t = 20 \times 0.693 = 13.86\text{ s}$$

Sol. 39 (B) We know that charging current in RC circuit is given as

$$i = i_0 e^{-t/\tau} = i_0 e^{-t/RC}$$

$$\Rightarrow \quad \ln i = \ln i_0 - \frac{t}{RC}$$

$$\Rightarrow \quad \ln i = \ln\left(\frac{\varepsilon}{R}\right) - \frac{t}{RC} \quad \ldots\text{(i)}$$

When resistance is doubled the equation will be

$$\ln i' = \ln\frac{\varepsilon}{2R} - \frac{t}{2RC} \quad \ldots\text{(ii)}$$

Thus Q represents the correct graph in which intercept is reduced and slope is also decreased.

Sol. 40 (C) After closing the switch circuit current is given as

$$i = \frac{9}{9} = 1\text{A}$$

Potential difference across the capacitors are given as

$$V_1 = 3 \times 1 = 3\text{ V}$$

and $\quad V_2 = 6 \times 1 = 6\text{ V}$

$$q_1 = 3 \times 3 = 9\ \mu\text{C}$$

and $\quad q_2 = 6 \times 6 = 36\ \mu\text{C}$

Charge at junction x on the two plates of capacitors is

$$\Delta q = -9 + 36 = 27\ \mu\text{C}$$

Initially when the switch was open charge at junction x at the two plates of capacitors was zero so the charge which is there on the two plates after closing the switch is flown through the switch from y to x when it is closed.

Sol. 41 (A) At any time, the level of liquid between the plates is given as

$$x_1 = \left(\frac{d}{3} - vt\right)$$

The thickness of the air capacitor above the liquid is

$$x_1 = d - \left(\frac{d}{3} - vt\right) = \left(\frac{2d}{3} + vt\right)$$

At any time the equivalent capacitance of the capacitor is given as

$$C=\frac{C_1C_2}{C_1+C_2}$$

Where $C_1=\frac{\epsilon_0 kA}{x_1}$, and $C_2=\frac{\epsilon_0 A}{x_2}$

Time constant $\tau=CR=\left[\frac{6\epsilon_0 R}{5d+3vt}\right]$

Sol. 42 (A) By short circuiting the battery the effective circuit across C is shown in figure below for calculation of Thevenin's resistance.

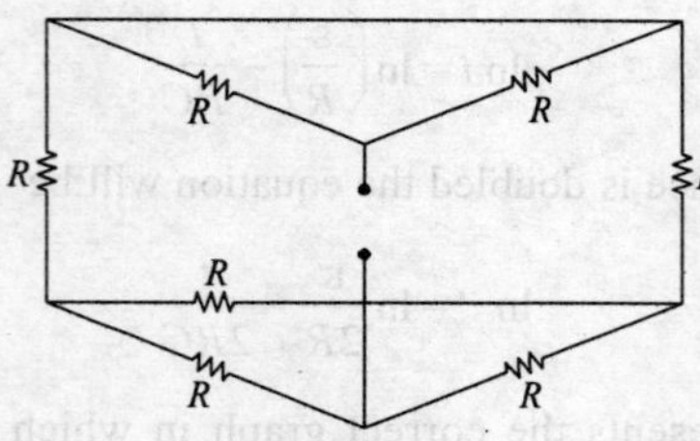

$$R_{eq}=\frac{3R}{2}=1.5R$$

$$\Rightarrow \quad \tau=C_{eq}R_{eq}=1.5CR$$

Sol. 43 (C) In steady state, the current in the resistors are shown in figure.

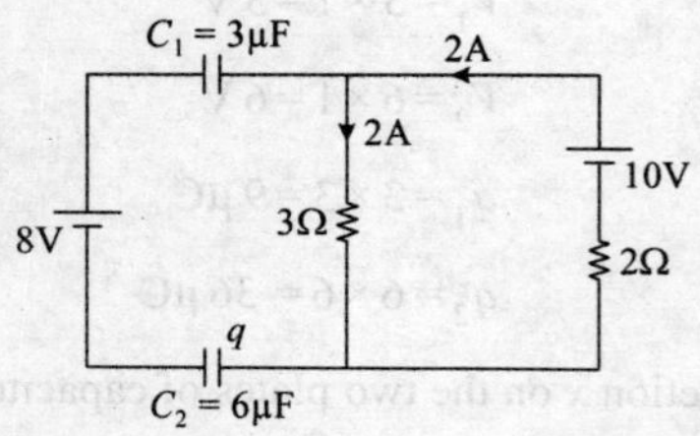

If q be the charge on each of the capacitor, then for the left loop we use

$$8-\frac{q}{3}-2\times3-\frac{q}{6}=0$$

$$\Rightarrow \quad q=4\,\mu C$$

Sol. 44 (D) For no current in galvanometer at any time including transient duration, then we use

$$\Rightarrow \quad \frac{2}{6}=\frac{\frac{1}{3}}{\frac{1}{C}}$$

$$\Rightarrow \quad C=1\,\mu F$$

Sol. 45 (A) Current in R_2 will be half of the current in transient duration which charges the capacitor and it is given as

$$i=\frac{1}{2}\times\frac{20}{3}e^{-\frac{t}{2\times3}}=\frac{10}{3}e^{-\frac{t}{6}}$$

Heat produced in resistor R_2 is given as

$$H=\int_0^\infty i^2 R\,dt$$

$$\Rightarrow \quad H=\frac{100}{9}\int_0^\infty e^{-\frac{t}{3}}\times 2dt$$

$$\Rightarrow \quad H=\frac{200}{9}\left|\frac{e^{-\frac{t}{3}}}{\left(-\frac{1}{3}\right)}\right|_0^\infty$$

$$\Rightarrow \quad H=\frac{200}{3}\,\mu J$$

Above heat can also be directly calculated as total heat dissipated is half of the work done by the battery in above case and heat is distributed in same ratio of resistances in the two resistances R_1 and $R_2/2$ in series. Students are advised to verify the result using this method also.

Sol. 46 (A) Across the capacitor internal resistance of the circuit is given as

$$R_{eq}=3\Omega$$

Thus time constant of the circuit is given as

$$\tau=R_{eq}C$$

$$\Rightarrow \quad \tau=6\times3=18\,\mu s$$

The current in resistance R_3 is given as

$$i=i_0e^{-t/\tau}$$

$$\Rightarrow \quad \frac{i_0}{e}=i_0e^{-t/\tau}$$

$$\Rightarrow \quad t=\tau=18\,\mu s$$

Sol. 47 (A) Just after closing the switch, uncharged capacitor behave like short circuit and charged capacitor behave like an ideal battery so current in circuit is given as

$$i=\frac{V}{3R}$$

Sol. 48 (B) For the given circuit effective time constant is given as

$$\tau=RC=6\times10^{-6}\times\left(\frac{8\times4}{8+4}\right)=16\times10^{-6}\,s$$

If i is the current in capacitor then it is given as

$$i = \frac{q_0}{RC} e^{-\frac{t}{RC}}$$

$$\Rightarrow \quad i = \frac{160}{16} e^{-\left(\frac{16\times10^{-6}}{16\times10^{-6}}\right)} = \frac{10}{e} A$$

If i_1 and i_2 are the currents in 4 Ω and 8 Ω respectively, then

$$i_1 + i_2 = \frac{10}{e} \quad \ldots(1)$$

and $$4i_1 = 8i_2 \quad \ldots(2)$$

Solving above equation gives

$$i_1 = \frac{20}{3e} \text{ A}$$

and $$i_2 = \frac{10}{3e} \text{ A}$$

Sol. 49 (D) If R is the resistance of the wire which was broken then we use

$$\frac{1}{1.2} = \frac{1}{R} + \frac{1}{2}$$

$$\Rightarrow \quad \frac{1}{R} = \frac{1}{1.2} - \frac{1}{2} = \frac{1}{3}$$

$$\Rightarrow \quad R = 3\,\Omega$$

Sol. 50 (B) The two resistances can be used either independently, in series or in parallel so the given values can be obtained by resistances of 4 Ω and 12 Ω resistances.

Sol. 51 (C) Current in the circuit is given as

$$i = \frac{3}{10+20} = 0.1 \text{ A}$$

Potential drop across the wire is given as

$$V = iR = 0.1 \times 20 = 2 \text{ V}$$

Thus potential gradient is given as

$$\lambda = \frac{V}{l} = \frac{2}{10} = 0.2 \text{ V/m}$$

Sol. 52 (A) The potential gradient across points B and C is given as

$$V_{BC} = \lambda l = 10 \times 0.3 = 3 \text{ V}$$

Sol. 53 (D) Resistance of bulb is given as

$$R_b = \frac{(1.5)^2}{4.5} = 0.5\,\Omega$$

The equivalent of 0.5 Ω and 1 Ω in parallel combination which is connected across the battery is given as

$$R = \frac{0.5\times1}{0.5+1} = 0.33\,\Omega$$

Current drawn from battery is given as

$$i = \frac{E}{2.67+0.33} = \frac{E}{3}$$

Current through the bulb is

$$i_b = \frac{E}{3} \times \frac{1}{1+0.5} = \frac{2E}{9}$$

For correct power dissipation in the bulb we use

$$\left(\frac{2E}{9}\right)^2 \times 0.5 = 4.5$$

$$\Rightarrow \quad E = 13.5 \text{ V}$$

Sol. 54 (B) At $t = 0$, when capacitor is undercharged it behaves like short circuit. In this case 6 Ω and 3 Ω will act as in parallel combination thus total resistance across battery is

$$R_{eq} = (1+2)\Omega = 3\,\Omega$$

Current through battery and 1Ω resistance is

$$i = \frac{12}{3} = 4 \text{ A}$$

Sol. 55 (A) In the circuit shown in figure if a current i is supplied by the battery then it is divided in resistances R and 3R in parallel as shown.

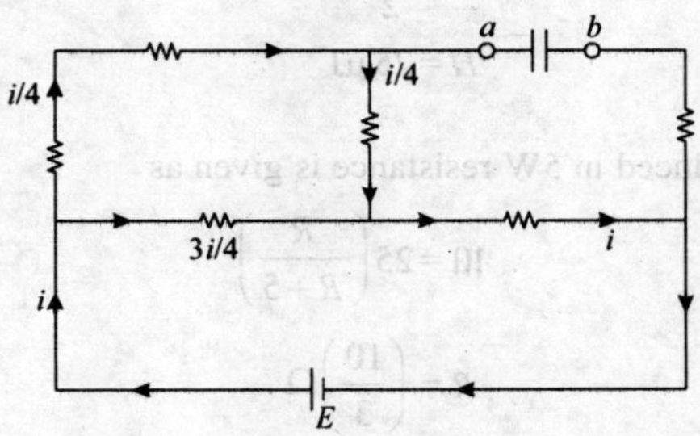

In steady state no current will flow through the branch of capacitor so equivalent resistance across the battery is given as

$$R_{eq} = R + \frac{(3R)(R)}{(3R+R)} = \frac{7}{4}R$$

Thus current through battery is given as

$$i = \frac{E}{(7/4)R} = \left(\frac{4E}{7R}\right)$$

In above circuit writing KVL equation from terminal a to b of capacitor gives

$$V_a - \frac{i}{4}R - iR = iR = V_b$$

$$\Rightarrow \quad V_a - V_b = \frac{5}{4} iR = 10$$

Substituting value of current in above equation, we get

$$\left(\frac{5}{4}\right)\left(\frac{4E}{7R}\right) = 10$$

$$\Rightarrow \quad E = 14\text{ V}$$

Sol. 56 (A) Writing equation of potential drop from terminal A to B gives

$$V_A - 6 - 3 \times 2 + \frac{9}{1} - 3 \times 3 = V_B$$

$$V_A - V_B = 12\text{ V}$$

Sol. 57 (D) Just after closing the switch capacitors behave as short circuit so all the current passes through the capacitors so no current will pass through PQ.

Sol. 58 (D) As for the capacitor given circuit is open and there is no return path or closed circuit is available so capacitor will not be charged.

Sol. 59 (C) When capacitor is discharged its total energy is dissipated as heat in the two resistances in inverse ratio. Total heat produced is given as

$$H = \frac{1}{2} CV^2$$

$$\Rightarrow \quad H = 25\ \mu\text{J}$$

Heat produced in 5W resistance is given as

$$10 = 25\left(\frac{R}{R+5}\right)$$

$$\Rightarrow \quad R = \left(\frac{10}{3}\right)\Omega$$

Sol. 60 (C) In position-1, maximum current is

$$i_0 = \frac{V}{R} = \frac{10}{5} = 2\text{ A}$$

At the given time when switch is shifted to position-2 current is 1 A or half of the above value. Thus at this instant capacitor is also charged to half of the final value of 5 V

Now it is shifted to position-2 where in steady state it is again charge to 5 V. but with opposite polarity. So in final steady state the energy stored in capacitor is same as it had at initial instant. Thus total work done by the lower battery is converted into heat. As battery polarity is reversed total charge supplied by the battery is 2 CV so total heat produced is given as

$$H = (\Delta q)V = (2CV)(V) = 2CV^2$$

$$\Rightarrow \quad H = 2 \times 2 \times 10^{-6} \times (5)^2$$

$$\Rightarrow \quad H = 100 \times 10^{-6}\text{ J}$$

$$\Rightarrow \quad H = 100\ \mu\text{J}$$

Sol. 61 (B) Initial rate of charging is fast so $Q_1 > Q_2$ and in second case as amount of charges are equal in the two intervals so $t_2 > t_1$.

Sol. 62 (B) Current in 1Ω resistance is given as

$$i_{1\Omega} = \frac{7}{1} = 7\text{ A}$$

Charge on 2μF capacitor is given as

$$q_{2\mu F} = CV = 12\ \mu\text{C}$$

Sol. 63 (A) Distributing currents in left and right loops of the circuit the currents are calculated as 3A in left loop and 3A in the right loop both clockwise respectively.

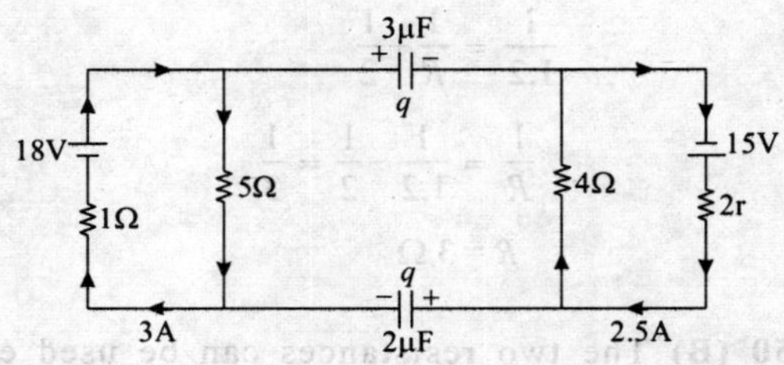

Charges on both the capacitors will be same. If the charge is q, we write KVL equation for the middle loop with capacitors as

$$-\frac{q}{3} + 15 - 2 \times 2.5 - \frac{q}{2} - 3 \times 1 + 18 = 0$$

$$\Rightarrow \quad q = 30\ \mu\text{C}$$

Sol. 64 (A) By changing the resistance only the time in which total heat is dissipated will increase. The total amount of heat remain the same as initial and final charges on the capacitors will be same in steady state of capacitors.

Sol. 65 (C) The given time can be considered as the half life time of the exponentially decreasing equation which is given as

$$t_{1/2} = (\ln 2)\tau_C = (\ln 2)RC$$

$$R = \frac{t}{(\ln 2)C}$$

$$R = \frac{2(\ln 2)\mu s}{(\ln 2)(0.5\mu F)} = 4\ \Omega$$

Thus resistance of ammeter is equal to 2 Ω.

Solutions of ADVANCE MCQs One or More Options Correct

Sol. 1 (A, B, D) When S is open equivalent capacitance is 2 μF and charge on the two capacitors is 36 μC and when S is closed current of 2 A flows in left loop and potential difference across 3 μF capacitor will be 6 V and that across 6 μF capacitor will be 12 V so their charges will become 12 μC and 72 μC. Thus options (A), (B) and (D) are correct.

Sol. 2 (All) At $t = 0$ just after closing the switch capacitor behaves like a short circuit so equivalent resistance across battery will be 3 kΩ.

So current in battery is 4 mA and that is equally divided in R_2 and R_3 so current in R_3 is 2 mA. After a long time in steady state current through battery will only be in left loop which is 3 mA and that in capacitor branch will become zero. Thus all the given options are correct.

Sol. 3 (A, D) In steady state the potential difference across capacitor is given as

$$V = Ed = 50 \times 0.05 = 2.5\text{ V}$$

Current through the battery in steady state is given as

$$i = \frac{E}{r+R} = \frac{E}{0.1+5} = \frac{E}{5.1} \qquad \ldots(1)$$

Potential difference across capacitor is given as

$$\frac{E}{5.1} \times 5 = 2.5$$

$$\Rightarrow \quad E = 2.55\text{ V}$$

Current through battery is given by equation-(1) as 0.05A

Charge on capacitor plates is given as

$$q = \epsilon_0 AE = 8.85 \times 10^{-12} \times 100 \times 10^{-4} \times 5000$$

$$\Rightarrow \quad q = 42.25 \times 10^{-11}\text{ C}$$

Force between plates of capacitor is given as

$$F = \frac{1}{2}qE = 0.5 \times 44.25 \times 10^{-11} \times 5000 = 1.1 \times 10^{-6}\text{ N}$$

Thus options (A) and (D) are correct.

Sol. 4 (A, C) H amount of heat is produced by first heater in time t_1 so we have

$$H = \frac{V^2}{R_1}t_1$$

$$\Rightarrow \quad R_1 = \frac{V^2 t_1}{H}$$

Similarly for second heater its resistance is given as

$$R_2 = \frac{V^2 t_2}{H}$$

In series combination same heat is produced in time given as

$$H = \left(\frac{V^2}{R_1 + R_2}\right)t$$

$$\Rightarrow \quad t = \frac{H(R_1 + R_2)}{V^2}$$

Substituting the values of R_1 and R_2, we get

$$t = t_1 + t_2$$

In parallel combination same heat is produced in time given as

$$H = \frac{V^2}{R_{\text{net}}}t$$

$$H = V^2 t\left(\frac{1}{R_1} + \frac{1}{R_2}\right)$$

$$H = V^2 t\left(\frac{H}{V^2 t_1} + \frac{H}{V^2 t_2}\right)$$

$$\Rightarrow \quad t = \frac{t_1 t_2}{t_1 + t_2}$$

Sol. 5 (B, C, D) Figure below shows the equivalent circuit of the two cells in parallel combination.

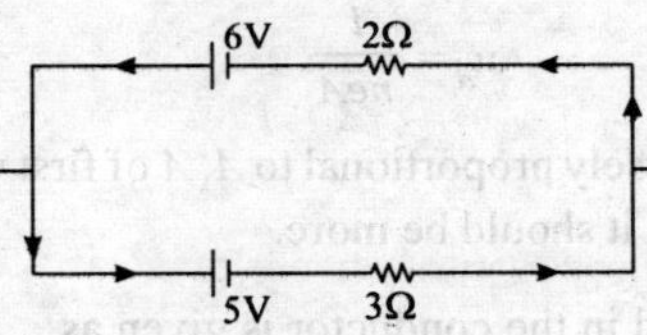

Circuit current is given as

$$i = \frac{6-5}{2+3} = 0.2\text{ A}$$

Terminal potential difference of cells is given as

$$V_1 = E_1 - ir_1 = 6 - 0.2 \times 2$$

$$\Rightarrow \quad V_1 = 5.6\text{ V}$$

When both cells are of equal EMF then no current will flow in the above circuit. Thus options (A), (C) and (D) are correct.

Sol. 6 (A, B, D) In series current is always same

$$\Rightarrow \quad I_A = I_B$$

Potential difference across terminals is given as

$$V_A + V_B = V_C$$

$$\Rightarrow \quad I_A R_A + I_B R_B = I_C R_C$$

In parallel current distributes in inverse ratio of resistance so we have

$$\Rightarrow \quad \frac{I_B}{I_C} = \frac{I_A}{I_C}$$

$$\Rightarrow \quad \frac{I_B}{I_C} = \frac{R_C}{R_A + R_B}$$

Thus options (A), (B) and (D) are correct.

Sol. 7 (B, C) In series current in same so we have

$$I_1 = I_2$$

As voltmeter resistances are different $V_1 \neq V_2$

Terminal potential difference is given as

$$V_A + V_B = V_C$$

Thus options (B) and (C) are correct.

Sol. 8 (A, B, C) As they are in series, current must be same so for equal resistances their potential difference must be same.

As resistance is given as $R = \frac{\rho l}{A}$ and R is same so cross sectional area should be smaller in first wire.

Drift speed in conductor is given as

$$v_d = \frac{i}{neA}$$

Thus v_d is inversely proportional to A. A of first wire is less. So drift velocity in it should be more.

As electric field in the conductor is given as

$$E = \frac{V}{l}$$

$$\Rightarrow \quad E \propto \frac{1}{l}$$

Thus electric field in second conductor will be less. Thus options (A), (B) and (C) are correct.

Sol. 9 (B, C, D) Depending upon the value of E the potential on right terminal of battery may be more, less or equal to 2 V that will decide the direction of current in the resistance r. Thus options (B), (C) and (D) are correct.

Sol. 10 (All) If switch S is open,

$$i_1 \rho l = E_2$$

where i_1 is the current in primary circuit and ρ is resistance per unit length of potentiometer wire.

Thus at null point balancing length is given as

$$l = \frac{E_2}{i_1 \rho}$$

If jockey is shifted towards right, resistance in primary circuit will increase so current i_1 will decrease and l will increase. If E_1 is increased, i_1 will also increase so l will decrease.

As $l \propto E_2$ with E_2 l will increase.

If switch is closed then null point will be obtained corresponding to the potential difference

$$V_2 = E_2 - i_2 r_2$$

Which is less than E_2 so null point balancing length will decrease. Thus all given options are correct.

Sol. 11 (A, C) By closing switch S_1, net external resistance will decrease this increases the circuit current so ammeter reading will increase.

By closing S_2, equivalent EMF will remain unchanged but equivalent internal resistance of battery will decrease and this increases the circuit current so ammeter reading will increase. Thus options (A) and (C) are correct.

Sol. 12 (A, D) If we consider current in circuit from b to a as shown in figure below, by writing equation of potential drop from b to a gives

$$V_b + 10 - 2i = V_a$$

$$\Rightarrow \quad V_b - V_a = 2i - 10 = 2\text{ V}$$

$$\Rightarrow \quad i = 6\text{ A}$$

$$\Rightarrow \quad V_c - V_a = 2 \times 6 = 12\text{ V}$$

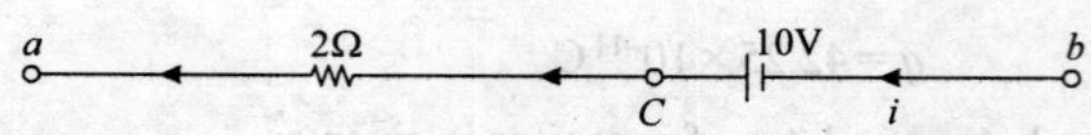

Sol. 13 (B, D) Between a and c, the Wheatstone bridge is balanced so equivalent resistance is r. Across all other points simple series and parallel grouping of resistors can be used. Thus options (B) and (D) are correct.

Sol. 14 (All) At $t = 0$ just after closing the switch capacitor behaves like EMF 6V and circuit current will be

$$i = \frac{6}{1+2} = 2\text{ A}$$

Half life time of the circuit can be given as

$$t_{1/2} = (\ln 2)\tau_C = RC(\ln 2) = 6 \ln(2)\text{ s}$$

In half-life time all circuit parameters get halved

Potential difference across capacitor will be

$$V_C = \frac{6}{2} = 3\text{ V}$$

Current in circuit will be

$$i = \frac{2}{1} = 1\text{ A}$$

Potential differences across 1 Ω and 2 Ω resistances will be

$$V_{1\Omega} = iR = 1\text{ V}$$

$$V_{2\Omega} = iR = 2\text{ V}$$

Sol. 15 (B, C, D) In steady state

$$q_C = EC \text{ and } q_{2C} = 2\text{ EC}$$

Time constant is same for both the circuits $\tau_C = 2$ RC

At time *t* charge on the two capacitors is given as

$$q_C = EC(1 - e^{t/\tau})$$

$$q_{2C} = 2EC(1 - e^{t/\tau})$$

$$\Rightarrow \quad \frac{q_C}{q_{2C}} = \frac{1}{2}$$

Thus options (B), (C) and (D) are correct.

Sol. 16 (B, D) The initial currents,

$$i_{01} = \frac{\varepsilon}{R}, \text{ and } i_{02} = \frac{\varepsilon}{R}, \text{ and so } i_{01} = i_{02}$$

Sol. 17 (B, C, D) In steady state current through branch of capacitor is zero. Thus current flows through 200 Ω and 900 Ω and ammeter A_2 in series combination.

Potential difference across the capacitor is given as

$$V_C = \frac{q}{C} = \frac{4\times 10^{-3}}{100\times 10^{-6}} = 40\text{ V}$$

This is also potential drop across 900 Ω resistance and 100 Ω ammeter A_2 in series of which the total resistance is 1000 Ω. This 1000 Ω and 200 Ω resistances are in series so we use

$$V_2 = V_{200\Omega} = \frac{V_{1000\Omega}}{5} = \frac{40}{5} = 8\text{ V}$$

Thus battery EMF is given as

$$E = V_{1000\Omega} + V_{200\Omega} = 48\text{ V}$$

Current through the battery is given as

$$i = \frac{E}{R}$$

$$\Rightarrow \quad i = \frac{48}{1200} = \frac{1}{25}\text{ A}$$

Thus options (B), (C) and (D) are correct.

* * * * *